Fifth Grade Math with Confidence

Instructor Guide

Fifth Grade Math with Confidence

Instructor Guide

KATE SNOW

WELL-TRAINED MIND PRESS

Names: Snow, Kate (Teacher), author.
Title: Fifth grade math with confidence. Instructor guide / Kate Snow.
Other titles: Instructor guide
Description: [Charles City, Virginia] : Well-Trained Mind Press, [2025] | Series: Snow, Kate (Teacher). Math with confidence. | For instructors of fifth grade math students.
Identifiers: ISBN: 9781944481735 (paperback) | 9781944481742 (eBook/EPUB)
Subjects: LCSH: Mathematics--Study and teaching (Elementary) | LCGFT: Teachers' guides. | BISAC: EDUCATION / Teaching / Subjects / Mathematics.
Classification: LCC: QA107.2 .S665 2025 | DCC: 372.7--dc23

3 4 5 6 7 8 9 Versa 30 29 28 27 26

Table of Contents

Welcome to *Fifth Grade Math* with Confidence!

Fifth Grade Math with Confidence is a **complete, hands-on, and fun** math curriculum that will give your child a solid foundation in math. Your child will learn the following fifth-grade math skills:

- multiplying and dividing multi-digit numbers
- adding and subtracting fractions and mixed numbers with different denominators
- multiplying and dividing fractions and mixed numbers
- adding, subtracting, multiplying, and dividing decimals
- fraction and decimal word problems
- using fractions and decimals to express measurements and solve measurement problems
- volume, geometry, line graphs, and the coordinate plane
- finding the mean and median of a data set

The incremental, confidence-building lessons will help your child develop a strong understanding of math, step by step. Plus, daily review ensures she fully masters what she has learned in previous lessons. With this blend of deep conceptual understanding and traditional skill practice, you'll give your child a thorough fifth-grade math education.

Like the earlier levels of *Math with Confidence*, you'll find many hands-on activities and fun games to help your child develop a positive attitude toward math. You'll also find more written explanations and printed examples to help your child develop math study skills and begin to complete her math lessons more independently.

Besides this Instructor Guide, *Fifth Grade Math with Confidence* also includes two colorful, engaging Student Workbooks. You'll need both workbooks to complete the program. Workbook Part A covers Units 1–7, and Workbook Part B covers Units 8–16.

Many parents worry about their ability to teach math as their children move into more challenging topics like fractions and decimals. If that's the case for you, don't worry: I promise to guide you every step of the way! *Fifth Grade Math with Confidence* is full of features that will help you teach math with confidence all year long:

- **Scripted, open-and-go lessons** help you clearly explain and teach new math concepts
- **Explanatory notes** help you understand more deeply how children learn math so you feel well-equipped to teach your child
- **Unit Wrap-ups and Checkpoints** at the end of each unit provide assessment and give you guidance on whether your child is ready to move on to the next unit

In the next section, you'll learn how the curriculum is organized and how to get your materials ready. Invest a little time reading this section now (and getting your Math Kit ready), and you'll be ready to teach math like a pro all year long.

Wishing you a joyful year of fifth grade math!
Kate Snow

Introduction

The Goals of *Fifth Grade Math with Confidence*

Fifth Grade Math with Confidence aims to help children become confident and capable math students, with a deep understanding of math concepts, proficiency and fluency with fundamental skills, and a positive attitude toward math.

Deep Conceptual Understanding

You'll focus on one main topic per unit so your child can build deep conceptual knowledge of the new material. (Educators call this a *mastery approach* to new content.) Each new lesson builds on the previous one so your child gradually develops thorough understanding.

Proficiency with Fundamental Skills

Children need lots of practice to master the basic skills necessary for proficiency in math. *Fifth Grade Math with Confidence* provides continual, ongoing review of these core skills so your child fully grasps them by the end of the year. (Educators call this a *spiral approach* to review, because children periodically revisit topics, just as the curve of a spiral returns to the same point on a circle.)

Positive Attitude

The lessons in *Fifth Grade Math with Confidence* include games, real-life applications, and lots of hands-on learning so your child enjoys and even looks forward to math time. Optional enrichment lessons at the end of each unit provide a break from the usual routine and help your child appreciate how math is used in everyday life.

What's New in Fifth Grade

If you used earlier levels of *Math with Confidence*, you'll find a few changes in *Fifth Grade Math with Confidence* to reflect your child's growing maturity.

- The Lesson Activities pages have more examples and text to read together, so that your child develops the ability to read and study math more independently.
- Each unit now includes a Unit Reference page that summarizes the core skills your child will learn in the unit. Your child can refer to these pages as she completes the practice and review workbook exercises. (You'll find these pages at the back of each workbook.)
- There is no longer a different picture book listed at the end of each unit. Instead, the enrichment lessons recommend buying one longer book and reading a few pages from the book at the end of each unit.

Overview

You'll need three books to teach *Fifth Grade Math with Confidence.* All three books are essential for the program.

- This Instructor Guide contains the scripted lesson plans for the entire year.
- Workbook Part A contains the workbook pages for the first half of the year (Units 1–7).
- Workbook Part B contains the workbook pages for the second half of the year (Units 8–16).

Units

Fifth Grade Math with Confidence is organized into 16 units. Each unit focuses on developing thorough understanding of one main concept, such as multiplying fractions, finding volume, or dividing decimals. Units vary in length from 6 to 13 lessons, and there are a total of 144 lessons. The final lesson in each unit is an optional enrichment lesson.

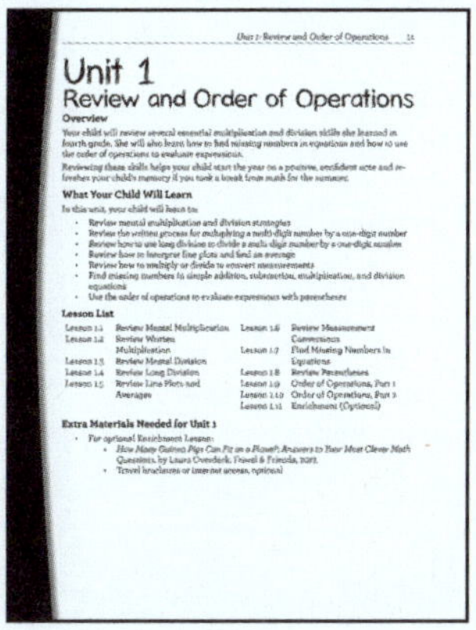
Unit 1
Review and Order of Operations

The preview for each unit includes the following:

- **Overview.** A brief summary of what you'll teach your child.
- **What Your Child Will Learn.** A detailed list of objectives for the unit.
- **Lesson List.** The full list of lessons included in the unit.
- **Extra Materials.** This section gives you a heads-up if you need any extra materials for the unit. You'll sometimes need to supplement your regular math materials with a few everyday household items, such as colored pencils, scissors, or a measuring tape. The optional enrichment lessons also usually require some extra materials.
- **Teaching Math with Confidence.** These notes help you understand more deeply how children learn math so that you're well-prepared to teach the new concepts.

Lessons

You'll need both the Instructor Guide and Student Workbook for every lesson. Most pilot families spent an average of 30-45 minutes on each lesson, with 10-15 minutes of parent-led instruction and 20-30 minutes of independent work. However, this will vary depending on your teaching style and your child's learning style—and whether you have any toddlers interrupting you!

The Instructor Guide contains the scripted, open-and-go lesson plans. Within the Instructor Guide:

- **Bold text** indicates what you are to say.
- *Italic text* provides sample answers.
- Gray-highlighted text indicates explanatory notes.

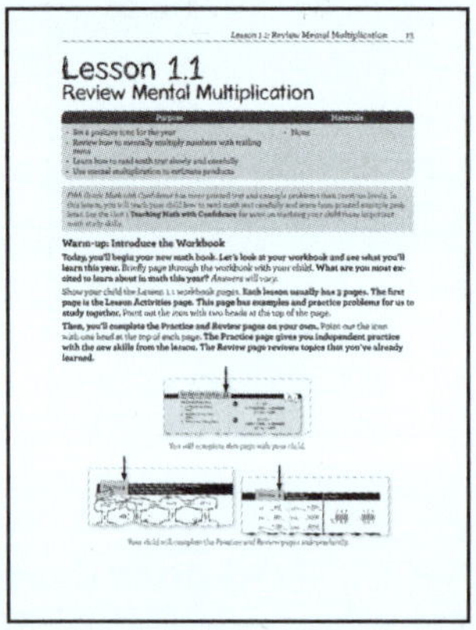

The Student Workbook includes three workbook pages for each lesson. First, you'll use the Lesson Activities page to teach your child the new concept or skill. Then, your child will complete the Practice and Review pages to reinforce what she learned in the lesson and review previously-learned skills.

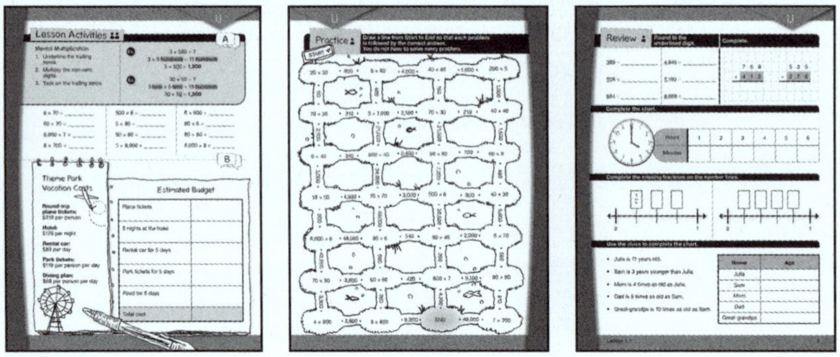

Memory work and warm-up activity with parent

Each lesson begins with a few memory work review questions and a quick warm-up activity. The memory work questions are listed at the top of each lesson. Reviewing a few questions daily helps your child master these important facts and vocabulary words. The warm-up activity eases your child into math time and helps start the lesson on a confident and positive note.

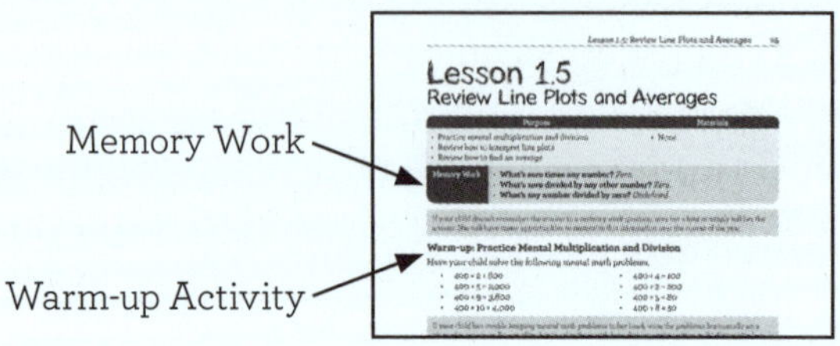

Lesson activities with parent

Next, you'll use the scripted lesson plan and Lesson Activities page to teach your child new concepts and skills. The Instructor Guide and Lesson Activities workbook pages are lettered so that it's easy to see how they align. Some activities are only in the Instructor Guide, without a matching section on the Lesson Activities page.

Instructor Guide

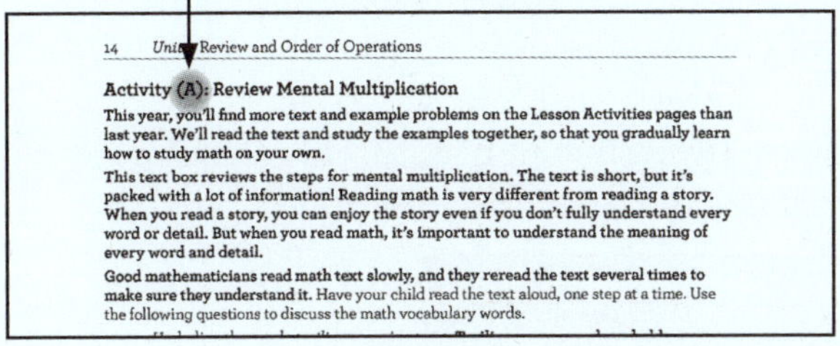

14 Unit 1: Review and Order of Operations

Activity (A): Review Mental Multiplication

This year, you'll find more text and example problems on the Lesson Activities pages than last year. We'll read the text and study the examples together, so that you gradually learn how to study math on your own.

This text box reviews the steps for mental multiplication. The text is short, but it's packed with a lot of information! Reading math is very different from reading a story. When you read a story, you can enjoy the story even if you don't fully understand every word or detail. But when you read math, it's important to understand the meaning of every word and detail.

Good mathematicians read math text slowly, and they reread the text several times to make sure they understand it. Have your child read the text aloud, one step at a time. Use the following questions to discuss the math vocabulary words.

Student Workbook

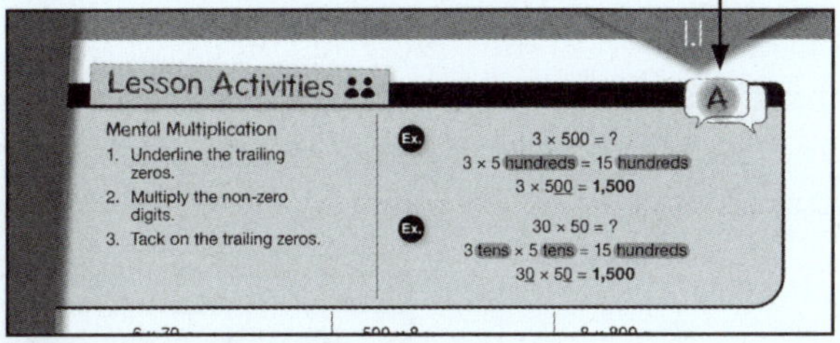

The activity headings and images in the Instructor Guide are lettered to help you find the matching activity in the Student Workbook.

Instructor Guide

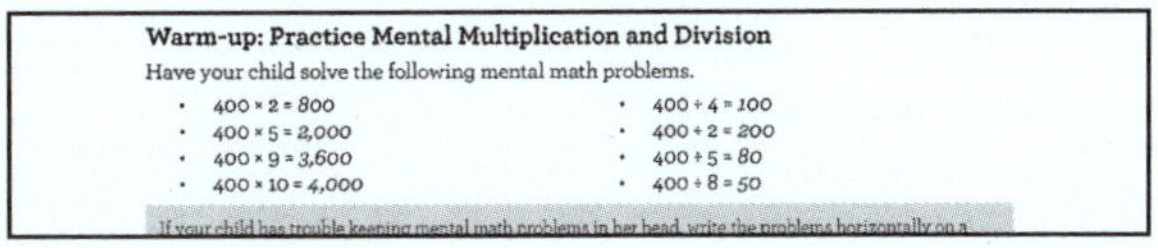

Warm-up: Practice Mental Multiplication and Division

Have your child solve the following mental math problems.

- 400 × 2 = *800*
- 400 × 5 = *2,000*
- 400 × 9 = *3,600*
- 400 × 10 = *4,000*
- 400 ÷ 4 = *100*
- 400 ÷ 2 = *200*
- 400 ÷ 5 = *80*
- 400 ÷ 8 = *50*

Some activity headings in the Instructor Guide do not have a letter. These activities do not have a matching section in the Student Workbook, and they are completed either orally or with hands-on materials instead.

As in the previous levels of *Math with Confidence*, the **lesson plans in the Instructor Guide are an essential part of the program.** Even if you don't follow the scripted lesson word-by-word, make sure you use this Instructor Guide alongside the Student Workbook. The text on the Lesson Activities page summarizes the core concept or skill in each lesson, but there are often warm-ups, games, and explanations in the Instructor Guide that aren't printed in the workbook.

Independent practice

Last, your child will complete the Practice and Review workbook pages on her own. You'll find answer keys for the Practice and Review pages at the end of each unit.

Enrichment Lessons (Optional)

Optional enrichment lessons are included at the end of each unit. The Instructor Guide provides enrichment activity directions, while the Student Workbook includes a two-page Unit Wrap-Up for your child to complete.

Many parents and children find that the enrichment lessons are their favorite part of the program. (Siblings often enjoy participating in them, too!) However, these lessons are completely optional. You are free to choose the ones that sound the most fun for your family, or skip them entirely if your schedule is too full.

Math enrichment book

Each enrichment lesson lists suggested pages to read from *How Many Guinea Pigs Can Fit on a Plane?: Answers to Your Most Clever Math Questions*, by Laura Overdeck. This book makes a fun companion to *Fifth Grade Math with Confidence*. It includes many real-life examples of the topics your child will study this year, including multiplication and division with large numbers, fractions, decimals, and measurements.

Enrichment activity

The enrichment activities help your child appreciate how math is used in everyday life. You'll find suggestions for art projects, cooking activities, real-world applications, and more to make math come alive for your child.

Unit Wrap-up (review and assessment)

The Unit Wrap-Ups provide two pages of additional exercises for the concepts and skills your child learned in the unit. You can use them to casually review the unit, or you can use them as tests to assess your child's progress more formally. Either way, children and parents often find it very satisfying to see this concrete evidence of growth. If you live in a state where you're required to provide evidence of learning, you may want to save them for your child's portfolio.

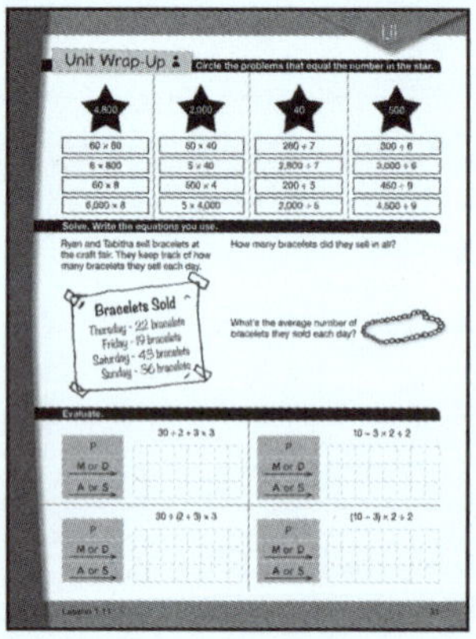

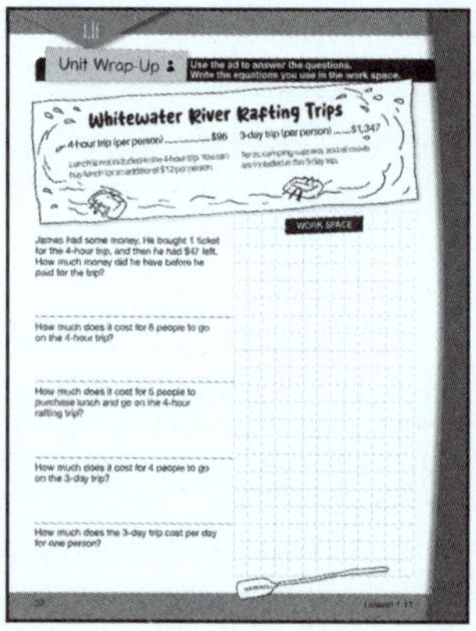

Your child is not expected to fully master every skill from every unit before moving on to the next unit. See below for more on pacing and assessing your child's progress.

Pacing and Checkpoints

Fifth Grade Math with Confidence provides lots of flexibility so your child can learn at his own pace. You know your child best, and you are always welcome to slow down or speed up the pace of the lessons based on your child's needs.

Is My Child Ready to Start *Fifth Grade Math with Confidence*?

Your child is ready to begin this program if he can:

- Understand place value in numbers to 1,000,000.
- Name answers to the multiplication and division facts (up to 10×10 and 100÷10). He should be able to recall the answers to most within 3 seconds or so.
- Solve multiplication problems with the traditional written process (up to four-digit numbers times one-digit numbers or two-digit numbers times two-digit numbers).
- Use long division to solve division problems (up to four-digit numbers divided by one-digit numbers).
- Find equivalent fractions and convert improper fractions to mixed numbers (and vice versa).
- Add and subtract fractions or mixed numbers with the same denominators.
- Read, write, and compare decimals to the hundredths place.
- Solve measurement problems and convert measurements within a system of measurement (for example, inches to feet, or kilograms to grams).
- Measure, compare, and reason about angles.

All of these skills are reviewed in the first few units, so don't worry if your child needs a refresher on a few of them. However, if your child is shaky on many of these skills, *Fourth Grade Math with Confidence* may be a better fit for him. Math skills build incrementally, and it will be difficult for your child to develop proficiency and confidence with the new fifth-grade skills if he has a weak foundation.

> If your child is not fluent with the multiplication facts but knows the rest of the skills listed above, she is probably ready to begin *Fifth Grade Math with Confidence*. Make sure to add 5 minutes of daily multiplication fact practice to each lesson until your child becomes more fluent with the facts. *Multiplication Facts that Stick* (also available from Well-Trained Mind Press) provides quick games to help your child master these essential skills. See the Unit 1 Checkpoint (page 51) for more guidance on assessing and developing multiplication fact fluency.

How Do I Know Whether to Stick with a Lesson (or Unit) or Move On?

Most children need lots of exposure to a new concept or skill before they fully grasp it. Each lesson in *Fifth Grade Math with Confidence* gently builds on the previous one, but your child doesn't need to completely master every lesson before moving on to the next. The program includes many opportunities for practice and review before your child is expected to achieve full proficiency with a topic.

In general, continue teaching new lessons until you reach the end of a unit. At the end of each unit, you'll find a Checkpoint that provides guidance on whether your child is ready to move on to the next unit.

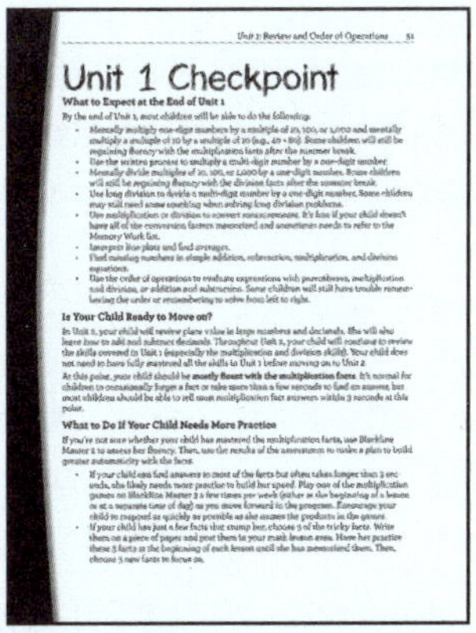
Unit 1 Checkpoint

The Checkpoints are divided into three parts:

- **What to Expect at the End of the Unit** This list of skills tells you what fifth graders typically are able to do at the end of each unit.
- **Is Your Child Ready to Move On?** This section tells you what your child needs to have mastered before moving on to the next unit.
- **What to Do if Your Child Needs More Practice** If your child isn't quite ready to move on, this section gives you options for reviewing and practicing the skills your child needs to master before the next unit. (This section is omitted if no specific skills are necessary for the next unit.)

Scheduling

Fifth Grade Math with Confidence includes 144 lessons. 128 are regular lessons, and 16 are optional enrichment lessons. You're welcome to adjust the number of lessons you teach per week to best fit your family's schedule. Some families prefer to teach math 5 days per week, while others prefer to teach math 4 days per week and leave one day open for co-ops, errands, or field trips.

Use the following guidelines to plan your year:

- If you teach 4 lessons per week and teach all the enrichment lessons, *Fifth Grade Math with Confidence* will take you 36 weeks.
- If you teach 4 lessons per week and skip the enrichment lessons, *Fifth Grade Math with Confidence* will take you 32 weeks.
- If you teach 5 lessons per week and teach all the enrichment lessons, *Fifth Grade Math with Confidence* will take you 29 weeks.
- If you teach 5 lessons per week and skip the enrichment lessons, *Fifth Grade Math with Confidence* will take you 26 weeks.

Use this list as a rough guide to planning your year, but don't set it in stone. You'll generally be able to cover one lesson per day, but you may occasionally find that you want to split a lesson over two days.

How Can I Adjust the Lessons to Best Fit My Child and My Schedule?

Children vary tremendously in how quickly they learn new math concepts and skills. Use these suggestions to adjust the lessons to best fit your child's needs and your family's schedule.

- If your student is a fast processor or picks up math skills quickly, you may be able to condense lessons and teach more than one lesson in one day. If so, teach the concepts that are new to your child. Then, have your child complete a selection of exercises on the corresponding Practice and Review pages.
- If your child has a slower processing speed or takes a while to grasp math concepts and skills, some lessons may take longer than you would like (or, longer than your child is able to stay engaged and attentive). If that's the case, set a timer for your desired lesson length, stop when the timer goes off, and continue the next day where you left off. In the elementary years, you are setting a foundation for a lifetime of proficiency and confidence in math. It's okay not to rush through these essential skills.
- If your child doesn't have the stamina to complete the Practice and Review pages at the same time, split the lesson into two parts. Do the Lesson Activities page and Practice page during one part of the day, and then have your child complete the Review page at a different time of the day.
- Adjust your use of manipulatives to fit your child's learning style. Some fifth graders are able to think abstractly about math concepts, but many still need concrete manipulatives to help them understand new topics. If your child readily understands a skill and doesn't enjoy using manipulatives, allow her to solve the problems without them. If your child learns best with a lot of visual and hands-on reinforcement, allow her to use manipulatives to model problems as much as she needs.
- If your child resists you "teaching" the lesson, come alongside him as a coach, working to understand the text and examples together.
- Games provide a fun way to practice math skills, and they can be a great way to bond with your child. However, if your child doesn't enjoy games, or you don't have time for a game on a particular day, choose a few problems from the game for your child to solve instead. That way, she'll still get the extra practice that the game was meant to provide.
- Don't worry if you have a bad day every once in a while. Extra tiredness, oncoming illness, or just plain grumpiness can make for a less-than-cheerful math lesson. It's perfectly normal for children to occasionally get frustrated, and it doesn't mean that you're a bad math teacher or need to change the way you teach. If emotions rise during math, just cut the lesson short and resume later in the day or the next day. Most of the time, you'll find that the next day goes much better.

Developing Independence in Math

Many fifth graders are eager for more independence, but that doesn't mean they're ready to go off and learn math on their own. Most still need direct instruction, lots of encouragement and accountability, and many opportunities to ask questions. Consider the next few years a gradual process of transferring responsibility to your child for her math learning, not an immediate or dramatic shift. And, don't be surprised if some days your child is ready to zoom through her Practice and Review pages on her own, while other days she needs you right by her side.

Use these tips to help your child develop age-appropriate independence in math this year:

- Encourage your child to refer to the Unit Reference pages (at the back of the workbook) if she can't remember how to solve a problem on a Practice or Review page. These pages provide a summary of the key teaching in each unit so that your child can refer to them rather than immediately asking you for help.
- When your child has a question about his independent work, have him write a question mark or place a small sticky note next to the tricky problem. Discuss the tricky problems *after* he finishes the rest of the page. Children often discover that they actually know how to find the answer if they wait a few minutes before asking for help.
- Teach your child how to check her own work with the answer keys in this Instructor Guide. Mark the matching answer key with a bookmark or sticky note to make it easier for her to find the correct page. Have her correct her work with a different colored pen or marker, and then ask her to try to figure out her mistakes before you help her with them.

What You'll Need

If you've used previous levels of *Math with Confidence*, you'll find that fifth grade has fewer manipulatives and Blackline Masters to manage. Most lessons only require materials from your Math Kit, but you'll also sometimes use everyday objects to enhance the lessons.

How to Create Your Math Kit

You'll use materials from your Math Kit in most core lessons. Stick the following materials in a box or basket so they're always ready to go, and keep them handy when you're teaching.

- **30 small counters (15 each of 2 different colors).** Any type of small object (such as plastic tiles, Legos, blocks, or plastic discs) is fine. You will mostly use these for game pieces.
- **Fraction bars.** These plastic bars are split into fractional parts. Look for a set that includes halves, thirds, fourths, fifths, sixths, eighths, tenths, and twelfths. Real bars are easiest to use, but you can copy and cut out Blackline Master 8 (page 571) if you don't have access to real fraction bars.

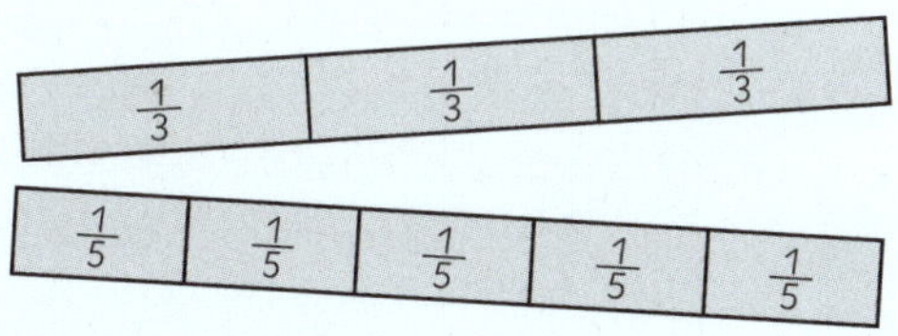

- **Fraction circles.** These plastic circles are another way to show fractional parts. As with fraction bars, look for a set that includes halves, thirds, fourths, fifths, sixths, eighths, tenths, and twelfths. Or, you can copy and cut out Blackline Master 14 (page 587).

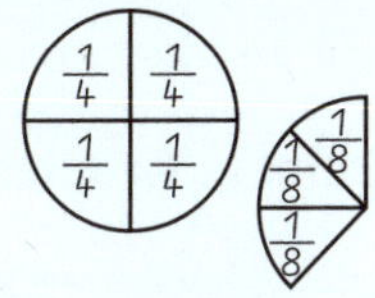

- **Base-ten blocks (30 unit blocks, 20 rods, 12 flats).** You will occasionally use base-ten blocks to represent decimal place-value. If you don't already own base-ten blocks, you may want to photocopy and color Blackline Master 15 (page 591) rather than buying a complete set.

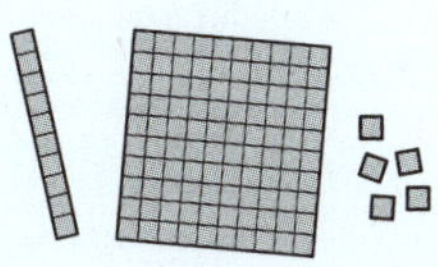

- **30 centimeter cubes (if you don't own base-ten blocks).** The small unit blocks in base-ten block sets are also known as centimeter cubes. Your child will use these blocks to explore volume this year. If you already own a set of base-ten blocks, you do not need to purchase any additional centimeter cubes. If you don't have a set of real base-ten blocks, make sure to buy a small set of centimeter cubes.
- **Play money (20 one-dollar bills, 20 ten-dollar bills, and 10 hundred-dollar bills).** You will only occasionally need play money this year. Play money from a toy cash register or board game works well. If you don't already have some, you can copy and cut out the play money on Blackline Master 16 (page 593).
- **1-foot (or 30-centimeter) ruler.**
- **Protractor.** Any clear plastic protractor is fine.
- **2 packs of playing cards and 2 dice.** You'll use playing cards and dice for some of the games in this book. Any standard 52-card decks and regular, six-sided dice will work fine.
- **Blank paper.** Your child may occasionally need scrap paper for extra space for solving problems. Any kind of paper is fine, including plain copy paper.
- **Pencils.** Keep sharp pencils on hand for lessons and workbook pages.
- **Highlighter.** Any color is fine.
- **1 plastic page protector and dry-erase marker.** You'll place one Blackline Master in a plastic page protector so that you can write on it with a dry-erase marker.

You will also sometimes use the rest of the Blackline Masters (from the back of this Instructor Guide or available online at welltrainedmind.com/mwc.) Most of the Blackline Masters are used for only a few lessons, but there are a few you may want to keep handy. See page 547 for more information.

You will occasionally need to save items for future lessons. This symbol will alert you if you need to save anything.

Other Supplies Needed

You'll only need your Math Kit for most lessons, but occasionally you'll need a few other common household items. You'll find these items listed in three different places in the curriculum to make sure you always know what you need:

- The preview for each unit lists all extra household items needed.
- The top of each lesson lists all supplies you'll need to teach that lesson. These lists include items from your Math Kit as well as extra household items. (Note that some lessons require scrap paper or a separate piece of paper. To save space, paper is not listed as a separate material.)
- You'll find the complete list of household items needed throughout the year on page 545.

Don't feel you have to gather the extra household items now. Most are common things like colored pencils, scissors, or a measuring tape you can grab right before you begin the lesson.

Helpful Resources

You'll find an appendix of helpful resources at the back of this book:

- Memory Work
- Scope and Sequence
- Materials List
- Blackline Masters

Unit 1
Review and Order of Operations

Overview

Your child will review several essential multiplication and division skills she learned in fourth grade. She will also learn how to find missing numbers in equations and how to use the order of operations to evaluate expressions.

Reviewing these skills helps your child start the year on a positive, confident note and refreshes your child's memory if you took a break from math for the summer.

What Your Child Will Learn

In this unit, your child will learn to:

- Review mental multiplication and division strategies
- Review the written process for multiplying a multi-digit number by a one-digit number
- Review how to use long division to divide a multi-digit number by a one-digit number
- Review how to interpret line plots and find an average
- Review how to multiply or divide to convert measurements
- Find missing numbers in simple addition, subtraction, multiplication, and division equations
- Use the order of operations to evaluate expressions with parentheses

Lesson List

Lesson 1.1	Review Mental Multiplication
Lesson 1.2	Review Written Multiplication
Lesson 1.3	Review Mental Division
Lesson 1.4	Review Long Division
Lesson 1.5	Review Line Plots and Averages
Lesson 1.6	Review Measurement Conversions
Lesson 1.7	Find Missing Numbers in Equations
Lesson 1.8	Review Parentheses
Lesson 1.9	Order of Operations, Part 1
Lesson 1.10	Order of Operations, Part 2
Lesson 1.11	Enrichment (Optional)

Extra Materials Needed for Unit 1

- For optional Enrichment Lesson:
  - *How Many Guinea Pigs Can Fit on a Plane?: Answers to Your Most Clever Math Questions*, by Laura Overdeck. Feiwel & Friends, 2017.
  - Travel brochures or internet access, optional

Teaching Math with Confidence: How to Teach Your Child to Read Math Text and Learn from Printed Examples

In *Third* and *Fourth Grade Math with Confidence,* the Lesson Activities pages in the Student Workbook included very little text or printed examples. Instead, the pages listed key words and provided space for you to demonstrate how to solve sample problems. *Fifth Grade Math with Confidence* includes more text and printed sample problems so that your child begins to learn how to read and study math books.

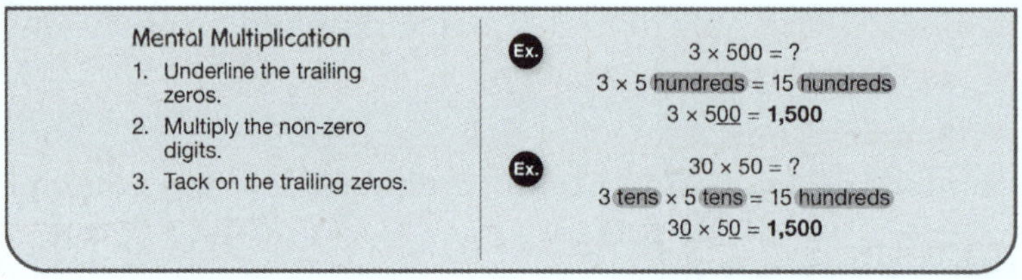

Mental Multiplication

1. Underline the trailing zeros.
2. Multiply the non-zero digits.
3. Tack on the trailing zeros.

Ex. $3 \times 500 = ?$
3×5 hundreds = 15 hundreds
$3 \times 5\underline{00} = \mathbf{1{,}500}$

Ex. $30 \times 50 = ?$
3 tens × 5 tens = 15 hundreds
$3\underline{0} \times 5\underline{0} = \mathbf{1{,}500}$

Sample text and example problems, from Lesson 1.1.

As in the previous levels of *Math with Confidence*, the **Instructor Guide is an essential part of the program.** Even if you don't follow the scripted lesson word-by-word, make sure you use the Instructor Guide alongside the Student Workbook. The text on the Lesson Activities page summarizes the core concept or skill in each lesson, but there are often warm-ups, games, and explanations in the Instructor Guide that aren't printed in the workbook.

In this unit, you'll teach your child how to read her math book slowly and carefully. Children are often under the mistaken impression that if they don't understand math explanations the first time, they're either not good at math or not a good reader. You'll correct this false assumption by teaching your child that math texts are different from narrative texts. When you read a story, you can enjoy the story even if you don't fully understand every word or detail. But when you read math, it's important to **read slowly**, make sure you **understand every vocabulary word**, and **check that you fully comprehend the text** before moving on. It's often helpful to **re-read** the text multiple times to help it sink in, too.

Besides teaching your child these important reading strategies, you'll also teach her how to study printed example problems. Children sometimes assume they can grasp the examples at a glance and want to rush past them. If this becomes a source of conflict with your child, use the following strategies to encourage her to slow down and discuss the examples with you.

- **Cover the rest of the page** with a piece of paper to help focus her attention on the example you're discussing.
- If your child is visually overwhelmed by the examples, **write out the example step-by-step on a separate piece of paper or whiteboard.** It's fine if you use the example on the page as a guide for yourself rather than as the main teaching tool for your child. Or, cover the example with a piece of paper and reveal only one line at a time.
- If your child is adamant that she understands the example and does not need it explained to her, **ask her to "be the teacher" and explain the example to you.** Then, check the Instructor Guide to make sure there aren't any additional teaching points to mention.

Developing math study skills is a gradual process. Just as with other skills, most children will need lots of direct teaching and coaching as they learn how to read and study math.

Lesson 1.1
Review Mental Multiplication

Purpose	Materials
• Set a positive tone for the year • Review how to mentally multiply numbers with trailing zeros • Learn how to read math text slowly and carefully • Use mental multiplication to estimate products	• None

Fifth Grade Math with Confidence has more printed text and example problems than previous levels. In this lesson, you will teach your child how to read math text carefully and learn from printed example problems. See the Unit 1 **Teaching Math with Confidence** for more on teaching your child these important math study skills.

Warm-up: Introduce the Workbook

Today, you'll begin your new math book. Let's look at your workbook and see what you'll learn this year. Briefly page through the workbook with your child. **What are you most excited to learn about in math this year?** *Answers will vary.*

Show your child the Lesson 1.1 workbook pages. **Each lesson usually has 3 pages. The first page is the Lesson Activities page. This page has examples and practice problems for us to study together.** Point out the icon with two heads at the top of the page.

Then, you'll complete the Practice and Review pages on your own. Point out the icon with one head at the top of each page. **The Practice page gives you independent practice with the new skills from the lesson. The Review page reviews topics that you've already learned.**

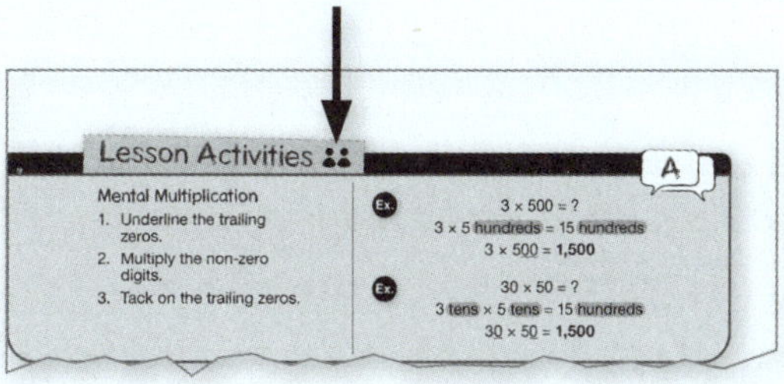

You will complete this page with your child.

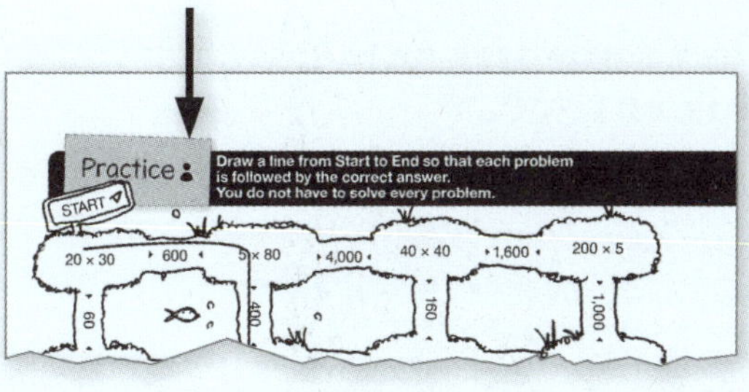

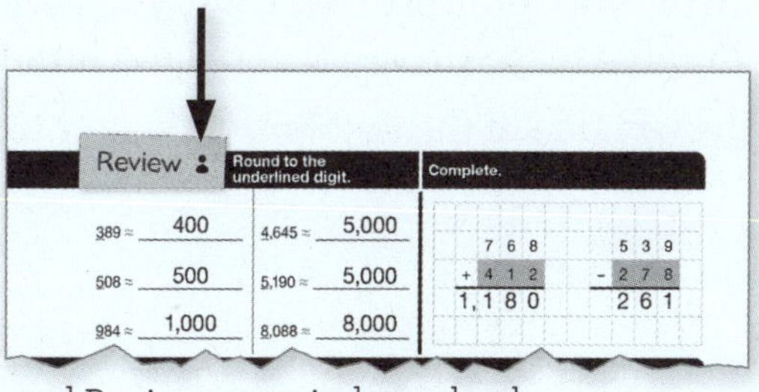

Your child will complete the Practice and Review pages independently.

Activity (A): Review Mental Multiplication

This year, you'll find more text and example problems on the Lesson Activities pages than last year. We'll read the text and study the examples together, so that you gradually learn how to study math on your own.

This text box reviews the steps for mental multiplication. The text is short, but it's packed with a lot of information! Reading math is very different from reading a story. When you read a story, you can enjoy the story even if you don't fully understand every word or detail. But when you read math, it's important to understand the meaning of every word and detail.

Good mathematicians read math text slowly, and they reread the text several times to make sure they understand it. Have your child read the text aloud, one step at a time. Use the following questions to discuss the math vocabulary words.

- Underline the words *trailing zeros* in step 1. **Trailing zeros are place-holder zeros that are to the right of the other digits in a number. For example, 500 has 2 trailing zeros.**
- Underline the words *non-zero digits* in step 2. **Non-zero digits are just digits that aren't zero, like 1, 7, or 8.**

A

Mental Multiplication
1. Underline the trailing zeros.
2. Multiply the non-zero digits.
3. Tack on the trailing zeros.

Ex. 3 × 500 = ?
3 × 5 hundreds = 15 hundreds
3 × 5<u>00</u> = **1,500**

Ex. 30 × 50 = ?
3 tens × 5 tens = 15 hundreds
3<u>0</u> × 5<u>0</u> = **1,500**

If this text (or any of the text in the book) is above your child's reading level, read it aloud to her instead.

The examples show how to use the steps to solve problems. When we study an example, we try to understand both how to follow the steps and why the steps work.

Read aloud the first example: ***3 times 500 equals what?***

- **3 times 5 *hundreds* equals 15 *hundreds*.**
- **500 has 2 trailing zeros, so you underline 2 zeros.**
- **After you multiply 3 times 5, you tack the 2 zeros back on to show that you have 15 hundreds. 3 times 500 equals 15 hundreds, or 1,500.**

Read aloud the second example: ***30 times 50 equals what?***

- **3 *tens* times 5 *tens* equals 15 *hundreds*, because 10 times 10 equals 100.**
- **30 has 1 trailing zero. 50 has 1 trailing zero. There are a total of 2 trailing zeros, so you underline 2 zeros.**
- **After you multiply 3 times 5, you tack the 2 zeros back on to show that you have 15 hundreds. 30 times 50 equals 15 hundreds, or 1,500.**

Cover the left side of the text box with your hand. **Can you explain the steps in your own words?** *Sample answer: Underline the zeros, multiply the other digits, then tack on the zeros you underlined.*

Restating mathematical text helps your child better understand and internalize it.

Have your child follow the steps to solve the practice problems.

A

6 × 70 = 420	500 × 8 = 4,000	8 × 800 = 6,400
60 × 70 = 4,200	5 × 80 = 400	80 × 8 = 640
6,000 × 7 = 42,000	50 × 80 = 4,000	80 × 80 = 6,400
6 × 700 = 4,200	5 × 8,000 = 40,000	8,000 × 8 = 64,000

Each column of problems has the same non-zero digits so that your child can focus on the place-value meaning of the trailing zeros rather than single-digit multiplication problems.

Activity (B): Create a Budget for a Theme Park Vacation

Have you ever been to a theme park or amusement park? *Answers will vary.* **Taking a vacation to a theme park can be very expensive! Whenever you make a big purchase like a vacation, it's a good idea to estimate the cost before you make a final decision about whether to go. We'll use mental multiplication to find the approximate cost for a theme park vacation for our family.**

Round-trip plane tickets cost $319 per person. What's $319 rounded to the nearest hundred? *$300.* **So, we'll multiply the number of people in our family by 300 to find the approximate cost for the plane tickets.** Write a multiplication problem to match and have your child find the product. For example, if you have 4 people in your family, write "4 × 300" in the left-hand column and write $1,200 in the right-hand column.

Plane tickets 4 × 300	$1,200

Sample answer for a family of 4. Use the number of people in your family as the first factor in the multiplication problem.

Have your child round the hotel price to the nearest hundred and multiply to find the approximate five-night cost. For the rental car, have your child round the price to the nearest ten.

5 nights at the hotel 5 × 200	$1,000
Rental car for 5 days 5 × 80	$400

Sample answers for a family of 4.

For the park tickets, have your child round $119 to the nearest hundred. **We multiply the number of people in our family by 100 to find the cost for one day. Then, we multiply that product by 5 to find the approximate cost for all 5 days.** Write a multiplication problem to match and have your child find the product. For example, if you have 4 people in your family, write "100 × 4 × 5" in the left-hand column and write $2,000 in the right-hand column.

Have her round the dining plan cost to the nearest ten and find the total dining plan cost for 5 days.

Park tickets for 5 days 100 × 4 × 5	$2,000
Food for 5 days 70 × 4 × 5	$1,400

Sample answers for a family of 4.

After your child completes the estimates, have her add the products (either mentally or on paper) to find the total approximate cost of the trip.

Independent Practice and Review

Have your child complete the Lesson 1.1 Practice and Review workbook pages.

Lesson 1.2
Review Written Multiplication

Purpose	Materials
• Introduce memory work • Review how to multiply a multi-digit number by a one-digit number with the multiplication algorithm • Estimate products and compare the estimate with the exact answer	• Deck of playing cards • Memory Work (Blackline Master 1)

In this lesson, you'll introduce your child to the Memory Work list (Blackline Master 1). Many families find it helpful to post the Memory Work pages near their lesson area to help their children gradually memorize the items over the course of the year.

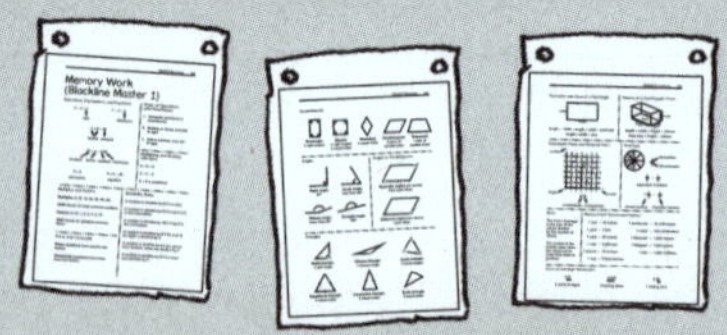

All Blackline Masters are available at the back of the book. **You can also find all Blackline Masters at welltrainedmind.com/mwc for easy printing.**

Warm-up: Introduce and Practice Memory Work

Show your child the Memory Work list (Blackline Master 1). **You'll memorize these important vocabulary words and facts this year. You already know many of them, and some of them are new. We'll practice them throughout the year so that you learn all of them.** Briefly look over the list with your child and have him point out a few facts he already knows.

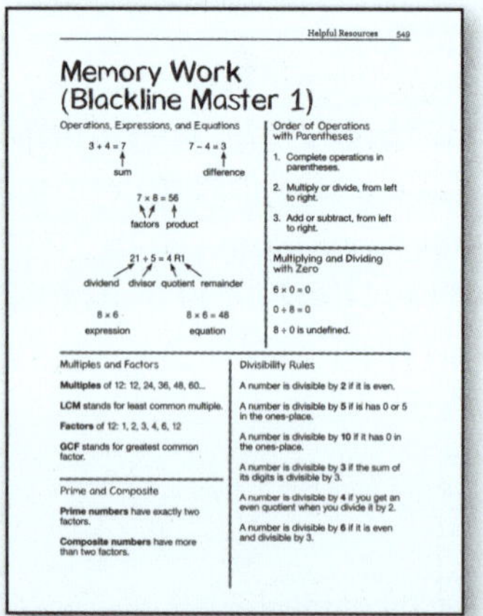

Helpful Resources 549

Memory Work (Blackline Master 1)

Operations, Expressions, and Equations

3 + 4 = 7 (sum)

7 − 4 = 3 (difference)

7 × 8 = 56 (factors, product)

21 ÷ 5 = 4 R1 (dividend, divisor, quotient, remainder)

8 × 6 (expression)

8 × 6 = 48 (equation)

Order of Operations with Parentheses

1. Complete operations in parentheses.
2. Multiply or divide, from left to right.
3. Add or subtract, from left to right.

Multiplying and Dividing with Zero

6 × 0 = 0

0 ÷ 8 = 0

8 ÷ 0 is undefined.

Multiples and Factors

Multiples of 12: 12, 24, 36, 48, 60...

LCM stands for least common multiple.

Factors of 12: 1, 2, 3, 4, 6, 12

GCF stands for greatest common factor.

Prime and Composite

Prime numbers have exactly two factors.

Composite numbers have more than two factors.

Divisibility Rules

A number is divisible by **2** if it is even.

A number is divisible by **5** if is has 0 or 5 in the ones-place.

A number is divisible by **10** if it has 0 in the ones-place.

A number is divisible by **3** if the sum of its digits is divisible by 3.

A number is divisible by **4** if you get an even quotient when you divide it by 2.

A number is divisible by **6** if it is even and divisible by 3.

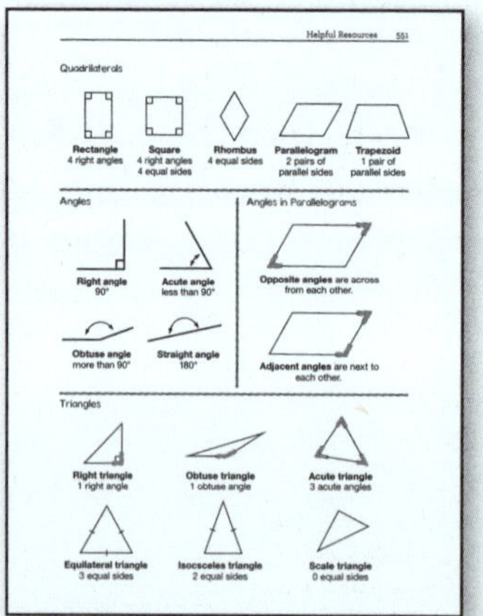

Helpful Resources 551

Quadrilaterals

Rectangle 4 right angles

Square 4 right angles 4 equal sides

Rhombus 4 equal sides

Parallelogram 2 pairs of parallel sides

Trapezoid 1 pair of parallel sides

Angles

Right angle 90°

Acute angle less than 90°

Obtuse angle more than 90°

Straight angle 180°

Angles in Parallelograms

Opposite angles are across from each other.

Adjacent angles are next to each other.

Triangles

Right triangle 1 right angle

Obtuse triangle 1 obtuse angle

Acute triangle 3 acute angles

Equilateral triangle 3 equal sides

Isocsceles triangle 2 equal sides

Scale triangle 0 equal sides

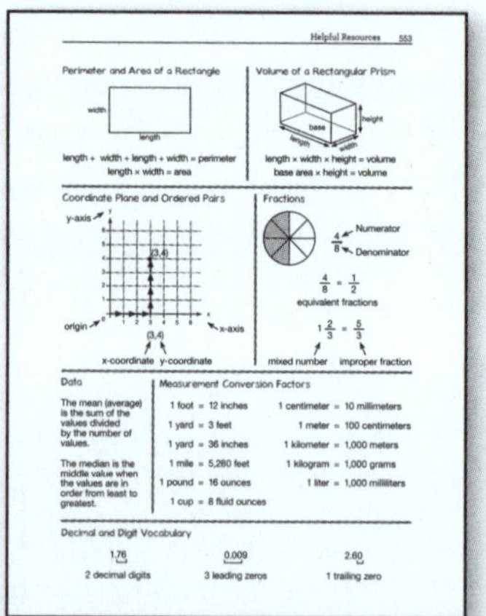

Helpful Resources 553

Perimeter and Area of a Rectangle

width, length

length + width + length + width = perimeter

length × width = area

Volume of a Rectangular Prism

height, base, length, width

length × width × height = volume

base area × height = volume

Coordinate Plane and Ordered Pairs

y-axis, origin, x-axis, (3,4)

(3,4): x-coordinate, y-coordinate

Fractions

$\frac{4}{8}$ Numerator, Denominator

$\frac{4}{8} = \frac{1}{2}$ equivalent fractions

$1\frac{2}{3} = \frac{5}{3}$ mixed number, improper fraction

Data

The mean (average) is the sum of the values divided by the number of values.

The median is the middle value when the values are in order from least to greatest.

Measurement Conversion Factors

1 foot = 12 inches

1 yard = 3 feet

1 yard = 36 inches

1 mile = 5,280 feet

1 pound = 16 ounces

1 cup = 8 fluid ounces

1 centimeter = 10 millimeters

1 meter = 100 centimeters

1 kilometer = 1,000 meters

1 kilogram = 1,000 grams

1 liter = 1,000 milliliters

Decimal and Digit Vocabulary

1.76 — 2 decimal digits

0.009 — 3 leading zeros

2.60 — 1 trailing zero

Children learned many of these items in *Fourth Grade Math with Confidence*. If you didn't use *Fourth Grade Math with Confidence*, you do not need to stop and help your child memorize all these items now. He'll have plenty of opportunities to learn them throughout fifth grade.

Activity (A): Review How to Multiply a Multi-Digit Number by a One-Digit Number

Last year, you learned how to multiply multi-digit numbers by one-digit numbers with the multiplication algorithm. Today, we'll review the process.

This text box demonstrates each step for multiplying a three-digit number by a one-digit number. Use the following questions to discuss the steps and example.

- **First, you multiply the 5 ones by 3. What's 5 times 3?** *15.* **15 ones equal 1 ten and 5 ones, so you write a 1 above the tens-place and 5 in the answer's ones-place.**
- **Second, you multiply 4 tens by 3. What's 4 times 3?** *12.* **Then, you add the 1 ten from the previous step. What's 12 tens plus 1 ten?** *13 tens.* **13 tens equal 1 hundred and 3 tens, so you write a 1 above the hundreds-place and 3 in the answer's tens-place.**
- **Last, you multiply 2 hundreds by 3. What's 2 times 3?** *6.* **Then, you add the 1 hundred from the previous step. What's 6 hundreds plus 1 hundred?** *7 hundreds.* **You write 7 in the answer's hundreds-place.**

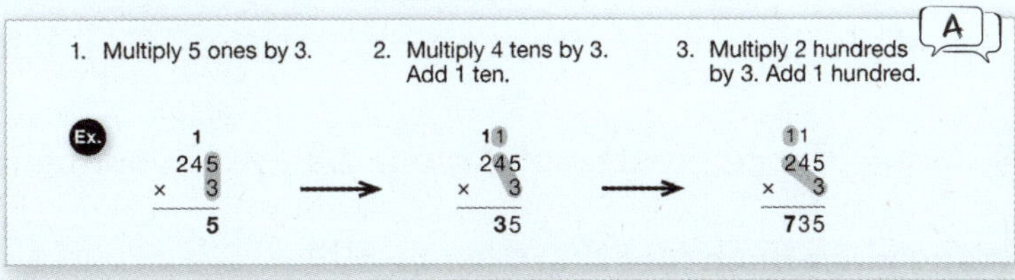

If your child is confused by the steps, model the problem with play money. Place 3 groups of 2 hundred-dollar bills, 4 ten-dollar bills, and 5 one-dollar bills on the table. Demonstrate each step with the bills, and trade as needed. For example: **The first step is to multiply 5 ones by 3. We have 3 groups of 5 one-dollar bills, so we have 15 one-dollar bills in all. We trade 10 one-dollar bills for 1 ten-dollar bill.**

Before you solve 417 times 4, let's estimate the answer. Estimating before you solve helps you know whether your answer is reasonable.

What's 417 rounded to the nearest hundred? *400.* Write 400 × 4 as shown. **What's 400 times 4?** *1,600.* Write 1,600 as shown. **Do you think the exact answer will be higher or lower than 1,600? Why?** *Sample answer: Higher. We rounded 417 down, so the estimate will be lower than the exact answer.*

Now, let's multiply to find the exact answer. Have your child multiply to find the exact product. Encourage him to refer to the example as needed.

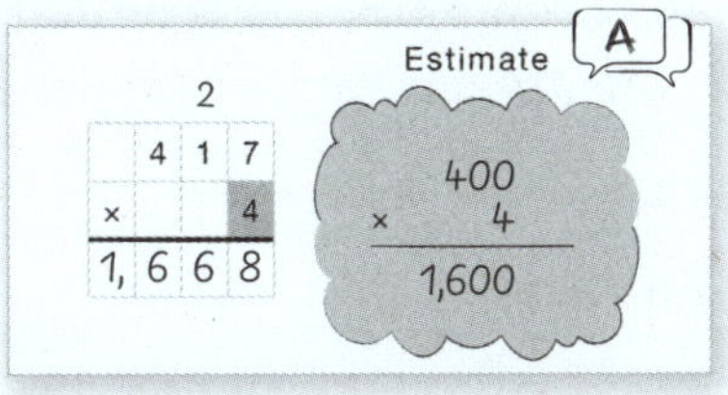

We estimated the product would be about 1,600. You found that the exact product is 1,668, so that seems like a reasonable answer. It's a little more than the estimate, since we rounded 417 down to 400.

Whether or not an answer is "reasonable" depends on the numbers involved. The product of a three-digit number times a one-digit number can be several hundred off from the estimate and still be a reasonable answer.

You can use this same process to multiply any multi-digit number times a one-digit number. You just keep multiplying until you have multiplied all the digits in the top number by the bottom number. Repeat with 2,981 × 5.

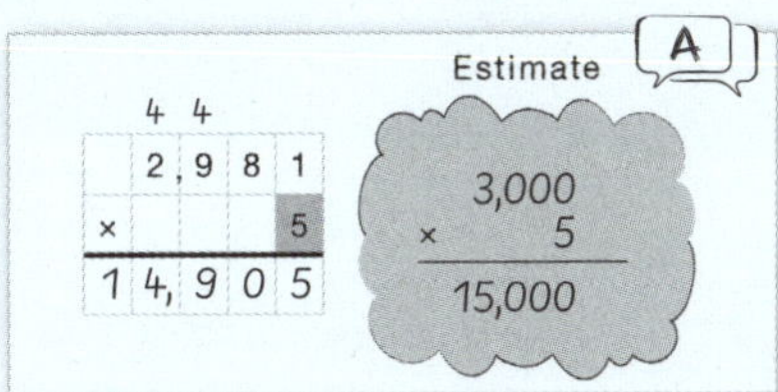

Activity (B): Play Multiplication War

Play Multiplication War.

Encourage your child to use estimation to arrange the cards to form the greatest product possible.

Multiplication War

Materials: Deck of playing cards, with 10s, jacks, queens, and kings removed (36 cards total)

Object of the Game: Have a greater total score than your opponent.

Shuffle the cards and place them face down in one pile.

Multiplication War has 3 rounds. On your turn, flip over the top 4 cards in the pile. Use the digits to make a three-digit number and a one-digit number. Write the numbers in your first multiplication grid and multiply to find the product.

For example, if you turn over a 5, 9, 2, and 1, you can create multiplication problems such as 129 × 5, 295 × 1, or 591 × 2. Try to arrange the numbers to create the greatest product possible. This product is your score for the round.

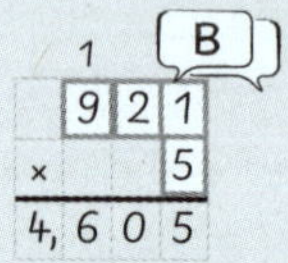

Make the greatest possible product from your cards.

Take turns until both players have completed all 3 rounds. Each player finds the sum of their 3 scores. Whoever has the greater total score wins.

Independent Practice and Review

Have your child complete the Lesson 1.2 Practice and Review workbook pages.

Lesson 1.3
Review Mental Division

Purpose	Materials
• Review two ways to interpret division equations • Review how to mentally divide numbers with trailing zeros by a one-digit number	• None

Memory Work

- **What do we call the number to be divided?** *The dividend.*
- **What do we call the number we divide by?** *The divisor.*
- **What do we call the result when we divide two numbers?** *The quotient.*
- **What do we call an amount that is left over after division?** *The remainder.*

You'll find suggested memory work review questions at the beginning of each lesson from this point forward. You'll review memory work daily, and you'll add new topics to the rotation as your child studies them. If you know your child already has a memory work item fully memorized, feel free to replace the suggested question with an item that she doesn't know as well. Or, if your child needs more practice with a particular fact, review it every day until she knows it more thoroughly.

Warm-up (A): Review Two Ways to Interpret Division Equations

In younger grades, you learned two different ways to interpret division equations. Division situations always involve splitting a total into equal groups. Sometimes, we use division to find the *size* of each group. Other times, we use division to find the *number* of equal groups. Read aloud both word problems in part A.

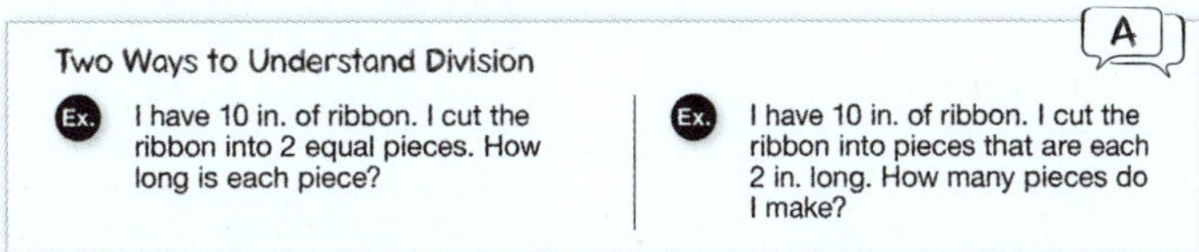

What do these word problems have in common? *Sample answers: Both involve cutting ribbon into parts. You divide 10 by 2 to find the answer for both problems.*

How are these problems different from each other? *Sample answer: One is about cutting the ribbon into 2 equal parts. The other is about cutting the ribbon into parts that are 2 inches long.*

Both of these problems involve cutting a ribbon into equal parts. In the first problem, we divide the total length by the number of groups or parts. The answer is the *size* of each group or part.

In the second problem, we divide the total by the size of each of group or part. The answer is the *number* of groups or parts.

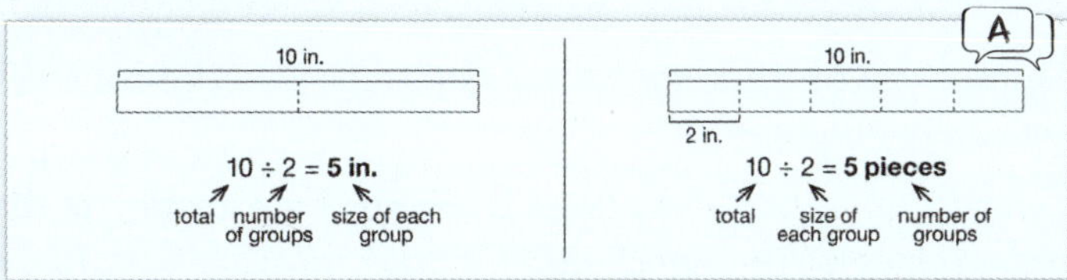

In the first problem, the answer is *5 inches*. In the second problem, the answer is *5 pieces*. Both problems have 5 as their numerical answer, but the 5 means something different in each problem. Always make sure to label your answers when you solve word problems and think about whether your answer makes sense.

> Understanding both interpretations of division will make it easier for your child to learn mental division strategies in Unit 6 and fraction division strategies in Unit 13.

Now, you get to write your own division word problems! Your first word problem should be about dividing 36 of something into 4 equal groups. Your second word problem should be about dividing 36 of something into equal groups of 4. Have your child write two word problems and label the quotients to match.

Sample word problems and labels.

If your child has trouble, suggest some topics for her word problems: **You could write your word problems about a group of 36 children. Or 36 pounds of jelly beans!**

Activity (B): Review Mental Division

Today, we'll review mental division. The text describes the steps for mentally dividing numbers with trailing zeros by one-digit numbers. Have your child read aloud the top section of the text.

B

Mental Division

1. Underline the trailing zeros.
2. Divide the other digits.
3. Tack on the underlined trailing zeros.

Ex. 18,000 ÷ 6 = ?
18 thousands ÷ 6 = 3 thousands
18,<u>000</u> ÷ 6 = **3,000**

Read aloud the first example: ***18,000 divided by 6 equals what?***

- **18 thousands divided by 6 equals 3 thousands.**
- **18,000 has 3 trailing zeros, so you underline 3 zeros.**
- **After you divide 18 thousands by 6, you tack the 3 zeros back on to show that you have 3 thousands.**
- **18,000 divided by 6 equals 3,000.**

> If your child has trouble understanding the connection between the steps and place-value, use play money to model the problem. Place 18 thousand-dollar bills on the table and have your child divide them into 6 equal groups. **We divide the 18 thousands into 6 equal groups. There are 3 thousands in each group.**

Have your child read aloud the bottom section of the text. Use the following questions to discuss the vocabulary words in the text.

- Underline the word *divisible*. **What does it mean if a number is divisible by another number?** *Sample answer: You can divide the first number evenly by the second number.* **So, if a number isn't divisible by another number, it means it can't be evenly divided by the number.**

- Underline the word *divisor.* **What is the divisor in a division problem?** *Sample answer: The number you divide by.*

If the non-zero digits aren't divisible by the divisor, try underlining fewer zeros.	Ex. 200 ÷ 4 = ? 2 hundreds ÷ 4 = ? 2 isn't divisible by 4. Try underlining only one zero. 200 ÷ 4 = ? 20 tens ÷ 4 = 5 tens 200 ÷ 4 = **50**

Point to the matching example. **Here's an example to help us understand what the text is saying. We want to divide 2 hundreds by 4, but 2 isn't divisible by 4. So, we underline just 1 zero and think of 200 as 20 tens. 20 tens divided by 4 equals 5 tens, or 50.**

If your child has trouble understanding this concept, model 200 with 2 hundred-dollar bills. **If 4 friends want to share this money, they need to trade the 2 hundred-dollar bills for 20 ten-dollar bills. Then, each of them can take 5 ten-dollar bills, or $50.**

Can you explain this idea in your own words? *Sample answer: If you can't divide the digits that aren't zero by the divisor, don't underline so many zeros. Think of the problem as dividing the next-smaller place instead.*

Have your child follow the steps to solve the practice problems.

		B
350 ÷ 7 = 50	6,400 ÷ 8 = 800	400 ÷ 5 = 80
3,500 ÷ 7 = 500	640 ÷ 8 = 80	40,000 ÷ 5 = 8,000
35,000 ÷ 7 = 5,000	64,000 ÷ 8 = 8,000	4,000 ÷ 5 = 800

Independent Practice and Review

Have your child complete the Lesson 1.3 Practice and Review workbook pages.

The workbook pages occasionally include optional starred problems. These problems provide extra challenge and give your child the chance to stretch her skills. If your child struggles with the challenge problems or feels frustrated by them, feel free to skip them.

Lesson 1.4
Review Long Division

Purpose	Materials
• Trade play money to concretely divide tens and ones • Review how to use the long division algorithm to divide by one-digit numbers	• Play money • Die

Memory Work	
	• **What do we call the result when we add numbers together?** *The sum.* • **What do we call the result when we subtract a number from another number?** *The difference.* • **What do we call the result when we multiply two numbers?** *The product.* • **What do we call the numbers in a multiplication equation that we multiply together?** *Factors.*

Warm-up (A): Trade Play Money to Divide

Today, we'll review long division. First, we'll do a hands-on review with play money. Then, we'll review the written steps.

If your child remembers and understands the steps in the long division algorithm, you can skip this warm-up activity. If you find later in the lesson that your child is confused or has forgotten the steps, return to the warm-up before continuing with the steps in the written process.

Let's pretend 3 friends work together to earn $85 and want to divide the money evenly. Put 8 ten-dollar bills and 5 one-dollar bills on the table. **How many ten-dollar bills does each friend get?** *2.* Arrange 6 of the ten-dollar bills in groups of 2. Leave the remaining bills off to the side.

There are still 2 ten-dollar bills and 5 one-dollar bills. How can you divide them as evenly as possible? *Trade the ten-dollar bills for one-dollar bills.* Trade the 2 ten-dollar bills for 20 one-dollar bills. **How many one-dollar bills does each friend get?** *8.* Place 8 one-dollar bills next to each group of ten-dollar bills. **So, how much money does each person earn in all?** *$28.* **How much money is left over?** *$1.*

What do you think the friends would do with the leftover $1? *Sample answer: Trade it for cents and divide the cents as evenly as possible.*

Now, let's pretend 5 friends work together to earn $115. Put 1 hundred-dollar bill, 1 ten-dollar bill, and 5 one-dollar bills on the table. **We don't have enough hundred-dollar bills for each person to get one, so we need to trade the hundred-dollar bill for 10 ten-dollar bills.** Trade the hundred-dollar bill for 10 ten-dollar bills.

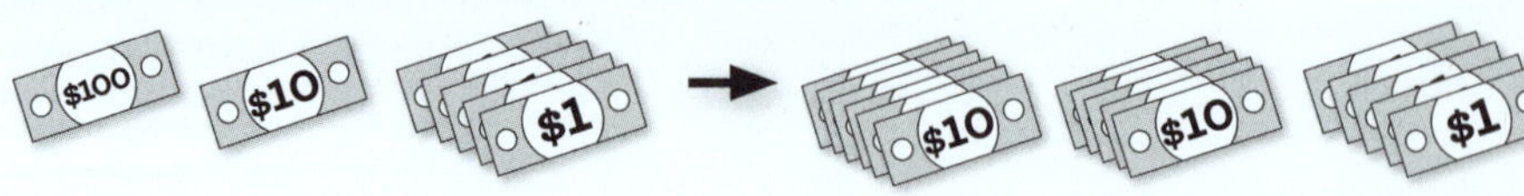

Have your child divide the ten-dollar bills as evenly as possible. **How many ten-dollar bills does each person get?** *2*.

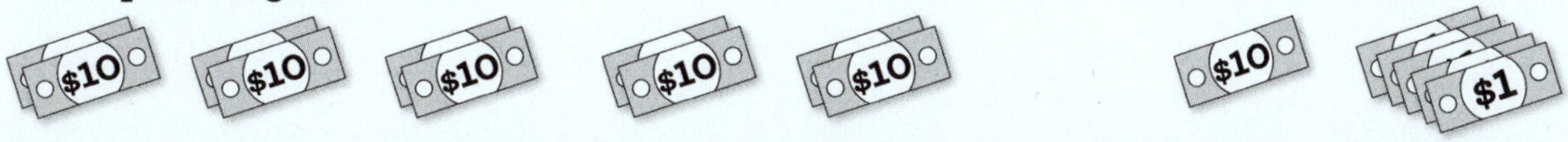

Trade the remaining 1 ten-dollar bill for 10 one-dollar bills. Have your child divide the resulting 15 one-dollar bills as evenly as possible. **How many one-dollar bills does each person get?** *3*.

So, how much money does each person earn in all? *$23*. **How much money is left over?** *$0*.

Activity (A): Review Long Division

Now, let's review the written steps for long division. Have your child read aloud the steps in part A. Point to the arrow alongside the steps. **When we divide with long division, we start with the largest place in the dividend. We repeat the steps until we have divided all the digits.**

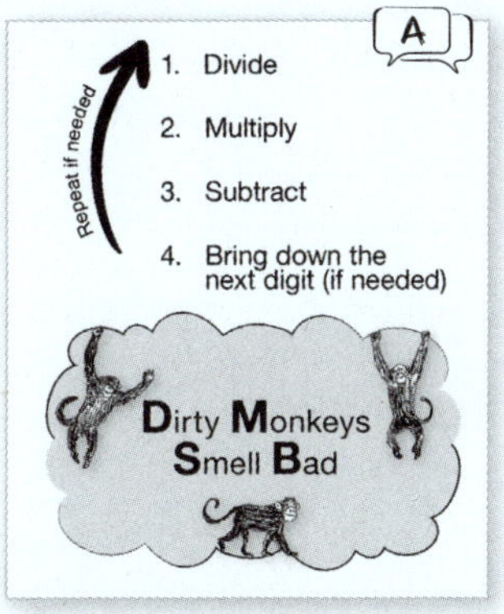

To remember the steps, just think, "Dirty Monkeys Smell Bad." The first letter of each word matches the first letter of each step.

The first example problem shows how to use long division to divide 85 by 3. It's the same as the first problem you solved in the warm-up.

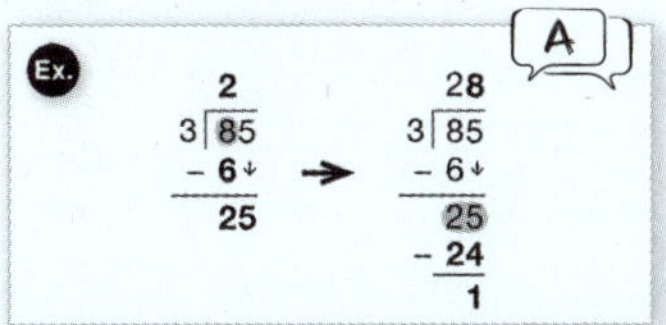

We start with the tens-place. Use the following questions to discuss how to divide the tens in the first example. Point to each number as you discuss it.

- **What's the first step?** *Divide.* **8 divided by 3 equals 2.**
- **What's the second step?** *Multiply.* **2 times 3 equals 6.**
- **What's the third step?** *Subtract.* **8 minus 6 equals 2.**
- **What's the fourth step?** *Bring down the next digit (if needed).* **We bring down the 5 ones.**

Then, we follow the steps again to divide the ones. We have 2 tens and 5 ones left to divide, so we have a total of 25 ones left to divide. Use the following questions to discuss how to divide the ones. Point to each number as you discuss it.

- **What's the first step?** *Divide.* **25 divided by 3 equals 8.**
- **What's the second step?** *Multiply.* **8 times 3 equals 24.**
- **What's the third step?** *Subtract.* **25 minus 24 equals 1.**

- **What's the fourth step?** *Bring down the next digit (if needed).* **There are no more digits to divide, so we're done. What's 85 divided by 3?** *28, with a remainder of 1.*

If your child has trouble understanding the written steps, use play money to model each step (as in the warm-up).

Now, let's review how to use the steps to divide 115 by 5. We only have 1 hundred, so we can't divide the hundreds into equal groups. Instead, we think of the 1 hundred as 10 tens. There are 11 tens in all, so we divide the 11 tens by 5. Discuss the second example step-by-step in the same way.

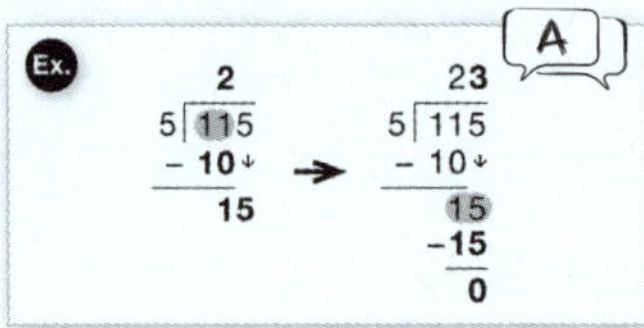

Activity (B): Play Roll and Divide

Play Roll and Divide.

Like many games in this program, Roll and Divide provides the opportunity for your child to both practice arithmetic and develop his logical reasoning skills. If your child is still developing fluency with long division, it's fine for him to write the divisors in the long division problems without much thought. But, if your child is mostly fluent with long division, encourage him to be more strategic and use estimation and mental math to figure out the high-scoring placements for his rolls.

Roll and Divide

Materials: Die

Object of the Game: Score more points than your opponent by creating larger remainders.

On your turn, roll the die. If you roll a 1, roll again until you roll a different number.

Choose a problem on your scorecard and write the number on the die as the divisor for the problem. (You do not have to complete the problems in order.) Then, solve the problem. The remainder is your score for that problem. If there is no remainder, your score is 0.

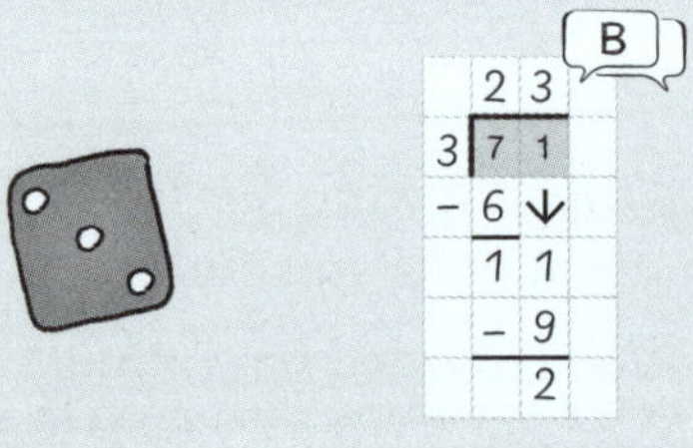

71 divided by 3 = 23 R2, so your score is 2.

Take turns rolling the die and completing the problems. Play until both players have completed their entire scorecard. Find the sum of each player's remainders. Whoever has the greater sum wins the game.

Independent Practice and Review

Have your child complete the Lesson 1.4 Practice and Review workbook pages.

Lesson 1.5
Review Line Plots and Averages

Purpose	Materials
• Practice mental multiplication and division • Review how to interpret line plots • Review how to find an average	• None
Memory Work	• **What's zero times any number?** *Zero.* • **What's zero divided by any other number?** *Zero.* • **What's any number divided by zero?** *Undefined.*

If your child doesn't remember the answer to a memory work question, give her a hint or simply tell her the answer. She will have many opportunities to memorize this information over the course of the year.

Warm-up: Practice Mental Multiplication and Division

Have your child solve the following mental math problems.

- 400 × 2 = *800*
- 400 × 5 = *2,000*
- 400 × 9 = *3,600*
- 400 × 10 = *4,000*
- 400 ÷ 4 = *100*
- 400 ÷ 2 = *200*
- 400 ÷ 5 = *80*
- 400 ÷ 8 = *50*

If your child has trouble keeping mental math problems in her head, write the problems horizontally on a piece of scrap paper. Do not allow her to solve them with long division or the written multi-digit multiplication algorithm.

Activity (A): Review How to Interpret Line Plots and Find Averages

Last year, you learned how to create and interpret line plots. We use line plots to organize data sets and make it easier to understand the data.

An apple farmer weighed baskets of apples to make this line plot. Each X stands for one basket of apples. The number below each X tells how much that basket weighed. The weight of each basket is called a value. Have your child read aloud the top part of the text box.

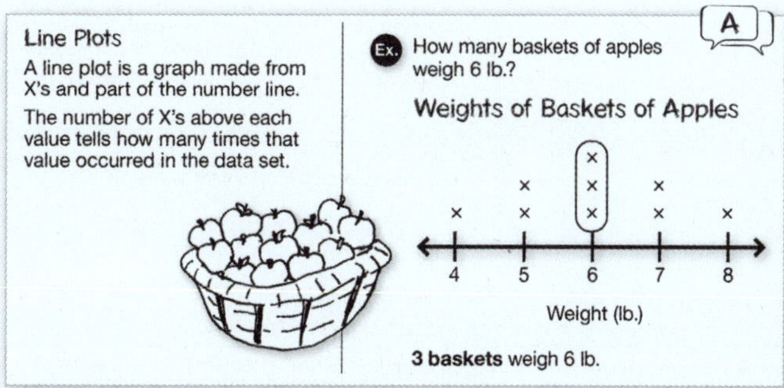

Read the example question aloud: **How many baskets of apples weigh 6 pounds?**

- Point to the 3 X's above the 6 on the line plot. **There are 3 X's above 6, so that means 3 baskets weigh 6 pounds.**
- **How many baskets weigh 4 pounds?** *1.*
- **How many baskets weigh 5 pounds?** *2.*
- **How many baskets weigh 7 pounds?** *2.*

- **How many baskets weigh 8 pounds?** *1.*
- **How many baskets did the farmer weigh in all?** *9.* If your child isn't sure, suggest she count the number of X's on the line plot.

You also learned how to find averages last year. We often use the word *average* in everyday life to describe the usual or most common value. For example, we might say that the average weight of an African elephant is 12,000 pounds. Does that mean that every elephant weighs 12,000 pounds? *No.* **It just means that a medium-sized elephant weighs about 12,000 pounds. Some are larger and some are smaller.**

To find an average in math, we divide the sum of the values by the number of values. Have your child read the bottom part of the text box aloud.

A

Averages

The average is one way to describe the "center" of a data set. To find the average:

1. Add up all the values in the data set.
2. Divide by the number of values in the data set.

Ex. What's the average weight of the baskets of apples?

4 + 5 + 5 + 6 + 6 + 6 + 7 + 7 + 8 = 54
54 ÷ 9 = **6 lb.**

If you split all the apples evenly into 9 baskets, each basket would weigh 6 lb.

The line plot in the first example tells how much each basket weighs.

- **To find the average, we first add up the weights of all the baskets. What's the sum of the weights?** *54 pounds.* **If you poured all the apples into one big basket, you would have 54 pounds of apples.**
- **Then, we divide by the number of values. The farmer weighed 9 baskets of apples, so there are 9 values in the data set. 54 divided by 9 equals 6, so the average weight is 6 pounds. If you split the apples into 9 baskets of equal weight, each basket would weigh 6 pounds.**

The farmer also recorded the weights of some pumpkins. Let's use the values in this data set to make a line plot. The first pumpkin weighed 9 pounds. Have your child draw a small X above the 9 on the line plot and cross out the 9 in the list (so she knows she's already drawn the matching X.) Repeat for the rest of the data. Encourage her to draw each X the same size. Then, help your child use the line plot to answer the questions.

A

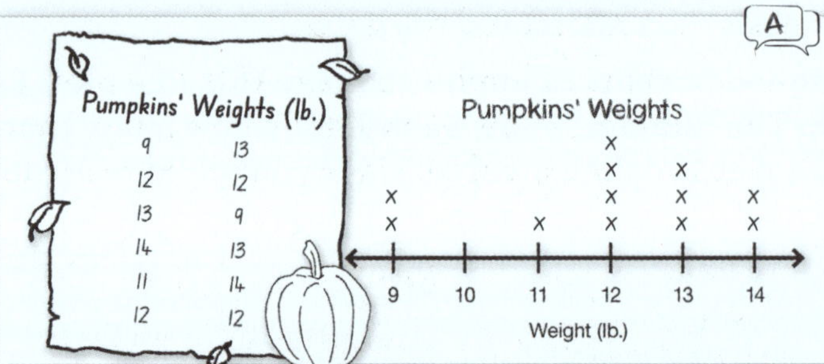

What's the total weight of all the pumpkins?	How many pumpkins' weights are represented in the data set?	What's the average weight of the pumpkins?
9 + 9 + 11 + 12 + 12 + 12 + 12 + 13 + 13 + 13 + 14 + 14 = 144 *lb.*	12	144 ÷ 12 = 12 *lb.*

Your child may complete the calculations on scrap paper if she needs more room than is provided on the Lesson Activities page.

Independent Practice and Review

Have your child complete the Lesson 1.5 Practice and Review workbook pages.

The Review pages review many of the skills covered in *Fourth Grade Math with Confidence*. If you find that your child has forgotten one of the skills included on the Review pages (or if you didn't use *Fourth Grade Math with Confidence*), briefly explain it to her.

It's normal for children to sometimes feel overwhelmed or tired by the length of the Practice and Review pages, especially at the beginning of the year. If needed, break up the work and have your child complete the Review page at a different time of day than the Practice page.

Lesson 1.6
Review Measurement Conversions

Purpose	Materials
• Review measurement units • Review how to multiply or divide to convert measurements	• Memory Work (Blackline Master 1)

Memory Work

- **How many inches equal 1 foot?** *12.*
- **How many feet equal 1 yard?** *3.*
- **How many inches equal 1 yard?** *36.*
- **How many feet equal 1 mile?** *5,280.*

This lesson begins with a scavenger hunt activity to review the concrete meanings of the measurement units covered in *Fourth Grade Math with Confidence*. If the scavenger hunt activity takes your child a long time, split the lesson over two days:

- Day 1: Complete the scavenger hunt in part A. Have your child complete the Review page.
- Day 2: Complete the teaching activity in part B. Have your child complete the Practice page.

Warm-up (A): Review Measurement Units with a Scavenger Hunt

In younger grades, you learned how to measure with both the U.S. customary system and the metric system. We'll warm up today with a measurement scavenger hunt.

Show your child part A. **The units in the top two rows are part of the U.S. customary system. They're used in the U.S., and sometimes in the United Kingdom and Canada. The units in the bottom two rows are part of the metric system. The metric system is the main measurement system in most of the world. It's also the main measurement system for scientists.**

Have your child find something in your home that matches each description. For the items marked with an asterisk, he can simply write a description of a distance that roughly matches the description. Help as needed, and accept any reasonable answer.

A

Measurement Scavenger Hunt

About 1 foot long *loaf of bread*	About 1 inch long *eraser*	About 1 yard long *desk*	* About 1 mile long *distance to the park*
Weighs about 1 pound *box of pasta*	Weighs about 1 ounce *glue stick*	Holds about 1 fluid ounce *medicine cup*	Holds about 1 cup *mug*
About 1 meter long *stove*	About 1 centimeter long *macaroni noodle*	About 1 millimeter long *pen tip*	* About 1 kilometer long *distance to the library*
Weighs about 1 gram *paper clip*	Weighs about 1 kilogram *cantaloupe*	Holds about 1 milliliter *eyedropper*	Holds about 1 liter *bottle of dish soap*

Sample answers.

Your child may use a ruler to help find matching items for the length units. Encourage him to use estimation to choose matching items for the weight and capacity units. Or, he can look at the labels of containers in your kitchen or bathroom to find items that fit the description.

Show your child the measurement section on the Memory Work list. **This list tells the conversion factor for each pair of units. A conversion factor is a number that we multiply or divide by to convert measurements. For example, the conversion factor for feet and inches is 12, because 1 foot equals 12 inches.** Leave the Memory Work list out for your child to refer to during the rest of the lesson.

Measurement Conversion Factors

1 foot = 12 inches	1 centimeter = 10 millimeters
1 yard = 3 feet	1 meter = 100 centimeters
1 yard = 36 inches	1 kilometer = 1,000 meters
1 mile = 5,280 feet	1 kilogram = 1,000 grams
1 pound = 16 ounces	1 liter = 1,000 milliliters
1 cup = 8 fluid ounces	

Your child does not need to memorize the term "conversion factor."

Activity (B): Multiply or Divide to Convert Measurements

Today, we'll review how to multiply or divide by conversion factors to convert measurements. Have your child read the text box aloud.

B

Multiply or Divide to Convert Measurements

To convert from a larger unit to a smaller unit, multiply by the conversion factor. Add on any extra smaller units.

Ex. 4 yd. 1 ft. = ______ ft.

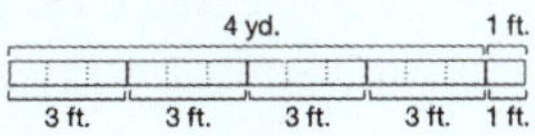

4 × 3 = 12
12 + 1 = 13
4 yd. 1 ft. = **13 ft.**

To convert from a smaller unit to a larger unit, divide by the conversion factor.

Ex. 37 mm = ______ cm

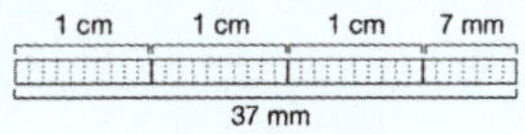

37 ÷ 10 = 3 R7
37 mm = **3 cm 7 mm**

In the first example, we want to convert 4 yards 1 foot to feet.

- **Which unit is larger, a yard or a foot?** *A yard.* If your child isn't sure, have him hold his hands 1 yard apart and then 1 foot apart. Or, have him look at the Memory Work list: **1 yard equals 3 feet, so 1 yard is larger than 1 foot.**
- **We're converting from a larger unit to a smaller unit, so we multiply first.**
- **There are 3 feet in each yard, so we start by multiplying 4 times 3. 4 yards equal 12 feet.**
- **Then, we add on the 1 extra foot. 12 plus 1 equals 13, so 4 yards 1 foot equals 13 feet.**

In the next example, we want to convert 37 millimeters to centimeters.

- **Which unit is larger, a millimeter or a centimeter?** *A centimeter.* If your child isn't sure, have him hold his fingers 1 millimeter apart and then 1 centimeter apart. Or, have him look at the Memory Work list: **1 centimeter equals 10 millimeters, so 1 millimeter is smaller than 1 centimeter.**
- **We're converting from a smaller unit to a larger unit, so we divide.**
- **Each group of 10 millimeters equals 1 centimeter, so we divide 37 by 10.**
- **37 divided by 10 is 3 with a remainder of 7. 37 millimeters equal 3 centimeters 7 millimeters.**

One way to remember whether to multiply or divide is to think of this rhyme: *Whole to parts? Multiply to start! Parts to whole? Division's in control!*

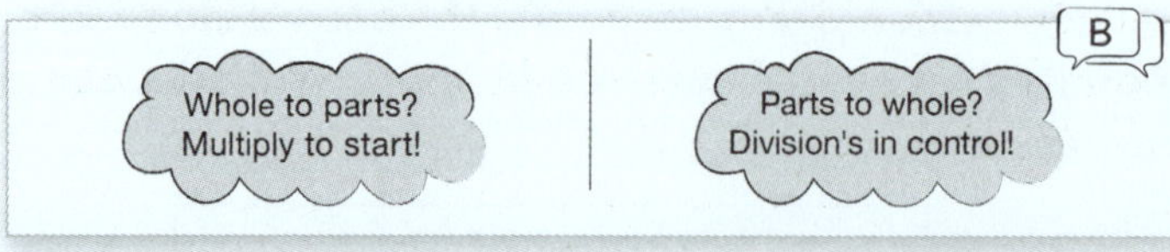

This rhyme uses "whole" and "parts" (rather than larger and smaller units) so that the rhyme can be generalized to other multiplication and division situations. If your child is confused by this terminology, explain that converting a larger unit to smaller units is like converting a whole unit to parts of the unit. Converting a smaller unit to a larger unit is like converting parts of a unit to the whole unit.

If your child enjoys hand motions, teach him these hand motions to help memorize the rhyme.

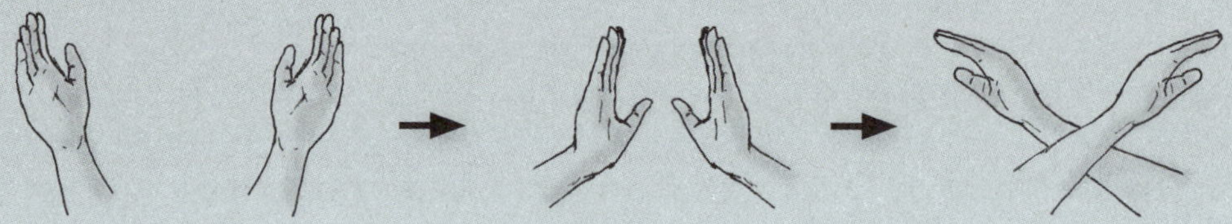

Whole... ...to parts? Multiply to start!

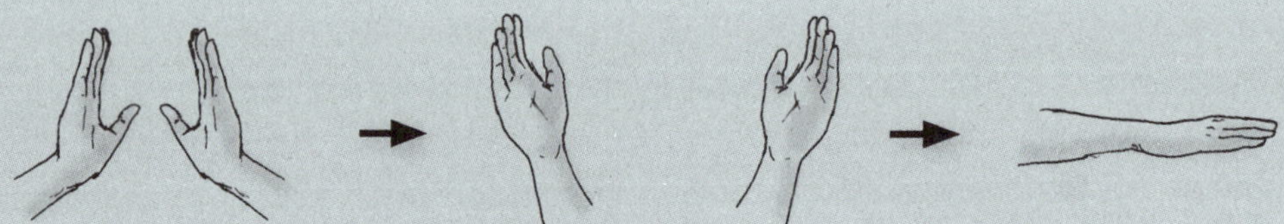

Parts... ...to whole? Division's in control!

Demonstrate how to solve the first practice problem.

- **We want to convert 5 cups to fluid ounces. Which unit is larger, a cup or a fluid ounce?** *A cup.* **We're converting from a larger unit to a smaller unit, so we multiply.**
- **What's the conversion factor?** *8.* If your child's not sure, have him look at the Memory Work list.
- Write "5 × 8 =" to begin an equation. **What's 5 times 8?** *40.* Write 40 to complete the equation and write 40 in the blank.

5 c. = 40 fl. oz.

$5 \times 8 = 40$

Have your child complete the rest of the practice problems in the same way.

2 kg 150 g = 2,150 g

$2 \times 1{,}000 = 2{,}000$

$2{,}000 + 150 = 2{,}150$

20 oz. = 1 lb. 4 oz.

$20 \div 16 = 1\ R4$

Independent Practice and Review

Have your child complete the Lesson 1.6 Practice and Review workbook pages.

If your child has trouble recalling measurement conversion factors, allow him to refer to the Memory Work list while he completes the Practice and Review pages.

Lesson 1.7
Find Missing Numbers in Equations

Purpose	Materials
• Think backwards to solve number riddles • Find missing numbers in equations	• None

Memory Work	
	• **How many ounces equal 1 pound?** *16.* • **How many fluid ounces equal 1 cup?** *8.*

Warm-up: Solve Number Riddles

Ask your child the following number riddles:

- **I'm thinking of a number. If you multiply my number by 6, you get 24. What's my number?** *4.* If your child's not sure, suggest she divide 24 by 4.
- **I'm thinking of a number. If you subtract 5 from my number, you get 30. What's my number?** *35.* If your child's not sure, suggest she add 5 plus 30.
- **I'm thinking of a number. If you divide my number by 4, you get 8. What's my number?** *32.* If your child's not sure, suggest she multiply 4 times 8.
- **I'm thinking of a number. If you add 20 to my number, you get 67. What's my number?** *47.* If your child's not sure, suggest she subtract 20 from 67.

Activity (A): Find Missing Numbers in Addition and Subtraction Equations

Today, we'll review how to find missing numbers in equations with all four basic operations. The four basic operations of math are addition, subtraction, multiplication, and division.

An equation is a number sentence with an equals sign. Equations combine numbers and operations to write a true mathematical statement. For example, 4 plus 3 equals 7 is an equation.

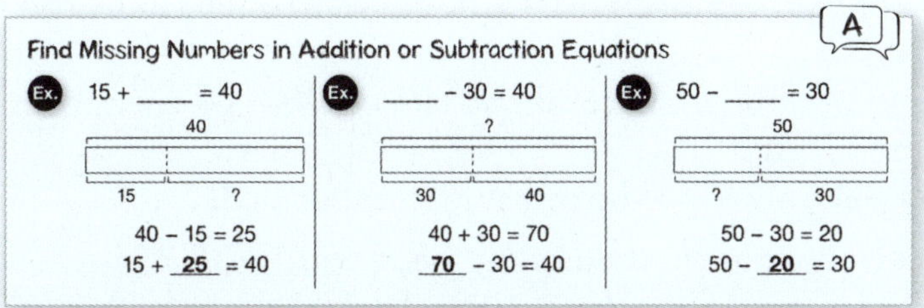

Read aloud the first example: ***15 plus what equals 40?***

- **When we add, we put together two parts to make a whole.**
- **In this problem, we know the whole and one part, so we can subtract to find the missing part.**
- **40 minus 15 equals 25, so the missing number is 25.**

Read aloud the second example: ***What minus 30 equals 40?***

- **When we subtract, we separate a whole quantity into two parts.**
- **We know the two parts and want to find the whole. So, we add the parts to find the whole.**
- **30 plus 40 equals 70, so the missing number is 70.**

Read aloud the third example: ***50 minus what equals 30?***

- **We know the whole and one of the parts. So, we subtract to find the other part.**
- **50 minus 30 equals 20, so the missing number is 20.**

If your child finds the bar diagrams confusing, use Part-Total diagrams (as in earlier levels of *Math with Confidence*) to represent the problems instead.

15 + ___ = 40   ___ − 30 = 40   50 − ___ = 30

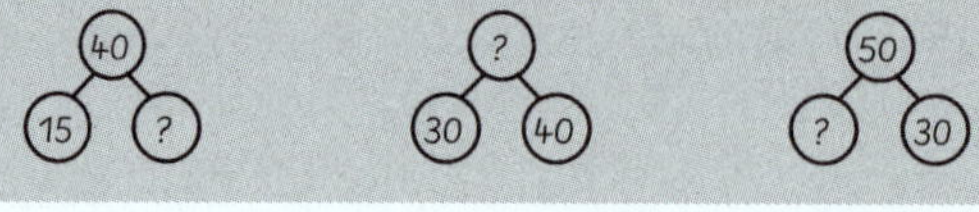

Have your child solve the practice problems. Have her write the equations she uses.

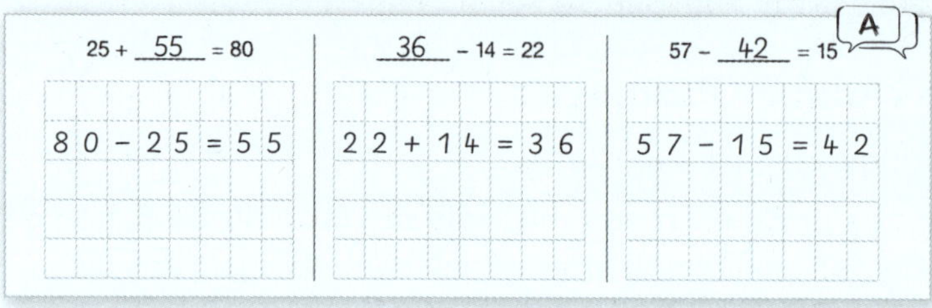

Writing the related equations helps your child think more deeply about the relationship between addition and subtraction.

Activity (B): Find Missing Numbers in Multiplication and Division Equations

Now, we'll find missing numbers in multiplication and division equations.

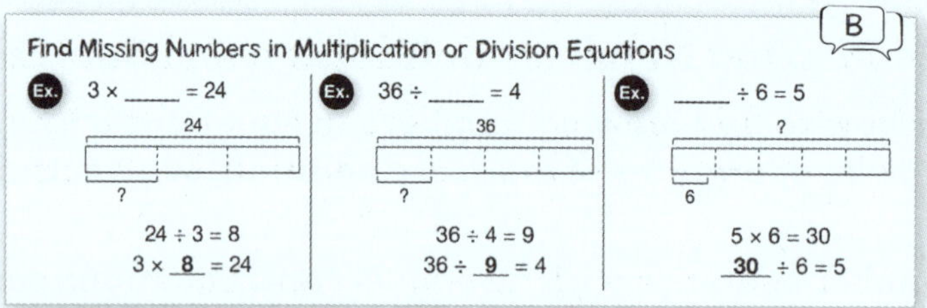

Read aloud the first example: ***3 times what equals 24?***

- **When we multiply, we multiply the number of groups times the size of each group to find the total.**
- **In this problem, we know the total and the number of groups. So, we divide to find the size of each group.**
- **24 divided by 3 equals 8, so the missing number is 8.**

Read aloud the second example: ***36 divided by what equals 4?***

- **We know the total and the number of groups.**
- **We divide the total by the number of groups to find the size of each group.**
- **36 divided by 4 equals 9, so the missing number is 9.**

Read aloud the third example: ***What divided by 6 equals 5?***

- **When we divide, we split a total into equal groups.**
- **In this problem, we know the number of groups and the size of each group. So, we multiply the number of groups times the size of each group to find the total.**
- **5 times 6 equals 30, so the missing number is 30.**

Have your child find the missing numbers in the practice problems. Have her write the equations she uses.

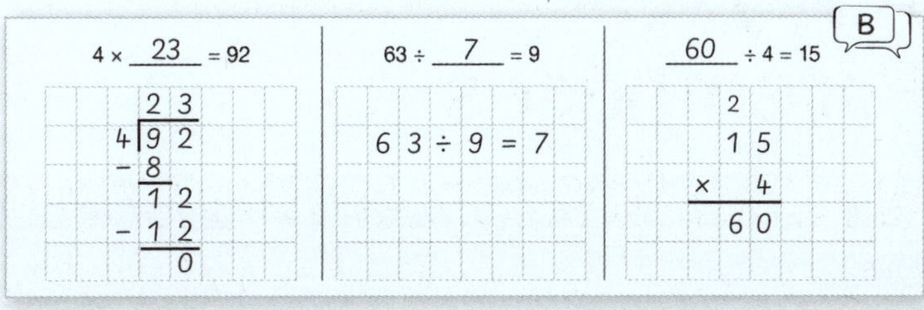

If you have time, have your child create a few equations with a missing number for you to solve.

Independent Practice and Review

Have your child complete the Lesson 1.7 Practice and Review workbook pages.

If possible, check your child's work as soon as she finishes, and have her correct any mistakes. Children benefit from immediate accountability, and your prompt attention shows that you value your child's work and effort.

Lesson 1.8
Review Parentheses

Purpose	Materials
• Introduce expressions • Find the value of expressions with parentheses	• Memory Work (Blackline Master 1)

Memory Work	
	• **How many millimeters equal 1 centimeter?** *10.* • **How many centimeters equal 1 meter?** *100.* • **How many meters equal 1 kilometer?** *1,000.* • **How many grams equal 1 kilogram?** *1,000.* • **How many milliliters equal 1 liter?** *1,000.*

Warm-up: Introduce Expressions

In the last lesson, you found missing numbers in equations. Today, you'll learn about expressions. In everyday life, when we talk about an expression, we mean the look on someone's face or a way that they share their thoughts and feelings. Have your child make a few different expressions with his face.

In math, the word *expression* means something very different! An expression is part of a number sentence that doesn't have an equals sign. Show your child the definitions of expressions and equations in the Memory Work list.

8×6	$8 \times 6 = 48$
expression	equation

Expressions can include any of the four basic operations. They can also include more than one operation. 3 plus 4, 10 divided by 2, or 5 times 7 plus 6 are all mathematical expressions.

> Expressions are "one side" of an equation. They cannot contain any of the following signs: =, <, >, ≤, or ≥. The memory work definition for fifth grade focuses on the fact that expressions cannot contain an equals sign. Your child will learn the more nuanced definition in future grades.

Activity (A): Evaluate Expressions with Parentheses

Today, we'll review how to find the value of expressions that have parentheses. Have your child read the left side of the text box aloud.

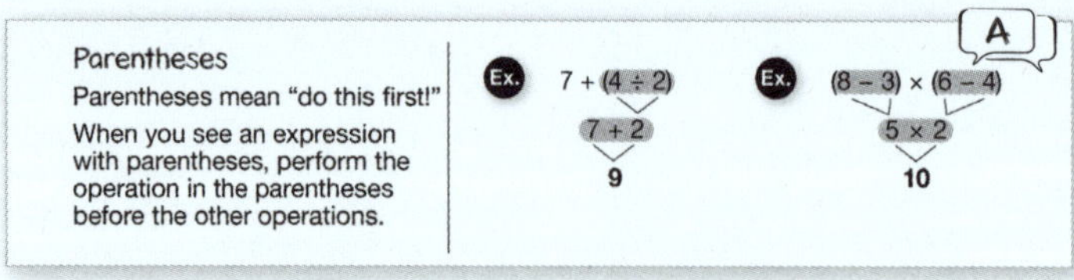

Read aloud the first example: ***7 plus the quantity 4 divided by 2.*** **When I say "the quantity," it means that the next part of the problem is in parentheses.**

- **4 divided by 2 is in parentheses, so you do that first. What's 4 divided by 2?** *2.* Point to the lines below 4 ÷ 2 that show how 4 ÷ 2 becomes 2 in the next line.
- **7 plus 2 equals 9, so the answer is 9.** Point to the lines below 7 + 2 that show how 7 + 2 becomes 9 in the final line.

Discuss the second example in the same way. Read it aloud as: ***The quantity 8 minus 3 times the quantity 6 minus 4.***

We call this process *evaluating* an expression. Listen to how the word *evaluate* has *value* in it. When you evaluate an expression, you find the value of the expression.

Cover the text box with your hand. **What do parentheses mean in a math problem?** *Do this first.*

When we evaluate expressions with multiple steps, we write each step on a new line, just like the examples. That helps prevent mistakes. Demonstrate how to solve the first practice problem.

- **8 divided by 4 is in parentheses, so I do that first. 8 divided by 4 is 2.** Draw lines below 8 and 4, and write 2 as shown.

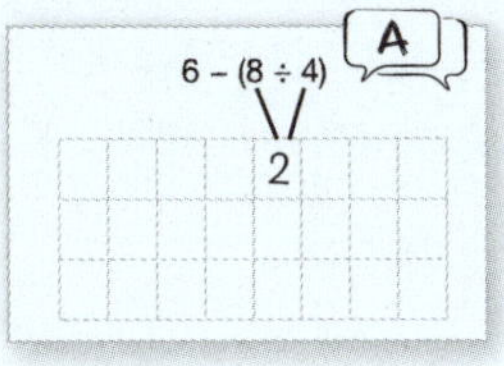

- **Then, I recopy the rest of the problem around it.** Write "6 –" before the 2.

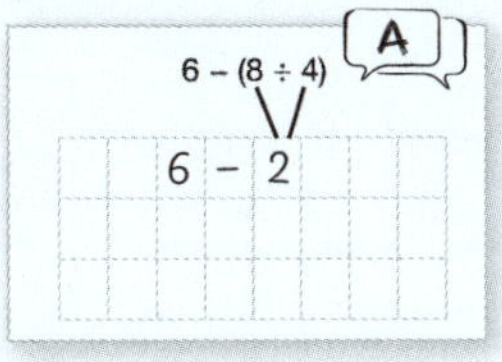

- **Last, I find 6 minus 2. 6 minus 2 is 4.** Draw lines below 6 and 2, and write 4 as shown.

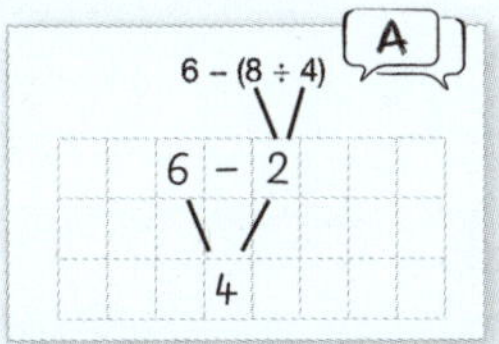

Have your child solve the practice problems in the same way.

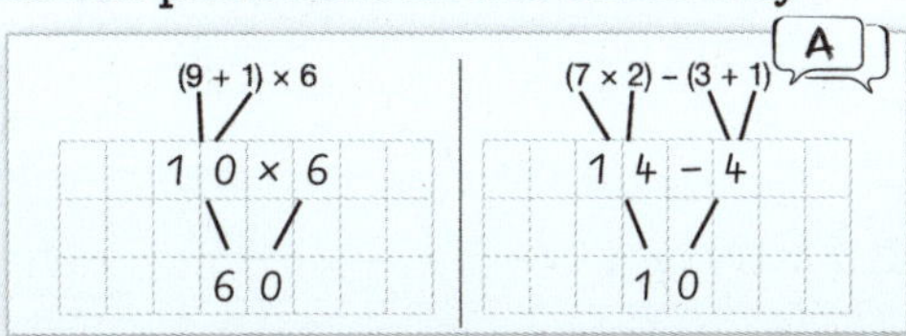

Even though your child can likely solve these problems mentally, require him to work downward and write each step on a new line. It may feel tedious and unnecessary, but it builds important habits for future grades when he'll solve algebraic equations in the same way. Drawing the lines connecting the steps (for example, from 6 – 2 to 4) is optional, and your child may skip this if he doesn't find these lines helpful.

If your child feels visually overwhelmed by these problems, have him use a highlighter to highlight each step before he completes it. For example, for (9 + 1) × 6, have him highlight 9 + 1 to remind him to complete that step first.

Activity (B): Play Parentheses Power (1-Player Game)

In this game, you insert parentheses into expressions to make their value as large as possible. Show your child the first problem. **Where could you put parentheses in this problem?** *Around 4 times 3 or around 3 plus 2.*

If you put parentheses around 4 times 3, what's the value of the expression? *14.* **If you put parentheses around 3 plus 2, what's the value of the expression?** *20.* **So, it's better to put the parentheses around 3 plus 2.**

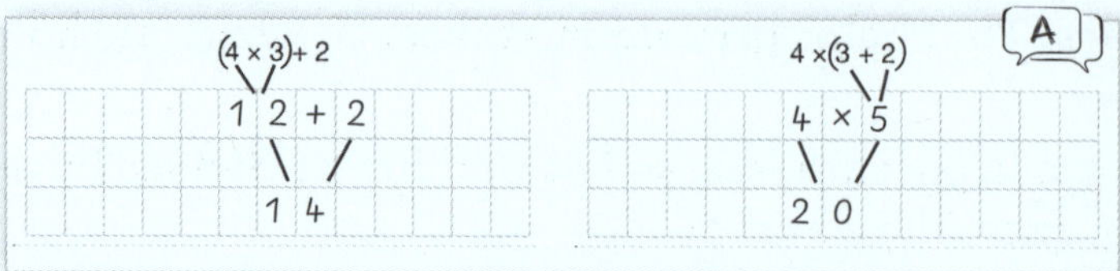

Sometimes in math, you just have to try things out! Have your child play Parentheses Power.

> *Fifth Grade Math with Confidence* includes a mix of one- and two-player games. If your child is ready for more independence in math, explain the directions for the one-player games to him and then have him complete these games independently.

Parentheses Power

Materials: None

Object of the Game: Insert parentheses into expressions to give the expressions as large a value as possible.

Write a pair of parentheses around one operation in each expression. Try to place the parentheses in the position that makes the value of the expression as large as possible. Then, evaluate the expression.

After you write parentheses and evaluate each expression, add up the value of all 6 expressions to find your total score. Use the scoring guide to see how well you did.

Independent Practice and Review

Have your child complete the Lesson 1.8 Practice and Review workbook pages.

Lesson 1.9
Order of Operations, Part 1

Purpose	Materials
• Understand the need for rules about the order of operations • Use the order of operations to evaluate expressions	• None

Memory Work	
	• **What are the four basic operations?** *Addition, subtraction, multiplication, and division.* • **What is an equation?** *A number sentence with an equals sign.* • **What is an expression?** *Part of a number sentence without an equals sign.*

This lesson teaches your child how to use the order of operations for expressions that contain addition, subtraction, multiplication, and division. Your child will learn how parentheses fit into the order of operations in Lesson 1.10. In *Sixth Grade Math with Confidence*, she'll learn about exponents and how they fit in the order of operations.

Warm-up (A): Why Do We Need Rules for the Order of Operations?

In the last lesson, you evaluated expressions with parentheses. You performed the operation in parentheses first. Show your child part A.

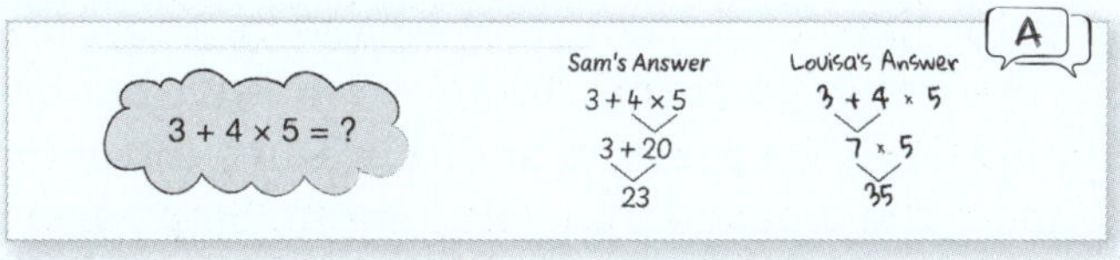

This expression doesn't have any parentheses. Sam and Louisa both evaluated this expression, but they got different answers!

- **What did Sam do first?** *Multiply 4 times 5.*
- **What did Sam do second?** *Add 3 plus 20.*
- **What answer did Sam get?** *23.*
- **What did Louisa do first?** *Add 3 plus 4.*
- **What did Louisa do second?** *Multiply 7 times 5.*
- **What answer did Louisa get?** *35.*
- **Why did Sam and Louisa get different answers?** *They chose different operations to do first.*

Today, you'll learn about the order of operations. By the end of the lesson, you'll know whether Sam or Louisa is right!

Activity (B): Learn the Order of Operations

Point to the number 9 at the top of the page (in the lesson number). **What number is this?** *9.* **Why does this symbol stand for the number 9?** *Sample answer: Because someone said so. I don't know!* **There's no particular reason that this number stands for 9. It's just something that everyone agrees on so we can communicate about numbers. I could make up my own number system if I wanted—but it wouldn't be very useful if no one else could understand it!**

Mathematicians have created a set of rules called the order of operations to use when they solve math problems with more than one operation. They could have chosen a different set of rules for the order of operations, but they decided to use this one. We follow the order of operations whenever we evaluate an expression so that everyone gets the same answer. Have your child read aloud the text.

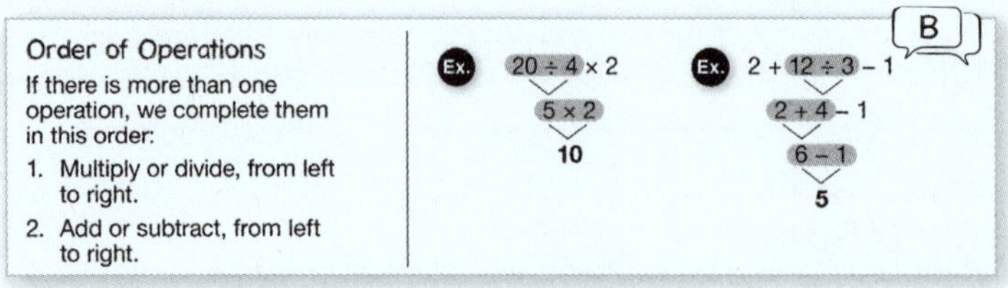

Read aloud the first example: ***20 divided by 4 times 2.***

- **What are the operations in this expression?** *Division and multiplication.*
- **In the order of operations, we perform multiplication and division in order from left to right.**
- Run your finger under the problem from left to right. Stop when you reach the division sign. **Does multiplication or division appear first in this problem?** *Division.*
- **So, we divide first.** Point to the lines under 20 ÷ 4. **20 divided by 4 equals 5.**
- **The only operation left is multiplication.** Point to the lines under 5 × 2. **5 times 2 equals 10.**

Read aloud the second example: ***2 plus 12 divided by 3 minus 1.***

- **What are the operations in this problem?** *Addition, division, and subtraction.*
- **In the order of operations, which of those operations comes first?** *Division.* **So, first we divide.** Point to the lines under 12 ÷ 3. *12 divided by 3 equals 4.*
- **What operations are left to perform?** *Addition and subtraction.*
- **In the order of operations, we perform addition and subtraction from left to right.**
- Run your finger under the problem from left to right. Stop when you reach the plus sign. **Does addition or subtraction appear first in this problem?** *Addition.*
- **So, next we add.** Point to the lines under 2 + 4. **2 plus 4 equals 6.**
- **Last, we subtract.** Point to the lines under 6 – 1. **6 minus 1 equals 5.**

Point at Sam and Louisa's answers in part A. **Who solved this problem correctly?** *Sam.* **Sam multiplied before he added, so he followed the order of operations correctly.**

Activity (B): Use the Order of Operations to Evaluate Expressions

Show your child the chart next to the first practice problem. **We'll use this chart to help perform the operations in the correct order. What do you think the M and D stand for?** *Multiplication and division.* **What do you think the A and S stand for?** *Addition and subtraction.* **The arrows remind you that you solve those pairs of operations in order from left to right.**

Demonstrate how to solve the first practice problem:

- Read the problem aloud: ***20 minus 10 plus 3.*** **What operations are in this problem?** *Subtraction and addition.* Circle S and A in the chart.
- **We perform addition and subtraction in the order we see them, from left to right.** Run your finger under the expression from left to right. Stop when you reach the minus sign. **The minus sign comes before the plus sign, so we subtract first. 20 minus 10 equals 10.** Draw lines below 20 and 10 and write 10 as shown. Write "+ 3" as shown.

- **Addition is the only operation left. 10 plus 3 equals 13.** Write 13 as shown.

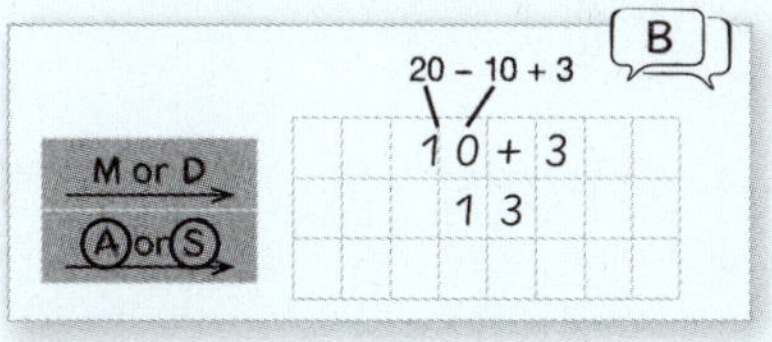

Always remember to perform addition and subtraction in whatever order they appear, from left to right. The same is true for multiplication and division.

Have your child solve the remaining practice problems in the same way. Make sure she writes out each step on a separate line.

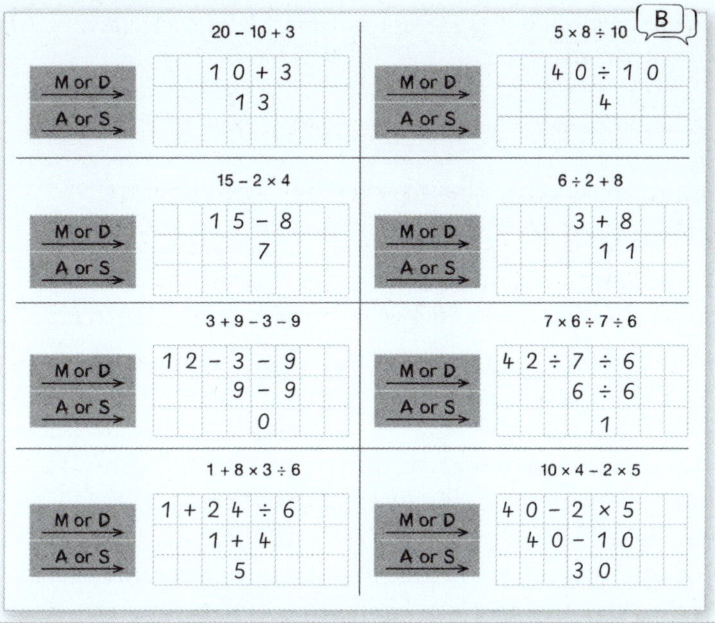

Many children will resist writing out steps they find unnecessary. This is a battle worth fighting! As these problems grow in complexity, it becomes very difficult to keep track of all the steps mentally. Writing out the steps also builds good habits for algebra in future grades.

Circling the letters on the chart or drawing lines between the expressions is optional, and your child may skip these steps if she doesn't find them helpful.

Independent Practice and Review

Have your child complete the Lesson 1.9 Practice and Review workbook pages.

Lesson 1.10
Order of Operations, Part 2

Purpose	Materials
• Practice using the order of operations to evaluate expressions • Use the order of operations to evaluate expressions with parentheses	• Playing cards • Unit Reference pages (pages 197-198 in Student Workbook A)

Memory Work
- **What are the four basic operations?** *Addition, subtraction, multiplication, and division.*
- **What is an equation?** *A number sentence with an equals sign.*
- **What is an expression?** *Part of a number sentence without an equals sign.*

Warm-up (A): Practice Using the Order of Operations

In the last lesson, you learned about the order of operations. These are the rules we use when we solve math problems with more than one operation. You learned that we multiply or divide, from left to right. Then, we add or subtract, from left to right.

Have your child use the order of operations to evaluate the expressions in part A. Have him circle the operations on the chart (as in Lesson 1.9) before he begins.

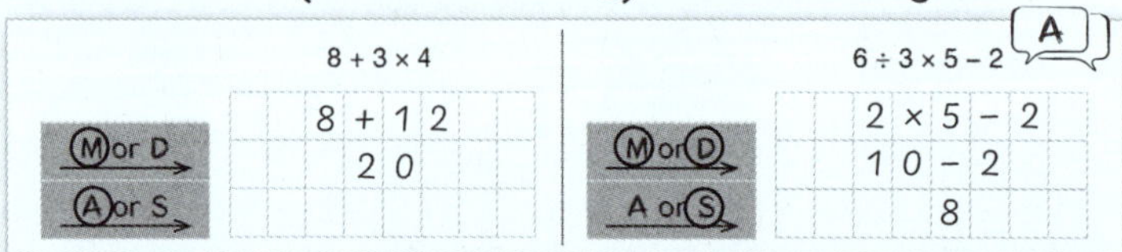

Activity (B): Use the Order of Operations with Parentheses

Today, you'll learn how to evaluate expressions with parentheses and multiple operations. Parentheses mean "do this first," so you complete the operations in parentheses before any other operations. Have your child read the text box aloud.

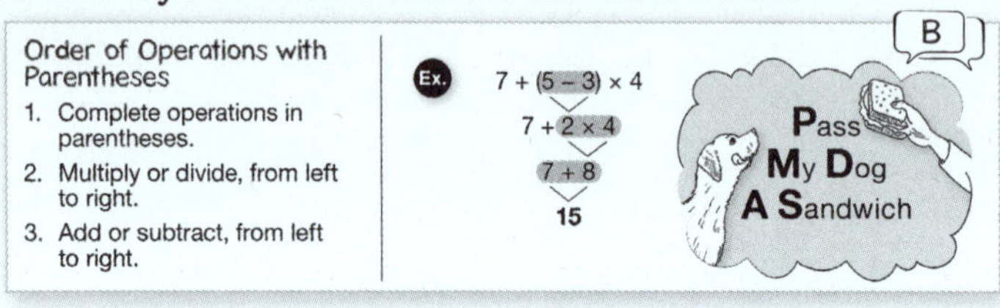

Read aloud the example: ***7 plus the quantity 5 minus 3, times 4.***

- **Are there parentheses in this expression?** *Yes.* **So, we perform the operation in parentheses first.** Point to the lines under 5 − 3. **5 minus 3 equals 2.**
- **What operations are left to perform in this problem?** *Addition and multiplication.*
- **In the order of operations, which comes first, addition or multiplication?** *Multiplication.*
- **So, we multiply next.** Point to the lines under 2 × 4. **2 times 4 equals 8.**
- **Last, we add.** Point to the lines under 7 + 8. **7 plus 8 equals 15.**

To remember the order of operations, just remember this silly sentence, "Pass my dog a sandwich." The first letter of each word matches one part of the order of operations.

Be careful though! You have to remember that multiplication *doesn't* come before division. Instead, we multiply or divide from left to right and do whichever comes first. The same is true for addition and subtraction.

Let's break up the silly sentence into chunks to help you remember which operations belong together. Pass. (Pause.) **My dog.** (Pause.) **A sandwich.**

Have your child repeat the sentence, with the pauses. Then, cover the order of operations list with your hand. **Can you name the operations in order?** *Sample answer: Parentheses, then multiplication and division, then addition and subtraction.* Allow your child to peek as needed.

Activity (C): Play Order of Operations War

Show your child the game board in part C. **In this game, you'll arrange digits in the blanks to create an expression with the greatest value possible.**

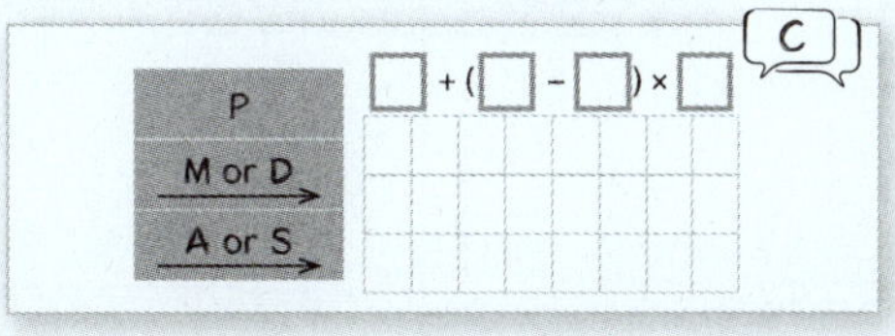

What do you think the P stands for in the order of operations charts? *Parentheses.* **When you circle the letters on these charts, don't circle the operation that's inside the parentheses. For example, in the first round of this game, don't circle the S for subtraction. That's because you'll do the subtraction when you evaluate the expression in parentheses. You don't need to circle it as a separate step.**

Play Order of Operations War.

Order of Operations War

Materials: Deck of playing cards, with 10s, jacks, queens, and kings removed (36 cards total)

Object of the Game: Have a greater total score than your opponent.

Shuffle the cards and place them face down in a pile.

Order of Operations War has 3 rounds. On your turn, flip over the top 4 cards in the pile. Use the digits to complete the blanks in the expression on your score card. (Complete the expressions in order from top to bottom.) Try to arrange the numbers to create an expression with the greatest value possible. Then, evaluate the expression. This value is your score for the round.

$5 + (9 - 2) \times 7$	$2 + (9 - 7) \times 5$	$9 + (5 - 2) \times 7$
$5 + 7 \times 7$	$2 + 2 \times 5$	$9 + 3 \times 7$
$5 + 49$	$2 + 10$	$9 + 21$
54	12	30

There are many possible plays for each combination of cards. These are some of the many possible plays if you draw a 2, 5, 7, and 9 for the first round. $5 + (9 - 2) \times 7$ yields the highest value, so that's the best play.

Take turns until both players have completed all 3 rounds. Each player finds the sum of their 3 scores, either mentally or on scrap paper. Whoever has the greater total score wins.

If part of the expression involves subtraction, you must arrange the numbers so that you subtract a smaller number from a larger number (and so the result is a positive number).

$5 + (2 - 9) \times 7$ (C)

You may not arrange the numbers in this way, since $2 - 9$ yields a negative number.

Activity: Introduce the Unit Reference Pages

Show your child the Unit 1 Reference pages (pages 197–198 in Workbook A). **These pages summarize what you learned in Unit 1. You will review what you learned in Unit 1 throughout the rest of the year. If you ever get stuck on a skill you learned in Unit 1, look back at these reference pages to help.**

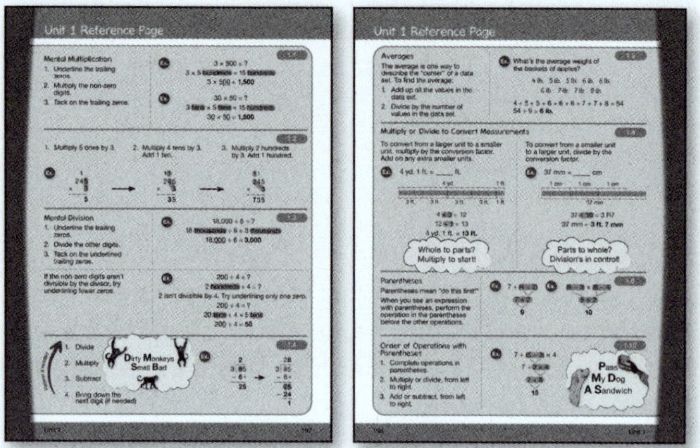

Each unit in *Fifth Grade Math with Confidence* has matching Unit Reference pages in the back of the workbook. If your child has trouble remembering how to complete a problem on the Review pages, encourage him to refer to these Unit Reference pages for help.

Independent Practice and Review

Have your child complete the Lesson 1.10 Practice and Review workbook pages. If needed, remind your child not to circle the letter on the chart that matches the operation within parentheses (since he will perform this operation when he evaluates the expression in parentheses).

Lesson 1.11
Enrichment (Optional)

Purpose	Materials
• Practice memory work • Appreciate how math can be used to answer real-life questions • Use mental multiplication to create a budget for a vacation • Summarize what your child has learned and assess your child's progress	• *How Many Guinea Pigs Can Fit on a Plane?: Answers to Your Most Clever Math Questions*, by Laura Overdeck • Travel brochures or internet access, optional

The final lesson in each unit is an optional enrichment lesson. These lessons assess your child's progress and help your child appreciate how math is used in everyday life.

Warm-up: Review Memory Work

Quiz your child on any of the memory work items that she struggled with during this unit.

Math Picture Book: *How Many Guinea Pigs Can Fit on a Plane?*

This year, we'll read a few pages from the book *How Many Guinea Pigs Can Fit on a Plane?* at the end of each unit. This fun book uses math to answer questions sent in by real kids. You'll be able to understand a lot of the calculations in the book, but it's okay if you don't understand every single one. Some of the topics are advanced for fifth grade, and you'll learn about them in the next few years.

Read pages 1–11 in *How Many Guinea Pigs Can Fit on a Plane?*

Some of the topics included in the book (such as the discussion of circles and pi on pages 2–3) are beyond fifth-grade level. Read these pages with your child as a preview of these advanced topics, and don't worry about your child fully understanding them.

Enrichment Activity: Estimate the Budget for a Vacation

In this activity, your child will estimate the budget for a vacation. Adjust this activity to fit your child and family. You can have her estimate the cost of a realistic family trip, an extravagant dream vacation, or something in-between.

In Lesson 1.1, we estimated the cost for a theme park vacation. Today, you get to choose a destination for an imaginary trip and estimate the cost of a vacation to that place.

Have your child choose a place she'd like to go and the number of days she'd like to stay. Help her brainstorm the types of expenses that the trip would involve, and then help her estimate the per-day or per-person cost for each expense. (Use the internet to find the approximate cost for each item, or simply tell her approximate numbers based on your experience.) Then, have her multiply and add to find the total estimated budget for the trip.

Grand Canyon Road Trip Budget

8 tanks of gas ($60 per tank) 8 × 60	$480
3 nights in the lodge ($400 per night) 3 × 400	$1,200
3 nights of camping ($50 per night) 3 × 50	$150
Groceries for camping and snacks $250	$250
Restaurant meals while staying at the lodge ($80 per person per day for 3 days) 5 × 80 × 3	$1,200
Souvenirs ($40 per person) 5 × 40	$200
Total cost	$3,480

Sample budget.

After your child completes the budget, discuss whether she's surprised by any of the costs. Also discuss the trade-offs between choices like camping versus staying in a hotel, or driving versus flying to a destination. For example: **Buying airplane tickets costs a lot more than driving, but you get to the destination much faster.** Or, **Restaurant meals for multiple people add up fast! Buying groceries and making your own meals saves a lot of money.**

> If your child would like to find the exact cost of the trip, she can use written multiplication or a calculator to find the total amount.

Unit Wrap-Up

Have your child complete the Unit 1 Wrap-Up.

> The final lesson in each unit includes an optional Unit Wrap-Up in the Student Workbook. You can use the Unit Wrap-Ups to informally review the material from the unit. Or, you can use them as tests to assess your child's progress more formally. (If you live in a state where you're required to provide evidence of learning, you may want to save them for your child's portfolio.) The Unit Wrap-Ups are completely optional, but children (and parents!) often find it very satisfying to see this concrete evidence of learning and growth.

Unit 1 Answer Key

1.1 Practice

Practice Draw a line from Start to End so that each problem is followed by the correct answer. You do not have to solve every problem.

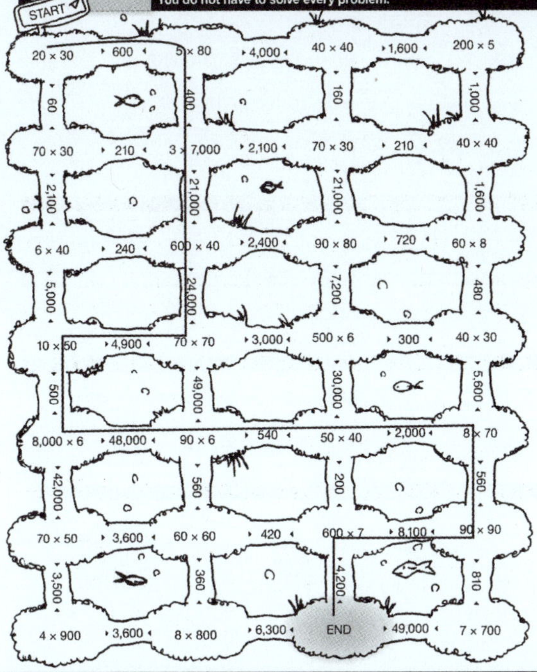

1.1 Review

Review Round to the underlined digit.

389 ≈ 400

508 ≈ 500

984 ≈ 1,000

4,645 ≈ 5,000

5,190 ≈ 5,000

8,088 ≈ 8,000

Complete.

$$\begin{array}{r} 768 \\ +\ 412 \\ \hline 1,180 \end{array} \qquad \begin{array}{r} 539 \\ -\ 278 \\ \hline 261 \end{array}$$

Complete the chart.

Hours	1	2	3	4	5	6
Minutes	60	120	180	240	300	360

Complete the missing fractions on the number lines.

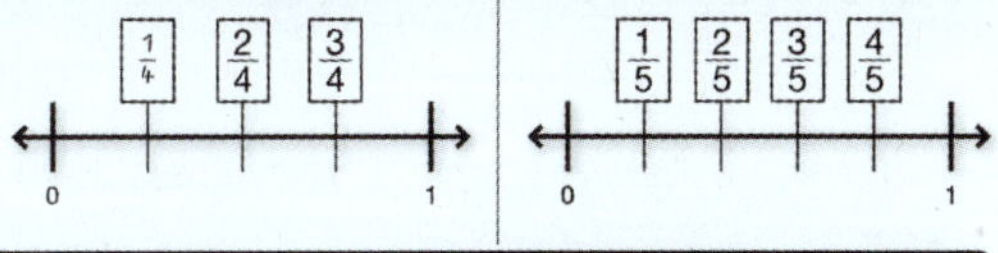

Use the clues to complete the chart.

- Julia is 11 years old.
- Sam is 3 years younger than Julia.
- Mom is 4 times as old as Julia.
- Dad is 5 times as old as Sam.
- Great-grandpa is 10 times as old as Sam.

Name	Age
Julia	11
Sam	8
Mom	44
Dad	40
Great-grandpa	80

1.2 Practice

Practice Find the products.

$$\begin{array}{r} 41 \\ \times\ 6 \\ \hline 246 \end{array} \quad \begin{array}{r} 73 \\ \times\ 5 \\ \hline 365 \end{array} \quad \begin{array}{r} 93 \\ \times\ 4 \\ \hline 372 \end{array} \quad \begin{array}{r} 86 \\ \times\ 3 \\ \hline 258 \end{array} \quad \begin{array}{r} 99 \\ \times\ 6 \\ \hline 594 \end{array}$$

$$\begin{array}{r} 343 \\ \times\ 2 \\ \hline 686 \end{array} \quad \begin{array}{r} 216 \\ \times\ 4 \\ \hline 864 \end{array} \quad \begin{array}{r} 1,027 \\ \times\ 3 \\ \hline 3,081 \end{array} \quad \begin{array}{r} 2,680 \\ \times\ 5 \\ \hline 13,400 \end{array}$$

Use the price list to answer the questions. Write the equations you use in the work space.

Airfare Sale

Seattle	$479
St. Louis	$406
Miami	$278
Boston	$390

WORK SPACE

How much do 3 tickets to St. Louis cost?

$1,218

$$\begin{array}{r} 406 \\ \times\ 3 \\ \hline 1,218 \end{array}$$

How much do 6 tickets to Boston cost?

$2,340

$$\begin{array}{r} 390 \\ \times\ 6 \\ \hline 2,340 \end{array}$$

How much do 4 tickets to Miami cost?

$1,112

$$\begin{array}{r} 278 \\ \times\ 4 \\ \hline 1,112 \end{array}$$

How much do 9 tickets to Seattle cost?

$4,311

$$\begin{array}{r} 479 \\ \times\ 9 \\ \hline 4,311 \end{array}$$

1.2 Review

Review Complete.

6 × 6 = 36	9 × 4 = 36	6 × 9 = 54
9 × 3 = 27	7 × 4 = 28	8 × 6 = 48
7 × 6 = 42	8 × 9 = 72	5 × 8 = 40
4 × 8 = 32	8 × 8 = 64	9 × 7 = 63

Complete the chart.

Meters	1	2	3	4	5	6
Centimeters	100	200	300	400	500	600

Find the area and perimeter.

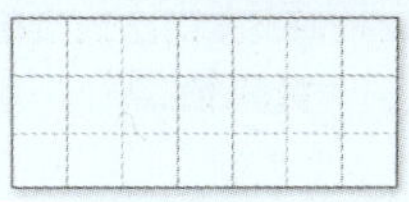

Perimeter: 20 cm

Area: 21 sq. cm

Write each number in expanded form.

789 = 700 + 80 + 9

708 = 700 + 8

7,080 = 7,000 + 80

7,890 = 7,000 + 800 + 90

Solve. Write the equations you use.

Harmony buys 3 tacos for $6 each and 2 burritos for $8 each. How much does she spend?

(3 × 6) + (2 × 8)
18 + 16
$34

Watson has $20. He buys 4 drinks for $3 each. How much money does he have left?

20 – (4 × 3)
20 – 12
$8

Unit 1 Answer Key

1.3 Practice

Practice Complete.

420 ÷ 7 = 60 4,200 ÷ 7 = 600	4,800 ÷ 6 = 800 48,000 ÷ 6 = 8,000	81,000 ÷ 9 = 9,000 810 ÷ 9 = 90
6,400 ÷ 8 = 800 640 ÷ 8 = 80	490 ÷ 7 = 70 49,000 ÷ 7 = 7,000	54,000 ÷ 6 = 9,000 5,400 ÷ 6 = 900
720 ÷ 9 = 80 7,200 ÷ 9 = 800	56,000 ÷ 8 = 7,000 5,600 ÷ 8 = 700	6,300 ÷ 7 = 900 630 ÷ 7 = 90
★ 450 ÷ 5 = 90	★ 3,200 ÷ 4 = 800	★ 25,000 ÷ 5 = 5,000

Solve. Write the equations you use.

Wyatt earns $160 for 8 hours of work. How much does he earn for each hour of work?

160 ÷ 8 = $20

Katelyn bakes 80 cupcakes. She puts 4 cupcakes in each box. How many boxes does she fill?

80 ÷ 4 = 20 boxes

Valentina has 40 cm of string. She cuts the string into pieces that are each 8 cm long. How many pieces of string does she make?

40 ÷ 8 = 5 pieces

Swim camp costs $200 for 5 days. How much does each day of camp cost?

200 ÷ 5 = $40

1.3 Review

Review Use mental math to complete.

35 + 5 = 40 35 + 6 = 41 35 + 7 = 42	48 + 20 = 68 48 + 22 = 70 48 + 25 = 73	65 + 15 = 80 65 + 25 = 90 65 + 35 = 100
73 − 3 = 70 73 − 4 = 69 73 − 5 = 68	86 − 3 = 83 86 − 13 = 73 86 − 23 = 63	91 − 90 = 1 91 − 89 = 2 91 − 88 = 3

Label the numbers on the number line.

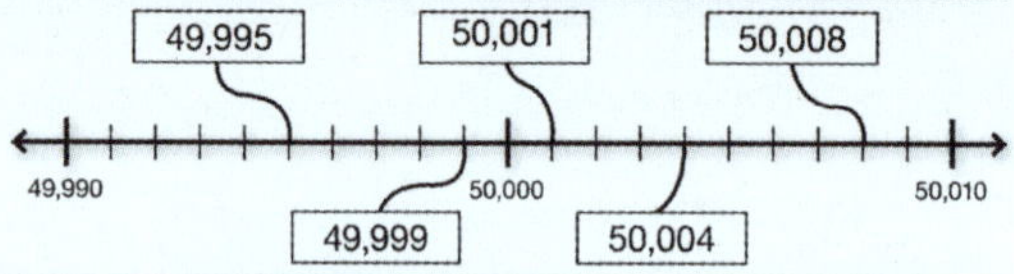

Complete the chart.

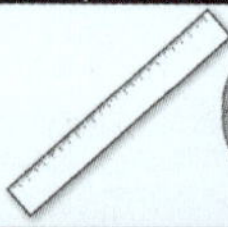

Feet	1	2	3	4	5	6	7	8
Inches	12	24	36	48	60	72	84	96

Complete.

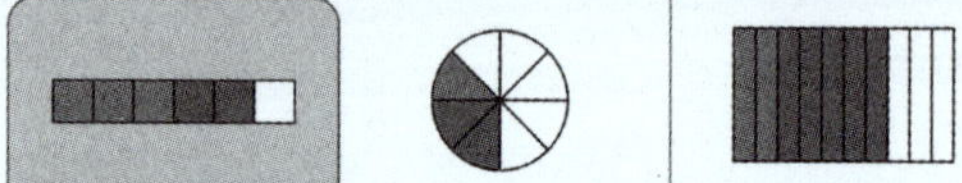

$\frac{3}{6} + \frac{2}{6} = \frac{5}{6}$ $\frac{1}{8} + \frac{2}{8} = \frac{3}{8}$ $\frac{2}{10} + \frac{5}{10} = \frac{7}{10}$

1.4 Practice

Practice Solve.

```
   46        22         63        219        141
2)93      3)67      4)253     3)658      5)706
 -8↓       -6↓       -24↓      -6↓        -5↓
  13        07         13       05         20
 -12        -6        -12       -3↓       -20↓
   1         1          1        28         06
                                -27         -5
                                  1          1

   17        13
5)89      6)80
 -5↓       -6↓
  39        20
 -35       -18
   4         2
```

Use long division to solve. Write the equations you use in the work space.

How much does the Alaska cruise cost per day?

$369

How much does the Greece cruise cost per day?

$516

WORK SPACE

```
    369            516
5)1,845        7)3,612
 -15↓           -35↓
   34             11
  -30↓            -7↓
    45             42
   -45            -42
     0              0
```

1.4 Review

Review

Round to the underlined digit.

5<u>3</u>9 ≈ 540
<u>5</u>39 ≈ 500
1,<u>5</u>08 ≈ 1,500
<u>1</u>,508 ≈ 2,000

Complete the missing factors in the factor pairs.

Factors of 24	Factors of 40
1 × 24	1 × 40
2 × 12	2 × 20
3 × 8	4 × 10
4 × 6	5 × 8

Choose the more reasonable measurement for each angle.

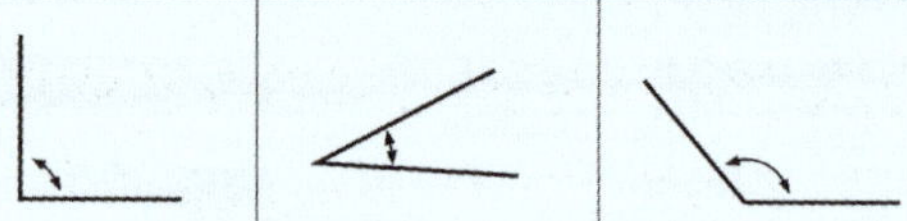

10° / (90°) (30°) / 130° 30° / (130°)

Complete the chart.

Cups	1	2	3	4	5	6	7	8
Fluid Ounces	8	16	24	32	40	48	56	64

Solve. Write the equations you use.

Gwen has 32 fl. oz. of juice. She pours 6 fl. oz. into each glass. How many glasses does she fill? How many fluid ounces does she have left?

32 ÷ 6 = 5R2
5 glasses
2 fl. oz. left

Charlie fills his water bottle with 24 fl. oz. of water. He drinks some water, and then he has 17 fl. oz. left. How many fluid ounces did he drink?

24 − ___ = 17
24 − 17 = 7 fl. oz.

Unit 1 Answer Key

1.5 Practice

Practice: Elisha and AJ are on different basketball teams. They kept track of how many points they scored in each game. Make a line plot for each data set. Then, answer the questions.

Elisha's Points

Sept. 23 - 4, Sept. 26 - 5, Sept. 27 - 2, Sept. 30 - 5, Oct. 2 - 6, Oct. 5 - 4, Oct. 8 - 5, Oct. 12 - 7, Oct. 13 - 6, Oct. 15 - 6

Elisha's Points

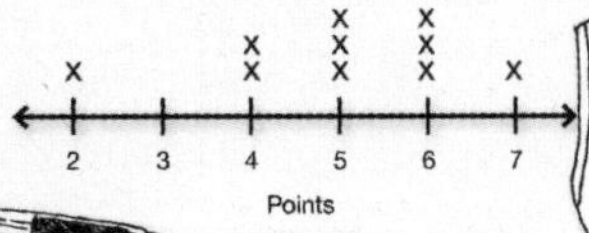

What's the total number of points Elisha scored in all the games?	How many games did Elisha play?	What's the average number of points Elisha scored per game?
2 + 4 + 4 + 5 + 5 + 5 + 6 + 6 + 6 + 7 = 50 points	10 games	50 ÷ 10 = 5 points

AJ's Points

Sept. 24 - 4, Sept. 25 - 5, Sept. 28 - 2, Sept. 30 - 6, Oct. 2 - 4, Oct. 7 - 5, Oct. 10 - 7, Oct. 14 - 7

AJ's Points

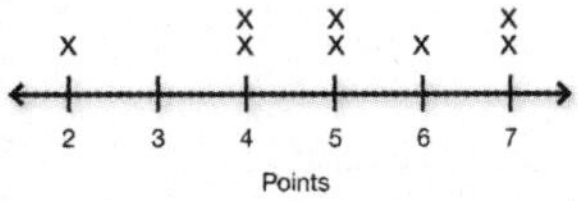

What's the total number of points AJ scored in all the games?	How many games did AJ play?	What's the average number of points AJ scored per game?
2 + 4 + 4 + 5 + 5 + 6 + 7 + 7 = 40 points	8 games	40 ÷ 8 = 5 points

Who scored more points in all?	Who played more games?	Who had the higher average number of points per game?
Elisha	Elisha	They tied.

1.5 Review

Review: Match.

- two hundred thousand five hundred — 200,500
- two hundred thousand fifty — 200,050
- two hundred five thousand — 205,000
- two hundred fifty thousand — 250,000

Use the pictures to complete the equivalent fractions.

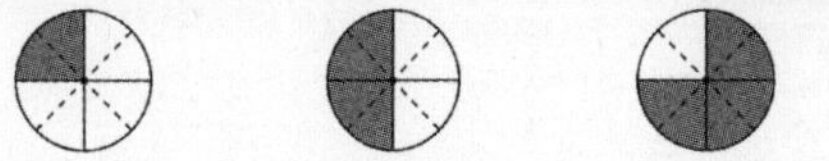

$\frac{1}{4} = \frac{2}{8}$ $\frac{2}{4} = \frac{4}{8}$ $\frac{3}{4} = \frac{6}{8}$

Complete the chart.

Liters	1	2	3	4	5	6
Milliliters	1,000	2,000	3,000	4,000	5,000	6,000

Solve. Write the equations you use.

Ryan buys a bottle of soda with 2 L. He divides it equally into 4 glasses. How many milliliters are in each glass?

2L = 2,000 mL
2,000 ÷ 4 = **500 mL**

Cora fills her water bottle with 1 L of water. She drinks 300 mL. How many milliliters does she have left?

1L = 1,000 mL
1,000 − 300 = **700 mL**

1.6 Practice

Practice: Match each unit with its abbreviation.

- meter — m
- millimeter — mm
- centimeter — cm
- kilometer — km
- liter — L
- milliliter — mL
- gram — g
- kilogram — kg
- yard — yd.
- foot — ft.
- mile — mi.
- inch — in.
- pound — lb.
- ounce — oz.
- fluid ounce — fl. oz.
- cup — c.

Complete.

1 km = 1,000 m	1 mi. = 5,280 ft.	1 week = 7 days
1 m = 100 cm	1 yd. = 3 ft.	1 day = 24 hr.
1 cm = 10 mm	1 ft. = 12 in.	1 hr. = 60 min.
1 L = 1,000 mL	1 lb. = 16 oz.	1 min. = 60 sec.
1 kg = 1,000 g	1 c. = 8 fl. oz.	

Complete. Write the equations you use.

3 hr. = 180 min.	29 in. = 2 ft. 5 in.	1 mi. 10 ft. = 5,290 ft.
3 × 60 = 180	29 ÷ 12 = 2 R5	1 × 5,280 = 5,280 5,280 + 10 = 5,290
235 cm = 2 m 35 cm	4,000 mL = 4 L	1 km 250 m = 1,250 m
235 ÷ 100 = 2 R35	4,000 ÷ 1,000 = 4	1 × 1,000 = 1,000 1,000 + 250 = 1,250

1.6 Review

Review: Complete the fact families.

7 + 6 = 13	7 × 9 = 63
6 + 7 = 13	9 × 7 = 63
13 − 6 = 7	63 ÷ 9 = 7
13 − 7 = 6	63 ÷ 7 = 9

Round to the underlined digit.

- 36,782 ≈ 37,000
- 89,905 ≈ 90,000
- 152,234 ≈ 152,000
- 476,500 ≈ 477,000

Match each fraction or mixed number to its place on the number line.

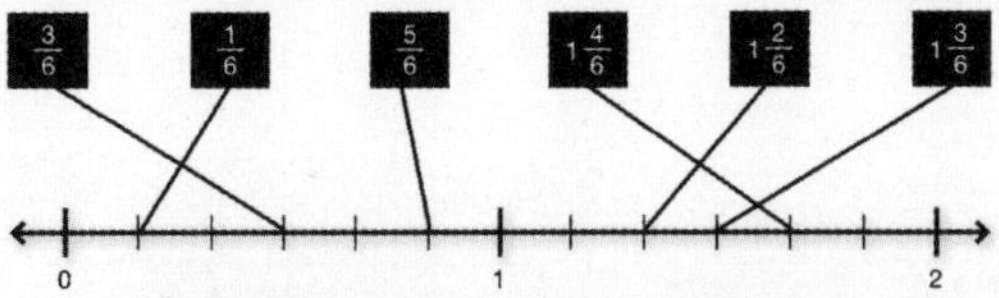

Complete the chart.

Kilograms	1	2	3	4	5	6
Grams	1,000	2,000	3,000	4,000	5,000	6,000

Solve. Write the equations you use.

Hattie has 1 kilogram of clay. She uses 800 grams to make a sculpture. How many grams of clay does she have left?

1,000 − 800 = **200 g**

Whitman has 1 kilogram of gummy bears. He divides the gummy bears equally into 2 bags. How many grams of gummy bears are in each bag?

1,000 ÷ 2 = **500 g**

Unit 1 Answer Key

1.7 Practice

Practice Circle the problem you can use to find the missing number. Then, solve the problem (with mental math or in the work space) to find the missing number.

		WORK SPACE
78 − <u>26</u> = 52	<u>90</u> − 36 = 54	78 − 52 = 26
78 + 52	(36 + 54) circled	36 + 54 = 90
(78 − 52) circled	54 − 36	
88 ÷ <u>11</u> = 8	<u>72</u> ÷ 12 = 6	88 ÷ 8 = 11
(88 ÷ 8) circled	(12 × 6) circled	12 × 6 = 72
88 × 8	12 ÷ 6	

Circle the equation that best matches the word problem. Then, use the equation to solve the word problem.

Theo had some money. He spent $16, and then he had $27 left. How much money did Theo start with?

(___ − 16 = 27) circled; 27 − ___ = 16

27 + 16 = **$43**

Molly had $27. She spent some money, and then she had $16 left. How much money did Molly spend?

___ − 16 = 27; (27 − ___ = 16) circled

27 − 16 = **$11**

There are 20 children at astronomy camp. The leaders divide the children into equal groups. There are 4 children in each group. How many groups did the leaders make?

(20 ÷ ___ = 4) circled; ___ ÷ 4 = 20

20 ÷ 4 = **5 groups**

The gymnastics camp leaders divide the children into 4 equal groups. They put 20 children in each group. How many children are at gymnastics camp?

20 ÷ ___ = 4; (___ ÷ 4 = 20) circled

20 × 4 = **80 children**

1.7 Review

Review Complete with <, >, or =.

- 43,560 (>) 43,000
- 43,560 (>) 43,500
- 43,560 (<) 43,600
- 43,560 (<) 45,460
- 43,560 (>) 43,559

Complete.

450 + <u>50</u> = 500	999 + <u>1</u> = 1,000
350 + <u>150</u> = 500	899 + <u>101</u> = 1,000
250 + <u>250</u> = 500	799 + <u>201</u> = 1,000
150 + <u>350</u> = 500	699 + <u>301</u> = 1,000
50 + <u>450</u> = 500	599 + <u>401</u> = 1,000

Complete the chart.

Pounds	1	2	3	4	5	6
Ounces	16	32	48	64	80	96

Use the line plot to answer the questions.

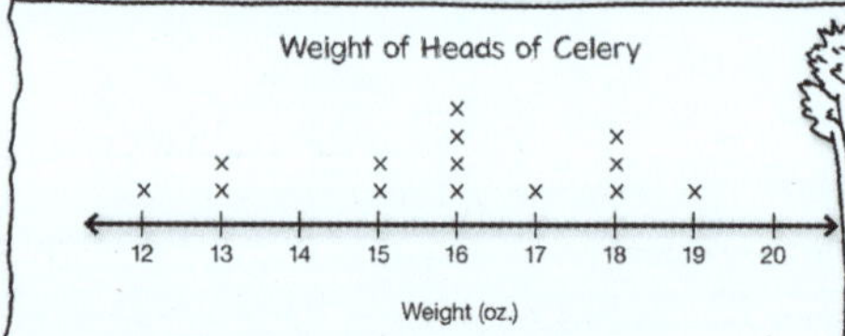

How much does the heaviest head of celery weigh? 19 oz.

How much does the lightest head of celery weigh? 12 oz.

How many heads of celery weigh exactly 1 pound (16 oz.)? 4

How many heads of celery weigh more than 1 pound (16 oz.)? 5

1.8 Practice

Practice Evaluate.

4 + (6 × 7) 4 + 42 46	3 × (12 ÷ 4) 3 × 3 9
(4 × 9) ÷ 9 36 ÷ 9 4	8 × (5 − 5) 8 × 0 0
(3 × 8) + (7 × 8) 24 + 56 80	(4 × 7) − (6 ÷ 6) 28 − 1 27
(30 + 6) ÷ (8 − 4) 36 ÷ 4 9	(17 − 7) × (4 + 6) 10 × 10 100

Circle the expression that best matches the word problem. Then, evaluate the expression to find the answer to the word problem.

Sarah's mom has $30. She buys a lamp at the garage sale for $12. Then, she splits the remaining money evenly between her 3 children. How much money does each child get?

((30 − 12) ÷ 3) circled; 30 − (12 ÷ 3)

(30 − 12) ÷ 3
18 ÷ 3
$6

Alex buys 5 mystery novels and 4 historical fiction novels at the garage sale. Each book costs $3. How much does he pay for all the books?

5 + (4 × 3); ((5 + 4) × 3) circled

(5 + 4) × 3
9 × 3
$27

1.8 Review

Review Write the multiples of each number in order. Then, answer the questions.

Multiples of 3	3	6	9	12	15	18	21	24	27	30
Multiples of 6	6	12	18	24	30	36	42	48	54	60
Multiples of 9	9	18	27	36	45	54	63	72	81	90

Which numbers appear on the list of multiples of 3 and the list of multiples of 6? 6, 12, 18, 24, 30

Which numbers appear on the list of multiples of 6 and the list of multiples of 9? 18, 36, 54

Which numbers appear on the list of multiples of 3 and the list of multiples of 9? 9, 18, 27

Complete. Write the equations you use.

5 min. = <u>300</u> sec.
5 × 60 = 300

4 km 75 m = <u>4,075</u> m
4 × 1,000 = 4,000
4,000 + 75 = 4,075

18 oz. = <u>1</u> lb. <u>2</u> oz.
18 ÷ 16 = 1 R2

Use long division to solve.

257 ÷ 7 = 36 R5
7)257
− 21
47
− 42
5

932 ÷ 7 = 133 R1
7)932
− 7
23
− 21
22
− 21
1

Find the average number of fish in the tanks at the pet store.

Number of Fish in Each Tank
7, 10, 9, 15, 6, 13, 3

7 + 10 + 9 + 15 + 6 + 13 + 3 = 63

63 ÷ 7 = **9 fish**

Unit 1 Answer Key

1.9 Practice

Practice: Evaluate. Then, find the blank that matches the answer. Write the matching letter in the blank to solve the riddle.

(A) 35 + 5 − 10
M or D / A or S
40 − 10
30

(D) 32 ÷ 4 × 2
M or D / A or S
8 × 2
16

(R) 20 − 2 × 6 + 1
M or D / A or S
20 − 12 + 1
8 + 1
9

(E) 4 × 10 − 3 × 2
M or D / A or S
40 − 3 × 2
40 − 6
34

(A) 4 + 3 + 15 ÷ 3
M or D / A or S
4 + 3 + 5
7 + 5
12

(D) 16 ÷ 4 × 2 + 3
M or D / A or S
4 × 2 + 3
8 + 3
11

What do you call a snake that solves equations?

A	N	A	D	D	E	R
30		12	11	16	34	9

Complete the expression to match the word problem. Then, evaluate the expression to find the answer to the word problem.

Laura sells 40 trading cards at the garage sale. She sells the trading cards in packs of 5. She charges $3 for each pack. How much money does she earn in all?

40 ÷ 5 × 3
8 × 3
$24

Paul has $28. Then, he buys a skateboard for $9 and 2 board games for $4 each. How much money does he have left?

28 − 9 − 2 × 4
28 − 9 − 8
19 − 8
$11

1.9 Review

Review: Use the pictures to complete the equivalent fractions.

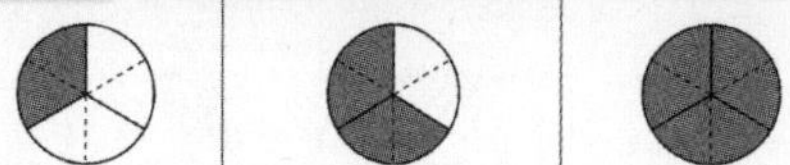

$\frac{1}{3} = \frac{2}{6}$ $\frac{2}{3} = \frac{4}{6}$ $\frac{3}{3} = \frac{6}{6}$

Complete. Write the equations you use.

10 days = 240 hr.
10 × 24 = 240

5 ft. 2 in. = 62 in.
5 × 12 + 2
60 + 2
62

2,300 mL = 2 L 300 mL
2,300 ÷ 1,000
= 2 R300

Circle the better estimate for each product.

6 × 415	2,078 × 9	32 × 47
(2,400) / 24,000	1,800 / (18,000)	150 / (1,500)

Circle the equation that best matches the word problem. Then, use the equation to solve the word problem.

I'm thinking of a number. The sum of my number and 47 is 93. What is my number?

___ − 47 = 93
(___ + 47 = 93)
93 − 47 = 46

★ I'm thinking of a number. If you divide my number by 6, you get 300. What is my number?

(___ ÷ 6 = 300)
300 ÷ 6 = ___
300 × 6 = 1,800

1.10 Practice

Practice: Evaluate.

20 − (3 + 1) × 2
P / M or D / A or S
20 − 4 × 2
20 − 8
12

15 − 3 × 4 + 6
P / M or D / A or S
15 − 12 + 6
3 + 6
9

4 + 3 × (5 + 2)
P / M or D / A or S
4 + 3 × 7
4 + 21
25

15 + 23 − (15 + 23)
P / M or D / A or S
15 + 23 − 38
38 − 38
0

7 − 6 ÷ 6 × 2
P / M or D / A or S
7 − 1 × 2
7 − 2
5

7 × (20 − 20) × 12
P / M or D / A or S
7 × 0 × 12
0 × 12
0

(50 − 10) ÷ (3 + 5)
P / M or D / A or S
40 ÷ (3 + 5)
40 ÷ 8
5

13 × (2 × 5)
P / M or D / A or S
13 × 10
130

Circle the expression that best matches the word problem. Then, evaluate the expression to find the answer to the word problem.

Mykah had $61. Then, she bought a movie ticket for $12 and a popcorn for $8. How much money does she have now?

61 − 12 + 8
(61 − (12 + 8))
61 − (12 + 8)
61 − 20
$41

Charlie had $32. He spent $7, and then he earned $20. How much money does he have now?

(32 − 7 + 20)
32 − (7 + 20)
32 − 7 + 20
25 + 20
$45

1.10 Review

Review: Choose the more reasonable measurement for each angle.

(100°) / 20°	120° / (20°)	(140°) / 40°

Complete.

1 km = 1,000 m	1 mi. = 5,280 ft.	1 week = 7 days
1 m = 100 cm	1 yd. = 3 ft.	1 day = 24 hr.
1 cm = 10 mm	1 ft. = 12 in.	1 hr. = 60 min.
1 L = 1,000 mL	1 lb. = 16 oz.	1 min. = 60 sec.
1 kg = 1,000 g	1 c. = 8 fl. oz.	

Complete. Write the equations you use.

2 hr. 15 min. = 135 min.
2 × 60 + 15
120 + 15
135

50 yd. = 150 ft.
50 × 3 = 150

17 kg = 17,000 g
17 × 1,000 = 17,000

Complete.

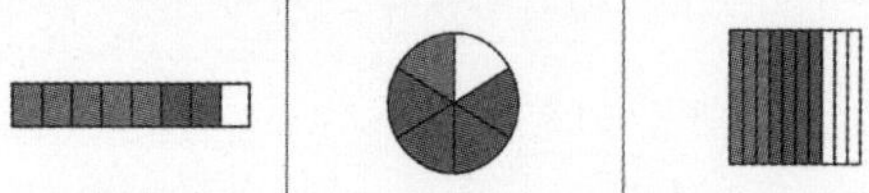

$\frac{5}{8} + \frac{2}{8} = \frac{7}{8}$ $\frac{1}{6} + \frac{4}{6} = \frac{5}{6}$ $\frac{3}{10} + \frac{4}{10} = \frac{7}{10}$

Unit 1 Answer Key

1.11 Unit Wrap-Up A

Unit Wrap-Up Circle the problems that equal the number in the star.

4,800	2,000	40	500
(60 × 80)	(50 × 40)	(280 ÷ 7)	300 ÷ 6
(6 × 800)	5 × 40	2,800 ÷ 7	(3,000 ÷ 6)
60 × 8	(500 × 4)	(200 ÷ 5)	450 ÷ 9
6,000 × 8	5 × 4,000	2,000 ÷ 5	(4,500 ÷ 9)

Solve. Write the equations you use.

Ryan and Tabitha sell bracelets at the craft fair. They keep track of how many bracelets they sell each day.

Bracelets Sold
Thursday - 22 bracelets
Friday - 19 bracelets
Saturday - 43 bracelets
Sunday - 36 bracelets

How many bracelets did they sell in all?

22 + 19 + 43 + 36 = **120 bracelets**

What's the average number of bracelets they sold each day?

120 ÷ 4 = **30 bracelets**

Evaluate.

P / M or D / A or S

30 ÷ 2 + 3 × 3
15 + 3 × 3
15 + 9
24

10 − 3 × 2 ÷ 2
10 − 6 ÷ 2
10 − 3
7

30 ÷ (2 + 3) × 3
30 ÷ 5 × 3
6 × 3
18

(10 − 3) × 2 ÷ 2
7 × 2 ÷ 2
14 ÷ 2
7

1.11 Unit Wrap-Up B

Unit Wrap-Up Use the ad to answer the questions. Write the equations you use in the work space.

Whitewater River Rafting Trips

4-hour trip (per person) $96
Lunch is not included in the 4-hour trip. You can buy lunch for an additional $12 per person.

3-day trip (per person) $1,347
Tents, camping supplies, and all meals are included in the 3-day trip.

WORK SPACE

James had some money. He bought 1 ticket for the 4-hour trip, and then he had $47 left. How much money did he have before he paid for the trip?

$143

96 + 47 = $143

How much does it cost for 8 people to go on the 4-hour trip?

$768

96 × 8 = $768

How much does it cost for 5 people to purchase lunch and go on the 4-hour rafting trip?

$540

96 × 5 = 480
12 × 5 = 60
480 + 60 = $540

How much does it cost for 4 people to go on the 3-day trip?

$5,388

1,347 × 4 = $5,388

How much does the 3-day trip cost per day for one person?

$449

1,347 ÷ 3 = 449
− 12 → 14
− 12 → 27
− 27 → 0

Unit 1 Checkpoint

What to Expect at the End of Unit 1

By the end of Unit 1, most children will be able to do the following:

- Mentally multiply one-digit numbers by a multiple of 10, 100, or 1,000 and mentally multiply a multiple of 10 by a multiple of 10 (e.g., 40 × 80). Some children will still be regaining fluency with the multiplication facts after the summer break.
- Use the written process to multiply a multi-digit number by a one-digit number.
- Mentally divide multiples of 10, 100, or 1,000 by a one-digit number. Some children will still be regaining fluency with the division facts after the summer break.
- Use long division to divide a multi-digit number by a one-digit number. Some children may still need some coaching when solving long division problems.
- Use multiplication or division to convert measurements. It's fine if your child doesn't have all of the conversion factors memorized and sometimes needs to refer to the Memory Work list.
- Interpret line plots and find averages.
- Find missing numbers in simple addition, subtraction, multiplication, and division equations.
- Use the order of operations to evaluate expressions with parentheses, multiplication and division, or addition and subtraction. Some children will still have trouble remembering the order or remembering to solve from left to right.

Is Your Child Ready to Move on?

In Unit 2, your child will review place value in large numbers and decimals. She will also learn how to add and subtract decimals. Throughout Unit 2, your child will continue to review the skills covered in Unit 1 (especially the multiplication and division skills). Your child does not need to have fully mastered all the skills in Unit 1 before moving on to Unit 2.

At this point, your child should be **mostly fluent with the multiplication facts**. It's normal for children to occasionally forget a fact or take more than a few seconds to find an answer, but most children should be able to tell most multiplication fact answers within 3 seconds at this point.

What to Do If Your Child Needs More Practice

If you're not sure whether your child has mastered the multiplication facts, use Blackline Master 2 to assess her fluency. Then, use the results of the assessment to make a plan to build greater automaticity with the facts.

- If your child can find answers to most of the facts but often takes longer than 3 seconds, she likely needs more practice to build her speed. Play one of the multiplication games on Blackline Master 3 a few times per week (either at the beginning of a lesson or at a separate time of day) as you move forward in the program. Encourage your child to respond as quickly as possible as she names the products in the games.
- If your child has just a few facts that stump her, choose 3 of the tricky facts. Write them on a piece of paper and post them in your math lesson area. Have her practice these 3 facts at the beginning of each lesson until she has memorized them. Then, choose 3 new facts to focus on.

- If your child has trouble finding answers to many of the multiplication facts, she likely needs more practice with them to be successful with *Fifth Grade Math with Confidence. Multiplication Facts that Stick* provides a systematic approach to mastering the facts. Use the activities from *Multiplication Facts that Stick* for 5–10 minutes per day outside of your regular math time.

If you find that your child's lack of fluency with the multiplication facts makes lessons long and frustrating, **allow her to use the multiplication chart** (Blackline Master 4) as she completes lessons from this point forward. This will allow her to continue to make progress with the new concepts in the program while she works to solidify the multiplication facts. For some children, using the multiplication chart for several months provides the reinforcement they need to solidify the multiplication facts.

Unit 2
Place Value and Decimals

Overview

Your child will deepen his understanding of place value as he studies both large and small numbers. In the first part of the unit, he will study whole-number place value to the billions-place and learn to round large numbers to any place. In the second part of the unit, your child will develop deeper number sense with decimals as he learns to read, write, and compare decimals to the thousandths-place. He'll learn how to write decimals as fractions or mixed numbers, how to round decimals to any place, and how to add and subtract decimals.

What Your Child Will Learn

In this unit, your child will learn to:

- Understand whole-number place value to the billions-place
- Round large numbers to any place
- Add and subtract numbers to the billions-place
- Understand decimal place value to the thousandths-place
- Compare decimals to the thousandths-place
- Write decimals in expanded form
- Write decimals as mixed numbers or fractions with base-ten denominators (i.e., understand that 4.372 equals 4 372/1,000)
- Round decimals to any place
- Add and subtract decimals to the thousandths-place

Lesson List

Lesson 2.1	Review Rounding
Lesson 2.2	Place Value to Billions
Lesson 2.3	Add and Subtract Large Numbers
Lesson 2.4	Review Decimals to the Hundredths-Place
Lesson 2.5	Mental Addition and Subtraction with Decimals
Lesson 2.6	Decimals on the Number Line and Rounding
Lesson 2.7	Add and Subtract Decimals to the Hundredths-Place
Lesson 2.8	Decimals to the Thousandths-Place
Lesson 2.9	Compare Decimals to the Thousandths-Place
Lesson 2.10	Write Decimals as Fractions or Mixed Numbers
Lesson 2.11	Add and Subtract Decimals to the Thousandths-Place
Lesson 2.12	Enrichment (Optional)

Extra Materials Needed for Unit 2

- World map, optional
- For optional Enrichment Lesson:
    - *How Many Guinea Pigs Can Fit on a Plane?: Answers to Your Most Clever Math Questions*, by Laura Overdeck. Feiwel & Friends, 2017.
    - 8-10 jars of spices, labeled in ounces

Teaching Math with Confidence: Using Base-Ten Blocks and Decimal Squares to Represent Decimals to the Thousandths-Place

In *Fourth Grade Math with Confidence*, you used printed decimal squares to teach your child how to read, write, and compare decimals to the hundredths-place. This year, you'll use both base-ten blocks and decimal squares as you teach your child about decimals to the thousandths-place.

First, you'll use base-ten blocks to represent decimals to the hundredths-place. You'll use flats to represent wholes, rods to represent tenths, and unit blocks to represent hundredths. These familiar place-value manipulatives remind your child that decimals are simply an extension of the place-value system. Each block is 1/10 the size of the next-larger block, just as each decimal place has 1/10 of the value of the next-larger place.

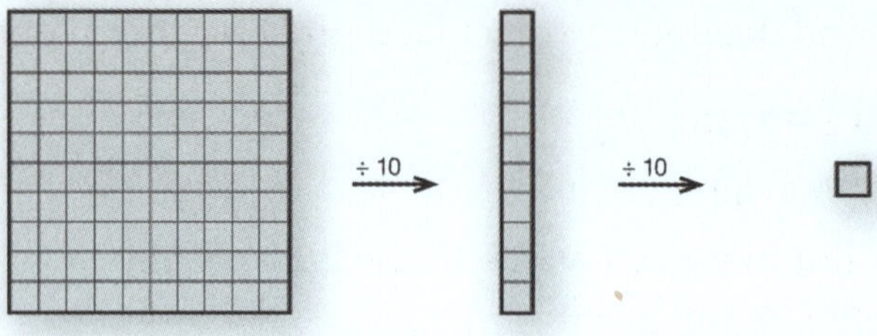

1 whole	1 tenth	1 hundredth
1	0.1	0.01

You'll also use the base-ten blocks to teach your child how to add and subtract decimals to the hundredths-place. Your child will see that he can add, subtract, and trade the blocks just as he did when he used them to model whole numbers.

Next, you'll teach your child how to extend these decimal concepts to the thousandths-place. Base-ten blocks don't come in such small pieces, so you'll use a printed decimal square (Blackline Master 7) to model them instead. In this model, each hundredth is split into 10 smaller parts to create thousandths.

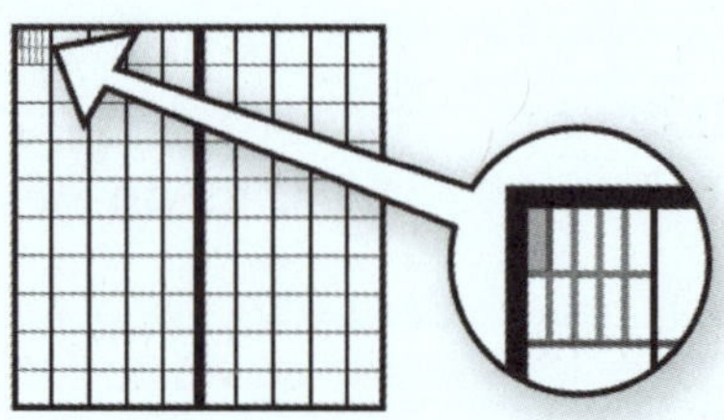

1 thousandth
0.001

Concrete experiences with base-ten blocks and decimal squares help your child develop decimal number sense so that he can understand real-world decimals. For example, 0.438 on the decimal square is a little less than half of the square. So, if you see 0.438 in a real-life context, you know that a 0.438 mile hike isn't very far, or that 0.438 pounds of ground beef might not be enough for a recipe that calls for half of a pound. As you teach your child about decimals in this unit, encourage him to think about the real-world meanings of the numbers and look for opportunities to discuss decimals that come up in your everyday life.

Lesson 2.1
Review Rounding

Purpose	Materials
• Review how to locate whole numbers on the number line • Review how to round large numbers to any place	• None
Memory Work	• **What is the order of operations?** *Parentheses, multiply or divide from left to right, add or subtract from left to right.*

Warm-up (A and C): Review Reading Multi-Digit Numbers and Finding Their Positions on the Number Line

Show your child the chart in part C. **This chart lists the diameters of the planets in our solar system. The diameter is the distance across the middle of the planet. Later in the lesson, you'll round these numbers to the nearest thousand.**

Have your child read aloud each number. Use the following questions to briefly discuss the chart.

- **Which planet has the smallest diameter?** *Mercury.*
- **Which planet has the greatest diameter?** *Jupiter.*
- **Which planet has about the same diameter as Earth?** *Venus.*

> If your child has trouble reading the numbers, remind her to use the comma to help. For example, for Jupiter: **First, read the part before the comma as one number: one hundred forty-two. Say "thousand" when you reach the comma. Then, read the part after the comma as one number: nine hundred eighty-four.**

Show your child the number lines in part A. **We'll warm up by finding the positions for the planets' diameters on these number lines. On the first number line, the distance between 0 and 5,000 is split into 5 parts. What's 5,000 divided by 5?** *1,000.* **So, we start at 0 and count by 1,000 to see what number each tick mark stands for.** Point to the first few tick marks as you name them: **0, 1,000, 2,000, 3,000, 4,000, 5,000.**

4,879 is between which multiples of 1,000? *4,000 and 5,000.* **Is 4,879 closer to 4,000 or 5,000?** *5,000.* Have your child draw a dot at the approximate position for 4,879 on the number line and connect the dot to the printed number. Repeat with the other numbers above the first number line.

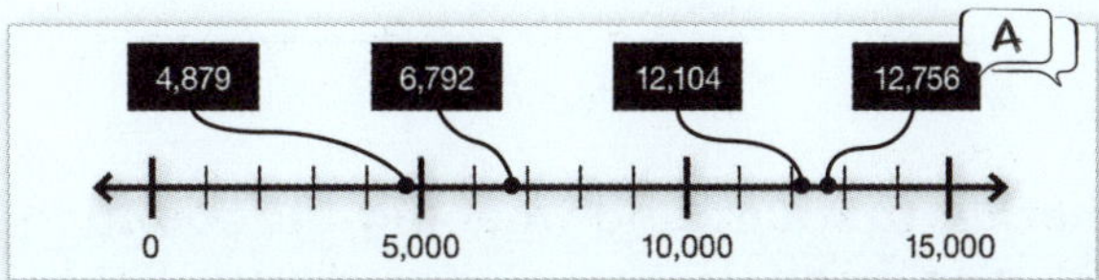

On the second number line, the distance between 0 and 50,000 is split into 5 parts. What's 50,000 divided by 5? *10,000.* **This time, we start at 0 and count by 10,000 to see what number each tick mark stands for.** Point to the first few tick marks as you name them: **0, 10,000, 20,000, 30,000, 40,000, 50,000.**

142,984 is between which multiples of 10,000? *140,000 and 150,000.* **Is 142,984 closer to 140,000 or 150,000?** *140,000.* Have your child draw a dot at the approximate position for 142,984 on the number line and connect the dot to the printed number. Repeat with the other numbers.

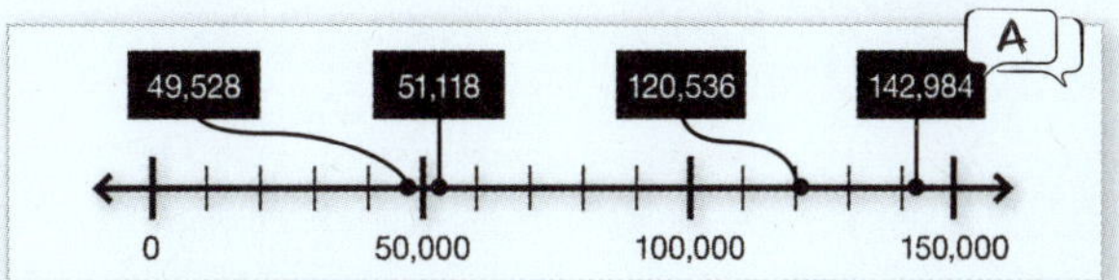

Activity (B): Review Rounding

Now, we'll review the steps for rounding. Have your child read aloud the steps.

B

How to Round Numbers

1. Underline the digit in the place you are rounding to.
2. Look at the digit in the next-smaller place.
   - If the digit is less than 5, round down. Keep the underlined digit the same, and change all the digits after it to zeros.
   - If the digit is 5 or greater, round up. Increase the underlined digit by 1. Change all the digits after it to zeros.

Ex. Round 12,756 to the nearest thousand.

12,756 ≈ **13,000**

The digit in the next-smaller place is 7.
7 is greater than 5, so you round up.

Ex. Round 12,756 to the nearest ten-thousand.

12,756 ≈ **10,000**

The digit in the next-smaller place is 2.
2 is less than 5, so you round down.

In the first example, we want to round 12,756 to the nearest thousand.

- **First, we underline the 2 in the thousands-place.**
- **Then, we look at the digit in the next-smaller place. What digit is in the next-smaller place?** *7.* **7 is greater than or equal to 5, so we round up.**
- **We increase the 2 to a 3 and change all the digits after it to zero. 12,756 rounded to the nearest thousand is 13,000.**

Look back at the number line in part A with your child. **The number line shows another way to think about why we round up instead of down. 12,756 is closer to 13,000 than 12,000 on the number line, so it rounds to 13,000. Earth has a diameter of about 13,000 kilometers.**

> If it's hard for your child to see this on the number line in part A, draw a quick number line sketch to illustrate.
>
> 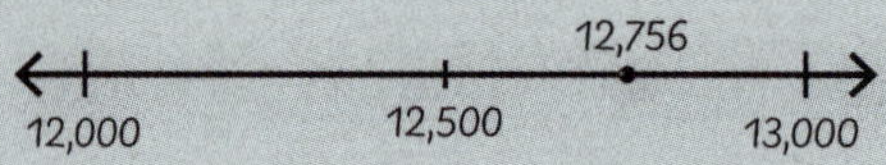
>

In the second example, we want to round 12,756 to the nearest ten-thousand.

- **First, we underline the 1 in the ten-thousands-place.**
- **Then, we look at the digit in the next-smaller place. What digit is in the next-smaller place?** *2.* **2 is less than 5, so we round down.**
- **We keep the 1 the same and change all the digits after it to zero. 12,756 rounded to the nearest ten-thousand is 10,000.**

> If your child has trouble understanding why 12,756 rounds to 10,000, draw a number line sketch like the following. **12,756 is between 10,000 and 20,000. It's closer to 10,000, so we round down.**
>
> 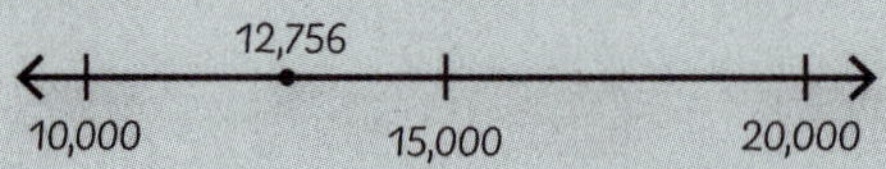
>

In real life, we choose whether to round and what digit to round to based on the situation. Knowing that Earth is about 10,000 kilometers across is probably close enough if you're just curious about how Earth's diameter compares to the moon's diameter or the sun's diameter. But if you're deciding how much fuel to put in a plane that's traveling around the world, you would want to use the exact number!

Activity (C): Round Planets' Diameters to the Nearest Thousand Kilometers

Have your child round each diameter in the chart to the nearest thousand kilometers. Write the rounded numbers in the chart.

Planet	Diameter (km)	Diameter Rounded to the Nearest Thousand (km)
Mercury	4,879	5,000
Venus	12,104	12,000
Earth	12,756	13,000
Mars	6,792	7,000
Jupiter	142,984	143,000
Saturn	120,536	121,000
Uranus	51,118	51,000
Neptune	49,528	50,000

If your child has trouble rounding Neptune's diameter, remind her to regroup 10 thousands as 1 ten-thousand: **There are 5 hundreds, so we round up. What's 9 increased by 1?** *10.* **When you have to increase a 9 to a 10, regroup and increase the next-larger digit. 10 thousands equal 1 ten-thousand, so 49,528 rounded to the nearest thousand is 50,000.** Or, draw a simple number line as shown to illustrate.

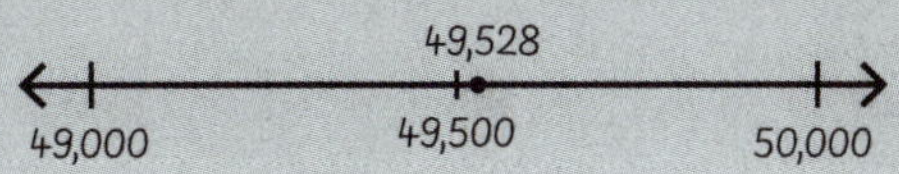

Use the following questions to discuss the planet's rounded diameters.

- **About how many thousands of kilometers less is Mercury's diameter than Earth's?** *Sample answer: 8,000 kilometers.* **How do you know?** *Sample answer: 13,000 minus 5,000 equals 8,000.* Accept any reasonable answer.
- **Which planet's diameter is about half of Earth's diameter?** *Mars.*
- **About how many thousands of kilometers more is Jupiter's diameter than Saturn's?** *Sample answer: 22,000 kilometers.* **How do you know?** *Sample answer: 143,000 minus 121,000 equals 22,000.* Accept any reasonable answer.

Questions like these help your child make sense of these large numbers.

Independent Practice and Review

Have your child complete the Lesson 2.1 Practice and Review workbook pages.

The dark line in the middle of each fraction square splits the fraction square in half and makes it easier for your child to count the narrow strips. Later in the unit, she'll use similar squares to review decimal place value.

The Review page asks children to write numbers in standard form. In British English, standard form refers to using the powers of 10 to express numbers. (For example: $3{,}217 = 3.217 \times 10^3$.) Your child will learn this way of writing numbers in future grades. If your family uses British English, simply tell your child to write the number the usual way when she sees a direction to write numbers in standard form.

Lesson 2.2
Place Value to Billions

Purpose	Materials
• Practice rounding • Introduce place value to the billions-place • Round large numbers	• None

Memory Work	• **What's zero times any number?** *Zero.* • **What's zero divided by any other number?** *Zero.* • **What's any number divided by zero?** *Undefined.*

Warm-up (A): Review Rounding

The sun is 1,391,400 kilometers across! To warm up, we'll round the diameter of the Sun to different places. Have your child complete the rounding exercises.

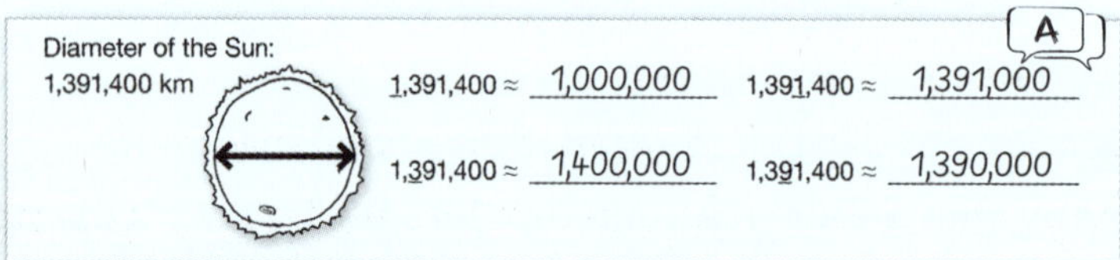

Activity (B): Introduce Place Value to the Billions

In younger grades, you learned about place value to the millions-place. Today, you'll learn about place value to the billions-place. We need large numbers in the billions when we measure distances in space. Pluto can be up to 7,304,326,000 kilometers away from the Sun!

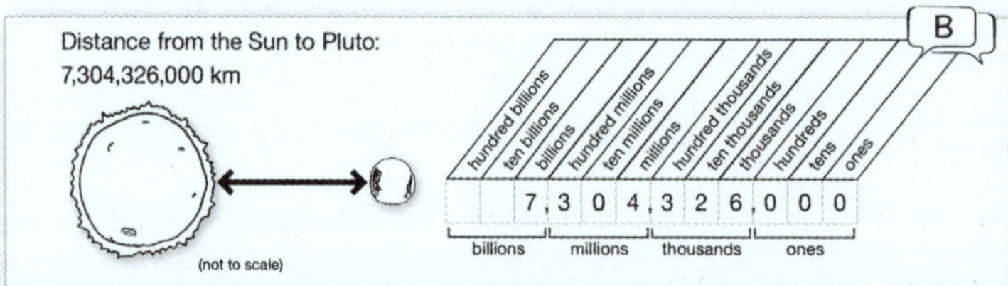

Orbits around the Sun aren't perfectly circular, so the celestial bodies' distances from the Sun can vary a great deal. In this lesson, all distances measure the aphelion, the farthest distance possible between the planet (or dwarf planet) and the Sun.

Each place in our place-value system is 10 times greater than the next-smaller place. 10 millions equal 1 ten-million. 10 ten-millions equal 1 hundred-million. 10 hundred-millions equal 1 billion! We can continue this pattern infinitely to make numbers as large as we want.

We write a comma after each group of three places to make it easier to read and write large numbers.

How many digits are in the number 7,304,326,000? *10.* Point to the 7 in the billions-place. **What place is this 7 in?** *The billions-place.* **The 7 is in the billions-place so it has a value of 7 billion.** Have your child identify the value of the rest of the digits in the number.

We round larger numbers the same way we round smaller numbers. Let's round the distance between Pluto and the sun to the billions-place. Demonstrate how to round 7,304,326,000 to the billions-place.

- **The 7 in the billions-place is already underlined. We look at the digit in the next-smaller place. What digit is in the next-smaller place?** *3.*
- **3 is less than 5, so we round down. We keep the underlined digit and the digits before it the same.**
- **We change all the digits after the underlined digit to zero.** Write 7,000,000,000 in the blank. **Pluto is about 7 billion kilometers from the sun.**

Have your child round the distance to the hundred-millions place in the same way.

B

7,304,326,000 ≈ 7,000,000,000   7,304,326,000 ≈ 7,300,000,000

Activity (C): Read Large Numbers and Round Distances to the Nearest Ten Million Kilometers

This chart shows the distance between each planet and the Sun in kilometers. Have your child read each distance aloud and then round it to the nearest ten million kilometers. Write the rounded numbers in the chart.

C

Planet	Distance from the Sun (km)	Distance from the Sun Rounded to the Nearest Ten Million (km)
Mercury	69,818,000	70,000,000
Venus	108,941,000	110,000,000
Earth	152,100,000	150,000,000
Mars	249,261,000	250,000,000
Jupiter	816,363,000	820,000,000
Saturn	1,506,527,000	1,510,000,000
Uranus	2,732,696,000	2,730,000,000
Neptune	4,471,050,000	4,470,000,000

If your child has trouble reading the numbers, remind him to use the commas to help. For example, for Mercury: **This number has two commas, so we say "million" when we reach the first comma, and we say "thousand" when we reach the second comma. This distance is 69 million, 818 thousand kilometers.**

For numbers with three commas, tell your child to say "billion" for the first comma, "million" for the second comma, and "thousand" for the third comma. For example, for Saturn: **One billion, five hundred six million, five hundred twenty-seven thousand.**

Then, use the following questions to discuss the distances.

- **Which planet is closest to the Sun?** *Mercury.*
- **Which planet is farthest from the Sun?** *Neptune.*
- **About how many million kilometers farther is Venus from the Sun than Mercury is?** *Sample answer: 40 million kilometers.* **How do you know?** *Sample answer: 110 million minus 70 million equals 40 million.*
- **About how many million kilometers farther is Mars from the Sun than Earth is?** *Sample answer: 100 million kilometers.* **How do you know?** *Sample answer: 250 million minus 150 million equals 100 million.* **If an astronaut traveled from Earth to Mars, they'd have to travel 100 million kilometers!**
- **About how many billion kilometers farther is Neptune from the Sun than Earth is?** *Sample answer: 4 billion kilometers.* **The Voyager 2 space probe traveled from Earth to Neptune to observe Neptune. The probe traveled about 70,000 kilometers every hour, but it still took 12 years to get to Neptune!**

Independent Practice and Review

Have your child complete the Lesson 2.2 Practice and Review workbook pages.

Lesson 2.3
Add and Subtract Large Numbers

Purpose	Materials
• Practice rounding large numbers • Add and subtract large numbers • Solve word problems with large numbers	• World map, optional

Memory Work

- **What do we call the top number in a fraction?** *The numerator.*
- **What do we call the bottom number in a fraction?** *The denominator.*
- **What do we call fractions that look different but have the same value?** *Equivalent fractions.*
- **What do we call numbers that have a whole number and a fraction?** *Mixed numbers.*

Warm-up (A): Round Countries' Populations to the Nearest Million

Do not show your child the Lesson Activities page yet.

In the last lesson, we used large numbers to measure distances in space. We also use large numbers to measure population. Today, we'll solve word problems about the four countries in the world with the greatest population.

Have your child guess which four countries in the world have the greatest population. Then, show her the chart in part A. Briefly discuss any background knowledge your child has about the countries. If you have time, find the countries on a world map.

Have your child read each number aloud. Then, have her round each number to the nearest million. Remind her as needed to underline the digit in the millions-place and look at the digit in the hundred-thousands-place to decide whether to round up or down.

A

	Population (2023)	Population Rounded to the Nearest Million
China	1,411,750,000	1,412,000,000
India	1,392,329,000	1,392,000,000
United States	335,167,000	335,000,000
Indonesia	277,750,000	278,000,000
World	8,051,404,000	8,051,000,000

These population figures are accurate as of 2023.

Activity (B): Solve Addition and Subtraction Word Problems with Large Numbers

When you were younger, you learned how to add and subtract with the addition and subtraction algorithms. We use the exact same steps to add and subtract numbers with millions or billions.

Have your child read the first word problem aloud. **What's the goal of the problem?** *Find about how many more people live in China than in the United States.*

B

About how many more people live in China than the United States? (Use the rounded numbers from part A.)

Problems with large numbers sometimes feel intimidating because there are so many digits to think about! If you ever feel overwhelmed by the numbers in a problem, just ignore them and think about how you would solve the problem if the numbers were smaller. For example, if 100 people lived in China and 40 people lived in the United States, how would you find the difference between the two populations? *Sample answer: I'd subtract 40 from 100.*

When we want to find the difference between two numbers, we subtract the smaller number from the larger number—no matter how large or small the numbers are!

Have your child use the rounded numbers from the chart to write a subtraction problem and solve. Point out that your child should align the digits with the same place value: **The population of China has more digits than the population of the United States. When you set up the subtraction problem, make sure you write the first digit for the United States under the digit in the same place in the number for China.**

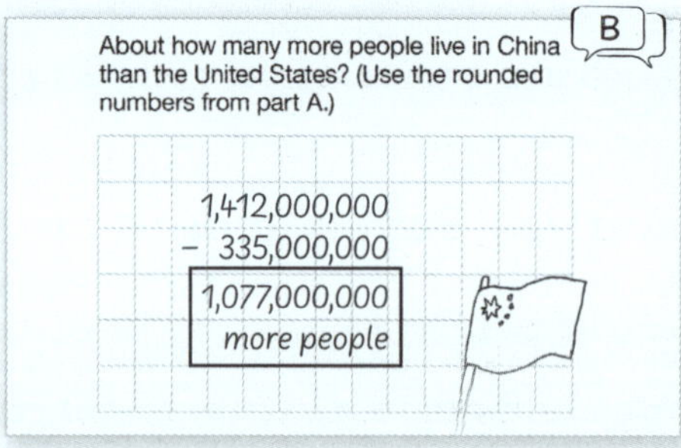

The 3 in the hundred-millions place in the population of the United States goes directly under the 4 in the hundred-millions place in the population of China.

> Using the rounded numbers makes these problems less tedious and time-consuming. If your child would like to find a more precise answer, she can use the printed numbers in the chart for her calculations.

Have your child solve the rest of the word problems in the same way. She should use the rounded numbers from the chart for each problem. For the final problem, point out that she can use the answer to the previous problem to help: **You already found the combined population of China and India. So, subtract that number from the total population of the world to find out how many people do not live in China or India.**

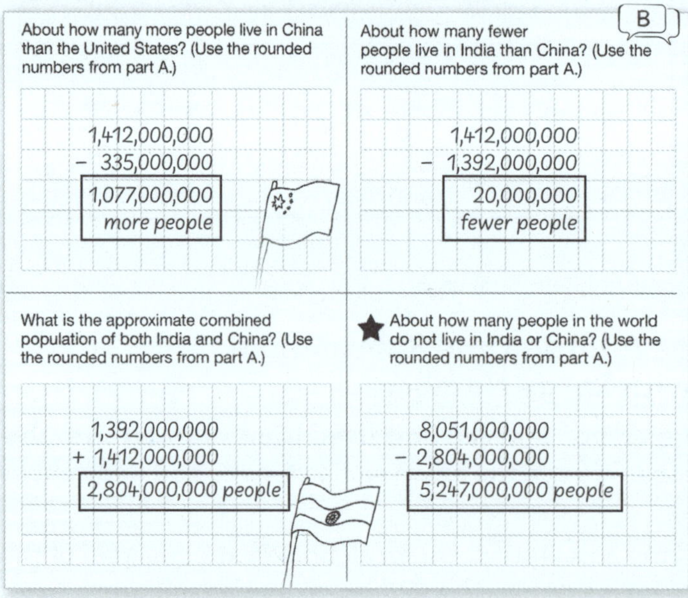

Independent Practice and Review

Have your child complete the Lesson 2.3 Practice and Review workbook pages.

Lesson 2.4
Review Decimals to the Hundredths-Place

Purpose	Materials
• Model decimal place value with base-ten blocks • Understand place value in decimals to the hundredths-place • Express decimals with fractions and mixed numbers • Express decimals in expanded form	• Base-ten blocks • Decimal cards (Blackline Master 5)

Memory Work

- **What does perimeter measure?** *The distance around the outside edge of a shape.*
- **What does area measure?** *The amount of space that a shape covers.*

Lessons 2.4 – 2.7 review decimals to the hundredths-place. In Lesson 2.8, your child will extend his understanding of decimals to the thousandths-place.

You will use base-ten blocks to model decimal place value in this lesson. See the Unit 2 **Teaching Math with Confidence** for an explanation of how using manipulatives helps your child develop deeper decimal number sense. You'll also need decimal cards (Blackline Master 5, cut apart on the dotted lines) for the first time in this lesson.

Warm-up (A): Use Base-Ten Blocks to Model Decimal Place-Value

Last year, you learned that decimal numbers are an extension of the usual place-value system. We divide by 10 to create places with a smaller value.

We will use base-ten blocks to represent decimals in this unit. A flat looks like a decimal square, so we'll use 1 flat to represent 1 whole. Place 1 flat on the table. Show your child the matching decimal square in part A.

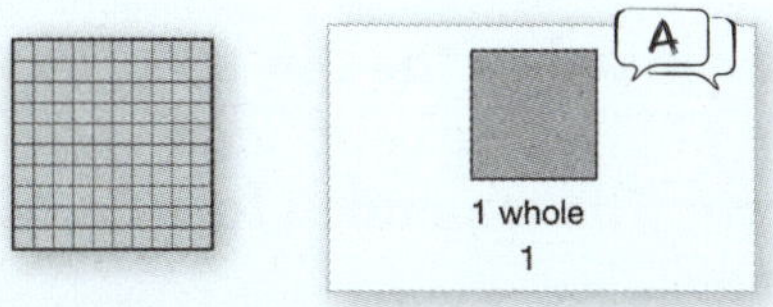

If you divide 1 whole into 10 equal parts, you get 10 tenths. The next-smaller place after the ones-place is called the *tenths-place*.

If you divide a flat into 10 equal parts, you get 10 rods. We will use rods to represent tenths. Place 1 rod on the table.

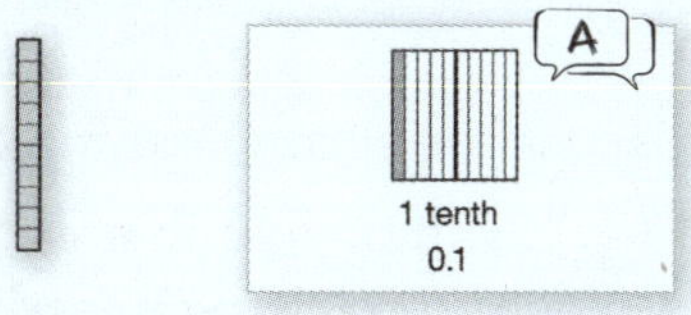

If you divide each tenth into 10 equal parts, you get 10 hundredths. The next-smaller place after the tenths-place is called the *hundredths-place.*

If you divide a rod into 10 equal parts, you get 10 unit blocks. We will use unit blocks to represent hundredths. Place 1 unit block on the table.

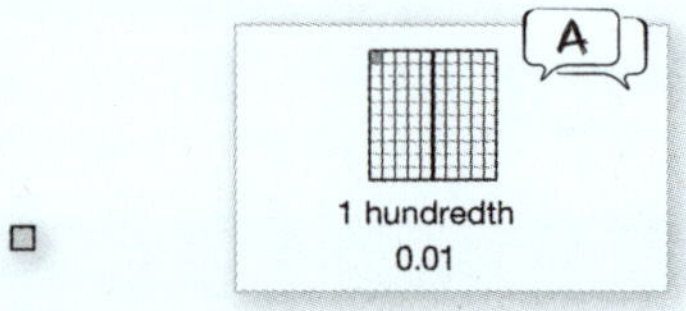

Can you guess what the place after the hundredths-place is called? *Thousandths.* **What about the place after that?** *Ten-thousandths.* **The decimal places follow the same pattern as whole number places. Just like with whole numbers, we can continue this pattern forever to make numbers as small as we want! You'll learn about the thousandths-place later in this unit.**

Activity (B): Review Representing Decimals in Multiple Ways

Today, you'll review how to use place-value thinking to represent decimals in multiple ways. Have your child read the text box aloud.

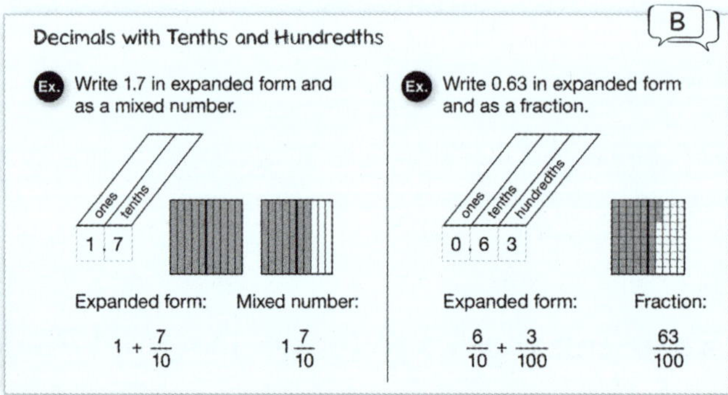

Use the following questions to discuss the first example:

- **The first number is 1.7.** (Read the number as "one point seven.")
- **What digit is in the ones-place?** *1.* **The 1 is in the ones-place, so it has a value of 1.**
- **What digit is in the tenths-place?** *7.* **The 7 is in the tenths-place, so it has a value of 7 tenths.**
- **Which part of the picture matches the 1 in 1.7?** *The whole square.*
- **Which part matches the 7?** *The 7 large strips.*
- Point to the expanded form. **The expanded form is the sum of the value of each digit: 1 plus 7 tenths.**
- Point to the mixed number. **1 plus 7 tenths equals 1 and seven-tenths.**

Read each individual digit in the decimals in your child's lessons. For example, in this activity, read 1.7 as "one point seven" rather than "one and seven tenths." Or, read 0.63 as "zero point six three" and not "sixty-three hundredths." Reading numbers in this way ensures that your child makes sense of the place-value meaning of the digits himself.

Use the following questions to discuss the second example:

- **The second number is 0.63.** (Read the number as "zero point six three.")
- **What digit is in the ones-place?** *0.* **Writing a leading zero in the ones-place makes it easier to see the decimal point.**
- **What digit is in the tenths-place?** *6.* **The 6 is in the tenths-place, so it has a value of 6 tenths.**

- **What digit is in the hundredths-place?** *3.* **The 3 is in the hundredths-place, so it has a value of 3 hundredths.**
- **Which part of the picture matches the 6?** *The 6 large strips.*
- **Which part of the picture matches the 3?** *The 3 small squares.*
- Point to the expanded form. **The expanded form of 0.63 is 6 tenths plus 3 hundredths.**
- Point to the fraction. **How many hundredths of this decimal square are shaded?** *63.* **6 tenths equal 60 hundredths, so 63 hundredths are shaded. 0.63 equals sixty-three-hundredths.**

Have your child model each example decimal with base-ten blocks. **Which is greater, 1.7 or 0.63?** *1.7.* **How do you know?** *Sample answer: 1.7 is more than one whole, and 0.63 is less than 1 whole.*

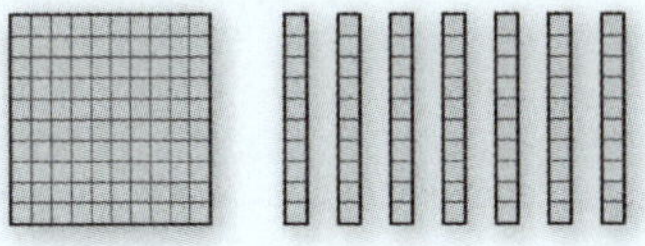

1.7 modeled with base-ten blocks.

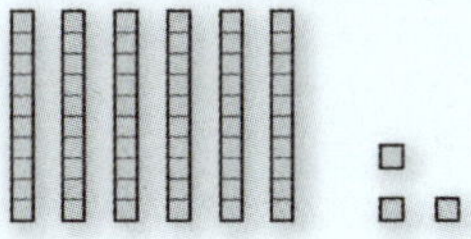

0.63 modeled with base-ten blocks.

Have your child color the decimal squares and complete the chart to match the decimal numbers.

Decimal	Decimal Squares	Expanded Form	Fraction or Mixed Number
0.27		$\frac{2}{10} + \frac{7}{100}$	$\frac{27}{100}$
1.3		$1 + \frac{3}{10}$	$1\frac{3}{10}$
1.45		$1 + \frac{4}{10} + \frac{5}{100}$	$1\frac{45}{100}$
1.06		$1 + \frac{6}{100}$	$1\frac{6}{100}$

It is also mathematically correct to write the expanded form for 1.7 as 1 + 0.7 or the expanded form for 0.63 as 0.6 + 0.03. *Math with Confidence* uses fractions for decimal expanded form to help your child better understand the connections between decimals and fractions.

Make sure your child writes a leading zero in the ones-place for decimals with a value less than 1. Developing this habit makes it easier to see the decimal point and helps prevent mistakes, especially when you align decimal places to add and subtract decimals.

Activity: Play Decimal War

Play Decimal War. If your child has trouble comparing the numbers, have him construct each number from base-ten blocks.

Decimal War

Materials: Decimal cards (cards with non-zero digits in the tenths-place and hundredths-place only, 18 cards total)

Object of the Game: Win the most cards.

Shuffle together the following decimal cards. (You will not need the cards with non-zero digits in the thousandths-place.)

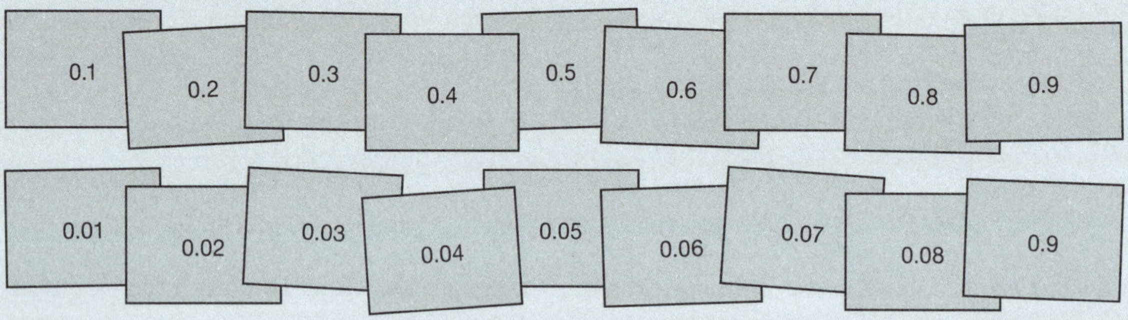

Use these decimal cards for this game.

Deal the cards face down into two equal piles. Give each player a pile. To play, both players flip over the top card in their piles. Whoever has the greater number wins both cards.

The player who flipped over 0.3 wins both cards, since 0.3 is greater than 0.07.

Play until the piles run out. Whoever has won more cards wins the game.

Independent Practice and Review

Have your child complete the Lesson 2.4 Practice and Review workbook pages.

Lesson 2.5
Mental Addition and Subtraction with Decimals

Purpose	Materials
• Review using place-value thinking to mentally add and subtract whole numbers • Understand that tacking a zero on to the end of a decimal does not change its value • Use place-value thinking to mentally add and subtract simple decimals • Find pairs of decimals whose sum is 1 whole	• Base-ten blocks • Counters

Memory Work

- **What are the four basic operations?** *Addition, subtraction, multiplication, and division.*
- **What is an equation?** *A number sentence with an equals sign.*
- **What is an expression?** *Part of a number sentence without an equals sign.*

In this lesson, you'll use mental math to help your child better understand decimal place value. Your child will learn how to add and subtract decimals with the vertical written process in Lesson 2.7.

Warm-up: Practice Mental Addition and Subtraction with Whole Numbers

When you were younger, you learned how to use place-value thinking to mentally add and subtract whole numbers. Ask your child the following oral mental math questions.

- **4 plus 3?** *7.*
- **40 plus 30?** *70.*
- **40 plus 3?** *43.*
- **4 plus 30?** *34.*
- **4 minus 3?** *1.*
- **40 minus 30?** *10.*
- **40 minus 3?** *37.*

If your child has trouble with any of these questions, model them with base-ten blocks.

Activity (A): Explore Equal Decimals

Have your child color the first two decimal squares to match the numbers printed below them.

- **What do you notice about the decimal squares for 0.6 and 0.60?** *Sample answer: The same amount is shaded in each pair.*
- **What fraction of each square is shaded?** *Six-tenths and sixty-hundredths.*
- **Six-tenths and sixty-hundredths are equivalent fractions. Both fractions mean the same part of the square.**
- **In the same way, 0.6 and 0.60 are equal to each other. Both decimals mean the same part of the square.**

Repeat with the other pair of decimals. **What fraction of each square is shaded?** *Four-tenths and forty-hundredths.*

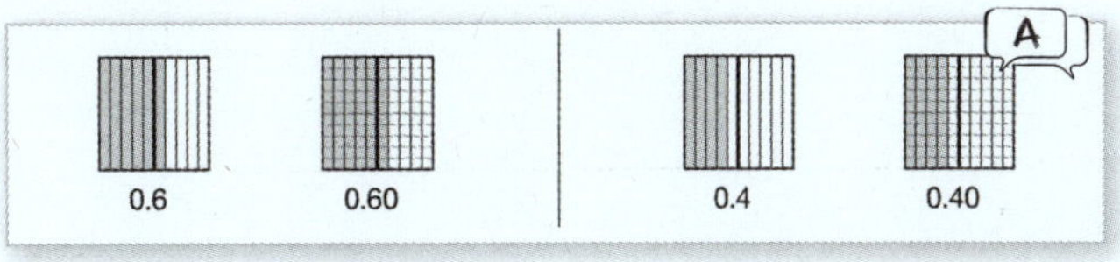

Tacking on a zero at the end of a decimal doesn't change its value. 0.6 equals 0.60, and 0.40 equals 0.4. Why doesn't the extra zero change the value of the decimals? *Sample answer: Because the extra zero doesn't add anything to the number.*

Tacking on zeros at the end of a decimal doesn't add any value, and it doesn't change the places of any of the digits. This is very different from whole numbers. If I tack on a zero at the end of 7, I move the 7 to the tens-place. I get 70, not 7!

Activity (B): Mentally Add and Subtract Simple Decimals

When you were younger, you learned how to use place-value thinking to mentally add and subtract whole numbers. You learned to add ones to ones or tens to tens, or to subtract ones from ones and tens from tens. Today, you'll learn how to use the same kind of place-value thinking to mentally add and subtract decimals.

Read aloud the first example: ***0.5 plus 0.4 equals what?*** (Read the decimals as "zero point five" and "zero point four.")

- **What place is the 5 in?** *The tenths-place.*
- **What place is the 4 in?** *The tenths-place.*
- **5 tenths plus 4 tenths equals 9 tenths, so the answer is 0.9.**

Discuss 0.07 – 0.03 in the same way.

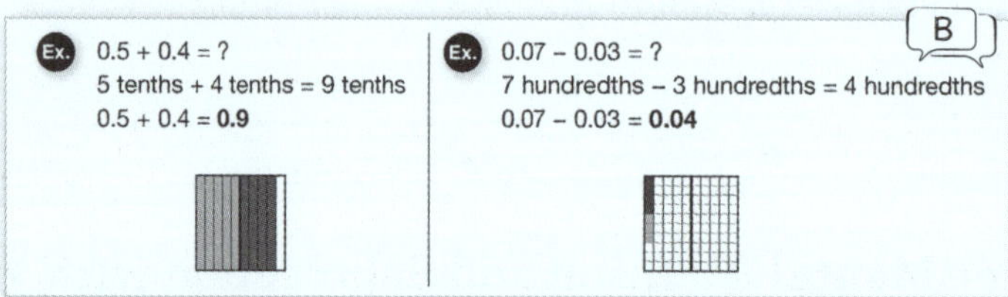

Read aloud the next example: ***0.3 plus 0.07 equals what?*** (Read the decimals as "zero point three" and "zero point zero seven.")

- **What place is the 3 in?** *The tenths-place.*
- **What place is the 7 in?** *The hundredths-place.*
- **The 3 and 7 are in different places, so we can't just add 3 plus 7 to find the answer.**
- **3 tenths equals 30 hundredths. So, we add 30 hundredths plus 7 hundredths to find that the answer is 37 hundredths, or 0.37.**

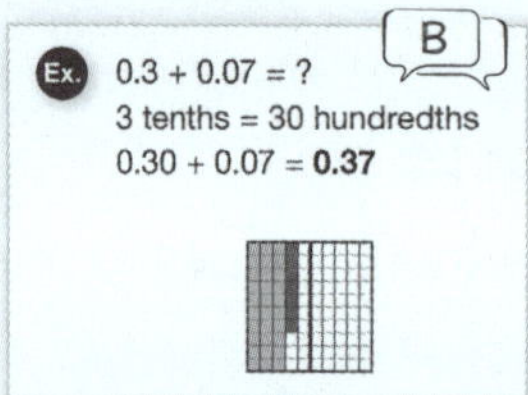

Read aloud the last example: ***0.5 minus 0.02 equals what?*** (Read the decimals as "zero point five" and "zero point zero two.")

- **What place is the 5 in?** *The tenths-place.*
- **What place is the 2 in?** *The hundredths-place.*
- **The 5 and 2 are in different places, so we can't just subtract 2 from 5 to find the answer.**
- **5 tenths equals 50 hundredths. So, we subtract 2 hundredths from 50 hundredths to find that the answer is 48 hundredths, or 0.48.**

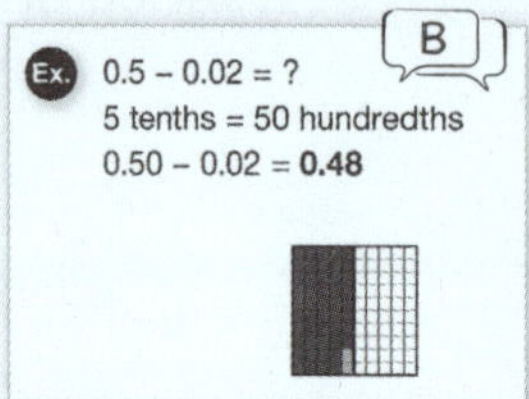

Have your child use place-value thinking to solve the practice problems.

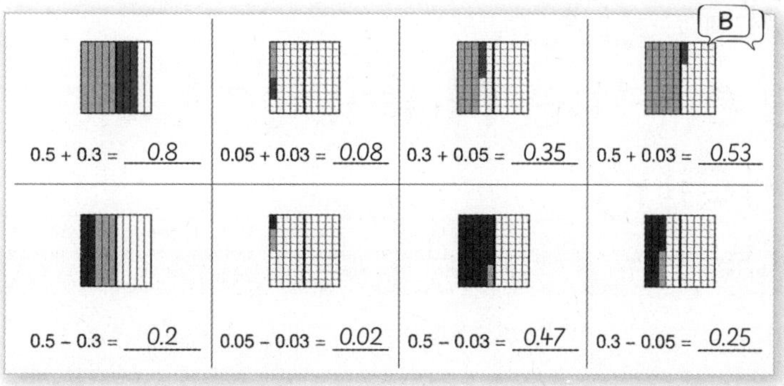

Activity (C): Play Four in a Row

Play Four in a Row.

If your child needs help visualizing the problems, place base-ten blocks on top of a flat to help find the matching numbers. For example, to find a match for 0.4, place 4 rods on top of a flat: **I need 6 tenths or 60 hundredths more to create 1 whole. So, I'm looking for 0.6 or 0.60.**

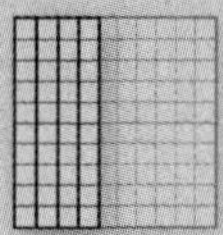

Four in a Row

Materials: 12 counters per player, with a different color for each player

Object of the Game: Be the first player to place counters in 4 boxes in a row, either horizontally, vertically, or diagonally.

On your turn, find a pair of numbers on the board whose sum is 1. Use 2 counters to cover both boxes. Play then passes to the other player.

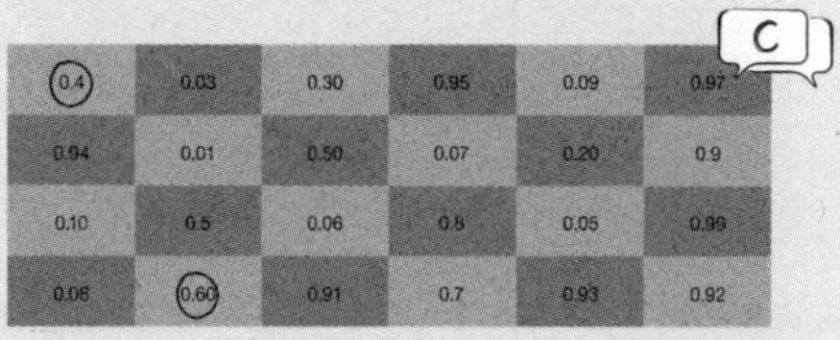

Sample play. 0.4 + 0.60 equals 1 whole.

Continue until one player covers 4 boxes in a row, either horizontally, vertically, or diagonally.

Answer Key:

- 0.4 and 0.60
- 0.7 and 0.30
- 0.20 and 0.8
- 0.9 and 0.10
- 0.5 and 0.50
- 0.99 and 0.01
- 0.95 and 0.05
- 0.92 and 0.08
- 0.94 and 0.06
- 0.93 and 0.07
- 0.91 and 0.09
- 0.97 and 0.03

Independent Practice and Review

Have your child complete the Lesson 2.5 Practice and Review workbook pages.

Lesson 2.6
Decimals on the Number Line and Rounding

Purpose	Materials
• Review mentally adding tenths and hundredths • Label decimals on number lines • Round decimals	• None

Memory Work	• **What is the order of operations?** *Parentheses, multiply or divide from left to right, add or subtract from left to right.*

Warm-up (A): Review Mentally Adding Tenths and Hundredths

In the last lesson, you learned to mentally add and subtract decimals. Have your child color the decimal squares to match each addition equation. Then, have him find the sum.

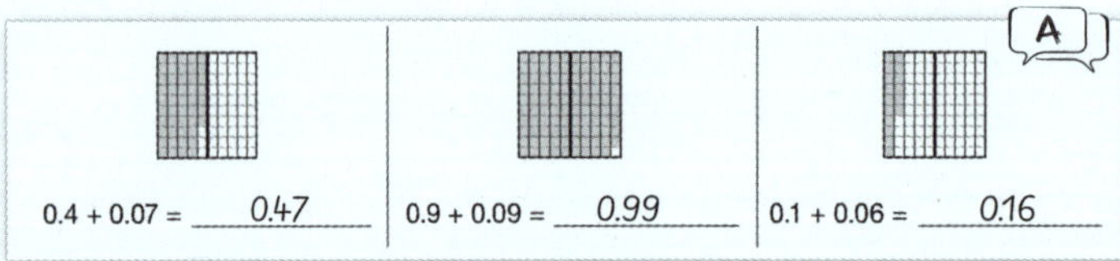

Adding tenths and hundredths prepares your child to use similar thinking to identify decimals on the number line in the next activity.

Activity (B): Identify Decimals on the Number Line

Today, you'll review how to label decimals on number lines. You'll also learn how to round decimals.

On the first number line, the distance between 0 and 1 is split into 10 parts. 1 whole divided by 10 equals 1 tenth. So, each interval is 1 tenth. We can start at 0 and count by tenths to see what number each tick mark stands for.

Explain as needed that "interval" means the space between tick marks on the number line.

The first two tick marks are already labeled. 1 tenth is 0.1. (Read 0.1 as "zero point 1.") **2 tenths is 0.2.** Have your child continue the pattern and label the rest of the tick marks.

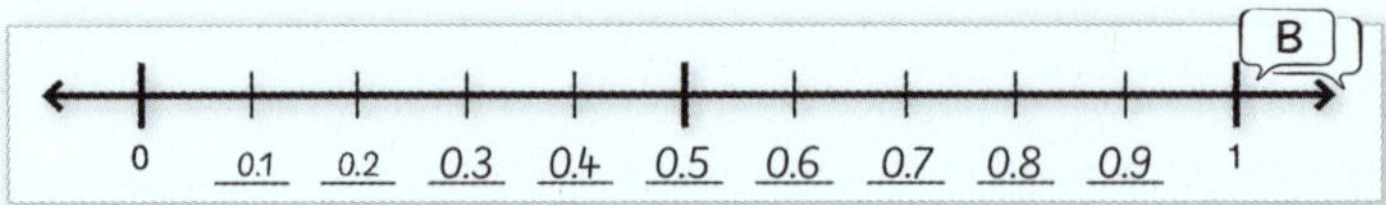

On the second number line, the distance between each tenth is split into 10 equal parts. 1 tenth divided by 10 equals 1 hundredth. So, each interval is 1 hundredth. We *could* start at 0 and count by hundredths to see what number each tick mark stands for. That could take a long time, though! Instead, we'll use the tick marks for tenths to help us identify the numbers.

Point to the first blank. **This tick mark is 1 hundredth more than 1 tenth. What's 1 tenth plus 1 hundredth?** *0.11.* Write 0.11 in the blank. Have your child label the other missing numbers in the same way.

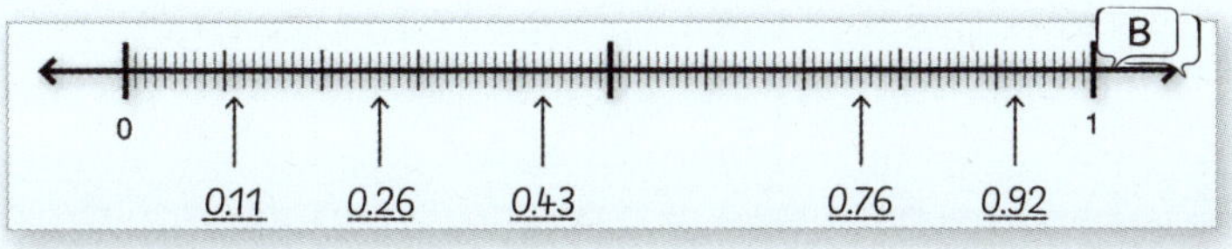

If your child has trouble labeling the numbers, use base-ten blocks to model the numbers. For example, for the first blank, place 1 rod and 1 unit block on the table: **1 tenth equals 10 hundredths. 10 plus 1 equals 11, so 1 tenth plus 1 hundredth equals 11 hundredths.**

0.1 + 0.01 = 0.11

Show your child the two shorter number lines. **These two number lines have the same *length* on the page, but that doesn't mean they stand for the same *distance* on the number line. When you read number lines, it's important to look closely at the labels and the number of intervals between the labels.**

Point to the number line that goes from 2 to 3. **On this number line, the distance between 2 and 3 is split into 10 equal parts. So, how large is each interval?** *1 tenth.* **How do you know?** *Sample answer. 3 minus 2 is 1, and 1 divided into 10 equal parts is 1 tenth.* Have your child label the missing number.

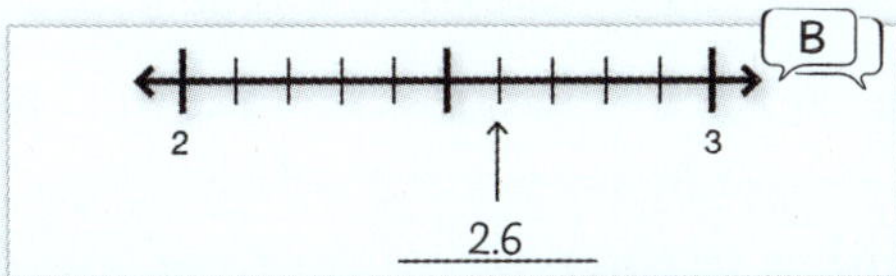

Point to the number line that goes from 1.7 to 1.8. **The next number line zooms in on the part of the number line from 1.7 to 1.8. On this number line, the distance between 1.7 and 1.8 is split into 10 equal parts. So, how large is each interval?** *1 hundredth.* **How do you know?** *Sample answer. 1.8 is 1 tenth greater than 1.7. 1 tenth divided into 10 equal parts is 1 hundredth.* Have your child label the missing number. If he's not sure, suggest he add 3 hundredths to 1.7.

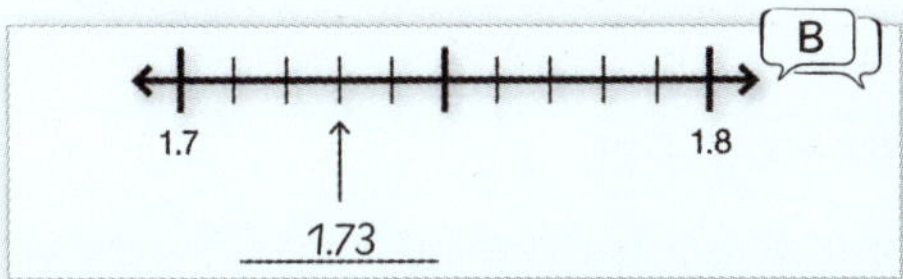

Activity (C): Round Decimals to the Ones-Place or Tenths-Place

We round decimals just like we round whole numbers. We underline the digit we're rounding to and look at the next-smaller place. If the digit is less than 5, we round down. If the digit is 5 or greater, we round up. When we round decimals, we drop the digits after the place we round to. Have your child read the text box aloud.

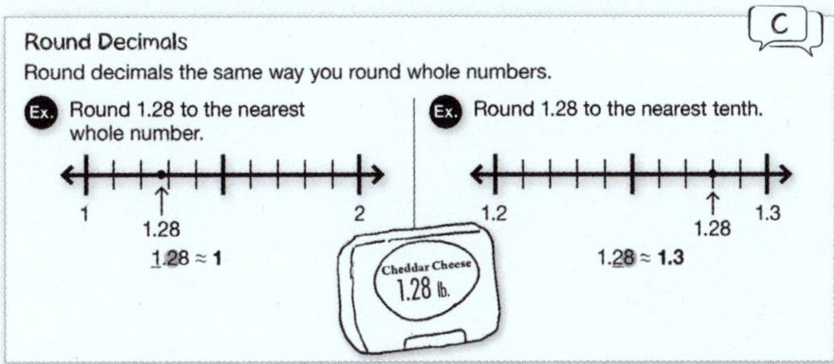

This block of cheese weighs 1.28 pounds. Use the following questions to discuss the examples.

- **To round 1.28 to the nearest whole number, we underline the 1. What digit is in the next-smaller place?** *2.* **2 is less than 5, so we round down.**
- **On the number line, 1.28 is between 1 and 2. It's closer to 1, so we round down to 1. 1.28 rounded to the nearest whole number is 1.**
- **To round 1.28 to the nearest tenth of a pound, we underline the 2. What digit is in the next-smaller place?** *8.* **8 is greater than 5, so we round up.**
- **On the number line, 1.28 is between 1.2 and 1.3. It's closer to 1.3, so we round up to 1.3.**

> If your child wonders why you drop the digits after the rounded place, explain that decimal digits in a measurement mean that the number is accurate to that place. For example, if you wrote 1.0, that would mean that the weight of the cheese is within 1 tenth of 1.0 pounds.

In everyday life, we choose whether to round and what digit to round to depending on the situation. If you want to serve cheese and crackers, it's probably fine to know that you have about 1 pound of cheese. If you're carefully following a recipe, you usually need to know the exact weight.

Have your child complete the practice exercises and round the numbers to the underlined places.

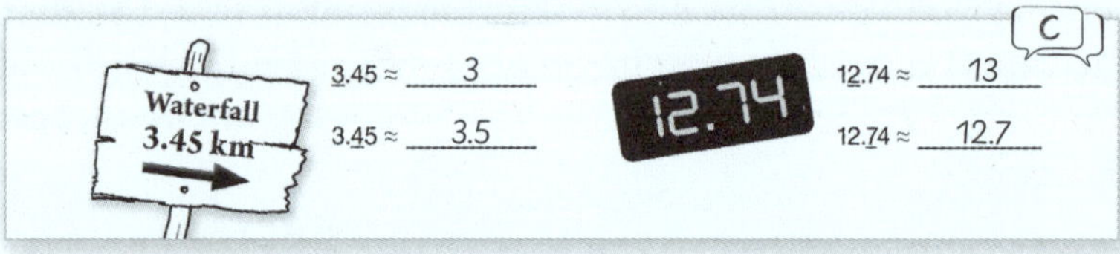

After your child completes the exercises, discuss the real-world advantages and disadvantages of rounding each number.

- For the trail sign: **Rounding to the nearest tenth of a kilometer tells you that the trail is about 3 and half kilometers long. Rounding to the nearest kilometer makes it seem like the trail is shorter than it is.**
- For the digital clock: **In track races, the runners' times are often very close together. Many runners might have a time that was close to 13 seconds. Race officials usually record the times to the hundredth of a second so that the scores reflect who won.**

Independent Practice and Review

Have your child complete the Lesson 2.6 Practice and Review workbook pages.

Lesson 2.7
Add and Subtract Decimals to the Hundredths-Place

Purpose	Materials
• Review adding and subtracting whole numbers with the written algorithms • Use the traditional written algorithms to add and subtract decimals with tenths and hundredths	• Base-ten blocks • Decimal Place-Value Chart (Blackline Master 6)

Memory Work

- **What do we call the number to be divided?** *The dividend.*
- **What do we call the number we divide by?** *The divisor.*
- **What do we call the result when we divide two numbers?** *The quotient.*
- **What do we call an amount that is left over after division?** *The remainder.*

Warm-up (A): Review Adding and Subtracting Whole Numbers

In younger grades, you learned how to use the written algorithms to add and subtract whole numbers. You stack the numbers on top of each other and line up the digits with the same place value. Then, you start with the ones-place and add or subtract.

Have your child complete the addition and subtraction problems in part A. If your child has trouble, use base-ten blocks to model the problems.

A

294 + 1,325

```
    1
  1,325
+   294
  1,619
```

702 − 45

```
     9
   6 10 12
   7  0  2
−     4  5
   6  5  7
```

Activity (B): Review Adding and Subtracting Money Amounts

Today, you'll learn how to add and subtract decimals with the written algorithms. We'll use base-ten blocks to model the problems.

Adding and subtracting decimals is a lot like adding and subtracting whole numbers. The only tricky part is making sure you line up the numbers correctly. Have your child read aloud the text in part B.

B

How to Add and Subtract Decimals

1. Line up the decimal points.
   - If one number is a whole number, write a decimal point after the whole number.
2. Tack on zeros until both numbers have the same number of decimal places.
3. Add or subtract like usual. Write a decimal point in the answer below the other decimal points.

Ex. 2.5 + 0.87 = ?

```
  2.50          1
+ 0.87   →    2.50
             +0.87
              3.37
```

Ex. 2 − 0.64 = ?

```
                9
              1 10 10
  2.00        2. 0  0
− 0.64   →   −0.64
              1.36
```

The first example shows how to add 2.5 and 0.87.

- Point to both decimal points. **Are the decimal points in both numbers lined up?** *Yes.*
- **How many decimal places does 2.5 have?** *1.*
- **How many decimal places does 0.87 have?** *2.*

- **So, we tack on a zero to 2.5 so that both numbers have the same number of decimal places.** Point to the highlighted 0 in 2.50.
- **Then, we add like usual. What does 2.5 plus 0.87 equal?** *3.37.*

Let's use base-ten blocks to check this answer. We'll put them on the Decimal Place-Value Chart to keep track of what decimal places they represent. Show your child the Decimal Place-Value Chart. **This chart has columns for each place. You'll learn about the thousandths-place in the next lesson.**

Arrange 2 flats and 5 rods on the chart to represent 2.5. Arrange 8 rods and 7 unit blocks on the chart to represent 0.87.

> Stack the blocks as needed to fit on the Decimal Place-Value Chart. To save space, these diagrams omit the thousandths-place.

Let's add. We'll start at the place with the lowest value, just like usual.

- **0 hundredths plus 7 hundredths equal 7 hundredths.** Point to the 7 in the printed example.

$$\begin{array}{r} 2.50 \\ +\,0.87 \\ \hline 7 \end{array}$$

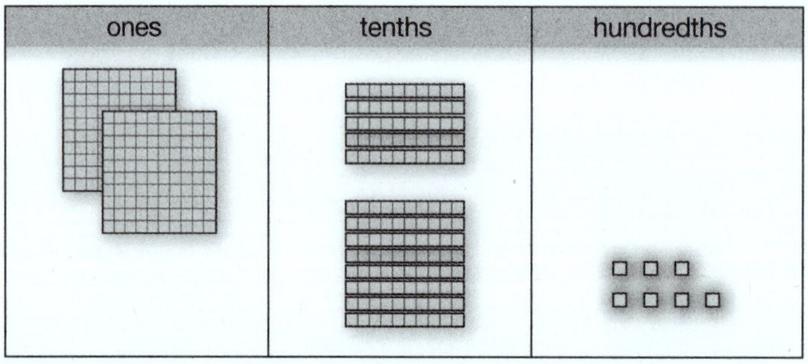

- **5 tenths plus 8 tenths equal 13 tenths. We trade 10 tenths for 1 whole.** Trade 10 rods for 1 flat and place it in the ones-column. **We show the trade by writing a 1 in the ones-column and a 3 in the answer's tenths-place.** Point to the 1 and 3.

$$\begin{array}{r} \mathbf{1} \\ 2.50 \\ +\,0.87 \\ \hline \mathbf{3}7 \end{array}$$

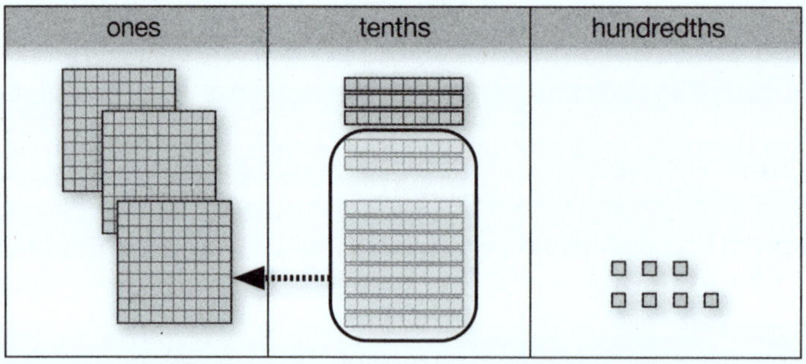

- **1 plus 2 plus 0 equals 3. We write 3 in the answer's ones-place. We write a decimal point directly below the other decimal points so that all the digits are in the correct places.** Point to the 3 and decimal point.

$$\begin{array}{r} 1 \\ 2.50 \\ +\,0.87 \\ \hline \mathbf{3.}37 \end{array}$$

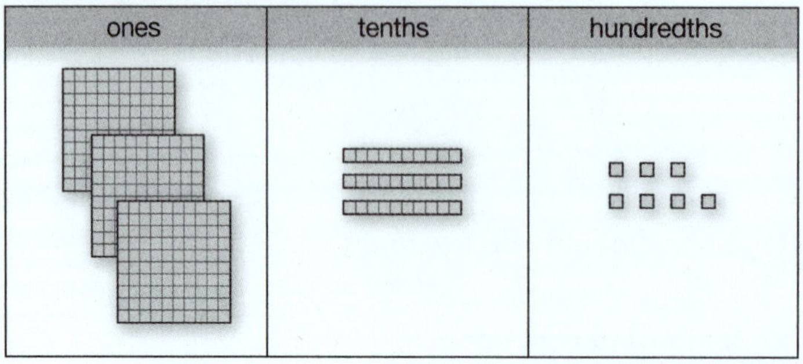

The second example shows how to subtract 0.64 from 2.

- **2 is a whole number, so we write a decimal point to show that the 2 is in the ones-place. We line up that decimal point with the decimal point in 0.64.** Point to both decimal points.
- **How many decimal places does 2 have?** *0.*
- **How many decimal places does 0.64 have?** *2.*
- **So, we tack on 2 zeros to 2 so that both numbers have the same number of decimal places.**
- **Then, we subtract like usual. What does 2 minus plus 0.64 equal?** *1.36.*

Let's use base-ten blocks to check this answer, too. Place 2 flats on the Decimal Place-Value Chart.

- **We start at the hundredths-place. We don't have any hundredths, so we need to trade. First, we trade 1 flat for 10 rods.** Trade 1 flat for 10 rods. Point to the crossed out 2 in the written example. **The 2 is crossed out and a 1 is written above it, because we only have 1 flat left.**
- Point to the crossed out 0 in the tenths-place, and the 10 written above it. **The 0 is crossed out and a 10 is written above it, because we now have 10 tenths.**

```
 1 10
 2.0 0   (2 and first 0 crossed out)
-0.6 4
```

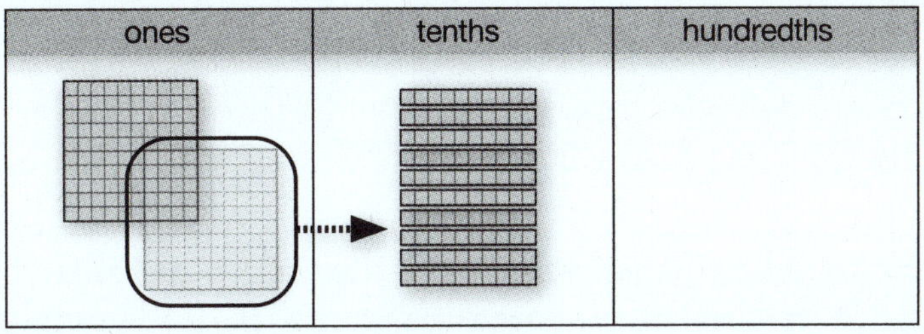

- **Next, we trade 1 tenth for 10 hundredths.** Trade 1 rod for 10 unit blocks. Point to the crossed out 10 above the tenths-place. **The 10 is crossed out and a 9 is written above it, because we only have 9 tenths left.**
- Point to the crossed out 0 in the hundredths-place, and the 10 written above it. **The 0 is crossed out and a 10 is written above it, because we now have 10 hundredths.**

```
    9
 1 10 10   (10 crossed out)
 2. 0  0   (2, 0, 0 crossed out)
-0. 6  4
```

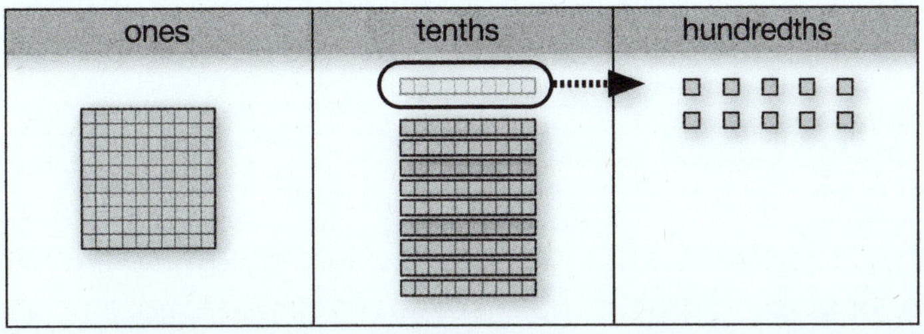

- **Now, we're ready to subtract. 10 hundredths minus 4 hundredths equal 6 hundredths.** Remove 4 unit blocks and point to the 6 in the example's answer.
- **9 tenths minus 6 tenths equal 3 tenths.** Remove 6 rods and point to the 3 in the example's answer.
- **1 minus 0 equals 1. We write 1 in the answer's ones-place. We write a decimal point directly below the other decimal points so that all the digits are in the correct places.** Point to the 1 and decimal point.

```
    9
 1 10 10   (10 crossed out)
 2. 0  0   (2, 0, 0 crossed out)
-0. 6  4
 1. 3  6
```

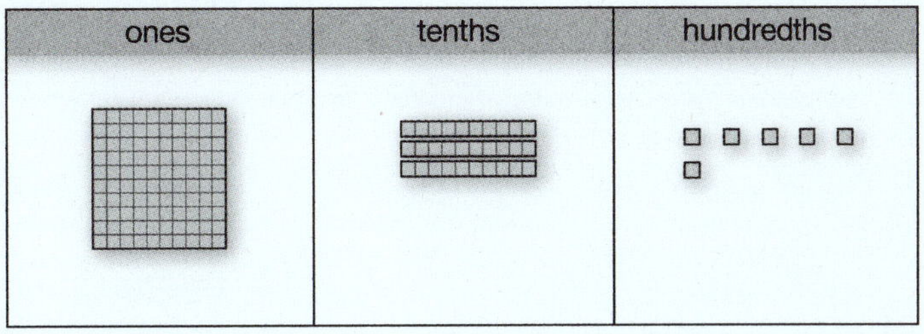

Activity (C): Play Leaf Fight

Play Leaf Fight. Help your child line up the numbers correctly and tack on zeros as needed. Use base-ten blocks on the Decimal Place-Value Chart to model the problems as needed.

The silliness of this activity makes solving these problems feel more relaxed and fun. But, if your child would rather not throw the papers (or if you're teaching this lesson in a place where it's not practical), put the paper wads in a bowl and draw 2 wads each turn instead. Replace the wads in the bowl after each turn.

Leaf Fight

Materials: 10 slips of paper

Object of the Game: Win the most points.

Write the following numbers on slips of paper. Crumple each wad of paper and place them on the table.

Both players count down in unison from 10 while throwing the crumpled wads of paper at each other. When you reach 1, both players stop and pick up the 2 closest wads of paper.

Both players unfold their paper wads and write their numbers in a blank problem on the scorecard. (Start with the first problem on the left, and complete the problems in order.) If the blank grids have a plus sign, each player finds the sum of the numbers they picked up. If the blank grids have a minus sign, each player finds the difference between the numbers they picked up. Whoever has the greater answer wins a point.

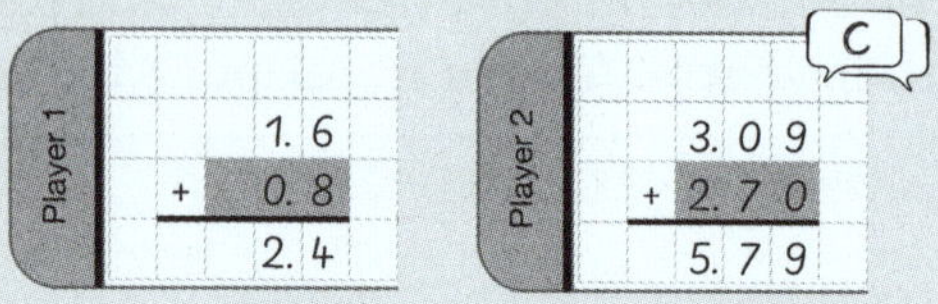

Sample first round. Player 2 wins the point, since 5.79 is greater than 2.4.

Crumple up your numbers and add them back to the pile of "leaves." Repeat until you have filled in all of the blank problems. Whoever wins more points wins the game.

Independent Practice and Review

Have your child complete the Lesson 2.7 Practice and Review workbook pages.

Lesson 2.8
Decimals to the Thousandths-Place

Purpose

- Introduce thousandths
- Write decimals to the thousandths-place in expanded form
- Compare decimals to the thousandths-place

Materials

- Base-ten blocks
- Decimal squares (Blackline Master 7, in a page protector)
- Decimal cards (Blackline Master 5)
- Dry-erase marker

Memory Work

- **What do we call the result when we multiply two numbers?** *The product.*
- **What do we call the numbers in a multiplication equation that we multiply together?** *Factors.*

Children often find decimals to the thousandths-place difficult to understand and read. You'll use the decimal squares on Blackline Master 7 to make these tiny amounts more concrete. Put the decimal squares in a page protector before the lesson (and make sure you have a dry erase marker handy) so that you can outline the decimal squares to represent different numbers.

Warm-up (A): Introduce Thousandths with Base-Ten Blocks and Decimal Squares

In the last few lessons, you've learned about decimals with digits in the tenths-place and hundredths-place. Today, you'll learn about decimals with digits in the thousandths-place.

In Lesson 2.4, we used base-ten blocks to model ones, tenths, and hundredths. Place 1 flat, 1 rod, and 1 unit cube on the table. **Each flat represents 1 whole. Each rod represents 1 tenth. Each unit cube represents 1 hundredth.**

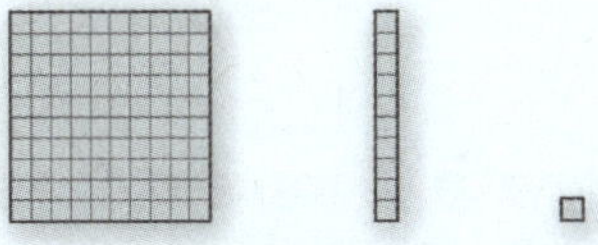

If we divide each hundredth into 10 equal parts, we get thousandths. Imagine you cut each unit cube into 10 parts. Each tiny piece would be one-thousandth of the flat. Those pieces would very hard to hold and count!

We don't have any base-ten blocks that small, so we'll use printed decimal squares to show thousandths instead. Show your child the decimal squares on Blackline Master 7.

That's a lot of lines! It's much easier to understand all the lines if you think of the decimal squares like base-ten blocks.

- **Each large square stands for 1 whole, just like we've used 1 flat to represent 1 whole.** Put a flat on top of the printed square to demonstrate. Have your child outline the whole square with a dry-erase marker. Then, erase the outline (to prepare for the next step.)

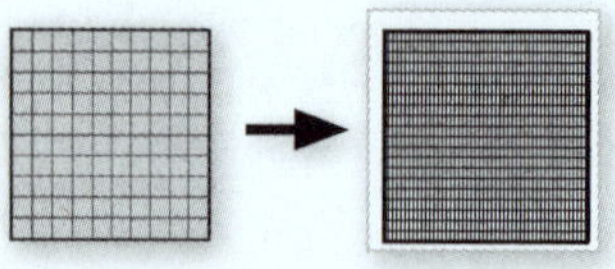

To save space, these diagrams include only one square from the blackline master unless both are needed.

- **Each large strip represents 1 tenth.** Put 1 rod on top of the left-most large strip to demonstrate. Have your child outline the matching strip as shown. Then, erase.

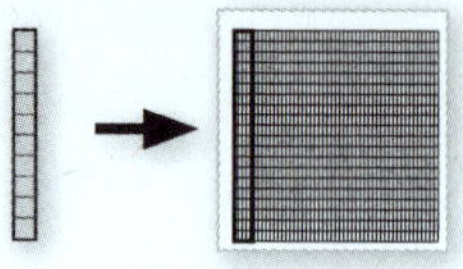

- **Each small square represents 1 hundredth.** Put 1 unit block in the top left corner to demonstrate. Have your child outline the small square as shown. Then, erase.

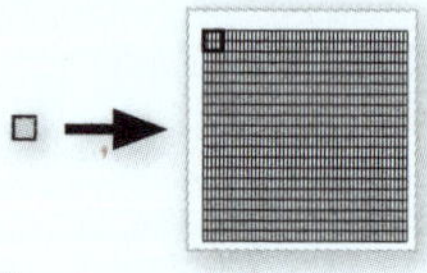

- **Each small strip represents 1 thousandth.** Have your child use a dry-erase marker to color the small strip in the top left corner. Then, erase.

Show your child the matching diagram in part A. Point to the picture of 1 thousandth. **We'll pretend the little circle next to the decimal square is like a magnifying glass. It zooms in on the decimal square so we can see the thousandths on the workbook pages.**

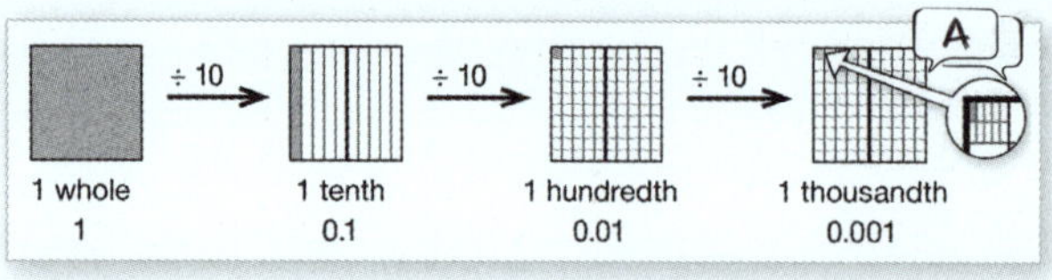

Activity (B): Write Decimals with Thousandths in Expanded Form

We often use decimals to the thousandths-place when we want to measure exact weights. This scale measures to the thousandth of a pound. Have your child read the text box aloud.

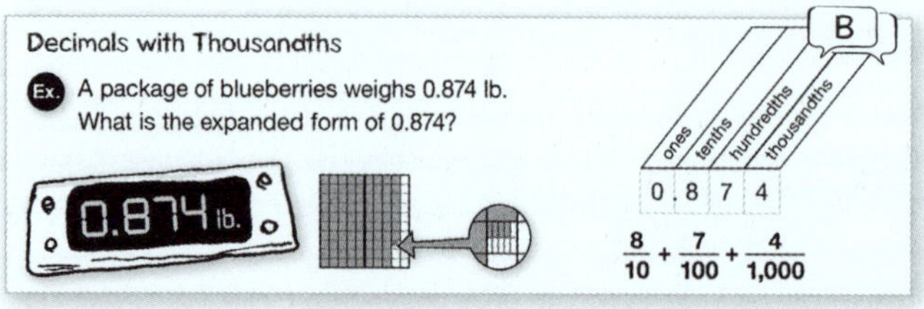

Use the following questions to discuss the place-value chart and decimal square.

- **What place is the zero in?** *The ones-place.*
- **What place is the 8 in?** *The tenths-place.* **Which part of the decimal square matches the 8?** *The 8 large strips.*

- **What place is the 7 in?** *The hundredths-place.* **Which part of the decimal square matches the 7?** *The 7 small squares.*
- **What place is the 4 in?** *The thousandths-place.* **Which part of the decimal square matches the 4?** *The 4 small strips.*

To write 0.874 in expanded form, we write the sum of the value of each digit: 8 tenths plus 7 hundredths plus 4 thousandths. Zeros don't add anything to the value of the number, so we don't include zeros in the expanded form.

Point to the decimal point in the place-value chart. **Sometimes, kids feel confused when they see so many digits in a number. If you ever feel confused by all the digits, remember that the decimal point separates the whole number part of the number from the fractional part of the number. The digits to the *left* of the decimal point tell the whole number. The digits to the *right* of the decimal point tell the fractional part.**

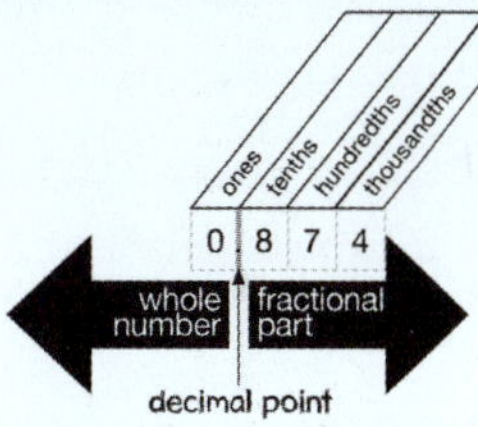

The digits to the left of the decimal point tell the whole number.
The digits to the right of the decimal point tell the fractional part.

This chart shows the weights of some other packages of blueberries. The first basket weighs 1.264 pounds.

- **What place is the 1 in?** *The ones-place.* Outline 1 whole decimal square.
- **What place is the 2 in?** *The tenths-place.* Outline 2 large strips.
- **What place is the 6 in?** *The hundredths-place.* Outline 6 small squares.
- **What place is the 4 in?** *The thousandths-place.* Color in 4 small strips.
- **So, how do we write 1.264 in expanded form?** *1 plus two-tenths plus six-hundredths plus four-thousandths.* Write "1 + 2/10 + 6/100 + 4/1,000" in the chart.

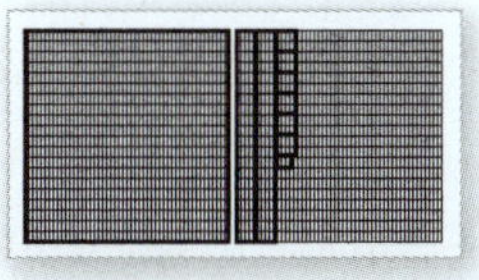

B

Weight (lbs.)	Expanded Form
1.264	$1 + \frac{2}{10} + \frac{6}{100} + \frac{4}{1,000}$

It's difficult to outline thousandths, so the lessons suggest coloring them instead. Always outline (or color) the decimal squares from left to right and top to bottom. Outline the tenths first, then the hundredths, and finally the thousandths.

If your child finds the lines on the decimal squares dizzying, have him represent the tenths and hundredths with real base-ten blocks. Put them directly on the decimal square, and then have him color only the thousandths on the blackline master.

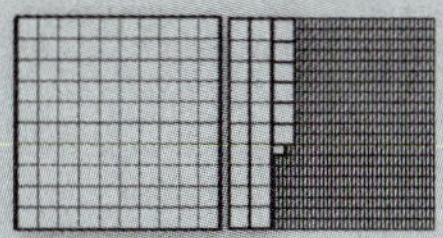

Have your child complete the rest of the chart in the same way. Have him represent each number on decimal squares before writing it in expanded form.

B

Weight (lbs.)	Expanded Form
1.264	$1 + \frac{2}{10} + \frac{6}{100} + \frac{4}{1,000}$
0.916	$\frac{9}{10} + \frac{1}{100} + \frac{6}{1,000}$
0.980	$\frac{9}{10} + \frac{8}{100}$
1.307	$1 + \frac{3}{10} + \frac{7}{1,000}$

> Make sure your child outlines the matching amounts even if he can easily write the numbers in expanded form. Outlining the matching amounts helps your child understand kinesthetically how small thousandths are compared to tenths and hundredths.

Which weights are greater than 1 pound? *1.264 and 1.307.* **Which weights are less than 1 pound?** *0.916 and 0.980.*

Which is the heaviest weight? *1.307 pounds.* **Which is the lightest weight?** *0.916 pounds.*

Activity (C): Play Decimal Compare

We're going to play a game called Decimal Compare. In this game, you get 3 decimal cards. One card has tenths, one card has hundredths, and one card has thousandths. You put the digits together to create one decimal number.

Place the following decimal cards (from Blackline Master 5) on the table: 0.4, 0.07, and 0.009.

- **0.4 is 4 tenths.** Use a dry erase marker to outline 4 large strips on a decimal square on Blackline Master 7.
- **0.07 is 7 hundredths.** Outline 7 small squares on the same decimal square.
- **0.009 is 9 thousandths.** Color 9 small strips on the same decimal square.
- **4 tenths plus 7 hundredths plus 9 thousandths equal 0.479. 0.479 is the standard form of the number.** Write 0.479 below the decimal square.

0.4 | 0.07 | 0.009

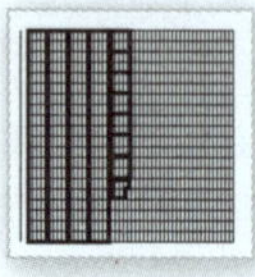

0.479

Play Decimal Compare.

Decimal Compare

Materials: Decimal cards (Blackline Master 5); decimal squares (Blackline Master 7)

Object of the Game: Win the most points.

Directions continued on next page.

Sort the decimal cards: place the cards with a non-zero digit in the tenths-place in one group, the cards with a non-zero digit in the hundredths-place in a different group, and the cards with a non-zero digit in the thousandths-place in a third group. Shuffle each group separately and place the cards in a face-down pile. Arrange the piles as shown.

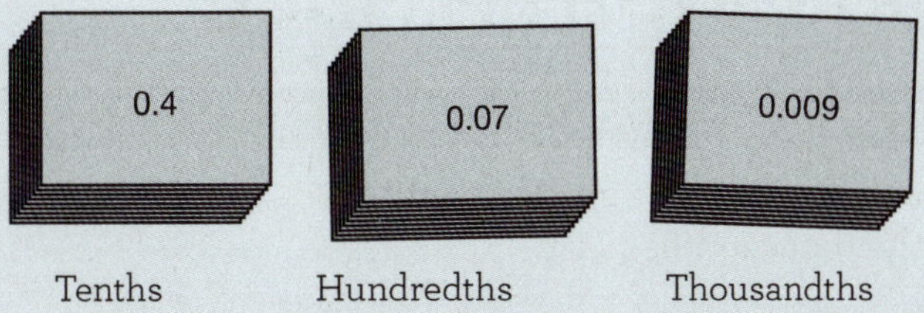

Decimal Compare is played in four rounds. On your turn, turn over the top card in each pile. Outline the value of each card on a decimal square. Write the total value of all three cards in your scorecard for the current round.

For example, if you turn over 0.3, 0.05, and 0.009 on your first turn, outline 3 tenths, 5 hundredths, and 9 thousandths on a decimal grid. Write 0.359 in the Round 1 space.

Then, the other player takes a turn in the same way. Whoever's number has the greater value wins a point for that round.

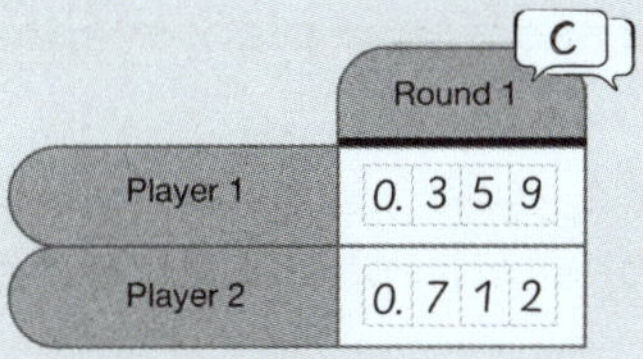

Player 2 wins, since he created the greater number.

Continue drawing cards off the top of the pile and play until you've completed all four rounds. Reshuffle the already-used cards as needed. Whoever has won more points wins. If both players have 2 points, play one additional tie-breaker round.

Save the decimal cards. You will need them again in Unit 14.

Independent Practice and Review

Have your child complete the Lesson 2.8 Practice and Review workbook pages.

Lesson 2.9
Compare Decimals to the Thousandths-Place

Purpose	Materials
• Review using place-value thinking to compare numbers • Compare numbers to the thousandths-place	• Decimal squares (Blackline Master 7), optional • 2 dice • Counters

Memory Work

- **How many millimeters equal 1 centimeter?** *10.*
- **How many centimeters equal 1 meter?** *100.*
- **How many meters equal 1 kilometer?** *1,000.*
- **How many grams equal 1 kilogram?** *1,000.*
- **How many milliliters equal 1 liter?** *1,000.*

Warm-up (A): Review Using Place-Value to Compare Numbers

When you were younger, you learned to use place-value thinking to compare whole numbers.

- **Which is greater, 3,209 or 2,999?** *3,209.* Write > in the circle. **Both of these numbers have a digit in the thousands-place. 3 is greater than 2, so 3,209 is greater than 2,999.**
- **Which is greater, 784 or 3,209?** *3,209.* Write < in the circle. **7 is greater than 3. But, the 7 is in the hundreds-place, while the 3 is in the thousands-place. So, 3,209 is greater.**

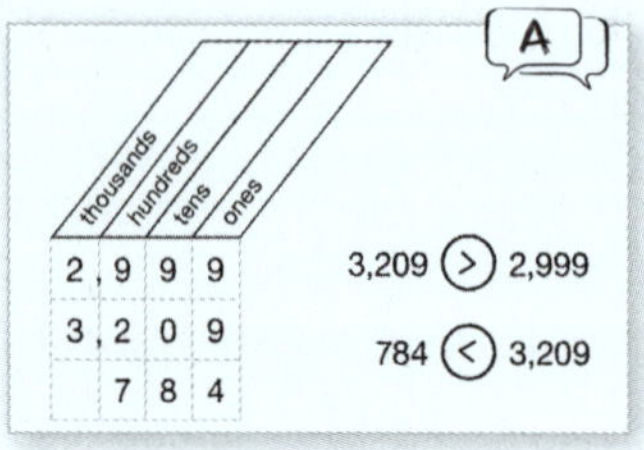

We also use place-thinking to compare decimals.

- **Which is greater, 0.29 or 0.8?** *0.8.* Write < in the circle. **Both of these numbers have a digit in the tenths-place. 8 is greater than 2, so 0.8 is greater than 0.29.**
- **Which is greater, 1 or 0.29?** *1.* Write > in the circle. **If you didn't know about decimal place-value, you might look at these numbers and think that 0.29 is greater, since 29 is greater than 1. But, the 1 is in the ones-place, and the 2 in 0.29 is in the tenths-place. So, 1 is greater than 0.29.**

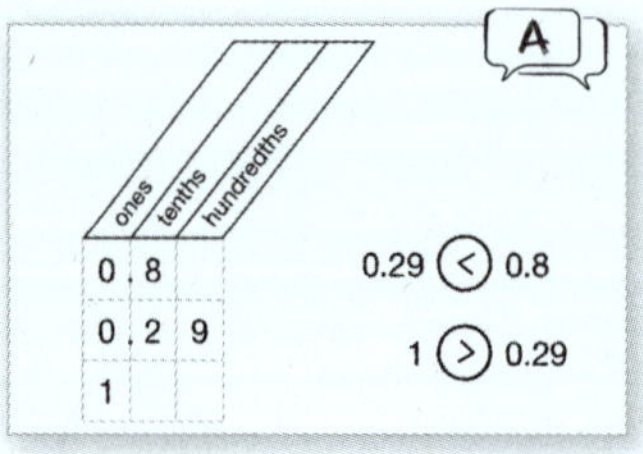

If your child has trouble understanding these comparisons, model the numbers with base-ten blocks or outline them on decimal squares.

Activity (B): Use Decimal Squares and Place-Value Thinking to Compare Decimals

Today, you'll learn how to use place-value thinking to compare decimals to the thousandths-place.

Race car drivers have to be able to react to the road very quickly. They do tests to see how quickly they can react to things. They want their reaction time to be as low as possible. Have your child read the text box aloud.

B

Compare Decimals

We can use place-value thinking or decimal squares to compare decimal numbers.

Ex. Max's reaction time is 0.219 seconds. Yuki's reaction time is 0.27 seconds. Who has the lower reaction time?

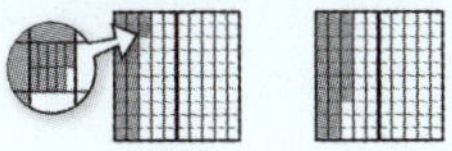

0.219 Max   0.27 Yuki

Max	0	.	2	1	9
Yuki	0	.	2	7	

0.219 < 0.27

Max has a lower reaction time than Yuki.

We can use place-value thinking to compare the times. Both numbers have a 2 in the tenths-place, so we look at the hundredths-place. 1 is less than 7, so 0.219 is less than 0.27.

The decimal squares also show that 0.219 is less than 0.27. 0.219 covers less of the decimal square than 0.27. So, Max has the lower reaction time.

If you didn't know about decimal place-value, you might look at these numbers and think that 0.27 is lower than 0.219, since 27 is less than 219. When you compare decimals, always look at where the decimal point is and make sure you compare digits with the same place-value.

Reaction time tests usually involve clicking a mouse (or pressing a button, or tapping a screen) as quickly as possible once prompted. If you have time, search for "reaction time test" online and give your child a chance to try a quick reaction time test before continuing with the lesson.

Have your child write <, >, or = in the circles in the practice problems. If she has trouble comparing the numbers, have her outline them on decimal squares. For 6.0 and 6, say: **6.0 and 6 are equal, because the zero in the tenths-place doesn't add any value to the 6 wholes.**

B

4 (>) 3.999   0.67 (>) 0.624   2.378 (<) 3.374

0.040 (=) 0.04   0.03 (>) 0.003   6.0 (=) 6

If your child wonders why someone would write 6.0 instead of 6, explain that the .0 means that the measurement is accurate to the nearest tenth. **If you bought a package of meat at the grocery store that was labeled 6.0 pounds, you'd know that its weight is within one-tenth of a pound of 6 pounds.** Your child does not need to fully grasp this concept, and she'll learn more about the significance of decimal digits in future math and science classes.

Activity (C): Play Dice Decimal War

Play Dice Decimal War. Encourage your child to use place-value thinking to compare the numbers. If she has trouble, have her outline the matching amounts on decimal squares.

Dice Decimal War

Materials: 2 dice; counters

Object of the Game: Win the most counters.

Give each player 10 counters.

To play, roll 2 dice and place a counter on the square whose label matches the sum of the dice. For example, if you roll a 5 and a 3, put a counter on the square labeled 8. Then, the other player rolls and places a counter on the square whose number matches the sum of the dice.

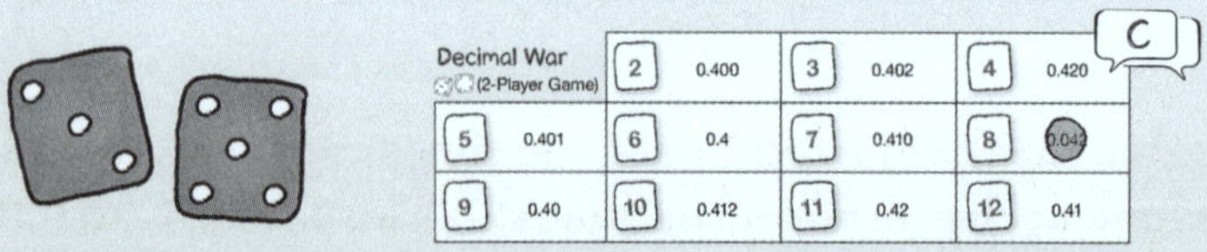

Have your child decide which player's counter is on a square with a greater decimal. The player whose counter is on the square with the greater decimal wins both counters and places them in her "Won" pile. Counters in the "Won" pile are now out of the game and cannot be used again.

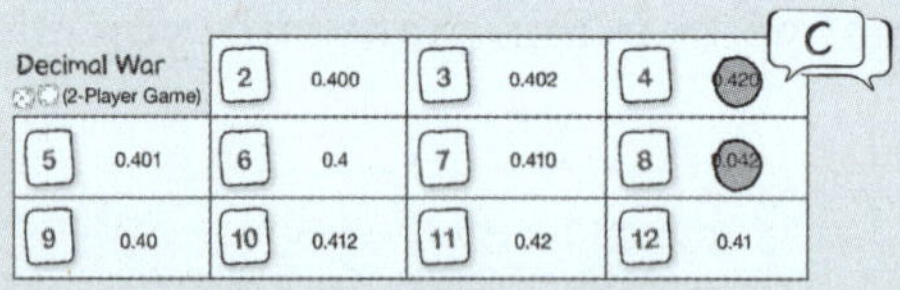

The player whose counter is on 0.420 wins, since 0.420 is greater than 0.042.

If both players' counters are on the same square (or if the squares have equal decimals), leave the counters where they are and play again. Whoever wins the next round wins all the counters on the board.

Play until both players use up their original pile of counters. Whoever has more counters in their "Won" pile wins the game.

Independent Practice and Review

Have your child complete the Lesson 2.9 Practice and Review workbook pages.

Lesson 2.10
Write Decimals as Fractions or Mixed Numbers

Purpose	Materials
• Identify decimals on the number line to the thousandths-place • Write decimals as mixed numbers or fractions • Write mixed numbers and fractions (with base-ten denominators) as decimals	• Decimal squares (Blackline Master 7) • Counters

Memory Work	
	• **What do we call an angle with a measure less than 90 degrees?** *Acute.* • **What do we call an angle with a measure equal to 90 degrees?** *Right.* • **What do we call an angle with a measure greater than 90 degrees and less than 180 degrees?** *Obtuse.* • **What do we call an angle with a measure equal to 180 degrees?** *Straight.*

Warm-up (A): Identify Decimals on the Number Line to the Thousandths-Place

In Lesson 2.6, you learned how to identify decimals on the number line to the hundredths-place. We'll warm up today by identifying decimals on the number line to the thousandths-place.

On the first number line, the distance between 0.4 and 0.5 is split into 10 parts. So, what is the size of each interval? *1 hundredth.* **What number does the arrow point to?** *0.48.* Write 0.48 in the blank.

The second number line zooms in on the distance between 0.48 and 0.49. The distance is split into 10 parts. So, what is the size of each interval? *1 thousandth.* **What number does the arrow point to?** *0.483.* Write 0.483 in the blank.

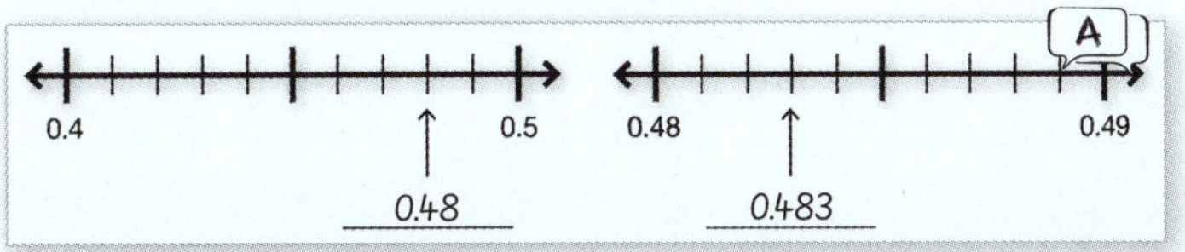

If your child has trouble understanding the number lines, show your child the matching numbers on decimal squares: **0.5 is 1 tenth more than 0.4. If I split 1 tenth into 10 equal parts, I get hundredths.** Or: **0.49 is 1 hundredth more than 0.48. If I split 1 hundredth into 10 equal parts, I get thousandths.**

Activity (B): Write Decimals as Fractions

We use both fractions and decimals to represent parts of things. When we have part of something, we can express the amount as either a fraction or a decimal. Today, you'll learn how to write decimals as fractions and fractions as decimals.

The left side of the box shows how to write decimals as fractions. Have your child read the steps aloud.

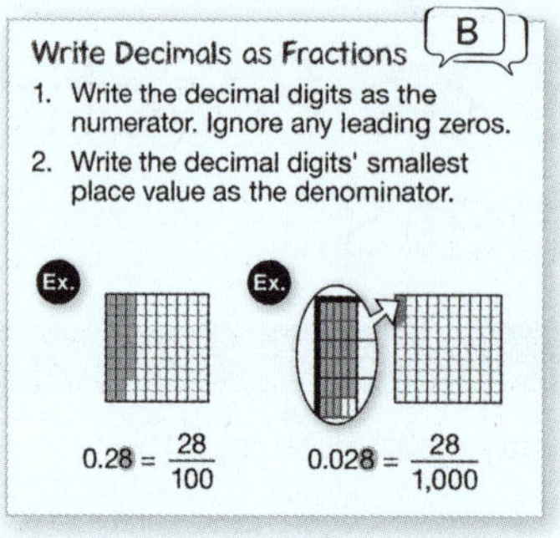

The first example shows how to write 0.28 as a fraction.

- **0.28 has two decimal digits, 2 and 8. We write 28 as the numerator.**
- Point to the 8 in 0.28. **What place is the 8 in?** *The hundredths-place.* **The smallest place value is the hundredths-place. So, we write 100 as the denominator.**
- **How does the decimal square show that 0.28 equals twenty-eight hundredths?** *Sample answer: 28 small squares are colored.* **Each tenth equals 10 hundredths, so 0.28 equals 20 hundredths plus 8 hundredths, or 28 hundredths.**

The second example shows how to write 0.028 as a fraction. How is this decimal similar to the decimal in the first example? *Sample answers: They both have a 0, 2, and 8. They have the same digits.* **How is this decimal different from the decimal in the first example?** *Sample answers: The digits are in different places. This decimal has a smaller value.*

- **0.028 has three decimal digits: 0, 2, and 8. The 0 is called a leading zero, because it's at the front of the non-zero decimal digits. We ignore the leading zero and write 28 as the numerator.**
- **Point to the 8 in 0.028. What place is the 8 in?** *The thousandths-place.* **The smallest place value is the thousandths-place. So, we write 1,000 as the denominator.**

How do the decimal squares show that 0.028 equals twenty-eight thousandths? *Sample answer: 28 small strips are colored.* **Each hundredth equals 10 thousandths, so 0.028 equals 20 thousandths plus 8 thousandths, or 28 thousandths.**

Have your child complete the practice exercises that involve writing decimals as fractions.

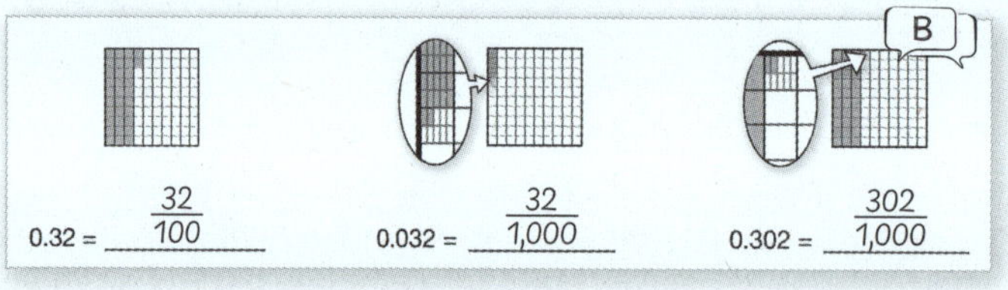

Activity (B): Write Fractions as Decimals

The right side of the box tells how to write fractions as decimals. Have your child read the steps aloud.

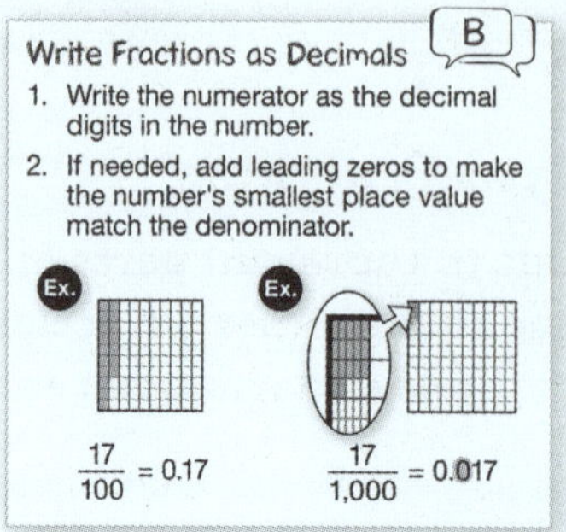

The first example shows how to write 17 hundredths as a decimal.

- **The numerator is 17, so we write 1 and 7 as the decimal digits.**
- **The denominator is 100, so we want the smallest place for the decimal to be the hundredths-place. We write a zero and decimal point before the 17 so that the 7 ends up in the hundredths-place.**

How do the decimal squares show that 17 hundredths equal 0.17? *Sample answer: 17 small squares equal 1 large strip plus 7 small squares.* **10 hundredths equal 1 tenth, so 17 hundredths equal 1 tenth and 7 hundredths, or 0.17.**

The second example shows how to write 17 thousandths as a decimal.

- **The numerator is 17, so we write 1 and 7 as the decimal digits again.**
- **This time, the denominator is 1,000, so we want the smallest place for the decimal to be the thousandths-place. We have to write a leading zero in front of the 17 before we write the decimal point and zero in the ones-place. That way, the 7 ends up in the thousandths-place.**

How do the decimal squares show that 17 thousandths equal 0.017? *Sample answer: 17 small strips equal 1 small square plus 7 small strips.* **10 thousandths equal 1 hundredth, so 17 thousandths equal 1 hundredth and 7 thousandths, or 0.017.**

Have your child complete the practice exercises that involve writing fractions as decimals.

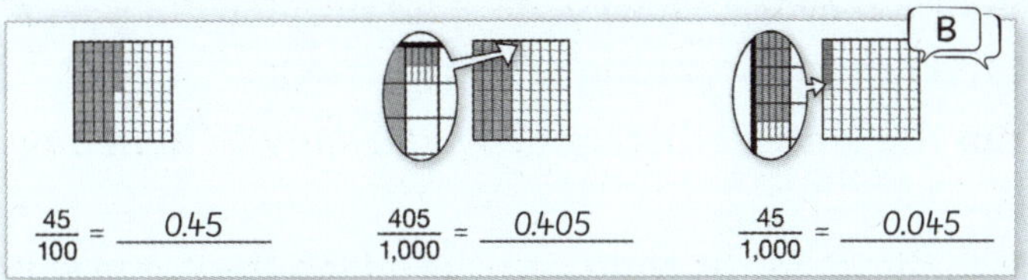

Activity (C): Play Four in a Row

Play Four in a Row.

Four in a Row

Materials: 12 counters per player, with a different color for each player

Object of the Game: Be the first player to place counters in 4 squares in a row, either horizontally, vertically, or diagonally.

On your turn, choose a decimal on the game board. Find the matching fraction or mixed number. Use 2 counters to cover both boxes. For example, if you choose 2.80 as your decimal, cover both 2.80 and 2 80/100 with counters. Play then passes to the other player.

One square in the game does not have a match. Neither player may play a counter on this square.

Continue until one player covers 4 boxes in a row, either horizontally, vertically, or diagonally.

Independent Practice and Review

Have your child complete the Lesson 2.10 Practice and Review workbook pages.

Lesson 2.11
Add and Subtract Decimals to the Thousandths-Place

Purpose	Materials
• Round decimals to the nearest whole number • Use the traditional written algorithms to add and subtract decimals to the thousandths-place • Estimate decimal sums or differences to check whether answers are reasonable	• None

Memory Work
- **How many ounces equal 1 pound?** *16.*
- **How many fluid ounces equal 1 cup?** *8.*

Warm-up (A): Round Decimals to the Nearest Whole Number

Kids who run track or cross-country often keep a running log to help them plan their workouts and check their progress. Show your child the chart in part A and briefly discuss any experience your child has with running or workout logs.

Which day did Nate run the longest distance? *Wednesday.* **Which day did he run the shortest distance?** *Tuesday.*

We round decimals with digits in the thousandths-place the same way we round other numbers. Have your child round each distance to the nearest mile. Remind her as needed to underline the digit in the ones-place and then look at the digit in the tenths-place to decide whether to round up or down.

A

Nate's Running Log

Day	Exact Distance (Miles)	Distance Rounded to the Nearest Mile
Monday	2.684	3
Tuesday	1.37	1
Wednesday	3.915	4
Thursday	2.7	3
Friday	1.826	2

Activity (B): Add and Subtract Decimals to the Thousandths-Place

Earlier in this unit, you learned how to add and subtract decimals with tenths and hundredths. Today, you'll use the same steps to add and subtract decimals to the thousandths-place. The text box lists the steps in case you need to review them.

B

How to Add and Subtract Decimals

1. Line up the decimal points.
2. Tack on zeros until both numbers have the same number of decimal places.
3. Add or subtract like usual. Write a decimal point in the answer below the other decimal points.

Ex. How far did Nate run on Tuesday and Wednesday?

```
  1.370           1
+ 3.915  ──→    1.370
               +3.915
               ──────
               5.285 miles
```

Read aloud the word problem in the example: ***How far did Nate run on Tuesday and Wednesday?*** **The example shows how to add 1.37 and 3.915 to find the total distance.** Point to both decimal points. **Are the decimal points in both numbers lined up?** *Yes.*

How many decimal places does 1.37 have? *2.* **How many decimal places does 3.915 have?** *3.* **So, we tack on one zero to 1.37 so that both numbers have the same number of decimal places.** Point to the highlighted 0 in 1.370. **Then, we add like usual. What does 1.37 plus 3.915 equal?** *5.285.* **Nate ran 5.285 miles on Tuesday and Wednesday.**

Activity (B): Estimate to Check Answers to Word Problems

Now, we'll use the running log from part A to solve more word problems. Read aloud the first word problem: ***How much farther did Nate run on Thursday than Friday?*** **What problem will you solve to find the answer?** *2.7 minus 1.826.* Help your child write the matching problem in the work space and solve.

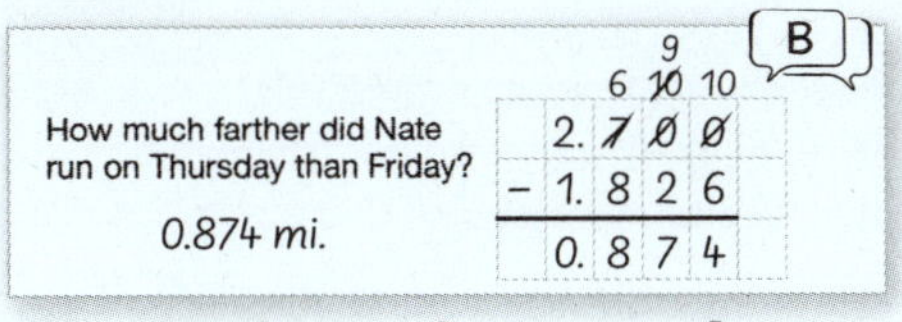

Sometimes, kids accidentally put the decimal point in the wrong place when they add and subtract decimals. You can use estimation to help check that your answer is reasonable. 2.7 miles is around 3 miles, and 1.826 miles is about 2 miles. 3 minus 2 equals 1, so we'd expect the answer to be around 1 mile. 0.874 is a reasonable answer.

If you accidentally wrote the final decimal point in the wrong spot, your answer might look like 0.0874 or 8.74 miles. Those aren't reasonable answers! If you ever get an answer that seems far off, check that you lined up the decimal points correctly and wrote the final decimal point in the correct spot.

0.0874 mi. *8.74 mi.*

Examples of incorrect decimal placement.

Have your child solve the other word problems. After she solves each problem, have her use estimation to check that her answer is reasonable.

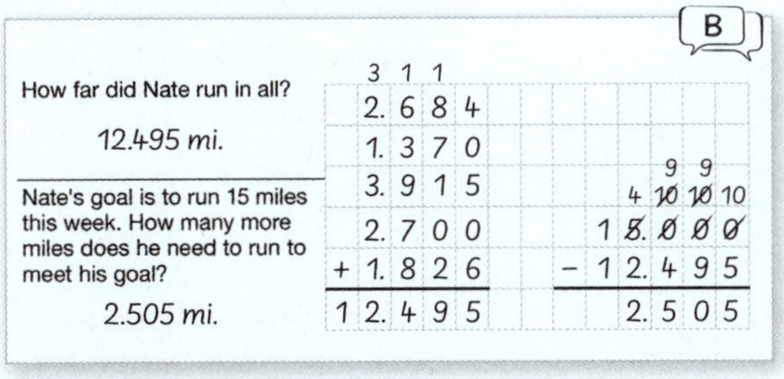

Independent Practice and Review

Have your child complete the Lesson 2.11 Practice and Review workbook pages.

Lesson 2.12
Enrichment (Optional)

Purpose	Materials
• Practice memory work • Appreciate how math can be used to answer real-life questions • Use decimals to compare weights • Summarize what your child has learned and assess your child's progress	• *How Many Guinea Pigs Can Fit on a Plane?: Answers to Your Most Clever Math Questions*, by Laura Overdeck • 8-10 jars of spices, labeled in ounces

For the enrichment activity, you'll need 8-10 jars of spices, labeled in ounces. Try to choose jars that are mostly full so your child can feel the difference between the weights. Also try to choose jars with varying weights, with some lighter than 1 ounce and some heavier than 1 ounce.

Warm-up: Review Memory Work

Quiz your child on any of the memory work items that he struggled with during this unit.

Math Picture Book: *How Many Guinea Pigs Can Fit on a Plane?*

Read pages 12-21 in *How Many Guinea Pigs Can Fit on a Plane?*

Enrichment Activity: Compare the Weights of Spice Jars

Today, we'll compare the weights of jars of spices. First, try to put the jars in order from lightest to heaviest. If we've already used some of the spices in the jars, just try to estimate how heavy you think the jar would be if it were full.

Place 8-10 jars of spices on the table. Have your child place the jars in order from lightest to heaviest, without looking at the printed weights on the labels.

Now, let's see how you did at putting the jars in order by weight! Have your child start with the lightest jar and read aloud the weight of each jar. Have him compare the jars' weights in order and fix the order for any jars that are in the wrong place.

Discuss how challenging it is to compare weights that are very light: **One ounce is pretty light, so parts of an ounce are very light. When two weights are very close, it can be hard to feel the difference.**

Unit Wrap-Up

Have your child complete the Unit 2 Wrap-Up.

Unit 2 Answer Key

2.1 Practice

Practice Label the number on the number line.

Number line 40–50 (45 marked): 47

Number line 100–200 (150 marked): 130

Number line 3,000–4,000 (3,500 marked): 3,100

Number line 70,000–80,000 (75,000 marked): 78,000

Circle the greatest number in each group.

57,498	(283,791)	47,890	99,909
56,921	280,791	4,789	(99,990)
(58,001)	282,791	(478,900)	99,900

Round to the underlined place.

15,894 ≈ 20,000
15,894 ≈ 16,000
15,894 ≈ 15,900
15,894 ≈ 15,890
329,708 ≈ 300,000
329,728 ≈ 330,000
329,728 ≈ 330,000
329,728 ≈ 329,700

Use the clues to solve the number riddle.

- I am greater than 520,000 and less than 530,000.
- The digit in my thousands-place is 4.
- The digit in my hundreds-place is the same as the digit in my hundred-thousands-place.
- The digit in my tens-place is 2 times the digit in my thousands-place.
- The digit in my ones-place is 4 less than the digit in my thousands-place.

5	2	4	5	8	0

2.1 Review

Review Complete the chart.

Standard Form	Expanded Form
4,291	4,000 + 200 + 90 + 1
3,685	3,000 + 600 + 80 + 5
25,290	20,000 + 5,000 + 200 + 90
30,018	30,000 + 10 + 8

Color the squares to match the fractions.

$\frac{1}{10}$ $\frac{3}{10}$ $\frac{5}{10}$ $\frac{8}{10}$ $\frac{10}{10}$

Find the sum or difference.

248 + 379: 379 + 248 = 627

379 − 166: 379 − 166 = 213

508 − 149: 508 − 149 = 359

Solve. Write the equations you use.

The bakery had some cookies. It sold 28 cookies and then had 54 cookies left. How many cookies were there at the start?

___ − 28 = 54
54 + 28 = 82 cookies

The bakery sold 16 chocolate chip cookies and 12 pumpkin spice cookies. Chocolate chip cookies cost $2 each. Pumpkin spice cookies cost $3 each. How much money did the bakery take in for all 28 cookies?

(16 × 2) + (12 × 3)
32 + 36
$68

2.2 Practice

Practice Match.

4,000,000	four million
4,000,000,000	four billion
4,040,000	four million forty thousand
4,040,000,000	four billion forty million
4,400,000	four million four hundred thousand
4,000,040,000	four billion forty thousand

Circle the greatest number in each group.

(4,067,208)	(1,567,893,200)	7,650,800	25,567,432,891
2,999,999	1,567,704,500	70,650,800	(25,567,432,894)
3,878,078	1,567,635,900	(7,650,800,000)	25,567,432,893

Round to the underlined place.

374,965,288 ≈ 400,000,000
374,965,288 ≈ 370,000,000
374,965,288 ≈ 375,000,000
374,965,288 ≈ 375,000,000
374,965,288 ≈ 374,970,000
374,965,288 ≈ 374,965,000
374,965,288 ≈ 374,965,300

Use the clues to solve the number riddle.

- I am greater than 367,000 and less than 368,000.
- The digit in my hundreds-place is 3 times the digit in my hundred-thousands-place.
- The digit in my tens-place is half of the digit in my ten-thousands-place.
- I am even.
- I am divisible by 10.

3	6	7	9	3	0

2.2 Review

Review Color the squares to match the fractions.

$\frac{9}{100}$ $\frac{50}{100}$ $\frac{99}{100}$ $\frac{90}{100}$ $\frac{76}{100}$

Complete. Write the equations you use.

3 hr. 15 min. = 195 min.
3 × 60 + 15
180 + 15
195

23 ft. = 7 yd. 2 ft.
23 ÷ 3 = 7 R2

4 L 200 mL = 4,200 mL
4 × 1,000 = 4,000
4,000 + 200
4,200

Complete the circles with +, −, ×, or ÷ to make the equations true.

★ (3 + 3) (−) (3 ÷ 3) = 5 ★ 3 + 3 + (3 (−) 3) = 6 ★ 3 + 3 + (3 (÷) 3) = 7

Solve. Write the equations you use in the work space.

Lukas' parents bought 6 dining chairs. They paid $1,128 in all for the chairs. Each chair had the same price. How much did each chair cost?

$188

They also bought a dining table for $874 and a cabinet for $1,039. How much more did the cabinet cost than the table?

$165

WORK SPACE

1,128 ÷ 6 = 188
− 6
52
− 48
48
− 48
0

1,039 − 874 = 165

Unit 2 Answer Key

2.3 Practice

Practice Use the chart to answer the questions. Write the equations you use in the work space.

Continent	Area (square miles)
Africa	11,724,000
Antarctica	5,500,000
Asia	17,226,000
Europe	3,900,000
North America	9,360,000
Oceania	3,286,000
South America	6,878,000

WORK SPACE

Which continent has the largest area?
Asia

Which continent has the smallest area?
Oceania

What's the total area of North America and South America?
16,238,000 sq. mi.

$$\begin{array}{r} 9,360,000 \\ +\ 6,878,000 \\ \hline 16,238,000 \end{array}$$

How much larger is North America than South America?
2,482,000 sq. mi.

$$\begin{array}{r} 9,360,000 \\ -\ 6,878,000 \\ \hline 2,482,000 \end{array}$$

How much larger is Africa than North America?
2,364,000 sq. mi.

$$\begin{array}{r} 11,724,000 \\ -\ 9,360,000 \\ \hline 2,364,000 \end{array}$$

2.3 Review

Review Write each money amount with a decimal point.

$2.34 | $4.05 | $4.50

Complete.

7 × 70 = 490
70 × 70 = 4,900
7,000 × 7 = 49,000

600 × 8 = 4,800
6 × 80 = 480
60 × 80 = 4,800

9 × 900 = 8,100
9,000 × 9 = 81,000
90 × 90 = 8,100

Complete the chart.

Yards	1	7	10	20	100	500
Feet	3	21	30	60	300	1,500

Oscar counted how many letters are in his friends' names. Use his data to make a line plot.

Oscar - 5
Charlotte - 9
Sarah - 5
Caleb - 5
John - 4
Willow - 6
Tia - 3
Madelyn - 7
Alex - 4
Mateo - 5
Oliver - 6
Anya - 4

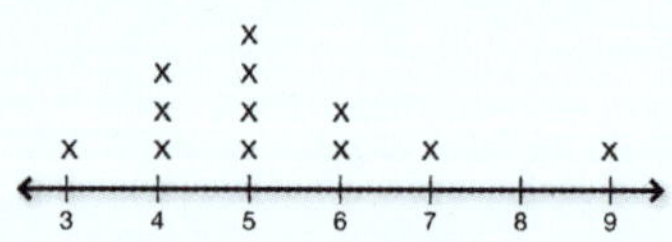

2.4 Practice

Practice Color the decimal squares to match. Then, write a fraction to match.

$0.1 = \frac{1}{10}$ | $0.07 = \frac{7}{100}$ | $0.17 = \frac{17}{100}$

$0.6 = \frac{6}{10}$ | $0.01 = \frac{1}{100}$ | $0.61 = \frac{61}{100}$

Color the decimal squares to match. Then, complete the circles with <, >, or =.

0.4 | 0.9 | 0.2

0.4 < 0.9
0.9 > 0.2
0.4 > 0.2

0.04 | 0.09 | 0.1

0.04 < 0.09
0.09 < 0.1
0.04 < 0.1

Use the charts to answer the questions.

Trail	Length (km)
Pine	3.89
Cedar	4.1
Hemlock	4.05

Which trail is the longest?
Cedar

Which trail is the shortest?
Pine

Name	Race Time (sec.)
Ravi	19.4
Emmy	18.72
Natasha	18.09

Whose time was shortest?
Natasha

Whose time was longest?
Ravi

2.4 Review

Review Complete the chart.

Minutes	1	5	10	30	60	90
Seconds	60	300	600	1,800	3,600	5,400

Complete.

2 pair(s) of parallel sides
4 right angles

2 pair(s) of parallel sides
0 right angles

1 pair(s) of parallel sides
2 right angles

Complete.

560 ÷ 7 = 80
5,600 ÷ 7 = 800
56,000 ÷ 7 = 8,000

7,200 ÷ 8 = 900
720 ÷ 8 = 90
72,000 ÷ 8 = 9,000

300 ÷ 5 = 60
30,000 ÷ 5 = 6,000
3,000 ÷ 5 = 600

Solve. Write the equations you use.

Liza biked 4 miles. Each mile equals 5,280 feet. How many feet did she bike?

$$\begin{array}{r} 5,280 \\ \times\ 4 \\ \hline 21,120 \text{ feet} \end{array}$$

Mitch ran 1,650 meters. John ran 3 times as far as Mitch. How far did John run?

$$\begin{array}{r} 1,650 \\ \times\ 3 \\ \hline 4,950 \text{ m} \end{array}$$

Unit 2 Answer Key

2.5 Practice

Four in a Row (2-Player Game)

0.4	0.03	0.30	0.95	0.09	0.97
0.94	0.01	0.50	0.07	0.20	0.9
0.10	0.5	0.06	0.8	0.05	0.99
0.08	0.60	0.91	0.7	0.93	0.92

Practice Complete. Use the pictures to help.

0.5 + 0.34 = 0.84

0.8 + 0.02 = 0.82

0.45 + 0.05 = 0.50

0.96 − 0.04 = 0.92

0.09 − 0.05 = 0.04

0.3 − 0.02 = 0.28

Use mental math to solve. Write the equations you use.

Mateo ran 0.8 miles on Friday and 0.5 miles on Saturday. How much farther did he run on Friday than on Saturday?

0.8 − 0.5 = 0.3 mi.

Isabella has 0.9 kg of clay. She uses 0.7 kg to make a mug. How much clay does she have left?

0.9 − 0.7 = 0.2 kg left

Sutton fills two water bottles for the soccer game. One water bottle holds 0.43 L. The other water bottle holds 0.4 L. How much water do the bottles hold in all?

0.43 + 0.4 = 0.83 L

Ruby swims 0.3 km on Tuesday and 0.4 km on Thursday. How far does she swim in all?

0.3 + 0.4 = 0.7 km

2.5 Review

Review Connect each number to its place on the number line.

$3\frac{3}{10}$, $3\frac{5}{10}$, $3\frac{9}{10}$, $4\frac{2}{10}$, $4\frac{8}{10}$

3 — 4 — 5

Evaluate.

4 × 2 + 8 ÷ 4
8 + 2
10

4 × (2 + 8) ÷ 4
4 × 10 ÷ 4
40 ÷ 4
10

Find the missing numbers. Write the equations you use.

42 + 39 = 81
81 − 42 = 39

62 − 27 = 35
27 + 35 = 62

7 × 20 = 140
140 ÷ 7 = 20

54 ÷ 6 = 9
54 ÷ 9 = 6

Round to the underlined digit.

3,964,382 ≈ 4,000,000

430,298 ≈ 430,000

41,087,360 ≈ 41,000,000

9,874,621 ≈ 10,000,000

29,999,999 ≈ 30,000,000

Find the average of the ages. Write the equations you use.

Ages: 14, 9, 6, 16, 9, 8, 8, 10

14 + 9 + 6 + 16 + 9 + 8 + 8 + 10 = 80

80 ÷ 8 = 10

2.6 Practice

Practice Connect each number to its place on the number line. Then, round each number to the underlined place.

3.4, 4.6, 4.1, 3.9 (number line 3 — 4 — 5)

4.6 ≈ 5

3.4 ≈ 3

4.1 ≈ 4

3.9 ≈ 4

2.13, 2.21, 2.28, 2.15 (number line 2.1 — 2.2 — 2.3)

2.13 ≈ 2.1

2.21 ≈ 2.2

2.28 ≈ 2.3

2.15 ≈ 2.2

Label the number on the number line.

1 — 2: 1.3

1.3 — 1.4: 1.37

6 — 7: 6.5

3.9 — 4: 3.96

0 — 1: 0.8

1 — 1.1: 1.04

2.6 Review

Review Use long division to solve.

$460 \div 7$: 7) 4 6 0 = 65; − 42, 40, − 35, 5

Use mental math to complete.

257 + 3 = 260

257 + 6 = 263

257 + 7 = 264

378 + 20 = 398

388 + 20 = 408

398 + 20 = 418

605 − 3 = 602

605 − 5 = 600

605 − 9 = 596

427 − 10 = 417

417 − 10 = 407

407 − 10 = 397

Find the sum or difference.

2,491 + 15,207 = 17,698

900 − 356 = 544

15,206 − 1,788 = 13,418

Write the multiples of each number in order. Then, answer the questions.

Multiples of 5: 5, 10, 15, 20, 25, 30, 35, 40, 45, 50

Multiples of 10: 10, 20, 30, 40, 50, 60, 70, 80, 90, 100

Multiples of 7: 7, 14, 21, 28, 35, 42, 49, 56, 63, 70

Which number(s) appear(s) on the list of multiples of 5 and the list of multiples of 10? 10, 20, 30, 40, and 50

Which number(s) appear(s) on the list of multiples of 5 and the list of multiples of 7? 35

Which number(s) appear(s) on the list of multiples of 10 and the list of multiples of 7? 70

Unit 2 Answer Key

2.7 Practice

Practice Find the sum or difference.

2.6 + 3.89	0.34 + 0.56	3 + 1.76
2.60 + 3.89 = 6.49	0.34 + 0.56 = 0.90	3.00 + 1.76 = 4.76

0.53 − 0.27	3.9 − 2.55	5 − 2.78
0.53 − 0.27 = 0.26	3.90 − 2.55 = 1.35	5.00 − 2.78 = 2.22

Solve. Write the equations you use.

David has $20.
He buys a picture frame for $16.47.
How much money does he have left?

20.00 − 16.47 = **$3.53**

Lynley was 0.49 m long when she was born. Now, she's 1.38 m tall.
How much has she grown?

1.38 − 0.49 = **0.89 m**

Elias uses 0.58 kg of white flour and 0.45 kg of wheat flour to make bread.
How much flour does he use in all?

0.58 + 0.45 = **1.03 kg**

The fun run race course is 3.1 miles long.
So far, Althea has run 1.65 miles.
How much farther does she have to run to finish the race?

3.10 − 1.65 = **1.45 mi.**

2.7 Review

Review Complete.

$\frac{5}{6} - \frac{2}{6} = \frac{3}{6}$

$\frac{4}{8} - \frac{1}{8} = \frac{3}{8}$

$\frac{8}{10} - \frac{3}{10} = \frac{5}{10}$

Round to the underlined place.

2.87 ≈ 3
2.87 ≈ 2.9
3.09 ≈ 3
3.09 ≈ 3.1

Complete.

637 × 9 = 5,733

8,104 × 8 = 64,832

Complete the chart. Then, use the chart to answer the questions.

Gallons	1	2	3	4	5	6
Quarts	4	8	12	16	20	24

James makes 1 gallon of tomato sauce.
His mom uses 1 quart of sauce for spaghetti.
How many quarts of tomato sauce are left?

1 × 4 = 4
4 − 1 = **3 qt.**

Harper makes 3 gallons of lemonade.
She pours the lemonade into 6 pitchers.
How many quarts of lemonade are in each pitcher?

3 × 4 = 12
12 ÷ 6 = **2 qt.**

2.8 Practice

Practice Color the decimal squares to match. Then, complete the circles with <, >, or =.

0.3 | 0.03 | 0.003

0.3 > 0.003
0.003 < 0.03
0.03 < 0.3

0.7 | 0.08 | 0.009

0.08 < 0.7
0.7 > 0.009
0.009 < 0.08

Complete the chart.

Standard Form	Expanded Form
0.325	$\frac{3}{10} + \frac{2}{100} + \frac{5}{1,000}$
0.76	$\frac{7}{10} + \frac{6}{100}$
1.061	$1 + \frac{6}{100} + \frac{1}{1,000}$
0.815	$\frac{8}{10} + \frac{1}{100} + \frac{5}{1,000}$
2.004	$2 + \frac{4}{1,000}$

Match.

0.6 — 6 tenths
0.07 — 7 hundredths
0.006 — 6 thousandths
0.7 — 7 tenths

2.8 Review

Review Complete the missing factors in the factor pairs. Then, answer the questions.

Factor Pairs of 24	Factor Pairs of 28	Factor Pairs of 35
1 × 24	1 × 28	1 × 35
2 × 12	2 × 14	5 × 7
3 × 8	4 × 7	
4 × 6		

What factors do 24 and 28 have in common? 1, 2, and 4

What factors do 28 and 35 have in common? 1 and 7

What factors do 24 and 35 have in common? 1

Match.

0.5 + 0.3 — 0.8
0.5 + 0.03 — 0.53
0.5 − 0.3 — 0.2
0.5 − 0.03 — 0.47
0.05 − 0.03 — 0.02

Label the numbers on the number line.

4 to 5: 4.1

3.7 to 3.8: 3.79

Solve. Write the equations you use.

Renting a bouncy house costs $279.99, plus $16.79 for sales tax.
What is the total cost?

279.99 + 16.79 = **$296.78**

Renting a cotton candy machine costs $116.99, plus $7.02 for sales tax and $26.78 for supplies. What is the total cost?

116.99 + 7.02 + 26.78 = **$150.79**

Unit 2 Answer Key

2.9 Practice

Practice Circle the greatest number in each group.

0.45	0.07	(6.4)	3.999
(0.5)	0.070	6.314	4.000
0.400	(0.7)	6.31	(4.001)

Circle the least number in each group.

0.39	0.082	3.20	(76.104)
(0.325)	(0.07)	2.7	76.7
0.378	0.4	(1.999)	76.32

Complete the circles with <, >, or =.

0.3 (>) 0.03	0.50 (=) 0.5	1.06 (=) 1.060
2.8 (=) 2.80	0.040 (>) 0.004	3.000 (<) 3.701
4 (=) 4.0	0.60 (<) 6	5.000 (=) 5.00

Use the chart to answer the questions.

Which gymnast had the highest score and won the gold medal?
Sunisa Lee

Which gymnast had the second-highest score and won the silver medal?
Rebeca Andrade

Which gymnast had the third-highest score and won the bronze medal?
Angelina Melnikova

2020 Olympics Women's All-Around Gymnastics Competition Top Scores

Name	Score
Angelina Melnikova	57.199
Mai Murakami	56.032
Sunisa Lee	57.433
Rebeca Andrade	57.298
Vladislava Urazova	56.996

2.9 Review

Review Write whether each angle is acute, right, obtuse, or straight.

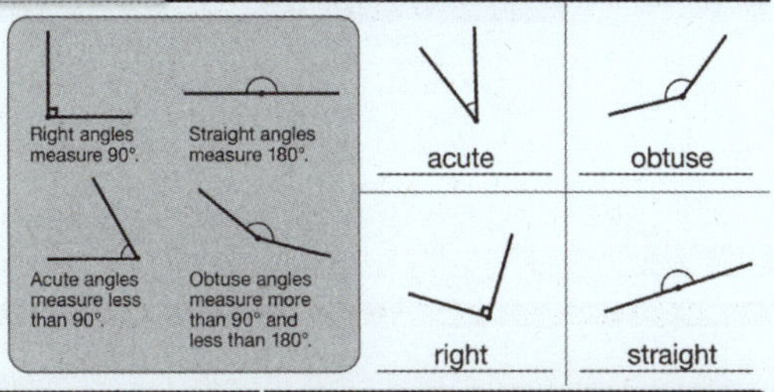

Round to the underlined place.

3.4 ≈	3
4.9 ≈	5
0.68 ≈	0.7
0.87 ≈	0.9
0.46 ≈	0
0.79 ≈	1

Use mental math to complete.

3,500 + 500 = 4,000	7,800 + 200 = 8,000
3,500 + 600 = 4,100	7,800 + 201 = 8,001
3,500 + 700 = 4,200	7,800 + 202 = 8,002
4,200 − 200 = 4,000	4,000 − 1 = 3,999
4,200 − 300 = 3,900	4,000 − 10 = 3,990
4,200 − 400 = 3,800	4,000 − 100 = 3,900

Write each length as a decimal.

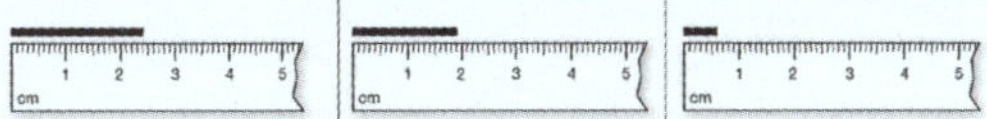

2.4 cm | 1.9 cm | 0.6 cm

2.10 Practice

Four in a Row (2-Player Game)

2.80	$\frac{4}{10}$	0.004	$2\frac{804}{1,000}$	2.08
$1\frac{9}{10}$	0.7	$\frac{36}{1,000}$	2.840	$\frac{7}{100}$
0.036	$1\frac{918}{1,000}$	1.91	$\frac{4}{1,000}$	0.36
$2\frac{80}{100}$	2.804	$2\frac{8}{100}$	1.918	$1\frac{91}{100}$
0.07	$\frac{36}{100}$	1.9	$\frac{7}{10}$	0.4

Practice Complete the charts.

Decimal	0.49	0.005	0.735	1.008	2.319	3.064
Fraction or Mixed Number	$\frac{49}{100}$	$\frac{5}{1,000}$	$\frac{735}{1,000}$	$1\frac{8}{1,000}$	$2\frac{319}{1,000}$	$3\frac{64}{1,000}$

Decimal	0.08	0.081	0.700	1.375	4.006	3.25
Fraction or Mixed Number	$\frac{8}{100}$	$\frac{81}{1,000}$	$\frac{700}{1,000}$	$1\frac{375}{1,000}$	$4\frac{6}{1,000}$	$3\frac{25}{100}$

Label the numbers on the number line.

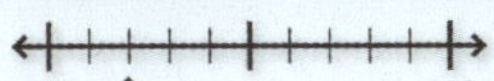

0.25 — 0.26: 0.252

2.08 — 2.09: 2.082

2.10 Review

Review Match each number to its dot on the number line.

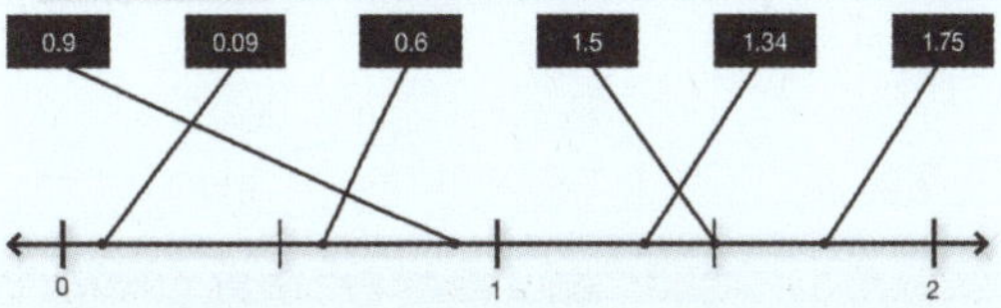

Use mental math to complete.

4 × 70 = 280	240 ÷ 6 = 40	300 ÷ 6 = 50
50 × 60 = 3,000	4,800 ÷ 8 = 600	2,000 ÷ 5 = 400
3,000 × 9 = 27,000	21,000 ÷ 7 = 3,000	1,400 ÷ 2 = 700

Find the sum, product, or difference.

0.74 + 2.6	3,284 × 7	3.5 − 1.84
2.60 + 0.74 = 3.34	3,284 × 7 = 22,988	3.50 − 1.84 = 1.66

Solve. Write the equations you use.

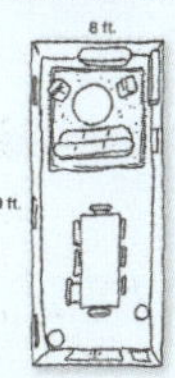

What is the perimeter of the room?

19 × 2 + 8 × 2
38 + 16
54 ft.

What is the area of the room?

19 × 8 = 152 sq. ft.

Unit 2 Answer Key

2.11 Practice

Practice: Use logical reasoning to circle the more reasonable answer for each problem.

1.999 + 0.999	0.005 + 2.381	0.68 + 1.14
(2.998) 2,998	(2.386) 23.86	0.182 (1.82)
1.623 − 0.582	**3 − 0.741**	**5.657 − 1**
10.41 (1.041)	(2.259) 0.259	(4.657) 5.557

Solve.

4.6 + 3.277	0.73 − 0.214	4 − 1.368
4.600 + 3.277 = 7.877	0.730 − 0.214 = 0.516	4.000 − 1.368 = 2.632

Use the map to answer the questions. Write the equations you use.

How much longer is the Rim Trail than the Rocky Flats Trail?

3.73 − 3.20 = **0.53 km**

How much shorter is the Buffalo Creek Trail than the Rocky Flats Trail?

3.200 − 1.934 = **1.266 km**

What is the total length of all three trails?

1.934 + 3.730 + 3.200 = **8.864 km**

2.11 Review

Review: Connect each number to its place on the number line. Then, round each number to the underlined place.

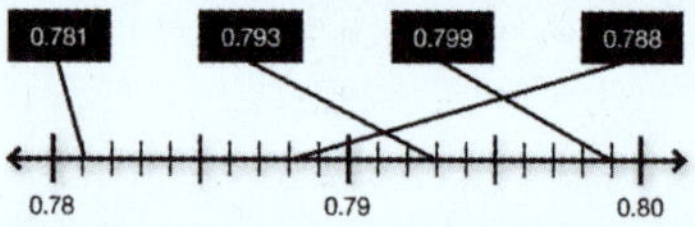

0.781 ≈ 0.78

0.793 ≈ 0.79

0.799 ≈ 0.80

0.788 ≈ 0.79

Complete. Write the equations you use.

410 cm = 4 m 10 cm	1 L 784 mL = 1,784 mL	3,250 g = 3 kg 250 g
410 ÷ 100 = 4 R10	1 × 1,000 + 784 = 1,784	3,250 ÷ 1,000 = 3 R250

Paisley asked her friends how many pets they have. Use her data to make a line plot and answer the questions.

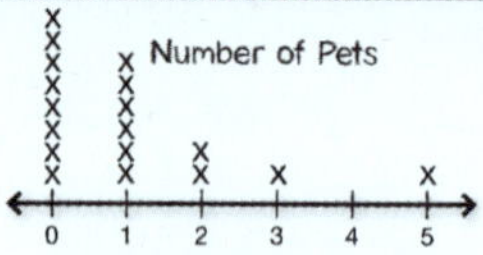

How many people have only one pet?

6

How many people do not have a pet?

8

What's the average number of pets Paisley's friends have?

1 + 2 + 0 + 0 + 3 + 1 + 1 + 0 + 0 + 1 + 1 + 0 + 1 + 5 + 0 + 0 + 2 + 0 = 18

18 ÷ 18 = **1 pet**

2.12 Unit Wrap-Up A

Unit Wrap-Up: Write a decimal to match each decimal square.

0.3

0.92

0.05

Write each number in expanded form.

4,670,208 = 4,000,000 + 600,000 + 70,000 + 200 + 8

0.053 = $\frac{5}{100} + \frac{3}{1{,}000}$

3.748 = $3 + \frac{7}{10} + \frac{4}{100} + \frac{8}{1{,}000}$

Round each number to the underlined place.

2,964,708,310 ≈ 3,000,000,000	1.749 ≈ 2
2,964,708,310 ≈ 3,000,000,000	1.749 ≈ 1.7
2,964,708,310 ≈ 2,960,000,000	1.749 ≈ 1.75

Circle the greatest number in each group.

27,098,432	0.06	(5.3)	7.999
5,678,325	0.006	5.213	(8)
(9,000,000,000)	(0.6)	5.21	7.597

Circle the least number in each group.

(5,000,000)	(0.075)	4.50	6.103
5,000,001	0.09	3.7	(6.102)
50,000,000	0.3	(2.977)	6.13

2.12 Unit Wrap-Up B

Unit Wrap-Up: Write each decimal as a fraction or mixed number. Write each fraction or mixed number as a decimal.

4.7 = $4\frac{7}{10}$	0.31 = $\frac{31}{100}$	6.093 = $6\frac{93}{1{,}000}$
$\frac{315}{1{,}000}$ = 0.315	$6\frac{74}{100}$ = 6.74	$2\frac{5}{100}$ = 2.05

Label the numbers on the number line.

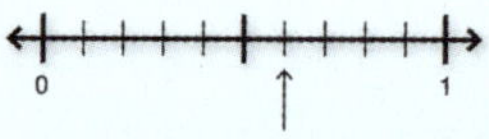

0.6

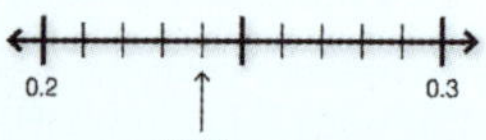

0.24

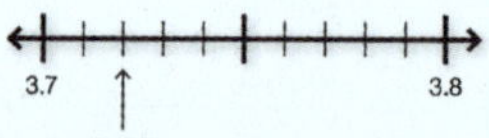

3.72

0.435

Use the scorecard from the robotics competition to answer the questions. Write the equations you use.

Team Name	Round 1 Score	Round 2 Score
Mega Bot	17.604	20.3
Nuts and Bolts	15.93	23.417

How many points did the Mega Bot team score in all?

17.604 + 20.300 = **37.904 points**

How many points did the Nuts and Bolts team score in all?

15.930 + 23.417 = **39.347 points**

Which team scored more points? How many more points did they score than the other team?

Nuts and Bolts

39.347 − 37.904 = **1.443 points**

Unit 2 Checkpoint

What to Expect at the End of Unit 2

By the end of Unit 2, most children will be able to do the following:

- Understand whole-number place value to the billions-place.
- Round large numbers to any place. Some children will need help when the rounding involves regrouping (for example, when rounding 369,480 to the thousands-place).
- Fluently add and subtract numbers to the billions-place.
- Understand decimal place value to the thousandths-place.
- Use place-value thinking to compare decimals to the thousandths-place.
- Write decimals in expanded form.
- Write decimals as mixed numbers or fractions with base-ten denominators, and vice versa (i.e., understand that 4.372 equals $4 \frac{372}{1,000}$ and vice versa). Many children will still have trouble with numbers with leading or trailing zeros.
- Round decimals to any place.
- Add and subtract decimals to the thousandths-place. Some children will still need help aligning digits or tacking on zeros before adding or subtracting.

Is Your Child Ready to Move on?

In Unit 3, your child will review the written multiplication algorithm and extend the algorithm to larger numbers. Before moving on to Unit 3, your child should be mostly fluent with the multiplication facts to 10×10. If you find that your child's lack of fluency with the multiplication facts makes lessons long or frustrating, **allow him to use the multiplication chart** (Blackline Master 4) as he completes the lessons in Unit 3. This will allow him to continue to make progress with new concepts while he works to solidify the multiplication facts. See the Unit 1 Checkpoint (page 52) for multiplication fact practice suggestions.

Your child does not need to have fully mastered the decimal skills in Unit 2 before moving on to Unit 3. He will review them in the Review pages before learning to multiply and divide decimals later in the year.

Unit 3
Whole Number Multiplication

Overview

In this unit, your child will review and strengthen her mental and written multiplication skills. In the first part of the unit, she will learn several new mental multiplication strategies, along with how to find the least common multiple for a pair of numbers. In the second part, your child will review the written multiplication algorithm and extend it to larger numbers.

What Your Child Will Learn

In this unit, your child will learn to:

- Find the least common multiple for a pair of numbers
- Use the "multiply and adjust" strategy to mentally multiply
- Use doubling to mentally multiply by 2 or 4
- Use the associative property to multiply three or more factors
- Multiply numbers with trailing zeros, either mentally or with the multiplication algorithm
- Use the box method to multiply two- or three-digit numbers
- Extend the multiplication algorithm to larger numbers (up to four-digit times two-digit or three-digit times three-digit)

Lesson List

Lesson 3.1	Find Least Common Multiples
Lesson 3.2	Multiply and Adjust
Lesson 3.3	Mentally Multiply by 2 or 4
Lesson 3.4	The Associative Property
Lesson 3.5	Place Value and Mental Multiplication
Lesson 3.6	Use the Multiplication Algorithm to Multiply Numbers with Trailing Zeros
Lesson 3.7	Multiply with the Box Method
Lesson 3.8	Use the Multiplication Algorithm to Multiply Two-Digit Numbers
Lesson 3.9	Use the Multiplication Algorithm to Multiply Larger Numbers
Lesson 3.10	Enrichment (Optional)

Extra Materials Needed for Unit 3

- For optional Enrichment Lesson:
    - *How Many Guinea Pigs Can Fit on a Plane?: Answers to Your Most Clever Math Questions*, by Laura Overdeck. Feiwel & Friends, 2017.
    - Stopwatch
    - Calculator or calculator app

Teaching Math with Confidence: Revisiting and Extending Multi-Digit Multiplication

In *Fourth Grade Math with Confidence,* your child learned two methods for multiplying two-digit numbers by two-digit numbers: the box method and the traditional written algorithm. Both methods use the distributive property to split numbers into tens and ones, multiply the parts separately, and add to find the final product.

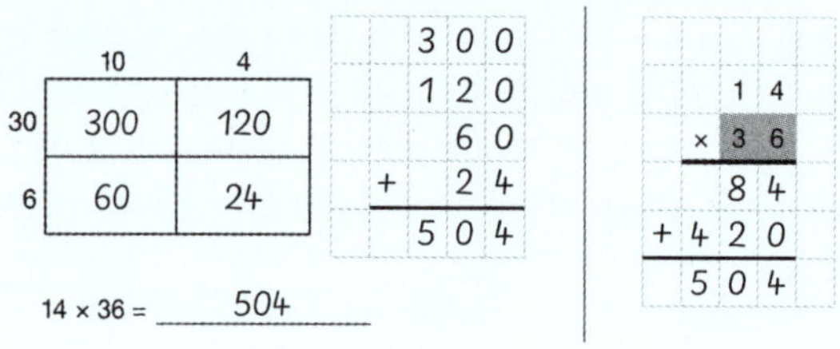

How to find 14 × 36 with the box method and the traditional algorithm.

In this unit, your child will review both methods and discover that they can be extended to multiply larger numbers. Finding the product of two three-digit numbers requires 9 separate multiplications, so multiplying these large numbers can be a slog. Use the following suggestions to help make multi-digit multiplication as painless as possible:

- If your child often needs more than a second or two to find answers to the multiplication facts, **allow her to use the multiplication chart** (Blackline Master 4) as she solves the problems. Otherwise, she'll spend so much energy figuring out the multiplication facts that she'll struggle to remember all the steps.
- Watch carefully as your child solves the problems on the Lesson Activities pages and help her **correct any errors immediately,** before she takes the next step in the problem. If you find that she needs lots of coaching and support, sit with her as she completes the Practice pages, too.
- Adjust the workload to match your child's stamina. It's more fruitful for your child to solve 3 problems with focused effort and concentration than it is for her to halfheartedly attempt 6 problems (and make a lot of mistakes in the process). **Split the lessons** over two days if there are too many problems for your child to solve in one sitting. Or, **cross out a few practice problems** if your child has already demonstrated fluency with the process.
- **Praise your child's persistence, and acknowledge that multi-digit multiplication is hard.** Let your child know that most kids find multi-step multiplication challenging, and that it's normal to sometimes get mixed up in the steps.
- **Celebrate your child's progress!** If your child is feeling discouraged, remind her how far she's come from first learning the multiplication facts.

Lesson 3.1
Find Least Common Multiples

Purpose	Materials
• Review multiples • Find the least common multiple for a pair of numbers	• Deck of playing cards

Memory Work	
	• **What does perimeter measure?** *The distance around the outside edge of a shape.* • **What does area measure?** *The amount of space that a shape covers.*

Knowing how to find least common multiples makes it much easier to find common denominators when adding and subtracting fractions. In this lesson, you'll teach your child how to find common multiples so that she's familiar with the technique before she needs to apply it to fractions in Unit 5.

Warm-up (A): Review Multiples

Last year, you learned about factors and multiples. Factors are the numbers that you multiply together to equal a target number. Multiples are what you get when you multiply the target number by a different number.

If your child has trouble remembering these vocabulary words, show her this illustration. **Factors are like the arrows in this picture. They're the multiplication facts that equal the target. Multiples are like the rings around the target number. If we multiply the target number by another whole number, we get a multiple of the target number.**

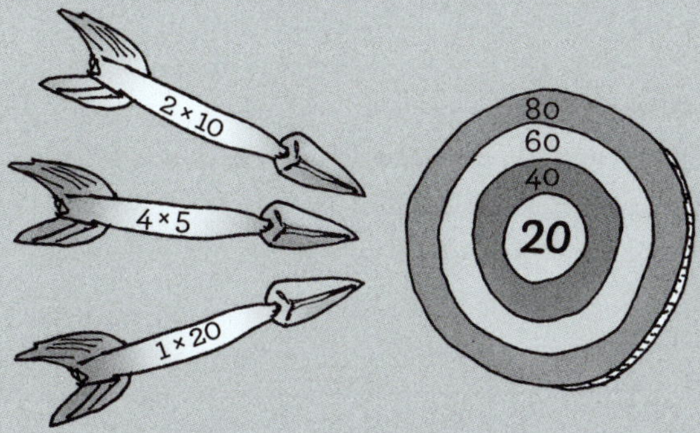

To warm up, we'll use hot dogs and hot dog buns to review multiples. These hot dogs come in packs of 8. What are the first 5 multiples of 8? *8, 16, 24, 32, 40.* Write the multiples in the blanks. **We could buy 8, 16, 24, 32, or 40 hot dogs.**

The hot dog buns come in packs of 6. What are the first 5 multiples of 6? *6, 12, 18, 24, 30.* Write the multiples in the blanks. **We could buy 6, 12, 18, 24, or 30 hot dog buns.**

If we want to buy the same number of hot dogs and hot dog buns, how many could we buy? *24 of each.* Circle 24 in both lists. **24 is called the least common multiple of 6 and 8, because it's the lowest multiple they have in common.**

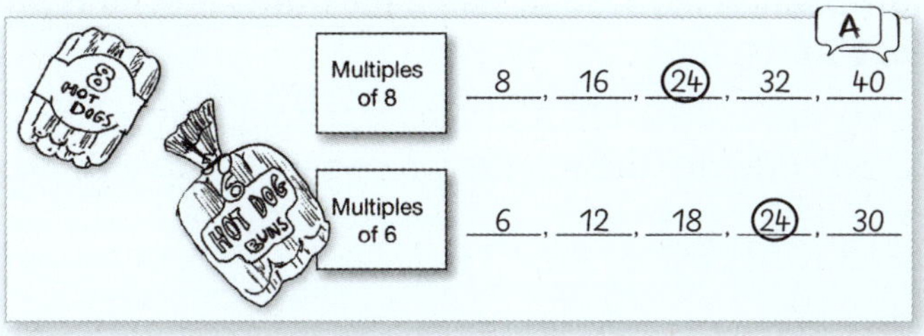

Activity (B): Introduce Common Multiples

Today, you'll learn how to find the least common multiple of two numbers. Have your child read the text in part B aloud.

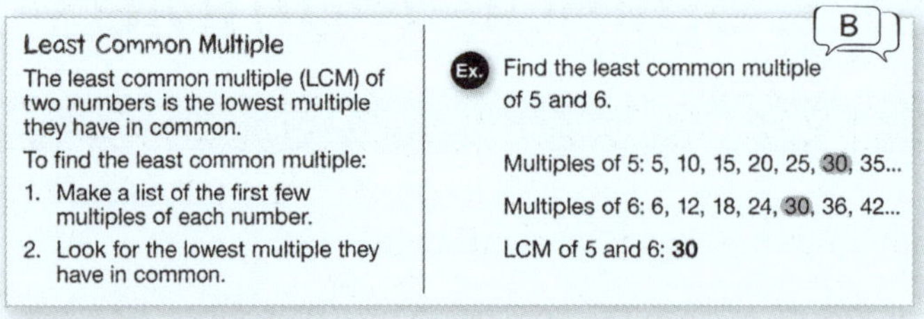

B

Least Common Multiple

The least common multiple (LCM) of two numbers is the lowest multiple they have in common.

To find the least common multiple:

1. Make a list of the first few multiples of each number.
2. Look for the lowest multiple they have in common.

Ex. Find the least common multiple of 5 and 6.

Multiples of 5: 5, 10, 15, 20, 25, 30, 35...

Multiples of 6: 6, 12, 18, 24, 30, 36, 42...

LCM of 5 and 6: **30**

Let's study the example to find the least common multiple of 5 and 6.

- **What are the multiples of 5?** *5, 10, 15, 20, 25, 30, 35.*
- **What are the multiples of 6?** *6, 12, 18, 24, 30, 36, and 42.*
- **What multiple do the two lists have in common?** *30.*

30 is the lowest multiple that they have in common, so 30 is the least common multiple of 5 and 6. If hamburger buns come in packs of 5 and hamburger patties come in packs of 6, you'd need to buy 30 buns and 30 patties if you want to have the same number of each.

Let's find the least common multiple of 4 and 2. Have your child create lists of the first 5 multiples of 2 and 4. **Which multiples do 4 and 2 have in common on this list?** *4 and 8.* Circle 4 and 8. **What's the least common multiple of 4 and 2?** *4.* **Sometimes, the least common multiple is one of the numbers. 4 is a multiple of 2, so it's the least common multiple of 2 and 4.**

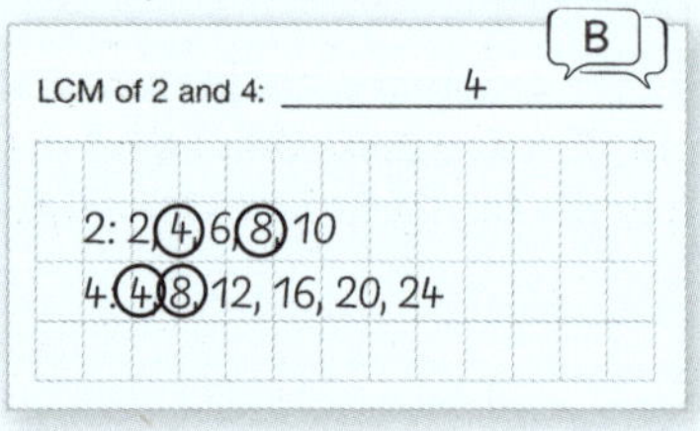

B

LCM of 2 and 4: 4

2: 2, 4, 6, 8, 10

4: 4, 8, 12, 16, 20, 24

Let's find the least common multiple of 9 and 6. Have your child create lists of the first 5 multiples of 9 and 6. **Which multiples do 9 and 6 have in common on this list?** *18.* Circle 18. **What's the least common multiple of 9 and 6?** *18.*

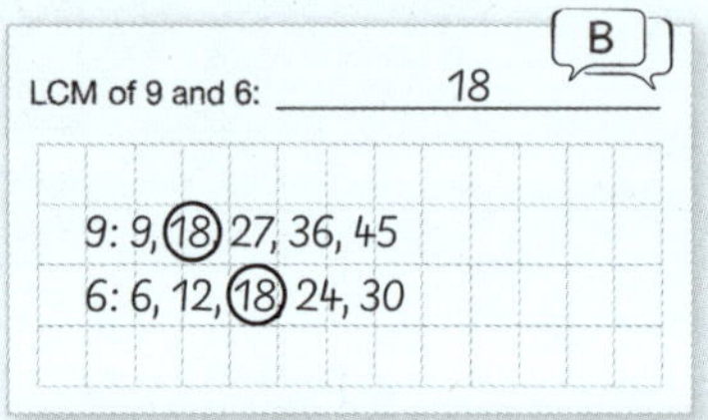

B

LCM of 9 and 6: 18

9: 9, 18, 27, 36, 45

6: 6, 12, 18, 24, 30

In these problems, we only needed to write the first 5 multiples of each number to find their least common multiple. You can write more multiples of each number if they don't have any multiples in common on the lists.

Another way to find the least common multiple of 2 numbers is to make a list of the multiples of the larger number and check whether each is also a multiple of the other number. For example, for 6 and 9, I would make a list of the multiples of 9.

- **The first multiple of 9 is 9. That's not a multiple of 6.**
- **The second multiple of 9 is 18. 18 is also a multiple of 6, so it must be the least common multiple of 6 and 9.**

Have your child try using this method to find the least common multiple of 3 and 5. (She can list the multiples of 5 orally or write them on scrap paper.) **What's the least common multiple of 3 and 5?** *15.*

Your child may use either approach to find least common multiples. Many children will need to use the first method for a while before they are ready to use the simpler method. You will revisit the simpler method in Unit 5.

Activity (C): Play Least Common Multiple War

Play Least Common Multiple War.

Encourage your child to find the least common multiples mentally if she can. Otherwise, have her write out the lists of multiples on scrap paper.

Least Common Multiple War

Materials: Deck of cards, with aces, jacks, queens, and kings removed (36 cards total)

Object of the Game: Have the lower total score.

Shuffle together the cards. Place them face down in a pile.

On your turn, flip over the top two cards in the pile. Write the numbers on your score card and find their least common multiple. For example, if you flip over a 3 and an 8, the least common multiple is 24. This LCM is your score for the round.

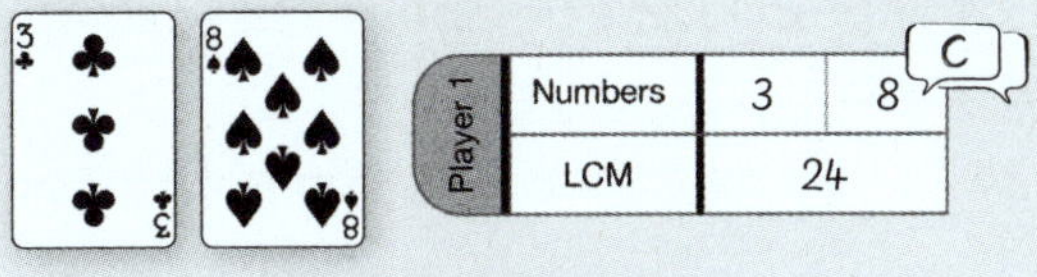

Sample play.

Take turns until both players have completed all 3 rounds. Then, each player finds the sum of their scores. Whoever has the lower total score wins the game.

Answer Key:

		First Card								
Second Card		2	3	4	5	6	7	8	9	10
	2	2	6	4	10	6	14	8	18	10
	3	6	3	12	15	6	21	24	9	30
	4	4	12	4	20	12	28	8	36	20
	5	10	15	20	5	30	35	40	45	10
	6	6	6	12	30	6	42	24	18	30
	7	14	21	28	35	42	7	56	63	70
	8	8	24	8	40	24	56	8	72	40
	9	18	9	36	45	18	63	72	9	90
	10	10	30	20	10	30	70	40	90	10

Independent Practice and Review

Have your child complete the Lesson 3.1 Practice and Review workbook pages.

Lesson 3.2
Multiply and Adjust

Purpose	Materials
• Use addition and subtraction to reason about multiples • Review the box method of multiplication • Use the "multiply and adjust" strategy to mentally multiply	• Die

Memory Work · **Name 4 multiples of 10.** *Sample answers: 20, 50, 160, 400.*

In this lesson, your child will learn to "multiply and adjust" to solve mental multiplication problems. These problems are challenging for many children, so don't be discouraged if he finds them difficult at first. He does not need to fully grasp the strategy now, and he will revisit it in Unit 6 with mental division problems.

Warm-up (A): Use Addition and Subtraction to Complete a Hot Dog Bun Chart

To warm up, let's pretend you are buying hot dog buns for a concession stand. The buns come in packs of 6. How many buns do you get if you buy 2 packs? *12.* **6 packs?** *36.* **10 packs?** *60.*

Concession stands need a lot of buns! Let's complete these charts to find out how many buns are in each number of packs.

- **20 times 6 equals 120. If you buy 20 packs, you get 120 buns.** Point to the matching column in the chart.
- **Let's say you have 20 packs and then buy 1 more pack. How many buns do you have now?** *126.* Write 126 in the chart. **20 packs hold 120 buns. 1 more pack holds 6 more buns. So, we add 120 plus 6 to find the total number of buns.** Write an arrow and "+6" as shown.
- **Let's say you have 21 packs and then buy 1 more pack. How many buns do you have now?** *132.* Write 132 in the chart. If your child's not sure, suggest he add 126 plus 6. Write an arrow and "+6" as shown.
- **Let's say you have 20 packs and then use up 1 pack. You have 19 packs left. How many buns do you have now?** *114.* Write 114 in the chart. **20 packs hold 120 buns. When you use 1 pack, you use 6 buns. So, we subtract 6 from 120 to find how many buns you have left.** Write an arrow and "-6" as shown.
- **Let's say you have 19 packs and then use up 1 pack. You have 18 packs left. How many buns do you have now?** *108.* Write 108 in the chart. If your child's not sure, suggest he subtract 6 from 114. Write an arrow and "-6" as shown.

A

Packs	18	19	20	21	22
Buns	108	114	120	126	132

−6 −6 +6 +6

Encourage your child to use mental addition and subtraction as he completes the chart. He may write vertical problems if needed.

Activity (B): Multiply and Adjust to Mentally Multiply

Last year, you learned how to use the box method to multiply numbers. Today, you'll review the box method and learn the "multiply and adjust" strategy for mental multiplication. The examples show how to solve the same problem with both methods.

Two Ways to Mentally Multiply (B)

Box Method

Ex. There are 6 buns in each pack. How many buns are in 43 packs?

	40	3
6	240	18

240 + 18 = 258
43 × 6 = **258 buns**

Multiply and Adjust

Ex. There are 6 buns in each pack. How many buns are in 43 packs?

40 packs: 40 × 6 = 240 (+6)
41 packs: 41 × 6 = 246 (+6)
42 packs: 42 × 6 = 252 (+6)
43 packs: 43 × 6 = 258

43 × 6 = **258 buns**

If you did not use *Fourth Grade Math with Confidence*, briefly read and discuss the box method example. Do not spend a lot of time making sure your child understands it at this point. For now, focus on the multiply and adjust strategy. Your child will study the box method more in Lesson 3.7.

Read aloud the example problem. **First, let's review how to use the box method to multiply 43 times 6. We'll find how many buns are in 40 packs and how many buns are in 3 packs. Then, we'll add to find the total number of buns.**

- Point to 40 and 6. **What's 40 times 6?** *240.* **There are 240 buns in 40 packs.**
- Point to 3 and 6. **What's 3 times 6?** *18.* **There are 18 buns in the remaining 3 packs.**
- **Last, we add the partial products to find the total product. 240 plus 18 equals 258, so there are 258 buns in 43 packs.**

The right side of the text box shows how to multiply and adjust to find the product. First, we multiply 40 times 6. Then, we add on the additional packs.

- **40 times 6 equals 240, so there are 240 buns in 40 packs.**
- **If we buy 1 more pack, we have 41 packs. So, to find the total number of buns, we add 6 to 240. What's 240 plus 6?** *246.* **There are 246 buns in 41 packs.**
- **If we buy 1 more pack, we have 42 packs. What's 246 plus 6?** *252.* **There are 252 buns in 42 packs.**
- **If we buy 1 more pack, we have 43 packs. What's 252 plus 6?** *258.* **There are 258 buns in 43 packs.**

This example demonstrates adding one pack at a time. You could also add on multiple packs at once.

Have your child complete the practice problems. He should use the first problem in each column to solve the second problem.

- For the first pair of problems, have him add 1 group of 4 to 280 to find 71 × 4.
- For the second pair of problems, have him subtract 1 group of 3 from 270 to find 89 × 3.
- For the third pair of problems, have him add 2 groups of 5 to 400 to find 82 × 5.

(B)

70 × 4 = 280 (+4)	90 × 3 = 270 (−3)	80 × 5 = 400 (+10)
71 × 4 = 284	89 × 3 = 267	82 × 5 = 410

The arrows are drawn only for clarity. Your child does not need to include them in his answers.

To make these problems more concrete, have him imagine objects that come in groups of 4, 3, or 5. For example, for the first problem, he might choose toys in a treat bag, wheels on cars, or hooves on horses: **I'll pretend there are 4 toys in each treat bag. 70 treat bags have 280 toys. 1 more treat bag has 4 more toys, so 71 treat bags have 284 toys.**

Activity (C): Play Climb the Ladder

In this game, we solve the problems in order, from the bottom of the ladder to the top. The goal is to be the first person to solve the problem at the top of each ladder. Play Climb the Ladder. Encourage your child to multiply and adjust to find the products.

Climb the Ladder

Materials: Die

Object of the Game: Win the most points by completing the multiplication problems at the top of the ladders.

On your turn, roll the die. Find the ladder that matches your roll and use the multiply-and-adjust strategy to solve the next blank multiplication problem. For example, if you roll a 3, complete the next blank multiplication problem in the middle ladder. After you solve one problem, play passes to the other player.

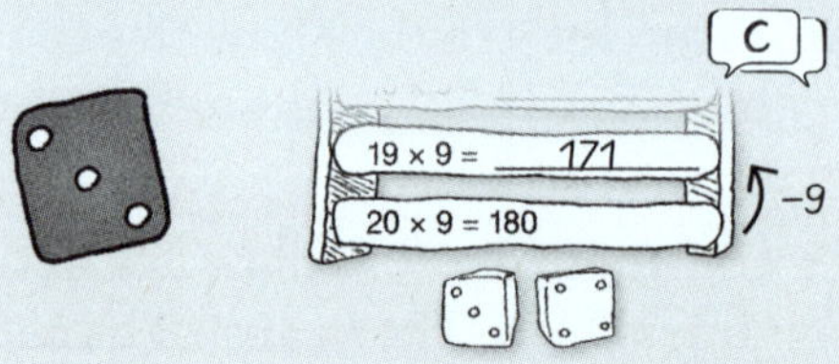

20 × 9 equals 180, so 19 × 9 is 9 less than 180, or 171.

Solve the problems in order from the bottom of the ladder to the top. The first person to solve the problem at the top of each ladder wins a point.

If the number on the die matches a completed ladder, play passes to the other player. Continue until all problems in all ladders are completed. The player with more points wins.

Answer Key:

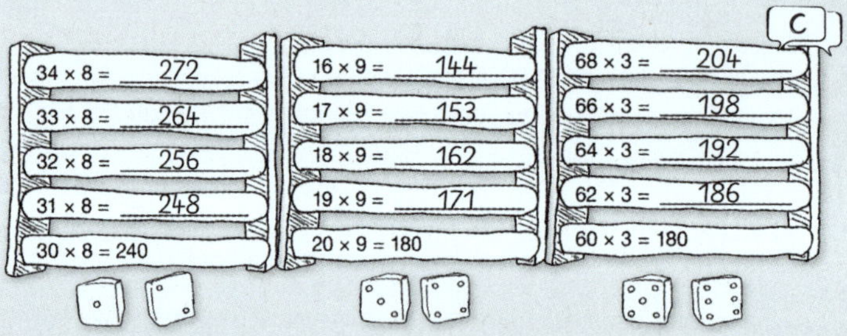

Independent Practice and Review

Have your child complete the Lesson 3.2 Practice and Review workbook pages.

Lesson 3.3
Mentally Multiply by 2 or 4

Purpose	Materials
• Review doubling numbers • Mentally multiply numbers by 2 or 4	• 2 decks of playing cards

Memory Work • **Name 4 factors of 15.** *1, 3, 5, 15. Your child may name the factors in any order.*

Warm-up (A): Review Doubling Numbers

When you were younger, you learned how to double numbers by adding the number to itself. For example, to double 25, you can add 25 plus 25. Have your child complete part A.

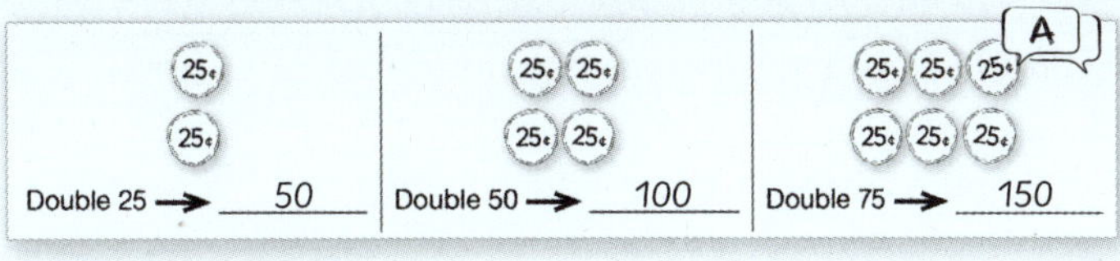

Activity (B): Mentally Multiply Numbers by 2 or 4

Today, you'll learn another way to double numbers and multiply them by 2. Have your child read the top section of the text box.

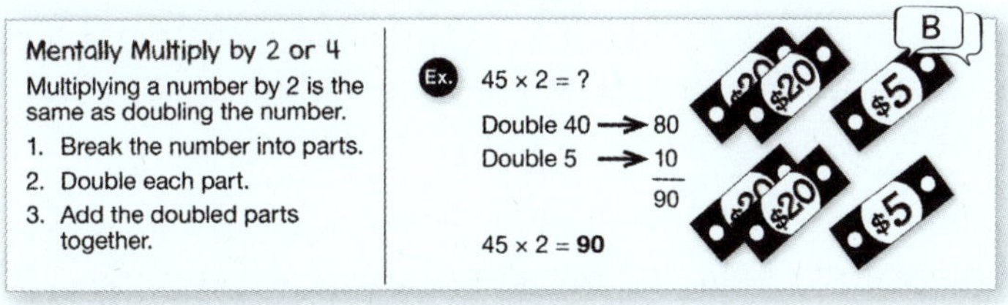

Read aloud the first example: ***45 times 2 equals what?***

- **First, we break the number into parts that are easy to double. The example breaks the number into 40 and 5.**
- **What's double 40?** *80.* **What's double 5?** *10.*
- **Then, we add the doubled parts together. 80 plus 10 is 90, so 45 times 2 equals 90.**

To multiply a number by 4, you double the number twice. Have your child read aloud the bottom part of the text box.

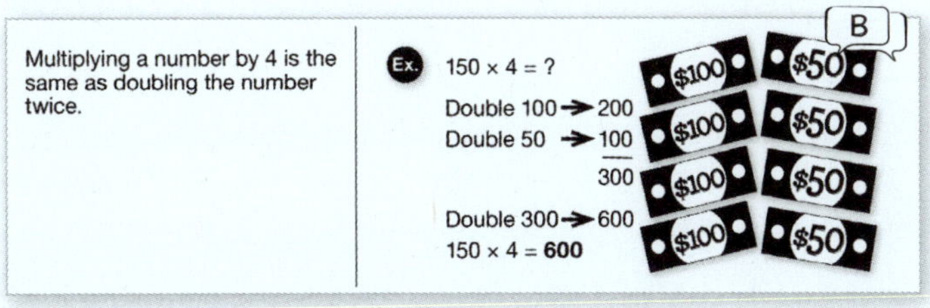

Read aloud the second example: ***150 times 4 equals what?***

- **First, we double 150. What's double 100?** *200.* **What's double 50?** *100.* **200 plus 100 is 300, so 150 times 2 equals 300.**
- **Next, we double 300. What's double 300?** *600.*
- **So, 150 times 4 equals 600.**

Have your child complete the practice problems. She should double the answer to the first problem in each column to help find the answer to the second problem in the column.

35 × 2 = 70	125 × 2 = 250	2,500 × 2 = 5,000
35 × 4 = 140 (×2)	125 × 4 = 500 (×2)	2,500 × 4 = 10,000 (×2)

B

The arrows are drawn only for clarity. Your child does not need to include them in her answers.

Activity (C): Play Flip and Multiply

Play Flip and Multiply.

Flip and Multiply

Materials: 2s and 4s from 2 decks of cards (16 cards total)

Object of the Game: Have the greater total sum of all your products.

Shuffle the cards and place them in a face-down pile.

On your turn, turn over the top card in the pile. Choose one of the multiplication problems on your scorecard and write the number on the card as the missing factor. (You may write the number in any of the multiplication equations.) Then, use mental math to find the product. The product is your score for that round.

For example, if you turn over a 4 on your first turn and write the 4 in the second multiplication problem, your product is 340 (since 85 × 4 = 340).

85 × 4 = 340

C

Take turns until both players have completed their scorecards. Each player adds up their products (either mentally or on scrap paper). Whoever has the greater total wins.

Independent Practice and Review

Have your child complete the Lesson 3.3 Practice and Review workbook pages.

Lesson 3.4
The Associative Property

Purpose	Materials
• Explore multiplying numbers with different orders and groupings • Introduce the associative property of multiplication • Use the associative property to make mental multiplication problems easier to solve	• Die • Counters

Memory Work

- **What do we call a quadrilateral with 4 right angles?** *A rectangle.*
- **What do we call a quadrilateral with 4 right angles and 4 equal sides?** *A square.*
- **What do we call a quadrilateral with 4 equal sides?** *A rhombus.*
- **What do we call a quadrilateral with 2 pairs of parallel sides?** *A parallelogram.*
- **What do we call a quadrilateral with exactly 1 pair of parallel sides?** *A trapezoid.*

Warm-up (A): Explore Multiplying the Same Numbers in Different Ways

Have your child complete the multiplication problems in part A. Make sure he follows the order of operations and completes the problem in parentheses first.

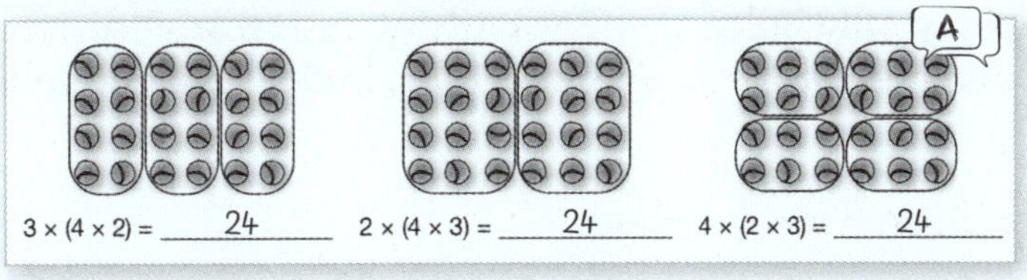

What 3 numbers get multiplied together in all of these expressions? *3, 4, and 2.*

- **In the first problem, there are 3 groups of tennis balls. Each group has 4 rows of 2 tennis balls.**
- **In the second problem, there are 2 groups of tennis balls. Each group has 4 rows of 3 tennis balls.**
- **In the third problem, there are 4 groups of tennis balls. Each group has 2 rows of 3 tennis balls.**

How many tennis balls are in each picture? *24.* **No matter how you group the factors, the product is always 24.**

Activity (B): Understand the Associative Property of Multiplication

When you were younger, you learned you can add numbers in any order or group them in any way and still get the same sum. The same is true for multiplication.

This property of addition and multiplication is called the associative property. The root word of associative is ***associate*****. When we associate with a person, it means we connect or spend time with them. The associative property of multiplication says that the numbers can associate with each other in different ways without changing the product.**

Have your child read the text aloud.

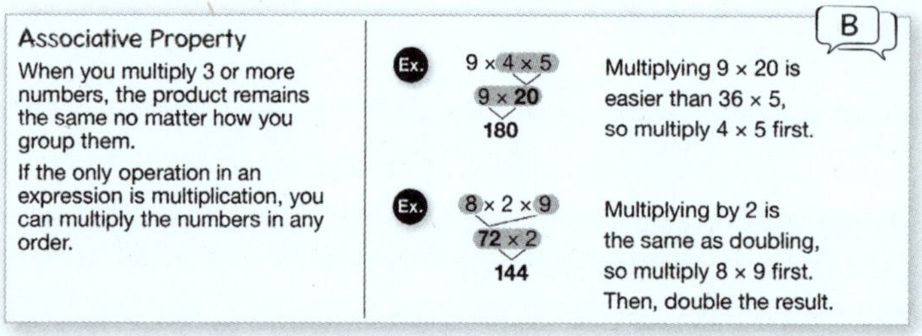

Let's study the examples to see how we can use the associative property to make mental multiplication easier.

- **The first example shows how to find the product of 9 times 4 times 5. 9 times 4 is 36. So, if we multiply 9 times 4 first, we'd have to multiply 36 times 5.**
- **Most people find it easier to multiply 4 times 5 first. 4 times 5 equals 20. 9 times 20 is 180, so the product is 180.**
- **The second example shows how to find the product of 8 times 2 times 9. 8 times 2 is 16. So, if we multiply 8 times 2 first, we'd have to multiply 16 times 9.**
- **Instead, it's easier to multiply 8 times 9 first. 8 times 9 equals 72. Multiplying a number by 2 is the same as doubling it, so we can double 72 to find the final product. Double 72 is 144.**

Cover the definition with your hand. **Can you say the associative property for multiplication in your own words?** *Sample answer: If you multiply more than 2 numbers together, you get the same product if you multiply them in a different order or group them in different ways.*

The associative property only holds true for multiplication or addition. If a problem involves subtraction, division, or a mix of operations, make sure you follow the order of operations.

Activity (C): Play Dice Tic-Tac-Toe

Play Dice Tic-Tac-Toe. Encourage your child to use the following strategies as he solves the problems in the game.

- **Check if the problem involves multiplying by zero.**

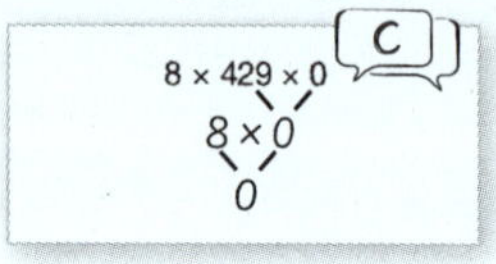

Any number times zero equals zero. So, if one of the factors is zero, the product will be zero.

- **Look for factors whose product has a trailing zero.**

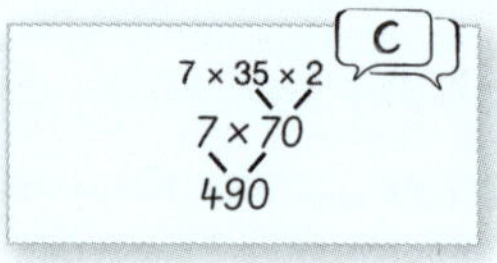

35 × 2 = 70. Then, it's easy to multiply 70 by 7.

- **If one of the factors is a 2, it's sometimes easier to multiply the other numbers first and then double their product.**

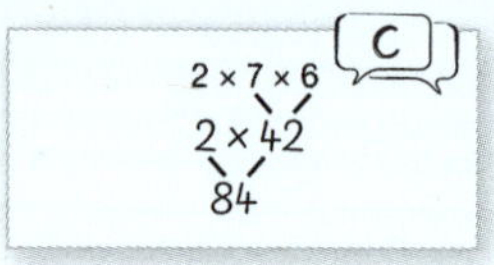

7 × 6 = 42. Then, double 42 to complete the problem.

If your child has trouble keeping track of the steps mentally, have him write the second step below the problem on the game board.

Dice Tic-Tac-Toe

Materials: Die; counters of two different colors

Object of the Game: Be the first player to fill three boxes in a row, either horizontally, vertically, or diagonally.

Give 10 counters of one color to one player and 10 counters of a different color to the other player.

On your turn, roll the die. Find the column in the game board that matches your roll, and choose a multiplication problem in that column. Name the answer and cover the problem with one of your counters. If you roll a 6, you may choose a problem in any column.

Play then passes to the other player. Continue until one player covers 3 boxes in a row, either horizontally, vertically, or diagonally.

Note that you only need to place 3 counters in a row to win, even though there are 5 rows and 5 columns on the gameboard. The extra rows and columns provide more opportunities to win.

Answer Key:

4 × 5 × 8 20 × 8 160	4 × 45 × 2 180 × 2 360	2 × 7 × 6 2 × 42 84	7 × 250 × 2 7 × 500 3,500	45 × 3 × 2 90 × 3 270
9 × 2 × 15 9 × 30 270	2 × 7 × 5 2 × 35 70	8 × 35 × 2 8 × 70 560	2 × 4 × 15 2 × 60 120	8 × 2 × 7 56 × 2 112
2 × 7 × 7 2 × 49 98	25 × 2 × 4 100 × 2 200	5 × 6 × 9 30 × 9 270	35 × 2 × 2 70 × 2 140	150 × 9 × 2 300 × 9 2,700
7 × 35 × 2 7 × 70 490	8 × 429 × 0 8 × 0 0	7 × 25 × 2 7 × 50 350	8 × 5 × 6 40 × 6 240	9 × 4 × 2 36 × 2 72
8 × 4 × 2 32 × 2 64	25 × 3 × 2 50 × 3 150	6 × 2 × 6 36 × 2 72	6 × 15 × 2 6 × 30 180	297 × 7 × 0 297 × 0 0

Independent Practice and Review

Have your child complete the Lesson 3.4 Practice and Review workbook pages.

Lesson 3.5
Place Value and Mental Multiplication

Purpose	Materials
• Model multiplying by 10 with bills • Understand that multiplying a number by 10 is the same as shifting the digits one place to the left on the place-value chart • Mentally multiply numbers by 10, 100, or 1,000 • Mentally multiply numbers with trailing zeros (i.e., 300 × 20)	• None

Memory Work	• **What is the order of operations?** *Parentheses, multiply or divide from left to right, add or subtract from left to right.*

Warm-up (A): Practice Multiplying by 10

For our warm-up today, we'll practice multiplying by 10. First, we'll multiply 13 times 10. When we multiply by 10, each ten-dollar bill becomes a hundred-dollar bill. Each one-dollar bill becomes a ten-dollar bill. What's 13 times 10? *130.* Write $130 as shown.

Next, we'll multiply 130 times 10. Each hundred-dollar bill becomes a thousand-dollar bill. Each ten-dollar bill becomes a hundred-dollar bill. What's 130 times 10? *1,300.* Write $1,300 as shown.

Repeat with 1,300 × 10. **Each thousand-dollar bill becomes a ten-thousand-dollar bill. Each hundred-dollar bill becomes a thousand-dollar bill. What's 1,300 times 10?** *13,000.* Write $13,000 as shown.

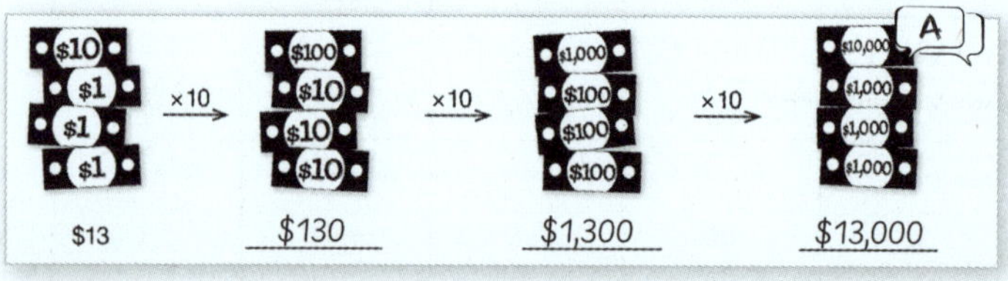

What pattern do you notice? *Sample answer: We tack on one more zero each time.*

Activity (B): Multiply by 10, 100, and 1,000 on the Place-Value Chart

We can also use a place-value chart to show multiplying by 10.

- **What is 13 times 10?** *130.* Write 130 in the place-value chart as shown.
- **What is 13 times 100?** *1,300.* If your child's not sure, say: **Multiplying by 100 is the same as multiplying by 10 twice. When you multiplied 13 by 10 twice in the warm-up, what answer did you get?** *1,300.* Write 1,300 in the place-value chart as shown.
- **What is 13 times 1,000?** *13,000.* If your child's not sure, say: **Multiplying by 1,000 is the same as multiplying by 10 three times. When you multiplied 13 by 10 three times in the warm-up, what answer did you get?** *13,000.* Write 13,000 in the place-value chart as shown.

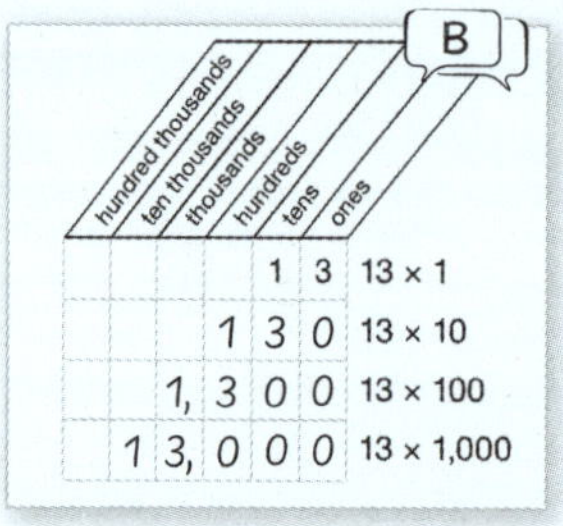

What pattern do you notice? *Sample answers: Each product has one more zero than the previous product. We tack on one more zero each time.*

Multiplying by 10 is the same as shifting the digits one place to the left on the place-value chart. We tack on 1 zero so that each digit is in the correct place.

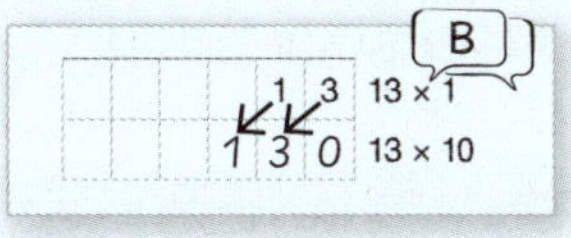

Multiplying by 100 is the same as shifting the digits two places to the left. Multiplying by 1,000 is the same as shifting the digits three places to the left.

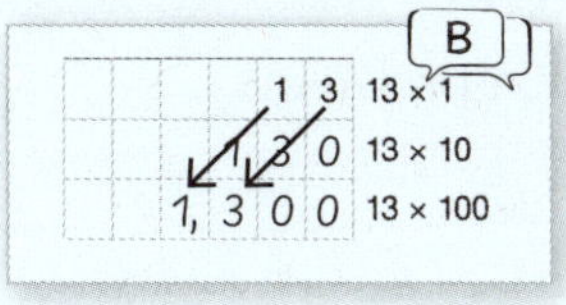

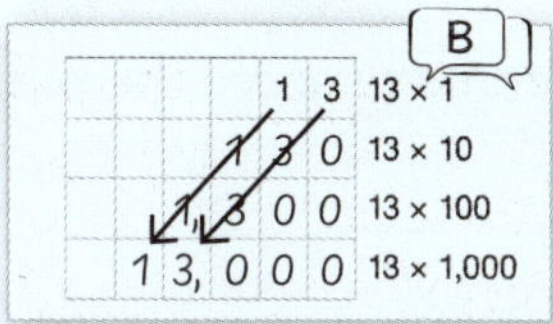

Have your child multiply 314 by 10, 100, and 1,000. Discuss how the digits shift one place to the left each time.

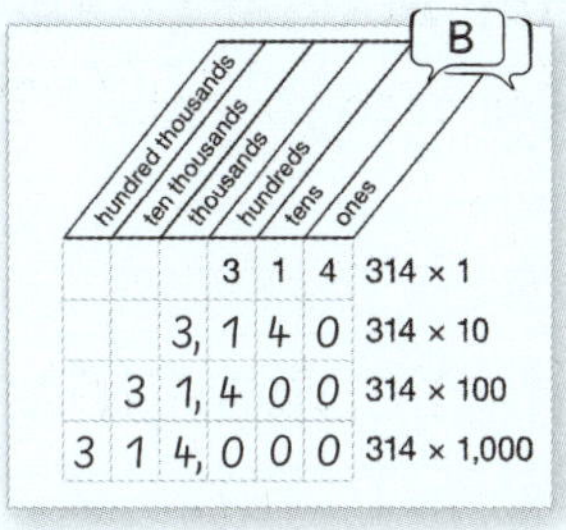

Activity (C): Mentally Multiply Numbers with Trailing Zeros

In Unit 1, we reviewed how to mentally multiply numbers with a few trailing zeros. You can use the same steps to multiply numbers with any number of trailing zeros. The steps are listed here in case you need to refer to them. Have your child read the top part of the text box aloud.

C

Mental Multiplication
1. Underline the trailing zeros.
2. Multiply the non-zero digits.
3. Tack on the trailing zeros.

Ex. 300 × 20 = ?
3 hundreds × 2 tens = 6 thousands
3<u>00</u> × 2<u>0</u> = **6,000**

Let's study the example to review how to use this technique.

- **300 has 2 trailing zeros, so you underline 2 zeros.**
- **20 has 1 trailing zero, so you underline 1 zero.**
- **3 times 2 equals 6. Then, you tack 3 zeros on to show that you have 6 thousands. 300 times 20 equals 6,000.**

In the last lesson, you learned about the associative property of multiplication. What does the associative property say about multiplication? *Sample answer: You can multiply numbers with any grouping or order and still get the same product.* Have your child read aloud the bottom part of the text box.

C

The associative property allows us to break numbers apart in this way to make multiplication easier.

Ex. 300 × 20 = ?
3 × 100 × 2 × 10
6 × 1,000
6,000

This next example shows why it works to underline the zeros and tack them back on. The associative property is the key. It allows us to break the numbers apart and multiply them with a different grouping.

- **300 equals 3 times 100. 20 equals 2 times 10.**
- **3 times 2 equals 6. 100 times 10 equals 1,000.**
- **6 times 1,000 equals 6,000.**

> Your child does not need to fully understand the connection between the associative property and the "tacking on zeros" technique for mental multiplication. What's most important is that she understands there is a logical (and mathematically-sound) reason behind the technique.

Have your child tack on zeros to solve the practice problems.

128 × 10 =	1,280	40 × 20 =	800
128 × 100 =	12,800	400 × 20 =	8,000
128 × 1,000 =	128,000	4,000 × 20 =	80,000

Activity (D): Play Multiplication Master (1-Player Game)

Explain the rules of Multiplication Master to your child. Then, have her play the game on her own.

Multiplication Master

Materials: None

Object of the Game: Place the factors in the multiplication problems to yield the greatest possible sum of the five products.

Multiplication Master has 5 rounds. In each round, choose one number from the circles above the game board. Write this number in one of the multiplication problems, and find the product. Try to place the numbers so that the total of the products will be as large as possible at the end of the game.

After you complete all 5 rounds, add all 5 products to find your total score (either mentally or on the grid). Use the scoring guide to see how close you got to the greatest possible score.

Answer Key:

This scorecard shows how to reach the highest possible score.

90 2,000 50 80 600

	Product
30 × 50	1,500
70 × 80	5,600
200 × 90	18,000
500 × 600	300,000
4,000 × 2,000	8,000,000
Total	8,325,100

Independent Practice and Review

Have your child complete the Lesson 3.5 Practice and Review workbook pages.

Lesson 3.6
Use the Multiplication Algorithm to Multiply Numbers with Trailing Zeros

Purpose	Materials
• Understand how multiplying by multiples of 10, 100, or 1,000 shifts products on the place-value chart • Use the multiplication algorithm to multiply numbers with trailing zeros	• None

Memory Work	
	• **What are the four basic operations?** *Addition, subtraction, multiplication, and division.* • **What is an equation?** *A number sentence with an equals sign.* • **What is an expression?** *Part of a number sentence without an equals sign.*

In the last lesson, your child used mental math to multiply numbers with trailing zeros. In these problems, it was easy for your child to mentally multiply the non-zero digits. For example, to multiply 400 × 20, your child multiplied 4 times 2 and then tacked on 3 zeros. In this lesson, your child will learn how to use the multiplication algorithm to multiply numbers whose non-zero digits are difficult to multiply mentally.

Warm-up (A): Shift Products on the Place-Value Chart

In the last lesson, you learned how to shift numbers on the place-value chart to multiply them by 10, 100, or 1,000. Have your child write the answers to 28 × 10, 28 × 100, and 28 × 1,000 on the place-value chart.

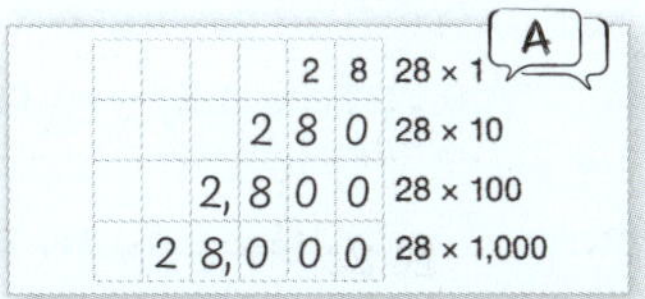

The next place-value chart shows that 28 times 3 equals 84. 28 times 30 is the same as 28 times 3 times 10. So, we can take the product of 28 times 3 and shift it one place to the left to find the answer to 28 times 30. We tack on 1 trailing zero so that the digits are all in the correct places. Write 840 in the chart as shown.

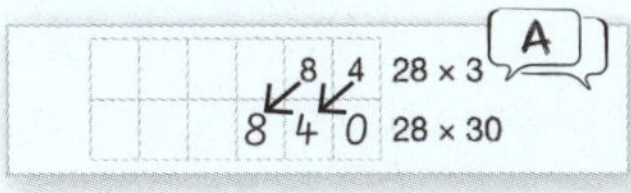

If 28 times 30 equals 840, what does 28 times 300 equal? *8,400.* Write 8,400 in the chart.

If 28 times 300 equals 8,400, what does 28 times 3,000 equal? *84,000.* Write 84,000 in the chart.

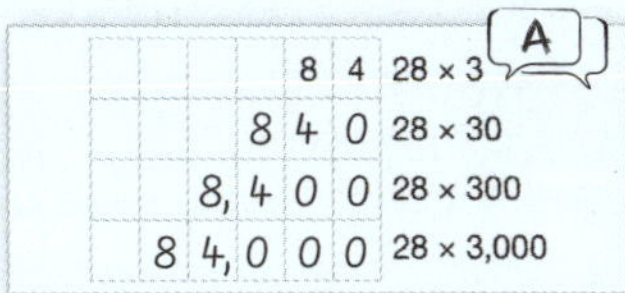

Have your child use the same approach to solve the other multiplication problems in part A. Remind him to write commas between the thousands-place and hundreds-place as needed.

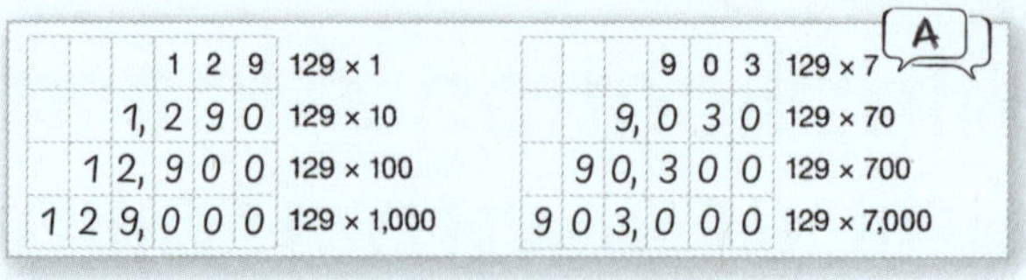

Activity (B): Use the Multiplication Algorithm to Multiply Numbers with Trailing Zeros

Last year, you learned how to multiply two-digit numbers by multiples of 10 with the multiplication algorithm. Today, you'll learn how to extend that skill to multiples of 100 or 1,000.

In part A, you knew that 28 times 3 equals 84. That made it easy to figure out 28 times 30. You shifted the digits one place to the left on the place-value chart and tacked on a zero.

When you use the multiplication algorithm to solve 28 times 30, you do these steps in reverse.

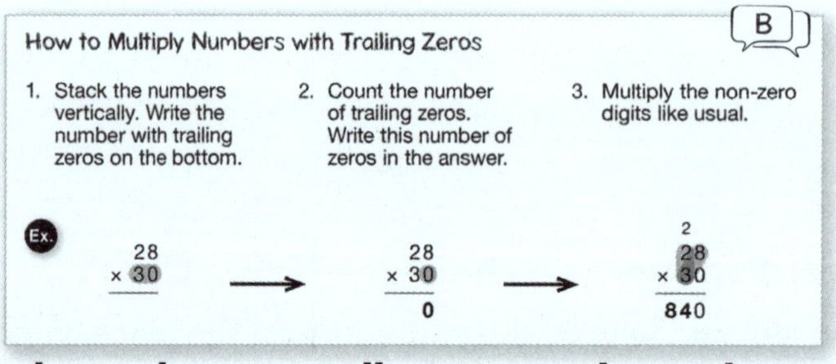

- **First, we stack the numbers vertically. We write the number with trailing zeros on the bottom. 30 has a trailing zero, so we write 30 on the bottom.**
- **Second, we count the number of trailing zeros in the bottom number. How many trailing zeros does 30 have?** *1.* **We write 1 zero in the ones-place of the answer. This shifts the digits in the next step to the left.**
- **Last, we multiply the non-zero digits like usual. 28 times 3 is 84. So, 28 times 30 is 840.**

If we multiplied 28 times 300, we would write 2 zeros in the answer. If we multiplied 28 times 3,000, we would write 3 zeros in the answer. Writing the correct number of trailing zeros makes sure that the other digits are shifted the correct number of places.

Have your child follow the steps to solve the practice problems. Remind him to write the trailing zeros in the answer before multiplying the non-zero digits.

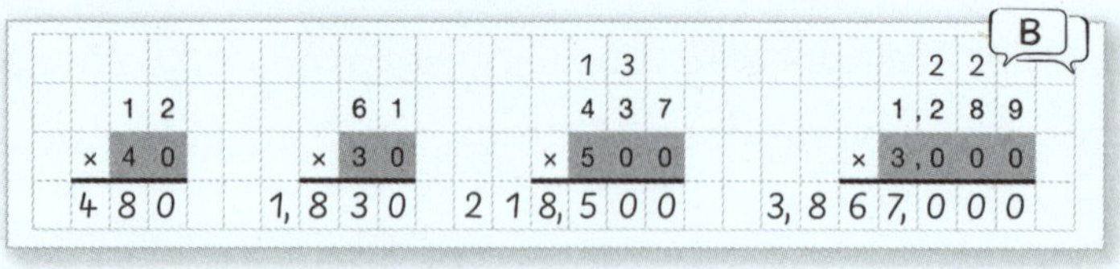

Independent Practice and Review

Have your child complete the Lesson 3.6 Practice and Review workbook pages.

Lesson 3.7
Multiply with the Box Method

Purpose	Materials
• Practice mentally multiplying numbers with trailing zeros • Review how to use the box method to multiply two-digit numbers by two-digit numbers • Learn how to use the box method to multiply three-digit numbers by two-digit numbers	• None

Memory Work	
	• **What do we call an angle with a measure less than 90 degrees?** *Acute.* • **What do we call an angle with a measure equal to 90 degrees?** *Right.* • **What do we call an angle with a measure greater than 90 degrees and less than 180 degrees?** *Obtuse.* • **What do we call an angle with a measure equal to 180 degrees?** *Straight.*

If you did not use *Fourth Grade Math with Confidence*, you may not be familiar with the box method. If so, use this lesson as a gentle introduction to the method, coach your child on the practice page as needed, and don't worry if your child doesn't fully master it by the end of the lesson.

Warm-up (A): Practice Mental Multiplication

Have your child complete the problems in part A. Remind her as needed to underline the trailing zeros, multiply the non-zero digits, and then tack on the underlined zeros.

A

90 × 40 = 3,600   300 × 20 = 6,000   900 × 200 = 180,000

Activity (B): Review How to Multiply Two-Digit Numbers with the Area Model and the Box Method

Last year, you learned how to use the area model to multiply two-digit numbers. You split the area into smaller parts, multiplied to find the area of each part, and then added the partial products.

This rectangle is 28 by 34. The numbers inside the rectangle show the area of each part.

- Point to 600. **20 times 30 equals 600.**
- Point to 80. **20 times 4 equals 80.**
- Point to 240. **8 times 30 equals 240.**
- Point to 32. **8 times 4 equals 32.**
- Point to the addition problem. **600 plus 80 plus 240 plus 32 equals 952. 34 times 28 equals 952.**

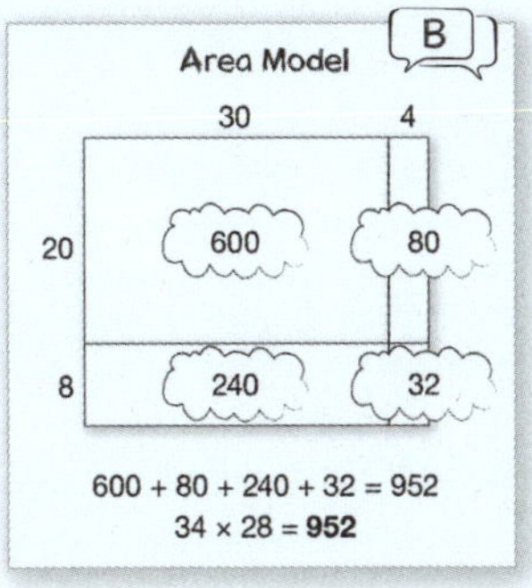

You also learned how to use the box method to multiply a two-digit number by a two-digit number. The box method is very similar to splitting a rectangle into parts to find its area. Here's how to multiply 34 times 28 with the box method.

- Point to 600. **20 times 30 equals 600.**
- Point to 80. **20 times 4 equals 80.**
- Point to 240. **8 times 30 equals 240.**
- Point to 32. **8 times 4 equals 32.**
- Point to the addition problem. **600 plus 80 plus 240 plus 32 equals 952. So, 34 times 28 equals 952.**

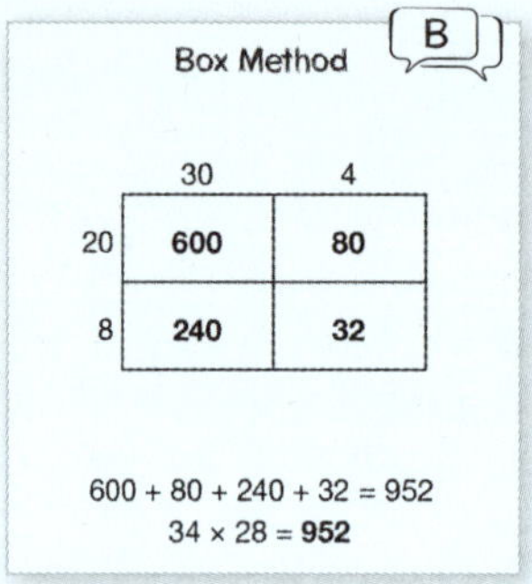

Both the box method and the area model involve the same steps and give you the same answer. The main difference is that the box method is easier to write out!

The next problem is 65 times 49. The factors are split into tens and ones to make the multiplying and adding steps as easy as possible. Have your child multiply to find the partial products. Then, have her add to find the total product. **What's 65 times 49?** *3,185.*

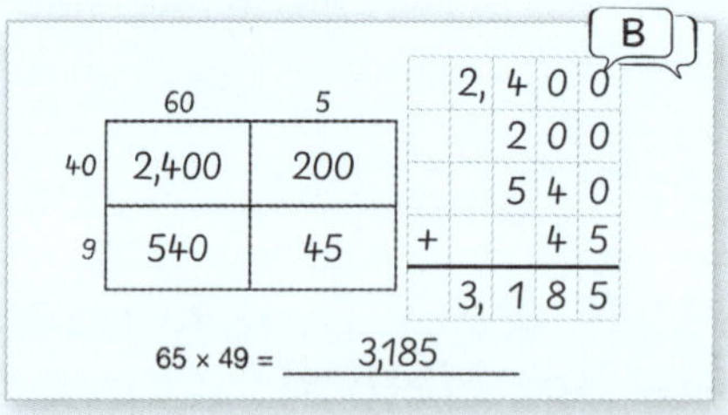

Your child may add the partial products mentally or write them in the grid and add with the written process.

For 73 times 54, you need to split the factors into tens and ones yourself. Help your child set up the problem as shown and solve.

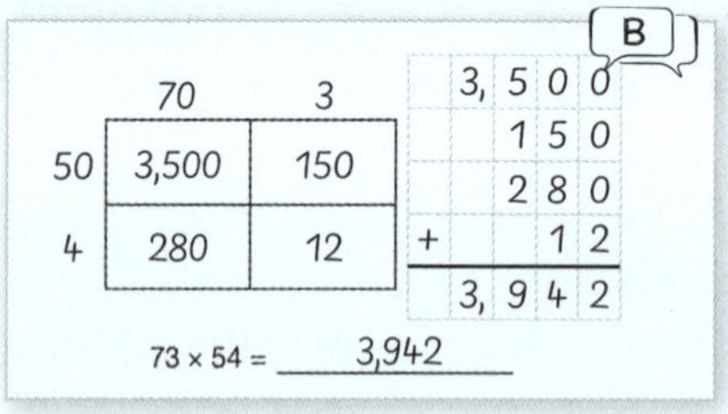

Activity (C): Use the Box Method to Multiply a Three-Digit Number by a Two-Digit Number

We can also use the box method to multiply larger numbers. Let's try using it to multiply a three-digit number by a two-digit number. We'll break the three-digit number into hundreds, tens, and ones. Have your child use the box method to complete the problem.

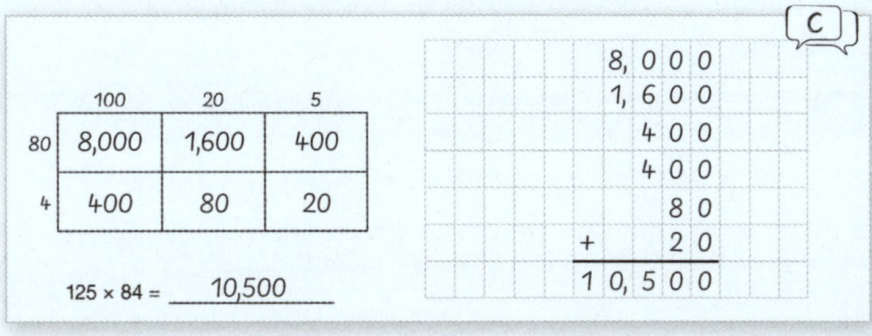

We could use the box method to multiply numbers with any number of digits, but it might take a lot of boxes!

Independent Practice and Review

Have your child complete the Lesson 3.7 Practice and Review workbook pages.

Lesson 3.8
Use the Multiplication Algorithm to Multiply Two-Digit Numbers

Purpose	Materials
• Practice multiplying in parts and adding to find the total area • Understand the meaning of the steps in the multiplication algorithm • Use the multiplication algorithm to multiply two-digit numbers	• 2 dice
Memory Work	• **What does LCM stand for?** *Least common multiple.*

In this lesson, you will review how to multiply two-digit numbers with the multiplication algorithm. If your child had trouble with this process last year or didn't learn it thoroughly, split the lesson over two days:

- Day 1: Do the Warm-up and Activity B. Then, have your child complete the Review page only.
- Day 2: Review the steps in Activity B and play Product Power (Activity C). Then, have your child complete the Practice page.

It's common for children to temporarily have trouble remembering the multiplication facts as they carry out the many steps in the multiplication algorithm. If your child struggles to remember the multiplication facts in this lesson, allow him to refer to the multiplication chart (Blackline Master 4). See the Unit 3 **Teaching Math with Confidence** for more tips on how to make multi-digit multiplication problems more manageable for your child.

Warm-up (A): Multiply in Parts to Find Total Area

Today, we'll review how to use the multiplication algorithm to multiply two-digit numbers by two-digit numbers. We'll warm up by solving a simpler problem.

Read aloud the first word problem: ***What is the area of the driveway?* The driveway is 42 feet long and 8 feet wide, so multiply 42 times 8 to find its area.** Have your child use the multiplication algorithm to multiply 42 × 8.

Read aloud the second word problem: ***What is the area of the lawn?* The lawn is 42 feet long and 30 feet wide, so multiply 42 times 30 to find its area.** Have your child use the multiplication algorithm to multiply 42 × 30.

Read aloud the last word problem: ***What is the total area of the driveway and lawn?* How can you find the total area?** *Add 336 plus 1,260.* Have your child find the sum of 336 and 1,260 to solve the problem.

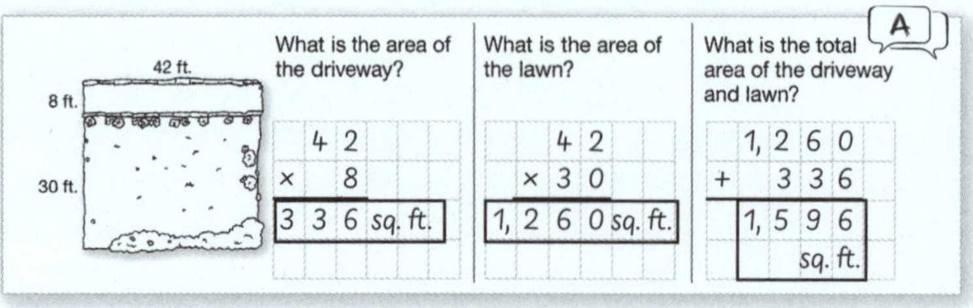

Activity (B): Understand the Big Picture of How the Multiplication Algorithm Works

Another way to find the total area of the yard is to use the multiplication algorithm to multiply 42 times 38. First, we'll review the big picture of how the algorithm works. Then, we'll take a closer look at the steps. Have your child read the top part of the text box aloud.

B

The Multiplication Algorithm

The multiplication algorithm breaks multiplication problems into parts. You multiply each part separately. Then, you add the parts to find the final product.

Ex.

```
     42
   × 38
  -----
    336  ←—— 42 × 8
+ 1,260  ←—— 42 × 30
  -----
  1,596  ←—— 42 × 38
```

Some children understand complex concepts better when they first grasp the big picture. Others understand the concepts better if they first study the details. If your child finds this discussion too general, go on to the next activity and then come back to this one.

When you use the multiplication algorithm, you first multiply the top number by the ones-place of the bottom number. In this problem, we multiply 42 times 8. We ignore the 3 in the tens-place while we do it. Use your finger to cover the 3 in 38. **Like you found in part A, 42 times 8 equals 336.**

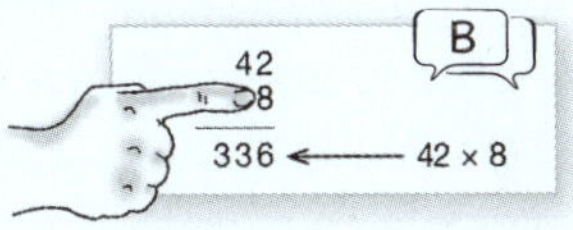

Then, you multiply the top number by the tens-place of the bottom number. In this problem, we multiply 42 times the 3 in 38. The 3 is in the tens-place, so we think of the 3 as 3 tens and ignore the 8 in the ones-place. Use your finger to cover the 8 in the ones-place. **We write a place-holder zero so that the digits are shifted one place to the left and in the correct place. Like you found in part A, 42 times 30 equals 1,260.**

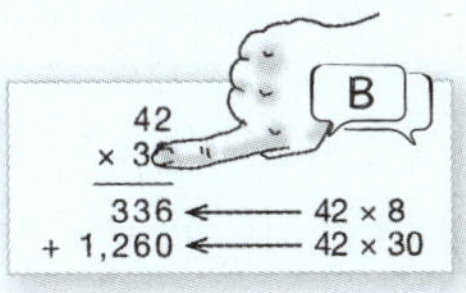

Last, you add the two partial products. 336 plus 1,260 equals 1,596.

B

```
     42
   × 38
  -----
    336  ←—— 42 × 8
+ 1,260  ←—— 42 × 30
  -----
  1,596  ←—— 42 × 38
```

This example leaves out any traded digits so that your child can focus on the overall meaning of the partial products in the problem. You will review how to record the traded digits when you discuss the steps in detail in the next activity.

Activity (B): Understand the Details of How to Use the Multiplication Algorithm

Now, let's review the details of the steps in the multiplication algorithm. The first step is to multiply the top number by the bottom number's ones-place. We ignore the 3 in the tens-place and multiply 42 times 8 like usual.

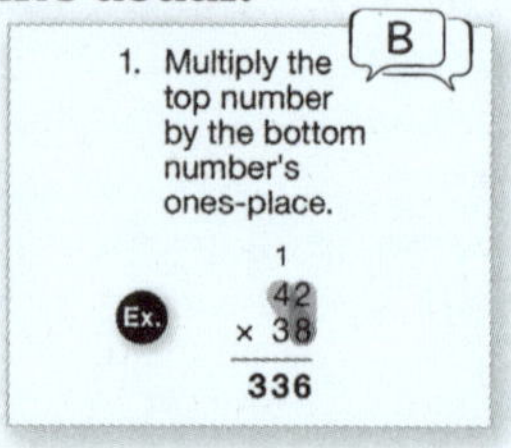

What's 2 times 8? *16.* **16 ones equal 1 ten and 6 ones, so we write a 1 above the tens-place and 6 in the partial product.**

What's 4 times 8? *32.* **Then, we add the 1 ten from the trade. 32 tens plus 1 ten equals 33 tens, so we write 33 in the partial product.**

You may have been taught to think of this process in the opposite order: multiplying each digit in the bottom number by the top number. It's fine to use this alternate way of describing the process if it's more natural for you.

The second step is to write a place-holder zero. We write the place-holder zero in the ones-place, directly below the first partial product. This zero will shift the digits in the second partial product to the correct place.

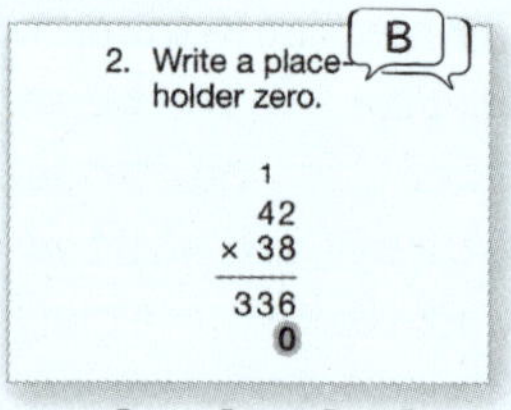

The third step is to multiply the top number by the bottom number's tens-place. We ignore the 8 in the ones-place and multiply 42 times 3. Use your finger to cover the 8 in 38.

What's 2 times 3? *6.* **We write 6 in the partial product. What's 4 times 3?** *12.* **We write 12 in the partial product.**

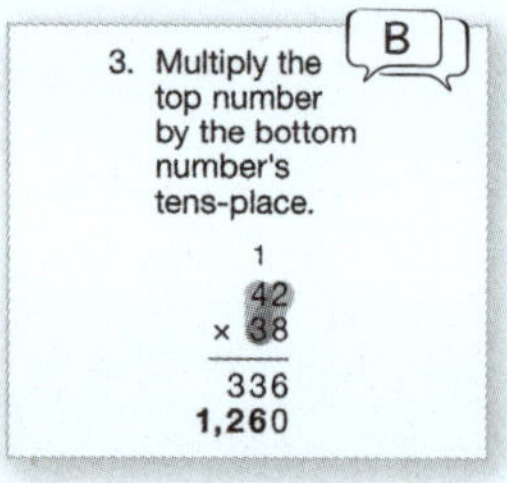

The fourth step is to add the partial products. 336 plus 1,260 equals 1,596, so 42 times 38 equals 1,596.

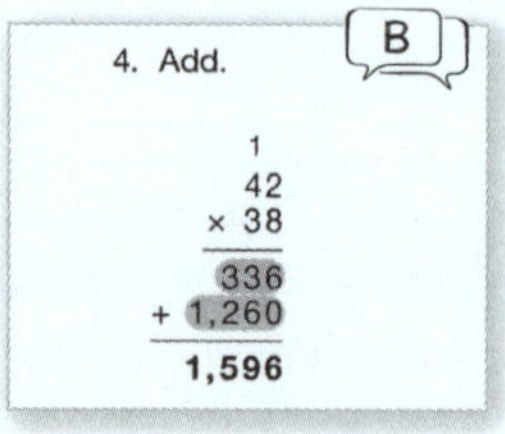

Demonstrate how to follow the steps to solve the first practice problem. Then, have your child complete the remaining problems.

$$\begin{array}{r} 61 \\ \times\ 43 \\ \hline 183 \\ +\ 2,440 \\ \hline \boxed{2,623} \end{array} \qquad \begin{array}{r} {\scriptstyle 1} \\ 32 \\ \times\ 74 \\ \hline 128 \\ +\ 2,240 \\ \hline \boxed{2,368} \end{array} \qquad \begin{array}{r} {\scriptstyle 1} \\ {\scriptstyle 3} \\ 45 \\ \times\ 37 \\ \hline 315 \\ +\ 1,350 \\ \hline \boxed{1,665} \end{array}$$

B

If your child has trouble keeping track of the steps, have him highlight or draw a ring around each pair of numbers before he multiplies them.

If your child has trouble remembering to add the traded digits, encourage him to cross out each traded digit after he adds it. The kinesthetic element of crossing out the digit often prevents forgetting about it. However, if your child finds the idea of crossing out the traded digit confusing, don't require him to do it.

Activity: (C): Play Product Power

Play Product Power.

Product Power

Materials: 2 dice

Object of the Game: Score more points than the other player by creating greater products.

Roll 2 dice. Use the numbers on the dice to create a two-digit number and write it on the top line of your first blank multiplication problem. You may write the digits in either order. The best strategy is to use the larger digit in the tens-place and the smaller digit in the ones-place.

Then, roll the 2 dice again. Use the numbers to create another two-digit number. Write this number on the next line of the multiplication problem. Find the product of the two numbers. This product is your score.

First roll: Second roll:

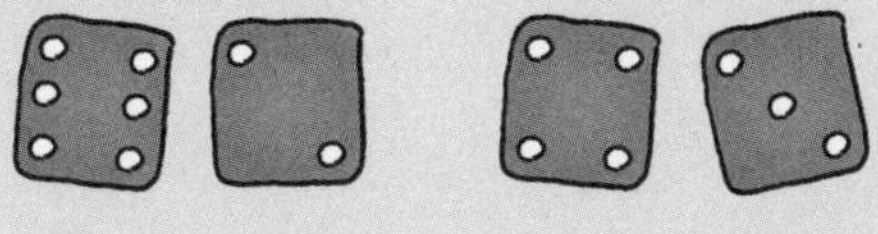

$$\begin{array}{r} 62 \\ \times\ 43 \\ \hline 186 \\ +\ 2,480 \\ \hline 2,666 \end{array}$$

C

Sample round.

Play then passes to the other player. Continue until both players have completed all 3 rounds. Add up each player's total points. The player with more points wins.

Independent Practice and Review

Have your child complete the Lesson 3.8 Practice and Review workbook pages.

Lesson 3.9
Use the Multiplication Algorithm to Multiply Larger Numbers

Purpose	Materials
• Compare and contrast the multiplication algorithm and box method • Use the multiplication algorithm to multiply numbers with more than two digits	• None

Memory Work
- **Name 4 factors of 8.** *1, 2, 4, 8.*
- **Name 4 multiples of 8.** *Sample answers: 16, 32, 40, 48.*

When you multiply large numbers, one small mistake means that the entire problem is incorrect. Children often find this very discouraging. Make sure to watch carefully as your child solves the problems on the Lesson Activities pages and help her correct any errors immediately. If you find that she needs lots of coaching and support, sit with her as she completes the Practice pages, too.

If this lesson takes your child a long time, split it over two days:

- Day 1: Do the Warm-up and Activity B. Then, have your child complete the Review page only.
- Day 2: Review the steps in Activity B and play Pick the Product (Activity C). Then, have your child complete the Practice page.

Warm-up (A): Compare and Contrast the Multiplication Algorithm and Box Method

In this unit, you've reviewed how to multiply two-digit numbers with both the multiplication algorithm and with the box method. To warm up, you'll use both methods to solve the same problem. As you work, think about what the two methods have in common. Have your child use both methods to find the product of 14 × 36.

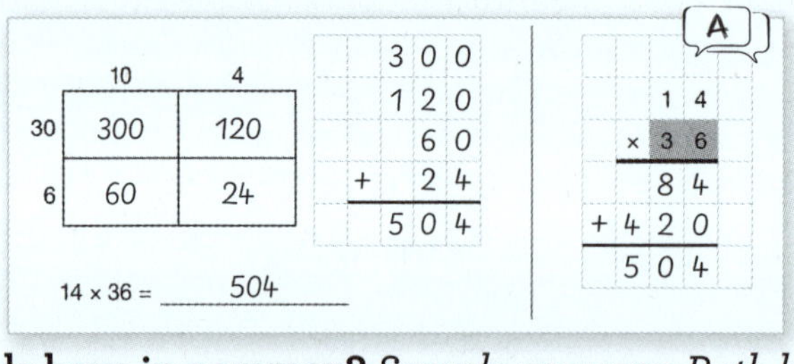

What do the two methods have in common? *Sample answers: Both have the same total product. You multiply the numbers in parts and then add them.*

How are the two ways different from each other? *Sample answers: You have to add 4 numbers when you use the box method, but you only have to add 2 numbers when you use the multiplication algorithm.*

When you use the box method, you find four partial products and add them. When you use the multiplication algorithm, you find two partial products and add them.

- Point to 84 in the multiplication algorithm problem. **Which partial products in the box method add up to 84?** *60 and 24.*

- Point to 420 in the multiplication algorithm problem. **Which partial products in the box method add up to 420?** *300 and 120.*

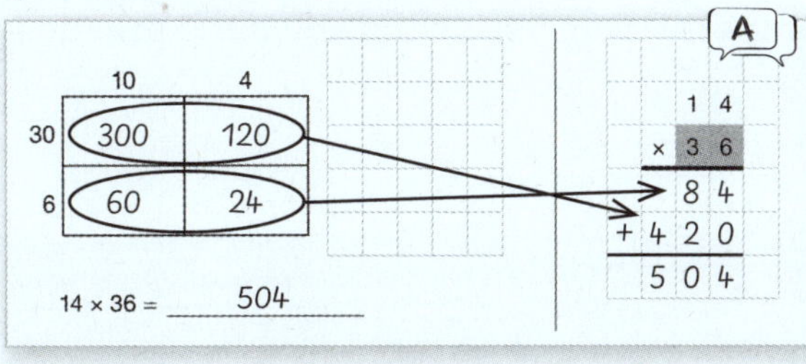

Both methods involve splitting the numbers into tens and ones, multiplying the parts, and then adding the parts. We just keep track of the parts differently.

Activity (B): Use the Multiplication Algorithm to Multiply Three-Digit Numbers

In the past few years, you've learned the step-by-step processes for adding, subtracting, multiplying, and dividing multi-digit numbers. These processes are called algorithms. What makes algorithms especially powerful is that we can extend them to numbers with any number of digits.

In Unit 2, you learned how to extend the addition and subtraction algorithms to numbers in the billions. Today, you'll extend the multiplication algorithm to multiply numbers with more than two digits. Have your child read the text in part B.

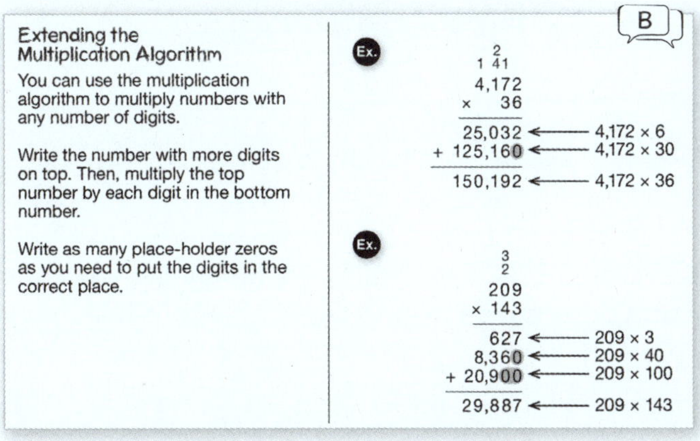

The first example shows how to multiply a four-digit number by a two-digit number. It's just like how you solved the problems in the last lesson.

- **First, you multiply the top number by the ones-place of the bottom number. 4,172 times 6 equals 25,032.**
- **Next, you write a place-holder zero in the ones-place and multiply the top number by the tens-place of the bottom number. The place-holder zero shifts the digits to the correct place. 4,172 times 30 equals 125,160.**
- **Last, you add the partial products. 25,032 plus 125,160 equals 150,192.**

The second example shows how to multiply a three-digit number by a three-digit number. It's a lot like the first example. The only difference is that you have to multiply the top number by the bottom number's hundreds-place as well.

- **First, you multiply the top number by the ones-place of the bottom number. 209 times 3 equals 627.**
- **Next, you write one place-holder zero and multiply the top number by the tens-place of the bottom number. 209 times 40 equals 8,360.**
- **Then, you write two place-holder zeros and multiply the top number by the hundreds-place of the bottom number. 209 times 100 equals 20,900.**
- **Last, you add the partial products. 627 plus 8,360 plus 20,900 equals 29,887.**

We could use the multiplication algorithm to multiply numbers with any number of digits, but it would take a lot of steps! In everyday life, adults usually use a calculator when they need to multiply large numbers. Have your child solve the practice problems.

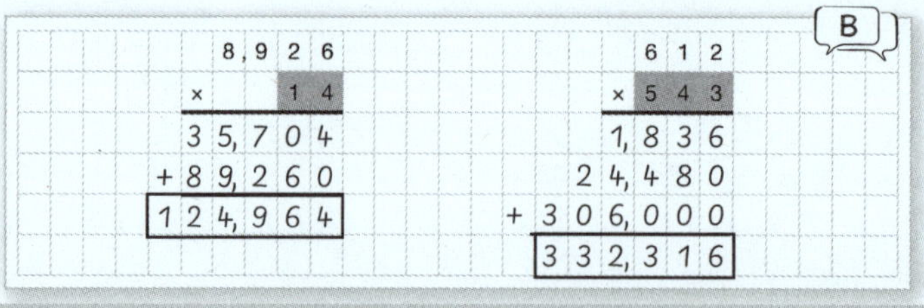

If you have time, show your child how to use a calculator to check her answers for the practice problems. Your child will explore multiplying with a calculator in the enrichment activity in Lesson 3.10.

Activity (C): Play Pick the Product

Play Pick the Product.

The multiplication problems in this game are chosen to produce answers that are very close to each other. This makes it very difficult to estimate which multiplication problems on the grid will yield greater products, so this game is mostly a game of luck.

Pick the Product

Materials: None

Object of the Game: Win the most points by choosing problems that yield the greater product.

Pick the Product has 3 rounds. In each round, each player chooses one of the problems on the game board and finds the answer to the problem. Whoever chooses the problem with a greater product wins one point.

Play until you've completed all the problems on the game board. Whoever has won more points wins the game.

Answer Key:

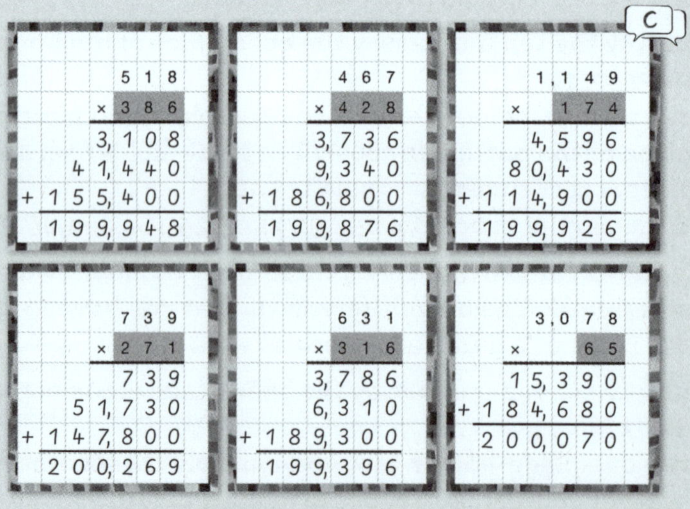

Independent Practice and Review

Have your child complete the Lesson 3.9 Practice and Review workbook pages.

Lesson 3.10
Enrichment (Optional)

Purpose	Materials
• Practice memory work • Appreciate how math can be used to answer real-life questions • Multiply to find how many times your heart beats in a minute, hour, day, or year • Summarize what your child has learned and assess your child's progress	• *How Many Guinea Pigs Can Fit on a Plane?: Answers to Your Most Clever Math Questions*, by Laura Overdeck • Stopwatch • Calculator or calculator app

Warm-up: Review Memory Work

Quiz your child on any of the memory work items that he struggled with during this unit.

Math Picture Book: *How Many Guinea Pigs Can Fit on a Plane?*

Read pages 22–31 in *How Many Guinea Pigs Can Fit on a Plane?*

Enrichment Activity: How Many Times Does Your Heart Beat in a Year?

Today, we'll figure out how many times your heart beats in a minute, an hour, a day, and a year.

As your heart pushes your blood around your body, it makes a little thump that we can feel. We call this little thump a pulse. You can feel your pulse each time your heart beats. Help your child find his pulse on his wrist. He should place his index finger and middle finger on the opposite wrist and press lightly below the base of his thumb.

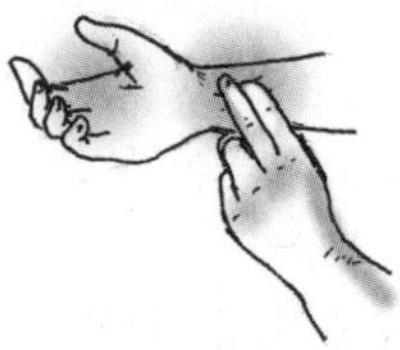

Set a timer for 15 seconds. Have your child count his pulse for 15 seconds. Start a simple chart like the following, and write his count in the chart.

Time Period	15 seconds	1 minute	1 hour	1 day	1 year
Number of Times My Heart Beats	23				

Sample chart.

There are 4 groups of 15 seconds in 1 minute. First we'll multiply your count by 4 to find how many times your heart beats each minute. Have your child multiply his count by 4 and record the number in the chart.

How many minutes are in 1 hour? *60.* **Multiply the number of times your heart beats in 1 minute by 60 to find how many times your heart beats in 1 hour.** Have your child multiply his previous number by 60 and record the number in the chart.

How many hours are in 1 day? *24.* **Multiply the number of times your heart beats in 1 hour by 24 to find how many times your heart beats in 1 day.** Have your child multiply his previous number by 24 and record the number in the chart.

How many days are usually in 1 year? *365.* **Multiply the number of times your heart beats in 1 day by 365 to find how many times your heart beats in 1 year. These numbers are getting pretty big, so let's use a calculator to find the final product.**

Help your child use a calculator to multiply his previous number by 365.

> If it's a leap year, your child can multiply by 366 instead of 365.

Time Period	*15 seconds*	*1 minute*	*1 hour*	*1 day*	*1 year*
Number of Times My Heart Beats	23	92	5,520	132,480	48,355,200

Sample completed chart.

Different animals' hearts beat at different rates, and small animals usually have faster heart rates than large animals. A horse usually has a heart rate of 28 to 40 beats per minute, and a hamster usually has a heart rate of 300 to 600 beats per minute!

> If your child is interested, he may add rows to his chart to find how many times a hamster or horse's heart beats in each time period.

Unit Wrap-Up

Have your child complete the Unit 3 Wrap-Up.

Unit 3 Answer Key

3.1 Practice

Practice Use the lists of multiples to find the least common multiple for each pair of numbers.

LCM of 3 and 4: 12
3, 6, 9, 12, 15
4, 8, 12, 16, 20

LCM of 9 and 3: 9
9, 18, 27, 36, 45
3, 6, 9, 12, 15

LCM of 6 and 10: 30
6, 12, 18, 24, 30
10, 20, 30, 40, 50

LCM of 6 and 15: 30
6, 12, 18, 24, 30
15, 30, 45, 60, 75

LCM of 100 and 20: 100
100, 200, 300, 400, 500, 600
20, 40, 60, 80, 100, 120

LCM of 25 and 30: 150
25, 50, 75, 100, 125, 150
30, 60, 90, 120, 150, 180

Find the least common multiple for each pair of numbers. Make your own lists of multiples.

LCM of 2 and 5: 10
2: 2, 4, 6, 8, 10, 12
5: 5, 10, 15, 20, 25

LCM of 6 and 12: 12
6: 6, 12, 18, 24, 30
12: 12, 24, 36, 48, 60

LCM of 8 and 10: 40
8: 8, 16, 24, 32, 40
10: 10, 20, 30, 40, 50

LCM of 5 and 7: 35
5: 5, 10, 15, 20, 25, 30, 35
7: 7, 14, 21, 28, 35

3.1 Review

Review Find the product.

$38 \times 9 = 342$ $87 \times 5 = 435$ $999 \times 6 = 5{,}994$ $4{,}036 \times 3 = 12{,}108$

Complete the chart.

	Double
20	40
50	100
100	200
500	1,000
5,000	10,000

Match each number to its dot on the number line.

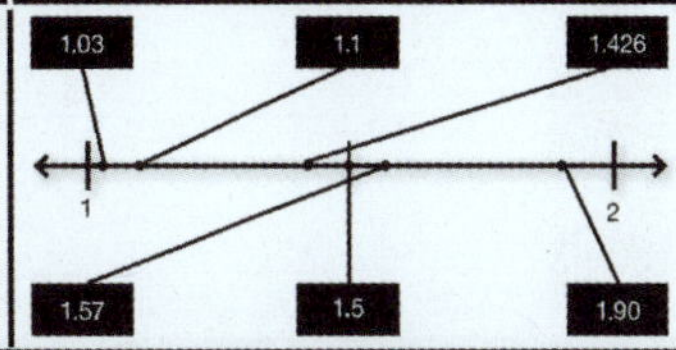

Color the diagrams to match the mixed numbers. Then, write <, >, or = to compare the mixed numbers.

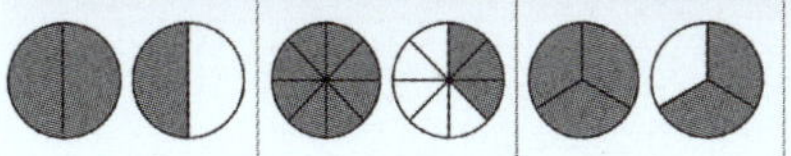

$1\frac{1}{2}$ $1\frac{3}{8}$ $1\frac{2}{3}$

$1\frac{1}{2} > 1\frac{3}{8}$

$1\frac{1}{2} < 1\frac{2}{3}$

$1\frac{2}{3} > 1\frac{3}{8}$

Solve. Write the equations you use.

What is the perimeter of the room?

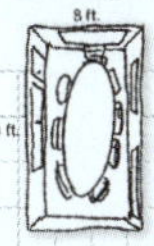

14 + 8 + 14 + 8 = **44 ft.**

The perimeter of the field is 800 m. All sides of the field are equal. What is the length of each side?

800 ÷ 4 = **200 m**

3.2 Practice

Practice Complete the charts. Use the completed boxes to help.

Packs	28	29	30	31	32
Hot Dogs	224	232	240	248	256

Packs	98	99	100	101	102
Hot Dogs	784	792	800	808	816

Find the products. Use the completed product to help.

40 × 3 = 120	30 × 5 = 150	50 × 6 = 300
41 × 3 = 123	29 × 5 = 145	51 × 6 = 306
42 × 3 = 126	28 × 5 = 140	★ 57 × 6 = 342

Use the box method to find the product.

	70	3
4	280	12

73 × 4 = 292

	90	9
7	630	63

99 × 7 = 693

Use any method to solve. Write the equations you use.

Yazmin is planning a party. She buys 24 packs of balloons. Each pack holds 8 balloons. How many balloons does she buy?

$24 \times 8 = 192$ **192 balloons**

Yazmin also buys 72 cupcakes. Each cupcake costs $3. What is the total cost of the cupcakes?

$72 \times 3 = 216$ **$216**

Yazmin decides to buy 1 more pack of balloons. How many balloons does she have now?

192 + 8 = **200 balloons**

Yazmin decides to buy 2 more cupcakes. What is the total cost of all the cupcakes now?

216 + 2 × 3
216 + 6
$222

3.2 Review

Review Write each decimal as a fraction or mixed number. Write each fraction or mixed number as a decimal.

$4.109 = 4\frac{109}{1{,}000}$	$0.87 = \frac{87}{100}$	$3.061 = 3\frac{61}{1{,}000}$
$1\frac{28}{100} = 1.28$	$6\frac{3}{10} = 6.3$	$2\frac{4}{1{,}000} = 2.004$

Color the diagrams to match the fractions. Then, write <, >, or = to compare the fractions.

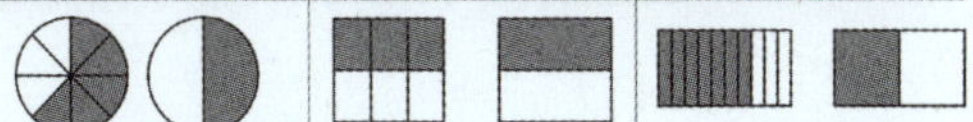

$\frac{5}{8} > \frac{1}{2}$ $\frac{3}{6} = \frac{1}{2}$ $\frac{7}{10} > \frac{1}{2}$

Write whether each angle is acute, right, obtuse, or straight.

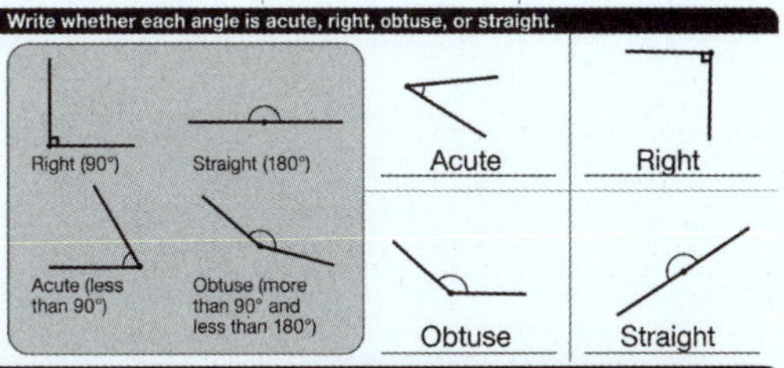

Solve. Write the equations you use.

Joan ran 3.39 miles on Monday. She ran 2.84 miles on Tuesday. How much farther did she run on Monday than Tuesday?

$3.39 - 2.84 = 0.55$ **0.55 mi.**

Otis' family drove 6.7 miles to swim practice. Then, they drove 4.54 miles to his grandparents' house. How far did they drive in all?

$6.7 + 4.54 = 11.24$ **11.24 mi.**

Unit 3 Answer Key

3.3 Practice

Practice Complete.

25 → ×2 → 50 → ×2 → 100 → ×2 → 200 → ×2 → 400

105 → ×2 → 210 → ×2 → 420 → ×2 → 840 → ×2 → 1,680

300 → ×2 → 600 → ×2 → 1,200 → ×2 → 2,400 → ×2 → 4,800

1,250 → ×2 → 2,500 → ×2 → 5,000 → ×2 → 10,000 → ×2 → 20,000

Find the products.

15 × 2 = 30	55 × 2 = 110	75 × 2 = 150
15 × 4 = 60	55 × 4 = 220	75 × 4 = 300
225 × 2 = 450	4,500 × 2 = 9,000	★ 4,501 × 2 = 9,002
225 × 4 = 900	4,500 × 4 = 18,000	★ 4,501 × 4 = 18,004

Solve. Write the equations you use.

Angelina's parents bought 4 kitchen chairs. Each chair cost $85. How much did the chairs cost in all?

85 × 4 = **$340**

Garrett's backyard is shaped like a square. Each side of the yard is 135 feet long. What is the perimeter of his backyard?

135 × 4 = **540 ft.**

3.3 Review

Review Find the least common multiple for each pair of numbers.

LCM of 5 and 3: 15

5: 5, 10, 15, 20
3: 3, 6, 9, 12, 15

LCM of 5 and 20: 20

5: 5, 10, 15, 20
20: 20, 40, 60

Color the diagram to match the fraction. Then, convert to a mixed number.

$\frac{7}{4} = 1\frac{3}{4}$ $\frac{7}{6} = 1\frac{1}{6}$ $\frac{7}{5} = 1\frac{2}{5}$

Match each shape to the name and definition that most specifically describe it.

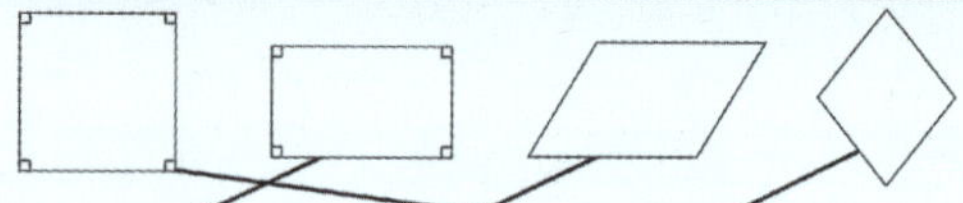

Rectangle (4 right angles) | Parallelogram (2 pairs of parallel sides) | Rhombus (2 pairs of parallel sides and 4 equal sides) | Square (4 equal sides and 4 right angles)

Solve. Write the equations you use.

Marcus had $5,682 in his savings account. Then, he used $4,599 to buy a used car. How much money did he have left?

5,682 − 4,599 = **$1,083**

3.4 Practice

Practice Draw a line from Start to End so that each problem is followed by the correct answer. You do not have to solve every problem.

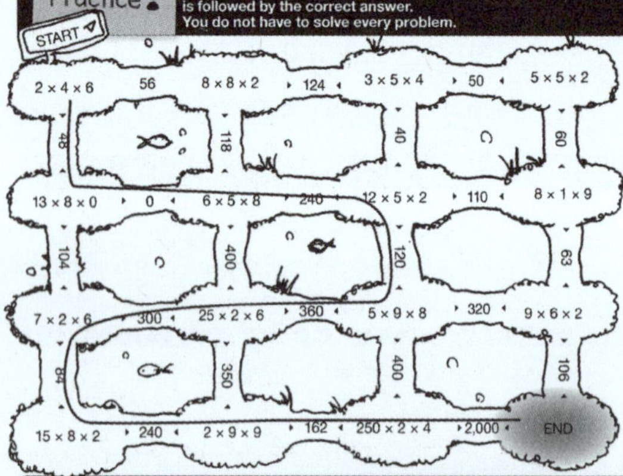

Solve. Write the equations you use.

Avery goes to 2 gymnastics lessons each week. Each lesson costs $15. How much do 8 weeks of lessons cost?

2 × 15 × 8
30 × 8
$240

Each box of graham crackers has 3 packs in it. Each pack holds 10 crackers. How many crackers are in 7 boxes?

3 × 10 × 7
30 × 7
210 crackers

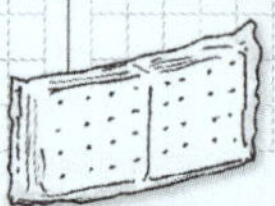

3.4 Review

Review Complete the missing addends. Use the pictures to help.

0.4 + 0.6 = 1 0.75 + 0.25 = 1 0.96 + 0.04 = 1

Use the pictures to complete the equivalent fractions.

$\frac{1}{3} = \frac{2}{6}$ $\frac{2}{3} = \frac{4}{6}$ $\frac{3}{3} = \frac{6}{6}$

Match.

70 × 7 → 490
600 × 5 → 3,000
50 × 80 → 4,000
300 × 9 → 2,700

4,000 → 4 × 1,000
2,700 → 27 × 100
490 → 49 × 10
3,000 → 3 × 1,000

Solve. Write the equations you use.

The ice cream stand earned $1,578 in May. It earned 3 times as much in June as it did in May. How much did it earn in June?

1,578 × 3 = **$4,734**

How much did the ice cream stand earn in all in May and June?

1,578 + 4,734 = **$6,312**

Unit 3 Answer Key

3.5 Practice

Multiplication Master (1-Player Game)

90 2,000 50 60 600

The highest possible total is 6,325,100. How close can you get?

	Product
30 ×	
70 ×	
200 ×	
500 ×	
4,000 ×	
Total	

Practice Complete.

367 × 10 = 3,670

367 × 100 = 36,700

367 × 1,000 = 367,000

60 × 70 = 4,200

600 × 70 = 42,000

6,000 × 70 = 420,00

10 × 508 = 5,080

100 × 508 = 50,800

1,000 × 508 = 508,000

50 × 40 = 2,000

50 × 400 = 20,000

50 × 4,000 = 200,000

Solve. Write the equations you use.

A party planner bought 40 rolls of streamers. Each roll was 100 feet long. How many feet of streamers did she buy?

40 × 100 = 4,000 ft.

A food pantry received 80 crates of apples to give away. Each crate contained 200 apples. How many apples did the food pantry receive?

80 × 200 = 16,000 apples

3.5 Review

Review Color the diagram to match the mixed number. Then, complete the missing numerator in the fraction.

$2\frac{1}{5} = \frac{11}{5}$ $2\frac{3}{4} = \frac{11}{4}$ $2\frac{3}{6} = \frac{15}{6}$

Find the product.

146 × 9 = 1,314

378 × 6 = 2,268

Evaluate.

P → M or D → A or S

10 − 3 × 2 ÷ 2

10 − 6 ÷ 2

10 − 3

7

Complete the chart. Use the completed box to help.

Pages	28	29	30	31	32
Trading Cards	252	261	270	279	288

Round each weight to the underlined place.

0.615g 0.017g 0.397g

0.615 ≈ 0.62 0.017 ≈ 0.02 0.397 ≈ 0.40

0.615 ≈ 0.6 0.017 ≈ 0.0 0.397 ≈ 0.4

3.6 Practice

Practice Complete each multiplication problem. Then, find the blanks that match the letter for each problem. Write the letter in the matching blanks to solve the riddle.

V: 82 × 30 = 2,460

M: 73 × 50 = 3,650

O: 541 × 600 = 324,600

H: 3,196 × 2,000 = 6,392,000

R: 97 × 40 = 3,880

E: 55 × 90 = 4,950

T: 208 × 700 = 145,600

S: 1,739 × 4,000 = 6,956,000

How do you make seven an even number?

R	E	M	O	V	E		T	H	E		S
3,880	4,950	3,650	324,600	2,460	4,950		145,600	6,392,000	4,950		6,956,000

Solve. Write the equations you use.

The animal shelter buys 32 bags of dog food. Each bag weighs 40 lb. How many pounds of dog food do they buy?

32 × 40 = 1,280 lb.

The animal shelter buys 20 bags of guinea pig pellets. Each bag weighs 14 kg. How many kilograms of guinea pig pellets do they buy?

14 × 20 = 280 kg

The animal shelter buys 30 cases of cat food. Each case contains 24 cans. How many cans of cat food do they buy?

24 × 30 = 720 cans

The animal shelter buys 20 dog collars. Each collar costs $18. How much do they spend?

18 × 20 = $360

3.6 Review

Review Circle yes or no to answer the questions.

12 ÷ 4 = 3
12 is divisible by 4.

12 ÷ 5 = 2 R2
12 is not divisible by 5.

Is 12 divisible by 3? **Yes**	Is 24 divisible by 3? **Yes**
Is 12 divisible by 6? **Yes**	Is 24 divisible by 6? **Yes**
Is 12 divisible by 8? **No**	Is 24 divisible by 8? **Yes**

Use the number lines to compare the fractions. Write <, >, or =.

$\frac{1}{4} > \frac{1}{8}$

$\frac{2}{4} = \frac{4}{8}$

$\frac{3}{4} < \frac{7}{8}$

$\frac{4}{4} = \frac{8}{8}$

Use the box method to solve.

	60	8
5	300	40

68 × 5 = 340

	30	7
9	270	63

37 × 9 = 333

Find the area.

5 ft. by 3 ft. — Area: 15 sq. ft.

15 cm by 10 cm — Area: 150 sq. cm

Unit 3 Answer Key

3.7 Practice

Practice Use the box method to find the products.

	20	6
90	1,800	540
5	100	30

1,800 + 540 + 100 + 30 = 2,470

26 × 95 = 2,470

	40	3
60	2,400	180
2	80	6

2,400 + 180 + 80 + 6 = 2,666

43 × 62 = 2,666

	100	50	3
60	6,000	3,000	180
4	400	200	12

6,000 + 3,000 + 180 + 400 + 200 + 12 = 9,792

153 × 64 = 9,792

Use the box method to find the area. Make sure to include the correct units.

The Olympic swimming pool is 164 ft. by 82 ft. What is its area?

164 ft. / 82 ft.

	100	60	4
80	8,000	4,800	320
2	200	120	8

8,000 + 4,800 + 320 + 200 + 120 + 8 = 13,448

164 × 82 = 13,448 sq. ft.

3.7 Review

Review Complete the missing fractions on the number line. Then, write <, >, or = to compare the numbers.

$\frac{6}{3}$, $\frac{7}{3}$, $\boxed{\frac{8}{3}}$, $\boxed{\frac{9}{3}}$, $\frac{10}{3}$, $\boxed{\frac{11}{3}}$, $\frac{12}{3}$ (2, 3, 4 marked on the number line)

$\frac{7}{3} > 2$	$\frac{8}{3} < 3$	$\frac{9}{3} = 3$
$\frac{10}{3} > 3$	$\frac{11}{3} < 4$	$\frac{12}{3} = 4$

Use mental math to complete.

35 × 2 = 70	80 × 9 = 720	7 × 25 × 2 = 350
35 × 4 = 140	81 × 9 = 729	8 × 2 × 15 = 240
300 × 20 = 6,000	50 × 6 = 300	17 × 6 × 0 = 0
300 × 200 = 60,000	49 × 6 = 294	1 × 54 × 1 = 54

Use the printed protractors to measure the angles.

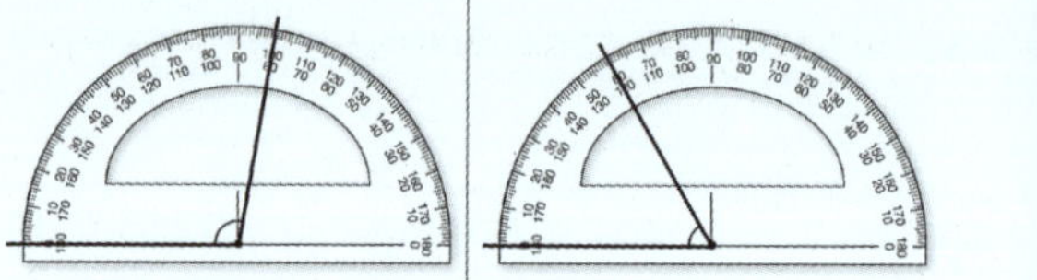

100° | 60°

3.8 Practice

Product Power (2-Player Game)

Player 1

Player 2

Practice Solve. Write the equations you use in the work space.

WORK SPACE

It takes 45 apples to make one gallon of apple cider. How many apples does it take to make 36 gallons of cider? 1,620 apples

45 × 36: 270 + 1,350 = 1,620

One medium pumpkin weighs about 18 pounds. How much do 75 pumpkins weigh? 1,350 lb.

18 × 75: 90 + 1,260 = 1,350

One day, the farm stand sells 18 trays of donuts. Each tray holds 32 donuts. How many donuts do they sell? 576 donuts

18 × 32: 36 + 540 = 576

3.8 Review

Review Use the pictures to complete the equivalent fractions.

$\frac{1}{2} = \frac{6}{12}$ | $\frac{2}{3} = \frac{8}{12}$ | $\frac{3}{4} = \frac{9}{12}$

Complete the circles with <, >, or =.

0.325 < 0.76	0.513 > 0.205
1.061 < 2.4	1.061 > 1.036
1.061 > 0.897	0.897 < 2.4

Use long division to solve.

97 ÷ 4 = 24 R1: 9 − 8 = 1; 17 − 16 = 1

387 ÷ 5 = 77 R2: 38 − 35 = 3; 37 − 35 = 2

Use the line plot to answer the questions.

Weight of Apples

Weight (lb.)	$\frac{1}{8}$	$\frac{2}{8}$	$\frac{3}{8}$	$\frac{4}{8}$	$\frac{5}{8}$	$\frac{6}{8}$
Apples	x	x	xxxx	xx	xxx	x

How much does the heaviest apple weigh? $\frac{6}{8}$ lb.

How much does the lightest apple weigh? $\frac{1}{8}$ lb.

How many apples weigh less than $\frac{4}{8}$ lb.? 6 apples

How many apples weigh more than $\frac{4}{8}$ lb.? 4 apples

Unit 3 Answer Key

3.9 Practice

Pick the Product (2-Player Game)

518 × 386	467 × 428	1,149 × 174
739 × 271	631 × 316	3,078 × 65

Practice Solve. Write the equations you use.

The food pantry gives away 3,475 kg of food each day. It is open 16 days per month. How much food does it give away each month?

```
   3,475
 ×    16
  20,850
+ 34,750
  55,600 kg
```

The recycling center processes 116 tons of recyclables each day. It is open 345 days per year. How many tons of recyclables does it process each year?

```
     116
   × 345
     580
   4,640
+ 34,800
  40,020 tons
```

3.9 Review

Review Round each number to the underlined place.

0.549 ≈ 0.55

0.814 ≈ 0.8

1.493 ≈ 1.5

3.275 ≈ 3

Circle the greatest number in each group.

0.04, 0.009, (0.1)	(0.62), 0.2, 0.602
2.5, (3.71), 1.894	4.47, 4.474, (4.7)

Find the least common multiple for each pair of numbers.

LCM of 4 and 3: 12

4: 4, 8, 12, 16, 20, 24
3: 3, 6, 9, 12, 15

LCM of 4 and 6: 12

4: 4, 8, 12, 16, 20
6: 6, 12, 18, 24

Use the printed rulers to measure the lines. Write each length as a decimal.

2.2 cm | 4.5 cm

0.1 m | 0.5 m

0.3 m | 0.9 m

3.10 Unit Wrap-Up A

Unit Wrap-Up Find the least common multiple for each pair of numbers.

LCM of 9 and 12: 36

9: 9, 18, 27, 36, 45
12: 12, 24, 36, 48

LCM of 5 and 8: 40

5: 5, 10, 15, 20, 25, 30, 35, 40
8: 8, 16, 24, 32, 40

Use mental math to complete.

9 × 6 × 2 = 108	45 × 2 = 90	80 × 6 = 480
8 × 25 × 2 = 400	45 × 4 = 180	81 × 6 = 486
200 × 70 = 14,000	9,185 × 10 = 91,850	17 × 6 × 0 = 0
8,000 × 30 = 240,000	1,000 × 486 = 486,000	1 × 14 × 1 = 14

Complete.

36 × 20 = 720

519 × 400 = 207,600

2,871 × 3,000 = 8,613,000

Use both the box method and the multiplication algorithm to find the product of 137 and 42.

	100	30	7
40	4,000	1,200	280
2	200	60	14

137 × 42 = 5,754

```
  4,000
  1,200
    280
    200
     60
+    14
  5,754
```

```
    137
  ×  42
    274
+ 5,480
  5,754
```

3.10 Unit Wrap-Up B

Unit Wrap-Up Use the brochure to answer the questions. Write your equations in the work space.

Board Your Horse at Meadowlark Farm!

Large 14 ft. by 12 ft. stall for each horse.

Daily outdoor time in our 125 ft. by 225 ft. exercise arena.

24 pounds of hay per day, plus grain, water, and clean bedding.

$379 per month

WORK SPACE

What is the area of each stall? 168 sq. ft.

```
    14
  × 12
    28
+  140
   168
```

There are 32 horses on the farm. How many pounds of hay do they eat each day? 768 lb.

```
    32
  × 24
   128
+  640
   768
```

How much hay does each horse eat in 1 year? (There are 365 days in 1 year.) 8,760 lb.

```
    365
  ×  24
  1,460
+ 7,300
  8,760
```

What is the area of the outdoor exercise arena? 28,125 sq. ft.

```
     225
   × 125
   1,125
   4,500
+ 22,500
  28,125
```

How much does it cost to board a horse at Meadowlark Farm for 1 year? $4,548

```
    379
  ×  12
    758
+ 3,790
  4,548
```

Unit 3 Checkpoint

What to Expect at the End of Unit 3

By the end of Unit 3, most children will be able to do the following:

- Find the least common multiple for a pair of numbers.
- Use the multiply-and-adjust strategy to mentally multiply two-digit numbers by one-digit numbers. Some children will be able to solve these problems mentally, but many will still struggle with them or be confused about which number to add or subtract.
- Double numbers (once or twice) to mentally multiply numbers by 2 or 4.
- Use the associative property to mentally multiply three or more factors. Some children will need help identifying which pair of numbers to multiply first.
- Multiply numbers with trailing zeros, both mentally and with the multiplication algorithm.
- Use the box method to multiply two- or three-digit numbers. Some children will make occasional mistakes with the mental multiplication step or need help setting up the boxes. If you did not use *Fourth Grade Math with Confidence*, it's fine if your child hasn't fully mastered this skill yet.
- Use the multiplication algorithm to multiply multi-digit numbers. Most children will be able to solve these problems independently, but some will still need a lot of coaching and support (especially when multiplying three-digit numbers by three-digit numbers). It's common for children to make occasional mistakes with the multiplication facts or get confused when solving problems that involve trading.

Is Your Child Ready to Move on?

In Unit 4, your child will study volume. Your child does not need to have fully mastered the skills in Unit 3 before moving on to Unit 4. She will practice the written process for multi-digit multiplication throughout the unit to help increase her fluency with this complex skill.

Unit 4
Volume

Overview

In Unit 4, you will introduce your child to volume. He'll first use centimeter cubes to build rectangular prisms (solids shaped like boxes) and find their volume. Then, he'll learn to use the volume formula to calculate their volume and find the volumes of complex shapes. He'll also learn how to use the volume formula "backwards" to find a missing dimension or the base area of a rectangular prism.

Children often find this unit a welcome break after the challenging multiplication lessons in Unit 3. Your child will continue to build fluency with written multiplication in the Review workbook pages.

What Your Child Will Learn

In this unit, your child will learn to:

- Understand that volume is the amount of space a solid takes up
- Use volume formulas (length × width × height or base area × height) to find volume
- Divide to find a missing dimension of a rectangular prism
- Divide to find the base area or height of a rectangular prism
- Split solids into rectangular prisms and add to find the total volume
- Solve volume word problems

Lesson List

Lesson 4.1	Introduce Volume
Lesson 4.2	Multiply to Find Volume
Lesson 4.3	Estimate and Measure Boxes' Volumes
Lesson 4.4	Find Missing Dimensions
Lesson 4.5	Cubic Meters
Lesson 4.6	Cubic Inches, Feet, and Yards
Lesson 4.7	Volume and Area, Part 1
Lesson 4.8	Volume and Area, Part 2
Lesson 4.9	Enrichment (Optional)

Extra Materials Needed for Unit 4

- 3 small boxes of different sizes (like boxes of pasta, rice, or pancake mix)
- 3 dice
- Meterstick, optional
- Measuring tape
- For optional Enrichment Lesson:
    - *How Many Guinea Pigs Can Fit on a Plane?: Answers to Your Most Clever Math Questions*, by Laura Overdeck. Feiwel & Friends, 2017.
    - Pillows, blankets, and furniture for building a fort
    - Measuring tape

Teaching Math with Confidence: Understanding 3-D Diagrams Before Finding Volume

In this unit, you'll teach your child how to find the volume of three-dimensional rectangular solids, such as boxes, pools, and rooms. Many of the volume problems are presented through 3-D diagrams like these:

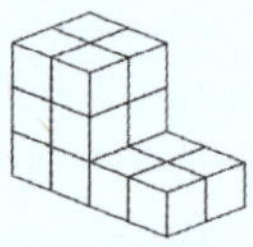

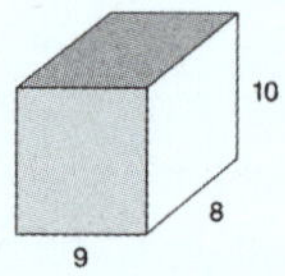

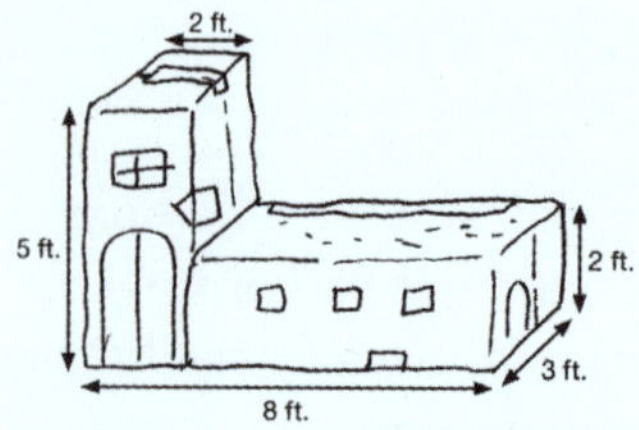

If your child often interprets 3-D diagrams (for example, to create Lego structures, assemble furniture, or build wood-working projects), he will likely find it easy to comprehend the diagrams. But, if he doesn't have much experience with 3-D diagrams, you'll need to teach him how to interpret them.

Throughout the unit, you'll find hands-on activities (like examining real boxes and building solids out of cubes) for building stronger 3-D spatial sense. You'll also find techniques for analyzing and interpreting 3-D diagrams (like splitting solids into parts or labeling important information). Most of these strategies are included only in the Instructor Guide, so make sure not to skip these important teaching activities.

Above all, encourage your child to stop and make sure he understands the 3-D diagram before he tackles the related volume problem. When children plunge right into solving, they often get confused by the many numbers and dimensions involved—especially in complex, multi-step problems. By analyzing the 3-D diagram first, he'll be ready to solve the problem in a logical and orderly way.

Lesson 4.1
Introduce Volume

Purpose	Materials
• Review one-dimensional, two-dimensional, and three-dimensional shapes • Develop spatial skills by building 3-D solids • Measure volume with cubic centimeters	• 1-foot (30-cm) ruler • Centimeter cubes (unit blocks from a set of base-ten blocks) • Small box (like a box of rice, pasta, or pancake mix)

Memory Work

- **What do we call the result when we add numbers together?** *The sum.*
- **What do we call the result when we subtract a number from another number?** *The difference.*
- **What do we call the result when we multiply two numbers?** *The product.*
- **What do we call the result when we divide two numbers?** *The quotient.*

Warm-up: Review the Difference Between 1-D, 2-D, and 3-D Shapes

When you were younger, you learned how to measure length and area. Have your child draw a 4 cm line on a piece of scrap paper. **We say that lines are *one-dimensional.* We measure lines with length units like inches, feet, centimeters, or meters. This line is 4 centimeters long.**

4 cm

Use the ruler to draw a 4 centimeter by 2 centimeter rectangle. (Use your child's line as one of the sides.) Draw lines inside the rectangle to split it into a 4 × 2 array. Label the length of each side.

We call flat shapes like this rectangle *two-dimensional.* We measure their area with square units, like square inches, square feet, square centimeters, or square meters. What's the area of this rectangle? *8 square centimeters.*

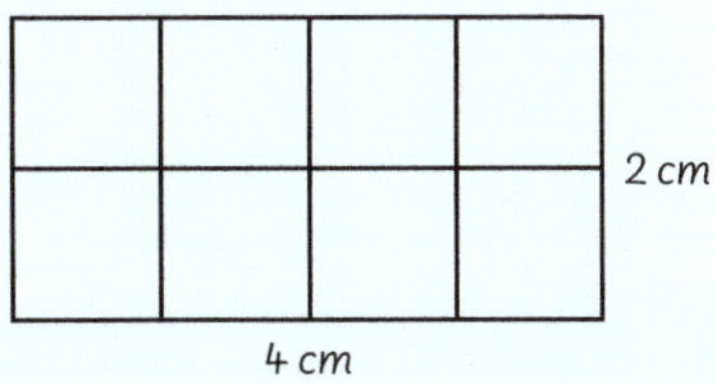

Stack 2 layers of 8 centimeter cubes (or unit blocks from your set of base-ten blocks) on top of the array. You will use 16 centimeter cubes in all. **We call solid shapes that take up space *three-dimensional.* We measure how much space they take up with cubic units. This solid has a volume of 16 cubic centimeters. Later in this unit, you'll learn how to measure volume with cubic inches, cubic feet, and cubic meters, too.**

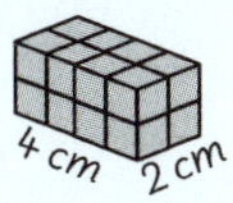

Activity (A): Build Solids from Centimeter Cubes and Find Their Volumes

We're starting a new unit on volume today. In this unit, you'll learn how to measure how much space solid shapes take up. Have your child read the text in part A.

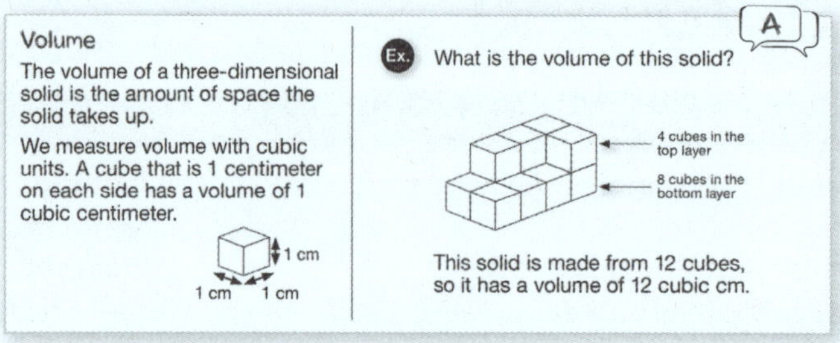

Show your child a centimeter cube. **One centimeter cube takes up a cube of space that is 1 centimeter on each side, so each block has a volume of 1 cubic centimeter.**

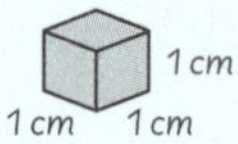

The word *volume* in math means something very different than the word *volume* on a speaker or remote control. In math, volume measures how much space a solid takes up, not how loud something is!

Let's use centimeter cubes to build the solid in the example. Have your child use centimeter cubes to build the solid. **It takes 12 cubes to build the solid. Each cube has a volume of 1 cubic centimeter, so the solid has a volume of 12 cubic centimeters.**

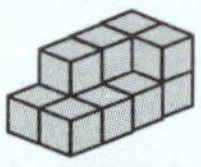

> Building the solid herself helps your child learn to interpret 3-D diagrams. If she has trouble, encourage her to start at the bottom and build one layer at a time. See the Unit 4 **Teaching Math with Confidence** for more tips on helping your child interpret 3-D diagrams.

Have your child build each solid in part A. After she builds each solid, have her count the number of centimeter cubes she used. Write the volume of each solid in the blank below it.

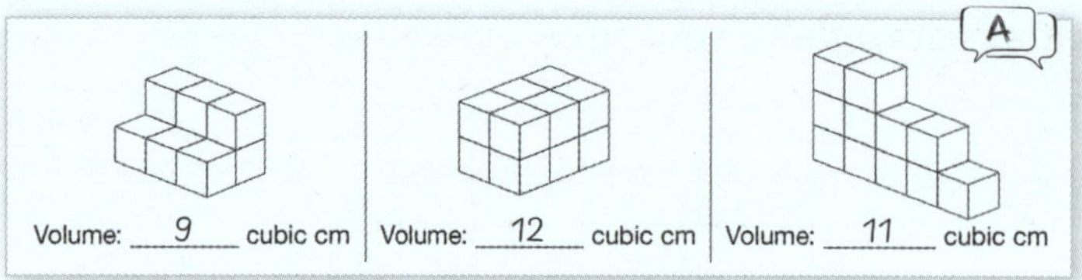

Activity (B): Find Volumes of Rectangular Prisms

All of the solids in part B are rectangular prisms. Rectangular prisms are like boxes. They have 6 sides, and each side is a rectangle. Have your child read the text box aloud.

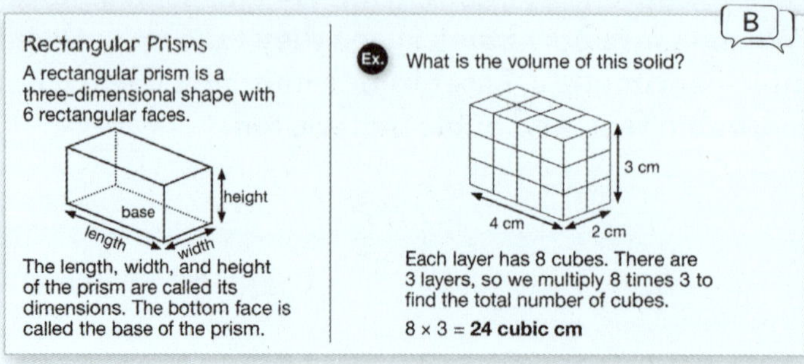

Show your child a small, closed box. Have your child identify the length, width, height, and base of the box. **The base of the box is the side that it sits on. The height is how tall the box is.**

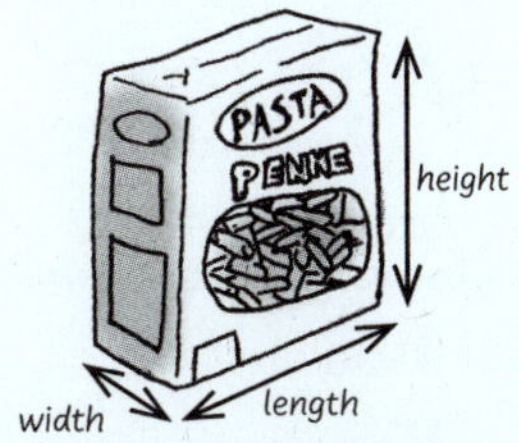

We typically call the base's longer side the length. In everyday life, we often use the terms length and width interchangeably to describe dimensions, so don't worry if you and your child sometimes mix them up.

Turn the box so that it lies on one of its sides. Have your child again identify the length, width, height, and base. **When we rotate the box, the dimensions rotate, too! But, we didn't change how much space the box takes up, so the volume doesn't change.** Repeat with the other side.

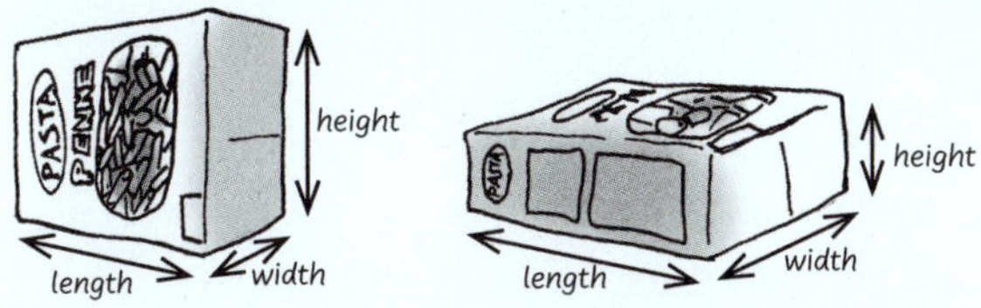

The example shows how to find the volume of a rectangular prism.

- **First, we find how many cubes are in each layer. How many cubes are in each layer of the rectangular prism?** *8.* If your child's not sure, have her build the bottom layer with centimeter cubes.
- **Then, we multiply the number of cubes in each layer by the number of layers to find the total number of cubes. How many layers of cubes are there?** *3.*
- **So, what's the volume of the rectangular prism?** *24.*

Have your child use this method to find the volume of each rectangular prism. If she has trouble identifying how many cubes are in each layer, have her construct the bottom layer of the prism from centimeter cubes.

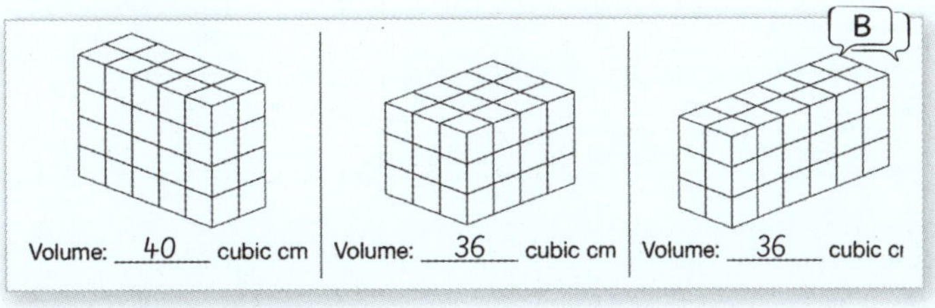

Independent Practice and Review

Have your child complete the Lesson 4.1 Practice and Review workbook pages.

Lesson 4.2
Multiply to Find Volume

Purpose	Materials
• Practice finding the volume of solids constructed from centimeter cubes • Use the volume formula (length × width × height) to find the volume of rectangular prisms	• 3 dice
Memory Work	• **What do we call the top number in a fraction?** *The numerator.* • **What do we call the bottom number in a fraction?** *The denominator.* • **What do we call fractions that look different but have the same value?** *Equivalent fractions.* • **What do we call numbers that have a whole number and a fraction?** *Mixed numbers.*

Warm-up (A): Find the Volume of 3-D Solids

In the last lesson, you learned how to use cubic centimeters to measure volume. Have your child find the volume of each solid in part A.

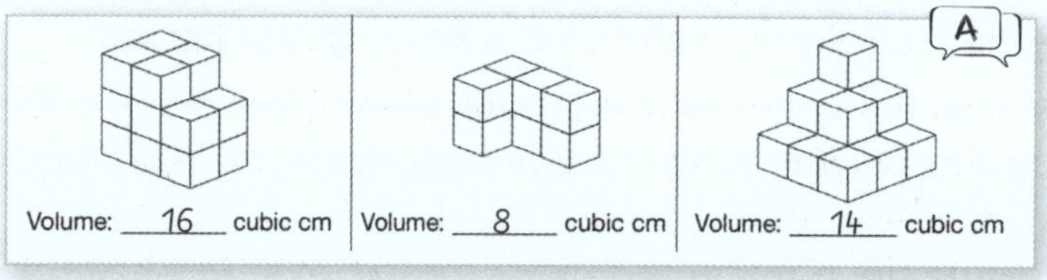

Your child does not need to build the solids out of centimeter cubes unless he has trouble finding their volumes.

Activity (B): Find the Volume of Rectangular Prisms

We can use multiplication to find the volume of rectangular prisms. Have your child read the text box.

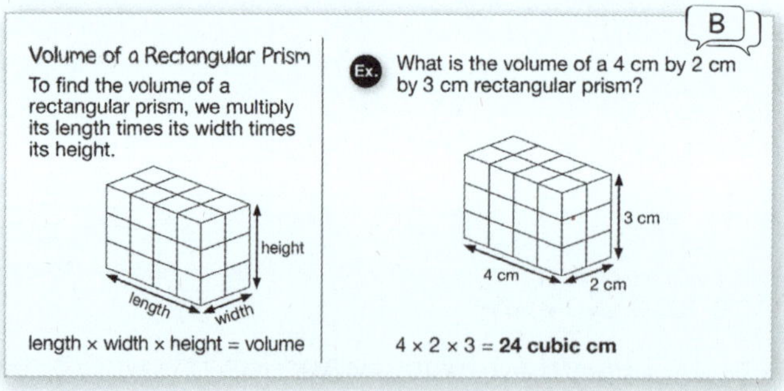

Point to the formula for volume. **This is called the formula for volume. It tells how to use multiplication to find the volume of any rectangular prism. Formulas are equations that describe mathematical rules. This formula only works for rectangular prisms. You can't use it to find the volume of a cone or a pyramid!**

Let's study the example to see how to use the formula.

- **What is the length of this rectangular prism?** *4 centimeters.*
- **What is its width?** *2 centimeters.*
- **What is its height?** *3 centimeters.*

Point to the written equation. **4 times 2 times 3 equals 24, so the volume is 24 cubic centimeters.**

Which part of the equation tells the number of cubes in each layer? *4 times 2.* **When we multiply length times width, we find the number of cubes in the bottom layer. Then, when we multiply 8 times 3, we multiply the number of cubes in each layer by the number of layers.**

With your child, label the dimensions of the solid in the first practice problem. **People sometimes use the word "by" to describe the dimensions of a rectangular prism. We could say that this solid is "2 by 4 by 2."**

Then, demonstrate how to write an equation for the volume on scrap paper: 2 × 4 × 2 = 16. Point to the left side of the equation. **You can write 2 times 4 times 2 as a short way to describe the solid's dimensions. We'll use this way to write dimensions in our game today.**

Have your child complete the other practice problems in the same way. Have your child write the equations on scrap paper if he needs more space.

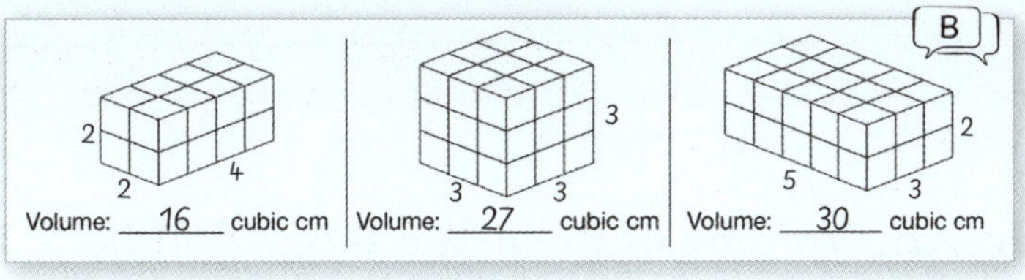

2 × 4 × 2 = 16 3 × 3 × 3 = 27 5 × 3 × 2 = 30

Activity (C): Play Build the Box

In this game, we'll pretend we're building boxes out of wood. We'll roll to find the dimensions of each box and then multiply to find the volume of the box. Play Build the Box.

If your child enjoys this game, play additional rounds and keep track of your scores on scrap paper.

Build the Box

Materials: 3 dice

Object of the Game: Score more points than the other player by creating boxes with a greater total volume.

Roll 3 dice. Write the numbers as the dimensions for your first box. (You may write the numbers in any order.) Multiply to find the volume of the prism and write it in the volume column. This product is your score.

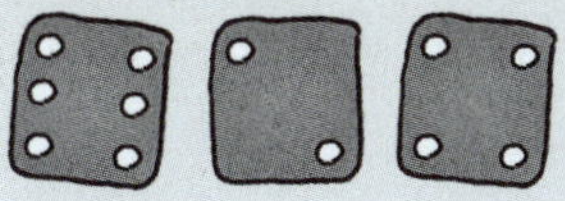

Dimensions (cm)	Volume (cubic cm)
6 × 2 × 4	48

Sample round.

Play then passes to the other player. Continue until both players have completed all 3 rounds. Add up each player's total points. The player with more points wins.

Independent Practice and Review

Have your child complete the Lesson 4.2 Practice and Review workbook pages.

Lesson 4.3
Estimate and Measure Boxes' Volumes

Purpose	Materials
• Practice multiplying to find volume • Estimate and measure the volume of real boxes • Understand that rectangular prisms can have different dimensions but the same volume	• Base-ten blocks • 3 small boxes of different sizes • 1-foot (30-cm) ruler

Memory Work

- **What does volume measure?** *The amount of space a solid occupies.*
- **What is the formula for the volume of a rectangular prism?** *Length times width times height.*

In this lesson, your child will estimate and measure the volume of 3 small boxes. Try to choose boxes whose length, width, and height are less than 30 cm, as this makes the measuring and multiplication easier. Boxes of rice, pasta, or pancake mix all work well for this activity.

Warm-up (A): Find the Volume of Base-Ten Block Solids

We used centimeter cubes to build 3-D solids in the last two lessons. We can also use larger base-ten blocks to build 3-D solids. Have your child use base-ten blocks to construct the solids in part A and find their volumes. Encourage her to use the largest possible base-ten blocks for each solid so she can build them more quickly.

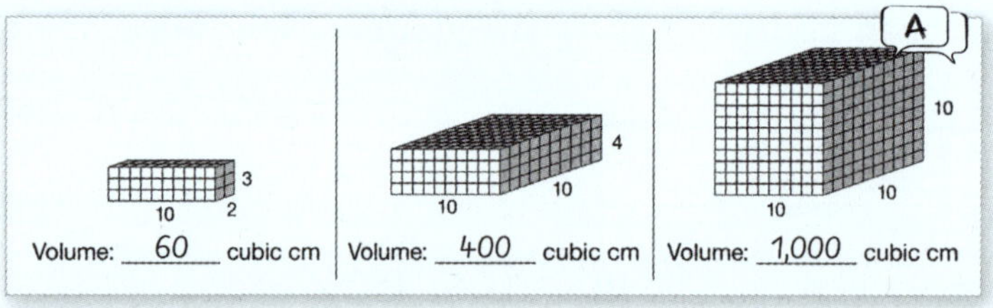

Use 6 rods for the first solid, 4 flats for the second solid, and 1 large cube (or 10 flats) for the third solid.

Activity (B): Use Measured Dimensions to Find Volume

When we build solids from base-ten blocks, we can see every cubic centimeter. When we find the volume of objects in real life, we can't always pack them full of centimeter cubes! Instead, we use their measurements to calculate their volumes.

Let's use the volume formula to find the volume of each box. Have your child multiply to find the volume of each box. **Which box has a greater volume?** *They're equal.* **Even though the boxes have different dimensions, they have the same volume and take up the same amount of space.**

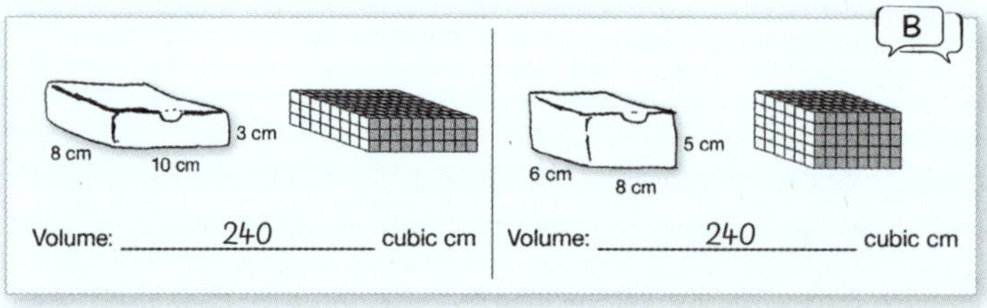

$10 \times 8 \times 3 = 240$ $\quad$ $8 \times 6 \times 5 = 240$

Activity (C): Measure Boxes' Sides to Find Their Volume

Show your child 3 small boxes with different dimensions. **Which box do you think has the smallest volume? Which has the next-larger volume? Which box do you think has the greatest volume?** *Answers will vary.* Write the name of each item in the chart in part C in the order your child arranged them.

Box
Rice
Pasta
Pancake Mix

In Unit 3, you learned about the associative property of multiplication. What does the associative property say? *You can multiply numbers in any order without changing the answer.* **To find the volume of a rectangular prism, we multiply the three dimensions together. It doesn't matter which dimensions we call the height, length, or width, as long as we include all three dimensions in the multiplication problem.**

Each corner of the box touches all three of its dimensions. So, if you point to one corner and measure the 3 edges that touch that corner, you'll measure all 3 dimensions of the box.

Point to one corner of the first box listed in the chart. Have your child run her finger along the three edges that touch the corner. Then, have her use a ruler to measure the 3 edges (in centimeters).

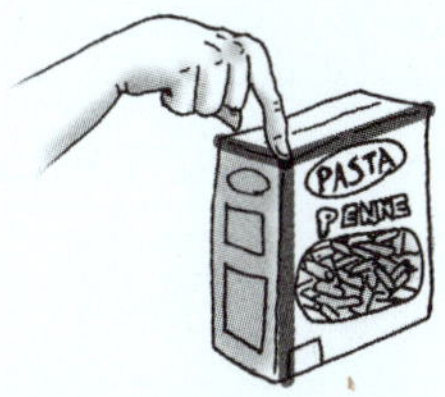

Help her round each length to the nearest centimeter and write the dimensions in the chart. Then, have her multiply (in the work space) to find the volume of the box. Repeat with the other two boxes.

Box	Dimensions (cm)	Volume (cubic cm)
Rice	15 × 3 × 21	945
Pasta	12 × 7 × 19	1,596
Pancake Mix	15 × 6 × 22	1,980

Once your child completes the chart, discuss whether she's surprised by any of the results. For example: **Did you expect that the pancake mix box would have a volume of almost 2,000 cubic centimeters?** Or: **The box of pasta is a little shorter than the box of rice, but it's a lot wider. That makes its volume greater than the volume of the box of rice.**

Independent Practice and Review

Have your child complete the Lesson 4.3 Practice and Review workbook pages.

Lesson 4.4
Find Missing Dimensions

Purpose	Materials
• Use centimeter cubes to reason about dimensions and volume • Use the volume formula to find a missing dimension	• Centimeter cubes (unit blocks)

Memory Work

- **What do we call a quadrilateral with 4 right angles?** *A rectangle.*
- **What do we call a quadrilateral with 4 right angles and 4 equal sides?** *A square.*
- **What do we call a quadrilateral with 4 equal sides?** *A rhombus.*
- **What do we call a quadrilateral with 2 pairs of parallel sides?** *A parallelogram.*
- **What do we call a quadrilateral with exactly 1 pair of parallel sides?** *A trapezoid.*

Warm-up: Solve Volume Riddles

In the last few lessons, you've learned how to find the volume of rectangular prisms. We'll warm up today with volume riddles.

These riddles preview using the volume formula to find missing dimensions.

- Arrange 6 centimeter cubes in a 2×3 array. **I'd like to build a rectangular prism with a volume of 18 cubic centimeters. How many layers like this do I need to build?** *3.* **How do you know?** *Sample answer: There are 6 cubes in your layer. 18 divided by 6 equals 3, so you need 3 layers.* **What will be the final dimensions of my rectangular prism?** *2 by 3 by 3.*

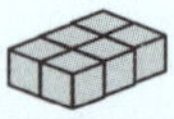

You do not need to build the full rectangular prism unless your child has trouble answering the questions.

- Arrange 10 cubes in a 2×5 upright wall. **I'd like to build a rectangular prism with a volume of 40 cubic centimeters. How many solids like this do I need to build and put together?** *4.* **How do you know?** *Sample answer: There are 10 cubes in your wall. 40 divided by 10 equals 4, so you need 4 slices like that one.* **What will be the final dimensions of my rectangular prism?** *5 by 4 by 2.*

- **I'd like to build a rectangular prism with a volume of 32 cubic centimeters. I'd like it to have 4 layers of cubes. How many cubes should be in each layer?** *8.* **How do you know?** *32 divided by 4 equals 8.* **What dimensions could I use for the layers?** *1 by 8 or 2 by 4.* If your child's not sure, give him 8 cubes and have him try arranging them until he finds both possible ways.

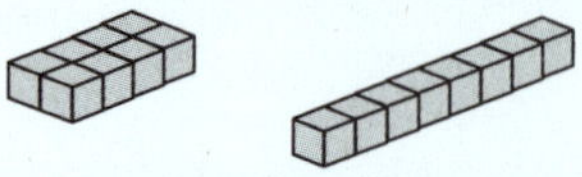

Activity (A): Use the Volume Formula to Find a Missing Dimension

Today, you'll learn how to use the volume formula to find a missing dimension for a rectangular prism. Have your child read the text.

A

How to Find a Missing Dimension

If you know the volume of a rectangular prism and two of its dimensions, you can use the volume formula to find the missing dimension.

1. Use the volume formula to write an equation. Write a blank for the missing dimension.
2. Multiply the two dimensions you know.
3. Divide the volume by the product of the two dimensions you know.

Ex. The box's volume is 30 cubic cm. What is its height?

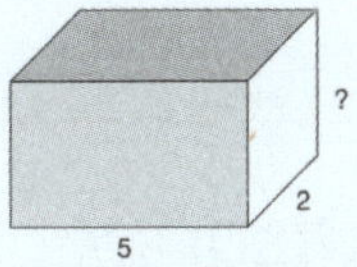

length × width × height = volume

5 × 2 × ____ = 30

10 × ____ = 30

30 ÷ 10 = **3 cm**

Let's study the example to see how to use the volume formula to find a missing dimension.

- **The box has a volume of 30 cubic centimeters. Which dimensions do we know?** *The length and the width.* **Which dimension do we want to find?** *The height.*
- **First, we write an equation for the volume of the rectangular prism. What's the volume formula for rectangular prisms?** *Length times width times height.* **In this solid, the length is 5, the width is 2, and the volume is 30. We want to find the height, so we write a blank for the height. This equation means "5 times 2 times what equals 30?"**
- **5 times 2 equals 10. 10 times the height equals 30.**
- **Division is the opposite of multiplication. So, 30 divided by 10 tells the missing number. 30 divided by 10 is 3, so the height is 3 centimeters.**

If your child is confused by this explanation, build a 5 × 2 array of cubes on the table. **I want to build a box with 30 cubes. I make the bottom layer 5 cubes long and 2 cubes wide. How many cubes are in the bottom layer?** *10.* **How many layers do I need to build in all?** *3.* **The total number of cubes divided by the number of cubes in each layer tells me the number of layers.**

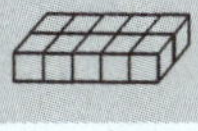

Have your child use the same method to solve the practice problems. He may solve the problems mentally or on scrap paper.

A

The box's volume is 70 cubic cm. What is its length?

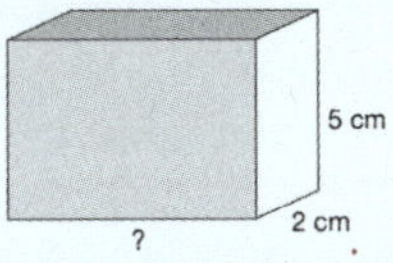

The box's volume is 56 cubic cm. What is its width?

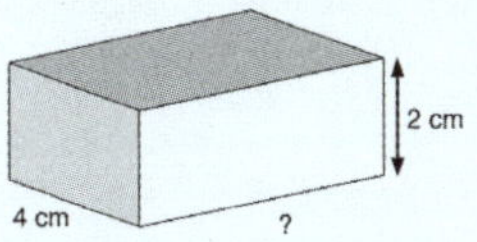

____ × 2 × 5 = 70

____ ×10 = 70

70 ÷ 10 = 7 cm

____ × 4 × 2 = 56

____ × 8 = 56

56 ÷ 8 = 7 cm

Activity (B): Play Disappearing Dimensions

Show your child the game board in part B. **This game board uses abbreviations. What do you think "vol." stands for?** *Volume.* **What do you think "cu. cm" stands for?** *Cubic centimeters.* **You can use these abbreviations when you solve problems, too.**

Play Disappearing Dimensions. Your child may write equations on scrap paper or use mental math to find the answers.

Disappearing Dimensions

Materials: None

Object of the Game: Complete missing dimensions to win the most points.

Start a scorecard on a separate piece of paper. Choose who will go first.

On your turn, choose a box on the gameboard. Find the missing dimension in the box. The missing number is your score. Add this score to your previous total.

For example, if you complete the following problem on your first turn, you score 6 points.

B

length: 6 cm width: 3 cm height: 2 cm vol.: 36 cu. cm

Cara	Mom
6	

Take turns until all problems have been completed. Whoever has the higher score wins the game.

Answer Key:

B

length: 6 cm width: 3 cm height: 2 cm vol.: 36 cu. cm	length: 3 cm width: 2 cm height: 9 cm vol.: 54 cu. cm	length: 5 cm width: 5 cm height: 4 cm vol.: 100 cu. cm	length: 2 cm width: 2 cm height: 6 cm vol.: 24 cu. cm
length: 2 cm width: 2 cm height: 10 cm vol.: 40 cu. cm	length: 4 cm width: 4 cm height: 3 cm vol.: 48 cu. cm	length: 8 cm width: 9 cm height: 1 cm vol.: 72 cu. cm	length: 6 cm width: 5 cm height: 2 cm vol.: 60 cu. cm

Independent Practice and Review

Have your child complete the Lesson 4.4 Practice and Review workbook pages.

Lesson 4.5
Cubic Meters

Purpose	Materials
• Review how to add to find total area • Introduce cubic meters • Split solids into rectangular prisms and add to find total volume	• Meterstick, optional

Memory Work	
	• **What's zero times any number?** *Zero.* • **What's zero divided by any other number?** *Zero.* • **What's any number divided by zero?** *Undefined.*

Warm-up (A): Review Adding Areas to Find Total Area

Show your child the first shape. **This shape is made of two rectangles. What's the area of the blue rectangle?** *15 square centimeters.* **What's the area of the tan rectangle?** *6 square centimeters.* **So, what's the area of the whole shape?** *21 square centimeters.* Write "21 sq. cm" in the blank. Have your child find the area of the other shape in the same way.

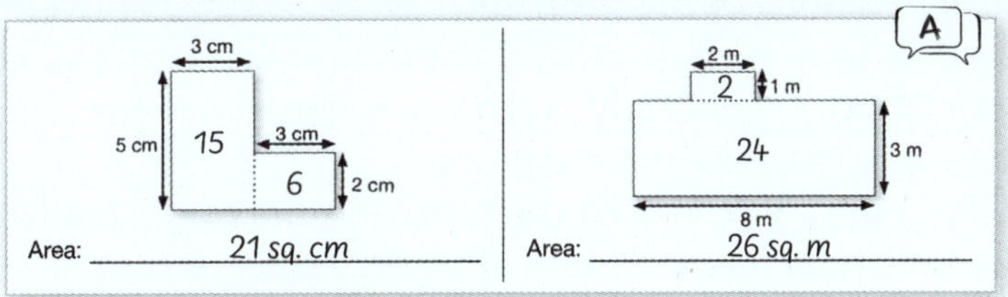

Activity (B): Introduce Cubic Meters

Today, you'll learn how to measure volume with cubic meters. You'll also learn how to add volumes to find the total volume of an object.

How many centimeters equal 1 meter? *100.* Use your hands or a meterstick to show your child the approximate length of a meter. (A meter is a little longer than a yard.)

A cube of space that is 1 meter on each side has a volume of 1 cubic meter. A large washing machine has a volume of about 1 cubic meter. Have your child read aloud the left side of the text box.

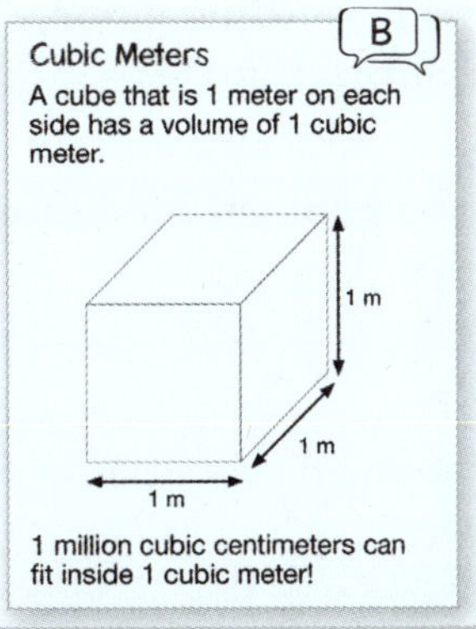

If your child wonders how 1 million cubic centimeters can fit inside 1 cubic meter, explain: **Each side of the cubic meter is 100 centimeters long. So, you multiply 100 times 100 times 100 to find its volume in cubic centimeters. 100 times 100 times 100 is 1 million, so the cubic meter has a volume of 1 million cubic centimeters.**

Activity (B): Add Volumes with Cubic Meters

Cubic meters are more useful than cubic centimeters when we find the volume of large objects. The example shows how to find the volume of the pool in cubic meters.

This pool is made of two rectangular prisms. So, we find the volume of each rectangular prism separately and then add the volumes to find the total volume of the pool. It's just like what you did to find area in the warm-up.

B

Ex. What is the total volume of the pool?

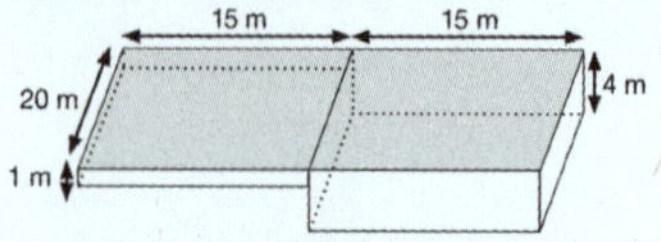

Volume of the shallow end:
20 × 15 × 1 = **300 cu. m**

Volume of the deep end:
20 × 15 × 4 = **1,200 cu. m**

Volume of the whole pool:
300 + 1,200 = **1,500 cu. m**

- **What are the dimensions of the shallow end?** *20 meters by 15 meters by 1 meter.* **So, we multiply 20 times 15 times 1 to find its volume. The volume of the shallow end is 300 cubic meters.**
- **What are the dimensions of the deep end?** *20 meters by 15 meters by 4 meters.* If your child isn't sure how to find the width, point out that the deep end has the same width as the shallow end. **So, we multiply 20 times 15 times 4 to find its volume. The volume of the deep end is 1,200 cubic meters.**
- **Last, we add 300 plus 1,200 to find the total volume of the pool. 300 plus 1,200 is 1,500, so the whole pool has a volume of 1,500 cubic meters.**

Let's use the same approach to solve the word problems. Have your child read the first word problem aloud. **We want to find the total volume of the pool. The pool is split into two parts. We'll find the volume of each part and add them.**

B

The pool is 2 m deep. What is its volume?

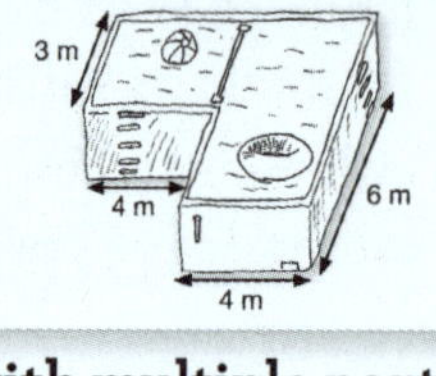

When you solve volume problems with multiple parts, there are a lot of different numbers to keep track of! It's important to identify the correct dimensions of each part before you start multiplying.

Let's start with the smaller part of the pool, on the left side.

- **What's the length of this part?** *4 meters.*
- **What's the width?** *3 meters.*
- **What's the height?** *2 meters.* If your child has trouble finding the height, point out that it is listed in the text of the word problem. Write it in next to the corresponding dimension of the pool as shown.

- Have your child write and solve a multiplication equation to find the volume of the smaller part of the pool: 4 × 3 × 2 = 24 cu. m

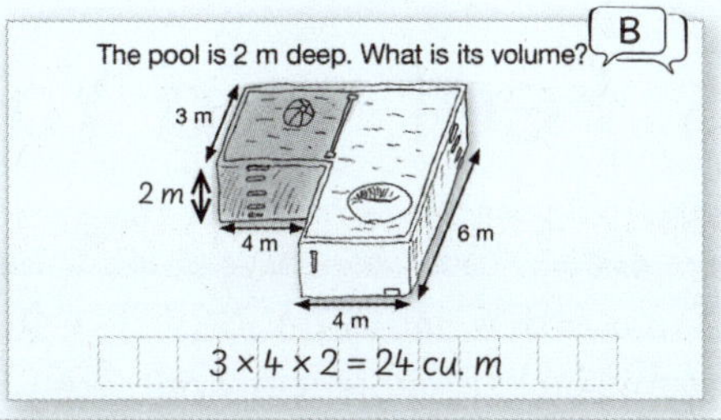

It's fine if your child identifies the 3-meter side as the length and 4-meter side as the width, as long as she includes both dimensions in her equation. We use the term "depth" rather than height when describing the dimensions of many real-life rectangular solids. Explain to your child that they mean the same thing, since the depth of the pool tells how high the water in the pool is.

Repeat with the larger part of the pool. Then, have your child add the volumes of each part to find the total volume of the pool.

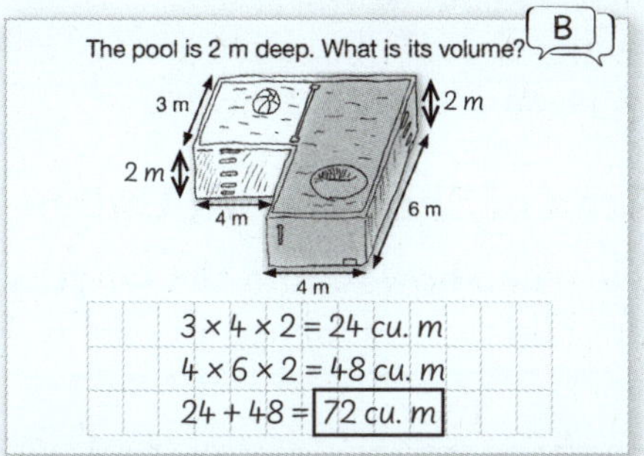

Children sometimes have trouble identifying the three dimensions in these complex diagrams. If this is the case for your child, say: **Each corner of the rectangular solid is connected to three edges. One edge is the length, one edge is the width, and one edge is the height.** Have your child put her finger on one corner of the pool. (Choose a corner whose connecting sides are visible in the diagram.) Then, have her trace the three edges that connect to the corner and name their dimensions.

Have your child solve the second word problem in the same way. Have her first find the volume of the top part of the stool and then find the volume of the bottom part of the stool.

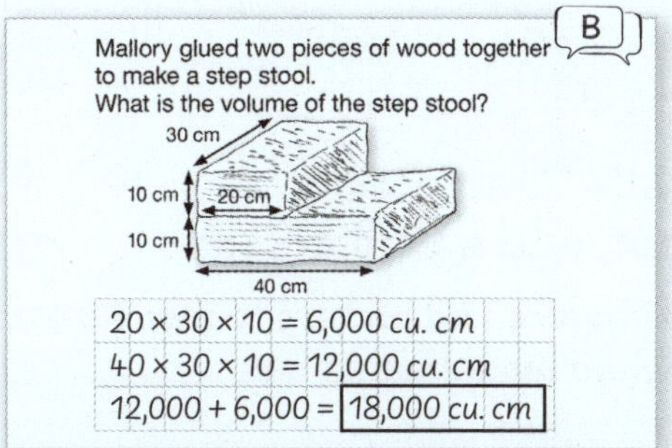

If your child has trouble finding the width of the bottom part of the stepstool, encourage her to look for a parallel edge in the diagram that is labeled.

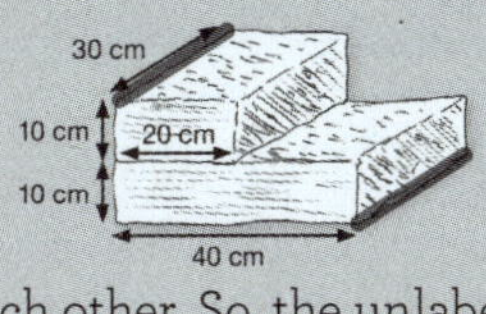

These two edges are parallel to each other. So, the unlabeled edge must also be 30 cm long.

Independent Practice and Review

Have your child complete the Lesson 4.5 Practice and Review workbook pages.

Lesson 4.6
Cubic Inches, Feet, and Yards

Purpose	Materials
• Find the area of rectangular shapes with unlabeled sides • Understand the magnitude of cubic inches, cubic feet, and cubic yards • Find missing dimensions in 3-D solids • Split solids into parts and add to find their total volume	• Ruler or measuring tape

Memory Work

- **How many inches equal 1 foot?** *12.*
- **How many feet equal 1 yard?** *3.*
- **How many inches equal 1 yard?** *36.*
- **How many feet equal 1 mile?** *5,280.*
- **How many ounces equal 1 pound?** *16.*
- **How many fluid ounces equal 1 cup?** *8.*

Warm-up (A): Find the Area of Shapes with Unlabeled Side Lengths

When you were younger, you learned how to find the lengths of missing sides in shapes made of rectangles. Show your child the first shape in part A. Have him find and label the lengths of the two unlabeled sides.

Then, have your child split each shape into rectangles, find the area of the rectangles, and add the rectangles' areas to find the total area of the shape.

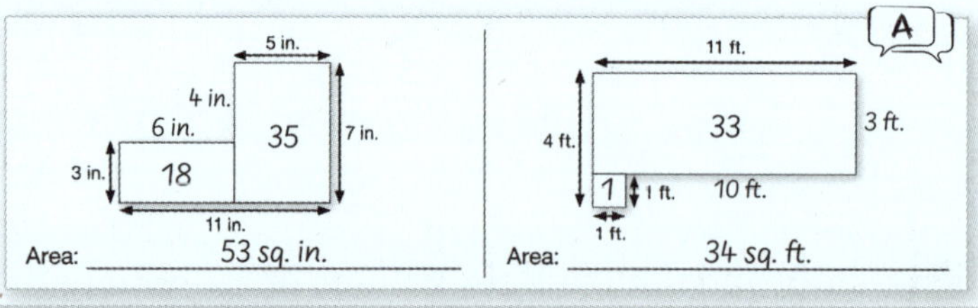

There are multiple ways to split the shapes into rectangles. If your child starts to split the shape into more than 2 rectangles, encourage him to find a simpler way.

Activity (B): Find Real-Life Examples of a Cubic Inch, a Cubic Foot, and a Cubic Yard

So far, we've used cubic centimeters and meters to measure volume. Today, we'll use U.S. customary units. Have your child read the text box.

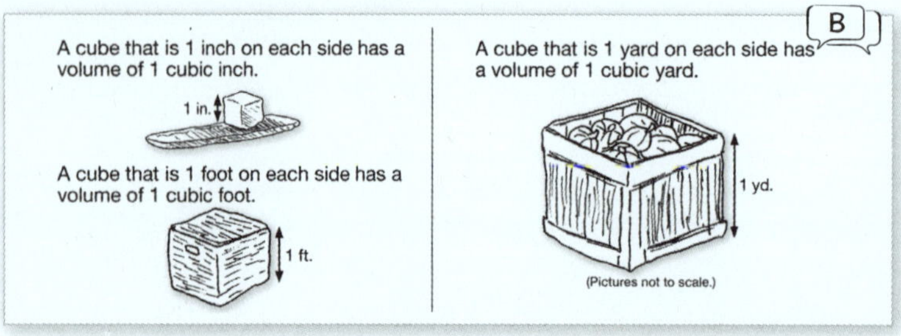

With your child, look around your home for objects with volumes of approximately 1 cubic inch, 1 cubic foot, and 1 cubic yard. Use a ruler or measuring tape to check their dimensions.

Sample items. They are not to scale.

You do not need to find objects with these exact volumes. This activity is simply meant to give your child a more concrete sense of the magnitude of each unit.

- Stacks of small sticky notes, small wooden or plastic blocks, or cubes of modeling clay often have a volume close to 1 cubic inch. You can also use a ruler to cut a stick of butter or an apple into a 1-inch cube.
- Storage baskets or cardboard boxes of food from wholesale clubs often have a volume close to one cubic foot. You can also stack textbooks or push cereal boxes together to create a shape with a volume of approximately one cubic foot.
- Many appliances (like dishwashers, stoves, washers, or dryers) are about 1 yard by 1 yard by 1 yard.

If your family does not use the U.S. customary system, you do not need to find real-life examples of cubic inches, feet, and yards. Instead, briefly discuss the magnitude of each unit and then move on to the word problems.

Activity (C): Solve Volume Word Problems

Have your child read the first word problem aloud. **We want to find the total volume of the fort. The fort is made from two boxes. We'll find the volume of each box and add them.**

Let's start by finding the volume of the tall box on the left side of the fort.

- **What's the length of this box?** *2 feet.*
- **What's the width?** *3 feet.* If your child has trouble finding this dimension, point out that it is the same as the width of the shorter box.
- **What's the height?** *5 feet.*

Then, have your child write a multiplication equation to find the volume of the box on the left.

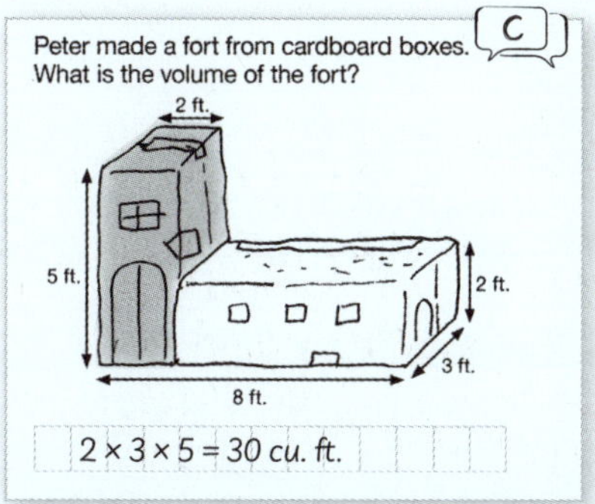

Now, we'll find the volume of the shorter box on the right side of the fort.

- **What's the length of this box?** *6 feet.* **How do you know?** *Sample answer: The length of this box plus the length of the tall box equals 8 feet. The tall box is 2 feet long, so we subtract 2 from 8 to find the length of this box.* **8 feet minus 6 feet equals 2 feet.** Have your child write "6 ft." along this dimension.
- **What's the width?** *3 feet.*
- **What's the height?** *2 feet.*

Have your child write a multiplication equation to find the volume of the box on the right. Finally, have him add the volumes of the two boxes to find the total volume of the fort.

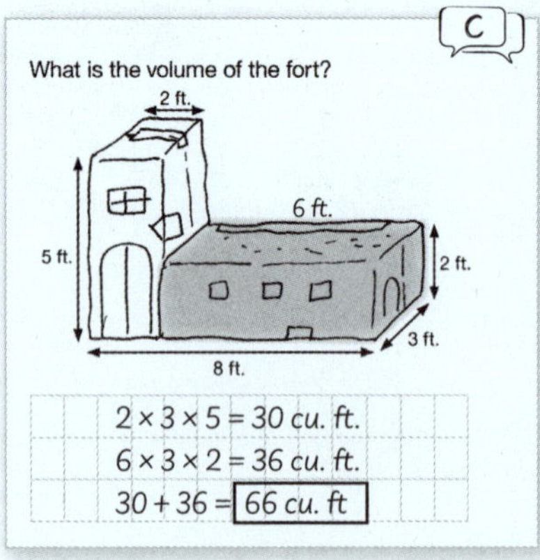

Have your child read the second word problem aloud. **What's the goal of this problem?** *Find the volume of the foam blocks.* **This problem is a little different than the other ones we've solved. Instead of finding the volume of the foam pit, you need to find the volume of the blocks in the foam pit.**

Let's split the foam pit into two rectangular prisms and then find the volume of the blocks in each part. Have your child draw a line to split the diagram into 2 rectangular prisms. If your child begins to split the shape into more than 2 rectangular prisms, encourage him to look for a simpler way.

Then, have him identify the dimensions of each part of the foam pit, find the volume of each part, and add to find the total volume. Make sure he uses 3 ft. as the height (not 4 ft.) so that he finds the volume of the blocks in the pit, not the pit itself.

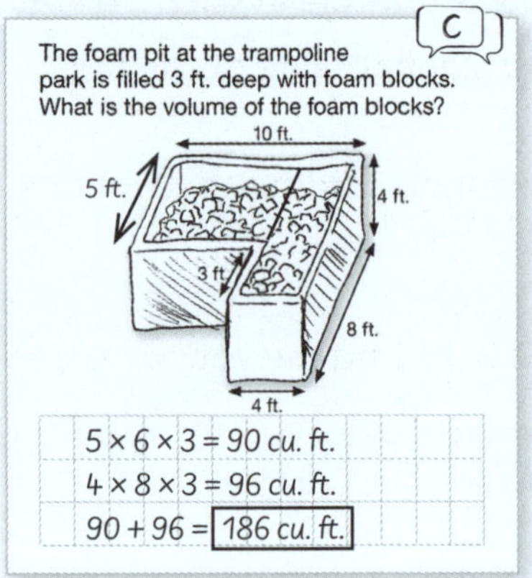

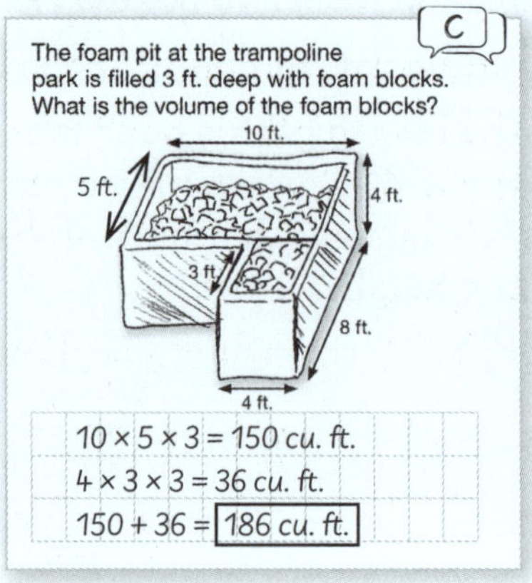

Your child may use either approach to find the volume.

Independent Practice and Review

Have your child complete the Lesson 4.6 Practice and Review workbook pages.

Lesson 4.7
Volume and Area, Part 1

Purpose	Materials
• Practice multiplying length times width to find area • Multiply base area by height to find volume • Find the volume of a room in your home	• Measuring tape

Memory Work	
	• **What does perimeter measure?** *The distance around the outside edge of a shape.* • **What does area measure?** *The amount of space that a shape covers.*

Warm-up (A): Practice Finding Area

In the last lesson, you learned about cubic feet, inches, and yards. Today, you'll learn about the connection between area and volume.

This floor plan shows the lengths and widths of the rooms in a new house. Have your child mentally multiply to find the area of each room.

A

length × width = area

Room	Area
Living Room	*160 sq. ft.*
Dining Room	*80 sq. ft.*
Kitchen	*100 sq. ft.*

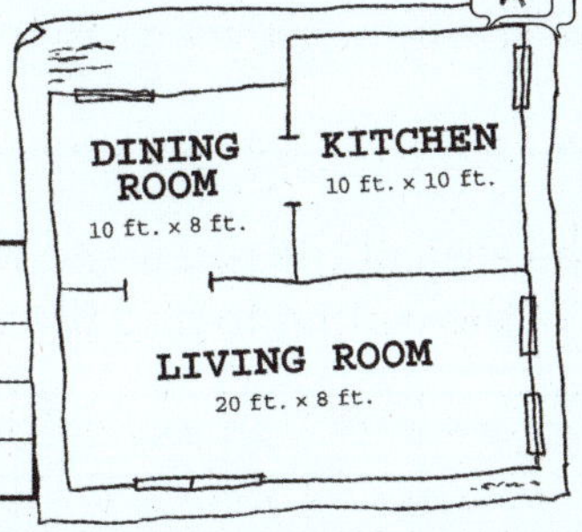

Activity (B): Use Area to Find Volume

People who fix and install furnaces, air conditioners, and ventilation systems are called HVAC technicians. HVAC stands for heating, ventilation, and air conditioning.

When HVAC technicians install new equipment, they find the volume of the house first. The volume tells them how much air needs to be heated or cooled in the house. Then, they can choose the right-size furnace or air conditioner for the house.

To find the volume, they sometimes use a shortcut. Instead of multiplying length times width times height for each room, they multiply the area of the room times the height. Have your child read the text in part B.

B

Area and Volume

If you know the area of the base of a rectangular prism, you've already found its length times its width.

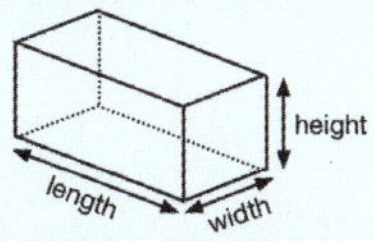

So, you can multiply the base area times its height to find its volume.

length × width × height = volume

base area × height = volume

Ex. The bathroom floor has an area of 54 sq. ft. The ceilings in the bathroom are 8 ft. high. What is the volume of the bathroom?

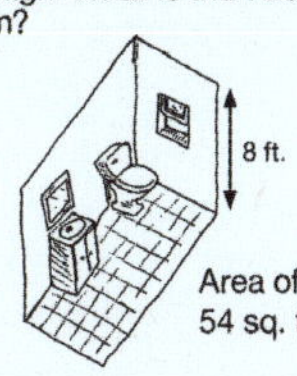

base area × height = volume

54 × 8 = **432 cu. feet**

Let's study the example to better understand why this works.

- **The bathroom has an area of 54 square feet. If you were going to fill the bathroom with cubic feet, it would take a layer of 54 1-foot boxes to cover the floor.**
- **How high are the ceilings in the bathroom?** *8 feet.* **You would need 8 layers of 54 cubic feet to fill the bathroom.**
- **So, you multiply 54 times 8 to find the volume. What's the volume of the bathroom?** *432 cubic feet.*

Now, let's find the volume of the rooms from the house in part A. Copy the area of each room (from part A) into the chart. Then, have your child multiply the area by the height to find the volume of each room (either mentally or on scrap paper).

B

Room	Area	Ceiling Height	Volume
Living Room	*160 sq. ft.*	20 ft.	*3,200 cu. ft.*
Dining Room	*80 sq. ft.*	10 ft.	*800 cu. ft.*
Kitchen	*100 sq. ft.*	8 ft.	*800 cu. ft.*

The final row in the chart is for us to find the volume of a room in our home. Have your child choose a room in your home. Help her use a measuring tape to measure the length, width, and height of the room.

If your family uses the U.S. customary system, measure the room's dimensions in feet and round to the nearest foot. If your family uses the metric system, measure in meters and round to the nearest meter.

If you're short on time, estimate the dimensions and tell them to your child rather than measuring.

Have your child find the area of the room and write it in the chart. Then, have her multiply the area by the height of the ceiling to find the volume of the room.

B

Room	Area	Ceiling Height	Volume
My bedroom	*208 sq. ft.*	*8 ft.*	*1,664 cu. ft.*

Sample answers for a room that is 13 by 16 by 8 feet.

Independent Practice and Review

Have your child complete the Lesson 4.7 Practice and Review workbook pages.

Lesson 4.8
Volume and Area, Part 2

Purpose	Materials
• Practice multiplying base area by height to find volume • Divide volume to find base area or height • Underline important information to solve volume word problems	• None

Memory Work • **What does LCM stand for?** *Least common multiple.*

Warm-up (A): Multiply Base Area by Height to Find Volume

In the last lesson, you learned how to multiply base area by height to find the volume of rectangular prisms. Have your child solve the word problems in part A.

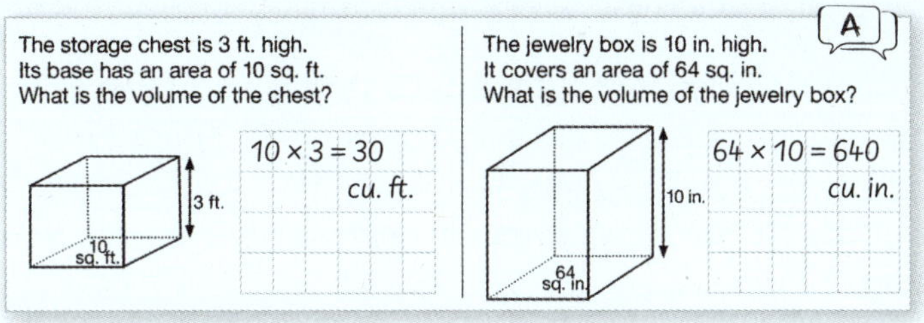

Activity (B): Divide to Find Base Area or Height

Today, you'll learn how to divide the volume to find the base area or height of a rectangular prism. Have your child read the top part of the text box aloud.

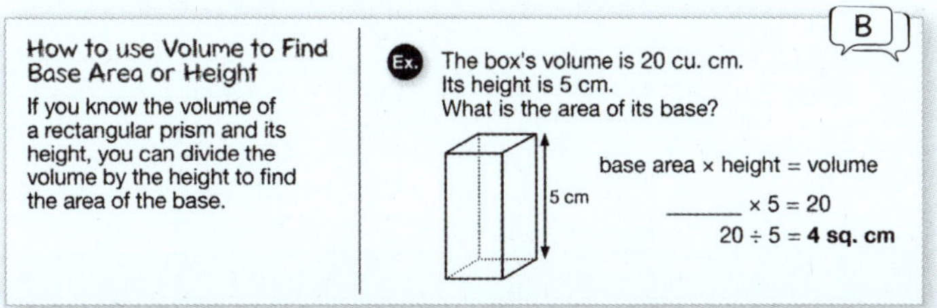

In the first example, we know the volume and height of the box. What do we want to find out? *The base area.* **Base area times height equals volume, so we divide volume by height to find the base area. What's the base area of the box?** *4 sq. cm.*

> If your child is confused by the example, explain the concept in terms of centimeter cubes: **Imagine you built a rectangular prism with a volume of 20 cubes. You use 5 layers of cubes, and you want to know how many cubes are in each layer. 20 divided by 5 equals 4, so there are 4 cubes in each layer.**

Why are the units for the answer square centimeters? *Sample answer: Because we use square units to measure area.* **Make sure to always use square units for your answer when you find area.**

Have your child read the bottom part of the text box aloud.

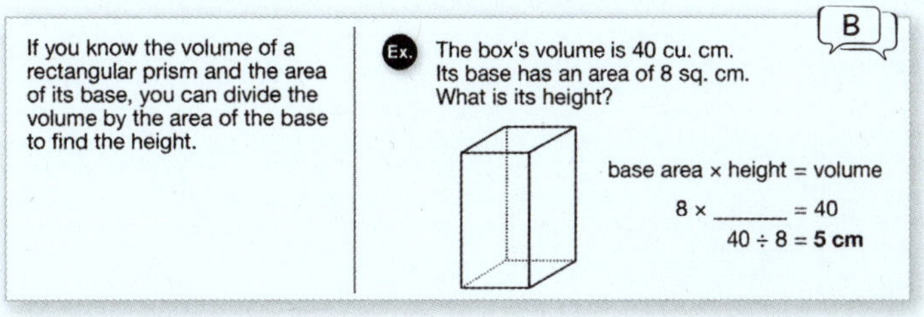

In the second example, we know the volume and base area of the box. What do we want to find out? *The height.* **Base area times height equals volume, so we divide volume by the base area to find the height. What's the height of the box?** *5 cm.*

> If your child is confused by the example, explain the concept in terms of centimeter cubes: **Imagine you built a rectangular prism with a volume of 40 cubes. You use 8 cubes in each layer. 40 divided by 8 equals 5, so there must be 5 layers.**

Why are the units for the answer regular centimeters instead of square centimeters or cubic centimeters? *Sample answer: Because we use regular units to measure length.* **Make sure to always use regular units for your answer when you find length.**

Activity (B): Underline Important Information to Solve Volume Word Problems

Have your child read the first word problem aloud. **What's the goal of this problem?** *Find the height of the dirt.* **What units will we use for our answer?** *Feet.* **How do you know?** *Sample answer: We measure height in regular units, not square or cubic units.*

> If needed, explain that garden dirt often comes in bags. The bags are usually labeled with the number of cubic feet they contain, so it's easy to know how many cubic feet you have used.

- **What information does the problem tell us that we can use to solve the problem?** *Sample answer: The garden bed covers 9 square feet. There are 18 cubic feet of dirt.* Have your child underline "9 square feet" and "18 cubic feet" in the problem.
- **Is 9 square feet the height, base area, or volume?** *Base area.* **Is 18 cubic feet the height or volume?** *Volume.*
- **We know the volume of the dirt and the base area of the garden bed. How can we use that information to find the height of the dirt?** *Divide the volume by the base area.* Write "18 ÷ 9 =" to begin an equation.
- Have your child complete the equation to solve the problem. **So, how high will the dirt fill the bed?** *2 feet.*

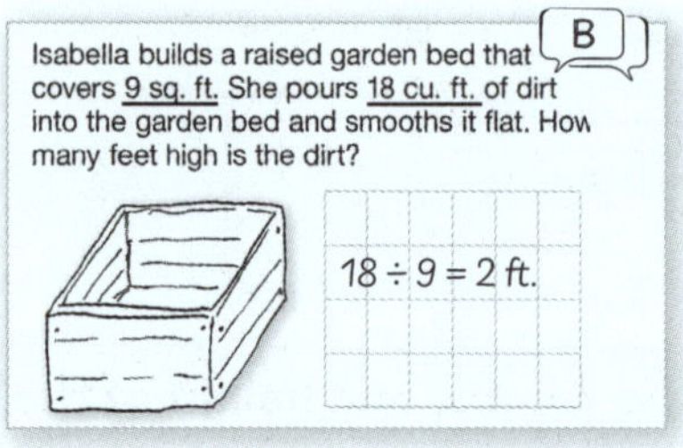

Have your child read the second word problem aloud. **What's the goal of this problem?** *Find how much floor area the cabinet will cover.* **What units will we use for our answer?** *Square feet.* **How do you know?** *Sample answer: We measure area in square units.*

- **What information does the problem tell us that we can use to solve the problem?** *Sample answer: The cabinet holds 80 cubic feet. The cabinet is 4 feet tall.* Have your child underline "80 cubic feet" and "4 feet" in the problem.
- **Is 80 cubic feet the height, base area, or volume?** *Volume.* **Is 4 feet the height or base area?** *Height.*
- **We know the volume of the cabinet and its height. How can we use that information to find the base area?** *Divide the volume by the height.*

- Have your child write and solve the matching equation. **So, how much floor area will the cabinet cover?** *20 square feet.*

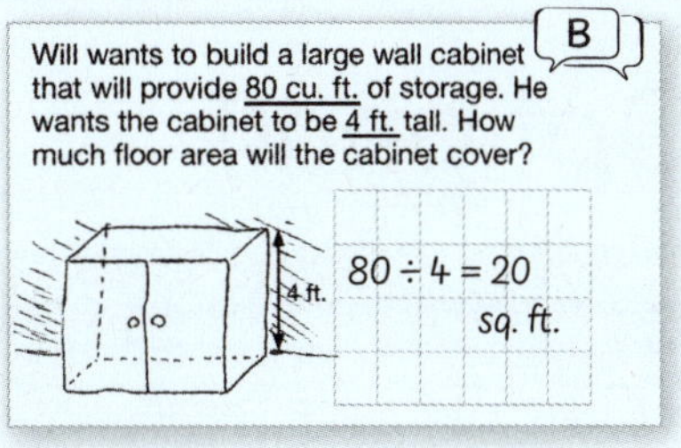

Independent Practice and Review

Have your child complete the Lesson 4.8 Practice and Review workbook pages.

Lesson 4.9
Enrichment (Optional)

Purpose	Materials
• Practice memory work • Appreciate how math can be used to answer real-life questions • Find the volume of a real-life fort • Summarize what your child has learned and assess your child's progress	• *How Many Guinea Pigs Can Fit on a Plane?: Answers to Your Most Clever Math Questions*, by Laura Overdeck • Pillows, blankets, and furniture for building a fort • Measuring tape

Warm-up: Review Memory Work

Quiz your child on any of the memory work items that she struggled with during this unit.

Math Picture Book: *How Many Guinea Pigs Can Fit on a Plane?*

Read pages 32–41 in *How Many Guinea Pigs Can Fit on a Plane?*

Enrichment Activity: Find the Volume of a Pillow Fort

Have your child use pillows, blankets, and furniture to build a fort. Encourage her to make the parts of the fort as rectangular as possible to make it easier to find the volume of the fort later. For example, she might arrange 2 chairs facing each other (about 4 feet apart) and drape a large blanket over them. Or, she might place chairs at the ends of a couch and drape a large blanket over both the couch and chairs.

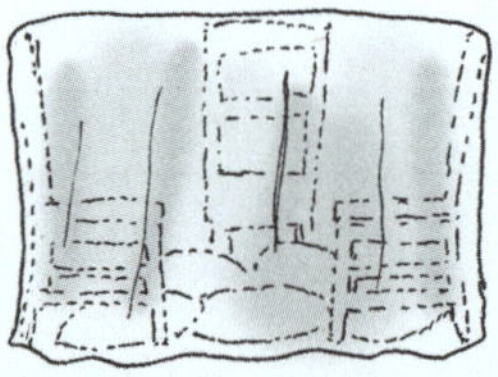

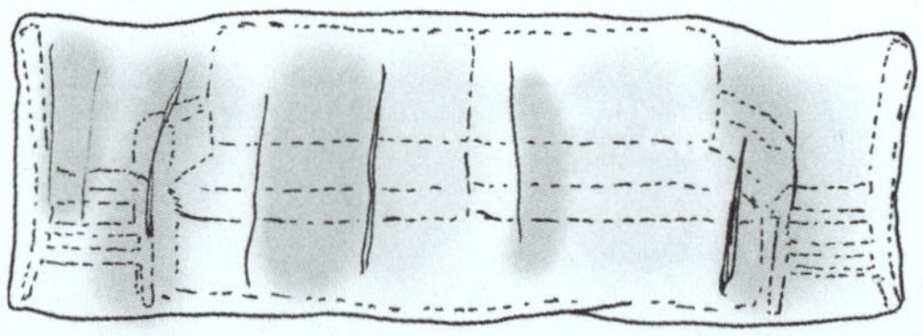

Feel free to get creative with your fort building. Large cardboard boxes are great for forts, or you can use pillows and blankets to enclose alcoves or nooks in your home.

After your child has constructed her fort, have her divide it into sections that are roughly shaped like rectangular prisms. Have her measure the length, width, and height and find the volume of each section. Then, have her add the volumes of each section to find the total volume of the fort.

If your family uses the U.S. customary system, measure in feet and round the lengths to the nearest foot. If your family uses the metric system, measure in meters and round to the nearest meter.

Unit Wrap-Up

Have your child complete the Unit 4 Wrap-Up.

Unit 4 Answer Key

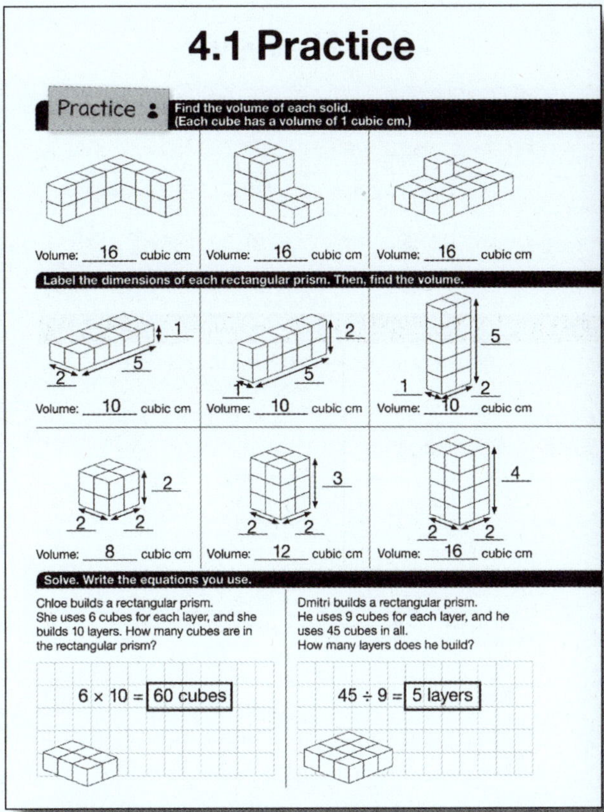

4.1 Practice

Practice Find the volume of each solid. (Each cube has a volume of 1 cubic cm.)

Volume: 16 cubic cm | Volume: 16 cubic cm | Volume: 16 cubic cm

Label the dimensions of each rectangular prism. Then, find the volume.

Volume: 10 cubic cm | Volume: 10 cubic cm | Volume: 10 cubic cm

Volume: 8 cubic cm | Volume: 12 cubic cm | Volume: 16 cubic cm

Solve. Write the equations you use.

Chloe builds a rectangular prism. She uses 6 cubes for each layer, and she builds 10 layers. How many cubes are in the rectangular prism?

6 × 10 = 60 cubes

Dmitri builds a rectangular prism. He uses 9 cubes for each layer, and he uses 45 cubes in all. How many layers does he build?

45 ÷ 9 = 5 layers

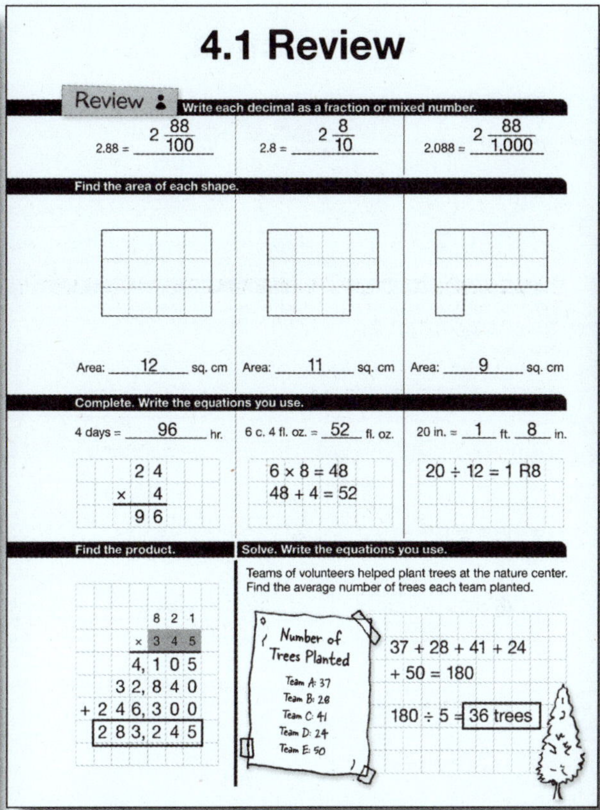

4.1 Review

Review Write each decimal as a fraction or mixed number.

2.88 = $2\frac{88}{100}$ | 2.8 = $2\frac{8}{10}$ | 2.088 = $2\frac{88}{1{,}000}$

Find the area of each shape.

Area: 12 sq. cm | Area: 11 sq. cm | Area: 9 sq. cm

Complete. Write the equations you use.

4 days = 96 hr. — 24 × 4 = 96

6 c. 4 fl. oz. = 52 fl. oz. — 6 × 8 = 48; 48 + 4 = 52

20 in. = 1 ft. 8 in. — 20 ÷ 12 = 1 R8

Find the product.

821 × 345: 4,105 + 32,840 + 246,300 = 283,245

Solve. Write the equations you use.

Teams of volunteers helped plant trees at the nature center. Find the average number of trees each team planted.

Number of Trees Planted: Team A: 37, Team B: 28, Team C: 41, Team D: 24, Team E: 50

37 + 28 + 41 + 24 + 50 = 180

180 ÷ 5 = 36 trees

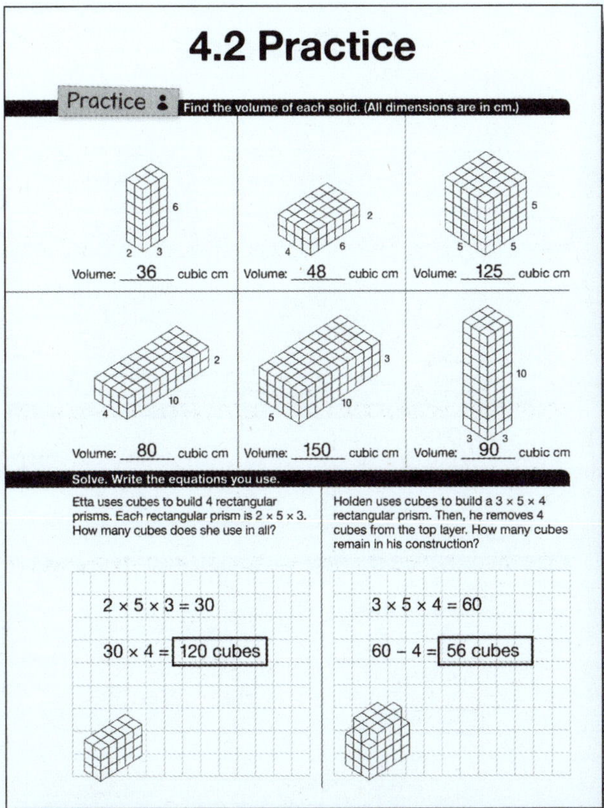

4.2 Practice

Practice Find the volume of each solid. (All dimensions are in cm.)

Volume: 36 cubic cm | Volume: 48 cubic cm | Volume: 125 cubic cm

Volume: 80 cubic cm | Volume: 150 cubic cm | Volume: 90 cubic cm

Solve. Write the equations you use.

Etta uses cubes to build 4 rectangular prisms. Each rectangular prism is 2 × 5 × 3. How many cubes does she use in all?

2 × 5 × 3 = 30

30 × 4 = 120 cubes

Holden uses cubes to build a 3 × 5 × 4 rectangular prism. Then, he removes 4 cubes from the top layer. How many cubes remain in his construction?

3 × 5 × 4 = 60

60 − 4 = 56 cubes

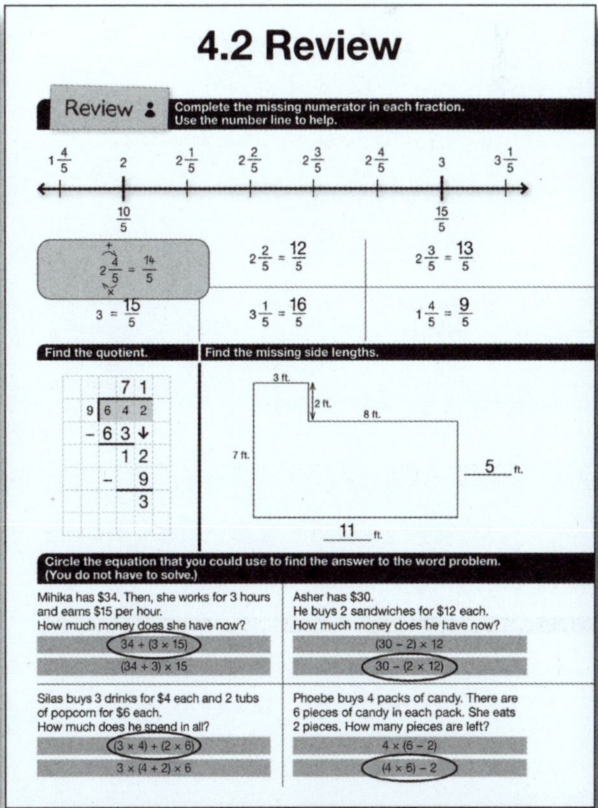

4.2 Review

Review Complete the missing numerator in each fraction. Use the number line to help.

$2\frac{4}{5} = \frac{14}{5}$ | $2\frac{2}{5} = \frac{12}{5}$ | $2\frac{3}{5} = \frac{13}{5}$

$3 = \frac{15}{5}$ | $3\frac{1}{5} = \frac{16}{5}$ | $1\frac{4}{5} = \frac{9}{5}$

Find the quotient.

642 ÷ 9 = 71 R3

Find the missing side lengths.

3 ft., 2 ft., 8 ft., 7 ft.; missing: 5 ft., 11 ft.

Circle the equation that you could use to find the answer to the word problem. (You do not have to solve.)

Mihika has $34. Then, she works for 3 hours and earns $15 per hour. How much money does she have now? — (circled) 34 + (3 × 15); (34 + 3) × 15

Asher has $30. He buys 2 sandwiches for $12 each. How much money does he have now? — (30 − 2) × 12; (circled) 30 − (2 × 12)

Silas buys 3 drinks for $4 each and 2 tubs of popcorn for $6 each. How much does he spend in all? — (circled) (3 × 4) + (2 × 6); 3 × (4 + 2) × 6

Phoebe buys 4 packs of candy. There are 6 pieces of candy in each pack. She eats 2 pieces. How many pieces are left? — 4 × (6 − 2); (circled) (4 × 6) − 2

Unit 4 Answer Key

4.3 Practice

Practice Find the volume of each solid. (All dimensions are in cm.)

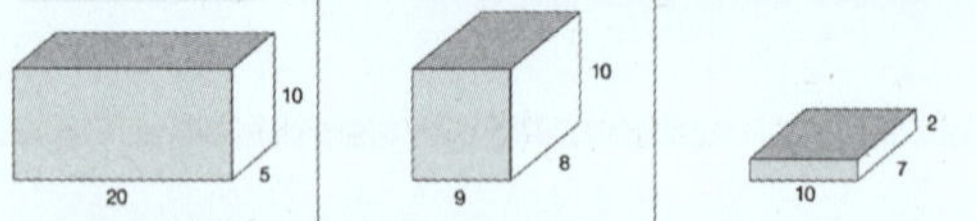

Volume: 1,000 cubic cm | Volume: 720 cubic cm | Volume: 140 cubic cm

Solve. Write the equations you use.

Willow buys a rectangular storage basket that is 25 cm long, 10 cm wide, and 20 cm high. What is the volume of the storage basket?

25 × 10 × 20 = **5,000 cubic cm**

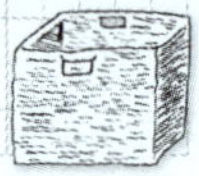

The cereal box is 20 cm long, 4 cm wide, and 30 cm high. What is its volume?

20 × 4 × 30 = **2,400 cubic cm**

Aven wants to fill this planter with dirt. How many cubic centimeters of dirt does he need?

30 × 20 × 100 = **60,000 cubic cm**

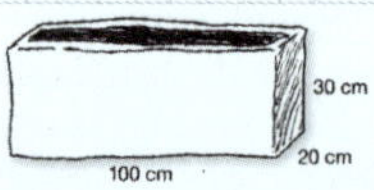

★ This planter is 10 cm wide and 10 cm long. It has a volume of 800 cubic cm. What is its height?

800 ÷ 10 = 80
80 ÷ 10 = **8 cm**

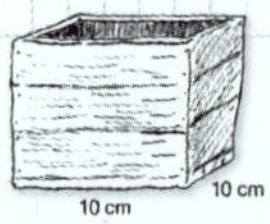

4.3 Review

Review Use mental math to complete.

4 × 8 × 2 = 64	205 × 2 = 410	70 × 7 = 490
6 × 8 × 5 = 240	205 × 4 = 820	71 × 7 = 497
900 × 60 = 54,000	420 ÷ 7 = 60	200 ÷ 4 = 50
9,000 × 60 = 540,000	4,200 ÷ 7 = 600	2,000 ÷ 4 = 500

Find the product.

```
      8 0 4
  ×   1 3 6
    4,8 2 4
   24,1 2 0
 + 80,4 0 0
 109,3 4 4
```

Find the least common multiple for each pair of numbers.

LCM of 5 and 6: 30
5: 5, 10, 15, 20, 25, 30
6: 6, 12, 18, 24, 30

LCM of 5 and 15: 15
5: 5, 10, 15
15: 15, 30

Solve. Write the equations you use.

The bucket holds 20 liters of water. It holds 4 times as many liters of water as the watering can. How many liters of water does the watering can hold?

20 ÷ 4 = **5 L**

How many milliliters of water does the watering can hold? (1 liter equals 1,000 milliliters.)

5 × 1,000 = **5,000 mL**

4.4 Practice

Practice Find the missing dimension for each solid. All measurements are in centimeters.

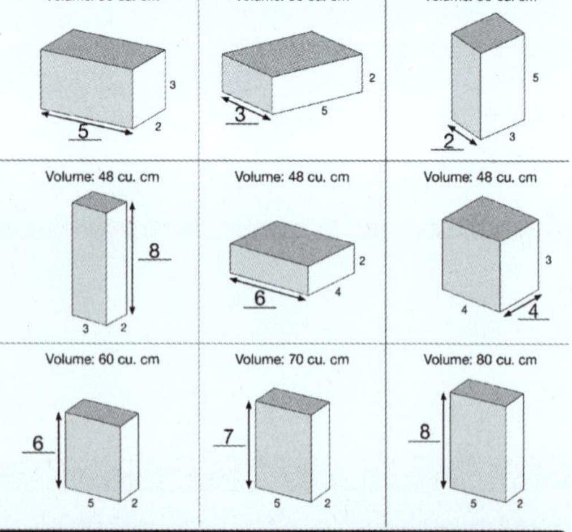

Use the clues to find the dimensions for each solid.

I have a volume of 36 cu. cm.
My length is 3 cm.
My length and width are the same.

Length: 3 cm
Width: 3 cm
Height: 4 cm

★ I have a volume of 40 cu. cm.
My length is 5 cm.
My height is twice my width.

Length: 5 cm
Width: 2 cm
Height: 4 cm

4.4 Review

Review Circle the more sensible measurement for each item.

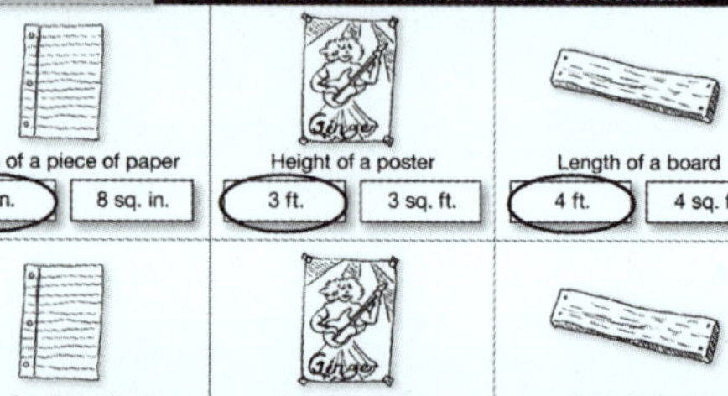

Width of a piece of paper	Height of a poster	Length of a board
8 in. (circled) / 8 sq. in.	**3 ft.** (circled) / 3 sq. ft.	**4 ft.** (circled) / 4 sq. ft.

Area of a piece of paper	Area of a poster	Area of a board
88 in. / **88 sq. in.** (circled)	6 ft. / **6 sq. ft.** (circled)	8 ft. / **8 sq. ft.** (circled)

Complete the circles with <, >, or =.

4.89 < 4.90
1.62 < 1.621
2.4 > 2.39
0.006 < 0.03

Find the product.

```
    7 8 1          4 2 9
  ×   6 0        × 8 0 0
 46,8 6 0      343,2 0 0
```

Solve. Write the equations you use.

Lilian's dog weighs 14.4 pounds. Her cat weighs 5.94 pounds. How much more does her dog weigh than her cat?

```
   1 4.4 0
 −   5.9 4
     8.4 6 lb.
```

Lilian buys 2 cases of cat food. Each case holds 12 cans. Each can holds 3 oz. of cat food. What is the total weight of the cat food?

2 × 12 × 3 = 72 oz.

Unit 4 Answer Key

4.5 Practice

Practice Find the total volume of each solid. Write the equations you use. All measurements are in meters.

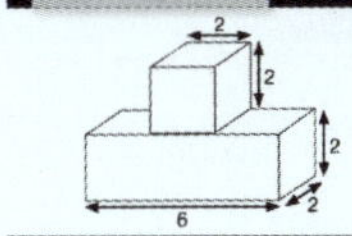

6 × 2 × 2 = 24 cu. m
2 × 2 × 2 = 8 cu. m

Volume: 32 cu. m

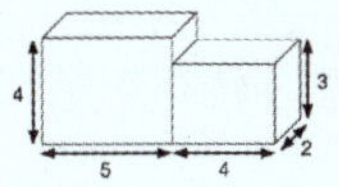

5 × 4 × 2 = 40 cu. m
4 × 3 × 2 = 24 cu. m

Volume: 64 cu. m

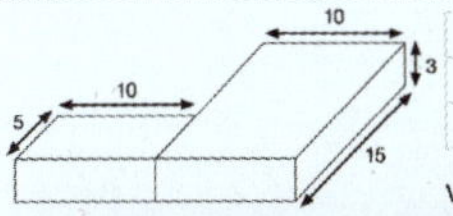

5 × 10 × 3 = 150 cu. m
15 × 10 × 3 = 450 cu. m

Volume: 600 cu. m

Choose dimensions for the shallow end and deep end of a pool. Then, use your dimensions to answer the questions.

	Length (m)	Width (m)	Depth (m)
Shallow End			
Deep End			

Design Your Own Pool!

What is the volume of the shallow end? | What is the volume of the deep end? | What is the total volume of the pool?

Answers will vary.

4.5 Review

Review Find the sum or difference.

$\frac{3}{10} + \frac{4}{10} = \frac{7}{10}$ | $\frac{2}{6} + \frac{3}{6} = \frac{5}{6}$ | $\frac{1}{4} + \frac{2}{4} = \frac{3}{4}$

$\frac{3}{5} - \frac{1}{5} = \frac{2}{5}$ | $\frac{7}{8} - \frac{2}{8} = \frac{5}{8}$ | $\frac{3}{3} - \frac{1}{3} = \frac{2}{3}$

Use the box method to find the product.

	70	4
30	2,100	120
1	70	4

2,100
120
70
+ 4
2,294

74 × 31 = 2,294

Round to the underlined digit.

254,018 ≈ 300,000
254,018 ≈ 250,000
254,018 ≈ 254,000
3.705 ≈ 4
3.705 ≈ 3.7
3.705 ≈ 3.71

Colton counted how many candies were in each pack. Use his data to create a line plot.

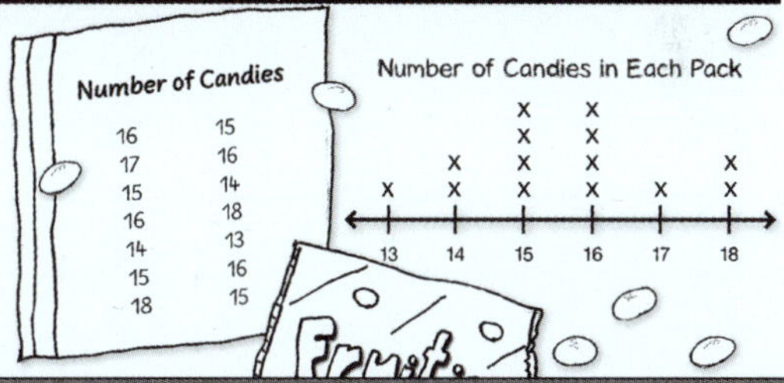

4.6 Practice

Practice Find the volume of each solid. Make sure to include the correct units.

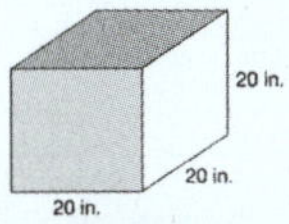

Volume: 8,000 cu. in.

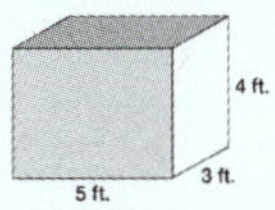

Volume: 60 cu. ft.

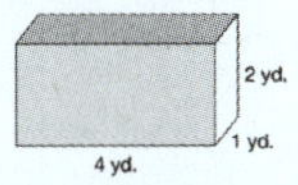

Volume: 8 cu. yd.

Solve. Write the equations you use.

Ahren fills the planter 6 inches high with dirt. What is the volume of the dirt?

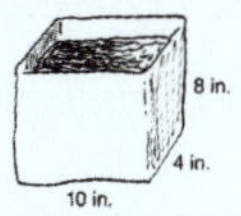

6 × 4 × 10 = 240 cu. in.

Poppy makes a robot sculpture from clay. She makes a 3-inch cube for the head. She makes a 5-inch cube for the body. How many cubic inches of clay does she use?

3 × 3 × 3 = 27 cu. in.
5 × 5 × 5 = 125 cu. in.
27 + 125 = 152 cu. in.

Reagan makes a fort out of cardboard. What is the volume of the fort?

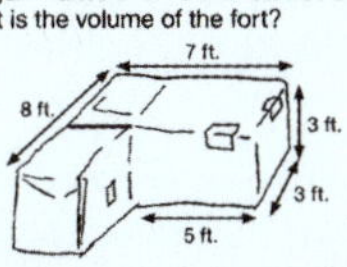

7 × 3 × 3 = 63 cu. ft.
5 × 3 × 2 = 30 cu. ft.
63 + 30 = 93 cu. ft.

4.6 Review

Review Connect each number to its place on the number line.

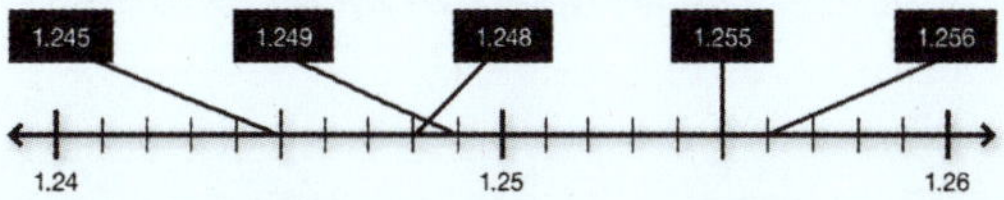

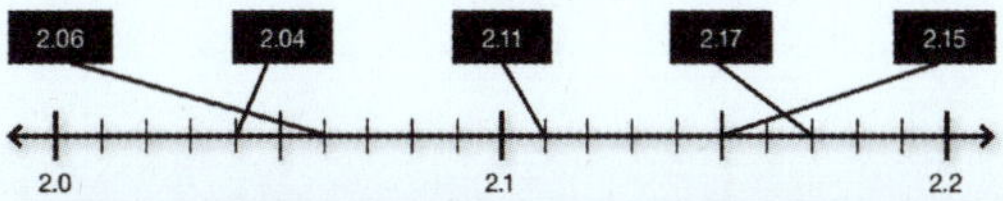

Complete the list of factors.

Factors of 30

1 × 30
2 × 15
3 × 10
5 × 6

Use mental math to complete the missing numbers.

5 + 8 = 9 + 4 | 2 × 8 = 4 × 4

15 − 7 = 10 − 2 | 5 × 4 × 3 = 60

★ 25 × 8 = 200 | ★ 300 × 20 = 6,000

Use the printed protractors to measure the angles.

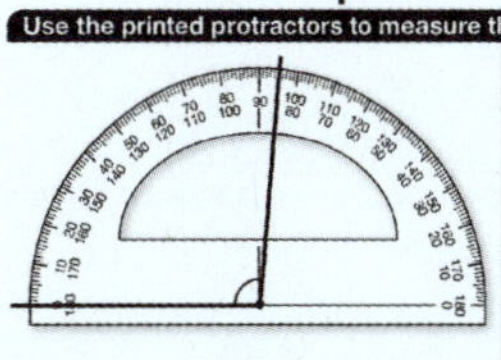

95 °

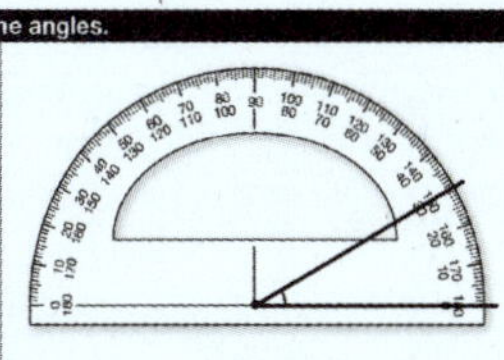

30 °

Unit 4 Answer Key

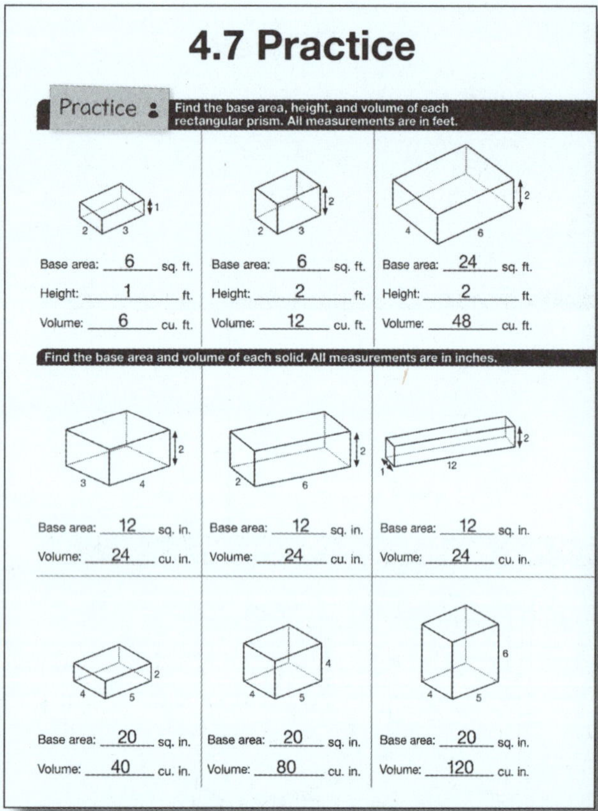

4.7 Practice

Practice: Find the base area, height, and volume of each rectangular prism. All measurements are in feet.

Base area: 6 sq. ft.	Base area: 6 sq. ft.	Base area: 24 sq. ft.
Height: 1 ft.	Height: 2 ft.	Height: 2 ft.
Volume: 6 cu. ft.	Volume: 12 cu. ft.	Volume: 48 cu. ft.

Find the base area and volume of each solid. All measurements are in inches.

Base area: 12 sq. in.	Base area: 12 sq. in.	Base area: 12 sq. in.
Volume: 24 cu. in.	Volume: 24 cu. in.	Volume: 24 cu. in.
Base area: 20 sq. in.	Base area: 20 sq. in.	Base area: 20 sq. in.
Volume: 40 cu. in.	Volume: 80 cu. in.	Volume: 120 cu. in.

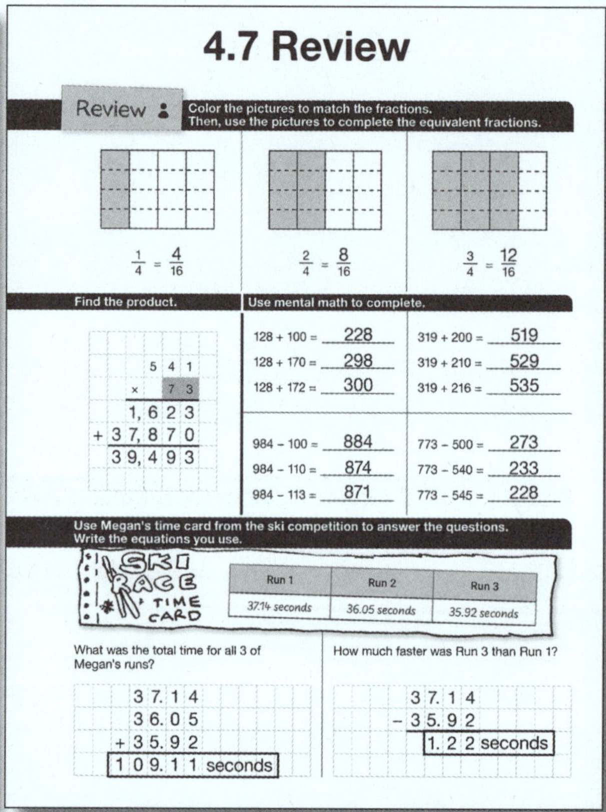

4.7 Review

Review: Color the pictures to match the fractions. Then, use the pictures to complete the equivalent fractions.

$\frac{1}{4} = \frac{4}{16}$ $\frac{2}{4} = \frac{8}{16}$ $\frac{3}{4} = \frac{12}{16}$

Find the product.

541×73: 1,623 + 37,870 = 39,493

Use mental math to complete.

128 + 100 = 228	319 + 200 = 519
128 + 170 = 298	319 + 210 = 529
128 + 172 = 300	319 + 216 = 535
984 − 100 = 884	773 − 500 = 273
984 − 110 = 874	773 − 540 = 233
984 − 113 = 871	773 − 545 = 228

Use Megan's time card from the ski competition to answer the questions. Write the equations you use.

SKI RACE TIME CARD

Run 1	Run 2	Run 3
37.14 seconds	36.05 seconds	35.92 seconds

What was the total time for all 3 of Megan's runs?

37.14 + 36.05 + 35.92 = 109.11 seconds

How much faster was Run 3 than Run 1?

37.14 − 35.92 = 1.22 seconds

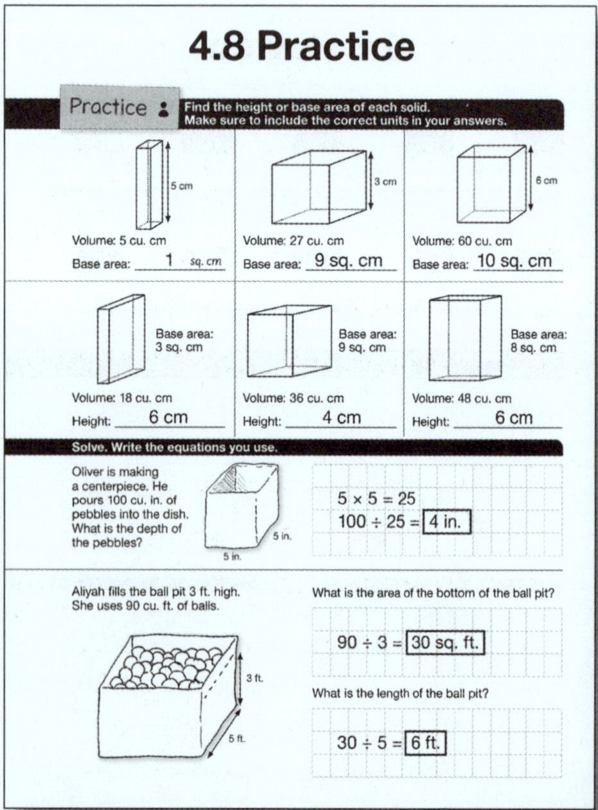

4.8 Practice

Practice: Find the height or base area of each solid. Make sure to include the correct units in your answers.

Volume: 5 cu. cm Base area: 1 sq. cm	Volume: 27 cu. cm Base area: 9 sq. cm	Volume: 60 cu. cm Base area: 10 sq. cm
Base area: 3 sq. cm Volume: 18 cu. cm Height: 6 cm	Base area: 9 sq. cm Volume: 36 cu. cm Height: 4 cm	Base area: 8 sq. cm Volume: 48 cu. cm Height: 6 cm

Solve. Write the equations you use.

Oliver is making a centerpiece. He pours 100 cu. in. of pebbles into the dish. What is the depth of the pebbles?

5 × 5 = 25
100 ÷ 25 = 4 in.

Aliyah fills the ball pit 3 ft. high. She uses 90 cu. ft. of balls.

What is the area of the bottom of the ball pit?

90 ÷ 3 = 30 sq. ft.

What is the length of the ball pit?

30 ÷ 5 = 6 ft.

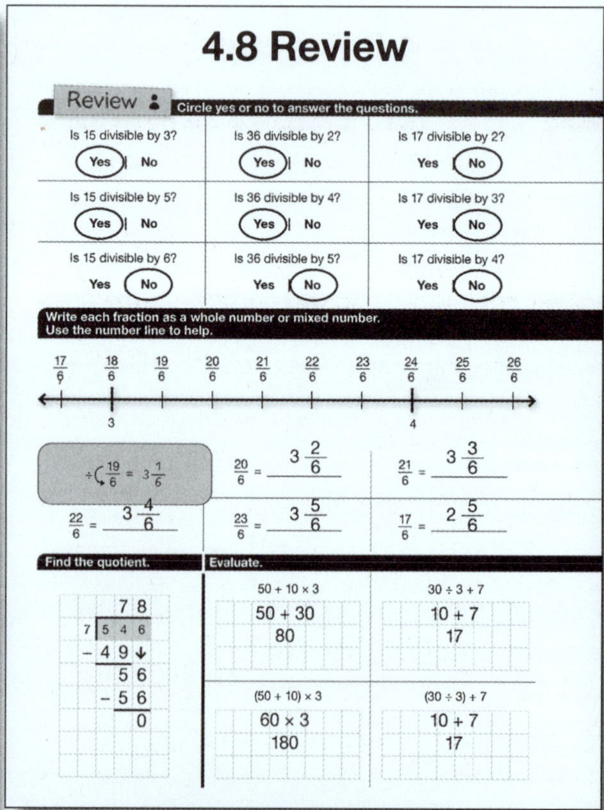

4.8 Review

Review: Circle yes or no to answer the questions.

Is 15 divisible by 3? **Yes**	Is 36 divisible by 2? **Yes**	Is 17 divisible by 2? **No**
Is 15 divisible by 5? **Yes**	Is 36 divisible by 4? **Yes**	Is 17 divisible by 3? **No**
Is 15 divisible by 6? **No**	Is 36 divisible by 5? **No**	Is 17 divisible by 4? **No**

Write each fraction as a whole number or mixed number. Use the number line to help.

$\frac{19}{6} = 3\frac{1}{6}$ $\frac{20}{6} = 3\frac{2}{6}$ $\frac{21}{6} = 3\frac{3}{6}$

$\frac{22}{6} = 3\frac{4}{6}$ $\frac{23}{6} = 3\frac{5}{6}$ $\frac{17}{6} = 2\frac{5}{6}$

Find the quotient.

$546 \div 7 = 78$: 54 − 49 = 5; 56 − 56 = 0

Evaluate.

50 + 10 × 3 50 + 30 80	30 ÷ 3 + 7 10 + 7 17
(50 + 10) × 3 60 × 3 180	(30 ÷ 3) + 7 10 + 7 17

Unit 4 Answer Key

4.9 Unit Wrap-Up A

Unit Wrap-Up — Choose the more sensible measurement for each volume.

Volume of a pool	Volume of a moving box	Volume of a box of rice
15 cu. cm / (15 cu. m)	3 cu. in. / (3 cu. ft.)	(48 cu. in.) / 48 cu. ft.

Find the missing information for each solid. Make sure to include the correct units in your answers.

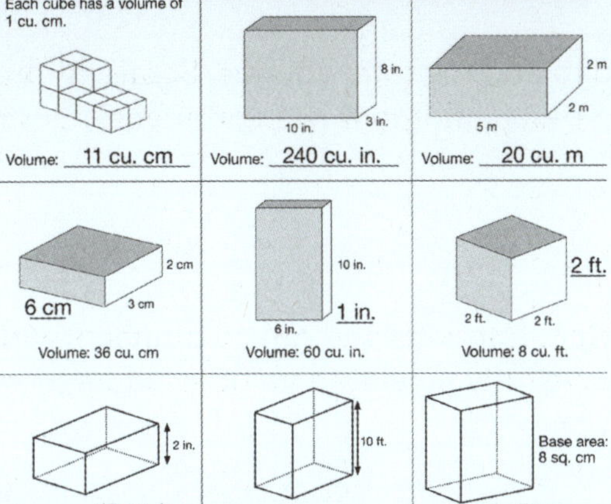

Each cube has a volume of 1 cu. cm.

Volume: 11 cu. cm

Volume: 240 cu. in.

Volume: 20 cu. m

6 cm — Volume: 36 cu. cm

1 in. — Volume: 60 cu. in.

2 ft. — Volume: 8 cu. ft.

Base area: 12 sq. in. — Volume: 24 cu. in.

Base area: 60 sq. ft. — Volume: 600 cu. ft.

Height: 5 cm — Volume: 40 cu. cm

4.9 Unit Wrap-Up B

Unit Wrap-Up — Solve. Write the equations you use.

Zaidee fills the aquarium to a depth of 10 in. What is the volume of the water?

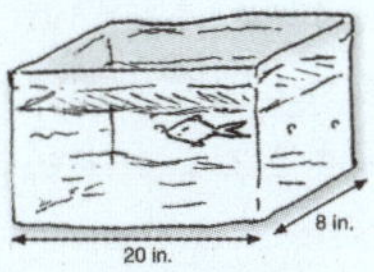

$20 \times 8 \times 10 =$ **1,600 cu. in.**

Quintin builds and sells scratching posts for cats. How many cubic inches of wood does he need for each scratching post?

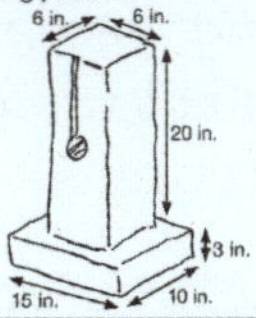

$15 \times 10 \times 3 =$ 450 cu. in.

$6 \times 6 \times 20 =$ 720 cu. in.

$720 + 450 =$ **1,170 cu. in.**

Rose's bedroom has a volume of 1,200 cu. ft. The ceilings are 8 ft. high. What is the area of the floor of her bedroom?

$1{,}200 \div 8 =$ **150 sq. ft.**

★ Rose's bedroom is 10 ft. wide. What is the length of her bedroom?

$150 \div 10 =$ **15 ft.**

Unit 4 Checkpoint

What to Expect at the End of Unit 4

By the end of Unit 4, most children will be able to do the following:

- Understand that volume is the amount of space a solid takes up, and understand that we use cubic units to measure volume.
- Use volume formulas (length × width × height or base area × height) to find volume.
- Divide to find a missing dimension of a rectangular prism.
- Divide to find the base area or height of a rectangular prism. The logic behind this process is quite abstract, and some children will still have trouble fully grasping why this method works.
- Split solids into rectangular prisms and add to find the total volume. Some children will need help breaking these problems into parts, finding missing dimensions, or keeping track of the steps while solving.
- Solve volume word problems.

Is Your Child Ready to Move on?

In Unit 5, your child will learn how to add and subtract fractions and mixed numbers with different denominators. Your child does not need to have fully mastered volume before moving on to Unit 5.

Unit 5
Add and Subtract Fractions and Mixed Numbers with Different Denominators

Overview

In *Fourth Grade Math with Confidence*, your child learned how to find equivalent fractions, use common denominators to compare fractions, and add and subtract fractions or mixed numbers with the same denominator. In this unit, she will combine these skills to add and subtract fractions and mixed numbers with different denominators.

You'll first review equivalent fractions and how to use common denominators to compare fractions. Then, you'll teach your child how to add and subtract fractions and mixed numbers with different denominators.

What Your Child Will Learn

In this unit, your child will learn to:

- Review how to convert mixed numbers to fractions and fractions to mixed numbers
- Review how to multiply to create equivalent fractions and find missing numbers in pairs of equivalent fractions
- Use common denominators to compare fractions with different denominators
- Add and subtract fractions or mixed numbers with different denominators
- Solve fraction and mixed number word problems
- Estimate the answers to mixed number addition and subtraction problems

Lesson List

Lesson 5.1	Review Fractions
Lesson 5.2	Review Mixed Numbers
Lesson 5.3	Review Equivalent Fractions
Lesson 5.4	Use Common Denominators to Compare Fractions
Lesson 5.5	Use Common Denominators to Add Fractions
Lesson 5.6	Use Common Denominators to Subtract Fractions
Lesson 5.7	Add and Subtract with Improper Fractions
Lesson 5.8	Add Mixed Numbers with Different Denominators
Lesson 5.9	Subtract Mixed Numbers with Different Denominators
Lesson 5.10	Estimate Mixed Number Sums and Differences
Lesson 5.11	Enrichment (Optional)

Extra Materials Needed for Unit 5

- Paper clip
- For optional Enrichment Lesson:
    - *How Many Guinea Pigs Can Fit on a Plane?: Answers to Your Most Clever Math Questions*, by Laura Overdeck. Feiwel & Friends, 2017.
    - Ingredients and supplies to make vegetable soup (optional)

Materials Note

You will use fraction bars to help your child visualize and understand fractions in this unit. If you don't own plastic, wooden, or foam fraction bars, you can use the paper fraction bars on Blackline Master 8 instead.

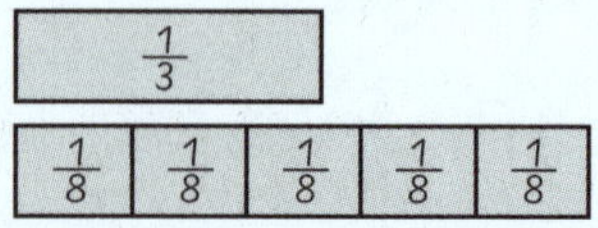

You will also need fraction cards (Blackline Master 9) to play games in this unit. To prepare the cards, copy them on sturdy paper, cut them apart and store them in a bag or envelope. You'll use these later in the year when your child studies fraction multiplication and division, too.

Teaching Math with Confidence: Learning to Organize Written Work in Math

In this unit, your child will learn how to add and subtract fractions and mixed numbers with different denominators. Most children grasp the general process easily. However, they often find the specifics more difficult—especially organizing their written work and keeping track of all the steps. Use these tips to help your child learn to organize her written work in this unit:

- When you demonstrate how to solve practice problems, follow the examples on the Lesson Activities pages carefully and organize your written work in the same way as shown in this Instructor Guide.
- When writing fractions and mixed numbers in the grids on the workbook pages, write the whole numbers so that they overlap two adjacent vertical boxes. Write the fraction bar between two boxes and write the numerator and denominator in the boxes above and below the bar. This makes it easier to visually distinguish the whole numbers from the fractions.

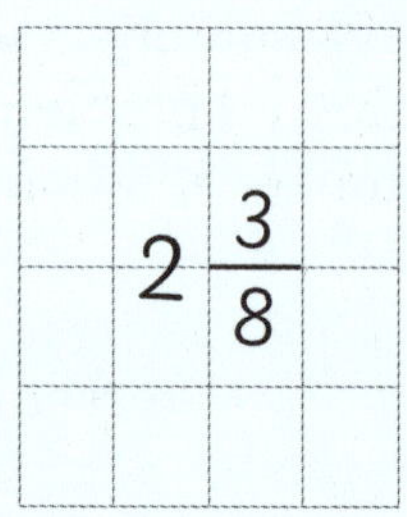

- Fraction and mixed number addition and subtraction problems can be written either horizontally or vertically. In the interest of space, problems involving only fractions are written horizontally in the workbook. If your child finds this confusing or has trouble organizing her work this way, allow her to rewrite the problems vertically on scrap paper. (If you do this, use lined paper turned sideways so that your child has columns to help organize her work.)
- Write equivalent fractions and mixed numbers directly next to the corresponding number, either vertically or horizontally.
- When you check your child's practice pages, check that her written work is organized. Praise any improvement in this area, and hold her accountable as needed. For some children, knowing that they'll have to recopy a messy problem provides all the incentive they need to solve it neatly in the first place.

Just as with other study skills, your child may need lots of direct teaching to learn how to organize her written work. That's okay! Your child's workbook pages don't need to be perfect. But, learning how to solve math problems neatly and carefully is an essential skill for success in math, especially as she moves into pre-algebra and algebra. It's worth the instructional time now to develop this habit.

Lesson 5.1
Review Fractions

Purpose	Materials
• Draw lines to split bars into fractional parts • Write fractions to match fraction bars • Identify fractions that are close to 0, 1/2, or 1 whole	• Fraction bars • Fraction cards (Blackline Master 9)

Memory Work	
	• **What does volume measure?** *The amount of space a solid occupies.* • **What is the formula for the volume of a rectangular prism?** *Multiply length times width times height.*

You will need fraction bars for the first time in this lesson. If you don't own plastic, wooden, or foam fraction bars, you can use the paper fraction bars on Blackline Master 8 instead.

Note that the word *fraction bar* can mean both these hands-on fraction pieces as well as the line we draw between the numerator and denominator in a fraction.

Warm-up (A): Introduce Fraction Bars and Draw Lines to Split Bars into Fractional Parts

We're beginning a unit on fractions today! What are 3 things you remember about fractions from last year? *Answers will vary.*

We will use fraction bars to model fractions in this unit. Show your child your set of fraction bars. **The longest bar stands for one whole. The colored bars show different fractional parts of the whole.** Have your child help you organize the bars by type as shown.

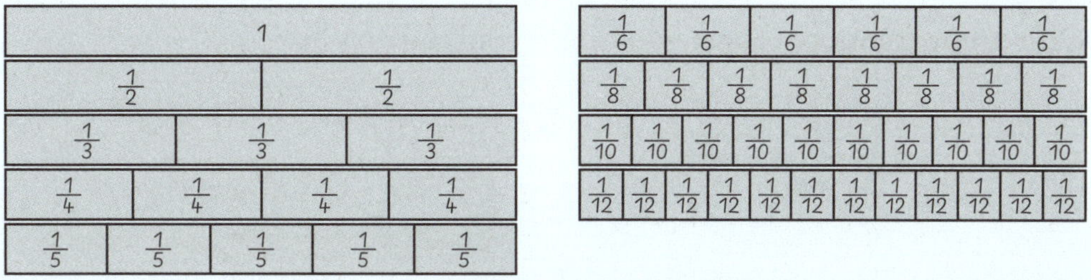

Show your child part A. **We're going to draw lines on these bars to match the fractional parts listed next to them.** Have your child draw a line to split the first bar into halves.

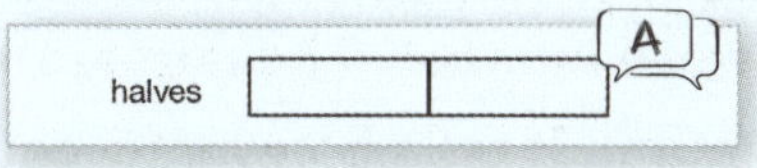

Draw lines on the next bar to divide it into fourths. Have your child first draw a line to divide the bar into 2 equal halves. Then, have her draw 2 more lines to divide each half into 2 equal parts.

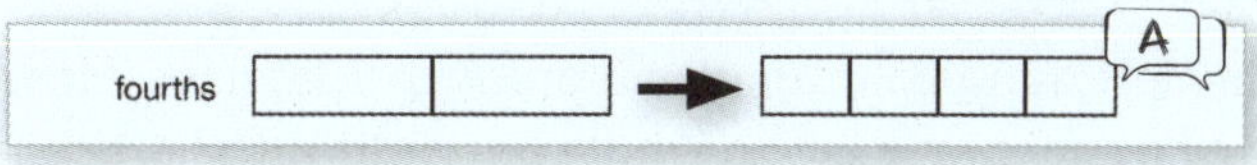

Step 1. Step 2.

Repeat with the next bar. Encourage your child to first divide the bar into halves, then fourths, and finally eighths.

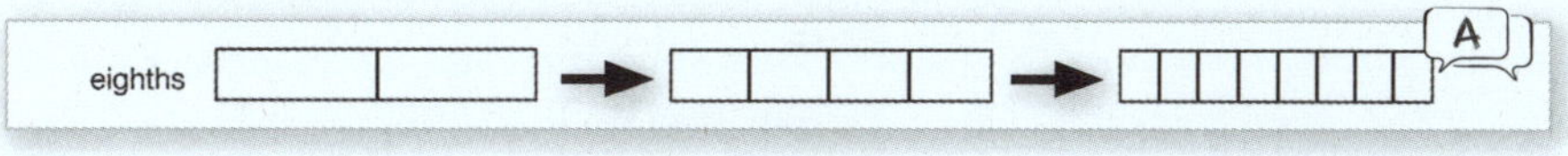

Step 1. Step 2. Step 3.

Draw lines on the next bar to divide it into thirds.

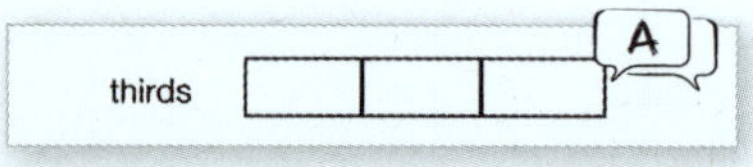

It's okay if the thirds aren't exactly equal to each other.

How many lines did you draw to split the bar into thirds? *2.* **To split a bar into 3 parts, you draw 2 lines. You always draw one line fewer than the number of parts you want to create.**

Draw lines on the next bar to divide it into sixths. Have your child first draw lines to divide the bar into thirds. Then, have her split each third into 2 parts to create sixths.

Step 1. Step 2.

Repeat with the next bar. Encourage your child to first divide the bar into thirds, then sixths, and finally twelfths.

Step 1. Step 2. Step 3.

Drawing the lines in this way (rather than simply drawing lines from left to right across the bar) makes it easier to draw equal parts. It also previews the idea of equivalent fractions. However, any strategy that helps your child divide the bar into roughly-equal pieces is fine. Another good strategy for dividing a bar into twelfths is to divide it into halves, then fourths, and finally twelfths.

After your child finishes splitting the bars into fractional parts, have her find the real fraction bars that match each diagram.

Activity (B): Review Fractions

Today, we'll review fractions. Have your child read the text box.

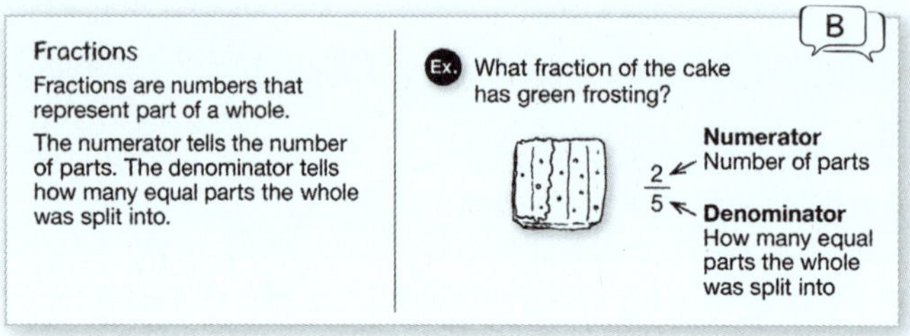

2 is the numerator in this fraction. To remember what the numerator means, think about how numerator starts like the word *number*. The numerator tells the number of parts.

5 is the denominator in this fraction. It tells how many equal parts the whole was split into. Denominator comes from the Latin word "nomen" that means "name." To remember what the denominator means, think about how it names what kind of parts the whole was split into, like fourths, halves, or sixths.

Point to the first bar in the left-hand column of the practice exercises. **How many parts of this bar are colored?** *4.* **How many equal parts is the whole bar split into?** *5.* **So, what fraction of the bar is colored?** *Four-fifths.* Write 4/5 in the blank. Repeat for the next two bars in the column.

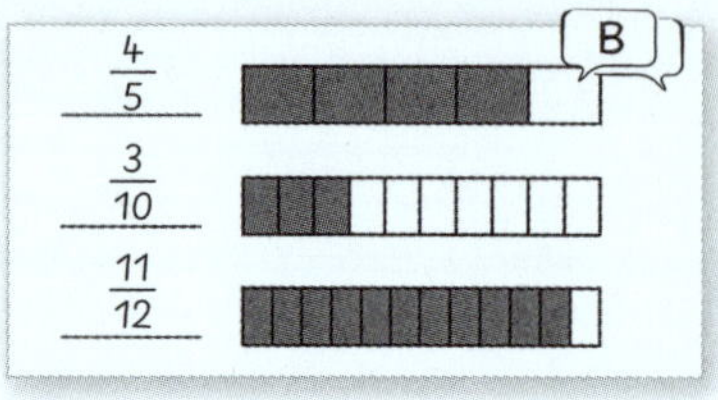

Point to the first bar in the right-hand column of the practice exercises. **To color two-thirds of the bar, first divide it into thirds. Then, color 2 of the parts.** Have your child color the bars to match the printed fractions. Encourage her to divide the bars as evenly as possible, but it's okay if they're not perfect.

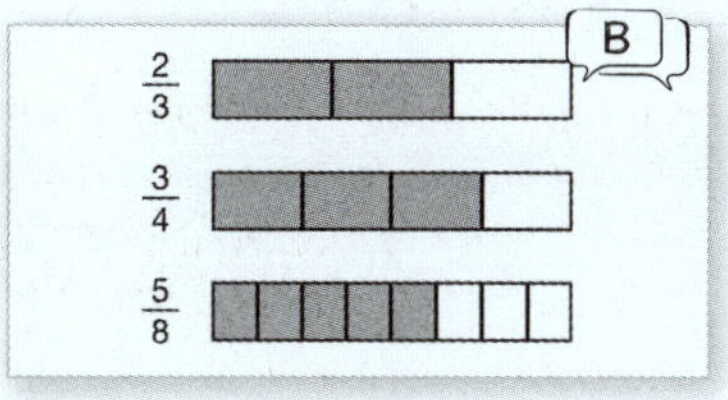

Activity (C): Play Hit the Target

Play Hit the Target.

Hit the Target

Materials: Fraction cards (Blackline Master 9); fraction bars

Object of the Game: Win more points by playing fractions that are closer to the target number than your opponent.

Shuffle the cards and place them face down in one pile. Deal 3 cards to each player.

Hit the Target has 6 rounds. In each round, both players choose one card from their hand and place it face-up on the table. Each player writes their fraction in the score card and models the fraction with fraction bars.

Then, use the fraction bars to determine whose fraction is closer to the target. Whoever's fraction is closer wins a point. If both fractions are equally close to the target, both players win a point.

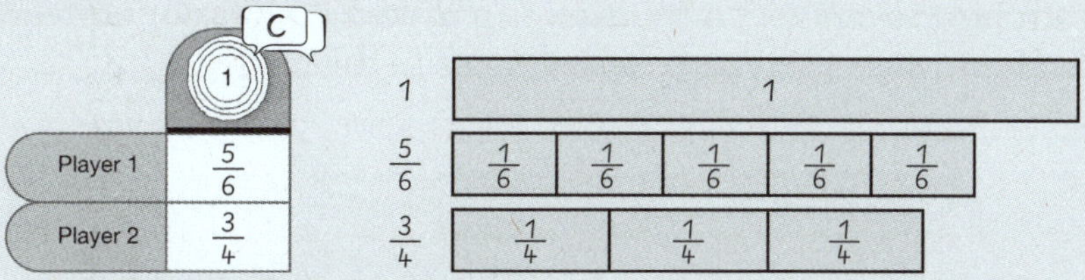

Sample first round. 5/6 is closer to 1 whole than 3/4 is, so Player 1 wins the point.

Each player takes a new card after each round (so that you always have 3 cards in your hand).

Play until you have completed all 6 rounds. Whoever wins more points wins the game.

Independent Practice and Review

Have your child complete the Lesson 5.1 Practice and Review workbook pages.

Lesson 5.2
Review Mixed Numbers

Purpose	Materials
• Practice writing mixed numbers • Review how to convert mixed numbers to improper fractions • Review how to convert improper fractions to mixed numbers	• Counters

Memory Work	
	• **What do we call the top number in a fraction?** *The numerator.* • **What does the numerator tell?** *The number of parts.* • **What do we call the bottom number in a fraction?** *The denominator.* • **What does the denominator tell?** *How many equal parts the whole was split into.*

Warm-up (A): Practice Writing Mixed Numbers

We'll review mixed numbers today. A mixed number is a combination of a whole number and a fraction. Have your child write a mixed number to match each diagram.

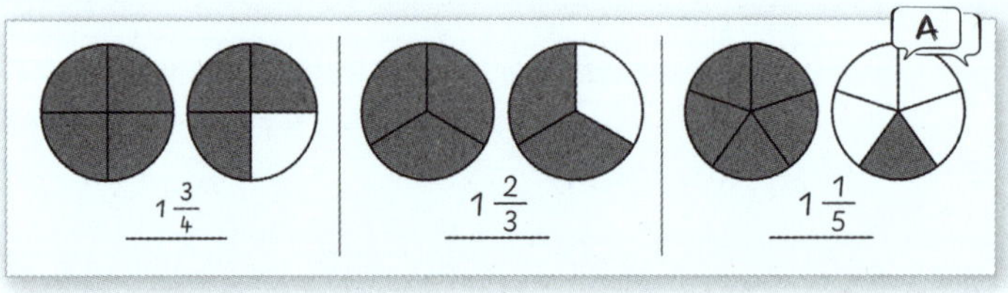

Activity (B): Review Improper Fractions and Mixed Numbers

Today, we'll review how to convert a fraction to a mixed number or convert a mixed number to a fraction. Have your child read the examples in the text box.

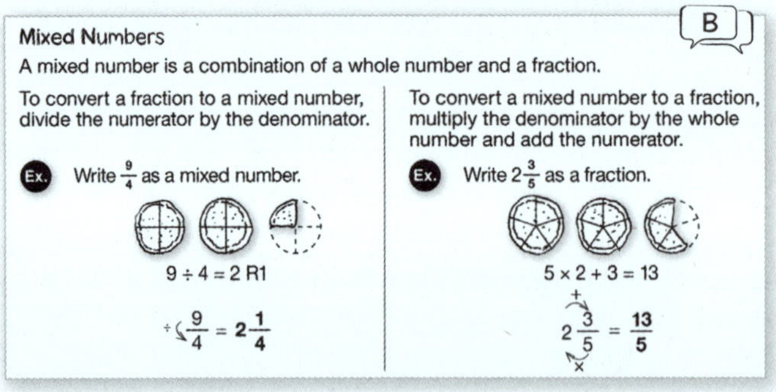

The first example shows how to convert nine-fourths to a mixed number.

How does the picture show that nine-fourths equals 2 and one-fourth? *Sample answer: Each slice of pizza is one-fourth of a pizza, and there are 9 slices. Each group of four-fourths equals 1 whole pizza, so nine-fourths equals 2 whole pizzas plus one-fourth of a pizza.*

One way to remember that you divide to convert fractional parts to mixed numbers is to think of this rhyme: ***Parts to whole? Division's in control!*** **This means that if you have fractional parts that you want to convert to a mixed number, start by dividing.**

The second example shows how to convert 2 and three-fifths to a fraction.

How does the picture show that 2 and three-fifths equals thirteen-fifths? *Sample answer: There are 2 whole pizzas plus three-fifths of a pizza. The 2 wholes each equal five-fifths. If you add up all the fifths, you get thirteen-fifths.*

One way to remember that you multiply to convert mixed numbers to fractions is to think of this rhyme: *Whole to parts? Multiply to start!* This means that if you have whole numbers that you want to convert to fractional parts, start by multiplying. Then, add on any extra fractional parts.

Remember, we can also call fractions like nine-fourths or twelve-fifths *improper fractions.* In improper fractions, the numerator is greater than or equal to the denominator. They're equal to or greater than 1 whole.

Fractions like two-thirds or one-tenth are called proper fractions. In *proper fractions,* the numerator is less than the denominator. They're less than 1 whole.

We see proper fractions more often in everyday life. But there's nothing wrong with improper fractions! They can be very helpful when you add, subtract, multiply, or divide fractions.
Have your child convert the fractions to mixed numbers and the mixed numbers to fractions.

$\frac{6}{5} = 1\frac{1}{5}$	$\frac{8}{5} = 1\frac{3}{5}$	$1\frac{1}{12} = \frac{13}{12}$	$1\frac{1}{4} = \frac{5}{4}$

B

Activity (C): Play Four in a Row

Play Four in a Row.

Four in a Row

Materials: 12 counters per player, with a different color for each player

Object of the Game: Be the first player to place counters in 4 boxes in a row, either horizontally, vertically, or diagonally.

On your turn, choose a mixed number on the game board. Find the matching fraction. Use 2 counters to cover both boxes. For example, if you choose 2 4/5 as your mixed number, cover both 2 4/5 and 14/5 with counters. Play then passes to the other player.

One box in the game (1 4/10) does not have a match. Neither player may play a counter on this box.

Continue until one player covers 4 boxes in a row, either horizontally, vertically, or diagonally.

Answer Key:

$3\frac{1}{2} = \frac{7}{2}$	$\frac{23}{12} = 1\frac{11}{12}$	$2\frac{5}{12} = \frac{29}{12}$	$\frac{27}{10} = 2\frac{7}{10}$	$2\frac{3}{6} = \frac{15}{6}$
$\frac{11}{8} = 1\frac{3}{8}$	$1\frac{3}{10} = \frac{13}{10}$	$\frac{7}{3} = 2\frac{1}{3}$	$1\frac{5}{6} = \frac{11}{6}$	$\frac{14}{5} = 2\frac{4}{5}$
$2\frac{7}{10} = \frac{27}{10}$	$\frac{11}{6} = 1\frac{5}{6}$	$3\frac{3}{4} = \frac{15}{4}$	$\frac{29}{12} = 2\frac{5}{12}$	$1\frac{3}{8} = \frac{11}{8}$
$\frac{15}{4} = 3\frac{3}{4}$	$2\frac{1}{3} = \frac{7}{3}$	$\frac{7}{2} = 3\frac{1}{2}$	$2\frac{7}{8} = \frac{23}{8}$	$\frac{13}{10} = 1\frac{3}{10}$
$2\frac{4}{5} = \frac{14}{5}$	$\frac{23}{8} = 2\frac{7}{8}$	$1\frac{11}{12} = \frac{23}{12}$	$\frac{15}{6} = 2\frac{3}{6}$	$1\frac{4}{10}$ *has no match*

Independent Practice and Review

Have your child complete the Lesson 5.2 Practice and Review workbook pages.

Lesson 5.3
Review Equivalent Fractions

Purpose	Materials
• Review equivalent fractions • Review how to multiply the numerator and denominator of a fraction by the same number to create an equivalent fraction • Review how to find missing numerators or denominators in pairs of equivalent fractions	• Fraction bars

Memory Work	
	• **What do we call numbers that have a whole number and a fraction?** *Mixed numbers.* • **What do we call a fraction whose numerator is greater than or equal to its denominator?** *An improper fraction.*

Warm-up: Review Equivalent Fractions with Fraction Bars

Today, we'll review equivalent fractions. What do you remember about equivalent fractions? *Sample answer: They look different but mean the same thing.*

Equivalent fractions are fractions that have different numerators and denominators but have the same value. Arrange fraction bars as shown to represent 2/6 and 1/3. Place the 1 whole bar on the table as well. **One-third and two-sixths are equivalent. They both represent the same amount of the whole bar, even though they have different numerators and denominators.**

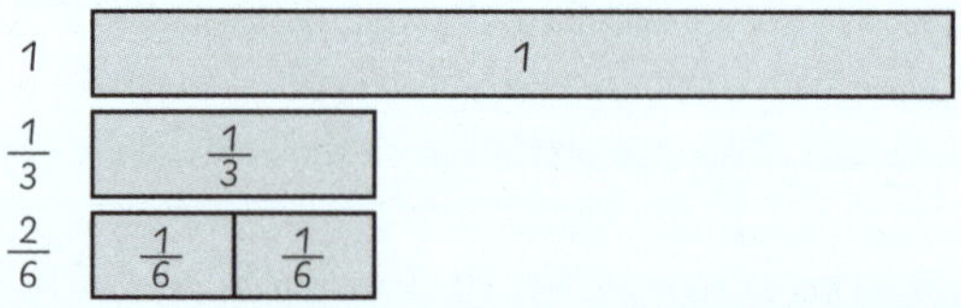

Arrange fraction bars as shown to represent 3/4 and 7/8. **Are three-fourths and seven-eighths equivalent?** *No.* **How do you know?** *Sample answer: Seven-eighths looks bigger than three-fourths.*

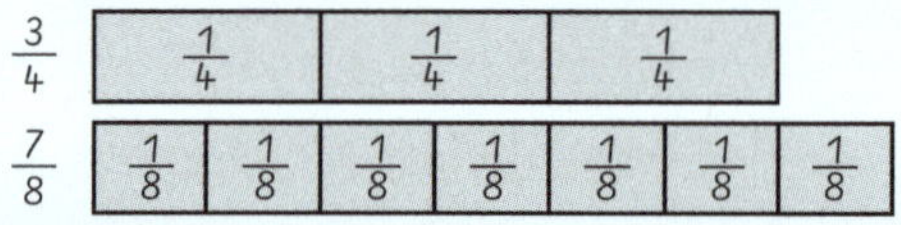

Three-fourths and seven-eighths are not equivalent. They don't represent the same amount of the whole bar.

Have your child experiment with the fraction bars to find 2 fractions equivalent to 3/4. She should find that 6/8 and 9/12 are both equivalent to 3/4.

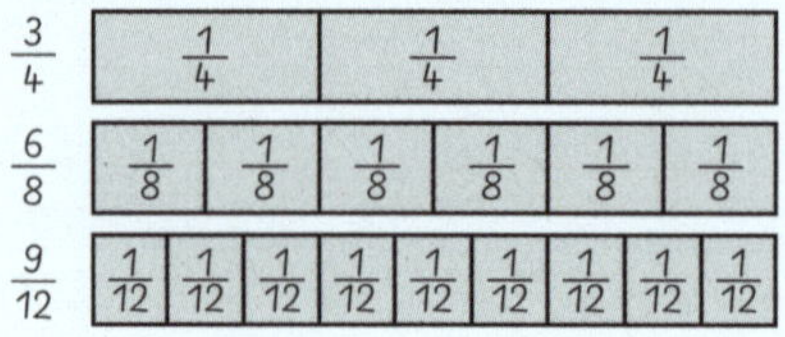

Activity (A): Review Multiplying to Find Equivalent Fractions

Now, let's review how to multiply to find equivalent fractions. Have your child read the text box.

A

Equivalent Fractions

Equivalent fractions are fractions that have different numerators and denominators but are equal to the same value.

One way to create an equivalent fraction is to make each fractional part into more equal parts. Multiply the numerator and denominator by the same number to find the equivalent fraction.

Ex. Trina has $\frac{1}{2}$ of a pizza.
She cuts the pizza into 4 equal slices.
What equivalent fraction does she create?

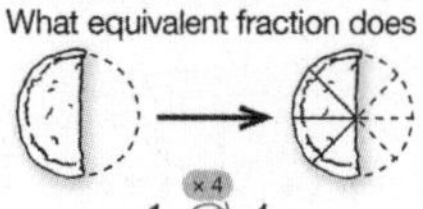

$$\frac{1}{2} \overset{\times 4}{=} \frac{4}{8}$$

Use the following questions to discuss the example problem.

- **Trina cuts one-half of the pizza into 4 equal parts.** Point to the "×4" above and below the equals sign. **4 is the multiplier in this problem. We multiply both the numerator and denominator by the multiplier to find the equivalent fraction.**
- Point to the numerators in both fractions: **1 times 4 equals 4.**
- Point to the denominators in both fractions: **2 times 4 equals 8.**
- **One-half equals four-eighths. Whether you have one-half of a pizza or four-eighths of a pizza, you have the same amount of pizza either way.**

When you multiply whole numbers, the product is always greater than either of the numbers. That's not always true when it comes to fractions! When you multiply the numerator and denominator by the same number, you don't change the value of the fraction.

It's like when you convert measurements. When you convert 2 feet to inches, you multiply 2 by 12 to get 24 inches. You don't make the measurement larger. You just change the units you use to describe it. 2 feet is equivalent to 24 inches, just like one-half is equivalent to four-eighths.

In Unit 10, your child will learn how to multiply fractions. She'll discover that multiplying the numerator and denominator by the same number is equivalent to multiplying the fraction by 1 whole. Any number times 1 equals the original number, so the value of the fraction doesn't change.

$$\frac{1}{4} \times \frac{3}{3} = \frac{3}{12}$$

Demonstrate how to complete the first practice problem.

- **Three-fourths of the bar is shaded.**
- **Each fourth becomes 3 equal parts, so the multiplier is 3.**
- Point to the numerator. **3 parts times 3 equals 9 parts. The 3 shaded parts become 9 shaded parts.**
- Point to the denominator. **4 parts times 3 equals 12 parts. Each part is one-twelfth of the bar.**
- **So, three-fourths equals nine-twelfths.**

A

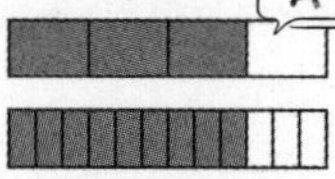

$$\frac{3}{4} \overset{\times 3}{=} \frac{9}{12}$$

If your child is confused, model both fractions with fraction bars to make the problem more concrete.

$\frac{3}{4}$	$\frac{1}{4}$	$\frac{1}{4}$	$\frac{1}{4}$						
$\frac{9}{12}$	$\frac{1}{12}$	$\frac{1}{12}$	$\frac{1}{12}$	$\frac{1}{12}$	$\frac{1}{12}$	$\frac{1}{12}$	$\frac{1}{12}$	$\frac{1}{12}$	$\frac{1}{12}$

Have your child complete the other two pairs of equivalent fractions in the same way.

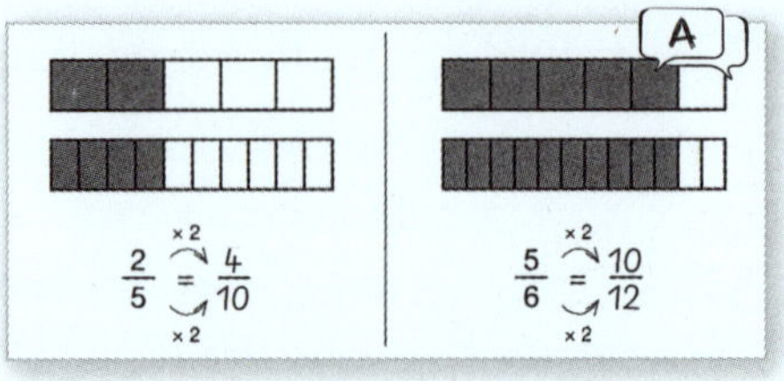

Activity (B): Find Missing Numbers in Equivalent Fractions

In part B, we'll use fraction squares to find missing numerators or denominators in pairs of equivalent fractions.

> Fraction squares provide more options for the denominator than fraction bars, so you'll use them for equivalent fraction problems with larger numbers.

In the first example, two-thirds of the fraction square is colored. The denominator for the equivalent fraction is 12. We need to find the numerator.

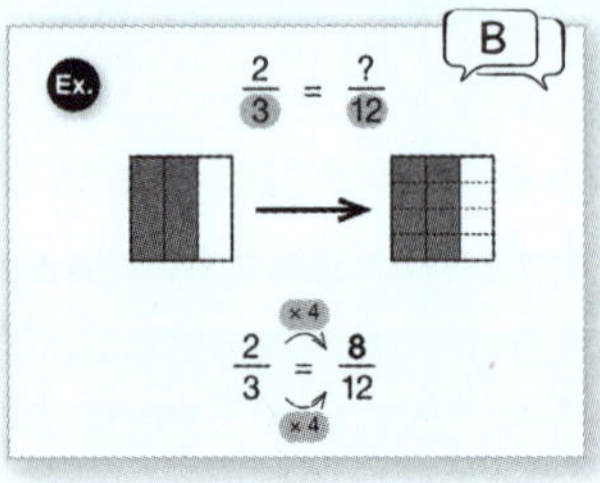

- **First, we find the multiplier. 3 times what equals 12?** *4.* **3 times 4 equals 12, so 4 is the multiplier.**
- **Each part became 4 equal parts. So, we have to multiply the numerator by 4. 2 times 4 equals 8, so the numerator is 8. Two-thirds equals eight-twelfths.**

In the second example, two-fifths of the fraction square is colored. The numerator for the equivalent fraction is 6. We need to find the denominator.

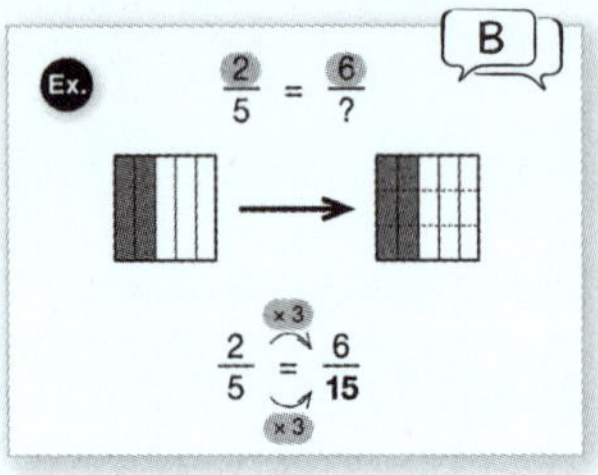

- **First, we find the multiplier. 2 times what equals 6?** *3.* **2 times 3 equals 6, so 3 is the multiplier.**
- **Each part became 3 equal parts. So, we have to multiply the denominator by 3. 5 times 3 equals 15, so the denominator is 15. Two-fifths equals six-fifteenths.**

Demonstrate how to solve the first practice problem.

- **First, we find the multiplier. 1 times what equals 2?** *2.* **1 times 2 equals 2, so 2 is the multiplier.** Write "×2" above and below the equals sign in the problem. Draw 1 horizontal line across the printed fraction square to match.
- **Each part becomes 2 equal parts, so we multiply the denominator by 2. What's 3 times 2?** *6.* Write 6 as the denominator. **One-third equals two-sixths.**

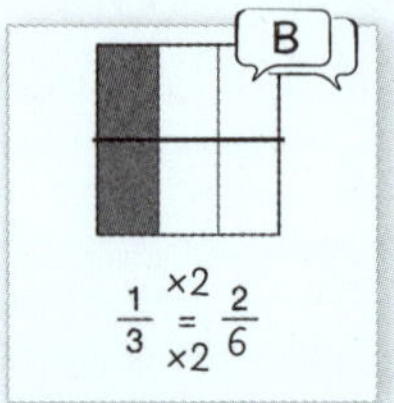

Have your child complete the other practice problems in the same way. After she finds the multiplier, have her draw horizontal lines on each fraction square to match.

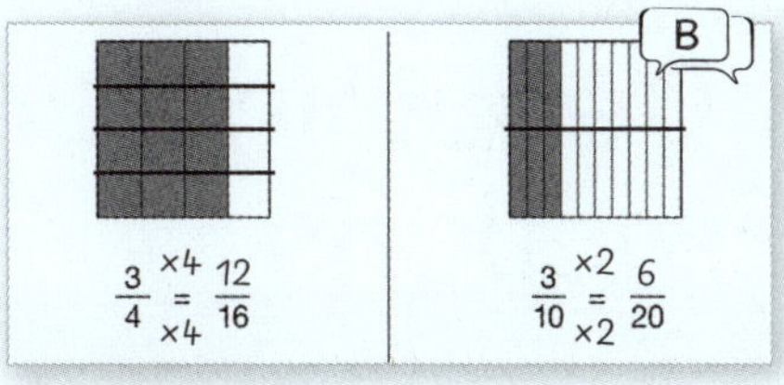

Activity (C): Play Fill the Fractions

In this game, you win as many points as the number you write. Keep that in mind as you choose which puzzles to complete!

Play Fill the Fractions. As your child solves each problem, have her first find the multiplier and write it above and below the equal sign. Then, have her multiply to find the missing number.

Fill the Fractions

Materials: None

Object of the Game: Complete equivalent fractions to win the most points.

Start a scorecard on a separate piece of paper. Choose who will go first.

On your turn, choose a puzzle on the gameboard. Find the missing number in the equivalent fraction. The missing number is your score. Add this score to your previous total.

For example, if you complete the following problem on your first turn, you score 21 points.

$$\frac{7}{8} \overset{\times 3}{\underset{\times 3}{=}} \frac{21}{24}$$

John	Mom
21	

Take turns until all problems have been completed. Whoever has the higher total score wins the game.

Answer Key:

$\frac{7}{8} = \frac{21}{24}$	$\frac{1}{2} = \frac{8}{16}$	$\frac{4}{5} = \frac{20}{25}$
$\frac{2}{5} = \frac{8}{20}$	$\frac{3}{8} = \frac{9}{24}$	$\frac{5}{12} = \frac{10}{24}$
$\frac{1}{3} = \frac{10}{30}$	$\frac{6}{10} = \frac{12}{20}$	$\frac{9}{12} = \frac{18}{24}$
$\frac{2}{3} = \frac{10}{15}$	$\frac{3}{6} = \frac{9}{18}$	$\frac{1}{2} = \frac{20}{40}$

Independent Practice and Review

Have your child complete the Lesson 5.3 Practice and Review workbook pages.

Lesson 5.4
Use Common Denominators to Compare Fractions

Purpose	Materials
• Learn a simpler way to find least common multiples • Use least common multiples to find common denominators • Use common denominators to compare fractions with different denominators	• Fraction bars • Fraction cards

Memory Work • **What does LCM stand for?** *Least common multiple.*

Warm-up (A): Learn a Simpler Way to Find Least Common Multiples

In Unit 3, you learned how to find least common multiples. One way is to make a list of the multiples of both numbers and then look for the lowest multiple they have in common.

Another way is to make a list of multiples of the larger number and check whether each is also a multiple of the smaller number. Demonstrate how to use this approach to find the LCM of 5 and 2.

- **5 is the larger number, so I'll start a list of the multiples of 5.**
- **The first multiple is 5.** Write 5 as shown. **5 is not a multiple of 2, so it's not the LCM. The second multiple is 10.** Write 10 as shown. **10 is also a multiple of 2, so 10 is the least common multiple.** Write 10 in the answer blank.

Have your child use this approach to find the least common multiple for each pair of numbers.

LCM of 5 and 2: *10*	LCM of 4 and 8: *8*	LCM of 4 and 10: *20* (A)
5, 10	*8*	*10, 20*

You'll need to find a lot of least common multiples in this lesson and in the rest of this unit. When the numbers are small, you may even be able to find the least common multiple mentally. Just think of the multiples of the larger number, and then check whether each multiple is also a multiple of the smaller number.

If your child has trouble finding multiples mentally, he may make lists of multiples on scrap paper instead.

Activity (B): Use Common Denominators to Compare Fractions

What does it mean when two people have something in common? *Sample answer: It means they are interested in the same things or have the same background.* Name a friend or family member and describe something your child has in common with that person. For example: **You and Brian both love to play basketball. That's something you have in common.**

When two fractions have a common denominator, it means they both have the same denominator. They have the denominator in common. We use common denominators to make it easier to compare fractions. Have your child read the text box.

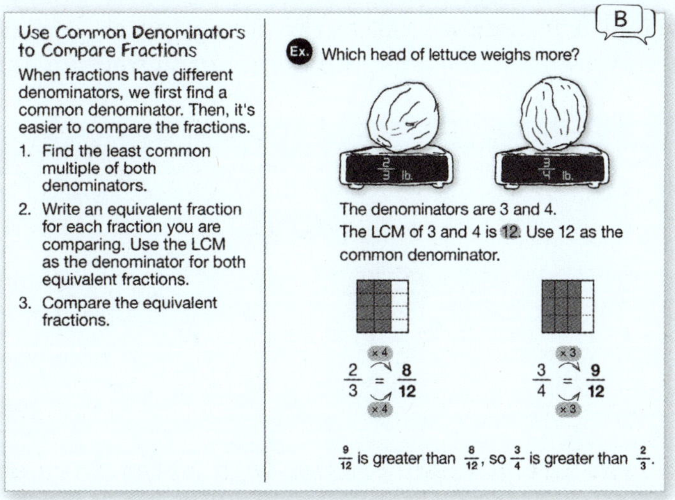

B

Use Common Denominators to Compare Fractions

When fractions have different denominators, we first find a common denominator. Then, it's easier to compare the fractions.

1. Find the least common multiple of both denominators.
2. Write an equivalent fraction for each fraction you are comparing. Use the LCM as the denominator for both equivalent fractions.
3. Compare the equivalent fractions.

Ex. Which head of lettuce weighs more?

The denominators are 3 and 4.
The LCM of 3 and 4 is 12. Use 12 as the common denominator.

$\frac{2}{3} = \frac{8}{12}$ (× 4)

$\frac{3}{4} = \frac{9}{12}$ (× 3)

$\frac{9}{12}$ is greater than $\frac{8}{12}$, so $\frac{3}{4}$ is greater than $\frac{2}{3}$.

Let's study the example to see how to use common denominators to compare fractions.

- **We want to find which head of lettuce weighs more. One weighs two-thirds of a pound, and the other weighs three-fourths of a pound.**
- **The first step is to find the least common multiple of the denominators. The denominators are 3 and 4. The least common multiple of 3 and 4 is 12.**
- **Next, we write equivalent fractions for both of the fractions we want to compare. We use the least common multiple as the common denominator. What fraction is equivalent to two-thirds?** *Eight-twelfths.* **What fraction is equivalent to three-fourths?** *Nine-twelfths.*
- **Which is greater, eight-twelfths or nine-twelfths?** *Nine-twelfths.* **So, three-fourths is greater than two-thirds.**

If your child has trouble understanding the fraction square diagrams, use fraction bars to model the sample problem.

$\frac{2}{3}$	$\frac{1}{3}$	$\frac{1}{3}$

$\frac{8}{12}$	$\frac{1}{12}$	$\frac{1}{12}$	$\frac{1}{12}$	$\frac{1}{12}$	$\frac{1}{12}$	$\frac{1}{12}$	$\frac{1}{12}$	$\frac{1}{12}$

$\frac{3}{4}$	$\frac{1}{4}$	$\frac{1}{4}$	$\frac{1}{4}$

$\frac{9}{12}$	$\frac{1}{12}$	$\frac{1}{12}$	$\frac{1}{12}$	$\frac{1}{12}$	$\frac{1}{12}$	$\frac{1}{12}$	$\frac{1}{12}$	$\frac{1}{12}$	$\frac{1}{12}$

8/12 is less than 9/12, so 2/3 is less than 3/4.

In the first problem, we want to find which apple weighs more. How much does each apple weigh? *Two-fifths of a pound and one-half of a pound.* Have your child model each fraction with fraction bars as shown. **Which is greater, one-half or two-fifths?** *One-half.*

$\frac{2}{5}$	$\frac{1}{5}$	$\frac{1}{5}$

$\frac{1}{2}$	$\frac{1}{2}$

We don't always have fraction bars handy when we need to solve fraction problems, so it's important to be able to compare fractions with common denominators. Let's practice with this pair of fractions.

The first step is to find the least common multiple of the denominators. What are the denominators in these fractions? *5 and 2.* **In the warm-up, we found that the least common multiple of 5 and 2 is 10.**

Next, we write equivalent fractions with 10 as the denominator. Write a fraction bar below each fraction as shown. Write 10 as the denominator for each fraction and leave the numerators blank.

Point to 2/5. **I want to write an equivalent fraction with tenths. 5 times what equals 10?** *2.* Point to the 5 and 10 as you name them. **So, I use 2 as the multiplier for the numerator, too. What's 2 times 2?** *4.* Write 4 as the numerator. Place 4 tenths-bars under the 2 fifths-bars to confirm your child's answer. **Two-fifths equals four-tenths.**

Point to 1/2. **I want to write an equivalent fraction with tenths. 2 times what equals 10?** *5.* Point to the 2 and 10 as you name them. **So, I use 5 as the multiplier for the numerator. What's 1 times 5?** *5.* Write 5 as the numerator. Place 5 tenths-bars under the 1 half-bar to confirm that the fractions are equivalent. **One-half equals five-tenths.**

Which is greater, four-tenths or five-tenths? *Five-tenths.* **So, which is greater, two-fifths or one-half?** *One half.* Write < in the circle to complete the problem.

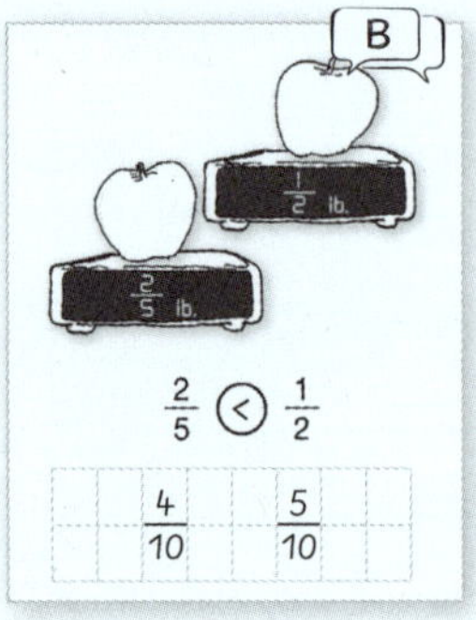

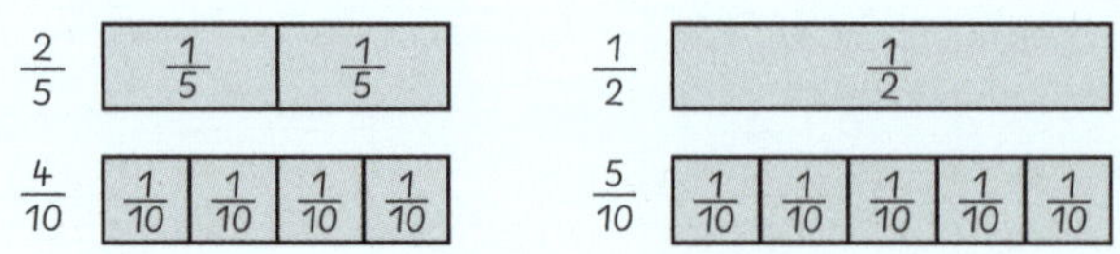

Have your child compare the weights of the tomatoes and garlic in the same way. Have him write out the equivalent fractions for each problem. Use fraction bars to model the problems as needed.

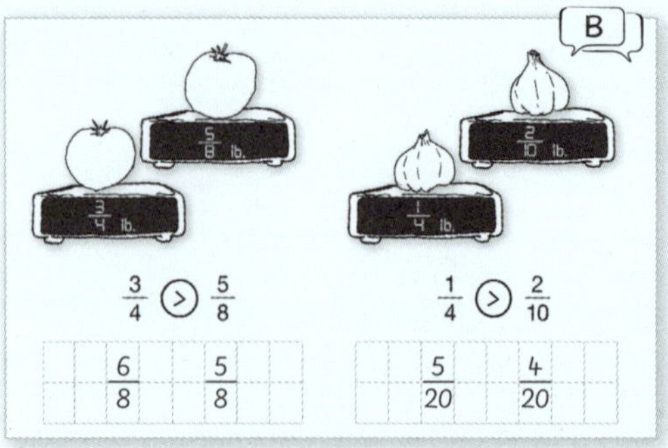

Activity (C): Play Fraction War

Play Fraction War.

Fraction War

Materials: Fraction cards with 2, 3, 4, 6, or 12 as the denominator (22 cards total)

Object of the Game: Win more points by playing greater fractions.

Shuffle the cards and place them face down in one pile.

Fraction War has 5 rounds. In each round, each player turns over a card from the pile and places it face-up on the table. Each player writes their fraction in the score card.

Then, have your child find a common denominator for the two fractions. Each player writes an equivalent fraction with the common denominator. Whoever has played the greater fraction wins a point.

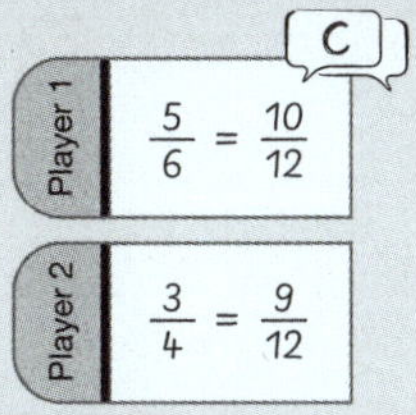

Sample round. The common denominator is 12, and the equivalent fractions are 10/12 and 9/12. 10/12 is greater than 9/12, so 5/6 is greater than 3/4. Player 1 wins the point.

Play until you have completed all 5 rounds. Whoever wins more points wins the game.

Independent Practice and Review

Have your child complete the Lesson 5.4 Practice and Review workbook pages.

Lesson 5.5
Use Common Denominators to Add Fractions

Purpose	Materials
• Review adding fractions with the same denominator • Use common denominators to add fractions with different denominators	• Fraction bars • Fraction cards

Memory Work
- **What is the order of operations?** *Parentheses, multiply or divide from left to right, add or subtract from left to right.*

Warm-up (A): Review Adding Fractions with the Same Denominator

Last year, you learned how to add fractions with the same denominator. Have your child complete the fraction addition problems.

A

$\frac{3}{8} + \frac{2}{8} = \frac{5}{8}$ | $\frac{6}{10} + \frac{3}{10} = \frac{9}{10}$ | $\frac{4}{12} + \frac{1}{12} = \frac{5}{12}$

If your child doesn't remember how to add fractions with the same denominator, model the fractions with fraction bars. Remind her to add the numerators and keep the denominators the same: **Just like 3 books plus 2 books equals 5 books, 3 eighths plus 2 eighths equals 5 eighths.**

$\frac{1}{8}$	$\frac{1}{8}$	$\frac{1}{8}$		$\frac{1}{8}$	$\frac{1}{8}$

$\frac{3}{8} + \frac{2}{8} = \frac{5}{8}$

Activity (B): Use Common Denominators to Add Fractions

In the warm-up, the fractions in each problem had the same denominator. Today, you'll learn how to add fractions with different denominators.

Adding fractions with different denominators is a lot like adding fractions with the same denominator. We just find equivalent fractions with a common denominator first. Have your child read the text box.

B

How to Use Common Denominators to Add Fractions

1. Find the least common multiple (LCM) of both denominators. You will use this number for the common denominator.
2. Rewrite each fraction as an equivalent fraction with the common denominator.
3. Add the fractions.

Ex. $\frac{2}{3} + \frac{1}{6} = ?$

The denominators are 3 and 6.
The LCM of 3 and 6 is 6.
So, use 6 as the common denominator.

$\frac{2}{3} + \frac{1}{6}$

$\downarrow \quad \downarrow$

$\frac{4}{6} + \frac{1}{6} = \frac{5}{6}$

Read aloud the example problem: ***Two-thirds plus one-sixth equals what?***

- Point to the pizza. **There is two-thirds of a cheese pizza and one-sixth of a pepperoni pizza. We want to add two-thirds and one-sixth to find the total amount of pizza.**
- **The first step is to find the least common multiple of the denominators. What are the denominators for these fractions?** *3 and 6.* **What is the least common multiple of 3 and 6?** *6.*
- **The second step is to rewrite each fraction with the common denominator. Two-thirds equal how many sixths?** *4.* **If you cut each third into 2 slices, you get four-sixths of a pizza. One-sixth already has 6 as its denominator.**

- **The last step is to add. What's four-sixths plus one-sixth?** *Five-sixths.* **There is a total of five-sixths of a pizza.**

You've learned in younger grades that we always add "like to like." When you add whole numbers, you add ones to ones and tens to tens. When you add measurements, you add feet to feet and inches to inches, or meters to meters and centimeters to centimeters.

Adding fractions with different denominators is the same. We can't add thirds to sixths. We first have to convert the thirds to sixths.

Demonstrate how to solve the first practice problem.

- **We want to add one-fourth and three-eighths.** Model the problem with fraction bars as shown.

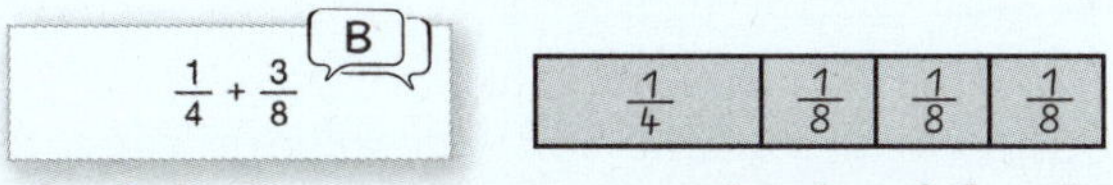

- **The first step is to find the least common multiple of the denominators. What are the denominators for these fractions?** *4 and 8.* **What is the least common multiple of 4 and 8?** *8.* **So, we'll use 8 as the common denominator.**
- **The second step is to rewrite each fraction with the common denominator.** Begin to rewrite the fractions as shown below the printed problem. Leave the numerators blank.

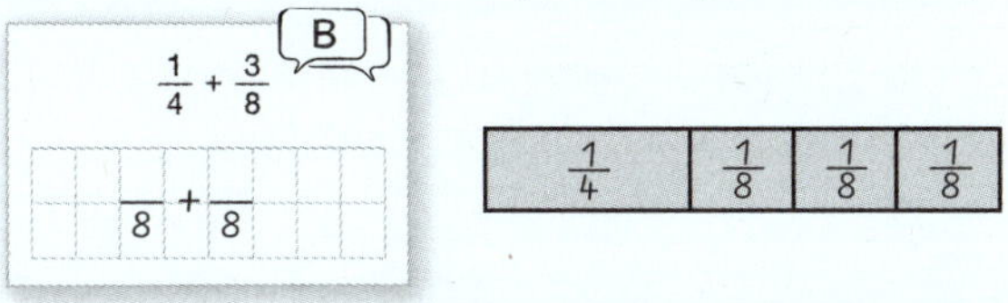

- **One-fourth equals how many eighths?** *2.* Write 2 as the numerator for the first fraction. Replace the 1 fourths-bar with 2 eighths-bars. **One-fourth equals two-eighths. Three-eighths already has 8 as a denominator.** Write 3 as the numerator for the second fraction.

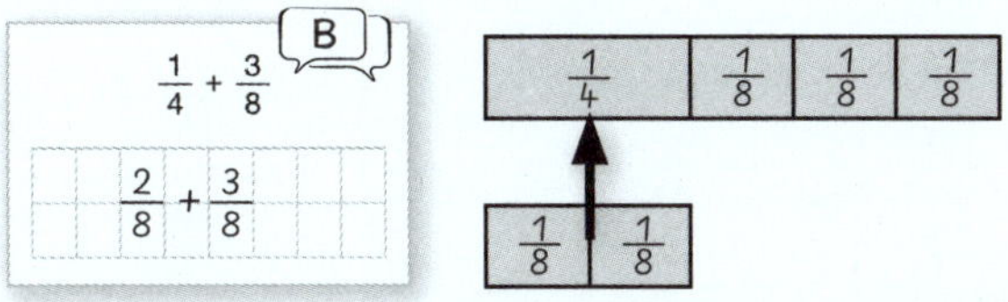

- **The last step is to add. What's two-eighths plus three-eighths?** *Five-eighths.* Write 5/8 to complete the equation.

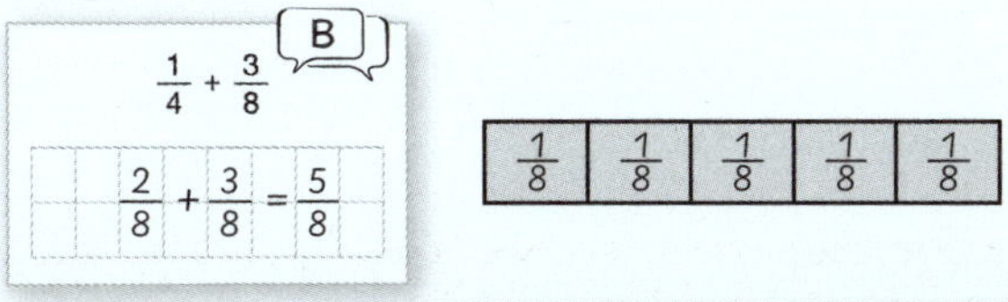

> Solving fraction arithmetic problems in this methodical and careful way helps prevent careless mistakes. Even if your child can find the answers to the problems mentally, make sure she writes out the equivalent fractions below each problem and follows this process. See the Unit 5 **Teaching Math with Confidence** for more tips on helping your child organize her written work.

Have your child use the same approach to complete the remaining practice problems. Make sure she rewrites each problem with equivalent fractions before solving. Model the problems with fraction bars as needed.

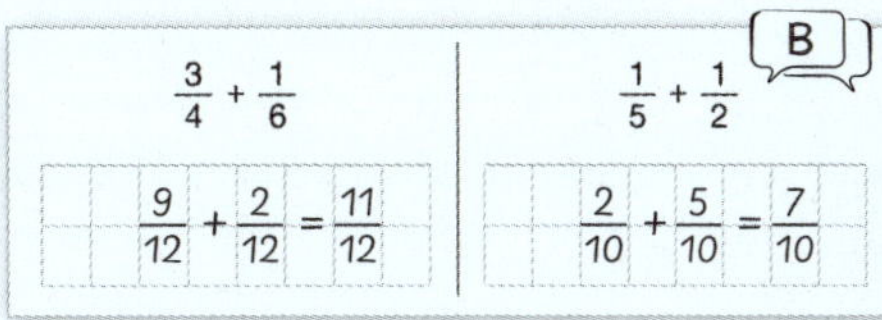

Activity (C): Play Fraction Addition War

Play Fraction Addition War.

> Your child does not need to simplify her answers (or reduce the fractions to lowest terms) in this unit. She will learn how to simplify fractions in Unit 8.

Fraction Addition War

Materials: Fraction cards

Object of the Game: Win the most points by creating greater sums.

Find the following fraction cards. Shuffle these cards and place them face down in a pile. (You will not use the rest of the fraction cards.)

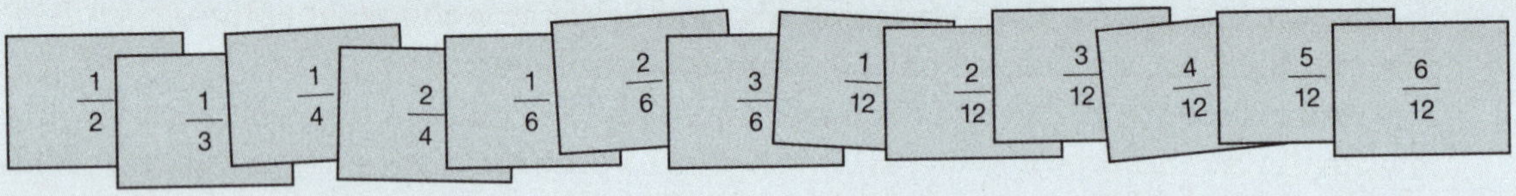

On your first turn, flip over the top 2 cards in the pile. Write the fractions in your score card. Use a common denominator to find their sum.

Then, the other player takes a turn in the same way. Whoever has the greater sum wins a point. (Use logical reasoning, fraction bars, or common denominators to compare the sums.) If the sums are equal, both players win a point.

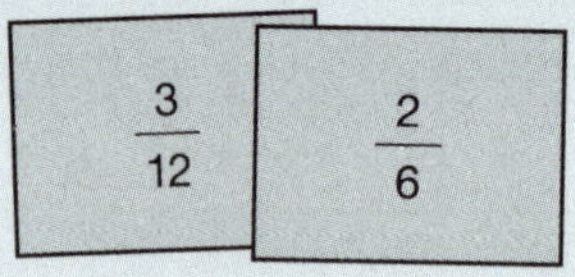

Player 1's cards.

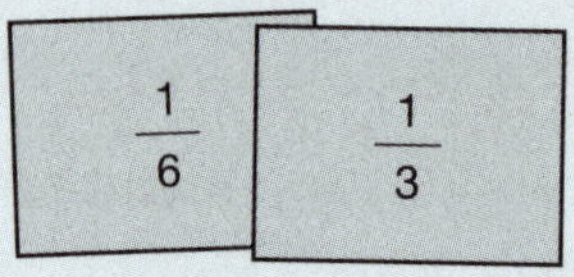

Player 2's cards.

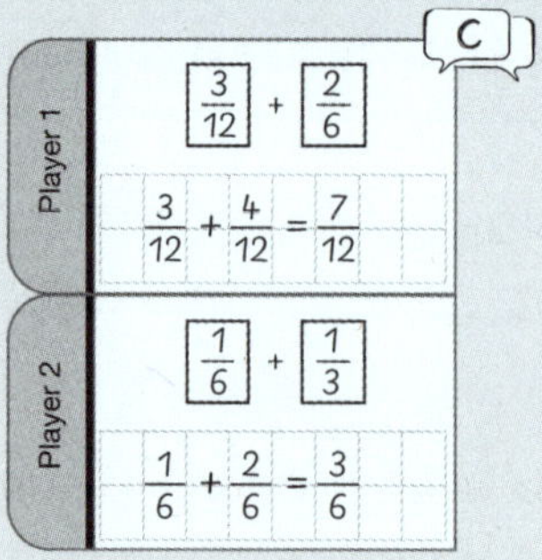

Sample round. 7/12 is greater than 3/6, so Player 1 wins the point.

Play until both players complete their scorecards. Whoever has won more points wins the game.

> **Advanced Variation:** Deal 3 cards to each player. On your turn, choose 2 of the cards to use. Then, take 2 new cards to replenish your hand. Reshuffle the discarded cards as needed.

Independent Practice and Review

Have your child complete the Lesson 5.5 Practice and Review workbook pages.

> If your child isn't sure what to write for the "find the mistake" exercises on the Practice page, say: **Imagine you were helping a friend with math and she made this mistake. What would you tell her to help her fix her mistake?** Your child may also tell you the mistake orally rather than writing it on the Practice page.

Lesson 5.6
Use Common Denominators to Subtract Fractions

Purpose	Materials
• Review subtracting fractions with the same denominator • Use common denominators to subtract fractions	• Fraction bars • Fraction cards

Memory Work	
	• **How many millimeters equal 1 centimeter?** *10.* • **How many centimeters equal 1 meter?** *100.* • **How many meters equal 1 kilometer?** *1,000.* • **How many grams equal 1 kilogram?** *1,000.* • **How many milliliters equal 1 liter?** *1,000.*

Warm-up (A): Review Subtracting Fractions with the Same Denominator

Last year, you learned how to subtract fractions with the same denominator. Have your child complete the fraction subtraction problems.

A

$\frac{5}{6} - \frac{3}{6} = \frac{2}{6}$ | $\frac{3}{8} - \frac{1}{8} = \frac{2}{8}$ | $\frac{11}{12} - \frac{3}{12} = \frac{8}{12}$

If your child doesn't remember how to subtract fractions with the same denominator, model the problems with fraction bars. Remind him to subtract the numerators and keep the denominators the same: **Just like 5 donuts minus 3 donuts equals 2 donuts, 5 sixths minus 3 sixths equals 2 sixths.**

$\frac{1}{6}$	$\frac{1}{6}$	~~$\frac{1}{6}$~~	~~$\frac{1}{6}$~~	~~$\frac{1}{6}$~~

$\frac{5}{6} - \frac{3}{6} = \frac{2}{6}$

Activity (B): Use Common Denominators to Subtract Fractions

In the last lesson, you learned how to add fractions with different denominators. Today, you'll learn how to subtract fractions with different denominators.

Subtracting fractions with different denominators is very similar to subtracting fractions with the same denominators. You just find equivalent fractions with common denominators before you subtract. Have your child read the text box.

B

How to Use Common Denominators to Subtract Fractions

1. Find the least common multiple (LCM) of both denominators. You will use this number for the common denominator.
2. Rewrite each fraction as an equivalent fraction with the common denominator.
3. Subtract the fractions.

Ex. $\frac{7}{8} - \frac{1}{4} = ?$

The denominators are 8 and 4.
The LCM of 8 and 4 is 8.
So, use 8 as the common denominator.

$\frac{7}{8} - \frac{1}{4}$

↓ ↓

$\frac{7}{8} - \frac{2}{8} = \frac{5}{8}$

Read aloud the example problem: ***Seven-eighths minus one-fourth equals what?***

- Point to the pizza. **Seven-eighths of the pizza is left over. Then, someone eats one-fourth of the whole pizza. We subtract one-fourth from seven-eighths to find how much pizza is left.**
- **The first step is to find the least common multiple of the denominators. What are the denominators for these fractions?** *8 and 4.* **What is the least common multiple of 8 and 4?** *8.*

- **The second step is to rewrite each fraction with the common denominator. Seven-eighths already has 8 as its denominator. One-fourth equals how many eighths?** *2.* **Eating two-eighths of the pizza is the same as eating one-fourth of the pizza.**
- **The last step is to subtract. What's seven-eighths minus two-eighths?** *Five-eighths.* **Five-eighths of the pizza is left.**

Demonstrate how to solve the first practice problem.

- **We want to subtract one-sixth from one-half.** Model the problem with a fraction bar as shown.

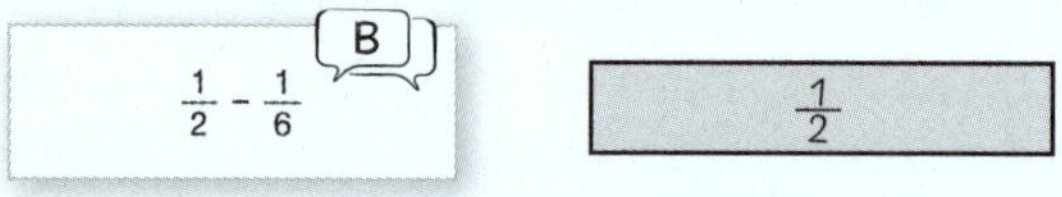

- **The first step is to find the least common multiple of the denominators. What are the denominators for these fractions?** *2 and 6.* **What is the least common multiple of 2 and 6?** *6.* **So, we'll use 6 as the common denominator.**
- **The second step is to rewrite each fraction with the common denominator.** Begin to rewrite the fractions as shown below the printed problem. Leave the numerators blank.

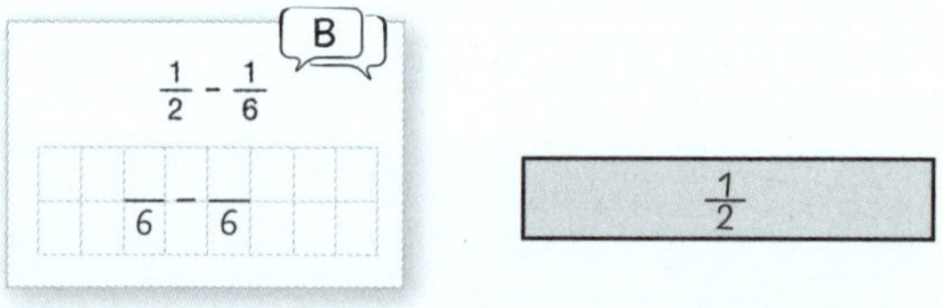

- **One-half equals how many sixths?** *3.* Write 3 as the numerator for the first fraction. Replace the 1 half-bar with 3 sixths-bars. **One-half equals three-sixths. One-sixth already has 6 as a denominator.** Write 1 as the numerator for the second fraction.

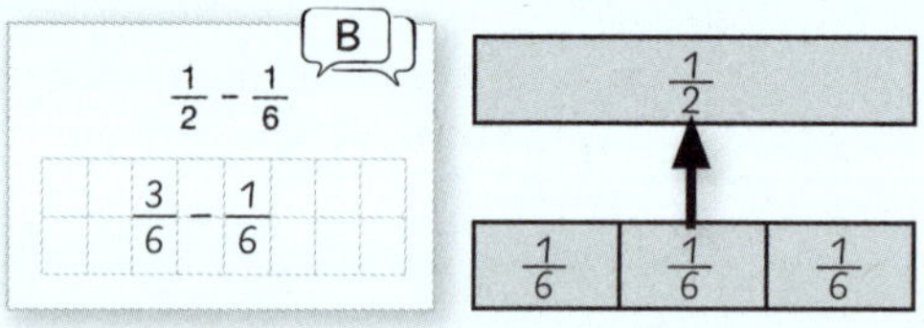

- **The last step is to subtract. What's three-sixths minus one-sixth?** *Two-sixths.* Write 2/6 to complete the equation. Remove 1 fraction bar as shown.

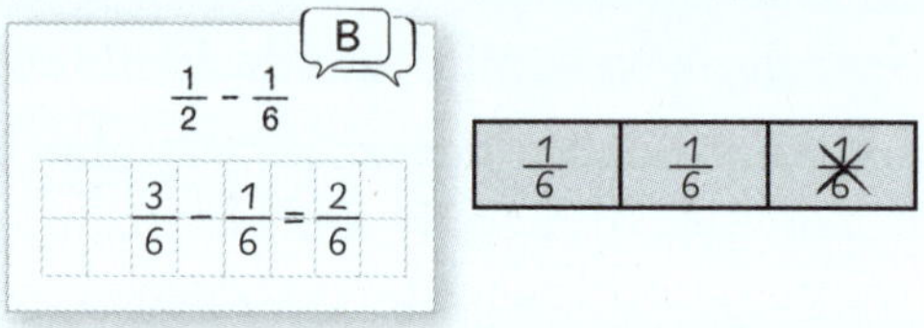

Your child does not need to simplify his answers (reduce the fractions to lowest terms) in this unit.

Have your child complete the remaining practice problems. Make sure he rewrites the problem with equivalent fractions before solving. Model the problems with fraction bars as needed.

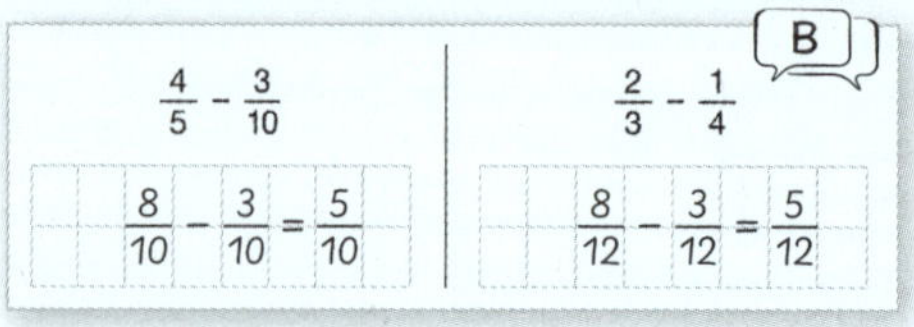

Activity (C): Play Fraction Difference War

Play Fraction Difference War.

Fraction Difference War

Materials: Fraction cards with 3, 6, or 12 as the denominator (18 cards total)

Object of the Game: Win the most points by creating greater differences.

Shuffle the cards and place them face down in a pile.

On your turn, flip over the top 2 cards in the pile. Write the fractions in your score card. (Use the larger fraction for the first number in the subtraction problem.) Use a common denominator to find their difference.

Then, the other player takes a turn in the same way. Whoever has the greater difference in each round wins a point. (Use logical reasoning, fraction bars, or common denominators to compare the differences.) If the differences are equal, both players win a point.

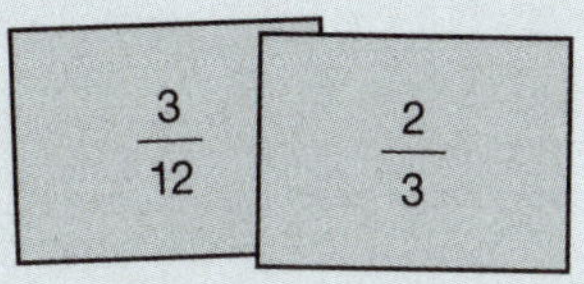

Player 1's cards.

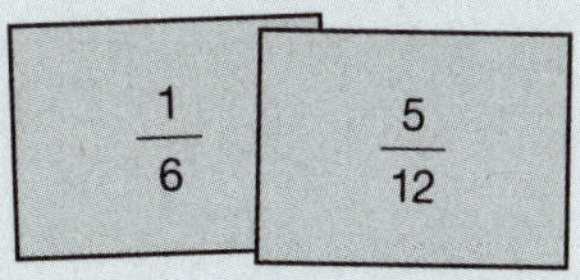

Player 2's cards.

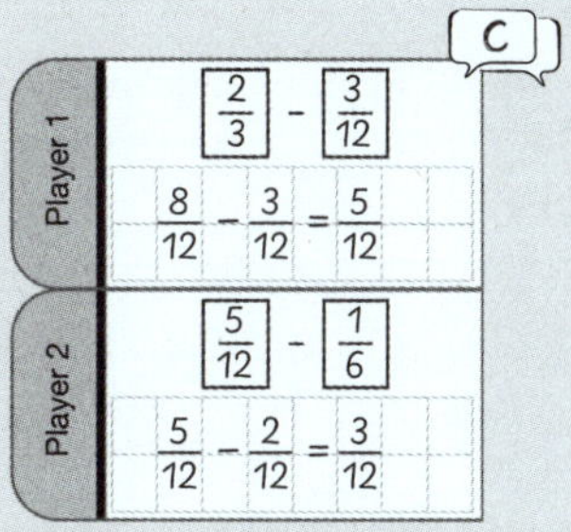

Sample round. 5/12 is greater than 3/12, so Player 1 wins the point.

Play until both players complete their scorecards. Whoever has won more points wins the game.

Advanced Variation: Deal 3 cards to each player. On your turn, choose 2 of the cards to use. Then, take 2 new cards to replenish your hand. Reshuffle the discarded cards as needed.

Independent Practice and Review

Have your child complete the Lesson 5.6 Practice and Review workbook pages.

Lesson 5.7
Add and Subtract with Improper Fractions

Purpose	Materials
• Practice converting improper fractions and mixed numbers • Practice converting an improper fraction to a mixed number after adding • Practice converting a mixed number to an improper fraction before subtracting	• Fraction bars, optional • Fraction cards

Memory Work

- **What do we call numbers that have a whole number and a fraction?** *Mixed numbers.*
- **What do we call a fraction whose numerator is greater than or equal to its denominator?** *An improper fraction.*

In Lessons 5.8 and 5.9, your child will learn how to add and subtract mixed numbers with different denominators. Children often make simple mistakes when solving these problems, because they feel overwhelmed by the sheer number of steps.

In this lesson, your child will practice converting mixed numbers and improper fractions when adding and subtracting fractions with different denominators. By gaining fluency with this simpler skill, she'll be better-equipped to solve the more complex problems in Lessons 5.8 and 5.9.

Warm-up: Practice Converting Improper Fractions and Mixed Numbers

In the last few lessons, you learned how to add and subtract fractions with different denominators. Today, you'll learn how to solve addition and subtraction problems that involve improper fractions.

- **What mixed number equals four-thirds?** *1 and one-third.*
- **What mixed number equals eleven-eighths?** *1 and three-eighths.*
- **1 and one-tenth equals what improper fraction?** *Eleven-tenths.*
- **1 and five-sixths equals what improper fraction?** *Eleven-sixths.*

Write the numbers on scrap paper if your child has trouble keeping them in her head.

Activity (A): Use Improper Fractions to Add and Subtract Fractions

When we add fractions, we sometimes get an improper fraction as the answer. In everyday life, we usually use mixed numbers more than improper fractions. So, if we get an improper fraction as an answer, we convert it to a mixed number.

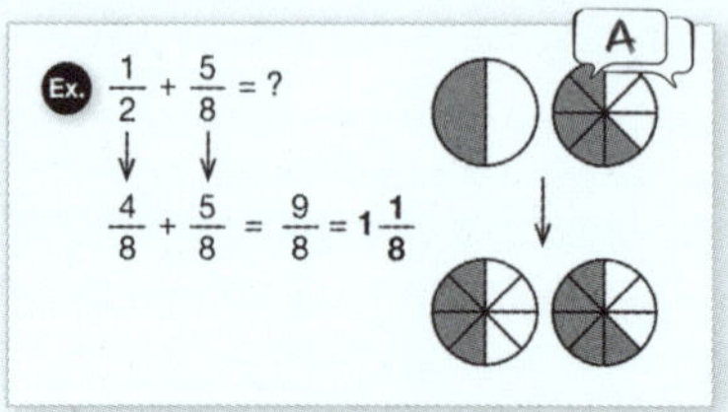

Use the following questions to discuss the first example:

- **We want to find the sum of one-half and five-eighths.**
- **First, we rewrite the problem with common denominators.**
- **Next, we add. Four-eighths plus five-eighths equals nine-eighths.**
- **Nine-eighths equals 1 and one-eighth, so the sum is 1 and one-eighth.**

We sometimes need to subtract a fraction from a mixed number. One way to do this is to convert the mixed number to an improper fraction before subtracting.

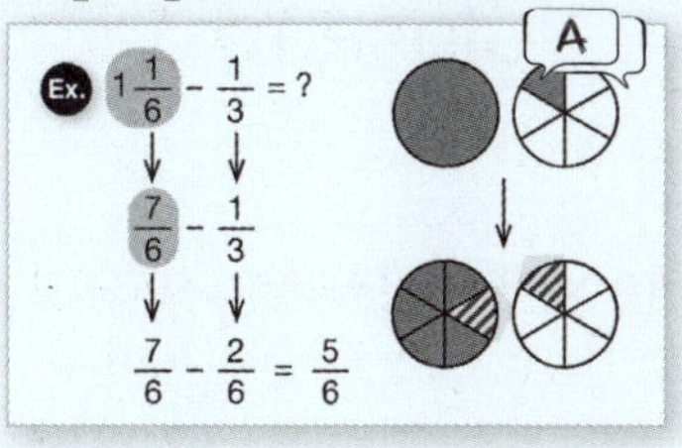

Use the following questions to discuss the second example:

- **We want to subtract one-third from 1 and one-sixth.**
- **First, we rewrite the mixed number as an improper fraction. 1 and one-sixth equals seven-sixths.**
- **Next, we rewrite the problem with common denominators.**
- **Last, we subtract. Seven-sixths minus two-sixths equals five-sixths.**

Have your child use the same steps to complete the practice problems.

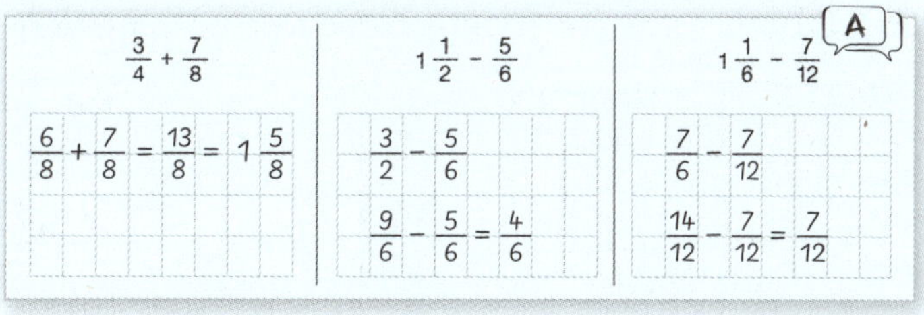

Activity (B): Prepare to Play Close to 1

Show your child the game board. **We're going to play a game called Close to 1. In this game, you choose cards from your hand whose sum is as close to 1 as possible.**

Put the fraction cards with 2/5, 1/2, and 1/10 on the table. **Which pair of cards has a sum as close to 1 whole as possible?** *Two-fifths and one-half.* **How do you know?** *Sample answer: Two-fifths is pretty close to one-half. So, when you add two-fifths and one-half, the sum must be about 1 whole.* If your child isn't sure, have her model each fraction with fraction bars before answering.

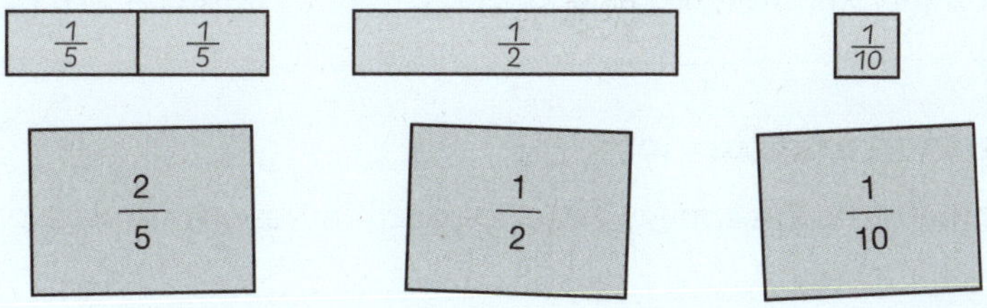

Activity (B): Play Close to 1

Play Close to 1. As you play, help your child use fraction number sense to decide how far each sum is from 1 whole. For example, if the sum is 7/8: **You'd need 1 more eighth to make 1 whole, so seven-eighths is one-eighth less than 1 whole.** Or, if the sum is 1 1/6: **One and one-sixth is one-sixth more than 1 whole.**

Close to 1

Materials: Fraction cards

Object of the Game: Score more points than the other player by creating sums as close as possible to 1 whole.

Shuffle the cards and place the stack face down on the table. Deal each player 3 cards.

On your turn, choose 2 cards from your hand. Try to choose cards whose sum is as close to 1 whole as possible. Write the fractions on the scorecard and find their sum. (If the sum is an improper fraction, convert it to a mixed number.) Then, figure out how close your sum is to 1 whole. Your sum may be greater than, less than, or equal to 1 whole.

Then, the other player takes a turn in the same way. Whoever's sum is closer to 1 whole wins the point. If both sums are equally close to 1, both players win a point.

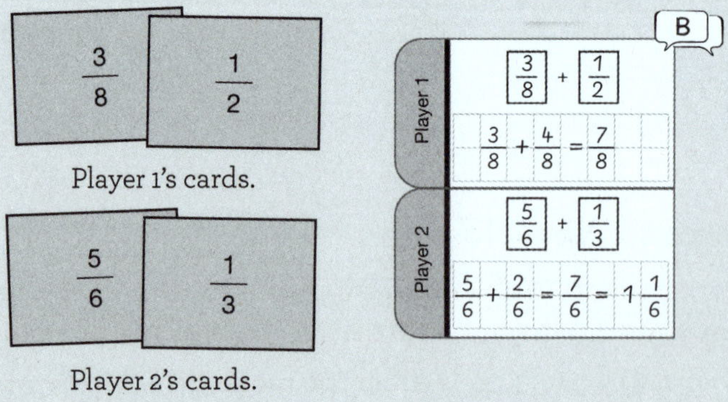

Sample round. 7/8 is closer to 1 whole than 1 1/6 (since 1/8 is less than 1/6). So, Player 1 wins the point.

Then, both players take 2 new cards from the face-down pile to replenish their hands.

Continue until you have completed all 3 rounds. Whoever has more points wins.

Independent Practice and Review

Have your child complete the Lesson 5.7 Practice and Review workbook pages.

Lesson 5.8
Add Mixed Numbers with Different Denominators

Purpose	Materials
• Review how to add mixed numbers with the same denominator • Use common denominators to add mixed numbers with different denominators	• Paper clip

Memory Work

- **What do we call an angle with a measure less than 90 degrees?** *Acute.*
- **What do we call an angle with a measure equal to 90 degrees?** *Right.*
- **What do we call an angle with a measure greater than 90 degrees and less than 180 degrees?** *Obtuse.*
- **What do we call an angle with a measure equal to 180 degrees?** *Straight.*

If this lesson takes your child a long time, split it over two days:

- Day 1: Do the Warm-up Activity A and Activity B. Then, have your child complete the Review page only.
- Day 2: Review the steps in Activity B and play Spin to Win (Activity C). Then, have your child complete the Practice page.

Warm-up (A): Review How to Add Mixed Numbers with the Same Denominator

Last year, you learned how to add mixed numbers with the same denominator. First, you add the fractions. Then, you add the whole numbers. Have your child complete the first problem. **What's 1 and one-sixth plus 2 and four-sixths?** *3 and five-sixths.*

Then, have your child complete the second problem. **Remember, if the sum of the fractions is greater than 1, you convert the fraction to a mixed number and add it to the whole number.** If needed, help your child convert the improper fraction to a mixed number: **Seven-fifths equals 1 and two-fifths, so you add 1 and two-fifths plus 3 to find the final sum.**

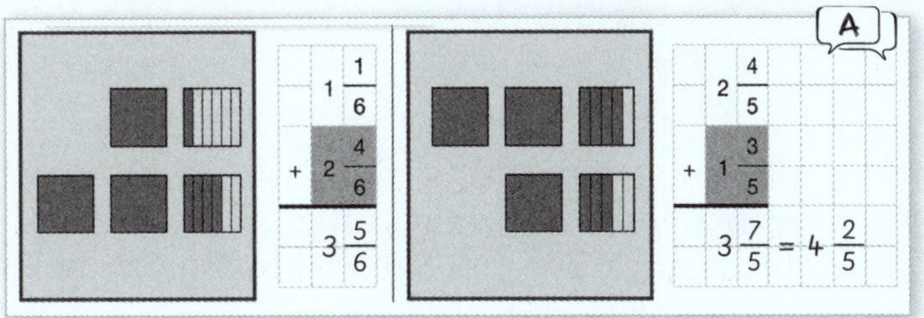

Activity (B): Use Common Denominators to Add Mixed Numbers

Today, you'll learn how to add mixed numbers where the fractions have different denominators. It's a lot like adding mixed numbers where the fractions have the same denominator. We just find equivalent fractions with a common denominator first. Have your child read the text box.

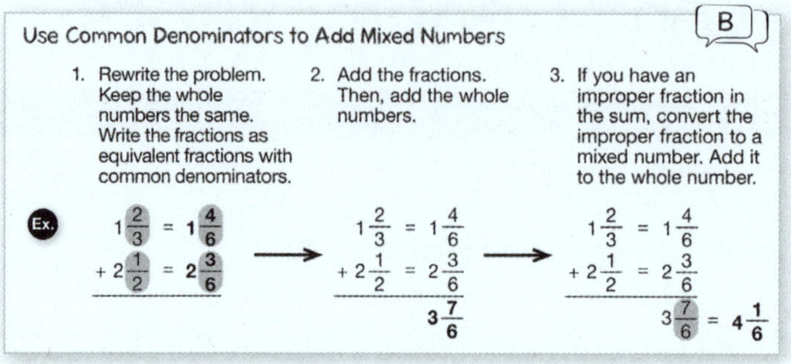

Let's study the example to see how to add fractions with different denominators.

- **We want to add 1 and two-thirds plus 2 and one-half. The first step is to rewrite the problem with common denominators. What is the common denominator for this problem?** *6.* **1 and two-thirds equals 1 and four-sixths. 2 and one-half equals 2 and three-sixths.**
- **Next, you add the fractions. What's four-sixths plus three-sixths?** *Seven-sixths.* **Then, you add the whole numbers. What's 1 plus 2?** *3.*
- **Last, you check if there is an improper fraction in the sum. Is there an improper fraction in the sum?** *Yes.* **What is the improper fraction?** *Seven-sixths.* **Seven-sixths equals 1 and one-sixth. So, we add 3 plus 1 and one-sixth to find that the final answer is 4 and one-sixth.**

Demonstrate how to use this approach to solve the first practice problem.

- **We want to add 1 and three-fourths plus 1 and one-eighth. The first step is to rewrite the problem with common denominators. What is the least common multiple of 4 and 8?** *8.* Begin to rewrite the mixed numbers as shown. Make sure to write an equals sign between the pairs of mixed numbers, and write the whole number so that it overlaps two boxes in the grid, as shown. Write 8 as the denominator for each fraction and leave the numerators blank.

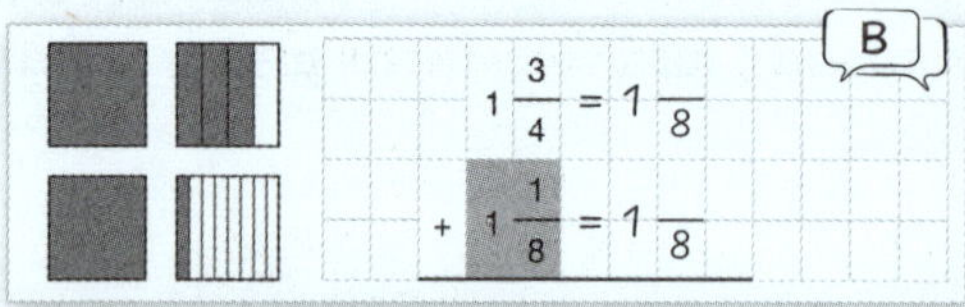

- **Three-fourths equals how many eighths?** *6.* Write 6 as the numerator for the top fraction. Draw a horizontal line across the printed fraction square to show that 3/4 equals 6/8. **One-eighth already has 8 as a denominator.** Write 1 as the numerator for the bottom fraction.

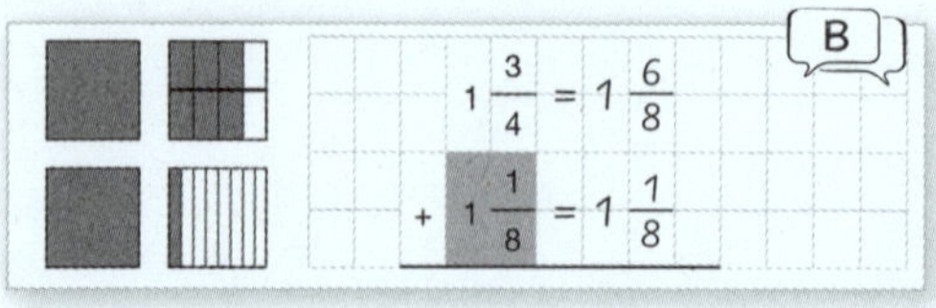

- **Next, we add the fractions. What's six-eighths plus one-eighth?** *Seven-eighths.* Write 7/8 directly below the fractions. **Then, you add the whole numbers. What's 1 plus 1?** *2.* Write 2 directly below the whole numbers. Write the 2 so that it overlaps two vertical boxes in the grid, as shown.

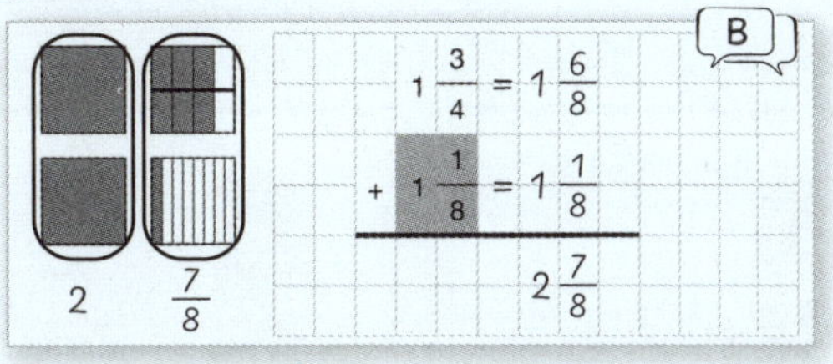

- **Is there an improper fraction in the sum?** *No.* **We're done! What does 1 and three-fourths plus 1 and one-eighth equal?** *2 and seven-eighths.*

> The squares that model 6/8 and 1/8 show the eighths in different ways. If your child is confused by this, have her count how many parts each square is cut into. **Both squares are cut into 8 equal parts, so each part is an eighth.**

There are a lot of steps in mixed number addition problems! Keeping your written work neat and organized makes it a lot easier to solve these problems without mistakes. What do you notice about how I organized my written work? *Sample answers: You wrote an equals sign between the equivalent mixed numbers. You lined up the whole numbers and fractions.*

When you solve the problems, make sure you rewrite both mixed numbers with the common denominator, and write an equals sign between the pairs of equivalent mixed numbers. This makes sure that the whole numbers and fractions are lined up for adding.

Have your child complete the remaining practice problem in the same way. Guide your child to organize his written work in the same way as you demonstrated.

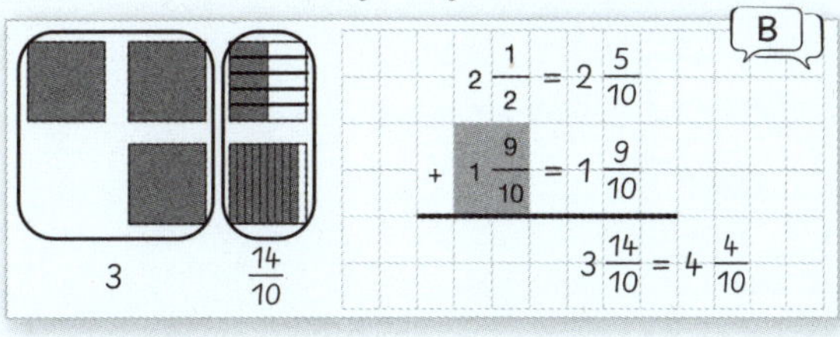

Activity (C): Play Spin to Win

Play Spin to Win. Help your child organize his written work in the same way as part B.

Spin to Win

Materials: Paper clip

Object of the Game: Win the most points.

To use the spinners, place one end of the paper clip in the middle of the spinner. Place the point of a pencil through the paper clip so that it touches the very middle of the circle. Hold the pencil upright and spin the paper clip so that it spins freely around the circle.

Spin to Win has 3 rounds. On your turn, spin both spinners. Write the number from the left-hand spinner as the top addend in your first blank addition problem. Write the number from the right-hand spinner as the bottom addend. Find the sum.

Directions continued on next page.

Then, have the other player spin twice and find the sum of his spins. Whoever has the greater sum wins a point for that round. If both players have the same sum, both players win a point.

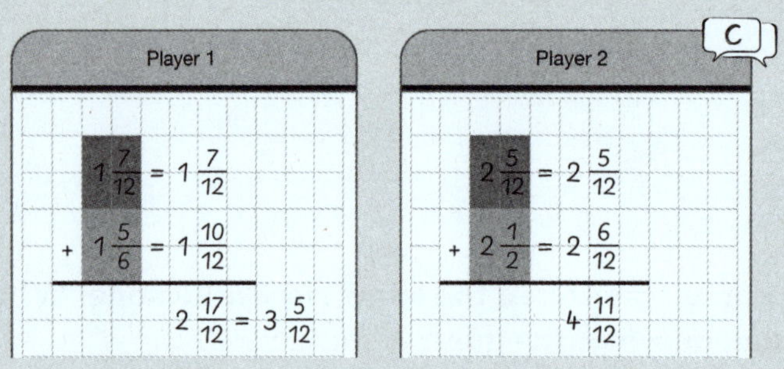

Sample round. Player 2 wins the point, since 4 11/12 is greater than 3 5/12.

Continue until you have completed 3 rounds. Whoever has won more points wins the game.

Independent Practice and Review

Have your child complete the Lesson 5.8 Practice and Review workbook page.

Lesson 5.9
Subtract Mixed Numbers with Different Denominators

Purpose	Materials
• Review how to subtract mixed numbers with the same denominator • Use common denominators to subtract mixed numbers with different denominators	• Paper clip

Memory Work	
	• **What are the four basic operations?** *Addition, subtraction, multiplication, and division.* • **What is an equation?** *A number sentence with an equals sign.* • **What is an expression?** *Part of a number sentence without an equals sign.*

If this lesson takes your child a long time, split it over two days:

- Day 1: Do the Warm-up Activity A and Activity B. Then, have your child complete the Review page only.
- Day 2: Review the steps in Activity B and play Spin to Win (Activity C). Then, have your child complete the Practice page.

Warm-up (A): Review How to Subtract Mixed Numbers with the Same Denominator

Last year, you learned how to subtract mixed numbers with the same denominator. First, you subtract the fractions. Then, you subtract the whole numbers.

Remember, if the top fraction is less than the bottom fraction, you trade 1 whole for fractional parts before subtracting. In the first problem, there is no top fraction, so we have to trade before subtracting. Demonstrate how to trade 1 whole for fractional parts:

- **We trade 1 whole for 3 thirds.** Cross out the 4 and write 3 above it as shown. Draw lines on one fraction square to split it into thirds.
- **1 whole equals three-thirds. So, now we have three-thirds.** Write 3/3 as shown. Then, have your child complete the problem.

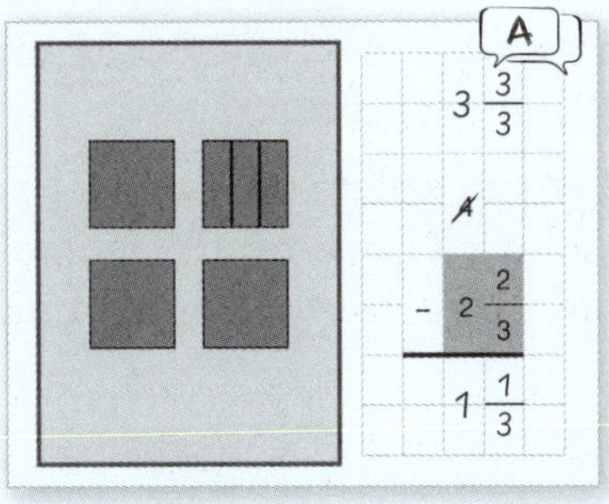

Have your child complete the second problem in the same way. Help her trade 1 whole for fractional parts as needed:

- **We trade 1 whole for fifths.** Cross out the 3 and write 2 above it as shown. Draw lines to split one fraction square into fifths.

- **1 whole equals five-fifths. We already had one-fifth, so now we have six-fifths.** Cross out 1/5 and write 6/5 above it as shown. Then, have your child complete the problem.

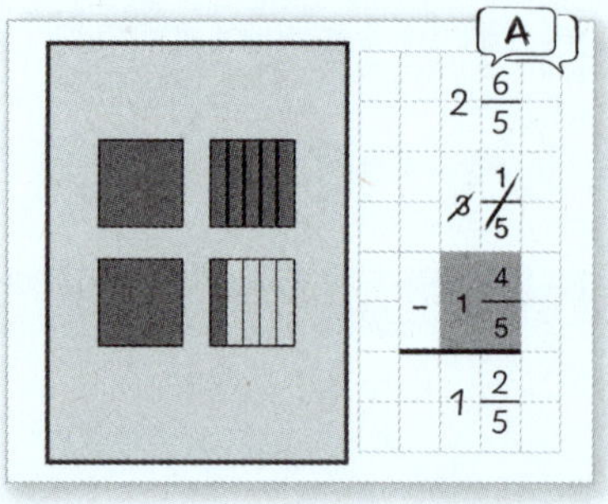

Activity (B): Use Common Denominators to Subtract Mixed Numbers

Today, you'll learn how to subtract mixed numbers where the fractions have different denominators. It's a lot like subtracting mixed numbers where the fractions have the same denominator. We just find equivalent fractions with a common denominator first. Have your child read the text box.

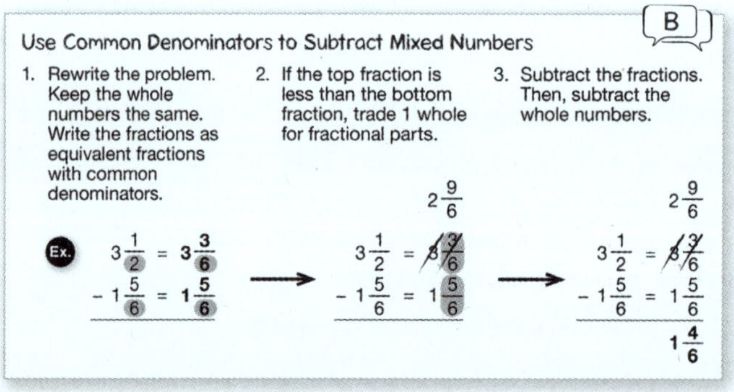

Let's study the example to see how to subtract fractions with different denominators.

- **We want to subtract 3 and one-half minus 1 and five-sixths. The first step is to rewrite the problem with common denominators. What is the common denominator for this problem?** *6.* **3 and one-half equals 3 and three-sixths. 1 and five-sixths already has 6 as its denominator.**
- **Next, you check whether the top fraction is greater than or equal to the bottom fraction. Three-sixths is less than five-sixths, so we need to trade 1 whole for six-sixths. We already have three-sixths. Six-sixths plus three-sixths equals nine-sixths.**
- **Last, you subtract the fractions and whole numbers. What's nine-sixths minus five-sixths?** *Four-sixths.* **What's 2 minus 1?** *1.*

Have your child use this approach to complete the practice problems. Guide her as needed with the trading in the second problem: **Three-tenths is less than six-tenths, so we need to trade 1 whole for ten-tenths. 2 and three-tenths equals 1 and thirteen-tenths.**

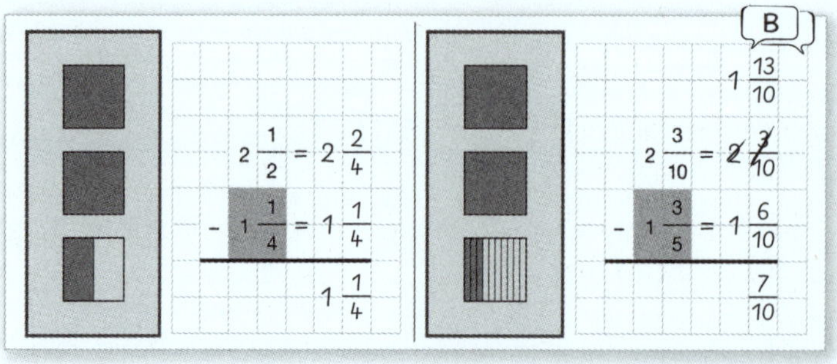

Activity (C): Play Spin to Win

Use the game board to play Spin to Win. See Lesson 5.8 (page 191) for directions. Write the number from the left-hand spinner as the top number in your subtraction problem and the number from the right-hand spinner as the bottom number. Whoever has the greater difference wins the point. If both players have the same difference, both players win a point.

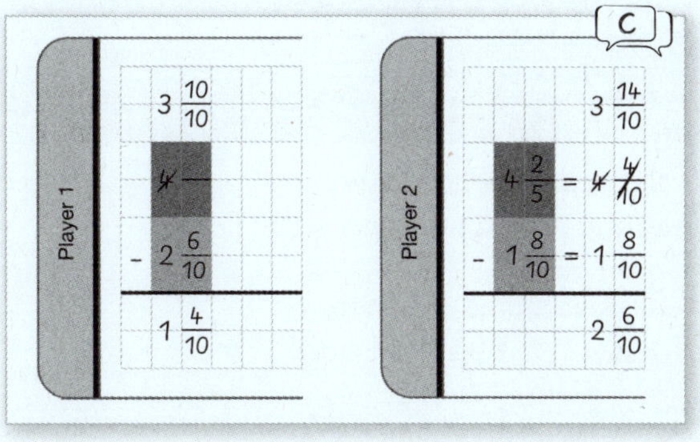

Sample round. Player 2's difference is greater, so Player 2 wins the point.

Independent Practice and Review

Have your child complete the Lesson 5.9 Practice and Review workbook pages.

Lesson 5.10
Estimate Mixed Number Sums and Differences

Purpose	Materials
• Round mixed numbers to the nearest whole number • Practice adding and subtracting mixed numbers with different denominators • Estimate sums and differences of mixed numbers • Solve mixed number addition and subtraction word problems	• None

Memory Work
- **What is a prime number?** *A number with exactly 2 factors.*
- **What is a composite number?** *A number with more than 2 factors.*

Warm-up (A): Use a Number Line to Round Mixed Numbers to the Nearest Whole Number

We'll warm up by rounding mixed numbers to the nearest whole number. Show your child the number line in part A. Point to the tick mark between 2 and 3. **What number does this tick mark represent?** *2 and one-half.* Point to the tick mark between 3 and 4. **What number does this tick mark represent?** *3 and one-half.*

Then, have your child use logical reasoning to connect each mixed number to its dot on the number line. If he has trouble, have him model the fractional part of the number with fraction bars first.

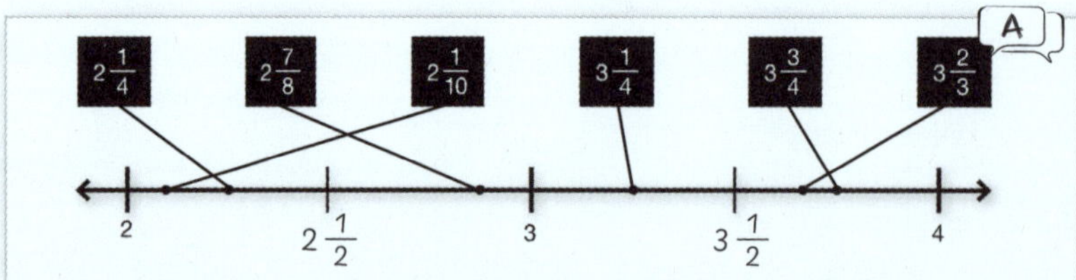

Then, have your child round each mixed number to the nearest whole number. Encourage him to use the number line to help. For example: **2 and 7/8 is between 2 1/2 and 3, so it's closer to 3 than to 2.**

A

$2\frac{1}{4} \approx$ 2 $\quad 2\frac{7}{8} \approx$ 3 $\quad 2\frac{1}{10} \approx$ 2

$3\frac{1}{4} \approx$ 3 $\quad 3\frac{3}{4} \approx$ 4 $\quad 3\frac{2}{3} \approx$ 4

Activity (B): Estimate Sums and Differences of Mixed Numbers

In the last two lessons, you learned how to add or subtract mixed numbers with different denominators. Today, you'll practice some more and learn how to estimate the sums and differences of mixed numbers.

To estimate the sums and differences, we'll round the mixed numbers to the nearest whole number. Point to the first problem. **Is 2 and seven-eighths closer to 2 or 3?** *3.* **Is 3 and three-fourths closer to 3 or 4?** *4.* Write 3 and 4 in the cloud as shown. **What's 3 plus 4?** *7.* **So, 7 is our estimate for this problem.** Write 7 as shown.

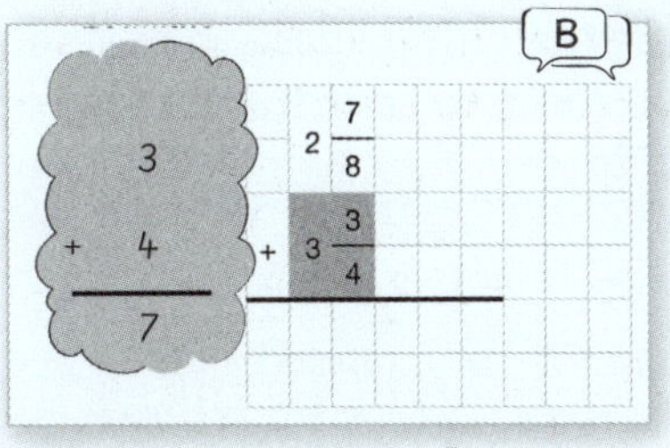

Do you think the sum will be less than or greater than 7? *Less.* **Why?** *Sample answer: We rounded both numbers up, so the sum won't actually be that high.*

> If your child is confused by this question, skip it for now and return to it after he's found the exact sum.

Then, have your child add to find the exact sum. **Is the exact sum less than 7 or greater than 7?** *Less than 7.* **We rounded both numbers up, so the actual sum wasn't as high as 7. For example, if you have 2 and seven-eighths pounds of blue clay and 3 and three-fourths pounds of red clay, you don't have a full 7 pounds of clay.**

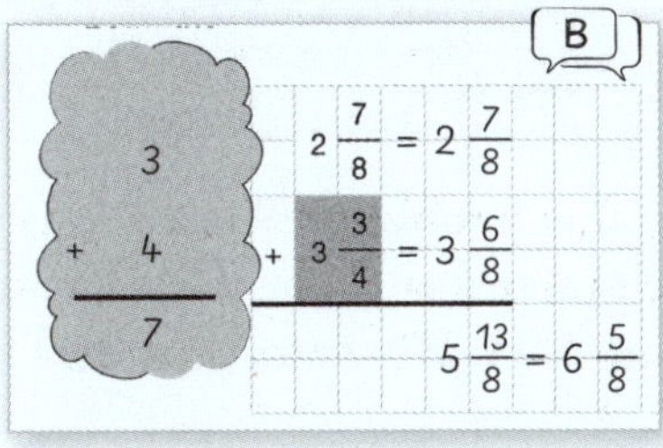

Have your child estimate the answer to the second problem in the same way. **Is 3 and one-fourth closer to 3 or 4?** *3.* **Is 2 and one-tenth closer to 2 or 3?** *2.* Write 3 and 2 in the cloud as shown. **What's 3 minus 2?** *1.* **So, 1 is our estimate for this problem. Do you expect the answer will be greater than 1 or less than 1?** *More than 1.* **Why?** *Sample answer: The difference between them is a little more than 1 whole. If I add 1 plus 2 and one-tenth, I only get 3 and one-tenth. That's not quite as much as 3 and one-fourth.*

> If your child is confused by this question, skip it for now and return to it after he's found the exact difference.

Then, have him subtract to find the exact difference. **Is the exact difference less than 1 or greater than 1?** *Greater than 1.* **3 minus 2 equals 1. One-fourth is greater than one-tenth. If you have 3 and one-fourth pounds of tomatoes and then use 2 and one-tenth pounds, you'll have a little more than 1 pound left.**

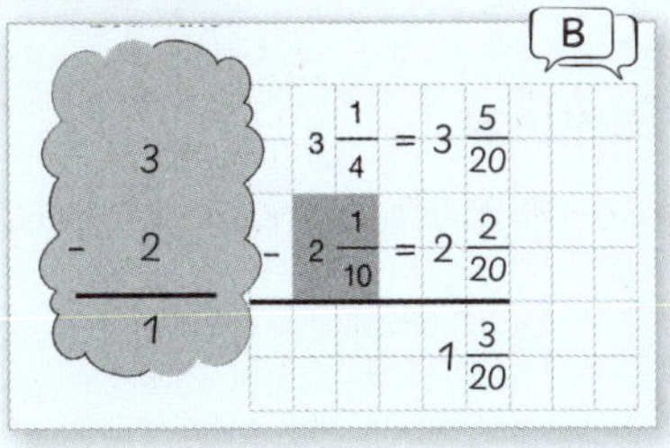

Activity (C): Estimate Answers to Mixed Number Word Problems

Have your child read aloud the first word problem. **What's the goal of this word problem?** *Find how many cups of fruit he used.*

> C
>
> Elliot uses $2\frac{1}{4}$ cups of strawberries and $3\frac{2}{3}$ cups of melon to make fruit salad. How many cups of fruit does he use in all?

Word problems with mixed numbers sometimes feel intimidating! If you ever feel confused by a mixed number word problem, just ignore the fractions for a minute. When we want to find a total amount, we add the two numbers together—no matter whether they're whole numbers, mixed numbers, or fractions!

Have your child write and solve the matching addition problem. **Write the problem on the left side of the grid so that you'll have room to rewrite the fractions with common denominators.**

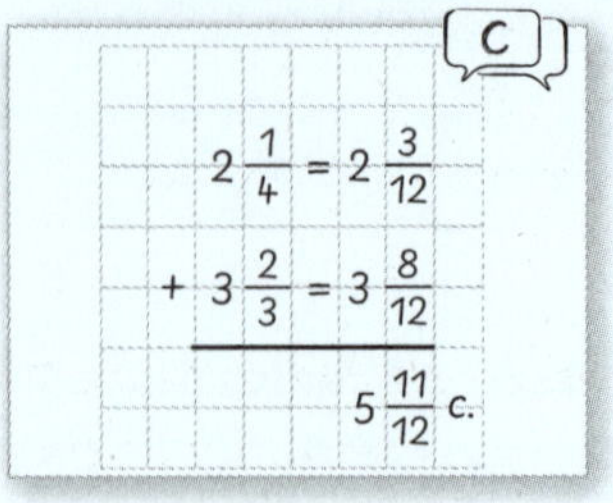

Let's use estimation to check that your answer is reasonable. 2 and one-fourth cups is about 2 cups. 3 and two-thirds is about 4 cups. 2 plus 4 is 6, so it makes sense that the answer would be close to 6 cups.

Have your child read aloud the second word problem. **What's the goal of this word problem?** *Find how many liters of water she drank.*

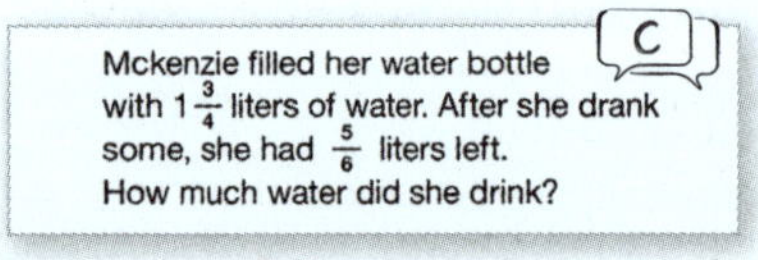

Will you add or subtract to solve this problem? *Subtract.* If your child's not sure, say: **We know how much water Mckenzie started with, and we know how much she had left at the end. So, we know the total and one part. How can you find the missing part?** *Subtract the part we know from the total.*

Have your child write and solve the matching subtraction problem. **Leave two rows of blank grid above the problem so that you'll have room to trade if you need to.**

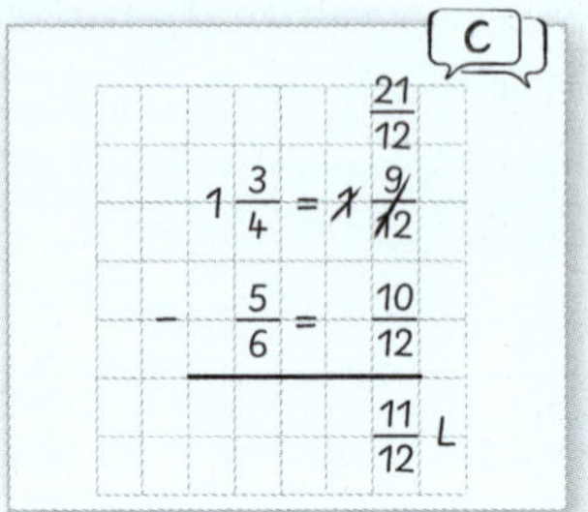

Let's use estimation to check that your answer is reasonable. 1 and three-fourths liters is about 2 liters. Five-sixths of a liter is about 1 liter. 2 minus 1 is 1, so it makes sense that the answer would be close to 1 liter.

Independent Practice and Review

Have your child complete the Lesson 5.10 Practice and Review workbook pages.

Lesson 5.11
Enrichment (Optional)

Purpose	Materials
• Practice memory work • Appreciate how math can be used to answer real-life questions • Add fractions and mixed numbers in a recipe • Summarize what your child has learned and assess your child's progress	• *How Many Guinea Pigs Can Fit on a Plane?: Answers to Your Most Clever Math Questions*, by Laura Overdeck • Ingredients and supplies to make vegetable soup (optional)

Warm-up: Review Memory Work

Quiz your child on any of the memory work items that she struggled with during this unit.

Math Picture Book: *How Many Guinea Pigs Can Fit on a Plane?*

Read pages 42-51 in *How Many Guinea Pigs Can Fit on a Plane?*

Enrichment Activity: Add Mixed Numbers in a Vegetable Soup Recipe

We often use mixed numbers in cooking. Show your child the following recipe.

Vegetable Soup

Ingredients:

- 2 tablespoons olive oil
- 1 1/3 cup chopped onions
- 3/4 cup chopped carrots
- 1 1/4 cup chopped celery
- 3 1/3 cups canned diced tomatoes (28-ounce can)
- 8 cups vegetable broth (64 fluid ounces)
- 2 1/2 cups diced potatoes
- 1 cup chopped green beans
- 2 bay leaves
- 1 teaspoon salt, or to taste
- 1/2 teaspoon ground black pepper
- 1 1/4 cup frozen corn, thawed
- 1 1/2 cup frozen peas, thawed

Heat the olive oil in a large pot over medium heat. Add the onions, carrots, and celery. Cook them for about 6 minutes, or until they are soft. Stir occasionally to keep them from burning.

Add the canned tomatoes, broth, potatoes, green beans, bay leaves, salt, and pepper. Bring the soup to a boil, then simmer for 30 minutes or until all the vegetables are tender.

Add the corn and peas. Cook for 5 more minutes. Check the seasoning and add more salt or pepper if needed. Serve. Makes 8 servings.

Let's find the total number of cups of vegetables in this recipe. We'll need a common denominator that works for all the mixed numbers. What denominators do the fractions have? *3, 4, and 2.* **What is the least common multiple for 3, 4, and 2?** *12.*

> If your child's not sure, point out that the least common multiple of 2 and 4 is 4. So, she can simply find the least common multiple of 3 and 4.

Help your child write a vertical addition problem that includes all the vegetables in the recipe. (Leave out the measurements for the olive oil, broth, bay leaves, salt, and pepper.) Then, have her rewrite the fractions with 12 as the common denominator. Finally, have her add to find the total number of cups of vegetables.

$$
\begin{aligned}
1\tfrac{1}{3} &= 1\tfrac{4}{12} \\
\tfrac{3}{4} &= \tfrac{9}{12} \\
1\tfrac{1}{4} &= 1\tfrac{3}{12} \\
3\tfrac{1}{3} &= 3\tfrac{4}{12} \\
8 &= 8 \\
2\tfrac{1}{2} &= 2\tfrac{6}{12} \\
1 &= 1 \\
1\tfrac{1}{4} &= 1\tfrac{3}{12} \\
+1\tfrac{1}{2} &= 1\tfrac{6}{12} \\
\hline
18\tfrac{35}{12} &= 20\tfrac{11}{12}
\end{aligned}
$$

If you have time, make the recipe with your child. Help her use measuring cups to measure out each ingredient, and discuss how the amounts compare to each other as you cook. For example: **Does the recipe include more chopped onions or chopped celery?** *Chopped onions.* **Does the recipe include more diced tomatoes or diced potatoes?** *Diced tomatoes.*

> This recipe is very adaptable. Feel free to change the ingredients if you have different vegetables on hand.

Unit Wrap-Up

Have your child complete the Unit 5 Wrap-Up.

Unit 5 Answer Key

5.1 Practice

Practice: Color the bars to match the fractions. Then, use the bars to compare the fractions.

$\frac{1}{2}$, $\frac{7}{8}$, $\frac{2}{4}$, $\frac{1}{5}$, $\frac{2}{5}$, $\frac{6}{6}$

$\frac{1}{2} < \frac{7}{8}$	$\frac{1}{2} > \frac{1}{5}$	$\frac{1}{2} = \frac{2}{4}$
$\frac{1}{5} < \frac{2}{5}$	$\frac{2}{4} > \frac{2}{5}$	$\frac{7}{8} > \frac{2}{5}$
$\frac{1}{2} < \frac{6}{6}$	$\frac{7}{8} < \frac{6}{6}$	$\frac{2}{5} < \frac{6}{6}$

Write the missing fraction in each equation.

$\frac{3}{4} + \frac{1}{4} = 1$	$\frac{1}{2} + \frac{1}{2} = 1$	$\frac{2}{3} + \frac{1}{3} = 1$
$\frac{5}{6} + \frac{1}{6} = 1$	$\frac{7}{12} + \frac{5}{12} = 1$	$\frac{1}{12} + \frac{11}{12} = 1$

Match each fraction to its dot on the number line.

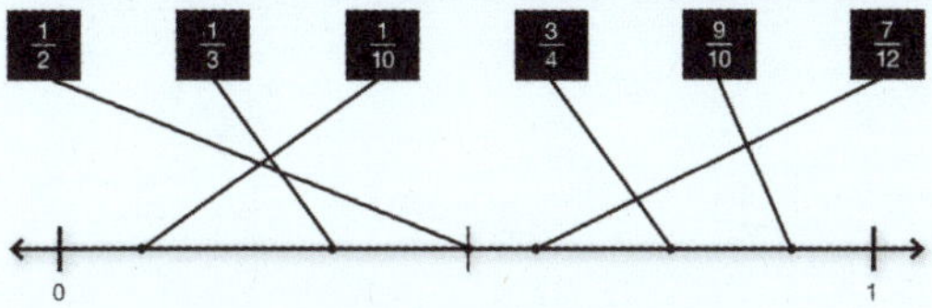

5.1 Review

Review: Complete.

0 right angle(s)	1 right angle(s)	0 right angle(s)
0 obtuse angle(s)	0 obtuse angle(s)	1 obtuse angle(s)
3 acute angle(s)	2 acute angle(s)	2 acute angle(s)

Use mental math to complete.

125 × 2 = 250	300 × 4 = 1,200	500 × 5 = 2,500
125 × 4 = 500	301 × 4 = 1,204	★ 499 × 5 = 2,495

Solve. Write your equations in the work space.

Michelle practiced piano for 270 minutes this week. She practiced 6 times, and she practiced the same amount each time. How long was each practice session?

45 min.

Katherine practiced piano for 245 minutes this week. She practiced 7 times, and she practiced the same amount each time. How long was each practice session?

35 min.

Who practiced more minutes in all?

Michelle

Whose practice sessions were longer?

Michelle

WORK SPACE

$270 \div 6 = 45$ (270 − 24 = 3; 30 − 30 = 0)

$245 \div 7 = 35$ (24 − 21 = 3; 35 − 35 = 0)

5.2 Practice

Practice: Complete the missing numbers in the chart. Use the circles to help.

Whole Number or Mixed Number	2	$2\frac{1}{3}$	$2\frac{2}{3}$	3	$3\frac{1}{3}$	$3\frac{2}{3}$	4	$4\frac{1}{3}$	$4\frac{2}{3}$
Fraction	$\frac{6}{3}$	$\frac{7}{3}$	$\frac{8}{3}$	$\frac{9}{3}$	$\frac{10}{3}$	$\frac{11}{3}$	$\frac{12}{3}$	$\frac{13}{3}$	$\frac{14}{3}$

Write each mixed number as a fraction. Write each fraction as a mixed number.

$2\frac{5}{8} = \frac{21}{8}$	$1\frac{2}{12} = \frac{14}{12}$	$1\frac{9}{10} = \frac{19}{10}$	$5\frac{1}{2} = \frac{11}{2}$
$\frac{7}{5} = 1\frac{2}{5}$	$\frac{7}{6} = 1\frac{1}{6}$	$\frac{25}{10} = 2\frac{5}{10}$	$\frac{17}{8} = 2\frac{1}{8}$

Solve. Write the equations you use.

Edith makes 4 loaves of pumpkin bread. She cuts each loaf into eighths. How many slices of pumpkin bread does she have?

$4 = \frac{32}{8}$ 32 slices

Levi's family has $1\frac{7}{8}$ pies left over after Thanksgiving. Each pie is cut into eighths. How many slices of pie do they have left?

$1\frac{7}{8} = \frac{15}{8}$ 15 slices left

Noah has 8 pieces of ribbon. Each piece of ribbon is $\frac{1}{3}$ of a meter long.

- How much ribbon does he have? Write your answer as a fraction. $\frac{8}{3}$ m
- How much ribbon does he have? Write your answer as a mixed number. $\frac{8}{3} = 2\frac{2}{3}$ m

The track is $\frac{1}{4}$ mile long. Jordyn runs 13 laps.

- How far does she run? Write your answer as a fraction. $\frac{13}{4}$ mi.
- How far does she run? Write your answer as a mixed number. $\frac{13}{4} = 3\frac{1}{4}$ mi.

5.2 Review

Review: Find the volume of each solid. Make sure to include the correct units in your answers.

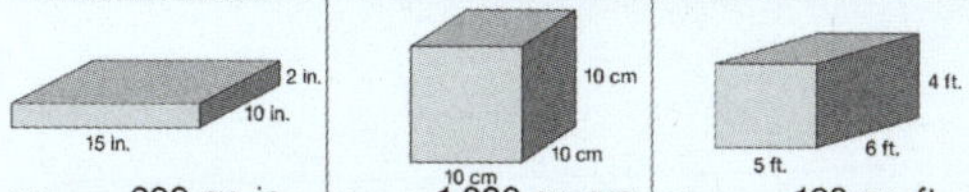

Volume: 300 cu. in.	Volume: 1,000 cu. cm	Volume: 120 cu. ft.

Use the printed rulers to measure the lines. Write each length as a mixed number.

$2\frac{3}{4}$ in. $1\frac{1}{4}$ in.

Solve. Write the equations you use.

Carpet costs $6 per square foot. How much does it cost to carpet the room?

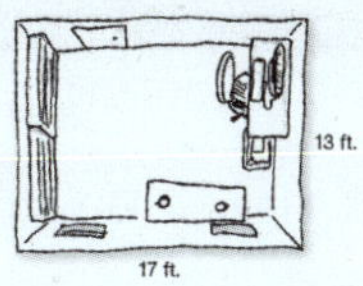

$17 \times 13 = 221$ (51 + 170 = 221); $221 \times 6 = \$1,326$

The perimeter of the garden is 92 feet. Each side is the same length. What is the length of each side?

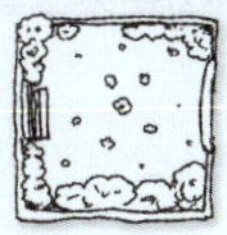

$92 \div 4 = 23$ (9 − 8 = 1; 12 − 12 = 0) 23 ft.

Unit 5 Answer Key

5.3 Practice

Fill the Fractions (2-Player Game)

$\frac{7}{8} = \frac{\ }{24}$	$\frac{1}{2} = \frac{6}{\ }$	$\frac{4}{5} = \frac{\ }{25}$
$\frac{2}{6} = \frac{8}{\ }$	$\frac{3}{8} = \frac{9}{\ }$	$\frac{5}{12} = \frac{\ }{24}$
$\frac{1}{3} = \frac{\ }{30}$	$\frac{6}{10} = \frac{12}{\ }$	$\frac{9}{12} = \frac{18}{\ }$
$\frac{2}{3} = \frac{10}{\ }$	$\frac{3}{6} = \frac{\ }{18}$	$\frac{1}{2} = \frac{\ }{40}$

Practice Complete the missing number in each pair of equivalent fractions. Then, find the blanks that match the answer for each problem. Write the matching letter in the blanks to solve the riddle.

V $\frac{2}{3} = \frac{6}{9}$	Y $\frac{1}{2} = \frac{40}{80}$	I $\frac{7}{8} = \frac{14}{16}$
R $\frac{3}{8} = \frac{6}{16}$	G $\frac{1}{4} = \frac{2}{8}$	S $\frac{4}{5} = \frac{80}{100}$
O $\frac{5}{10} = \frac{50}{100}$	T $\frac{5}{6} = \frac{10}{12}$	N $\frac{3}{4} = \frac{15}{20}$
D $\frac{4}{4} = \frac{36}{36}$	E $\frac{1}{3} = \frac{7}{21}$	

Why did the obtuse angle go to the beach?
Because it was...

O (50) V (9) E (7) R (16) N (20) I (14) N (20) E (7) T (10) Y (80)

D (36) E (7) G (2) R (16) E (7) E (7) S (100)

5.3 Review

Review Find the least common multiple for each pair of numbers.

LCM of 3 and 2: 6 3: 3, 6, 9, 12, 15 2: 2, 4, 6, 8, 10	LCM of 3 and 4: 12 3: 3, 6, 9, 12, 15 4: 4, 8, 12, 16, 20	LCM of 3 and 5: 15 3: 3, 6, 9, 12, 15 5: 5, 10, 15, 20, 25
LCM of 4 and 5: 20 4: 4, 8, 12, 16, 20 5: 5, 10, 15, 20, 25	LCM of 4 and 6: 12 4: 4, 8, 12, 16, 20 6: 6, 12, 18, 24, 30	LCM of 4 and 8: 8 4: 4, 8, 12, 16, 20 8: 8, 16, 24, 32, 40

Complete the chart.

	Half
10	5
16	8
20	10
30	15
32	16
100	50

Complete the circles with <, >, or =.

$\frac{1}{12} < \frac{5}{12}$ $3\frac{3}{8} > 2\frac{7}{8}$

$\frac{3}{6} < \frac{7}{6}$ $1\frac{9}{10} > 1\frac{8}{10}$

$\frac{4}{5} > \frac{2}{5}$ $2\frac{1}{2} = 2\frac{2}{4}$

$\frac{3}{8} < \frac{8}{3}$ $2 = \frac{12}{6}$

$\frac{5}{4} > \frac{5}{5}$ $2 < \frac{13}{6}$

Solve. Write the equations you use.

The playground is 38 meters long and 24 meters wide. What is its perimeter?

38 × 2 + 24 × 2
76 + 48
124 m

The playground is 38 meters long and 24 meters wide. What is its area?

$$\begin{array}{r} 38 \\ \times\ 24 \\ \hline 152 \\ +\ 760 \\ \hline 912 \end{array}$$

912 sq. m

5.4 Practice

Fraction War (2-Player Game)

Player 1

Player 2

Practice Find the least common multiple for each pair of numbers.

LCM of 3 and 8: 24 8, 16, (24)	LCM of 4 and 16: 16 (16)	LCM of 6 and 15: 30 15, (30)

Write equivalent fractions with common denominators for each pair of fractions. Use the LCMs (above) to help find the common denominators. Then, write <, >, or = to compare the fractions.

$\frac{3}{8} > \frac{1}{3}$ $\frac{9}{24}$ $\frac{8}{24}$	$\frac{7}{16} < \frac{3}{4}$ $\frac{7}{16}$ $\frac{12}{16}$	$\frac{2}{6} = \frac{5}{15}$ $\frac{10}{30}$ $\frac{10}{30}$

Solve. Write the equivalent fractions you use to answer the questions.

Sammy ran $\frac{2}{5}$ of a kilometer. Mina ran $\frac{3}{10}$ of a kilometer. Who ran farther?

$\frac{2}{5} = \frac{4}{10}$

$\frac{2}{5} > \frac{3}{10}$ Sammy

Milo has $\frac{2}{3}$ cup of sugar. He needs $\frac{3}{4}$ cup to make cookies. Does he have enough sugar?

$\frac{2}{3} = \frac{8}{12}$ $\frac{3}{4} = \frac{9}{12}$

$\frac{2}{3} < \frac{3}{4}$ No

5.4 Review

Review Use the clues to complete the chart.

- The platypus weighs 1 kg.
- The koala weighs 11 kg more than the platypus.
- The emu's weight is 4 times the koala's weight.
- The kangaroo weighs twice as much as the emu.

Animal	Weight (kg)
Platypus	1
Koala	12
Emu	48
Kangaroo	96

Round to the underlined digit.	Use mental math to complete.	
4.579 ≈ 5	63 ÷ 9 = 7	54 ÷ 9 = 6
4.579 ≈ 4.6	630 ÷ 9 = 70	540 ÷ 9 = 60
4.579 ≈ 4.58	6,300 ÷ 9 = 700	5,400 ÷ 9 = 600
297,845 ≈ 300,000	40 ÷ 8 = 5	30 ÷ 5 = 6
297,845 ≈ 300,000	400 ÷ 8 = 50	300 ÷ 5 = 60
297,845 ≈ 298,000	4,000 ÷ 8 = 500	3,000 ÷ 5 = 600

Find the volume of the solid. Write the equations you use.

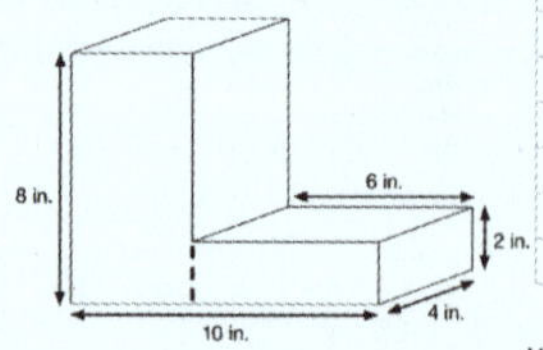

8 × 4 × 4 = 128 cu. in.
6 × 4 × 2 = 48 cu. in.
128 + 48 = 176 cu. in.

Volume: 176 cu. in.

Unit 5 Answer Key

5.5 Practice

Practice Find the sum.

$\frac{3}{10}+\frac{2}{5}$	$\frac{1}{4}+\frac{1}{8}$	$\frac{1}{2}+\frac{1}{3}$
$\frac{3}{10}+\frac{4}{10}=\frac{7}{10}$	$\frac{2}{8}+\frac{1}{8}=\frac{3}{8}$	$\frac{3}{6}+\frac{2}{6}=\frac{5}{6}$

Describe the mistake in each problem. Then, solve it correctly.

Incorrect	What is the mistake?	Correct solution:
$\frac{3}{8}+\frac{1}{2}$ → $\frac{3}{8}+\frac{1}{8}=\frac{4}{8}$	$\frac{1}{2}$ does not equal $\frac{1}{8}$	$\frac{3}{8}+\frac{4}{8}=\frac{7}{8}$
$\frac{2}{5}+\frac{1}{3}$ → $\frac{6}{15}+\frac{5}{15}=\frac{11}{30}$	You don't add the denominators when you add fractions.	$\frac{6}{15}+\frac{5}{15}=\frac{11}{15}$

Solve. Write the equations you use.

Ava makes granola with $\frac{2}{3}$ cup of dried cherries and $\frac{1}{4}$ cup of dried cranberries. How much dried fruit does she use in all?

$\frac{2}{3}+\frac{1}{4}$

$\frac{8}{12}+\frac{3}{12}=\frac{11}{12}$ c.

Gideon makes a smoothie with $\frac{1}{6}$ pound of blueberries and $\frac{1}{4}$ pound of chopped pineapple. How much fruit does he put in the smoothie in all?

$\frac{1}{6}+\frac{1}{4}$

$\frac{2}{12}+\frac{3}{12}=\frac{5}{12}$ lb.

5.5 Review

Review Draw a triangle that matches each description.

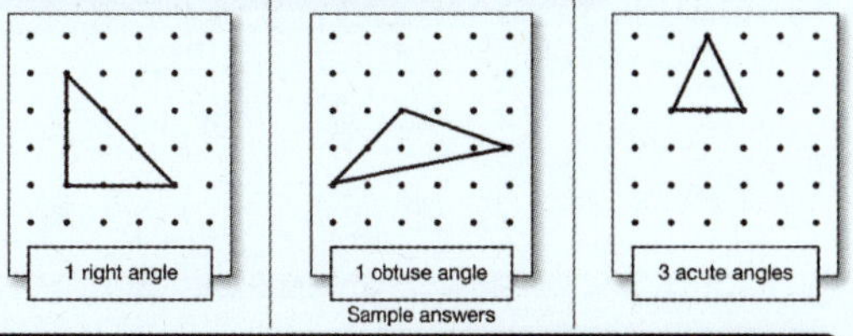

Write the numbers in order from least to greatest.

1.01, 0.999, 1, 0.90 → 0.90 (least), 0.999, 1, 1.01 (greatest)

0.04, 0.041, 0.004, 0.40 → 0.004 (least), 0.04, 0.041, 0.40 (greatest)

Circle the words that describe the answer to each problem. You do not need to find the exact answers.

Problem	Answer circled
358 + 315	greater than 600
217 + 345	less than 600
153 + 439	less than 600
642 − 96	greater than 500
975 − 507	less than 500
850 − 328	greater than 500

5.6 Practice

Practice Find the difference.

$\frac{5}{8}-\frac{1}{4}$	$\frac{8}{10}-\frac{1}{2}$	$\frac{2}{3}-\frac{1}{12}$
$\frac{5}{8}-\frac{2}{8}=\frac{3}{8}$	$\frac{8}{10}-\frac{5}{10}=\frac{3}{10}$	$\frac{8}{12}-\frac{1}{12}=\frac{7}{12}$

Find the missing numbers to complete the problems.

	★	★
$\frac{2}{3}-\frac{1}{9}$ → $\frac{[6]}{9}-\frac{1}{9}=\frac{[5]}{9}$	$\frac{1}{[2]}-\frac{[1]}{5}$ → $\frac{5}{10}-\frac{2}{10}=\frac{[3]}{10}$	$\frac{[3]}{4}-\frac{[1]}{5}$ → $\frac{15}{20}-\frac{[4]}{20}=\frac{11}{20}$

Use the clues to find the missing weights for the bars of soap. Write the equations you use.

- The lavender soap weighs $\frac{1}{3}$ lb. less than the rosemary soap.
- The lemon soap weighs $\frac{1}{6}$ lb. more than the lavender soap.
- The peppermint soap weighs $\frac{1}{4}$ lb. less than the lemon soap.

Rosemary soap $\frac{3}{4}$ lb. Lavender soap $\frac{5}{12}$ lb. Lemon soap $\frac{7}{12}$ lb. Peppermint soap $\frac{4}{12}$ lb.

$\frac{3}{4}-\frac{1}{3}$

$\frac{9}{12}-\frac{4}{12}=\frac{5}{12}$

$\frac{5}{12}+\frac{1}{6}$

$\frac{5}{12}+\frac{2}{12}=\frac{7}{12}$

$\frac{7}{12}-\frac{1}{4}$

$\frac{7}{12}-\frac{3}{12}=\frac{4}{12}$

5.6 Review

Review Connect each number to its position on the number line.

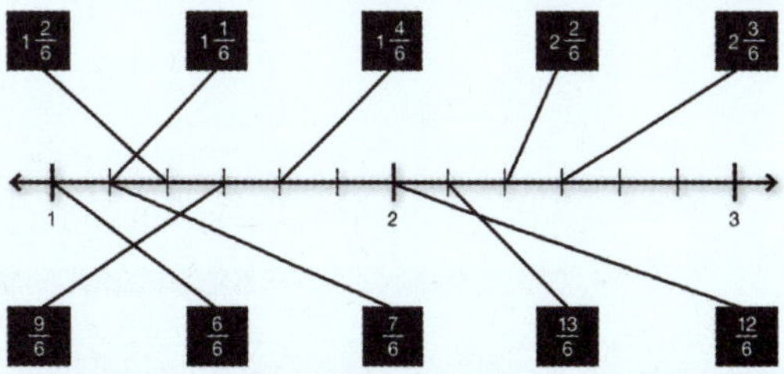

Use long division to solve.

$67 \div 4 = 16$ R3 (67 − 4 = 27; 27 − 24 = 3)

$109 \div 7 = 15$ R4 (10 − 7 = 39; 39 − 35 = 4)

$571 \div 4 = 142$ R3 (5 − 4 = 17; 17 − 16 = 11; 11 − 8 = 3)

$538 \div 5 = 107$ R3 (5 − 5 = 03; 3 − 0 = 38; 38 − 35 = 3)

Solve. Write the equations you use.

The storage unit is 15 feet long, 12 feet wide and 8 feet tall. What is the volume of the storage unit?

15 × 12 × 8 = 1,440 cu. ft.

Zachary has 3 kg of rice. Then, he uses 1.7 kg. How much rice is left?

3.0 − 1.7 = 1.3 kg

Unit 5 Answer Key

5.7 Practice

Practice: Circle the fractions that match the description. X the fractions that do not match the description.

Less than 1	Equal to 1	Greater than 1
(circled) $\frac{3}{4}$, X, X, X, (circled) $\frac{8}{10}$, X	(circled) $\frac{5}{5}$, X, X, X, X, (circled) $\frac{4}{4}$	X, (circled) $\frac{11}{10}$, X, (circled) $\frac{3}{2}$, (circled) $\frac{5}{3}$, X

Find the sum or difference.

$\frac{3}{5}+\frac{9}{10}$: $\frac{6}{10}+\frac{9}{10}=\frac{15}{10}=1\frac{5}{10}$

$1\frac{1}{4}-\frac{5}{12}$: $\frac{5}{4}-\frac{5}{12}$; $\frac{15}{12}-\frac{5}{12}=\frac{10}{12}$

$1\frac{1}{3}-\frac{11}{12}$: $\frac{4}{3}-\frac{11}{12}$; $\frac{16}{12}-\frac{11}{12}=\frac{5}{12}$

Use the recipe to answer the questions. Write the equations you use.

What is the total amount of raisins and flaked coconut called for in the recipe?

$\frac{2}{3}+\frac{1}{2}$

$\frac{4}{6}+\frac{3}{6}=\frac{7}{6}=1\frac{1}{6}$

How many more cups of oats than raisins does the recipe call for?

$1\frac{1}{4}-\frac{2}{3}$ $\frac{5}{4}-\frac{2}{3}$

$\frac{15}{12}-\frac{8}{12}=\frac{7}{12}$ c.

Oatmeal Raisin Cookies
- $\frac{3}{4}$ cup all-purpose flour
- $\frac{1}{2}$ teaspoon baking soda
- $\frac{1}{4}$ teaspoon salt
- $\frac{1}{2}$ cup butter
- $\frac{3}{8}$ cup brown sugar
- $\frac{3}{8}$ cup white sugar
- $1\frac{1}{4}$ cups oats
- 1 egg
- $\frac{2}{3}$ cup raisins
- $\frac{1}{2}$ cup flaked coconut

5.7 Review

Review: Find the missing information for each rectangular prism. Make sure to include the correct units.

Base area: 9 sq. cm	Base area: 30 sq. ft.	Base area: 10 sq. m
Height: 4 cm	Height: 3 ft.	Height: 4 m
Volume: 36 cu. cm	Volume: 90 cubic ft.	Volume: 40 cubic m

Find the product.

$$\begin{array}{r} 749 \\ \times\ 58 \\ \hline 5{,}992 \\ +\ 37{,}450 \\ \hline 43{,}442 \end{array}$$

Write each decimal as a mixed number.

- $3.2 = 3\frac{2}{10}$
- $1.54 = 1\frac{54}{100}$
- $3.02 = 3\frac{2}{100}$
- $1.837 = 1\frac{837}{1{,}000}$
- $3.020 = 3\frac{20}{1{,}000}$
- $2.019 = 2\frac{19}{1{,}000}$

Solve. Write the equations you use.

Seth ran the race in 20.74 seconds. Ian ran the race in 23.06 seconds. How many seconds shorter was Seth's time than Ian's time?

$23.06 - 20.74 = 2.32$ sec.

The fund-raising committee wants to raise $20,000 for new playground equipment. They have raised $12,675 so far. How much money do they have left to raise?

$20{,}000 - 12{,}675 = \$7{,}325$

5.8 Practice/Review

Practice: Complete.

$$3\frac{2}{5}=3\frac{4}{10},\quad +1\frac{3}{10}=1\frac{3}{10},\quad 4\frac{7}{10}$$

$$2\frac{2}{3}=2\frac{4}{6},\quad +3\frac{5}{6}=3\frac{5}{6},\quad 5\frac{9}{6}=6\frac{3}{6}$$

$$1\frac{7}{8}=1\frac{7}{8},\quad +2\frac{1}{4}=2\frac{2}{8},\quad 3\frac{9}{8}=4\frac{1}{8}$$

Review: Label the numbers on the number line.

- 2.5 to 2.6: 2.57
- 3.01 to 3.02: 3.015

Find the missing dimension for each solid. All measurements are in centimeters.

Volume: 36 cubic cm	Volume: 36 cubic cm	Volume: 36 cubic cm
2, 2, 9	3, 4, 3	3, 2, 6

Solve. Write the equations you use.

Caleb has a block of clay that weighs 3 kilograms. He splits the clay into 5 equal balls. How heavy is each ball in grams? (1 kg equals 1,000 grams.)

$1{,}000 \times 3 = 3{,}000$ g

$3{,}000 \div 5 = 600$ g

The art teacher buys 4 cases of markers. Each case holds 10 boxes. Each box holds 8 markers. How many markers does the art teacher buy?

$4 \times 10 \times 8 = 320$ markers

5.9 Practice/Review

Practice: Complete.

$$3\frac{1}{2}=3\frac{2}{4}\ (\text{renamed } 2\frac{6}{4}),\quad -1\frac{3}{4}=1\frac{3}{4},\quad 1\frac{3}{4}$$

$$4\frac{1}{3}=4\frac{2}{6}\ (\text{renamed } 3\frac{8}{6}),\quad -1\frac{5}{6}=1\frac{5}{6},\quad 2\frac{3}{6}$$

$$5\ (\text{renamed } 4\frac{3}{3}),\quad -2\frac{2}{3},\quad 2\frac{1}{3}$$

Review: Answer the questions about the numbers. Write your answers as whole numbers or decimals.

3,489,620	2.751
What is the value of the 9? 9,000	What is the value of the 7? 0.7
What is the value of the 4? 400,000	What is the value of the 5? 0.05
What is the value of the 8? 80,000	What is the value of the 2? 2
What is the value of the 3? 3,000,000	What is the value of the 1? 0.001

Solve. Write the equations you use.

Windsor's family hiked 4 miles through the forest. How long was their hike in feet? (1 mile equals 5,280 feet.)

$5{,}280 \times 4 = 21{,}120$ ft.

Daniel's family has 2 gallons of milk. They drink 2 quarts of milk per day. How many days will their milk last? (1 gallon equals 4 quarts.)

$2 \times 4 = 8$ quarts

$8 \div 2 = 4$ days

Unit 5 Answer Key

5.10 Practice

Practice: Round each number to the nearest whole number. Then, circle the better estimate for the sum or difference. You do not need to find the exact answers.

Problem	Choices	Circled
$1\frac{7}{8} + 1\frac{5}{6}$	3, 4	4
$2\frac{1}{10} + 2\frac{1}{5}$	4, 5	4
$1\frac{1}{4} + 1\frac{11}{12}$	3, 4	3
$5 - 2\frac{10}{12}$	2, 3	2
$5\frac{1}{5} - 2\frac{1}{8}$	2, 3	3
$5\frac{1}{5} - 2\frac{7}{8}$	2, 3	2

Solve. Write the equations you use.

Aaron and Lewis ran a relay race together. Aaron ran $1\frac{8}{10}$ km, and Lewis ran the rest of the race. The total length of the race was $5\frac{1}{5}$ km. How far did Lewis run?

$$5\frac{1}{5} = 5\frac{2}{10} = 4\frac{12}{10}$$
$$-\,1\frac{8}{10} = 1\frac{8}{10}$$
$$3\frac{4}{10}\text{ km}$$

Owen's pet turtle weighs $2\frac{3}{8}$ pounds. His pet guinea pig weighs $\frac{3}{4}$ pounds less than his turtle. How much does his guinea pig weigh?

$$2\frac{3}{8} = 2\frac{3}{8} = 1\frac{11}{8}$$
$$-\,\frac{3}{4} = \frac{6}{8}$$
$$1\frac{5}{8}\text{ lb.}$$

5.10 Review

Review: Complete the chart.

Cups	1	5	10	20	25	40	50	100
Fluid Ounces	8	40	80	160	200	320	400	800

Find the volume of each solid. Make sure to include the correct units.

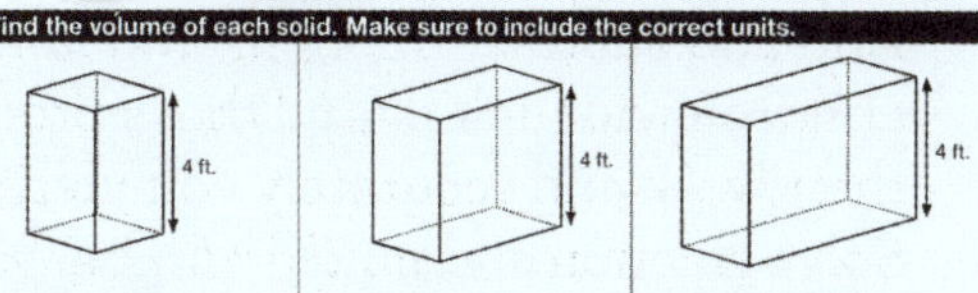

Base area: 4 sq. ft. Volume: 16 cu. ft.

Base area: 8 sq. ft. Volume: 32 cu. ft.

Base area: 10 sq. ft. Volume: 40 cu. ft.

Draw a line to connect the numbers in order from Start to End. Follow the rule.

Rule: Add 0.3 (Start → End)

0.4	0.7	1.0	1.7	2.0
0.3	0.2	1.3	2.4	2.5
0.5	0.6	1.6	1.9	2.2
0.8	1.4	2.0	2.3	2.5
1.5	1.8	2.2	2.7	2.8

Rule: Subtract 0.4 (Start → End)

5.8	5.5	2.6	2.2	1.8
5.4	5.1	3.0	1.9	1.4
5.0	4.5	3.4	3.5	1.0
4.6	4.2	3.8	0.7	0.6
4.4	3.9	3.6	0.4	0.2

Write one pair of parentheses in each equation to make the equation true.

★ $6 + (8 \div 1) \times 2 = 22$

★ $6 + 8 \div (1 \times 2) = 10$

★ $(6 + 8) \div 1 \times 2 = 28$

5.11 Unit Wrap-Up A

Unit Wrap-Up: Use the words from the word bank to complete the sentence.

A mixed number is a number with a whole number and a fraction.

Equivalent fractions look different but have the same value.

The numerator is the top number in a fraction.

The denominator is the bottom number in a fraction.

Word bank: denominator • mixed number • numerator • equivalent

Write equivalent fractions with common denominators for each pair of fractions. Then, write <, >, or = to compare the fractions.

$\frac{7}{12} < \frac{2}{3}$: $\frac{7}{12}$, $\frac{8}{12}$

$\frac{7}{10} > \frac{3}{5}$: $\frac{7}{10}$, $\frac{6}{10}$

$\frac{2}{5} > \frac{1}{4}$: $\frac{8}{20}$, $\frac{5}{20}$

Find the sum or difference.

$\frac{3}{8} + \frac{3}{4}$: $\frac{3}{8} + \frac{6}{8} = \frac{9}{8} = 1\frac{1}{8}$

$\frac{9}{10} - \frac{2}{5}$: $\frac{9}{10} - \frac{4}{10} = \frac{5}{10}$

$\frac{5}{6} - \frac{1}{4}$: $\frac{10}{12} - \frac{3}{12} = \frac{7}{12}$

Round each number to the nearest whole number. Then, circle the better estimate for the sum or difference.

Problem	Choices	Circled
$3\frac{2}{3} + 2\frac{3}{4}$	6, 7	7
$1\frac{1}{4} + 2\frac{5}{8}$	3, 4	4
$2\frac{1}{8} - 1\frac{1}{10}$	1, 2	1

5.11 Unit Wrap-Up B

Unit Wrap-Up: Miri wants to make this quilt. Use the quilt pattern to answer the questions.

Star Quilt Pattern

Fabric at the fabric store comes in rolls. You'll need the following lengths of each color of fabric.

- $\frac{3}{4}$ yd. dark blue fabric
- $1\frac{5}{8}$ yd. light blue fabric
- $3\frac{1}{4}$ yd. white fabric
- $1\frac{2}{3}$ yd. green fabric
- $4\frac{5}{6}$ yd. gray fabric for the back of the quilt

How much blue fabric does Miri need in all? (Include both the dark blue fabric and light blue fabric.)

$$\frac{3}{4} = \frac{6}{8}$$
$$+\,1\frac{5}{8} = 1\frac{5}{8}$$
$$1\frac{11}{8} = 2\frac{3}{8}\text{ yd.}$$

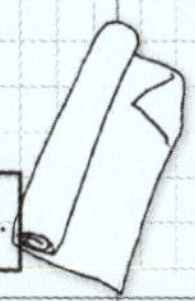

Miri already has two pieces of gray fabric. One piece is $1\frac{1}{2}$ yd. long. The other piece is $3\frac{2}{3}$ yd. long. Does she have enough gray fabric?

$$1\frac{1}{2} = 1\frac{3}{6}$$
$$+\,3\frac{2}{3} = 3\frac{4}{6}$$
$$4\frac{7}{6} = 5\frac{1}{6}\text{ yd.}$$

yes

How much more white fabric than green fabric does Miri need?

$$3\frac{1}{4} = 3\frac{3}{12} = 2\frac{15}{12}$$
$$-\,1\frac{2}{3} = 1\frac{8}{12}$$
$$1\frac{7}{12}\text{ yd.}$$

Miri already has $2\frac{1}{3}$ yd. of white fabric. How much more white fabric does she need?

$$3\frac{1}{4} = 3\frac{3}{12} = 2\frac{15}{12}$$
$$-\,2\frac{1}{3} = 2\frac{4}{12}$$
$$\frac{11}{12}\text{ yd.}$$

Unit 5 Checkpoint

What to Expect at the End of Unit 5

By the end of Unit 5, most children will be able to do the following:

- Convert mixed numbers to fractions and fractions to mixed numbers.
- Multiply to find a missing number in a pair of equivalent fractions.
- Use common denominators to compare fractions with different denominators.
- Add and subtract fractions and mixed numbers with different denominators. Most children will understand these processes well, but some will have trouble organizing their work and accurately completing the full sequence of steps.
- Solve fraction and mixed number word problems. Some children will still need help writing out and solving the matching addition or subtraction problems.
- Estimate sums or differences of mixed numbers. Children will vary in how accurately they can predict the sums or differences, and many children will still be working on this skill.

Is Your Child Ready to Move on?

In Unit 6, your child will learn strategies for mental division.

Before moving on to Unit 6, your child should be mostly fluent with the multiplication and division facts up to 10×10 and 100÷10. If you find that your child's lack of fluency with the multiplication or division facts makes the lessons long or frustrating, **allow her to use the multiplication chart** (Blackline Master 4) as she completes the lessons in Unit 6.

Your child does not need to have fully mastered the fraction addition and subtraction skills in Unit 5 before moving on to Unit 6. She will practice them in the Review pages before learning to multiply and divide fractions later in the year.

Unit 6
Mental Division

Overview

Your child will learn a variety of mental division techniques in this unit, with a focus on dividing numbers to 100 and finding all factors of numbers to 100. He'll also learn divisibility rules for 3, 4, and 6, how to find the greatest common factor for a pair of numbers, and how to mentally divide larger numbers by multiples of 10 or 100.

What Your Child Will Learn

In this unit, your child will learn to:

- Mentally divide by 15, 25, and 35
- Use divisibility rules to tell whether numbers are divisible by 2, 3, 4, 5, or 6
- Mentally divide by 2 by splitting numbers in half
- Mentally divide by 4 by dividing by 2 twice
- Use the "multiply and adjust" strategy to mentally divide two-digit numbers by one-digit numbers
- Use mental division and divisibility rules to find all factors of numbers to 100
- Find the greatest common factor (GCF) of two numbers
- Mentally divide by multiples of 10 or 100 (for example, 600 ÷ 30 or 3,000 ÷ 500)

Lesson List

Lesson 6.1	Mentally Divide by 15, 25, and 35	Lesson 6.6	Find All Factors for Numbers to 100
Lesson 6.2	Mentally Divide by 2 and 5	Lesson 6.7	Find Greatest Common Factors
Lesson 6.3	Mentally Divide by 3	Lesson 6.8	Mentally Divide by Multiples of 10 or 100
Lesson 6.4	Mentally Divide by 6	Lesson 6.9	Enrichment (Optional)
Lesson 6.5	Mentally Divide by 4		

Extra Materials Needed for Unit 6

- 4 small slips of paper
- For optional Enrichment Lesson:
  - *How Many Guinea Pigs Can Fit on a Plane?: Answers to Your Most Clever Math Questions,* by Laura Overdeck. Feiwel & Friends, 2017.

Teaching Math with Confidence: Two Ways to Visualize Mental Division Problems

When your child first learned to divide, he learned that we use division to find answers in two different types of equal-groups contexts. Sometimes, we want to find the size of each equal group. Other times, we want to find the number of equal groups. For example:

I have 20 ft. of rope. I cut the rope into 5 equal pieces. How long is each piece?

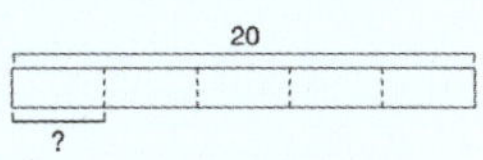

20 ÷ 5 = 4 ft.

This problem asks you to find the size of each equal group.

I have 20 ft. of rope. I cut the rope into pieces that are each 5 ft. long. How many pieces do I make?

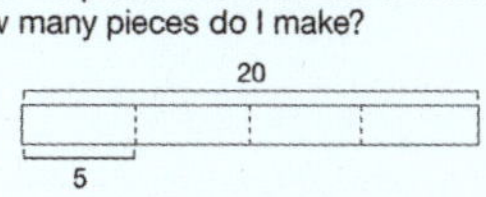

20 ÷ 5 = 4 pieces

This problem asks you to find the number of equal groups.

Both problems have 4 as an answer, but the 4 means something different in each problem. The answer to the first problem is *4 feet*, but the answer to the second problem is *4 pieces*. You find the *size of each group* in the first problem, and you find the *number of groups* in the second problem.

In this unit, your child will learn strategies for mentally dividing numbers to 100. Some of these mental division strategies are more intuitive if you visualize finding the size of each group. For example, dividing by 2 is usually easier if you imagine splitting the quantity into 2 equal groups.

Other mental division strategies are more intuitive if you imagine dividing the quantity into groups of a certain size. For example, it's very difficult to imagine dividing most quantities into 5 equal groups. It's usually easier if you instead imagine measuring out as many groups of 5 from the quantity as possible.

Wrestling with mental division helps your child develop a stronger understanding of the two meanings of division. It also strengthens his understanding of divisibility, the distributive property, and the relationship between multiplication and division. However, some children find mental division very difficult, regardless of how they visualize the problems. If you find that this is true for your child, use the following suggestions to adjust the mental division lessons to your child's needs. That way, he can reap the benefits of mental division without feeling overwhelmed:

- **Use the concrete situations** presented on the Lesson Activities pages to help your child visualize the practice problems. For example, most children find it much easier to imagine splitting 208 children into 4 equal groups than trying to solve 208 ÷ 4 without any additional context.
- Model the strategies presented in the lesson, but **allow your child to use any efficient and accurate strategy** that makes sense to him. Children often make up their own strategies for solving mental math problems, and that's perfectly fine.
- If your child finds mental division very taxing, **don't require him to solve every practice problem** on the Lesson Activities and Practice pages. Or, split the lessons over two days.
- Mental math is meant to help your child develop his number sense, not develop a memory champion. **Always allow him to write down any in-between steps** in his solving process.
- **Don't allow your child to rewrite mental division problems as written long division problems.** Skipping mental math and going straight to the algorithm short-circuits all the number sense growth that mental math provides.
- **Don't worry if your child doesn't become fully fluent with mental division** by the end of the unit. Even if he doesn't completely master these strategies now, the exposure to these challenging concepts will help prepare him to tackle fraction and decimal division later in the year.

Lesson 6.1
Mentally Divide by 15, 25, and 35

Purpose	Materials
• Skip-count by 15, 25, and 35 to create lists of multiples • Mentally divide by 15, 25, or 35	• 4 small slips of paper

Memory Work	
	• **What do we call the number to be divided?** *The dividend.* • **What do we call the number we divide by?** *The divisor.* • **What do we call the result when we divide two numbers?** *The quotient.* • **What do we call an amount that is left over after division?** *The remainder.*

Warm-up (A): Skip-Count to Create Lists of Multiples of 15, 25, or 35

Have you ever been to an arcade? *Answers will vary.* Briefly discuss your child's experiences with arcades. **At some arcades, you win tickets with different point values when you play the games. Then, you use the points to earn prizes.**

We'll warm up today by making a chart to show how many points you get from different numbers of tickets. We'll use skip-counting to complete the rows in the chart. Have your child skip-count to find the value of each number of tickets.

A

Number of Tickets	1	2	3	4	5	6	7	8
15	15	30	45	60	75	90	105	120
25	25	50	75	100	125	150	175	200
35	35	70	105	140	175	210	245	280

Your child is not expected to have these skip-counting sequences memorized. Encourage her to use repeated mental addition to find the values. For example: **Two 15-point tickets are worth 30 points, so three 15-point tickets are worth 15 points more. What's 30 plus 15?** *45 points.*

Number of Tickets	1	2	3
15	15	30	45

+15

Activity (B): Use Skip-Counting or Reasoning to Mentally Divide by 15, 25, or 35

Today, you'll learn how to mentally divide by 15, 25, or 35. We'll cover the charts in part A, but you can peek at them if you need to. Use a piece of scrap paper to cover part A.

Have your child read the text box aloud.

Mental Division (B)

We can use skip-counting to mentally divide by numbers like 15, 25, and 35.
Or, we can think about equal groups within the dividend.

Ex. Andrew wants to buy a prize that costs 60 points. How many 15-point tickets does he need?

Skip-Counting

60 ÷ 15 = ?

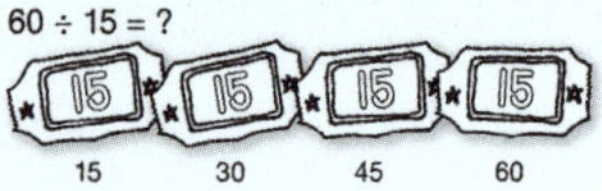

60 is the fourth multiple of 15.
So, there are 4 groups of 15 in 60.
60 ÷ 15 = **4**

Think about Equal Groups

60 ÷ 15 = ?

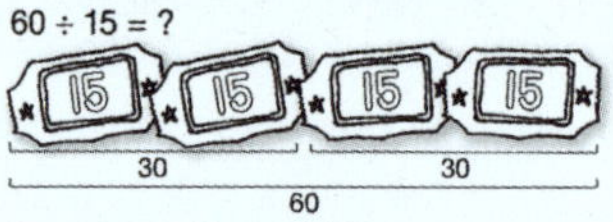

2 groups of 15 equal 30.
2 groups of 30 equal 60.
So, there are 4 groups of 15 in 60.
60 ÷ 15 = **4**

The first example shows how to use skip-counting to divide 60 by 15. When people count out money or arcade tickets, they often skip-count aloud to keep track of how many bills or tickets they need to give the cashier.

We'll use pretend tickets to help understand how to divide by these numbers. Write 15 on 4 small slips of paper. Count by 15s as you place one ticket at a time on the table: **15, 30, 45, 60. 4 groups of 15 equal 60, so 60 divided by 15 equals 4.**

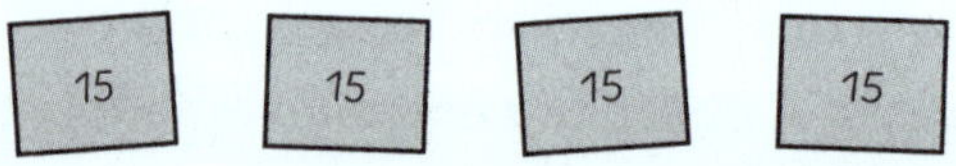

The second example shows how to think about equal groups to divide 60 by 15. Split the tickets into 2 pairs. **Every pair of 2 tickets is worth 30 points. I know that 2 groups of 30 equal 60. So, 2 pairs of 2 tickets are worth 60 points.**

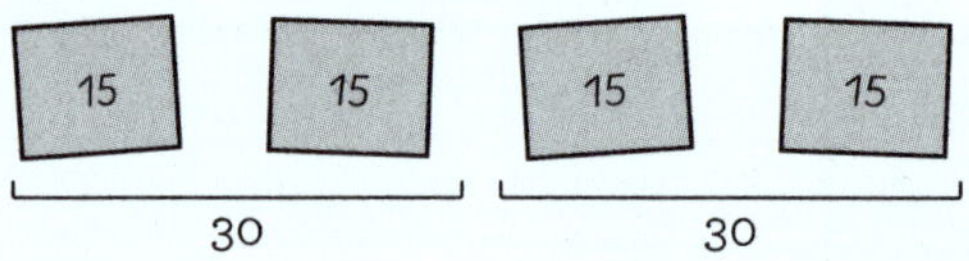

Have your child write a division problem to match each of the questions about the arcade prizes. Then, have her use mental math to solve the problems. She may use either of the sample approaches to find the answers.

(B)

How many 35-point tickets do you need to buy a dinosaur? 105 ÷ 35 = 3 *tickets*	How many 15-point tickets do you need to buy a box of candy? 120 ÷ 15 = 8 *tickets*
How many 25-point tickets do you need to buy a teddy bear? 200 ÷ 25 = 8 *tickets*	★ How many 250-point tickets do you need to buy a speaker? 1,250 ÷ 250 = 5 *tickets*

If your child has trouble with the problems, make more pretend tickets to make the problems more concrete. For example, for the dinosaur problem, write 35 on several slips of paper and encourage her to count by 35s as she pretends to pay for the dinosaur.

Encourage your child to count by 250s to solve the starred problem: 250, 500, 750, 1,000, 1,250.

Independent Practice and Review

Have your child complete the Lesson 6.1 Practice and Review workbook pages.

Lesson 6.2
Mentally Divide by 2 and 5

Purpose	Materials
• Review two ways to interpret division • Review divisibility rules for 2 and 5 • Split quantities in half to mentally divide by 2 • Use the "multiply and adjust" strategy to mentally divide numbers by 5	• None

Memory Work

- **How do you know if a number is divisible by 2?** *It is even. It has a 0, 2, 4, 6, or 8 in the ones-place.*
- **How do you know if a number is divisible by 5?** *It has a 0 or 5 in the ones-place.*
- **How do you know if a number is divisible by 10?** *It has a 0 in the ones-place.*

Warm-up (A): Review Two Ways to Interpret Division

You have learned two different ways to interpret division equations. Division situations always involve splitting a total into equal groups. Sometimes, we use division to find the number of equal groups. Other times, we use division to find the size of each group.

See the Unit 6 **Teaching Math with Confidence** for more on these two ways to interpret division, along with tips on teaching mental division.

Have your child read aloud and solve both word problems in part A. Make sure he labels his answers correctly.

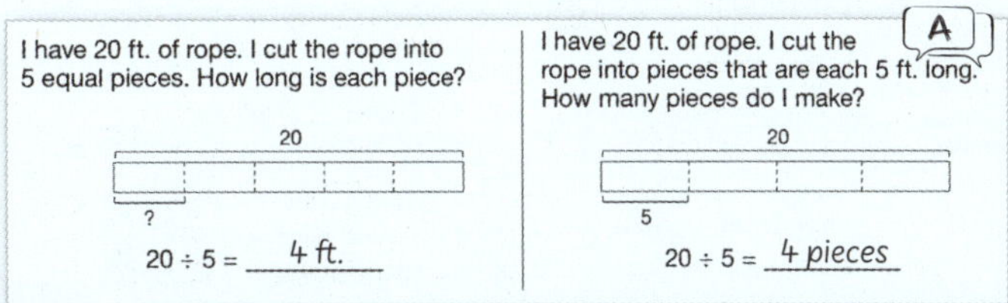

These problems are purposely simple so your child can focus on the underlying concept rather than the numbers.

In the first problem, did you find the number of equal groups or the size of each group? *The size of each group.* **In the second problem, did you find the number of equal groups or the size of each group?** *The number of equal groups.* **Today, you'll use these two interpretations of division to mentally divide by 2 or 5.**

Activity (B): Mentally Divide by 2 or 5

What does it mean if a number is divisible by another number? *Sample answer: It means the second number evenly divides the first number.* **Is 12 divisible by 2?** *Yes.* **How do you know?** *Sample answer: 12 divided by 2 equals 6.* **Is 12 divisible by 5?** *No.* **How do you know?** *Sample answer: 12 divided by 5 has a remainder.*

When you were younger, you learned divisibility rules for 2 and 5. Today, you'll review these rules and mentally divide by 2 and 5.

When we mentally divide by 2, it's usually easiest to imagine you're splitting a quantity into 2 equal groups and finding the size of each group. Have your child read the top part of the text box aloud.

B

Divide by 2 or 5

A number is divisible by 2 if it is even.

To mentally divide a number by 2, break the number into parts and split each part in half.

Ex. Simon won 38 tickets at the arcade. He shared the tickets equally with his brother. How many did they each get?

38 ÷ 2 = ?

Half of 30 → 15

Half of 8 → 4

19

38 ÷ 2 = **19 tickets**

Read aloud the first example word problem. **In this problem, we want to divide 38 tickets into 2 equal groups.**

- **First, we split 38 into 30 and 8.**
- **Half of 30 is 15.**
- **Half of 8 is 4.**
- **15 plus 4 is 19, so 38 divided by 2 equals 19. Each person gets 19 tickets.**
- Point to the illustration. **How do you think they could divide these tickets evenly?** *Sample answer: They could trade 1 ten for 2 fives and 1 five for 5 ones. Then, each person could get 1 ten, 1 five, and 4 ones.*

We could also have broken 38 in a different way. For example, you could also break 38 into 20 and 18 and find half of each part. Either way, you still get the same answer.

In Unit 3, you learned how to use related multiples to mentally multiply. We'll use a similar approach to mentally divide by 5. When we mentally divide by 5, it's usually easiest to imagine you're splitting a quantity into groups of 5 and finding the number of equal groups. Have your child read aloud the bottom part of the text box.

B

A number is divisible by 5 if it has 0 or 5 in its ones-place.

To mentally divide a number by 5, write the problem as a missing factor problem. Then, multiply and adjust to find the missing factor.

Ex. Isabella won 65 tickets at the arcade. Each bracelet costs 5 tickets. How many bracelets can she buy?

65 ÷ 5 = ? → ____ × 5 = 65

10 × 5 = 50. Too low.

11 × 5 = 55. Too low.

12 × 5 = 60. Too low.

13 × 5 = 65. Just right!

65 ÷ 5 = **13 bracelets**

Read aloud the second example word problem. **In this problem, we want to divide 65 tickets into equal groups of 5.**

- **First, we rewrite the division problem as a missing factor problem: What times 5 equals 65?**
- **In the example, the first estimate is 10. 10 times 5 equals 50, so that's too low. Isabella can buy more than 10 bracelets.**
- **The second estimate is 11. 11 times 5 is 55, so that's still too low.**
- **The third estimate is 12. 12 times 5 is 60, so that's still too low.**
- **The fourth estimate is 13. 13 times 5 is 65. That's just right!**
- **65 divided by 5 equals 13, so Isabella can buy 13 bracelets.**

Now, you get to choose some prizes at the arcade! Have your child use the "multiply and adjust" strategy to complete the problems. If he has trouble getting started, suggest he try multiplying 20 × 5. After he solves each problem, ask him what prizes he would pick.

If you have 105 tickets, how many prizes can you get?

20 × 5 = 100
21 × 5 = 105

105 ÷ 5 = 21 prizes

If you have 90 tickets, how many prizes can you get?

20 × 5 = 100
19 × 5 = 95
18 × 5 = 90
90 ÷ 5 = 18 prizes

Sample solutions. Your child may use different multiplication problems to find the answers.

Independent Practice and Review

Have your child complete the Lesson 6.2 Practice and Review workbook pages.

Lesson 6.3
Mentally Divide by 3

Purpose	Materials
• Explore patterns in the multiples of 3 • Learn the divisibility rule for 3 • Mentally divide by 3	• Playing cards • Counters

Memory Work	
	• **What do we call the number to be divided?** *The dividend.* • **What do we call the number we divide by?** *The divisor.* • **What do we call the result when we divide two numbers?** *The quotient.* • **What do we call an amount that is left over after division?** *The remainder.*

Warm-up (A): Explore Patterns in Multiples of 3

In this activity, your child will look for patterns in the multiples of 3 to explore the divisibility rule for 3. Cover part B with a piece of paper so that your child has the opportunity to discover the divisibility rule for 3 on her own.

In the last lesson, we reviewed the divisibility rules for 2 and 5 and mentally divided by 2 and 5. Today, you'll learn the divisibility rule for 3 and mentally divide by 3.

The divisibility rule for 3 is very different than the rules for 2 and 5. We'll warm up by exploring patterns in the multiples of 3. You might even discover the divisibility rule for yourself!

The first row in each chart lists the multiples of 3 in order. The second row lists the sum of the digits in the multiples. The first few are already completed. Point to the column with 15 in it. **What are the digits in 15?** *1 and 5.* **What is the sum of those digits?** *6.* Write 6 in the box below 15. Continue in the same way with the rest of the multiples of 3.

A

Multiple of 3	3	6	9	12	15	18	21	24	27	30
Sum of digits	3	6	9	3	6	9	3	6	9	3

Multiple of 3	33	36	39	42	45	48	51	54	57	60
Sum of digits	6	9	12	6	9	12	6	9	12	6

What do you notice about the sums of the digits? *Sample answers: They repeat in patterns. All of the sums are multiples of 3. All of the sums are divisible by 3.*

When you add up the digits in the multiples of 3, the sum is always divisible by 3!

This informal exploration is meant to help your child understand the divisibility rule for 3 and see that it holds true up to 60. Formally proving that this rule is true for all numbers requires an understanding of algebra, so it is not included here.

Activity (B): Mentally Divide by 3

Have your child read the top part of the text box aloud.

B

Divide by 3	
A number is divisible by 3 if the sum of its digits is divisible by 3.	Ex. Is 96 divisible by 3? 9 + 6 = 15 15 is divisible by 3, so 96 is divisible by 3.

Cover the divisibility rule with your hand. **How do we know whether a number is divisible by 3?** *The sum of its digits is divisible by 3.*

In the last lesson, you used the multiply-and-adjust strategy to divide by 5. Today, we'll use a similar approach to mentally divide by 3. Have your child read aloud the bottom part of the text box.

To mentally divide a number by 3, write the problem as a missing factor problem. Then, multiply and adjust to find the missing factor.	**Ex.** Sasha has 57 tickets. Each game at the fair costs 3 tickets. How many games can he play? 57 ÷ 3 = ? → ____ × 3 = 57 20 × 3 = 60. Too high. 19 × 3 = 57. Just right! 57 ÷ 3 = **19 games**

Read aloud the second example word problem. **In this problem, we want to divide 57 tickets into equal groups of 3.**

- **First, we rewrite the division problem as a missing factor problem: What times 3 equals 57?**
- **In the example, the first estimate is 20. 20 times 3 equals 60, so that's too high. Sasha can't play 20 games.**
- **The second estimate is 19. 19 times 3 is 57, so that's just right.**
- **57 divided by 3 equals 19, so Sasha can play 19 games.**

Have your child use the "multiply and adjust" strategy to complete the problems.

72 ÷ 3 = 24	93 ÷ 3 = 31	84 ÷ 3 = 28
20 × 3 = 60	30 × 3 = 90	30 × 3 = 90
22 × 3 = 66	31 × 3 = 93	29 × 3 = 87
24 × 3 = 72		28 × 3 = 84

Sample solutions. Your child may use different multiplication problems to find the answers.

Activity (C): Play Division Tic-Tac-Toe

Play Division Tic-Tac-Toe. Encourage your child to multiply and adjust to find the answers to the division problems.

If your child has trouble solving the problems mentally, have her write her multiplication equations on scrap paper.

Division Tic-Tac-Toe

Materials: 2s, 3s, and 5s from a deck of cards (12 cards total); counters of two different colors

Object of the Game: Be the first player to fill three boxes in a row, either horizontally, vertically, or diagonally.

Shuffle the cards and place them face down in one pile. Give 8 counters of one color to one player and 8 counters of a different color to the other player.

On your turn, flip over a card. Find a number on the game board that is divisible by the number on the card. Divide the number on the game board by the number on the card. Name the answer and place a counter on the number.

Directions continued on next page.

For example, if you flip over a 5, you can choose any number on the board that is divisible by 5. If you choose 75, say "75 divided by 5 equals 15" and place a counter on 75.

Sample play. You may choose any number that is divisible by the number on your card.

Play then passes to the other player. If you draw a card and all the multiples of the card are already covered, you lose your turn and play passes to the other player. If you run out of cards, reshuffle the cards you've already used. Continue until one player covers 3 boxes in a row, either horizontally, vertically, or diagonally.

Note that you only need to place 3 counters in a row to win, even though there are 4 rows and 4 columns on the gameboard. The extra row and columns provide more opportunities to win.

Independent Practice and Review

Have your child complete the Lesson 6.3 Practice and Review workbook pages.

Lesson 6.4
Mentally Divide by 6

Purpose	Materials
• Explore divisibility patterns in the multiples of 6 • Learn the divisibility rule for 6 • Mentally divide by 6	• None

Memory Work	
	• **How do you know if a number is divisible by 2?** *It is even. It has a 0, 2, 4, 6, or 8 in the ones-place.* • **How do you know if a number is divisible by 3?** *The sum of its digits is divisible by 3.* • **How do you know if a number is divisible by 5?** *It has a 0 or 5 in the ones-place.*

Warm-up (A): Explore Multiples of 6 with Dot Patterns

In this activity, your child will explore the divisibility rule for 6. Cover part B with a piece of paper so that your child has the opportunity to understand the divisibility rule for 6 on his own before reading it.

Today, you'll learn the divisibility rule for 6 and mentally divide by 6. We'll use these dot patterns to explore divisibility in the multiples of 6. You might even discover the divisibility rule for yourself!

Point to the dot diagram above the 6.

- **Is 6 divisible by 2?** *Yes.* **In the dot diagram, each row has 2 dots, so we can see that 6 is divisible by 2.** Write a check mark in the box below 6.
- **Is 6 divisible by 3?** *Yes.* **In the dot diagram, each column has 3 dots, so we can see that 6 is divisible by 3.** Write a check mark in the box.

Repeat with the dot diagram for 12. **12 is made from 2 blocks of 6 dots. Each block is divisible by both 2 and 3, so 12 must be divisible by both 2 and 3 as well.**

Repeat with the dot diagram for 18. **18 is made from 3 blocks of 6 dots. Again, each block is divisible by both 2 and 3, so 18 must be divisible by both 2 and 3 as well.**

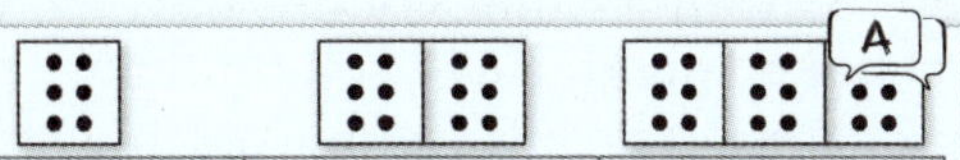

	6	12	18
Divisible by 2?	√	√	√
Divisible by 3?	√	√	√
Divisible by 6?	√	√	√

Can you predict what the divisibility rule for 6 is? *Sample answer: The number has to be divisible by both 2 and 3.* **If a number is divisible by both 2 and 3, it is divisible by 6, too!**

We can use a similar principle to create other divisibility rules. This overall principle holds true for any 2 numbers that have no factor (other than 1) in common. For example, if a number is divisible by both 4 and 5, it is also divisible by 20. However, if a number is divisible by both 2 and 4, that does not automatically mean the number is divisible by 8, since 2 and 4 share the common factor of 2. For example, 12 is divisible by both 2 and 4, but it is not divisible by 8.

Activity (B): Mentally Divide by 6

Have your child read the top part of the text box aloud.

Divide by 6 A number is divisible by 6 if it is divisible by 2 and divisible by 3.	B Ex. Is 78 divisible by 6? 78 is an even number, so it is divisible by 2. 7 + 8 = 15. 15 is divisible by 3, so 78 is divisible by 3. 78 is divisible by both 2 and 3, so it is divisible by 6.

What are the digits in 78? *7 and 8.* **7 plus 8 equals 15. Is 15 divisible by 3?** *Yes.* **How do you know?** *15 divided by 3 equals 5. 1 plus 5 equals 6, and 6 is divisible by 3.* **The sum of the digits in 78 is divisible by 3, so 78 is divisible by 3.**

Cover the divisibility rule with your hand. **How do we know whether a number is divisible by 6?** *The number is divisible by both 2 and 3.*

In the last lesson, you used the multiply-and-adjust strategy to divide by 3. We can use the same strategy to mentally divide by 6. Have your child read aloud the bottom part of the text box.

To mentally divide a number by 6, write the problem as a missing factor problem. Then, multiply and adjust to find the missing factor.	B Ex. The bakery packs its products in boxes of 6. If they pack 78 donuts, how many boxes of donuts do they fill? 78 ÷ 6 = ? → _____ × 6 = 78 10 × 6 = 60. Too low. 11 × 6 = 66. Too low. 12 × 6 = 72. Too low. 13 × 6 = 78. Just right! 78 ÷ 6 = **13**

Read aloud the word problem. **In this problem, we want to divide 78 donuts into equal groups of 6.**

- **First, we rewrite the division problem as a missing factor problem: What times 6 equals 78?**
- **In the example, the first estimate is 10. 10 times 6 equals 60, so that's too low. If you pack 10 boxes, you still have more donuts.**
- **The second estimate is 11. 11 times 6 is 66, so that's still too low.**
- **The next estimate is 12. 12 times 6 is 72, so we're close!**
- **13 times 6 equals 78.**
- **So, 78 divided by 6 equals 13. The bakery can fill 13 boxes of donuts.**

The bakery also baked 132 cookies and 114 muffins. Let's figure out how many boxes of 6 they can pack for each baked good. Have your child use the "multiply and adjust" strategy to solve the practice problems. If he has trouble getting started, suggest he begin with 20 × 6 for both problems.

B

132 ÷ 6 = 22

20 × 6 = 120
21 × 6 = 126
22 × 6 = 132

114 ÷ 6 = 19

20 × 6 = 120
19 × 6 = 114

Sample solutions. Your child may use different multiplication problems to find the answers.

Independent Practice and Review

Have your child complete the Lesson 6.4 Practice and Review workbook pages.

Lesson 6.5
Mentally Divide by 4

Purpose	Materials
• Practice mentally dividing by 2 • Learn the divisibility rule for 4 • Split quantities in half twice to mentally divide by 4 • Practice mentally dividing by 2, 3, 4, 5, and 6	• Die • Counters

Memory Work	
	• **How do you know if a number is divisible by 2?** *It is even. It has a 0, 2, 4, 6, or 8 in the ones-place.* • **How do you know if a number is divisible by 3?** *The sum of its digits is divisible by 3.* • **How do you know if a number is divisible by 5?** *It has a 0 or 5 in the ones-place.* • **How do you know if a number is divisible by 6?** *It is even and divisible by 3.*

Warm-up: Practice Mentally Dividing by 2

In Lesson 6.1, you practiced splitting numbers in half to mentally divide by 2. Ask your child the following questions orally.

- **What's 128 divided by 2?** *64.*
- **What's 64 divided by 2?** *32.*
- **What's 32 divided by 2?** *16.*
- **What's 16 divided by 2?** *8.*
- **What's 8 divided by 2?** *4.*
- **What's 4 divided by 2?** *2.*
- **What's 2 divided by 2?** *1.*

This activity prepares your child to divide by 2 twice in the next activity.

Activity (A): Mentally Divide by 4

Today, you'll first learn how to mentally divide numbers by 4. Then, you'll learn the divisibility rule for 4. Have your child read aloud the top part of the text box.

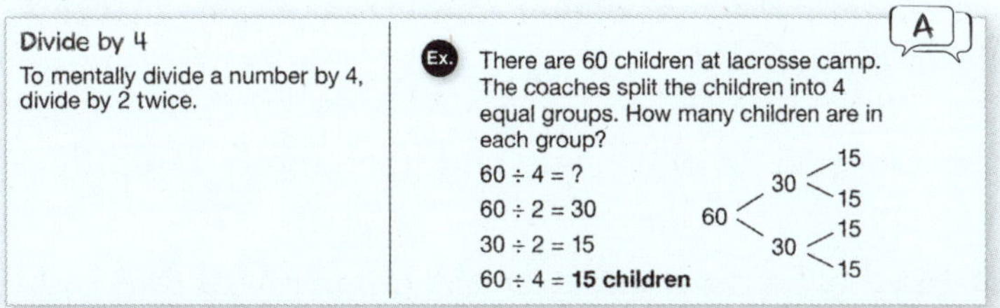

Read aloud the example word problem. **In this problem, we want to divide 60 children into 4 equal groups.**

- **First, we split the children into 2 equal groups. 60 divided by 2 equals 30.**
- **Then, we split each group into 2 smaller groups. 30 divided by 2 equals 15. So, there are 15 children in each group.**

You could also use the multiply-and-adjust strategy to solve this problem. However, dividing by 2 twice is usually a more efficient strategy.

The divisibility rule for 4 is related to the divisibility rule for 2. How do we know whether a number is divisible by 2? *If a number is even, it is divisible by 2.* Have your child read the bottom part of the text box aloud.

A number is divisible by 4 if you get an even number when you divide the number by 2.

Ex. Is 60 divisible by 4?
60 ÷ 2 = 30
30 is an even number. That means you can divide it by 2 and get another whole number.
So, 60 is divisible by 4.

60 divided by 2 is 30. 30 is an even number, so we can divide it by 2 again and get a whole number.

Dividing by 4 is like dividing by 2 twice. So, if you divide a number by 2 and get an even number, you know you can divide it by 2 again and still get a whole number.

Cover the divisibility rule with your hand. **How do we know whether a number is divisible by 4?** *You get an even number when you divide it by 2.*

Have your child complete the practice problems. Encourage her to divide by 2 twice to solve each problem.

84 ÷ 4 = 21
84 ÷ 2 = 42
42 ÷ 2 = 21

208 ÷ 4 = 52
208 ÷ 2 = 104
104 ÷ 2 = 52

Activity (B): Play Division Tic-Tac-Toe

Play Division Tic-Tac-Toe. Encourage your child to use the strategies she has learned in Lessons 6.1 – 6.4 as she finds the answers.

Division Tic-Tac-Toe

Materials: Die; counters of two different colors

Object of the Game: Be the first player to fill three boxes in a row, either horizontally, vertically, or diagonally.

Give 10 counters of one color to one player and 10 counters of a different color to the other player.

On your turn, roll the die. Find a number on the game board that is divisible by the number on the die. Divide the number on the game board by the number on the die. Name the answer and place a counter on the number.

For example, if you roll a 2, you can choose any number on the board that is divisible by 2. If you choose 52, say "52 divided by 2 equals 26" and place a counter on 52.

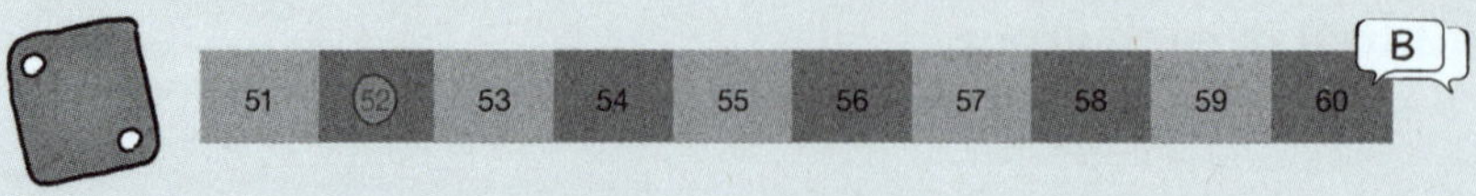

Sample play. You may choose any number that is divisible by the number on your card.

Directions continued on next page.

All numbers are divisible by 1. So, if you roll a 1, you may place a counter anywhere on the board.

Play then passes to the other player. Continue until one player covers 3 boxes in a row, either horizontally, vertically, or diagonally.

Independent Practice and Review

Have your child complete the Lesson 6.5 Practice and Review workbook pages.

Lesson 6.6
Find All Factors for Numbers to 100

Purpose	Materials
• Find factors in a real-life context • Use mental division to find all factors for numbers less than 100	• None

Memory Work
- **Name 4 multiples of 10.** *Sample answers: 30, 70, 300, 4,000.*
- **Name 4 factors of 10.** *1, 2, 5, 10.*

In *Fourth Grade Math with Confidence*, your child learned how to use the division facts to find factor pairs for numbers less than 50. In this lesson, he'll learn how to use his mental division skills to find all factors for any number up to 100.

Warm-up (A): Review Factor Pairs

Last year, you learned how to find the factor pairs of a number. Factor pairs are the pairs of factors that you multiply together to equal a certain number.

Let's review by finding all the factor pairs of 24. We'll check every number from 1 to 9 to see if it's a factor of 24. Point to the list of numbers 1-9. **We'll use this list to make sure we check every number.**

Is 1 a factor of 24? *Yes.* **1 times what equals 24?** *24.* Write "1 × 24." Cross out the 1 in the chart.

Is 2 a factor of 24? *Yes.* **2 times what equals 24?** *12.* Write "2 × 12." Cross out the 2 in the chart. If your child has trouble finding the matching factor for 2, suggest he split 24 in half.

Go through each number from 1-9 in the same way until your child has found all the factor pairs.

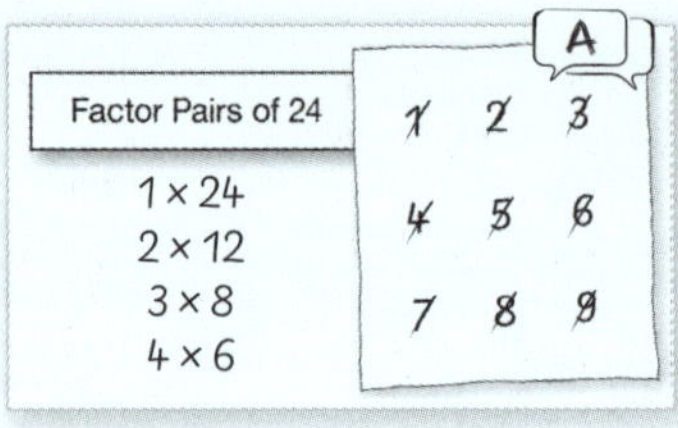

How do you know that 24 isn't divisible by 7? *Sample answers: You get a remainder if you divide 24 by 7. 7 times 3 equals 21, and 7 times 4 equals 28.* **You can always use your knowledge of division and the multiplication facts to check whether a number is divisible by another number, even if you haven't learned a specific divisibility rule for the divisor.**

Have your child find all factor pairs of 23 in the same way. **23 only has 1 factor pair! Any number divided by 1 equals the number, so 1 times the number is always one of the factor pairs.**

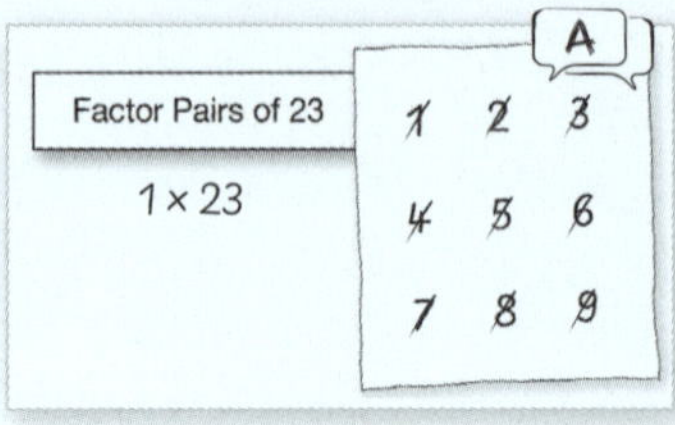

Activity (B): Find All Factors for Numbers Less than 100

In the last few lessons, you have learned how to mentally divide numbers. Today, you'll use this skill to find all factors for numbers up to 100. We check whether the number is divisible by the numbers from 1 to 9, just like in the warm-up. Have your child read the text box.

How to Find All Factors of a Number Less Than 100	B
To find all factors of a number less than 100, check to see whether the target number is divisible by the numbers 1 to 9. If the target number is divisible by one of the numbers, write the matching factor pair. Once you find all the factor pairs, write all the factors in order from least to greatest.	**Ex.** Find all the factors of 68. 68 ÷ 1 = 68. 1 × 68 is a factor pair. 68 ÷ 2 = 34. 2 × 34 is a factor pair. 68 is not divisible by 3, so 3 is not a factor of 68. 68 ÷ 4 = 17. 4 × 17 is a factor pair. 68 is not divisible by 5, 6, 7, 8, or 9. So, 5, 6, 7, 8, and 9 are not factors of 68. Factors of 68: **1, 2, 4, 17, 34, and 68.**

The example shows that 68 is divisible by 1, 2, and 4. Let's check that 68 isn't divisible by the other numbers from 1 to 9.

- **How do you know 68 isn't divisible by 3?** *Sample answer: The sum of the digits is 14. 14 isn't divisible by 3, so 68 isn't divisible by 3.*
- **How do you know 68 isn't divisible by 5?** *Sample answer: The digit in its ones-place isn't 0 or 5.*
- **How do you know 68 isn't divisible by 6?** *Sample answer: It's not divisible by 3, so it's not divisible by 6.*
- **How do you know 68 isn't divisible by 7?** *Sample answer: 10 times 7 is 70. That's only 2 more than 68, so 68 isn't a multiple of 7.*
- **How do you know 68 isn't divisible by 8?** *Sample answer: 8 times 8 equals 64. That's 4 less than 68, so 68 isn't a multiple of 8.*
- **How do you know 68 isn't divisible by 9?** *9 times 7 equals 63. That's 5 less than 68, so 68 isn't a multiple of 9.*

In the final answer, the answers are written in order from least to greatest. When an answer tells you to find all the factors of a number, write them in this order.

> Writing the factors in order from least to greatest is simply a convention. It sometimes proves helpful to have the factors listed in order when finding common denominators, simplifying fractions, or factoring polynomials in algebra.

Not all numbers have so many factors! Some numbers only have 2 factors: 1 and the number. Have your child read the bottom part of the text box aloud.

	B
Prime numbers have exactly 2 factors: 1 and the number itself. Composite numbers have more than 2 factors.	**Ex.** Is 68 prime or composite? 68 has more than 2 factors, so it is composite. **Ex.** Is 23 prime or composite? 23 has exactly 2 factors, so it is prime.

Use the following questions to briefly discuss prime and composite numbers:

- **Why is 68 composite?** *It has more than 2 factors.*
- **Why is 23 prime?** *It only has 2 factors.*
- **Is 2 prime or composite?** *Prime.* **How do you know?** *Sample answer: Its only factor pair is 1 times 2.*
- **Is 9 prime or composite?** *Composite.* **How do you know?** *Sample answer: Its factor pairs are 1 times 9 and 3 times 3.*
- **What are the factors of 1?** *1.* **1 has only one factor, so it's neither prime nor composite!**

Have your child read the word problem aloud. **What's the goal of this problem?** *Find how many chairs she can put in each row.* **We'll find all the factors of 60 to see how many chairs she could put in each row.**

Help your child check whether 60 is divisible by the numbers from 1 to 9.

- **What's 60 divided by 1?** *60.* **So, 1 and 60 are factors of 60.** Write "1 × 60." **She could make 60 rows of 1, or 1 row of 60. They both might look pretty silly, though!**
- **Is 60 divisible by 2?** *Yes.* **What's 60 divided by 2?** *30.* Write "2 × 30." **She could make 30 rows of 2, or 2 rows of 30.**
- **Is 60 divisible by 3?** *Yes.* **What's 60 divided by 3?** *20.* Write "3 × 20." **She could make 20 rows of 3, or 3 rows of 20.**
- **Is 60 divisible by 4?** *Yes.* **What's 60 divided by 4?** *15.* Write "4 × 15." **She could make 4 rows of 15, or 15 rows of 4.**
- **Is 60 divisible by 5?** *Yes.* **What's 60 divided by 5?** *12.* Write "5 × 12." **She could make 5 rows of 12, or 12 rows of 5.**
- **Is 60 divisible by 6?** *Yes.* **What's 60 divided by 6?** *10.* Write "6 × 10." **She could make 10 rows of 6, or 6 rows of 10.**
- **Is 60 divisible by 7?** *No.* **How do you know?** *Sample answer: 60 divided by 7 equals 8, with a remainder of 4.*
- **Is 60 divisible by 8?** *No.* **How do you know?** *Sample answer: 60 divided by 8 equals 7, with a remainder of 4.*
- **Is 60 divisible by 9?** *No.* **How do you know?** *Sample answer: 60 divided by 9 equals 6, with a remainder of 6.*

To complete the problem, we write the factors in order from least to greatest. Write "1, 2, 3, 4, 5, 6, 10, 12, 15, 20, 30, or 60 chairs."

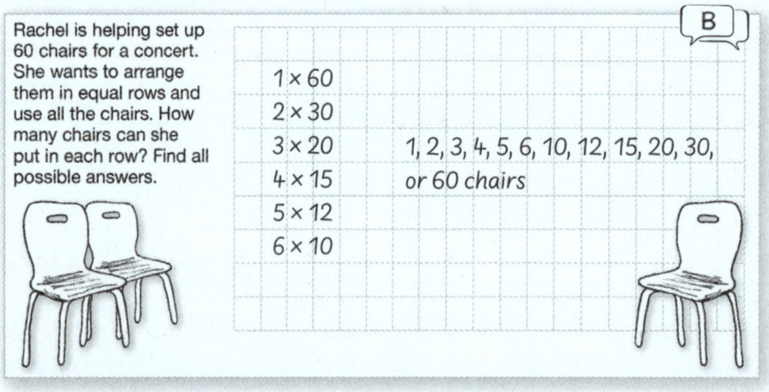

Independent Practice and Review

Have your child complete the Lesson 6.6 Practice and Review workbook pages.

Lesson 6.7
Find Greatest Common Factors

Purpose	Materials
• Practice finding all factor pairs for a number • Find the greatest common factor for a pair of numbers	• None

Memory Work
- **What is a prime number?** *A number with exactly 2 factors.*
- **What is a composite number?** *A number with more than 2 factors.*

Warm-up (A): Practice Finding All Factors of a Number

In the last lesson, you reviewed how to find all factors of numbers to 100. You check whether the number is divisible by each of the numbers from 1 to 9. Have your child solve the problems in part A. She should find all factors of 24 for the first problem and all factors of 28 for the second problem.

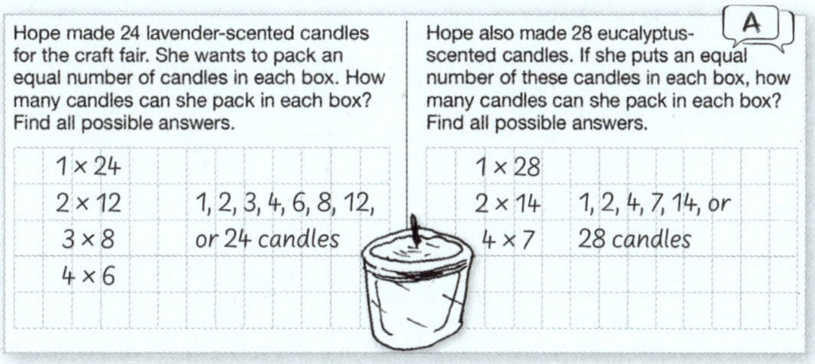
A

Hope made 24 lavender-scented candles for the craft fair. She wants to pack an equal number of candles in each box. How many candles can she pack in each box? Find all possible answers.

1 × 24
2 × 12
3 × 8
4 × 6

1, 2, 3, 4, 6, 8, 12, or 24 candles

Hope also made 28 eucalyptus-scented candles. If she puts an equal number of these candles in each box, how many candles can she pack in each box? Find all possible answers.

1 × 28
2 × 14
4 × 7

1, 2, 4, 7, 14, or 28 candles

Activity (B): Find the Greatest Common Factor for a Pair of Numbers

Today, you'll learn how to find the greatest common factor for a pair of numbers. We can find common factors just like we find common multiples. We make a list of all the factor pairs for both numbers and then look for the greatest factor they have in common. Have your child read the text in part B aloud.

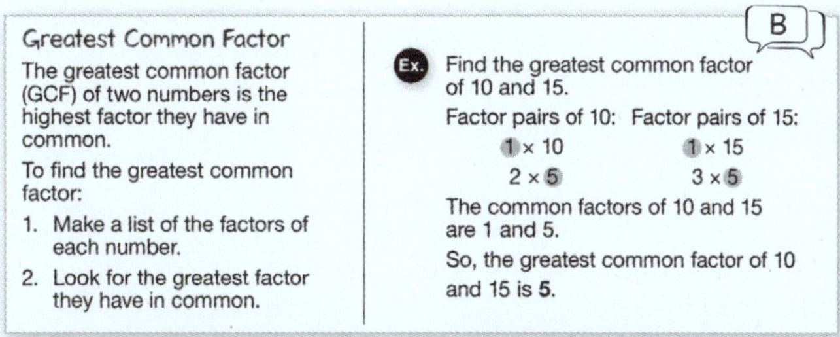
B

Greatest Common Factor

The greatest common factor (GCF) of two numbers is the highest factor they have in common.

To find the greatest common factor:

1. Make a list of the factors of each number.
2. Look for the greatest factor they have in common.

Ex. Find the greatest common factor of 10 and 15.

Factor pairs of 10: 1 × 10, 2 × 5
Factor pairs of 15: 1 × 15, 3 × 5

The common factors of 10 and 15 are 1 and 5.

So, the greatest common factor of 10 and 15 is **5**.

Let's study the example to see how to find the greatest common factor of 10 and 15.

- **What are the factor pairs of 10?** *1 times 10 and 2 times 5.*
- **What are the factor pairs of 15?** *1 times 15 and 3 times 5.*
- **What factors do the two lists have in common?** *1 and 5.*
- **What is the greatest factor they have in common?** *5.*

British English generally uses the term "highest common factor" instead of "greatest common factor." If you live in a country that uses British English rather than American English, feel free to substitute this term as you teach the lesson.

Let's complete these charts so we can find the greatest common factor of the different number pairs. You already found all the factor pairs of 24 and 28 in the warm-up. Have your child write all the factor pairs of 24 and 28 as shown. Then, have her find all the factor pairs of 30.

Factor Pairs of 24	Factor Pairs of 28	Factor Pairs of 30 (B)
1 × 24	1 × 28	1 × 30
2 × 12	2 × 14	2 × 15
3 × 8	4 × 7	3 × 10
4 × 6		5 × 6

What factors do 24 and 28 have in common? *1, 2, and 4.* Write "1, 2, 4" in the space. **Which of the common factors is the greatest?** *4.* **So, the GCF of 24 and 28 is 4.** Write 4 in the blank. Repeat for the other questions.

What factor(s) do 24 and 28 have in common?	What factor(s) do 28 and 30 have in common?	What factor(s) do 24 and 30 have in common? (B)
1, 2, 4	1, 2	1, 2, 3, 6
GCF of 24 and 28: 4	GCF of 28 and 30: 2	GCF of 24 and 30: 6

Independent Practice and Review

Have your child complete the Lesson 6.7 Practice and Review workbook pages.

Lesson 6.8
Mentally Divide by Multiples of 10 or 100

Purpose	Materials
• Review using place-value thinking to mentally divide • Learn to mentally divide when both the dividend and divisor have trailing zeros • Review how to multiply to check answers to division problems	• None
Memory Work	• **What does GCF stand for?** *Greatest common factor.* • **Name 4 factors of 30.** *Possible answers: 1, 2, 3, 5, 6, 10, 15, 30.*

Warm-up (A): Review Mental Division by One-Digit Numbers

In Unit 1, we reviewed how to use place-value thinking to mentally divide numbers with trailing zeros. Have your child use this method to complete the problems in part A.

A

240 ÷ 8 = 30	300 ÷ 6 = 50	600 ÷ 3 = 200
800 ÷ 2 = 400	2,700 ÷ 3 = 900	4,000 ÷ 2 = 2,000

If needed, your child may underline the trailing zeros in the dividend and then tack them on to the quotient, as in Lesson 1.3. If he doesn't need this strategy, don't require it.

Activity (B): Mentally Divide by Multiples of 10 or 100

Today, you'll learn how to mentally divide by multiples of 10 or 100, like 40, 80, or 300. Have your child read the left side of the text box aloud.

B

Mental Division with Trailing Zeros

Cross out the trailing zeros the numbers have in common. Then, divide the other digits.

Ex. The winter festival decorating committee wants to buy 1,200 ornaments. The ornaments come in packs of 40. How many packs should the committee buy?

1,200 ÷ 40 = ?

120 tens ÷ 4 tens = 30

1,20~~0~~ ÷ 4~~0~~ = **30**

Read aloud the example: ***1,200 divided by 40 equals what?* How many trailing zeros do 1,200 and 40 have in common?** *1.* **So, we'll think of both numbers as groups of tens. 1,200 equals 120 tens, and 40 equals 4 tens.**

We cross out 1 trailing zero in each number to show that we're dividing 120 tens by 4 tens. 120 tens divided into groups of 4 tens makes 30 groups. 1,200 divided by 40 equals 30.

Children often wonder why the answer to this problem is 30 rather than 30 tens. To help your child understand why, have him imagine using play money to model the problem. **Imagine you have 120 ten-dollar bills. If you divide them groups of 4 tens, how many groups do you make?** *30.* Or, have him multiply to see that the answer must be 30, not 300: **300 times 40 is 12,000. 30 times 40 is 1,200, so 30 is the correct quotient.**

Have your child solve the practice problems. Make sure he first identifies and crosses out any trailing zeros the numbers have in common. For example: **300 has 2 trailing zeros. 60 has 1 trailing zero. They have 1 trailing zero in common, so cross out 1 zero in each problem.**

B

24~~0~~ ÷ 8~~0~~ = 3	30~~0~~ ÷ 6~~0~~ = 5	60~~0~~ ÷ 3~~0~~ = 20
8~~00~~ ÷ 2~~00~~ = 4	2,7~~00~~ ÷ 3~~00~~ = 9	4,0~~00~~ ÷ 2~~00~~ = 20

Activity (C): Multiply to Check Answers to Word Problems

These word problems are all about a winter festival. The planning team made a shopping list of the supplies they need.

Have your child read the first word problem aloud, write a matching division equation, and solve.

Candy canes come in packs of 40. How many packs should the planning team buy?

320 ÷ 40 = 8 packs

Winter Festival Shopping List
- 320 candy canes
- 400 cookies
- 1,500 sheets of sparkly paper (for making snowflakes)

How can you use multiplication to check your answer? *Multiply 40 times 8.* **Multiplication and division are the opposite of each other, so we can use multiplication to check answers to division problems.** Have your child write the matching multiplication equation and solve to check his answer.

Check: *8 × 40 = 320*

Repeat with the final two word problems.

Cookies come in boxes of 80. How many boxes should the planning team buy?

400 ÷ 80 = 5 boxes

Check: *80 × 5 = 400*

Sparkly paper comes in packs of 30 sheets. How many packs should the planning team buy?

1,500 ÷ 30 = 50 packs

Check: *30 × 50 = 1,500*

Independent Practice and Review

Have your child complete the Lesson 6.8 Practice and Review workbook pages.

Lesson 6.9
Enrichment (Optional)

Purpose	Materials
• Practice memory work • Appreciate how math can be used to answer real-life questions • Use mental division to plan a booth at a festival or market • Summarize what your child has learned and assess your child's progress	• *How Many Guinea Pigs Can Fit on a Plane?: Answers to Your Most Clever Math Questions*, by Laura Overdeck

Warm-up: Review Memory Work

Quiz your child on any of the memory work items that she struggled with during this unit.

Math Picture Book: *How Many Guinea Pigs Can Fit on a Plane?*

Read pages 52-61 in *How Many Guinea Pigs Can Fit on a Plane?*

Enrichment Activity: Plan a Booth at a Festival or Market

In Lesson 6.8, we used division to figure out how many supplies to buy for refreshments and activities at a winter festival. Today, you get to plan your own booth at a festival and figure out what supplies you would need for your booth.

What kind of festival or market would you like to have a booth at? *Sample answers: craft fair, harvest festival, farmer's market, carnival.* **What kind of activity or product would you like to sell at your booth?** *Sample answers: A booth where you can tie-dye a shirt. A booth that sells pudding. A booth where you can buy honey. A booth where you can play the ring toss.*

Help your child brainstorm what supplies she would need and choose a target number of customers. Then, have her use multiplication or division to figure out how much she needs of each item on the supply list. Estimate or round the quantities as needed or search online for any specific numbers you need.

Plop and Jiggle Pudding Booth (for 150 customers)

- *Each box of pudding mix makes 6 servings.*

  $150 \div 6 = 25$ boxes

- *I need 2 cups of milk for each box of pudding mix.*

  $25 \times 2 = 50$ c. of milk

- *Disposable spoons come in boxes of 50.*

  $150 \div 50 = 3$ boxes of spoons

- *Disposable bowls come in packs of 30.*

  $150 \div 30 = 5$ packs

Sample supply list for 150 customers at a pudding booth.

If your child would like to take the activity further, help her estimate the approximate cost for each item on the supply list. Help her set a fair price for her product or activity, and then help her calculate how much profit she would make.

Unit Wrap-Up

Have your child complete the Unit 6 Wrap-Up.

Unit 6 Answer Key

6.1 Practice

Practice: Find the quotients.

15 ÷ 15 = 1	25 ÷ 25 = 1	35 ÷ 35 = 1
30 ÷ 15 = 2	50 ÷ 25 = 2	70 ÷ 35 = 2
45 ÷ 15 = 3	75 ÷ 25 = 3	105 ÷ 35 = 3
60 ÷ 15 = 4	100 ÷ 25 = 4	140 ÷ 35 = 4
120 ÷ 15 = 8	200 ÷ 25 = 8	★ 90 ÷ 45 = 2
150 ÷ 15 = 10	300 ÷ 25 = 12	★ 180 ÷ 45 = 4
180 ÷ 15 = 12	400 ÷ 25 = 16	★ 270 ÷ 45 = 6

Write the missing dividend in each division problem.

150 ÷ 25 = 6 | 75 ÷ 15 = 5 | ★ 135 ÷ 45 = 3

Solve. Write the equations you use.

There are 175 children at softball camp. The coaches split them into teams of 25. How many teams do they make?

175 ÷ 25 = 7 teams

Jazz dance lessons cost $105 for the winter term. Each lesson costs $15. How many lessons are in the winter term?

105 ÷ 15 = 7 lessons

The library has $115 to buy board games. Each board game costs $25. How many board games can they buy?

115 ÷ 25 = 4 R15
[4 games]

How much money will they have left?

[$15]

Asher's family set aside $150 to buy tickets to a show. Each ticket costs $35. How many tickets can they buy?

150 ÷ 35 = 4 R10
[4 tickets]

How much money will they have left?

[$10]

6.1 Review

Review: Find the products. Use the completed product to help.

30 × 3 = 90	50 × 4 = 200	70 × 5 = 350
31 × 3 = 93	49 × 4 = 196	72 × 5 = 360
32 × 3 = 96	48 × 4 = 192	74 × 5 = 370
34 × 3 = 102	45 × 4 = 180	76 × 5 = 380

Complete the chart.

	× 2
25	50
35	70
55	110
75	150
45	90
65	130
85	170

Find the sum or difference. If your answer is an improper fraction, convert the improper fraction to a mixed number.

$\frac{1}{6} + \frac{11}{12}$: $\frac{2}{12} + \frac{11}{12} = \frac{13}{12} = 1\frac{1}{12}$

$\frac{3}{4} - \frac{1}{6}$: $\frac{9}{12} - \frac{2}{12} = \frac{7}{12}$

$\frac{7}{9} - \frac{1}{3}$: $\frac{7}{9} - \frac{3}{9} = \frac{4}{9}$

$\frac{7}{10} + \frac{3}{5}$: $\frac{7}{10} + \frac{6}{10} = \frac{13}{10} = 1\frac{3}{10}$

Find the volume of the box. Write the equations you use in the work space.

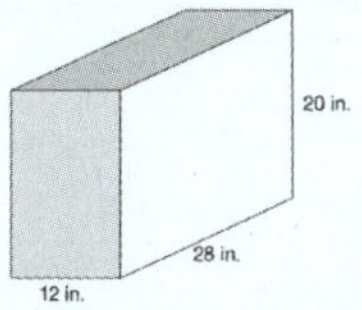

WORK SPACE

```
   2 8
 × 1 2
   5 6
+2 8 0
 3 3 6
```

```
   3 3 6
 ×   2 0
 6,7 2 0  cu. in.
```

6.2 Practice

Practice: Circle the numbers that match the description. X the numbers that do not match the description.

Divisible by 2	Divisible by 5	Divisible by 10
X 85, (90), (92)	(85), (90), X 92	X 85, (90), X 92
X 95, (100), X 105	(95), (100), (105)	X 95, (100), X 105

Complete.

80 ÷2→ 40 ÷2→ 20 ÷2→ 10 ÷2→ 5

144 ÷2→ 72 ÷2→ 36 ÷2→ 18 ÷2→ 9

400 ÷2→ 200 ÷2→ 100 ÷2→ 50 ÷2→ 25

Use mental math to find the quotient.

70 ÷ 5 = 14 | 85 ÷ 5 = 17 | 120 ÷ 5 = 24

Solve. Write the equations you use.

Abigail bakes 103 cookies to give away. She packs 5 cookies in each box. How many boxes does she fill?

103 ÷ 5 = ? [20 boxes]
20 × 5 = 100

How many cookies does she have left?

103 − 100 = [3 cookies]

The books at the library sale cost $5 each. Carlos has $67 to spend on books. How many books can he buy?

67 ÷ 5 = ? [13 books]
13 × 5 = 65

If he buys as many books as possible, how much money will he have left?

67 − 65 = [$2]

6.2 Review

Review: Complete.

$2\frac{1}{3} = 2\frac{4}{12}$
$+ 1\frac{1}{4} = 1\frac{3}{12}$
$3\frac{7}{12}$

$3\frac{4}{5} = 3\frac{8}{10}$
$+ 2\frac{7}{10} = 2\frac{7}{10}$
$5\frac{15}{10} = 6\frac{5}{10}$

$4\frac{1}{2} = 4\frac{4}{8}$
$+ 5\frac{7}{8} = 5\frac{7}{8}$
$9\frac{11}{8} = 10\frac{3}{8}$

Draw a line that connects the numbers in order from Start to End. Follow the rule.

Rule: Add 0.07 (Start → End)

0.07	0.14	0.3	0.70	0.77
0.014	0.21	0.25	0.63	0.69
0.24	0.28	0.41	0.56	0.6
0.32	0.35	0.42	0.49	0.55
0.36	0.4	0.19	0.52	0.38

Rule: Subtract 0.03 (Start → End)

0.8	0.77	0.74	0.69	0.38
0.07	0.7	0.71	0.54	0.44
0.79	0.75	0.68	0.4	0.5
0.83	0.86	0.65	0.57	0.53
0.99	0.84	0.62	0.59	0.56

Solve. Write the equations you use.

Elijah swam 45 laps on Monday. He swam 25 fewer laps on Tuesday than he swam on Monday. How many laps did he swim on Tuesday?

45 − 25 = [20 laps]

How many laps did he swim in all on Monday and Tuesday?

45 + 20 = [65 laps]

Katelyn played 3 times as many basketball games in November as she played in October. She played 18 basketball games in November. How many basketball games did she play in October?

18 ÷ 3 = [6 games]

How many more basketball games did she play in November than October?

18 − 6 = [12 games]

Unit 6 Answer Key

6.3 Practice

Practice Circle the numbers that are divisible by 3. X the numbers that are not divisible by 3.

✗ 49	◯ 51	✗ 37	◯ 75	◯ 96	✗ 97
◯ 267	◯ 672	✗ 101	◯ 102	✗ 1,001	◯ 1,002

Find the quotients.

60 ÷ 3 = 20	90 ÷ 3 = 30	120 ÷ 3 = 40
63 ÷ 3 = 21	87 ÷ 3 = 29	123 ÷ 3 = 41
66 ÷ 3 = 22	84 ÷ 3 = 28	126 ÷ 3 = 42
69 ÷ 3 = 23	81 ÷ 3 = 27	129 ÷ 3 = 43
72 ÷ 3 = 24	78 ÷ 3 = 26	132 ÷ 3 = 44

Complete the price chart. Use the completed box to help.

Number of tacos	48	49	50	51	52
Total price	\$144	\$147	\$150	\$153	\$156

Write a number that matches each description. (Many answers are possible.)

- This number has 3 digits.
- This number is greater than 200 and less than 500.
- This number is divisible by 2.
- This number is divisible by 3.

2 3 4
Sample answer

- This number has 4 digits.
- This number is less than 2,000.
- This number is divisible by 5.
- Thie number is divisible by 3.

1, 2 1 5
Sample answer

6.3 Review

Review Complete.

$$3\frac{4}{5} = 3\frac{8}{10} \qquad -\ 2\frac{3}{10} = 2\frac{3}{10} \qquad 1\frac{5}{10}$$

$$4\frac{1}{8} = \cancel{4}\,\cancel{\tfrac{1}{8}}\ \ 3\frac{9}{8} \qquad -\ 2\frac{1}{2} = 2\frac{4}{8} \qquad 1\frac{5}{8}$$

$$\cancel{6}\ \ 5\frac{6}{6} \qquad -\ 3\frac{5}{6} \qquad 2\frac{1}{6}$$

Circle the problems that equal the number in the star.

★ 2	★ 20	★ 5	★ 50
80 ÷ 4	◯ 80 ÷ 4	150 ÷ 3	◯ 150 ÷ 3
◯ 80 ÷ 40	80 ÷ 40	◯ 150 ÷ 30	150 ÷ 30
140 ÷ 7	◯ 140 ÷ 7	400 ÷ 8	◯ 400 ÷ 8
◯ 140 ÷ 70	140 ÷ 70	◯ 400 ÷ 80	400 ÷ 80

Find the least common multiple for each pair of numbers.

LCM of 5 and 6: 30	LCM of 5 and 7: 35	LCM of 5 and 10: 10
6, 12, 18, 24, (30)	7, 14, 21, 28, (35)	(10)

6.4 Practice

Practice Circle the numbers that match the description. X the numbers that do not match the description.

Divisible by 2			Divisible by 3			Divisible by 6		
◯ 90	◯ 92	✗ 93	◯ 90	✗ 92	◯ 93	◯ 90	✗ 92	✗ 93
◯ 96	✗ 99	◯ 100	◯ 96	◯ 99	✗ 100	◯ 96	✗ 99	✗ 100
◯ 102	✗ 105	◯ 108	◯ 102	◯ 105	◯ 108	◯ 102	✗ 105	◯ 108

Arrange the digits to create a number that matches the description at the top of the column. (More than one answer is possible for some of the problems.)

	Divisible by 2	Divisible by 3	Divisible by 6
5 6 1	1 5 6	5 6 1	5 1 6
2 9 4	4 9 2	9 2 4	2 9 4
0 7 2	7 2 0	2 0 7	2 7 0

Use mental math to find the quotient.

84 ÷ 6 = 14 | 126 ÷ 6 = 21 | ★ 294 ÷ 6 = 49

6.4 Review

Review Write equivalent fractions with common denominators for each pair of fractions. Then, write <, >, or = to compare the fractions.

$\frac{5}{12}$ (>) $\frac{1}{3}$	$\frac{6}{10}$ (=) $\frac{3}{5}$	$\frac{3}{5}$ (<) $\frac{3}{4}$
$\frac{5}{12}$ $\frac{4}{12}$	$\frac{6}{10}$ $\frac{6}{10}$	$\frac{12}{20}$ $\frac{15}{20}$

Use long division to solve.

```
    6 6
6 ) 3 9 7
  - 3 6 ↓
      3 7
    - 3 6
        1
```

Use mental math to solve.

23 × 2 = 46	4 × 8 × 2 = 64
23 × 4 = 92	4 × 8 × 4 = 128
51 × 2 = 102	2 × 15 × 6 = 180
51 × 4 = 204	4 × 15 × 6 = 360
75 × 2 = 150	2 × 25 × 8 = 400
75 × 4 = 300	4 × 25 × 8 = 800

Complete.

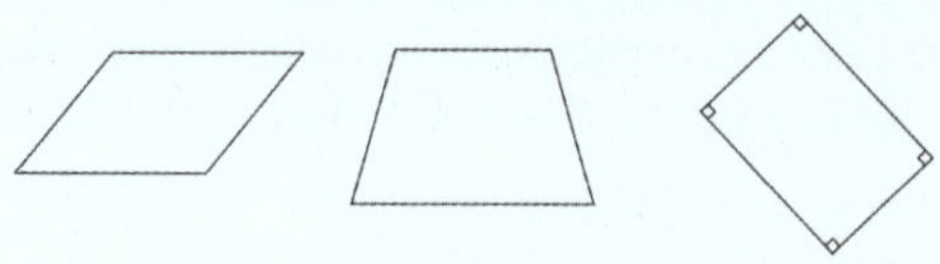

2 pair(s) of parallel sides	1 pair(s) of parallel sides	2 pair(s) of parallel sides
0 right angle(s)	0 right angle(s)	4 right angle(s)

Unit 6 Answer Key

6.5 Practice

Practice Circle the numbers that match the description. X the numbers that do not match the description.

Divisible by 2			
(90)	(92)	X 93	(94)
(96)	(98)	X 99	(100)
X 103	(104)	(106)	(108)

Divisible by 4			
X 90	(92)	X 93	X 94
(96)	X 98	X 99	(100)
X 103	(104)	X 106	(108)

Find the quotients.

48 ÷ 2 = 24	68 ÷ 2 = 34	84 ÷ 2 = 42
48 ÷ 4 = 12	68 ÷ 4 = 17	84 ÷ 4 = 21
100 ÷ 2 = 50	116 ÷ 2 = 58	★ 536 ÷ 2 = 268
100 ÷ 4 = 25	116 ÷ 4 = 29	536 ÷ 4 = 134

Use the numbers to solve the number riddles. You will use each number once.

75 | 90 | 109 | 130 | 140 | 162

- I am a two-digit number.
- I am divisible by 5.
- I am not divisible by 10.

75

- I am a two-digit number.
- I am divisible by 6.

90

- I am a three-digit number.
- I am divisible by 10.
- I am divisible by 4.

140

- I am a three-digit number.
- I am divisible by 10.
- I am not divisible by 4.

130

- I am a three-digit number.
- I am divisible by 6.

162

- I am a three-digit number.
- I am not divisible by 10.
- I am not divisible by 6.

109

6.5 Review

Review Circle yes or no to answer the questions.

Is 70 divisible by 7? (Yes) | No	Is 64 divisible by 8? (Yes) | No	Is 81 divisible by 9? (Yes) | No
Is 75 divisible by 7? Yes | (No)	Is 72 divisible by 8? (Yes) | No	Is 85 divisible by 9? Yes | (No)
Is 77 divisible by 7? (Yes) | No	Is 74 divisible by 8? Yes | (No)	Is 90 divisible by 9? (Yes) | No

Complete the circles with <, >, or =.

0.8 (>) 0.08

0.7 (=) 0.70

0.060 (=) 0.06

0.005 (<) 0.050

0.040 (=) 0.04

Complete the missing factors in the factor pairs.

Factor Pairs of 30	Factor Pairs of 40
1 × 30	1 × 40
2 × 15	2 × 20
3 × 10	4 × 10
5 × 6	5 × 8

Solve. Write the equations you use.

The tennis coach has 164 tennis balls. She splits them evenly into 4 baskets. How many tennis balls are in each basket?

41 balls

$164 \div 4 = 41$ (4 | 164: − 16, 04, − 4, 0)

WORK SPACE

6 tennis lessons cost $216. How much does each lesson cost?

$36

$216 \div 6 = 36$ (6 | 216: − 18, 36, − 36, 0)

6.6 Practice

Practice Find all factors of each number. Use mental or written division to check whether each number is divisible by the numbers from 1 to 9. Then, answer the questions.

Factor Pairs of 64	Factor Pairs of 67
1 × 64 2 × 32 4 × 16 8 × 8	1 × 67
Is 64 prime or composite? composite	Is 67 prime or composite? prime

Factor Pairs of 89	Factor Pairs of 93
1 × 89	1 × 93 3 × 31
Is 89 prime or composite? prime	Is 93 prime or composite? composite

Solve.

David baked 90 cookies to give away. He wants to pack the cookies in boxes, and he wants to put the same number of cookies in each box. How many cookies can he pack in each box? Find all possible answers.

1 × 90
2 × 45
3 × 30
5 × 18
6 × 15
9 × 10

1, 2, 3, 5, 6, 9, 10, 15, 18, 30, 45, or 90 cookies

6.6 Review

Review Complete the equivalent fractions. Then, write each fraction as a decimal. Use the pictures to help.

$\frac{1}{2} = \frac{5}{10} = 0.5$

$\frac{1}{4} = \frac{25}{100} = 0.25$

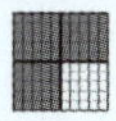
$\frac{3}{4} = \frac{75}{100} = 0.75$

$\frac{1}{5} = \frac{2}{10} = 0.2$

$\frac{2}{5} = \frac{4}{10} = 0.4$

$\frac{4}{5} = \frac{8}{10} = 0.8$

Complete.

90 × 90 = 8,100
9 × 900 = 8,100
900 × 900 = 810,000
90 × 9,000 = 810,000
900 × 90 = 81,000
9,000 × 9 = 81,000

Find the missing information for each rectangular prism.

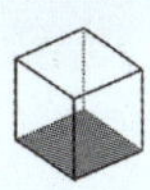

Volume: 64 cubic cm
Height: 4 cm
Base area: 16 sq. cm

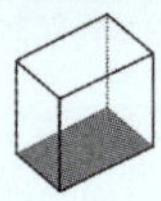

Volume: 75 cubic cm
Height: 5 cm
Base area: 15 sq. cm

Solve. Write the equations you use.

Moira had $3\frac{5}{12}$ chocolate bars. She gave $1\frac{2}{3}$ chocolate bars to her sister. How many chocolate bars did she have left?

$3\frac{5}{12} = 2\frac{17}{12}$

$-1\frac{2}{3} = 1\frac{8}{12}$

$1\frac{9}{12}$ bars

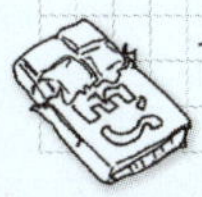

Steven's baby sister weighed 5.45 kg. Then, she gained 0.87 kg. How much did she weigh then?

$5.45 + 0.87 = 6.32$ kg

Unit 6 Answer Key

6.7 Practice

Practice Find all factor pairs for each number. Then, answer the questions.

Factor Pairs of 12	Factor Pairs of 15	What factors do 12 and 15 have in common?
1 × 12 2 × 6 3 × 4	1 × 15 3 × 5	1 and 3 GCF of 12 and 15: 3

Factor Pairs of 16	Factor Pairs of 32	What factors do 16 and 32 have in common?
1 × 16 2 × 8 4 × 4	1 × 32 2 × 16 4 × 8	1, 2, 4, 8, 16 GCF of 16 and 32: 16

Factor Pairs of 25	Factor Pairs of 45	What factors do 25 and 45 have in common?
1 × 25 5 × 5	1 × 45 3 × 15 5 × 9	1 and 5 GCF of 25 and 45: 5

Find the greatest common factor for each pair of numbers. Make your own lists of factors.

GCF of 8 and 9: 1

8	9
1 × 8 2 × 4	1 × 9 3 × 3

GCF of 18 and 27: 9

18	27
1 × 18 2 × 9 3 × 6	1 × 27 3 × 9

6.7 Review

Review Choose the more sensible measurement for each volume.

Volume of a thimble: (3 cu. cm) / 3 cu. m

Volume of a bathtub: 6 cu. in. / (6 cu. ft.)

Volume of a small pool: 16 cu. km / (16 cu. m)

Complete.

240 ÷ 3 = 80
240 ÷ 4 = 60
240 ÷ 6 = 40

2,400 ÷ 3 = 800
2,400 ÷ 4 = 600
2,400 ÷ 6 = 400

Use mental math to find the quotients.

72 ÷ 3 = 24
92 ÷ 2 = 46
72 ÷ 6 = 12
92 ÷ 4 = 23

Circle the word that describes each number.

8	prime | (composite)
9	prime | (composite)
12	prime | (composite)
17	(prime) | composite
20	prime | (composite)
21	prime | (composite)
24	prime | (composite)
27	prime | (composite)
29	(prime) | composite

6.8 Practice

Practice Match.

150 ÷ 30	5
210 ÷ 70	3
160 ÷ 40	4
1,800 ÷ 60	30
2,800 ÷ 70	40
450 ÷ 9	50
360 ÷ 60	6
2,400 ÷ 600	4
1,800 ÷ 300	6
2,700 ÷ 900	3
1,200 ÷ 40	30
3,500 ÷ 700	5
250 ÷ 5	50
2,000 ÷ 50	40

Solve. Write the equations you use.

Winter Festival Shopping List
- 350 napkins
- 2,400 twinkle lights
- Enough cocoa mix to make 300 cups of cocoa

Napkins come in packs of 70. How many packs should the planning team buy?

350 ÷ 70 = 5 packs

Twinkle lights come in boxes of 200. How many boxes of twinkle lights should the planning team buy?

2,400 ÷ 200 = 12 boxes

★ Each tub of cocoa mix makes 80 cups of cocoa. How many tubs should the planning team buy?

4 × 80 = 320
4 tubs

6.8 Review

Review Find the greatest common factor for each pair of numbers. Make your own lists of factors.

GCF of 25 and 35: 5

25	35
1 × 25 5 × 5	1 × 35 5 × 7

GCF of 28 and 40: 4

28	40
1 × 28 2 × 14 4 × 7	1 × 40 2 × 20 4 × 10 5 × 8

Circle the numbers that match the description. X the numbers that do not match the description.

Divisible by 3	Divisible by 4	Divisible by 6
(120) X180 (132) (144) (150) (156)	(120) X180 (132) (144) X150 (156)	(120) X180 (132) (144) (150) (156)

Solve. Write the equations you use.

Elizabeth's family has $1\frac{3}{8}$ sausage pizzas and $1\frac{3}{4}$ vegetable pizzas left over after a party. How much more vegetable pizza than sausage pizza do they have?

$$1\frac{3}{4} = 1\frac{6}{8}$$
$$-\,1\frac{3}{8} = 1\frac{3}{8}$$
$\frac{3}{8}$ of a pizza

Preston had 1.36 kg of gummy worms. He ate some of the gummy worms and then he had 0.742 kg left. How many kilograms of gummy worms did he eat?

$$1.360 - 0.742 = 0.618$$
0.618 kg

Unit 6 Answer Key

6.9 Unit Wrap-Up A

Unit Wrap-Up Write the number that makes the statement true. You will use each number once.

2 3 4 5 6 10

A number is divisible by 2 if it is even.	A number is divisible by 10 if it has 0 in its ones-place.
A number is divisible by 4 if you get an even number when you divide the number by 2.	A number is divisible by 6 if it is divisible by 2 and divisible by 3.
A number is divisible by 5 if it has 0 or 5 in its ones-place.	A number is divisible by 3 if the sum of its digits is divisible by 3.

Match.

45 ÷ 15	2	150 ÷ 50
70 ÷ 35	3	320 ÷ 80
100 ÷ 25	4	180 ÷ 90
75 ÷ 15	5	300 ÷ 60

Use mental math to find the quotients.

90 ÷ 3 = 30	100 ÷ 5 = 20	120 ÷ 6 = 20
93 ÷ 3 = 31	95 ÷ 5 = 19	126 ÷ 6 = 21
96 ÷ 3 = 32	90 ÷ 5 = 18	132 ÷ 6 = 22
99 ÷ 3 = 33	85 ÷ 5 = 17	138 ÷ 6 = 23
44 ÷ 2 = 22	96 ÷ 2 = 48	4,800 ÷ 60 = 80
44 ÷ 4 = 11	96 ÷ 4 = 24	4,800 ÷ 600 = 8

6.9 Unit Wrap-Up B

Unit Wrap-Up Find all factors of each number. Then, answer the questions.

Factor Pairs of 63	Factor Pairs of 75
1 × 63	1 × 75
3 × 21	3 × 25
7 × 9	5 x 15

Is 63 prime or composite? composite

Is 75 prime or composite? composite

What factors do 63 and 75 have in common? 1 and 3

GCF of 63 and 75: 3

Use the numbers to solve the number riddles. You will use each number once.

65 70 72 81 225 349 357 468

• I am a two-digit number. • I am divisible by 5. • I am divisible by 2. 70	• I am a two-digit number. • I am divisible by 5. • I am not divisible by 2. 65
• I am a two-digit number. • I am divisible by 6. • I am divisible by 4. 72	• I am a two-digit number. • I am divisible by 3. • I am not divisible by 2. 81
• I am a three-digit number. • I am divisible by 5. 225	• I am a three-digit number. • I am divisible by 6. 468
• I am a three-digit number. • I am divisible by 3. • I am not divisible by 5. • I am not divisible by 4. 357	• I am a three-digit number. • I am not divisible by 2. • I am not divisible by 5. • I am not divisible by 3. 349

Unit 6 Checkpoint

What to Expect at the End of Unit 6

By the end of Unit 6, most children will be able to do the following:

- Use skip-counting or equal-groups reasoning to mentally divide by 15, 25, or 35.
- Know the divisibility rules for 3, 4, and 6, and tell whether numbers are divisible by 3, 4, and 6.
- Mentally divide by 2 by splitting numbers in half, and mentally divide by 4 by dividing by 2 twice.
- Use the "multiply and adjust" strategy to mentally divide two-digit numbers. Many children will still find this strategy challenging, so don't worry if your child hasn't fully mastered it.
- Use mental division and divisibility rules to find all factors of numbers to 100. Some children will still need to be reminded to check every factor from 1 to 9, and some will still struggle with some of the mental division required.
- Make lists of factors to find the greatest common factor of two numbers.
- Mentally divide by multiples of 10 or 100 by crossing out common trailing zeros.

Is Your Child Ready to Move on?

In Unit 7, your child will review long division and learn how to perform long division with two-digit divisors.

Before moving on to Unit 7, your child should be mostly fluent with the multiplication and division facts up to 10×10 and 100÷10. If you find that your child's lack of fluency with the multiplication or division facts makes the lessons long or frustrating, **allow her to use the multiplication chart** (Blackline Master 4) as she completes the lessons in Unit 7.

Unit 7
Long Division

Overview

Your child will review long division with one-digit divisors and learn to perform long division with two-digit divisors. She'll also review how to use multiplication and addition to check long division, and she will apply long division to real-life situations and word problems.

What Your Child Will Learn

In this unit, your child will learn to:

- Review how to use long division to divide by one-digit numbers
- Use long division to divide by multiples of 10 and two-digit numbers
- Use long division to solve word problems

Lesson List

Lesson 7.1	Review Long Division with One-Digit Divisors
Lesson 7.2	Introduce Long Division with Two-Digit Divisors
Lesson 7.3	Divide by Two-Digit Multiples of 10
Lesson 7.4	Divide by Two-Digit Divisors
Lesson 7.5	Long Division with Four-Digit Dividends
Lesson 7.6	Enrichment (Optional)

Extra Materials Needed for Unit 7

- For optional Enrichment Lesson:
  - *How Many Guinea Pigs Can Fit on a Plane?: Answers to Your Most Clever Math Questions*, by Laura Overdeck. Feiwel & Friends, 2017.
  - Map app

Teaching Math with Confidence: How Multiplication Tables Take the Stress out of Long Division with Two-Digit Divisors

In *Fourth Grade Math with Confidence*, your child learned how to perform long division with one-digit divisors. In this unit, she'll learn how to perform long division with two-digit divisors.

In theory, dividing by a two-digit divisor is very similar to dividing by a one-digit divisor. No matter how many digits are in the divisor, you follow the usual steps and repeat the steps until you've divided all the digits in the dividend. In actual practice, dividing by a two-digit divisor is much more difficult than dividing by a one-digit divisor. The larger numbers involved make both the dividing and multiplying steps much harder.

When you divide by a one-digit divisor, the multiplication and division facts make it relatively easy to complete the divide and multiply steps. But when you divide by a two-digit divisor, you have to perform more challenging estimations and calculations. For example, when you divide 7,052 by 82, the first step is to divide 705 by 82. That's not a division fact that most people have memorized!

$$5\overline{)7{,}052}\quad\text{quotient: } 1$$

> The first step is to divide. 7 ÷ 5 = 1 R2, so I write 1 in the quotient.

$$82\overline{)7{,}052}\quad\text{quotient: } ?$$

> The first step is to divide. What's 705 divided by 82!?

These calculations take a lot of estimation skills, stamina, and working memory. By the time you find the quotient, you may not remember where you are in the division problem or have much mental energy left to complete the rest of the problem. And, if you estimate the quotient incorrectly, you'll have to erase everything you've done so far and start over.

In order to make long division with two-digit divisors more manageable, *Math with Confidence* provides printed multiplication tables for these problems. (Sometimes, your child will complete the multiplication table herself. Other times, the products will already be provided.) When your child needs to estimate a challenging quotient or find the product of the quotient and two-digit divisor, she can simply look at the table. That way, she can concentrate on the steps in the long division process without getting bogged down by the many intermediate calculations. It takes a little time to create the table, but the effort pays off quickly once you start the long division process.

$$82\overline{)7{,}052}\quad\text{quotient: } 8$$

> The table shows that 8 times 82 equals 656. That's as close as I can get to 705 without going over, so I write 8 in the quotient.

	1	2	3	4	5	6	7	8	9
× 82	82	164	246	328	410	492	574	656	738

Math with Confidence does not require children to learn how to perform these problems without a multiplication table. The minor benefit of learning to estimate the quotients is simply not worth the tedium and frustration. (After all, most adults reach for a calculator any time they need to divide a multi-digit number by a two-digit divisor.) If your child doesn't have a calculator handy in a real-life division situation, she can simply jot down a quick multiplication table before beginning to divide.

Lesson 7.1
Review Long Division with One-Digit Divisors

Purpose	Materials
• Review the steps in long division • Practice long division with one-digit divisors • Estimate quotients	• Play money • Highlighter

Memory Work

- **What do we call the number to be divided?** *The dividend.*
- **What do we call the number we divide by?** *The divisor.*
- **What do we call the result when we divide two numbers?** *The quotient.*
- **What do we call an amount that is left over after division?** *The remainder.*

In this lesson, you will review two important details of long division: choosing how many digits to divide and correctly placing the digits in the quotient. These seemingly-minor points are essential for success with two-digit divisors. Make sure to teach this lesson, even if your child is already fluent with long division with one-digit divisors.

Warm-up: Review Long Division Steps

In Unit 1, we reviewed long division. What are the steps in long division? *Divide, multiply, subtract, bring down.* **What silly sentence helps us remember the steps?** *Dirty monkeys smell bad.* **The first letter of each word matches the first letter of each step.**

If your child has trouble remembering the steps in long division, have her jot them in the margin of the workbook page or on a separate slip of paper for easy reference.

Activity (A): Review Long Division with One-Digit Divisors

Today, we'll review long division with one-digit divisors. This lesson will prepare you to perform long division with two-digit divisors in the next lesson.

We'll pretend you run a lemonade stand with four friends. Which four friends would you like to run the lemonade stand with? *Answers will vary.* **The five of you agree to evenly split the money you earn each day. If there are any dollars left over, you leave them in your money box to use as change the next day.**

You will highlight numbers throughout the unit to help your child identify how many digits to divide and place the digits in the quotient correctly. Make sure to do it here even if your child doesn't need the extra support.

On the first day, the lemonade stand earns $38. Place 3 ten-dollar bills and 8 one-dollar bills on the table. **Can you divide 3 ten-dollar bills between 5 people without trading?** *No.* **3 is less than 5, so we can't divide 3 tens by 5 without trading. Instead, we think of the 3 tens as 30 ones. The first step is to divide 38 ones by 5.** Highlight the 38.

Have your child use long division to complete the problem. **How much money does each person earn?** *$7.* **How much money is left over?** *$3.*

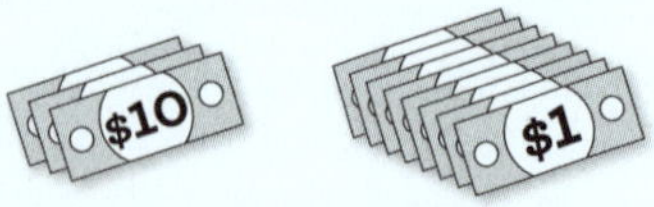

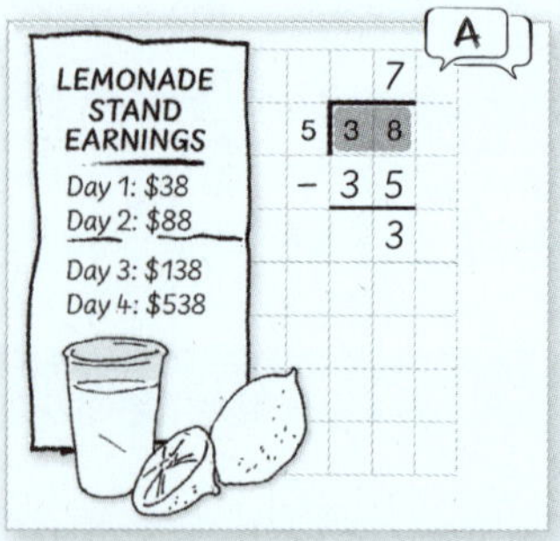

You do not need to trade the 3 ten-dollar bills for 30 one-dollar bills unless your child has trouble understanding how to complete the problem.

Why did you write the 7 in the ones-place and not the tens-place? *Sample answers: Each person gets 7 one-dollar bills. If I wrote it in the tens-place, that would mean each person gets $70—that's more than the lemonade stand earned!*

Always write the digit in the quotient directly above the rightmost digit in the digits you divide. You divided 38 by 5. The rightmost digit in 38 is 8, so you write the 7 directly above the 8. 38 ones divided by 5 equals 7 ones.

Discussing this detail prepares your child to divide by two-digit divisors in the next lesson.

On the second day, the lemonade stand earns $88. Place 8 ten-dollar bills and 8 one-dollar bills on the table. **Can you divide 8 ten-dollar bills between 5 people without trading?** *Yes.* **8 is greater than 5, so we can divide 8 tens by 5 without trading. The first step is to divide 8 tens by 5.** Highlight the 8.

Have your child use long division to divide 8 by 5. **How do you know that the 1 in the quotient belongs in the tens-place?** *Sample answer: I divided 8 tens by 5, so my answer was a number of tens.* **You divided 8 by 5. The rightmost digit in 8 is 8, so you write the 1 directly above the 8. 8 tens divided by 5 equals 1 ten.**

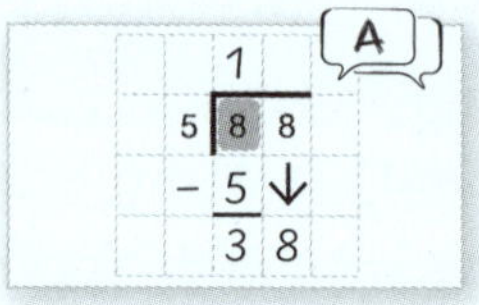

What's the next step? *Divide 38 by 5.* Highlight the 38, and have your child use long division to complete the problem. **How much money does each person earn?** *$17.* **How much money is left over?** *$3.*

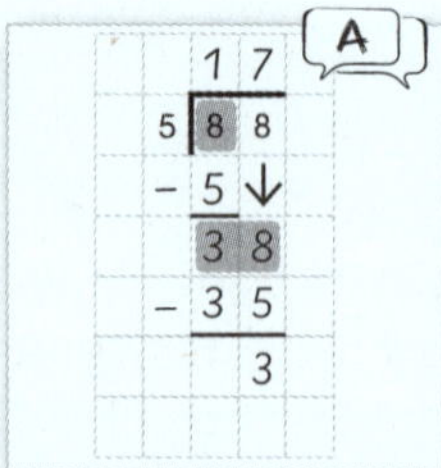

Repeat for the final two problems. Model the problems with play money as needed to make them more concrete. Make sure your child writes the digits in the correct places in the quotients.

- For 138 ÷ 5, highlight the 1 and 3 before your child solves the problem (since the first step is to divide 13 tens by 5). After she brings down the 8, highlight the 38.

- For 538 ÷ 5, highlight the 5 before your child solves the problem (since the first step is to divide 5 hundreds by 5). After she brings down the 3, highlight the 3. After she brings down the 8, highlight the 38.

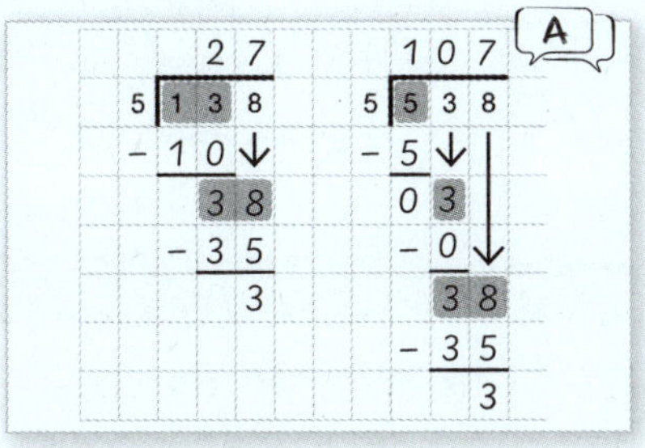

Activity (B): Play the Quotient Game

In this game, you get to choose which long division problems to solve. You score as many points as the quotient, so try to choose problems with as large a quotient as possible. Play the Quotient Game.

As you play, model how to use estimation to choose problems with as large a quotient as possible. For example, for 234 ÷ 6: **6 times 40 is 240, so the quotient will be a little less than 40. I'll pick a problem with a larger quotient.** Or, for 908 ÷ 4: **4 times 200 is 800, so the quotient must be larger than 200! That's a good problem to pick.**

The Quotient Game

Materials: None

Object of the Game: Score more points than the other player by creating greater quotients.

On your turn, choose one of the long division problems in part B. Write the problem on your scorecard and solve it. The quotient is your score. Cross out the problem you solved. Each problem may only be solved once.

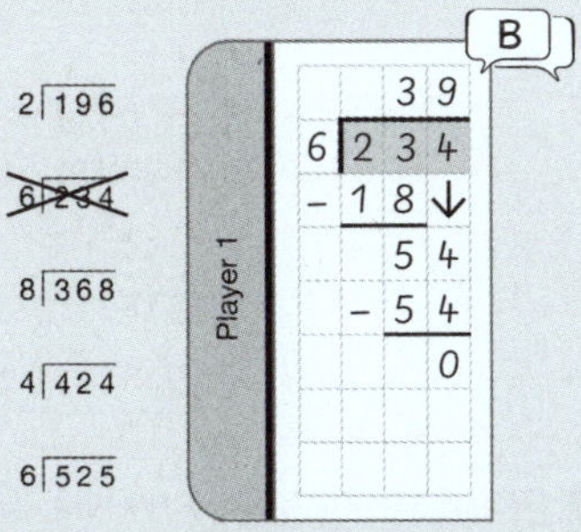

You score 39 points, since the quotient is 39.

Play then passes to the other player. Continue until both players have completed all 3 rounds. (You will not complete every division problem.) Add up each player's total points. The player with more points wins.

Independent Practice and Review

Have your child complete the Lesson 7.1 Practice and Review workbook pages.

Lesson 7.2
Introduce Long Division with Two-Digit Divisors

Purpose	Materials
• Use a multiplication table to mentally find quotients and remainders • Use long division to divide by two-digit divisors	• Playing cards

Memory Work

- **What does volume measure?** *The amount of space a solid occupies.*
- **What is the formula for the volume of a rectangular prism?** *Multiply length times width times height.*

In this lesson, your child will use a multiplication table to divide by two-digit divisors. See the Unit 7 **Teaching Math with Confidence** for the benefits of using a multiplication table to solve these challenging problems.

In this lesson, you'll focus on problems where you only go through the long division steps once. In the next lesson, your child will learn how to solve problems where you go through the long division steps more than once.

Warm-up (A): Use a Multiplication Table to Mentally Divide by 15

In the last lesson, you reviewed how to use long division to divide by one-digit divisors. Today, you'll learn how to use long division to divide with two-digit divisors.

All of the problems on this page involve dividing by 15. Let's complete the ×15 multiplication table to help solve these problems. Have your child complete the multiplication table.

	1	2	3	4	5	6	7	8	9
× 15	15	30	45	60	75	90	105	120	135

Your child may use whatever technique he would like to complete this multiplication table (and the other two-digit multiplication tables in this unit). Most children find it easiest to use mental repeated addition, but he may also use mental multiplication or write out vertical addition or multiplication problems on scrap paper.

Let's pretend you're making treat bags for a party with 15 guests. You have 68 bouncy balls, and you want to give each guest an equal number of bouncy balls.

Which product on the chart is as close to 68 as possible, without going over? *60.* **The chart shows that 15 groups of 4 equal 60. So, how many bouncy balls does each person get?** *4.*

If you give each guest 4 bouncy balls, how many will be left over? *8.* **How do you know?** *Sample answer: 68 minus 60 equals 8, so you'd have 8 bouncy balls left.*

	1	2	3	4	5	6	7	8	9
× 15	15	30	45	60	75	90	105	120	135

Ask your child the following questions. Have him use the chart to find the answers.

- **If you have 91 bouncy balls, how many will each guest get?** *6.* **How many bouncy balls would you have left?** *1.*
- **If you have 120 bouncy balls, how many will each guest get?** *8.* **How many bouncy balls would you have left?** *0.*
- **If you have 143 bouncy balls, how many will each guest get?** *9.* **How many bouncy balls would you have left?** *8.*

Activity (B): Use Long Division to Divide by 15

In the warm-up, you used mental math to find how many bouncy balls you could give each guest. We could also use long division to solve these problems.

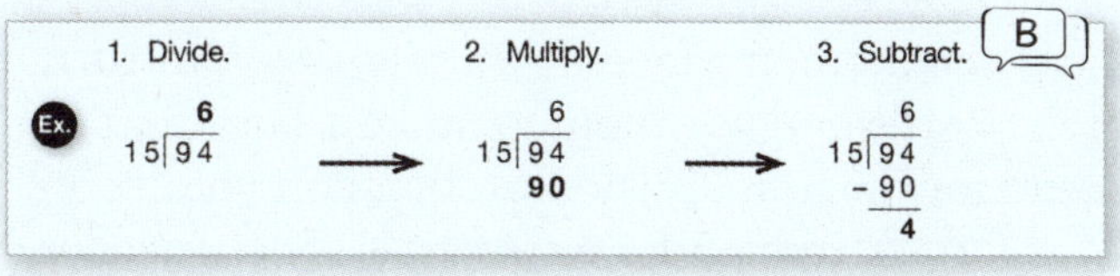

The example shows how to use long division to divide 94 by 15.

- **The first step is to divide.** Point to the 9. **Can you divide 9 by 15?** *No.* **9 is less than 15, so the first step is to divide 94 by 15.**
- **The multiplication table shows that 90 is as close as you can get to 94 without going over. 6 times 15 equals 90, so 94 divided by 15 equals 6. The 6 goes directly over the 4, since it's the rightmost digit in the digits we divided.**
- **Next, you multiply. 6 times 15 equals 90. We write 90 directly below 94.**
- **Then, you subtract. 94 minus 90 equals 4.**
- **Last, you bring down the next digit, if needed. We have already divided all the digits in 94, so we're done. If you have 94 bouncy balls, how many does each guest get?** *6.* **How many would you have left?** *4.*

Have your child use long division to complete the practice problems. Encourage him to use the multiplication table in part A to help.

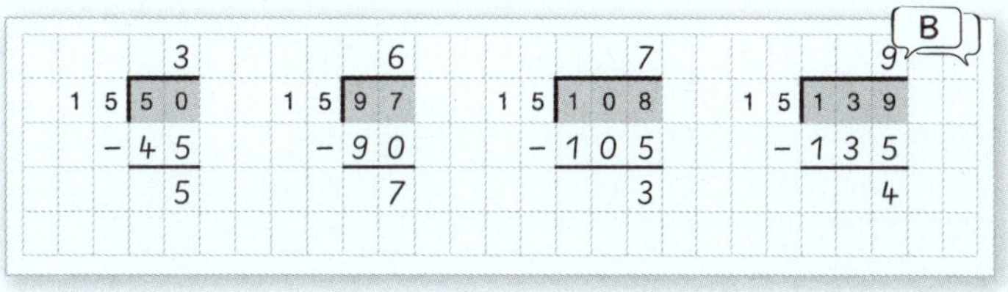

Activity (C): Play Flip and Divide

Play Flip and Divide.

Flip and Divide

Materials: Deck of playing cards with 10s, jacks, queens, and kings removed (36 cards total)

Object of the Game: Score the most points by creating the greatest possible remainders.

Shuffle the cards and place them in a face-down pile. On your turn, flip over the top 3 cards. Choose 2 of the cards and use them to make a two-digit number. Write the number as the dividend for the first division problem on your scorecard. Try to choose digits that will yield as large a remainder as possible. Then, use long division to solve the problem. The remainder is your score for that round. If there is no remainder, your score is 0.

For example, if you flip over a 2, 4, and 7 on your first turn, you may write 24, 27, 47, 42, 72, or 74 as the dividend for your first division problem. 74 ÷ 15 yields the greatest possible remainder, so writing 74 as the dividend is the best play. 74 ÷ 15 = 4 R14, so your score is 14.

Play until both players have completed their scorecards. Find the sum of each player's remainders. Whoever has the greater total sum wins the game.

Cooperative Variation: Play together on just one game board. After you finish one round, play again on the other game board. See if you can beat your first score.

Independent Practice and Review

Have your child complete the Lesson 7.2 Practice and Review workbook pages.

Lesson 7.3
Divide by Two-Digit Multiples of 10

Purpose	Materials
• Review how to multiply and add to check long division • Use long division to divide by two-digit multiples of 10	• Highlighter

Memory Work	
	• **What do we call a quadrilateral with 4 right angles?** *A rectangle.* • **What do we call a quadrilateral with 4 right angles and 4 equal sides?** *A square.* • **What do we call a quadrilateral with 4 equal sides?** *A rhombus.* • **What do we call a quadrilateral with 2 pairs of parallel sides?** *A parallelogram.* • **What do we call a quadrilateral with exactly 1 pair of parallel sides?** *A trapezoid.*

This lesson uses divisors that are multiples of 10 to make the division, multiplication, and subtraction steps as simple as possible. Your child will divide by other two-digit numbers in the next lesson.

Warm-up (A): Review How to Multiply and Add to Check Long Division

In the last lesson, you learned how to use long division to divide with two-digit divisors.

Read aloud the word problem. **What's the goal?** *Find how many balloons are in each group.*

We want to divide 223 by 30. We'll use the multiplication chart in part B to help. Which product on the chart is as close to 223 as possible, without going over? *210.* **7 times 30 equals 210, so the party planner can put 7 balloons in each group.** Have your child use long division to complete the problem.

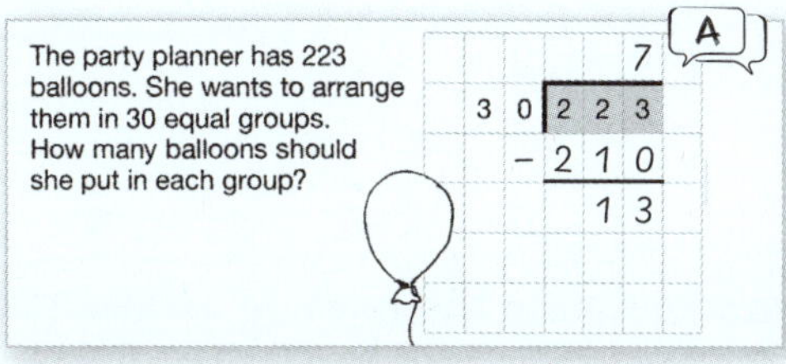

How many balloons are in each group? *7.* **How many balloons are left over?** *13.* **What do you think the party planner might do with the extra balloons?** *Sample answers: Give them to someone else. Take them home. Add 1 extra balloon to 13 of the groups.*

Let's multiply and add to check the answer. Write 30 × 7 vertically in the grid. Have your child complete the problem. **There are 210 balloons in the 30 groups of 7.**

Now, we add on the 13 leftover balloons. Write 13 below the multiplication problem as shown. Write a plus sign and horizontal line. Have your child complete the addition problem. **30 times 7 plus 13 equals 223, so the answer is correct.**

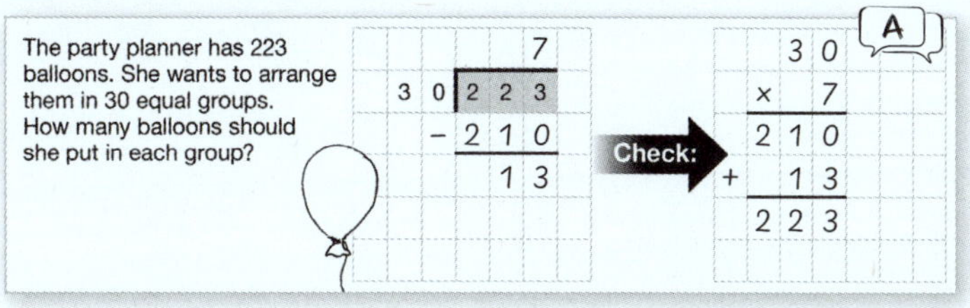

Activity (B): Use Long Division to Divide by Two-Digit Multiples of 10

In the last lesson and the warm-up, you only had to go through the long division steps once. Today, you'll learn how to solve problems where you go through the long division steps more than once.

For the next party, the party planner had 518 balloons to arrange in 30 equal groups. Point to the ×30 multiplication table in part B. **518 is much greater than 270, so we can't simply read the quotient off the table. We'll need to go through the long division steps more than once to divide 518 by 30.**

First, we choose how many digits in the dividend to divide.

- **Let's try 1 digit. 5 is less than 30, so we can't divide 5 hundreds by 30.**
- **Let's try 2 digits. We have 51 tens. 51 is greater than 30, so we can divide the 51 tens into 30 equal groups.**

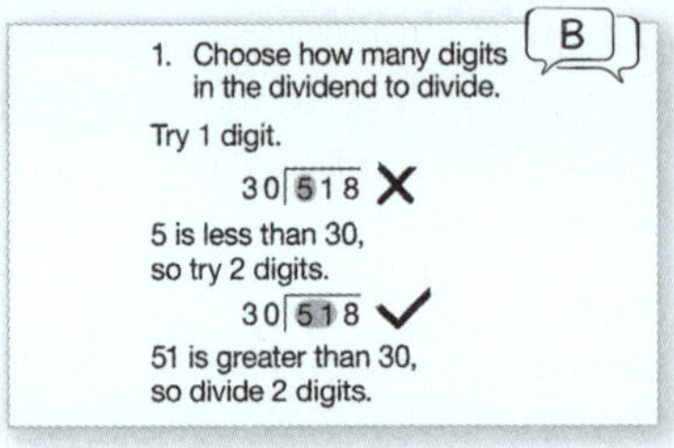

Next, we follow the long division steps for the digits we chose. Point to each number as you discuss it.

- **What's the first step?** *Divide.* **51 divided by 30 equals 1. The 1 goes directly above the 1 in 51.**
- **What's the second step?** *Multiply.* **1 times 30 equals 30.**
- **What's the third step?** *Subtract.* **51 minus 30 equals 21.**
- **What's the fourth step?** *Bring down the next digit (if needed).* **We bring down the 8.**

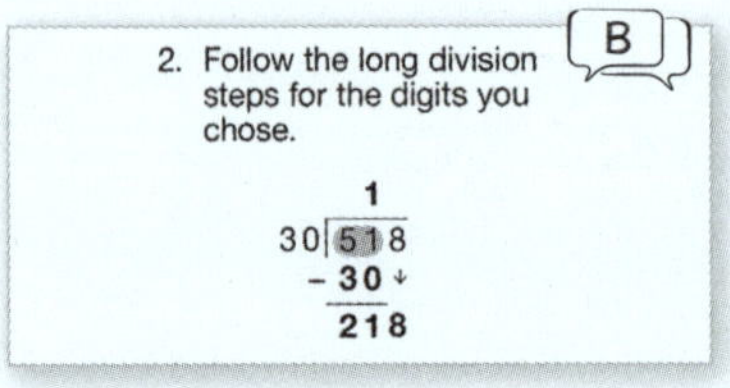

Then, we follow the steps again to divide the ones. We have 21 tens and 8 ones left to divide, so we have a total of 218 ones left to divide. Use the following questions to discuss how to complete the problem. Point to each number as you discuss it.

- **What's the first step?** *Divide.* **The multiplication chart shows that 7 times 30 equals 210. That's as close as we can get to 218 without going over, so 218 divided by 30 has a quotient of 7.**
- **What's the second step?** *Multiply.* **7 times 30 equals 210.**
- **What's the third step?** *Subtract.* **218 minus 210 equals 8.**
- **What's the fourth step?** *Bring down the next digit (if needed).* **There are no more digits to divide, so we're done. What's 518 divided by 30?** *17, with a remainder of 8.*

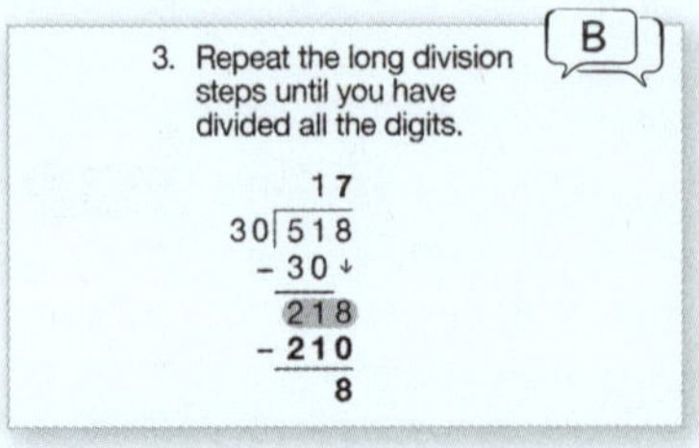

How many balloons can the party planner put in each group? *17.* **How many balloons are left over?** *8.*

Have your child use long division to solve the practice problems. Help her choose how many digits to divide and highlight these digits each time she divides. Remind your child as needed to write the digits in the quotient directly above the rightmost digit she divided.

- For 654 ÷ 30: **Is 6 greater than 30?** *No.* **Is 65 greater than 30?** *Yes.* Have your child highlight the 6 and 5. After she brings down the 4, have her highlight the 54 and repeat the long division steps.
- For 245 ÷ 30: **Is 2 greater than 30?** *No.* **Is 24 greater than 30?** *No.* **Is 245 greater than 30?** *Yes.* Have your child highlight 245 and solve.
- For 875 ÷ 30: **Is 8 greater than 30?** *No.* **Is 87 greater than 30?** *Yes.* Have your child highlight the 8 and 7. After she brings down the 5, have her highlight the 275 and repeat the steps.

	× 30
1	30
2	60
3	90
4	120
5	150
6	180
7	210
8	240
9	270

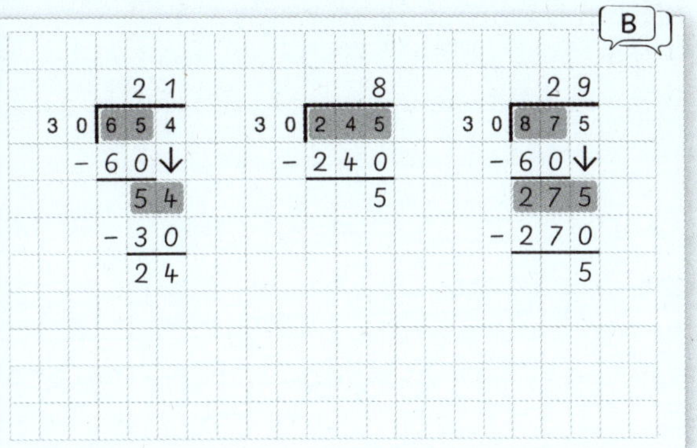

Independent Practice and Review

Have your child complete the Lesson 7.3 Practice and Review workbook pages.

Lesson 7.4
Divide by Two-Digit Divisors

Purpose	Materials
• Complete a ×24 multiplication table • Use long division to divide by two-digit divisors • Reason about remainders	• Highlighter

Memory Work

- **What do we call the top number in a fraction?** *The numerator.*
- **What does the numerator tell?** *The number of parts.*
- **What do we call the bottom number in a fraction?** *The denominator.*
- **What does the denominator tell?** *How many equal parts the whole was split into.*

Warm-up (A): Complete a ×24 Multiplication Table

In the last few lessons, you learned how to perform long division with two-digit divisors. Today, you'll practice more as we help an Adventure Club see whether it's raised enough money for everyone in the club to go ziplining. Have you ever participated in a fundraiser? *Answers will vary.*

There are 24 members in the Adventure Club, so we'll be dividing by 24 a lot today. Let's finish the ×24 multiplication table to help. Have your child complete the multiplication table.

	1	2	3	4	5	6	7	8	9
× 24	24	48	72	96	120	144	168	192	216

Activity (B): Practice Long Division with Two-Digit Divisors

Show your child the poster and chart. **Ziplining costs $64 per person, so the club is trying to raise $64 for each of the 24 members. This chart shows how much money the club raised at each of its fundraisers. We'll use long division to see how much the adventure club made per member in each fundraiser. At the end of the lesson, we'll add up how much they made per person to see if they met their goal of $64 per person.**

Fundraiser	Total Amount of Money Raised	Amount Raised Per Member	Remainder
Car Wash	$290		
Pancake Breakfast	$570		
Raffle	$230		
Chili Cook-Off	$449		
	Total:		

Another way to find out whether the Adventure Club met the goal is to add up the proceeds of all 4 fundraisers and divide the total by 24. If your child points this out, praise him for finding a more efficient way to solve the problem. Explain that dividing the proceeds of each fundraiser separately gives him more practice with long division.

The Adventure Club earned $290 at the car wash fundraiser. Let's use long division to find out how much money the car wash raised for each club member. Write 290 ÷ 24 as a long division problem in the work space. Have your child use long division to solve. Help as needed.

```
       12
  24)290
    -24↓
      50
     -48
       2
```

How much money did the adventure club earn at the carwash for each member? *$12.* **How much money is left over?** *$2.* **The members of the adventure club decided to put the extra $2 in the club's bank account for now.** Write $12 and $2 in the chart as shown.

Fundraiser	Total Amount of Money Raised	Amount Raised Per Member	Remainder
Car Wash	$290	$12	$2

Let's use long division to see how much the adventure club raised in the other fundraisers. Have your child write and complete long division problems to find how much the club raised per member at the other fundraisers. Write the amount raised per member and remainder in the chart after your child completes each long division problem. After he finishes, have him add to find the total amount raised per member and the total sum of the remainders.

Fundraiser	Total Amount of Money Raised	Amount Raised Per Member	Remainder
Car Wash	$290	$12	$2
Pancake Breakfast	$570	$23	$18
Raffle	$230	$9	$14
Chili Cook-Off	$449	$18	$17
	Total:	62	51

```
       23            9           18
  24)570       24)230       24)449
    -48↓         -216         -24↓
      90           14          209
     -72                      -192
      18                        17
```

How much did the Adventure Club raise per member? *$62.* **They're very close to the goal! The club members decided to see if they had enough money left over from the fundraiser remainders. There is $51 in the club bank account from the fundraisers. Is that enough to give each member $2 more?** *Yes.* **How do you know?** *Sample answer: 2 times 24 is 48, and 48 is less than 51.* **The club raised enough money to pay for all the members' ziplining trips!**

Independent Practice and Review

Have your child complete the Lesson 7.4 Practice and Review workbook pages.

Lesson 7.5
Long Division with Four-Digit Dividends

Purpose	Materials
• Use long division to divide four-digit numbers by two-digit numbers • Solve division word problems and interpret remainders	• Highlighter, optional

Memory Work	
	• **How do you know if a number is divisible by 2?** *It is even. It has a 0, 2, 4, 6, or 8 in the ones-place.* • **How do you know if a number is divisible by 3?** *The sum of its digits is divisible by 3.* • **How do you know if a number is divisible by 4?** *When you divide it by 2, the quotient is even.* • **How do you know if a number is divisible by 6?** *It is even and divisible by 3.*

In this lesson, your child will suggest words to create silly division word problems (as in the game Mad Libs). This makes these lengthy long division problems feel more relaxed and fun.

Warm-up (B): Fill in the Blanks to Create Silly Division Word Problems

In this warm-up, you will prepare Activity B for use later in the lesson. Keep the Lesson Activities page hidden from your child as you complete this warm-up.

Have you ever played the game Mad Libs? *Answers will vary.* **In this game, people suggest words to complete the blanks in a story. They don't know what the story is about, so the story often ends up pretty silly.**

I'm going to ask you to tell me some words, and I'll write your answers in the blanks in the word problems. We'll solve the problems later in the lesson.

First, tell me the name of a person. *Sample answer: Gertrude.* Write the name in the first blank in the first word problem in part B. **Next, tell me an object. It can be any sort of object.** *Sample answer: Jelly donut.* Write the plural form of the object (for example, "jelly donuts") in the next blank.

B

Gertrude (NAME) splits
4,950 jelly donuts (OBJECTS) into
27 equal groups.
How many are in each group?
How many are left over?

Sample completed problem.

Fill in the blanks for the second word problem in the same way. Keep the page hidden while you complete the blanks so that your child doesn't know the context for each problem.

Once you've completed all four blanks, show your child the page and give her a few minutes to read and enjoy the completed word problems.

Activity (A): Extend Long Division to Four-Digit Dividends

In the last lesson, you learned how to divide three-digit numbers by two-digit numbers. Today, you'll learn how to divide four-digit numbers by two-digit numbers. We use the same steps.

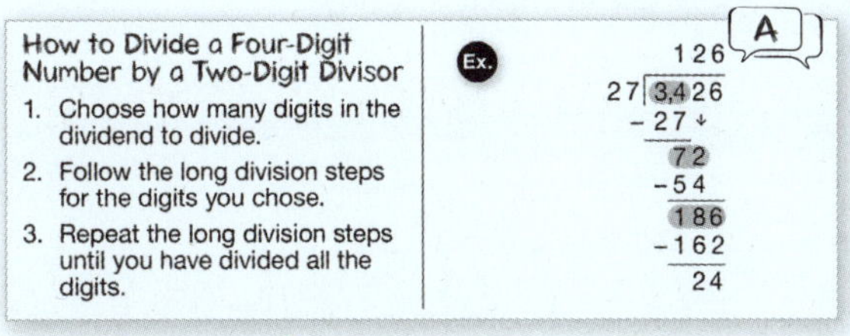

Use the following questions to discuss the example.

- **Which digits in the dividend are divided first in this example?** *The 3 and 4.*
- **How many times do you have to repeat the long division steps to complete this problem?** *3 times.*
- **What is 3,426 divided by 27?** *126, with a remainder of 24.*

Activity (B): Divide Four-Digit Numbers to Solve Silly Word Problems

Now, let's use long division to solve the silly word problems we created in the warm-up.

Read the first completed word problem aloud. Have your child use long division to write and solve the matching problem. Encourage her to use the ×27 table to help, and highlight the digits to be divided as needed. Once she completes the division problem, have her use the quotient and remainder to answer the word problem. For example: *Gertrude has 183 jelly donuts in each group, with 9 left over.* Have your child complete the second problem in the same way.

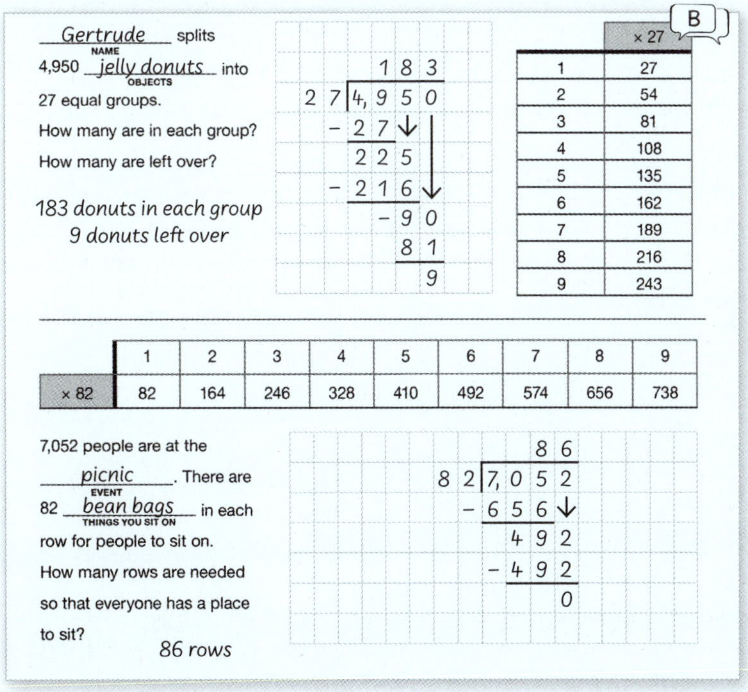

Sample completed word problems and long division problems.

Independent Practice and Review

Have your child complete the Lesson 7.5 Practice and Review workbook pages.

Lesson 7.6
Enrichment (Optional)

Purpose	Materials
• Practice memory work • Appreciate how math can be used to answer real-life questions • Use long division to approximate the length of a road trip • Summarize what your child has learned and assess your child's progress	• *How Many Guinea Pigs Can Fit on a Plane?: Answers to Your Most Clever Math Questions*, by Laura Overdeck • Map app

Warm-up: Review Memory Work

Quiz your child on any of the memory work items that he struggled with during this unit.

Math Picture Book: *How Many Guinea Pigs Can Fit on a Plane?*

Read pages 62-69 in *How Many Guinea Pigs Can Fit on a Plane?*

Enrichment Activity: How Long Will It Take to Drive?

Today, you get to choose a destination for an imaginary road trip. We'll use long division to estimate how long it would take to drive to that place.

Have your child choose a road trip destination. Use a map app to find the distance from your home to the destination. If needed, round the distance to the nearest mile.

Highways in the United States usually have a speed limit around 70 miles per hour. So, we can divide the distance by 70 to find roughly how many hours it would take to drive this distance.

Have your child make a multiplication table for 70 as shown. Then, have him use long division to divide the distance by 70. For example: *It's 915 miles from our house to Niagara Falls. 915 divided by 70 is 13 with a remainder of 5. That means it would take about 13 hours of driving to drive to Niagara Falls.*

```
      1 3
 70 | 9 1 5
    - 7 0 ↓
      2 1 5
    - 2 1 0
          5
```

	×70		×70
1	70	6	420
2	140	7	490
3	210	8	560
4	280	9	630
5	350		

Sample long division problem for a destination 915 miles away.

Compare your child's estimate to the map app's prediction. Help your child understand that both numbers only provide an estimate of how long the trip would take. **If we ran into traffic or drove on slower roads, the trip would take longer. We'd probably need to take some rest stops, too!**

> Feel free to adjust this activity to your family's average driving speed. If your family uses the metric system, help him divide the distance in kilometers by your country's speed limit or your family's average driving speed.

Unit Wrap-Up

Have your child complete the Unit 7 Wrap-Up.

Unit 7 Answer Key

7.1 Practice

Practice — Describe the mistake in each problem. Then, solve it correctly.

Incorrect	What is the mistake?	Correct solution:
$374 \div 5$: quotient 73; $374 - 35 = 24$, $24 - 15 = 9$	Sample answer: The remainder is greater than the divisor.	$374 \div 5 = 74$; $37 - 35 = 2$, bring down 4: $24 - 20 = 4$ (remainder 4)
$229 \div 3$: quotient 760; $22 - 21 = 1$, $19 - 18 = 1$, $1 - 0 = 1$	Sample answer: The 7 is in the wrong column.	$229 \div 3 = 76$; $22 - 21 = 1$, bring down 9: $19 - 18 = 1$ (remainder 1)

Use long division to solve. Write the equations you use in the work space. Think carefully about how to interpret the remainder.

185 people are in line for the amusement park ride. Each car on the ride holds 4 people. How many cars does it take to hold all the people?

47 cars

WORK SPACE

$185 \div 4 = 46$; $18 - 16 = 2$, bring down 5: $25 - 24 = 1$ (remainder 1)

307 visitors are registered to tour the historic village. There are 8 tour guides. The guides try to divide the visitors into groups as evenly as possible. How many visitors will be in each tour group?

38 or 39 visitors

$307 \div 8 = 38$; $30 - 24 = 6$, bring down 7: $67 - 64 = 3$ (remainder 3)

7.1 Review

Review — Match.

- Factors of 30 — 1, 2, 3, 5, 6, 10, 15, 30
- Multiples of 30 — 30, 60, 90, 120, 150
- Prime numbers — 3, 5, 7, 11, 19
- Numbers divisible by 4 — 16, 28, 40, 48, 100

Complete the chart.

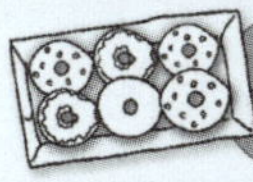

Boxes	10	12	13	14	15	17	18	20
Donuts	60	72	78	84	90	102	108	120

Complete.

1 km = 1,000 m	1 mi. = 5,280 ft.	1 week = 7 days
1 m = 100 cm	1 yd. = 3 ft.	1 day = 24 hr.
1 cm = 10 mm	1 ft. = 12 in.	1 hr. = 60 min.
1 L = 1,000 mL	1 lb. = 16 oz.	1 min. = 60 sec.
1 kg = 1,000 g	1 c. = 8 fl. oz.	

Solve. Write the equations you use.

Ian had some money. He spent \$25, and then he had \$35 left. How much money did he start with?

? – 25 = 35
35 + 25 = **\$60**

★ Sylvia had \$80. She bought 2 lamps at a thrift store, and then she had \$36 left. Both lamps cost the same amount. How much did each lamp cost?

80 – 36 = 44
44 ÷ 2 = **\$22**

7.2 Practice

Practice — Complete the multiplication tables.

	1	2	3	4	5	6	7	8	9
× 70	70	140	210	280	350	420	490	560	630

	1	2	3	4	5	6	7	8	9
× 25	25	50	75	100	125	150	175	200	225

Use long division to solve. Use the multiplication tables (above) to help. Then, find the blanks that match the letter for each problem. Write the letter in the matching blanks to solve the riddle.

- R: $199 \div 70 = 2$; $199 - 140 = 59$
- H: $393 \div 70 = 5$; $393 - 350 = 43$
- V: $432 \div 70 = 6$; $432 - 420 = 12$
- S: $645 \div 70 = 9$; $645 - 630 = 15$
- N: $78 \div 25 = 3$; $78 - 75 = 3$
- O: $80 \div 25 = 3$; $80 - 75 = 5$
- E: $97 \div 25 = 3$; $97 - 75 = 22$
- D: $188 \div 25 = 7$; $188 - 175 = 13$
- I: $206 \div 25 = 8$; $206 - 200 = 6$

Why did the student wear glasses for her math lesson?
Because it improves...

H	E	R		D	I	V	I	S	I	O	N
5 R43	3 R22	2 R59		7 R13	8 R6	6 R12	8 R6	9 R15	8 R6	3 R5	3 R3

7.2 Review

Review — Find the missing numbers in the equations.

36; ? — 3 × 12 = 36	48; ? — 48 ÷ 8 = 6	?; 7 — 28 ÷ 4 = 7
120; ? — 120 ÷ 30 = 4	?; 50 — 200 ÷ 50 = 4	180; ? — 3 × 60 = 180

Complete the chart.

Cups	1	5	8	10	11	20	21	19
Fluid Ounces	8	40	64	80	88	160	168	152

Find the average number of children in each cabin at nature camp.

Cabin List

- **Red Maple:** 14 campers
- **White Oak:** 12 campers
- **Blue Spruce:** 9 campers
- **Silver Birch:** 11 campers
- **White Pine:** 14 campers

14 + 12 + 9 + 11 + 14 = 60
60 ÷ 5 = **12 campers**

Unit 7 Answer Key

7.3 Practice

Practice Use long division to find the quotient. Then, multiply (or multiply and add) to check your answers. Use the multiplication table to help.

	× 40
1	40
2	80
3	120
4	160
5	200
6	240
7	280
8	320
9	360

```
      7          1 3          2 4
40 )3 0 5    40 )5 2 7    40 )9 9 9
  - 2 8 0      - 4 0↓       - 8 0↓
      2 5        1 2 7        1 9 9
               - 1 2 0      - 1 6 0
                     7          3 9
```

Check

```
     4 0         1 3         2 4
   ×   7       × 4 0       × 4 0
   2 8 0       5 2 0       9 6 0
 +   2 5     +     7     +   3 9
   3 0 5       5 2 7       9 9 9
```

Use long division to solve. Use the multiplication table to help.

Ella has 837 stickers. She arranges 60 stickers on each page in her sticker book. How many pages does she fill?

13 pages

After Ella fills as many pages as possible, she puts the leftover stickers on their own page. How many stickers are on this page?

57 stickers

```
       1 3
60 )8 3 7
  - 6 0↓
    2 3 7
  - 1 8 0
      5 7
```

	× 60
1	60
2	120
3	180
4	240
5	300
6	360
7	420
8	480
9	540

7.3 Review

Review Find the greatest common factor for each pair of numbers. Make your own lists of factors.

GCF of 9 and 12: 3

9	12
1 × 9	1 × 12
3 × 3	2 × 6
	3 × 4

GCF of 12 and 16: 4

12	16
1 × 12	1 × 16
2 × 6	2 × 8
3 × 4	4 × 4

Complete.

360 ÷ 90 = 4 | 500 ÷ 50 = 10 | 2,400 ÷ 40 = 60

1,000 ÷ 200 = 5 | 3,500 ÷ 700 = 5 | 3,000 ÷ 600 = 5

Use the printed protractors to measure the angles.

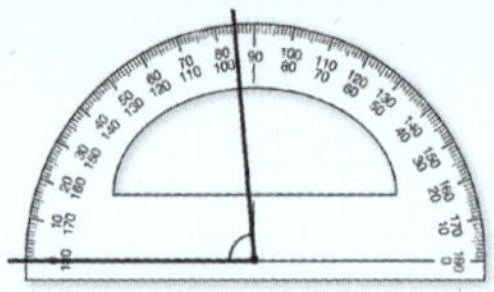

85°

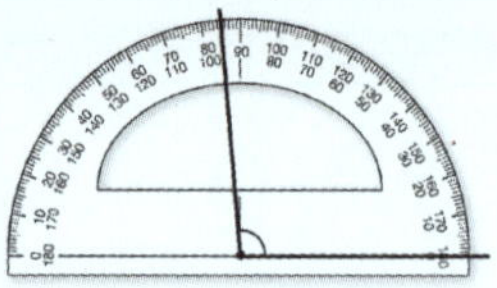

95°

Solve. Write the equations you use.

Norah read 60 pages on Saturday. She read 3 times as many pages on Saturday as she read on Sunday. How many pages did she read on Sunday?

60 ÷ 3 = 20 pages

Shawn practiced the piano for 15 minutes on Monday. He practiced for 3 times as long on Tuesday as he practiced on Monday. How long did he practice the piano on Tuesday?

15 × 3 = 45 minutes

7.4 Practice/Review

Practice Use long division to find the quotients. Use the multiplication tables to help.

	× 45
1	45
2	90
3	135
4	180
5	225
6	270
7	315
8	360
9	405

```
       1 3
45 )5 9 7
  - 4 5
    1 4 7
  - 1 3 5
      1 2
```

	× 67
1	67
2	134
3	201
4	268
5	335
6	402
7	469
8	536
9	603

```
       1 3
67 )8 8 3
  - 6 7
    2 1 3
  - 2 0 1
      1 2
```

Review Complete the chart.

Boxes	10	13	15	16	18	19	20
Cookies	50	65	75	80	90	95	100

Find the missing information for each rectangular prism. Make sure to include the correct units.

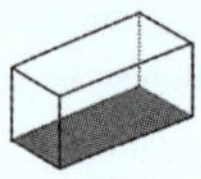

Base area: 10 sq. cm

Height: 3 cm

Volume: 30 cu. cm

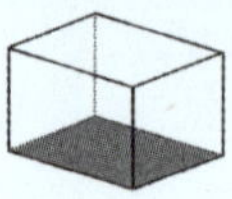

Base area: 20 sq. ft.

Height: 4 ft.

Volume: 80 cu. ft.

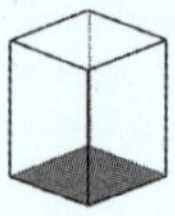

Base area: 9 sq. m

Height: 5 m

Volume: 45 cu. m

Unit 7 Answer Key

7.5 Practice

Practice Complete the multiplication table.

	1	2	3	4	5	6	7	8	9
× 12	12	24	36	48	60	72	84	96	108

Use long division to solve the word problems. Use the multiplication table (above) to help.

Ezra's family has 8 chickens. Last year, they gathered 1,980 eggs from their chickens. How many dozens of eggs did they gather? (12 eggs equal 1 dozen.)

165 dozens

$$\begin{array}{r} 165 \\ 12\,\overline{)1,980} \\ -12\downarrow \\ 78 \\ -72\downarrow \\ 60 \\ -60 \\ 0 \end{array}$$

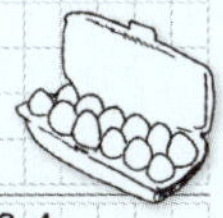

Benjamin Franklin lived for 1,011 months. How many years and months did he live?

84 years, 3 months

$$\begin{array}{r} 84 \\ 12\,\overline{)1,011} \\ -96\downarrow \\ 51 \\ -48 \\ 3 \end{array}$$

The Great Pyramid of Giza is 5,448 inches tall. How many feet tall is it?

454 ft.

$$\begin{array}{r} 454 \\ 12\,\overline{)5,448} \\ -48\downarrow \\ 64 \\ -60\downarrow \\ 48 \\ -48 \\ 0 \end{array}$$

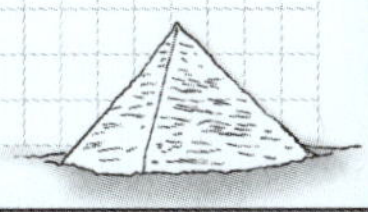

7.5 Review

Review Draw lines to divide the bars into the fractional part listed.

halves, thirds, fourths, sixths, eighths, twelfths

Complete the missing numbers in the equivalent fractions.

$\frac{1}{2} = \frac{4}{8}$	$\frac{3}{4} = \frac{6}{8}$	$\frac{1}{4} = \frac{2}{8}$
$\frac{1}{3} = \frac{2}{6}$	$\frac{2}{3} = \frac{4}{6}$	$\frac{3}{3} = \frac{6}{6}$
$\frac{1}{3} = \frac{4}{12}$	$\frac{2}{3} = \frac{8}{12}$	$\frac{3}{3} = \frac{12}{12}$
$\frac{1}{6} = \frac{2}{12}$	$\frac{3}{6} = \frac{6}{12}$	$\frac{5}{6} = \frac{10}{12}$

Find all factors of each number. Then, answer the questions.

Factors of 23: 1, 23

1 × 23

Is 23 prime or composite? prime

Factors of 25: 1, 5, 25

1 × 25
5 × 5

Is 25 prime or composite? composite

7.6 Unit Wrap-Up A

Unit Wrap-Up Use the words in the word bank to label the numbers in the division problem.

$$\begin{array}{r} 9 \\ 7\,\overline{)65} \\ -63 \\ 2 \end{array}$$

9 ← quotient; 65 ← dividend; divisor → 7; remainder → 2

Word bank: divisor, remainder, quotient, dividend

Write the long division steps in order.

1. divide
2. multiply
3. subtract
4. bring down

Use long division to find the quotient. Then, multiply (or multiply and add) to check your answers. Use the multiplication table to help.

	× 30
1	30
2	60
3	90
4	120
5	150
6	180
7	210
8	240
9	270

$$\begin{array}{r} 9 \\ 30\,\overline{)286} \\ -270 \\ 16 \end{array} \qquad \begin{array}{r} 16 \\ 30\,\overline{)480} \\ -30\downarrow \\ 180 \\ -180 \\ 0 \end{array} \qquad \begin{array}{r} 18 \\ 30\,\overline{)565} \\ -30\downarrow \\ 265 \\ -240 \\ 25 \end{array}$$

Check

$$\begin{array}{r} 30 \\ \times\ 9 \\ \hline 270 \\ +\ 16 \\ \hline 286 \end{array} \qquad \begin{array}{r} 16 \\ \times\ 30 \\ \hline 480 \end{array} \qquad \begin{array}{r} 18 \\ \times\ 30 \\ \hline 540 \\ +\ 25 \\ \hline 565 \end{array}$$

7.6 Unit Wrap-Up B

Unit Wrap-Up Use long division to solve the word problems. Use the multiplication tables to help.

Charlie has a bracelet-making business. He uses 40 cm of string for each bracelet. How many bracelets can he make from 683 cm of string?

17 bracelets

$$\begin{array}{r} 17 \\ 40\,\overline{)683} \\ -40 \\ 283 \\ -280 \\ 3 \end{array}$$

	× 40
1	40
2	80
3	120
4	160
5	200
6	240
7	280
8	320
9	360

Charlie uses 34 beads for each bracelet. How many bracelets can he make from a pack of 1,500 beads?

44 bracelets

$$\begin{array}{r} 44 \\ 34\,\overline{)1,500} \\ -136\downarrow \\ 140 \\ -136 \\ 4 \end{array}$$

	× 34
1	34
2	68
3	102
4	136
5	170
6	204
7	238
8	272
9	306

Charlie charges $15 per bracelet. Last year, he earned $1,875. How many bracelets did he sell?

125 bracelets

$$\begin{array}{r} 125 \\ 15\,\overline{)1,875} \\ -15\downarrow \\ 37 \\ -30\downarrow \\ 75 \\ -75 \\ 0 \end{array}$$

	× 15
1	15
2	30
3	45
4	60
5	75
6	90
7	105
8	120
9	135

Unit 7 Checkpoint

What to Expect at the End of Unit 7

By the end of Unit 7, most children will be able to do the following:

- Use long division to solve division problems (up to four digits divided by two digits). Most children will be able to use the steps to solve long division problems independently, but some will still need coaching and support. Many children will make occasional mistakes.

Is Your Child Ready to Move on?

In Unit 8, your child will learn how to find fractions of a set. Your child does not need to have fully mastered long division before moving on to Unit 8. If she is struggling to solve long division problems independently, look for the long division problems on the Review pages in Unit 8. Coach your child through solving these problems as needed, and remind her to refer to the examples on the Unit 7 Reference pages in the back of the workbook.

Unit 8
Fractions of Sets and Simplest Form

Overview

In the first part of the unit, your child will learn to find fractions of sets and measures. For example, he'll learn to answer questions like "What's 3/4 of 1 foot?" or "If 5 of the 15 marbles are striped, what fraction of the marbles are striped?" He'll also learn to simplify fractions. In the second part of the unit, your child will learn to use bar models to solve word problems about fractional parts of sets.

What Your Child Will Learn

In this unit, your child will learn to:

- Describe part of a set with a fraction
- Write fractions in simplest form
- Describe part of a set or measurement unit with a fraction and find fractional parts of measurement units
- Find the number of objects in a fractional part of a set
- Use bar models to solve find-the-part, comparison, and find-the-whole fraction word problems

Lesson List

Lesson 8.1	Represent Part of a Set with a Fraction	Lesson 8.7	Find a Fractional Part of a Unit of Measure
Lesson 8.2	Divide to Create Equivalent Fractions	Lesson 8.8	Find-the-Part Word Problems
		Lesson 8.9	Comparison Word Problems, Part 1
Lesson 8.3	Divide by Common Factors to Simplify Fractions	Lesson 8.10	Comparison Word Problems, Part 2
Lesson 8.4	Use the GCF to Simplify Fractions	Lesson 8.11	Comparison Word Problems, Part 3
Lesson 8.5	Represent Units of Measure with Fractions or Mixed Numbers	Lesson 8.12	Find-the-Whole Word Problems
		Lesson 8.13	Enrichment (Optional)
Lesson 8.6	Find a Fractional Part of a Set		

Extra Materials Needed for Unit 8

- Paper clip
- Highlighter
- 5 craft sticks or writing utensils (any kind)
- For optional Enrichment Lesson:
  - *How Many Guinea Pigs Can Fit on a Plane?: Answers to Your Most Clever Math Questions*, by Laura Overdeck. Feiwel & Friends, 2017.
  - Collection of 20-30 objects

Teaching Math with Confidence: Using Bar Models to Solve Word Problems about Fractional Parts of Sets

In this unit, your child will solve word problems about fractional parts of sets. He'll tackle three different types of problems: find-the-part, comparison, and find-the-whole problems. Some of these problems ask him to find the size of part of a set, while others ask him to find the size of a whole set.

Children often have trouble understanding and visualizing these problems, especially problems that ask them to find the size of the whole set. You'll use bar models to help your child understand the structure of these problems and solve them.

Niall's family is driving to visit his cousins. The cousins live 40 kilometers away. So far, Niall's family has driven $\frac{3}{4}$ of the distance. How far have they driven?

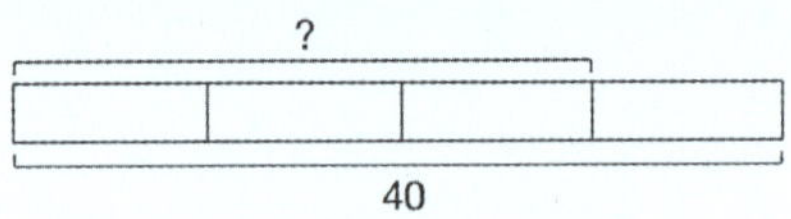

Sample find-the-part problem.

In a survey, 24 people said they like strawberry ice cream best. These 24 people were $\frac{3}{8}$ of all the people who answered the survey. How many people answered the survey?

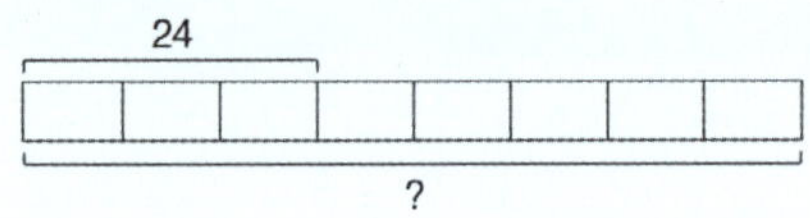

Sample find-the-whole problem.

While the bar models may seem confusing or complicated at first, they become extremely helpful once your child understands how to use them. Use the following suggestions to help him become more comfortable with this powerful way of representing fractional relationships.

- Children often want to jump straight to solving before they even understand the word problem. If your child tends to rush, use these three key questions to slow him down before he starts solving.
  - **What is the goal?**
  - **What do you know?**
  - **Will your answer be greater or less than the number you know?** (This question nudges your child to consider whether the known quantity is part of the set or the whole set.)
- When you read through the examples with your child, make sure your child fully understands the problem before you analyze the sample bar model. Cover the bar model with a piece of paper or sticky note if you find he always wants to jump ahead.
- Your child may immediately know the answers to some of the word problems in the earlier lessons and not need a bar model to solve them. If this happens, have him explain to you how he found the answer. Then, ask him to pretend to "be the teacher" and show you how you could use a bar model to solve the problem. The bar model examples in the earlier lessons lay the groundwork for the more-difficult bar models in the later lessons, so it's important he understand them.
- Explain to your child that you value careful reasoning more than quick answers, and that it's okay if it takes him some time to solve these challenging word problems. Most of the lessons include only 5 or 6 word problems (split between the Lesson Activities and Practice pages) to encourage your child to think deeply about the problems.
- Help your child as much as he needs, and don't worry if he can't solve these tricky word problems entirely independently by the end of the unit. He'll have more opportunities to practice them throughout the year.

Lesson 8.1
Represent Part of a Set with a Fraction

Purpose	Materials
• Use counters to find a fraction of a set • Represent part of a set with a fraction	• Counters • Highlighter

Memory Work	
	• **What do we call the top number in a fraction?** *The numerator.* • **What does the numerator tell?** *The number of parts.* • **What do we call the bottom number in a fraction?** *The denominator.* • **What does the denominator tell?** *How many equal parts the whole was split into.*

In this lesson, your child will begin using Student Workbook B. Keep Student Workbook A handy so that your child can refer to the Unit Reference pages at the back of the workbook as she completes the Review pages. (Or, tear out the Unit Reference pages and place them in plastic page protectors in a binder.)

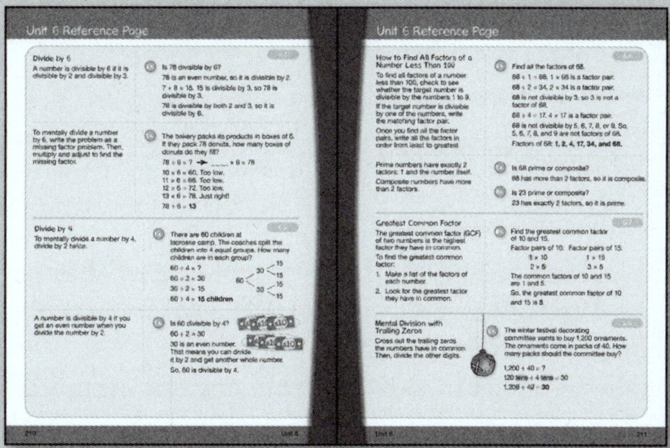

Warm-up: Find a Fraction for Part of a Set of Counters

You've learned that we can use fractions to describe parts of many different types of wholes. For example, we might say we have one-fourth of a pizza left, or that I ate two-fifths of a candy bar. We also use fractions to describe parts of measures, like one-third of a cup or nine-tenths of a kilogram. In each of these examples, the fraction describes part of a whole. The whole might be a pizza, a candy bar, a cup, or a kilogram.

Today, you'll learn how to use a fraction to describe part of a set of objects. In these problems, the entire set of objects is the whole.

The following activity uses red and blue counters. If your counters are different colors, substitute their colors as you arrange the counters and read the questions.

Put 1 red counter and 2 blue counters on the table. **There are 3 counters in this set, so each counter is one-third of the set. 1 counter is red, so one-third of the set is red. 2 of the counters are blue, so two-thirds of the set is blue.**

Repeat with the following sets of counters:

- Put 1 red counter and 5 blue counters on the table. **What fraction of this set is red?** *One-sixth.* **What fraction of this set is blue?** *Five-sixths.*

- Put 3 red counters and 1 blue counter on the table. **What fraction of this set is red?** *Three-fourths.* **What fraction of this set is blue?** *One-fourth.*

- Put 2 red counters and 2 blue counters on the table. **What fraction of the set is red?** *Two-fourths. One-half.* **Each counter is one-fourth of the set, so two-fourths of the set is red. Two-fourths is equivalent to one-half, so we can also say that one-half of the set is red.**

Activity (A): Represent Part of a Set with a Fraction

Read aloud the examples with your child.

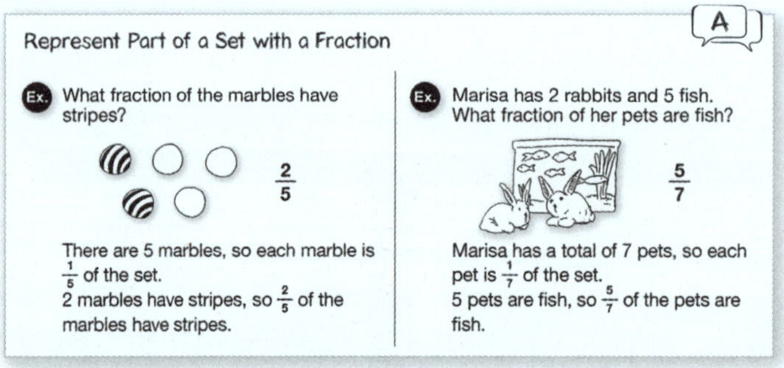

Use these questions to discuss the examples:

- **In the first example, there are a total of 5 marbles. 2 of them are striped.**
- **Each marble is one-fifth of the set, so two-fifths of the marbles have stripes.**
- **How many marbles do not have stripes?** *3.*
- **What fraction of the marbles in this example are not striped?** *Three-fifths.*
- **In the second example, Marisa has 7 pets. 5 of the pets are fish, so five-sevenths of the pets are fish.**
- **What fraction of her pets are rabbits?** *Two-sevenths.*
- **If Marisa got another rabbit, then how many pets would she have?** *8.* **What fraction of her pets would be rabbits then?** *Three-eighths.* If your child has trouble understanding this question, have her first draw an additional rabbit on the page.

Have your child write fractions to answer the questions about the treat bags.

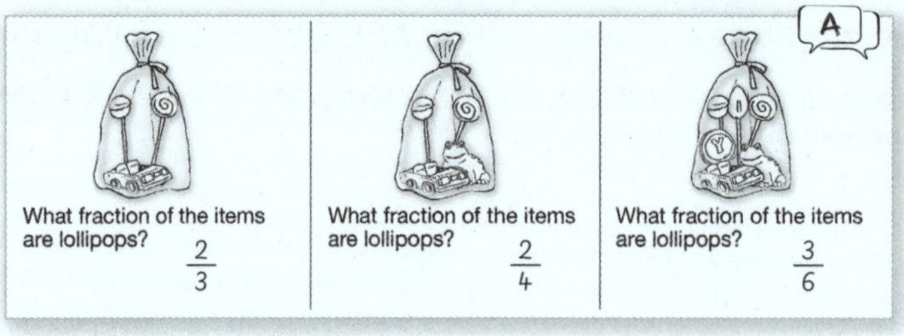

Activity (B): Find the Fraction of Consonants and Vowels in Your Child's Name

Now, we'll write fractions to describe the letters in your name. Have your child write her first and last name in the blanks. Have her highlight the vowels in both names.

Jane — MY FIRST NAME

Doe — MY LAST NAME

> If needed, remind your child that the vowels are a, e, i, o, and u. The letter y counts as a vowel if it makes a vowel sound. All other letters are consonants.

How many letters in your first name are vowels? *Sample answer: 2.* **How many letters are there in all in your first name?** *Sample answer: 4.* **So, what fraction of the letters in your first name are vowels?** *Sample answer: Two-fourths. One-half.* Have your child write this fraction in the chart. Repeat with the rest of the blanks in the chart.

	What fraction of the letters are vowels?	What fraction of the letters are consonants?
First name	$\frac{2}{4}$	$\frac{2}{4}$
Last name	$\frac{2}{3}$	$\frac{1}{3}$
Both names	$\frac{4}{7}$	$\frac{3}{7}$

Sample answers.

> Your child will learn how to simplify fractions in Lessons 8.2-8.4. She does not need to simplify any of the fractions in this chart unless she would like to.

What do the fractions of vowels and consonants in each row add up to? *1 whole.* **Why do the fractions in each row add up to 1 whole?** *Sample answer: All the letters are either vowels or consonants. So, the fraction of vowels plus the fraction of consonants must add up to the whole word.*

Does your first or last name have more vowels? *Answers will vary.* **Does your first or last name have a greater fraction of vowels?** *Answers will vary.*

Independent Practice and Review

Have your child complete the Lesson 8.1 Practice and Review workbook pages.

Lesson 8.2
Divide to Create Equivalent Fractions

Purpose	Materials
• Practice writing fractions to describe part of a set • Divide the numerator and denominator by the same number to create equivalent fractions • Choose divisors to create equivalent fractions	• None

Memory Work	
	• **What do we call fractions that look different but have the same value?** *Equivalent fractions.* • **What do we call numbers that have a whole number and a fraction?** *Mixed numbers.* • **What do we call a fraction whose numerator is greater than or equal to its denominator?** *An improper fraction.*

Warm-up (A): Practice Representing Part of a Set with Fractions

In the last lesson, you learned how to represent part of a set with a fraction. Point to the first exercise. **How many marbles are striped?** *4.* **How many marbles are there in all?** *8.* **So, what fraction of the marbles are striped?** *Four-eighths.* Write 4/8 in the blank. Have your child complete the other exercises in the same way.

What do all 3 sets of marbles have in common? *Half of the marbles are striped.* **Four-eighths, three-sixths, and five-tenths are all equivalent to one-half.**

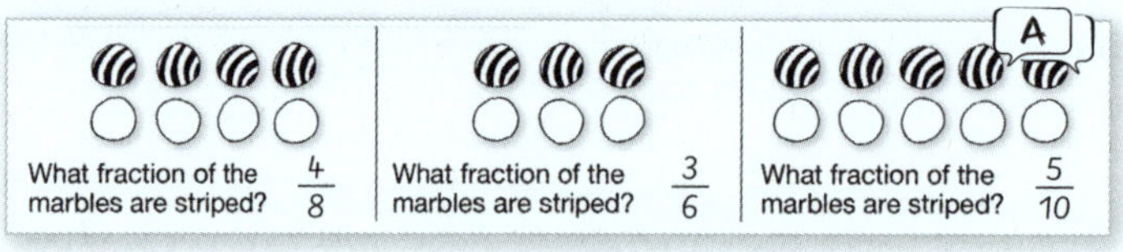

Activity (B): Divide to Create Equivalent Fractions

You already know how to create equivalent fractions by multiplying the numerator and denominator by the same number. Today, you'll learn how to divide the numerator and denominator by the same number to create an equivalent fraction. Have your child read the text box aloud.

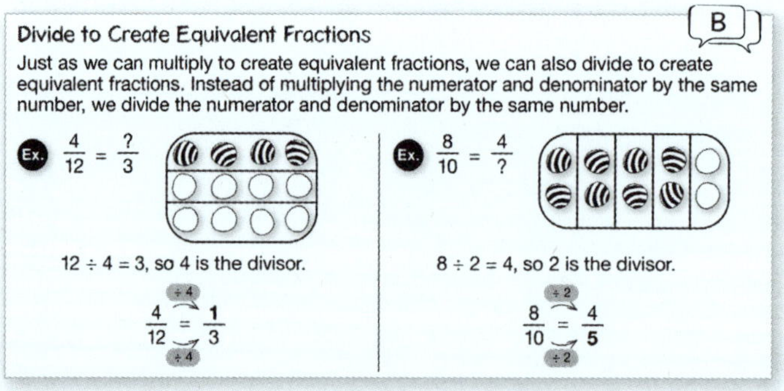

In the first example, four-twelfths of the marbles are striped. We need to find the numerator in the equivalent fraction.

- **First, we find the divisor. 12 divided by what equals 3?** *4.* **12 divided by 4 equals 3, so 4 is the divisor. We divide the 12 marbles into groups of 4 and make 3 groups.**
- **4 divided by 4 equals 1, so the numerator is 1. If you divide 4 marbles into groups of 4, you get 1 group. Four-twelfths equals one-third.**

In the second example, eight-tenths of the marbles are striped. We need to find the denominator in the equivalent fraction.

- **First, we find the divisor. 8 divided by what equals 4?** *2.* **8 divided by 2 equals 4, so 2 is the divisor. We divide the marbles into groups of 2, and 4 of the groups have stripes.**
- **10 divided by 2 equals 5, so the denominator is 5. If you divide all 10 marbles into groups of 2, you get 5 groups. Eight-tenths equals four-fifths.**

In the first practice problem, there are 10 marbles. 6 of them are striped. We want to find the missing denominator.

First, we find the divisor. 6 divided by what equals 3? *2.* **2 is the divisor. We divide the marbles into groups of 2.** Write "÷2" above and below the equals sign in the problem. Draw circles around each group of 2 marbles as shown.

Now, we divide the denominator by 2. What's 10 divided by 2? *5.* Write 5 as the denominator. **Three-fifths of the groups have striped marbles.**

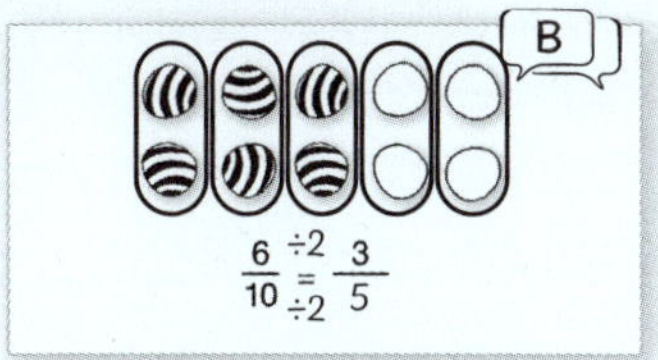

Have your child complete the other practice problems in the same way.

- For the second problem: **10 divided by 5 equals 2.** Outline the groups of 5 as shown.
- For the third problem: **40 divided by 20 equals 2.** Outline the groups of 20 as shown.

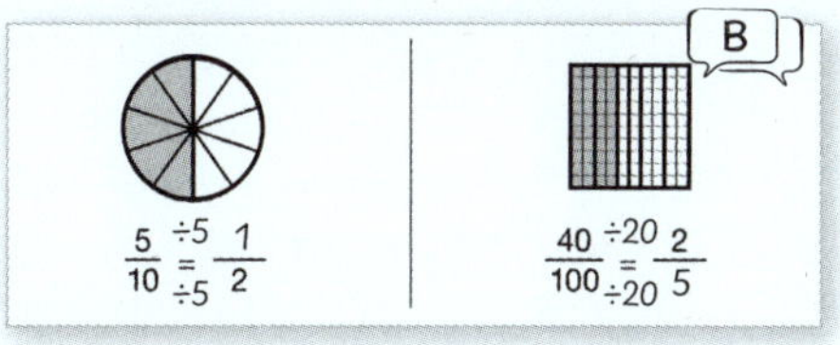

Activity (C): Play Fill the Fractions

In this game, you win as many points as the number you write, and you want to get the lowest score possible. Keep that in mind as you choose which puzzles to complete!

Play Fill the Fractions. As your child solves each problem, have him first find the divisor and write it above and below the equals sign. Then, have him divide to find the missing number in the equivalent fraction.

> Use counters as needed to model the problems. For example, for 3/15, place 3 counters of one color and 12 counters of another color on the table. **We have 15 counters. We want to create 5 groups, so how many counters go in each group?** *3.* **So, 3 is the divisor.**

Fill the Fractions

Materials: None

Object of the Game: Complete equivalent fractions to win fewer points than your opponent.

Choose who will go first.

Directions continued on next page.

On your turn, choose a puzzle on the gameboard. Find the missing number in the equivalent fraction. The missing number is your score. Write your initials in the box. For example, if you complete the following problem on your first turn, you score 1 point.

ZP C

$$\frac{3}{15} \underset{\div 3}{\overset{\div 3}{=}} \frac{1}{5}$$

Take turns until all problems have been completed. Each player adds up all of their points. Whoever has the lower score wins the game.

Answer Key:

$\frac{3}{15} = \frac{1}{5}$	$\frac{8}{12} = \frac{2}{3}$	$\frac{10}{30} = \frac{2}{6}$	$\frac{6}{8} = \frac{3}{4}$
$\frac{14}{20} = \frac{7}{10}$	$\frac{6}{20} = \frac{3}{10}$	$\frac{21}{30} = \frac{7}{10}$	$\frac{20}{40} = \frac{1}{2}$
$\frac{6}{16} = \frac{3}{8}$	$\frac{6}{24} = \frac{1}{4}$	$\frac{5}{15} = \frac{1}{3}$	$\frac{10}{18} = \frac{5}{9}$

Independent Practice and Review

Have your child complete the Lesson 8.2 Practice and Review workbook pages.

Lesson 8.3
Divide by Common Factors to Simplify Fractions

Purpose	Materials
• Practice dividing to find missing numbers in equivalent fractions • Divide by common factors to simplify fractions • Understand that the simplest form of a fraction is the equivalent fraction with the smallest numerator and denominator possible	• Playing cards

Memory Work

- **How do you know if a number is divisible by 2?** *It is even. It has 0, 2, 4, 6, or 8 in the ones-place.*
- **How do you know if a number is divisible by 3?** *The sum of its digits is divisible by 3.*
- **How do you know if a number is divisible by 4?** *When you divide it by 2, the quotient is even.*
- **How do you know if a number is divisible by 5?** *It has a 0 or 5 in the ones-place.*
- **How do you know if a number is divisible by 6?** *It is even and divisible by 3.*

In this lesson, your child will learn to simplify fractions and express them in simplest form. (For example, the simplest form of 3/6 is 1/2.) You may have been taught this process as "reducing fractions" or "putting fractions in lowest terms." Children are often confused by these descriptions, since the words "reducing" or "lowest" imply that the value of the fraction has gotten smaller. *Math with Confidence* describes this process as simplifying to better convey that the fractions' values do not change.

Warm-up (A): Practice Dividing to Create Equivalent Fractions

In the last lesson, you learned how to divide the numerator and the denominator of a fraction by the same number to create an equivalent fraction. Have your child find the missing numbers in the pairs of equivalent fractions.

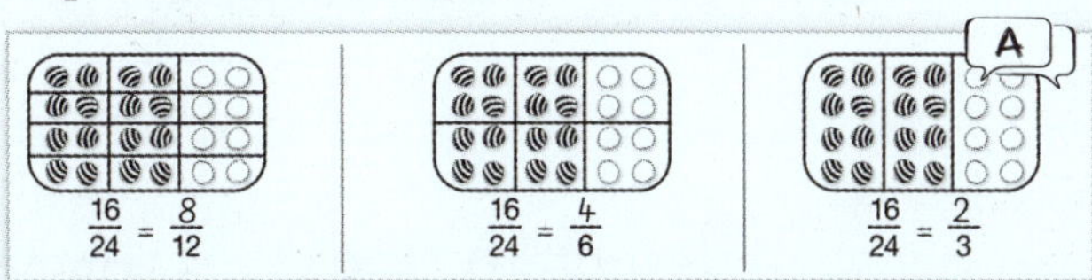

What do these three problems have in common? *They all have the same number of marbles.* **Sixteen-twenty-fourths, eight-twelfths, four-sixths, and two-thirds are all equivalent to each other. You could use any of these fractions to describe what fraction of the set is striped. Which fraction would be simplest to use in everyday life?** *Two-thirds.*

Activity (B): Divide by Common Factors to Simplify Fractions

Today, you will learn how to find the simplest form of a fraction. The simplest form is the equivalent fraction with the smallest numerator and denominator possible. It's usually more convenient to use fractions when they're in simplest form. For example, it's much easier to measure out two-thirds of a yard of ribbon than sixteen-twenty-fourths of a yard! Have your child read the text box aloud.

B

Divide by Common Factors to Simplify Fractions

The simplest form of a fraction is the equivalent fraction with the smallest numerator and denominator possible.

To find the simplest form of a fraction, divide the numerator and denominator by a common factor. Keep dividing until the numerator and denominator have no common factors (other than 1).

Ex. Express $\frac{18}{24}$ in simplest form.

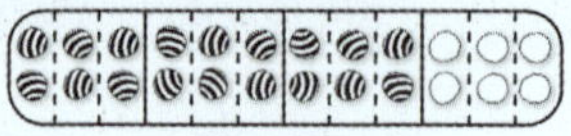

$$\frac{18}{24} \overset{\div 2}{\underset{\div 2}{=}} \frac{9}{12} \overset{\div 3}{\underset{\div 3}{=}} \frac{3}{4}$$

3 and 4 have no common factors (other than 1).
So, $\frac{3}{4}$ is the simplest form of $\frac{18}{24}$.

Let's study the example to learn how to simplify eighteen-twenty-fourths and write it in simplest form.

- **18 and 24 are both even and divisible by 2, so we'll divide 18 and 24 by 2 first. What's 18 divided by 2?** *9.* **What's 24 divided by 2?** *12.* **So, eighteen-twenty-fourths is equivalent to nine-twelfths.**
- **Nine-twelfths is simpler than eighteen-twenty-fourths, but we can simplify it even further. 9 and 12 both have 3 as a factor, so we divide both numbers by 3. What's 9 divided by 3?** *3.* **What's 12 divided by 3?** *4.* **So, nine-twelfths is equivalent to three-fourths.**
- **Do 3 and 4 have any factors in common other than 1?** *No.* **We can't divide any further. The simplest form of eighteen-twenty-fourths is three-fourths.**

Is eighteen-twenty-fourths less than, greater than, or equal to three-fourths? *Equal.* **Even though the fractions have different numerators and denominators, they still have the same value. When you simplify a fraction, you change the numerator and denominator. But, you don't change the overall value of the fraction.**

> You could also simplify 18/24 in one step by dividing both the numerator and denominator by 6.

Demonstrate how to solve the first practice problem.

- **We want to simplify sixteen-twentieths. Both 16 and 20 have 4 as a factor, so I'll start by dividing by 4.** Write "÷4" above and below the equals sign in the problem.
- **What's 16 divided by 4?** *4.* Write 4 as the numerator. **What's 20 divided by 4?** *5.* Write 5 as the denominator.
- **Do 4 and 5 have any common factors other than 1?** *No.* **We can't divide 4 and 5 by the same number. So, we've found that four-fifths is the simplest form of sixteen-twentieths.**

B

$$\frac{16}{20} \overset{\div 4}{\underset{\div 4}{=}} \frac{4}{5}$$

> You could also simplify 16/20 by dividing by 2 twice.

Have your child complete the other practice problems in the same way. She may divide once or multiple times as she simplifies the fractions in this lesson, as long as the final fraction is in simplest form.

B

$$\frac{9}{27} \overset{\div 9}{\underset{\div 9}{=}} \frac{1}{3} \qquad \frac{20}{30} \overset{\div 10}{\underset{\div 10}{=}} \frac{2}{3}$$

Activity (C): Play Flip and Simplify

Play Flip and Simplify.

Flip and Simplify

Materials: 2s, 3s, 4s, and 5s from 1 deck of cards (16 cards total)

Object of the Game: Write the most fractions in simplest form.

Shuffle the cards and place them in a face-down pile.

On your turn, flip over a card. Choose a fraction on the game board. Divide the numerator and denominator by the number on the card. (You must choose a fraction where both the numerator and denominator are divisible by the number on the card.)

After you divide the numerator and denominator by the number on the card, check whether the resulting fraction is in simplest form. If it is in simplest form, circle the final fraction and write your initials in the box. For example, if you turn over a 3:

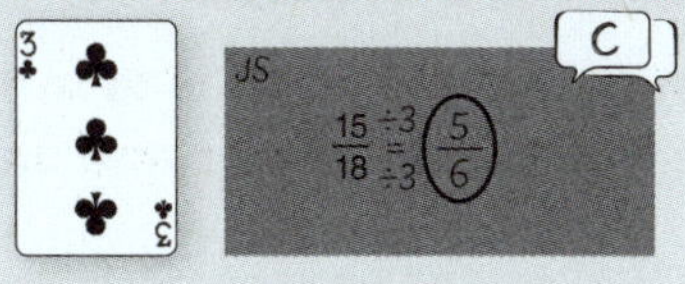

Sample play. 5/6 is in simplest form, so the player circles the fraction and writes their initials in the box.

If the resulting fraction is not in simplest form, leave the fraction to be simplified further on a different turn. Either player may eventually simplify it.

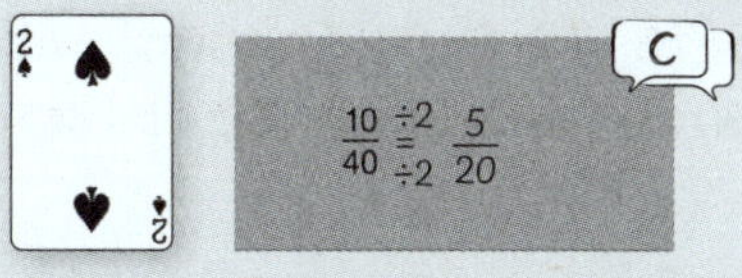

Sample play. 5/20 is not in simplest form. Either player may simplify it further on a future turn.

If you flip over a card and find that you cannot use the number on the card as a divisor for any of the fractions, you lose your turn and play passes to the other player.

Take turns flipping over cards and simplifying the fractions until all the fractions are in simplest form. Whoever has written their initials on more boxes wins the game. If you run out of cards, shuffle and re-use the already-played cards.

Answer Key:

The answer key shows the simplest form for each fraction. It may take several steps before you find this simplest form of the fraction.

$\frac{10}{40} = \frac{1}{4}$	$\frac{15}{30} = \frac{1}{2}$	$\frac{24}{60} = \frac{2}{5}$
$\frac{40}{48} = \frac{5}{6}$	$\frac{6}{18} = \frac{1}{3}$	$\frac{15}{18} = \frac{5}{6}$
$\frac{8}{20} = \frac{2}{5}$	$\frac{24}{36} = \frac{2}{3}$	$\frac{25}{40} = \frac{5}{8}$

Independent Practice and Review

Have your child complete the Lesson 8.3 Practice and Review workbook pages.

Lesson 8.4
Use the GCF to Simplify Fractions

Purpose	Materials
• Learn a simpler way to find greatest common factors • Divide by the greatest common factor of the numerator and denominator to simplify a fraction or mixed number	• None

Memory Work	• **What does GCF stand for?** *Greatest common factor.* • **Name 4 factors of 28.** *Possible answers: 1, 2, 4, 7, 14, 28.*

Warm-up (A): Learn a Simpler Way to Find Greatest Common Factors

In Unit 3, you learned how to find the greatest common factor for a pair of numbers. You made a list of the factors of both numbers and then looked for the greatest factor they have in common.

A simpler way to find the greatest common factor is to make a list of the factors of the smaller number. Then, start with the largest factor and check whether it is also a factor of the other number.

Demonstrate how to use this approach to find the GCF of 16 and 24.

- **16 is the smaller number, so I'll start with a list of the factor pairs of 16.**
- **What are the factor pairs of 16?** *1 and 16, 2 and 8, 4 and 4.* Write 1 × 16, 2 × 8, and 4 × 4.
- **The largest factor of 16 is 16. Is 16 a factor of 24?** *No.* Cross out 16.
- **The next-largest factor of 16 is 8. Is 8 a factor of 24?** *Yes.* **So, 8 is the greatest common factor.** Circle 8 and write 8 in the answer blank.

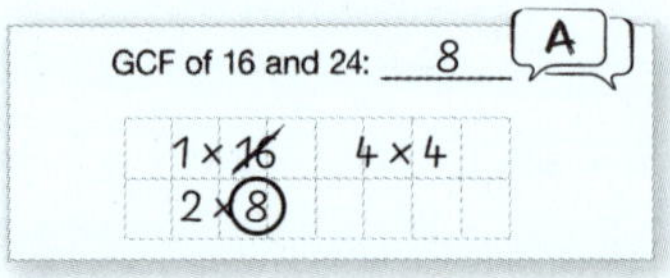

Have your child use this approach to find the greatest common factor for 20 and 28. For 7 and 8, point out that the only factor pair of 7 is 1 and 7. **7 isn't a factor of 8, so the only factor they have in common is 1.**

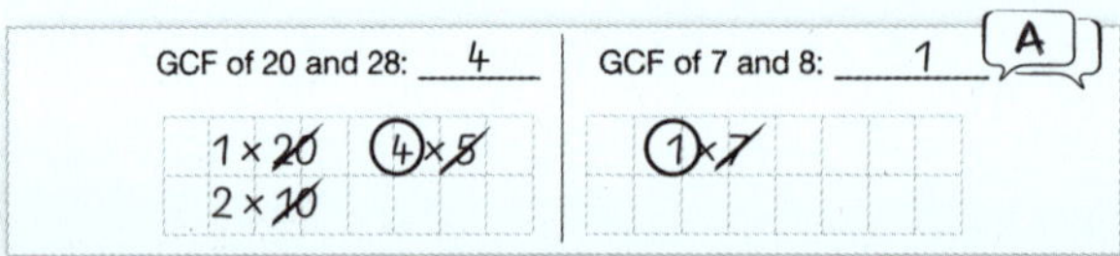

When the numbers are small, you may even be able to find the greatest common factor mentally. Just think of the factors of the smaller number and check whether each is also a factor of the larger number.

Activity (B): Divide by the Greatest Common Factor to Simplify Fractions

In the last lesson, you learned how to find the simplest form of a fraction. How do you know when you've found the simplest form of a fraction? *Sample answer: There aren't any more numbers that divide both the numerator and denominator.* Have your child read the text box aloud.

> B
>
> **Divide by the Greatest Common Factor to Simplify Fractions**
>
> Divide the numerator and denominator by the greatest common factor (GCF) to simplify the fraction in one step.
>
> Ex. Express $\frac{14}{28}$ in simplest form.
>
> $$\frac{14}{28} \overset{\div 2}{\underset{\div 2}{=}} \frac{7}{14} \overset{\div 7}{\underset{\div 7}{=}} \frac{1}{2}$$
>
> Ex. Express $\frac{14}{28}$ in simplest form.
>
> The greatest common factor of 14 and 28 is 14. So, divide both 14 and 28 by 14.
>
> $$\frac{14}{28} \overset{\div 14}{\underset{\div 14}{=}} \frac{1}{2}$$

One way to find the simplest form is to divide until the numerator and denominator have no common factors other than 1. The first example shows how to use this method to express fourteen-twenty-eighths in simplest form.

- **14 and 28 both have 2 as a factor, so we divide both numbers by 2.**
- **Seven-fourteenths is simpler than fourteen-twenty-eighths, but we can simplify it even further. 7 and 14 both have 7 as a factor, so we divide both numbers by 7. Seven-fourteenths is equivalent to one-half.**
- **Do 1 and 2 have any factors in common other than 1?** *No.* **We can't divide any further. The simplest form of fourteen-twenty-eighths is one-half.**

The second example shows how to use the greatest common factor to simplify fourteen-twenty-eighths. The greatest common factor of 14 and 28 is 14, so we divide both numbers by 14 to simplify it in one step.

Which approach do you like better? *Answers will vary.* **If you can quickly find the greatest common factor, dividing by the greatest common factor is usually more efficient. But if you're not sure what the greatest common factor is, it's fine to start by dividing both the numerator and denominator by any common factor.**

Demonstrate how to simplify 16/24 and 1 16/24:

- **In part A, we found that the greatest common factor of 16 and 24 is 8.** Write "÷8" above and below the equals sign.
- **What's 16 divided by 8?** *2.* **What's 24 divided by 8?** *3.* Write 2/3.
- **To write a mixed number in simplest form, we leave the whole number the same and simplify the fraction. The simplest form of sixteen-twenty-fourths is two-thirds, so the simplest form of 1 and sixteen-twenty-fourths is 1 and two-thirds.**

> B
>
> $$\frac{16}{24} \overset{\div 8}{\underset{\div 8}{=}} \frac{2}{3}$$
>
> $$1\frac{16}{24} = 1\frac{2}{3}$$

Have your child simplify the other fractions and mixed numbers in the same way. For 7/8, say: **The greatest common factor of 7 and 8 is 1, so they don't have any other common factors. Seven-eighths is already in simplest form.**

> B
>
> $$\frac{20}{28} \overset{\div 4}{\underset{\div 4}{=}} \frac{5}{7} \qquad \frac{7}{8} = \frac{7}{8}$$
>
> $$3\frac{20}{28} = 3\frac{5}{7} \qquad 4\frac{7}{8} = 4\frac{7}{8}$$

Activity (C): Simplify Fractions for a Sewing Project

Writing fractions in simplest form makes it easier to use them in everyday life. Let's simplify the materials list for this tote bag to make the directions easier to follow. Have your child simplify each fraction or mixed number in the tote bag directions. Have him write the problems on scrap paper if he needs more space.

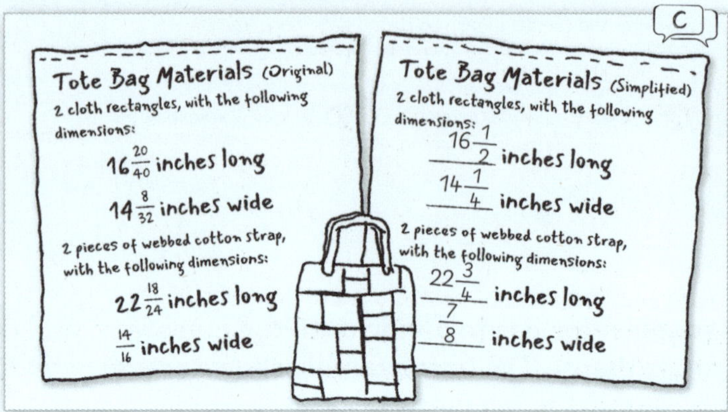

Independent Practice and Review

Have your child complete the Lesson 8.4 Practice and Review workbook pages.

Lesson 8.5

Represent Units of Measure with Fractions or Mixed Numbers

Purpose	Materials
• Explore splitting 1 foot into fractional parts • Represent units of measure with fractions or mixed numbers	• 1-foot ruler • 5 craft sticks or writing utensils (any kind) • Die

Memory Work

- **1 foot equals how many inches?** *12.*
- **1 hour equals how many minutes?** *60.*
- **1 pound equals how many ounces?** *16.*
- **1 meter equals how many centimeters?** *100.*
- **1 centimeter equals how many millimeters?** *10.*
- **1 liter equals how many milliliters?** *1,000.*
- **1 cup equals how many fluid ounces?** *8.*

The above memory work reviews the measurement equivalencies your child will use in this lesson. If your child has trouble recalling these equivalencies, jot them on a piece of scrap paper for her to refer to as she completes the lesson activities and practice page.

Warm-up: Split 1 Foot into Fractional Parts

Show your child a 1-foot ruler. **There are 12 inches in 1 foot.**

- **If I split 1 foot into 2 equal parts, how many inches are in each part?** *6.* **One-half of a foot equals 6 inches.** Place a craft stick (or writing utensil) in the middle of the ruler to split it into halves.
- **If I split 1 foot into 3 equal parts, how many inches are in each part?** *4.* **One-third of a foot equals 4 inches.** Place 2 craft sticks on the ruler to split it into thirds.
- **If I split 1 foot into 4 equal parts, how many inches are in each part?** *3.* **One-fourth of a foot equals 3 inches.** Place 3 craft sticks on the ruler to split it into fourths.
- **If I split 1 foot into 6 equal parts, how many inches are in each part?** *2.* **One-sixth of a foot equals 2 inches.** Place 5 craft sticks on the ruler to split it into sixths.
- **If I split 1 foot into 12 equal parts, how many inches are in each part?** *1.* **One-twelfth of a foot equals 1 inch.** (You do not need to place craft sticks on the ruler to split it into twelfths.)

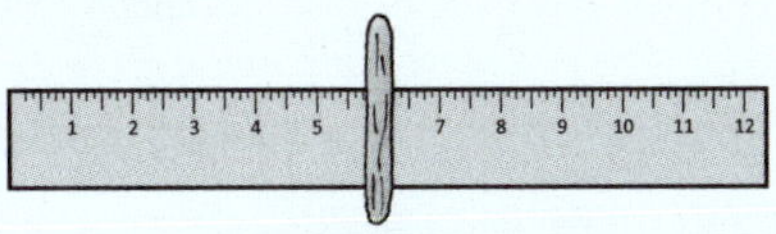

1/2 ft. = 6 in.

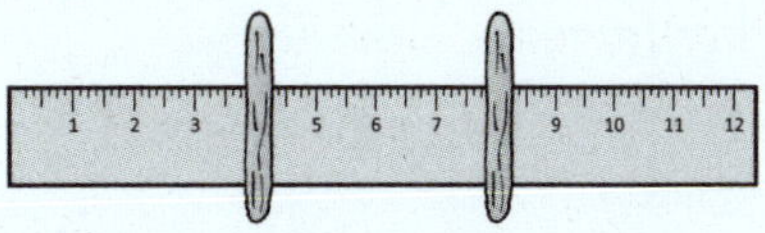

1/3 ft. = 4 in.

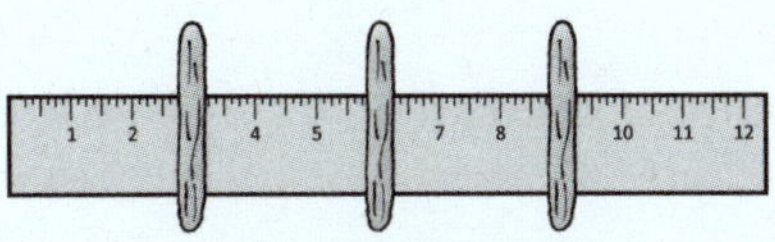

1/4 ft. = 3 in.

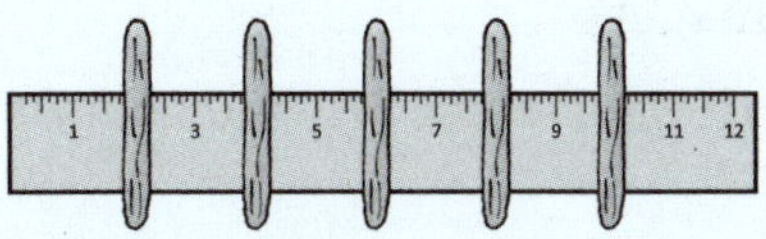

1/6 ft. = 2 in.

Activity (A): Represent Units of Measure with Fractions or Mixed Numbers

Today, you'll learn how to write a fraction to represent part of a unit of measure.

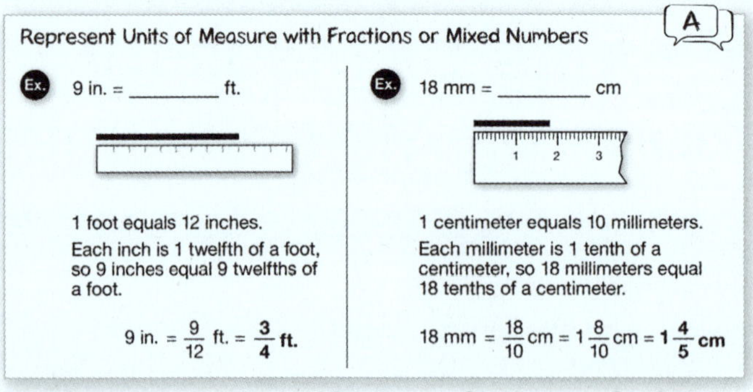

The first example shows how to write 9 inches as a fraction of a foot.

- **How many inches equal 1 foot?** *12.* **A whole foot is 12 inches, so each inch is one-twelfth of a whole foot. 9 inches are nine-twelfths of the whole foot.**
- **9 and 12 are both divisible by 3, so we divide by 3 to simplify the fraction. What's the simplified fraction?** *Three-fourths.*
- **9 inches equals three-fourths of a foot.**

The second example shows how to write 18 millimeters as a mixed number of centimeters.

- **How many millimeters equal 1 centimeter?** *10.* **Each millimeter is one-tenth of a centimeter. 18 millimeters are eighteen-tenths of a centimeter.**
- **Eighteen-tenths is an improper fraction, so we divide 18 by 10 to create a mixed number. 18 divided by 10 equals 1 with a remainder of 8, so the mixed number is 1 and eight-tenths.**
- **8 and 10 are both divisible by 2, so we divide by 2 to simplify the fraction. What's the simplified fraction?** *Four-fifths.*
- **18 millimeters equal 1 and four-fifths centimeters.**

Have your child complete the practice problems in the same way. Remind her to simplify the fractions as needed.

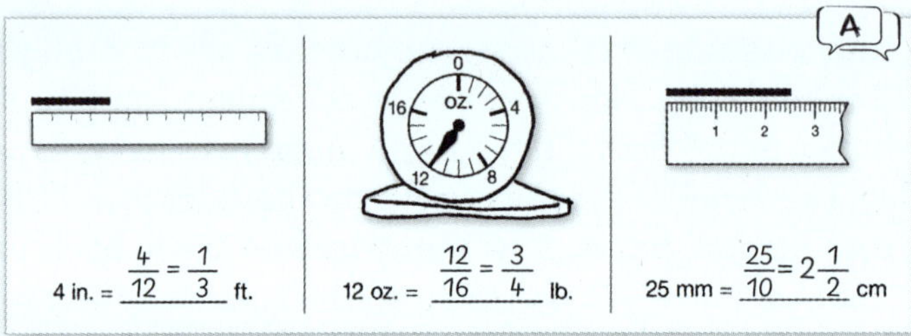

Activity (B): Play Ant Race

In this game, we pretend we're ants crawling along a meterstick. The first ant to reach 1 meter wins. Play Race to 1 Meter.

Ant Race

Materials: Die

Object of the Game: Be the first player to reach 1 meter.

Directions continued on next page.

Begin a simple scorecard as shown on a separate piece of paper. Each player should have one column labeled "cm" and another labeled "m."

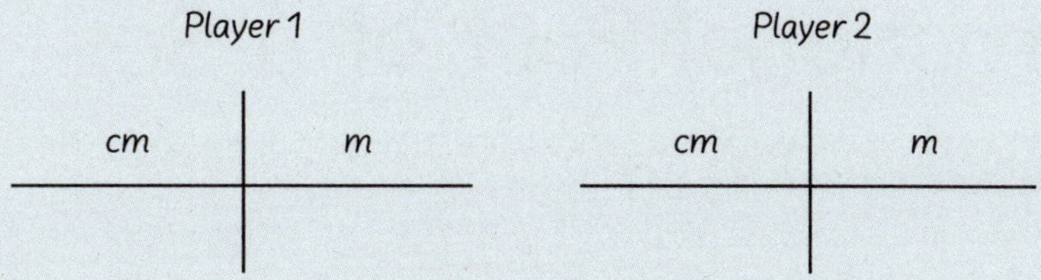

Sample scorecard.

On your first turn, roll the die. Find the matching number of centimeters on the chart and write this number in the centimeter column of your chart. (This distance is how far your ant advances along the meterstick.) Draw a line along the meterstick to show how far your ant travels. Write the matching fraction of a meter in the meter column. Simplify the fraction.

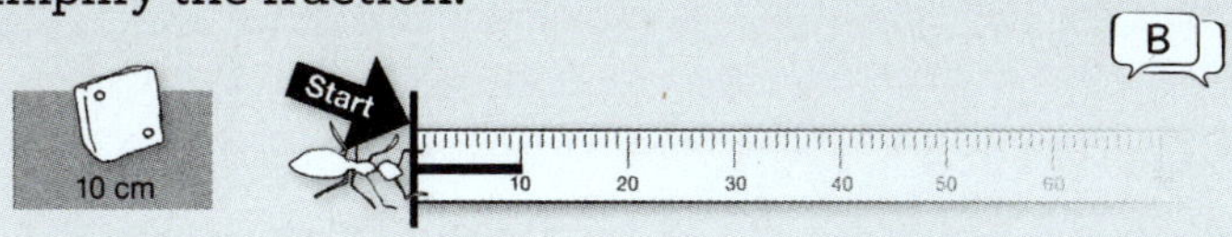

cm	m
10 cm	$\frac{10}{100} = \frac{1}{10}$ m

Sample first turn if you roll a 2.

On subsequent turns, add the new number of centimeters to your previous number of centimeters to find the total distance your ant has traveled along the meterstick. Continue your line along the meterstick to show the total distance your ant has traveled. Then, record the total distance in your scorecard as a fraction of a meter. Simplify the fraction.

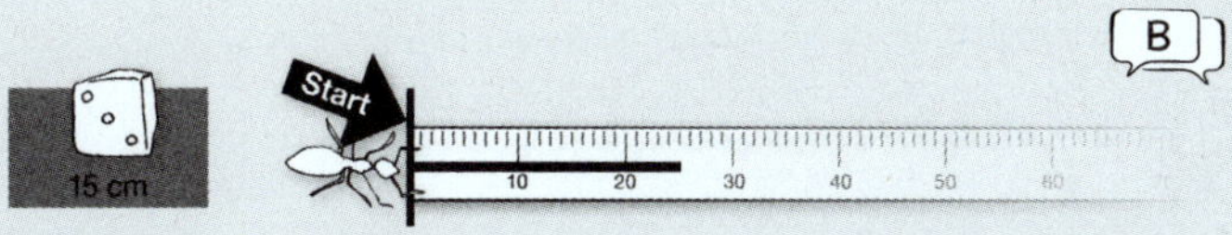

cm	m
10 cm	$\frac{10}{100} = \frac{1}{10}$ m
25 cm	$\frac{25}{100} = \frac{1}{4}$ m

Sample second turn if you roll a 3.

Take turns rolling the die, adding the new number of centimeters to your previous distance, and writing the resulting number of centimeters as a fraction of a meter. If you go past 1 meter, write the measurement as a mixed number.

The first player to reach 1 whole meter (or go past it) wins the game.

Answer Key:

$\frac{5}{100} = \frac{1}{20}$	$\frac{10}{100} = \frac{1}{10}$	$\frac{15}{100} = \frac{3}{20}$	$\frac{20}{100} = \frac{1}{5}$	$\frac{25}{100} = \frac{1}{4}$
$\frac{30}{100} = \frac{3}{10}$	$\frac{35}{100} = \frac{7}{20}$	$\frac{40}{100} = \frac{2}{5}$	$\frac{45}{100} = \frac{9}{20}$	$\frac{50}{100} = \frac{1}{2}$
$\frac{55}{100} = \frac{11}{20}$	$\frac{60}{100} = \frac{3}{5}$	$\frac{65}{100} = \frac{13}{20}$	$\frac{70}{100} = \frac{7}{10}$	$\frac{75}{100} = \frac{3}{4}$
$\frac{80}{100} = \frac{4}{5}$	$\frac{85}{100} = \frac{17}{20}$	$\frac{90}{100} = \frac{9}{10}$	$\frac{95}{100} = \frac{19}{20}$	$\frac{100}{100} = 1$

Independent Practice and Review

Have your child complete the Lesson 8.5 Practice and Review workbook pages.

Lesson 8.6
Find a Fractional Part of a Set

Purpose	Materials
• Split a set of counters into fractional parts • Find the number of objects in a fraction of a set	• Counters • Paper clip

Memory Work	• **What is the order of operations?** *Parentheses, multiply or divide from left to right, add or subtract from left to right.*

In this lesson, your child will learn how to use whole-number arithmetic to find a fraction of a set. For example, to find 3/8 of 16, he'll first divide 16 into 8 equal parts to find the size of 1 eighth. Then, he'll multiply the answer by 3 to find the size of 3 eighths. This approach encourages him to think deeply about the size of the fractional parts and the relationship between the part and whole.

Warm-up: Find Part of a Set of Counters

Place 12 counters on the table. Arrange the counters in 2 rows of 6. **Let's pretend that the counters are candies. I want to give you two-thirds of the candies and keep one-third for myself.**

Dividing the counters into thirds is the same as splitting the set into 3 equal groups. Split the counters into 3 groups as shown. **How many candies are in each third?** *4.*

If I give you two-thirds of the set, how many candies do you get? *8.* **How do you know?** *Sample answers: 2 groups of 4 equal 8. 2 times 4 equals 8.* **If I keep one-third of the set, how many candies do I get?** *4.*

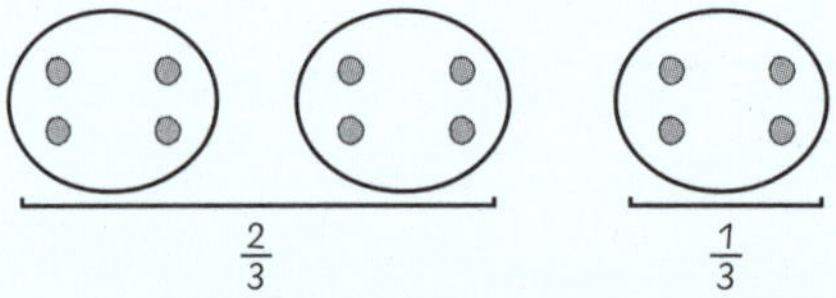

Push the counters back together. **Let's say I want to keep five-sixths of the candies and give you one-sixth. Dividing the counters into sixths is the same as splitting the set into 6 equal groups.** Split the counters into 6 groups as shown. **How many candies are in each sixth?** *2.*

If I keep five-sixths of the set, how many candies do I keep? *10.* **How do you know?** *Sample answers: 5 groups of 2 equal 10. 5 times 2 equals 10.* **If I give you one-sixth of the set, how many candies do you get?** *2.*

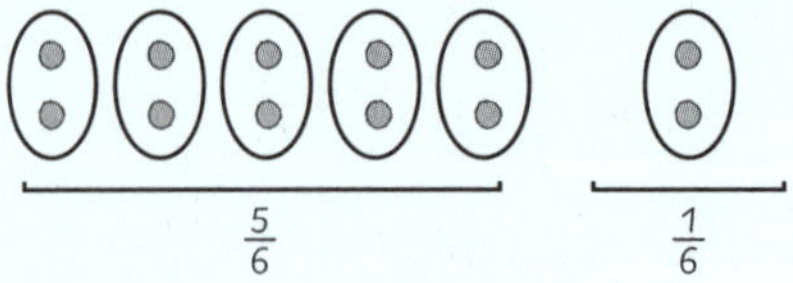

Activity (A): Find Part of a Set

In Lesson 8.1, you learned how to write a fraction to describe part of a set. Today, you'll learn how to find a fractional part of a set. The text box shows how to divide and multiply to find a fraction of a set. It's just like what you did in the warm-up. Have your child read the top part of the text box.

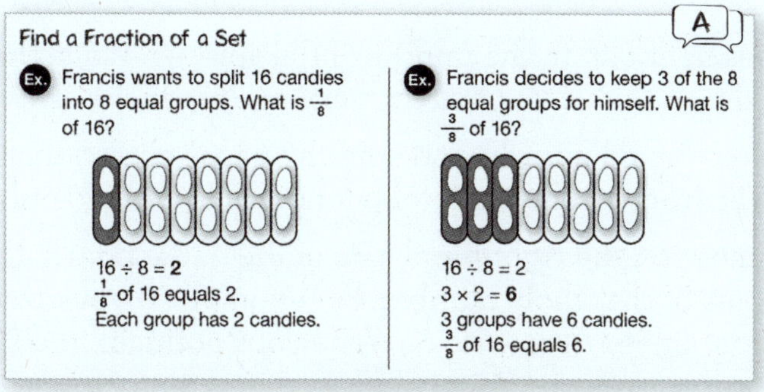

The first example shows how to find one-eighth of 16. We split the 16 candies into 8 equal groups. 16 divided by 8 equals 2, so one-eighth of 16 equals 2.

The second example shows how to find three-eighths of 16. We already found that one-eighth of 16 is 2. We want *three*-eighths of the set, so we multiply 3 times 2. 3 times 2 equals 6. Three-eighths of 16 equals 6.

If your child has trouble understanding the examples, use fraction bars and counters to make the problems more concrete. Place 8 eighth-bars on the table. Then, take 16 counters. **We want to split the 16 counters into eighths. 16 divided by 8 equals 2.** Put 2 counters under each eighth-bar. **If I take three-eighths of the counters, I take 3 groups of 2.**

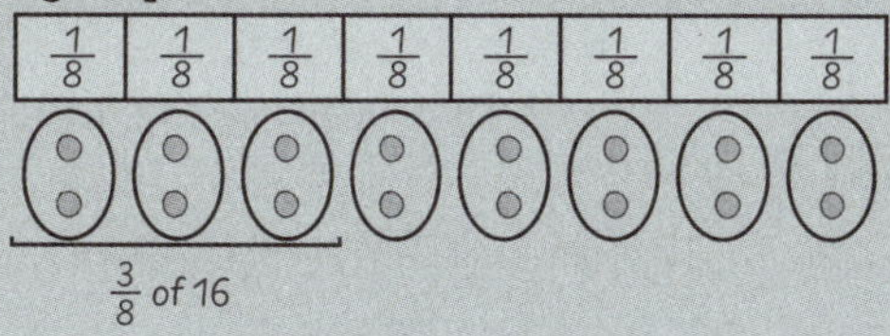

For the practice problems, have your child first draw lines to split each set into the fractional part indicated. Then, have him divide and multiply to complete the problems. (He may write out the equations or solve them mentally.)

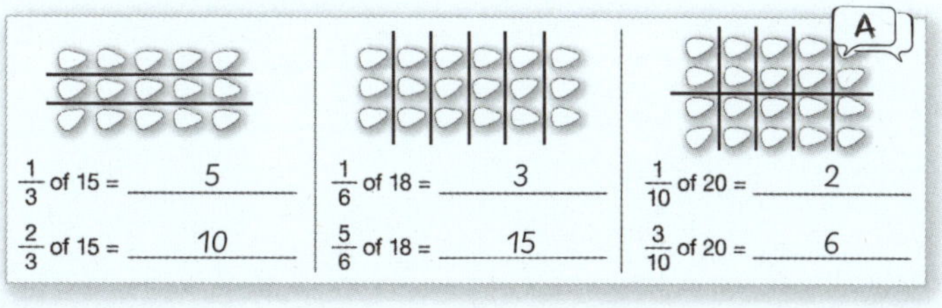

Activity (B): Play Spin a Set

Play Spin a Set.

Encourage your child to find the answers mentally in this game. For example, if he spins 3/5 and chooses 20: **What's one-fifth of 20?** *4.* **So, what's three-fifths of 20?** *12.* If he has trouble keeping the numbers in his head, it's fine for him to write the equations on paper instead.

Spin a Set

Materials: Paper clip

Object of the Game: Win the most points.

Place one end of the paper clip in the middle of the spinner. Place the point of a pencil through the paper clip so that it touches the very middle of the circle.

On your turn, hold the pencil upright and spin the paper clip so that it spins freely around the circle. The fraction the paper clip lands on is your fraction for the round.

Choose a whole number on the right-hand side of the game board. Use the fraction to find the matching part of the whole number. For example, if you spin 1/5 and choose 30, you score 6 points, since 1/5 of 30 is 6. Write your points in the scorecard.

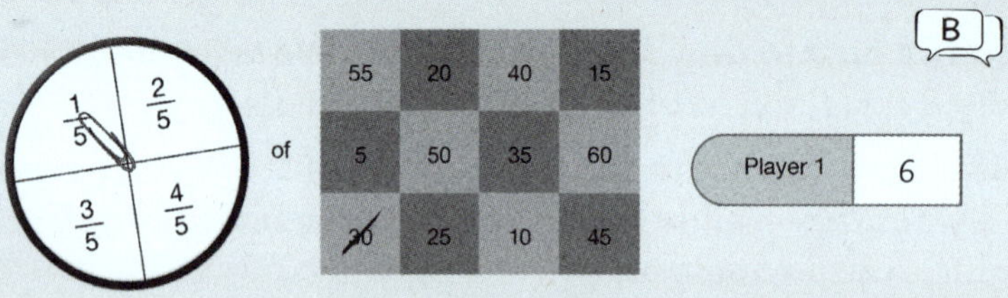

Cross out the whole number you chose. Neither player may use this number again.

Take turns until both players have filled their scorecards. Then, both players find the sum of their points. Whoever has the higher total number of points wins the game.

Independent Practice and Review

Have your child complete the Lesson 8.6 Practice and Review workbook pages.

Lesson 8.7
Find a Fractional Part of a Unit of Measure

Purpose	Materials
• Find fractional parts of 1 foot • Find fractional parts of measurement units	• 1-foot ruler • 5 craft sticks or writing utensils (any kind)

Memory Work

- **What do we call a quadrilateral with 4 right angles?** *A rectangle.*
- **What do we call a quadrilateral with 4 right angles and 4 equal sides?** *A square.*
- **What do we call a quadrilateral with 4 equal sides?** *A rhombus.*
- **What do we call a quadrilateral with 2 pairs of parallel sides?** *A parallelogram.*
- **What do we call a quadrilateral with exactly 1 pair of parallel sides?** *A trapezoid.*

Warm-up: Find Fractional Parts of a Foot with a Ruler

In the last lesson, you learned how to find a fractional part of a set. Today, you'll learn how to find a fractional part of a measurement unit.

We'll warm up by finding fractional parts of 1 foot. Place a 1-foot ruler on the table. **12 inches equal 1 foot.** Place 5 craft sticks (or writing utensils) on the ruler to split it into sixths.

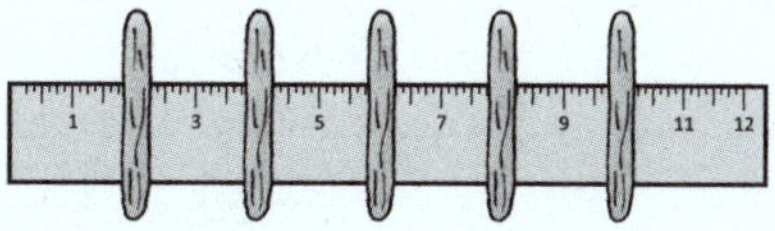

- **How many inches equal one-sixth of a foot?** *2.* If your child's not sure, suggest she divide 12 by 6.
- **How many inches equal two-sixths of a foot?** *4.* If your child's not sure, say: **One-sixth of a foot equals 2 inches. So multiply 2 inches by 2 to find two-sixths of a foot.**
- **How many inches equal three-sixths of a foot?** *6.* If your child's not sure, suggest she multiply 3 times 2.
- **How many inches equal four-sixths of a foot?** *8.* If your child's not sure, suggest she multiply 4 times 2.
- **How many inches equal five-sixths of a foot?** *10.* If your child's not sure, suggest she multiply 5 times 2.
- **How many inches equal six-sixths of a foot?** *12.* If your child's not sure, suggest she multiply 6 times 2. **Six-sixths equal 1 whole, so six-sixths of a foot equal the whole foot.**

Activity (A): Use Multiplication and Division to Find Fractional Parts of a Foot

Point to the example. **We read this question as "Two-thirds of a foot equals how many inches?" We read it that way to help make sense of the question, even though the words *of* and *a* aren't printed.**

Find Part of a Unit (A)

Ex. $\frac{2}{3}$ ft. equals how many inches?

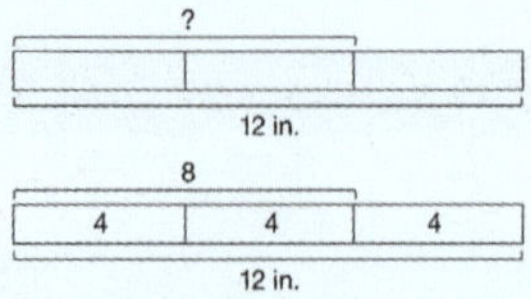

12 in. ÷ 3 = 4 in.
$\frac{1}{3}$ ft. = **4 in.**

2 × 4 in. = 8 in.
$\frac{2}{3}$ ft. = **8 in.**

Finding a fractional part of a foot is a lot like finding a fractional part of a set. We just treat the 12 inches like a set of 12 objects.

- **First, we find one-third of 12. We split the 12 inches into 3 equal groups. 12 divided by 3 equals 4, so one-third of 12 equals 4.**
- **We want to find two-thirds of 1 foot, so we multiply 2 times 4. 2 times 4 equals 8. Two-thirds of 1 foot equals 8 inches.**

Have your child divide and multiply to complete the problems. (She may write out equations or perform the calculations mentally.) Make sure to read each practice problem aloud. For example, for the first problem: ***One-fourth of a foot equals how many inches?***

(A)

$\frac{1}{4}$ ft. = 3 in.	$\frac{5}{6}$ ft. = 10 in.	$\frac{7}{12}$ ft. = 7 in.
12 ÷ 4 = 3	12 ÷ 6 = 2 5 × 2 = 10	12 ÷ 12 = 1 7 × 1 = 7

If your child has trouble, use the 1-foot ruler to model the problems. For example, for 1/4 ft.: **First, let's split the 12 inches into 4 equal parts. How many inches are in each fourth?** *3.* **So, one-fourth of a foot equals 3 inches.**

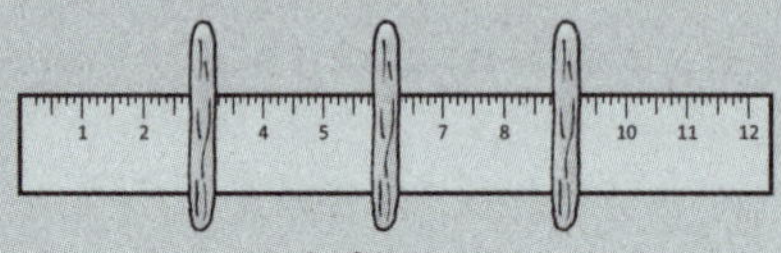

1/4 ft. = 3 in.

Activity (B): Find Part of a Pound and Liter

We often need to find parts of measurement units when we measure food. Some recipes use fractions of larger units, while others use whole numbers of smaller units. So, it's helpful to know how to convert between them.

How many ounces equal 1 pound? *16.* **For these exercises, you need to find fractions of 16 ounces.** Have your child write each fraction of a pound as a number of ounces. For example, for the first problem: **We want to find half of 16 ounces, so divide 16 by 2.**

(B)

$\frac{1}{2}$ lb. = 8 oz.	$\frac{5}{8}$ lb. = 10 oz.
16 ÷ 2 = 8	16 ÷ 8 = 2 5 × 2 = 10
$\frac{3}{4}$ lb. = 12 oz.	$\frac{15}{16}$ lb. = 15 oz.
16 ÷ 4 = 4 3 × 4 = 12	16 ÷ 16 = 1 15 × 1 = 15

How many milliliters equal 1 liter? *1,000.* **For these exercises, you need to find fractions of 1,000 milliliters.** Have your child write each fraction of a liter as a number of milliliters. For example, for the first problem: **We want to find half of 1,000 milliliters, so divide 1,000 by 2.**

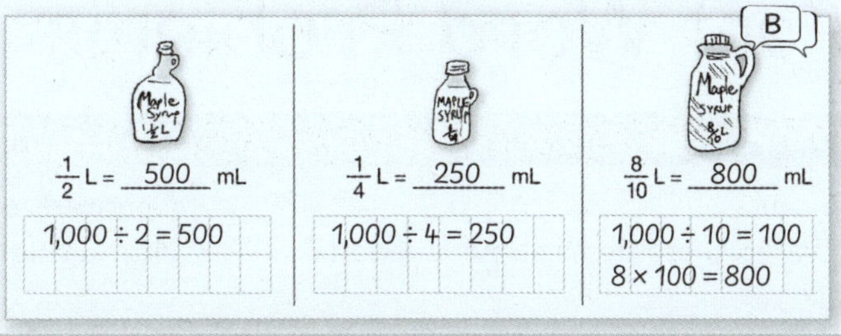

Help your child divide mentally as needed. For example, for ¼ of 1,000: **To divide 1,000 by 4, divide it in half twice. What's 1,000 divided by 2?** *500.* **What's 500 divided by 2?** *250.* **So, 1,000 divided by 4 equals 250.**

Independent Practice and Review

Have your child complete the Lesson 8.7 Practice and Review workbook pages.

Lesson 8.8
Find-the-Part Word Problems

Purpose	Materials
• Mentally find parts of sets • Use bar models to solve word problems about fractional parts of sets	• Counters, optional • Highlighter

Memory Work	
	• **What do we call an angle with a measure less than 90 degrees?** *Acute.* • **What do we call an angle with a measure equal to 90 degrees?** *Right.* • **What do we call an angle with a measure greater than 90 degrees and less than 180 degrees?** *Obtuse.* • **What do we call an angle with a measure equal to 180 degrees?** *Straight.*

This lesson begins a series of lessons on solving word problems about fractional parts of a set. The word problems mostly involve small numbers (or problems that are easy to solve with mental math) so that your child can focus on the structure of the problems rather than arithmetic. See the Unit 8 **Teaching Math with Confidence** for an overview of these types of problems.

Warm-up: Mentally Find Part of a Set

Ask your child the following questions orally. Model the questions with counters as needed (as in Lesson 8.6). Encourage him to find the answers mentally, but allow him to write the numbers down as needed.

- **What's one-third of 21?** *7.*
- **What's two-thirds of 21?** *14.*
- **What's one-fifth of 15?** *3.*
- **What's four-fifths of 15?** *12.*
- **What's one-fourth of 40?** *10.*
- **What's three-fourths of 40?** *30.*

Activity (A): Use Bar Models to Solve Find-the-Part Word Problems

Today, we'll use bar models to help find a fractional part of a set. When we solve these types of word problems, we break the process into three steps: understand the problem, draw a bar model, and use the bar model to solve.

First, let's read the problem carefully and make sure we understand it. Read the example problem aloud. **What's the goal?** *Find how many of the animals are cats.* **In this problem, we know the size of the whole set and the fraction.** Highlight 60 and 2/3 in the problem.

Ex. Norah has 60 miniature animal figures. $\frac{2}{3}$ of the animals are cats. (A)
How many cats does she have?

Will our answer be greater than or less than 60? *Less.* **How do you know?** *Sample answer: 60 is the total number of Norah's animals, and we're finding part of it.*

Next, let's see how the bar model matches the problem. The bar represents the whole set of animal figures. Norah has 60 animal figures in all. Point to the bracket labeled 60.

Three-thirds equal one whole, so the bar is split into 3 equal parts to show thirds. We want to find how many animal figures are in two-thirds of the set. Point to the bracket labeled with a question mark.

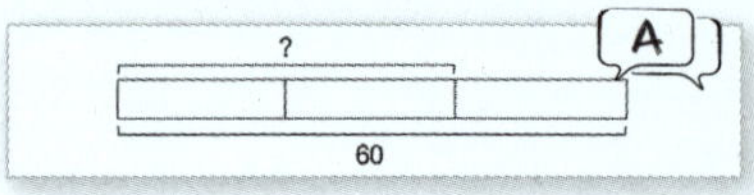

Last, let's study the example to see how to use the bar model to solve the problem. We know that the whole bar represents 60 animals. It's split into 3 small bars called unit bars. We divide 60 by 3 to find the value of each unit bar. 60 divided by 3 equals 20. Each unit bar stands for 20 animals.

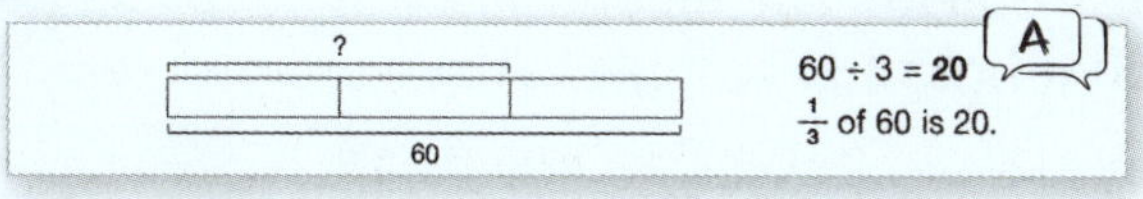

2 unit bars equal two-thirds of the set. So, we multiply 2 times 20 to find the number of animal figures in two-thirds of the set. 2 times 20 equals 40. Norah has 40 cat figures.

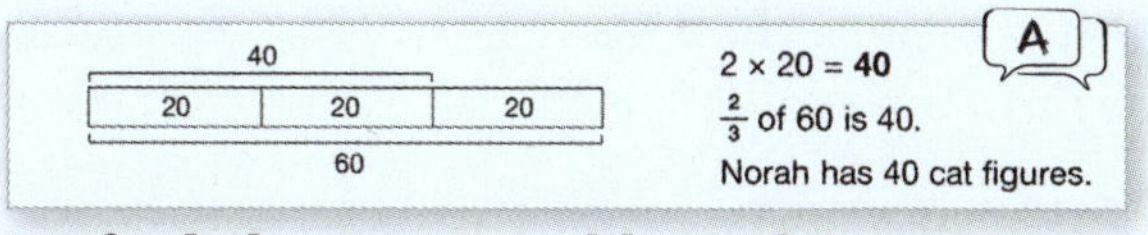

We call problems like this "find-the-part" problems, because we want to find part of a whole amount. We draw one bar to represent the whole amount. Then, we split the bar into fractional parts to match the problem.

Read aloud the first practice problem. **This problem has two goals. What is the first goal?** *Find how far Niall's family has driven.* **What is the second goal?** *Find how far they have left to drive.* **What do we know in this problem?** *The trip is 40 km long. Niall's family has already driven 3/4 of the distance.* Highlight 40 and 3/4 in the word problem.

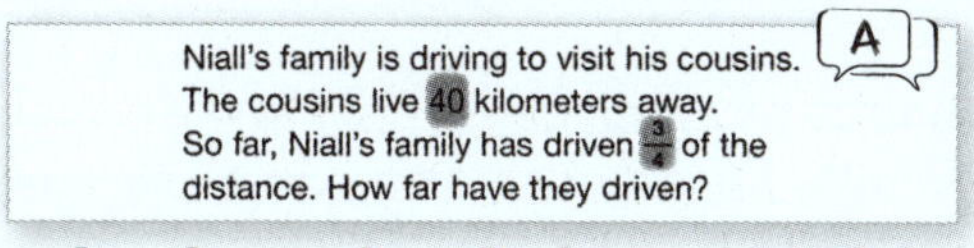

We want to find the distance they have already driven. Will the answer be greater than or less than 40? *Less.* **How do you know?** *Sample answers: They haven't driven the whole distance yet. We know the whole distance, and we're finding a part.*

In this problem, the bar model is already drawn for us. The bar represents the whole distance, so it's labeled 40. The bar is split into 4 unit bars. Each unit bar is one-fourth of the whole distance.

We want to find three-fourths of the distance, so there's a bracket over three-fourths of the bar. The question mark reminds us that this is the quantity we want to find.

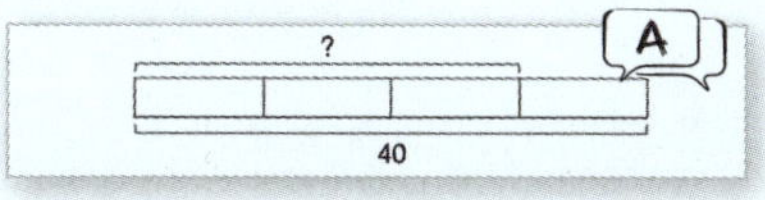

The third step is to use the bar model to solve the problem. We start by finding the value of each unit bar. How many kilometers does each unit bar represent? *10.* **How do you know?** *40 divided by 4 equals 10.* Write "40 ÷ 4 = 10." Write 10 inside each unit bar.

How far has Niall's family already driven? *30 kilometers.* **How do you know?** *3 times 10 equals 30.* Write "3 × 10 = 30." Write "30 km" below the first question. **Three-fourths of 40 equals 30.**

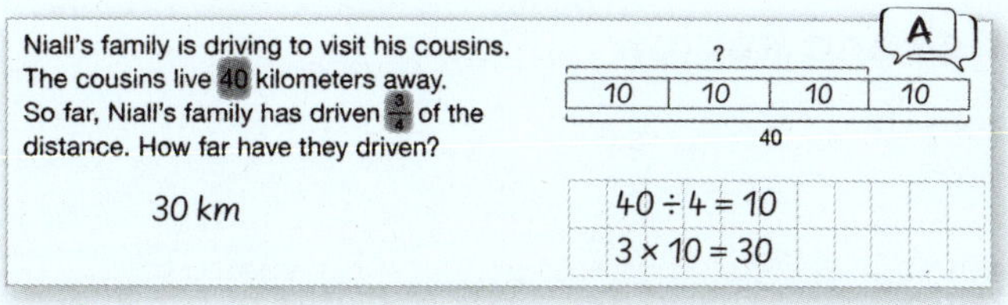

How far does Niall's family have left to drive? *10 kilometers.* **How do you know?** *Possible answers: They have one unit bar left to drive, and each unit bar equals 10 kilometers. 40 minus 30 equals 10.* Write "40 − 30 = 10." Write "10 km" below the second question.

Read aloud the second practice problem. **This problem has two goals. What is the first goal?** *Find how many dollars the store will take off the price.* **What is the second goal?** *Find how much the stuffed snake costs.*

What do we know in this problem? *The regular price of the snake and the fraction of the price that is subtracted.* Highlight $20 and 1/4 in the word problem.

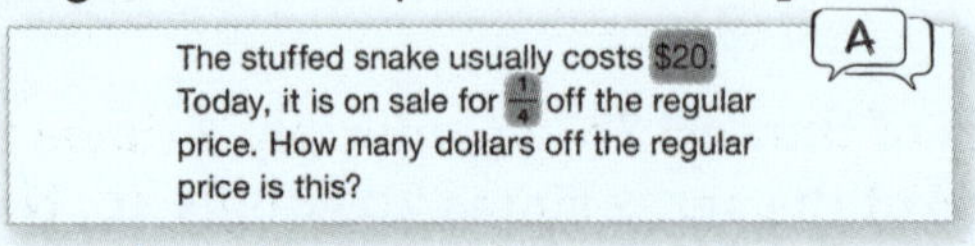

Will the sale price be greater or less than $20? *Less.* **How do you know?** *Sample answer: Sale prices are always less than the regular price! We'll subtract part of the price from the regular price.*

Next, we label the bar model. The whole bar stands for $20. Draw a bracket below the bar and label it 20.

We want to find one-fourth of the whole amount, so split the whole bar into fourths. Have your child draw lines to split the bar into fourths. Draw a bracket above 1 unit bar and label it with a question mark.

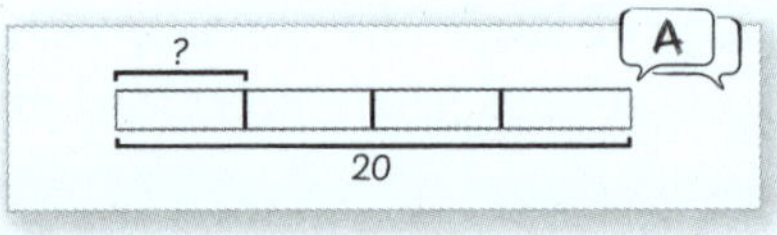

How many dollars does each unit bar represent? *5.* **How do you know?** *20 divided by 4 equals 5.* Write "20 ÷ 4 = 5." Write 5 inside each unit bar. **How many dollars will the store take off the regular price?** *$5.* Write "$5" below the first question.

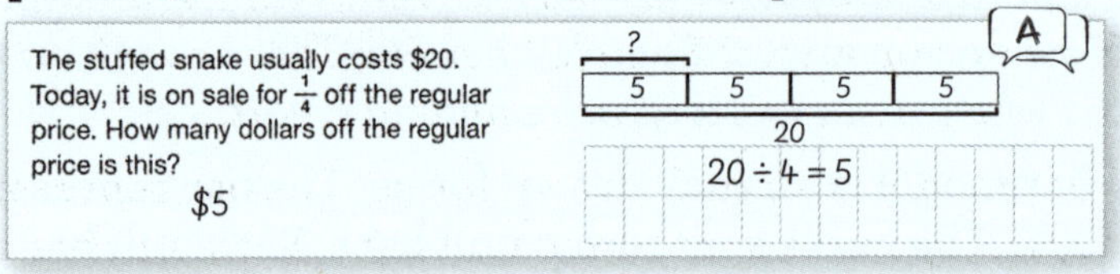

What is the sale price for the snake? *$15.* **How do you know?** *Possible answers: 20 minus 5 equals 15. Each unit bar equals $5, and the snake's price equals 3 unit bars.* Write "20 − 5 = 15" and write "$15" below the second question.

Make sure to label and discuss the bar model even if your child quickly finds the answer mentally. The bar models in this lesson lay the groundwork for more challenging problems, so it's important that your child is familiar with them.

Independent Practice and Review

Have your child complete the Lesson 8.8 Practice and Review workbook pages.

The Practice pages in Lessons 8.8-8.12 are designed to help your child gradually become more independent at drawing and labeling bar models. They start with a fully-labeled bar model and then gradually reduce the level of labeling.

Lesson 8.9
Comparison Word Problems, Part 1

Purpose	Materials
• Mentally find parts of measurement units • Solve comparison word problems where one quantity is a fraction of another quantity and you know the larger quantity	• Highlighter

Memory Work	
	• **What does perimeter measure?** *The distance around the outside edge of a shape.* • **What does area measure?** *The amount of space that a shape covers.* • **What does volume measure?** *The amount of space a solid occupies.*

Warm-up: Mentally Find Part of a Measurement Unit

Ask your child the following questions orally. Encourage her to find the answers mentally, but allow her to write the numbers down as needed.

- **One-fourth of a foot equals how many inches?** *3 inches.*
- **Three-fourths of a foot equals how many inches?** *9 inches.*
- **One-tenth of a meter equals how many centimeters?** *10 centimeters.*
- **Seven-tenths of a meter equals how many centimeters?** *70 centimeters.*
- **One-fifth of a kilogram equals how many grams?** *200 grams.*
- **Three-fifths of a kilogram equals how many grams?** *600 grams.*

Activity (A): Use Bar Models to Solve Comparison Word Problems

In the last lesson, you used bar models to find part of a whole. You drew one bar to stand for the whole amount, and you split it up to find the fractional part.

Today, we'll use bar models to solve comparison word problems. We'll draw two bars for each problem because we'll have two quantities to compare in each problem.

Read the example problem aloud. **What's the goal in the problem?** *Find how many cards Rowan has.* **What do we know in this problem?** *Jonny has 80 trading cards. Rowan has seven-eighths as many cards as Jonny.* Highlight 80 and 7/8 in the problem.

Ex. Jonny and Rowan both collect trading cards.
Jonny has 80 trading cards. Rowan has $\frac{7}{8}$ as many cards as Jonny.
How many trading cards does Rowan have? (A)

Will the answer be greater or less than 80? *Less.* **How do you know?** *Rowan has only a fraction of the cards that Jonny has.*

> Discussing the problem in detail helps your child make sense of the problem (and encourages her to stop and think rather than rush to multiply or divide!) If your child has trouble focusing on this step, cover the bar model and equations with a slip of paper while you discuss the problem. See the Unit 8 **Teaching Math with Confidence** for more tips on teaching your child to solve these problems with bar models.

We know Jonny has 80 trading cards, so his whole bar has a value of 80. Rowan has seven-eighths as many cards as Jonny, so his bar is seven-eighths as long as Jonny's.

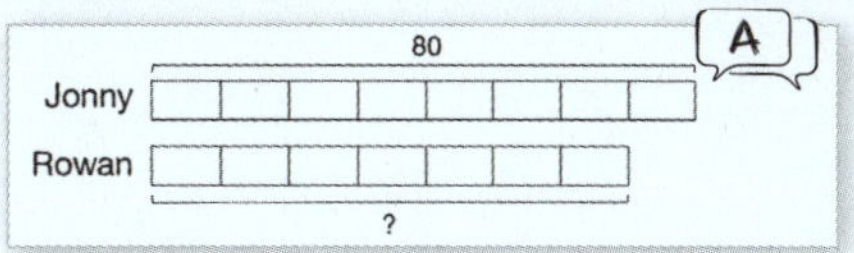

We know that the whole bar represents 80 trading cards. It's split into eight-eighths, so we divide 80 by 8 to find the value of each unit bar. 80 divided by 8 equals 10. Each unit bar stands for 10 cards.

7 unit bars equal seven-eighths of the set. So, we multiply 7 times 10 to find how many cards Rowan has. 7 times 10 equals 70. Rowan has 70 cards.

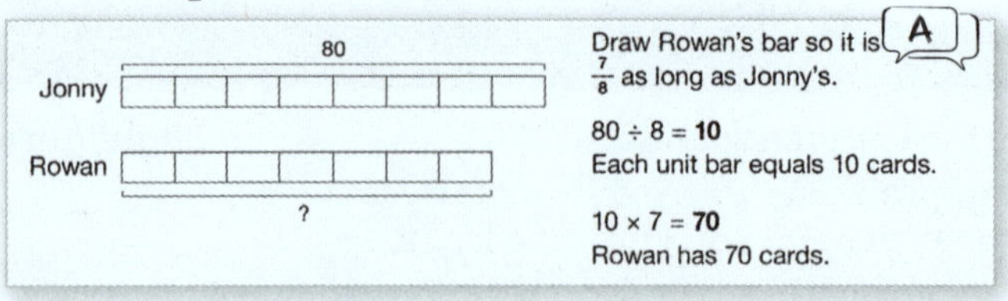

Read aloud the first practice problem. **This problem has two goals. What is the first goal?** *Find how much Oscar earned on Saturday.* **What is the second goal?** *Find how much Oscar earned in all.*

In this problem, we know how much Oscar earned on Friday night. We also know he earned two-thirds as much on Saturday as on Friday. Highlight 60 and 2/3 in the word problem.

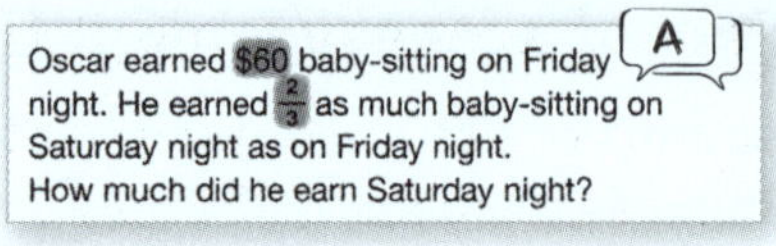

We want to find how much he earned on Saturday. Will the answer be greater or less than $60? *Less.* **How do you know?** *He didn't earn as much on Saturday as Friday.*

The bar model is already printed for us. The bar for Friday has a value of 60. He earned 2/3 as much on Saturday. So, the bar for Friday is split into 3 thirds. The bar for Saturday is made of 2 unit bars. It's two-thirds as long as the bar for Friday.

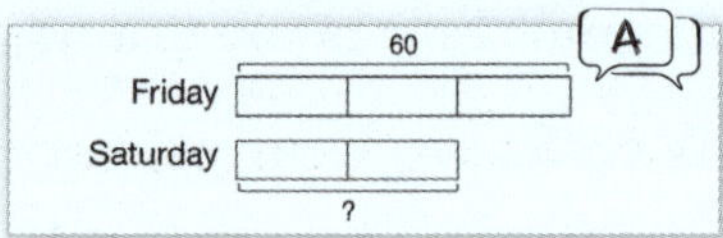

How many dollars does each unit bar represent? *20.* **How do you know?** *60 divided by 3 equals 20.* Write "60 ÷ 3 = 20." Write 20 inside each unit bar.

How much did Oscar earn on Saturday? *$40.* **How do you know?** *2 times 20 equals 40.* Write "2 × 20 = 40." Write "$40" below the first question.

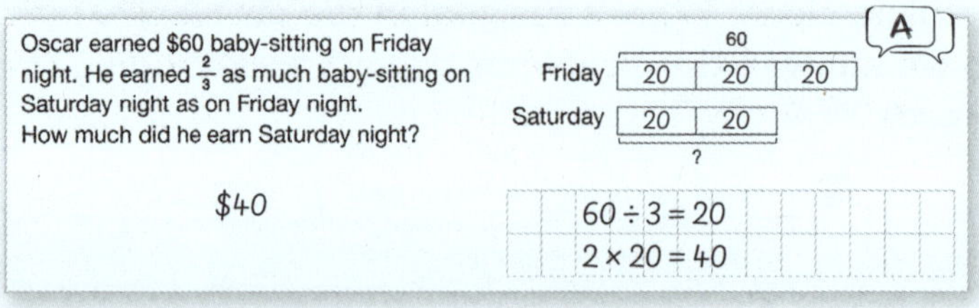

How much did he earn in all? *$100.* **How do you know?** *Sample answer: 60 plus 40 equals 100.* Write "60 + 40 = 100" and write "$100" below the second question.

Read aloud the second practice problem. **This problem has two goals. What is the first goal?** *Find how many laps Liam ran.* **What is the second goal?** *Find how many more laps Abby ran than Liam.*

In this problem, we know how many laps Abby ran. We also know Liam ran four-fifths as many laps as Abby. Highlight 40 and 4/5 in the word problem.

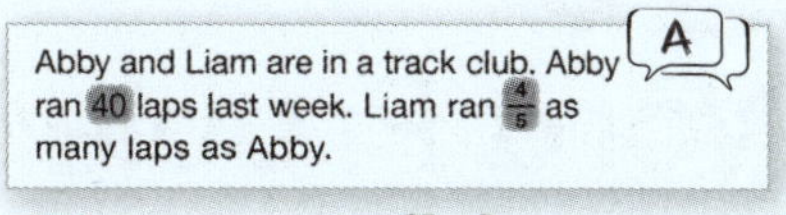

We want to find how many laps Liam ran. Will the answer be greater or less than 40 laps? *Less.* **How do you know?** *Sample answer: Liam ran a fraction of the number of laps that Abby ran.*

Now, we draw the bar model. We'll start by drawing a bar to represent Abby's laps. Draw a bar and label it 40 as shown. **We want to find four-fifths of Abby's number of laps. Her bar represents the whole amount, so I'll split her bar into five-fifths.** Draw lines to split Abby's bar into 5 equal parts.

Liam ran four-fifths as many laps as Abby, so I'll draw 4 unit bars to make his bar. Draw 4 unit bars as shown. Make sure each bar is roughly the same length as the unit bars in Abby's bar, and that the total bar is about 4/5 of Abby's. Label the bar with a bracket and question mark.

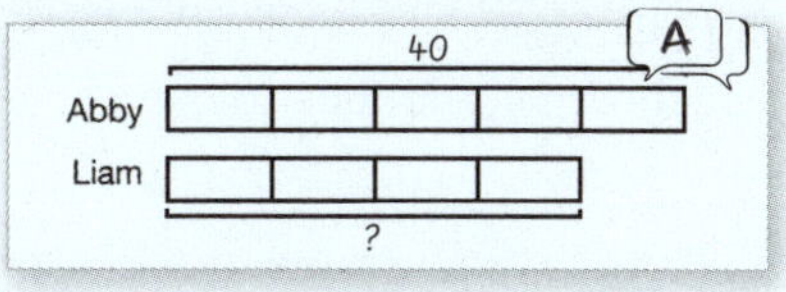

How many laps does each unit bar represent? *8.* **How do you know?** *40 divided by 5 equals 8.* Write "40 ÷ 5 = 8." Write 8 inside each unit bar.

How many laps did Liam run? *32.* **How do you know?** *4 times 8 equals 32.* Write "32 laps" below the first question.

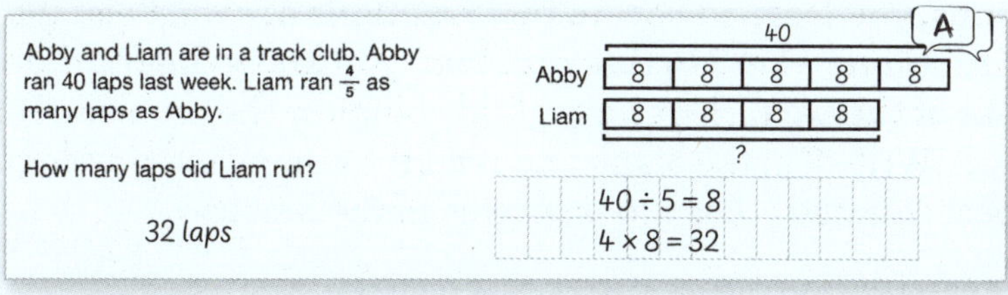

How many more laps did Abby run than Liam? *8.* **How do you know?** *Possible answers: 40 minus 32 equals 8. Each unit bar equals 8 laps, and Abby's bar is one unit bar longer than Liam's.* Write "8 laps" below the second question.

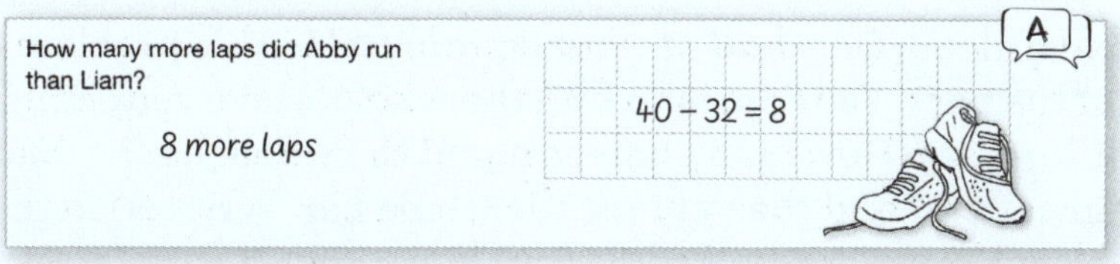

Independent Practice and Review

Have your child complete the Lesson 8.9 Practice and Review workbook pages.

Lesson 8.10
Comparison Word Problems, Part 2

Purpose	Materials
• Use bar diagrams to find parts and wholes • Solve comparison word problems where one quantity is a fraction of another quantity and you know the smaller quantity	• Highlighter

Memory Work	
	• **What's zero times any number?** *Zero.* • **What's zero divided by any other number?** *Zero.* • **What's any number divided by zero?** *Undefined.*

In the last lesson, your child solved comparison word problems where one quantity was a fraction of a larger quantity. In this lesson, your child will solve similar comparison word problems. However, instead of finding the smaller quantity, he'll use the fractional relationship to find the larger quantity. He'll find the "whole" instead of the "part."

This lesson focuses on problems that involve unit fractions (fractions with 1 as their numerator), since they're usually easiest for children to grasp at first. In the next lesson, your child will learn how to solve problems with other fractions, too.

Warm-up (A): Use Bar Diagrams to Find Parts and Wholes

In the last few lessons, you learned how to find fractions of sets. Read the first problem aloud: ***One-half of 16 equals what?*** **In this problem, you know the fraction and whole. Your job is to find the size of the part.** Have your child complete the problem. If he's not sure, suggest he divide 16 by 2. Write 8 in the blank and read the completed problem aloud: **One-half of 16 equals 8.** Repeat with the other two problems in the first row.

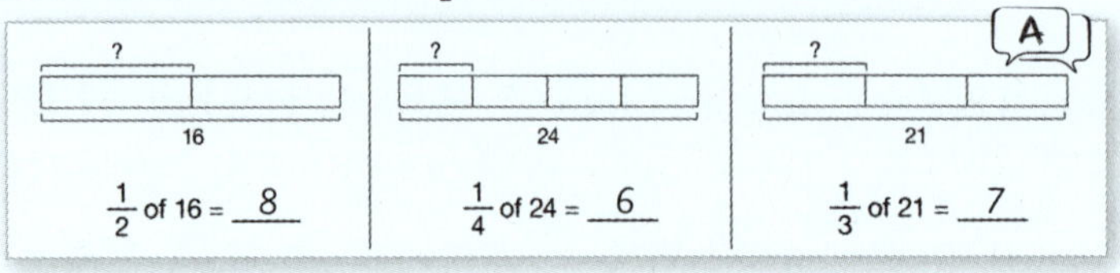

Read the next problem aloud: ***One-half of what equals 10?*** **In this problem, you know the fraction and size of the part. Your job is to find the whole.** Have your child complete the problem. If he's not sure, say: **How many halves equal the whole bar?** *2.* **Each unit bar equals 10, so multiply 2 times 10 to find the value of the whole bar.** Write 20 in the blank and read the completed problem aloud: **One-half of 20 equals 10.** Repeat with the other problems.

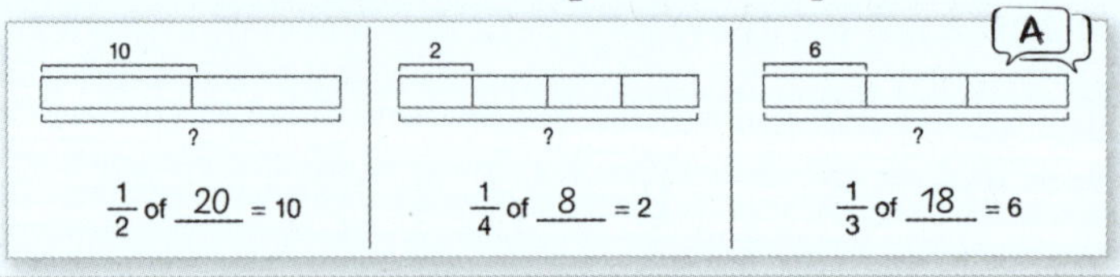

If your child has trouble understanding the structure of this problem, frame it in a more concrete way: **Let's pretend I gave you half of a pack of candy, and you got 10 pieces of candy. How many pieces of candy are in the whole pack?** *20.*

Activity (B): Find the Larger Quantity in Comparison Word Problems

In the last lesson, we used bar models to solve comparison word problems. We knew the value of the larger quantity, and we found the value of the smaller quantity.

Today, we'll use bar models to solve comparison word problems again. In these problems, we'll know the value of the smaller quantity. We'll use it to find the value of the larger quantity. We'll draw two bars for each problem again, because we'll have two quantities to compare in each problem.

Read the example problem aloud. **What is the goal?** *Find how old his grandmother is.*

What do we know in this problem? *Apollos is 10 years old. He's one-sixth as old as his grandma.* Highlight 10 and 1/6 in the problem.

> Ex. Apollos is 10 years old. His age is $\frac{1}{6}$ of his grandma's age. How old is his grandma?

Will the answer be greater or less than 10? *Greater.* **How do you know?** *His age is a fraction of his grandma's. His grandma has to be older than him!*

Apollos is 10. Apollos' age is one-sixth of his grandma's age. Six-sixths equal 1 whole, so we draw 6 unit bars to make his grandma's bar.

Each unit bar stands for 10 years, so we multiply 6 times 10 to find his grandma's age. 6 times 10 is 60, so his grandma is 60.

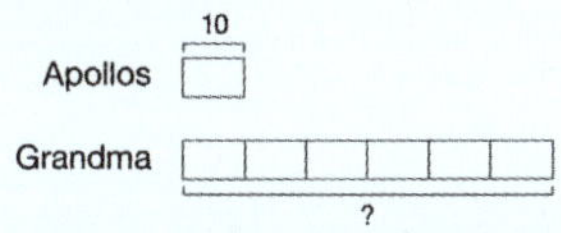

6 sixths equal 1 whole. Draw 6 copies of Apollos' bar to make Grandma's bar.

$6 \times 10 =$ **60 years**

Read aloud the first practice problem. **What's the goal?** *Find how many laps Elena swam.* **What do we know in this problem?** *Charlotte swam 10 laps. She swam one-third as many laps as Elena.* Highlight 10 and 1/3.

> Charlotte swam 10 laps. She swam $\frac{1}{3}$ as many laps as Elena. How many laps did Elena swim?

Will the answer be greater or less than 10? *Greater.* **How do you know?** *Charlotte only swam a fraction of the laps that Elena swam.*

Charlotte swam one-third as many laps as Elena. Three-thirds equal one whole, so we use 3 copies of the unit bar to make Elena's bar.

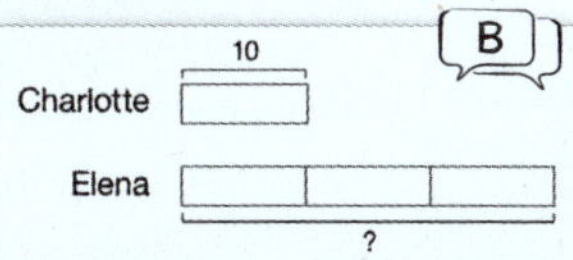

How many laps did Elena swim? *30.* **How do you know?** *3 times 10 equals 30.* Write "3 × 10 = 30 laps."

> $3 \times 10 = 30$ laps

Read aloud the second practice problem. **What's the goal?** *Find how much money he earned on Friday.*

What do we know? *Scander earned \$8 on Thursday. He earned one-fourth as much on Thursday as on Friday.* Highlight \$8 and 1/4.

> Scander rakes leaves to earn money. He earned \$8 on Thursday. He earned $\frac{1}{4}$ as many dollars on Thursday as he earned on Friday. How many dollars did he earn on Friday?

Will the answer be greater or less than 8? *Greater.* **How do you know?** *He earned more on Friday than Thursday.*

First, I'll draw the bar for Thursday. I know this bar will be a lot shorter than the Friday bar, so I'll make it small. Draw 1 unit bar next to Thursday. Label it as shown.

Scander earned one-fourth as much on Thursday as on Friday. How many fourths equal 1 whole? *4.* **So, we draw 4 copies of the unit bar to make the Friday bar.** Draw 4 copies of the unit bar to make the Friday bar. Label it as shown.

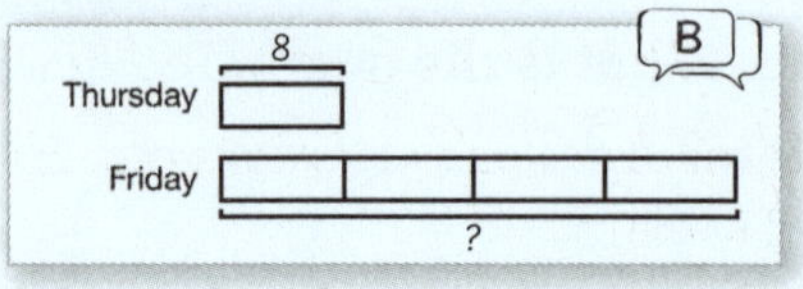

Have your child use the bar model to solve the problem. **How much did Scander earn on Friday?** *32.* **How do you know?** *4 times 8 equals 32.* Write "4 × 8 = \$32."

$$4 \times 8 = \$32$$

Independent Practice and Review

Have your child complete the Lesson 8.10 Practice and Review workbook pages.

Lesson 8.11
Comparison Word Problems, Part 3

Purpose	Materials
• Use bar diagrams to find wholes • Solve comparison word problems where one quantity is a fraction of another quantity and you know the smaller quantity	• Highlighter

Memory Work
- **What is a prime number?** *A number with exactly 2 factors.*
- **What is a composite number?** *A number with more than 2 factors.*

In the last lesson, your child solved comparison word problems where one quantity was a fraction of another quantity. All of the problems involved unit fractions (fractions with 1 as their numerator) to help her grasp this challenging concept.

In this lesson, your child will learn how to solve similar problems with non-unit fractions. Many children find this concept one of the most difficult to learn in fifth grade, so don't worry if your child struggles with these problems at first. Provide as much support and coaching as your child needs, and help her with the problems on the Practice page if needed.

Warm-up (A): Use Bar Diagrams to Find Wholes

Read the first problem aloud: ***One-third of what equals 5?*** Have your child complete the problem. If she's not sure, say: **Each unit bar is one-third of the whole bar. How many thirds equal the whole bar?** *3.* **Each unit bar has a value of 5, so multiply 3 times 5 to find the value of the whole bar.** Write 15 in the blank and read the completed problem aloud: **One-third of 15 equals 5.** Repeat with the other problems.

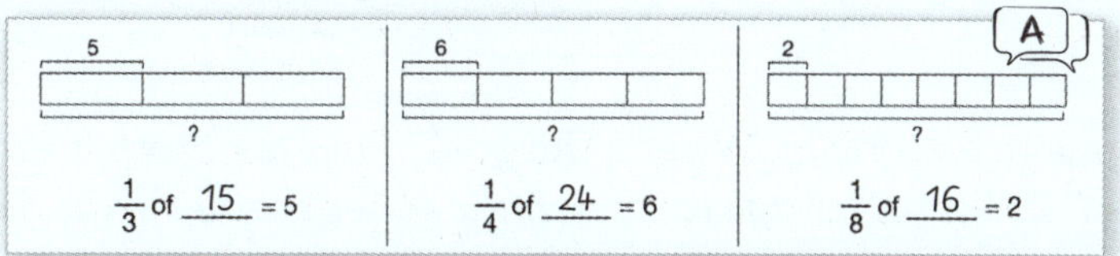

Read the next problem aloud: ***Two-thirds of what is 8?*** **2 unit bars have a value of 8. So, what's the value of 1 unit bar?** *4.* **How do you know?** *8 divided by 2 equals 4.* Write 4 on each of the unit bars.

What's the value of the whole bar? *12.* **How do you know?** *3 times 4 equals 12.* Write 12 in the blank and read the completed problem aloud: **Two-thirds of 12 equals 8.** Repeat with the other problems.

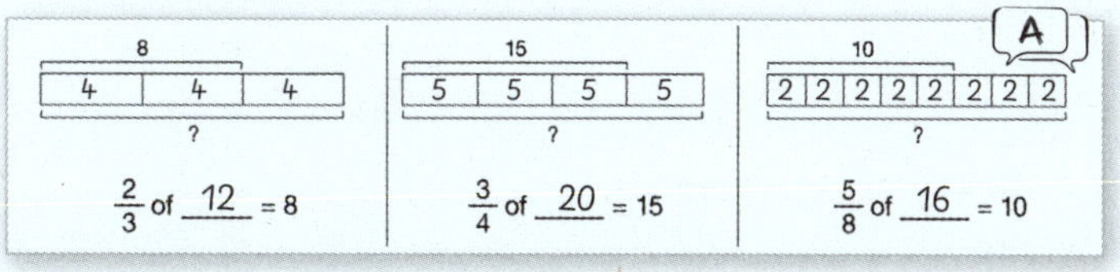

Activity (B): Find the Larger Quantity in Comparison Word Problems

In the last lesson, we used bar models to solve comparison word problems. Point to the first row of problems in part A. **All of the problems were like these. You knew the value of one fractional part, and then you multiplied to find the value of the larger quantity.**

Point to the second row of problems in part A. **Today, you'll learn how to solve word problems like these. In these problems, you know the value of multiple fractional parts. You divide to find the value of one fractional part and then multiply to find the total value of the larger quantity.**

We'll draw two bars for each problem again today, because we'll have two quantities to compare in each problem. We'll use the same three steps as before: understand the problem, draw a bar model, and use the bar model to solve.

Have your child read aloud the example problem. **What's the goal?** *Find how many points Wyatt scored.*

What do we know in this problem? *Austin scored two-thirds as many points as Wyatt. Austin scored 10 points.* Highlight 2/3 and 10 in the problem.

Will the answer be greater or less than 10? *Greater.* **How do you know?** *Austin scored a fraction of the points that Wyatt scored.*

Ex. Austin scored $\frac{2}{3}$ as many points as Wyatt. Austin scored 10 points. How many points did Wyatt score?

Austin scored 10 points. Austin scored two-thirds as many points as Wyatt. Austin's bar is split into 2 parts so that each unit bar stands for 1 third. Three-thirds equal one whole, so we draw 3 copies of the unit bar to make Wyatt's bar.

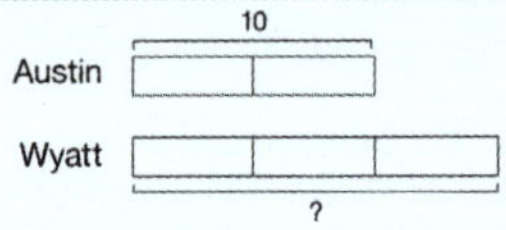

Split Austin's bar into 2 parts so each unit bar stands for 1 third.

3 thirds equal 1 whole, so draw 3 copies of the unit bar to make Wyatt's bar.

2 unit bars stand for 10 points. What's 10 divided by 2? *5.* **Each unit bar stands for 5 points. What's 3 times 5?** *15.* **Wyatt scored 15 points.**

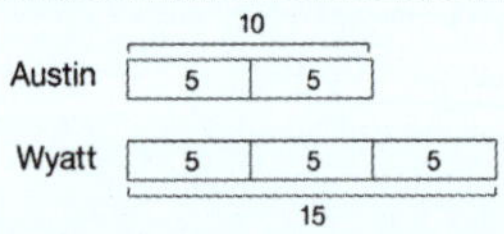

$10 \div 2 = 5$

$3 \times 5 =$ **15 points**

Read aloud the first practice problem. **What's the goal?** *Find her brother's age.* **What do we know in this problem?** *Ilse is 9. Her age is three-fifths of her brother's age.* Highlight 9 and 3/5.

Ilse is 9. Her age is $\frac{3}{5}$ of her brother's age. How old is her brother?

Will the answer be greater or less than 9? *Greater.* **How do you know?** *She's only part of her brother's age.*

Ilse's age is three-fifths of her brother's age. We split Ilse's bar into 3 parts so that each unit bar stands for 1 fifth. Five-fifths equal one whole, so we draw 5 copies of the unit bar to make the brother's bar.

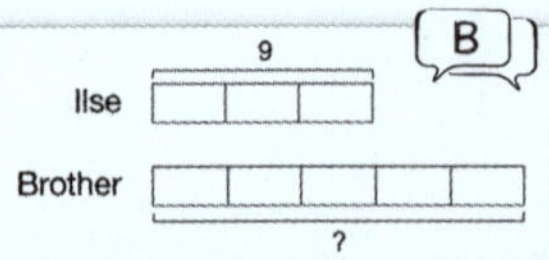

How many years does each unit bar stand for? *3 years.* **How do you know?** *9 divided by 3 equals 3.* Write "9 ÷ 3 = 3." Write 3 on each unit bar.

How old is Ilse's brother? *15.* **How do you know?** *3 times 5 equals 15.* Write "3 × 5 = 15 years old."

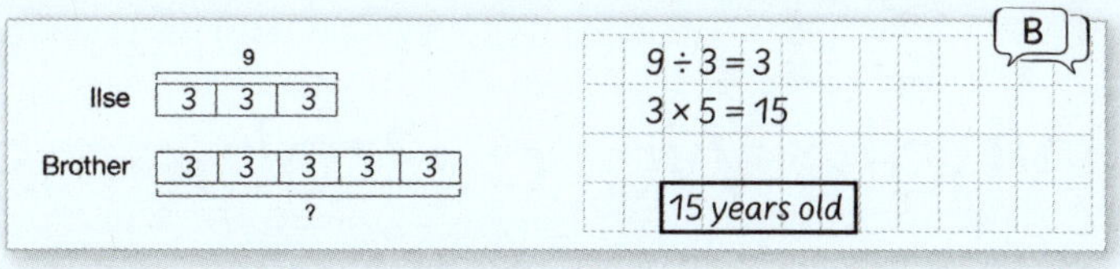

Read aloud the final practice problem. **What's the goal?** *Find how much money his sister has.* **What do we know in this problem?** *Harry has $30. He has five-eighths as much money as his sister.* Highlight $30 and 5/8.

> Harry has $30. He has $\frac{5}{8}$ as much money as his sister. How much money does his sister have?

Who has more money, Harry or his sister? *His sister.* **Will the answer be greater or less than $30?** *Greater.* **How do you know?** *Harry only has a fraction of the money his sister has.*

I'll start by drawing a bar for Harry. He has five-eighths as much money as his sister, so I'll draw 5 unit bars. Draw 5 small unit bars as shown.

How many eighths equal one whole? *8.* **So, we draw 8 copies of the unit bar to make Harry's sister's bar.** Draw 8 copies of the unit bar to make the sister's bar. Label it as shown.

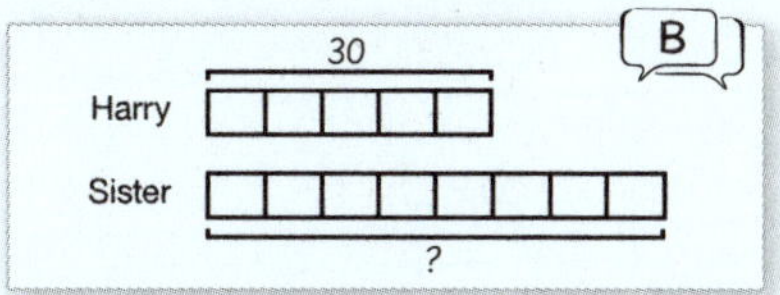

How many dollars does each unit bar stand for? *$6.* **How do you know?** *30 divided by 5 equals 6.* Write "30 ÷ 5 = 6." Write 6 on each unit bar.

How much money does Harry's sister have? *$48.* **How do you know?** *8 times 6 equals 48.* Write "8 × 6 = $48."

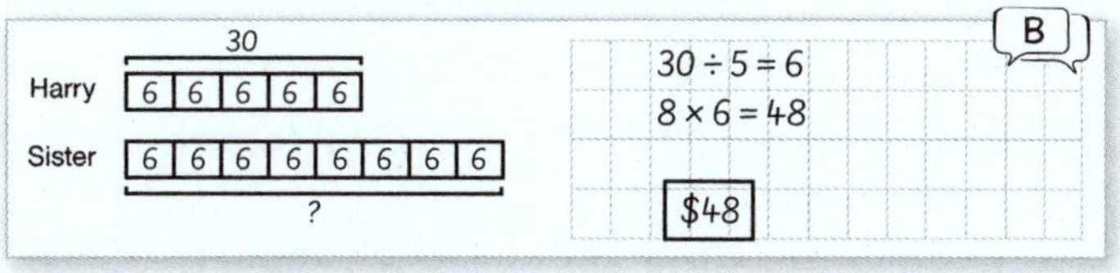

Independent Practice and Review

Have your child complete the Lesson 8.11 Practice and Review workbook pages.

Lesson 8.12
Find-the-Whole Word Problems

Purpose	Materials
• Mentally find the number of objects in a whole set, given a fractional part • Use bar models to solve word problems that involve finding the number of objects in a whole set, given a fractional part	• Highlighter

Memory Work

- **What are the four basic operations?** *Addition, subtraction, multiplication, and division.*
- **What is an equation?** *A number sentence with an equals sign.*
- **What is an expression?** *Part of a number sentence without an equals sign.*

In Lessons 8.10 and 8.11, your child solved comparison word problems where one quantity was a fraction of another quantity. He knew the smaller quantity and used the fractional relationship to find the larger quantity.

In this lesson, your child will use bar models to solve similar problems. Instead of comparing two quantities, your child will use the size of a fractional part of a set to find the size of the whole set. These problems can be very difficult for children to grasp at first, so give your child lots of support and coaching and help him with the Practice page as needed.

Warm-up: Mentally Find the Size of the Whole Set

Ask your child the following questions orally. If he has trouble, draw a simple bar model for each problem (as in part A of Lesson 8.11). Encourage him to find the answers in his head, but allow him to write down the bar models and equations as needed.

- **One-half of what number equals 3?** *6.*
- **One-half of what number equals 10?** *20.*
- **One-third of what number equals 5?** *15.*
- **One-third of what number equals 7?** *21.*
- **One-fourth of what number equals 2?** *8.*
- **One-fourth of what number equals 8?** *32.*

These problems only involve unit fractions (with a numerator of 1) to make them easier to visualize.

Activity (A): Use Bar Models to Solve Find-the-Whole Word Problems

In the last two lessons, you solved comparison word problems. You used the value of the smaller quantity to find the value of the larger quantity. We compared two quantities, so we drew two bars for each problem.

Today, we'll use bar models to solve word problems where you know the size of part of a set, and you want to find the size of the whole set. We call these "find-the-whole" problems. For these problems, we'll draw just one bar to represent the whole set. Then, we'll split the bar into fractional parts and use the size of the part to figure out the size of the whole.

Have your child read the example problem aloud. **What's the goal?** *Find the number of coins in the whole collection.* **What do we know in this problem?** *60 coins are from the U.S. They're 3/4 of the set.* Highlight 3/4 and 60 in the problem.

A

Ex. Jacob collects coins. $\frac{3}{4}$ of his coins are from the United States, and the rest are from other countries. Jacob has 60 coins from the United States. How many coins are in his whole collection?

Will the answer be greater or less than 60? *Greater.* **How do you know?** *The 60 U.S. coins are only part of the collection.*

The bar represents the whole collection. The bar is split into 4 parts so that each unit bar stands for one-fourth of the collection. Three-fourths of Jacob's coins are from the United States, so three-fourths of the bar has a value of 60. We want to find the size of the whole collection.

We know that the 3 unit bars represent 60 coins. So, we divide 60 by 3 to find the value of each unit bar. What's 60 divided by 3? *20.* **Each unit bar stands for 20 coins.**

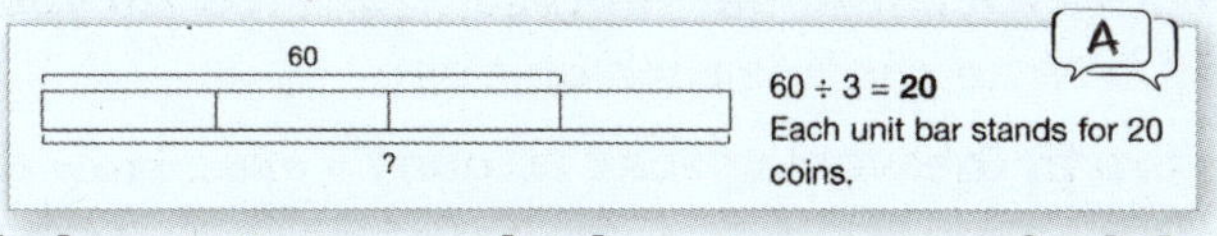

4 unit bars equal the whole set. So, we multiply 4 times 20 to find the size of the whole collection. What's 4 times 20? *80.* **Jacob has 80 coins in his collection.**

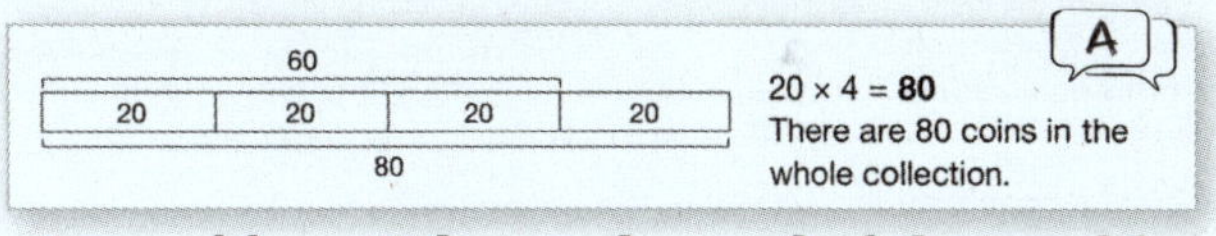

Read aloud the first practice problem. **What is the goal of this problem?** *Find the total number of people who answered the survey.* **What do we know in this problem?** *24 people chose strawberry. They're 3/8 of the set.* Highlight 24 and 3/8 in the word problem.

In a survey, 24 people said they like strawberry ice cream best.
These 24 people were $\frac{3}{8}$ of all the people who answered the survey.
How many people answered the survey?

Will the answer be greater or less than 24? *Greater.* **How do you know?** *The 24 people are only part of the set.*

This bar stands for all the people who answered the survey. The bar is split into 8 equal parts so that each unit bar stands for one-eighth of the people.

We know that three-eighths of the people chose strawberry, so three-eighths of the bar has a value of 24. We want to find the total number of people who answered the survey.

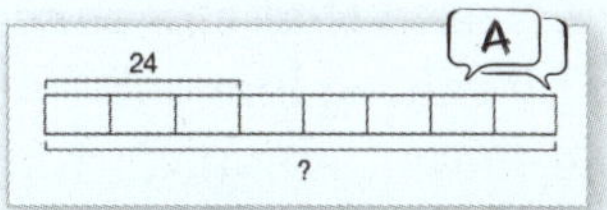

How many people does each unit bar represent? *8.* **How do you know?** *24 divided by 3 equals 8.* Write "24 ÷ 3 = 8." Write 8 in each unit bar.

How many people answered the survey in all? *64 people.* **How do you know?** *8 times 8 equals 64.* Write "8 × 8 = 64."

Read aloud the second practice problem. **What is the goal?** *Find how many googly eyes were in the whole pack.* **What do we know?** *He used 16 googly eyes. They're four-fifths of the pack.* Highlight 16 and 4/5 in the word problem.

Will the answer be greater or less than 16? *Greater.* **How do you know?** *He only used part of the pack.*

Sam had a pack of googly eyes.
He used $\frac{4}{5}$ of the pack to make puppets.
He used 16 googly eyes.
How many googly eyes were in the pack to start?

The bar stands for the whole pack of googly eyes. We know the part is four-fifths of the pack, so I'll split the bar into fifths. Split the bar into 5 equal parts.

We know that four-fifths of the pack equals 16 googly eyes. Draw a bracket above 4 of the unit bars and label it 16. **We want to find the total number of googly eyes in the pack.** Draw a bracket below the bar and label it with a question mark.

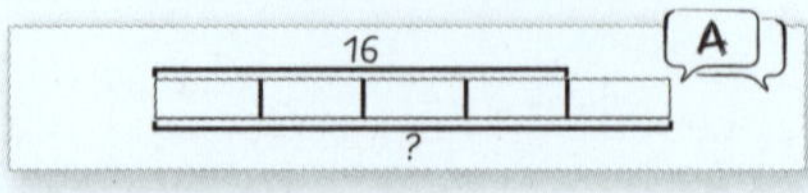

How many googly eyes does each unit bar represent? *4.* **How do you know?** *16 divided by 4 equals 4.* Write "16 ÷ 4 = 4." Write 4 inside each unit bar.

How many googly eyes are in the whole pack? *20 googly eyes.* **How do you know?** *5 times 4 equals 20.* Write "5 × 4 = 20."

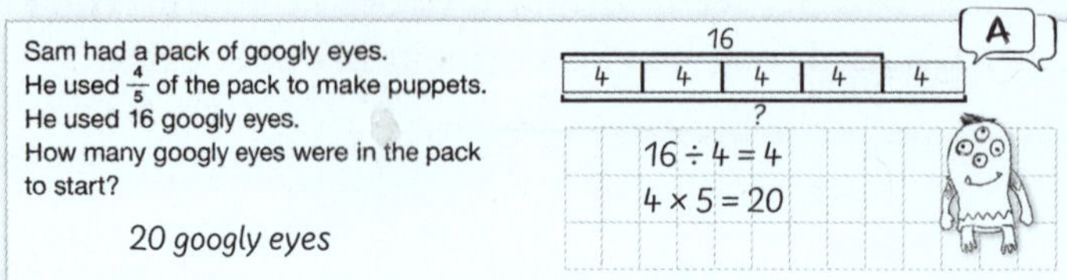

Read aloud the third practice problem. **What is the goal of this problem?** *Find how much money Emery has.* **What do we know?** *She earned two-thirds of the money by mowing lawns. She earned $50 raking leaves.* Highlight 50 and 2/3 in the word problem.

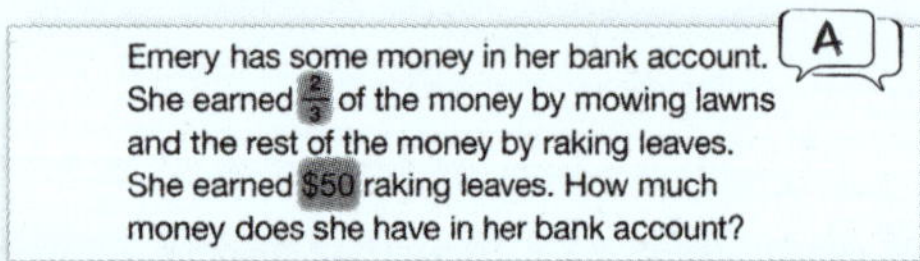

Will the answer be greater or less than $50? *Greater.* **How do you know?** *She only earned part of the money raking leaves.*

The bar stands for all the money in Emery's bank account. We know she earned two-thirds of the money mowing lawns, so I'll split the bar into thirds. Split the bar into 3 equal parts.

This problem is a little different than the other ones! We know that Emery earned two-thirds of the money by mowing lawns, and that she earned $50 raking leaves. So, what fraction of her money did she earn by raking leaves? *One-third.* **How do you know?** *Sample answer: Three-thirds equal one whole, and three-thirds minus two-thirds equals one-third.* Draw a bracket above 1/3 of the bar and label it 50. Draw a bracket below the bar and label it with a question mark.

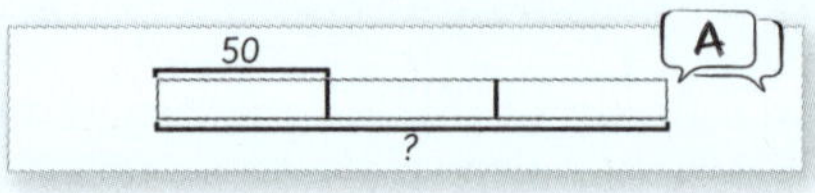

How many dollars does each unit bar represent? *50.* Write 50 inside each unit bar. **How much money does Emery have in her bank account?** *$150.* **How do you know?** *3 times 50 equals 150.* Write "3 × 50 = 150."

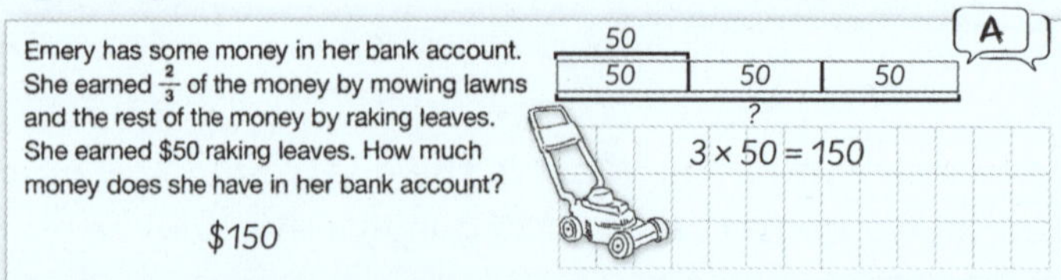

Independent Practice and Review

Have your child complete the Lesson 8.12 Practice and Review workbook pages.

Lesson 8.13
Enrichment (Optional)

Purpose	Materials
• Practice memory work • Appreciate how math can be used to answer real-life questions • Write fractions and word problems to describe a collection • Summarize what your child has learned and assess your child's progress	• *How Many Guinea Pigs Can Fit on a Plane?: Answers to Your Most Clever Math Questions*, by Laura Overdeck • Collection of 20-30 objects

Warm-up: Review Memory Work

Quiz your child on any of the memory work items that she struggled with during this unit.

Math Picture Book: *How Many Guinea Pigs Can Fit on a Plane?*

Read pages 70-81 in *How Many Guinea Pigs Can Fit on a Plane?*

Enrichment Activity: Write Fractions and Word Problems for a Collection

In this unit, you've used fractions to describe many different types of sets. Today, you'll write fractions and word problems for a collection or set that you choose.

Have your child choose a collection of 20-30 objects from your home. The objects should be related to each other in some way, but not identical. She can choose to use a personal favorite collection (such as race cars, stuffed animals, or rocks) or a set of household objects (such as silverware, Christmas ornaments, or books).

> This activity works best if the number of objects is not prime and has several different factors, like 20, 24, 28, or 30.

Have your child categorize the collection in several different ways. Then, have her use the number of items in each category and the number of objects in the total set to describe each category with a fraction. For example: *Only one-fourth of my rocks are metamorphic. Three-sevenths of my rocks are igneous rocks. That's a little less than half.*

Also have her write several word problems about her set. Challenge her to try to create a find-the-part, comparison, and find-the-whole word problem. For example:

- Find-the-part: *One-fourth of my rocks are metamorphic. There are 28 rocks in the whole collection. How many are metamorphic?*
- Comparison: *I have three-fourths as many sedimentary rocks as igneous rocks. I have 9 sedimentary rocks. How many igneous rocks do I have?*
- Find-the-whole: *Three-sevenths of my rocks are igneous rocks. I have 12 igneous rocks. How many rocks are in the whole collection?*

Unit Wrap-Up

Have your child complete the Unit 8 Wrap-Up.

The Unit Wrap-Up includes a mix of different types of word problems (find-the-part, find-the-whole, and comparison). If your child struggles with the mix of problems, use the following tips to help her solve them.

- Use the same questions you used throughout the unit to make sure she understands the word problem: **What's the goal? What do you know? Will the answer be greater or less than the number you already know?**
- Help your child identify whether the problem is a comparison problem or not. If two quantities are being compared, she should draw 2 bars. If she's finding a part or whole of just one quantity, she should draw just 1 bar.
- If it's not a comparison problem, help your child identify whether she's looking for the part or whole. For example, for the first word problem on the second page: **You're trying to find how many people chose pepperoni. Is that the whole set or part of the set?** *Part.* **So, this is a find-the-part problem.**

Unit 8 Answer Key

8.1 Practice

Practice Use the pictures to answer the questions.

What fraction of the blocks are squares? $\frac{9}{13}$

What fraction of the blocks are triangles? $\frac{4}{13}$

What fraction of the blocks are solid-colored? $\frac{8}{13}$

What fraction of the blocks are striped squares? $\frac{3}{13}$

What fraction of the blocks are striped? $\frac{5}{13}$

What fraction of the blocks are striped triangles? $\frac{2}{13}$

Use the chart to answer the questions.

Favorite Season Survey Results

Season	Number of People
Fall	5
Winter	3
Spring	7
Summer	8
Total	23

What fraction of the people said fall is their favorite season? $\frac{5}{23}$

What fraction of the people said winter is their favorite season? $\frac{3}{23}$

What fraction of the people said spring is their favorite season? $\frac{7}{23}$

What fraction of the people said summer is their favorite season? $\frac{8}{23}$

8.1 Review

Review Complete the equivalent fractions.

$\frac{4}{4}$ = 1 whole

$\frac{12}{6}$ = 2 wholes

$\frac{15}{5}$ = 3 wholes

Complete the chart.

Centimeters	1	7	10	11	45	86
Millimeters	10	70	100	110	450	860

Use long division to solve. Use the multiplication table to help.

$$4{,}248 \div 35 = 121 \text{ R } 13$$

35)4,248 → 121
− 35
74
− 70
48
− 35
13

	× 35
1	35
2	70
3	105
4	140
5	175
6	210
7	245
8	280
9	315

Round to the underlined digit.

3,467,829 ≈ 3,467,800

3,467,829 ≈ 3,500,000

3,467,829 ≈ 3,000,000

2.746 ≈ 2.75

2.746 ≈ 2.7

2.746 ≈ 3

Solve. Write the equations you use.

Aubrey bakes 72 cupcakes. She divides the cupcakes equally into 8 boxes. Then, she brings 3 boxes to a party. How many cupcakes does she bring to the party?

72 ÷ 8 = 9
9 × 3 = 27
27 cupcakes

Ivan makes 42 cookies. He divides the cookies equally into 7 bags. Then, he gives 2 of the bags to his friend. How many cookies does he give his friend?

42 ÷ 7 = 6
6 × 2 = 12
12 cookies

8.2 Practice

Practice Complete the missing number in each pair of equivalent fractions.

$\frac{6}{12} = \frac{1}{2}$ $\frac{3}{12} = \frac{1}{4}$ $\frac{2}{12} = \frac{1}{6}$

$\frac{8}{12} = \frac{2}{3}$ $\frac{9}{12} = \frac{3}{4}$ $\frac{10}{12} = \frac{5}{6}$

$\frac{2}{16} = \frac{1}{8}$ $\frac{4}{16} = \frac{1}{4}$ $\frac{6}{16} = \frac{3}{8}$

$\frac{10}{16} = \frac{5}{8}$ $\frac{12}{16} = \frac{3}{4}$ $\frac{14}{16} = \frac{7}{8}$

$\frac{10}{100} = \frac{1}{10}$ $\frac{25}{100} = \frac{1}{4}$ $\frac{50}{100} = \frac{1}{2}$

$\frac{20}{100} = \frac{1}{5}$ $\frac{80}{100} = \frac{4}{5}$ $\frac{70}{100} = \frac{7}{10}$

8.2 Review

Review Find the factor pairs for each number. Then, use the lists to find the greatest common factors.

Factor Pairs of 30	Factor Pairs of 32	Factor Pairs of 36
1 × 30	1 × 32	1 × 36, 6 × 6
2 × 15	2 × 16	2 × 18
3 × 10	4 × 8	3 × 12
5 × 6		4 × 9

GCF of 30 and 32: 2 GCF of 32 and 36: 4 GCF of 30 and 36: 6

Find the base area of each rectangular prism. Make sure to include the correct units.

4 ft. — Volume: 16 cu. ft. Base area: 4 sq. ft.

2 ft. — Volume: 16 cu. ft. Base area: 8 sq. ft.

Complete.

  381
× 45
 1905
+15240
17,145

Circle the prime numbers. (There is one in each row.)

9, **11**, 14, 16

21, 24, 27, **29**

35, 36, **37**, 38

40, 42, **43**, 45

Complete the circles with <, >, or =.

0.47 < 0.74

0.328 < 0.329

0.019 < 0.2

0.51 > 0.501

3.62 < 4.8

Unit 8 Answer Key

8.3 Practice

Practice Write each fraction in simplest form. If the fraction is already in simplest form, circle the fraction.

$\frac{4}{8} = \frac{1}{2}$	($\frac{5}{8}$) circled	$\frac{6}{8} = \frac{3}{4}$
$\frac{5}{10} = \frac{1}{2}$	$\frac{6}{10} = \frac{3}{5}$	($\frac{7}{10}$) circled
$\frac{10}{16} = \frac{5}{8}$	$\frac{12}{16} = \frac{3}{4}$	$\frac{14}{16} = \frac{7}{8}$
($\frac{8}{15}$) circled	$\frac{9}{15} = \frac{3}{5}$	$\frac{10}{15} = \frac{2}{3}$
$\frac{10}{100} = \frac{1}{10}$	$\frac{50}{100} = \frac{1}{2}$	$\frac{80}{100} = \frac{4}{5}$

Use the chart to answer the questions. Write your answers in simplest form.

What fraction of the people chose peanut butter and jelly?
$\frac{6}{24} = \frac{1}{4}$

What fraction of the people chose bacon, lettuce, and tomato?
$\frac{3}{24} = \frac{1}{8}$

What fraction of the people chose grilled cheese?
$\frac{8}{24} = \frac{1}{3}$

What fraction of the people chose other?
$\frac{7}{24}$

Favorite Type of Sandwich
Survey Results

Sandwich	Number of People
Peanut Butter and Jelly	6
Bacon, Lettuce, and Tomato	3
Grilled Cheese	8
Other	7
Total	24

8.3 Review

Review Find the perimeter of each shape.

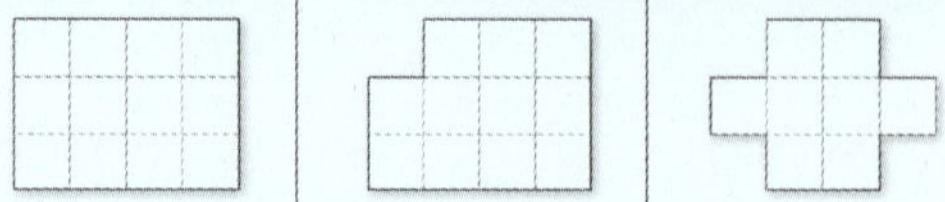

Perimeter: 14 cm | Perimeter: 14 cm | Perimeter: 14 cm

Complete.

90 ÷ 9 = 10	100 ÷ 5 = 20	100 ÷ 50 = 2
99 ÷ 9 = 11	110 ÷ 5 = 22	200 ÷ 50 = 4
108 ÷ 9 = 12	120 ÷ 5 = 24	300 ÷ 50 = 6
117 ÷ 9 = 13	130 ÷ 5 = 26	400 ÷ 50 = 8
126 ÷ 9 = 14	140 ÷ 5 = 28	500 ÷ 50 = 10
135 ÷ 9 = 15	150 ÷ 5 = 30	600 ÷ 50 = 12

Solve. Write the equations you use.

Ayesha's grandma has $4\frac{3}{10}$ lb. of apples. She uses $2\frac{1}{2}$ lb. to make applesauce. She uses the rest of the apples to make a pie. How many pounds of apples does she use for the pie?

$4\frac{3}{10} = 3\frac{13}{10}$

$-\ 2\frac{1}{2} = 2\frac{5}{10}$

$1\frac{8}{10} = \boxed{1\frac{4}{5}\text{ lb.}}$

The granola recipe calls for $\frac{2}{3}$ c. of walnuts and $1\frac{1}{2}$ c. of almonds. How many cups of nuts are there in all in the recipe?

$\frac{2}{3} = \frac{4}{6}$

$+\ 1\frac{1}{2} = 1\frac{3}{6}$

$1\frac{7}{6} = \boxed{2\frac{1}{6}\text{ c.}}$

8.4 Practice

Practice Find the greatest common factor (GCF) for each pair of numbers.

GCF of 7 and 21: 7 7: 1, 7 21: 1, 3, 7, 21	GCF of 20 and 32: 4 20: 1, 2, 4, 5, 10, 20 32: 1, 2, 4, 8, 16, 32	GCF of 4 and 24: 4 4: 1, 2, 4 24: 1, 2, 3, 4, 6, 8, 12, 24
GCF of 15 and 30: 15 15: 1, 3, 5, 15, 30 30: 1, 2, 3, 5, 6, 10, 15	GCF of 13 and 20: 1 13: 1, 13 20: 1, 2, 4, 5, 10, 20	GCF of 10 and 16: 2 10: 1, 2, 5, 10 16: 1, 2, 4, 8, 16

Use the GCFs you found above to write each fraction in simplest form. If the fraction is already in simplest form, circle the fraction.

$\frac{7}{21} = \frac{1}{3}$	$\frac{20}{32} = \frac{5}{8}$	$\frac{4}{24} = \frac{1}{6}$
$\frac{15}{30} = \frac{1}{2}$	($\frac{13}{20}$) circled	$\frac{10}{16} = \frac{5}{8}$

Write the simplest form for each fraction or mixed number in the matching blank.

Grandma's Famous Sugar Cookies (Original)
- $2\frac{6}{10}$ cups of flour
- $\frac{8}{12}$ cups of sugar
- $\frac{15}{30}$ teaspoons of baking powder
- $\frac{10}{40}$ teaspoons of salt
- $\frac{14}{16}$ cups of butter
- 1 egg
- $2\frac{7}{28}$ teaspoons of vanilla

Grandma's Famous Sugar Cookies (Simplified)
- $2\frac{3}{5}$ cups of flour
- $\frac{2}{3}$ cups of sugar
- $\frac{1}{2}$ teaspoons of baking powder
- $\frac{1}{4}$ teaspoons of salt
- $\frac{7}{8}$ cups of butter
- 1 egg
- $2\frac{1}{4}$ teaspoons of vanilla

8.4 Review

Review Find the products.

43 × 90 = 3,870 | 28 × 50 = 1,400 | 415 × 700 = 290,500 | 3,047 × 6,000 = 18,282,000

Convert the improper fractions to mixed numbers. Simplify the fraction if possible.

$\frac{9}{6} = 1\frac{3}{6} = 1\frac{1}{2}$	$\frac{10}{4} = 2\frac{2}{4} = 2\frac{1}{2}$	$\frac{12}{5} = 2\frac{2}{5}$
$\frac{20}{3} = 6\frac{2}{3}$	$\frac{25}{10} = 2\frac{5}{10} = 2\frac{1}{2}$	$\frac{15}{12} = 1\frac{3}{12} = 1\frac{1}{4}$

Complete the chart. Then, use the chart to answer the questions.

Feet	1	5	3	7	10	9	4	6
Inches	12	60	36	84	120	108	48	72

Des has 7 feet of yarn. He uses 40 inches to make a craft. How many inches of yarn does he have left?

7 ft. = 84 in.

84 − 40 = $\boxed{44\text{ in.}}$

Ellie has 10 feet of yarn. She splits the yarn into 4 equal pieces. How many inches long is each piece?

10 ft. = 120 in.

120 ÷ 4 = $\boxed{30\text{ in.}}$

Unit 8 Answer Key

8.5 Practice

Practice Write each measurement as a fraction or mixed number. Write your answers in simplest form.

20 min. = $\frac{20}{60} = \frac{1}{3}$ hr.

35 min. = $\frac{35}{60} = \frac{7}{12}$ hr.

75 min. = $\frac{75}{60} = 1\frac{15}{60} = 1\frac{1}{4}$ hr.

200 mL = $\frac{200}{1{,}000} = \frac{1}{5}$ L

400 mL = $\frac{400}{1{,}000} = \frac{2}{5}$ L

1,600 mL = $\frac{1{,}600}{1{,}000} = 1\frac{600}{1{,}000} = 1\frac{3}{5}$ L

1 fl. oz. = $\frac{1}{8}$ c.

4 fl. oz. = $\frac{4}{8} = \frac{1}{2}$ c.

14 fl. oz. = $\frac{14}{8} = 1\frac{6}{8} = 1\frac{3}{4}$ c.

Answer the questions. Write your answers in simplest form.

Harper swam 750 meters. What fraction of a kilometer did she swim?

$\frac{750}{1{,}000} = \boxed{\frac{3}{4}\text{ km}}$

Lucas used 600 grams of flour to make scones. What fraction of a kilogram did he use?

$\frac{600}{1{,}000} = \boxed{\frac{3}{5}\text{ km}}$

Mia ran 2,250 meters. How many kilometers did she run? Write your answer as a mixed number.

$\frac{2{,}250}{1{,}000} = 2\frac{250}{1{,}000} = \boxed{2\frac{1}{4}\text{ km}}$

Theodore watched a movie that was 130 minutes long. How many hours long was the movie? Write your answer as a mixed number.

$\frac{130}{60} = 2\frac{10}{60} = \boxed{2\frac{1}{6}\text{ hr.}}$

8.5 Review

Review Find all factors of each number. Then, answer the questions.

Factors of 75: 1, 3, 5, 15, 25, 75

1 × 75
3 × 25
5 × 15

Factors of 50: 1, 2, 5, 10, 25, 50

1 × 50
2 × 25
5 × 10

What factors do 75 and 50 have in common? 1, 5, 25

What is the greatest common factor of 75 and 50? 25

Evaluate. Make sure you use the order of operations.

3 + (10 × 6) – 5
3 + 60 – 5
63 – 5
58

6 + 9 – 3 × 2
6 + 9 – 6
15 – 6
9

36 ÷ 4 × 3
9 × 3
27

Complete the chart.

Yards	1	20	19	21	24	25	30	32
Feet	3	60	57	63	72	75	90	96

Use long division to solve.

```
     2 9
30 ) 8 8 9
   - 6 0↓
     2 8 9
   - 2 7 0
       1 9
```

	× 30
1	30
2	60
3	90
4	120
5	150
6	180
7	210
8	240
9	270

Write as a fraction.

0.98 = $\frac{98}{100}$

0.375 = $\frac{375}{1{,}000}$

0.089 = $\frac{89}{1{,}000}$

0.4 = $\frac{4}{10}$

8.6 Practice

Practice Complete.

$\frac{1}{5}$ of 10 = 2
$\frac{2}{5}$ of 10 = 4
$\frac{3}{5}$ of 10 = 6
$\frac{4}{5}$ of 10 = 8
$\frac{5}{5}$ of 10 = 10

$\frac{1}{4}$ of 12 = 3
$\frac{2}{4}$ of 12 = 6
$\frac{3}{4}$ of 12 = 9
$\frac{4}{4}$ of 12 = 12

$\frac{1}{3}$ of 21 = 7
$\frac{2}{3}$ of 21 = 14
$\frac{3}{3}$ of 21 = 21

$\frac{1}{8}$ of 16 = 2
$\frac{5}{8}$ of 16 = 10

$\frac{1}{9}$ of 9 = 1
$\frac{4}{9}$ of 9 = 4

$\frac{1}{6}$ of 12 = 2
$\frac{3}{6}$ of 12 = 6

$\frac{1}{4}$ of 16 = 4
$\frac{3}{4}$ of 16 = 12
$\frac{0}{4}$ of 16 = 0
$\frac{4}{4}$ of 16 = 16

$\frac{1}{5}$ of 15 = 3
$\frac{3}{5}$ of 15 = 9
$\frac{0}{5}$ of 15 = 0
$\frac{5}{5}$ of 15 = 15

$\frac{1}{11}$ of 11 = 1
$\frac{8}{11}$ of 11 = 8
$\frac{0}{11}$ of 11 = 0
$\frac{11}{11}$ of 11 = 11

8.6 Review

Review Write each fraction or mixed number in simplest form. If the fraction or mixed number is already in simplest form, circle it.

$\frac{7}{28} = \frac{1}{4}$

$\frac{16}{32} = \frac{1}{2}$

$\frac{11}{24}$ (circled)

$2\frac{17}{30}$ (circled)

$3\frac{15}{20} = 3\frac{3}{4}$

$1\frac{44}{55} = 1\frac{4}{5}$

Complete the chart.

Hours	1	3	5	8	10	20
Minutes	60	180	300	480	600	1,200

Solve. Write your answers in simplest form.

$\frac{3}{6} - \frac{1}{6} = \frac{2}{6} = \frac{1}{3}$

$\frac{4}{9} + \frac{2}{9} = \frac{6}{9} = \frac{2}{3}$

$\frac{1}{10} + \frac{3}{10} = \frac{4}{10} = \frac{2}{5}$

$\frac{7}{8} - \frac{3}{8} = \frac{4}{8} = \frac{1}{2}$

$\frac{11}{12} - \frac{2}{12} = \frac{9}{12} = \frac{3}{4}$

$\frac{7}{12} - \frac{3}{12} = \frac{4}{12} = \frac{1}{3}$

Solve. Write the equations you use.

Bodie has 35 meters of rope. He cuts the rope into 5 equal pieces. Then, he uses 2 pieces to make a rope ladder. How many meters of rope does he use for the rope ladder?

35 ÷ 5 = 7
7 × 2 = **14 m**

Eliana has 100 fossils in her collection. She splits the fossils into 5 equal groups. Then, she puts 3 of the groups on a shelf. How many fossils are on the shelf?

100 ÷ 5 = 20
20 × 3 = **60 fossils**

Unit 8 Answer Key

8.7 Practice

Practice Complete.

$\frac{1}{2}$ ft. = 6 in.
12 ÷ 2 = 6

$\frac{3}{4}$ ft. = 9 in.
12 ÷ 4 = 3
3 × 3 = 9

$\frac{1}{2}$ m = 50 cm
100 ÷ 2 = 50

$\frac{1}{4}$ m = 25 cm
100 ÷ 4 = 25

$\frac{3}{4}$ m = 75 cm
100 ÷ 4 = 25
3 × 25 = 75

$\frac{4}{5}$ m = 80 cm
100 ÷ 5 = 20
4 × 20 = 80

$\frac{1}{2}$ hr. = 30 min.
60 ÷ 2 = 30

$\frac{3}{4}$ hr. = 45 min.
60 ÷ 4 = 15
3 × 15 = 45

$\frac{2}{3}$ hr. = 40 min.
60 ÷ 3 = 20
2 × 20 = 40

$\frac{9}{10}$ hr. = 54 min.
60 ÷ 10 = 6
9 × 6 = 54

Solve. Write the equations you use.

Lions often sleep for $\frac{5}{6}$ of the day. How many hours is this? (1 day = 24 hours)

24 ÷ 6 = 4
5 × 4 = **20 hours**

Cotton-top tamarin monkeys weigh about $\frac{2}{5}$ kg. How many grams is this? (1 kg = 1,000 g)

1,000 ÷ 5 = 200
2 × 200 = **400 g**

8.7 Review

Review Complete. Write your answers in simplest form.

$1\frac{1}{6} = 1\frac{1}{6}$
$+\ 2\frac{1}{2} = 2\frac{3}{6}$
$3\frac{4}{6} = 3\frac{2}{3}$

$4\frac{1}{8} = 4\frac{1}{8}$
$+\ 2\frac{1}{4} = 2\frac{2}{8}$
$6\frac{3}{8}$

$3\frac{1}{2} = 3\frac{5}{10}$
$+\ 1\frac{7}{10} = 1\frac{7}{10}$
$4\frac{12}{10} = 5\frac{1}{5}$

Label the numbers on the number line.

0 to 1: 0.6

2.5 to 2.6: 2.52

0.49 to 0.5: 0.495

0 to 0.1: 0.04

Answer the questions. Write your answers in simplest form.

Juniper runs track. Her favorite race is 800 m long. What fraction of a kilometer is her favorite race?

$\frac{800}{1{,}000} = \frac{4}{5}$ **km**

Asher asks 20 people whether they have a pet. 8 of the people have a dog and 4 of the people have a cat. The rest don't have a pet. What fraction of the people don't have a pet?

8 + 4 = 12
20 − 12 = 8
$\frac{8}{20} = \frac{2}{5}$ **of the people**

8.8 Practice

Practice Use bar models to solve.

Ruth has 64 inches of string. Then, she uses $\frac{5}{8}$ of the string to make a craft. How many inches of string does she use to make the craft?

40 in.

64 ÷ 8 = 8
5 × 8 = 40

How many inches of string does Ruth have left?

24 in.

64 − 40 = 24

Luke has \$40. He spends $\frac{2}{5}$ of his money at the arcade. How much money does he spend?

\$16

40 ÷ 5 = 8
2 × 8 = 16

How much money does Luke have left?

\$24

40 − 16 = 24

★ Samantha's library book has 150 pages. She read $\frac{2}{3}$ of her book this week. How many pages did Samantha read?

100 pages

150 ÷ 3 = 50
2 × 50 = 100

Cannon's library book has 120 pages. He read $\frac{3}{4}$ of his book this week. How many pages did Cannon read?

90 pages

120 ÷ 4 = 30
3 × 30 = 90

Who read more pages? How many more?

Samantha
10 more pages

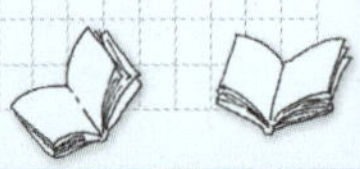

8.8 Review

Review Circle the numbers that match the description. X the numbers that do not match the description.

Divisible by 3			Divisible by 4			Divisible by 6		
X 200	(201)	X 202	(200)	X 201	X 202	X 200	X 201	X 202
X 203	(204)	X 205	X 203	(204)	X 205	X 203	(204)	X 205
X 206	(207)	X 208	X 206	X 207	(208)	X 206	X 207	X 208

Complete. Write your answers in simplest form.

$3\frac{1}{3} = 2\frac{8}{6}$
$-\ 1\frac{5}{6} = 1\frac{5}{6}$
$1\frac{3}{6} = 1\frac{1}{2}$

$4\frac{5}{12} = 3\frac{17}{12}$
$-\ 2\frac{2}{3} = 2\frac{8}{12}$
$1\frac{9}{12} = 1\frac{3}{4}$

$7\frac{3}{10} = 6\frac{13}{10}$
$-\ 3\frac{1}{2} = 3\frac{5}{10}$
$3\frac{8}{10} = 3\frac{4}{5}$

Find the volume of the foam pit. Write the equations you use.

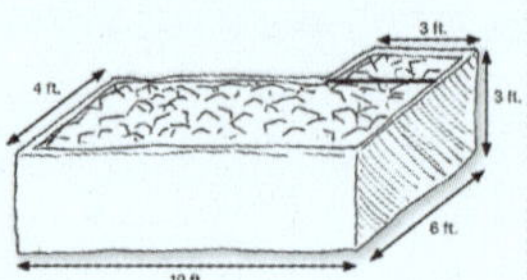

4 × 10 × 3 = 120
2 × 3 × 3 = 18
120 + 18 = **138 cu. ft.**

Unit 8 Answer Key

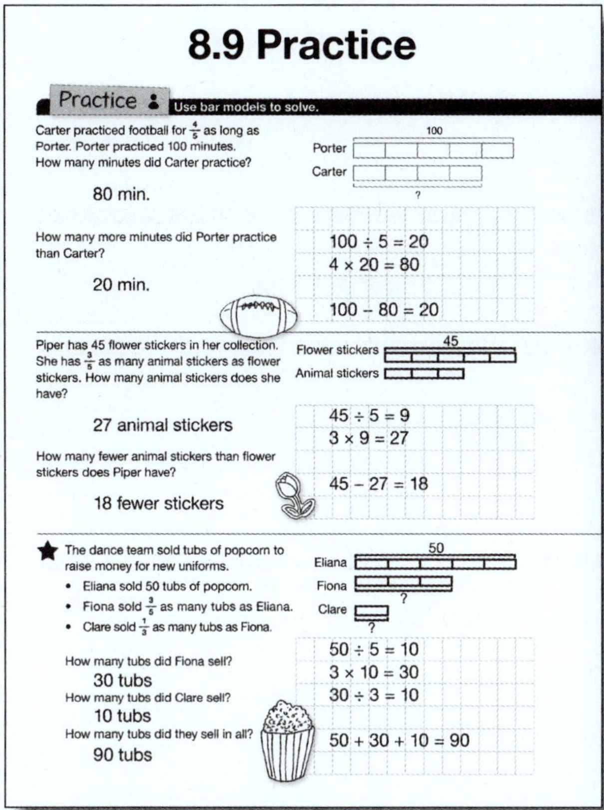

8.9 Practice

Practice Use bar models to solve.

Carter practiced football for $\frac{4}{5}$ as long as Porter. Porter practiced 100 minutes. How many minutes did Carter practice?

Porter / Carter (bar model: 100, ?)

80 min.

How many more minutes did Porter practice than Carter?

20 min.

100 ÷ 5 = 20
4 × 20 = 80
100 − 80 = 20

Piper has 45 flower stickers in her collection. She has $\frac{3}{5}$ as many animal stickers as flower stickers. How many animal stickers does she have?

Flower stickers / Animal stickers (bar model: 45)

27 animal stickers

How many fewer animal stickers than flower stickers does Piper have?

18 fewer stickers

45 ÷ 5 = 9
3 × 9 = 27
45 − 27 = 18

★ The dance team sold tubs of popcorn to raise money for new uniforms.

- Eliana sold 50 tubs of popcorn.
- Fiona sold $\frac{3}{5}$ as many tubs as Eliana.
- Clare sold $\frac{1}{3}$ as many tubs as Fiona.

Eliana / Fiona / Clare (bar model: 50, ?, ?)

How many tubs did Fiona sell?
30 tubs
How many tubs did Clare sell?
10 tubs
How many tubs did they sell in all?
90 tubs

50 ÷ 5 = 10
3 × 10 = 30
30 ÷ 3 = 10
50 + 30 + 10 = 90

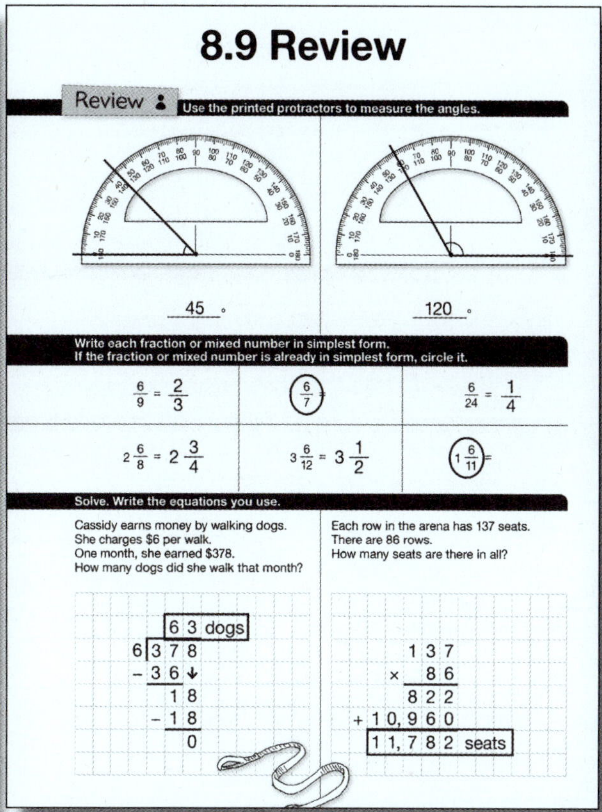

8.9 Review

Review Use the printed protractors to measure the angles.

45 ° 120 °

Write each fraction or mixed number in simplest form. If the fraction or mixed number is already in simplest form, circle it.

$\frac{6}{9} = \frac{2}{3}$ ($\frac{6}{7}$ circled) $\frac{6}{24} = \frac{1}{4}$

$2\frac{6}{8} = 2\frac{3}{4}$ $3\frac{6}{12} = 3\frac{1}{2}$ ($1\frac{6}{11}$ circled)

Solve. Write the equations you use.

Cassidy earns money by walking dogs. She charges $6 per walk. One month, she earned $378. How many dogs did she walk that month?

378 ÷ 6 = 63 dogs (6 | 378; −36; 18; −18; 0)

Each row in the arena has 137 seats. There are 86 rows. How many seats are there in all?

137 × 86: 822 + 10,960 = 11,782 seats

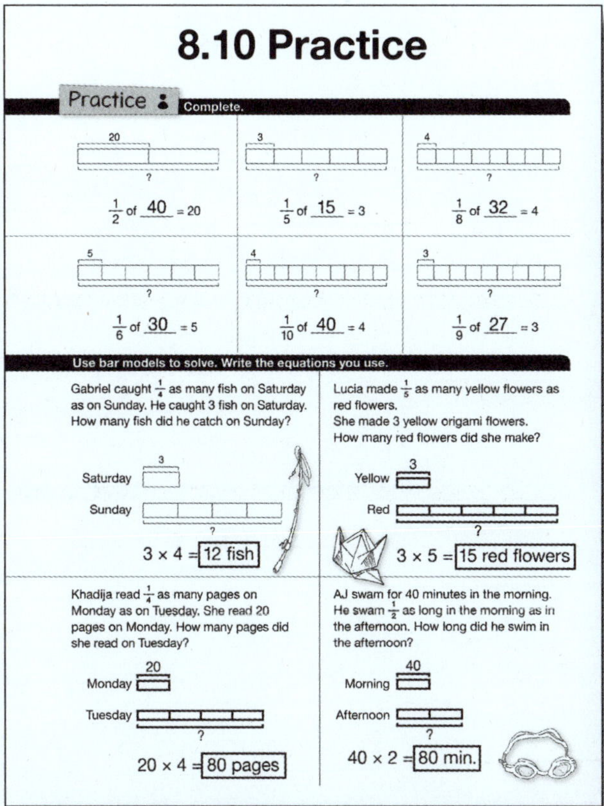

8.10 Practice

Practice Complete.

$\frac{1}{2}$ of 40 = 20 $\frac{1}{5}$ of 15 = 3 $\frac{1}{8}$ of 32 = 4

$\frac{1}{6}$ of 30 = 5 $\frac{1}{10}$ of 40 = 4 $\frac{1}{9}$ of 27 = 3

Use bar models to solve. Write the equations you use.

Gabriel caught $\frac{1}{4}$ as many fish on Saturday as on Sunday. He caught 3 fish on Saturday. How many fish did he catch on Sunday?

Saturday / Sunday (bar model: 3, ?)

3 × 4 = 12 fish

Lucia made $\frac{1}{5}$ as many yellow flowers as red flowers. She made 3 yellow origami flowers. How many red flowers did she make?

Yellow / Red (bar model: 3, ?)

3 × 5 = 15 red flowers

Khadija read $\frac{1}{4}$ as many pages on Monday as on Tuesday. She read 20 pages on Monday. How many pages did she read on Tuesday?

Monday / Tuesday (bar model: 20, ?)

20 × 4 = 80 pages

AJ swam for 40 minutes in the morning. He swam $\frac{1}{2}$ as long in the morning as in the afternoon. How long did he swim in the afternoon?

Morning / Afternoon (bar model: 40, ?)

40 × 2 = 80 min.

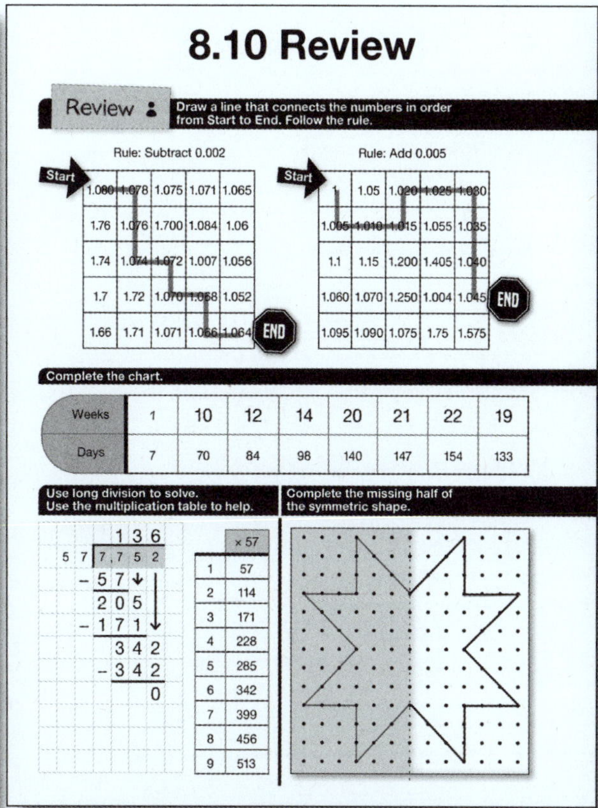

8.10 Review

Review Draw a line that connects the numbers in order from Start to End. Follow the rule.

Rule: Subtract 0.002

1.080	1.078	1.075	1.071	1.065
1.76	1.076	1.700	1.084	1.06
1.74	1.074	1.072	1.007	1.056
1.7	1.72	1.070	1.068	1.052
1.66	1.71	1.071	1.066	1.064

Rule: Add 0.005

1	1.05	1.020	1.025	1.030
1.005	1.010	1.015	1.055	1.035
1.1	1.15	1.200	1.405	1.040
1.060	1.070	1.250	1.004	1.045
1.095	1.090	1.075	1.75	1.575

Complete the chart.

Weeks	1	10	12	14	20	21	22	19
Days	7	70	84	98	140	147	154	133

Use long division to solve. Use the multiplication table to help.

7,752 ÷ 57 = 136 (−571; 205; −171; 342; −342; 0)

× 57	
1	57
2	114
3	171
4	228
5	285
6	342
7	399
8	456
9	513

Complete the missing half of the symmetric shape.

Unit 8 Answer Key

8.11 Practice

Harry has $30. He has $\frac{5}{6}$ as much money as his sister. How much money does his sister have?

Harry

Sister

Practice Complete.

$\frac{3}{5}$ of 30 = 18

$\frac{5}{6}$ of 12 = 10

$\frac{4}{10}$ of 100 = 40

Use bar models to solve. Write the equations you use.

Cora took her horse for an 8-mile trail ride on Monday. She rode $\frac{2}{3}$ as far on Monday as on Wednesday. How far did she ride on Wednesday?

Monday (8)

Wednesday (?)

8 ÷ 2 = 4
3 × 4 = 12

12 miles

George bought a baseball glove and bat. The glove cost $21. It cost $\frac{3}{5}$ as much as the bat. How much did the bat cost?

Glove (21)

Bat (?)

21 ÷ 3 = 7
5 × 7 = 35

$35

8.11 Review

Review Use mental math to complete.

160 ÷ 40 = 4	2,500 ÷ 500 = 5	10,000 ÷ 2,000 = 5
320 ÷ 80 = 4	3,000 ÷ 600 = 5	14,000 ÷ 7,000 = 2
490 ÷ 70 = 7	7,200 ÷ 800 = 9	24,000 ÷ 6,000 = 4

Complete the chart.

Gallons	1	10	20	21	30	29
Quarts	4	40	80	84	120	116

Draw a triangle that matches each description.

Sample answers.

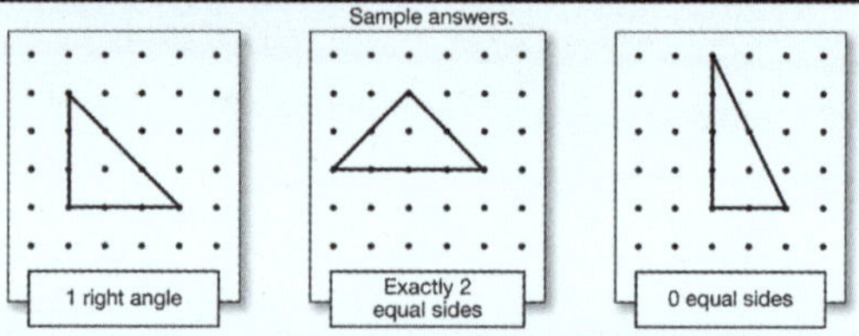

1 right angle | Exactly 2 equal sides | 0 equal sides

Solve. Write the equations you use.

Annaliese's family buys two hams to serve at a party. One ham weighs 5.93 kg, and the other ham weighs 8.6 kg. What is the total weight of both hams?

  5.93
+ 8.60
14.53 kg

One turkey at the store weighs 15.48 pounds. Another turkey weighs 18.3 pounds. How much more does the heavier turkey weigh than the lighter turkey?

  18.30
− 15.48
  2.82 lb.

8.12 Practice

Practice Use bar models to solve.

Marleigh bought a pack of candy. She gave Safiyya $\frac{1}{4}$ of the pieces of candy. Safiyya got 12 pieces of candy. How many pieces of candy were in the pack when Marleigh opened it?

48 pieces

12 × 4 = 48

How many pieces of candy does Marleigh have left?

36 pieces

48 − 12 = 36

Brandon spent $\frac{3}{5}$ of his money on a model plane. The model plane cost $18. How much money did he start with?

$30

18 ÷ 3 = 6
5 × 6 = 30

How much money does Brandon have left?

$12

30 − 18 = 12

★ John spent $\frac{1}{3}$ of his free time playing video games. He spent the rest of his free time playing basketball. He spent 100 minutes playing basketball. How much free time did he have in all?

150 min.

100 ÷ 2 = 50
3 × 50 = 150

How much time did he spend playing video games?

50 min.

8.12 Review

Review Use mental math to complete.

30 × 70 = 2,100	30 × 700 = 21,000	300 × 700 = 210,000
90 × 50 = 4,500	90 × 500 = 45,000	900 × 500 = 450,000
10 × 80 = 800	10 × 800 = 8,000	100 × 80 = 8,000
50 × 60 = 3,000	50 × 600 = 30,000	500 × 600 = 300,000

Draw a line parallel to each printed line.

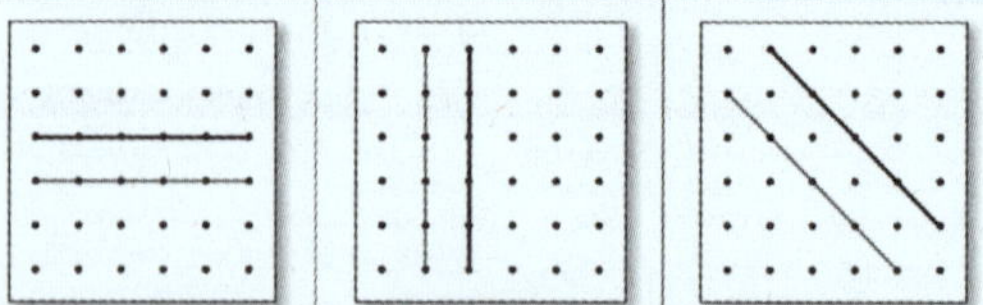

Sample answers

Complete the chart. Then, write the numbers in order from least to greatest.

Standard Form	Expanded Form
3.06	$3 + \frac{6}{100}$
3.601	$3 + \frac{6}{10} + \frac{1}{1,000}$
3.6	$3 + \frac{6}{10}$
3.061	$3 + \frac{6}{100} + \frac{1}{1,000}$

3.06 (least), 3.061, 3.6, 3.601 (greatest)

Unit 8 Answer Key

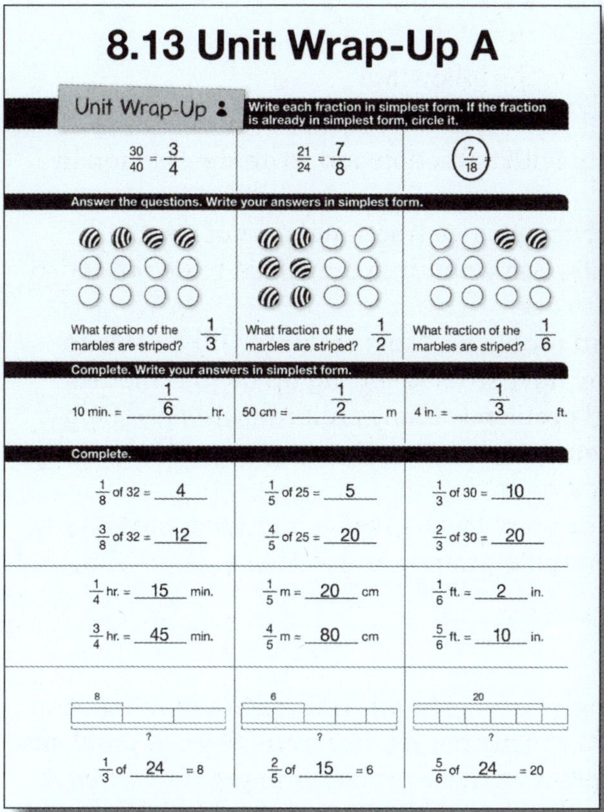

8.13 Unit Wrap-Up A

Unit Wrap-Up — Write each fraction in simplest form. If the fraction is already in simplest form, circle it.

$\frac{30}{40} = \frac{3}{4}$	$\frac{21}{24} = \frac{7}{8}$	$\frac{7}{18}$ (circled)

Answer the questions. Write your answers in simplest form.

What fraction of the marbles are striped? $\frac{1}{3}$	What fraction of the marbles are striped? $\frac{1}{2}$	What fraction of the marbles are striped? $\frac{1}{6}$

Complete. Write your answers in simplest form.

10 min. = $\frac{1}{6}$ hr.	50 cm = $\frac{1}{2}$ m	4 in. = $\frac{1}{3}$ ft.

Complete.

$\frac{1}{8}$ of 32 = 4	$\frac{1}{5}$ of 25 = 5	$\frac{1}{3}$ of 30 = 10
$\frac{3}{8}$ of 32 = 12	$\frac{4}{5}$ of 25 = 20	$\frac{2}{3}$ of 30 = 20
$\frac{1}{4}$ hr. = 15 min.	$\frac{1}{5}$ m = 20 cm	$\frac{1}{6}$ ft. = 2 in.
$\frac{3}{4}$ hr. = 45 min.	$\frac{4}{5}$ m = 80 cm	$\frac{5}{6}$ ft. = 10 in.
$\frac{1}{3}$ of 24 = 8	$\frac{2}{5}$ of 15 = 6	$\frac{5}{6}$ of 24 = 20

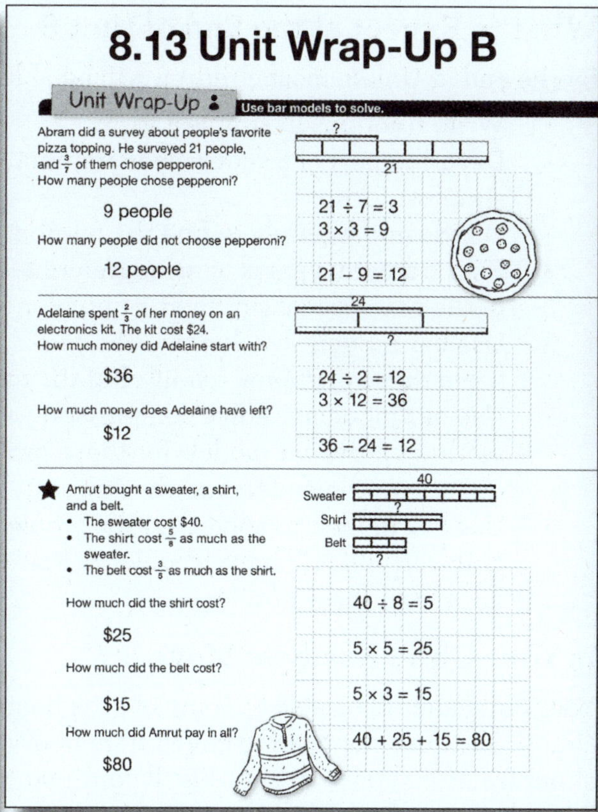

8.13 Unit Wrap-Up B

Unit Wrap-Up — Use bar models to solve.

Abram did a survey about people's favorite pizza topping. He surveyed 21 people, and $\frac{3}{7}$ of them chose pepperoni.
How many people chose pepperoni?

9 people

$21 \div 7 = 3$
$3 \times 3 = 9$

How many people did not choose pepperoni?

12 people

$21 - 9 = 12$

Adelaine spent $\frac{2}{3}$ of her money on an electronics kit. The kit cost $24.
How much money did Adelaine start with?

$36

$24 \div 2 = 12$
$3 \times 12 = 36$

How much money does Adelaine have left?

$12

$36 - 24 = 12$

★ Amrut bought a sweater, a shirt, and a belt.

- The sweater cost $40.
- The shirt cost $\frac{5}{8}$ as much as the sweater.
- The belt cost $\frac{3}{5}$ as much as the shirt.

How much did the shirt cost?

$25

How much did the belt cost?

$15

How much did Amrut pay in all?

$80

$40 \div 8 = 5$
$5 \times 5 = 25$
$5 \times 3 = 15$
$40 + 25 + 15 = 80$

Unit 8 Checkpoint

What to Expect at the End of Unit 8

By the end of Unit 8, most children will be able to do the following:

- Write fractions in simplest form.
- Describe part of a set or measurement unit with a fraction and write the fraction in simplest form.
- Divide and multiply to find the number of objects in a fractional part of a set.
- Find fractional parts of measurement units. Some children may need to be reminded of the correct measurement equivalency to use.
- Use bar models to solve find-the-part word problems. Most children will be able to solve these problems readily, but they may have trouble setting up the bar models.
- Use bar models to solve comparison word problems. Many children will need help setting up the bar models for these problems, especially when they know the smaller quantity and need to find the larger quantity.
- Use bar models to solve find-the-whole word problems, given a fractional part. Many children will still have trouble with these problems and need a lot of support and guidance with these problems.

Is Your Child Ready to Move on?

Your child should be able to complete the basic calculations in this unit before moving on to Unit 9. She does not need to have full mastery over using bar models to solve word problems about fractional parts of sets. She'll continue to practice these problems in the Review pages. Provide as much coaching and support as she needs when she tackles these problems.

Unit 9
The Coordinate Plane and Line Graphs

Overview

Your child will learn how to identify and plot ordered pairs on the coordinate plane. She will also learn how to create line graphs based on real-world data and number patterns.

This year, your child will learn to plot ordered pairs with positive coordinates only. In sixth grade, she will learn how to plot ordered pairs with negative coordinates as well.

What Your Child Will Learn

In this unit, your child will learn to:

- Identify and plot points on the coordinate plane (positive coordinates only)
- Identify the slope of lines on the coordinate plane as upward, downward, horizontal, or vertical
- Create and interpret line graphs based on real-world data
- Make a table of values based on a real-life number pattern, plot the resulting ordered pairs, and use the graph to draw conclusions about the number pattern

Lesson List

Lesson 9.1	Plot Points on the Coordinate Plane	Lesson 9.4	Graph Number Patterns on the Coordinate Plane
Lesson 9.2	Draw Line Segments on the Coordinate Plane	Lesson 9.5	Use Line Graphs to Draw Conclusions
Lesson 9.3	Create and Interpret Real-World Line Graphs	Lesson 9.6	Enrichment (Optional)

Extra Materials Needed for Unit 9

- Colored pencils or markers
- For optional Enrichment Lesson:
    - × *How Many Guinea Pigs Can Fit on a Plane?: Answers to Your Most Clever Math Questions,* by Laura Overdeck. Feiwel & Friends, 2017.
    - × World map or globe with latitude and longitude lines, optional

Teaching Math with Confidence: Introducing Slope and Linear Relationships

In this brief unit, you'll teach your child to plot points and draw line graphs on the coordinate plane. You'll especially focus on graphing addition and subtraction patterns on the coordinate plane. All of these patterns in this unit are based on real-world situations. Basing the graphs on real-world situations helps your child concretely understand the meaning of each ordered pair as well as the slope of the resulting line.

For example, in Lesson 9.4, your child will make a graph to describe how a total amount of money changes as more money is earned. Each ordered pair refers to the total amount of money on a particular day. The line slopes upward because the amount of money increases each day.

Tireni has $20. He gets a job feeding his neighbor's cats for $3 per day.

Day	Dollars
0	20
1	23
2	26
3	29
4	32
5	35

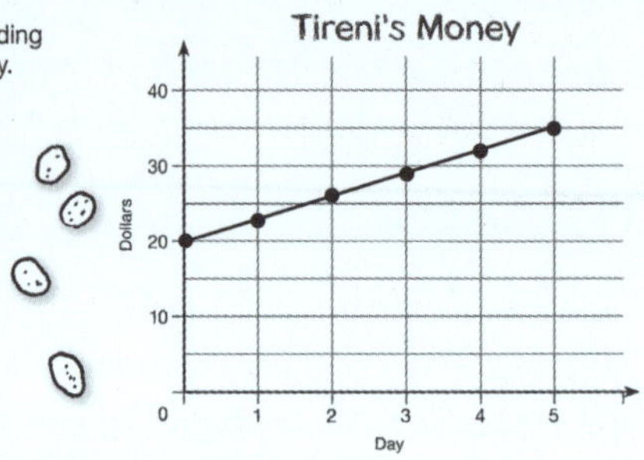

Each ordered pair tells a day and amount of money.
For example, the point (2,26) means that on day 2, Tireni has $26.

Addition and subtraction number patterns like this one are called linear relationships. In linear relationships, the same amount is added or subtracted to a quantity over and over. (You may remember from your own algebra classes that linear relationships can be expressed with equations in the form $y = mx + b$. For example, the above graph matches the equation $y = 3x + 20$.)

Linear relationships are a foundational algebra topic, so becoming familiar with them now prepares your child to understand them more abstractly later. In this unit, focus on helping your child understand how the graphs relate to the matching real-life situations. She'll have plenty of time in future grades to master the complexities of using variables and equations to describe linear relationships.

Lesson 9.1
Plot Points on the Coordinate Plane

Purpose	Materials
• Preview the idea of traveling on a coordinate plane • Learn coordinate plane vocabulary • Use ordered pairs to identify locations and plot points on the coordinate plane	• None

Memory Work	
	• **What does LCM stand for?** *Least common multiple.* • **Name 4 multiples of 8.** *Sample answers: 8, 16, 32, 64.*

Warm-up (A): Follow Directions to Find the Treasure

This pirate map has a grid and starting point. The treasure is hidden under one of the palm trees on the map, and the numbers and arrows show how to move on the grid to find the treasure.

Have your child put the tip of her pencil on the starting point. **The first direction is to move 1 unit down.** Have your child draw a line 1 unit long (along the vertical grid line) as shown. Repeat with the rest of the directions until your child reaches the end and finds the correct palm tree. **You found the treasure!**

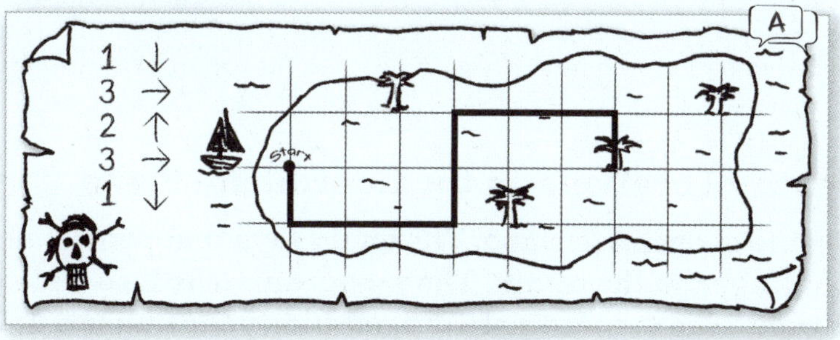

Activity (B): Introduce the Coordinate Plane

We're beginning a new unit today. You'll learn how to plot points and identify locations on the coordinate plane. You'll find that the coordinate plane is a lot like the grid you used to find the pirate treasure in the warm-up.

> In math, coordinate is pronounced "co-OR-din-it" (and not "co-or-din-ATE," as in the verb that means to work together).

Show your child the coordinate plane in part B. **The coordinate plane is like a map made from two perpendicular number lines. We can use the numbers from the number lines to identify any location on the map.**

> Remind your child as needed that lines that are perpendicular to each other meet to form a right angle.

In math, the word *plane* means a flat, two-dimensional surface. What does it mean when two people coordinate? *It means they work together to do something.* **On the coordinate plane, two numbers work together to name a location on a flat surface.** Have your child read the text box aloud.

Ordered Pairs and the Coordinate Plane

(3,4) is called an ordered pair. It tells a location on the coordinate plane.

(3,4)
x-coordinate y-coordinate

The x-coordinate tells the horizontal distance from the origin. The y-coordinate tells the vertical distance from the origin.

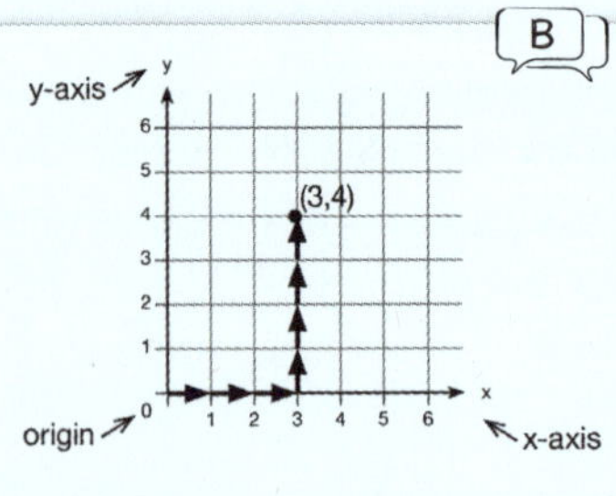

Highlight the following features of the coordinate plane:

- Point to the point labeled "origin." **This point is called the origin. It's the 0-mark for both of the number lines.**
- **The number lines on either side are called the axes. The horizontal line is called the x-axis. The vertical line is called the y-axis.**
- Point to the labeled point. **We say that the coordinates of this ordered pair are (3,4). If you start at the origin, move 3 units to the right, and 4 units up, you land at this point. 3 is the x-coordinate, and 4 is the y-coordinate.**

Axes (pronounced AK-sees) is the plural form of axis. Calling them the x-axis and y-axis is simply a mathematical convention.

When you name an ordered pair, read only the two numbers in the ordered pair (and not the comma or parentheses). For example, read (3,4) as "three four."

Activity (C): Identify Locations on the Coordinate Plane

Let's plot point A on the coordinate plane. The chart says that point A should be at (1,6). To graph it, put your finger on the origin. The x-coordinate is 1, so slide your finger 1 unit horizontally to the right. The y-coordinate is 6, so slide your finger 6 units up vertically. Have your child draw a point at this location and label it A. Repeat with points B and C.

Point	Ordered Pair
A	(1,6)
B	(5,8)
C	(0,4)

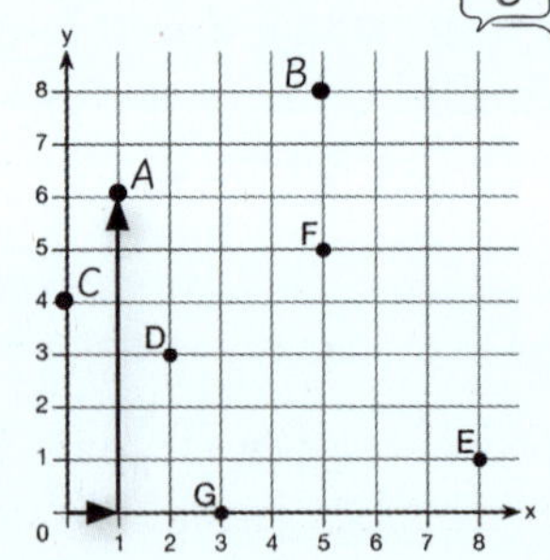

Moving step-by-step from the origin helps your child understand that ordered pairs identify the horizontal and vertical distance from the origin.

Now, let's find the ordered pair that identifies the location of point D.

- **First, I put my finger on the point. Then, I slide it down to the x-axis.** Put your finger on the point and slide it down to the x-axis. **I land on 2, so the x-coordinate is 2.**

- **Next, I put my finger back on the point. This time, I slide it across to the y-axis.** Put your finger on the point and slide it across to the y-axis. **I land on 3, so the y-coordinate is 3.** Write (2,3) in the chart.

D	(2,3)

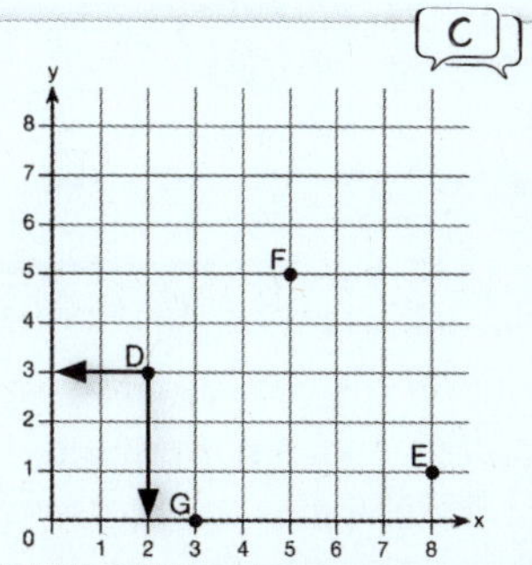

We always write the x-coordinate first and then the y-coordinate so that we know which is which. We write a comma between the two numbers and write parentheses around them.

Have your child identify the locations of points E, F, and G and write the matching ordered pairs in the chart.

Point	Ordered Pair
A	(1,6)
B	(5,8)
C	(0,4)
D	(2,3)
E	(8,1)
F	(5,5)
G	(3,0)

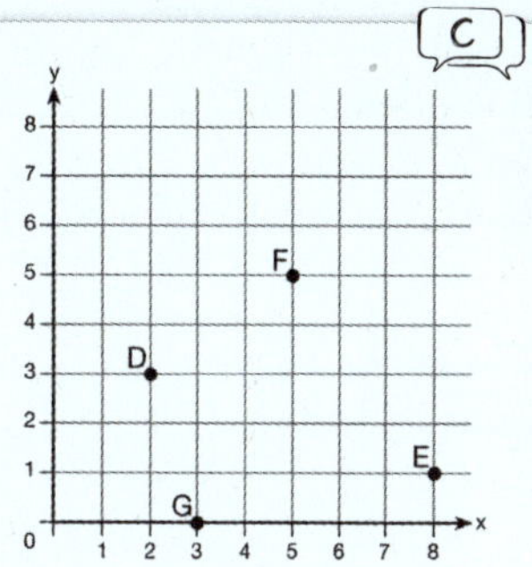

Activity (D): Play Hot and Cold on the Coordinate Plane

Now, we'll play Hot and Cold. I'll choose a secret location on the coordinate plane. You'll guess a location, draw a point there, and tell me the coordinates. If you're far away from my secret point, I'll say, "Cold." If you're close to my secret point, I'll say, "Hot."

> You can also use other words for hot and cold to express how close your child is to your secret location. **You're ice cold. You're getting warmer. You're burning up!**

Secretly choose a point on the first coordinate plane and write its coordinates on a piece of scrap paper. Then, have your child guess a location on the coordinate plane, draw a point at the location, and tell you the matching ordered pair.

For example, if you chose (0,5) as your secret location:

- *Is your secret location (4,2)?* **Cold.**
- *Is your secret location (2,3)?* **Getting warmer.**
- *Is your secret location (1,5)?* **Hot.**
- *Is your secret location (0, 5)?* **You found it!**

Continue until your child guesses your secret location. Then, reverse roles and play again on the second coordinate plane.

> If your child would like to play multiple rounds, re-use the coordinate planes and use a different colored marker or colored pencil to record the new locations.

Independent Practice and Review

Have your child complete the Lesson 9.1 Practice and Review workbook pages.

Lesson 9.2
Draw Line Segments on the Coordinate Plane

Purpose	Materials
• Practice plotting points on the coordinate plane • Draw line segments on the coordinate plane • Describe a line segment's slope as upwards, downwards, vertical, or horizontal	• 2 dice • Counters
Memory Work	• **What do we call the horizontal axis?** *The x-axis.* • **What do we call the vertical axis?** *The y-axis.* • **What do we call the (0,0) point?** *The origin.* • **What is an ordered pair?** *A pair of numbers that identify the location of a point.* • **In an ordered pair, what do we call the first number?** *The x-coordinate.* **What does it tell?** *The point's horizontal distance.* • **In an ordered pair, what do we call the second number?** *The y-coordinate.* **What does it tell?** *The point's vertical distance.*

In this lesson, your child will learn to observe and describe line segments' slopes with informal terms like *vertical, horizontal, upwards,* and *downwards.* In future grades, your child will learn to use numbers to describe and measure slope.

Warm-up (A): Practice Drawing Points on the Coordinate Plane

In the last lesson, you learned that the coordinate plane is like a map made from two perpendicular number lines. We use the numbers on the number lines to identify the locations on the map. Have your child follow the directions in part A.

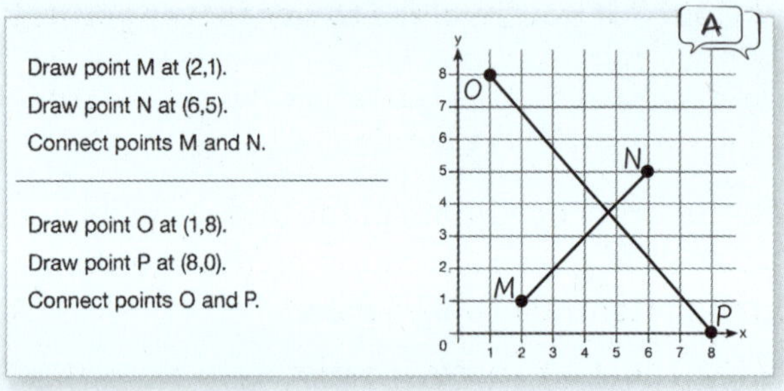

Activity (B): Identify Line Segments' Slope

In the warm-up you drew points on the coordinate plane and connected them with a line to create a line segment. Today, you'll learn how to describe a line segment's slope.

In geometry, a *line* continues forever, while a *line segment* is a finite part of a line. In everyday conversation, we often use the word *line* to describe both.

Hold your left arm vertically in front of you, as shown. Have your child sit next to you so he sees your arm from the same direction as you do. **When a line segment is completely up-and-down, we say it's vertical.** Have your child hold his arm vertically, too. Show him the vertical line segment in part B.

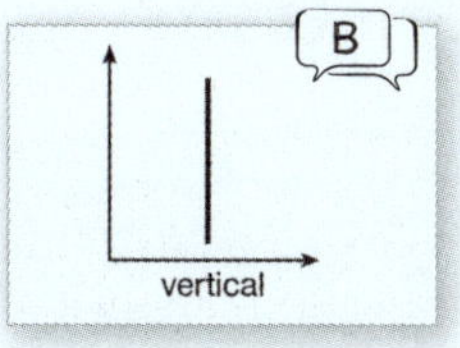

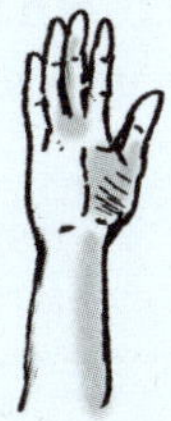

Hold your left arm horizontally in front of you. **When a line segment is completely flat, we say it's horizontal.** Have your child hold his arm horizontally, too. Show him the horizontal line segment in part B.

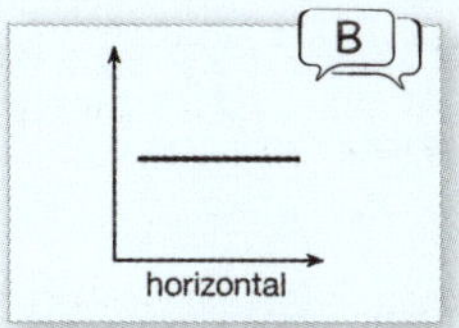

When I lift my hand and leave my elbow where it is, my arm slopes upward. If I put a ball on my elbow, I'd have to push it upward along my arm. Lift your hand (and keep your elbow stationary) to demonstrate upward slope. Have your child demonstrate upward slope with his arm and show him the line segment with an upward slope.

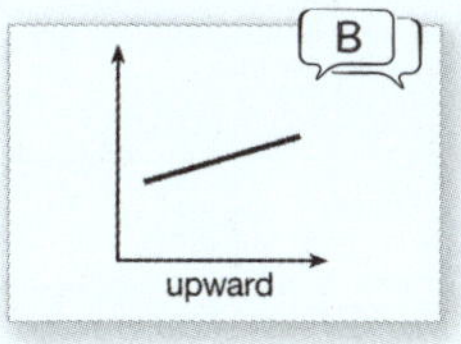

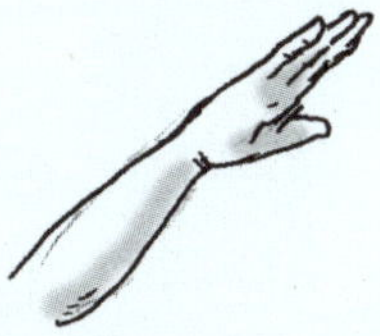

Return your arm to horizontal. **When I drop my hand down and leave my elbow where it is, my arm slopes downward. If I put a ball on my elbow, it would roll downward along my arm.** Drop your hand (and keep your elbow stationary) to demonstrate downward slope. Have your child demonstrate downward slope with his arm as well.

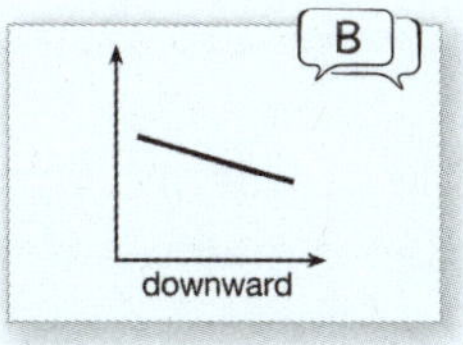

We think of slope from left to right, just like the numbers on the horizontal axis increase from left to right. In part A, what kind of slope does line segment MN have? *Upward.* **What kind of slope does line segment OP have?** *Downward.*

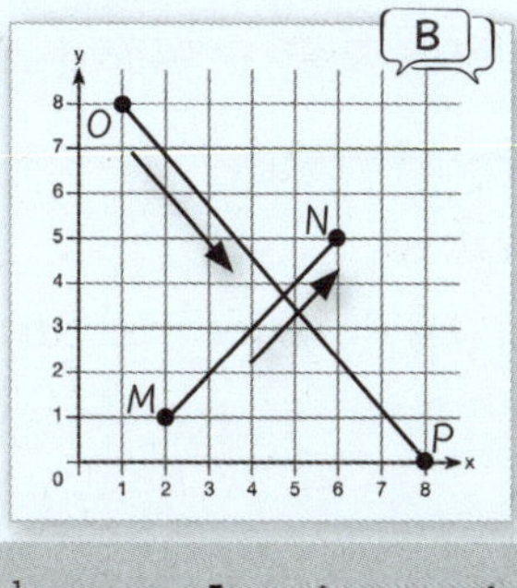

If your child has trouble identifying the slope, say: **Imagine putting a ball on the left end of the line segment. Would it roll downward or would you have to push it upward?**

Activity (C): Play What's the Slope?

In this game, we'll roll dice to create ordered pairs. For example, if you roll a 6 and 2, you could create the ordered pair (2,6) or (6,2). In each turn, we'll roll the dice twice to create two ordered pairs and connect them with a line segment. You win more counters if you create line segments that slope upward, so try to choose your ordered pairs wisely!

Play What's the Slope?

In this game, you can nearly always avoid creating a vertical or horizontal line segment. If your child begins to draw a vertical or horizontal line, encourage him to think about whether a better play is available.

What's the Slope?

Materials: 2 dice, counters

Object of the Game: Win the most counters.

On your turn, roll 2 dice. Use the numbers to create an ordered pair. For example, if you roll 4 and 3, you may create the ordered pair (3,4) or (4,3). Plot a point at this location on your gameboard. Then, roll the 2 dice again. Create another ordered pair and graph a point at the new location. Connect the two points with a line segment.

Then, use the key to determine how many counters you win (or whether you lose your counters).

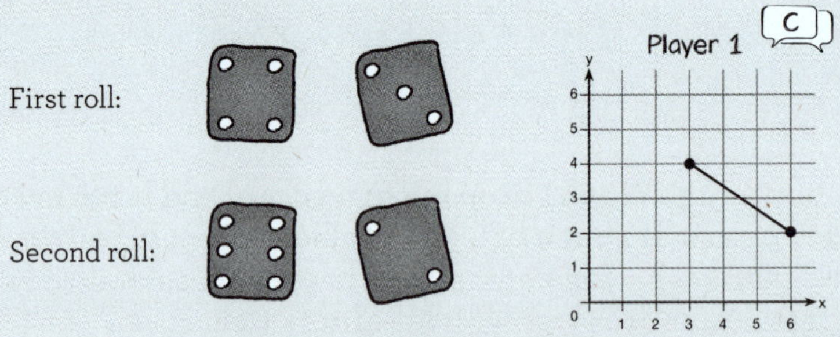

Sample play. This line segment slopes downward, so you take 1 counter.

Take turns rolling the dice and creating new line segments. Draw a new line segment each time, with 2 new endpoints. The line segments may overlap and cross.

If you roll the same doubles for both ordered pairs, reroll your second ordered pair. For example, if you roll double 3s for both ordered pairs, re-roll to create your second ordered pair.

Repeat until both players have taken 5 turns and drawn 5 separate line segments on their game boards. Whoever has won more counters wins the game.

Independent Practice and Review

Have your child complete the Lesson 9.2 Practice and Review workbook pages.

Lesson 9.3
Create and Interpret Real-World Line Graphs

Purpose	Materials
• Review ways to describe slope • Interpret a real-world line graph • Create a real-world line graph and choose an appropriate scale • Understand how slope shows change in line graphs	• None

Memory Work	
	• **What do we call the horizontal axis?** *The x-axis.* • **What do we call the vertical axis?** *The y-axis.* • **What do we call the (0,0) point?** *The origin.* • **What is an ordered pair?** *A pair of numbers that identify the location of a point.* • **In an ordered pair, what do we call the first number?** *The x-coordinate.* **What does it tell?** *The point's horizontal distance.* • **In an ordered pair, what do we call the second number?** *The y-coordinate.* **What does it tell?** *The point's vertical distance.*

Warm-up: Review Slope

In the last lesson, you learned how to draw and describe line segments on the coordinate plane.

- **Use your left arm to show me what a horizontal line segment looks like.** *Child holds her arm horizontally.*
- **Show me what a vertical line segment looks like.** *Child holds her arm vertically.*
- **Show me what a line segment with an upward slope looks like.** *Child holds her arm so that it slopes upward towards the right.* Remind your child as needed that we think of slope from left to right: **If I put a ball on your left elbow, you would need to push it upward along your arm.**
- **Show me what a line segment with a downward slope looks like.** *Child holds her arm so that it slopes downward towards the right.* **If I put a ball on your left elbow, it would roll downward along your arm.**

Horizontal.

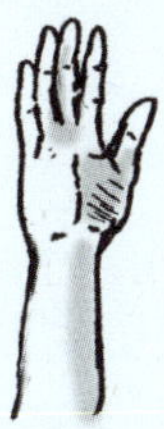

Vertical.

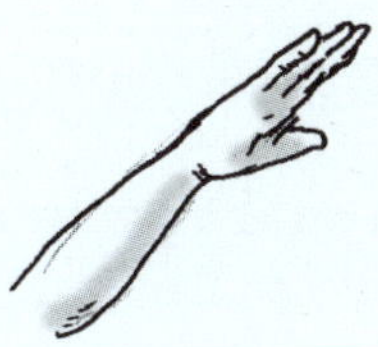

Upward.

Downward.

Activity (A): Interpret a Temperature Line Graph

Today, you'll learn how to create and interpret line graphs. Line graphs use points on the coordinate plane to organize data and make it easier to understand.

Let's look at the title and labels to see what information this graph shows.

- **What is the title?** *Daily Temperature at Noon.* **The temperature varies over the course of the day, so this graph shows only what the temperature was at noon each day.**
- **What is the x-axis labeled?** *Day.*
- **What is the y-axis labeled?** *Temperature.*
- Point to the °F along the vertical axis. **The little circle means degrees, and the F means that the temperature was measured with the Fahrenheit scale. That's the temperature measurement scale used in the United States.**

Each point on the coordinate plane stands for the temperature for one day. The x-coordinate tells the day, and the y-coordinate tells the temperature. Where is the point for day 1? *Child points to left-most point.* **The graph doesn't show the exact temperature, but we can use the numbers along the y-axis to estimate the temperature. About what temperature was it that day?** *37 degrees.* **37 degrees is pretty cold! Water freezes at 32 degrees Fahrenheit, so it's just a little warmer than that.**

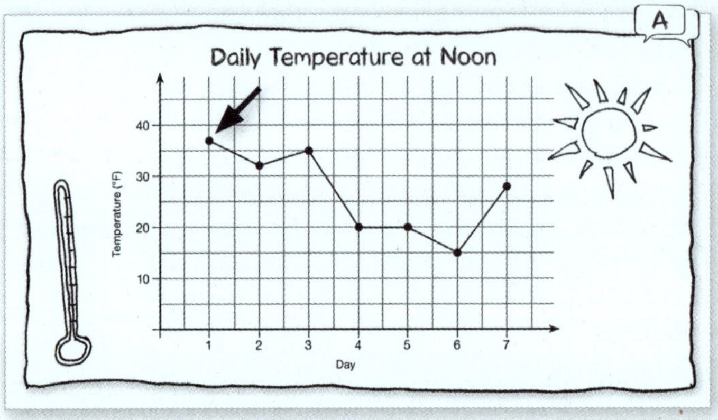

If your family uses the Celsius system to measure temperature, explain that 37° F is approximately 3° C.

Briefly discuss how this temperature compares to temperatures where you live. For example, if you live in a warmer climate: **It never gets that cold here!** Or, if you live in a colder climate: **Our temperature is usually around 37 degrees in November and December.**

Have your child trace her finger along the line from Day 1 to Day 7. Have her tell the approximate temperature for each day. Accept any reasonable approximation.

- Day 1: *37 °F.*
- Day 2: *32 °F.*
- Day 3: *35 °F.*
- Day 4: *20 °F.*
- Day 5: *20 °F.*
- Day 6: *15 °F.*
- Day 7: *28 °F.*

Your finger moves up and down on the paper as you trace the line. Have your child trace her finger along the line from Day 1 to Day 7 again. This time, have her describe the slope of each line segment as she traces it.

- Day 1 to Day 2: *Downward slope.*
- Day 2 to Day 3: *Upward slope.*
- Day 3 to Day 4: *Downward slope.*
- Day 4 to Day 5: *Horizontal.*
- Day 5 to Day 6: *Downward slope.*
- Day 6 to Day 7: *Upward slope.*

How does the temperature change when the line segment has an upward slope? *Sample answers: It goes up. It increases. It gets warmer.*

How does the temperature change when the line segment has a downward slope? *Sample answers: It goes down. It decreases. It gets colder.*

Why is the line segment from Day 4 to Day 5 horizontal? *The temperature at noon was the same both days.*

Then, have your child answer the questions in part A.

Which day had the highest temperature?	How many days had a temperature warmer than 30°?	Between which two consecutive days did the temperature decrease the most?
Day 1	3 days	Days 3 and 4
Which day had the lowest temperature?	How many days had a temperature colder than 30°?	Between which two consecutive days did the temperature increase the most?
Day 6	4 days	Days 6 and 7

Explain as needed that *consecutive* means "in a row."

Activity (B): Choose an Appropriate Scale and Make a Line Graph

This chart shows how tall a birch tree was each year. We'll use this chart to make a line graph. First, let's write the title. Write "Birch Tree Height" above the graph.

Second, we need to label the axes. When we make line graphs about time, we put the time increment on the horizontal axis. Write "Age (years)" below the horizontal axis. **We put the other measurement on the vertical axis.** Write "Height (ft.)" next to the vertical axis.

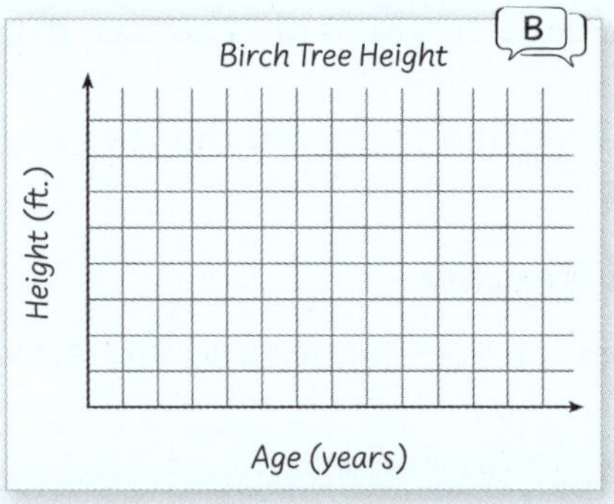

If your child wonders why time goes on the horizontal axis, explain that it's customary to put the independent variable on the horizontal axis and the dependent variable on the vertical axis. Time isn't affected by how fast the birch tree grows, so it is called the *independent variable* in this problem. The tree's height depends on how much time has passed, so it's the *dependent variable* in this problem.

Third, we need to choose how far to space the tick marks for the number lines on the x-axis and y-axis. This spacing is called the *scale*. The tick marks must be evenly spaced, but we can use a different scale on each axis.

The age of the tree goes up to 6 years old. We want to show every year, so we need room for 6 tick marks on the x-axis. We could space them 1 box apart on the grid, but then the tick marks would be very crowded. Instead, let's space them 2 boxes apart. Draw tick marks and label them as shown.

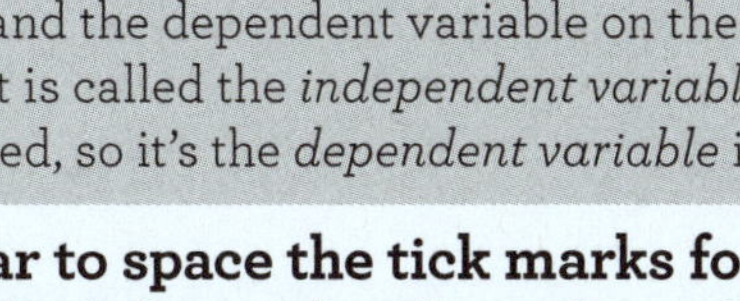

The tree's height goes up to 15 feet. If we space the tick marks 1 box apart, do we have room for 15 tick marks on the y-axis? *No.* **How do you know?** *There are only 8 horizontal lines along the y-axis.* **What would work better?** *Sample answers: Draw tick marks 1 box apart, but label them with the multiples of 2. Draw tick marks 2 boxes apart and label them with the multiples of 4.* Accept any answer that spaces the tick marks evenly and mostly fills the y-axis. Have your child label the y-axis accordingly.

Then, help your child plot the numbers in each row in the chart as an ordered pair. After she plots all 6 points, have her connect each pair of neighboring points with a line.

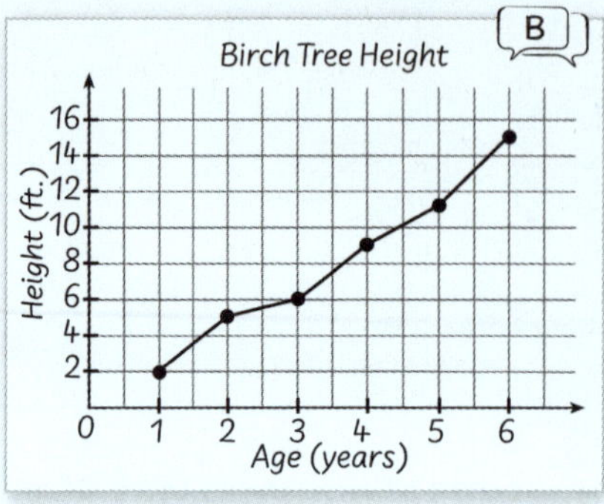

Sample answer. Your child may choose to label the y-axis in a different way.

Have your child trace her finger along the line from Year 1 to Year 6.

- **What do you notice about the slope of all of the line segments?** *They all slope upward.*
- **Why do all the line segments slope upward?** *The tree grows taller every year.*
- **Between which two consecutive years did the tree grow the least?** *Year 2 to 3.* **How much did it grow?** *1 foot.*
- **Between which two consecutive years did the tree grow the most?** *Year 5 to 6.* **How much did it grow?** *4 feet.*

Independent Practice and Review

Have your child complete the Lesson 9.3 Practice and Review workbook pages.

Lesson 9.4
Graph Number Patterns on the Coordinate Plane

Purpose	Materials
• Identify and continue addition and subtraction patterns • Graph addition and subtraction patterns on the coordinate plane • Understand that slope shows whether the numbers in a number pattern increase, decrease, or stay the same	• None

Memory Work	
	• **What do we call the horizontal axis?** *The x-axis.* • **What do we call the vertical axis?** *The y-axis.* • **What do we call the (0,0) point?** *The origin.* • **What is an ordered pair?** *A pair of numbers that identify the location of a point.* • **In an ordered pair, what do we call the first number?** *The x-coordinate.* **What does it tell?** *The point's horizontal distance.* • **In an ordered pair, what do we call the second number?** *The y-coordinate.* **What does it tell?** *The point's vertical distance.*

In this lesson, your child will graph addition and subtraction number patterns on the coordinate plane. This activity previews graphing linear equations, which is a fundamental algebra concept. See the Unit 9 **Teaching Math with Confidence** for more on how this unit prepares your child for algebraic thinking in future grades.

Warm-up: Continue Addition and Subtraction Patterns

We'll warm up with some addition and subtraction number patterns today. I'll tell you the first few numbers in the pattern, and then you tell me the next number.

- **5, 15, 25, 35....** *45.* **What's the pattern?** *Add 10.*
- **1, 4, 7, 10....** *13.* **What's the pattern?** *Add 3.*
- **7, 107, 207, 307....** *407.* **What's the pattern?** *Add 100.*
- **19, 15, 11, 7....** *3.* **What's the pattern?** *Subtract 4.*
- **68, 58, 48, 38....** *28.* **What's the pattern?** *Subtract 10.*
- **90, 70, 50, 30....** *10.* **What's the pattern?** *Subtract 20.*

If your child has trouble keeping track of the numbers in his head, write them on a piece of scrap paper.

Activity (A): Create Number Pattern Graphs and Analyze Their Slope

In the last lesson, you created and interpreted real-world line graphs. Today, you'll learn how to create line graphs about addition and subtraction patterns.

Read aloud the first situation: ***Tireni has $20. He gets a job feeding his neighbor's cats for $3 per day.*** **First, we'll make a chart to see how much money he has after each day.**

Day 0 is the day before he starts the job. At the end of day 0, he has $20. How much money does he have at the end of Day 1 of the job? *$23.* **How do you know?** *20 plus 3 equals 23.* Write 23 in the chart as shown. Have your child complete the chart in the same way.

Day	Dollars
0	20
1	23
2	26
3	29
4	32
5	35

Now, we'll graph the information from the chart. On Day 0, Tireni has $20. So, the first ordered pair is (0,20). Draw a point at (0,20) as shown. Have your child plot points to match the ordered pairs for the other rows of the chart. (He should approximate the points' positions as needed.) Then, have him draw a line connecting the points.

Tireni has $20. He gets a job feeding his neighbor's cats for $3 per day.

Day	Dollars
0	20
1	23
2	26
3	29
4	32
5	35

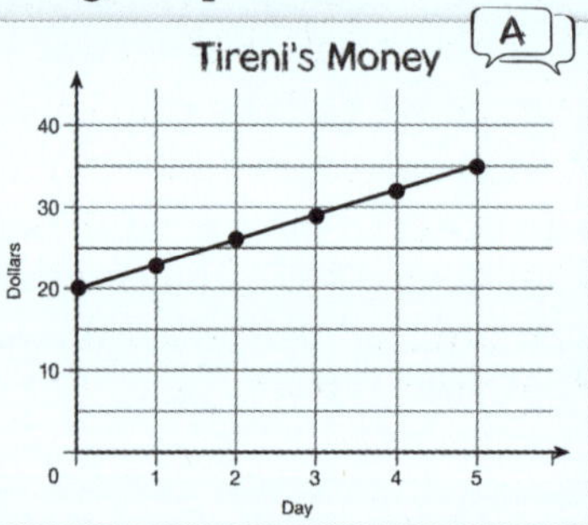

Does this line have an upward or downward slope? *Upward.* **As the days pass, Tireni has more money. So, the line slopes upward. He earns the same amount of money each day, so the line always has the same slope.**

Repeat for the next situation. **Which word best describe the slope of this line: upward, downward, horizontal, or vertical?** *Horizontal.* **As the days pass, nothing changes about how much money Lily has. So, the line stays flat and has a horizontal slope.**

Lily has $20. She doesn't spend any money or earn any money.

Day	Dollars
0	20
1	20
2	20
3	20
4	20
5	20

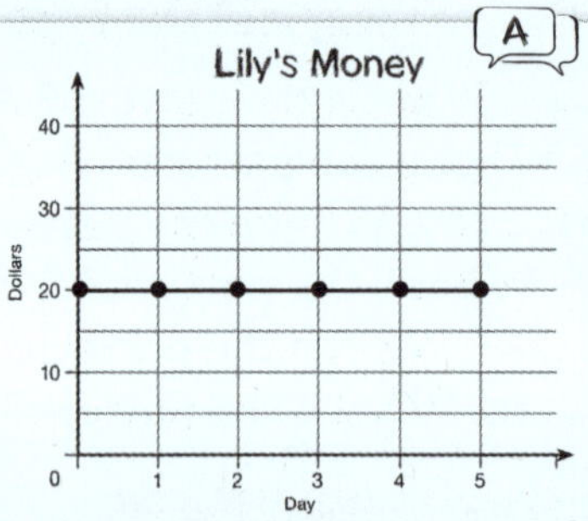

Repeat for the final situation. Point to (4,0) on the graph. **What does this point mean for Brayden?** *He runs out of money on Day 4.*

Brayden has $20. He spends $5 per day on candy.

Day	Dollars
0	20
1	15
2	10
3	5
4	0
5	0

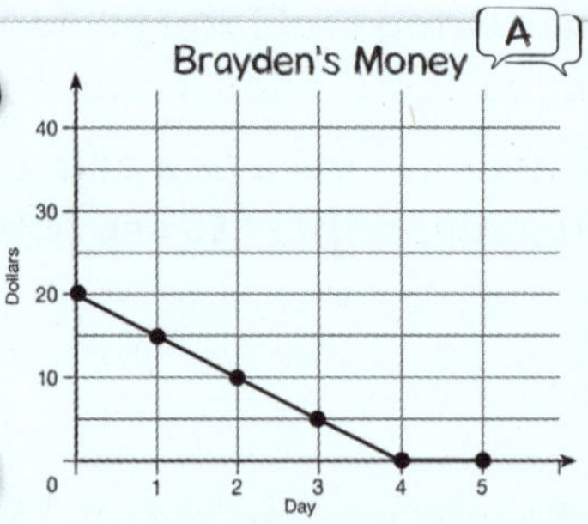

From Days 0 to 4, does the line have an upward or downward slope? *Downward.* **As the days pass, Brayden has less and less money. So, the line slopes downward.**

From Day 4 to Day 5, does the line have an upward or downward slope? *Neither.* **Once Brayden is out of money, nothing changes, so the line stays horizontal.**

Independent Practice and Review

Have your child complete the Lesson 9.4 Practice and Review workbook pages.

If your child has trouble with any of the questions on the Practice page, explain that the tick marks represent the *end* of each unit of time. The intervals between the tick marks represent the time as it passes.

For the dog food problem, the tick marks represent the end of each week, and the interval between the tick marks represents the passing time. For example: **The interval between from 0 and 1 represents the 7 days the dog spends eating the first 5 pounds of food. When you get to the tick mark for Week 1, the first week has passed and 25 pounds of food are left.**

For the reading problem, the tick marks represent the end of each day's reading time. For example: **When Katya starts reading on Day 1, she starts on page 11. After Day 1, Katya has read 30 pages of her book. That means she reads pages 31 through 50 on Day 2, and she reads pages 51 through 70 on Day 3.**

Lesson 9.5
Use Line Graphs to Draw Conclusions

Purpose	Materials
• Continue addition and subtraction patterns • Use number patterns to create a double line graph • Use a double line graph to draw conclusions	• Colored pencils or markers

Memory Work

- **What do we call the horizontal axis?** *The x-axis.*
- **What do we call the vertical axis?** *The y-axis.*
- **What do we call the (0,0) point?** *The origin.*
- **What is an ordered pair?** *A pair of numbers that identify the location of a point.*
- **In an ordered pair, what do we call the first number?** *The x-coordinate.* **What does it tell?** *The point's horizontal distance.*
- **In an ordered pair, what do we call the second number?** *The y-coordinate.* **What does it tell?** *The point's vertical distance.*

Warm-up: Continue Addition and Subtraction Patterns

We'll warm up with more addition and subtraction number patterns today. I'll tell you the first few numbers in the pattern, and then you tell me the next number.

- **9, 18, 27, 36....** *45.* **What's the pattern?** *Add 9.*
- **105, 109, 113, 117....** *121.* **What's the pattern?** *Add 4.*
- **104, 304, 504, 704....** *904.* **What's the pattern?** *Add 200.*
- **40, 34, 28, 22....** *16.* **What's the pattern?** *Subtract 6.*
- **189, 179, 169, 159....** *149.* **What's the pattern?** *Subtract 10.*
- **1,000, 800, 600, 400....** *200.* **What's the pattern?** *Subtract 200.*

If your child has trouble keeping track of the numbers in her head, write them on a piece of scrap paper.

Activity (A): Create Charts for Kayak Rental Prices

In the last lesson, you learned how to create line graphs about children earning and spending money. Today, you'll learn how to create line graphs to answer questions about the cost of renting a kayak. Have you ever paddled a kayak or rented a boat? *Answers will vary.*

Some boat rental companies offer different prices depending on how long you rent the boat. At Dave's Kayak Rental, it costs $10 per hour to rent a kayak. Let's complete this price chart to see how much you pay for each number of hours at Dave's. Have your child complete the chart.

A

Hours	1	2	3	4	5	6	7	8
Cost ($)	10	20	30	40	50	60	70	80

At Bob's Kayak Rental, it costs $16 for the first hour. It costs $8 for every hour after the first hour. Let's complete the chart to see how much you pay for each number of hours at Bob's. Have your child complete the chart.

Hours	1	2	3	4	5	6	7	8
Cost ($)	16	24	32	40	48	56	64	72

Then, have your child use the charts to answer the questions.

Which company costs less if you kayak for 1 hour?	Which company costs less if you kayak for 3 hours?	Which company costs less if you kayak for 5 hours?
Dave's	*Dave's*	*Bob's*

Activity (B): Create a Double Line Graph

Now, we'll make a double line graph to compare the costs of renting from each place. We'll use a different color to graph each number pattern.

First, we'll make a line graph to show how much you pay if you rent from Dave's. Have your child use a colored pencil or marker to plot the ordered pairs from the chart for Dave's. Then, have her draw a straight line connecting the points and label the line with "Dave's" as shown.

Next, we'll make a line graph to show how much you pay if you rent from Bob's. We'll draw it on the same coordinate plane so we can compare the costs. Have your child use a different colored pencil or marker to plot the ordered pairs from the chart for Bob's. Then, have her draw a straight line connecting the points and label the line with "Bob's" as shown.

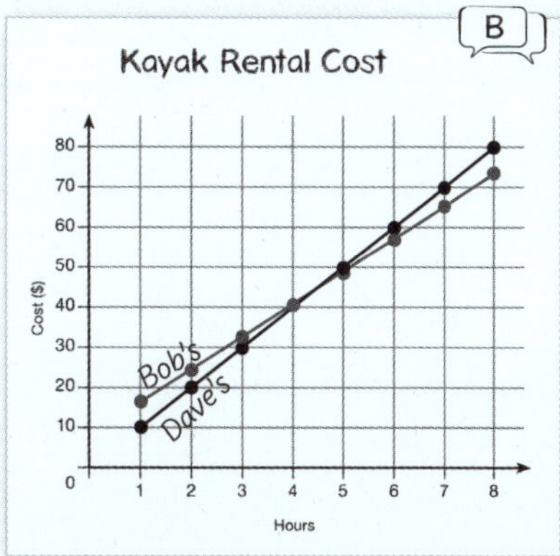

Does the line for Dave's have an upward or downward slope? *Upward.* **Does the line for Bob's have an upward or downward slope?** *Upward.* **You pay more money if you keep the kayak longer. So, both lines always slope upward.**

Which line is steeper and goes up more quickly? *Dave's.* **The line for Dave's goes up $10 each hour. The line for Bob's goes up only $8 each hour after the first hour. So, the line for Dave's slopes upward more quickly and is steeper.**

Why do the two lines intersect at the point (4,40)? *Sample answer: Both companies cost $40 for 4 hours.*

Activity (B): Use a Double Line Graph to Draw Conclusions

In part A, you used the charts to compare the costs for the two companies. We can also use the graph to compare the costs. Cover part A with a piece of paper.

Covering the chart requires your child to use the line graph to answer the questions. This nudges her to think more deeply about the real-world meaning of the lines on the graph.

Read aloud the first word problem: ***Which company costs less if you kayak for less than 4 hours?*** *Dave's.* **For less than 4 hours, the line for Dave's is below the line for Bob's. So, Dave's costs less.** Write "Dave's" in the blank.

Read aloud the next word problem: ***Which company costs less if you kayak for 4 hours?*** *Both cost the same amount.* **The lines for Dave's and Bob's intersect at 4 hours, because both companies cost the same amount.** Write "They cost the same." in the blank.

Read aloud the last word problem: ***Which company costs less if you kayak for more than 4 hours?*** *Bob's.* **For more than 4 hours, the line for Bob's is below the line for Dave's. So, Bob's costs less.** Write "Bob's" in the blank.

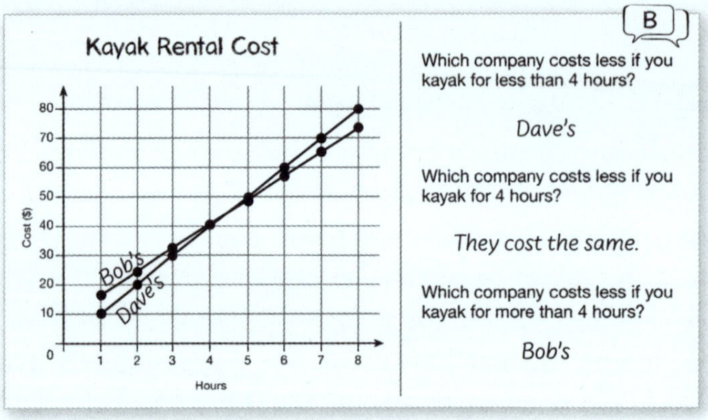

Independent Practice and Review

Have your child complete the Lesson 9.5 Practice and Review workbook pages.

Lesson 9.6
Enrichment (Optional)

Purpose	Materials
• Practice memory work • Appreciate how math can be used to answer real-life questions • Identify locations based on their latitude and longitude • Summarize what your child has learned and assess your child's progress	• *How Many Guinea Pigs Can Fit on a Plane?: Answers to Your Most Clever Math Questions*, by Laura Overdeck • World map or globe with latitude and longitude lines, optional

Warm-up: Review Memory Work

Quiz your child on any of the memory work items that he struggled with during this unit.

Math Picture Book: *How Many Guinea Pigs Can Fit on a Plane?*

Read pages 82-91 in *How Many Guinea Pigs Can Fit on a Plane?*

Enrichment Activity: Identify Latitude and Longitude

Latitude and longitude are like an imaginary coordinate plane over the whole world. If you know the latitude and longitude of a location, you can find where it is in the world, even if you've never heard of it.

Show your child a world map or globe with latitude and longitude lines. (Or, use the map on the following page instead.) **The dark horizontal line is called the Equator, and the dark vertical line is called the Prime Meridian. The place where these imaginary lines intersect is the origin for the latitude and longitude system.**

The longitude for a location is like the x-coordinate. It tells the horizontal distance from the Prime Meridian to the east or to the west. The latitude for a location is like the y-coordinate. It tells the vertical distance from the Equator to the north or south. The longitude lines in this map are curved, because they follow the curve of the earth.

Here's how to find the location for 150° east and 30° south. I put my finger on the origin and slide it east horizontally until I reach the 150° line. Then, I slide my finger downwards along the line until I hit the 30° line. What continent do I land on? *Australia.*

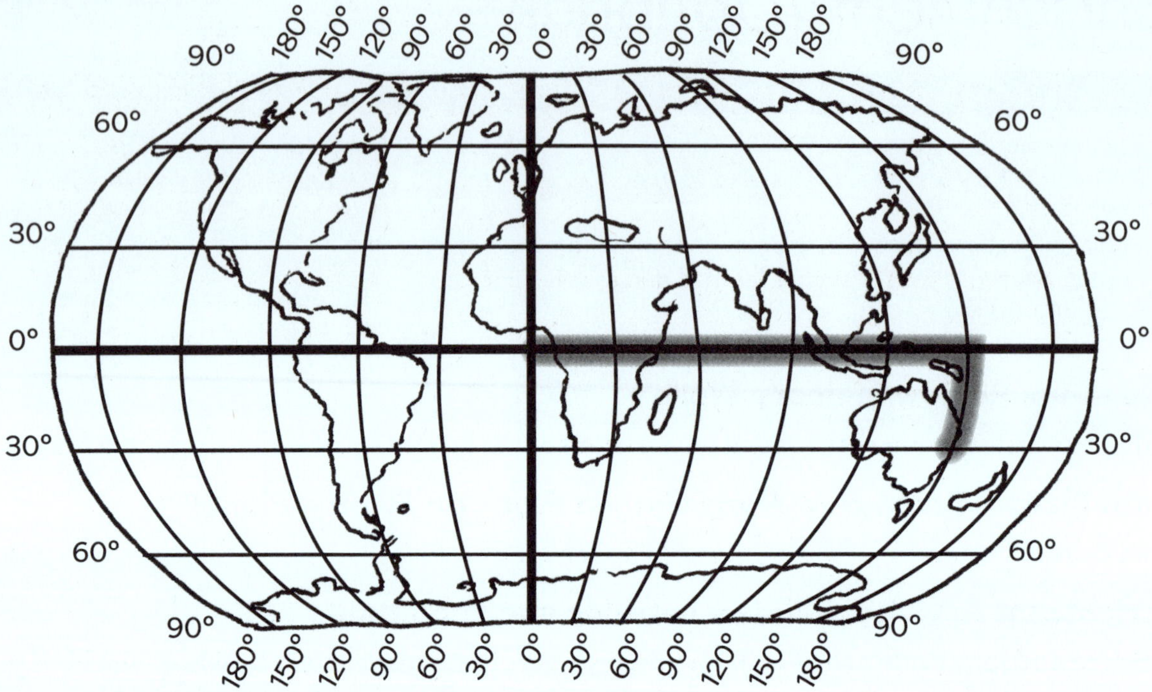

Have your child identify the continent for the following locations. Help your child with the continent names as needed.

- **120° east, 60° north.** *Asia.*
- **30° east, 30° south.** *Africa.*
- **120° west, 60° north.** *North America.*
- **60° west, 30° south.** *South America.*
- **90° west, 90° south.** *Antarctica.*

Then, use the map to find the approximate longitude and latitude for where you live.

> If your child is interested, search online to find your exact latitude and longitude. Explain that the decimal part of the numbers makes them more exact. For example: **Grand Rapids is at 42.9634° north and 85.6681° west. That's about 43° north and 86° west.**

Unit Wrap-Up

Have your child complete the Unit 9 Wrap-Up.

Unit 9 Answer Key

9.1 Practice

Hot and Cold (2-Player Game)

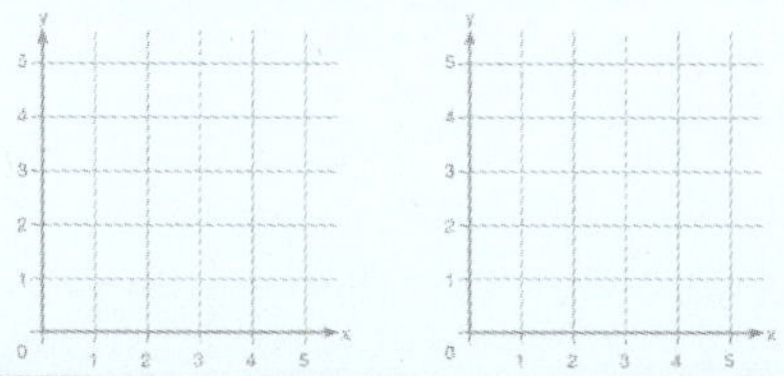

Practice Write the ordered pair that describes the location of each point.

Point	Ordered Pair
L	(3,2)
M	(4,5)
N	(1,0)
O	(5,3)
P	(0,4)

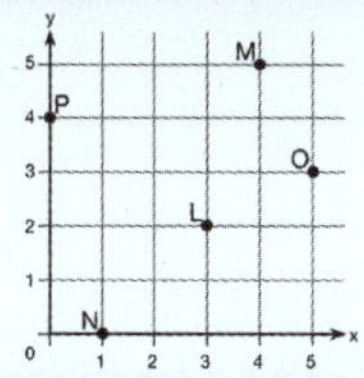

Draw and label each point in the correct location on the coordinate plane.

Point	Ordered Pair
Q	(2,4)
R	(4,2)
S	(0,3)
T	(3,0)
U	(5,1)

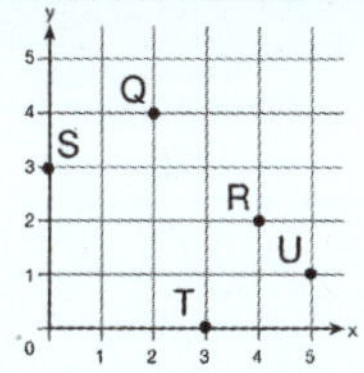

9.1 Review

Review Write each measurement as a fraction. Write your answers in simplest form.

8 mm = $\frac{8}{10} = \frac{4}{5}$ cm

8 in. = $\frac{8}{12} = \frac{2}{3}$ ft.

8 fl. oz. = 1 c.

10 min. = $\frac{10}{60} = \frac{1}{6}$ hr.

10 cm = $\frac{10}{100} = \frac{1}{10}$ m

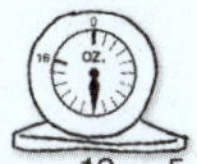

10 oz. = $\frac{10}{16} = \frac{5}{8}$ lbs.

Complete the missing numbers.

5 + 4 = 10 − 1

12 − 8 = 16 ÷ 4

10 + 30 = 8 × 5

20 − 8 = 6 × 2

100 ÷ 5 = 15 + 5

24 − 10 = 5 + 9

Find the product.

```
      4 2 5
  ×   2 1 3
    1,2 7 5
    4,2 5 0
+ 8 5,0 0 0
  9 0,5 2 5
```

Use the bar model to solve.

In a survey, 10 people chose green as their favorite color. These 10 people were $\frac{1}{6}$ of all the people who answered the survey. How many people answered the survey?

60 people

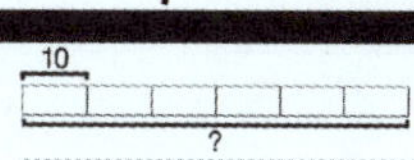

6 × 10 = 60

How many people did not choose green?

50 people

60 − 10 = 50

9.2 Practice

Practice Follow the directions to draw a line segment. Then, circle the word that best describes the slope of each line segment.

- Draw a point at (0,4).
- Draw a point at (5,4).
- Connect the points.

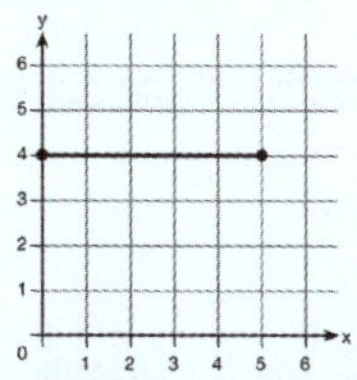

Upward | Downward | **(Horizontal)** | Vertical

- Draw a point at (1,2).
- Draw a point at (4,5).
- Connect the points.

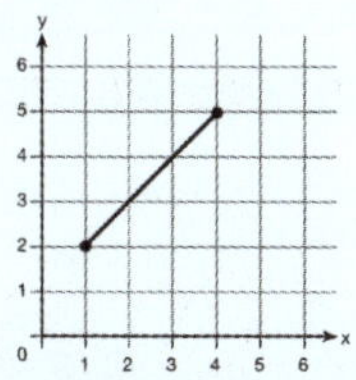

(Upward) | Downward | Horizontal | Vertical

- Draw a point at (1,5).
- Draw a point at (5,0).
- Connect the points.

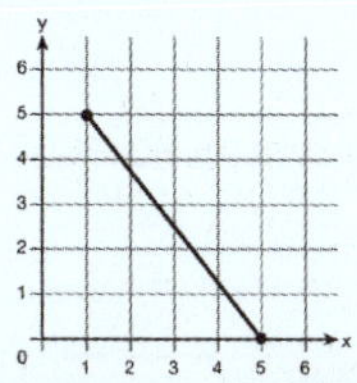

Upward | **(Downward)** | Horizontal | Vertical

- Draw a point at (2,0).
- Draw a point at (2,5).
- Connect the points.

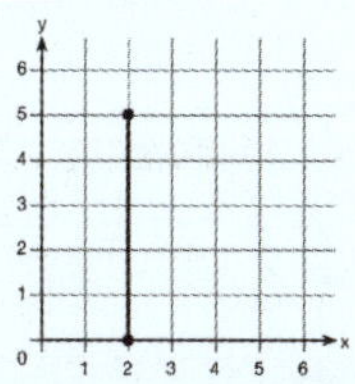

Upward | Downward | Horizontal | **(Vertical)**

9.2 Review

Review Complete.

$\frac{1}{3}$ hr. = 20 min.

$\frac{1}{2}$ m = 50 cm

$\frac{1}{6}$ ft. = 2 in.

$\frac{1}{4}$ m = 25 cm

$\frac{9}{10}$ L = 900 mL

$\frac{3}{4}$ lbs. = 12 oz.

Use long division to solve. Use the multiplication table to help.

```
        3 0
99 ) 2,9 8 5
   − 2 9 7 ↓
         1 5
       −   0
         1 5
```

	× 99
1	99
2	198
3	297
4	396
5	495
6	594
7	693
8	792
9	891

Use mental math to complete.

4 × 3 × 2 = 24

5 × 8 × 7 = 280

2 × 25 × 3 = 150

30 × 50 × 6 = 9,000

7 × 5 × 20 = 700

Use the bar model to solve.

Michael had $40. Then, he spent $\frac{4}{5}$ of his money on a video game. How much did the video game cost?

$32

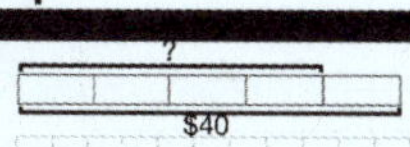

How much money did he have left?

$8

40 ÷ 5 = 8
8 × 4 = 32
40 − 32 = 8

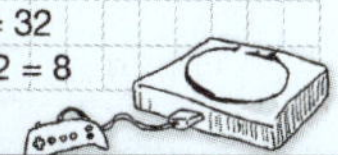

Unit 9 Answer Key

9.3 Practice

Practice: Lila sold lemonade at a lemonade stand for 5 days. Use the information in the chart to make a line graph. Choose a scale that fills most of the grid paper. Make sure to include a title for your graph and labels for the axes.

Day	Cups of Lemonade
1	15
2	25
3	21
4	40
5	32

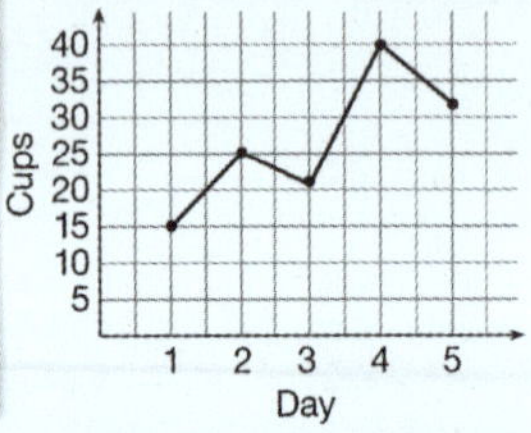

Circle the word that best describes the slope of each line segment.

Day 1 to Day 2	Day 2 to Day 3	Day 3 to Day 4	Day 4 to Day 5
(Upward)	Upward	(Upward)	Upward
Downward	(Downward)	Downward	(Downward)
Horizontal	Horizontal	Horizontal	Horizontal
Vertical	Vertical	Vertical	Vertical

Use the chart and line graph to answer the questions.

Which day did Lila sell the most cups of lemonade?

Day 4

Between which two consecutive days did sales increase the most?

Days 3 and 4

Which day did Lila sell the fewest cups of lemonade?

Day 1

Between which two consecutive days did sales decrease the most?

Days 4 and 5

9.3 Review

Review: Continue the patterns.

Rule + 5: 24, 29, 34, 39, 44, 49, 54, 59

Rule + 7: 24, 31, 38, 45, 52, 59, 66, 73

Rule − 8: 80, 72, 64, 56, 48, 40, 32, 24

Rule − 6: 80, 74, 68, 62, 56, 50, 44, 38

Complete.

$\frac{1}{8}$ of 80 = 10	$\frac{1}{5}$ of 100 = 20	$\frac{1}{3}$ of 60 = 20
$\frac{5}{8}$ of 80 = 50	$\frac{3}{5}$ of 100 = 60	$\frac{2}{3}$ of 60 = 40
$\frac{1}{4}$ of 100 = 25	$\frac{1}{6}$ of 30 = 5	$\frac{1}{10}$ of 150 = 15
$\frac{3}{4}$ of 100 = 75	$\frac{3}{6}$ of 30 = 15	$\frac{2}{10}$ of 150 = 30

Use bar models to solve.

Evie bought a leotard and ballet slippers. The leotard cost $24. It cost $\frac{3}{4}$ as much as the ballet slippers cost. How much did the ballet slippers cost?

$32

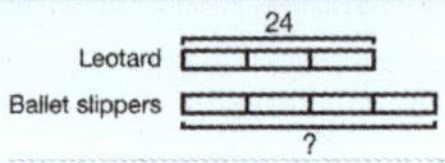

How much did she pay in all?

$56

24 ÷ 3 = 8
8 × 4 = 32   32 + 24 = 56

9.4 Practice

Practice: Use the information to complete the chart. Then, use the chart to make a line graph and answer the questions.

Krispin's family buys a bag of dog food that weighs 30 pounds. His dog eats 5 pounds of dog food per week.

Week	Pounds of Dog Food Left
0	30
1	25
2	20
3	15
4	10
5	5
6	0

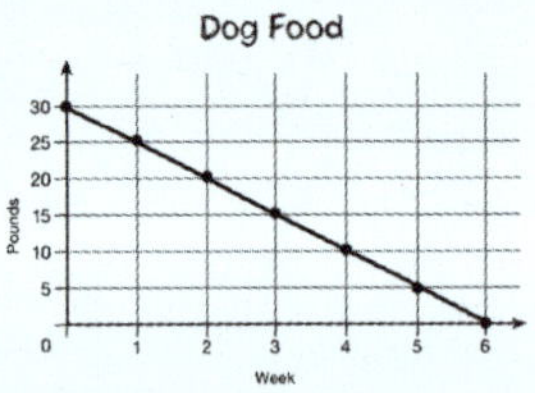

Does the graph slope upward or downward?

downward

How many pounds of dog food are left after week 4?

10 pounds

How many weeks does 1 bag of dog food last for Krispin's dog?

6 weeks

Katya has already read 10 pages in her library book. She plans to read 20 pages per day.

Day	Pages Read
0	10
1	30
2	50
3	70
4	90
5	110

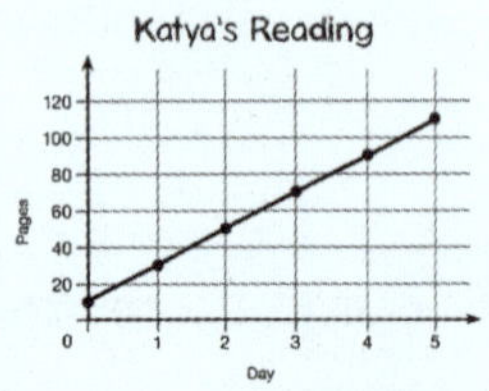

Does the graph slope upward or downward?

upward

Which day will Katya read page 70 in her book?

Day 3

Katya's book has 150 pages. After day 5, how many more days will it take Katya to finish her book?

2 more days

9.4 Review

Review: Write each mixed number as a fraction. Write each fraction as a mixed number.

$1\frac{3}{8} = \frac{11}{8}$	$2\frac{1}{12} = \frac{25}{12}$	$3\frac{7}{10} = \frac{37}{10}$	$6\frac{1}{2} = \frac{13}{2}$
$\frac{7}{6} = 1\frac{1}{6}$	$\frac{17}{6} = 2\frac{5}{6}$	$\frac{49}{10} = 4\frac{9}{10}$	$\frac{25}{8} = 3\frac{1}{8}$

Use the box method to find the product.

	20	8
90	1,800	720
6	120	48

1,800
720
120
+ 48
2,688

28 × 96 = 2,688

Round to the underlined digit.

8.972 ≈ 9
8.972 ≈ 9.0
8.972 ≈ 8.97
3,482,906 ≈ 3,000,000
3,482,906 ≈ 3,483,000
3,482,906 ≈ 3,500,000

Find the volume of each solid. Each solid is made of centimeter cubes.

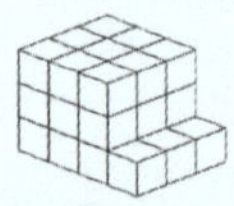

Volume: 30 cubic cm

Volume: 26 cubic cm

Volume: 14 cubic cm

Solve. Write your answers in simplest form.

Graham had a ribbon that was 30 inches long. He used 25 inches of the ribbon to make a craft. What fraction of the ribbon did he use?

$\frac{25}{30} = \frac{5}{6}$ of the ribbon

Kascia spent 40 minutes playing the drums. What fraction of an hour did she spend playing the drums?

$\frac{40}{60} = \frac{2}{3}$ of an hour

Unit 9 Answer Key

9.5 Practice

Practice Use the information to complete the charts.

Week	0	1	2	3	4	5	6	7
Savings ($)	15	18	21	24	27	30	33	36

Week	0	1	2	3	4	5	6	7
Savings ($)	0	6	12	18	24	30	36	42

Use the charts to create a line graph that shows how much money Connor and Rylie have each week. Label the lines with the person's name. Then, answer the questions.

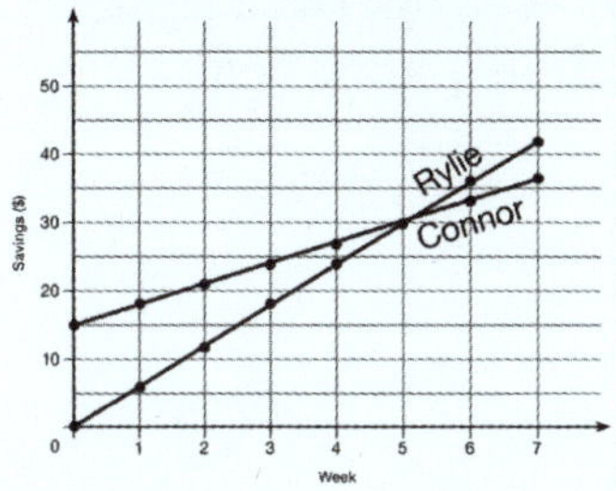

Which weeks does Connor have more money than Rylie?

weeks 1, 2, 3, and 4

Which week do Connor and Rylie have the same amount of money?

week 5

Which weeks does Rylie have more money than Connor?

weeks 6 and 7

9.5 Review

Review Write each decimal as a fraction or mixed number. Write each fraction or mixed number as a decimal.

$4.29 = 4\frac{29}{100}$ | $0.351 = \frac{351}{1,000}$ | $6.07 = 6\frac{7}{100}$

$2\frac{6}{10} = 2.6$ | $3\frac{207}{1,000} = 3.207$ | $\frac{36}{100} = 0.36$

Complete the blanks with fractions. Write the fractions in simplest form.

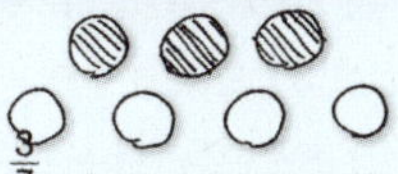

$\frac{3}{7}$ of the circles have stripes.

$\frac{4}{7}$ of the circles do not have stripes.

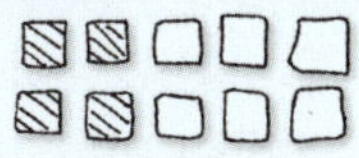

$\frac{2}{5}$ of the squares have stripes.

$\frac{3}{5}$ of the squares do not have stripes.

Complete the chart.

Words	Standard Form
eight billion	8,000,000,000
eight billion two hundred seventy-eight million	8,278,000,000
eight billion two hundred seventy-eight million three hundred ninety-four thousand	8,278,394,000

Use bar models to solve.

Emilia has $18. She has $\frac{2}{3}$ as much money as her brother. How much money does her brother have?

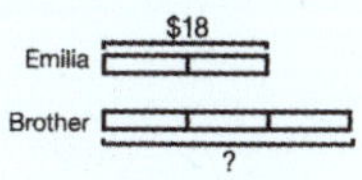

$18 \div 2 = 9$

$9 \times 3 = 27$

Emilia's brother has $27

9.6 Unit Wrap-Up A

Unit Wrap-Up Use the words and phrases in the word bank to fill the blanks. You will use each word or phrase once.

(4,2) is called an ordered pair.

In (4,2), the 4 is the x-coordinate.

In (4,2), the 2 is the y-coordinate.

The point (0,0) is called the origin.

The horizontal axis is called the x-axis.

The vertical axis is called the y-axis.

Word bank: x-axis, y-axis, origin, ordered pair, x-coordinate, y-coordinate

Write the ordered pair that describes the location of each point.

Point	Ordered Pair
L	(5,2)
M	(1,4)
N	(3,0)
O	(0,2)

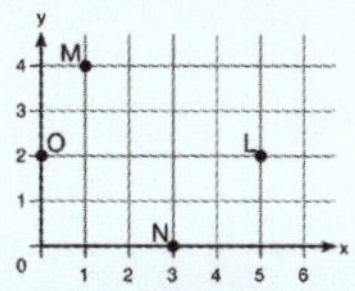

Harrison's family keeps chickens and collects eggs each day. Use the information in the chart to make a line graph. Choose a scale that fills most of the grid paper. Make sure to include a title for your graph and labels for the axes.

Day	Number of Eggs
1	8
2	12
3	11
4	7
5	13

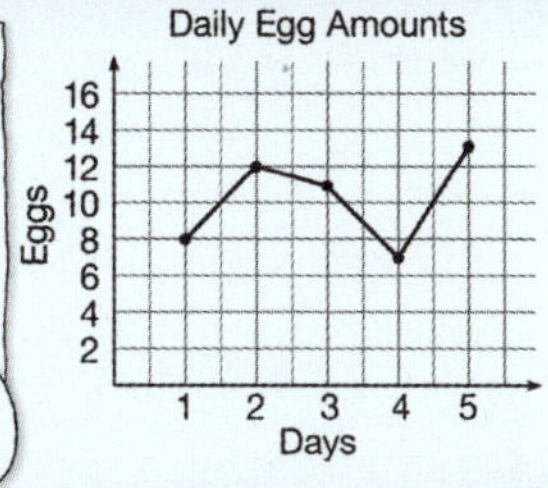

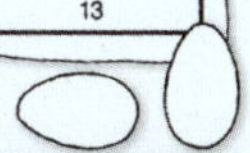

9.6 Unit Wrap-Up B

Unit Wrap-Up Use the information to complete the charts.

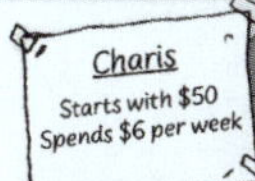

Week	0	1	2	3	4	5	6	7
Savings ($)	50	44	38	32	26	20	14	8

Week	0	1	2	3	4	5	6	7
Savings ($)	10	16	22	28	34	40	46	52

Use the charts to create a line graph that shows how much money Nikola and Charis have each week. Label the lines with the person's name. Then, answer the questions.

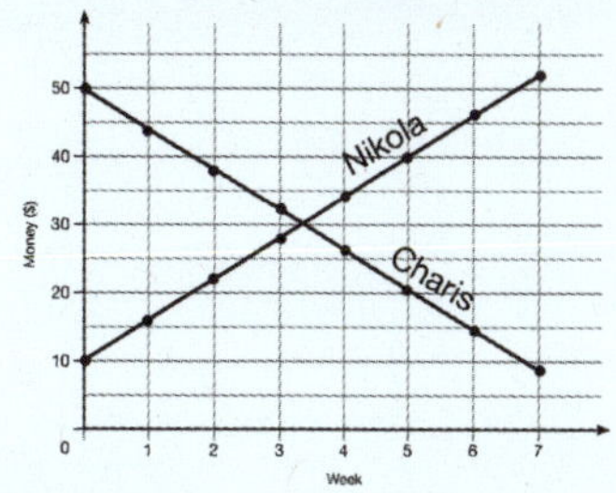

Does Charis' line slope upward or downward?

downward

Does Nikola's line slope upward or downward?

upward

Which weeks does Charis have more money than Nikola?

weeks 1, 2, and 3

Which weeks does Nikola have more money than Charis?

weeks 4, 5, 6, and 7

Unit 9 Checkpoint

What to Expect at the End of Unit 9

By the end of Unit 9, most children will be able to do the following:

- Identify and draw points on the coordinate plane. Some children will occasionally confuse the x-coordinate and y-coordinate.
- Identify the slope of lines on the coordinate plane as upward, downward, horizontal, or vertical.
- Create and interpret line graphs based on real-world data.
- Make a table of values based on a real-life number pattern, plot the resulting ordered pairs, and use the graph to draw conclusions about the number pattern. Some children will still be confused about how to draw conclusions from a line graph only.

Is Your Child Ready to Move on?

In Unit 10, your child will learn how to multiply fractions. Your child does not need to have fully mastered plotting points on the coordinate plane and creating line graphs before moving on.

Unit 10
Multiply Fractions

Overview

Your child will learn how to multiply fractions in order to find a fraction of a fraction. He will also reason about fraction multiplication, compare products, and learn how to multiply to find the area of rectangles with fractional sides.

This short unit focuses on multiplying fractions with a value less than 1. Your child will learn how to multiply with fractions, whole numbers, and mixed numbers in Unit 11. He'll also learn how to apply fraction multiplication to a greater variety of situations. Then, in *Sixth Grade Math with Confidence*, your child will learn how to use cancelling to solve more complex fraction multiplication problems.

What Your Child Will Learn

In this unit, your child will learn to:

- Multiply to find a fraction of a fraction
- Reason about fraction multiplication and compare products of fraction multiplication
- Solve fraction multiplication word problems
- Multiply to find the area of rectangles with fractional lengths

Lesson List

Lesson 10.1	Find a Fraction of a Fraction
Lesson 10.2	Multiply Fractions by Fractions
Lesson 10.3	Fraction Multiplication Word Problems
Lesson 10.4	Compare Products of Fractions
Lesson 10.5	Find Fractional Areas
Lesson 10.6	Enrichment (Optional)

Extra Materials Needed for Unit 10

- 3 paper half-circles
- Scissors
- Paper square foot
- 10 in. by 8 in. paper rectangle
- Rectangular object whose length and width are less than 1 foot (such as a book or picture)
- For optional Enrichment Lesson:
  - × *How Many Guinea Pigs Can Fit on a Plane?: Answers to Your Most Clever Math Questions*, by Laura Overdeck. Feiwel & Friends, 2017.
  - × Rectangular chocolate bar with lines that split it into fractional parts (such as a Hershey bar or Cadbury Dairy Milk bar)

See Lesson 10.1 for directions on how to prepare the paper half-circles. See Lesson 10.5 for directions on how to prepare the paper square foot and 10 in. by 8 in. rectangle.

Teaching Math with Confidence: Developing Conceptual Understanding of Fraction Multiplication

Over the past few years, your child has learned to find fractions of many different things: pizzas, chocolate bars, measurement units, distances on the number line, sets of objects, and more. In this unit, your child will learn that we can also find fractions of fractions. Just as you can find 1/2 of a whole pizza, you can also find 1/2 of part of a pizza.

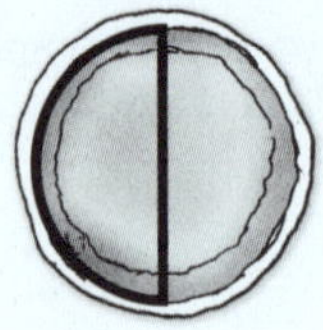

1/2 of 1 pizza.

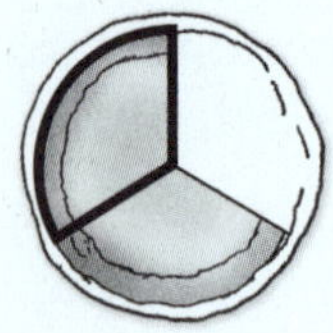

1/2 of 2/3 of a pizza.

Children often struggle to understand what it means to find a fraction of a fraction. That's because finding a fraction of a fraction requires children to toggle between two different frames of reference. For example, in Lesson 10.1, your child will fold sheets of paper to find 3/4 of 1/2. In this problem, he first needs to "zoom in" on 1/2 of the paper and find three-fourths of this part. Then, once he's identified the correct amount, he needs to "zoom out" and write this amount as a fraction of the whole paper.

3/4 of 1/2 of the paper equals 3/8 of the whole paper.

Once your child understands this foundational concept, you'll teach him how to multiply to solve these problems. For example, to find 3/4 of 1/2, we multiply 3/4 × 1/2. We multiply the numerators and denominators separately and simplify if needed. Just as in Unit 5, the product's numerator tells the number of parts, while the product's denominator tells how many equal parts the whole was split into.

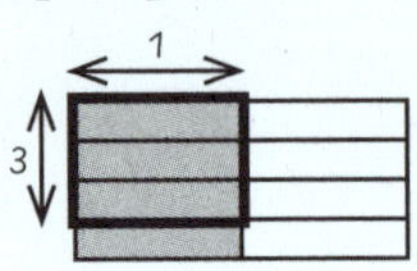

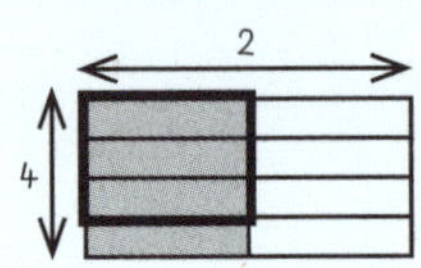

$$\frac{3}{4} \times \frac{1}{2} = \frac{3 \times 1}{4 \times 2} = \frac{3}{8}$$

Number of parts (numerator)

How many parts the whole was split into (denominator)

Your child will study "part of a part" problems in many different contexts in his math studies in the next few years: decimals, percentages, ratios, proportions and more. As you teach this unit, make sure to keep the focus on understanding the conceptual meaning of fraction-of-a-fraction problems (and not on zipping through the arithmetic). You'll find drawing exercises, real-world applications, and comparison questions throughout the unit to nudge your child to think deeply about this fundamental concept.

Lesson 10.1
Find a Fraction of a Fraction

Purpose	Materials
• Use hands-on materials to concretely find a fraction of a fraction • Understand that you can find a fractional part of a fraction • Use pictures to find a fractional part of a fraction	• 3 paper half-circles • Scissors • Highlighter, optional

Memory Work

- **What do we call the top number in a fraction?** *The numerator.*
- **What does the numerator tell?** *The number of parts.*
- **What do we call the bottom number in a fraction?** *The denominator.*
- **What does the denominator tell?** *How many equal parts the whole was split into.*

This lesson helps your child develop conceptual understanding of what it means to find a fraction of a fraction. She will learn how to use fraction multiplication to solve these problems in Lesson 10.2. See the Unit 10 **Teaching Math with Confidence** for more on why it's important to develop both conceptual understanding and procedural fluency with fraction multiplication.

You'll need 3 paper half-circles for the hands-on warm-up for this lesson. To make the half-circles, trace a round object (like a bowl or cup) to create 2 whole circles. Cut out each whole circle and then cut it in half.

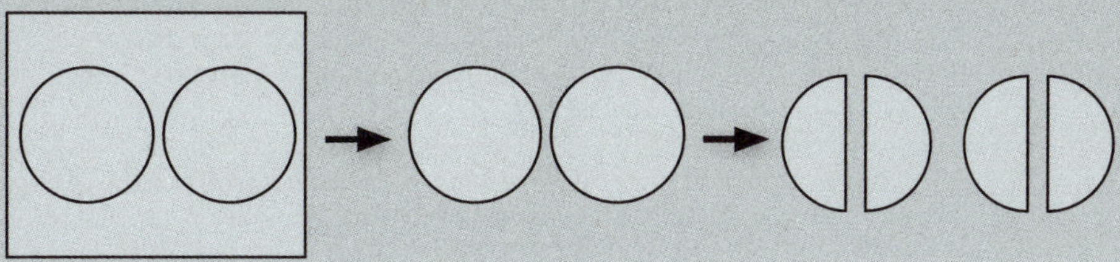

Warm-up (A): Cut Paper Circles to Find a Fraction of a Fraction

Today, you'll learn how to find a fractional part of a fraction. We'll warm up by cutting paper circles into fractional parts to match the problems in part A.

Give your child a half-circle. **Let's pretend we have half of a pizza left over. You decide to eat one-half of the leftover amount.** Have your child cut the half-circle into 2 roughly-equal parts. **If you eat one of these parts, what fraction of the whole pizza do you eat?** *One-fourth.* Write 1/4 as shown. Outline the matching part of the printed pizza.

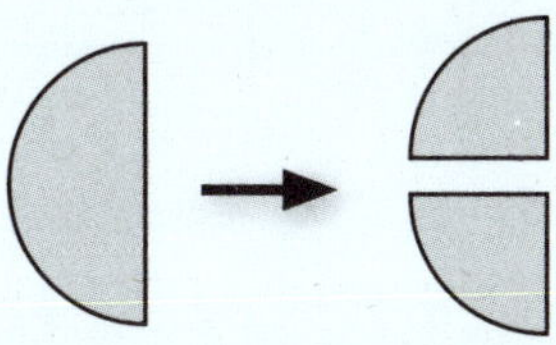

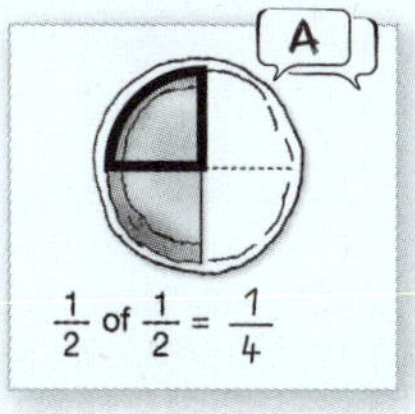

Give your child another half-circle. **This time, you decide to eat one-third of the leftover**

amount. Have your child cut the half-circle into 3 roughly-equal parts. **If you eat one of these parts, what fraction of the whole pizza do you eat?** *One-sixth.* Write 1/6 as shown. Outline the matching part of the printed pizza.

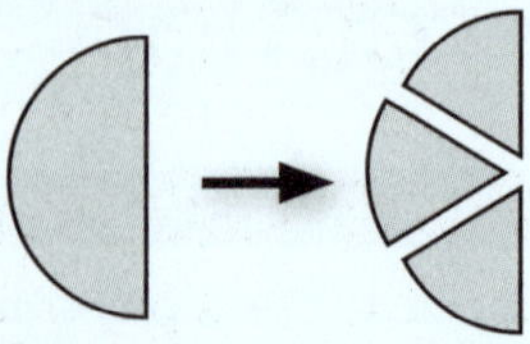

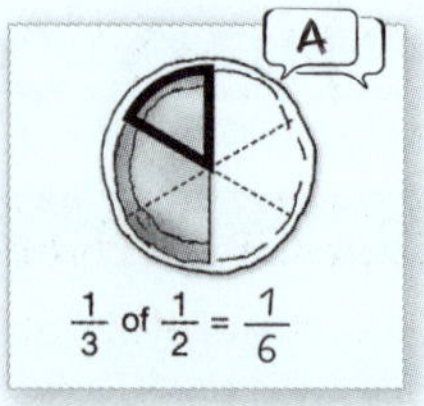

Give your child another half-circle. **This time, you decide to eat one-fourth of the leftover amount.** Have your child cut the half-circle into 4 roughly-equal parts. **If you eat one of these parts, what fraction of the whole pizza do you eat?** *One-eighth.* Write 1/8 as shown. Outline the matching part of the printed pizza.

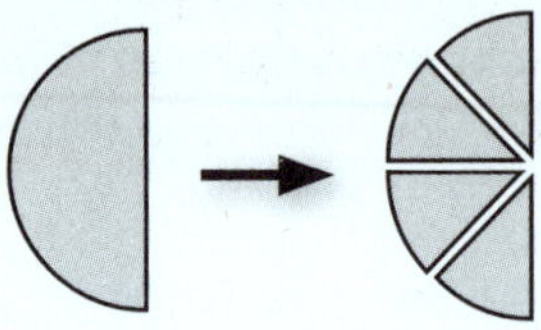

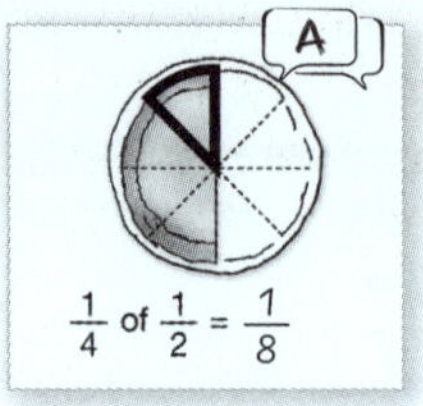

Activity (B): Fold a Paper Rectangle to Find a Fraction of a Fraction

Earlier in the year you solved problems like "What's three-fourths of 8 marbles?" You split the 8 marbles into 4 equal groups and then you took 3 of the groups. Today, you'll learn how to find a fraction of a fraction. Instead of finding a fraction of a whole number of objects, you'll find a fraction of a fractional part.

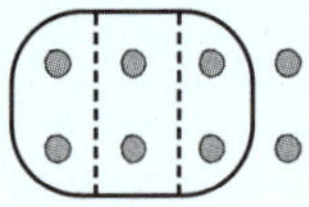

$\frac{3}{4}$ of 8 = 6

To find 3/4 of 8 marbles, you split the 8 marbles into 4 groups and take 3 of the groups. Finding a fraction of a fraction is similar.

We'll use sheet cakes to learn how to find a fraction of a fraction today. Have you ever eaten a sheet cake from a bakery? *Answers will vary.* **Sheet cakes are rectangular cakes that feed a lot of people. People often have part of a sheet cake left over after an event.** Have your child read the text box aloud.

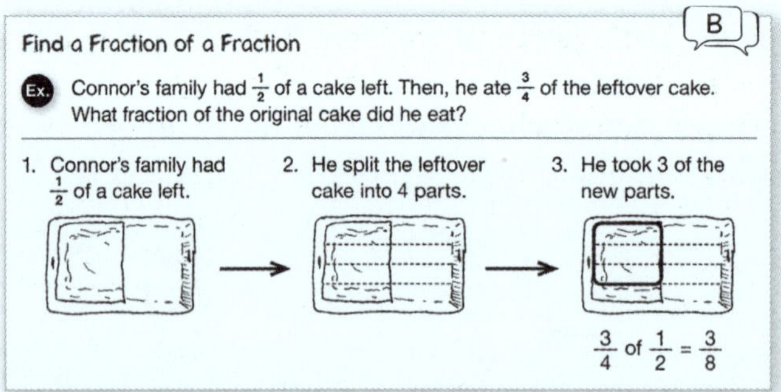

Let's model this problem with paper. We'll use one piece of paper to stand for the whole sheet cake. How much sheet cake is left over? *One-half of the cake.* Fold a piece of paper in half to match the diagram. Have your child color the left side of the paper to stand for the leftover cake. (A quick scribble is fine.)

Connor eats three-fourths of the leftover cake, so let's split the leftover cake into fourths. Fold the paper into fourths in the opposite direction.

How many of the new fourths does Connor take? *3.* Outline 3 of the fourths as shown. **What fraction of the whole cake is this?** *Three-eighths.* If your child's not sure, point out that the fold lines split the whole cake into 8 equal parts, and that Connor takes 3 of them.

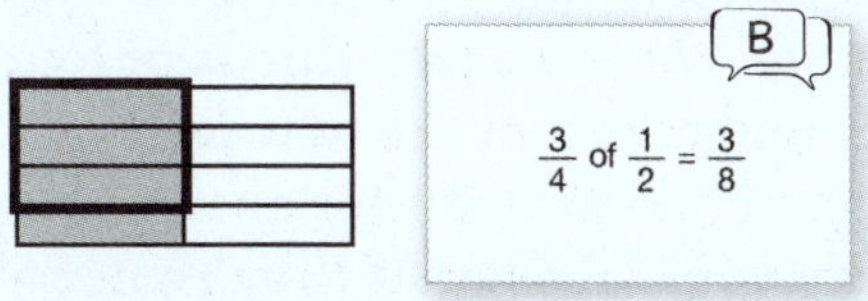

Point to the written equation. **We read this equation as "three-fourths of one-half equals three-eighths."**

If your child has trouble with this, fold the blank half of the paper underneath so that you can only see the "leftover" cake. **We need to find three-fourths of the leftover cake, so we zoom in to look at just the leftover cake.** Outline 3/4 of the visible part of the paper.

Then, we zoom out and think about what fraction of the whole cake we have. Unfold the paper so your child can see the whole piece of paper. **This amount is three-eighths of the whole cake.**

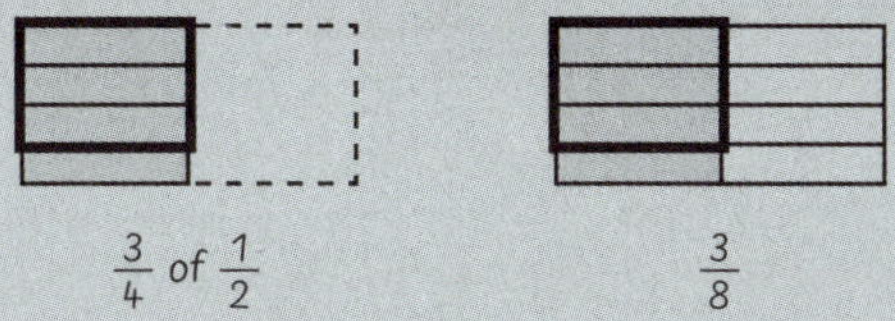

3/4 of the leftover part equals 3/8 of the original whole cake.

Read aloud the first practice problem: ***One-fourth of one-fifth is what?***

- **We want to find one-fourth of one-fifth of the rectangle. We'll follow the same 3 steps as in the example.**
- **First, we identify how much we *have*. What fraction of the rectangle is colored?** *One-fifth.* Highlight or circle 1/5.
- **Second, we *split* the amount we have into smaller fractional parts to match the denominator of the first fraction. We want one-fourth of one-fifth, so we split the rectangle into fourths in the other direction.** Point to the dotted lines that split the rectangle into fourths.
- **Last, we *take* the number of new fractional parts that we want. We want one-fourth of one-fifth, so we take 1 of the new fourths.** Point to the outlined section of the rectangle.
- **What fraction of the whole rectangle do we take?** *One-twentieth.* Write 1/20 as the answer.

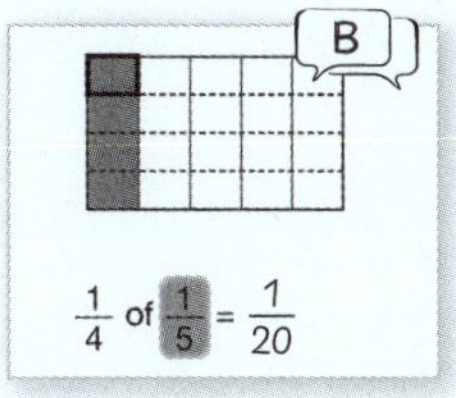

Have your child complete the rest of the practice problems in the same way. Encourage her to think "have, split, take" to help break the problems into steps. Make sure she highlights or circles the starting amount before drawing horizontal lines and outlining the matching part of the rectangle.

- For 1/3 of 4/5, explain as needed that your child should outline 1 of the new thirds (and not 1 of the fifteenths): **We want one-third of four-fifths. So, we split the four-fifths into 3 equal parts and take 1 of the new parts.**
- For 2/3 of 4/5, explain as needed that your child should outline 2 of the new thirds (and not 2 of the fifteenths): **We want two-thirds of four-fifths. So, we split the four-fifths into 3 equal parts and take 2 of the new parts.**
- For 2/3 of 1/4, remind your child to write her answer in simplest form. **From this point forward, always simplify your answers if they're not already in simplest form.**

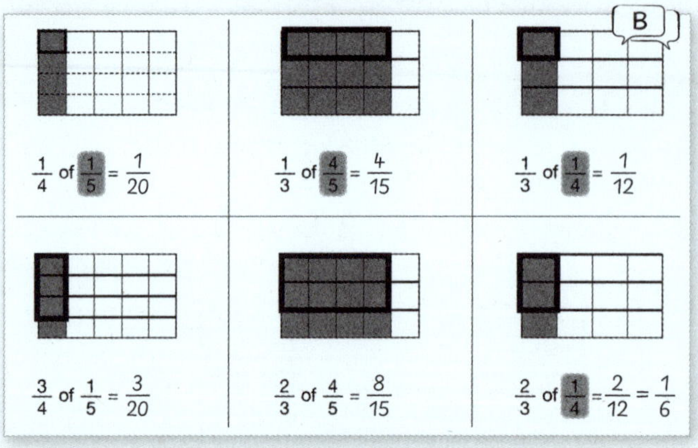

To make these problems more concrete, fold and color pieces of paper to match them as in the example problem discussion.

In the next lesson, your child will learn how to multiply fractions to find a fraction of a fraction. For now, encourage her to use the pictures to visually identify the fractional parts. If your child notices that she can multiply the numerators and denominators to find the answers, praise her for noticing the pattern. Allow her to use the pattern to complete the products, but make sure to also discuss how the product matches the meaning of the problem.

Independent Practice and Review

Have your child complete the Lesson 10.1 Practice and Review workbook pages.

Lesson 10.2
Multiply Fractions by Fractions

Purpose	Materials
• Practice using pictures to visually find a fraction of a fraction • Multiply fractions by fractions	• Fraction cards • Highlighter, optional

Memory Work
- **What do we call the result when we multiply two numbers?** *The product.*
- **What do we call the numbers in a multiplication equation that we multiply together?** *Factors.*

In this lesson, your child will learn how to multiply a fraction by a fraction. The numerators and denominators in the fractions are small numbers so that your child can focus on the conceptual meaning of fraction multiplication and not get bogged down by the arithmetic.

Warm-up (A): Practice Finding a Fraction of a Fraction

In the last lesson, you learned how to find a fraction of a fraction. Read aloud the first problem: ***One-fourth of three-fourths is what?* We want to find one-fourth of three-fourths of the rectangle. Let's practice following the same 3 steps as in the last lesson.**

- **First, we identify how much we *have*. What fraction of the rectangle is colored?** *Three-fourths.* Highlight or circle 3/4.
- **Second, we *split* the amount we have into smaller fractional parts to match the denominator of the first fraction. We want one-fourth of three-fourths, so we split the rectangle into fourths in the other direction.** Draw lines to split the rectangle into fourths as shown.
- **Last, we *take* the number of fractional parts that we want. We want one-fourth of three-fourths, so we take 1 of the new fourths.** Outline the section of the rectangle shown below.
- **What fraction of the whole rectangle do we take?** *Three-sixteenths.* Write 3/16 as the answer.

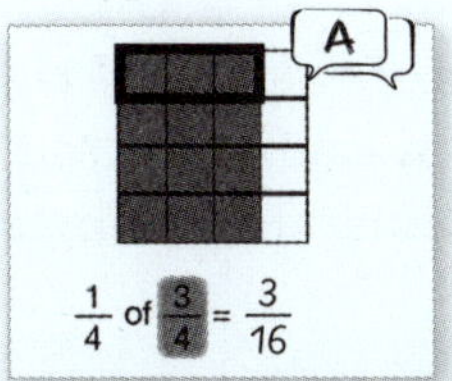

Have your child complete the rest of the practice problems in the same way. Encourage him to think "have, split, take" to help break the problems into steps.

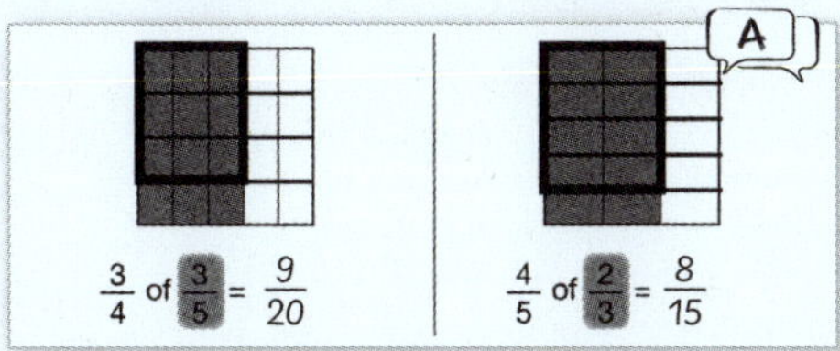

What relationship do you notice between the numerators in each equation? *Sample answer: The third numerator is the product of the first and second numerators.* If your child isn't sure, point out this relationship.

$\frac{1}{4}$ of $\frac{3}{4}$ = $\frac{3}{16}$	$\frac{3}{4}$ of $\frac{3}{5}$ = $\frac{9}{20}$	$\frac{4}{5}$ of $\frac{2}{3}$ = $\frac{8}{15}$

$1 \times 3 = 3$. $3 \times 3 = 9$. $4 \times 2 = 8$.

What relationship do you notice between the denominators in each equation? *Sample answer: The third denominator is the product of the first and second denominators.* If your child isn't sure, point out this relationship.

$\frac{1}{4}$ of $\frac{3}{4}$ = $\frac{3}{16}$	$\frac{3}{4}$ of $\frac{3}{5}$ = $\frac{9}{20}$	$\frac{4}{5}$ of $\frac{2}{3}$ = $\frac{8}{15}$

$4 \times 4 = 16$. $4 \times 5 = 20$. $5 \times 3 = 15$.

Activity (B): Multiply a Fraction by a Fraction

In math, the word "of" often means *multiply*. For example, if I want 3 boxes *of* 4 cupcakes, I multiply 3 times 4 to find how many cupcakes I get. If I set up 6 rows *of* 8 chairs, I multiply 6 times 8 to find how many chairs I set up. If I want to find three-fifths *of* seven-eighths, I multiply three-fifths times seven-eighths.

In the warm-up, you drew lines to visually find a fraction of a fraction. We can also use multiplication to find a fraction of a fraction. Today, you'll learn how. Have your child read the steps in the text box aloud.

Multiply a Fraction by a Fraction

In math, "of" usually means multiply. To find a fraction of a fraction, multiply the fractions.

1. Multiply the numerators.
2. Multiply the denominators.
3. Simplify if needed.

Ex. Aria's family had $\frac{7}{8}$ of a cake left. Then, she ate $\frac{3}{5}$ of the leftover cake. What fraction of the whole cake did she eat?

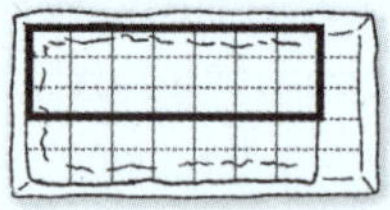

$$\frac{3}{5} \times \frac{7}{8} = \frac{3 \times 7}{5 \times 8} = \frac{21}{40}$$

Read aloud the example problem. **Imagine we had seven-eighths of a sheet cake left. If you ate three-fifths of the leftover cake, would you eat a little or a lot of cake?** *A lot.* **I think Aria might get a stomachache!**

Look at the picture. How many slices of cake did Aria eat? *21.* **How do you know?** *3 times 7 is 21.* **There were 7 slices of cake left in each row, and Aria ate 3 of the rows. So, Aria ate 21 slices of cake.** Point to the answer's numerator. **3 times 7 equals 21, so 21 is the numerator for the answer.**

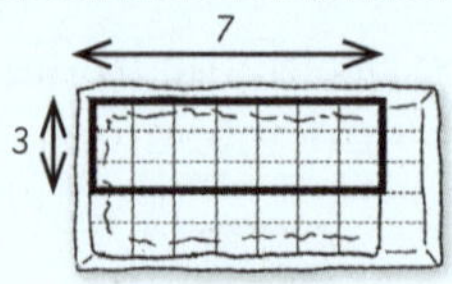

$$\frac{3}{5} \times \frac{7}{8} = \frac{3 \times 7}{5 \times 8} = \frac{21}{40}$$ ← Number of parts

How many slices was the whole cake cut into? *40.* **How do you know?** *5 times 8 is 40.* **The whole cake was split into 40 parts, so each slice is one-fortieth of the cake.** Point to the answer's denominator. **5 times 8 equals 40, so 40 is the denominator for the answer.**

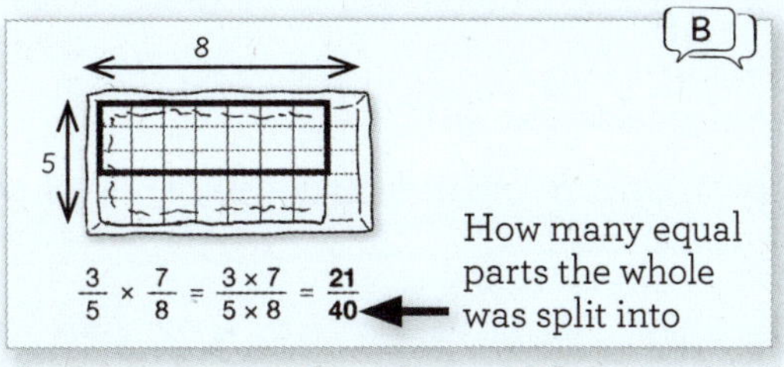

Most kids find multiplying fractions simpler than adding and subtracting fractions. You don't need any common denominators or equivalent fractions. All you have to do is multiply the numerators, multiply the denominators, and then simplify if needed.

Have your child multiply to complete the practice problems. Remind him to simplify his answers if needed. Outline the matching part of the cake.

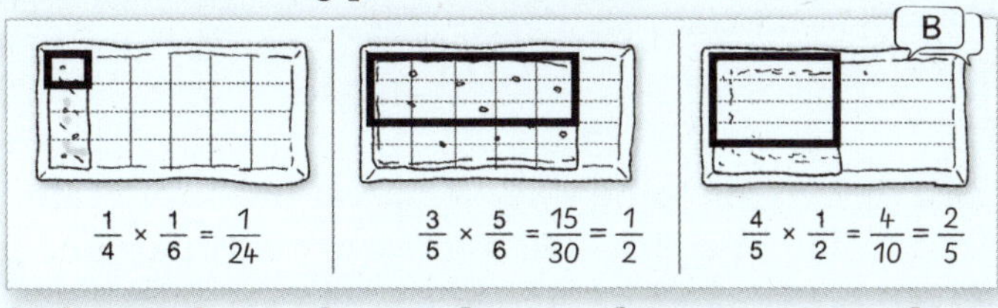

When we multiply whole numbers, the product is always *greater* than the factors. For example, 2 times 3 is 6, which is greater than both 2 and 3.

When we multiply fractions less than 1 whole, the product is always *less* than either of the factors. Since we're finding a fraction of a fraction, the answer is less than either fraction. Have your child look at the completed practice problems and confirm that the product is less than either factor.

Activity (C): Play Too Much Cake!

Play Too Much Cake! As you play, frame each fraction multiplication problem in terms of cake (like the example problem in part B). For example, if you turn over 1/3 and 4/5: **Four-fifths of the cake was left, and I ate one-third of it. One-third times four-fifths is four-fifteenths, so I ate four-fifteenths of the whole cake.** Sketch rectangles to model the problems if needed.

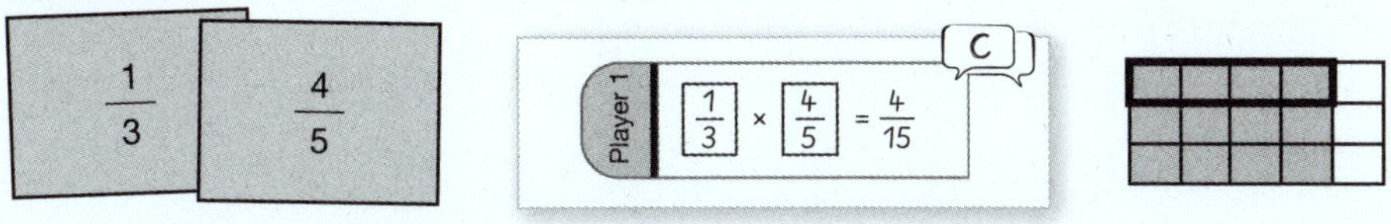

Sample play and matching rectangle sketch.

This game uses only the fraction cards with low denominators so that your child doesn't have to simplify fractions with large numbers.

Too Much Cake!

Materials: 1/2, 1/4, 2/4, 3/4, 1/5, 2/5, 3/5, 4/5, 1/6, 2/6, 3/6, 4/6, 5/6 cards from set of fraction cards (Blackline Master 9)

Object of the Game: Score more points than the other player by creating greater products.

Shuffle the cards and place the stack face down on the table.

Player 1 flips over the top 2 cards from the stack of cards. He writes the fractions in the first blank multiplication problem on his score card, finds the product, and simplifies the answer if possible.

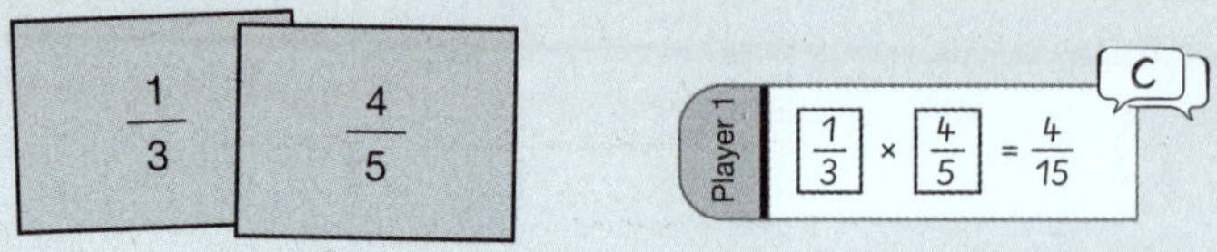

Then, Player 2 takes a turn in the same way. Whoever has the greater product wins a point. (Use logical reasoning or equivalent fractions to compare the fractions.)

Repeat until you have completed 3 rounds. Whoever has more points wins.

Independent Practice and Review

Have your child complete the Lesson 10.2 Practice and Review workbook pages.

Lesson 10.3
Fraction Multiplication Word Problems

Purpose	Materials
• Use fraction bars to understand the meaning of the answers to fraction multiplication problems • Write and solve multiplication equations for fraction-of-a-fraction word problems	• Fraction bars

Memory Work

- **What do we call the horizontal axis?** *The x-axis.*
- **What do we call the vertical axis?** *The y-axis.*
- **What do we call the (0,0) point?** *The origin.*
- **What is an ordered pair?** *A pair of numbers that identify the location of a point.*
- **In an ordered pair, what do we call the first number?** *The x-coordinate.* **What does it tell?** *The point's horizontal distance.*
- **In an ordered pair, what do we call the second number?** *The y-coordinate.* **What does it tell?** *The point's vertical distance.*

Warm-up (A): Use Fraction Bars to Understand Fraction Multiplication

In the last lesson, you learned that we can multiply to find a fraction of a fraction. We used rectangles to understand what the problems meant. We can also use fraction bars to understand the answers to fraction multiplication problems.

Using a different model helps your child think about fraction multiplication more flexibly and develop a deeper understanding of what the answers mean. If she finds this new model confusing, it's fine to draw rectangle sketches or simply have her perform the calculations instead.

In the first problem, we want to find one-half of two-fifths. How much do we have? *Two-fifths.* Arrange 2 fifth-bars on the table as shown. **Split the fraction bars into 2 equal parts.** *Child separates the fraction bars as shown.* **Take 1 of the parts.** *Child takes 1 fifth-bar.* **How much did you take?** *One-fifth.* Have your child multiply to complete the problem.

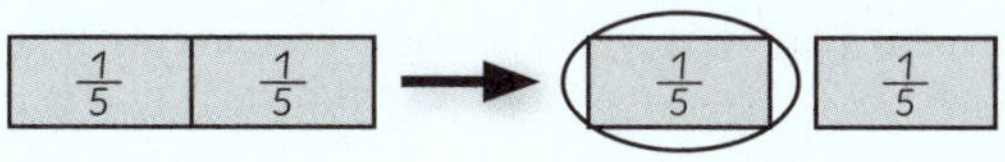

A

$\frac{1}{2}$ of $\frac{2}{5}$

$\frac{1}{2} \times \frac{2}{5} = \frac{2}{10} = \frac{1}{5}$

In the second problem, we want to find one-half of three-fifths. How much do we have? *Three-fifths.* Arrange 3 fifth-bars on the table as shown. **We don't have an even number of bars. Instead, let's experiment with the fraction bars to see if we can find one-half of three-fifths.** Give your child a moment to experiment with the bars. If she's stuck, suggest she try tenths. **6 tenths equal 3 fifths. 6 divided by 2 equals 3, so one-half of three-fifths equals three-tenths.** Have your child multiply to complete the problem.

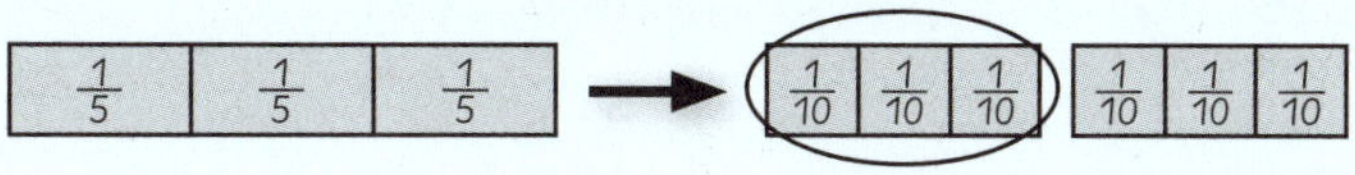

A

$\frac{1}{2}$ of $\frac{3}{5}$

$\frac{1}{2} \times \frac{3}{5} = \frac{3}{10}$

In the last problem, we want to find five-sixths of one-half. How much do we have? *One-half.* Arrange 1 half-bar on the table as shown. **Let's experiment with the fraction bars to see if we can find five-sixths of one-half.** Give your child a moment to experiment with the bars. If she's stuck, suggest she try twelfths. **6 twelfths equal 1 half. So, five-sixths of one-half equals five-twelfths.** Have your child multiply to complete the problem.

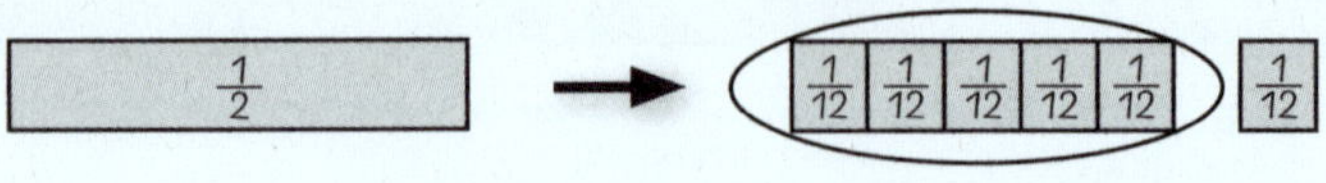

A

$\frac{5}{6}$ of $\frac{1}{2}$

$\frac{5}{6} \times \frac{1}{2} = \frac{5}{12}$

Activity (B): Write Multiplication Equations to Solve Fraction-of-a-Fraction Word Problems

In the last lesson, you learned how to multiply fractions to find a fraction of a fraction. In word problems, the word "of" is often an important clue that you should multiply. Have your child read the text box aloud.

B

"Of" Means Multiply

In math, "of" usually means multiply. We multiply to find a fraction of a fraction.

To solve a fraction-of-a-fraction word problem, first imagine the problem and describe what you're trying to find in words. Then, write a fraction multiplication problem to match.

Ex. The trail is $\frac{3}{5}$ km long. Matthew ran $\frac{1}{2}$ of the trail and walked the rest. How far did he run?

We want to find $\frac{1}{2}$ of $\frac{3}{5}$.

$\frac{1}{2}$ of $\frac{3}{5}$ → $\frac{1}{2} \times \frac{3}{5}$

$\frac{1}{2} \times \frac{3}{5} = \frac{3}{10}$ **km**

Read aloud the problem. Demonstrate how to imagine the problem: **I'm imagining a trail in the woods. It's only three-fifths of a kilometer, so it's not that long. Now, I imagine a boy running along it. He runs halfway and gets tired, so he walks the rest.**

Visualizing word problems helps make them more concrete. It also helps prevent your child from simply pulling the fractions out of the problem and multiplying them without thinking.

The whole trail is three-fifths of a kilometer. Matthew runs one-half of the trail, so we want to find one-half of three-fifths. Point to the matching words.

We want to find a fraction of a fraction, so "of" means multiply. One-half times three-fifths equals three-tenths of a kilometer.

Have your child use this approach to complete the word problems. Have her first describe each situation as a fraction of a fraction and complete the blanks. Then, have her write and solve the matching multiplication problem.

B

Genevieve poured $\frac{2}{3}$ L of lemonade into a pitcher. Then, she drank $\frac{1}{4}$ of the lemonade in the pitcher. What fraction of a liter did she drink?

$\frac{1}{4}$ of $\frac{2}{3}$

$\frac{1}{4} \times \frac{2}{3} = \frac{2}{12} = \frac{1}{6}$ L

Tristan had a board $\frac{3}{4}$ yard long. He used $\frac{5}{6}$ of the board to make a shelf. What fraction of a yard did he use?

$\frac{5}{6}$ of $\frac{3}{4}$

$\frac{5}{6} \times \frac{3}{4} = \frac{15}{24} = \frac{5}{8}$ yd.

Francis had $\frac{9}{10}$ kg of clay. He used $\frac{1}{3}$ of the clay to make a sculpture. What fraction of a kilogram did he use?

$\frac{1}{3}$ of $\frac{9}{10}$

$\frac{1}{3} \times \frac{9}{10} = \frac{9}{30} = \frac{3}{10}$ kg

The track is $\frac{1}{4}$ mi. long. Rory ran $\frac{2}{3}$ of the way around the track. What fraction of a mile did she run?

$\frac{2}{3}$ of $\frac{1}{4}$

$\frac{2}{3} \times \frac{1}{4} = \frac{2}{12} = \frac{1}{6}$ mi.

Writing the factors in the same order as the "of" statement helps your child pay attention to the real-life meaning of the problem.

Activity (C): Create a Word Problem to Match a Fraction Multiplication Problem

Creating her own word problem helps your child better understand the meaning of fraction multiplication.

Now, you get to create your own word problem to match five-sixths times one-third. We can interpret five-sixths times one-third as "five-sixths of one-third," so your problem should be about finding five-sixths of one-third of something. Have your child create a word problem that matches the multiplication problem. Then, have her solve the problem and label the answer to match her word problem.

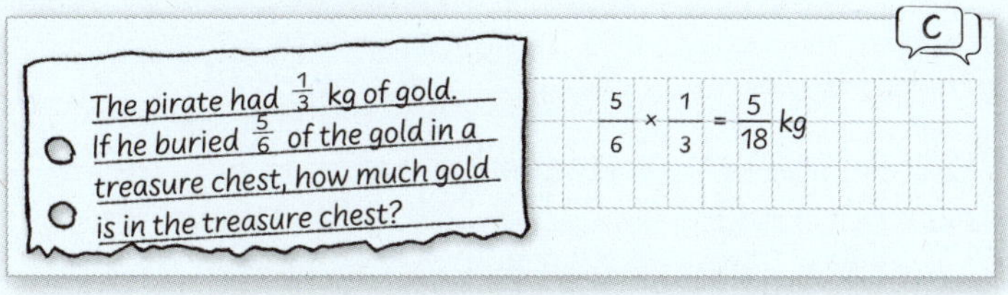

Sample word problem and solution.

If your child has trouble, encourage her to first choose a measurement unit for one-third, such as meters or pounds.

Independent Practice and Review

Have your child complete the Lesson 10.3 Practice and Review workbook pages.

Lesson 10.4
Compare Products of Fractions

Purpose	Materials
• Review the properties of multiplication by comparing products • Use the properties of multiplication to compare products of fractions • Practice multiplying fractions	• None

Memory Work	
	• **What's zero times any number?** *Zero.* • **What's zero divided by any other number?** *Zero.* • **What's any number divided by zero?** *Undefined.*

In this lesson, your child will apply his understanding of the properties of whole-number multiplication to fraction multiplication. This will help him develop a deeper conceptual understanding of fraction multiplication and begin to reason about fraction multiplication problems more abstractly.

Warm-up (A): Review Properties of Multiplication

We'll warm up by comparing products of whole numbers. In these problems, you don't have to actually find any of the products. Instead, you can use the properties of multiplication to decide whether a greater-than, less-than, or equals sign belongs in each circle.

- **Which is greater, 492 times 0 or 492?** *492.* **How do you know?** *Sample answer: Any number times 0 equals 0, so 492 times 0 is 0. That's less than 492.* Write < in the circle.
- **Which is greater, 39 times 1 or 39?** *They're equal.* **How do you know?** *Sample answer: Any number times 1 equals the number, so 39 times 1 equals 39.* Write = in the circle.
- **Which is greater, 7 times 94 or 94?** *7 times 94.* **How do you know?** *Sample answer: 7 groups of 94 is greater than 1 group of 94.* Write > in the circle.
- **Which is greater, 27 times 132, or 26 times 132?** *27 times 132.* **How do you know?** *Sample answer: 27 groups of 132 is more than 26 groups of 132.* Write > in the circle.
- **Which is greater, 48 times 36 or 48 times 37?** *48 times 37.* **How do you know?** *Sample answer: 48 groups of 36 is less than 48 groups of 37.* Write < in the circle.
- **Which is greater, 55 times 33 or 33 times 55?** *They're equal.* **How do you know?** *Sample answer: We can multiply in any order without changing the product.* Write = in the circle.

492×0 (<) 492	39×1 (=) 39	7×94 (>) 94
27×132 (>) 26×132	48×36 (<) 48×37	55×33 (=) 33×55

Activity (B): Compare Fraction Products with "Would You Rather..." Questions

Now, we'll use fraction multiplication to answer "Would You Rather?" questions. These questions present two different scenarios, and you get to decide which scenario you prefer. There's no right answer to these questions as long as you have a good reason for your answer.

Read aloud the first question: ***Would you rather have three-fourths of three-eighths of a pizza or three-fourths of five-eighths of a pizza?*** **Which product do you predict will be greater?** *Three-fourths times five-eighths.* **Why?** *Sample answer: There is more pizza to start.*

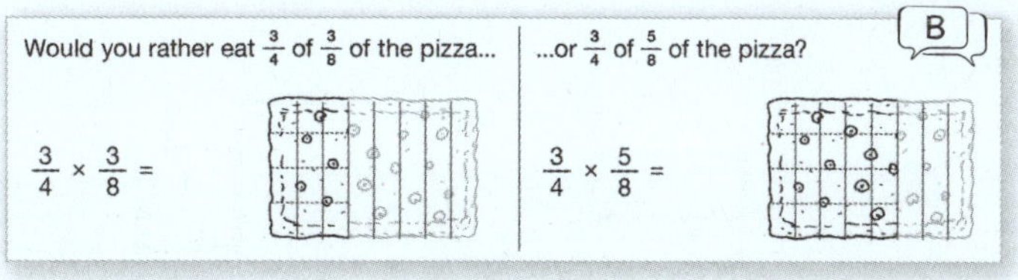

There are two different ways to predict which answer will be greater. One way is to think about the meaning of the problem. Five-eighths of a pizza is more than three-eighths of a pizza. So, if you take three-fourths of each pizza, you get more if you start with more.

Or, you can use what you know about multiplication to predict which answer will be greater. In both problems, we multiply three-fourths times a number. Five-eighths is greater than three-eighths, so the product of three-fourths and five-eighths will be greater than the product of three-fourths and three-eighths.

Have your child multiply to find both products and outline the matching parts on the pictures. **Which pizza would you rather have? Why?** *Sample answers: I'd rather get three-fourths of five-eighths, so that I'd have more pizza. I'd rather get three-fourths of three-eighths, because I don't like pizza.*

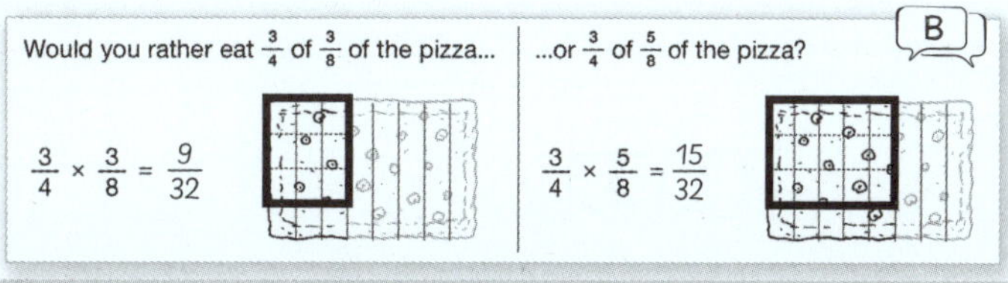

Accept any reasonable answer for this question and the other "Would you rather...?" questions in the lesson.

The problems in this lesson assume that the same whole item (pizza, lawn, etc.) is under consideration in each comparison. If the sizes were different, these comparisons wouldn't necessarily be valid. For example, if you take 3/4 of 3/8 of a large pizza, you might get more than if you take 3/4 of 5/8 of a small pizza.

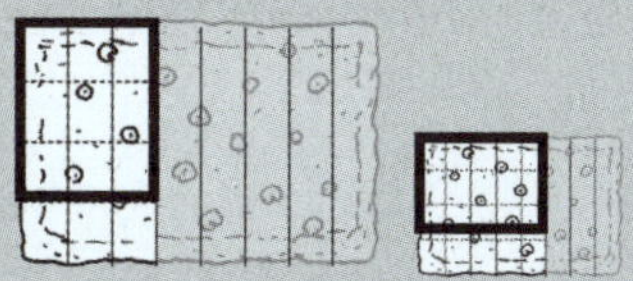

Read aloud the second question and have your child predict which product will be greater. **In both problems, you find a fraction of five-sixths. Two-thirds is greater than one-third, so two-thirds of five-sixths is greater than one-third of five-sixths. Or, you can think about the properties of multiplication. In both problems, we multiply a number times five-sixths. Two-thirds is greater than one-third, so the product of two-thirds and five-sixths will be greater than the product of one-third and five-sixths.**

Then, have him find both products and outline the matching parts of the diagrams.

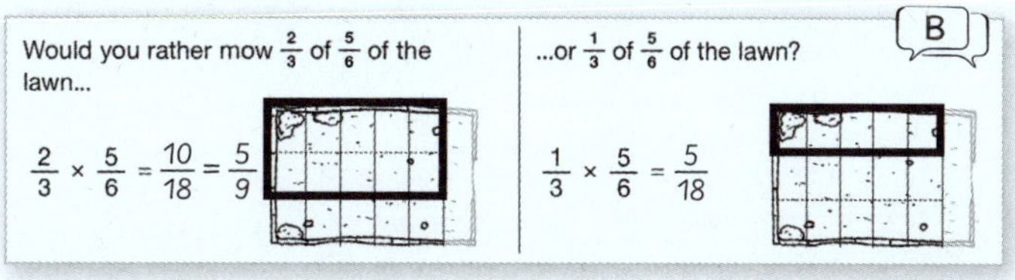

Which lawn mowing job would you rather do? Why? Sample answers: *I'd rather mow two-thirds of five-sixths of the lawn, because I think I'd get paid more. I'd rather mow one-third of five-sixths of the lawn so I don't have to mow as much.*

Repeat with the third question. **Which product do you predict will be greater?** *They will be equal.* **Why?** *Sample answer: We can multiply in any order.* **Changing the order of the factors doesn't change the product. So, these two products should be equal to each other.** Have your child find both products.

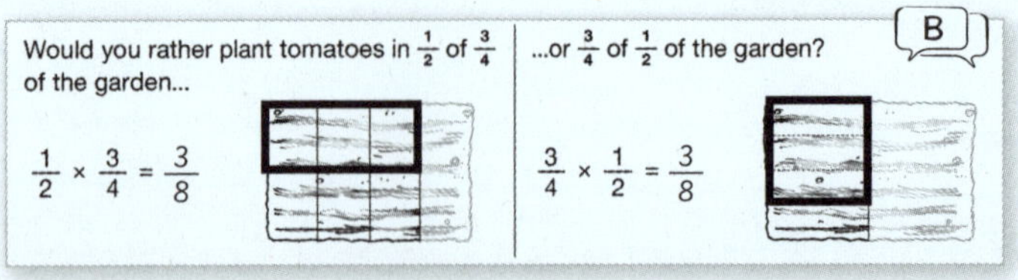

Would you rather plant tomatoes in one-half of three-fourths of the garden, or would you rather plant tomatoes in three-fourths of one-half of the garden? Why? *Sample answer: It doesn't matter, since they're the same amount.*

Repeat with the fourth question. **Which product do you predict will be greater?** *Two-thirds times five-fifths.* **Why?** *Sample answer: Zero-fifths equals zero, and any number times zero equals zero.*

What whole number does five-fifths equal? *1.* **Any number times 1 equals the number, so two-thirds times five-fifths equals two-thirds. What whole number does zero-fifths equal?** *Zero.* **Any number times zero equals zero, so two-thirds times zero-fifths equals zero.** Have your child find both products.

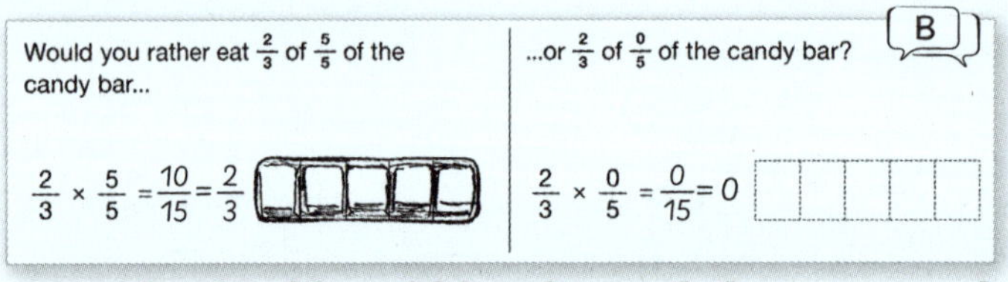

Would you rather eat two-thirds of five-fifths of a candy bar, or two-thirds of zero-fifths of a candy bar? *Sample answers: I'd rather get two-thirds of five-fifths, since I like candy bars. I'd rather get two-thirds of zero-fifths, since I don't like candy bars.*

Independent Practice and Review

Have your child complete the Lesson 10.4 Practice and Review workbook pages.

Lesson 10.5
Find Fractional Areas

Purpose

- Find fractions of a square foot
- Multiply fractions to find area
- Find the area of real-life objects as fractions of a square foot

Materials

- Paper square foot
- 10 in. by 8 in. paper rectangle
- 1-foot ruler
- Rectangular object whose length and width are less than 1 foot (such as a book or picture)

Memory Work

- **What does perimeter measure?** *The distance around the outside edge of a shape.*
- **What does area measure?** *The amount of space that a shape covers.*
- **What does volume measure?** *The amount of space a solid occupies.*
- **What is the formula for the volume of a rectangular prism?** *Multiply length times width times height.*

You'll use a paper square foot to help your child concretely understand the idea of a fractional part of a square foot in this lesson. Use wrapping paper, newspaper, or scrapbooking paper to make a paper square that is 1 foot long on each side before the lesson.

You'll also need a 10 in. by 8 in. paper rectangle. To make the rectangle, cut 1/2 inch off the short side and 1 inch off the long side of a standard piece of copy paper (U.S. letter size).

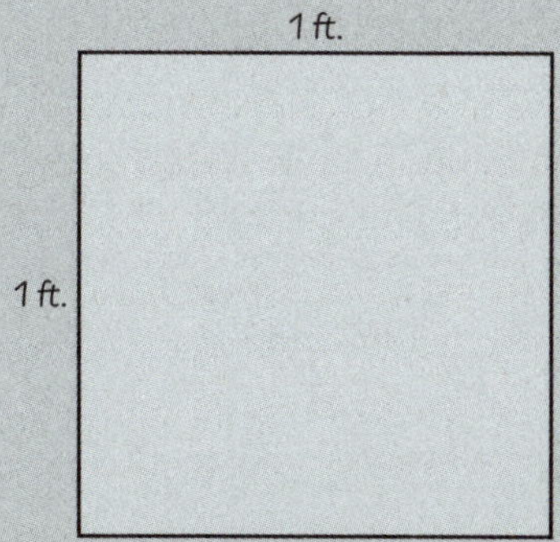

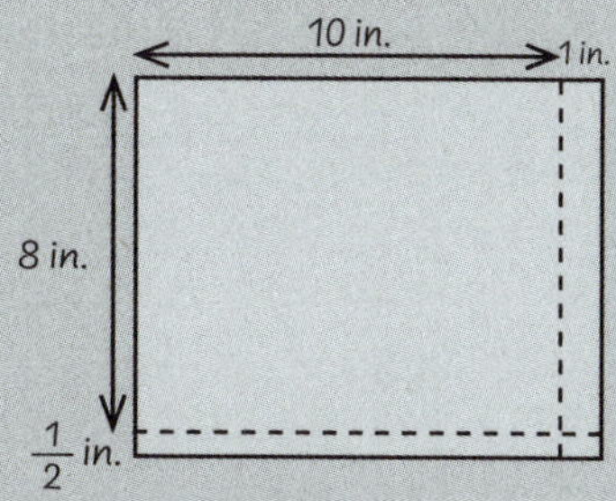

Warm-up (A): Find Fractions of a Square Foot

In younger grades, you learned how to find the area of rectangles. How do you find the area of a rectangle? *Multiply length times width.* **What are three different units we use to measure area?** *Sample answers: Square inches, square centimeters, square miles.*

Show your child a paper square that is 1 foot long on each side. **This paper square is 1 foot long on each side, so it covers an area of 1 square foot.**

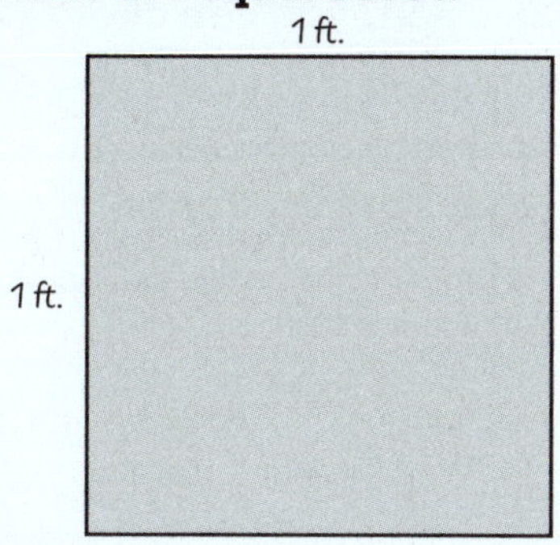

Have your child complete the fractions in part A. After your child completes each fraction, use your hands to show her the approximate matching part of the paper square foot.

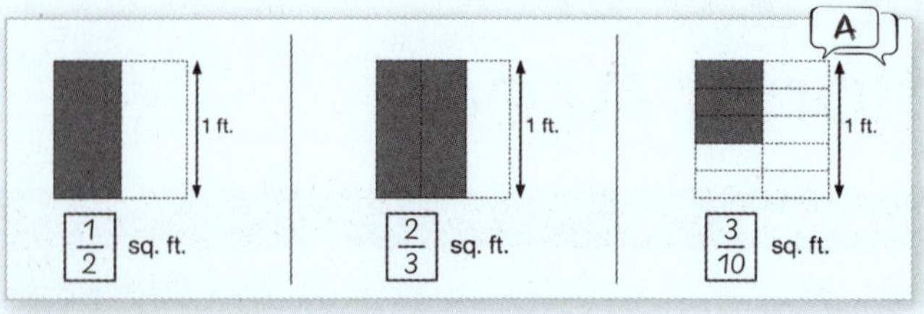

Activity (B): Multiply Fractions to Find Area

Today, you'll learn how to multiply fractions to find the area of rectangles. We multiply length times width, just like usual.

This example shows how to find the area of a postcard. Have you ever gotten a postcard in the mail? *Answers will vary.* **Postcards are pretty small.** Use your hands to show your child the approximate size of a postcard.

The postcard is one-half of a foot long and one-third of a foot wide, so we multiply one-half times one-third. What's one-half times one-third? *One-sixth.* **The postcard has an area of one-sixth of a square foot.**

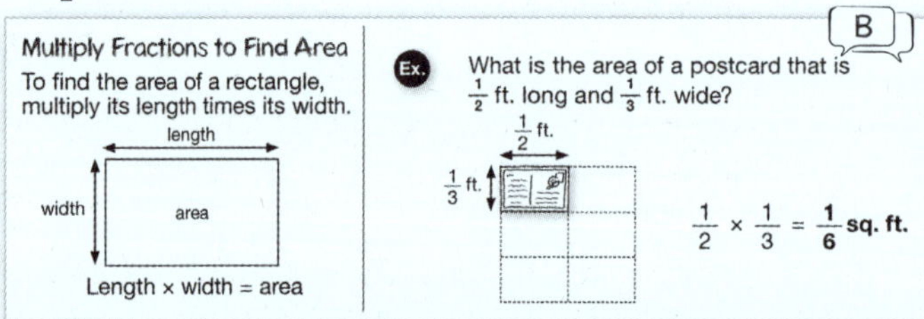

How many postcards would it take to cover one whole square foot? *6.* If your child's not sure, point to the 3 × 2 grid in the printed square foot.

Have your child find the area of the objects in the practice problems. Remind her to label her answers with the correct square units and simplify her answers as needed.

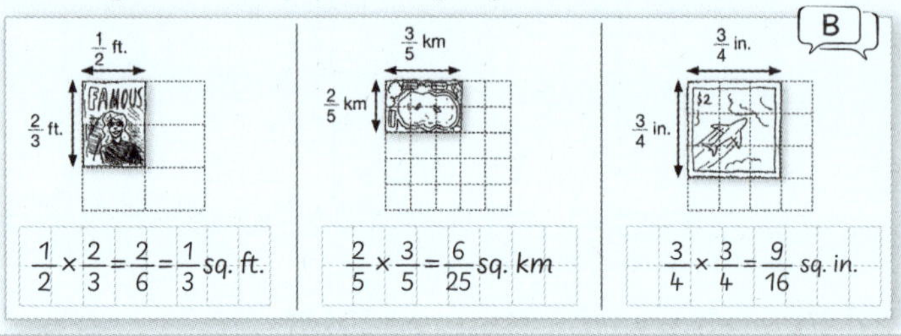

Your child may write the factors in these problems in either order, since length and width are interchangeable in the formula for the area of a rectangle.

Activity (C): Multiply Fractions to Find the Area of Real-Life Objects

Now, we'll find the area of some real objects as a fraction of a square foot. First, we'll find the area of a paper rectangle. Then, you can choose a rectangular object, and we'll find its area.

Show your child a 10 in. by 8 in. paper rectangle. This **rectangle is 10 inches long and 8 inches wide. What is its area in square inches?** *80 square inches.*

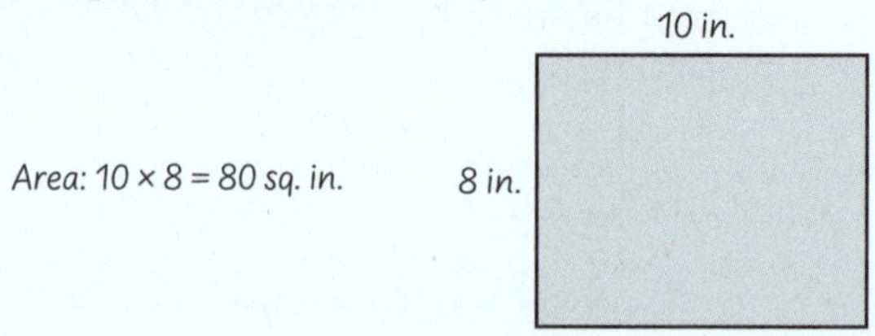

Place the rectangle on top of the paper square foot. **Is the area of this paper rectangle greater than or less than 1 square foot?** *Less.* **How do you know?** *Sample answer: It fits inside the paper square foot.* **About what fraction of a square foot do you think it is?** *Sample answer: About one-half. A little more than one-half.* Accept any reasonable answer.

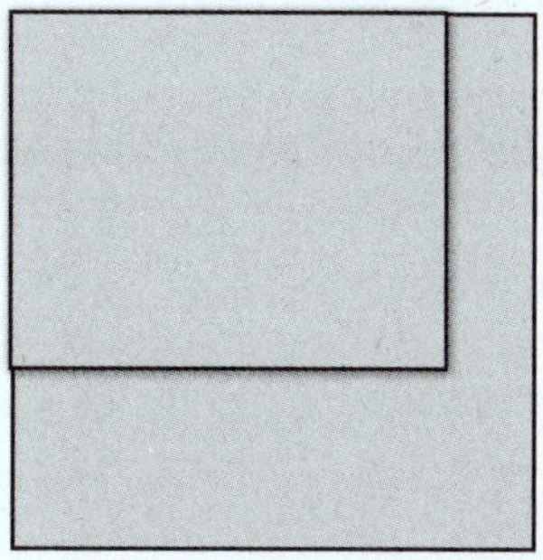

When we measure the rectangle's area in square inches, the area is a whole number. When we measure its area in square feet, the area will be a fraction.

The printed large square in part C stands for 1 square foot. Each side is divided into 12 equal lengths, so each small square stands for 1 square inch. Have your child draw a 10 by 8 rectangle in the grid to match the paper rectangle's dimensions.

We know that the long side of the rectangle is 10 inches. In simplest form, what fraction of a foot is that? *Five-sixths.* Label the left side of the rectangle with "5/6 ft." Repeat with the 8-inch side.

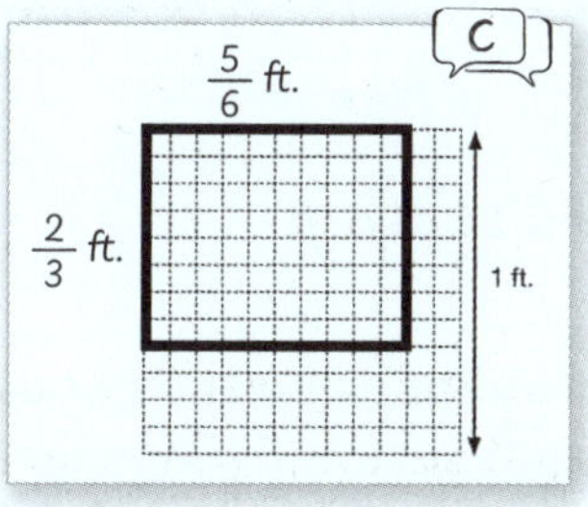

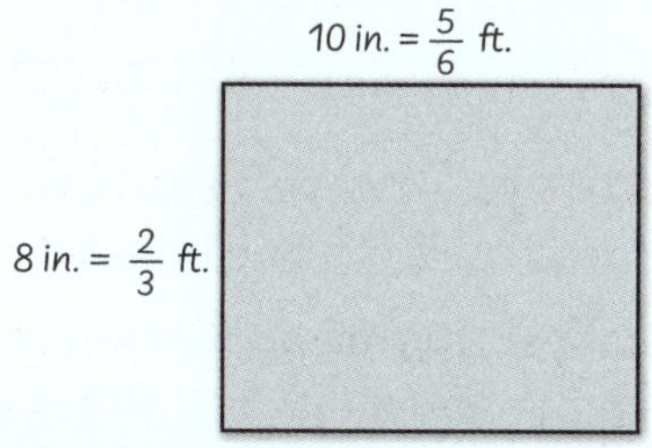

How do we find the area of the rectangle? *Multiply five-sixths times two-thirds.* Write "5/6 × 2/3 =" and have your child complete the multiplication problem. Remind her to simplify and label her answer.

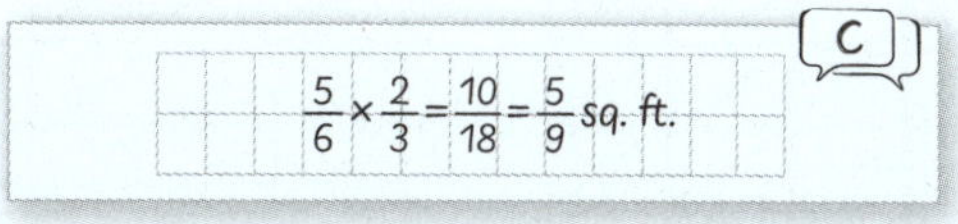

What fraction of a square foot does the paper rectangle cover? *Five-ninths.* **So, the paper rectangle has an area of five-ninths of a square foot.**

For the second problem, you get to choose something around the house whose area you'd like to find. The object must be a rectangle. Both of its dimensions must be greater than 1 inch and less than 12 inches. Have your child choose an object that matches this description, such as a book or picture. To find its area, have your child first measure its length and width in inches and sketch the dimensions on the grid. Then, have her convert the dimensions to fractions of a foot and multiply to find the area as a fraction of a square foot.

If the object's length and width are not whole numbers of inches, help your child round the measurements to the nearest inch.

Independent Practice and Review

Have your child complete the Lesson 10.5 Practice and Review workbook pages.

Lesson 10.6
Enrichment (Optional)

Purpose	Materials
• Practice memory work • Appreciate how math can be used to answer real-life questions • Create fraction-of-a-fraction word problems for a real-life situation • Summarize what your child has learned and assess your child's progress	• *How Many Guinea Pigs Can Fit on a Plane?: Answers to Your Most Clever Math Questions*, by Laura Overdeck • Rectangular chocolate bar with lines that split it into fractional parts

For the enrichment activity, you will need a rectangular chocolate bar with lines that split it into smaller rectangles, such as a Hershey bar or Cadbury Dairy Milk bar. If you don't have a chocolate bar, use a paper rectangle or a rectangular baked treat (like a pan of brownies or cake) instead.

Warm-up: Review Memory Work

Quiz your child on any of the memory work items that he struggled with during this unit.

Math Picture Book: *How Many Guinea Pigs Can Fit on a Plane?*

Read pages 92-101 in *How Many Guinea Pigs Can Fit on a Plane?*

Enrichment Activity: Create Fraction-of-a-Fraction Word Problems about a Chocolate Bar

Today, you'll create fraction-of-a-fraction word problems about a chocolate bar! Show your child a rectangular chocolate bar. **What kind of fractional parts do the vertical lines split the chocolate bar into?** *Sample answer: Fourths.* **What kind of fractional parts do the horizontal lines split the chocolate bar into?** *Sample answer: Thirds.*

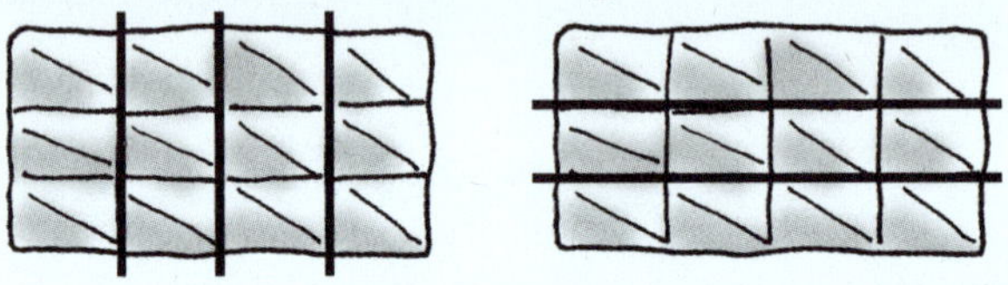

Have your child use the fractional parts to make up and solve several fraction-of-a-fraction word problems about the chocolate bar. Then, enjoy the chocolate bar together.

If I eat $\frac{2}{3}$ of $\frac{1}{4}$ of the chocolate bar, how much of the whole bar do I eat?

$\frac{2}{3} \times \frac{1}{4} = \frac{2}{12} = \frac{1}{6}$

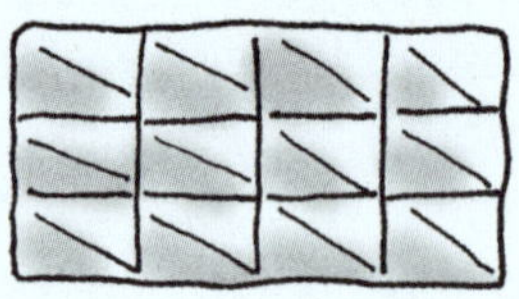

Sample word problem.

Unit Wrap-Up

Have your child complete the Unit 10 Wrap-Up.

Unit 10 Answer Key

10.1 Practice

Practice: Draw lines to split the rectangle so that it matches the problem. Then, outline the matching part of the rectangle and complete the blank. Write your answers in simplest form.

$\frac{1}{2}$ of $\frac{1}{4}$ = $\frac{1}{8}$	$\frac{1}{2}$ of $\frac{3}{5}$ = $\frac{3}{10}$	$\frac{1}{2}$ of $\frac{5}{8}$ = $\frac{5}{16}$
$\frac{1}{3}$ of $\frac{1}{3}$ = $\frac{1}{9}$	$\frac{1}{3}$ of $\frac{2}{5}$ = $\frac{2}{15}$	$\frac{1}{3}$ of $\frac{7}{8}$ = $\frac{7}{24}$
$\frac{2}{3}$ of $\frac{1}{3}$ = $\frac{2}{9}$	$\frac{2}{3}$ of $\frac{2}{5}$ = $\frac{4}{15}$	$\frac{2}{3}$ of $\frac{7}{8}$ = $\frac{14}{24}$ = $\frac{7}{12}$

Answer the questions. Use the pictures to help.

★ Connor's family had $\frac{1}{3}$ of a pie left over. Connor eats $\frac{1}{4}$ of the leftover pie. What fraction of a whole pie does he eat?

$\frac{1}{4}$ of $\frac{1}{3}$ = $\frac{1}{12}$ of the whole pie

★ Helene's dad gives her $\frac{1}{2}$ of a chocolate bar. She eats $\frac{3}{4}$ of the chocolate and saves the rest for later. What fraction of a whole chocolate bar does she eat?

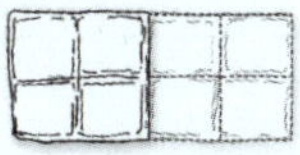

$\frac{3}{4}$ of $\frac{1}{2}$ = $\frac{3}{8}$ of a whole bar

10.1 Review

Review: Write each fraction or mixed number in simplest form. If the fraction or mixed number is already in simplest form, circle it.

$\frac{6}{8} = \frac{3}{4}$	($\frac{3}{5}$)	$\frac{8}{20} = \frac{2}{5}$
$1\frac{5}{10} = 1\frac{1}{2}$	$2\frac{4}{12} = 2\frac{1}{3}$	($3\frac{5}{9}$)

Use logical reasoning to complete the circles with <, >, or =. (You do not need to find the answers to the problems.)

491 + 275 (>) 491 − 275	37 × 85 (<) 37 × 86	648 ÷ 18 (>) 522 ÷ 18
351 − 284 (<) 352 − 284	94 × 62 (<) 95 × 62	575 ÷ 23 (>) 575 ÷ 25
106 − 28 (<) 106 − 27	48 × 87 (=) 87 × 48	102 × 34 (>) 102 ÷ 34

Write whether each angle is acute, right, obtuse, or straight.

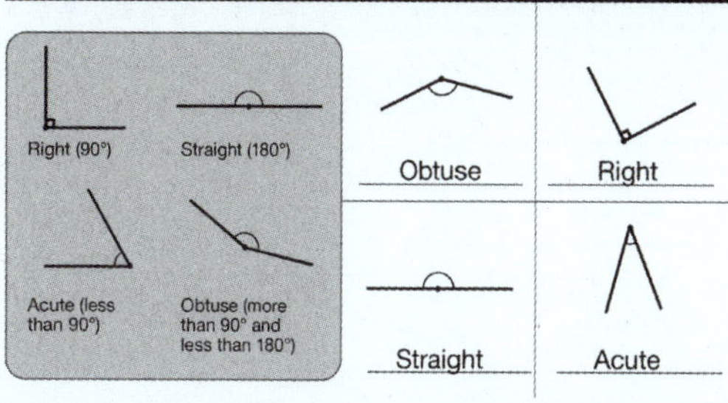

10.2 Practice

Practice: Find the product. Write each product in simplest form. Then, find the blank that matches the product. Write the matching letter in the blank to solve the riddle.

E $\frac{1}{3} \times \frac{1}{4} = \frac{1}{12}$	N $\frac{2}{3} \times \frac{1}{2} = \frac{2}{6} = \frac{1}{3}$	E $\frac{1}{3} \times \frac{4}{5} = \frac{4}{15}$
O $\frac{1}{2} \times \frac{4}{5} = \frac{4}{10} = \frac{2}{5}$	S $\frac{1}{8} \times \frac{3}{5} = \frac{3}{40}$	N $\frac{1}{3} \times \frac{1}{10} = \frac{1}{30}$
M $\frac{2}{3} \times \frac{1}{5} = \frac{2}{15}$	W $\frac{3}{4} \times \frac{4}{5} = \frac{12}{20} = \frac{3}{5}$	G $\frac{2}{3} \times \frac{7}{8} = \frac{14}{24} = \frac{7}{12}$
A $\frac{5}{6} \times \frac{1}{5} = \frac{5}{30} = \frac{1}{6}$	A $\frac{9}{10} \times \frac{1}{2} = \frac{9}{20}$	K $\frac{7}{10} \times \frac{1}{10} = \frac{7}{100}$
S $\frac{3}{4} \times \frac{3}{4} = \frac{9}{16}$	L $\frac{2}{3} \times \frac{2}{3} = \frac{4}{9}$	! $\frac{5}{6} \times \frac{5}{6} = \frac{25}{36}$

What do mathematicians do after a blizzard?

M	A	K	E		S	N	O	W
$\frac{2}{15}$	$\frac{1}{6}$	$\frac{7}{100}$	$\frac{1}{12}$		$\frac{9}{16}$	$\frac{1}{30}$	$\frac{2}{5}$	$\frac{3}{5}$

A	N	G	L	E	S	!
$\frac{9}{20}$	$\frac{1}{3}$	$\frac{7}{12}$	$\frac{4}{9}$	$\frac{4}{15}$	$\frac{3}{40}$	$\frac{25}{36}$

10.2 Review

Review: Draw and label each point in the correct location on the coordinate plane.

Point	Ordered Pair
A	(3,4)
B	(5,2)
C	(1,6)
D	(0,3)
E	(4,0)

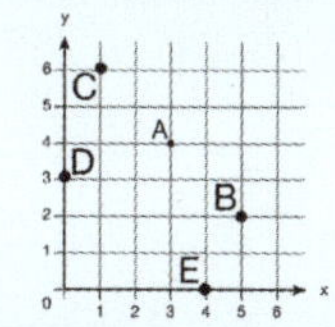

Use long division to solve. Use the multiplication table to help.

$$964 \div 35 = 27 \text{ R}19$$

```
      2 7
35 ) 9 6 4
   - 7 0 ↓
     2 6 4
   - 2 4 5
       1 9
```

× 35	
1	35
2	70
3	105
4	140
5	175
6	210
7	245
8	280
9	315

Use mental math to complete.

80 × 300 = 24,000

500 × 6 = 3,000

90 × 80 = 7,200

6,000 × 7 = 42,000

900 × 900 = 810,000

Use bar models to solve.

Noah biked 12 miles on Saturday. He biked $\frac{3}{4}$ as much on Sunday as on Saturday. How far did he bike on Sunday?

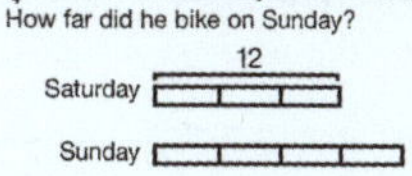

12 ÷ 3 = 4

4 × 4 = 16

16 miles

Unit 10 Answer Key

10.3 Practice

Practice Complete the missing numbers in the multiplication equations.

$\frac{1}{2} \times \frac{1}{4} = \frac{1}{\boxed{8}}$ | $\frac{2}{3} \times \frac{4}{5} = \frac{\boxed{8}}{15}$ | $\frac{3}{5} \times \frac{\boxed{7}}{10} = \frac{21}{50}$

$\frac{1}{3} \times \frac{1}{\boxed{4}} = \frac{1}{12}$ | $\frac{1}{\boxed{2}} \times \frac{7}{10} = \frac{\boxed{7}}{20}$ | $\frac{\boxed{1}}{5} \times \frac{3}{\boxed{4}} = \frac{3}{20}$

Write a multiplication problem to match. Then, solve. Write the product in simplest form.

$\frac{1}{2}$ of $\frac{9}{10}$: $\frac{1}{2} \times \frac{9}{10} = \frac{9}{20}$

$\frac{3}{4}$ of $\frac{5}{6}$: $\frac{3}{4} \times \frac{5}{6} = \frac{15}{24} = \frac{5}{8}$

$\frac{2}{5}$ of $\frac{1}{4}$: $\frac{2}{5} \times \frac{1}{4} = \frac{2}{20} = \frac{1}{10}$

Complete the blanks to match the word problem. Then, write and solve the matching multiplication problem. Write the product in simplest form.

Kayla worked in the yard for $\frac{3}{4}$ hr. She spent $\frac{1}{3}$ of the time raking. What fraction of an hour did she spend raking?

$\frac{1}{3}$ of $\frac{3}{4}$

$\frac{1}{3} \times \frac{3}{4} = \frac{3}{12} = \boxed{\frac{1}{4}\text{ hr.}}$

Obadiah had $\frac{8}{10}$ of a meter of string. He used $\frac{2}{3}$ of the string to make a pulley. What fraction of a meter did he use?

$\frac{2}{3}$ of $\frac{8}{10}$

$\frac{2}{3} \times \frac{8}{10} = \frac{16}{30} = \boxed{\frac{8}{15}\text{ m}}$

Quinn made $\frac{3}{8}$ gal. of bubble solution. Then, she used $\frac{1}{4}$ of the bubble solution to blow bubbles for her little sister. What fraction of a gallon did she use?

$\frac{1}{4}$ of $\frac{3}{8}$

$\frac{1}{4} \times \frac{3}{8} = \boxed{\frac{3}{32}\text{ gal.}}$

Maddox had $\frac{1}{2}$ lb. of blueberries. He used $\frac{4}{5}$ of the blueberries to make muffins. What fraction of a pound did he use?

$\frac{4}{5}$ of $\frac{1}{2}$

$\frac{4}{5} \times \frac{1}{2} = \frac{4}{10} = \boxed{\frac{2}{5}\text{ lb.}}$

10.3 Review

Review Write each fraction as a whole number or mixed number.

$\frac{15}{8} = 1\frac{7}{8}$ | $\frac{16}{8} = 2$ | $\frac{19}{8} = 2\frac{3}{8}$ | $\frac{21}{8} = 2\frac{5}{8}$

$\frac{20}{4} = 5$ | $\frac{20}{5} = 4$ | $\frac{20}{10} = 2$ | $\frac{20}{2} = 10$

The chart shows how much it snowed each day. Use the information in the chart to make a line graph. Choose a scale that fills most of the grid paper. Make sure to include a title for your graph and labels for the axes.

Day	Snowfall (in.)
1	3
2	8
3	0
4	1
5	10

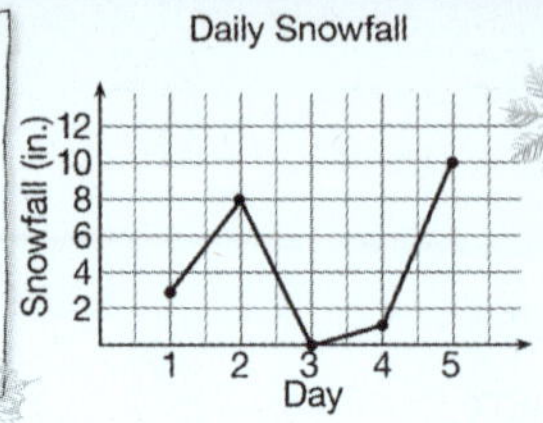

Circle the word that best describes the slope of each line segment.

Day 1 to Day 2	Day 2 to Day 3	Day 3 to Day 4	Day 4 to Day 5
(Upward)	Upward	(Upward)	(Upward)
Downward	(Downward)	Downward	Downward
Horizontal	Horizontal	Horizontal	Horizontal
Vertical	Vertical	Vertical	Vertical

Solve. Write your answers in simplest form.

There are 20 chocolate candies in the pack. 7 of them are red. What fraction of the candies are red?

$\boxed{\frac{7}{20}\text{ of the candies}}$

There are 20 chocolate candies in the pack. 8 of them are blue. What fraction of the candies are blue?

$\frac{8}{20} = \boxed{\frac{2}{5}\text{ of the candies}}$

10.4 Practice

Practice Find the products. Write your answers in simplest form.

$\frac{1}{5} \times \frac{1}{2} = \frac{1}{10}$

$\frac{2}{5} \times \frac{1}{2} = \frac{2}{10} = \frac{1}{5}$

$\frac{3}{5} \times \frac{1}{2} = \frac{3}{10}$

$\frac{4}{5} \times \frac{1}{2} = \frac{4}{10} = \frac{2}{5}$

$\frac{5}{5} \times \frac{1}{2} = \frac{5}{10} = \frac{1}{2}$

$\frac{1}{3} \times \frac{0}{8} = \frac{0}{24} = 0$

$\frac{1}{3} \times \frac{1}{8} = \frac{1}{24}$

$\frac{1}{3} \times \frac{4}{8} = \frac{4}{24} = \frac{1}{6}$

$\frac{1}{3} \times \frac{7}{8} = \frac{7}{24}$

$\frac{1}{3} \times \frac{8}{8} = \frac{8}{24} = \frac{1}{3}$

$\frac{1}{4} \times \frac{1}{5} = \frac{1}{20}$

$\frac{1}{5} \times \frac{1}{4} = \frac{1}{20}$

$\frac{3}{4} \times \frac{4}{5} = \frac{12}{20} = \frac{3}{5}$

$\frac{4}{5} \times \frac{3}{4} = \frac{12}{20} = \frac{3}{5}$

Use logical reasoning to complete the circles with <, >, or =. (You do not need to find the answers to the problems.)

$\frac{1}{3} \times \frac{1}{4} < \frac{1}{3} \times \frac{3}{4}$ | $\frac{1}{6} \times \frac{3}{8} < \frac{5}{6} \times \frac{3}{8}$ | $\frac{1}{2} \times \frac{1}{10} < \frac{1}{2} \times \frac{7}{8}$

$\frac{4}{5} \times \frac{9}{10} = \frac{9}{10} \times \frac{4}{5}$ | $\frac{1}{6} \times \frac{10}{10} > \frac{1}{6} \times \frac{5}{10}$ | $\frac{7}{8} \times \frac{0}{3} < \frac{7}{8} \times \frac{3}{3}$

Solve. Write your answers in simplest form.

Austin colored $\frac{1}{3}$ of the flag blue. Then, he drew stars on $\frac{3}{5}$ of the blue part. What fraction of the flag has stars?

$\frac{3}{5} \times \frac{1}{3} = \frac{3}{15} = \boxed{\frac{1}{5}\text{ of the flag}}$

Avonlea colored $\frac{3}{5}$ of the flag blue. Then, she drew stars on $\frac{1}{3}$ of the blue part. What fraction of the flag has stars?

$\frac{1}{3} \times \frac{3}{5} = \frac{3}{15} = \boxed{\frac{1}{5}\text{ of the flag}}$

10.4 Review

Review Choose the more sensible measurement for each item.

Area of an envelope: $\frac{1}{4}$ sq. in. / ($\frac{1}{4}$ sq. ft.)

Area of a postage stamp: ($\frac{3}{5}$ sq. in.) / $\frac{3}{5}$ sq. ft.

Area of a window: $\frac{7}{8}$ sq. cm / ($\frac{7}{8}$ sq. m)

Complete the chart. Write the fractions in simplest form.

Inches	1	2	3	4	5	6
Fractions of a foot	$\frac{1}{12}$	$\frac{1}{6}$	$\frac{1}{4}$	$\frac{1}{3}$	$\frac{5}{12}$	$\frac{1}{2}$

Evaluate. Make sure you use the order of operations.

1 × 2 × 3 + 4
2 × 3 + 4
6 + 4
10

1 × 2 + 3 × 4
2 + 12
14

1 + 2 × 3 × 4
1 + 6 × 4
1 + 24
25

Solve. Write the equations you use.

Maddie caught two fish. One fish weighed 4.5 kg and the other fish weighed 3.72 kg. What was the total weight of the fish?

4.50 + 3.72 = **8.22 kg**

How much more did the heavier fish weigh than the lighter fish?

4.50 − 3.72 = **0.78 kg more**

Unit 10 Answer Key

10.5 Practice

Practice: Label the dimensions of each rectangle. Then, use the dimensions to find the area. Make sure to use the correct units.

$\frac{1}{4} \times \frac{1}{5} = \frac{1}{20}$ sq. ft.

$\frac{2}{3} \times \frac{2}{3} = \frac{4}{9}$ sq. m

$\frac{1}{2} \times \frac{3}{4} = \frac{3}{8}$ sq. ft.

$\frac{2}{3} \times \frac{1}{4} = \frac{2}{12} = \frac{1}{6}$ sq. ft.

$\frac{5}{6} \times \frac{4}{5} = \frac{20}{30} = \frac{2}{3}$ sq. m

$\frac{1}{2} \times \frac{2}{5} = \frac{2}{10} = \frac{1}{5}$ sq. yd.

Solve. Write the equations you use.

The postage stamp is $\frac{7}{8}$ in. long and $\frac{3}{4}$ in. wide. What is its area?

$\frac{7}{8} \times \frac{3}{4} = \frac{21}{32}$ sq. in.

The botanical garden is $\frac{6}{10}$ km long and $\frac{3}{10}$ km wide. What is its area?

$\frac{6}{10} \times \frac{3}{10} = \frac{18}{100} = \frac{9}{50}$ sq. km

10.5 Review

Review: Use the information to complete the chart. Then, use the chart to make a line graph.

PARKING $8 for the first hour, then $6 per hour

Hours	Cost ($)
1	8
2	14
3	20
4	26
5	32
6	38
7	44
8	50

Parking Cost

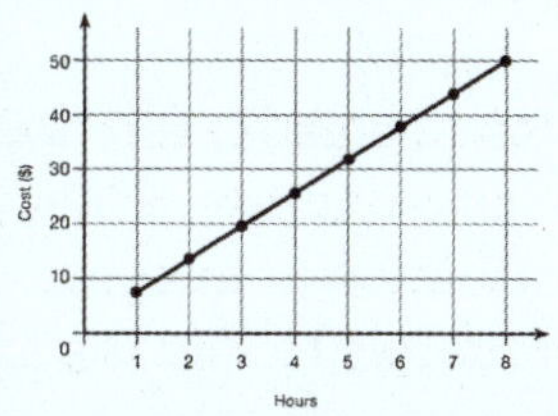

Find the sum or difference. If your answer is an improper fraction, convert the improper fraction to a mixed number. Write your answers in simplest form.

$\frac{4}{5} + \frac{7}{10}$: $\frac{8}{10} + \frac{7}{10}$, $\frac{15}{10} = 1\frac{5}{10} = 1\frac{1}{2}$

$\frac{4}{5} - \frac{7}{10}$: $\frac{8}{10} - \frac{7}{10}$, $\frac{1}{10}$

$\frac{3}{4} - \frac{1}{12}$: $\frac{9}{12} - \frac{1}{12}$, $\frac{8}{12} = \frac{2}{3}$

Use bar models to solve.

Annabelle scored $\frac{4}{5}$ as many points as Mishi. Annabelle scored 12 points. How many points did Mishi score?

Annabelle (12) / Mishi

$12 \div 4 = 3$

$3 \times 5 = 15$

15 points

10.6 Unit Wrap-Up A

Unit Wrap-Up: Follow the directions to color the flag and answer the questions.

- Draw stars on $\frac{1}{3}$ of the yellow stripe. What fraction of the flag has stars?
  $\frac{1}{3} \times \frac{1}{2} = \frac{1}{6}$ of the flag
- Draw dots on $\frac{1}{2}$ of the green stripe. What fraction of the flag has dots?
  $\frac{1}{2} \times \frac{1}{2} = \frac{1}{4}$ of the flag

Write a multiplication problem to match. Then, solve. Write the product in simplest form.

$\frac{1}{3}$ of $\frac{9}{10}$: $\frac{1}{3} \times \frac{9}{10} = \frac{9}{30} = \frac{3}{10}$

$\frac{3}{4}$ of $\frac{4}{5}$: $\frac{3}{4} \times \frac{4}{5} = \frac{12}{20} = \frac{3}{5}$

$\frac{1}{2}$ of $\frac{5}{6}$: $\frac{1}{2} \times \frac{5}{6} = \frac{5}{12}$

Complete the missing numbers in the multiplication equations.

$\frac{1}{6} \times \frac{1}{\boxed{2}} = \frac{1}{12}$

$\frac{1}{\boxed{2}} \times \frac{\boxed{7}}{10} = \frac{7}{20}$

$\frac{\boxed{1}}{3} \times \frac{5}{\boxed{8}} = \frac{5}{24}$

$\frac{\boxed{1}}{3} \times \frac{4}{\boxed{5}} = \frac{4}{15}$

$\frac{3}{\boxed{5}} \times \frac{2}{5} = \frac{\boxed{6}}{25}$

$\frac{1}{6} \times \frac{\boxed{1}}{\boxed{6}} = \frac{1}{36}$

Use logical reasoning to complete the circles with <, >, or =. (You do not need to find the answers to the problems.)

$\frac{1}{5} \times \frac{1}{4} < \frac{1}{5} \times \frac{3}{4}$

$\frac{3}{5} \times \frac{3}{4} < \frac{4}{5} \times \frac{3}{4}$

$\frac{1}{2} \times \frac{1}{8} < \frac{1}{2} \times \frac{5}{6}$

$\frac{2}{3} \times \frac{1}{2} = \frac{1}{2} \times \frac{2}{3}$

$\frac{1}{4} \times \frac{8}{8} > \frac{1}{4} \times \frac{3}{8}$

$\frac{7}{10} \times \frac{0}{4} < \frac{7}{10} \times \frac{4}{4}$

10.6 Unit Wrap-Up B

Unit Wrap-Up: Label the dimensions of each rectangle. Then, use the dimensions to find the area. Make sure to use the correct units.

$\frac{1}{2} \times \frac{1}{2} = \frac{1}{4}$ sq. m

$\frac{2}{3} \times \frac{5}{6} = \frac{10}{18} = \frac{5}{9}$ sq. ft.

$\frac{3}{3} \times \frac{3}{4} = \frac{9}{12} = \frac{3}{4}$ sq. yd.

Solve. Write the equations you use. Write your answers in simplest form. (Watch out! Not all problems are multiplication problems.)

Matthias put sausage on $\frac{2}{3}$ of the pizza. Then, he put mushrooms on $\frac{1}{4}$ of the slices with sausage. What fraction of the whole pizza has mushrooms?

$\frac{1}{4} \times \frac{2}{3} = \frac{2}{12} = \frac{1}{6}$ of the pizza

Becket used $\frac{2}{3}$ lb. of strawberries and $\frac{1}{5}$ lb. of grapes to make fruit salad. How much fruit did he use in all?

$\frac{2}{3} + \frac{1}{5}$, $\frac{10}{15} + \frac{3}{15} = \frac{13}{15}$ lb.

The nature trail is $\frac{9}{10}$ km long. $\frac{1}{3}$ of the trail is uphill, and the rest is downhill. How long is the uphill part of the trail?

$\frac{1}{3} \times \frac{9}{10} = \frac{9}{30} = \frac{3}{10}$ km

The sign is $\frac{3}{4}$ ft. long and $\frac{1}{3}$ ft. wide. What is its area?

$\frac{3}{4} \times \frac{1}{3} = \frac{3}{12} = \frac{1}{4}$ sq. ft.

Adalyn made $\frac{3}{4}$ L of soup. Then, her family ate $\frac{5}{8}$ L. How much soup was left?

$\frac{3}{4} - \frac{5}{8}$, $\frac{6}{8} - \frac{5}{8} = \frac{1}{8}$ L

Henry's family had $\frac{1}{3}$ of a cake left. Henry ate $\frac{2}{5}$ of the leftover cake. What fraction of the whole cake did he eat?

$\frac{2}{5} \times \frac{1}{3} = \frac{2}{15}$ of the cake

Unit 10 Checkpoint

What to Expect at the End of Unit 10

By the end of Unit 10, most children will be able to do the following:

- Multiply to find a fraction of a fraction and simplify the result if needed.
- Write and solve fraction multiplication problems to solve fraction-of-a-fraction word problems. Some children may need help imagining the situation and describing it with "of."
- Reason about fraction multiplication and compare products of fraction multiplication. Some children will still have trouble with this, especially if they don't have a concrete situation to imagine.
- Multiply to find the area of rectangles with fractional lengths.

Is Your Child Ready to Move on?

In Unit 11, your child will learn how to multiply fractions, mixed numbers, and whole numbers. Before moving on to Unit 11, your child should be very comfortable multiplying fractions. If your child is having trouble multiplying fractions, review the steps (from Lesson 10.2) at the beginning of each lesson and make up a few simple fraction multiplication problems for him to complete.

Unit 11
Multiply Mixed Numbers

Overview

In Unit 10, your child learned how to multiply fractions. In this unit, she will extend these skills to find products of fractions, whole numbers, or mixed numbers. She'll apply these skills to a variety of real-life situations, including scaling recipes down or finding area.

What Your Child Will Learn

In this unit, your child will learn to:

- Multiply whole numbers by fractions or mixed numbers to find the total of equal groups
- Multiply to find fractions of whole numbers or mixed numbers
- Estimate products of mixed numbers and products of whole numbers and mixed numbers
- Reason about fraction multiplication and predict whether a product will be greater than, less than, or equal to one of the factors
- Solve multiplication word problems that involve multiplying fractions, whole numbers, or mixed numbers
- Multiply fractions, whole numbers, or mixed numbers to find the area of rectangles

Lesson List

Lesson 11.1	Multiply Whole Numbers by Fractions	Lesson 11.5	Multiply Fractions by Whole Numbers
Lesson 11.2	Multiply Whole Numbers by Mixed Numbers	Lesson 11.6	Multiply Fractions by Mixed Numbers
Lesson 11.3	Estimate Products of Whole Numbers and Mixed Numbers	Lesson 11.7	Solve Multiplicative Comparison Problems and Predict Products
Lesson 11.4	Estimate and Find Products of Mixed Numbers	Lesson 11.8	Multiply Mixed Numbers to Find Rectangles' Areas
		Lesson 11.9	Enrichment (Optional)

Extra Materials Needed for Unit 11

- Measuring cups and spoons, optional
- 4 one-inch paper squares
- Scissors
- For optional Enrichment Lesson:
  - *How Many Guinea Pigs Can Fit on a Plane?: Answers to Your Most Clever Math Questions*, by Laura Overdeck. Feiwel & Friends, 2017.
  - Recipe with fractions and mixed numbers

Teaching Math with Confidence: Applying Fraction and Mixed Number Multiplication to Real-World Problems

In this unit, you'll teach your child how to multiply fractions, whole numbers, or mixed numbers (in varying combinations). All of these problems can be solved with the same simple process:

1. Write any whole numbers or mixed numbers as improper fractions.
2. Multiply the fractions.
3. If needed, simplify the answer, or convert it to a whole number or mixed number.

Ex. Micah uses $1\frac{3}{4}$ bags of potting soil to fill the planter. Each bag weighs $2\frac{1}{3}$ kg. Exactly how much soil does he use?

$1\frac{3}{4} \times 2\frac{1}{3} = ?$

$\frac{7}{4} \times \frac{7}{3} = \frac{7 \times 7}{4 \times 3} = \frac{49}{12}$

$\frac{49}{12} = \mathbf{4\frac{1}{12}}$ **kg**

Sample mixed number multiplication problem from Lesson 11.4.

Children who can proficiently solve textbook multiplication problems often have little idea how to apply their skills to everyday situations. To prevent this, you'll work methodically through several common real-world contexts so that your child knows not only *how* to multiply to solve these problems but also *when* to multiply.

- **Equal groups:** In Lessons 11.1-11.4, your child will multiply to find the total of equal groups of fractional amounts. For example: *Easton's dog eats 1 1/3 cups of dog food each day. How much food does his dog eat in 4 days?*
- **Fraction of a total:** In Lessons 11.5 and 11.6, your child will extend the skills she learned in Unit 10 to find a fraction of a whole number or mixed number. For example: *The fried rice recipe calls for 2 1/2 cups of cooked rice. Ryland only wants to make 2/3 of the recipe. How much rice should he use?*
- **Multiplicative comparison:** In Lesson 11.7, your child will solve problems where one quantity is compared to another with multiplication. For example: *The wood frog is 1 3/4 in. long. The bullfrog is 3 times as long as the wood frog. How long is the bullfrog?*
- **Area:** In Lesson 11.8, your child will multiply to find the area of rectangles whose sides are fractions, whole numbers, or mixed numbers. For example: *What is the area of a rectangle that is 2 1/2 in. long and 1 1/2 in. wide?*

Lesson 11.1
Multiply Whole Numbers by Fractions

Purpose	Materials
• Write whole numbers as fractions with 1 as the denominator • Multiply a whole number by a fraction to find the total of equal groups	• 2 dice

Memory Work	
	• **What do we call the top number in a fraction?** *The numerator.* • **What does the numerator tell?** *The number of parts.* • **What do we call the bottom number in a fraction?** *The denominator.* • **What does the denominator tell?** *How many equal parts the whole was split into.*

In *Fourth Grade Math with Confidence*, your child learned how to multiply a whole number by a fraction to find the total of equal groups. In this lesson, she'll learn how to use fraction multiplication procedures to solve these problems.

Warm-up (A): Write Whole Numbers as Fractions with 1 as the Denominator

Show your child the example in part A. **We can write 3 wholes as a fraction with 3 as the numerator and 1 as the denominator.**

Point to the 1 in 3/1. **In a fraction, the denominator tells how many equal parts the whole was divided into. When we write 1 as the denominator, it means that each whole is simply divided into 1 part and that it's still whole. We read this fraction as "3 wholes" or "3 over 1."** Have your child write fractions with 1 as the denominator for the other exercises.

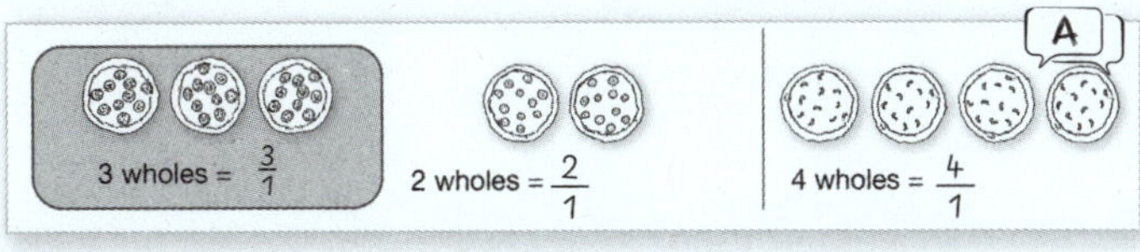

Activity (B): Multiply Whole Numbers by Fractions

In the last unit, you learned how to multiply fractions. In this unit, you'll learn how to use the same process to multiply fractions, whole numbers, or mixed numbers.

Today, you'll learn how to multiply a whole number by a fraction to find the total of equal groups. You write the whole number as a fraction with 1 as the denominator, and then you multiply like usual. Have your child read the text box aloud.

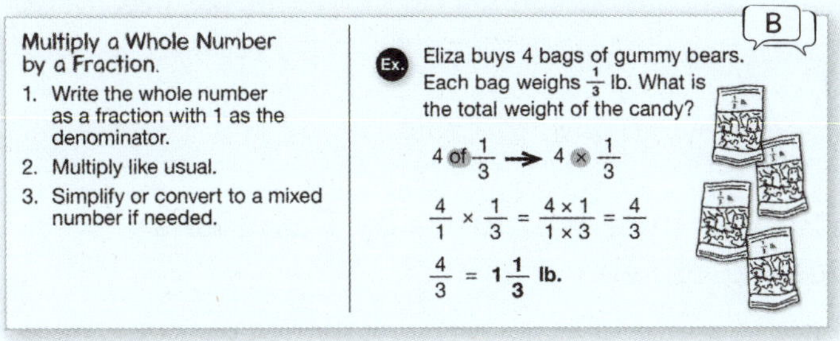

The example shows how to use multiplication to find the weight of 4 bags of gummy bears.

- **Each bag weighs one-third of a pound, so we multiply 4 times one-third to find the total weight.**
- **First, we write the whole number as a fraction. 4 wholes equal 4 over 1.**
- **Then, we follow the usual steps in fraction multiplication. We multiply the numerators, and then we multiply the denominators.**
- **Four-thirds is an improper fraction, so we convert it to a mixed number. Four-thirds equal 1 and one-third pounds.**

Draw a circle around 3 of the bags in the picture. **3 thirds equal 1 whole, so 3 bags weigh 1 pound. The last bag weighs one-third of a pound, so there's a total of 1 and one-third pounds of candy.**

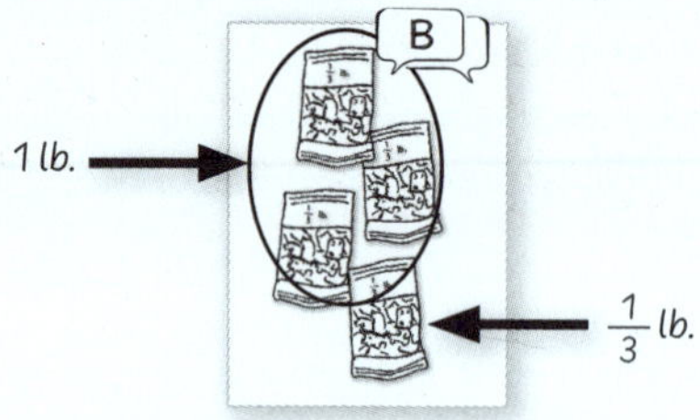

The next customer wants 3 bags of gummy worms. What multiplication problem can we solve to find the total weight of the candy? *3 times one-fourth.* Write "3 × 1/4" and have your child multiply to find the product.

Repeat with the second practice problem: **This customer wants 4 bags of jelly beans. What multiplication problem can we solve to find the total weight of the candy?** *4 times three-eighths.*

To make these problems more concrete, model them with fraction bars.

- For the first problem, place 3 fourth-bars on the table. **3 times one-fourth equals three-fourths.**
- For the second problem, a standard set of fraction bars doesn't include enough eighth-bars to represent all 4 bags of candy. Instead, place 3 eighth-bars on the table to represent one bag of candy. **Imagine if we had 4 groups like this one. We'd have 12 eighth-bars, or twelve-eighths.**

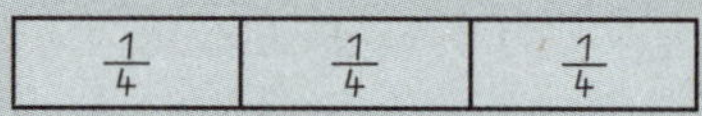

Each bar represents 1 bag of candy. 3 × 1/4 = 3/4.

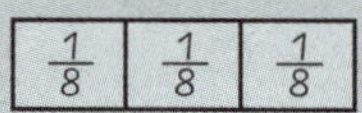

If you had 4 groups like this, you'd have 12 eighth-bars. 4 × 3/8 = 12/8, or 1 1/2.

Activity (C): Multiply Whole Numbers by Fractions at the Candy Shopping Spree

You're a lucky customer at a candy store today, because you've won a candy shopping spree! You get to roll 2 dice to find how many bags of each type of candy you get. Then, you'll multiply to find the weight of the candy.

Have your child roll 2 dice. Write the sum of the numbers she rolls as the numerator in the first problem. Write 1 as the denominator. **Each bag of gummy bears weighs one-third of a pound. Multiply to find out how many pounds of gummy bears you won.** Help your child multiply to find the answer. If she needs to convert the fraction to a mixed number, have her write an equals sign and the mixed number to the right of the problem as shown. Repeat with the remaining bags of candy.

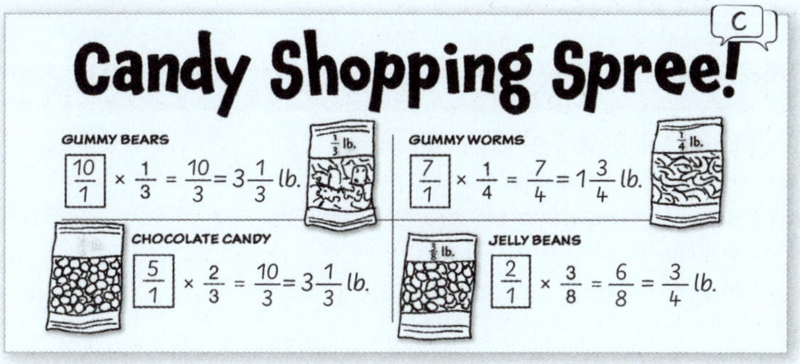

Sample answers.

Independent Practice and Review

Have your child complete the Lesson 11.1 Practice and Review workbook pages.

Lesson 11.2
Multiply Whole Numbers by Mixed Numbers

Purpose	Materials
• Practice repeated addition with mixed numbers and improper fractions • Use fraction multiplication or the distributive property to multiply whole numbers by mixed numbers • Multiply whole numbers by mixed numbers to find the total of equal groups	• Measuring cups, optional
Memory Work	• **What is the order of operations?** *Parentheses, multiply or divide from left to right, add or subtract from left to right.*

This unit sometimes uses measuring cups (1-cup, 1/2-cup, 1/3-cup, and 1/4-cup measures) to make the examples more concrete. If you don't have measuring cups available, refer to the printed pictures in the Student Workbook or show your child the printed pictures in the Instructor Guide instead.

Warm-up (A): Practice Repeated Addition with Mixed Numbers and Improper Fractions

Today, we're going to solve a problem about a boy named Easton and his dog. He feeds his dog 1 and one-third cups of dog food each day. Show your child a 1-cup measure and 1/3-cup measure.

How many cups of food does his dog eat in 2 days? *2 and two-third cups.* Write 2 2/3 in the chart. Have your child complete the blanks for 3 days in the same way. If he's not sure, suggest he add 1 1/3 to the previous amount.

We could also use improper fractions to complete the chart. 1 and one-third equals how many thirds? *4.* **If Easton lost the 1-cup measure, he could use the one-third-cup measure instead and give his dog 4 small scoops each day.** Write 4/3 in the chart as shown. Then, have your child complete the remaining blanks with improper fractions. If he has trouble, suggest he add 4/3 to the previous amount.

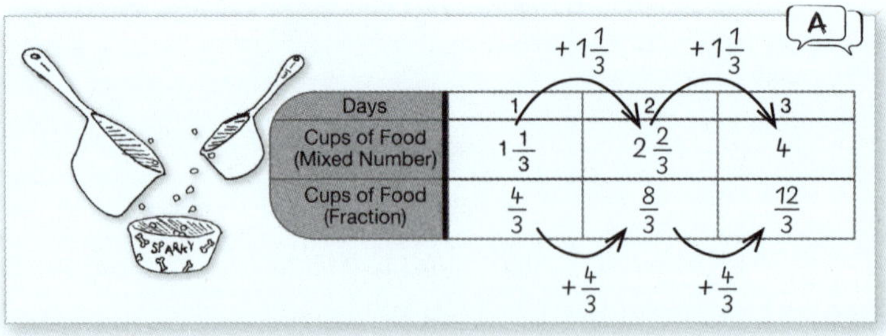

Activity (B): Use Fraction Multiplication or the Distributive Property to Multiply Whole Numbers by Mixed Numbers

Today, you'll learn two ways to multiply a whole number by a mixed number to find the total of equal groups. We can write both numbers as fractions, or we can use the distributive property.

Refresh your child's memory of the distributive property as needed: **We use the distributive property when we split a number into parts, multiply the parts by a number, and then add the products. For example, let's say you want to buy 12 books, and each book costs $7. Instead of multiplying 7 times 12, we can split 12 into 10 and 2. First, we can multiply 7 times 10 to find the cost of 10 books. Then, we multiply 7 times 2 to find the cost of 2 books. Last, we can add the products to find the total cost.**

$$7 \times 12 = (7 \times 10) + (7 \times 2) = 70 + 14 = 84$$

Read the word problem aloud. **We want to find how much food Easton's dog eats in 4 days. The dog eats 1 and one-third cups each day, so, we multiply 4 times 1 and one-third to find the total amount.**

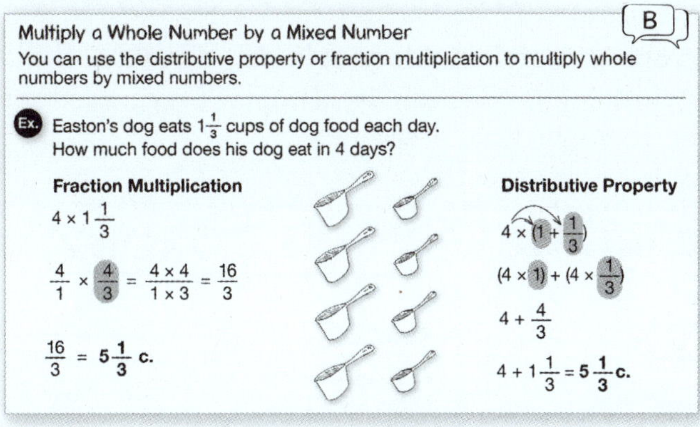

The first example shows how to use fraction multiplication to multiply 4 times 1 and one-third. We write both numbers as fractions and then multiply as usual.

- **What fraction equals 4 wholes?** *4 over 1.* **What fraction equals 1 and one-third?** *Four-thirds.*
- **4 times 4 equals 16. 1 times 3 equals 3. Sixteen-thirds equals 5 and one-third.**

The second example shows how to use the distributive property to multiply 4 times 1 and one-third. We split 1 and one-third into 1 plus one-third and then multiply 4 times both parts.

- **First, we multiply 4 times 1. What part of the picture matches 4 times 1?** *The 4 one-cup measures.*
- **Then, we multiply 4 times one-third. What part of the picture matches 4 times one-third?** *The 4 one-third-cup measures.*
- **The parentheses in the equation remind us to multiply before we add the partial products. What's 4 times 1?** *4.* **What's 4 times one-third?** *Four-thirds.* Draw rings as shown to demonstrate how 4 × 1 equals 4 and 4 × 1/3 equals 4/3.
- **Four-thirds equals 1 and one-third. 4 plus 1 and one-third equals 5 and one-third, so that's the final answer.**

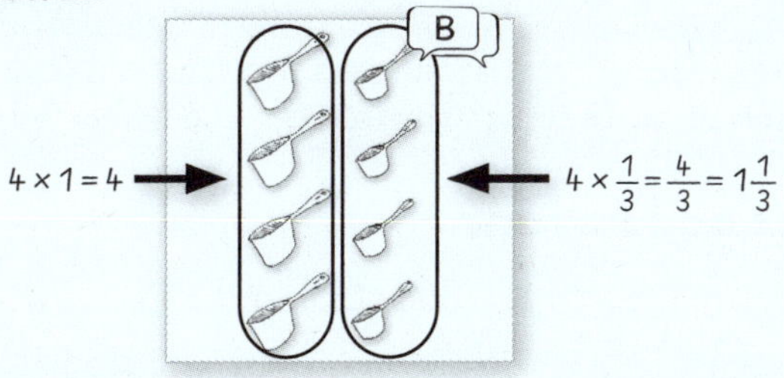

Which way do you like better? *Answers will vary.* **You can use either method when you multiply a whole number times a mixed number.**

Don't worry if your child doesn't fully understand how to use the distributive property to solve these problems. It's fine for him to use fraction multiplication instead.

Read aloud the first practice word problem. Use real measuring cups to show your child how large 2 1/2 cups is. **One way to measure 2 and one-half cups of flour is to scoop 2 whole cups and then a half-cup. 2 and one-half equals what improper fraction?** *Five-halves.* **If you lost your 1 cup measure, you could scoop 5 half-cups of flour instead.**

B

Evelyn uses $2\frac{1}{2}$ c. of flour for each batch of cookies. How many cups of flour does she need to make 3 batches?

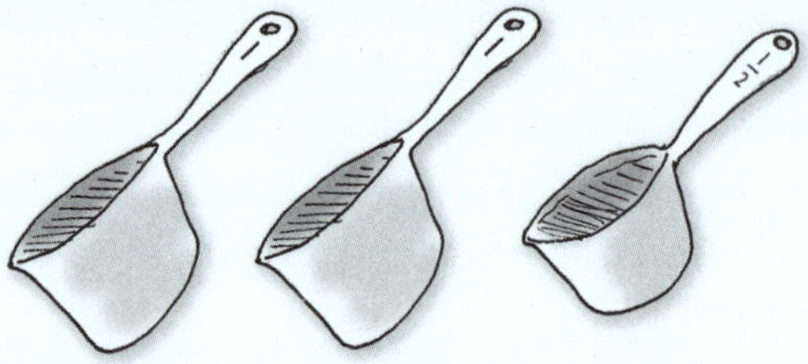

What multiplication problem matches this problem? *3 times 2 and one-half.* Have your child write and solve the matching multiplication problem. He may use either method to find the product. Then, have him solve the final problem.

B

Evelyn uses $2\frac{1}{2}$ c. of flour for each batch of cookies. How many cups of flour does she need to make 3 batches?

$3 \times 2\frac{1}{2}$

$\frac{3}{1} \times \frac{5}{2} = \frac{15}{2} = 7\frac{1}{2}$ c.

Sebastian cuts 4 pieces of plastic string to make a bracelet. Each piece is $1\frac{2}{3}$ ft. long. How many feet of plastic string does he use in all?

$4 \times 1\frac{2}{3}$

$\frac{4}{1} \times \frac{5}{3} = \frac{20}{3} = 6\frac{2}{3}$ ft.

Activity (C): Create a Word Problem to Match a Multiplication Problem

Creating his own word problem helps your child better understand what it means to multiply a whole number by a mixed number.

Now, you get to create your own word problem to match 3 times 2 and three-fourths! Have your child create a word problem that matches the multiplication problem. Remind him as needed that his problem should be about 3 groups, and that each group should have a size of 2 3/4 units. Then, have him solve the problem and label the answer to match his word problem.

C

Each pitcher holds $2\frac{3}{4}$ L of water. How much do 3 pitchers hold?

$3 \times 2\frac{3}{4} = ?$

$\frac{3}{1} \times \frac{11}{4} = \frac{33}{4} = 8\frac{1}{4}$ L

Sample word problem and solution.

If your child has trouble, encourage him to first choose a unit for 2 3/4: **How about you make up a problem that involves using 2 and three-fourths meters? Or 2 and three-fourths pizzas?**

Independent Practice and Review

Have your child complete the Lesson 11.2 Practice and Review workbook pages.

Lesson 11.3
Estimate Products of Whole Numbers and Mixed Numbers

Purpose	Materials
• Practice rounding mixed numbers to the nearest whole number • Estimate products of whole numbers and mixed numbers • Practice multiplying whole numbers by mixed numbers	• None
Memory Work	• **How do you know if a number is divisible by 3?** *The sum of its digits is divisible by 3.* • **How do you know if a number is divisible by 4?** *When you divide it by 2, the quotient is even.* • **How do you know if a number is divisible by 6?** *It is even and divisible by 3.*

Warm-up (A): Round Mixed Numbers to the Nearest Whole Number

We'll warm up by rounding these mixed numbers to the nearest whole number. Have your child round each number to the nearest whole number.

(A)

$3\frac{2}{3} \approx$ 4	$1\frac{1}{2} \approx$ 2	$4\frac{1}{5} \approx$ 4

If needed, remind your child to think about whether the fractional part of the number is less than, equal to, or greater than 1/2. **If the fraction is less than one-half, you round down. If the fraction is equal to or greater than one-half, you round up.**

Activity (B): Estimate Products of Whole Numbers and Mixed Numbers

In the last few lessons, you learned how to multiply a whole number by a mixed number to find the total of equal groups. Today, you'll learn how to estimate these products. Have your child read aloud the top part of the text box.

(B)

Estimate Products of Whole Numbers and Mixed Numbers

To estimate the product of a whole number and a mixed number, round the mixed number to the nearest whole number.

Ex. Maddie runs $2\frac{1}{4}$ mi. each day. About how far does she run in 3 days?

$3 \times 2\frac{1}{4} \approx ?$

$3 \times 2 = 6$

Maddie runs about 6 miles in 3 days.

Ex. Maddie runs $2\frac{1}{4}$ mi. each day. Exactly how far does she run in 3 days?

$3 \times 2\frac{1}{4} = ?$

$\frac{3}{1} \times \frac{9}{4} = \frac{3 \times 9}{1 \times 4} = \frac{27}{4}$

$\frac{27}{4} = 6\frac{3}{4}$ **mi.**

The first example shows how to estimate the product of a whole number and mixed number. Read the word problem aloud.

- **We want to find the product of 3 and 2 and one-fourth.**
- **What's 2 and one-fourth rounded to the nearest whole number?** *2.*
- **So, we multiply 3 times 2 to estimate the product. 3 times 2 is 6, so she ran about 6 miles.**
- **Do you expect that the exact answer will be greater than or less than 6?** *Greater than 6.* **Why?** *Sample answer: 2 and one-fourth is greater than 2, so we're missing part of the exact answer in the estimate.*

The second example shows how to find the exact product.

- **What fraction equals 3 wholes?** *3 over 1.*
- **What fraction equals 2 and one-fourth?** *Nine-fourths.*
- **3 times 9 equals 27. 1 times 4 equals 4. Twenty-seven-fourths equals 6 and three-fourths.**

Show your child the first practice problem in part B. **What is 1 and two-thirds rounded to the nearest whole number?** *2.* **What's 4 times 2?** *8.* **So, 8 is a good estimate for this problem.** Write "4 × 2 = 8" in the cloud.

Do you predict the answer will be greater than 8 or less than 8? Why? *Sample answer: The answer will be less than 8. 1 and two-thirds is less than 2, so the estimate is a little too much.*

Then, have your child find the exact product (either with the distributive property or fraction multiplication). **Is the product greater than or less than 8?** *Less.* Repeat with the other two problems.

Activity (C): Play Pop the Product (1-Player Game)

Explain to your child how to play Pop the Product. Then, have her complete this one-player game. Encourage her to round the mixed numbers in the problems to the nearest whole number to help estimate the products.

Pop the Product

Materials: None

Object of the Game: Write factors in the multiplication problems so that each problem yields the target product in the balloons.

For each problem, choose a number from the boxes on the left. Write the number in a multiplication problem so that the problem's product matches the description in the balloon. Then, solve the problem to check whether you are correct. If you are correct, draw an X on the balloon to "pop" it.

For example, the target product for the first problem is "greater than 3 and less than 4." Look for a number that you can multiply by 1 1/6 to yield a product between 3 and 4. Repeat until you've popped all the balloons.

Answer Key:

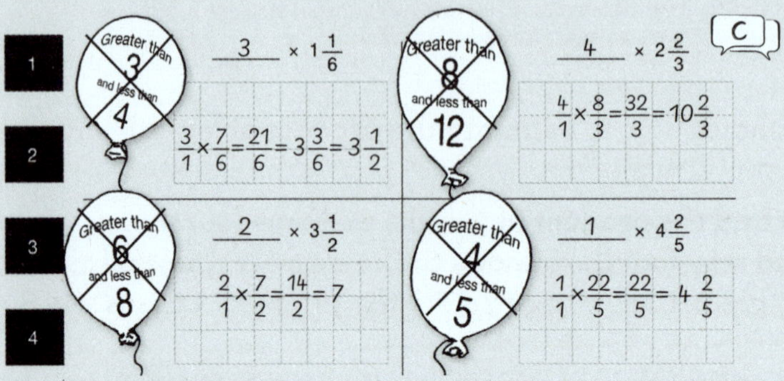

Independent Practice and Review

Have your child complete the Lesson 11.3 Practice and Review workbook pages.

Lesson 11.4
Estimate and Find Products of Mixed Numbers

Purpose	Materials
• Practice converting mixed numbers and improper fractions • Estimate products of mixed numbers • Multiply mixed numbers	• 2 dice

Memory Work	
	• **What do we call numbers that have a whole number and a fraction?** *Mixed numbers.* • **What do we call a fraction whose numerator is greater than or equal to its denominator?** *An improper fraction.*

Warm-up (A): Practice Converting Mixed Numbers and Improper Fractions

Have your child convert the mixed numbers to improper fractions and the improper fractions to mixed numbers.

A

$1\frac{2}{3} = \frac{5}{3}$	$3\frac{9}{10} = \frac{39}{10}$	$\frac{31}{15} = 2\frac{1}{15}$	$\frac{78}{25} = 3\frac{3}{25}$

If needed, help your child multiply and adjust to perform the mental division. For example, for 31/15:

- **We want to divide 31 by 15. 1 times 15 is 15, so that's too low.**
- **What's 2 times 15?** *30.* **That's as close as we can get to 31 without going over, so the quotient is 2. What's the remainder?** *1.*
- **So, thirty-one-fifteenths equals 2 and one-fifteenth.**

Activity (B): Estimate and Find Products of Mixed Numbers

In the last few lessons, you learned how to multiply a whole number by a fraction or mixed number. Today, you'll learn how to multiply a mixed number by a mixed number and estimate the product.

B

Estimate and Find Products of Mixed Numbers

Ex. Micah uses $1\frac{3}{4}$ bags of potting soil to fill the planter. Each bag weighs $2\frac{1}{3}$ kg. About how much soil does he use?

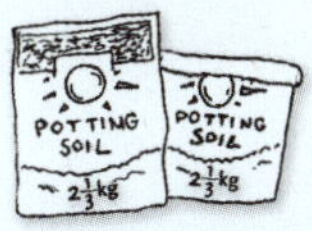

$1\frac{3}{4} \times 2\frac{1}{3} \approx ?$

$2 \times 2 = \mathbf{4}$

Micah uses about 4 kg of potting soil.

Ex. Micah uses $1\frac{3}{4}$ bags of potting soil to fill the planter. Each bag weighs $2\frac{1}{3}$ kg. Exactly how much soil does he use?

$1\frac{3}{4} \times 2\frac{1}{3} = ?$

$\frac{7}{4} \times \frac{7}{3} = \frac{7 \times 7}{4 \times 3} = \frac{49}{12}$

$\frac{49}{12} = \mathbf{4\frac{1}{12}\ kg}$

The first example shows how to estimate the product of two mixed numbers. Read the word problem aloud.

- **We want to estimate the product of 1 and three-fourths times 2 and one-third. What's 1 and three-fourths rounded to the nearest whole number?** *2.* **He used about 2 bags.**
- **What's 2 and one-third rounded to the nearest whole number?** *2.* **Each bag weighs about 2 kilograms.**
- **2 times 2 is 4, so he used about 4 kilograms of potting soil.**

The second example shows how to find the exact product. We convert both numbers to fractions and then multiply like usual.

- **What fraction equals 1 and three-fourths?** *Seven-fourths.*
- **What fraction equals 2 and one-third?** *Seven-thirds.*
- **7 times 7 equals 49. 4 times 3 equals 12.**
- **Forty-nine-twelfths equals 4 and one-twelfth. He used 4 and one-twelfth kilograms of potting soil.**

Show your child the first practice problem in part A. **To imagine this problem, let's say Micah used 1 and one-fourth bags of dirt, and that each bag weighed 2 and two-thirds kilograms. What is 1 and one-fourth rounded to the nearest whole number?** *1.* **What's 2 and two-thirds rounded to the nearest whole number?** *3.* **What's 1 times 3?** *3.* Write "1 × 3 = 3" in the estimate cloud. **So, 3 is a good estimate for this problem. Micah used about 3 bags of dirt.** Have your child find the exact product. Repeat with the other two problems.

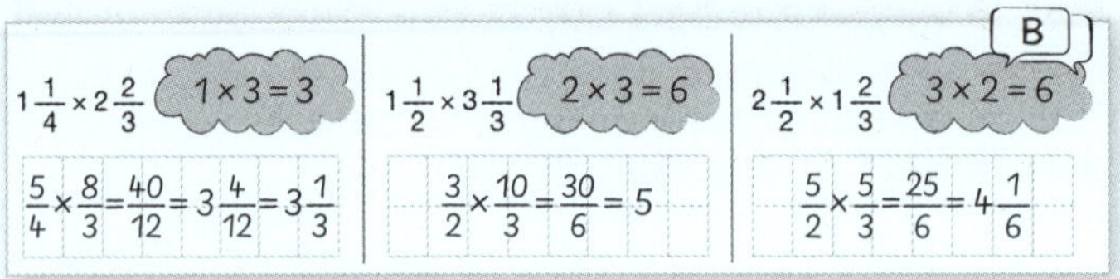

Activity (C): Play Roll and Multiply

Play Roll and Multiply. If your child needs more space, have him solve the problems on scrap paper.

Roll and Multiply

Materials: 2 dice

Object of the Game: Win the most points.

Roll and Multiply has 3 rounds. On your turn, roll both dice. Find the mixed numbers in the table on the left that match the numbers on the dice and write them as the factors in a multiplication problem. (For example, if you roll a 1 and 4, your multiplication problem is 2 2/3 × 2 2/5.) Find the product.

Then, have the other player roll and find the product of the matching mixed numbers. Whoever has the greater product wins a point for that round.

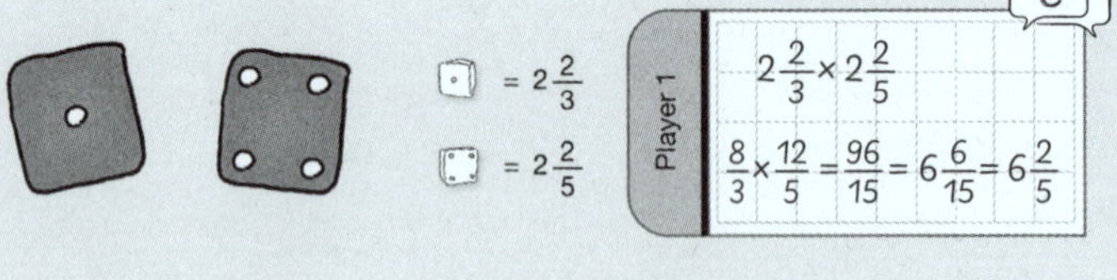

Sample play.

Continue until you have completed 3 rounds. Whoever has won more points wins the game.

Independent Practice and Review

Have your child complete the Lesson 11.4 Practice and Review workbook pages.

Lesson 11.5
Multiply Fractions by Whole Numbers

Purpose	Materials
• Practice finding a fraction of a fraction • Multiply to find a fraction of a whole number	• Highlighter

Memory Work
- **Name 4 factors of 18.** *Possible answers: 1, 2, 3, 6, 9, 18.*
- **What does GCF stand for?** *Greatest common factor.*

In Lessons 11.1-11.4, your child used multiplication to find the total of equal groups. In Lessons 11.5 and 11.6, she will use multiplication to find fractions of quantities. See the Unit 11 **Teaching Math with Confidence** for more on why *Math with Confidence* addresses these skills separately, even though the problems are solved with the same techniques.

Warm-up (A): Practice Finding a Fraction of a Fraction

In Unit 10, you learned how to find a fraction of a fraction. Read aloud the first problem: ***One-third of one-half.***

When you solved these problems with pictures, you used 3 steps to find the answer: have, split, take.

- **First, we identify how much we *have*. What fraction of the rectangle is colored?** *One-half.* Highlight 1/2.
- **Second, we *split* the amount we have into smaller fractional parts to match the denominator of the first fraction. We want one-third of one-half, so we split the rectangle into thirds in the other direction.**
- **Last, we *take* the number of fractional parts that we want. We want one-third of one-half, so we take 1 of the new thirds.** Outline one of the fractional parts as shown.
- **What fraction of the whole rectangle do we take?** *One-sixth.*

We could also multiply 1/3 times 1/2 to find the answer. Have your child find the product.

Repeat with the other problems. First, have your child draw lines to find the answer visually. Then, have her write and solve the matching multiplication problem.

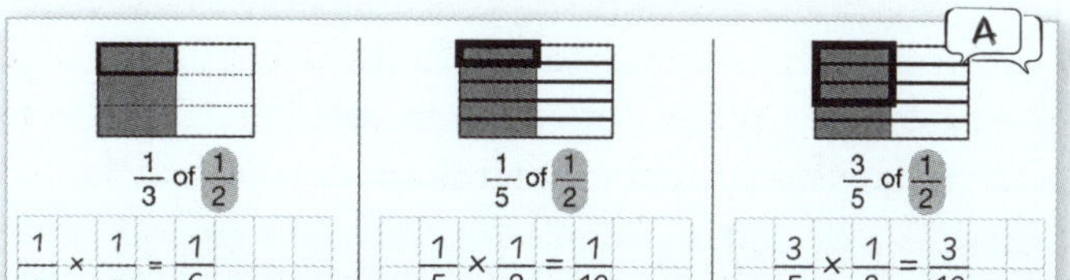

Solving the problems in part A with both methods prepares your child to find a fraction of a whole number in part B.

Activity (B): Multiply to Find a Fraction of a Whole Number

Today, you'll learn how to find a fraction of a whole number. Have your child read the text box aloud.

Multiply a Fraction by a Whole Number (B)

In math, "of" usually means multiply. To find a fraction of a whole number, multiply the fraction by the whole number.

Ex. Amanda's family bought 2 one-pound slabs of fudge while they were on vacation. They still have $\frac{3}{5}$ of the fudge left. How many pounds of fudge do they have left?

$\frac{3}{5}$ of 2 → $\frac{3}{5} \times 2$

$\frac{3}{5} \times \frac{2}{1} = \frac{3 \times 2}{5 \times 1} = \frac{6}{5}$

$\frac{6}{5} = 1\frac{1}{5}$ lb.

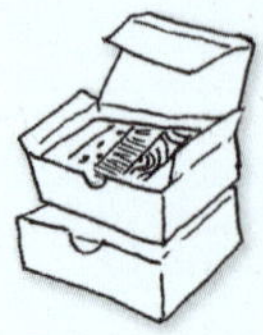

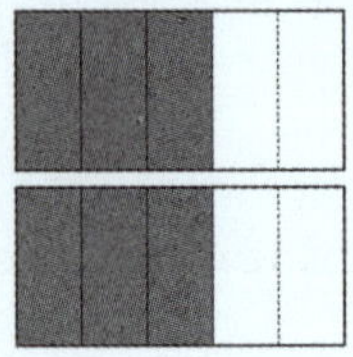

The example shows how to use multiplication to find three-fifths of 2.

- Read aloud the problem. **We want to find a fraction of a number, so "of" means multiply. We multiply three-fifths times 2 to find three-fifths of 2 pounds.**
- **How do we write the whole number as a fraction?** *2 over 1.*
- **Then, we follow the usual steps in fraction multiplication. 3 times 2 is 6. 5 times 1 is 5.**
- **Six-fifths is an improper fraction, so we convert it to a mixed number. Six-fifths equals what mixed number?** *1 and one-fifth.* **How much fudge does Amanda's family have left?** *1 and one-fifth pounds.*

If your child has trouble understanding how the diagram matches the problem, draw lines on the printed example as shown. **Amanda's family has 2 pounds of fudge. We split the fudge into 5 equal parts and take 3 of the parts. We get 1 and one-fifth pounds of fudge.**

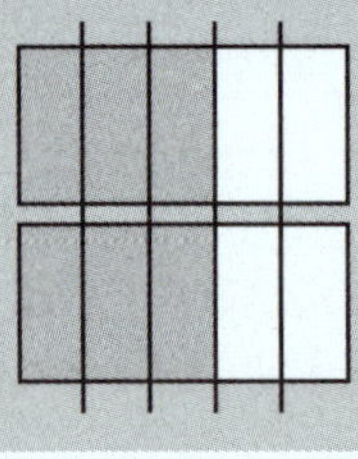

When you were younger, you learned that we can multiply in any order without changing the answer. We could also think of this problem as finding the weight of 2 slabs of fudge that each weigh three-fifths of a pound. Either way we get the same answer.

When you solve the practice problems, write the factors in the multiplication problems in the same order as the numbers in the "of" statement. Writing the factors in the same order helps us remember what the problem means in everyday life.

Your child may notice that the example problem doesn't specify what fraction of each slab Amanda's family has left. They may have more of one slab left than the other. (For example, they may have eaten 4/5 lb. of one slab and still have 1 whole slab plus 1/5 lb. left.) Regardless, the family has 1 1/5 lb. of fudge left, even if it's unevenly shared between the two slabs.

Have your child use the word "of" to describe what she's trying to find in each practice problem. Then, have her complete the blanks and solve the matching multiplication problem.

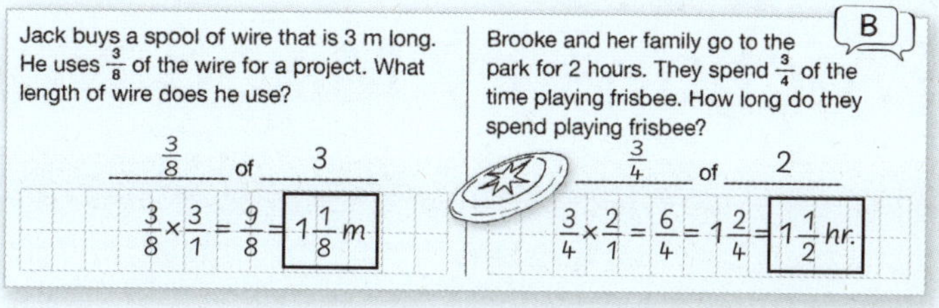

Activity (C): Create a Word Problem to Match a Multiplication Problem

Now, you get to write your own word problem to match five-sixths times 3. Have your child create a word problem that matches the multiplication problem. If needed, explain that her problem should be about finding 5/6 of 3 wholes. Then, have her solve the problem and label the answer to match the word problem.

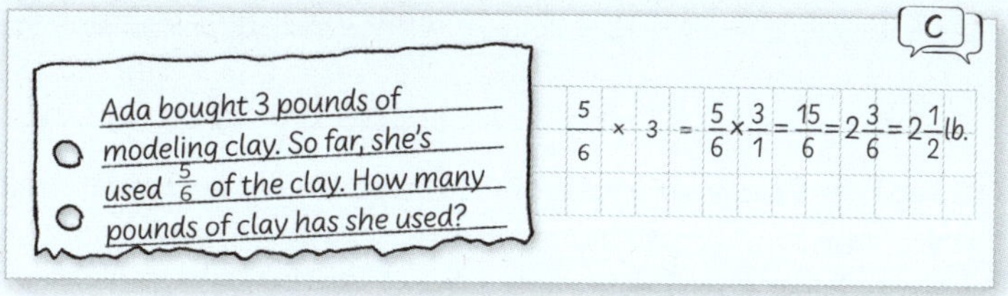

Sample word problem and solution.

> If your child has trouble, encourage her to first choose a unit for the 3 wholes that can be split into parts. She can choose objects that can be cut (like 3 pizzas or 3 candy bars) or measurement units (like 3 kilograms of rice or 3 feet of string).

Independent Practice and Review

Have your child complete the Lesson 11.5 Practice and Review workbook pages.

Lesson 11.6
Multiply Fractions by Mixed Numbers

Purpose	Materials
• Practice multiplying fractions by whole numbers • Multiply fractions by mixed numbers • Use fraction multiplication to scale down a recipe	• Measuring cups and spoons, optional

Memory Work	
	• **What do we call an angle with a measure less than 90 degrees?** *Acute.* • **What do we call an angle with a measure equal to 90 degrees?** *Right.* • **What do we call an angle with a measure greater than 90 degrees and less than 180 degrees?** *Obtuse.* • **What do we call an angle with a measure equal to 180 degrees?** *Straight.*

Warm-up (A): Practice Multiplying Fractions by Whole Numbers

In the last lesson, you learned how to multiply a fraction by a whole number. Have your child write each "of" statement as a multiplication problem and find the product. If needed, remind him to rewrite the whole number as a fraction with 1 as the denominator.

A

$\frac{1}{6}$ of 3	$\frac{3}{5}$ of 4	$\frac{7}{8}$ of 2
$\frac{1}{6} \times \frac{3}{1} = \frac{3}{6} = \frac{1}{2}$	$\frac{3}{5} \times \frac{4}{1} = \frac{12}{5} = 2\frac{2}{5}$	$\frac{7}{8} \times \frac{2}{1} = \frac{14}{8} = 1\frac{6}{8} = 1\frac{3}{4}$

Activity (B): Multiply a Fraction by a Mixed Number to Scale Down a Recipe

Today, you'll learn how to multiply a fraction by a mixed number to find fractions of amounts in recipes. Have your child read the text box aloud.

B

Multiply a Fraction by a Mixed Number

To multiply a fraction by a mixed number, convert the mixed number to a fraction. Then, multiply like usual.

Ex. The fried rice recipe calls for $2\frac{1}{2}$ cups of cooked rice. Ryland only wants to make $\frac{2}{3}$ of the recipe. How much rice should he use?

$$\frac{2}{3} \times 2\frac{1}{2}$$

$$\frac{2}{3} \times \frac{5}{2} = \frac{2 \times 5}{3 \times 2} = \frac{10}{6}$$

$$\frac{10}{6} = 1\frac{4}{6} = \mathbf{1\frac{2}{3}\ c.}$$

Does Ryland want to make more or less fried rice than the original recipe makes? *Less.* **When we want to make less of a recipe, we multiply all the ingredients by the same fraction. This is called "scaling down" a recipe. When we want to make more of a recipe, we multiply all the ingredients by the same whole number or mixed number. This is called "scaling up" a recipe. Scaling the recipe makes sure that the ingredients stay in balance with each other so the food tastes good.**

Use the following questions to discuss the example:

- Show your child a 1-cup measure and 1/2-cup measure. **To measure 2 and one-half cups, we use 2 whole cups plus one-half of a cup.**
- **We want to find two-thirds of 2 and one-half, so we multiply two-thirds times 2 and one-half. We rewrite the mixed number as an improper fraction and then multiply like usual.**

- **What fraction equals 2 and one-half?** *Five-halves.*
- **Two-thirds times five-halves equals ten-sixths. Then, we convert ten-sixths to a fraction and simplify.**
- **How much rice should Ryland use?** *1 and two-thirds cups.* Show your child a 1-cup measure and 1/3-cup measure. **To measure 1 and two-thirds cups, we use 1 whole cup and 2 one-third cups.**

Let's scale down the rest of the ingredients in this recipe. We'll find two-thirds of all the amounts. Help your child write and solve multiplication problems to scale down the rest of the ingredients in the recipe. Use real measuring cups and spoons to show both the original and scaled-down amounts. For 5/6 c. of frozen peas and carrots, say: **Measuring cup sets don't usually have one-sixth cups, so I'd probably just estimate and use a little less than 1 full cup.**

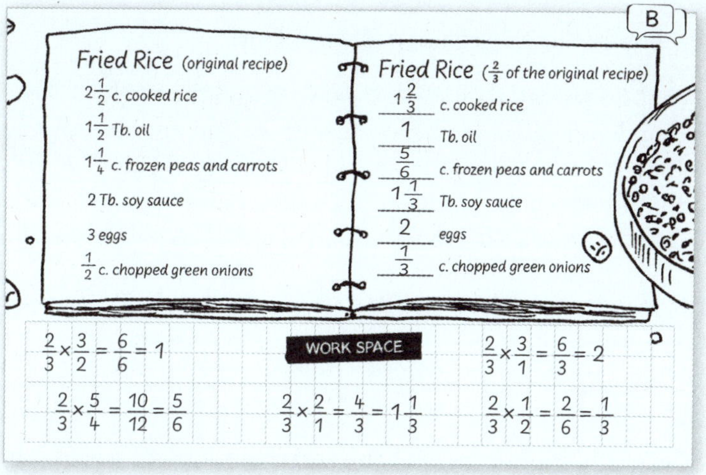

Why are all the quantities less than the original quantities? *Sample answers: We scaled the recipe down. We multiplied all the quantities by two-thirds.* **When you multiply a number by a fraction less than 1, the product is always less than the original number.**

You can also use the distributive property to multiply a fraction by a mixed number (as in Lesson 11.2). However, the resulting arithmetic is often more complicated and error-prone than simply converting the mixed number to an improper fraction. If your child is interested, ask him to try multiplying 2/3 times 2 1/2 with the distributive property and compare the results to the example problem.

$$\frac{2}{3} \times 2\frac{1}{2}$$

$$(\frac{2}{3} \times 2) + (\frac{2}{3} \times \frac{1}{2})$$

$$\frac{4}{3} + \frac{2}{6}$$

$$1\frac{1}{3} + \frac{1}{3}$$

$$1\frac{2}{3}$$

Independent Practice and Review

Have your child complete the Lesson 11.6 Practice and Review workbook pages.

Lesson 11.7
Solve Multiplicative Comparison Problems and Predict Products

Purpose	Materials
• Preview multiplicative comparison problems by drawing lines of different lengths • Use fraction multiplication to solve multiplicative comparison problems • Predict the products of multiplicative comparison problems	• None

Memory Work

- **What do we call a quadrilateral with 4 right angles?** *A rectangle.*
- **What do we call a quadrilateral with 4 right angles and 4 equal sides?** *A square.*
- **What do we call a quadrilateral with 4 equal sides?** *A rhombus.*
- **What do we call a quadrilateral with 2 pairs of parallel sides?** *A parallelogram.*
- **What do we call a quadrilateral with exactly 1 pair of parallel sides?** *A trapezoid.*

Warm-up: Use a Reference Line to Draw Lines with Different Lengths

In this lesson, your child will investigate multiplying a number by a fraction less than 1, a fraction equal to 1, and a mixed number greater than 1. The warm-up activity previews this concept.

Draw a reference line about 4 inches long at the top of a piece of scrap paper as shown. (You do not need to measure the length exactly.) **I'm going to give you directions for drawing some lines. The lines may be shorter than, longer than, or the same length as my line. Start all your lines below mine, along the left side of the paper.** Have your child draw the following lines in order, below your line.

- **Draw a line that is about half as long as my line.**
- **Draw a line that is the same length as my line.**
- **Draw a line that is 2 times as long as my line.**
- **Draw a line that is about 1 and one-half times as long as my line.** If your child is unsure, suggest she start by drawing a line that matches your line. Then, have her extend it by half the length of the original line.

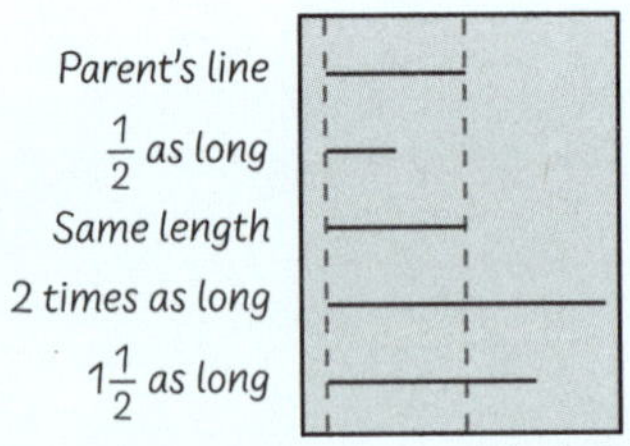

The dotted lines are included for visual reference. Your child does not need to include them.

Your child should simply eyeball the lines' lengths. She does not need to measure anything or perform any fraction arithmetic.

Activity (A): Solve Multiplicative Comparison Problems and Predict Products

In this unit, you've learned how to multiply fractions, whole numbers, and mixed numbers. Today, you'll use your multiplication skills to solve comparison problems and predict their products.

Show your child part A. **The wood frog is 1 and three-fourths of an inch long. We'll use the clues in part A to find the lengths of the other frogs at the nature center.**

Read aloud the first clue: ***The spring peeper is two-thirds as long as the wood frog.* Is the spring peeper shorter, longer, or the same length as the wood frog?** *Shorter.*

Hold your fingers as shown to match the length of the wood frog. **Two-thirds of the length of the wood frog is a little more than half the length of the wood frog.** Narrow the distance between your fingers to show the approximate length of the spring peeper. **About how long do you think the spring peeper is?** *Sample answer: 1 inch.*

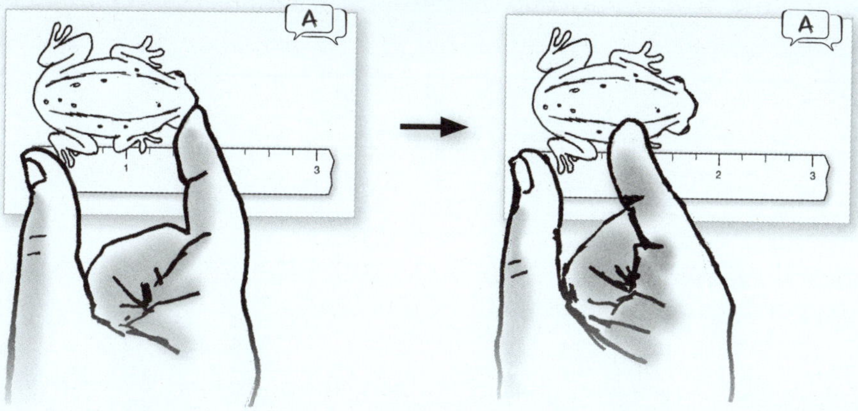

What multiplication problem can you use to find the spring peeper's exact length? *Two-thirds times 1 and three-fourths.* Have your child write and solve the matching problem. **How long is the spring peeper?** *1 and one-sixth inches.* Write "1 1/6" in the chart.

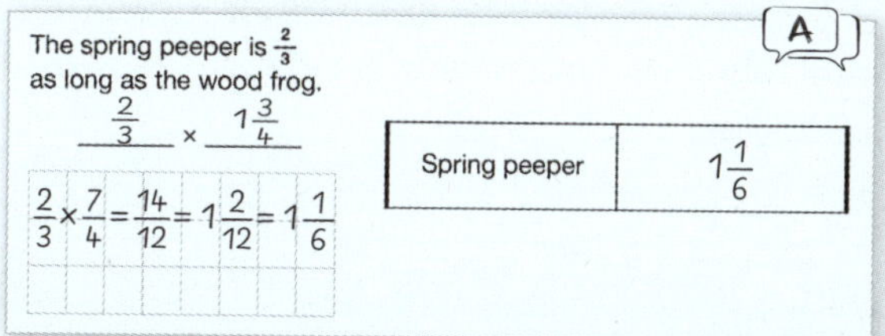

Repeat with the next clue: ***The gray tree frog is four-fourths as long as the wood frog.* Is the gray tree frog shorter, longer, or the same length as the wood frog?** *The same length.* **How do you know?** *Sample answer: Four-fourths equals 1, and any number times 1 equals the number.*

What multiplication problem can you use to find the gray tree frog's length? *Four-fourths times 1 and three-fourths.* Have your child write and solve the matching problem. **How long is the gray tree frog?** *1 and three-fourths inches.* Write "1 3/4" in the chart.

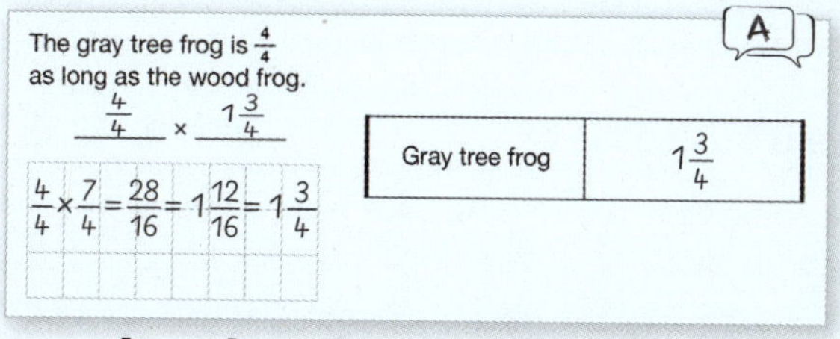

The gray tree frog is the same length as the wood frog! Four-fourths equals 1 whole, and multiplying a number by 1 always equals the original number.

Repeat with the final clue: ***The bullfrog is 3 times as long as the wood frog.*** **Is the bullfrog shorter, longer, or the same length as the wood frog?** *Longer.* **The wood frog is about 2 inches long, so about how long do you think the bullfrog is?** *Sample answer: 6 inches.*

What multiplication problem can you use to find the bullfrog's exact length? *3 times 1 and three-fourths.* Have your child write and solve the matching problem. **How long is the bullfrog?** *5 and one-fourth inches.* Write "5 1/4" in the chart.

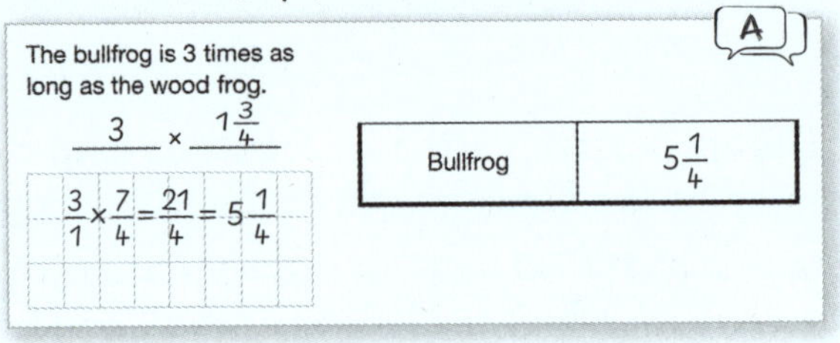

Activity (B): Play Pop the Product (1-Player Game)

Explain to your child how to play Pop the Product. Then, have her complete this one-player game.

Pop the Product

Materials: None

Object of the Game: Write factors in the multiplication problems so that each problem yields the target product in the balloons.

For each problem, choose a number from the boxes on the left. Write the number in a multiplication problem so that the problem's product matches the description in the balloon. Then, solve the problem to check whether you are correct. If you are correct, draw an X on the balloon to "pop" it.

For example, the target product for the first problem is "less than 2 1/2." Look for a number that you can multiply by 2 1/2 to yield a product less than 2 1/2. Repeat until you've popped all the balloons.

Answer Key:

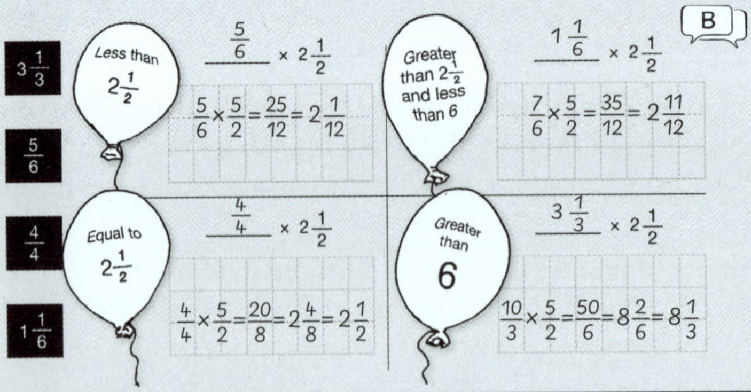

Independent Practice and Review

Have your child complete the Lesson 11.7 Practice and Review workbook pages.

Lesson 11.8
Multiply Mixed Numbers to Find Rectangles' Areas

Purpose	Materials
• Use paper square inches to find the area of a rectangle • Multiply mixed numbers to find the area of rectangles • Draw rectangles to match dimensions in a scale drawing and find their areas	• 1-foot ruler • 4 one-inch paper squares • Scissors

Memory Work

- **What do we call the horizontal axis?** *The x-axis.*
- **What do we call the vertical axis?** *The y-axis.*
- **What do we call the (0,0) point?** *The origin.*
- **What is an ordered pair?** *A pair of numbers that identify the location of a point.*
- **In an ordered pair, what do we call the first number?** *The x-coordinate.* **What does it tell?** *The point's horizontal distance.*
- **In an ordered pair, what do we call the second number?** *The y-coordinate.* **What does it tell?** *The point's vertical distance.*

You will need 4 one-inch paper squares for the warm-up activity. To make the paper squares, cut a piece of paper into a 2-inch by 2-inch square. (Or, use a 2-inch square sticky note.) Then, cut the square into 4 roughly equal squares.

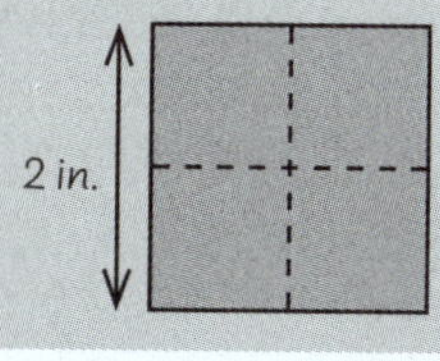

Warm-up: Use Paper Squares to Measure the Area of a Rectangle

This hands-on activity provides concrete experience with "tiling" a rectangle with whole square inches and fractions of square inches. Tiling rectangles in this way helps your child understand the real-life meaning of areas expressed with mixed numbers.

Today, we'll warm up by using paper squares to measure the area of a rectangle. Have your child use the ruler to draw a rectangle 2 1/2 inches long and 1 1/2 inches wide on a piece of scrap paper. (Help as needed. It's okay if the rectangle is a little crooked or its angles aren't exactly 90°.)

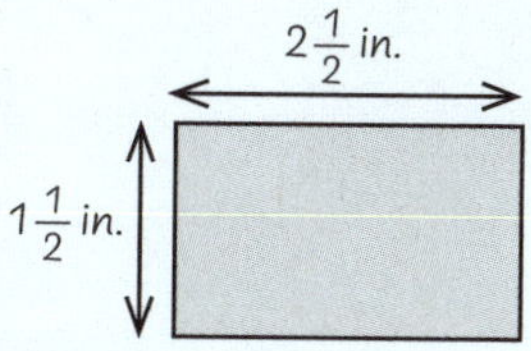

How many square inches do you think it would take to cover this rectangle? *Sample answer: 3.* **How do you know?** *Sample answer: It looks like about 3 square inches would fit.*

Give your child 4 one-inch paper squares. **Let's use these paper squares to find the exact area of the rectangle. The sides of the squares are 1 inch, so each square has an area of 1 square inch.** Give your child a chance to experiment with covering the rectangle with the paper squares. **How many whole squares fit in the rectangle?** *2.*

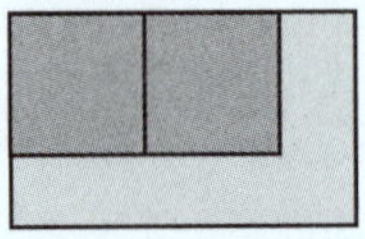

How could you use the paper squares to cover the rest of the rectangle? *Sample answer: Cut the paper squares into smaller parts.* Help your child cut the remaining paper squares in half and use the halves to cover as much of the uncovered area as possible.

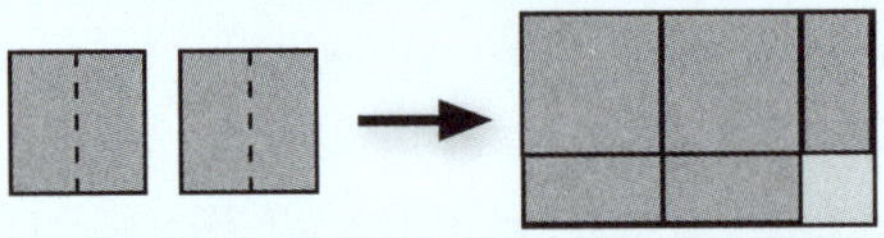

How can you cover the last little part of the rectangle? *Sample answer: Cut one of the halves in half.* Help your child cut the remaining half into 2 equal parts. Use one of the resulting squares to cover the final part of the rectangle.

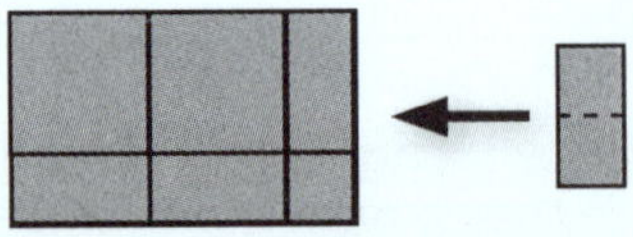

How many square inches did it take to cover the whole rectangle? *3 and three-fourths square inches.* **How do you know?** *Sample answers: We used 2 whole squares, 3 half-squares, and 1 quarter-square to cover the rectangle. They add up to 3 and three-fourths. Or: We had 4 whole squares, and we used all but one-fourth of one square. So, we must have used 3 and three-fourths square inches.* If your child isn't sure, have him identify the area of each piece of paper he used to cover the rectangle and then add to find the sum.

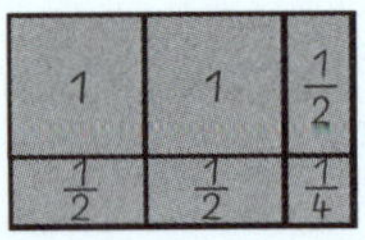

$1+1+\frac{1}{2}+\frac{1}{2}+\frac{1}{2}+\frac{1}{4}=3\frac{3}{4}$ sq. in.

Activity (A): Multiply Mixed Numbers to Find Area

In the warm-up, we used paper squares to measure the area of a rectangle that was 2 and one-half by 1 and one-half inches long. We could also multiply the length by the width to find the area. We just convert both mixed numbers to fractions and then multiply like usual.

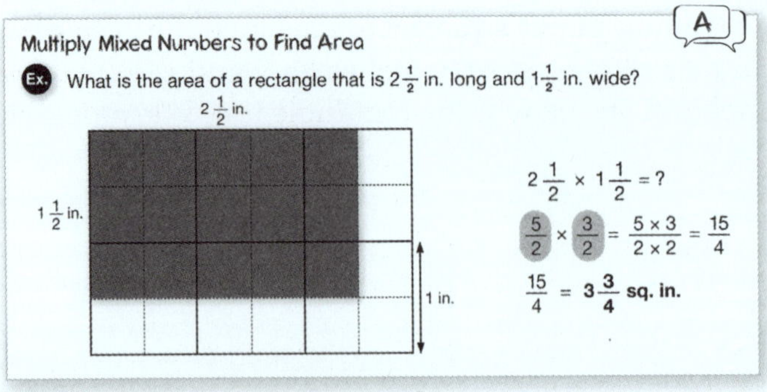

Use the following questions to discuss the example:

- **What fraction equals 2 and one-half?** *Five-halves.*
- **What fraction equals 1 and one-half?** *Three-halves.* **Five-halves times three-halves equals fifteen-fourths.**
- **Each small square in the diagram is what fraction of a square inch?** *One-fourth.* If your child isn't sure, point out that it takes 4 small squares to cover 1 square inch.

- **If you had tiny tiles the same size as the small squares, how many would it take to cover the rectangle?** *15.* **How do you know?** *Sample answer: There are 3 rows of 5 small squares.*
- **Fifteen-fourths equals 3 and three-fourths square inches, just like we found in the warm-up.**

Activity (B): Multiply to Find Area in a Bedroom Floor Plan

People use diagrams like this to plan how to fit the furniture in a room. Point to the key below the floor plan. **In this bedroom floor plan, each square stands for 1 square foot. The narrow rectangles along the top and left edge stand for windows. The two lines along the bottom edge stand for a door.** Briefly discuss any experience your child has with drawing or interpreting floor plans.

You get to decide where the furniture goes in this bedroom floor plan. Have your child choose where he'd like to place the furniture in the room. (He may want to place the bed first, since it's the largest item.) Encourage him to think about what a logical bedroom layout would look like. For example: **You probably don't want the bed right in front of the door!**

Then, help him draw rectangles on the floor plan to represent each piece of furniture. For example: **The dresser is 4 and one-half feet long and 1 and one-fourth of a foot wide. So, the rectangle should be 4 and one-half squares long and 1 and one-fourth squares wide.** It's fine for your child to approximate the fractional lengths.

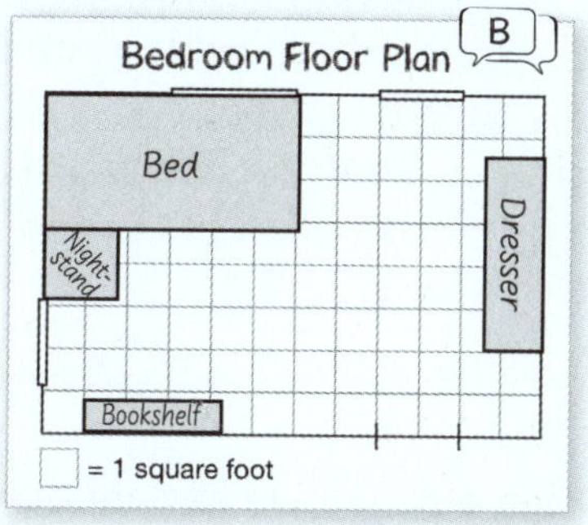

Have your child multiply to find the area that each item would cover in the bedroom. If he runs out of space for equations in the work space, have him write them on scrap paper.

Furniture Dimensions (B)

Item	Length (ft.)	Width (ft.)	Area (sq. ft.)
Bookshelf	$3\frac{1}{3}$	$\frac{3}{4}$	$2\frac{1}{2}$
Dresser	$4\frac{1}{2}$	$1\frac{1}{4}$	$5\frac{5}{8}$
Nightstand	$1\frac{3}{4}$	$1\frac{3}{4}$	$3\frac{1}{16}$
★ Bed	6	$3\frac{1}{4}$	$19\frac{1}{2}$

WORK SPACE (B)

$3\frac{1}{3} \times \frac{3}{4}$

$\frac{10}{3} \times \frac{3}{4} = \frac{30}{12} = 2\frac{6}{12} = 2\frac{1}{2}$

$1\frac{3}{4} \times 1\frac{3}{4}$

$\frac{7}{4} \times \frac{7}{4} = \frac{49}{16} = 3\frac{1}{16}$

$4\frac{1}{2} \times 1\frac{1}{4}$

$\frac{9}{2} \times \frac{5}{4} = \frac{45}{8} = 5\frac{5}{8}$

$6 \times 3\frac{1}{4}$

$\frac{6}{1} \times \frac{13}{4} = \frac{78}{4} = 19\frac{2}{4} = 19\frac{1}{2}$

> Finding the area of the bed requires multiplying 13 by 6 and dividing 78 by 4. Your child may use mental math or the written algorithm for these steps.

Independent Practice and Review

Have your child complete the Lesson 11.8 Practice and Review workbook pages.

Lesson 11.9
Enrichment (Optional)

Purpose	Materials
• Practice memory work • Appreciate how math can be used to answer real-life questions • Multiply to scale a recipe up or down • Summarize what your child has learned and assess your child's progress	• *How Many Guinea Pigs Can Fit on a Plane?: Answers to Your Most Clever Math Questions*, by Laura Overdeck • Recipe with fractions and mixed numbers

Warm-up: Review Memory Work

Quiz your child on any of the memory work items that she struggled with during this unit.

Math Picture Book: *How Many Guinea Pigs Can Fit on a Plane?*

Read pages 102-109 in *How Many Guinea Pigs Can Fit on a Plane?*

Enrichment Activity: Use Multiplication to Scale a Recipe Up or Down

In this unit, you've learned how to multiply to scale recipes. Show your child a recipe with fractions and mixed numbers. Discuss reasons you might want to scale the recipe up or down. For example: **If I wanted to make this cheesy potato recipe for a holiday dinner, I'd probably multiply this recipe by 3 or 4.** Or: **This bread recipe makes 2 loaves. If I only wanted 1 loaf, I'd multiply the recipe by 1/2.**

Have your child decide whether she'd like to scale the recipe up or down. Then, have her choose a number to use to scale the recipe.

- If she'd like to scale the recipe down, have her choose a fraction less than 1 (like 1/3, 1/2, or 3/4) to multiply by the original quantities.
- If she'd like to scale the recipe up, have her choose a whole number or mixed number greater than 1 (like 1 2/3, 2, or 3 1/2) to multiply by the original quantities.

Then, have her multiply to scale the recipe by her chosen factor.

Unit Wrap-Up

Have your child complete the Unit 11 Wrap-Up.

Unit 11 Answer Key

11.1 Practice

Practice: Find the product. Write your answers in simplest form. If your answer is an improper fraction, convert it to a mixed number.

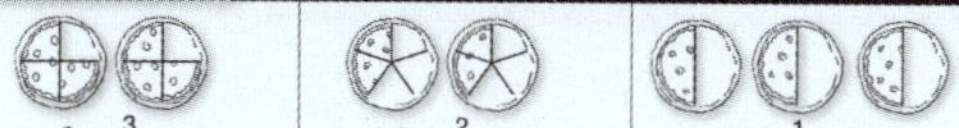

$2 \times \frac{3}{4} =$ $\frac{2}{1} \times \frac{3}{4} = \frac{6}{4} = 1\frac{2}{4} = 1\frac{1}{2}$

$2 \times \frac{2}{5} =$ $\frac{2}{1} \times \frac{2}{5} = \frac{4}{5}$

$3 \times \frac{1}{2} =$ $\frac{3}{1} \times \frac{1}{2} = \frac{3}{2} = 1\frac{1}{2}$

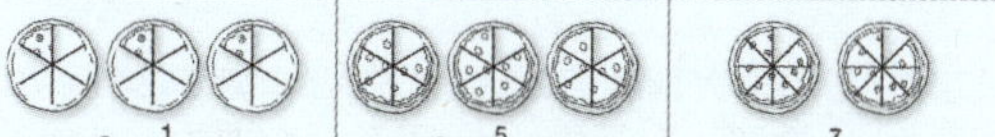

$3 \times \frac{1}{6} =$ $\frac{3}{1} \times \frac{1}{6} = \frac{3}{6} = \frac{1}{2}$

$3 \times \frac{5}{6} =$ $\frac{3}{1} \times \frac{5}{6} = \frac{15}{6} = 2\frac{3}{6} = 2\frac{1}{2}$

$2 \times \frac{7}{8} =$ $\frac{2}{1} \times \frac{7}{8} = \frac{14}{8} = 1\frac{6}{8} = 1\frac{3}{4}$

Complete the blanks to match each word problem. Then, write and solve the matching multiplication equation. Write your answers in simplest form.

Sadie made 15 bars of scented soap to give as gifts. Each bar weighed $\frac{1}{4}$ lb. How many pounds of soap did she make?

15 of $\frac{1}{4}$

$\frac{15}{1} \times \frac{1}{4} = \frac{15}{4} = 3\frac{3}{4}$ lb.

Nasir has 8 pieces of ribbon. Each ribbon is $\frac{2}{3}$ ft. long. How many feet of ribbon does he have in all?

8 of $\frac{2}{3}$

$\frac{8}{1} \times \frac{2}{3} = \frac{16}{3} = 5\frac{1}{3}$ ft.

Sawyer made a big batch of fudge to give as gifts. He cut the fudge into 4 pieces, and each piece weighed $\frac{3}{10}$ kg. How many kilograms of fudge did he make?

4 of $\frac{3}{10}$

$\frac{4}{1} \times \frac{3}{10} = \frac{12}{10} = 1\frac{2}{10} = 1\frac{1}{5}$ kg

Selah practices the trumpet for $\frac{1}{2}$ hr. each day. How many hours does she practice each week?

7 of $\frac{1}{2}$

$\frac{7}{1} \times \frac{1}{2} = \frac{7}{2} = 3\frac{1}{2}$ hr.

11.1 Review

Review: Write the ordered pair that describes the location of each point.

Point	Ordered Pair
V	(1,5)
W	(4,4)
X	(5,1)
Y	(0,0)
Z	(3,6)

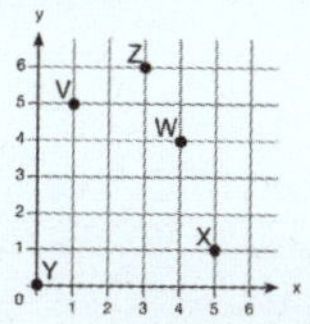

Find the missing information for each rectangular prism. Make sure to include the correct units.

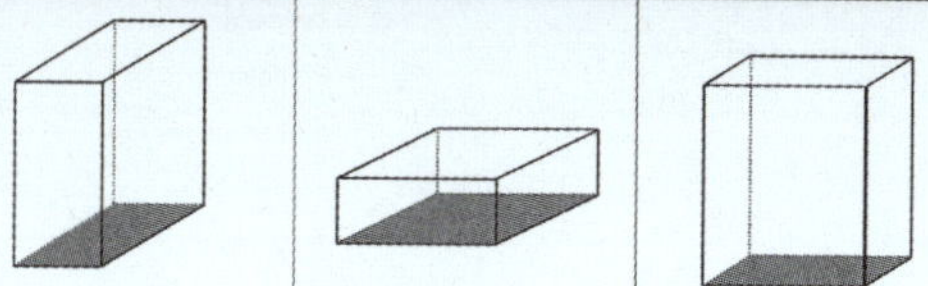

Base area: 6 sq. cm
Height: 4 cm
Volume: 24 cu. cm

Base area: 20 sq. ft.
Height: 2 ft.
Volume: 40 cubic ft.

Base area: 10 sq. m
Height: 6 m
Volume: 60 cubic m

Use mental math to complete the division problems.

150 ÷ 3 = 50
150 ÷ 30 = 5
240 ÷ 8 = 30
240 ÷ 80 = 3
360 ÷ 9 = 40
360 ÷ 90 = 4

490 ÷ 7 = 70
490 ÷ 70 = 7
640 ÷ 8 = 80
640 ÷ 80 = 8
720 ÷ 9 = 80
720 ÷ 90 = 8

Find the product.

$$\begin{array}{r} 768 \\ \times\ 351 \\ \hline 768 \\ 38{,}400 \\ +\ 230{,}400 \\ \hline 269{,}568 \end{array}$$

11.2 Practice

Practice: Use the distributive property or fraction multiplication to find the products. Write your answers as whole numbers or mixed numbers in simplest form.

$3 \times 2\frac{1}{4}$: $\frac{3}{1} \times \frac{9}{4} = \frac{27}{4} = 6\frac{3}{4}$

$2 \times 3\frac{1}{5}$: $\frac{2}{1} \times \frac{16}{5} = \frac{32}{5} = 6\frac{2}{5}$

$4 \times 1\frac{3}{4}$: $\frac{4}{1} \times \frac{7}{4} = \frac{28}{4} = 7$

$2 \times 2\frac{3}{5}$: $\frac{2}{1} \times \frac{13}{5} = \frac{26}{5} = 5\frac{1}{5}$

$2 \times 1\frac{2}{3}$: $\frac{2}{1} \times \frac{5}{3} = \frac{10}{3} = 3\frac{1}{3}$

$5 \times 3\frac{1}{10}$: $\frac{5}{1} \times \frac{31}{10} = \frac{155}{10} = 15\frac{5}{10} = 15\frac{1}{2}$

Complete the blanks to match each word problem. Then, write and solve the matching multiplication equation. Write your answers as whole numbers or mixed numbers in simplest form.

Laurel has 3 hockey practices each week. Each practice is $1\frac{1}{2}$ hr. long. How many hours does she spend practicing hockey each week?

3 of $1\frac{1}{2}$

$\frac{3}{1} \times \frac{3}{2} = \frac{9}{2} = 4\frac{1}{2}$ hr.

Josiah makes 5 pitchers of punch for a party. He puts $2\frac{1}{4}$ liters in each pitcher. How many liters of punch does he make in all?

5 of $2\frac{1}{4}$

$\frac{5}{1} \times \frac{9}{4} = \frac{45}{4} = 11\frac{1}{4}$ L

11.2 Review

Review: Estimate the answer to each problem. Then, circle the words that match the answer. You do not need to find the exact answers.

Problem	Circled answer
3 × 201	greater than 600
3 × 199	less than 600
2 × 295	less than 600
388 ÷ 2	less than 200
432 ÷ 2	greater than 200
415 ÷ 4	greater than 100

Use mental math to complete.

80 ÷ 20 = 4
100 ÷ 20 = 5
120 ÷ 20 = 6
140 ÷ 20 = 7
160 ÷ 20 = 8

70 ÷ 7 = 10
77 ÷ 7 = 11
84 ÷ 7 = 12
91 ÷ 7 = 13
98 ÷ 7 = 14

100 ÷ 50 = 2
150 ÷ 50 = 3
200 ÷ 50 = 4
250 ÷ 50 = 5
300 ÷ 50 = 6

Use the clues to complete the chart.

- Mom is 40 years old.
- Jackson's age is $\frac{1}{8}$ of Mom's age.
- Dad is 9 times as old as Jackson.
- Jackson's age is $\frac{1}{2}$ of Vivian's age.
- ★ Mom's age is $\frac{2}{3}$ of Grandma's age.

Name	Age
Mom	40
Dad	45
Jackson	5
Vivian	10
Grandma	60

Unit 11 Answer Key

11.3 Practice

Practice: Estimate the answer to each problem. Then, circle the words that match the answer. You do not need to find the exact answers.

- $2 \times 1\frac{7}{8}$: **(less than 4)** / greater than 4
- $4 \times 2\frac{1}{5}$: less than 8 / **(greater than 8)**
- $3 \times 1\frac{2}{3}$: less than 3 / **(greater than 3)**

Betty's dad wants to make a triple batch of chili. Multiply the amount for each ingredient by 3 to find how much of each ingredient he needs. Write your equations in the workspace.

Dad's Delicious Chili (Makes 8 servings)
- $1\frac{1}{2}$ tablespoons of oil
- 2 cups of onions, chopped
- $\frac{1}{4}$ cup of chili powder
- $\frac{3}{4}$ teaspoon cumin
- $1\frac{1}{4}$ teaspoon garlic powder
- $1\frac{3}{4}$ pounds of ground beef
- $3\frac{1}{3}$ cups of canned diced tomatoes
- $3\frac{2}{3}$ cups of canned tomato puree

Dad's Delicious Chili (Makes 24 servings)
- $4\frac{1}{2}$ tablespoons of oil
- 6 cups of onions, chopped
- $\frac{3}{4}$ cup of chili powder
- $2\frac{1}{4}$ teaspoon cumin
- $3\frac{3}{4}$ teaspoon garlic powder
- $5\frac{1}{4}$ pounds of ground beef
- 10 cups of canned diced tomatoes
- 11 cups of canned tomato puree

WORK SPACE

$\frac{3}{1}\times\frac{3}{2}=\frac{9}{2}=4\frac{1}{2}$

$3 \times 2 = 6$

$\frac{3}{1}\times\frac{1}{4}=\frac{3}{4}$

$\frac{3}{1}\times\frac{3}{4}=\frac{9}{4}=2\frac{1}{4}$

$\frac{3}{1}\times\frac{5}{4}=\frac{15}{4}=3\frac{3}{4}$

$\frac{3}{1}\times\frac{7}{4}=\frac{21}{4}=5\frac{1}{4}$

$\frac{3}{1}\times\frac{10}{3}=\frac{30}{3}=10$

$\frac{3}{1}\times\frac{11}{3}=\frac{33}{3}=11$

11.3 Review

Review: Find all factors of each number. Then, answer the question.

Factors of 64: 1, 2, 4, 8, 16, 32, 64

1 × 64
2 × 32
4 × 16
8 × 8

Factors of 80: 1,2,4,5,8,10,16,20,40,80

1 × 80
2 × 40
4 × 20
5 × 16
8 × 10

What is the GCF of 64 and 80? 16

Connect each mixed number to its place on the number line.

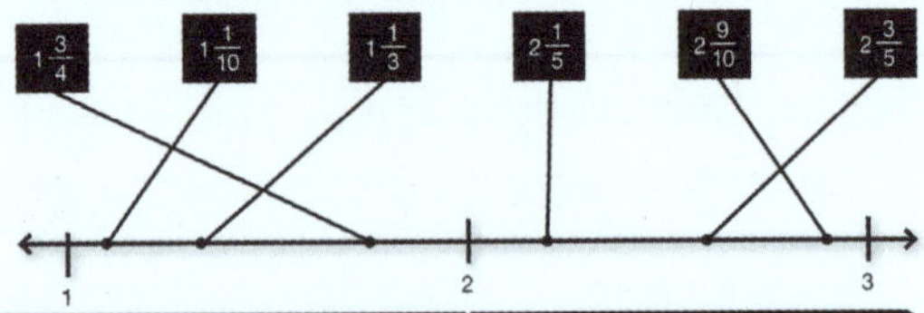

Use long division to solve. Use the multiplication table to help.

$$709 \div 27 = 26 \text{ R } 7$$

```
     2 6
2 7 )7 0 9
   - 5 4
     1 6 9
   - 1 6 2
         7
```

	× 27
1	27
2	54
3	81
4	108
5	135
6	162
7	189
8	216
9	243

Complete.

1 meter = 100 centimeters

1 centimeter = 10 millimeters

1 liter = 1,000 milliliters

1 kilometer = 1,000 meters

1 kilogram = 1,000 grams

11.4 Practice

Practice: Circle the most reasonable estimate for each problem. You do not need to find the exact answers.

- $3\frac{1}{6} \times 4\frac{5}{8}$: 12 / **(15)** / 18
- $2\frac{3}{4} \times 4\frac{1}{3}$: 8 / 10 / **(12)**
- $1\frac{7}{8} \times 3\frac{1}{4}$: 3 / **(6)** / 9
- $1\frac{1}{9} \times 3$: **(3)** / 6 / 9
- $2 \times 4\frac{5}{6}$: 8 / **(10)** / 12
- $4 \times 1\frac{1}{4}$: **(4)** / 8 / 12

Find the exact product. Write your answers in simplest form. If your answer is an improper fraction, convert to a whole number or mixed number.

$1\frac{1}{6} \times 2\frac{1}{2}$: $\frac{7}{6}\times\frac{5}{2}=\frac{35}{12}=2\frac{11}{12}$

$3\frac{1}{3} \times 2\frac{2}{3}$: $\frac{10}{3}\times\frac{8}{3}=\frac{80}{9}=8\frac{8}{9}$

$1\frac{4}{5} \times 4\frac{1}{2}$: $\frac{9}{5}\times\frac{9}{2}=\frac{81}{10}=8\frac{1}{10}$

$2\frac{1}{4} \times 1\frac{3}{5}$: $\frac{9}{4}\times\frac{8}{5}=\frac{72}{20}=3\frac{12}{20}=3\frac{3}{5}$

Solve. Write your answers in simplest form. If your answer is an improper fraction, convert to a mixed number.

The art students use $4\frac{1}{2}$ bottles of paint. Each bottle holds $1\frac{3}{4}$ cups of paint. How many cups of paint do the students use in all?

$1\frac{3}{4}\times 4\frac{1}{2}$

$\frac{7}{4}\times\frac{9}{2}=\frac{63}{8}=$ **$7\frac{7}{8}$ cups**

The puppy weighs $3\frac{1}{4}$ kg. Its mother weighs $3\frac{1}{3}$ times as much as the puppy. How much does the mother dog weigh?

$3\frac{1}{3}\times 3\frac{1}{4}$

$\frac{10}{3}\times\frac{13}{4}=\frac{130}{12}=10\frac{10}{12}$ **$10\frac{5}{6}$ kg**

11.4 Review

Review: Write parallel or perpendicular to complete the blanks.

$\overleftrightarrow{MN}$ and $\overleftrightarrow{NO}$ are perpendicular

$\overleftrightarrow{OP}$ and $\overleftrightarrow{NO}$ are perpendicular

$\overleftrightarrow{MN}$ and $\overleftrightarrow{OP}$ are parallel

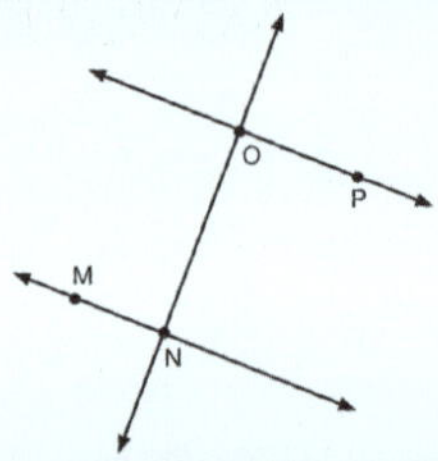

Plot and label each point on the coordinate plane.

Point	Ordered Pair
Q	(5,1)
R	(2,4)
S	(3,0)
T	(4,4)
U	(0,1)

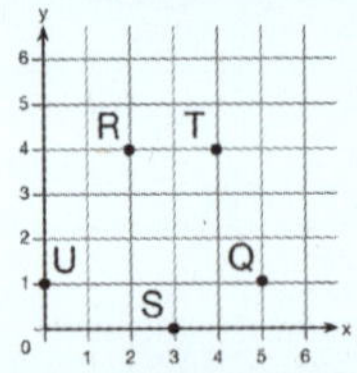

Find the product.

```
      4 9 8
  ×     3 7
    3,4 8 6
+ 1 4,9 4 0
  1 8,4 2 6
```

Use mental math to complete.

430 + 200 = 630
430 + 270 = 700
430 + 280 = 710

950 + 50 = 1,000
950 + 250 = 1,200
950 + 550 = 1,500

840 − 30 = 810
840 − 230 = 610
840 − 530 = 310

620 − 20 = 600
620 − 70 = 550
620 − 170 = 450

Unit 11 Answer Key

11.5 Practice

Practice Roman's mom wants to make a small batch of snack mix. Find $\frac{3}{4}$ of each amount to find how much of each ingredient she needs. Write your equations in the workspace.

Snack Mix (Original)

- 8 c. popcorn
- 5 c. pretzels
- 4 c. peanuts
- 2 c. chocolate candy
- 3 c. mini marshmallows

Snack Mix ($\frac{3}{4}$ of the original recipe)

- 6 c. popcorn
- $3\frac{3}{4}$ c. pretzels
- 3 c. peanuts
- $1\frac{1}{2}$ c. chocolate candy
- $2\frac{1}{4}$ c. mini marshmallows

WORK SPACE

$\frac{3}{4} \times \frac{8}{1} = \frac{24}{4} = 6$

$\frac{3}{4} \times \frac{5}{1} = \frac{15}{4} = 3\frac{3}{4}$

$\frac{3}{4} \times \frac{4}{1} = \frac{12}{4} = 3$

$\frac{3}{4} \times \frac{2}{1} = \frac{6}{4} = 1\frac{2}{4} = 1\frac{1}{2}$

$\frac{3}{4} \times \frac{3}{1} = \frac{9}{4} = 2\frac{1}{4}$

Complete the blanks to match each word problem. Then, write and solve the matching multiplication equation. Write your answers as whole numbers or mixed numbers in simplest form.

Harley and his dad have a 5-pound bag of potatoes. They peel and chop $\frac{1}{3}$ of the potatoes in the bag. How many pounds of potatoes do they prepare?

$\frac{1}{3}$ of 5

$\frac{1}{3} \times \frac{5}{1} = \frac{5}{3} = 1\frac{2}{3}$ lb.

Sania and her friends order 4 pizzas. They eat $\frac{4}{5}$ of the pizzas. How much pizza do they eat?

$\frac{4}{5}$ of 4

$\frac{4}{5} \times \frac{4}{1} = \frac{16}{5} = 3\frac{1}{5}$ pizzas

11.5 Review

Review Write each fraction as a mixed number in simplest form.

$\frac{25}{12} = 2\frac{1}{12}$	$\frac{35}{12} = 2\frac{11}{12}$	$\frac{50}{12} = 4\frac{2}{12} = 4\frac{1}{6}$
$\frac{45}{20} = 2\frac{5}{20} = 2\frac{1}{4}$	$\frac{27}{25} = 1\frac{2}{25}$	$\frac{33}{15} = 2\frac{3}{15} = 2\frac{1}{5}$

Circle the word that best describes the slope of each line.

Graph 1	Graph 2	Graph 3
(Upward) circled	Upward	Upward
Downward	(Downward) circled	Downward
Horizontal	Horizontal	Horizontal
Vertical	Vertical	(Vertical) circled

Find the least common multiple for each pair of numbers.

LCM of 10 and 15: 30 — 15, (30)

LCM of 12 and 18: 36 — 18, (36), 54

LCM of 5 and 7: 35 — 7, 14, 21, 28, (35)

Solve. Write the equations you use.

25 teams are playing in the volleyball tournament. There are 18 players on each team. How many players are at the tournament?

450 players

$$\begin{array}{r} 25 \\ \times\ 18 \\ \hline 200 \\ +\ 250 \\ \hline 450 \end{array}$$

11.6 Practice

Practice Find the product. Then, find the blank that matches the product. Write the matching letter in the blank to solve the riddle.

N: $\frac{1}{2} \times 2\frac{1}{5}$ $\frac{1}{2} \times \frac{11}{5} = \frac{11}{10} = 1\frac{1}{10}$	F: $\frac{1}{2} \times 2\frac{2}{5}$ $\frac{1}{2} \times \frac{12}{5} = \frac{12}{10} = 1\frac{2}{10} = 1\frac{1}{5}$	I: $\frac{1}{2} \times 2\frac{3}{5}$ $\frac{1}{2} \times \frac{13}{5} = \frac{13}{10} = 1\frac{3}{10}$
Y: $\frac{1}{3} \times 2\frac{1}{4}$ $\frac{1}{3} \times \frac{9}{4} = \frac{9}{12} = \frac{3}{4}$	K: $\frac{2}{3} \times 2\frac{1}{4}$ $\frac{2}{3} \times \frac{9}{4} = \frac{18}{12} = 1\frac{6}{12} = 1\frac{1}{2}$	L: $\frac{3}{3} \times 2\frac{1}{4}$ $\frac{3}{3} \times \frac{9}{4} = \frac{27}{12} = 2\frac{3}{12} = 2\frac{1}{4}$
O: $\frac{3}{4} \times 1\frac{1}{4}$ $\frac{3}{4} \times \frac{5}{4} = \frac{15}{16}$	T: $\frac{3}{4} \times 2\frac{1}{2}$ $\frac{3}{4} \times \frac{5}{2} = \frac{15}{8} = 1\frac{7}{8}$	E: $\frac{3}{4} \times 5$ $\frac{3}{4} \times \frac{5}{1} = \frac{15}{4} = 3\frac{3}{4}$
M: $1 \times 3\frac{1}{2}$ $\frac{1}{1} \times \frac{7}{2} = \frac{7}{2} = 3\frac{1}{2}$	P: $2 \times 3\frac{1}{2}$ $\frac{2}{1} \times \frac{7}{2} = \frac{14}{2} = 7$	L: $4 \times 3\frac{1}{2}$ $\frac{4}{1} \times \frac{7}{2} = \frac{28}{2} = 14$

If you have 27 goats and 19 cows, what do you have?

P	L	E	N	T	Y
7	$2\frac{1}{4}$	$3\frac{3}{4}$	$1\frac{1}{10}$	$1\frac{7}{8}$	$\frac{3}{4}$

O	F		M	I	L	K
$\frac{15}{16}$	$1\frac{1}{5}$		$3\frac{1}{2}$	$1\frac{3}{10}$	14	$1\frac{1}{2}$

11.6 Review

Review Choose the more sensible measurement for each item.

Volume of a baby pool	Volume of a jewelry box	Volume of a box of cereal
20 cu. in. / (20 cu. ft.) circled	(16 cu. in.) circled / 16 cu. ft.	(150 cu. in.) circled / 150 cu. ft.

Use the information to complete the chart. Then, use the chart to make a line graph.

Each box of cookies costs $5.

Boxes	Cost ($)
0	0
1	5
2	10
3	15
4	20
5	25
6	30

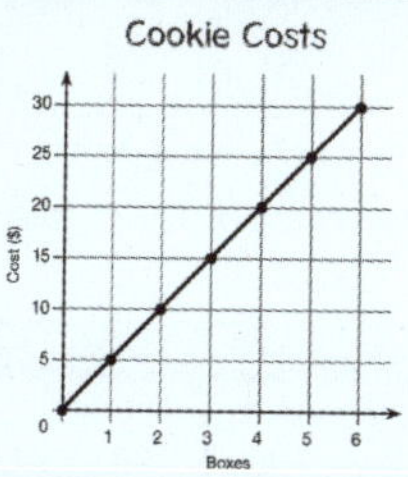

Evaluate.

20 + 20 × 2 − 4 20 + 40 − 4 60 − 4 56	8 − 3 × 2 + 6 8 − 6 + 6 2 + 6 8	20 ÷ 4 + 6 ÷ 2 5 + 3 8
(20 + 20) × 2 − 4 40 × 2 − 4 80 − 4 76	(8 − 3) × (2 + 6) 5 × 8 40	20 ÷ (4 + 6) ÷ 2 20 ÷ 10 ÷ 2 2 ÷ 2 1

Unit 11 Answer Key

11.7 Practice

Practice Find the products. Write your answers in simplest form.

$\frac{4}{5} \times 1\frac{1}{2}$	$\frac{5}{5} \times 1\frac{1}{2}$	$1\frac{4}{5} \times 1\frac{1}{2}$
$\frac{4}{5} \times \frac{3}{2} = \frac{12}{10} = 1\frac{2}{10} = 1\frac{1}{5}$	$\frac{5}{5} \times \frac{3}{2} = \frac{15}{10} = 1\frac{5}{10} = 1\frac{1}{2}$	$\frac{9}{5} \times \frac{3}{2} = \frac{27}{10} = 2\frac{7}{10}$
$\frac{3}{8} \times 2$	$\frac{8}{8} \times 2$	$1\frac{3}{8} \times 2$
$\frac{3}{8} \times \frac{2}{1} = \frac{6}{8} = \frac{3}{4}$	$\frac{8}{8} \times \frac{2}{1} = \frac{16}{8} = 2$	$\frac{11}{8} \times \frac{2}{1} = \frac{22}{8} = 2\frac{6}{8} = 2\frac{3}{4}$

Use logical reasoning to complete the circles with <, >, or =.
(You do not need to find the exact answers to the multiplication problems.)

$6\frac{1}{2} > 1$	$\frac{6}{6} = 1$	$\frac{1}{6} < 1$
$6\frac{1}{2} \times 2\frac{7}{10} > 2\frac{7}{10}$	$\frac{6}{6} \times 2\frac{7}{10} = 2\frac{7}{10}$	$\frac{1}{6} \times 2\frac{7}{10} < 2\frac{7}{10}$

Use the clues to find how much each person's fish weighed. Write your answers in simplest form. Convert any improper fractions to whole numbers or mixed numbers.

- David's fish weighed 2 times the weight of Caylee's fish.
- Annie's fish weighed $\frac{2}{3}$ as much as David's fish.
- Hawthorn's fish weighed $1\frac{1}{2}$ times as much as Caylee's fish.

$\frac{2}{1} \times \frac{4}{3} = \frac{8}{3} = 2\frac{2}{3}$

$\frac{2}{3} \times \frac{8}{3} = \frac{16}{9} = 1\frac{7}{9}$

$\frac{3}{2} \times \frac{4}{3} = \frac{12}{6} = 2$

Fishing Contest Results	
Caylee	$1\frac{1}{3}$ kg
David	$2\frac{2}{3}$ kg
Annie	$1\frac{7}{9}$ kg
Hawthorn	2 kg

11.7 Review

Review Find the area of each rectangle. Write your answers in simplest form.

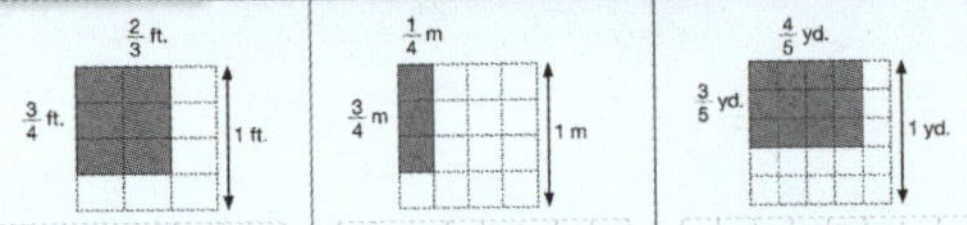

$\frac{2}{3} \times \frac{3}{4} = \frac{6}{12} = \frac{1}{2}$ sq. ft.	$\frac{1}{4} \times \frac{3}{4} = \frac{3}{16}$ sq. m	$\frac{4}{5} \times \frac{3}{5} = \frac{12}{25}$ sq. yd.

Complete.

1 foot = 12 inches
1 yard = 3 feet
1 yard = 36 inches
1 mile = 5,280 feet
1 pound = 16 ounces
1 cup = 8 fluid ounces

Circle the numbers that match the description. X the numbers that do not match the description.

Divisible by 2	Divisible by 3
(90) (92) (94) (96) (98) (100)	(90) X92 X94 (96) X98 X100

Divisible by 4	Divisible by 6
X90 (92) X94 (96) X98 (100)	(90) X92 X94 (96) X98 X100

Solve. Write the equations you use.

Magnus helped his mom make $2\frac{1}{4}$ liters of soup. Then, his family ate $1\frac{5}{8}$ liters. How many liters of soup did they have left?

$2\frac{1}{4} = 2\frac{2}{8} = 1\frac{10}{8}$

$-\ 1\frac{5}{8} = 1\frac{5}{8}$

$\boxed{\frac{5}{8}\text{ L}}$

Kira owns 40 model trains. She displays $\frac{1}{4}$ of her trains, and she keeps the other $\frac{3}{4}$ in storage. How many trains does she have in storage?

$\frac{3}{4} \times \frac{40}{1} = \frac{120}{4} = \boxed{30\text{ trains}}$

11.8 Practice

Practice Label the dimensions of each rectangle. Then, find the area. Make sure to use the correct units.

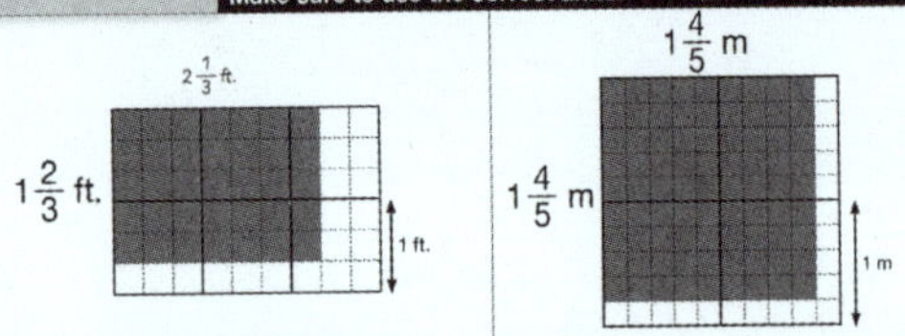

$\frac{7}{3} \times \frac{5}{3} = \frac{35}{9} = 3\frac{8}{9}$ sq. ft.	$\frac{9}{5} \times \frac{9}{5} = \frac{81}{25} = 3\frac{6}{25}$ sq. m

Outline a rectangle to match the dimensions. Then, find the area of the rectangle. Make sure to use the correct units.

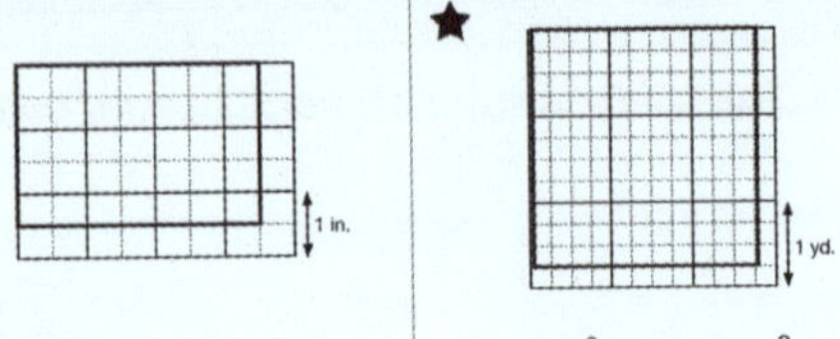

Length: $3\frac{1}{2}$ in. Width: $2\frac{1}{2}$ in.	★ Length: $2\frac{3}{4}$ yd. Width: $2\frac{3}{4}$ yd.
$\frac{7}{2} \times \frac{5}{2} = \frac{35}{4} = 8\frac{3}{4}$ sq. in.	$\frac{11}{4} \times \frac{11}{4} = \frac{121}{16} = 7\frac{9}{16}$ sq. yd.

11.8 Review

Review Complete.

30 ÷ 15 = 2	60 ÷ 20 = 3	25 ÷ 25 = 1
31 ÷ 15 = 2 R1	64 ÷ 20 = 3 R4	27 ÷ 25 = 1 R2
35 ÷ 15 = 2 R5	68 ÷ 20 = 3 R8	30 ÷ 25 = 1 R5
45 ÷ 15 = 3	75 ÷ 20 = 3 R15	40 ÷ 25 = 1 R15
47 ÷ 15 = 3 R2	76 ÷ 20 = 3 R16	50 ÷ 25 = 2
59 ÷ 15 = 3 R14	79 ÷ 20 = 3 R19	53 ÷ 25 = 2 R3

Find the missing dimension for each solid. All measurements are in inches.

Volume: 27 cu. in.	Volume: 24 cu. in.	Volume: 20 cu. in.

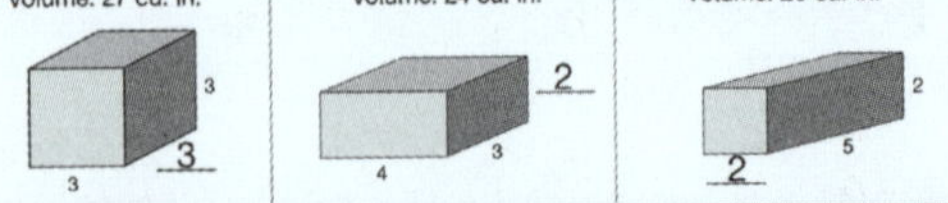

Write each measurement as a fraction. Write your answers in simplest form.

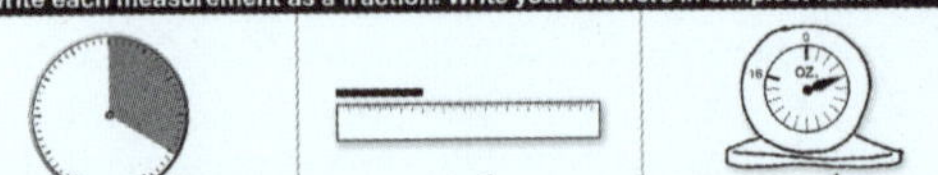

20 min. = $\frac{1}{3}$ hr.	4 in. = $\frac{1}{3}$ ft.	4 oz. = $\frac{1}{4}$ lb.

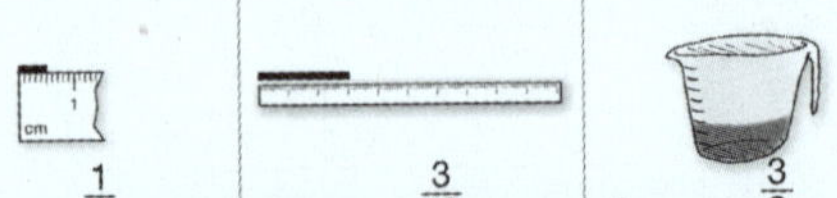

5 mm = $\frac{1}{2}$ cm	30 cm = $\frac{3}{10}$ m	3 fl. oz. = $\frac{3}{8}$ c.

Unit 11 Answer Key

11.9 Unit Wrap-Up A

Unit Wrap-Up Find the products. Write your answers in simplest form. If the answer is an improper fraction, convert it to a mixed number or whole number.

$\frac{1}{4} \times 1\frac{2}{3}$	$\frac{3}{4} \times 1\frac{2}{3}$	$\frac{4}{4} \times 1\frac{2}{3}$
$\frac{1}{4} \times \frac{5}{3} = \frac{5}{12}$	$\frac{3}{4} \times \frac{5}{3} = \frac{15}{12} = 1\frac{3}{12} = 1\frac{1}{4}$	$\frac{4}{4} \times \frac{5}{3} = \frac{20}{12} = 1\frac{8}{12} = 1\frac{2}{3}$
$1\frac{1}{4} \times 1\frac{2}{3}$	$1\frac{3}{4} \times 1\frac{2}{3}$	$4 \times 1\frac{2}{3}$
$\frac{5}{4} \times \frac{5}{3} = \frac{25}{12} = 2\frac{1}{12}$	$\frac{7}{4} \times \frac{5}{3} = \frac{35}{12} = 2\frac{11}{12}$	$\frac{4}{1} \times \frac{5}{3} = \frac{20}{3} = 6\frac{2}{3}$

Circle the most reasonable estimate for each problem. You do not need to find the exact answers.

$2\frac{1}{5} \times 3\frac{7}{8}$	$1\frac{1}{10} \times 4$	$3 \times 2\frac{3}{4}$
6 (8) 10	(4) 6 8	6 (9) 12

Use logical reasoning to complete the circles with <, >, or =. (You do not need to find the answers to the problems.)

$\frac{5}{8} < 1$	$2\frac{5}{8} > 1$	$\frac{8}{8} = 1$
$\frac{5}{8} \times 4\frac{1}{3} < 4\frac{1}{3}$	$2\frac{5}{8} \times \frac{1}{2} > \frac{1}{2}$	$\frac{8}{8} \times 5\frac{1}{4} = 5\frac{1}{4}$

Label the dimensions. Then, find the area of the rectangle.

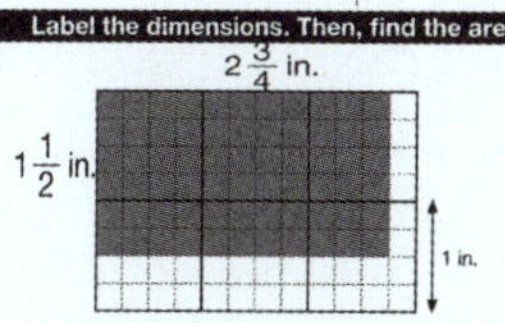

$\frac{11}{4} \times \frac{3}{2} = \frac{33}{8} = 4\frac{1}{8}$ sq. in.

11.9 Unit Wrap-Up B

Unit Wrap-Up Solve. Write the equations you use. Write your answers in simplest form. If the answer is an improper fraction, convert it to a mixed number or whole number.

You're invited to a Valentine's Party!

What: We'll decorate cookies, make Valentine's cards, and play games.

Where: Marcus and Hannah's house

When: February 14, from 2:00 P.M. to 4:30 P.M.

Marcus and Hannah bought 7 boxes of candy hearts for the party. Each box holds $1\frac{1}{4}$ oz. What was the total weight of the candy?

$\frac{7}{1} \times \frac{5}{4} = \frac{35}{4} = \boxed{8\frac{3}{4} \text{ oz.}}$

The guests used $1\frac{3}{4}$ spools of ribbon to decorate the Valentine's cards. Each spool held $3\frac{1}{2}$ m of ribbon. How much ribbon did they use?

$\frac{7}{4} \times \frac{7}{2} = \frac{49}{8} = \boxed{6\frac{1}{8} \text{ m}}$

The original cookie frosting recipe called for $2\frac{1}{3}$ c. of powdered sugar. Marcus and Hannah decided to make $1\frac{1}{2}$ times the recipe to make sure they had enough frosting. How much powdered sugar did they use?

$\frac{7}{3} \times \frac{3}{2} = \frac{21}{6} = 3\frac{3}{6} = \boxed{3\frac{1}{2} \text{ c.}}$

Marcus and Hannah made punch. They used $\frac{2}{3}$ as much orange juice as lemon-lime soda. They used $2\frac{3}{4}$ L of lemon-lime soda. How much orange juice did they use?

$\frac{2}{3} \times \frac{11}{4} = \frac{22}{12} = 1\frac{10}{12} = \boxed{1\frac{5}{6} \text{ L}}$

Unit 11 Checkpoint

What to Expect at the End of Unit 11

By the end of Unit 11, most children will be able to do the following:

- Multiply whole numbers by fractions or mixed numbers to find the total of equal groups. Your child may use fraction multiplication or the distributive property to solve these problems.
- Multiply to find fractions of whole numbers or mixed numbers.
- Estimate products of mixed numbers (or products of whole numbers and mixed numbers). Most children will be able to round both factors to the nearest whole number and multiply. Many will have trouble predicting whether the exact answer will be greater than or less than the estimate.
- Reason about fraction multiplication and predict whether a product will be greater than, less than, or equal to one the factors. Some children will still have trouble with this, especially if they don't have a concrete situation to imagine.
- Solve multiplication word problems that involve multiplying fractions, whole numbers, or mixed numbers. Some children may still have trouble interpreting and understanding these word problems.
- Multiply fractions, whole numbers, or mixed numbers to find the area of rectangles.

Is Your Child Ready to Move on?

In Unit 12, your child will study geometry. She does not need to have fully mastered multiplying fractions, whole numbers, and mixed numbers before moving on.

Unit 12
Geometry

Overview

Your child will learn to find the measure of missing angles in triangles and identify triangles based on both their sides and angles. He will also learn to find the measure of missing angles in parallelograms and rhombuses.

Many children find this unit a pleasant change of pace after the intense focus on multiplying fractions and mixed numbers in Units 10 and 11. Your child will practice those skills in the Review pages so that he's ready to tackle fraction division in Unit 13.

What Your Child Will Learn

In this unit, your child will learn to:

- Review how to measure and draw angles with a protractor
- Identify acute, right, and obtuse triangles
- Identify equilateral, isosceles, and scalene triangles
- Categorize triangles based on both their angles and sides
- Find the measure of a missing angle in a triangle
- Identify quadrilaterals
- Build and draw triangles and quadrilaterals
- Find the measure of missing angles in parallelograms and rhombuses

Lesson List

Lesson 12.1	Review Angles
Lesson 12.2	Draw Angles and Solve Angle Puzzles
Lesson 12.3	Acute, Right, and Obtuse Triangles
Lesson 12.4	Find Missing Angles in Triangles
Lesson 12.5	Equilateral, Isosceles, and Scalene Triangles
Lesson 12.6	Categorize Triangles by Their Angles and Sides
Lesson 12.7	Review Quadrilaterals
Lesson 12.8	Opposite and Adjacent Angles in Parallelograms and Rhombuses
Lesson 12.9	Enrichment (Optional)

Extra Materials Needed for Unit 12

- 2 pencils
- Scissors
- For optional Enrichment Lesson:
  - *How Many Guinea Pigs Can Fit on a Plane?: Answers to Your Most Clever Math Questions*, by Laura Overdeck. Feiwel & Friends, 2017.
  - Small piece of cardstock or cardboard (about 3 inches square)
  - Paper
  - Black marker
  - Colored pencils, markers, or watercolor paints

You will also need a protractor and the following blackline masters:

- Paper Strips (Blackline Master 10)
- Paper Triangles (Blackline Master 11)
- Paper Parallelogram (Blackline Master 12)

Teaching Math with Confidence: Using Hands-On Exploration to Understand Side and Angle Relationships in Triangles

In *Fourth Grade Math with Confidence,* your child learned to classify triangles by their angles. This year, your child will also learn to classify triangles by their sides.

Your child will construct many paper triangles in this unit. He'll build triangles from paper strips to explore the relationships between the sides and angles, fold paper triangles to explore symmetry, and tear the corners off paper triangles to study the sum of their angles.

One important principle he'll explore is that once you choose two side lengths and set an angle between them, the length of the third side is determined. All other triangles with the same two sides and angle will be identical to the original triangle. (You may remember this as the side-angle-side or SAS theorem in your high school geometry class.)

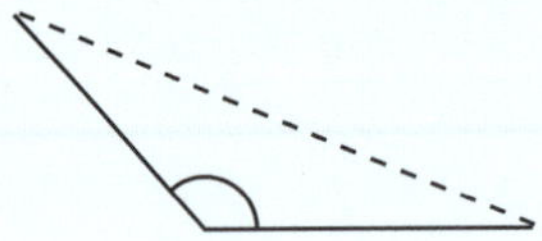

Once you determine the lengths of the two solid sides of this triangle and choose an angle between them, you also determine the length of the dotted side. No other length for the dotted side is possible.

He'll also explore the related fact that the sum of the two shorter sides of the triangle must be greater than the length of the longer side of the triangle. (You may remember this as the Triangle Inequality Theorem.) If the sum of the two shorter sides is less than the length of the longer side, the two shorter sides won't be able to reach each other.

The two shorter sides are not long enough to reach each other, no matter what angle is between them.

These hands-on activities help your child go beyond simply memorizing the definitions so that he develops deeper geometric intuition about triangles. He'll revisit these principles more formally when he studies geometry in middle school and high school.

Lesson 12.1
Review Angles

Purpose	Materials
• Review the definitions of acute, right, obtuse, and straight angles • Review how to measure angles with a protractor • Identify whether angles are acute, right, obtuse, or straight	• 2 pencils • Protractor
Memory Work	• **What is a prime number?** *A number with exactly 2 factors.* • **What is a composite number?** *A number with more than 2 factors.*

Lessons 12.1 and 12.2 review angle concepts your child learned in *Fourth Grade Math with Confidence*: identifying types of angles, measuring and drawing angles with a protractor, and adding and subtracting angle measures to find unknown angles. If your child remembers these concepts well and flies through this lesson, you may want to combine it with Lesson 12.2. Have your child complete both of the quick Practice pages, and then choose a selection of problems from the Review pages.

Warm-up: Review Acute, Right, Obtuse, and Straight Angles

Last year, you learned about types of angles.

- Arrange 2 pencils on the table to form a right angle. **What do we call an angle with a measure equal to 90 degrees?** *Right.*
- Rotate one pencil to form an obtuse angle. **What do we call an angle with a measure greater than 90 degrees and less than 180 degrees?** *Obtuse.*
- Rotate one pencil to form an acute angle. **What do we call an angle with a measure less than 90 degrees?** *Acute.*
- Arrange the 2 pencils in a straight line. **What do we call an angle with a measure equal to 180 degrees?** *Straight.*

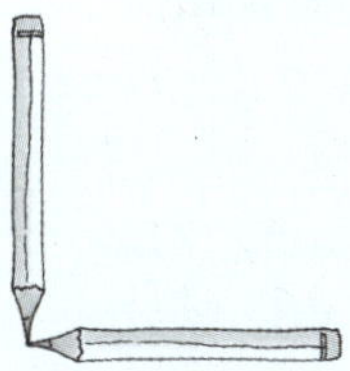

Right angle.

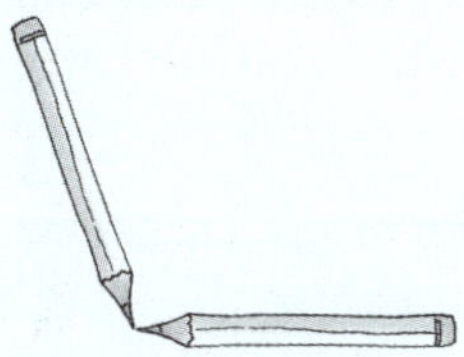

Obtuse angle.

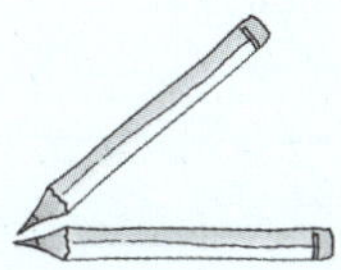

Acute angle.

Straight angle.

Activity (A): Review How to Measure Angles with a Protractor

Today, we'll review how to measure angles with a protractor. Remember, a protractor is like a curved ruler. Instead of measuring in inches or centimeters, it measures in degrees! Show your child a protractor and review the following features:

- Point to the midpoint. **This is the protractor's midpoint. We put the angle's vertex here.**
- Point to the zero line (the line that connects the two 0° marks on either side of the protractor). **This is the protractor's zero line. We line up one side of the angle with the zero line.**
- Point to the numbers and tick marks along the edge of the protractor. **After we line up one side of the angle with the zero line, we find where the other side intersects these numbers and tick marks. The numbers and tick marks are the scale. They tell us the angle's measure.**

- If your protractor has numbers and tick marks for measuring inches or centimeters, point them out. **These numbers and tick marks are for measuring inches and centimeters, not degrees. We ignore them when we measure angles.**

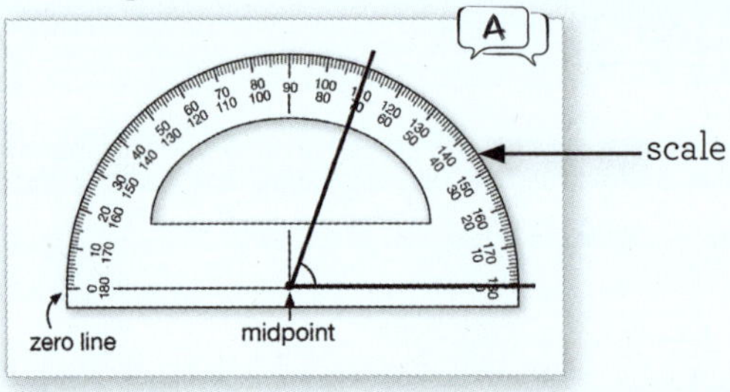

The text box tells the steps for measuring an angle with a protractor. Have your child read the text box aloud.

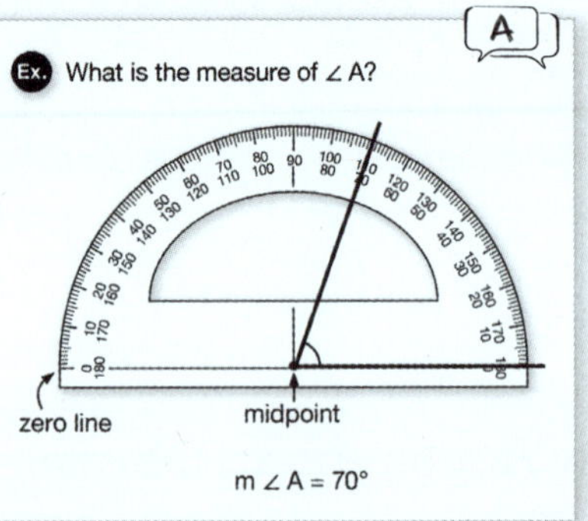

How to Measure an Angle with a Protractor

An **angle** is formed when two lines meet. The point where the lines meet is the **vertex** of the angle.

To measure an angle:

1. Line up the protractor's midpoint with the angle's vertex.
2. Line up the protractor's zero line with one side of the angle.
3. Choose the correct scale.
4. Find where the other side of the angle intersects the scale.

Ex. What is the measure of ∠ A?

zero line

midpoint

m ∠ A = 70°

The tricky part of using a protractor is that protractors have two scales. The printed angle intersects one scale at 110 degrees and the other scale at 70 degrees. We have to decide which scale to use.

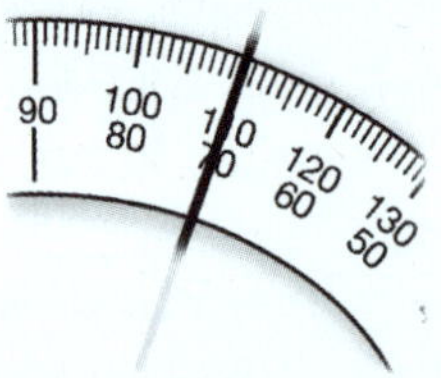

One way to tell is to use estimation. Is this angle acute, right, or obtuse? *Acute.* **Acute angles have a measure less than 90 degrees, so this angle couldn't measure 110 degrees. It must measure 70 degrees.**

Another way is to look for where the bottom side of the angle intersects the scale. The bottom side of the angle touches the 0-degree mark of the scale on the right side of the protractor. So, we use the scale that starts with zero on the right side. Point to the 0° mark on the right side of the protractor.

I move my finger along the scale from the 0-degree mark until it reaches the place where the other side of the angle intersects this scale. Point to the 0-degree mark and sweep your finger along the scale until you reach the other side of the angle. **The other side of the angle intersects this scale at the 70-degree mark. So, this angle measures 70 degrees, not 110 degrees.**

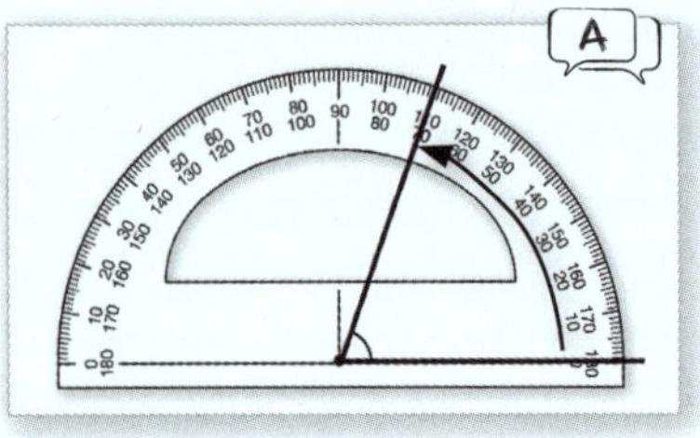

Point to the final equation in the teaching box. **The lower-case m is the abbreviation for measure. We read this equation as "The measure of angle A equals 70 degrees."**

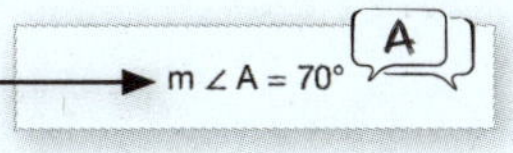

Activity (B): Measure Angles with a Protractor

Point to ∠B. **Is angle B acute, obtuse, right, or straight?** *Obtuse.* **How do you know?** *Sample answer: It looks wider than a right angle.* Write "obtuse" in the chart. Then, have your child measure the angle with the protractor. Help as needed, especially with choosing the correct scale. **What is the measure of angle B?** *120 degrees.* Write 120° in the chart.

	∠B
Type of Angle	obtuse
Measure	120°

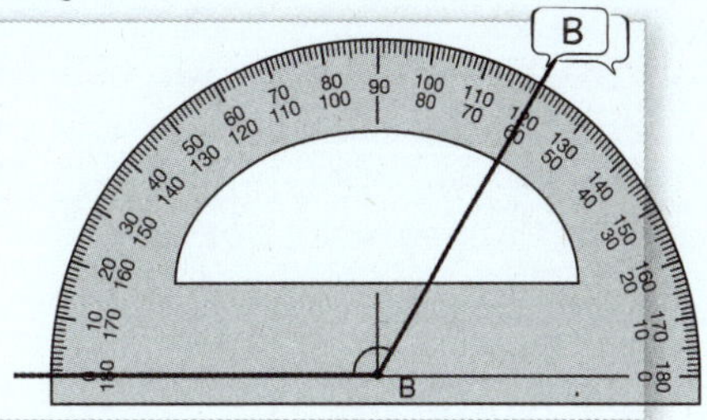

Repeat with the other angles.

	∠B	∠C	∠D	∠E
Type of Angle	obtuse	acute	acute	obtuse
Measure	120°	40°	20°	145°

> If the side of the printed angle doesn't reach the protractor's scale, demonstrate how to align the straight edge of the protractor along this side of the angle. Draw a line along the protractor to extend the side until it reaches the scale.

Independent Practice and Review

Have your child complete the Lesson 12.1 Practice and Review workbook pages.

Lesson 12.2
Draw Angles and Solve Angle Puzzles

Purpose	Materials
• Use pencils to create angles with an approximate measure • Use a protractor to draw angles • Add or subtract to find the measure of unknown angles	• 2 pencils • Protractor

Memory Work	
	• **What do we call an angle with a measure less than 90 degrees?** *Acute.* • **What do we call an angle with a measure equal to 90 degrees?** *Right.* • **What do we call an angle with a measure greater than 90 degrees and less than 180 degrees?** *Obtuse.* • **What do we call an angle with a measure equal to 180 degrees?** *Straight.*

Warm-up: Estimate Angle Measures with Pencils

In this activity, your child will approximate different angle measures by arranging pencils on the table. Accept any reasonable answer, and use a protractor if you're not sure whether an angle is close to the correct measure.

Arrange 2 pencils in a V on the table with their points together. **I'm going to describe some angles. Move the pencils to match the angle that I describe.**

- **Make a 90-degree angle.** *Child makes a right angle.*
- **Make an angle with a measure of about 40 degrees.** *Child makes an angle with a measure of about 40°.* If he's not sure, say: **40 is about half of 90, so make your angle about half as wide as a right angle.**
- **Make an angle with a measure of about 20 degrees.** *Child makes an angle with a measure of about 20°.* If he's not sure, say: **20 is half of 40, so make your angle about half as wide as your previous angle.**
- **Make an angle with a measure of 180 degrees.** *Child makes a straight line with the pencils.* If he's not sure, say: **Remember, a 180-degree is a straight angle, so arrange the pencils in a straight line.**
- **Make an angle with a measure of about 130 degrees.** *Child makes an angle with a measure of about 130°.* If he's not sure, say: **130 is about halfway between 180 and 90, so your angle should be about halfway between a straight angle and right angle.**

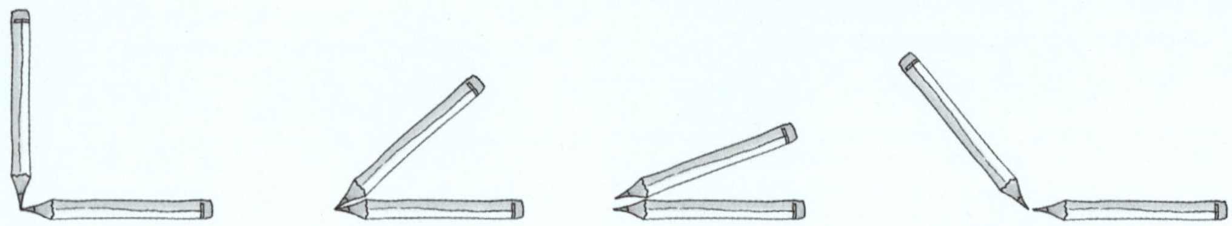

90° angle. 40° angle. 20° angle. 130° angle.

180° angle.

Sample angles. Your child's angles may also face a different direction.

Activity (A): Review How to Draw Angles with a Protractor

In the last lesson, we reviewed how to measure angles with a protractor. Today, we'll review how to draw angles with a protractor. Have your child read the text box aloud.

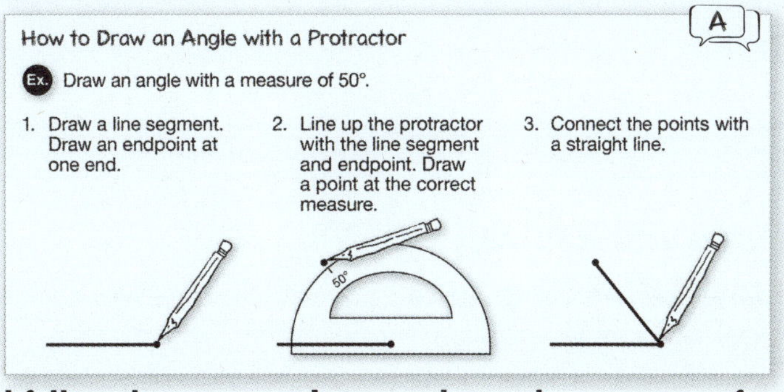

Then, have your child follow the steps to draw angles with measures of 35° and 123°. Encourage him to draw a horizontal line about 3 inches long as the first step for each angle.

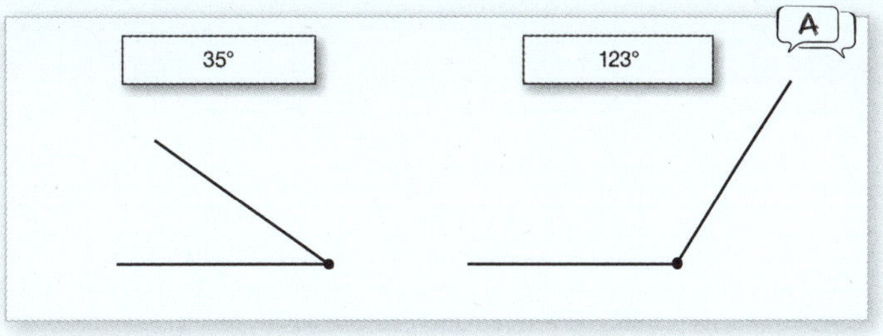

Sample angles. Your child's angles may be oriented differently or open in a different direction.

If your child has trouble finding the correct tick mark for 123°, encourage him to use what he knows about the number line to find it: **Each tick mark stands for 1 degree. So, look for the tick mark that is 3 tick marks past 120 degrees.**

Activity (B): Solve Angle Puzzles

Last year, you also learned how to add and subtract angles to solve angle puzzles. In these puzzles, some of the angles are marked. Your job is to use the marked angles to figure out the measure of the unknown angle.

In the first puzzle, two angles are put together to make a larger angle. How can you find the measure of this larger angle? *Add the two smaller angles together.* Have your child add 27 plus 25 to find the measure of the larger angle. He may use mental math or write a vertical addition problem on scrap paper. **What is the measure of the larger angle?** *52 degrees.* Write 52° in the blank.

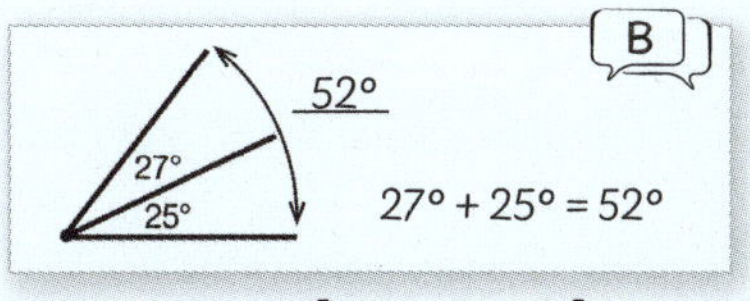

In the next puzzle, two angles are put together to make a right angle. What is the measure of a right angle? *90 degrees.* **How can you find the measure of the unknown angle?** *Subtract 31 from 90.* **What's the measure of the unknown angle?** *59 degrees.* Write 59° in the blank.

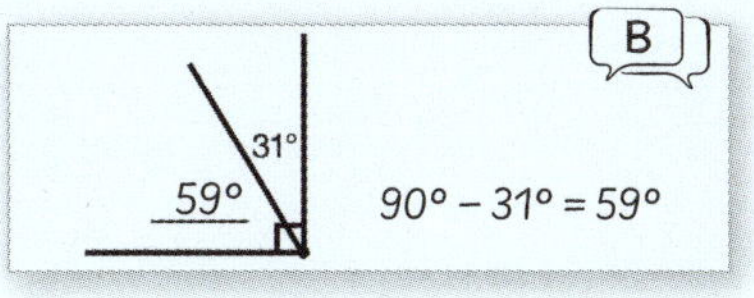

In the next puzzle, two angles are put together to make a straight angle. What is the measure of a straight angle? *180 degrees.* **How can you find the measure of the unknown angle?** *Subtract 42 from 180.* **What's the measure of the unknown angle?** *138 degrees.* Write 138° in the blank.

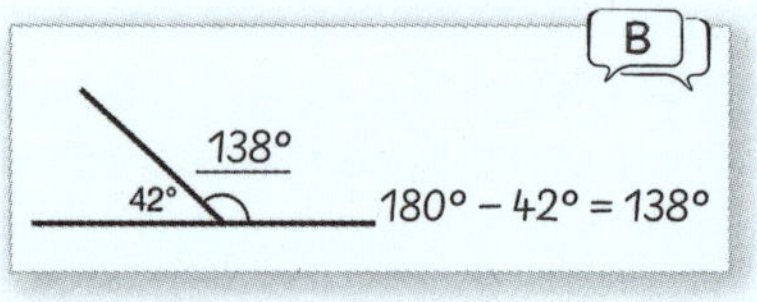

Independent Practice and Review

Have your child complete the Lesson 12.2 Practice and Review workbook pages.

Lesson 12.3
Acute, Right, and Obtuse Triangles

Purpose	Materials
• Make triangles from paper strips • Name triangles by their vertices • Identify acute, right, and obtuse triangles • Draw acute, right, and obtuse triangles on the coordinate plane	• Paper Strips (Blackline Master 10)
Memory Work	• **What is an acute triangle?** *A triangle with 3 acute angles.* • **What is a right triangle?** *A triangle with a right angle.* • **What is an obtuse triangle?** *A triangle with an obtuse angle.*

In this lesson, you will review how to identify triangles by their angles. In Lesson 12.5, your child will learn how to identify triangles by their side lengths.

Warm-up: Build Triangles with Paper Strips

We'll focus on the angles in triangles today. We'll warm up by creating triangles from paper strips.

See the Unit 12 **Teaching Math with Confidence** to learn how hands-on building activities like this one help your child understand side and angle relationships in triangles.

Show your child the paper strips from Blackline Master 10. Take three 10-cm strips and arrange them to make a triangle. **When we create triangles from the paper strips, we use the edges of the paper strips as the sides of the triangle. The vertices of the triangle are the points where the corners of the paper strips meet.** Point to each angle in the triangle and have your child identify whether it is acute, right, or obtuse.

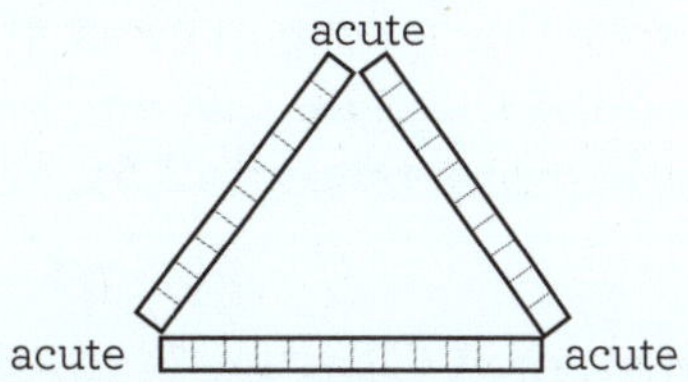

If the paper strips are sliding too much, place them on a piece of paper or piece of felt rather than the table. Use a contrasting color (not white) to help your child see the triangle within the strips more easily.

Give your child one 12-cm strip, one 16-cm strip, and one 20-cm strip and have her make a triangle from the strips. Point to each angle in the triangle and have your child identify whether it is acute, right, or obtuse.

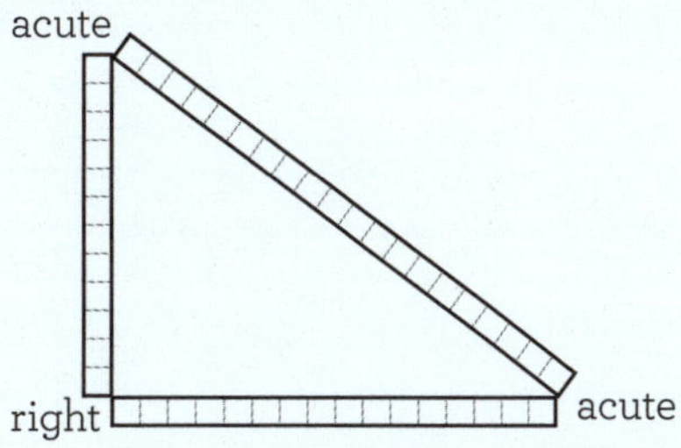

Give your child two 12-cm strips and one 18-cm strip, and have her make a triangle from them. Point to each angle in the triangle and have your child identify whether it is acute, right, or obtuse.

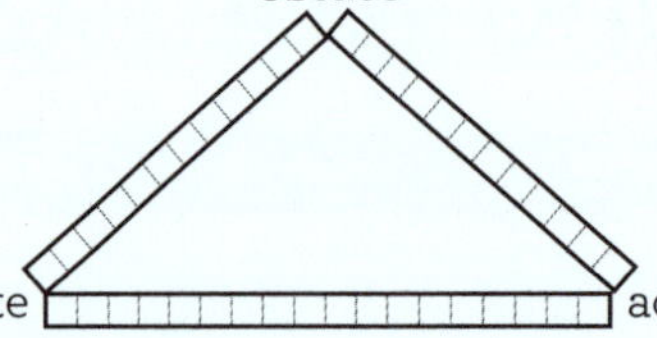

Save these paper strips for Lessons 12.6 and 12.7.

Activity (A): Review Acute, Right, and Obtuse Triangles

Last year, you learned that we can use triangles' angles to sort them into different groups. Today, we'll review how to identify triangles by their angles. Have your child read the definitions in the text box aloud.

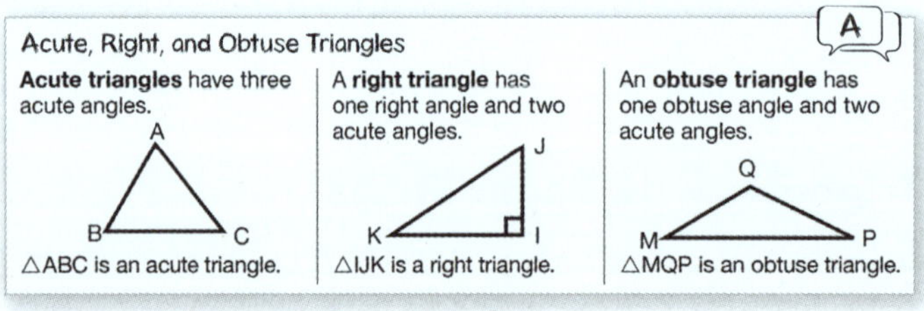

Use the following questions to discuss the triangles:

- Point to the sentence below the acute triangle. **We read this sentence as, "Triangle ABC is an acute triangle." Triangle ABC means the triangle that has points A, B, and C as its vertices. Which angles are acute in triangle ABC?** *Angles A, B, and C.*
- **Triangle IJK is a right triangle. Which angle is right?** *Angle I.* **Which angles are acute?** *Angles K and J.*
- **Triangle MQP is an obtuse triangle. Which angle is obtuse?** *Angle Q.* **Which angles are acute?** *Angles M and P.*

When we name a triangle with its vertices, we can start at any letter. We move either clockwise or counterclockwise around the triangle, and we name the vertices in order. What are some other ways we could name triangle ABC? *Possible answers: Triangle ACB, BAC, BCA, CAB, or CBA.*

Activity (B): Draw Acute, Right, and Obtuse Triangles on the Coordinate Plane

Now, you'll draw different types of triangles on the coordinate plane. There are many different ways to draw these triangles. For each triangle, you'll draw one point. Then, you'll connect the 3 points to form a triangle.

These exercises nudge your child to think more deeply about the relationships between the sides and angles in a triangle. It also helps her become more comfortable with drawing shapes on the coordinate plane. Make sure your child uses a pencil for these exercises so that she can erase any incorrect guesses.

In future grades, your child will learn that she can draw points between grid lines to show fractional coordinates. For now, ask her to draw her points only at whole-number coordinates (where two grid lines intersect).

Read aloud the direction for the first row of exercises: ***Draw point F so that triangle DEF is an acute triangle.*** Have your child choose a point on the first coordinate plane that she thinks will form an acute triangle with points D and E. Then, have her connect the points and check that the triangle has 3 acute angles. If the triangle doesn't have 3 acute triangles, have her erase her work and try again.

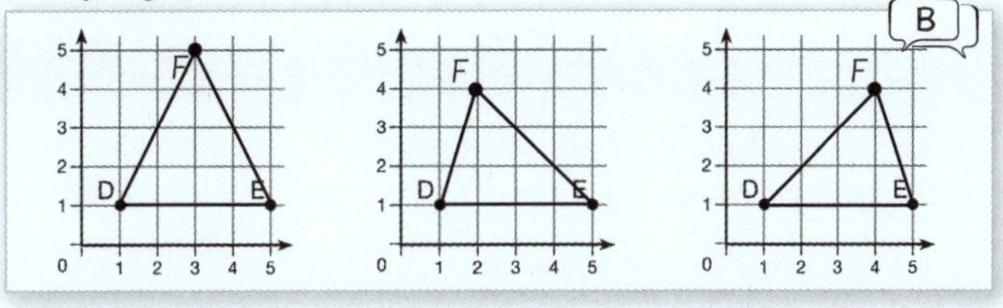

Sample answers. Your child may draw the point anywhere that forms an acute triangle.

Repeat with the other exercises in the row.

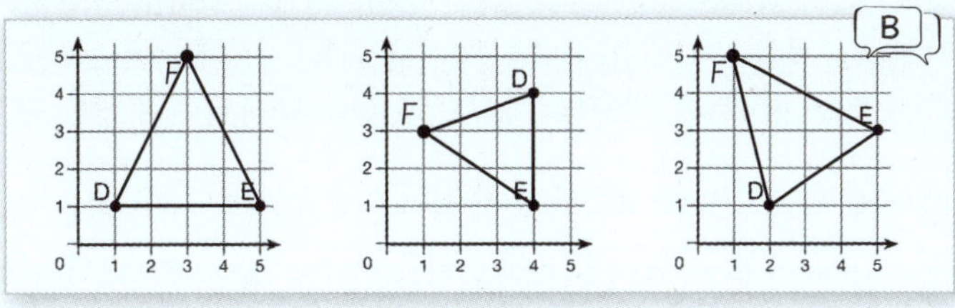

Sample answers.

Read aloud the direction for the second row of exercises: ***Draw point R so that triangle RST is a right triangle.*** Have your child choose a point that she thinks will form a right triangle with points S and T. If she has trouble, suggest that she start by making ∠T the right angle: **Where could you place point R so that angle T is right?**

Then, have her connect the points and check that the triangle has 1 right angle and 2 acute angles. If not, have her erase her work and try again. Repeat for all 3 exercises.

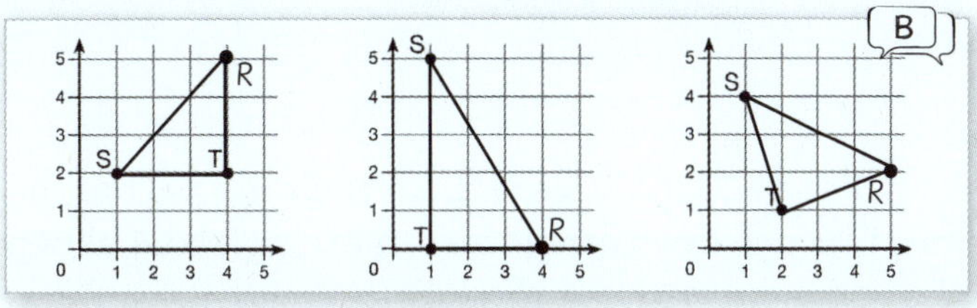

Sample answers.

Read aloud the direction for the final row of exercises: ***Draw point Y so that triangle XYZ is an obtuse triangle.*** Have your child choose a point on the grid that she thinks will form an obtuse triangle with points X and Z. If she has trouble, suggest that she start by making ∠Z the obtuse angle: **Where could you place point Y so that angle Z is obtuse?**

Then, have her connect the points and check that the triangle has 1 obtuse angle and 2 acute angles. If not, have her erase her work and try again. Repeat for all 3 exercises.

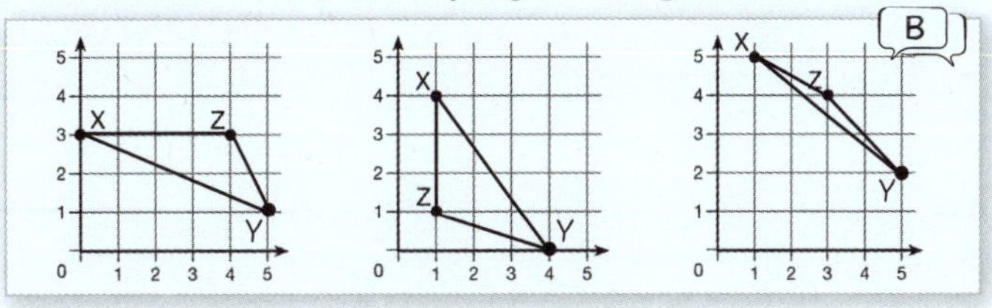

Sample answers.

Independent Practice and Review

Have your child complete the Lesson 12.3 Practice and Review workbook pages.

Lesson 12.4
Find Missing Angles in Triangles

Purpose	Materials
• Create acute, right, and obtuse triangles from paper • Investigate the sum of angles in different kinds of triangles • Learn that the sum of the angles in a triangle always equals 180° • Find the measure of an unknown angle in a triangle	• Paper • Scissors • Ruler
Memory Work	• **What is an acute triangle?** *A triangle with 3 acute angles.* • **What is a right triangle?** *A triangle with a right angle.* • **What is an obtuse triangle?** *A triangle with an obtuse angle.*

Warm-up: Investigate the Sum of Angles in Paper Triangles

In the last lesson, we reviewed how to identify triangles based on their angles. To warm up today, we'll create triangles out of paper and investigate the sum of their angles.

Have your child create a right triangle from a piece of paper. Encourage him to use the corner of the piece of paper as the right angle and then use a ruler to draw the opposite side. The other angles and sides may have any measure.

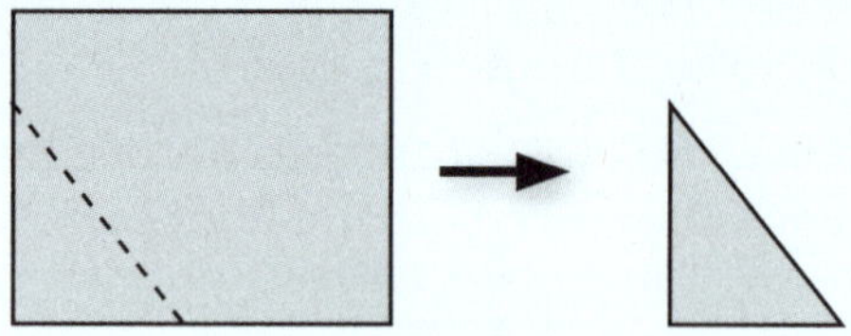

Sample right triangle.

Have your child create an obtuse triangle from the remaining part of the paper. Encourage him to use a ruler to draw just one line across the remaining piece of paper to create the obtuse triangle.

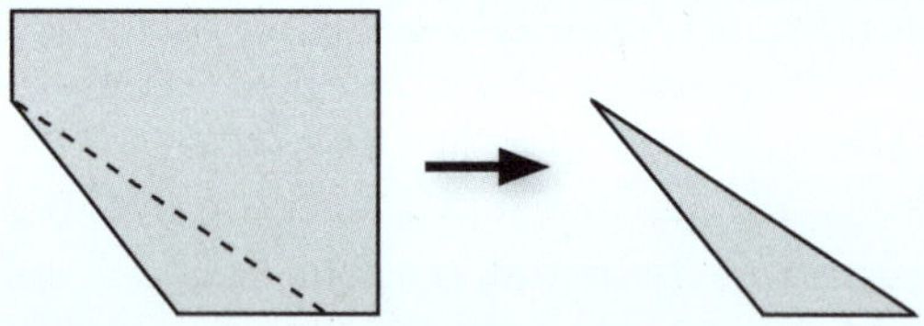

Sample obtuse triangle.

Have your child create an acute triangle from the remaining part of the paper. He may need to use the ruler to draw one or two lines, depending on how he cut the previous triangles.

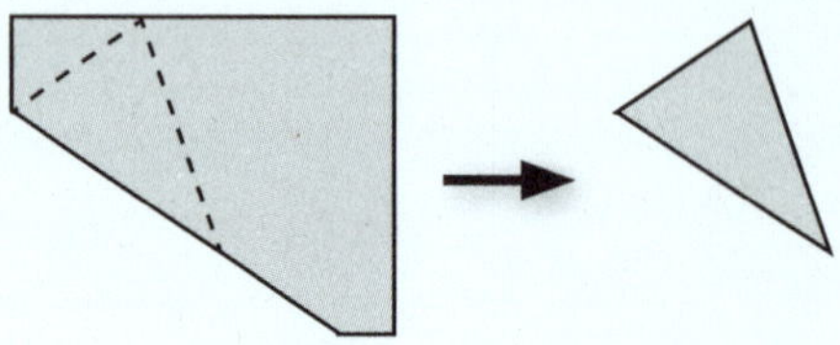

Sample acute triangle.

Now, let's investigate the sum of the angles in each triangle. Tear off the 3 corners of the right triangle and place them together as shown. **The three angles form a straight angle! So, what must the sum of the three angles equal?** *180 degrees.*

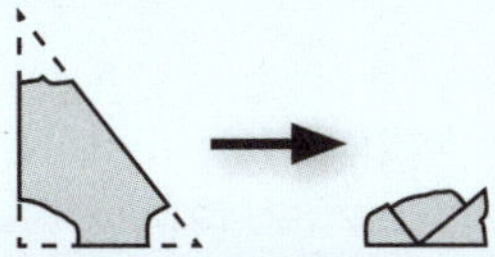

Make sure to roughly tear the corners rather than cutting them with scissors. The "shaggy" edges make it easier to see which corners to put together to form a straight angle.

Have your child repeat with the obtuse and acute triangles. **The sums of the angles in these triangles equal 180 degrees, too!**

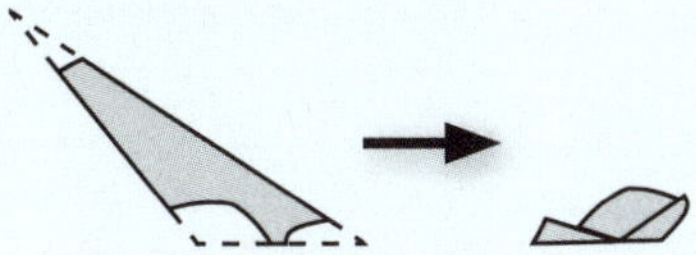

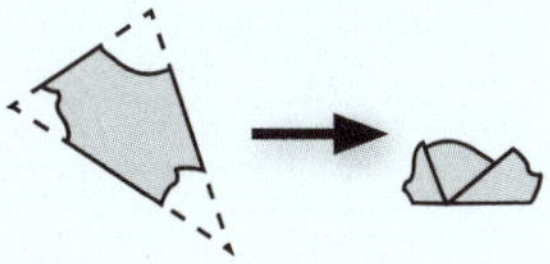

Activity (A): Find a Missing Angle in a Triangle

In the warm-up, we saw that the sum of the angles in each triangle was 180 degrees. This is always true for all triangles. We can use this fact to find a missing angle in a triangle. Have your child read the text box aloud.

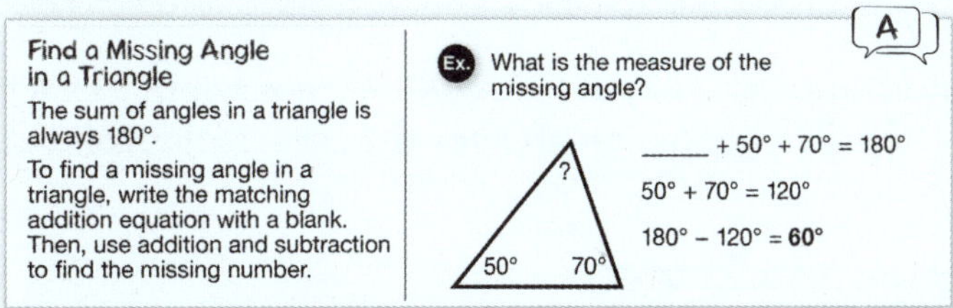

A

Find a Missing Angle in a Triangle

The sum of angles in a triangle is always 180°.

To find a missing angle in a triangle, write the matching addition equation with a blank. Then, use addition and subtraction to find the missing number.

Ex. What is the measure of the missing angle?

_____ + 50° + 70° = 180°

50° + 70° = 120°

180° − 120° = **60°**

In the example, we know that one angle measures 50 degrees and another angle measures 70 degrees. We want to find the measure of the third angle.

50 plus 70 equals 120. So, we can subtract 120 from 180 to find the measure of the third angle. What's 180 minus 120? *60.* **The third angle measures 60 degrees.**

Have your child use this method to find the measure of the missing angles in the triangles in part A. He may use mental math or write out his equations on scrap paper.

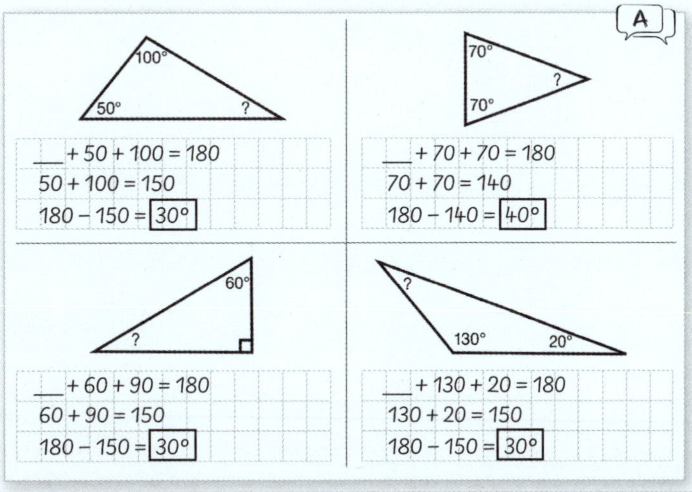

If your child has trouble with the bottom left exercise, point out that the right angle measures 90°.

Activity (B): Draw a Triangle and Find a Missing Angle

Read aloud the word problem in part B. **This word problem tells the degree measures for two of the angles in a triangle, but there's no drawing. Let's make a quick sketch to help visualize the problem.**

Will this triangle be acute, obtuse, or right? *Obtuse.* **How do you know?** *The 107-degree angle is obtuse.* **So, draw a sketch of an obtuse triangle. It's okay if the angles don't exactly match the measurements.** Have your child draw an obtuse triangle, label the vertices to match the problem, and label the measures for the known angles. Have him draw a question mark inside ∠C.

Have your child write the matching addition equation with a blank to show the sum of the angles. Then, have him find the measure of the missing angle. **What's the measure of angle C?** *25 degrees.*

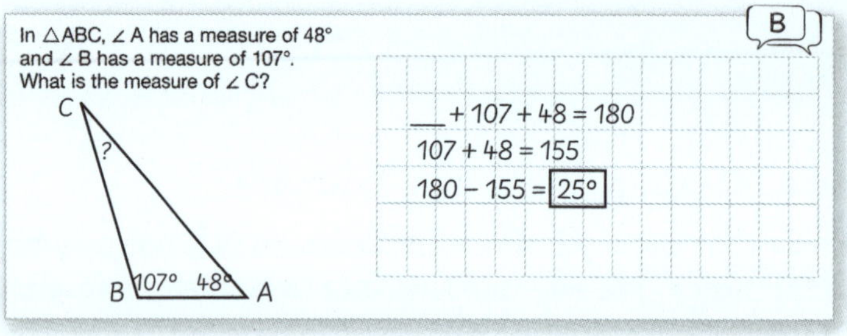

Sample drawing. Your child's drawing may look different.

Look back at the drawing with your child. **Does 25 degrees seem like a reasonable measurement for angle C?** *Yes.* **If you'd gotten an answer that seemed unreasonable, you'd want to check your work!**

Independent Practice and Review

Have your child complete the Lesson 12.4 Practice and Review workbook pages.

Lesson 12.5
Equilateral, Isosceles, and Scalene Triangles

Purpose	Materials
• Review symmetry in triangles • Identify equilateral, isosceles, and scalene triangles • Identify equal sides and angles in triangles	• Paper Triangles (Blackline Master 11)

Memory Work	• **What is the sum of the angles in a triangle?** *180°.*

Warm-up (A): Fold Paper Triangles to Review Symmetry

When you were younger, you learned about symmetry. Do you remember what makes a shape symmetric? *Sample answers: The two sides line up with each other. The two sides are a mirror image of each other.*

Shapes and objects are symmetric if they have two halves that exactly mirror each other. Fold Triangle 1 (from Blackline Master 11) in half as shown. Then, unfold the triangle. **This fold line is a line of symmetry. It splits the triangle into two identical halves, and each half is a mirror image of the other.** Draw a matching line on the printed triangle in part A.

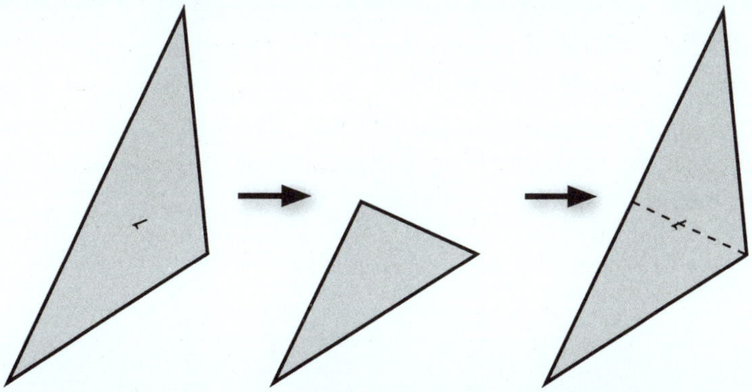

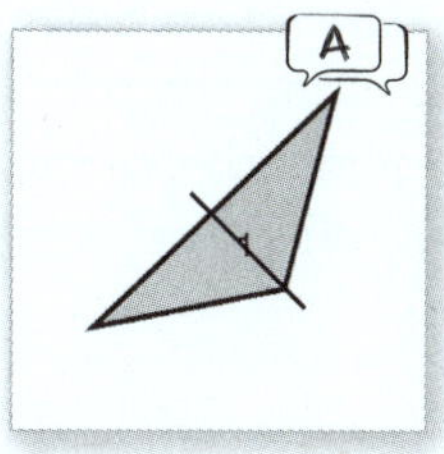

Does this triangle have any other lines of symmetry? *No.* If your child's not sure, have her try folding the triangle in half in other ways and see if the halves line up.

Repeat with the other paper triangles. Draw the matching lines of symmetry on the printed triangles. (Not all triangles will have a line of symmetry.)

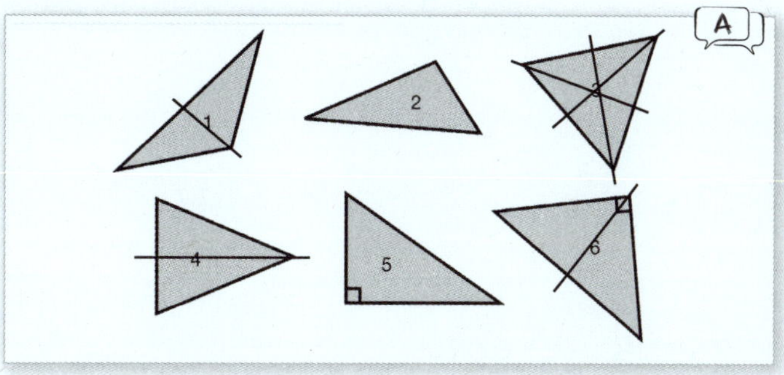

Activity (B): Introduce Equilateral, Isosceles, and Scalene Triangles

In Lesson 12.3, we reviewed how to identify triangles based on their angles. We can also identify triangles by the lengths of their sides. Read the text box aloud to your child. Then, have her practice pronouncing equilateral, isosceles, and scalene.

> This lesson suggests that you read the text box to your child (rather than having her read the text box aloud to you) so that you can demonstrate how to pronounce these challenging vocabulary words.
>
> - Equilateral: "ee-qui-LAT-er-ul"
> - Isosceles: "eye-SAH-suh-leez"
> - Scalene: "SKAY-leen"

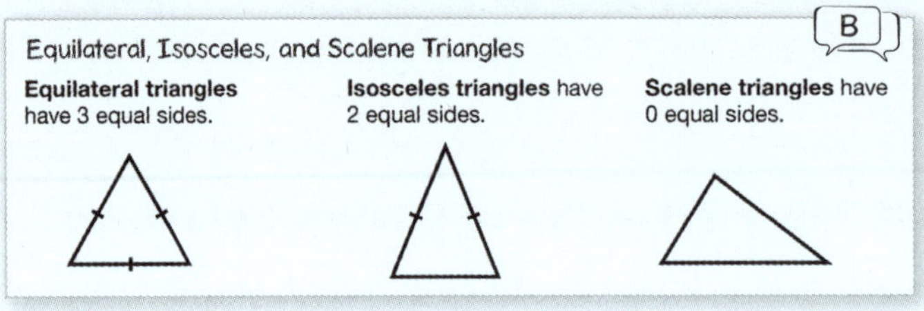

The tick marks on the sides of the triangle mean that the marked sides have the same length. In the equilateral triangle, all 3 sides have the same length, so all 3 sides have a tick mark. In the isosceles triangle, only 2 sides have the same length, so only these sides have a tick mark.

Activity (B): Identify Equilateral, Isosceles, and Scalene Triangles

Now, let's identify whether the paper triangles are equilateral, isosceles, or scalene.

In part A, we found that triangle 1 has 1 line of symmetry. Take Triangle 1 and fold it as shown. **These two halves are mirror images of each other, so the sides that match up must have the same length. The third side is longer than the others.** Draw tick marks as shown on the equal sides of the printed triangle. **Is this triangle equilateral, isosceles, or scalene?** *Isosceles.* Write "isosceles" in the blank.

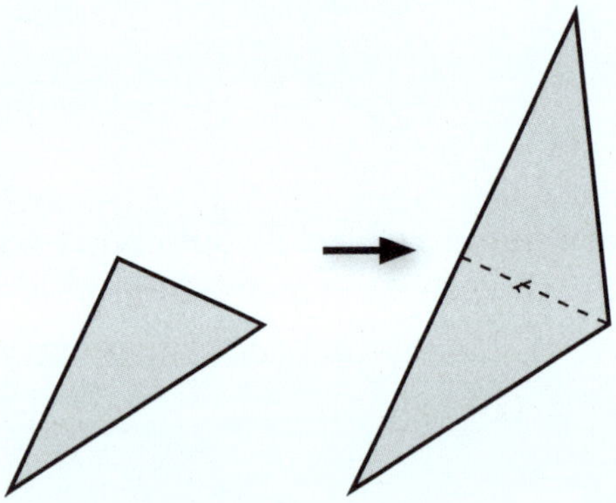

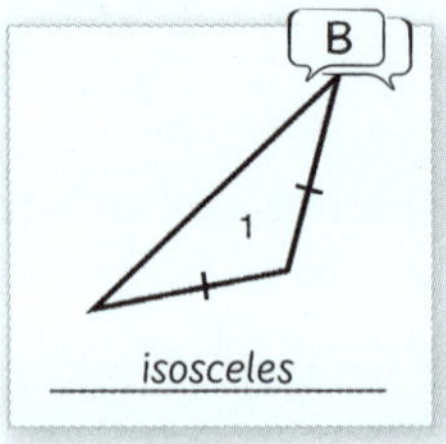

Repeat with the rest of the triangles. For each triangle, have your child identify and mark any equal sides. Then, have her identify whether the triangle is equilateral, isosceles, or scalene.

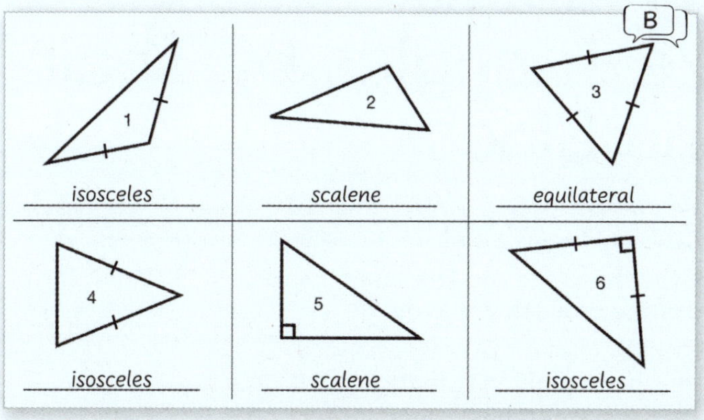

Some of these triangles also have equal angles. Take Triangle 1 and fold it as shown. **These two halves are mirror images of each other, so the angles that match up must be equal to each other. We define isosceles triangles as having two equal sides, but they automatically have two equal angles, too.** Draw an arc in each angle. Draw one tick mark through each arc, as shown. **We can use arcs with tick marks to show that two angles are equal.**

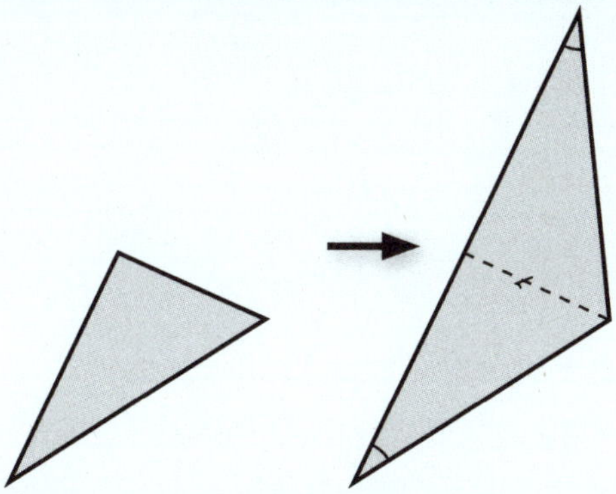

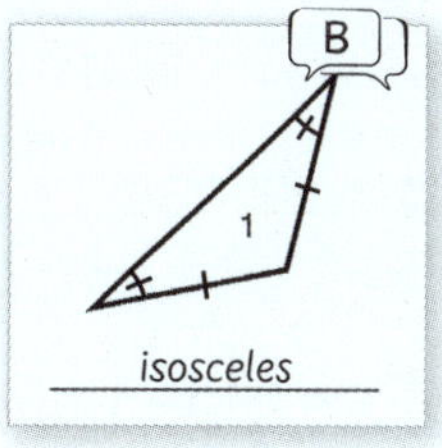

Have your child add arcs with tick marks to the equal angles in the rest of the triangles.

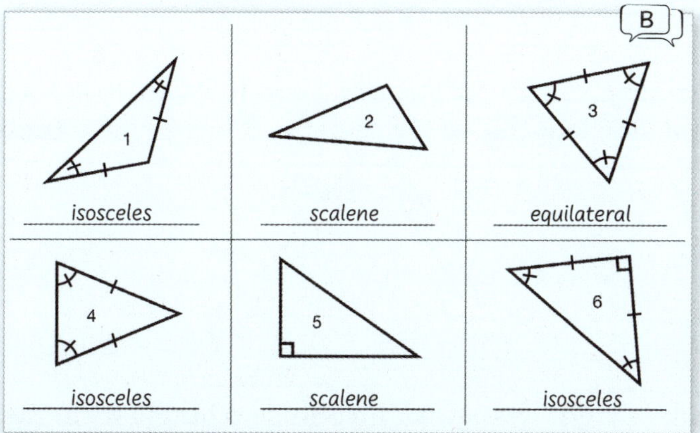

Look back at the triangles in part B and ask the following questions:

- **Which triangles are obtuse triangles?** *1 and 2.*
- **Which triangles are right triangles?** *5 and 6.*
- **Which triangles are acute?** *3 and 4.*

We can label triangles based on either their sides or their angles. In the next lesson, you'll learn how to categorize triangles in both ways.

Independent Practice and Review

Have your child complete the Lesson 12.5 Practice and Review workbook pages.

Lesson 12.6
Categorize Triangles by Their Angles and Sides

Purpose	Materials
• Preview the idea that the third side of a triangle must be shorter than the sum of the other two sides • Review triangle definitions • Build and draw triangles to fit a given category • Categorize triangles by both their angles and sides	• Paper Strips (Blackline Master 10)

Memory Work

- **What is an equilateral triangle?** *A triangle with 3 equal sides.*
- **What is an isosceles triangle?** *A triangle with 2 equal sides.*
- **What is a scalene triangle?** *A triangle with no equal sides.*

This lesson provides valuable hands-on experience with constructing triangles, but it may take longer than a usual lesson. If you find that the lesson runs long, split it over two days.

- Day 1: Complete the warm-up. Have your child build and draw the triangles in the Isosceles row in the chart on the Lesson Activities page. Then, have your child complete the Review page.
- Day 2: Have your child build and draw the triangles in the Scalene and Equilateral rows in the chart on the Lesson Activities page. Then, have your child complete the Practice page.

Warm-up: Explore Side Lengths in Paper Strip Triangles

Organize the paper strips (from Blackline Master 10) on the table as shown to make it easier to find a strip of a given length.

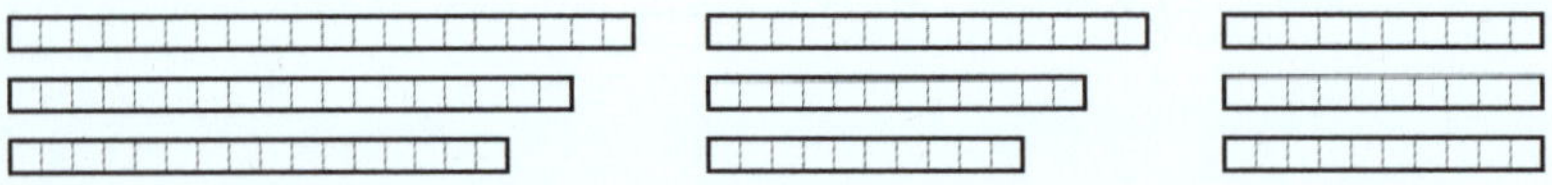

Put together one 14-cm strip, one 16-cm strip, and one 18-cm strip to form a triangle. **This triangle has 3 different side lengths, so it's scalene. It has 3 acute angles, so it's also acute.**

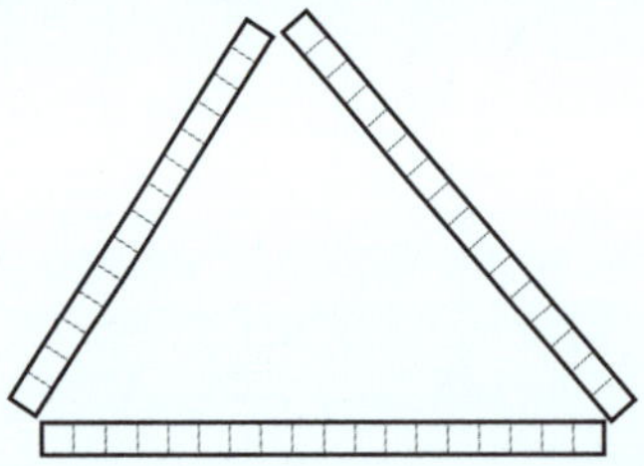

Let's see if we can make a right triangle or an obtuse triangle from these 3 paper strips. Give your child a moment to try rearranging the strips. **Can you make a right triangle or an obtuse triangle from these 3 side lengths?** *No.* **Why not?** *Sample answer: If I make a right angle or obtuse angle between two of the strips, the third strip doesn't reach.*

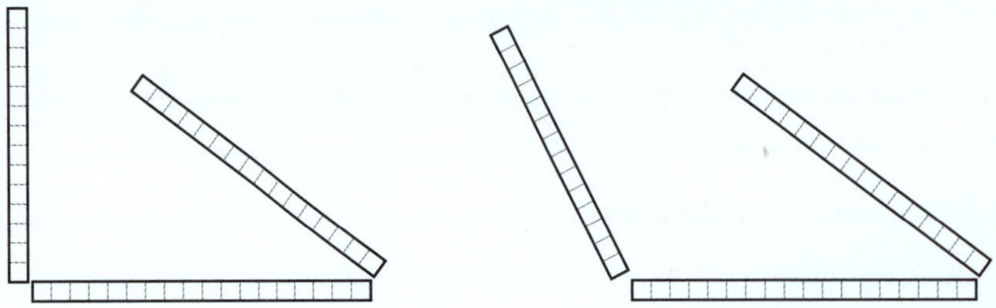

There's only one triangle you can make from any 3 side lengths! You can arrange the paper strips so that the triangle flips or turns, but the side lengths and angles won't change. Give your child a minute or two to experiment with the paper strips and see that any group of 3 paper strips can only be arranged to form 1 triangle.

Give your child one 20-cm strip and two 10-cm strips. **Try to put these paper strips together to create a triangle. What happens?** *Sample answer: The 10-centimeter strips just lie on top of the 20-cm strip. The sides aren't long enough to make a triangle.*

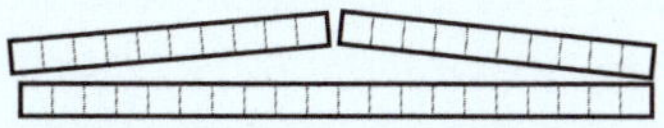

In a triangle, the sum of the two shorter sides must be longer than the longest side. Otherwise, it's not possible to make a triangle.

Activity (A): Build and Draw Triangles to Fit Given Categories

You have learned how to identify triangles by their angles or by their sides. Today, we'll investigate how these categories overlap.

Show your child the chart on the Lesson Activities page. **The labels across the top of the chart are the words we use to identify triangles based on their angles. The labels along the left side of the chart are the words we use to identify triangles based on their sides.**

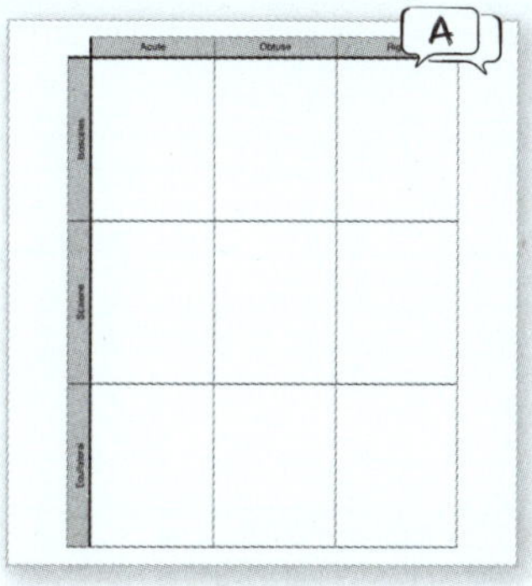

You'll build triangles out of paper strips to fit the categories on this chart today. After you create a triangle from the paper strips, you'll draw it in the matching box in the chart. You'll find that it's impossible to build triangles for two of the categories.

Point to the top left box in the chart. Have your child use the paper strips to create a triangle that is both isosceles and acute. If he's stuck, encourage him to think about the meaning of each word: **Isosceles means the triangle has 2 equal sides. So, start with 2 strips of the same length. Acute means that all the angles in the triangle must be acute. So, arrange the strips to form an acute angle.**

Once your child creates a triangle that is both isosceles and acute, have him sketch the triangle in the matching box on the chart. (This sketch does not need to be precise, and he does not need to use a protractor or ruler.) Have him label the lengths of the sides to match the paper strips and add tick marks to the two equal sides to show that they are equal.

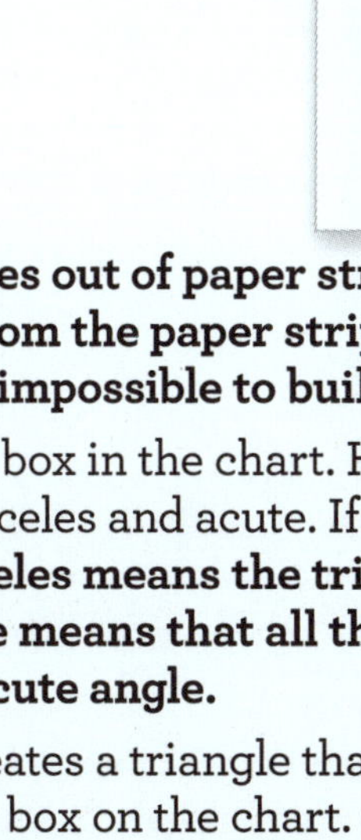

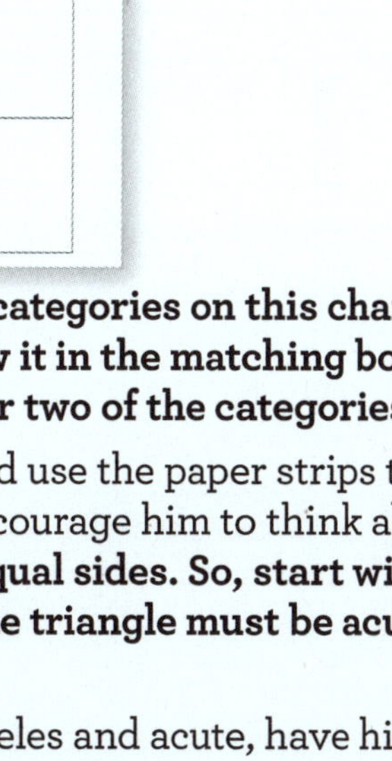

Sample isosceles acute triangle.

The hands-on building is more important than the sketching in this activity. If your child has trouble sketching the triangles or feels frustrated by it, simply make a check mark in each box to show that your child has found a triangle that fits the category.

Encourage your child to use trial and error to create the triangles. He may need to experiment with several different combinations of strips before finding a triangle that fits the category.

Repeat for the other boxes in the Isosceles and Scalene rows.

- If your child has trouble creating an isosceles right triangle, suggest he form a right angle with two 10-cm strips and then look for a third strip to use for the final side.
- If your child has trouble creating a scalene right triangle, suggest he form a right angle between the 12-cm and 16-cm strips and then look for a third strip to use for the final side.

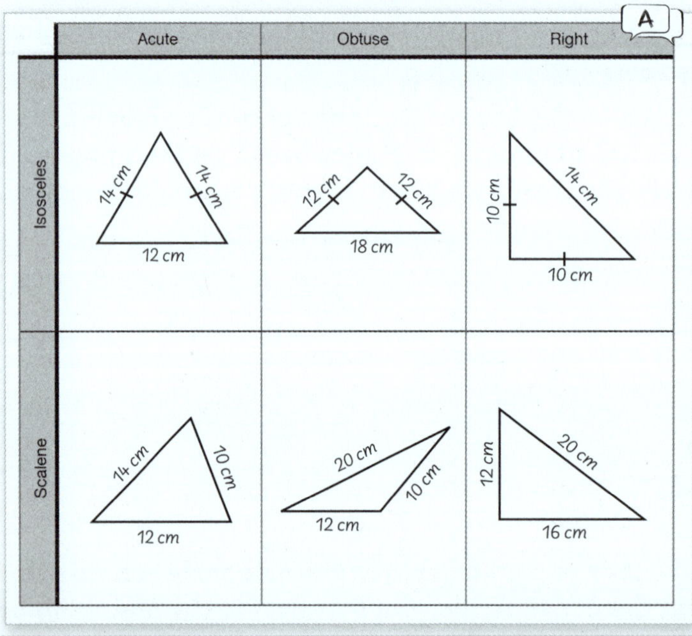

The paper strip lengths are chosen so that your child can form a right scalene triangle with a 12-cm, 16-cm, and 20-cm strip, and so he can form a right isosceles triangle with a 10-cm, 10-cm, and 14-cm strip. According to the Pythagorean theorem, the third side of the right isosceles triangle should technically be 14.14 cm rather than 14 cm, but this margin of error is reasonable when working with paper strips. Your child will learn more about the relationships between the sides of right triangles when he studies the Pythagorean theorem and trigonometry in future grades.

Point to the box for an equilateral acute triangle. **How many equal sides do equilateral triangles have?** *3.* **So, you'll need to use 3 strips with the same length to build this triangle.** Have your child use three 10-cm strips to create an equilateral acute triangle. Then, have him draw the triangle in the chart and label the equal sides with tick marks.

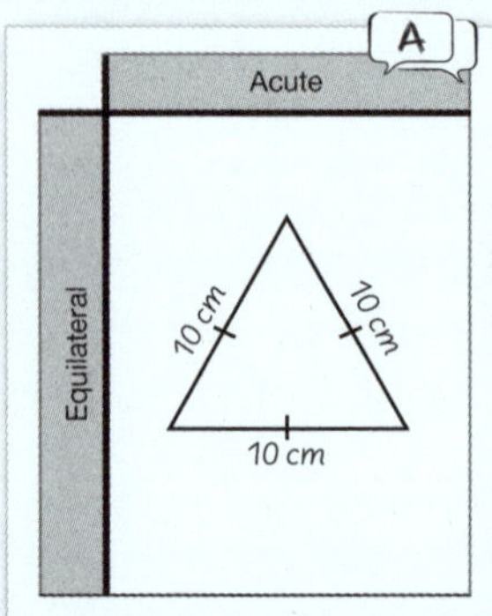

Have your child try to create an obtuse equilateral triangle. **Why can't you make an obtuse equilateral triangle?** *Sample answer: If I make an obtuse angle between two of the strips, the other strip doesn't reach.* Have your child try to create a right equilateral triangle as well.

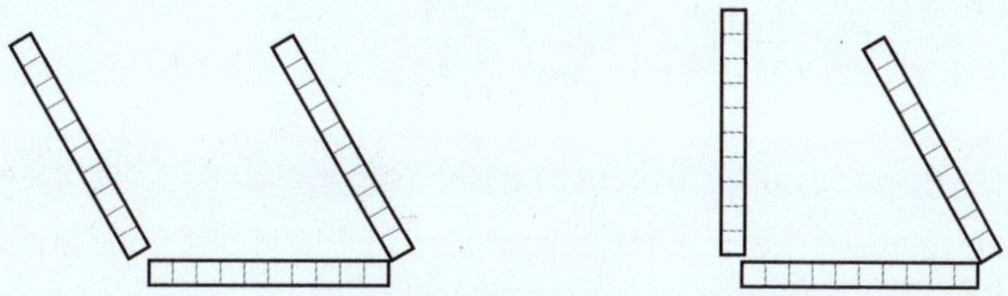

It's impossible to create an obtuse equilateral triangle or right equilateral triangle. Draw an X in both of these boxes. **If you have 3 equal sides, there's only one way to arrange the sides. All equilateral triangles are acute.**

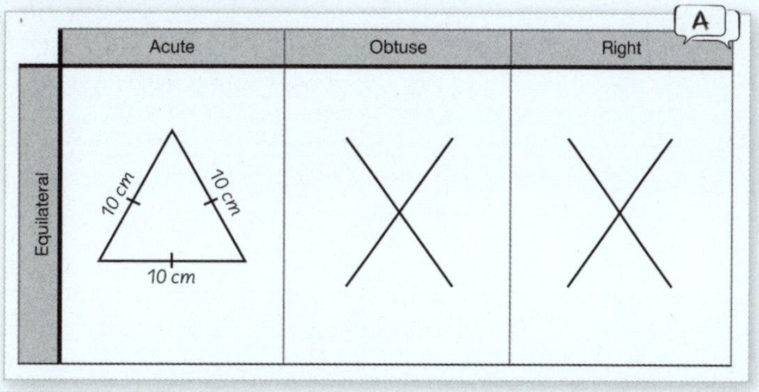

If your child is interested, challenge him to figure out the measure of each angle in an equilateral triangle: **The angles in equilateral triangles are all equal. The sum of the angles in a triangle is always 180 degrees. So, what's the measure of each angle in an equilateral triangle?** *60 degrees.* **How do you know?** *180 divided by 3 equals 60.*

Save these paper strips for Lesson 12.7.

Independent Practice and Review

Have your child complete the Lesson 12.6 Practice and Review workbook pages.

Lesson 12.7
Review Quadrilaterals

Purpose	Materials
• Review parallel, intersecting, and perpendicular lines • Review definitions of different types of quadrilaterals • Build and draw different types of quadrilaterals	• Paper Strips (Blackline Master 10)

Memory Work
- **What is an equilateral triangle?** *A triangle with 3 equal sides.*
- **What is an isosceles triangle?** *A triangle with 2 equal sides.*
- **What is a scalene triangle?** *A triangle with no equal sides.*

In this lesson, you will review the definition of trapezoids. In the U.S. and Canada, some math books define trapezoids as quadrilaterals with at least 1 pair of parallel sides, while others define them as quadrilaterals with exactly 1 pair of parallel sides. *Math with Confidence* uses this second definition.

In British English, a *trapezoid* is defined as a quadrilateral with no pairs of parallel sides, while *trapezium* is used to describe quadrilaterals with at least 1 pair of parallel sides. If you live in the U.K. or another country that uses British English, explain both meanings to your child.

Warm-up: Review Parallel, Perpendicular, and Intersecting Lines with Paper Strips

In younger grades, you learned about parallel, perpendicular, and intersecting lines.

- **Parallel lines are always the same distance apart, like railroad tracks. No matter how far you continue the lines, they never cross.** Have your child arrange two paper strips parallel to each other.
- **Intersecting lines cross each other to create 4 angles.** Have your child arrange two paper strips so that they intersect to form an X.
- **Perpendicular lines intersect to create 4 right angles.** Have your child arrange two paper strips so that they intersect to form 4 right angles.

Parallel lines.

Intersecting lines.

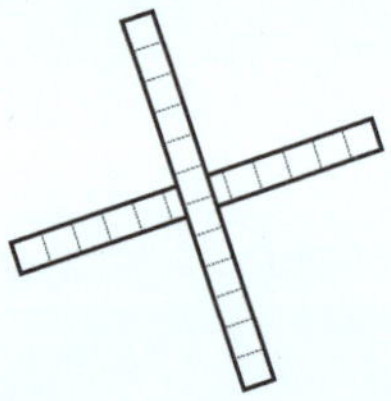
Perpendicular lines.

Activity (A): Review Quadrilateral Definitions

In younger grades, you learned about quadrilaterals. Quadrilaterals are shapes with 4 sides and 4 angles. Today, we'll review the definitions of different types of quadrilaterals. Have your child read the definitions in the text box aloud.

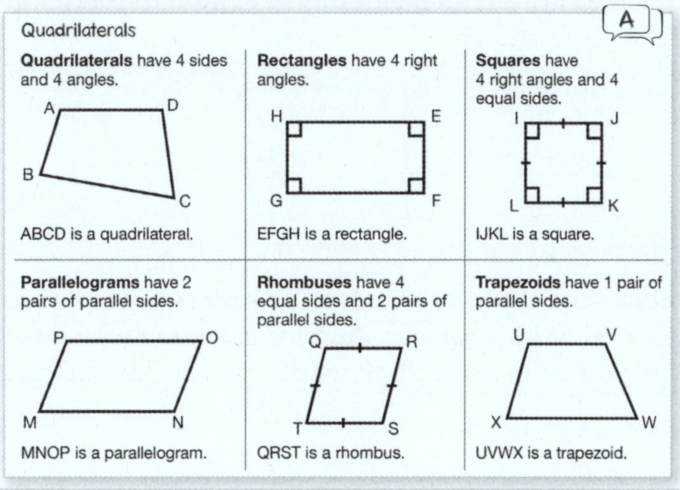

In these diagrams, only the equal sides relevant to the definition are marked. In the next activity, your child will explore equal sides in rectangles and parallelograms as well.

When we name a quadrilateral with its vertices, we can start at any letter. Then, we move either clockwise or counterclockwise around the quadrilateral, and we name the vertices in order. What are some other ways we could name quadrilateral ABCD? *Possible answers: DCBA, CBAD, BADC, ADCB, BCDA, CDAB, DABC.*

Activity (B): Create and Draw Quadrilaterals

We'll use paper strips to create shapes to fit every category on this chart. After you build a quadrilateral, you'll draw it in the matching box in the chart and mark any equal sides you notice.

What must all quadrilaterals have? *4 sides and 4 angles.* Have your child create a quadrilateral from the paper strips. Encourage her to create a quadrilateral that doesn't fit any of the other categories listed in part A.

Then, have her sketch the quadrilateral in the matching box on the chart and label the lengths of the sides. (This sketch does not need to be precise, and she does not need to use a protractor or ruler.) Repeat with the other quadrilaterals in part B.

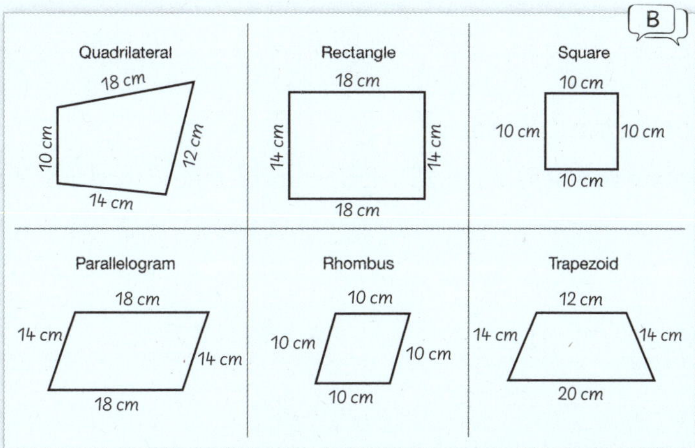

Sample answers.

The sides that are across from each other in quadrilaterals are called opposite sides. What do you notice about the opposite sides in the rectangle? *Sample answers: They are parallel to each other. They are the same length.* **When we have two pairs of equal sides in a shape, we label each side in one pair with 1 tick mark. We label each side in the other pair with 2 tick marks. That way, it's clear that all 4 sides aren't equal to each other.** Demonstrate how to label the rectangle's sides as shown.

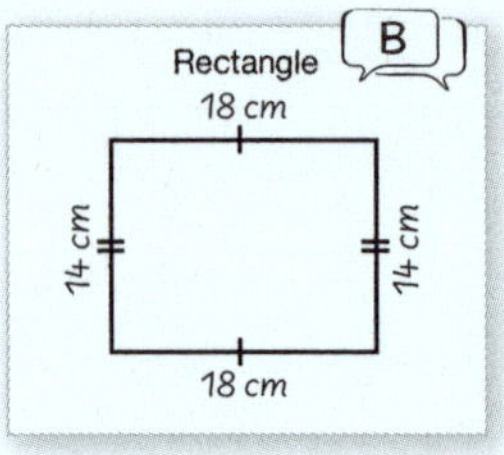

What do you notice about the opposite sides in the square? *Sample answers: They are parallel to each other. They are the same length.* **All four sides are equal, so we label each side with 1 tick mark.** Have your child mark 1 tick mark on each side of the square.

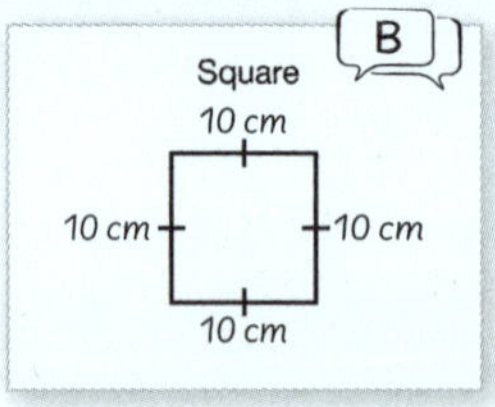

Have your child label the pairs of equal sides in the parallelogram, rhombus, and trapezoid in the same way.

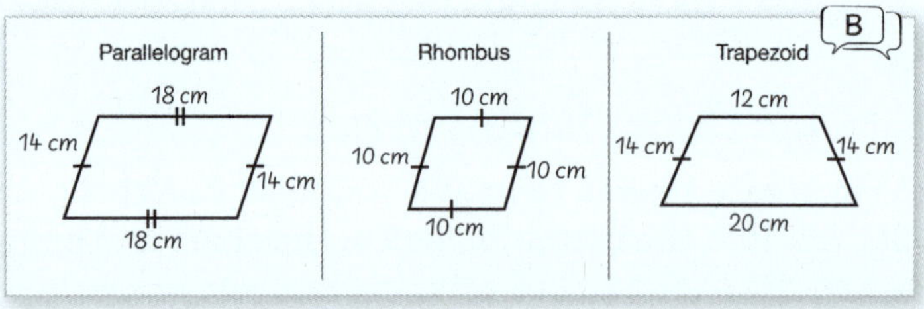

Your child's trapezoid may or may not have a pair of equal sides, depending on how she constructed her trapezoid from the paper strips.

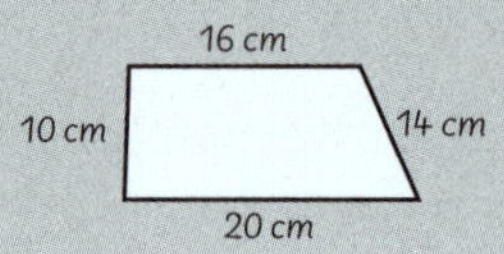

Sample trapezoid with no pairs of equal sides.

You will not use the paper strips again after this lesson, and you do not need to save them.

Independent Practice and Review

Have your child complete the Lesson 12.7 Practice and Review workbook pages.

Lesson 12.8
Opposite and Adjacent Angles in Parallelograms and Rhombuses

Purpose	Materials
• Explore the relationships between angles in a paper parallelogram • Identify opposite and adjacent angles in parallelograms and rhombuses • Use angle relationships to find the measures of missing angles in parallelograms and rhombuses	• Paper Parallelogram (Blackline Master 12)

Memory Work	
	• **What do we call a quadrilateral with 4 right angles?** *A rectangle.* • **What do we call a quadrilateral with 4 right angles and 4 equal sides?** *A square.* • **What do we call a quadrilateral with 4 equal sides?** *A rhombus.* • **What do we call a quadrilateral with 2 pairs of parallel sides?** *A parallelogram.* • **What do we call a quadrilateral with exactly 1 pair of parallel sides?** *A trapezoid.*

Warm-up: Explore the Relationships Between Angles in a Paper Parallelogram

In the last lesson, we reviewed the definitions of quadrilaterals. Today, you'll learn about angles in parallelograms and rhombuses. To warm up, we'll investigate the angles in a parallelogram.

The angles in the parallelogram are labeled with numbers inside the angles to make it easier to discuss the angles.

The angles that are across from each other in a parallelogram are called *opposite angles*. Show your child the paper parallelogram (from Blackline Master 12). **Angle 4 and angle 2 are opposite angles.** Tear off ∠4. Place it inside ∠2. **What do you notice about angle 4 and angle 2?** *They're equal.*

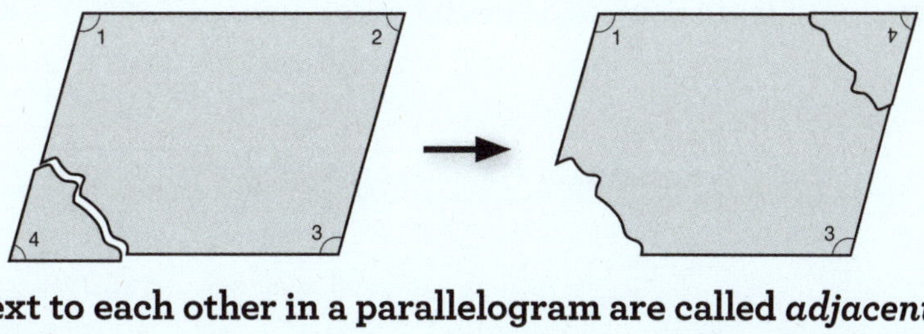

Angles that are next to each other in a parallelogram are called *adjacent angles*. Angles 1 and 4 are adjacent. Place the torn ∠4 next to ∠1 as shown. **What do you notice about angle 1 and angle 4?** *Sample answer: They make a straight angle. They add up to 180 degrees.*

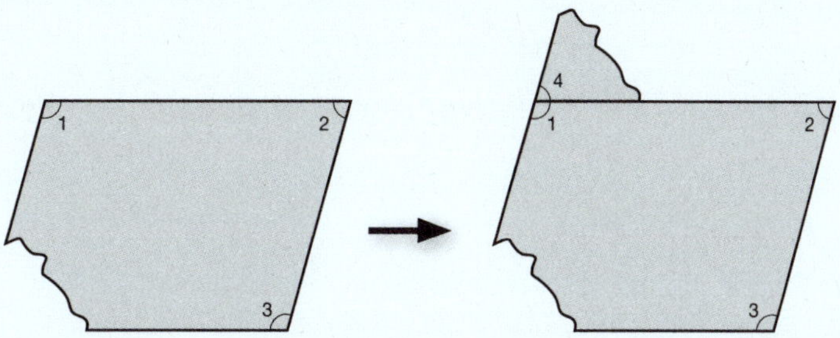

Activity (A): Use Opposite and Adjacent Angles to Find Missing Angles in Parallelograms and Rhombuses

Today, you'll learn how to use opposite and adjacent angles to find missing angles in parallelograms. It can be tricky to remember these terms, so first we'll practice them with our bodies.

Have your child sit or stand across from you (so that you're looking straight at each other). **Opposite angles are across from each other, just like we are opposite each other. They can look across the parallelogram and see each other.**

Then, have your child sit or stand next to you. **Adjacent means "next to." Adjacent angles are next to each other around the parallelogram, just like we are adjacent to each other.**

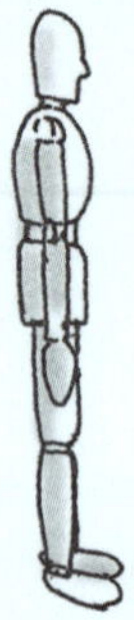

Opposite.

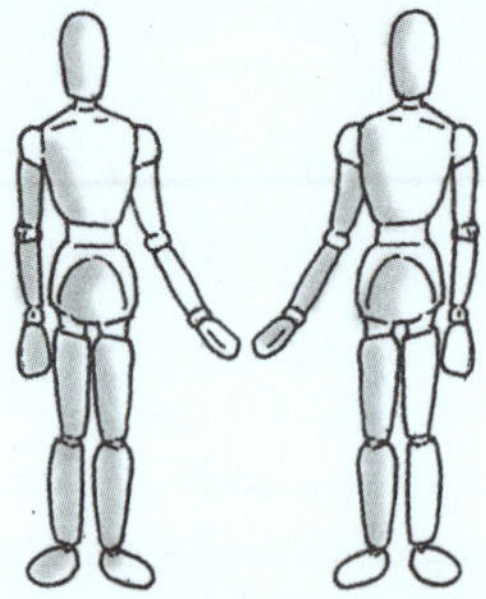

Adjacent.

In the warm-up, we found that opposite angles in parallelograms are equal, and that adjacent angles have a sum of 180 degrees. This is true for all parallelograms. Rhombuses are a special kind of parallelogram, so this is true for all rhombuses, too. Have your child read aloud the left side of the text box.

A

Opposite angles are across from each other diagonally. In parallelograms and rhombuses, opposite angles are always equal to each other.

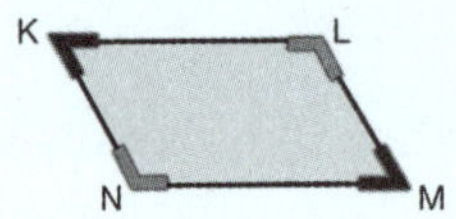

$m\angle K = m\angle M$

$m\angle N = m\angle L$

Which angles are opposite from each other in parallelogram KLMN? *Angles K and M. Angles L and N.*

Have your child read aloud the right side of the text box.

A

Adjacent angles are next to each other. In parallelograms and rhombuses, the sum of two adjacent angles is always 180°.

Ex. $\angle K$ is 60°. What is the measure of $\angle N$?

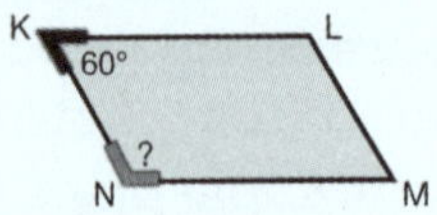

60° + ______ = 180°

180° − 60° = **120°**

Which angles are adjacent to angle K? *Angles L or N.* **Which angles are adjacent to angle L?** *Angles K or M.*

In the example, we know that angle K measures 60 degrees. We want to find the measure of angle N. Angle K and angle N are adjacent, so the sum of their measures must equal 180 degrees. We subtract 60 from 180 to find the measure of angle N. What's 180 minus 60? *120.* **Angle N measures 120 degrees.**

What is the measure of angle L? *120 degrees.* **How do you know?** *Sample answer: Angles N and L are opposite angles, so angle L has the same measure as angle N.*

What is the measure of angle M? *60 degrees.* **How do you know?** *Sample answer: Angles M and K are opposite angles, so angle M has the same measure as angle K.*

Have your child find the measures of the missing angles in parallelogram ABCD and rhombus EFGH.

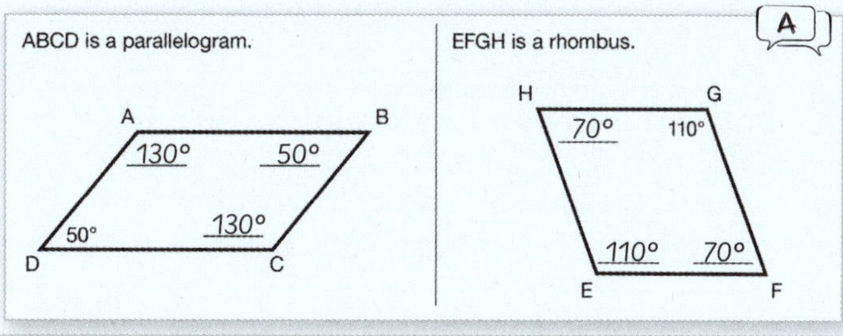

These theorems about opposite and adjacent angles only hold true for quadrilaterals with 2 pairs of parallel sides, like parallelograms and rhombuses. They do not necessarily hold true for all quadrilaterals.

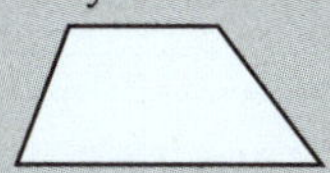

Opposite sides are not necessarily equal (and adjacent angles do not necessarily add up to 180°) in shapes that don't have 2 pairs of parallel sides.

Activity (B): Find Unknown Angles in Parallelograms

Part B has two puzzles to solve. In the first puzzle, what is the measure of angle W? *125 degrees.* If your child's not sure, say: **The right angle measures 90 degrees, and the marked angle is 35 degrees. So, you add them to find the total measure of angle W.** Draw an arc and label the angle as shown.

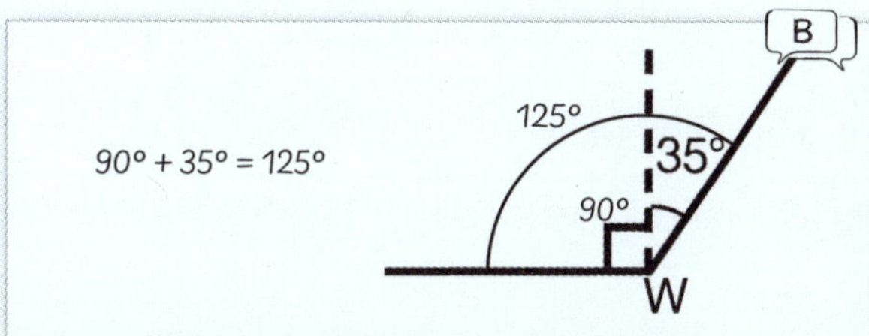

So, what must the measure of angle Y be? *125 degrees.* Have your child then complete the other missing angle measures in parallelogram WXYZ.

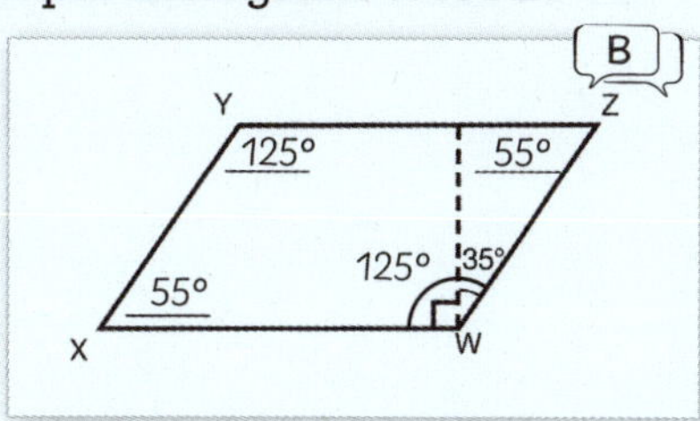

In the next puzzle, two angles are put together at point R to make a straight angle. What is the measure of a straight angle? *180 degrees.* **How can you find the measure of the unknown angle at point R?** *Subtract 80 from 180.* If your child isn't sure, say: **The sum of the two angles equals 180 degrees. So, we can subtract 80 from 180 to find the measure of the unknown angle. What's 180 degrees minus 80 degrees?** *100 degrees.* Write 100° in the blank at point R.

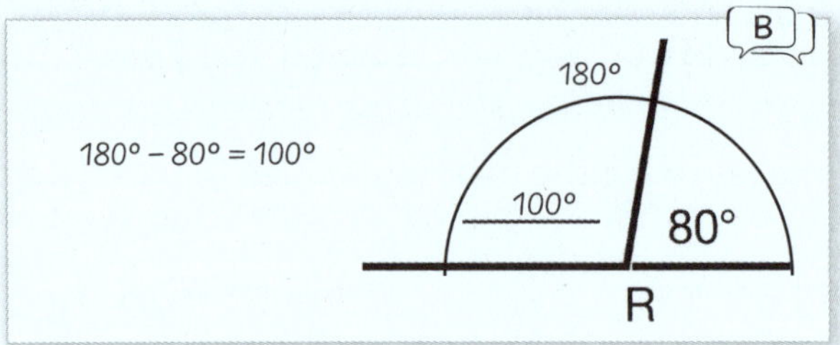

Then, have your child complete the other missing angle measures.

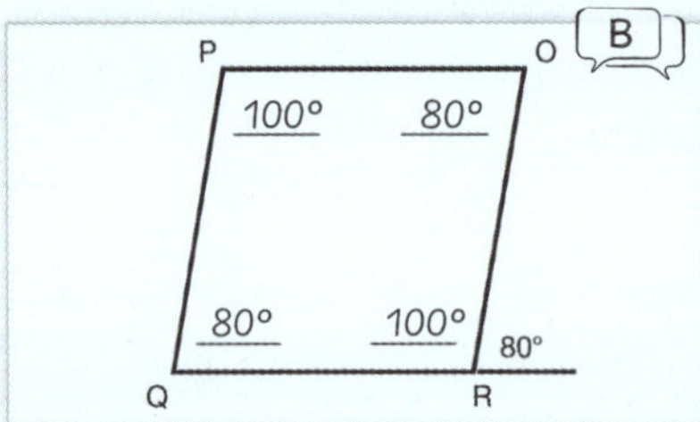

Have your child find the sum of the angles in each parallelogram, either mentally or on paper. **What is the sum of the angles in each parallelogram?** *360 degrees.* **The angles in a quadrilateral always add up to 360 degrees! You'll learn more about that in older grades, and you'll learn how to use that fact to solve more complicated angle puzzles.**

If your child wonders why this is true, explain that any quadrilateral can be cut along a diagonal to form 2 triangles: **The angles in each triangle have a sum of 180°, so the sum of the angles in both triangles will always equal 360°.**

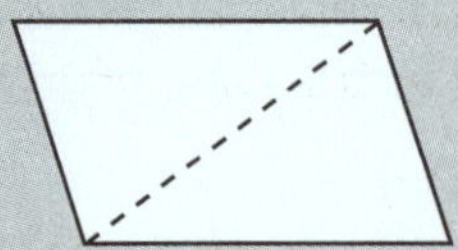

Independent Practice and Review

Have your child complete the Lesson 12.8 Practice and Review workbook pages.

Lesson 12.9
Enrichment (Optional)

Purpose	Materials
• Practice memory work • Appreciate how math can be used to answer real-life questions • Tessellate a triangle or quadrilateral to make an art project • Summarize what your child has learned and assess your child's progress	• *How Many Guinea Pigs Can Fit on a Plane?: Answers to Your Most Clever Math Questions*, by Laura Overdeck • Small piece of cardstock or cardboard (about 3 inches square) • Paper • Black marker • Colored pencils, markers, or watercolor paints

Warm-up: Review Memory Work

Quiz your child on any of the memory work items that she struggled with during this unit.

Math Picture Book: *How Many Guinea Pigs Can Fit on a Plane?*

Read pages 110-119 in *How Many Guinea Pigs Can Fit on a Plane?*

Enrichment Activity: Make Tessellations with a Triangle or Quadrilateral

In this unit, you've studied triangles and quadrilaterals. Today, we'll use triangles or quadrilaterals to make an art project called a tessellation.

A tessellation is a pattern made by repeating a shape over and over to cover a flat surface. The copies of the shapes must fit together with no gaps or overlaps. For example, tile floors are often tessellations. The tiles fit together to completely cover the floor, without any gaps. Look around your home with your child for examples of tessellations.

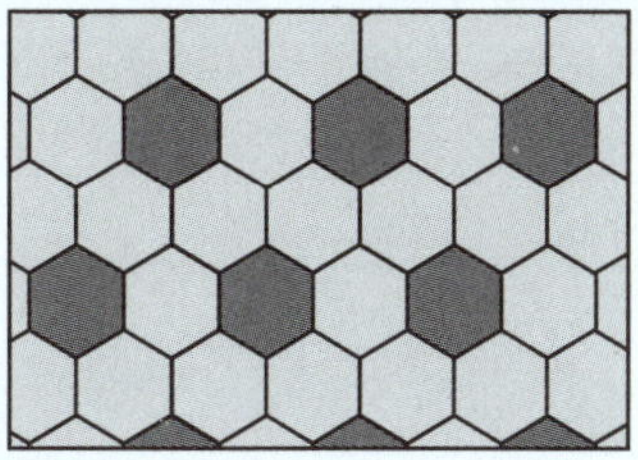

Sample tessellations.

Give your child a small piece of cardboard or cardstock (about 3 inches square). Have her use a ruler to draw a triangle or quadrilateral on the cardstock. Then, have her cut out the shape to make a template.

Sample templates.

Your child can make any kind of triangle or quadrilateral, as all triangles or quadrilaterals will form a tessellation. Encourage your child to draw the shape to fill most of the piece of cardboard, so that the template is easy to handle.

Tessellations are usually made by flipping or turning the base shape. Let's see how you can tessellate your shape. On a piece of scrap paper, have your child trace the template with a pencil. Then, have her experiment with flipping or turning the template to create an arrangement that fully fills in the space, with no gaps or overlaps. There may be more than one way to flip or turn the shape to create a tessellation.

Once your child has found an arrangement she likes, have her trace the template on the final piece of paper for her art project. Have her cover the paper completely with the tessellation. Have her outline each shape in black marker, then color the shapes with colored pencils, markers, or watercolor paint.

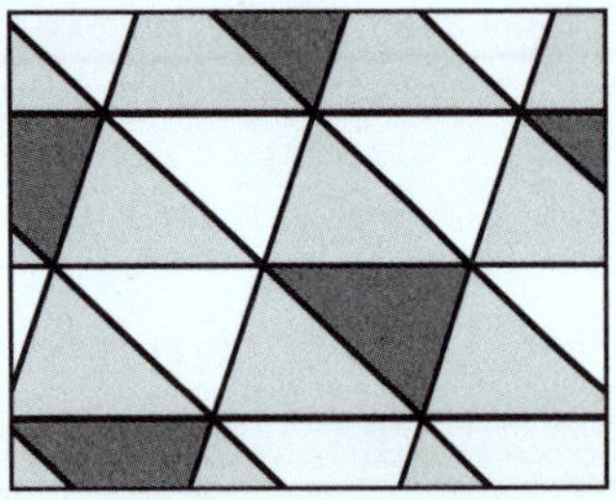

If your child has trouble creating a tessellation with her shape, use these tips to guide her:

- If your child made a triangle, she can turn the template 180 degrees (around the midpoint of one side) to create a parallelogram. Then, she can "stack" the parallelograms.

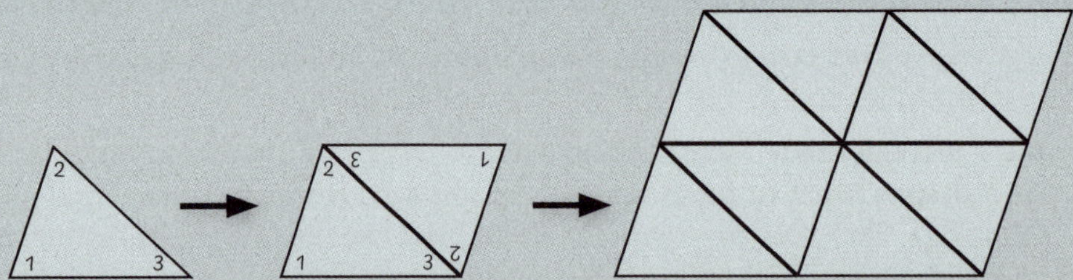

- If your child made a quadrilateral, have her turn the template 180 degrees (around the midpoint of one side) to draw the second, third, and fourth shapes. She will need to use the midpoint of a different side each time.

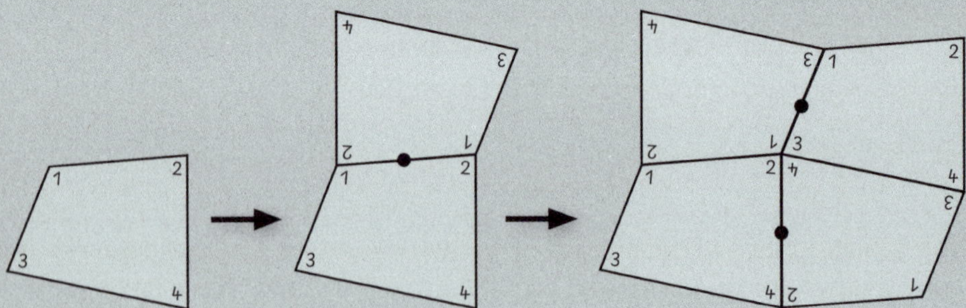

Unit Wrap-Up

Have your child complete the Unit 12 Wrap-Up.

Unit 12 Answer Key

12.1 Practice

Practice: Choose the more reasonable measurement for each angle.

75° / **(90°)**	**(75°)** / 90°	90° / **(100°)**
(30°) / 60°	**(120°)** / 160°	180° / **(160°)**

Write whether each angle is acute, right, obtuse, or straight. Then, use a protractor to measure each angle.

	∠M	∠N	∠O	∠P
Type of Angle	obtuse	obtuse	right	acute
Measure	100°	155°	90°	30°

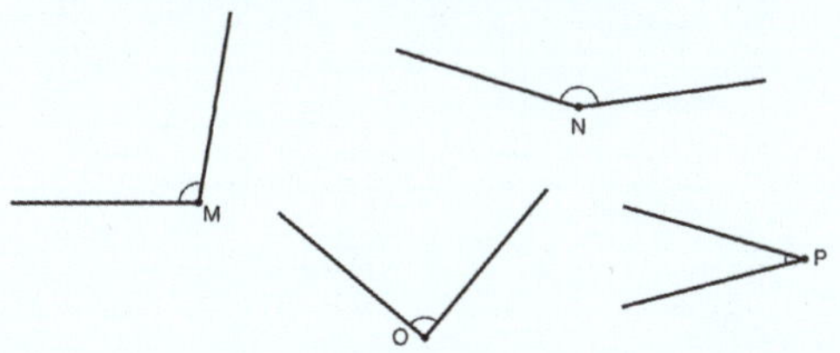

12.1 Review

Review: Complete the chart. Write the fractions in simplest form.

1 hr. = 60 min.

Minutes	10	20	30	40	50	60
Fractions of an hour	$\frac{1}{6}$	$\frac{1}{3}$	$\frac{1}{2}$	$\frac{2}{3}$	$\frac{5}{6}$	1

Find the products. Write your answers in simplest form. If the answer is an improper fraction, convert it to a mixed number or whole number.

$\frac{2}{3} \times \frac{3}{5}$	$\frac{2}{3} \times 1\frac{3}{5}$	$\frac{2}{3} \times 2\frac{3}{5}$
$\frac{2}{3} \times \frac{3}{5} = \frac{6}{15} = \frac{2}{5}$	$\frac{2}{3} \times \frac{8}{5} = \frac{16}{15} = 1\frac{1}{15}$	$\frac{2}{3} \times \frac{13}{5} = \frac{26}{15} = 1\frac{11}{15}$
$2 \times \frac{3}{5}$	$2 \times 1\frac{3}{5}$	$2 \times 2\frac{3}{5}$
$\frac{2}{1} \times \frac{3}{5} = \frac{6}{5} = 1\frac{1}{5}$	$\frac{2}{1} \times \frac{8}{5} = \frac{16}{5} = 3\frac{1}{5}$	$\frac{2}{1} \times \frac{13}{5} = \frac{26}{5} = 5\frac{1}{5}$

Solve. Write the equations you use.

The baseball cap costs $23.79. The t-shirt costs $14.99. How much more does the baseball cap cost than the t-shirt?

23.79
− 14.99
$8.80

What is the volume of the wooden step?

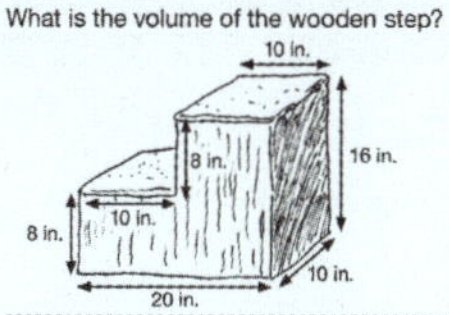

20 × 8 × 10 = 1,600
8 × 10 × 10 = 800
1,600 + 800 = **2,400 cu. in.**

12.2 Practice

Practice: Use a protractor to draw an angle with the given measure.

80° 135°

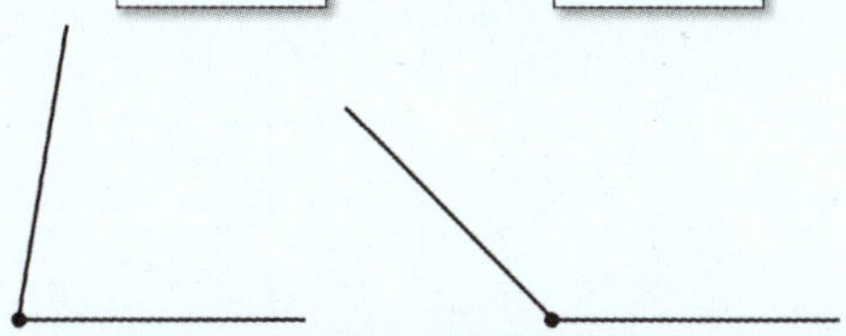

Find the missing angle measures. If needed, write your equations in the work space.

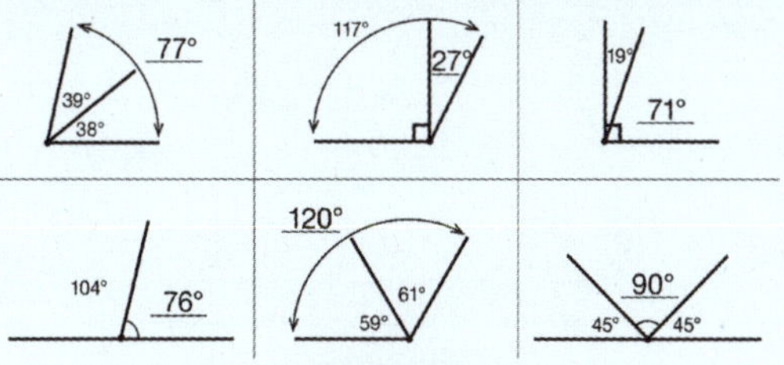

WORK SPACE

39 + 38 = 77
117 − 90 = 27
90 − 19 = 71
180 − 104 = 76
59 + 61 = 120
180 − 45 − 45 = 90

12.2 Review

Review: Label the dimensions. Then, find the area of the rectangle. Make sure to use the correct units.

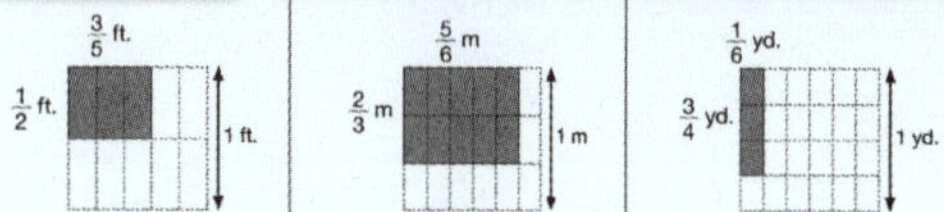

$\frac{3}{5} \times \frac{1}{2} = \frac{3}{10}$ sq. ft.	$\frac{5}{6} \times \frac{2}{3} = \frac{10}{18} = \frac{5}{9}$ sq. ft.	$\frac{1}{6} \times \frac{3}{4} = \frac{3}{24} = \frac{1}{8}$ sq. yd.

Complete the circles with <, >, or =.

1.3 (>) 1.03
0.7 (>) 0.07
3.004 (<) 3.01
5.102 (>) 5.012
4.300 (=) 4.3

Use long division to solve.

313 ÷ 8 = 39 R1: 8)313, − 24, 73, − 72, 1

504 ÷ 7 = 72: 7)504, − 49, 14, − 14, 0

685 ÷ 9 = 76 R1: 9)685, − 63, 55, − 54, 1

Solve. Write the equations you use.

Lilia's family has $\frac{3}{8}$ of a pie left over. Then, Lilia eats $\frac{3}{4}$ of the leftover pie. What fraction of the whole pie does she eat?

$\frac{3}{4} \times \frac{3}{8} =$ **$\frac{9}{32}$ of the pie**

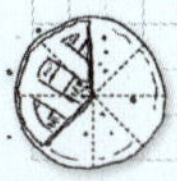

Peter's family has $\frac{5}{8}$ of a pepperoni pizza and $\frac{2}{3}$ of a cheese pizza left over after a party. How much pizza do they have in all?

$\frac{5}{8} = \frac{15}{24}$
$+ \frac{2}{3} = \frac{16}{24}$
$\frac{31}{24} =$ **$1\frac{7}{24}$ pizzas**

Unit 12 Answer Key

12.3 Practice

Practice Write whether each triangle is acute, right, or obtuse.

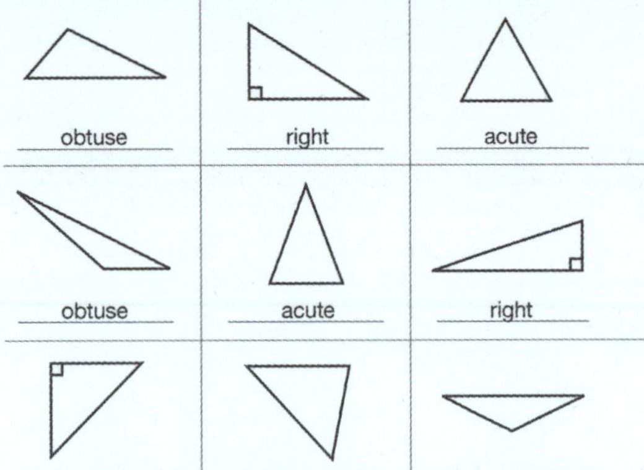

obtuse	right	acute
obtuse	acute	right
right	acute	obtuse

Follow the directions. Then, connect the points to form a triangle.

Draw point A so that △ABC is an acute triangle.

Draw point E so that △DEF is a right triangle.

Draw point I so that △GHI is an obtuse triangle.

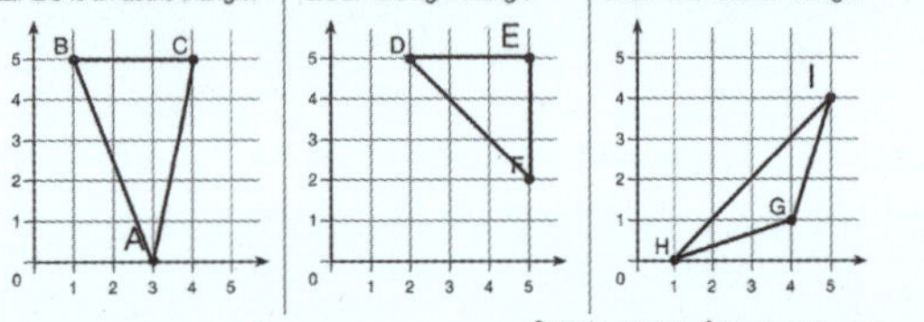

Sample answers. Answers may vary

12.3 Review

Review Complete the chart. Write the fractions in simplest form.

1 m = 100 cm

Centimeters	25	50	75	100	125	150
Fraction of a meter	$\frac{1}{4}$	$\frac{1}{2}$	$\frac{3}{4}$	1	$1\frac{1}{4}$	$1\frac{1}{2}$

Find the products. Write your answers in simplest form. If the answer is an improper fraction, convert it to a mixed number or whole number.

$3 \times \frac{3}{4}$: $\frac{3}{1} \times \frac{3}{4} = \frac{9}{4} = 2\frac{1}{4}$

$4 \times \frac{3}{4}$: $\frac{4}{1} \times \frac{3}{4} = \frac{12}{4} = 3$

$5 \times \frac{3}{4}$: $\frac{5}{1} \times \frac{3}{4} = \frac{15}{4} = 3\frac{3}{4}$

$3\frac{1}{2} \times \frac{3}{4}$: $\frac{7}{2} \times \frac{3}{4} = \frac{21}{8} = 2\frac{5}{8}$

$4\frac{1}{2} \times \frac{3}{4}$: $\frac{9}{2} \times \frac{3}{4} = \frac{27}{8} = 3\frac{3}{8}$

$5\frac{1}{2} \times \frac{3}{4}$: $\frac{11}{2} \times \frac{3}{4} = \frac{33}{8} = 4\frac{1}{8}$

Find the area of each rug.

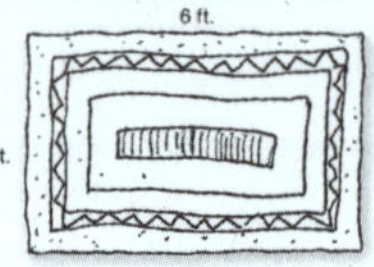

6 ft., 4 ft.

$4 \times 6 = 24$ sq. ft.

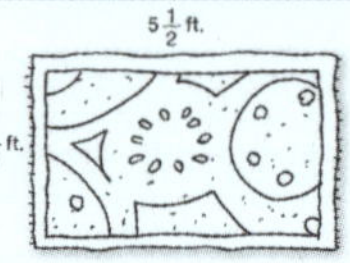

$5\frac{1}{2}$ ft., $3\frac{1}{2}$ ft.

$3\frac{1}{2} \times 5\frac{1}{2}$

$\frac{7}{2} \times \frac{11}{2} = \frac{77}{4} = 19\frac{1}{4}$ sq. ft.

12.4 Practice

Practice Find the missing angle in each triangle.

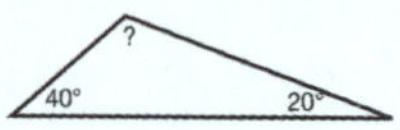

40°, 20°, ?

__ + 40 + 20 = 180
40 + 20 = 60
180 − 60 = 120°

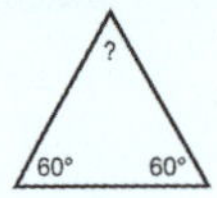

60°, 60°, ?

__ + 60 + 60 = 180
60 + 60 = 120
180 − 120 = 60°

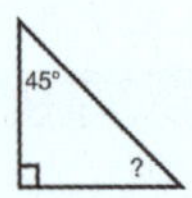

45°, ?

__ + 45 + 90 = 180
45 + 90 = 135
180 − 135 = 45°

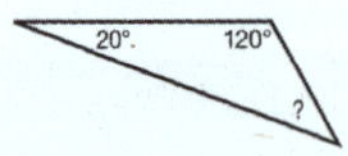

20°, 120°, ?

__ + 20 + 120 = 180
120 + 20 = 140
180 − 140 = 40°

Use the clues to find the measures of the missing angles.

The measure of angle M is 40° greater than the measure of angle L.

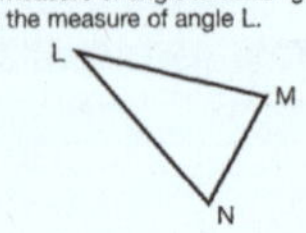

35 + 40 = 75
35 + 75 = 110
180 − 110 = 70

m∠L = 35°
m∠M = 75°
m∠N = 70°

The measure of angle Q is 2 times the measure of angle P.

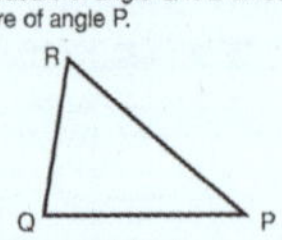

2 × 40 = 80
40 + 80 = 120
180 − 120 = 60

m∠P = 40°
m∠Q = 80°
m∠R = 60°

12.4 Review

Review Write each number in expanded form.

2.35 = $2 + \frac{3}{10} + \frac{5}{100}$

1.742 = $1 + \frac{7}{10} + \frac{4}{100} + \frac{2}{1,000}$

0.73 = $\frac{7}{10} + \frac{3}{100}$

3.401 = $3 + \frac{4}{10} + \frac{1}{1,000}$

52.6 = $50 + 2 + \frac{6}{10}$

39.05 = $30 + 9 + \frac{5}{100}$

Solve.

38 ÷ 6 = 6 R2

37 ÷ 8 = 4 R5

46 ÷ 7 = 6 R4

55 ÷ 8 = 6 R7

60 ÷ 9 = 6 R6

67 ÷ 8 = 8 R3

Estimate the answer to each problem. Then, circle the words that match the answer. You do not need to find the exact answers.

$4 \times 1\frac{5}{6}$: (less than 8) circled; greater than 8

$3 \times 2\frac{1}{5}$: less than 6; (greater than 6) circled

$2 \times 4\frac{1}{2}$: (less than 10) circled; greater than 10

$\frac{3}{4} \times 3\frac{7}{8}$: (less than $3\frac{7}{8}$) circled; greater than $3\frac{7}{8}$

$2 \times 3\frac{7}{8}$: less than $3\frac{7}{8}$; (greater than $3\frac{7}{8}$) circled

$2\frac{3}{4} \times 3\frac{7}{8}$: less than $3\frac{7}{8}$; (greater than $3\frac{7}{8}$) circled

Solve. Write the equations you use. Write your answers in simplest form. If the answer is an improper fraction, convert it to a mixed number or whole number.

The recipe calls for $1\frac{2}{3}$ c. oats for each batch of oatmeal cookies. Wilder wants to make 4 batches. How many cups of oats does he need?

$4 \times 1\frac{2}{3}$

$\frac{4}{1} \times \frac{5}{3} = \frac{20}{3} = 6\frac{2}{3}$ c.

The recipe calls for $\frac{3}{4}$ c. of raisins for each batch of oatmeal cookies. AnnMarie only wants to make $\frac{1}{2}$ of the recipe. How many cups of raisins does she need?

$\frac{1}{2} \times \frac{3}{4} = \frac{3}{8}$ c.

Unit 12 Answer Key

12.5 Practice

Practice Write whether each triangle is equilateral, isosceles, or scalene. All equal sides are labeled.

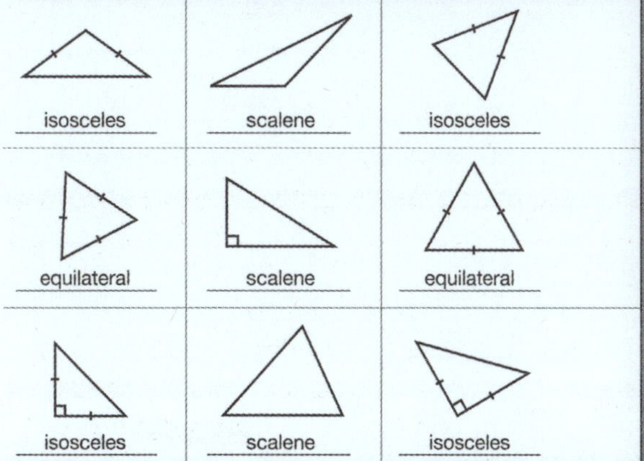

isosceles	scalene	isosceles
equilateral	scalene	equilateral
isosceles	scalene	isosceles

Use the descriptions to add tick marks to the sides of the triangles. Then, draw as many lines of symmetry as possible.

$\overline{JK}$ is the same length as $\overline{KL}$.

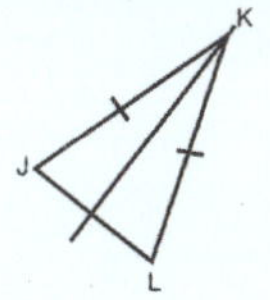

$\overline{AB}$ is the same length as $\overline{BC}$.
$\overline{BC}$ is the same length as $\overline{CA}$.

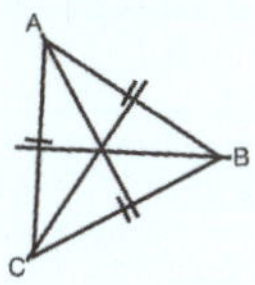

12.5 Review

Review Find the products. Write your answers in simplest form. If the answer is an improper fraction, convert it to a mixed number or whole number.

$\frac{1}{3} \times \frac{3}{8}$: $\frac{1}{3} \times \frac{3}{8} = \frac{3}{24} = \frac{1}{8}$

$\frac{2}{3} \times \frac{3}{8}$: $\frac{2}{3} \times \frac{3}{8} = \frac{6}{24} = \frac{1}{4}$

$\frac{3}{3} \times \frac{3}{8}$: $\frac{3}{3} \times \frac{3}{8} = \frac{9}{24} = \frac{3}{8}$

$3 \times \frac{3}{8}$: $\frac{3}{1} \times \frac{3}{8} = \frac{9}{8} = 1\frac{1}{8}$

$3\frac{2}{3} \times \frac{3}{8}$: $\frac{11}{3} \times \frac{3}{8} = \frac{33}{24} = 1\frac{9}{24} = 1\frac{3}{8}$

$8 \times \frac{3}{8}$: $\frac{8}{1} \times \frac{3}{8} = \frac{24}{8} = 3$

Complete the missing numbers.

$10 \times 5 \times 2 =$ 100
$5 \times 5 \times 4 =$ 100
$2 \times 2 \times 25 =$ 100
$20 \times 5 \times 2 =$ 200
$5 \times 10 \times 4 =$ 200
$2 \times 2 \times 50 =$ 200

Write a decimal number to match each grid.

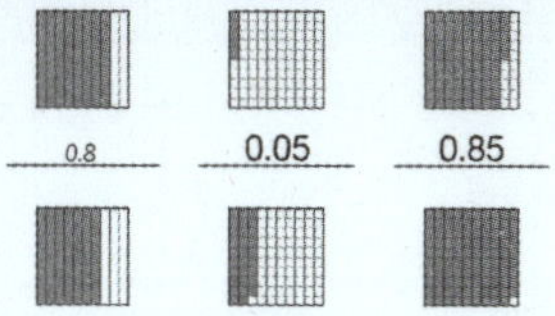

0.8 0.05 0.85
0.7 0.29 0.99

Solve. Write the equations you use. Write your answers in simplest form. If the answer is an improper fraction, convert it to a mixed number or whole number.

Each bag of pasta weighs $\frac{7}{8}$ lb. Sekani uses $1\frac{1}{3}$ bags. How many pounds of pasta does he use?

$1\frac{1}{3} \times \frac{7}{8}$

$\frac{4}{3} \times \frac{7}{8} = \frac{28}{24} = 1\frac{4}{24} =$ **$1\frac{1}{6}$ lb**

Shoshana runs $4\frac{7}{10}$ km. Emily runs twice as far as Shoshana. How far does Emily run?

$2 \times 4\frac{7}{10}$

$\frac{2}{1} \times \frac{47}{10} = \frac{94}{10} = 9\frac{4}{10} =$ **$9\frac{2}{5}$ km**

12.6 Practice

Practice Write the letter for each triangle in the correct space in the chart.

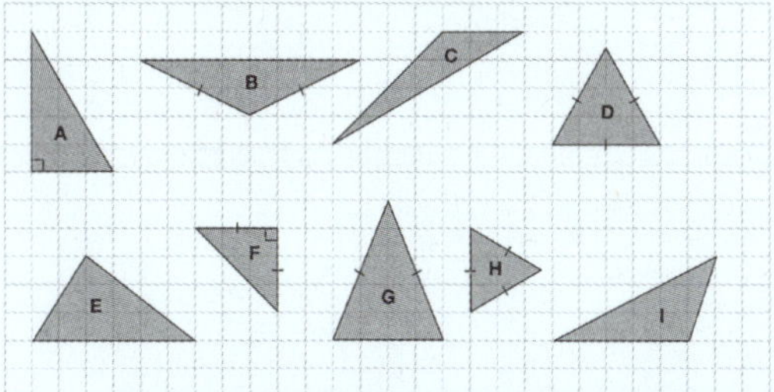

	Acute	Obtuse	Right
Isosceles	G	B	F
Scalene	E	C, I	A
Equilateral	H, D		

Answer the questions.

Can an isosceles triangle also be a right triangle? yes

Can an equilateral triangle also be acute? yes

Can an obtuse triangle also be isosceles? yes

Can a scalene triangle also be isosceles? no

Can an equilateral triangle also be obtuse? no

Can a scalene triangle also be acute? yes

12.6 Review

Review Connect each number to its place on the number line.

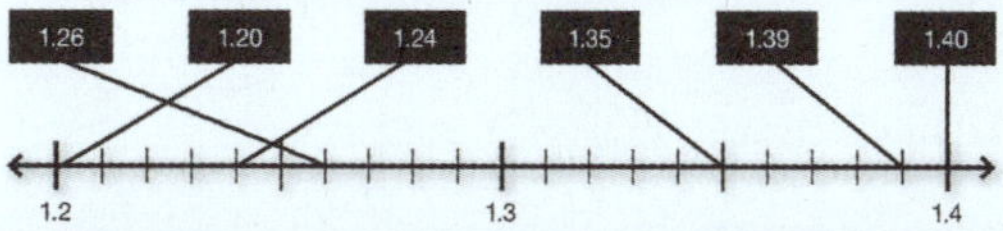

Find the products. Write your answers in simplest form. If the answer is an improper fraction, convert it to a mixed number or whole number.

$5 \times 1\frac{3}{4}$: $\frac{5}{1} \times \frac{7}{4} = \frac{35}{4} = 8\frac{3}{4}$

$2\frac{2}{3} \times 1\frac{1}{8}$: $\frac{8}{3} \times \frac{9}{8} = \frac{72}{24} = 3$

$\frac{2}{5} \times \frac{3}{4}$: $\frac{2}{5} \times \frac{3}{4} = \frac{6}{20} = \frac{3}{10}$

Find the missing angle.

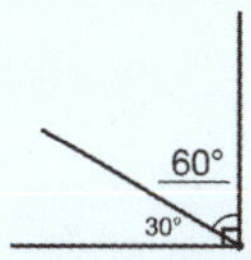

Find the product.

```
  2 8 1
×     4
-------
1,1 2 4
```

```
     2 8 1
×      3 4
----------
   1,1 2 4
 + 8,4 3 0
----------
   9,5 5 4
```

```
       2 8 1
×      5 3 4
------------
     1,1 2 4
     8,4 3 0
+ 1 4 0,5 0 0
------------
  1 5 0,0 5 4
```

Solve. Write the equations you use. Write your answers in simplest form. If the answer is an improper fraction, convert it to a mixed number or whole number.

There are 28 children in the choir. $\frac{3}{4}$ of the children are ten years old, and the rest are eleven years old. How many children are ten years old?

$\frac{3}{4}$ of 28

$28 \div 4 = 7$

$3 \times 7 =$ **21 children**

Lennox's dad is $5\frac{5}{6}$ ft. tall. Lennox's height is $\frac{3}{4}$ of her dad's height. How tall is Lennox?

$\frac{3}{4} \times 5\frac{5}{6}$

$\frac{3}{4} \times \frac{35}{6} = \frac{105}{24} = 4\frac{9}{24} =$ **$4\frac{3}{8}$ ft.**

Unit 12 Answer Key

12.7 Practice

Practice Write the most specific name possible for each quadrilateral. Use the words in the word bank.

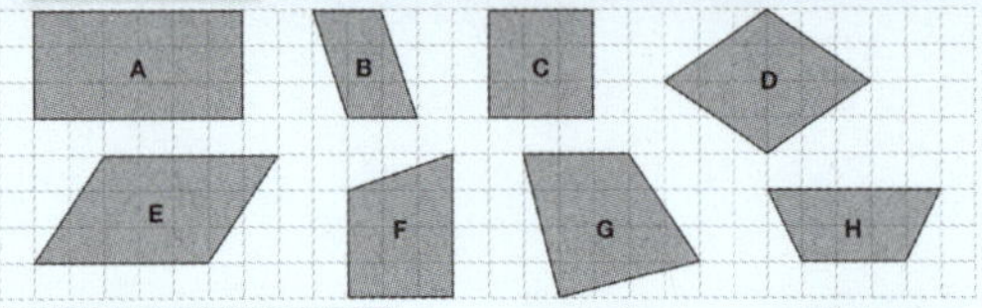

Parallelogram	Rhombus
Quadrilateral	Square
Rectangle	Trapezoid

A: rectangle
B: parallelogram
C: square
D: rhombus
E: parallelogram
F: trapezoid
G: quadrilateral
H: trapezoid

Follow the directions. Then, connect the points to form a quadrilateral.

Draw point D so that ABCD is a quadrilateral.
Draw point E so that EFGH is a rectangle.
Draw point J so that IJKL is a square.

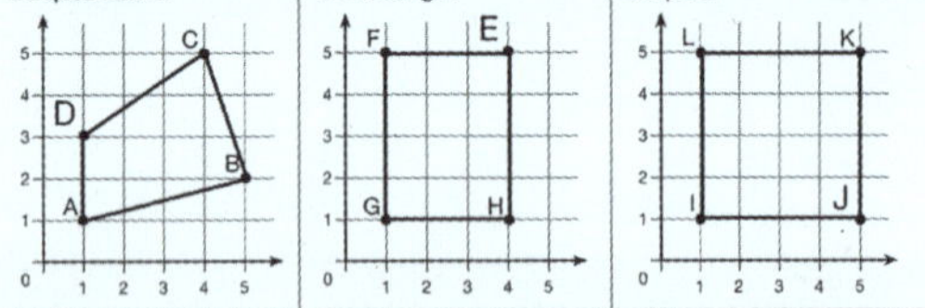

Draw point O so that MNOP is a parallelogram.
Draw point Q so that QRST is a rhombus.
Draw point V so that UVWX is a trapezoid.

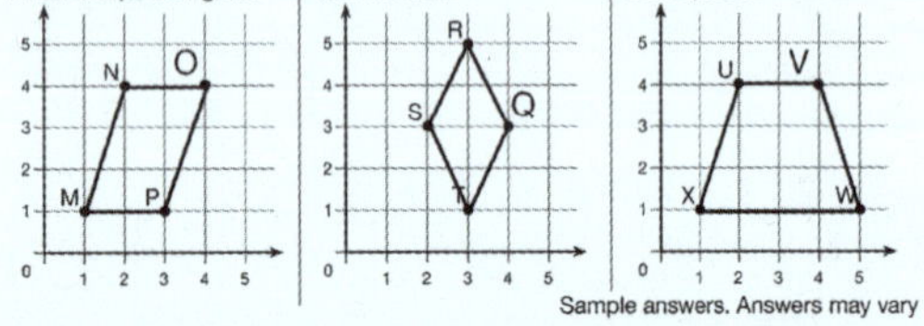

Sample answers. Answers may vary

12.7 Review

Review Complete.

$\frac{1}{4}$ of 40 = 10	$\frac{1}{5}$ of 25 = 5	$\frac{1}{3}$ of 45 = 15
$\frac{3}{4}$ of 40 = 30	$\frac{3}{5}$ of 25 = 15	$\frac{2}{3}$ of 45 = 30
$\frac{1}{5}$ of 100 = 20	$\frac{1}{6}$ of 48 = 8	$\frac{1}{10}$ of 120 = 12
$\frac{4}{5}$ of 100 = 80	$\frac{5}{6}$ of 48 = 40	$\frac{2}{10}$ of 120 = 24

Find the missing angle.

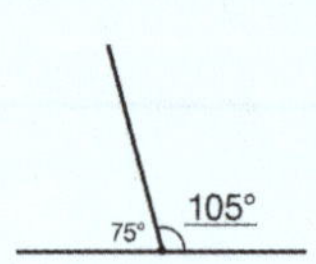

Find the product.

$\frac{1}{2} \times \frac{1}{3} = \frac{1}{6}$

$\frac{1}{2} \times \frac{1}{4} = \frac{1}{8}$

$\frac{1}{2} \times \frac{1}{5} = \frac{1}{10}$

$\frac{2}{3} \times \frac{1}{8} = \frac{2}{24} = \frac{1}{12}$

$\frac{2}{3} \times \frac{3}{8} = \frac{6}{24} = \frac{1}{4}$

$\frac{2}{3} \times \frac{5}{8} = \frac{10}{24} = \frac{5}{12}$

Solve. Write the equations you use in the work space.

3 friends work together to earn $276. They split the money evenly. How much does each friend get?

$92

The bakery bakes 350 cupcakes. They pack the cupcakes in boxes of 6. How many boxes do they fill?

58 boxes

There are 129 children at drama camp. The leaders split them as equally as possible into 9 groups. How many children are in each group?

14 or 15 children

WORK SPACE

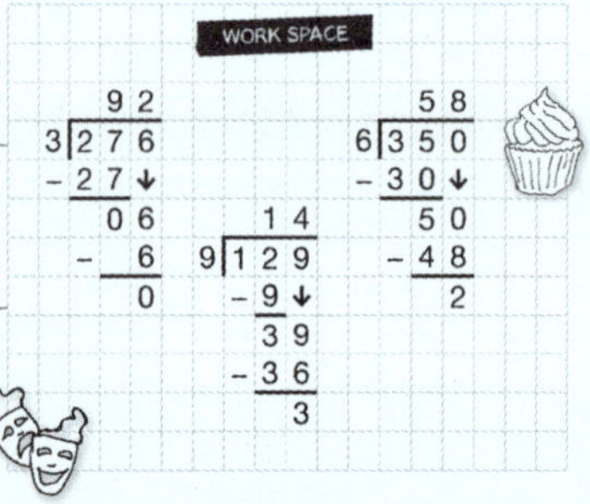

12.8 Practice

Practice Circle the word that describes the relationship between the angles.

∠G and ∠H	∠G and ∠I	∠G and ∠J
Opposite / **Adjacent** (circled)	**Opposite** (circled) / Adjacent	Opposite / **Adjacent** (circled)

∠H and ∠I	∠H and ∠J	∠I and ∠J
Opposite / **Adjacent** (circled)	**Opposite** (circled) / Adjacent	Opposite / **Adjacent** (circled)

GHIJ is a parallelogram.

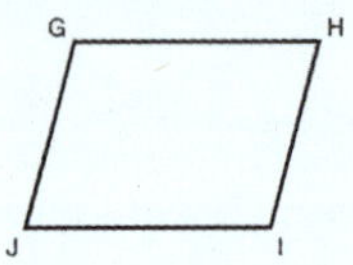

Use the marked angle to find the measure of the other angles.

CDEF is a rhombus.

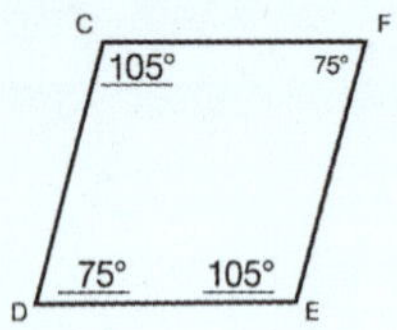

KLMN is a parallelogram.

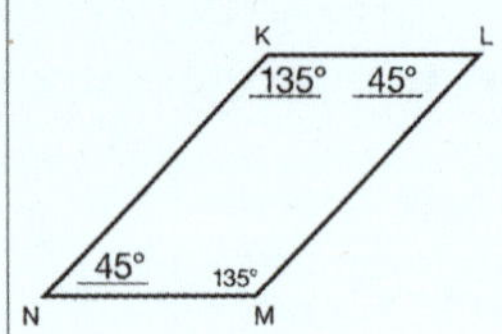

OPQR is a rhombus.

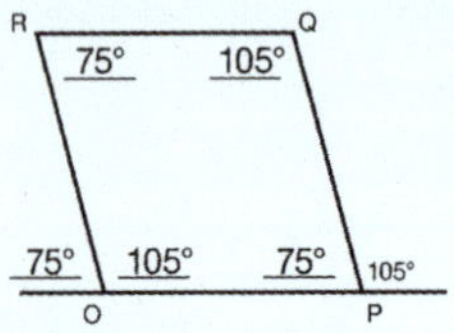

STUV is a parallelogram.

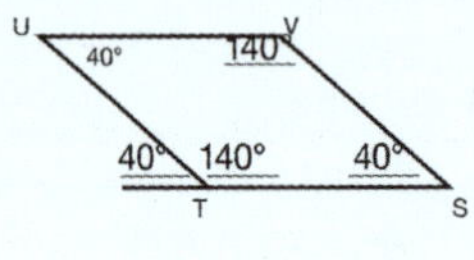

12.8 Review

Review Complete the chart. Write the fractions in simplest form.

1 c. = 8 oz.

Fluid ounces	1	2	3	4	5	6	7	8
Cups	$\frac{1}{8}$	$\frac{1}{4}$	$\frac{3}{8}$	$\frac{1}{2}$	$\frac{5}{8}$	$\frac{3}{4}$	$\frac{7}{8}$	1

Write the ordered pair for each point.

Point	Ordered Pair
A	(2,4)
B	(5,1)
C	(5,5)
D	(0,4)
E	(4,0)

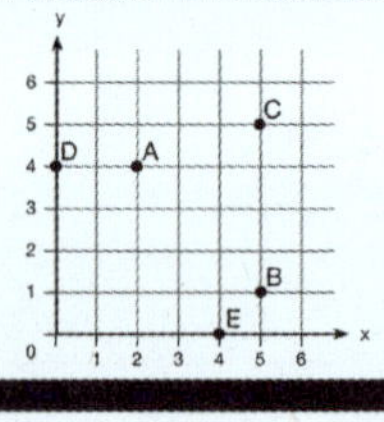

Solve. Write the equations you use.

At the fun run, the volunteers make $5\frac{1}{3}$ gallons of red sports drink and $3\frac{3}{4}$ gallons of blue sports drink. How many gallons of sports drink do they make in all?

$5\frac{1}{3} + 3\frac{3}{4}$

$5\frac{4}{12} + 3\frac{9}{12} = 8\frac{13}{12} =$ $9\frac{1}{12}$ gal.

Penelope runs 4.87 km. Cicely runs 3.9 km. How much farther does Penelope run than Cicely?

4.87 − 3.90 = 0.97 km

The announcer's platform is 2 feet high. It has a volume of 160 cubic feet. What area does the platform cover?

160 ÷ 2 = 80 sq. ft.

The finish line banner is 10 ft. long and $\frac{3}{4}$ ft. wide. What is the area of the banner?

$\frac{10}{1} \times \frac{3}{4} = \frac{30}{4} = 7\frac{2}{4} = 7\frac{1}{2}$ sq. ft.

Unit 12 Answer Key

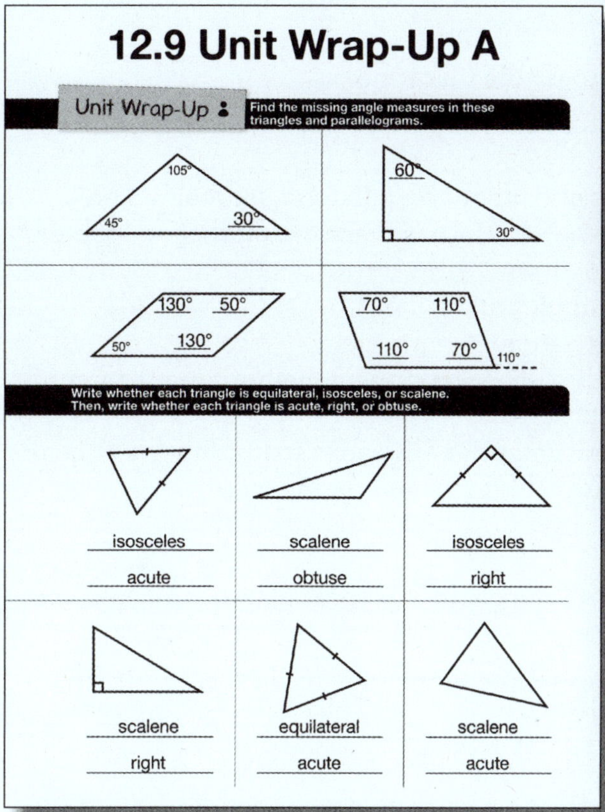

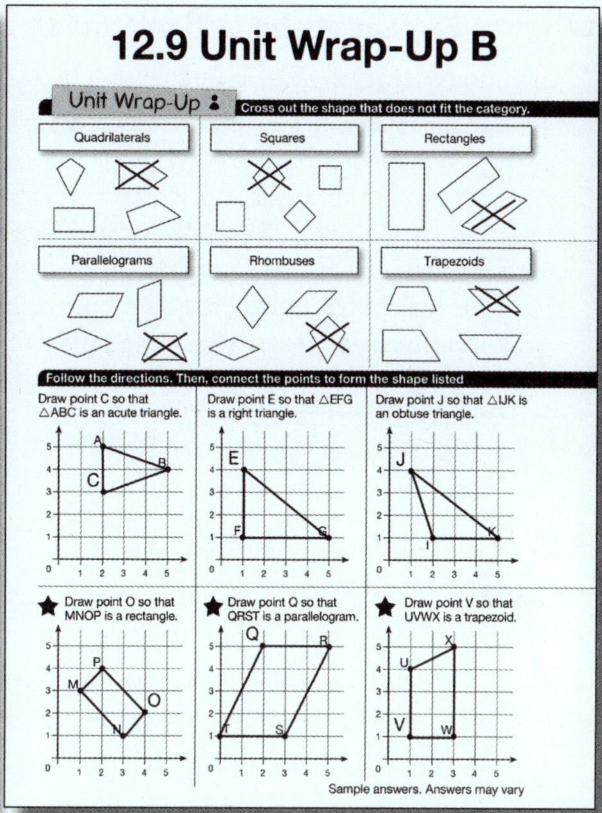

Unit 12 Checkpoint

What to Expect at the End of Unit 12

By the end of Unit 12, most children will be able to do the following:

- Measure and draw angles with a protractor. Some children will still need help lining up the protractor correctly.
- Identify acute, right, and obtuse triangles and identify equilateral, isosceles, and scalene triangles. Some children will still be working on memorizing these vocabulary words.
- Categorize triangles based on both their angles and sides.
- Find the measure of a missing angle in a triangle.
- Identify quadrilaterals. Some children will still be working on memorizing the definitions of quadrilaterals.
- Build different kinds of triangles and quadrilaterals with paper strips and draw them.
- Find the measure of missing angles in parallelograms and rhombuses.

Is Your Child Ready to Move on?

Your child does not need to have fully mastered all the geometry vocabulary words and concepts in Unit 12.

In Unit 13, your child will learn to divide fractions. Before moving on to Unit 13, your child should have already mastered the following skills:

- Finding a fraction of a whole number
- Multiplying a fraction by a fraction

What to Do If Your Child Needs More Practice

If your child is having trouble with any of the above skills, spend a day or two practicing the corresponding review activities below before moving on to Unit 13.

- Spin a Set (Lesson 8.6)
- Too Much Cake! (Lesson 10.2)

Unit 13
Divide Fractions

Overview

You will introduce your child to fraction division in this unit. She will learn how to express quotients of whole numbers as fractions, divide fractions by whole numbers, and divide whole numbers by unit fractions (like 1/3 or 1/8).

This unit is meant as a gentle introduction to this challenging concept. In *Sixth Grade Math with Confidence,* your child will go deeper and learn how to solve a wider variety of fraction division problems.

What Your Child Will Learn

In this unit, your child will learn to:

- Understand that the fraction bar is another way to represent division
- Divide small whole numbers by small whole numbers and write the result as a fraction or mixed number (for example, 6 ÷ 5 = 1 1/5 or 3 ÷ 4 = 3/4)
- Write remainders as fractions
- Divide fractions by whole numbers (for example, 2/3 ÷ 4)
- Divide whole numbers by unit fractions (for example, 3 ÷ 1/2)
- Solve word problems that involve dividing fractions and whole numbers

Lesson List

Lesson 13.1	Use the Fraction Bar to Show Division	Lesson 13.6	Divide Fractions by Whole Numbers
Lesson 13.2	Division Word Problems with Fractional Quotients	Lesson 13.7	Fraction Division Word Problems
Lesson 13.3	Write Remainders as Fractions	Lesson 13.8	Divide Whole Numbers by Unit Fractions
Lesson 13.4	Use Pictures to Divide Fractions by Whole Numbers	Lesson 13.9	More Fraction Division Word Problems
Lesson 13.5	Divide Unit Fractions by Whole Numbers	Lesson 13.10	Enrichment (Optional)

Extra Materials Needed for Unit 13

- Red colored pencil or marker
- Scissors
- For optional Enrichment Lesson:
    - *How Many Guinea Pigs Can Fit on a Plane?: Answers to Your Most Clever Math Questions,* by Laura Overdeck. Feiwel & Friends, 2017.
    - Paper
    - Scissors
- die

You will also use fraction circles from your math kit in this unit. If you don't have fraction circles, you can use the paper fraction circles on Blackline Master 14 instead.

Teaching Math with Confidence: Using Simple Problems to Build Conceptual Understanding of Fraction Division

Fraction division is one of the most poorly-understood concepts in elementary arithmetic. Children usually have no trouble learning the procedure for solving numerical fraction division problems, but they usually have little idea of when or how to apply fraction division to real-world situations. In fact, this concept has proven so daunting to generations of children that the traditional rhyme for teaching fraction division even admits defeat: "Ours is not to wonder why, just invert and multiply!"

Math with Confidence splits fraction division between fifth and sixth grades to help your child understand and develop confidence with this challenging topic. You'll use hands-on materials and familiar contexts to help your child understand the meaning of the problems.

This year, your child will learn to divide fractions by whole numbers and divide whole numbers by unit fractions (fractions with a numerator of 1, like 1/4 or 1/6). Studying just these two categories keeps the numbers simple so she can focus on understanding the underlying meaning of the equations.

The limited range of problems also makes it easier for your child to understand why we rewrite fraction division problems as multiplication problems before solving. Most fifth-graders aren't ready to wade into the abstractions of reciprocals, so instead you'll focus on one simple concept: Dividing by a whole number is the same as multiplying by the matching unit fraction (and vice versa).

For example, say you want to split 3/4 of a pizza between 3 people. Dividing by 3 is the same as multiplying by 1/3 (that is, finding 1/3 of the quantity). So, you can multiply 3/4 × 1/3 to find the answer.

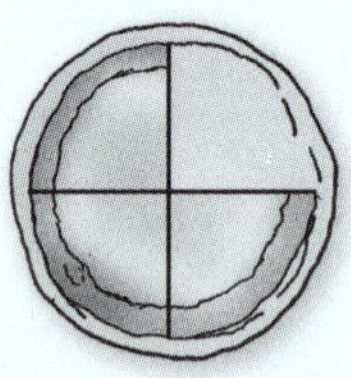

$\frac{3}{4} \div 3 = ?$

$\frac{3}{4} \times \frac{1}{3} = \frac{3}{12} = \frac{1}{4}$ *of the pizza*

If 3 people share 3/4 of a pizza, each person gets 1/4 of the whole pizza.

Or, say you want to split 3 pizzas into fourths. There are 4 fourths in each whole pizza, so you can multiply 3 × 4 to find the answer.

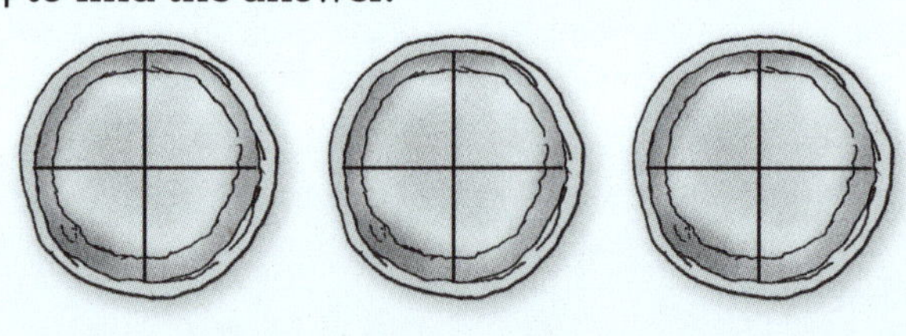

$3 \div \frac{1}{4} = ?$

$3 \times 4 = 12$ *slices*

If you cut 3 pizzas into fourths, you make 12 slices.

By focusing on just these two types of problems, your child will develop a strong conceptual understanding of what it means to divide with fractions. She'll also begin to develop procedural fluency with rewriting fraction division problems as multiplication problems. In *Sixth Grade Math with Confidence*, she'll learn about reciprocals and how to use this approach to solve a wider variety of fraction division problems.

If you never learned the conceptual basis for fraction division, you're not alone. Many parents never learned the meaning of fraction division, so this unit may feel challenging to teach. If so, read the scripted lessons word for word and make sure to look closely at the diagrams to see how they match the explanation. Fraction division can be difficult for both children and adults, so try to be patient with both your student and yourself.

Lesson 13.1
Use the Fraction Bar to Show Division

Purpose	Materials
• Use paper chocolate bars to concretely divide small whole numbers into equal parts • Use the fraction bar to write and solve whole-number division problems • Solve division problems with mixed number or fractional quotients	• Paper chocolate bars (Blackline Master 13) • Scissors

Memory Work	
	• **What do we call the number to be divided?** *The dividend.* • **What do we call the number we divide by?** *The divisor.* • **What do we call the result when we divide two numbers?** *The quotient.*

Warm-up (A): Use Paper Chocolate Bars to Solve Division Problems with Small Whole Numbers

We'll use these paper chocolate bars to model the problems in today's lesson. The lines on the chocolate bar split it into 12 small pieces. Place 4 paper chocolate bars (from Blackline Master 13) on the table. **Let's pretend we want to evenly share these 4 chocolate bars. How many do we each get?** *2.* Write 2 in the blank.

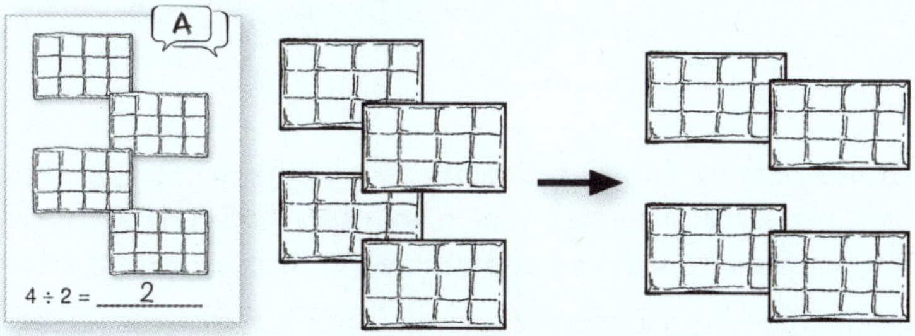

Remove 1 chocolate bar and leave 3 on the table. **Now we have 3 chocolate bars to share. How many do we each get?** *1 and one-half.* If your child's not sure, say: **We could each get 1 whole chocolate bar, and then there would be 1 chocolate bar left to split. How could we share it equally?** *Sample answer: Break it in half.* Write 1 1/2 in the blank.

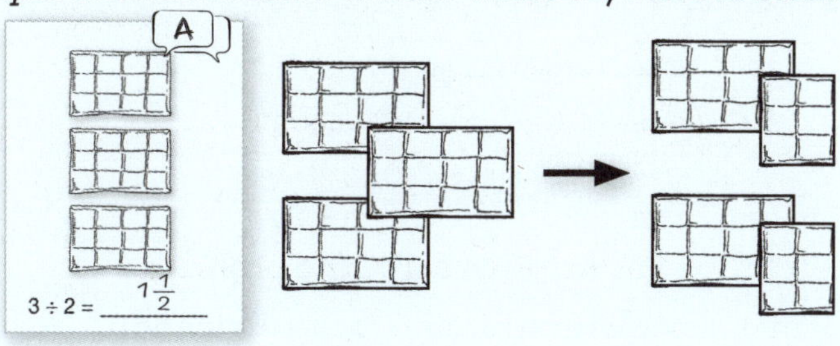

Repeat with the final 2 exercises.

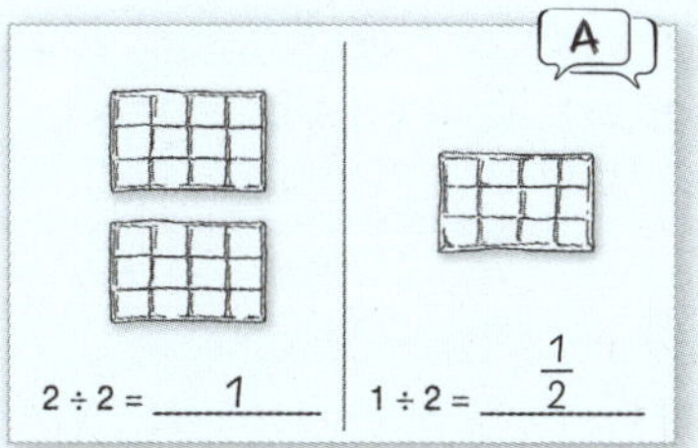

Activity (B): Use the Fraction Bar to Show Division and Write Quotients with Fractions

Some items can't be cut into smaller parts, like marbles, people, or puppies. When we divide them into equal groups, we sometimes have a remainder. For example, if 2 children want to share 3 puppies, they don't each get 1 and one-half puppies! They each get 1 puppy, and there's 1 puppy left over.

But, there are other items that can be cut into smaller parts, like chocolate bars, pizzas, or ribbons. We can cut them into smaller parts to divide them equally. If 2 children want to share 3 chocolate bars, they each get 1 and one-half chocolate bars.

Today, you'll learn how to solve division problems where we cut items into fractional parts to divide them evenly. We use the fraction bar to help us. The fraction bar is the horizontal line that separates the numerator from the denominator in a fraction. We can also use it to show division. Have your child read the left side of the text box aloud.

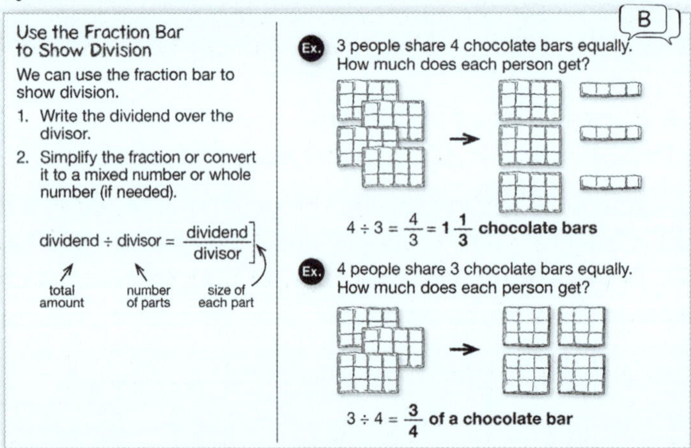

Use the Fraction Bar to Show Division

We can use the fraction bar to show division.

1. Write the dividend over the divisor.
2. Simplify the fraction or convert it to a mixed number or whole number (if needed).

$\text{dividend} \div \text{divisor} = \frac{\text{dividend}}{\text{divisor}}$

total amount — number of parts — size of each part

B

Ex. 3 people share 4 chocolate bars equally. How much does each person get?

$4 \div 3 = \frac{4}{3} = 1\frac{1}{3}$ **chocolate bars**

Ex. 4 people share 3 chocolate bars equally. How much does each person get?

$3 \div 4 = \frac{3}{4}$ **of a chocolate bar**

The first example shows how to divide 4 chocolate bars between 3 people. Place 4 paper chocolate bars on the table. **Each person gets 1 chocolate bar. Then, there's one chocolate bar left over for the 3 people to share, so they break it into 3 equal parts.**

Have your child use scissors to cut 1 paper chocolate bar into thirds. Arrange the paper chocolate bars in 3 equal groups to match the picture. **How many chocolate bars does each person get?** *1 and one-third.*

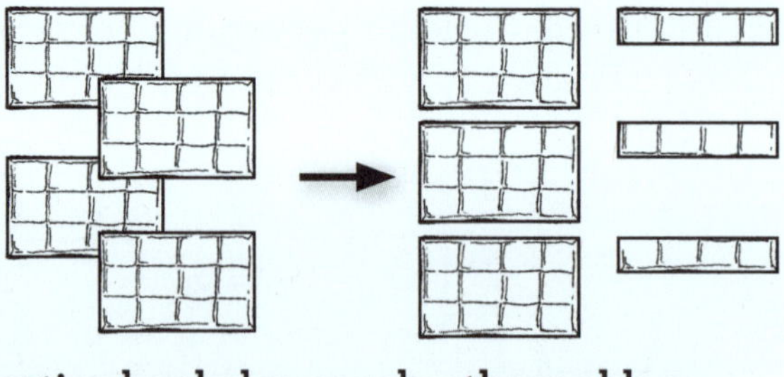

Now, let's see how the fraction bar helps us solve the problem.

- **We have a total of 4 chocolate bars, so 4 is the dividend.**
- **We want to split the chocolate bars into 3 equal groups, so 3 is the divisor.**
- **When you write the dividend over the divisor, you get 4 over 3, or four-thirds.**
- **Four-thirds equals 1 and one-third, so 4 divided by 3 equals 1 and one-third.**

$4 \div 3 = \frac{4}{3} = 1\frac{1}{3}$ **chocolate bars**

dividend divisor

Point to 4/3. **We can think of this as a fraction and read it as "four-thirds." Or, we can think of it as a division problem and read it "4 divided by 3." Either way, we get the same answer.**

Point to the division symbol in 4 ÷ 3. **The division symbol even looks like a fraction bar, with dots in place of the numbers!**

The second example shows how to divide 3 chocolate bars between 4 people. Place 3 paper chocolate bars on the table. **Uh-oh, we don't have enough chocolate bars for each person to get a whole bar! Instead, let's break each chocolate bar into 4 equal parts. That way, each person gets 1 piece from each chocolate bar.**

Have your child use scissors to cut each of the 3 paper chocolate bars into fourths. **Each person gets 1 piece of each chocolate bar, so each person gets 3 pieces.** Have your child arrange the pieces into 4 equal groups. **What fraction of a chocolate bar does each person get?** *Three-fourths.*

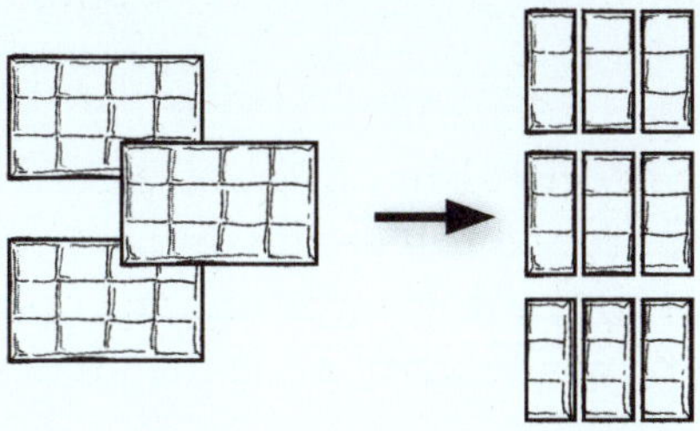

Now, let's see how the fraction bar helps us solve the problem.

- **We have a total of 3 chocolate bars, so 3 is the dividend.**
- **We want to split the chocolate bars into 4 equal groups, so 4 is the divisor.**
- **When you write the dividend over the divisor, you get 3 over 4, or three-fourths. Each person gets three-fourths of a chocolate bar.**
- Point to 3/4. **We can read 3 over 4 as "three-fourths" or as "3 divided by 4."**

$3 \div 4 = \frac{3}{4}$ of a chocolate bar

dividend divisor

Have your child write the dividend over the divisor to solve the practice problems. Model each problem with paper chocolate bars as in the example. Have your child cut the paper chocolate bars apart as needed to help understand the answers.

$4 \div 1 = \frac{4}{1} = 4$	$6 \div 2 = \frac{6}{2} = 3$	$5 \div 3 = \frac{5}{3} = 1\frac{2}{3}$
$1 \div 4 = \frac{1}{4}$	$2 \div 6 = \frac{2}{6} = \frac{1}{3}$	$3 \div 5 = \frac{3}{5}$

The final problem (3 ÷ 5) is difficult to model with the paper chocolate bars, since the bars don't have lines that divide them into fifths. Instead, draw 3 rectangles on scrap paper. Have your child draw lines on the rectangles to divide them into fifths. **Each person gets 1 fifth from each chocolate bar. So, each person gets three-fifths of a chocolate bar.**

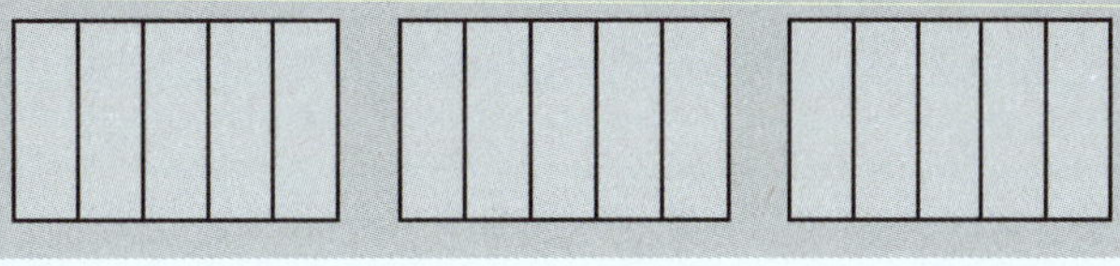

Activity (C): Play Not Enough Chocolate!

Play Not Enough Chocolate! As you play, frame each division problem in terms of chocolate bars (like the example problems in part B). For example, if you roll a 4 and then a 5: **I have 4 chocolate bars, and I need to split them equally between 5 people.** Use paper chocolate bars or draw rectangles to model the problems as needed (as explained in the above gray box).

You do not need to save the paper chocolate bars after this lesson.

Not Enough Chocolate!

Materials: Die

Object of the Game: Score more points than the other player by creating greater quotients.

Player 1 rolls the die twice. She writes her first roll as the dividend in her first division problem. She writes her second roll as the divisor in the same division problem. Then, she finds the quotient. (If the answer is an improper fraction, convert the fraction to a mixed number or whole number. If the answer is not in simplest form, simplify the fraction.)

Sample play.

Then, Player 2 takes a turn in the same way. Whoever has the greater quotient wins a point. (Use logical reasoning or equivalent fractions to compare the fractions.)

Repeat until you have completed 3 rounds. Whoever has more points wins.

Independent Practice and Review

Have your child complete the Lesson 13.1 Practice and Review workbook pages.

Lesson 13.2
Division Word Problems with Fractional Quotients

Purpose	Materials
• Practice dividing whole numbers and naming the quotient as a fraction or mixed number • Write and solve division equations to match word problems that involve dividing small numbers	• None

Memory Work	
	• **What do we call numbers that have a whole number and a fraction?** *Mixed numbers.* • **What do we call a fraction whose numerator is greater than or equal to its denominator?** *An improper fraction.*

Warm-up (A): Make a Cookie-Sharing Chart for Your Family

In the last lesson, you learned how to solve problems where we cut items into fractional parts to divide them evenly. Discuss a time when your family tried to share food items equally. For example: **Remember when there were 3 cupcakes left over after the party, and we had to figure out how to share them between the 4 of us?**

To warm up, we're going to make a chart to show how our family can share different numbers of cookies. How many people live in our home? *Answers will vary.* **We'll divide each of these numbers of cookies by the number of people who live in our home.**

> Feel free to define "the number of people who live in our home" in whatever way makes the most sense for your family and for this context.

Draw lines on the first printed cookie in Activity A to split it into the same number of parts as people in your family. For example, if you have 5 people in your family, draw lines to split the cookie into fifths. **If we share one cookie evenly, what fraction of the cookie does each of us get?** *Sample answer (for a family of 5): One-fifth.*

Write the number of people in your home as the divisor for the first division problem. Then, have your child write the dividend over the divisor to complete the equation. Read the completed equation aloud. For example, for a family of 5: **One divided by 5 equals one-fifth.**

$1 \div \underline{\ 5\ } = \frac{1}{5}$ (A)

Sample answer. Replace the 5 with the number of people in your family.

Repeat with the rest of the problems. Draw lines on each additional cookie to show how you would split it into fractional parts to match the number of people in your family. Then, have your child look at all the divided cookies and complete the matching division problem.

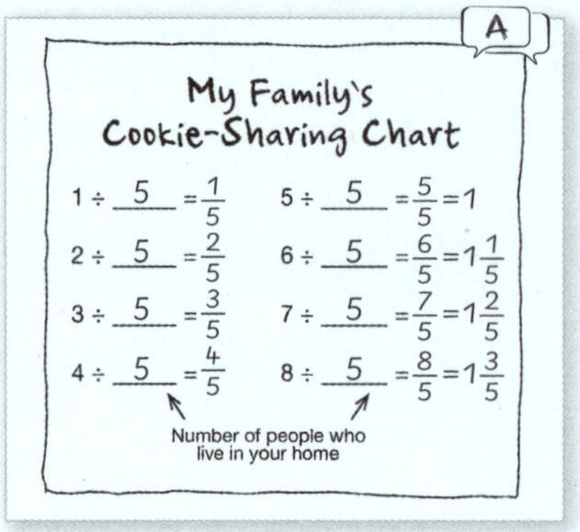

Sample answers for a family of 5. Your child should use the number of people who live in your house as the divisor for each division problem.

Use the following questions to discuss the chart with your child.

- **Which dividend means each person gets 1 whole cookie?** *Sample answer (for a family of 5): 5 cookies.* **If the dividend and divisor are equal, the quotient is 1.**
- **Which dividends mean each person gets more than 1 whole cookie?** *Sample answer (for a family of 5): 6 cookies or more.* **If the dividend is greater than the divisor, the quotient is greater than 1.**
- **Which dividends mean each person gets less than 1 whole cookie?** *Sample answer (for a family of 5): 4 cookies or less.* **If the dividend is less than the divisor, the quotient is less than 1.**

Activity (B): Write Division Equations to Match Word Problems

In younger grades, you learned how to divide to solve word problems. You didn't have to think too hard about which number was the dividend and which number was the divisor, because you always divided the larger number by the smaller number.

Today, you'll learn how to solve division word problems with small numbers. Writing the matching equation for these problems can be tricky! You'll need to think carefully about which number tells the total amount and which number tells the number of equal parts.

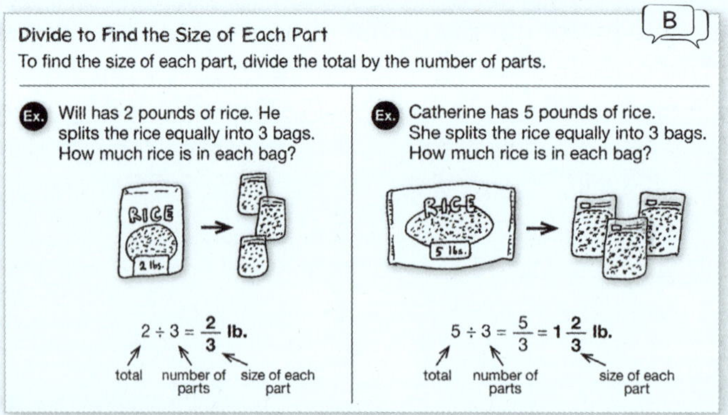

Read aloud the first example problem.

- **What's the total amount of rice in this problem?** *2 pounds.*
- **How many equal parts does Will split the rice into?** *3.*
- **So, we divide 2 by 3 to find the answer. 2 divided by 3 equals 2 over 3, or two-thirds of a pound.**

- **In this problem, is the dividend greater than, less than, or equal to the divisor?** *Less.* **If the dividend is less than the divisor, the numerator is less than the denominator. So, the quotient must be less than 1.**

Read aloud the second example problem.

- **What's the total amount of rice in this problem?** *5 pounds.*
- **How many equal parts does Catherine split the rice into?** *3.*
- **This time, we divide 5 by 3 to find the answer. 5 divided by 3 equals 5 over 3, or 1 and two-thirds of a pound.**
- **In this problem, is the dividend greater than, less than, or equal to the divisor?** *Greater.* **If the dividend is greater than the divisor, the numerator is greater than the denominator. So, the quotient must be greater than 1.**

Have your child solve the practice word problems in the same way. Ask him to identify the total amount and number of equal parts before he writes the matching equation for each problem.

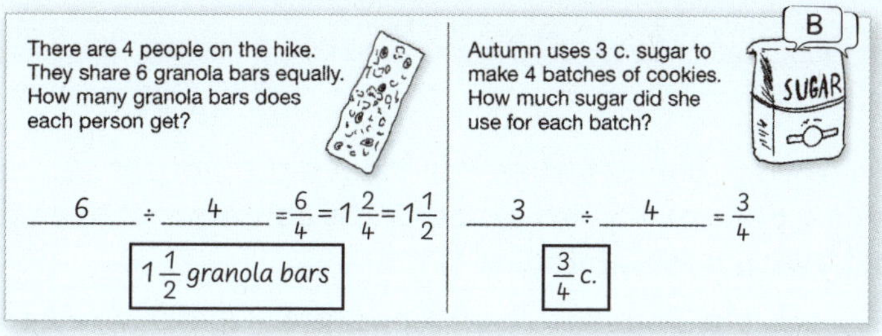
There are 4 people on the hike. They share 6 granola bars equally. How many granola bars does each person get?

$6 \div 4 = \frac{6}{4} = 1\frac{2}{4} = 1\frac{1}{2}$

$1\frac{1}{2}$ granola bars

B

Autumn uses 3 c. sugar to make 4 batches of cookies. How much sugar did she use for each batch?

$3 \div 4 = \frac{3}{4}$

$\frac{3}{4}$ c.

Independent Practice and Review

Have your child complete the Lesson 13.2 Practice and Review workbook pages.

Lesson 13.3
Write Remainders as Fractions

Purpose	Materials
• Use a visual model to interpret a remainder as a fraction • Write remainders as fractions	• Red colored pencil or marker

Memory Work

- **What are opposite angles in a parallelogram?** *Angles that are across from each other.*
- **What are adjacent angles in a parallelogram?** *Angles that are next to each other.*

Warm-up (A): Color Measuring Cups to Find a Fractional Remainder

This warm-up activity provides a visual preview of the strategy your child will use to write remainders as fractions in the next activity.

We'll warm up with a word problem today. Read aloud the word problem. **In this problem, Maddy wants to divide 9 cups of tomato sauce into 4 containers. If we divide 9 by 4 with long division, we get 2, with a remainder of 1.**

How many whole cups can she pour into each container? *2.* Use a red colored pencil or marker to color each jar up to the 2-cup line.

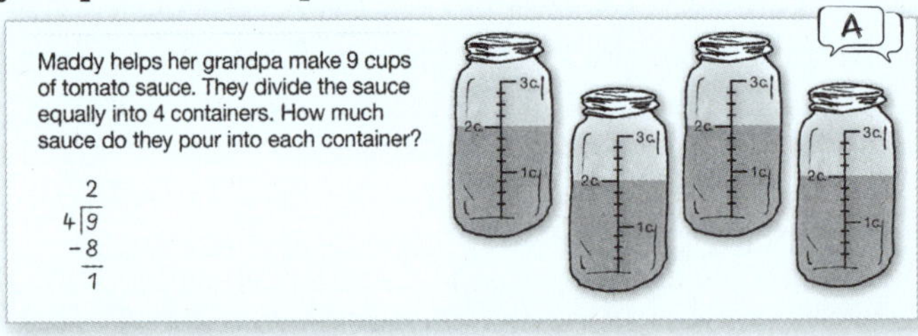

After she pours 2 whole cups into each container, how much sauce does she have left? *1 cup.* **How do you know?** *Sample answer: There's a remainder of 1. She's already poured out 8 cups, so there is 1 cup left.* **What's 1 divided by 4?** *One-fourth.* **She can pour one-fourth of a cup of sauce into each container.** Use a red colored pencil or marker to color each jar up to the line for 2 1/4 cups.

There are 2 and one-fourth cups of sauce in each container. 9 divided by 4 equals 2 and one-fourth. Write "2 1/4 c." in the space below the problem.

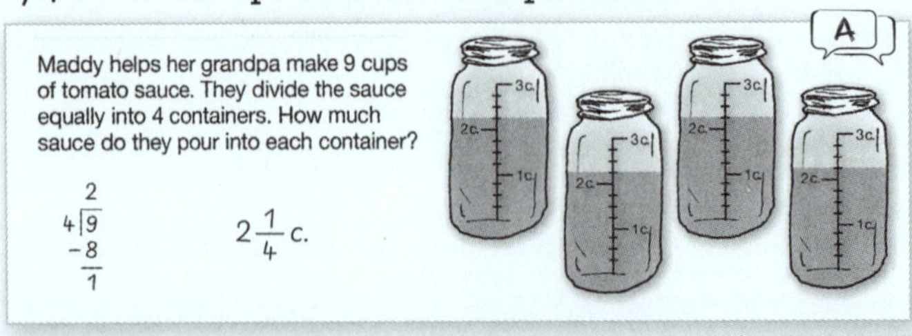

If your child is interested, demonstrate how to solve this problem by writing the dividend over the divisor: **We could also write a horizontal equation to solve this problem.** Write "9 ÷ 4 = 9/4" on a piece of scrap paper. **What mixed number does nine-fourths equal?** *2 and one-fourth.* **Either way, we get the same answer.**

$$9 \div 4 = \frac{9}{4} = 2\frac{1}{4}$$

Activity (B): Divide Remainders into Fractional Parts

In the warm-up, we divided up the leftover cup of tomato sauce so that we could write the quotient as a mixed number. Today, you'll learn how to write long division quotients as mixed numbers. Have your child read the text box aloud.

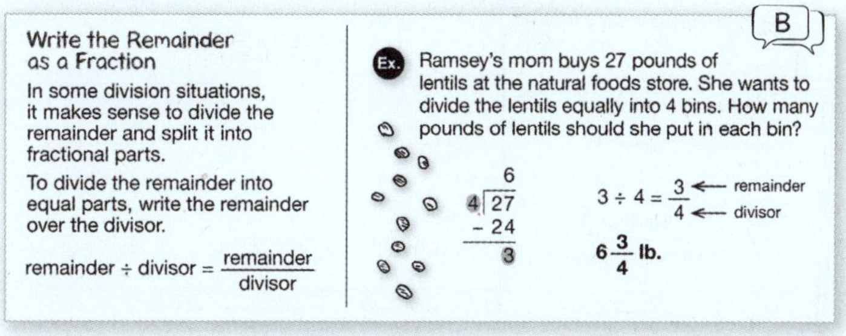

The example problem shows how to split up the remainder and write the quotient as a mixed number. Read aloud the example problem.

- **Ramsey's mom wants to divide 27 by 4. This long division problem shows that the answer is 6, with a remainder of 3.**
- **How many whole pounds of lentils can Ramsey's mom pour into each bin?** *6 pounds.* **How many pounds are left for her to divide up?** *3 pounds.*
- **There are 3 pounds of lentils left to divide between the 4 bins. What's 3 divided by 4?** *Three-fourths.* **So, she can pour three-fourths of a pound of lentils into each of the bins to finish dividing the lentils.**
- **What's the total weight of the lentils in each bin?** *6 and three-fourths pounds.*

This chart shows the rest of the food Ramsey's mom bought and how many bins she wants to store it in. We'll use long division to find how much she should put in each bin.

She bought 10 kilograms of raisins, and she wants to split the raisins evenly between 3 bins. What division equation can we use to find how much she should put in each bin? *10 divided by 3.* Write 10 ÷ 3 as a long division problem and have your child solve it.

10 divided by 3 equals 3 with a remainder of 1. After she puts 3 kilograms in each bin, she'll have 1 kilogram left over. What's 1 divided by 3? *One-third.* **So, she should put 3 and one-third kilograms of raisins in each bin.** Write 3 1/3 in the blank in the list.

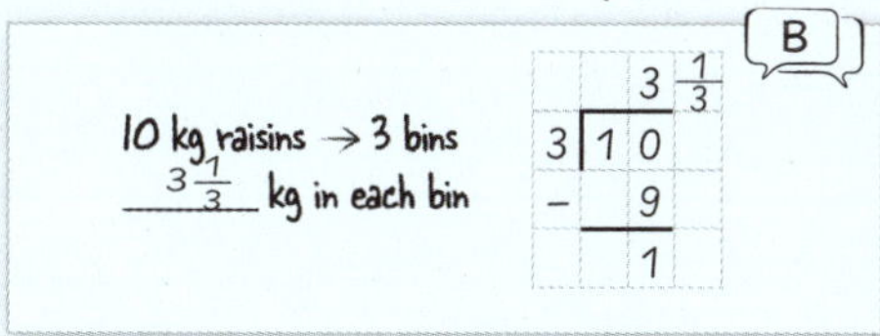

Have your child write and solve long division problems to complete the other blanks in the chart. Remind her as needed to write the remainder over the divisor to find the fractional part of each mixed number. For the final problem, have her simplify her answer before writing it in the chart.

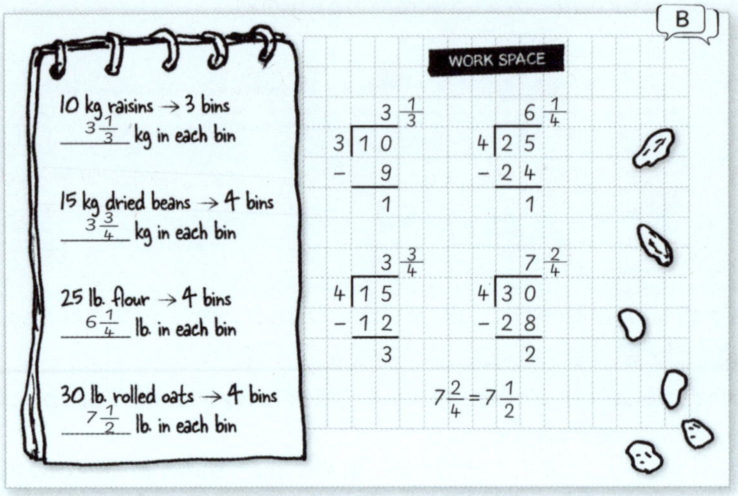

Independent Practice and Review

Have your child complete the Lesson 13.3 Practice and Review workbook pages.

Lesson 13.4
Use Pictures to Divide Fractions by Whole Numbers

Purpose	Materials
• Review two ways to interpret division equations • Use pictures to visually find the answers to fraction division problems	• Fraction circles

Memory Work	
	• **What is an equilateral triangle?** *A triangle with 3 equal sides.* • **What is an isosceles triangle?** *A triangle with 2 equal sides.* • **What is a scalene triangle?** *A triangle with no equal sides.*

If you were never taught the conceptual meaning of fraction division, this lesson and the rest of the unit may feel challenging to teach. If so, see the Unit 13 **Teaching Math with Confidence** for a preview of the two categories of problems that your child will study. Make sure to read the lessons word for word and examine the diagrams carefully so that you learn this challenging concept along with your child.

This lesson provides a visual and hands-on introduction to the concept of dividing fractions. He will learn the process for calculating the answers to these problems in Lesson 13.5. If your child easily grasps the concept, you may want to combine this lesson with Lesson 13.5.

You will need fraction circles for the first time in this lesson. If you don't own plastic, wood, or foam fraction circles, color and cut out the fraction circles on Blackline Master 14 before the lesson.

Warm-up (A): Review Two Ways to Interpret Division Problems

In younger grades, you learned that we can use division to answer two different kinds of questions about equal parts.

If you'd like to make this activity more hands-on, cut two 8-inch strips of paper and have your child cut the strips to match the word problems.

Have your child read aloud and complete the first word problem. Make sure your child labels his answer. **In this problem, we divide the total by the *number* of equal parts. The answer is the *size* of each part.** Draw a line as shown on the printed ribbon. **Kylan split the ribbon into 2 equal pieces. Each piece is 4 inches long.**

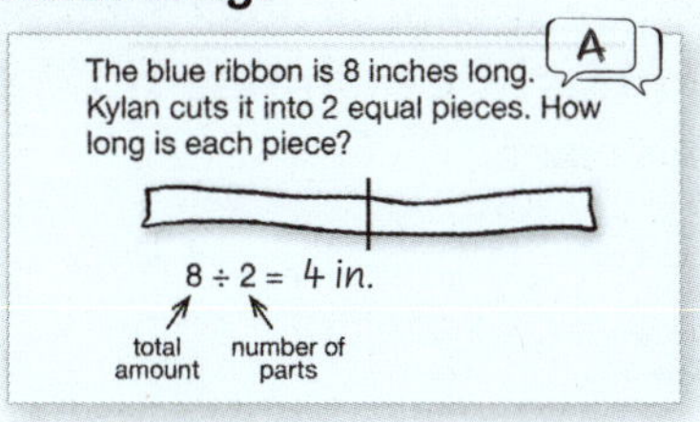

Repeat with the second problem. **In this problem, we divide the total by the *size* of each part. The answer is the *number* of parts.** Draw lines as shown on the printed ribbon. **Allie split the ribbon into 2-inch pieces. She made 4 pieces.**

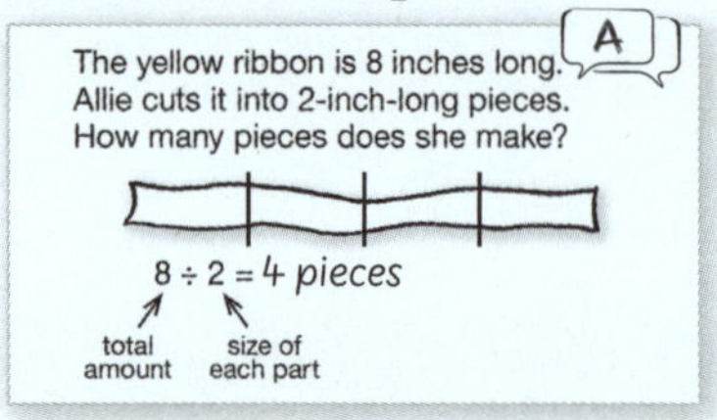
A

The yellow ribbon is 8 inches long. Allie cuts it into 2-inch-long pieces. How many pieces does she make?

$8 \div 2 = 4$ pieces

total amount; size of each part

Activity (B): Use Pictures to Divide Fractions by Whole Numbers

Today, we'll use fraction circles to divide fractions by whole numbers. Understanding what fraction division problems mean can be challenging, so we'll use fraction circles to model the problems. Arrange the fraction circles on the table as shown.

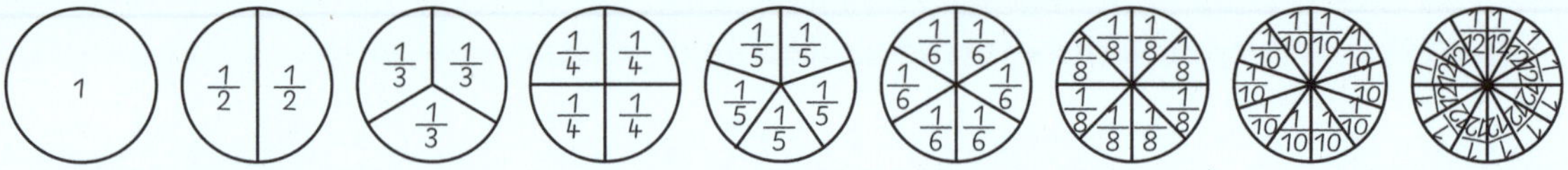

Arranging the fraction circles this way makes it easier to find the pieces you need as you teach the lesson.

All of the problems today are like the problem about the blue ribbon in the warm-up. The problems will tell you the total amount and the number of equal parts. You'll divide to find the size of the parts.

Read aloud the first example word problem. **How much pizza does Juliana's family have?** *Three-fourths of a pizza.* Place 3 fourths (from your set of fraction circles) on the table. **3 people share the pizza evenly.** Separate the fraction circles as shown. **What fraction of the whole pizza does each person get?** *One-fourth.*

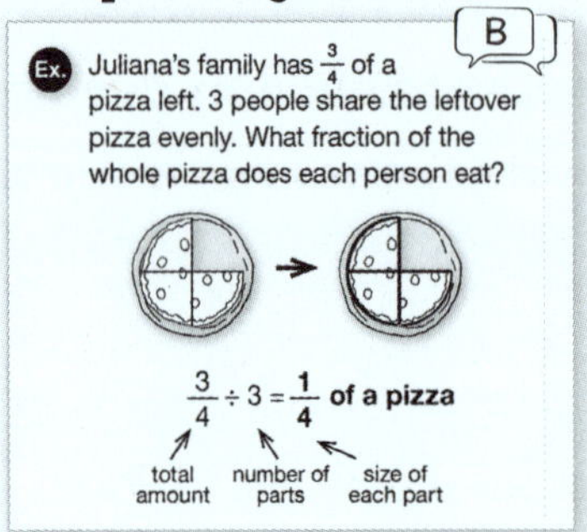
B

Ex. Juliana's family has $\frac{3}{4}$ of a pizza left. 3 people share the leftover pizza evenly. What fraction of the whole pizza does each person eat?

$\frac{3}{4} \div 3 = \frac{1}{4}$ **of a pizza**

total amount; number of parts; size of each part

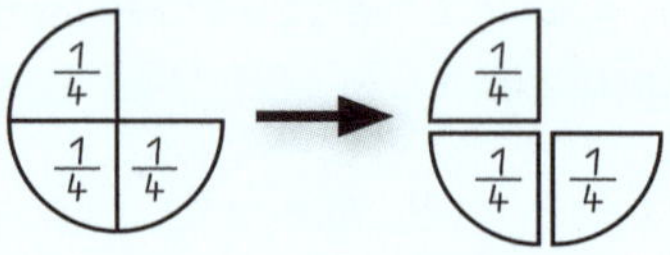

Read aloud the second example word problem. **How much pizza does Zeke's family have?** *Six-tenths of a pizza.* Place 6 tenths on the table. **3 people share the pizza evenly.** Separate the fraction circles as shown. **How many tenths does each person get?** *2 tenths.* **Each person gets two-tenths of the pizza. Two-tenths equals one-fifth, so we could also say that each person gets one-fifth of the whole pizza.**

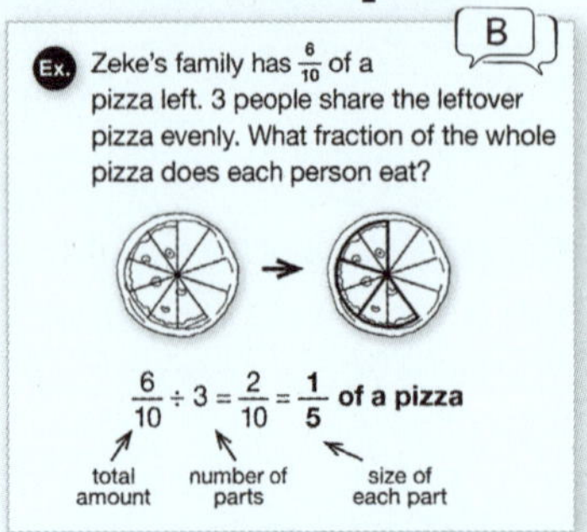
B

Ex. Zeke's family has $\frac{6}{10}$ of a pizza left. 3 people share the leftover pizza evenly. What fraction of the whole pizza does each person eat?

$\frac{6}{10} \div 3 = \frac{2}{10} = \frac{1}{5}$ **of a pizza**

total amount; number of parts; size of each part

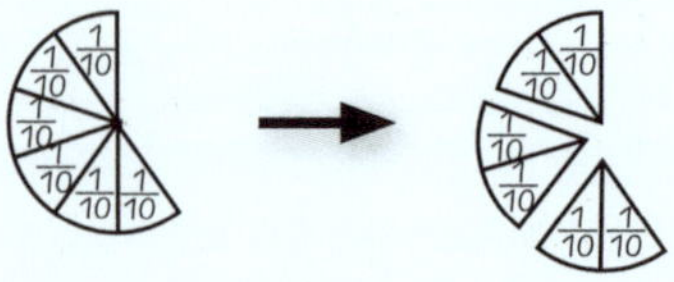

Have your child use similar reasoning to solve the practice problems. Encourage him to use the pictures to find the answers, and model the problems with fraction circles as needed. Have him simplify his answers as needed.

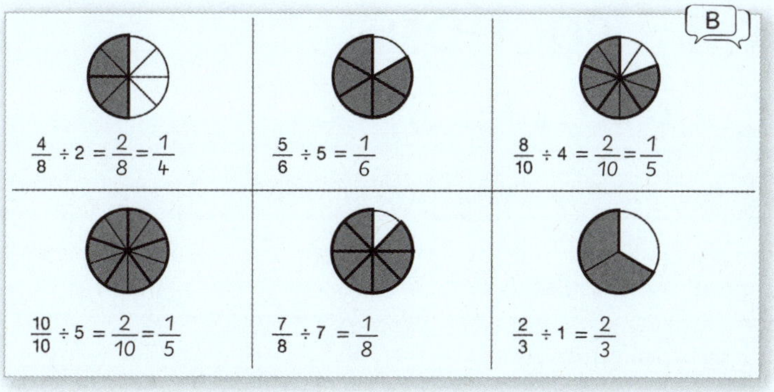

The dark lines show how to split the total amount into the correct number of equal parts. Your child does not need to draw these lines.

Independent Practice and Review

Have your child complete the Lesson 13.4 Practice and Review workbook pages.

Lesson 13.5
Divide Unit Fractions by Whole Numbers

Purpose	Materials
• Explore the relationship between dividing by a whole number and multiplying by the related unit fraction • Rewrite division problems as multiplication problems to divide unit fractions by whole numbers	• Fraction circles • Die

Memory Work

- **What do we call the top number in a fraction?** *The numerator.*
- **What does the numerator tell?** *The number of parts.*
- **What do we call the bottom number in a fraction?** *The denominator.*
- **What does the denominator tell?** *How many equal parts the whole was split into.*

Warm-up (A): Explore the Relationship Between Multiplying by a Fraction and Dividing by a Whole Number

Unit fractions are fractions with 1 as the numerator. Today, you'll learn how to divide a unit fraction by a whole number.

We'll warm up by exploring the relationship between multiplying by a unit fraction and dividing by a whole number.

What's one-third of 6 marbles? *2 marbles.* **The problems in the first column show 3 different ways to find one-third of 6.** Have your child solve the problems in the first column.

- **What do you notice about the answers to these problems?** *They're all equal!*
- Point to 1/3 × 6/1 and 6/1 × 1/3. **We can multiply in any order without changing the product. One-third times 6 and 6 times one-third both equal 2.**
- Point to 1/3 × 6/1 and 6 ÷ 3. **To find one-third of 6, we divide 6 into 3 equal parts. One-third of 6 and 6 divided by 3 both equal 2.**
- Point to all 3 problems. **If we want to split 6 marbles into 3 equal parts, we can use any of these equations to help us find the size of each part.**

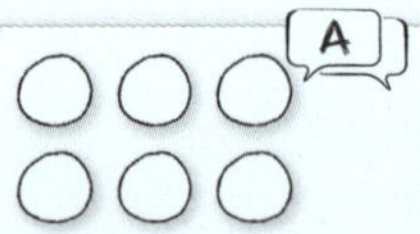

$\frac{1}{3} \times \frac{6}{1} = \frac{6}{3} = 2$

$\frac{6}{1} \times \frac{1}{3} = \frac{6}{3} = 2$

$6 \div 3 = 2$

Have your child solve the problems in the second column. Encourage her to use the picture to solve 4/5 ÷ 2. **If we want to split four-fifths of a pizza into 2 equal parts, we can use any of these equations to help us find the size of each part. What fraction of the whole pizza does each person get?** *Two-fifths.*

Repeat with the final column. **If we split one-half of a pizza between 4 people, what fraction of the whole pizza does each person get?** *One-eighth.*

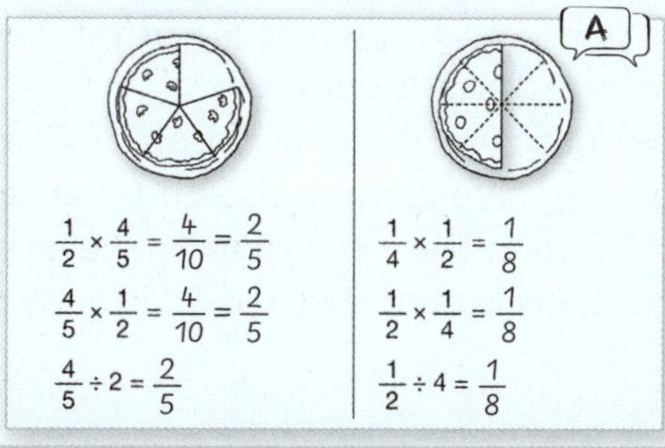

If your child has trouble with the fraction division problems, use fraction circles to model them. For 4/5 ÷ 2, place 4 fifths on the table and separate them into 2 groups of 2 fifths. For 1/2 ÷ 4, trade 1 half for 4 eighths. **If we have half of a pizza, we can cut it into 4 equal parts to split it between 4 people.**

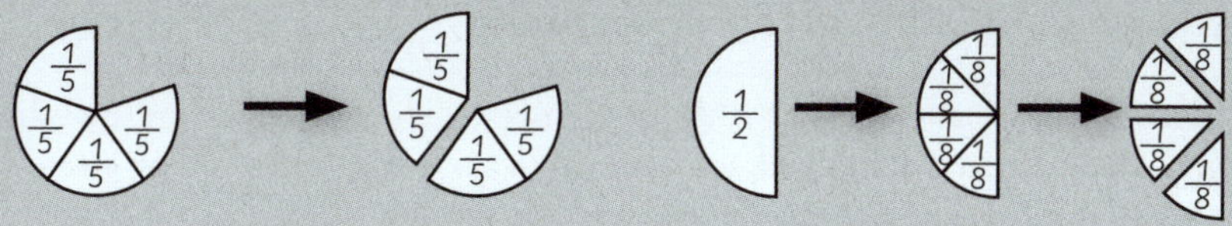

4/5 ÷ 2 = 2/5 1/2 ÷ 4 = 1/8

Activity (B): Use "Keep, Change, Flip" to Divide a Unit Fraction by a Whole Number

In the warm-up you saw that dividing by a whole number is the same as multiplying by the matching unit fraction.

- **If you want to divide a quantity by 2, you can multiply the quantity by what fraction?** *One-half.*
- **If you want to divide a quantity by 3, you can multiply the quantity by what fraction?** *One-third.*
- **If you want to divide a quantity by 4, you can multiply the quantity by what fraction?** *One-fourth.*

If your child has trouble answering these questions, point to the corresponding problems in part A.

To divide a fraction by a whole number, we rewrite the division problem as a multiplication problem. There are three steps for rewriting the division problem as a multiplication problem: keep, change, and flip! Have your child read the text box aloud.

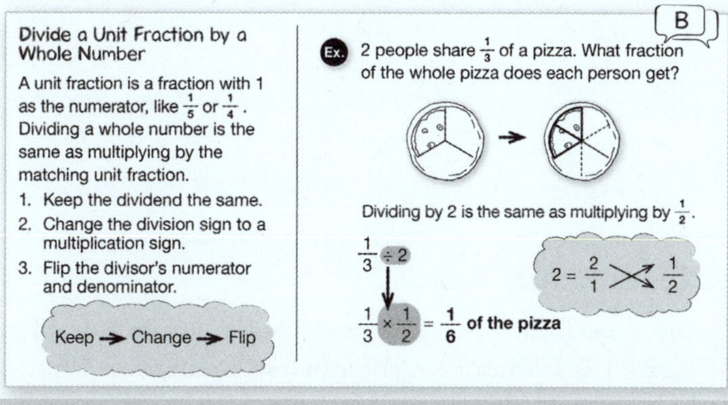

You may have learned this process as "multiplying by the reciprocal." In *Sixth Grade Math with Confidence*, your child will learn about reciprocals and how to extend "keep, change, flip" to a wider variety of fraction division problems.

Let's study the example to learn how to use "keep, change, flip" to rewrite a division problem as a multiplication problem.

- **We have one-third of a pizza, and we want to split it between 2 people. The matching division problem is one-third divided by 2.**
- **The first step for rewriting the problem is "keep." We keep one-third.**
- **The second step is "change." We change the division sign to a multiplication sign.**
- **The third step is "flip."** Point to the cloud. **2 equals 2 over 1. We flip the numerator and denominator and write one-half, since dividing by 2 is the same as multiplying by one-half.**

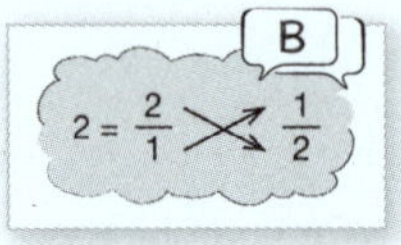

- **One-third times one-half is one-sixth, so one-third divided by 2 equals one-sixth. Each person gets one-sixth of the whole pizza.**

To make the problem more concrete, model it with fraction circles. Place 1 third on the table, then trade it for 2 sixths. **If we have one-third of a pizza, we can cut the pizza into 2 smaller slices. Each person would get 1 of the smaller slices, or one-sixth of the whole pizza.**

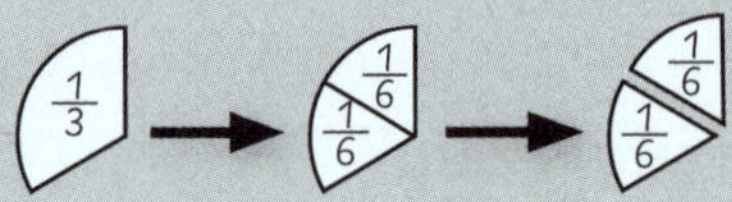

1/3 ÷ 2 = 1/6

Cover the text box with your hand.

- **What are the three steps for rewriting a division problem as a multiplication problem?** *Keep, change, flip.*
- **Which part of the equation do we keep?** *The dividend.*
- **Which part of the equation do we change?** *The division sign.* **What do we change it to?** *A multiplication sign.*
- **Which part of the equation do we flip?** *The divisor.*

Have your child use "keep, change, flip" to rewrite the division problems as multiplication problems and solve. After your child solves the problems, draw lines on the circle to match her answer. For example, for 1/2 ÷ 5, draw lines on the shaded part of the circle to split it into 5 equal pieces. **If you have one-half of a pizza and cut it into 5 equal slices, each slice is one-tenth of a whole pizza.**

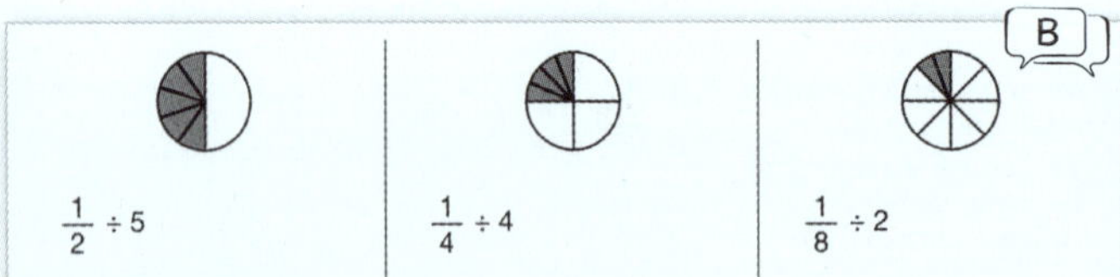

Activity (C): Play Not Enough Pizza!

Show your child the game board. **In this game, we'll roll a die to find out how many people share the pizza. We'll write the number on the die as the divisor. Then, we'll divide to find what fraction of the whole pizza each person gets.**

Whichever player has the greater quotient wins the round. Is it better to roll a higher number or a lower number? *Lower number.* **How do you know?** *Sample answer: If you roll a high number, you have to split the pizza into a lot of parts, so the parts will be pretty small. If you roll a low number, you don't have to split the pizza into so many parts, so the parts will be larger.*

> If your child's not sure, make the question more concrete: **Imagine you have one-third of a pizza and want to get as big a piece as possible. Would you rather split it with 2 people or with 5 people?** *2 people*. **When you split the pizza with fewer people, each person gets a larger piece.**

Play Not Enough Pizza!

Not Enough Pizza!

Materials: Die

Object of the Game: Score more points than the other player by creating greater quotients.

Player 1 rolls the die and writes the number on the die as the divisor in her first division problem. Then, she rewrites the problem as a multiplication problem and solves.

Then, Player 2 takes a turn in the same way. Whoever has the greater answer wins a point. (Use logical reasoning or equivalent fractions to compare the fractions.)

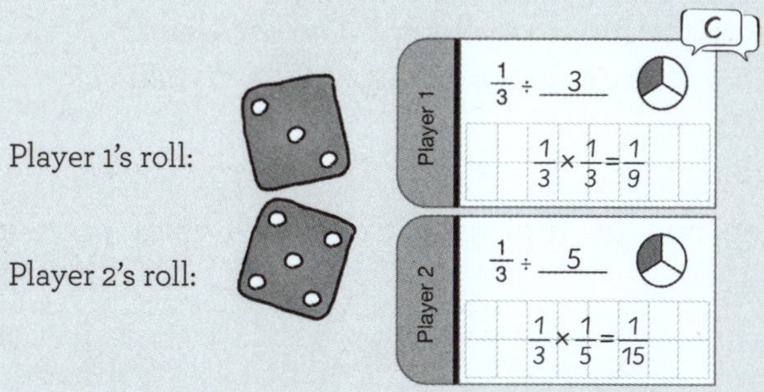

Sample round. Player 1 wins the point, since 1/9 is greater than 1/15.

Repeat until you have completed 3 rounds. Whoever has more points wins.

Independent Practice and Review

Have your child complete the Lesson 13.5 Practice and Review workbook pages.

Lesson 13.6
Divide Fractions by Whole Numbers

Purpose	Materials
• Practice dividing unit fractions by whole numbers • Rewrite division problems as multiplication problems to divide fractions by whole numbers	• Fraction circles • Die
Memory Work	• **What is an acute triangle?** *A triangle with 3 acute angles.* • **What is a right triangle?** *A triangle with a right angle.* • **What is an obtuse triangle?** *A triangle with an obtuse angle.*

In Lesson 13.5, your child used "keep, change, flip" to divide unit fractions by whole numbers. In this lesson, he will use the same process to divide any fraction by a whole number.

Warm-up (A): Use "Keep, Change, Flip" to Divide Unit Fractions by Whole Numbers

In the last lesson, you learned how to rewrite fraction division problems as multiplication problems.

- **What are the three steps?** *Keep, change, flip.*
- **Which part of the equation do we keep?** *The dividend.*
- **Which part of the equation do we change?** *The division sign.* **What do we change it to?** *A multiplication sign.*
- **Which part of the equation do we flip?** *The divisor.*

Have your child use "keep, change, flip" to rewrite the division problems as multiplication problems and solve.

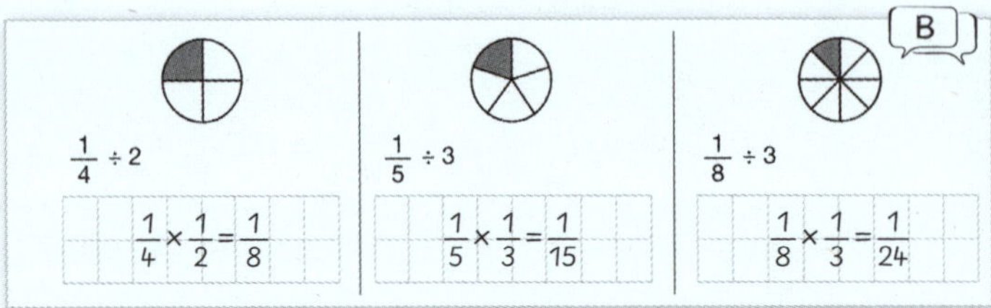

If your child has trouble remembering "keep, change, flip" have him create a silly acronym with the letters K, C, and F to help remember the order.

Kevin	*Koalas*
Chases	*Climb*
Frisbees	*Fences*

Activity (B): Use "Keep, Change, Flip" to Divide Any Fraction by a Whole Number

Today, you'll learn how to use "keep, change, flip" to divide any fraction by a whole number. Have your child read the text box aloud.

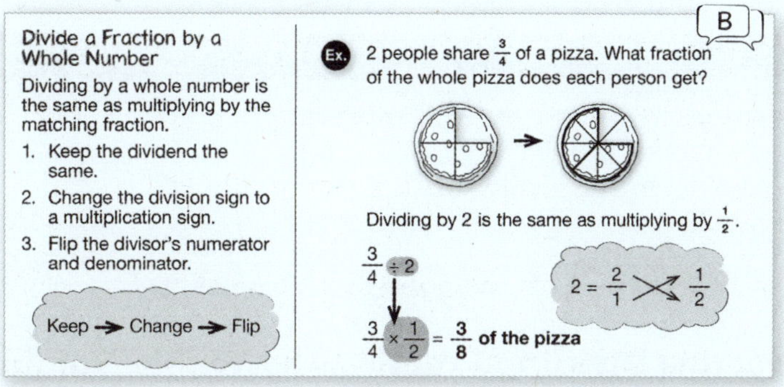

Let's study the example to learn how to use "keep, change, flip" to solve this problem.

- **We have three-fourths of a pizza, and we want to split the pizza between 2 people. The matching division problem is three-fourths divided by 2.**
- **The first step for rewriting the problem is "keep." We keep three-fourths.**
- **The second step is "change." We change the division sign to a multiplication sign.**
- **The third step is "flip."** Point to the cloud. **2 equals 2 over 1. We flip the numerator and denominator and write one-half, since dividing by 2 is the same as multiplying by one-half.**
- **Three-fourths times one-half is three-eighths, so three-fourths divided by 2 equals three-eighths. Each person gets three-eighths of the whole pizza.**

To make the problem more concrete, model it with fraction circles. Place 3 fourths on the table, then trade them for 6 eighths. **If we have three-fourths of a pizza, we can cut each slice into 2 smaller slices. Each person would get 3 of the smaller slices, so each person would get three-eighths of the whole pizza.**

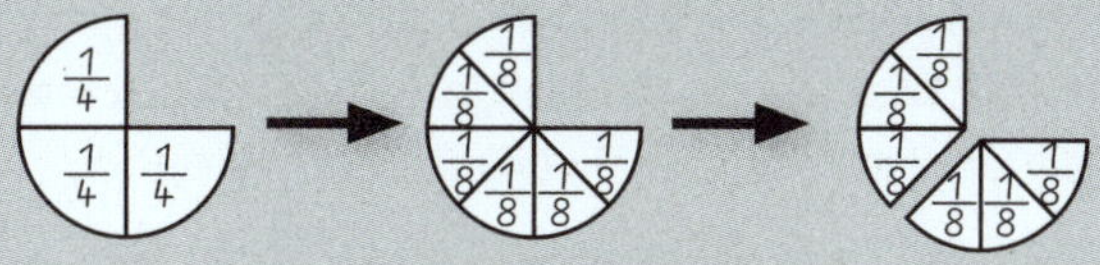

3/4 ÷ 2 = 3/4 × 1/2 = 3/8

Activity (C): Play Not Enough Pizza!

We'll play Not Enough Pizza! again today to practice dividing fractions by whole numbers. Play Not Enough Pizza! See Lesson 13.5 (page 437) for directions. Simplify the answers if needed.

Player 1's roll:

Player 2's roll:

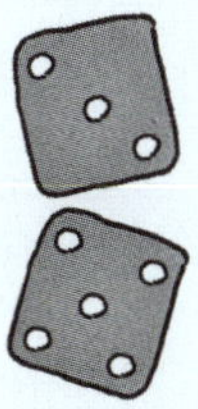

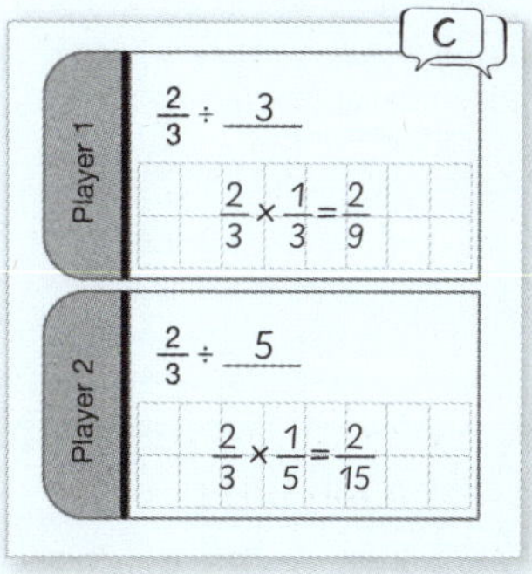

Sample first round. Player 1 wins the point, because 2/9 is greater than 2/15.

Independent Practice and Review

Have your child complete the Lesson 13.6 Practice and Review workbook pages.

Lesson 13.7
Fraction Division Word Problems

Purpose	Materials
• Practice dividing fractions by whole numbers by rewriting the problems as multiplication problems • Solve division word problems that involve dividing a fraction by a whole number	• None

Memory Work • **What is the sum of the angles in a triangle?** *180°.*

Warm-up (A): Practice Dividing Fractions by Whole Numbers

In the last few lessons, you learned how to divide a fraction by a whole number. You learned how to use "keep, change, flip" to rewrite these problems as multiplication problems. Have your child rewrite each division problem as a multiplication problem and solve. If needed, remind her to simplify her answers.

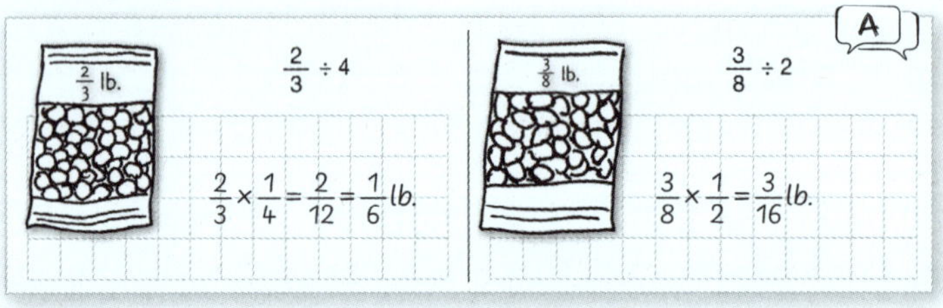

After your child completes the problems, ask the following questions to help her make sense of the quotients:

- **If you divide two-thirds of a pound of chocolate candy between 4 people, how much candy does each person get?** *One-sixth of a pound.*
- **If you divide three-eighths of a pound of jelly beans between 2 people, how much candy does each person get?** *Three-sixteenths of a pound.*

Activity (B): Divide Fractions by Whole Numbers to Find the Size of Each Part

Today, you'll solve word problems that involve dividing a fraction by a whole number. Have your child read aloud the text box.

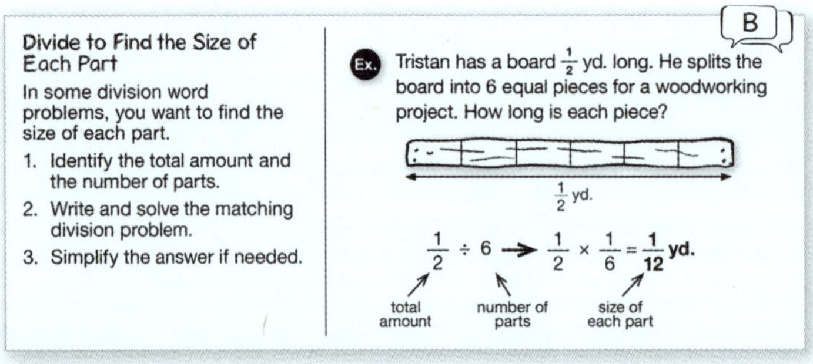

Read aloud the example problem. **In this problem, we know the total and number of parts. We want to find the size of each part.**

- **What's the total length of the board?** *One-half of a yard.*
- **How many equal pieces does Tristan split the board into?** *6 pieces.*
- **The total amount is one-half, and we want to divide the total amount into 6 equal parts. So, we divide one-half by 6 to find the answer.**

- **Dividing by 6 is the same as multiplying by one-sixth. We use "keep, change, flip" to rewrite the problem as a multiplication problem.**
- **One-half times one-sixth equals one-twelfth. Each piece is one-twelfth of a yard long.**

Have your child solve the practice word problems in the same way. Ask her to identify the total amount and number of parts before she writes the matching division equation for each problem. Then, have her rewrite the problem as a multiplication problem and solve.

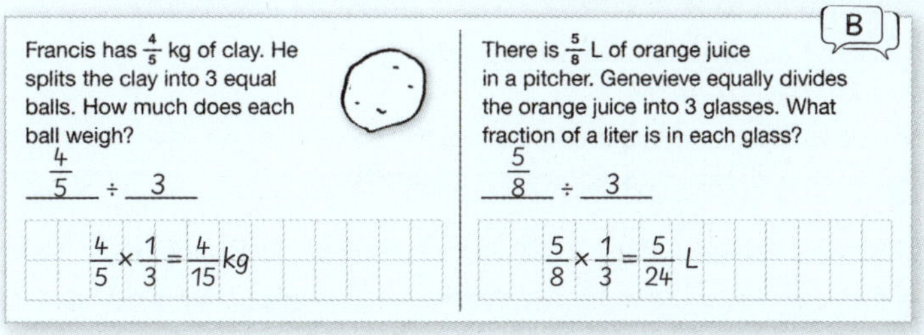

Activity (C): Create a Word Problem to Match a Division Problem

Now, you get to write your own word problem to match two-thirds divided by 4. Have your child create a word problem that matches the division problem. If needed, explain that her problem should involve splitting a total of two-thirds into 4 equal parts. Then, have her solve the problem and label the answer to match the word problem.

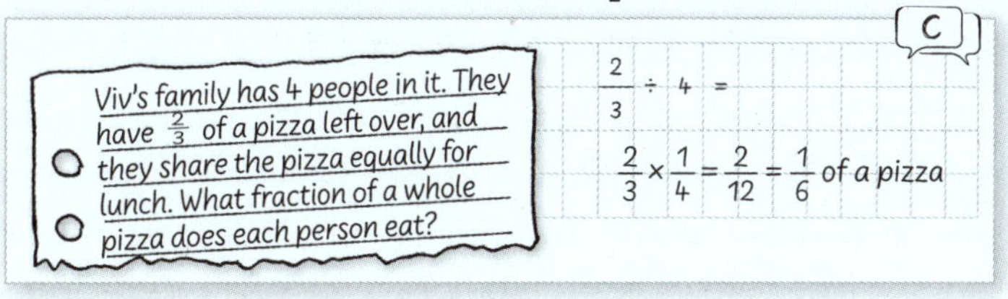

Sample word problem and solution.

Independent Practice and Review

Have your child complete the Lesson 13.7 Practice and Review workbook pages.

Lesson 13.8
Divide Whole Numbers by Unit Fractions

Purpose	Materials
• Explore dividing 1 whole by a unit fraction • Rewrite division problems as multiplication problems to divide whole numbers by unit fractions • Understand that the quotient can be greater than the dividend when you divide a whole number by a fraction	• None

Memory Work	
	• **What do we call a quadrilateral with 4 right angles?** *A rectangle.* • **What do we call a quadrilateral with 4 right angles and 4 equal sides?** *A square.* • **What do we call a quadrilateral with 4 equal sides?** *A rhombus.* • **What do we call a quadrilateral with 2 pairs of parallel sides?** *A parallelogram.* • **What do we call a quadrilateral with exactly 1 pair of parallel sides?** *A trapezoid.*

Warm-up (A): Use Pictures to Divide 1 Whole by a Unit Fraction

In the last few lessons, you divided a fractional amount into equal parts. You knew the total amount and the number of equal parts, and you divided to find the size of each part.

Today, you'll learn how to divide a whole number by a unit fraction. In these problems, you know the total amount and the size of each part. You divide to find the number of equal parts.

We'll warm up today by dividing 1 whole by unit fractions. Read aloud the first word problem. **The matching division problem is 1 divided by one-fifth. How many times does one-fifth go into 1 whole?** *5.* Write 5 in the blank. **There are 5 fifths in 1 whole, so dividing 1 whole by one-fifth is the same as multiplying 1 whole by 5.**

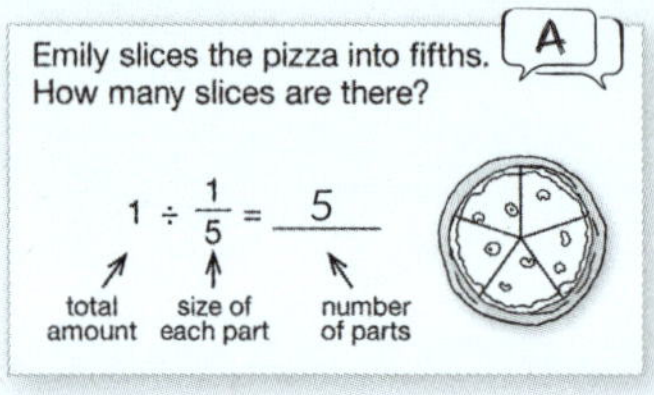

Repeat with the second problem. **There are 4 fourths in 1 whole, so dividing 1 whole by one-fourth is the same as multiplying 1 whole by 4. 1 divided by one-fourth equals 4.**

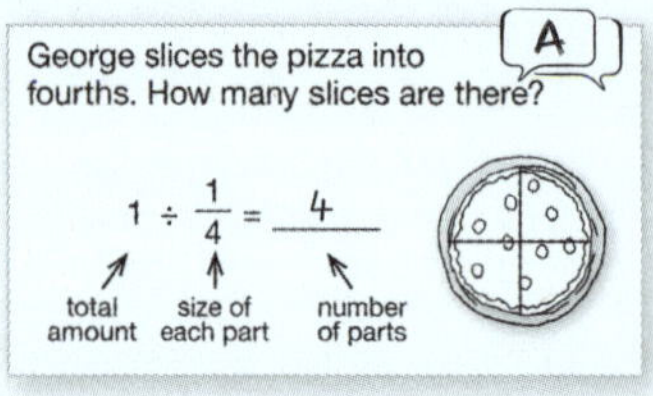

To make these problems more concrete, model them with fraction circles.

Activity (B): Divide Whole Numbers by Unit Fractions

Today, you'll learn how to divide a whole number by a unit fraction. Just like in the previous lessons, we use "keep, change, flip" to rewrite the problems as multiplication problems. We flip the unit fraction's numerator and denominator and write the matching whole number. Have your child read the text box aloud.

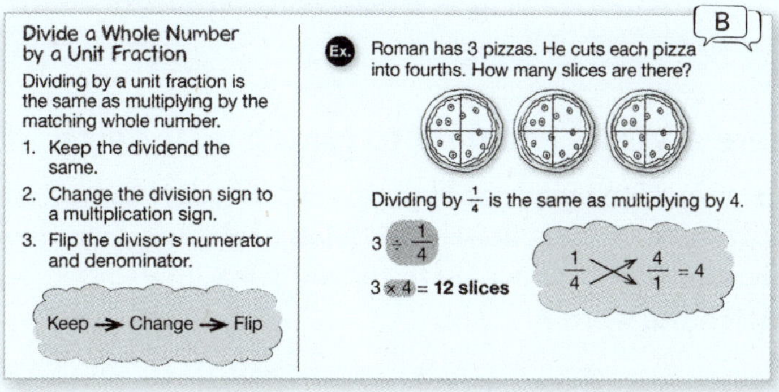

Read the example problem to your child.

- **Roman has 3 pizzas. He cuts each pizza into fourths, so the matching division problem is 3 divided by one-fourth.**
- **The first step for rewriting the problem is "keep." We keep the 3.**
- **The second step is "change." We change the division sign to a multiplication sign.**
- **The third step is "flip." There are 4 fourths in each whole, so dividing 3 wholes by one-fourth is the same as multiplying 3 wholes by 4.** Point to the cloud. **We flip the numerator and denominator and write 4.**

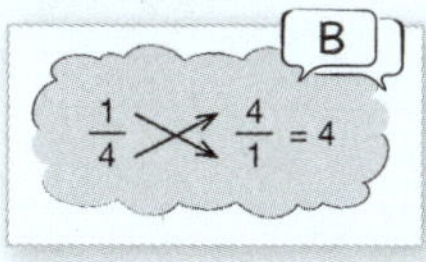

- **3 times 4 equals 12, so 3 divided by one-fourth equals 12. There are 12 slices of pizza. Let's number the slices to make sure there are really 12.** Write the numbers 1-12 on the slices of pizza as shown.

- **Why is the quotient greater than the dividend?** *Sample answer: Each pizza got cut into multiple slices, so we end up with more slices than the original number of pizzas.*

Up until this point, your child has solved division problems in which the quotient was always less than the dividend. However, when you divide a whole number by a fraction less than 1, the quotient is always greater than the dividend.

$6 \div 3 = 2$	$3 \div \frac{1}{4} = 12$
↑ dividend ↑ quotient	↑ dividend ↑ quotient
Your child is used to problems like this, where the quotient is less than the dividend.	In fraction division problems, the quotient is sometimes greater than the dividend.

Children often find this confusing at first. If so, remind your child that the quotient in these problems tells the number of parts, not the size of each part. To make this concept more concrete, give your child a piece of paper and have him cut it into eighths as shown. **When we divide 1 whole into eighths, we get 8 pieces.**

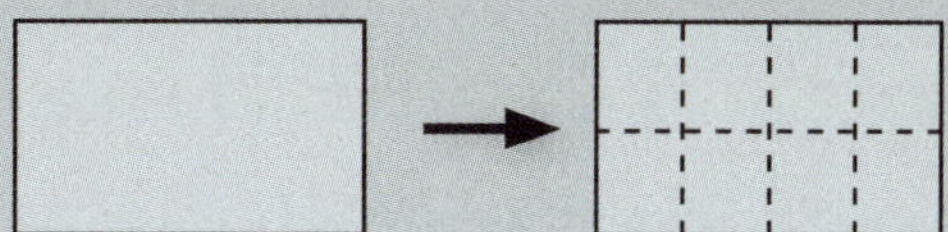

$1 \div \frac{1}{8} = 8$

Have your child use “keep, change, flip” to rewrite the division problems as multiplication problems and solve.

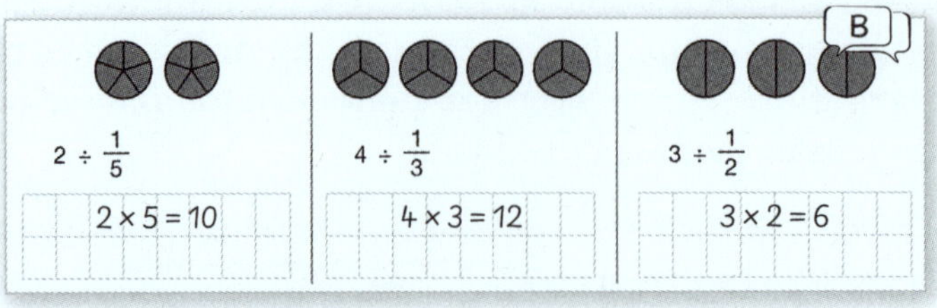

Activity (C): Create a Word Problem to Match a Division Problem

Now, you get to write your own word problem to match 5 divided by one-third. Have your child create a word problem that matches the division problem. If needed, explain that his problem should involve splitting 5 wholes into thirds. Then, have him solve the problem and label the answer to match the word problem.

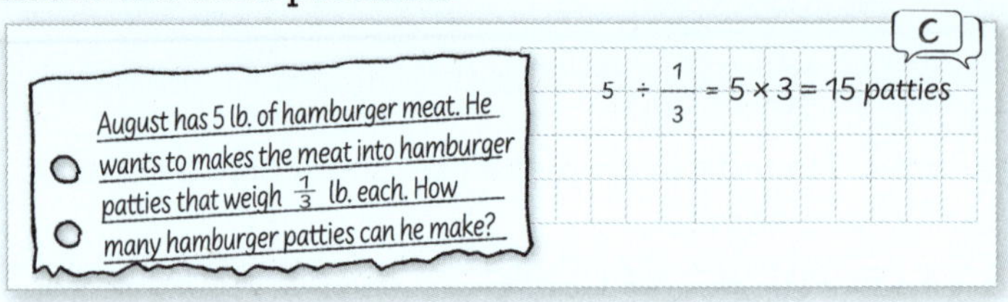

Sample word problem and solution.

Independent Practice and Review

Have your child complete the Lesson 13.8 Practice and Review workbook pages.

Lesson 13.9
More Fraction Division Word Problems

Purpose	Materials
• Practice "flipping" whole numbers and unit fractions • Solve word problems that involve dividing a unit fraction by a whole number or a whole number by a unit fraction • Practice dividing whole numbers by unit fractions and unit fractions by whole numbers	• Counters

Memory Work

- **What do we call the horizontal axis?** *The x-axis.*
- **What do we call the vertical axis?** *The y-axis.*
- **What do we call the (0,0) point?** *The origin.*
- **What is an ordered pair?** *A pair of numbers that identify the location of a point.*
- **In an ordered pair, what do we call the first number?** *The x-coordinate.* **What does it tell?** *The point's horizontal distance.*
- **In an ordered pair, what do we call the second number?** *The y-coordinate.* **What does it tell?** *The point's vertical distance.*

Warm-up: Practice "Flipping" Whole Number and Unit Fractions

In this unit, you've learned how to rewrite division problems as multiplication problems. You learned that dividing by a whole number is the same as multiplying by the matching unit fraction.

- **Dividing by 2 is the same as multiplying by what fraction?** *One-half.*
- **Dividing by 4 is the same as multiplying by what fraction?** *One-fourth.*
- **Dividing by 5 is the same as multiplying by what fraction?** *One-fifth.*

You also learned that dividing by a unit fraction is the same as multiplying by the matching whole number.

- **Dividing by one-third is the same as multiplying by what whole number?** *3.*
- **Dividing by one-sixth is the same as multiplying by what whole number?** *6.*
- **Dividing by one-eighth is the same as multiplying by what whole number?** *8.*

If your child has trouble with these questions, write the numbers on scrap paper and have your child flip the numerator and denominator. (Write whole numbers over 1.)

$$\frac{2}{1} \rightarrow \frac{1}{2}$$

Dividing by 2 is the same as multiplying by 1/2.

$$\frac{1}{3} \rightarrow \frac{3}{1}$$

Dividing by 1/3 is the same as multiplying by 3.

If your child struggles to understand the second set of questions, use fraction circles to remind her of the meaning of the answers. For example, for the first question, place 3 thirds on the table. **There are 3 thirds in 1 whole, so dividing a total amount by one-third is the same as multiplying the amount by 3.** It's okay if your child is still hazy on exactly why this works.

Activity (A): Write Division Equations to Match Word Problems

Today, you'll solve a mix of fraction division word problems. Make sure you think carefully about which number tells the total amount and which number tells the number of equal parts or size of the equal parts.

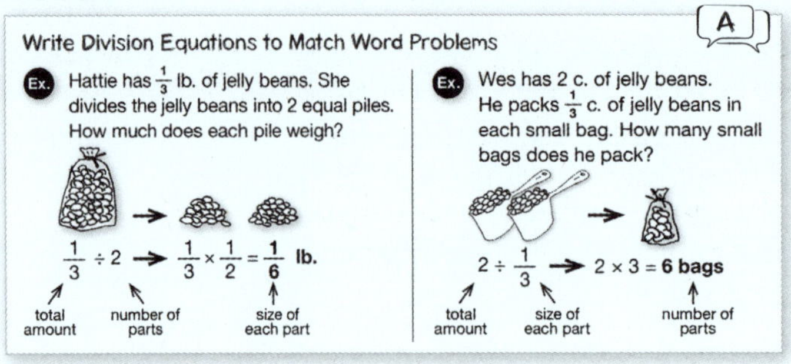

Read aloud the first example problem.

- **What's the total weight of the jelly beans?** *One-third of a pound.*
- **Do we know the number of piles that Hattie makes or the size of each pile?** *The number of piles.*
- **How many equal piles does Hattie make?** *2 piles.*
- **So, we divide one-third by 2 to find the answer. One-third divided by 2 equals one-sixth of a pound. Each pile weighs one-sixth of a pound.**

Read aloud the second example problem.

- **How many total cups of jelly beans does Wes have?** *2 cups.*
- **Do we know the number of bags that Wes packs or the size of each bag?** *The size of each bag.*
- **How many cups of jelly beans does Wes pack in each bag?** *One-third of a cup.*
- **This time, we divide 2 by one-third. 2 divided by one-third equals 6. Wes packs 6 bags.**

Have your child solve the word problems. For each problem:

- Read the problem aloud.
- Ask: **What's the total amount?** Have your child underline the total amount.
- Ask: **Do you know the number of equal parts or size of each equal part?** Have her underline this amount.
- Have her write a division equation to match the problem. Then, have her rewrite the division problem as a multiplication problem and solve.

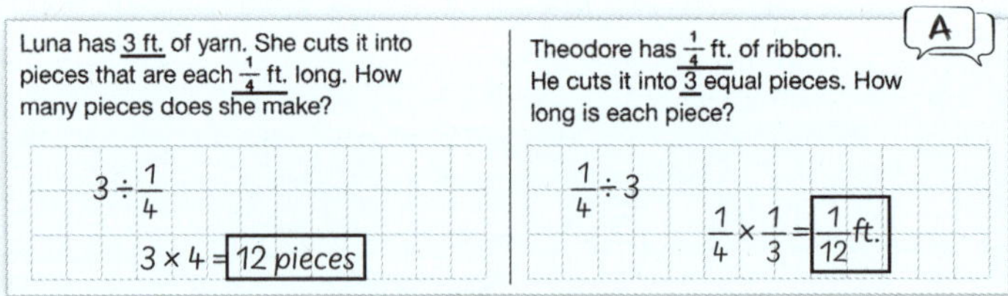

Activity (B): Play Four in a Row

Play Four in a Row. Your child may solve the problems mentally, or she may rewrite the division problems as multiplication problems on a piece of scrap paper and solve.

Four in a Row

Materials: 12 counters per player, with a different color for each player

Object of the Game: Be the first player to place counters in 4 boxes in a row, either horizontally, vertically, or diagonally.

On your turn, choose a division problem on the game board. Find the matching quotient. Use 2 counters to cover both boxes. For example, if you choose 1/3 ÷ 4 as your division problem, cover both the problem and 1/12 with counters. Play then passes to the other player.

One box in the game does not have a match. This box is a "stopper," and neither player may play a counter on this square. If you find the stopper, choose a different box.

Continue until one player covers 4 boxes in a row, either horizontally, vertically, or diagonally.

Answer Key:

- 1/3 ÷ 4 = 1/12
- 5 ÷ 1/2 = 10
- 2 ÷ 1/4 = 8
- 1/3 ÷ 5 = 1/15
- 2 ÷ 1/8 = 16
- 5 ÷ 1/4 = stopper
- 5 ÷ 1/3 = 15
- 1/3 ÷ 3 = 1/9
- 3 ÷ 1/3 = 9
- 4 ÷ 1/3 = 12
- 1/4 ÷ 2 = 1/8
- 1/8 ÷ 2 = 1/16
- 1/2 ÷ 5 = 1/10

Independent Practice and Review

Have your child complete the Lesson 13.9 Practice and Review workbook pages.

Lesson 13.10
Enrichment (Optional)

Purpose

- Practice memory work
- Learn mental math tricks
- Explore repeated division by 2 by cutting a piece of paper in half as many times as possible
- Summarize what your child has learned and assess your child's progress

Materials

- *How Many Guinea Pigs Can Fit on a Plane?: Answers to Your Most Clever Math Questions,* by Laura Overdeck
- Paper
- Scissors

Warm-up: Review Memory Work

Quiz your child on any of the memory work items that he struggled with during this unit.

Math Picture Book: *How Many Guinea Pigs Can Fit on a Plane?*

Read pages 120-123 in *How Many Guinea Pigs Can Fit on a Plane?*

Enrichment Activity: How Many Times Can You Divide a Piece of Paper by 2?

In this unit, you learned how to divide fractions by whole numbers. Today, we'll cut a piece of paper into 2 equal parts. Then, we'll take one of those parts and cut it into 2 equal parts. We'll do this over and over until we can't cut the paper any smaller. How many times do you think we'll be able to cut the paper into 2 equal parts? *Answers will vary.*

Give your child a piece of paper and have him cut it into 2 roughly equal pieces. (He may fold the paper in half to find where to cut it, or he may estimate where to cut.) **What fraction of the whole paper is one of these pieces?** *One-half.* Write 1/2 on one of the pieces and set it aside.

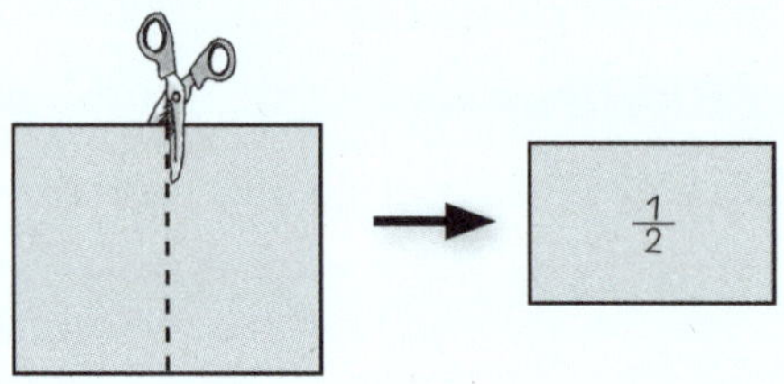

Then, have your child take the other piece and cut it into 2 equal pieces. **What fraction of the whole paper is one of these pieces?** *One-fourth.* If he's not sure, write "1/2 ÷ 2 =" on a scrap piece of paper and have him solve. Write 1/4 on one of the pieces and set it next to the piece labeled 1/2.

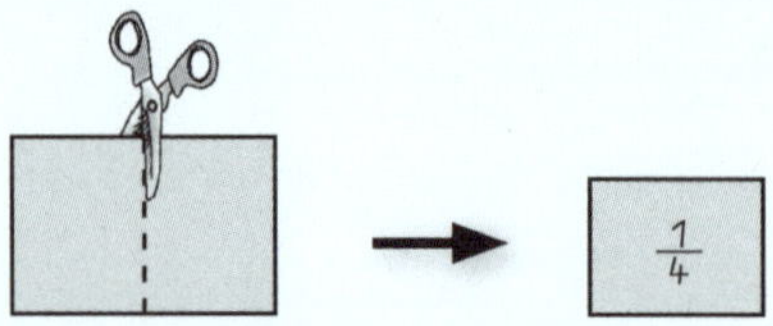

Have your child continue in this way until the paper can no longer be cut in half. (If some of the pieces are too small for you to write a fraction on them, use a sticky note or slip of paper to create a label for these pieces.)

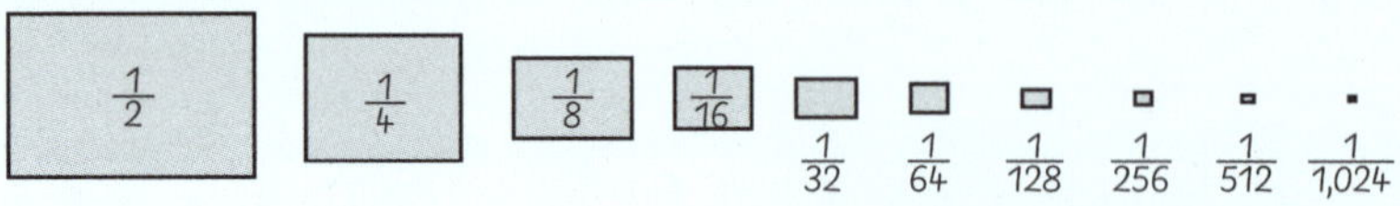

How many times were you able to cut the paper into 2 equal parts? *Sample answer: 10 times.* **What fraction of the whole piece of paper is your smallest piece?** *Sample answer: One-one-thousand-and-twenty-fourth!*

Unit Wrap-Up

Have your child complete the Unit 13 Wrap-Up.

Unit 13 Answer Key

13.1 Practice

Not Enough Chocolate! (2-Player Game)

Player 1	___ ÷ ___ =	___ ÷ ___ =	___ ÷ ___ =
Player 2	___ ÷ ___ =	___ ÷ ___ =	___ ÷ ___ =

Practice Write a fraction to complete each division problem. If needed, simplify the fraction or convert it to a whole number or mixed number.

$2 \div 5 = \frac{2}{5}$	$5 \div 5 = \frac{5}{5} = 1$	$6 \div 5 = \frac{6}{5} = 1\frac{1}{5}$
$2 \div 2 = \frac{2}{2} = 1$	$2 \div 3 = \frac{2}{3}$	$2 \div 4 = \frac{2}{4} = \frac{1}{2}$
$0 \div 6 = \frac{0}{6} = 0$	$1 \div 6 = \frac{1}{6}$	$6 \div 1 = \frac{6}{1} = 6$

13.1 Review

Review Complete the chart.

1 m = 100 cm

Centimeters	50	25	75	20	40	60	80	100
Meters	$\frac{1}{2}$	$\frac{1}{4}$	$\frac{3}{4}$	$\frac{1}{5}$	$\frac{2}{5}$	$\frac{3}{5}$	$\frac{4}{5}$	$\frac{5}{5}$

Use the marked angle to find the measure of the other angles in the parallelogram.

Parallelogram 1: 45°, 135°, 135°, 45°

Parallelogram 2: 75°, 105°, 105°, 75°, 105°

Use the completed division problem to answer the questions. Think carefully about how to interpret the remainder in each problem.

17 ÷ 3 = 5 R2

17 children want to ride the Ferris Wheel. 3 children fit in each pod. How many pods do they need so that all the children can ride at the same time?

6 pods

17 children go to the amusement park together. They divide into 3 groups as equally as possible. How many children are in each group?

5 or 6 children

The kettle corn seller has 17 cups of popcorn kernels. He uses 3 cups for each batch of kettle corn. How many full batches of kettle corn can he make?

5 batches

After he makes as many full batches as possible, how many cups of popcorn kernels does he have left?

2 cups

There are 17 chicken nuggets in the jumbo order. 3 children split the chicken nuggets equally. How many whole chicken nuggets does each child get?

5 nuggets

After each child takes as many whole nuggets as possible, how many are left over?

2 nuggets

13.2 Practice

Practice Estimate the answer to each problem. Then, circle the words that match the answer. You do not need to find the exact answers.

Problem	Answer (circled)
6 ÷ 8	less than 1
5 ÷ 2	greater than 1
10 ÷ 7	greater than 1
3 ÷ 9	less than 1
0 ÷ 7	less than 1
4 ÷ 9	less than 1

Complete the blanks to match each word problem. Then, solve the matching division problem. If needed, simplify the fraction, or convert to a whole number or mixed number.

3 friends want to share 4 packs of candy equally. How much candy does each person get?

$3 \div 4 = \frac{3}{4}$ of a pack

Grant's family buys 2 pies for a party. There are 12 people at the party. If they divide the pies equally, how much pie is there for each person?

$2 \div 12 = \frac{2}{12} = \frac{1}{6}$ of a pie

Kylie has 5 lb. of almonds. She divides the almonds equally into 4 bags. How many pounds of almonds are in each bag?

$5 \div 4 = \frac{5}{4} = 1\frac{1}{4}$ lb.

Scout has 2 kg of peanuts. She divides the peanuts equally into 8 bags. How many kilograms of peanuts are in each bag?

$2 \div 8 = \frac{2}{8} = \frac{1}{4}$ kg

Thomas makes 3 liters of lemonade. He divides it equally into 6 glasses. How much lemonade is in each glass?

$3 \div 6 = \frac{3}{6} = \frac{1}{2}$ L

Esperanza wants to serve punch to 8 people. She makes 1 gallon of punch and splits it equally into their glasses. How much punch is in each glass?

$1 \div 8 = \frac{1}{8}$ gal.

Val has a length of rope 8 meters long. If he cuts the rope into 3 equal parts, how long will each piece be?

$8 \div 3 = \frac{8}{3} = 2\frac{2}{3}$ m

★ Sam practices the oboe for the same amount of time each day. He practices 3 hours each week. What fraction of an hour does he practice each day?

$3 \div 7 = \frac{3}{7}$ hr.

13.2 Review

Review Use long division to solve. Use the multiplication table to help.

46) 389: 8; − 368; remainder 21

46) 473: 10; − 46↓; 13; − 0; 13

46) 1,505: 32; − 138↓; 125; − 92; 33

× 46	
1	46
2	92
3	138
4	184
5	230
6	276
7	322
8	368
9	414

Write the most specific name possible for each quadrilateral. Use the words in the word bank.

Parallelogram, Quadrilateral, Square, Trapezoid, Rhombus, Rectangle

Word bank: Parallelogram, Quadrilateral, Rectangle, Rhombus, Square, Trapezoid

Answer the questions. Write your equations in the work space.

Garden: $3\frac{1}{3}$ m by $2\frac{1}{2}$ m

What is the perimeter of the garden?

$11\frac{2}{3}$ m

What is the area of the garden?

$8\frac{1}{3}$ sq. m

WORK SPACE

$3\frac{1}{3} + 2\frac{1}{2} + 3\frac{1}{3} + 2\frac{1}{2} = 11\frac{2}{3}$

$2\frac{1}{2} \times 3\frac{1}{3}$

$\frac{5}{2} \times \frac{10}{3} = \frac{50}{6} = 8\frac{2}{6} = 8\frac{1}{3}$

Unit 13 Answer Key

13.3 Practice

Practice: Use mental math or long division to solve. Write the quotients as mixed numbers in simplest form.

$21 \div 5 = 4\frac{1}{5}$

$53 \div 10 = 5\frac{3}{10}$

$85 \div 6 = 14\frac{1}{6}$

$137 \div 3 = 45\frac{2}{3}$

WORK SPACE

$137 \div 3$: 3 into 137 = 45; − 12 ↓; 17; − 15; 2

$85 \div 6$: 6 into 85 = 14; − 6 ↓; 25; − 24; 1

Match each division problem to the words that best describe its quotient. You do not need to find the exact quotients.

31 ÷ 6 → between 5 and 6	between 4 and 5	38 ÷ 5 → between 7 and 8
43 ÷ 10 → between 4 and 5	between 5 and 6	50 ÷ 8 → between 6 and 7
37 ÷ 6 → between 6 and 7	between 6 and 7	38 ÷ 9 → between 4 and 5
30 ÷ 4 → between 7 and 8	between 7 and 8	36 ÷ 7 → between 5 and 6

Use the completed division problem to answer the questions in a sensible way. Think carefully about how to interpret the remainder in each problem.

13 ÷ 4 = 3 R1

4 children evenly share 13 cookies. How many cookies does each child get?
$3\frac{1}{4}$ cookies

Simone has 13 stuffed koalas. She divides them as equally as possible on 4 shelves. How many koalas are on each shelf?
3 or 4 koalas

Matthew has 13 fluid ounces of paint. He divides the paint evenly into 4 containers. How many fluid ounces are in each container?
$3\frac{1}{4}$ fl. oz.

Travis has 13 feet of rope. He cuts the rope into 4 equal pieces. How long is each piece?
$3\frac{1}{4}$ ft.

13.3 Review

Review: Complete the chart.

1 hr. = 60 min.

Minutes	30	20	40	15	45	6	18	54
Hours	$\frac{1}{2}$	$\frac{1}{3}$	$\frac{2}{3}$	$\frac{1}{4}$	$\frac{3}{4}$	$\frac{1}{10}$	$\frac{3}{10}$	$\frac{9}{10}$

Draw a line to connect the numbers in order from Start to End. Follow the rule.

Rule: Subtract $\frac{1}{4}$ (Start → End)

5	$4\frac{3}{4}$	$4\frac{1}{2}$	$4\frac{3}{5}$	$3\frac{1}{8}$
$4\frac{1}{3}$	$4\frac{2}{3}$	$4\frac{1}{4}$	$4\frac{4}{5}$	$3\frac{7}{8}$
$3\frac{2}{3}$	$3\frac{1}{8}$	4	$3\frac{3}{4}$	$3\frac{5}{8}$
$3\frac{1}{3}$	3	$3\frac{1}{4}$	$3\frac{1}{2}$	$2\frac{1}{5}$
$2\frac{5}{6}$	$2\frac{3}{4}$	$2\frac{1}{2}$	$2\frac{1}{4}$	2

Rule: Subtract 0.25 (Start → End)

5	4.75	4.5	4.45	4.3
4.35	4.6	4.25	4.2	4.15
3.6	3.12	4	3.75	3.65
3.3	3	3.25	3.5	3.15
2.85	2.75	2.5	2.25	2

Complete the missing numbers.

$(3 + 2) \times 6 = 30$ | $2 \times (2 + 4) = 12$ | ★ $8 \times (5 - 2) = 24$

$5 \times (4 + 3) = 35$ | $7 \times (3 + 1) = 28$ | ★ $6 \times (4 - 1) = 18$

Solve. Write the equations you use in the work space.

Molly has 147 books. She arranges them on 3 shelves and puts the same number of books on each shelf. How many books are on each shelf?
49 books

Seth runs 3 miles per day. How many days does it take for him to run 108 miles?
36 days

WORK SPACE

$147 \div 3$: 3 into 147 = 49; − 12 ↓; 27; − 27; 0

$108 \div 3$: 3 into 108 = 36; − 9 ↓; 18; − 18; 0

13.4 Practice

Practice: Use the pictures to solve. Write your answers in simplest form.

$\frac{6}{12} \div 2 = \frac{3}{12} = \frac{1}{4}$ | $\frac{6}{12} \div 3 = \frac{2}{12} = \frac{1}{6}$ | $\frac{6}{12} \div 6 = \frac{1}{12}$

$\frac{8}{12} \div 2 = \frac{4}{12} = \frac{1}{3}$ | $\frac{8}{12} \div 4 = \frac{2}{12} = \frac{1}{6}$ | $\frac{8}{12} \div 8 = \frac{1}{12}$

$\frac{9}{12} \div 9 = \frac{1}{12}$ | $\frac{9}{12} \div 3 = \frac{3}{12} = \frac{1}{4}$ | $\frac{9}{12} \div 1 = \frac{9}{12} = \frac{3}{4}$

$\frac{10}{12} \div 10 = \frac{1}{12}$ | $\frac{10}{12} \div 5 = \frac{2}{12} = \frac{1}{6}$ | $\frac{10}{12} \div 2 = \frac{5}{12}$

$\frac{4}{12} \div 4 = \frac{1}{12}$ | $\frac{4}{12} \div 2 = \frac{2}{12} = \frac{1}{6}$ | $\frac{4}{12} \div 1 = \frac{4}{12} = \frac{1}{3}$

$\frac{12}{12} \div 4 = \frac{3}{12} = \frac{1}{4}$ | $\frac{12}{12} \div 3 = \frac{4}{12} = \frac{1}{3}$ | $\frac{12}{12} \div 6 = \frac{2}{12} = \frac{1}{6}$

13.4 Review

Review: Complete the chart.

1 ft. = 12 in.

Inches	1	11	2	10	3	9	4	8
Feet	$\frac{1}{12}$	$\frac{11}{12}$	$\frac{1}{6}$	$\frac{5}{6}$	$\frac{1}{4}$	$\frac{3}{4}$	$\frac{1}{3}$	$\frac{2}{3}$

Find the missing angle in each triangle.

Triangle with angles 68°, right angle, ?:
90 + 68 = 158
180 − 158 = 22°

Triangle with angles 32°, 32°, ?:
32 + 32 = 64
180 − 64 = 116°

Use mental math to complete.

$400 \times 60 = 24{,}000$ | $2{,}700 \div 900 = 3$ | $900 \times 700 = 630{,}000$

$9{,}000 \div 30 = 300$ | $50 \times 8{,}000 = 400{,}000$ | $20{,}000 \div 500 = 40$

$5{,}000 \times 40 = 200{,}000$ | $35{,}000 \div 7 = 5{,}000$ | $7 \times 7{,}000 = 49{,}000$

Use the clues to complete the chart.

- There are 40 animals in the aquarium in all.
- $\frac{4}{5}$ of the animals are fish.
- $\frac{1}{8}$ of the animals are sting rays.
- $\frac{1}{20}$ of the animals are sharks.
- The rest of the animals are turtles.

Type of Animal	Number
Fish	32
Sting rays	5
Sharks	2
Turtles	1

Unit 13 Answer Key

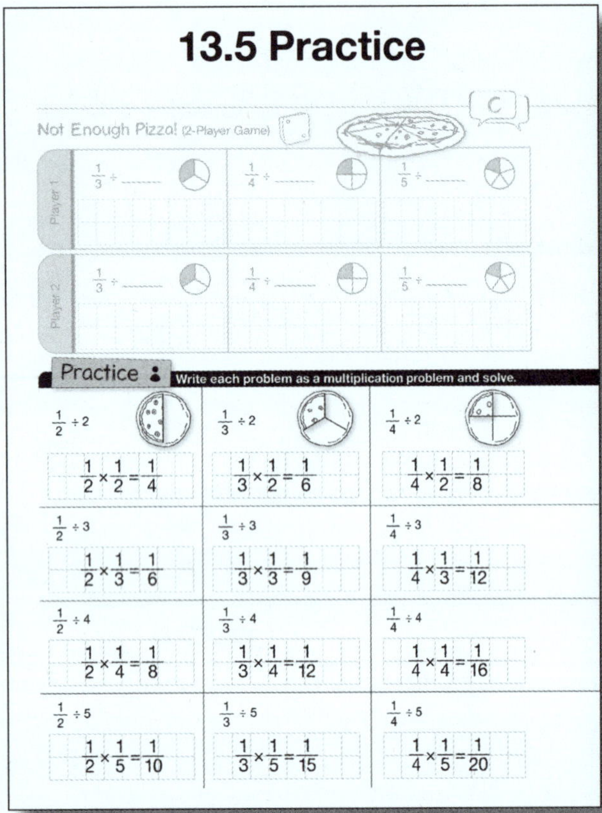

13.5 Practice

Not Enough Pizza! (2-Player Game)

Player 1: $\frac{1}{3}\div$ ___ | $\frac{1}{4}\div$ ___ | $\frac{1}{5}\div$ ___

Player 2: $\frac{1}{3}\div$ ___ | $\frac{1}{4}\div$ ___ | $\frac{1}{5}\div$ ___

Practice Write each problem as a multiplication problem and solve.

$\frac{1}{2}\div 2$ $\frac{1}{2}\times\frac{1}{2}=\frac{1}{4}$	$\frac{1}{3}\div 2$ $\frac{1}{3}\times\frac{1}{2}=\frac{1}{6}$	$\frac{1}{4}\div 2$ $\frac{1}{4}\times\frac{1}{2}=\frac{1}{8}$
$\frac{1}{2}\div 3$ $\frac{1}{2}\times\frac{1}{3}=\frac{1}{6}$	$\frac{1}{3}\div 3$ $\frac{1}{3}\times\frac{1}{3}=\frac{1}{9}$	$\frac{1}{4}\div 3$ $\frac{1}{4}\times\frac{1}{3}=\frac{1}{12}$
$\frac{1}{2}\div 4$ $\frac{1}{2}\times\frac{1}{4}=\frac{1}{8}$	$\frac{1}{3}\div 4$ $\frac{1}{3}\times\frac{1}{4}=\frac{1}{12}$	$\frac{1}{4}\div 4$ $\frac{1}{4}\times\frac{1}{4}=\frac{1}{16}$
$\frac{1}{2}\div 5$ $\frac{1}{2}\times\frac{1}{5}=\frac{1}{10}$	$\frac{1}{3}\div 5$ $\frac{1}{3}\times\frac{1}{5}=\frac{1}{15}$	$\frac{1}{4}\div 5$ $\frac{1}{4}\times\frac{1}{5}=\frac{1}{20}$

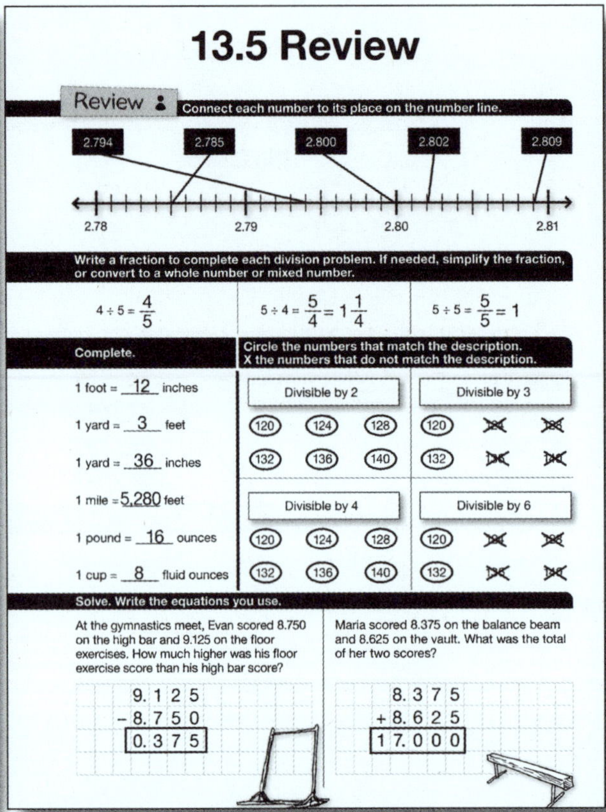

13.5 Review

Review Connect each number to its place on the number line.

2.794 | 2.785 | 2.800 | 2.802 | 2.809

2.78 | 2.79 | 2.80 | 2.81

Write a fraction to complete each division problem. If needed, simplify the fraction, or convert to a whole number or mixed number.

$4\div 5=\frac{4}{5}$ | $5\div 4=\frac{5}{4}=1\frac{1}{4}$ | $5\div 5=\frac{5}{5}=1$

Complete.

1 foot = 12 inches
1 yard = 3 feet
1 yard = 36 inches
1 mile = 5,280 feet
1 pound = 16 ounces
1 cup = 8 fluid ounces

Circle the numbers that match the description. X the numbers that do not match the description.

Divisible by 2: 120, 124, 128, 132, 136, 140 (all circled)

Divisible by 3: 120, 132 (circled); 124, 128, 136, 140 (X)

Divisible by 4: 120, 124, 128, 132, 136, 140 (all circled)

Divisible by 6: 120, 132 (circled); 124, 128, 136, 140 (X)

Solve. Write the equations you use.

At the gymnastics meet, Evan scored 8.750 on the high bar and 9.125 on the floor exercises. How much higher was his floor exercise score than his high bar score?

$9.125 - 8.750 = \boxed{0.375}$

Maria scored 8.375 on the balance beam and 8.625 on the vault. What was the total of her two scores?

$8.375 + 8.625 = \boxed{17.000}$

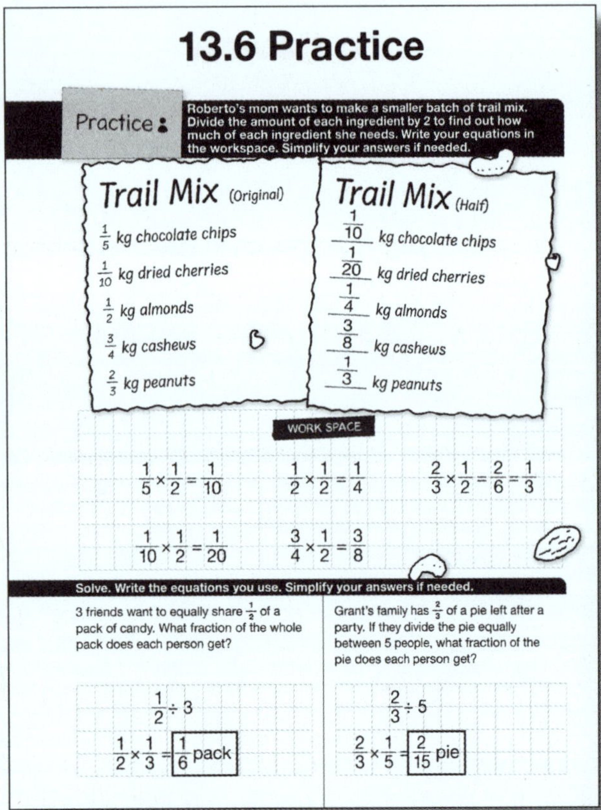

13.6 Practice

Practice Roberto's mom wants to make a smaller batch of trail mix. Divide the amount of each ingredient by 2 to find out how much of each ingredient she needs. Write your equations in the workspace. Simplify your answers if needed.

Trail Mix (Original)

$\frac{1}{5}$ kg chocolate chips
$\frac{1}{10}$ kg dried cherries
$\frac{1}{2}$ kg almonds
$\frac{3}{4}$ kg cashews
$\frac{2}{3}$ kg peanuts

Trail Mix (Half)

$\frac{1}{10}$ kg chocolate chips
$\frac{1}{20}$ kg dried cherries
$\frac{1}{4}$ kg almonds
$\frac{3}{8}$ kg cashews
$\frac{1}{3}$ kg peanuts

WORK SPACE

$\frac{1}{5}\times\frac{1}{2}=\frac{1}{10}$ | $\frac{1}{2}\times\frac{1}{2}=\frac{1}{4}$ | $\frac{2}{3}\times\frac{1}{2}=\frac{2}{6}=\frac{1}{3}$

$\frac{1}{10}\times\frac{1}{2}=\frac{1}{20}$ | $\frac{3}{4}\times\frac{1}{2}=\frac{3}{8}$

Solve. Write the equations you use. Simplify your answers if needed.

3 friends want to equally share $\frac{1}{2}$ of a pack of candy. What fraction of the whole pack does each person get?

$\frac{1}{2}\div 3$

$\frac{1}{2}\times\frac{1}{3}=\boxed{\frac{1}{6}\text{ pack}}$

Grant's family has $\frac{2}{3}$ of a pie left after a party. If they divide the pie equally between 5 people, what fraction of the pie does each person get?

$\frac{2}{3}\div 5$

$\frac{2}{3}\times\frac{1}{5}=\boxed{\frac{2}{15}\text{ pie}}$

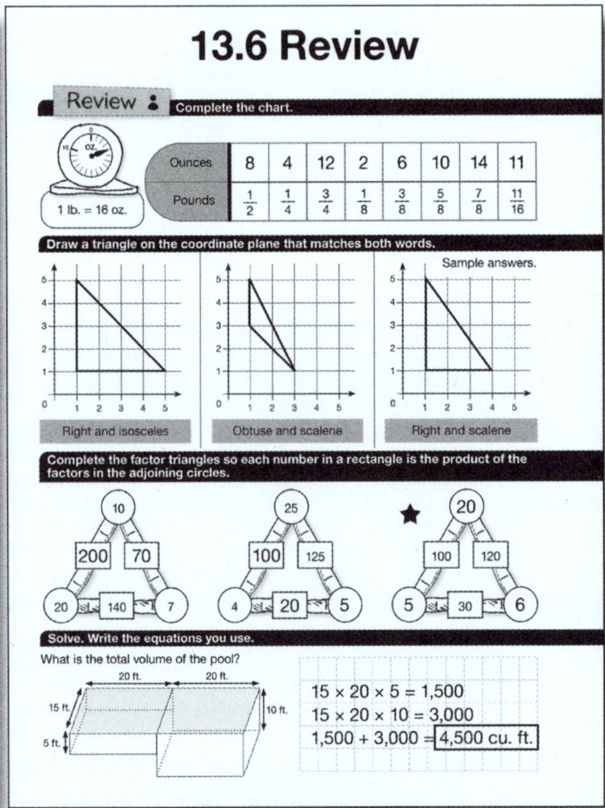

13.6 Review

Review Complete the chart.

1 lb. = 16 oz.

Ounces	8	4	12	2	6	10	14	11
Pounds	$\frac{1}{2}$	$\frac{1}{4}$	$\frac{3}{4}$	$\frac{1}{8}$	$\frac{3}{8}$	$\frac{5}{8}$	$\frac{7}{8}$	$\frac{11}{16}$

Draw a triangle on the coordinate plane that matches both words.

Sample answers.

Right and isosceles | Obtuse and scalene | Right and scalene

Complete the factor triangles so each number in a rectangle is the product of the factors in the adjoining circles.

Circles 10, 20, 7; rectangles 200, 70, 140

Circles 25, 4, 5; rectangles 100, 125, 20

★ Circles 20, 5, 6; rectangles 100, 120, 30

Solve. Write the equations you use.

What is the total volume of the pool?

20 ft. | 20 ft. | 15 ft. | 5 ft. | 10 ft.

$15\times 20\times 5=1{,}500$
$15\times 20\times 10=3{,}000$
$1{,}500+3{,}000=\boxed{4{,}500\text{ cu. ft.}}$

Unit 13 Answer Key

13.7 Practice

Practice: Rewrite each problem as a multiplication problem and solve. Simplify your answer if needed. Then, find the blank that matches the product. Write the matching letter in the blank to solve the riddle.

C $\frac{1}{8} \div 2$ $\frac{1}{8} \times \frac{1}{2} = \frac{1}{16}$	E $\frac{1}{5} \div 3$ $\frac{1}{5} \times \frac{1}{3} = \frac{1}{15}$	I $\frac{1}{10} \div 4$ $\frac{1}{10} \times \frac{1}{4} = \frac{1}{40}$
L $\frac{3}{4} \div 2$ $\frac{3}{4} \times \frac{1}{2} = \frac{3}{8}$	N $\frac{2}{3} \div 3$ $\frac{2}{3} \times \frac{1}{3} = \frac{2}{9}$	T $\frac{3}{10} \div 2$ $\frac{3}{10} \times \frac{1}{2} = \frac{3}{20}$
E $\frac{4}{5} \div 3$ $\frac{4}{5} \times \frac{1}{3} = \frac{4}{15}$	! $\frac{3}{8} \div 3$ $\frac{3}{8} \times \frac{1}{3} = \frac{3}{24} = \frac{1}{8}$	B $\frac{9}{10} \div 3$ $\frac{9}{10} \times \frac{1}{3} = \frac{9}{30} = \frac{3}{10}$

What did the zero say to the eight? 100

N	I	C	E		B	E	L	T	!
$\frac{2}{9}$	$\frac{1}{40}$	$\frac{1}{16}$	$\frac{4}{15}$		$\frac{3}{10}$	$\frac{1}{15}$	$\frac{3}{8}$	$\frac{3}{20}$	$\frac{1}{8}$

Solve. Write the equations you use. Simplify your answer if needed.

Kylie has $\frac{3}{4}$ lb. of almonds. She divides the almonds equally into 4 bags. How many pounds of almonds are in each bag?

$\frac{3}{4} \div 4$

$\frac{3}{4} \times \frac{1}{4} = \frac{3}{16}$ lb.

Scout has $\frac{7}{10}$ kg of peanuts. She divides the peanuts equally into 2 bags. How many kilograms of peanuts are in each bag?

$\frac{7}{10} \div 2$

$\frac{7}{10} \times \frac{1}{2} = \frac{7}{20}$ kg

13.7 Review

Review: Choose the more sensible measurement for each item.

Area of a piece of paper	Area of a poster	Area of a sticky note
$\frac{3}{4}$ sq. in. / **($\frac{3}{4}$ sq. ft.)**	$\frac{1}{2}$ sq. cm / **($\frac{1}{2}$ sq. m)**	$\frac{1}{16}$ sq. in. / **($\frac{1}{16}$ sq. ft.)**

Draw a line to connect the numbers in order from Start to End. Follow the rule.

Rule: Add 0.5

1.2	0.7	3.0	1.7	2.0
1.7	2.2	2.3	2.4	6.5
1.5	2.7	3.1	3.9	6.2
2.8	3.2	3.7	4.3	5.7
2.5	3.8	4.2	4.7	5.2

Start → 1.2, 1.7, 2.2, 2.7, 3.2, 3.7, 4.2, 4.7, 5.2, 5.7, 6.2 → END

Rule: Subtract 0.3

3.6	3.4	3.1	1.5	1.2
3.3	3.0	2.9	1.8	0.9
2.0	2.7	2.4	2.1	0.6
4.6	2.5	1.1	1.4	0.3
3.5	2.3	0.7	0.4	0

Start → 3.6, 3.3, 3.0, 2.7, 2.4, 2.1, 1.8, 1.5, 1.2, 0.9, 0.6, 0.3, 0 → END

Use long division to solve. Write the remainder as a fraction. Use the example to help.

Example: $73 \div 6 = 12\frac{1}{6}$ (6)73; − 6; 13; − 12; 1 (1 ← remainder, 6 ← divisor)

$163 \div 4 = 40\frac{3}{4}$: − 16; 03; − 0; 3

$487 \div 3 = 162\frac{1}{3}$: − 3; 18; − 18; 07; − 6; 1

$702 \div 5 = 140\frac{2}{5}$: − 5; 20; − 20; 02; − 0; 2

13.8 Practice

Practice: Rewrite each problem as a multiplication problem and solve.

$3 \div \frac{1}{6}$ 3 × 6 = 18	$4 \div \frac{1}{2}$ 4 × 2 = 8	$2 \div \frac{1}{4}$ 2 × 4 = 8
$3 \div \frac{1}{10}$ 3 × 10 = 30	$4 \div \frac{1}{5}$ 4 × 5 = 20	$2 \div \frac{1}{8}$ 2 × 8 = 16

Solve. Write the equations you use.

Luke makes 4 lb. of granola. He packages the granola in bags that each weigh $\frac{1}{4}$ lb. How many bags can he fill?

$4 \div \frac{1}{4}$

4 × 4 = 16 bags

Anna makes 3 kg of trail mix. She packages the trail mix in bags that each weigh $\frac{1}{8}$ kg. How many bags can she pack?

$3 \div \frac{1}{8}$

3 × 8 = 24 bags

Matthew has 2 pounds of hamburger. He uses it to make hamburger patties that weigh $\frac{1}{4}$ lb. each. How many hamburger patties can he make?

$2 \div \frac{1}{4}$

2 × 4 = 8 patties

Quinn makes 3 liters of hot chocolate. She pours $\frac{1}{4}$ liter in each mug. How many mugs does she fill?

$3 \div \frac{1}{4}$

3 × 4 = 12 mugs

13.8 Review

Review: Find the products. Write your answers in simplest form. If the answer is an improper fraction, convert it to a mixed number or whole number.

$3 \times 1\frac{2}{5}$ $\frac{3}{1} \times \frac{7}{5} = \frac{21}{5} = 4\frac{1}{5}$	$1\frac{1}{3} \times 1\frac{1}{8}$ $\frac{4}{3} \times \frac{9}{8} = \frac{36}{24} = 1\frac{12}{24} = 1\frac{1}{2}$	$\frac{3}{5} \times \frac{3}{5}$ $\frac{3}{5} \times \frac{3}{5} = \frac{9}{25}$
$\frac{1}{5} \times 3$ $\frac{1}{5} \times \frac{3}{1} = \frac{3}{5}$	$2\frac{1}{4} \times \frac{7}{8}$ $\frac{9}{4} \times \frac{7}{8} = \frac{63}{32} = 1\frac{31}{32}$	$\frac{2}{3} \times \frac{2}{3}$ $\frac{2}{3} \times \frac{2}{3} = \frac{4}{9}$

Use the information to complete the chart. Then, use the chart to make a line graph.

Parking costs $12 for the first hour. Each additional hour costs $8.

Hours	Cost ($)
1	12
2	20
3	28
4	36
5	44
6	52

Use bar models to solve. Write the equations you use.

Kristina spent $\frac{7}{8}$ of her money on a puzzle. The puzzle cost $35. How much money did Kristina have to start?

$40

How much money does she have left?

$5

35 ÷ 7 = 5 40 − 35 = 5

5 × 8 = 40

Unit 13 Answer Key

13.9 Practice

Practice: Draw a line from Start to End so that each problem is followed by the correct answer. You do not have to solve every problem.

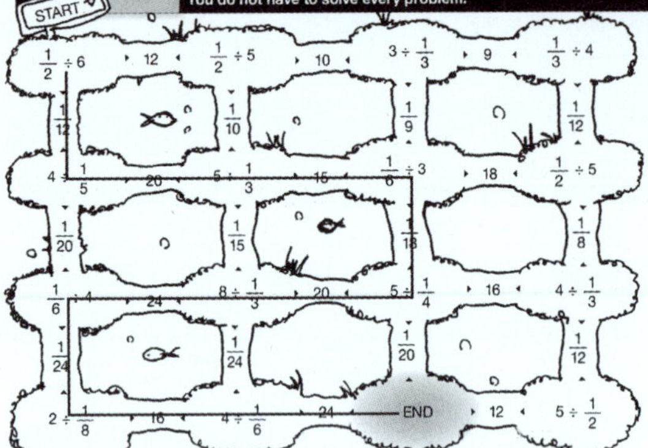

Solve. Write the equations you use. Simplify if needed.

Elijah has $\frac{1}{3}$ of a candy bar. He breaks it into 4 pieces. What fraction of the whole candy bar is each piece?

$\frac{1}{3} \div 4 = \frac{1}{3} \times \frac{1}{4} = \frac{1}{12}$ bar

Liam runs 5 km around the outdoor track. Each lap is $\frac{1}{3}$ km long. How many laps does he run?

$5 \div \frac{1}{3}$ $5 \times 3 = 15$ laps

Olivia has 4 muffins to share. She gives each person $\frac{1}{4}$ of a muffin. How many people get a piece of muffin?

$4 \div \frac{1}{4} = 4 \times 4 = 16$ people

Mia has $\frac{1}{10}$ m of wire. She cuts the wire into 3 equal pieces. What fraction of a meter is each piece?

$\frac{1}{10} \div 3 = \frac{1}{10} \times \frac{1}{3} = \frac{1}{30}$ m

13.9 Review

Review: Use mental math to find the quotients.

75 ÷ 25 = 3	60 ÷ 15 = 4	90 ÷ 45 = 2
125 ÷ 25 = 5	45 ÷ 15 = 3	180 ÷ 45 = 4
64 ÷ 2 = 32	120 ÷ 3 = 40	300 ÷ 6 = 50
64 ÷ 4 = 16	126 ÷ 3 = 42	294 ÷ 6 = 49

Use the key to color the fractions and create a winter scene.

Light blue: fractions equivalent to $\frac{1}{2}$

Brown: fractions equivalent to $\frac{1}{3}$

Green: fractions equivalent to $\frac{1}{4}$

Leave all other fractions white

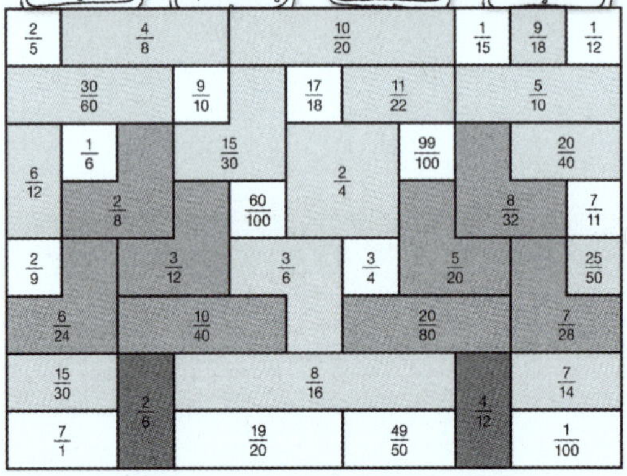

13.10 Unit Wrap-Up A

Unit Wrap-Up: Complete. If needed, simplify your answer or convert it to a whole number or mixed number.

$1 \div 3 = \frac{1}{3}$

$5 \div 3 = \frac{5}{3} = 1\frac{2}{3}$

$6 \div 3 = \frac{6}{3} = 2$

Rewrite each problem as a multiplication problem and solve. Simplify your answer if needed.

$\frac{1}{2} \div 4$: $\frac{1}{2} \times \frac{1}{4} = \frac{1}{8}$

$\frac{4}{5} \div 4$: $\frac{4}{5} \times \frac{1}{4} = \frac{4}{20} = \frac{1}{5}$

$2 \div \frac{1}{5}$: $2 \times 5 = 10$

$\frac{1}{2} \div 5$: $\frac{1}{2} \times \frac{1}{5} = \frac{1}{10}$

$\frac{2}{5} \div 4$: $\frac{2}{5} \times \frac{1}{4} = \frac{2}{20} = \frac{1}{10}$

$2 \div \frac{1}{4}$: $2 \times 4 = 8$

13.10 Unit Wrap-Up B

Unit Wrap-Up: Peter's family is preparing for a backpacking trip. Use their shopping list to answer the questions. Write the equations you use. Write your answers in simplest form.

Backpacking Trip Shopping List

- 2 lb. rice
- $\frac{3}{4}$ lb. salami
- 4 c. pancake mix
- 2 c. hot cocoa mix
- 8 granola bars
- 3 packs of macaroni and cheese

Trail mix ingredients:

- $\frac{1}{4}$ lb. almonds
- $\frac{1}{2}$ lb. raisins
- $\frac{2}{3}$ lb. peanuts
- $\frac{1}{4}$ lb. chocolate candies
- $\frac{1}{3}$ lb. dried apricots

It takes $\frac{1}{6}$ c. of pancake mix to make one pancake. How many pancakes can they make?

$4 \div \frac{1}{6}$ $4 \times 6 = 24$ pancakes

There are 5 people in Peter's family. If they split the granola bars equally, how many granola bars will each person get?

$8 \div 5 = \frac{8}{5} = 1\frac{3}{5}$ bars

Peter's mom cuts the salami into 5 equal pieces. How much does each piece weigh?

$\frac{3}{4} \div 5$ $\frac{3}{4} \times \frac{1}{5} = \frac{3}{20}$ lb.

Each pack of macaroni and cheese weighs $\frac{3}{4}$ lb. What is the total weight of all the packs of macaroni and cheese?

$3 \times \frac{3}{4}$ $\frac{3}{1} \times \frac{3}{4} = \frac{9}{4} = 2\frac{1}{4}$ lb.

It takes $\frac{1}{4}$ c. of hot cocoa mix to make one mug of cocoa. How many mugs of hot cocoa can they make?

$2 \div \frac{1}{4}$ $2 \times 4 = 8$ mugs

★ Peter's dad mixes together all of the trail mix ingredients. Then, he packs the trail mix into smaller bags. Each bag weighs $\frac{1}{8}$ lb. How many bags does he pack?

$\frac{1}{4} + \frac{1}{2} + \frac{2}{3} + \frac{1}{4} + \frac{1}{3} = 2$

$2 \div \frac{1}{8}$ $2 \times 8 = 16$ bags

Unit 13 Checkpoint

What to Expect at the End of Unit 13

By the end of Unit 13, most children will be able to do the following:

- Understand that the fraction bar is another way to show division.
- Divide small whole numbers by small whole numbers and write the result as a fraction or mixed number.
- Use fractions to express remainders in long division problems.
- Divide fractions by whole numbers by rewriting the problem as a multiplication problem.
- Divide whole numbers by unit fractions by rewriting the problem as a multiplication problem.
- Solve word problems that involve dividing fractions and whole numbers. Some children will still need help identifying which number to write as the dividend and which number to write as the divisor.

Is Your Child Ready to Move on?

Many children find fraction division very difficult to grasp. Don't worry if your child sometimes gets mixed up as she solves fraction division problems. This unit is meant simply as an introduction to fraction division, and your child will study this concept in greater depth in sixth grade.

Unit 14
Multiply Whole Numbers by Decimals

Overview

In Unit 2, your child studied place value in decimal numbers and learned how to add and subtract decimals. In this unit, he will learn how to multiply whole numbers by decimals, both with mental math and the written algorithm. He will also learn how to move the decimal point to multiply decimals by 10, 100, or 1,000 and convert measurements within the metric system.

In *Sixth Grade Math with Confidence*, your child will learn how to multiply decimals by decimals.

What Your Child Will Learn

In this unit, your child will learn to:

- Write decimals as groups of tenths, hundredths, or thousandths
- Use place-value thinking to mentally multiply whole numbers by simple decimals
- Move the decimal point to multiply decimals by 10, 100, or 1,000
- Multiply to convert metric measures
- Multiply whole numbers by decimals with written multiplication
- Estimate answers to decimal multiplication problems
- Solve decimal multiplication word problems, including problems with money

Lesson List

Lesson 14.1	Review Decimal Place-Value and Vocabulary
Lesson 14.2	Write Decimals as Groups of Tenths, Hundredths, or Thousandths
Lesson 14.3	Use Place-Value Thinking to Multiply Whole Numbers by Decimals
Lesson 14.4	Multiply Decimals by One-Digit Whole Numbers
Lesson 14.5	Multiply Decimals by 10, 100, or 1,000
Lesson 14.6	Multiply to Convert Metric Measurements
Lesson 14.7	Multiply Decimals by Whole Numbers with Trailing Zeros
Lesson 14.8	Multiply Decimals by Two-Digit Whole Numbers
Lesson 14.9	Enrichment (Optional)

Extra Materials Needed for Unit 14

- For optional Enrichment Lesson:
  - × *How Many Guinea Pigs Can Fit on a Plane?: Answers to Your Most Clever Math Questions*, by Laura Overdeck. Feiwel & Friends, 2017.
  - × Grocery store flyer or website
  - × Family recipe that makes a large batch

Teaching Math with Confidence: Using Equal-Groups Multiplication to Introduce Decimal Multiplication

When your child first learned how to multiply whole numbers, you used equal groups of objects to help him understand the meaning of multiplication. He learned that one factor in a multiplication problem tells the number of groups, while the other factor tells the size of each group. The product tells the total.

$3 \times 4 = 12$

number of groups — size of each group — total

In this unit, you'll teach your child how to multiply whole numbers by decimals. You'll use this same equal-groups model to help him understand what the problems mean. The whole number in each problem represents the number of items, and the decimal number represents the size of each item. The product represents the total quantity.

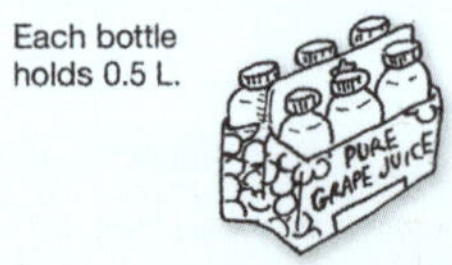

$6 \times 0.5 = 3$ L

number of items — size of each item — total quantity

Thinking of decimal multiplication this way will help your child estimate answers to decimal multiplication problems and develop deeper decimal number sense. In sixth grade, he'll learn how to multiply decimals by decimals and learn other ways to interpret decimal multiplication problems.

Lesson 14.1
Review Decimal Place-Value and Vocabulary

Purpose	Materials
• Review decimal place-value and expanded form • Identify decimal digits, leading zeros, and trailing zeros in decimal numbers	• Die • Counters

Memory Work

- **What are opposite angles in a parallelogram?** *Angles that are across from each other.*
- **What are adjacent angles in a parallelogram?** *Angles that are next to each other.*

This short lesson introduces key vocabulary words that your child will use as she learns to multiply and divide decimals. If your child flies through the lesson, combine it with Lesson 14.2.

Warm-up (A): Review Decimal Place-Value

Earlier this year, you learned about decimal place-value to the thousandths-place. You learned how to write decimals in expanded form.

Have your child write each decimal in expanded form. Encourage her to use the place-value chart to help. For example, for 0.045: **What place is the 4 in?** *The hundredths-place.* **So, the 4 has a value of four-hundredths.**

A

ones	tenths	hundredths	thousandths
1.	7	6	8
0.	0	4	5
3.	6	0	
5.	2	0	4

$1.768 = 1 + \frac{7}{10} + \frac{6}{100} + \frac{8}{1{,}000}$

$0.045 = \frac{4}{100} + \frac{5}{1{,}000}$

$3.60 = 3 + \frac{6}{10}$

$5.204 = 5 + \frac{2}{10} + \frac{4}{1{,}000}$

Read each individual decimal digit in decimal numbers. For example, read 0.045 as "zero point zero four five" rather than "forty-five thousandths." Reading numbers in this way ensures that your child makes sense of the place-value meaning of the digits herself.

Activity (B): Learn Decimal Digit Vocabulary

Today, you'll learn some vocabulary words we use to describe the digits in decimal numbers. We'll use these words often as you learn how to multiply and divide decimals, so it's helpful to know them. Have your child read the text box aloud.

B

Decimal Vocabulary

Decimal digits are the digits to the right of the decimal point. They stand for the fractional part of the number.	**Leading zeros** are zeros that come before the first non-zero digit. They make sure the non-zero digits are in the correct place.	**Trailing zeros** are zeros that come after the final non-zero digit. They do not change the value of the number.
1.768 3 decimal digits	0.045 2 leading zeros	3.60 1 trailing zero

Use the following questions to discuss the examples.

- **The digits to the left of the decimal point tell the whole number part of the number. The digits to the right of the decimal point are the decimal digits. They tell the fractional part of the number.**
- **How many decimal digits are in 1.768?** *3.*
- **Leading zeros are the digits that are to the left of the first non-zero digit. We call them that because they lead us to the first digit in the number that has value.**
- **0.045 has two leading zeros. One of the leading zeros is before the decimal point and one is after the decimal point. The leading zeros are important, because they make sure that the 4 and 5 are in the correct places.**
- **Trailing zeros are the digits to the right of the last non-zero digit. They trail along after the digits that add value to the number.**
- **3.60 has 1 trailing zero. We often use trailing zeros for measurements, because they show that the measurement is accurate to that digit.**

Make sure your child always writes a leading zero in the ones-place for decimals with a value less than 1. Developing this habit makes it easier to see the decimal point and helps prevent mistakes.

If your child wonders why someone would write 3.60 instead of 3.6, explain that the 0 in the hundredths-place means that the measurement is accurate to the nearest hundredth. If you bought a package of flour at the grocery store that was labeled 3.60 pounds, you'd know that its weight is within one-hundredth of 3.60 pounds. Your child does not need to fully grasp this concept, and she'll learn more about the significance of decimal digits in future math and science classes.

Activity (C): Play Decimal Digit Tic-Tac-Toe

Play Decimal Digit Tic-Tac-Toe.

Decimal Digit Tic-Tac-Toe

Materials: Die; counters of two different colors

Object of the Game: Be the first player to fill three boxes in a row, either horizontally, vertically, or diagonally.

Give 8 counters of one color to one player and 8 counters of a different color to the other player.

On your turn, roll the die. Find the description that matches your roll, and then put a counter on a number that fits the description. For example, if you roll a 4, the matching description is "3 leading zeros." So, you could put your counter on 0.009, 0.007, or 0.001.

If you roll a number and all the matching numbers are covered, you lose your turn and play passes to the other player.

Take turns until one player covers 3 boxes in a row, either horizontally, vertically, or diagonally.

Independent Practice and Review

Have your child complete the Lesson 14.1 Practice and Review workbook pages.

Lesson 14.2
Write Decimals as Groups of Tenths, Hundredths, or Thousandths

Purpose	Materials
• Practice writing fractions with base-ten denominators as decimals • Write decimals as groups of tenths, hundredths, or thousandths	• Counters

Memory Work	
	• **How do you know if a number is divisible by 2?** *It is even. It has 0, 2, 4, 6, or 8 in the ones-place.* • **How do you know if a number is divisible by 3?** *The sum of its digits is divisible by 3.* • **How do you know if a number is divisible by 4?** *When you divide it by 2, the quotient is even.* • **How do you know if a number is divisible by 5?** *It has a 0 or 5 in the ones-place.* • **How do you know if a number is divisible by 6?** *It is even and divisible by 3.*

This lesson prepares your child to understand the regrouping sometimes necessary when multiplying whole numbers by decimals.

Warm-up (A): Write Fractions as Decimals

Each decimal square represents 1 whole. We can use both fractions and decimals to represent the shaded part. Have your child write each fraction as a decimal.

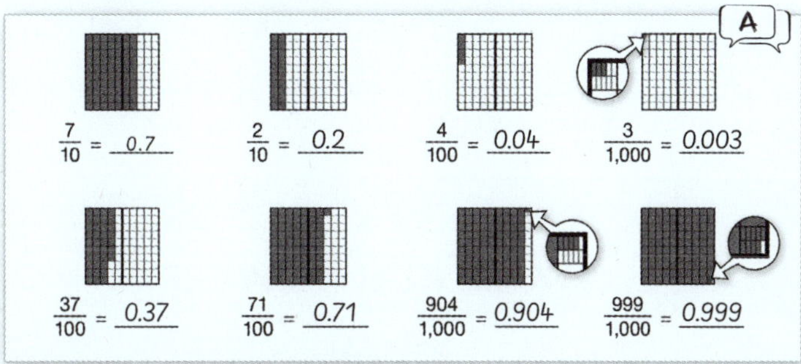

Activity (B): Write Decimals as Groups of Tenths, Hundredths, or Thousandths

When you were younger, you learned how to regroup ones, tens, hundreds, and thousands. For example, you learned that 40 ones equal 4 tens, or that 2 hundreds equal 20 tens.

Today, you'll learn how to write decimals as groups of tenths, hundredths, or thousandths. Knowing how to write them this way will help you understand decimal multiplication in the next lesson.

The first example shows how to write 1.24 as a group of hundredths.

- **First, we write the decimal as a mixed number. 1.24 equals 1 and 24 hundredths.**
- **Next, we write the mixed number as an improper fraction. 1 and 24 hundredths equals what improper fraction?** *124 hundredths.*
- **Last, we translate the improper fraction to words.**

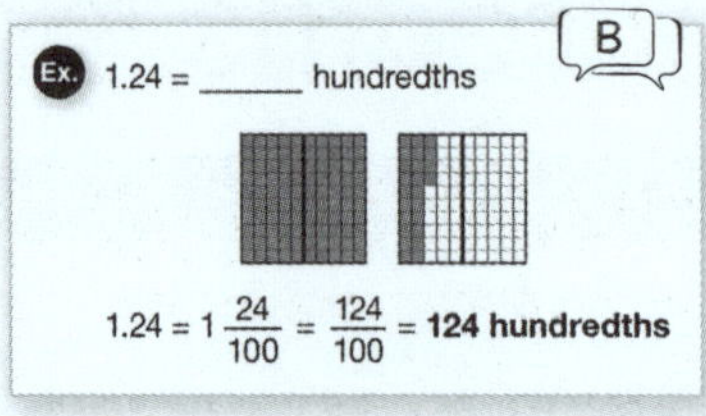

The second example shows how to write 17 tenths as a decimal.

- **First, we translate the words into a fraction and write 17 tenths as an improper fraction.**
- **Then, we convert 17 tenths to a mixed number. What mixed number equals 17 tenths?** *1 and seven-tenths.*
- **Last, we write the mixed number as a decimal. 1 and seven-tenths equals what decimal?** *1.7.*

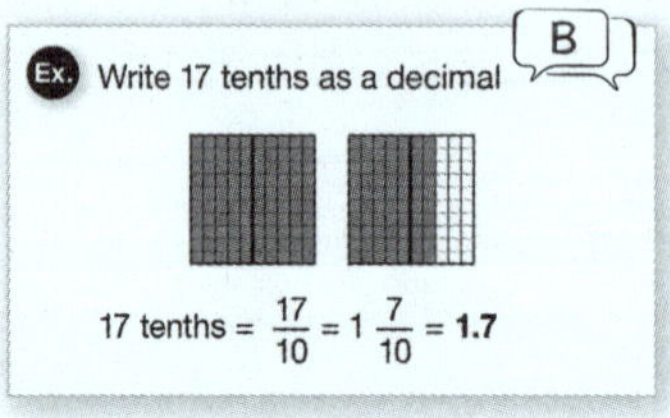

Activity (C): Play Four in a Row

Play Four in a Row. Your child may find the matching boxes mentally, or he may write out improper fractions and mixed numbers on a separate piece of paper.

The boxes on this Four in a Row game board are smaller than usual. If your counters don't fit, have each player use a different-colored marker and X the boxes instead.

Four in a Row

Materials: 12 counters per player, with a different color for each player

Object of the Game: Be the first player to place counters in 4 boxes in a row, either horizontally, vertically, or diagonally.

On your turn, choose one of the light-colored boxes on the game board. Find the matching number in a dark-colored box. Use 2 counters to cover both boxes. For example, if you choose the box with 38 tenths, cover that box and the box with 3.8. Play then passes to the other player.

Continue until one player covers 4 boxes in a row, either horizontally, vertically, or diagonally.

Directions continued on next page.

Answer Key:

- 38 tenths = 3.8
- 129 thousandths = 0.129
- 45 thousandths = 0.045
- 45 tenths = 4.5
- 600 hundredths = 6
- 38 hundredths = 0.38
- 129 tenths = 12.9
- 38 thousandths = 0.038
- 600 thousandths = 0.6
- 45 hundredths = 0.45
- 129 hundredths = 1.29
- 600 tenths = 60

Independent Practice and Review

Have your child complete the Lesson 14.2 Practice and Review workbook pages.

Lesson 14.3
Use Place-Value Thinking to Multiply Whole Numbers by Decimals

Purpose	Materials
• Color pictures to introduce decimal multiplication • Use mental math to multiply whole numbers by decimals	• Base-ten blocks • Decimal cards (Blackline Master 5) • Die

Memory Work

- **What do we call the digits to the right of the decimal point?** *Decimal digits.*
- **What do we call zeros that come before the first non-zero digit in a number?** *Leading zeros.*
- **What do we call zeros that come after the final non-zero digit in a number?** *Trailing zeros.*

In this lesson, your child will use mental math to multiply whole numbers by simple decimals. In the next lesson, your child will learn how to use the written algorithm to multiply whole numbers by more-complex decimals.

You'll need decimal cards (Blackline Master 5, cut apart on the dotted lines) again in this lesson. You will not need them again after this lesson.

Warm-up (A): Introduce Decimal Multiplication

Earlier in the year, you learned how to add and subtract decimals. Today, you'll learn how to multiply whole numbers by decimals. In these problems, we use multiplication to quickly find the total of a number of equal groups or items.

See the Unit 14 **Teaching Math with Confidence** for more on how to use whole-number multiplication to help your child understand decimal multiplication.

In the first picture, each ball of clay weighs 0.2 kilograms. We multiply 4 times 0.2 to find the weight of 4 balls of clay. The 4 tells the number of items, and the 0.2 tells the size of each item.

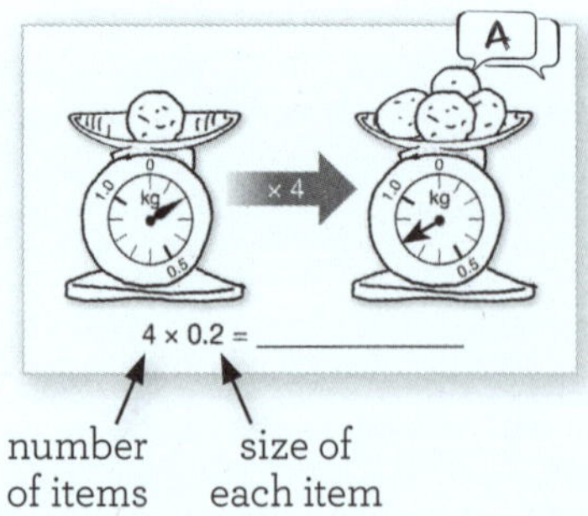

Let's use base-ten blocks to model the problem. Place 4 groups of 2 rods on the table. **Each rod represents 0.1, or one-tenth of a flat. 4 times 2 equals 8, so what does 4 times 0.2 equal?** *0.8.* If your child's not sure, say: **4 times two-tenths equals eight-tenths, so 4 times 0.2 equals 0.8.** Write 0.8 in the blank and have your child draw a hand on the right-hand scale to show 0.8 kg.

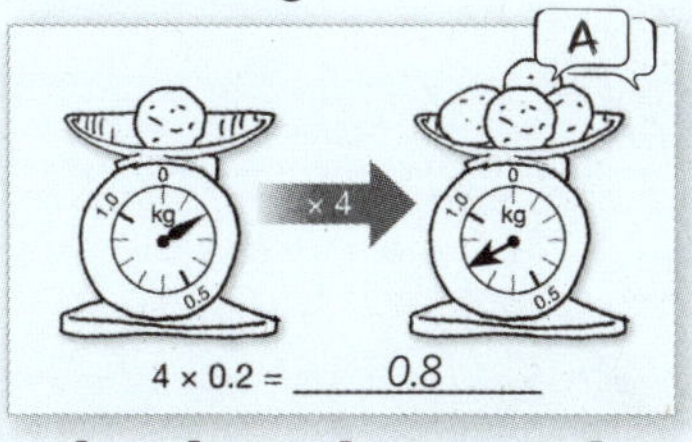

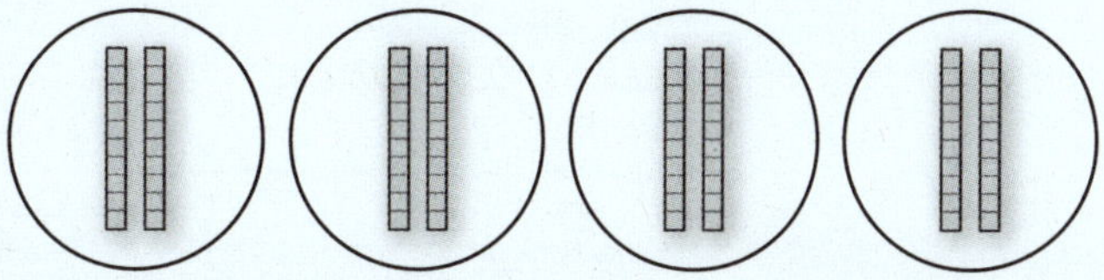

The water bottle in the second picture has 0.6 liters of water in it. We multiply 3 times 0.6 to find how much water we get if we pour 0.6 liters into the empty bottles 3 times.

Place 3 groups of 6 rods on the table. **3 times 6 equals 18, so what does 3 times 0.6 equal?** *1.8.* If your child's not sure, say: **3 times six-tenths equals eighteen-tenths, so 3 times 0.6 equals 1.8.**

Write 1.8 in the blank. Have your child color the first empty bottle up to the 1 liter line and the second empty bottle up to the 0.8 liter line.

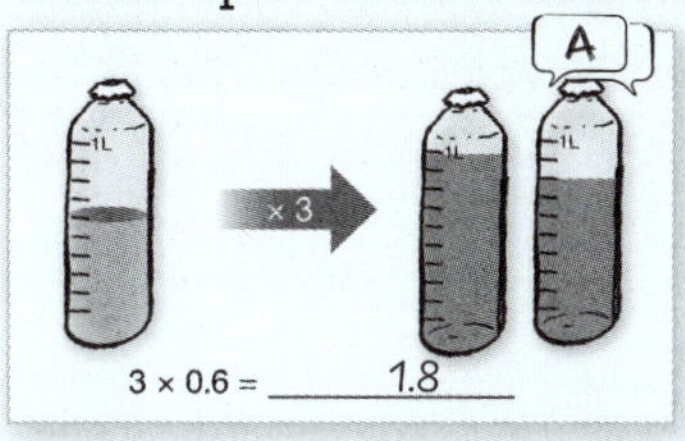

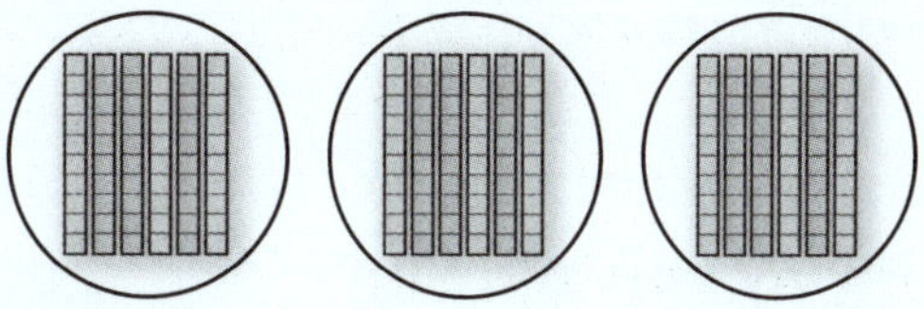

Activity (B): Use Place-Value Thinking to Multiply Whole Numbers by Decimals

Today, you'll learn how to use place-value thinking to multiply whole numbers by decimals. It's a lot like how we use place-value thinking to multiply whole numbers.

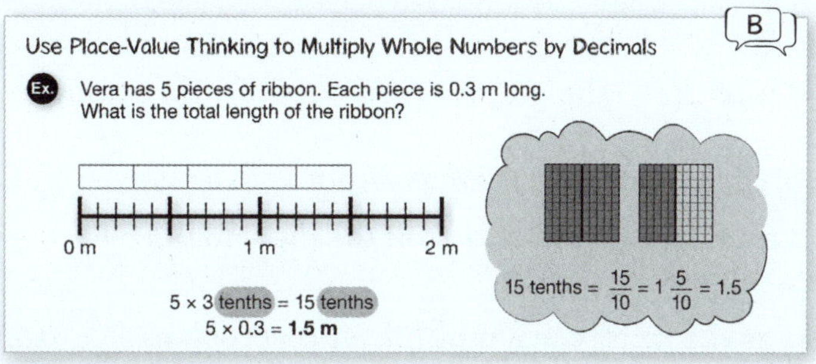

Read aloud the example problem.

- **The example shows how to multiply 5 times 0.3. The 5 tells the number of pieces, and the 0.3 tells the size of each piece.** Place 5 groups of 3 rods on the table.
- **5 groups of 3 tenths equals how many tenths?** *15.*
- **15 tenths equal 1 and five-tenths, or 1.5.** Push together 10 of the rods as shown. **Vera has 1.5 meters of ribbon.**

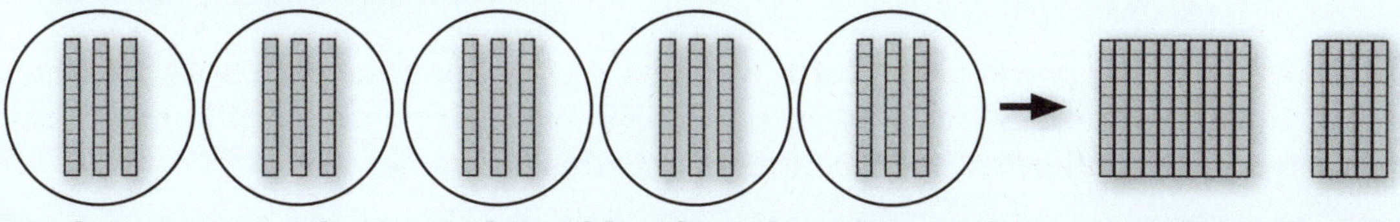

Why is the answer to the example problem less than 5? *Sample answer: Each of the ribbons is less than 1 meter long. So, if you have 5 of them, you don't have a full 5 meters of ribbon.* **When we multiply a whole number by a number less than 1, the product is always less than the whole number.**

It's okay if your child doesn't fully understand this idea yet.

Have your child use place-value thinking to solve the practice problems.

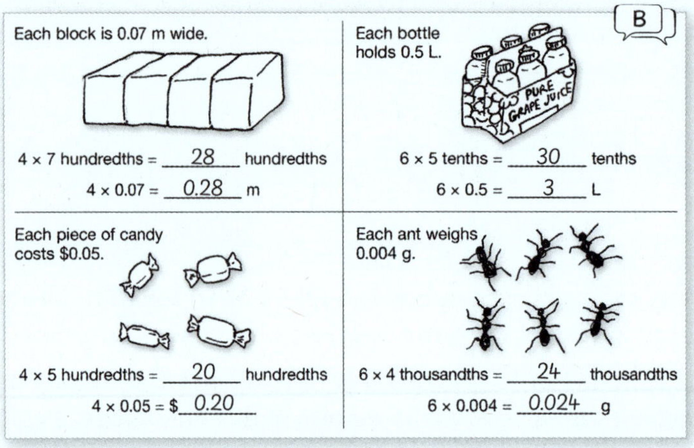

Use base-ten blocks (or the Decimal Squares on Blackline Master 7) to model the problems as needed. Your child may also find it helpful to see how fraction multiplication yields the same answer as place-value thinking. For example, for the first practice problem: **0.07 equals seven-hundredths. When I multiply 4 times 7 hundredths, I get 28 hundredths.**

$$\frac{4}{1} \times \frac{7}{100} = \frac{28}{100} = 0.28$$

Activity (C): Play Roll and Flip

Play Roll and Flip.

Roll and Flip

Materials: Die; decimal cards

Object of the Game: Have the greater total sum of your products.

Shuffle the decimal cards and place them face-down in a pile.

Roll and Flip has 4 rounds. On your turn, roll the die and flip over the top card in the pile. (If you roll a 1, roll again.)

Write the numbers as the factors in a multiplication problem. For example, if you roll a 4 and flip over 0.08, your multiplication problem is 4 × 0.08. Find the product.

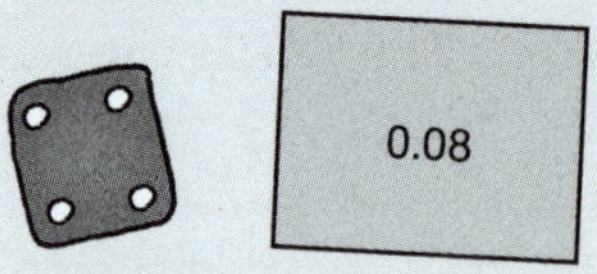

C

4 × 0.08 = 0.32

Sample turn.

Then, have the other player take a turn in the same way. Continue until both players have completed 4 rounds. Each player finds the sum of their products (either mentally or on scrap paper). Whoever has the higher sum wins the game.

Independent Practice and Review

Have your child complete the Lesson 14.3 Practice and Review workbook pages.

Lesson 14.4
Multiply Decimals by One-Digit Whole Numbers

Purpose	Materials
• Preview decimal multiplication by adding equal decimal amounts • Use the written algorithm to multiply a decimal by a one-digit whole number	• Base-ten blocks • Decimal Place-Value Chart (Blackline Master 6) • Die

Memory Work

- **What do we call the result when we multiply two numbers?** *The product.*
- **What do we call the numbers in a multiplication equation that we multiply together?** *Factors.*

Warm-up (A): Add Equal Decimals

Earlier this year, you learned how to add decimals. Have your child complete the problems.

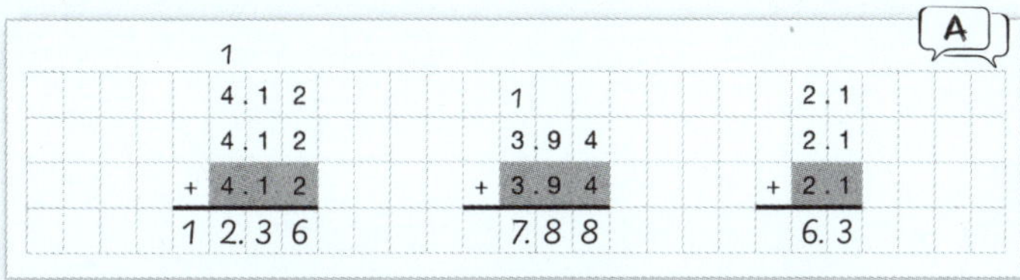

Activity (B): Multiply Decimals by Whole Numbers with the Written Multiplication Algorithm

In the warm-up, you added to find the sum of equal decimal amounts. What operation do we use to add equal groups more quickly? *Multiplication.* **Today, you'll learn how to use written multiplication to find the total of equal decimal amounts.**

Have your child read the text box aloud.

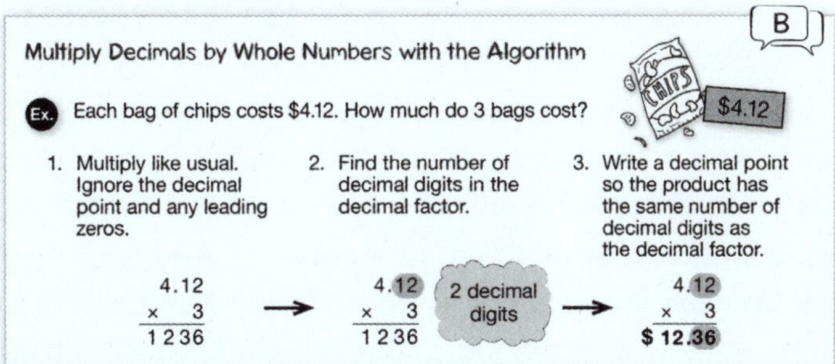

The example shows how to multiply 4.12 times 3.

- **First, we multiply the digits like usual with the multiplication algorithm, starting with the ones-place.**
- **Then, we count the decimal digits in the decimal factor. How many decimal digits does 4.12 have?** *2.*
- **Last, we write the decimal point so the product has the same number of decimal digits as the decimal factor. In this problem, 4.12 has 2 decimal digits, so the product has 2 decimal digits as well.**

Placing the decimal point in this way makes sure that each digit ends up in the correct place. Let's use base-ten blocks to check that each digit is in the correct place. Arrange 3 groups of 4 flats, 1 rod, and 2 unit blocks on the Decimal Place-Value Chart.

- **2 hundredths times 3 equals 6 hundredths, so the 6 belongs in the hundredths-place.**
- **1 tenth times 3 equals 3 tenths, so the 3 belongs in the tenths-place.**
- **4 ones times 3 equals 12 ones. 12 ones equals 1 ten and 2 ones, so the 1 belongs in the tens-place and 2 belongs in the ones-place.**

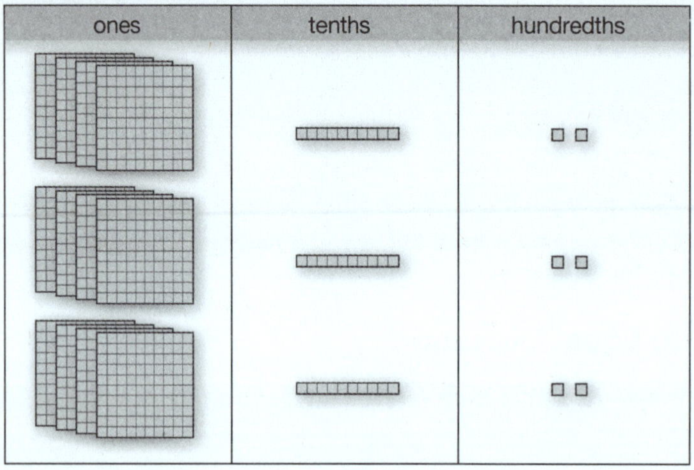

4 × 3 = 12 0.1 × 3 = 0.3 0.02 × 3 = 0.06

Stack the flats as needed to fit on the Decimal Place-Value Chart.

Point back to the matching addition problem in part A. **Multiplying 4.12 times 3 is just like adding 4.12 plus 4.12 plus 4.12.**

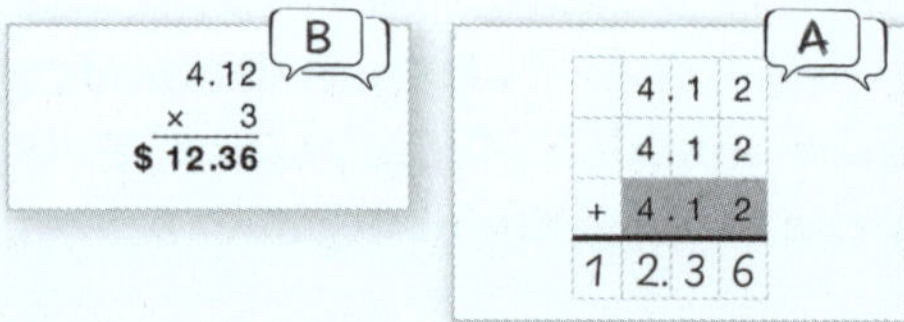

When we add decimals, we line up the decimal points so that we add the digits with the same place value. We add hundredths to hundredths, tenths to tenths, and ones to ones.

When we multiply a decimal by a whole number, we don't need to line up the decimal points. That's because the whole number simply tells us how many groups or copies of the decimal amount we have. In this problem, the 3 tells us that we have 3 groups of $4.12.

In the first practice problem, you multiply 3.94 times 2 to find how much 2 boxes of cereal cost. Have your child follow the steps to solve the problem. Use base-ten blocks to model the problem as needed. After your child solves it, point back at the matching addition problem in part A. **Whether you add or multiply, 2 boxes of cereal cost $7.88.**

In the second problem, each bag of sugar weighs 2.1 kilograms. So, we'll multiply 2.1 by 3 to find how much 3 bags weigh. After your child solves it, point back at the matching addition problem in part A. **How much do 3 bags of sugar weigh?** *6.3 kg.*

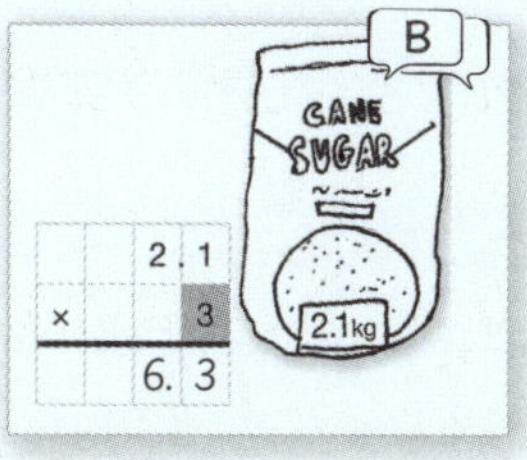

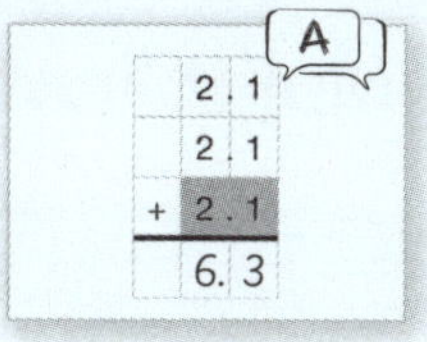

In the last problem, each spool of wire is 0.734 meters long. Let's multiply 0.734 by 4 to find out how much wire is on 4 spools. Remind your child as needed to ignore the leading zero. **If we wanted to use addition to check the multiplication, what addition problem would we use?** *0.734 plus 0.734 plus 0.734 plus 0.734.* (Your child does not need to find this sum.)

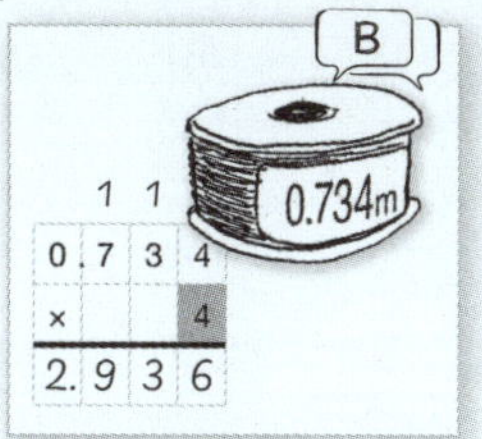

Activity (C): Play Decimal Multiplication Least to Greatest (1-Player Game)

To play this game, you roll a die. You write the number on the die as the missing factor in one of the multiplication problems and find the product. Your goal is to complete your game board so that the products are in order from least to greatest. Be careful, though! Once you write a factor, you can't change it.

Let's pretend I rolled a 6 and wrote it in the first problem on the left side of the gameboard. Do you think that would be a good play? Why or why not? *Sample answer: That wouldn't be a good play, because the product would be around 12. That means all the other products would have to be greater than 12.* **If you write 6 in the first problem, all the other problems' products have to be greater than that product. You probably want to write the 6 on the right side of the game board and wait until you roll smaller numbers for the left side.**

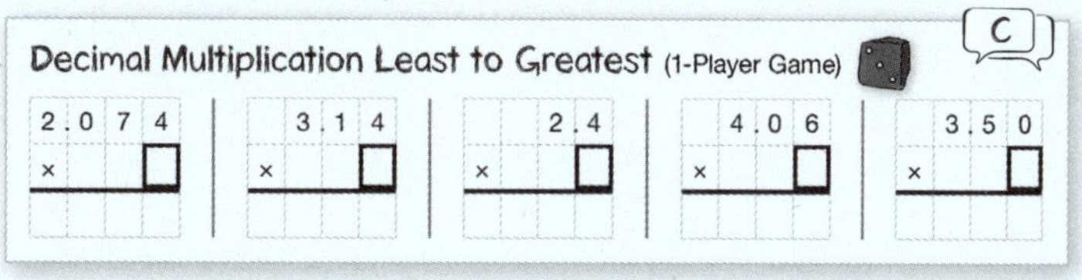

The goal of the game is for the products to end up in order from least to greatest (from left to right). So, it's better to place lower rolls on the left side of the board and higher rolls on the right side.

Have your child play Decimal Multiplication Least to Greatest. Encourage him to use estimation as he decides where to place the factors.

Decimal Multiplication Least to Greatest

Materials: Die

Object of the Game: Complete the multiplication problems so that the products are in order from least to greatest.

Roll the die. Write the number you roll as the missing factor in one of the multiplication problems. (If you roll a 1, roll again.) Then, multiply to find the product.

After you complete all the multiplication problems, count how many of the products are in order from least to greatest (with no out-of-order products between them). Use the scoring guide to see how well you did.

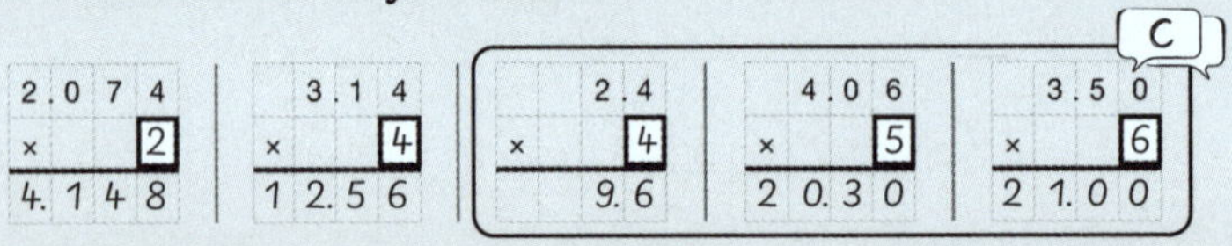

Sample completed game board. This player has 3 products in a row from least to greatest.

Independent Practice and Review

Have your child complete the Lesson 14.4 Practice and Review workbook pages.

Lesson 14.5
Multiply Decimals by 10, 100, or 1,000

Purpose	Materials
• Understand that multiplying a number by 10, 100, or 1,000 is the same as shifting the digits to the left on the place-value chart • Multiply decimals by 10, 100, or 1,000 by moving the decimal point	• Base-ten blocks • Decimal Place-Value Chart (Blackline Master 6)

Memory Work	
	• **What do we call the digits to the right of the decimal point?** *Decimal digits.* • **What do we call zeros that come before the first non-zero digit in a number?** *Leading zeros.* • **What do we call zeros that come after the final non-zero digit in a number?** *Trailing zeros.*

Warm-up (A): Multiply Whole Numbers and Decimals by 10, 100, and 1,000 on the Place-Value Chart

In Unit 3, we used the place-value chart to multiply numbers by 10, 100, and 1,000.

- **3 times 1 equals 3. What is 3 times 10?** *30.* Write 30 in the place-value chart as shown. **Multiplying by 10 is the same as shifting the 3 one place to the left on the place-value chart. We tack on 1 trailing zero so that the 3 is in the correct place.**
- **What is 3 times 100?** *300.* Write 300 in the place-value chart. **Multiplying by 100 is the same as multiplying by 10 twice. We shift the 3 two places to the left and tack on 2 trailing zeros.**
- **What is 3 times 1,000?** *3,000.* Write 3,000 in the chart. **Multiplying by 1,000 is the same as multiplying by 10 three times. We shift the 3 three places to the left and tack on 3 trailing zeros.**

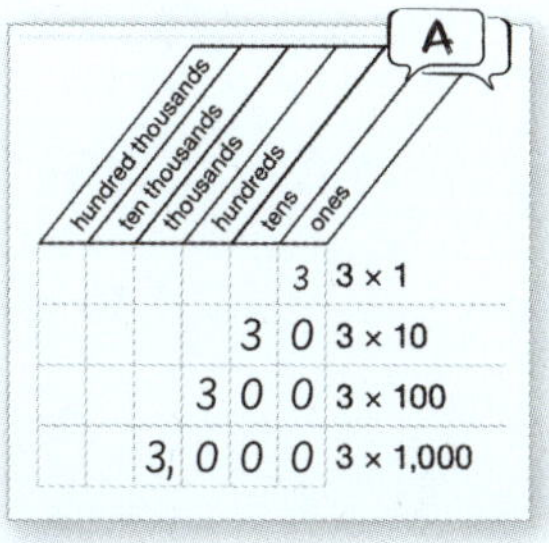

We can use the same approach to multiply a decimal number by 10, 100, or 1,000. We'll use base-ten blocks to see how.

Place 2 unit blocks in the hundredths-column on the Decimal Place-Value Chart. **We have 0.02, or 2 hundredths.**

0.02 times 1 equals 0.02. When we multiply 0.02 by 10, each hundredth is multiplied by 10. Each unit block becomes a rod. Shift the 2 unit blocks to the tenths-column and replace them with 2 rods. **We shift the 2 one place to the left. 0.02 times 10 equals 0.2.** Write 0.2 in the place-value chart.

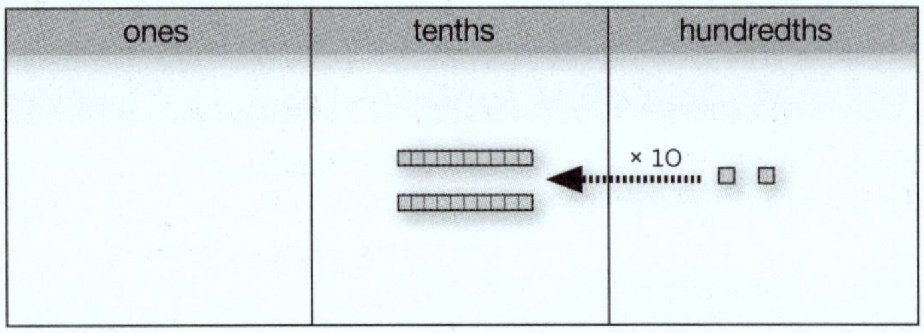

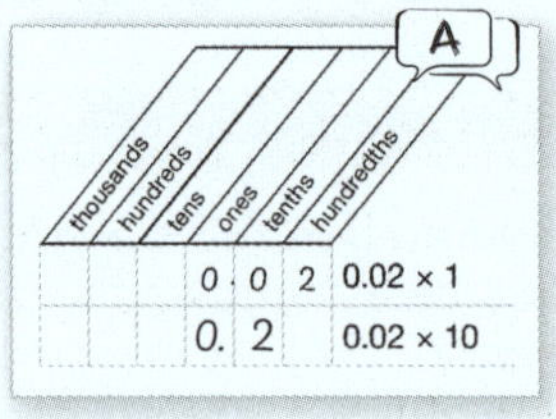

Clear the blocks off the chart. Then, place 2 unit blocks in the hundredths-column again. **When we multiply 0.02 by 100, each hundredth is multiplied by 100. Each unit block becomes a flat.** Shift the 2 unit blocks to the ones-column and replace them with 2 flats. **We shift the 2 two places to the left. 0.02 times 100 equals 2.** Write 2 in the place-value chart.

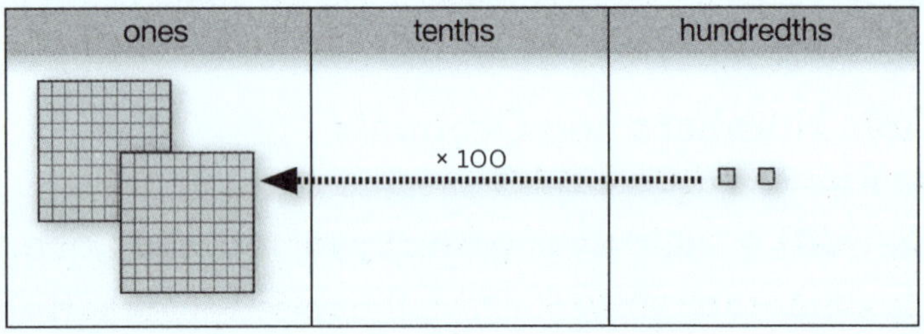

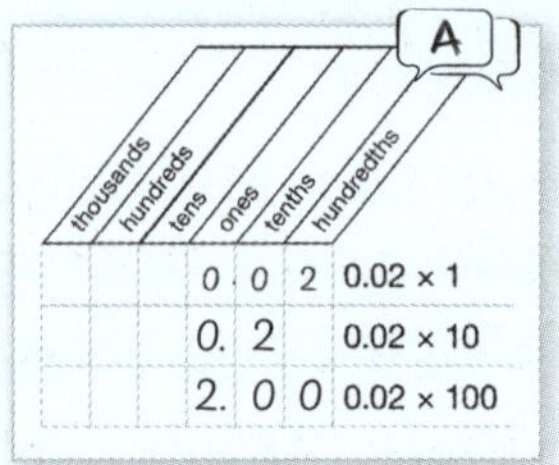

When we multiply 0.02 by 1,000, each hundredth is multiplied by 1,000. We shift the 2 three places to the left. 0.02 times 1,000 equals 20.

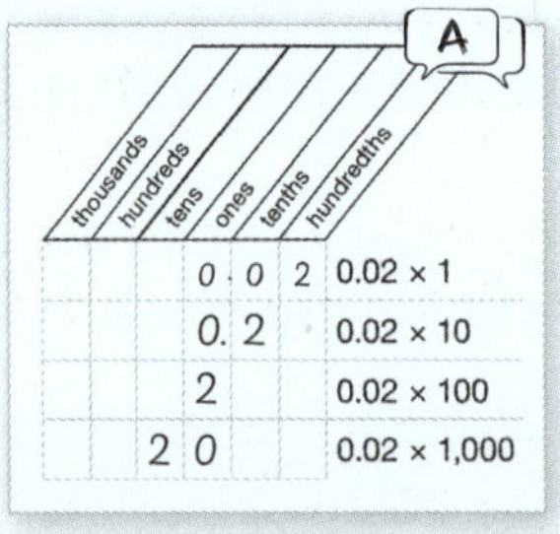

The base-ten blocks do not lend themselves well to modeling 0.02 times 1,000. To make this problem more concrete, use play money. Place 2 pennies, 2 dimes, 2 one-dollar bills, and 2 ten-dollar bills on the table. **If we multiply 2 pennies by 10 three times, we get 2 ten-dollar bills! 2 cents times 1,000 equals 20 dollars.**

Activity (B): Move the Decimal Point to Multiply Decimals by 10, 100, or 1,000

In the warm-up, you shifted the digits on the place-value chart to multiply numbers by 10, 100, or 1,000. In everyday life, we don't usually have a place-value chart handy if we need to mentally multiply a decimal by 10, 100, or 1,000. Instead, we use a shortcut. We move the decimal point instead! Have your child read the text box aloud.

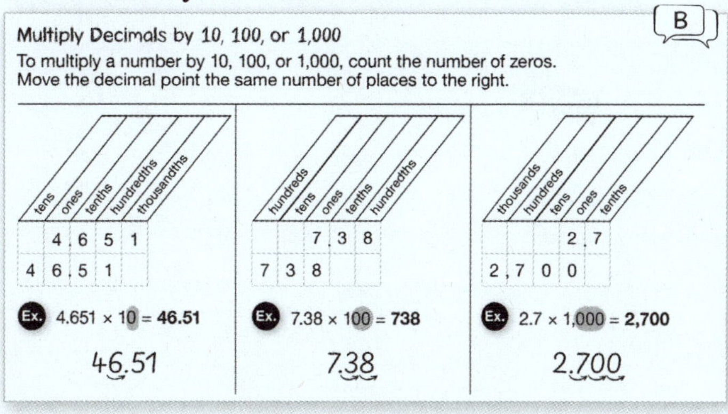

The first example shows how to multiply 4.651 times 10.

- **First, we copy the decimal number without the decimal point.**
- **Next, we count the number of zeros in 10, 100, or 1,000. 10 has 1 zero.**
- **Then, we put the pencil at the decimal point's original position, between the 4 and 6. 10 has 1 zero, so we move the pencil 1 place to the right and write the decimal point there.**

We could also use estimation to check that this answer makes sense. What's 4.65 rounded to the nearest whole number? *5.* **What's 5 times 10?** *50.* **46.51 is close to 50, so that's a reasonable answer.**

If we put the decimal point in the wrong place, we might get an answer of 4,651 or 0.4651. Those answers are very far away from our estimate, so we'd know we had the wrong answer.

Discuss the other examples in the same way.

- For 7.38 × 100, point out that you do not need to write a decimal point in the final answer: **738 is a whole number. Writing a decimal point after the 8 isn't necessary, since we already know what place each digit is in.**
- For 2.7 × 1,000, point out that you need to tack on two trailing zeros in the tens-place and ones-place: **We need to tack on trailing zeros in the tens-place and ones-place. Otherwise, the answer would look like 27.**

If your child has trouble understanding the idea of moving the decimal point, write the digits in each number on a piece of scrap paper. Write a decimal point on a small slip of paper and physically move the decimal point as you discuss the example problems.

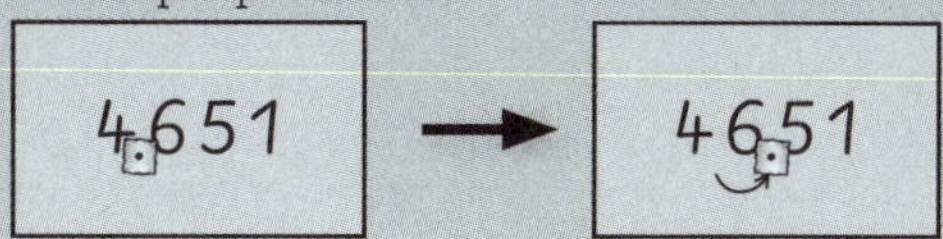

Point to the first column of practice problems. **Each bouncy ball costs $1.83. What's $1.83 rounded to the nearest dollar?** *$2.* **So, about how much do 10 bouncy balls cost?** *$20.* **100 bouncy balls?** *$200.* **1,000 bouncy balls?** *$2,000.* Have your child follow the steps to complete the problems. Repeat with the spool of ribbon and pack of cotton candy.

B

1.83 × 10 = 18.3

1.83 × 100 = 183

1.83 × 1,000 = 1,830

3.9 × 10 = 39

3.9 × 100 = 390

3.9 × 1,000 = 3,900

0.472 × 10 = 4.72

0.472 × 100 = 47.2

0.472 × 1,000 = 472

Your child may tack on a trailing zero to 18.3, since we typically write prices with 2 decimal digits. Either way is fine.

Independent Practice and Review

Have your child complete the Lesson 14.5 Practice and Review workbook pages.

Lesson 14.6
Multiply to Convert Metric Measurements

Purpose	Materials
• Review metric prefixes and conversion factors • Multiply by 10, 100, or 1,000 to convert measurements within the metric system	• None

Memory Work	
	• **How many millimeters equal 1 centimeter?** *10.* • **How many centimeters equal 1 meter?** *100.* • **How many meters equal 1 kilometer?** *1,000.* • **How many grams equal 1 kilogram?** *1,000.* • **How many milliliters equal 1 liter?** *1,000.*

In this lesson, your child will learn how to multiply by 10, 100, or 1,000 to convert from larger metric units to smaller metric units. He will learn how to divide to convert smaller units to larger units in Lesson 15.3.

Warm-up (A): Review Metric Prefixes and Conversion Factors

This chart shows the conversion factors for metric measurement units. Conversion factors are the numbers we multiply or divide by to convert measurements.

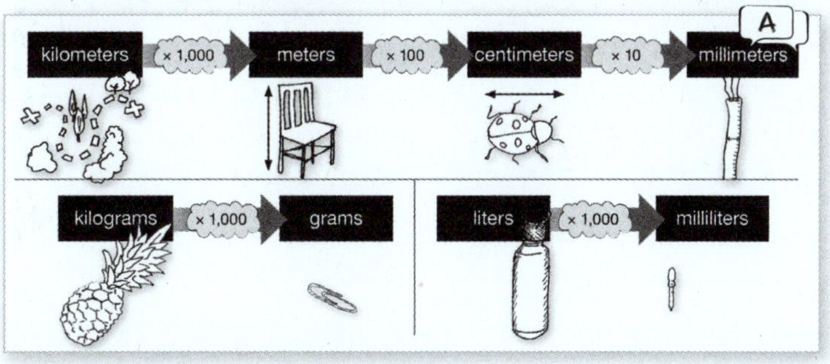

Use the following questions to discuss the chart.

- **The prefix *kilo-* means thousand. There are 1,000 meters in a kilometer. So, if we want to convert kilometers to meters, we multiply the number of kilometers by 1,000. 5 kilometers equal how many meters?** *5,000.*
- **The prefix *centi-* means hundredth. Each centimeter is one-hundredth of a meter, and there are 100 centimeters in a meter. To convert meters to centimeters, we multiply the number of meters by 100. 3 meters equal how many centimeters?** *300.*
- **The prefix *milli-* means thousandth. Each millimeter is one-thousandth of a meter. There are 10 millimeters in each centimeter. To convert centimeters to millimeters, we multiply the number of centimeters by 10. 15 centimeters equal how many millimeters?** *150.*
- **There are 1,000 grams in a kilogram. So, if we want to convert kilograms to grams, we multiply the number of kilograms by 1,000. 8 kilograms equal how many grams?** *8,000.*
- **Each milliliter is one-thousandth of a liter. There are 1,000 milliliters in each liter. To convert liters to milliliters, we multiply the number of liters by 1,000. 20 liters equal how many milliliters?** *20,000.*

Activity (B): Move the Decimal Point to Convert Metric Measures

In the last lesson, you learned how to move the decimal point to multiply decimals by 10, 100, or 1,000.

Today, you'll learn how to convert decimal measurements in the metric system. When we convert from a larger unit to a smaller unit in the metric system, we multiply by 10, 100, or 1,000. So, we can move the decimal point to perform the multiplication. Have your child read the text box aloud.

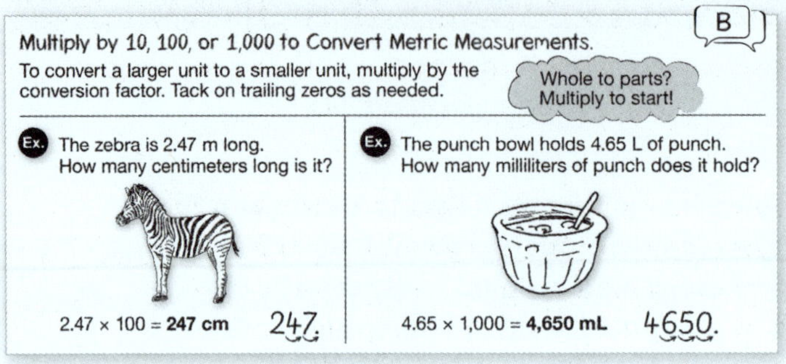

Use the following questions to discuss the examples.

- **The zebra is 2.47 meters long. How many centimeters are in 1 meter?** *100.* **So, we multiply by 100 to convert meters to centimeters.**
- **What's 2.47 times 100?** *247.* **We are multiplying by 100, so we move the decimal point 2 places to the right. The zebra is 247 centimeters long.**
- **The punch bowl holds 4.65 liters of punch. How many milliliters are in 1 liter?** *1,000.* **So, we multiply by 1,000 to convert liters to milliliters.**
- **What's 4.65 times 1,000?** *4,650.* **We are multiplying by 1,000, so we move the decimal point 3 places to the right. The punch bowl holds 4,650 milliliters of punch.**

Have your child complete the practice problems. Have him write out a multiplication problem for each conversion and then move the decimal point to find the answer. If he has trouble remembering the conversion factors, encourage him to use the chart in part A.

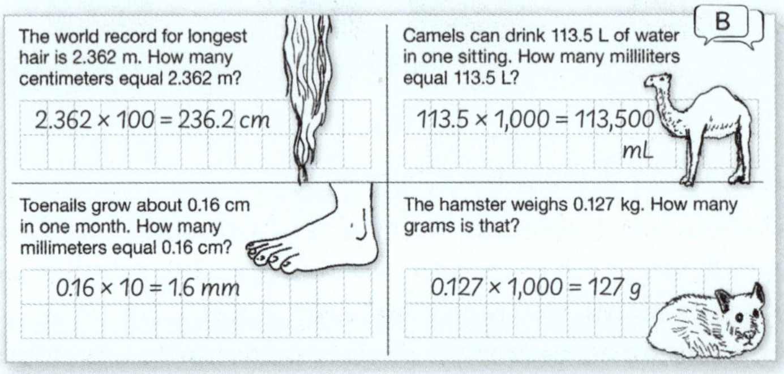

Independent Practice and Review

Have your child complete the Lesson 14.6 Practice and Review workbook pages.

Lesson 14.7
Multiply Decimals by Whole Numbers with Trailing Zeros

Purpose	Materials
• Practice multiplying whole numbers by numbers with trailing zeros • Use the written algorithm to multiply decimals by whole numbers with trailing zeros	• None

Memory Work
- **What is an equilateral triangle?** *A triangle with 3 equal sides.*
- **What is an isosceles triangle?** *A triangle with 2 equal sides.*
- **What is a scalene triangle?** *A triangle with no equal sides.*

Warm-up (A): Review How to Use the Multiplication Algorithm to Multiply Numbers with Trailing Zeros

Earlier in the year, you learned how to multiply whole numbers by numbers with trailing zeros. You count the number of trailing zeros in the bottom number and write the same number of zeros in the product. Then, you multiply the non-zero digits like usual.

Point to 47 × 60. **How many trailing zeros does 60 have?** *1.* **So, write 1 zero in the product. Then, multiply 47 times 6 like usual.** Have your child find 47 × 60. Then, have her find the other products in the same way.

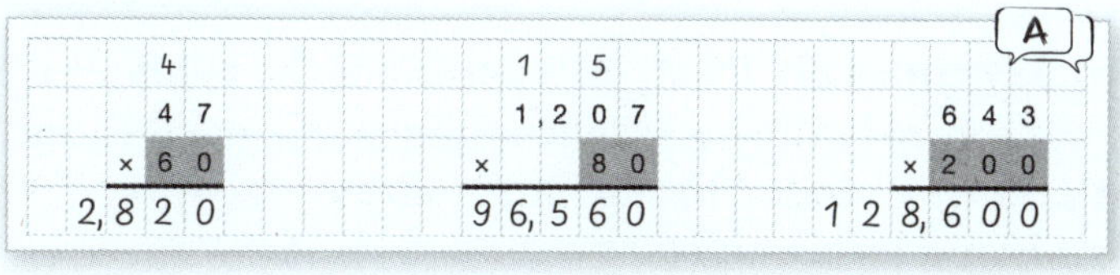

Activity (B): Multiply Decimals by Whole Numbers with Trailing Zeros

Today, you'll learn how to use the written multiplication algorithm to multiply decimals by whole numbers with trailing zeros. Just like in Lesson 14.4, you multiply like usual and then decide where to put the decimal point. Have your child read the text box aloud.

B

Multiply Decimals by Whole Numbers with Trailing Zeros

1. Multiply like usual. Ignore any leading zeros.
2. Count the decimal digits in the decimal factor.
3. Place the decimal point in the product so the product has the same number of decimal digits as the decimal factor.

Ex. Each rubber duck costs $2.89. How much do 30 rubber ducks cost?

```
   2 2
   2.89
 ×   30
 $86.70
```

Read aloud the example problem. **We need to multiply $2.89 times 30 to find the cost of 30 rubber ducks.**

- **First, we multiply the digits like usual with the multiplication algorithm.**
- **Then, we count the decimal digits in the decimal factor. How many decimal digits does 2.89 have?** *2.*
- **2.89 has 2 decimal digits, so the product must have 2 decimal digits, too. We place the decimal point between the 6 and 7 so that the product has 2 decimal digits. $2.89 times 30 equals $86.70. 30 rubber ducks cost $86.70.**

We could also use estimation to check that this answer makes sense. What's \$2.89 rounded to the nearest dollar? *\$3.* **What's \$3 times 30?** *\$90.* **\$86.70 is close to \$90, so that's a reasonable answer.**

Another way to understand why this process works is to think about cents. \$2.89 equals 289 cents. 289 cents times 30 equals 8,670 cents, and 8,670 cents equals \$86.70.

Show your child the practice problems in part B. **These problems have the same digits as the problems in part A. You can use the whole-number products from part A to solve them.**

> Since your child already knows how to perform multi-digit multiplication, these exercises focus on placing the decimal point in the correct spot. On the practice page, your child will solve problems that require her to both multiply and place the decimal point.

The first problem is 4.7 times 60. First, let's estimate the product. What's 4.7 rounded to the nearest whole number? *5.* **What's 5 times 60?** *300.* **So, the product should be around 300.**

Now, let's find the exact answer. First, we multiply like usual. In part A, you found that 47 times 60 equals 2,820. Write 2820 as the product. (Do not write a comma.) **I don't write a comma, because I'm not sure what place each digit is in yet.**

How many decimal digits are in the decimal factor? *1.* **So, the answer should have one decimal digit.** Write a decimal point between the 2 and 0 as shown. **What's 4.7 times 60?** *282.0.* **We estimated the answer would be around 300, so that's reasonable.**

The next problem is 0.047 times 60. First, let's estimate the product again. The greatest place in 0.047 that's not a zero is the hundredths-place. So, we'll round 0.047 to the hundredths-place. What's 0.047 rounded to the hundredths-place? *0.05.* **What's 0.05 times 60?** *3.* **So, the product should be around 3.**

> If your child has trouble mentally multiplying 0.05 times 60, remind her how to use place-value thinking to find the answer: **5 hundredths times 60 equals 300 hundredths, or 3.**

Have your child follow the steps to find 0.047 × 60. Repeat with 0.47 × 60.

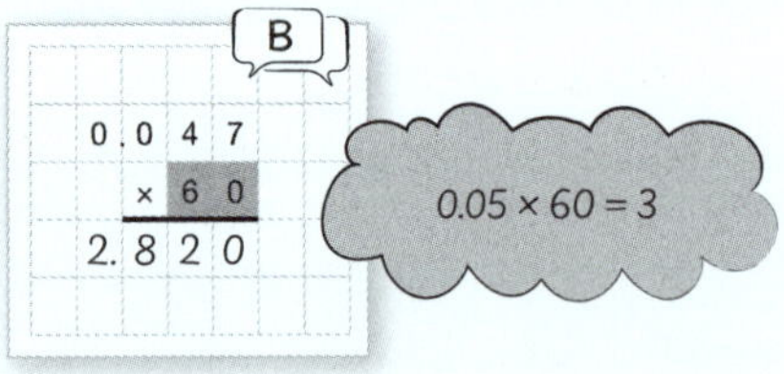

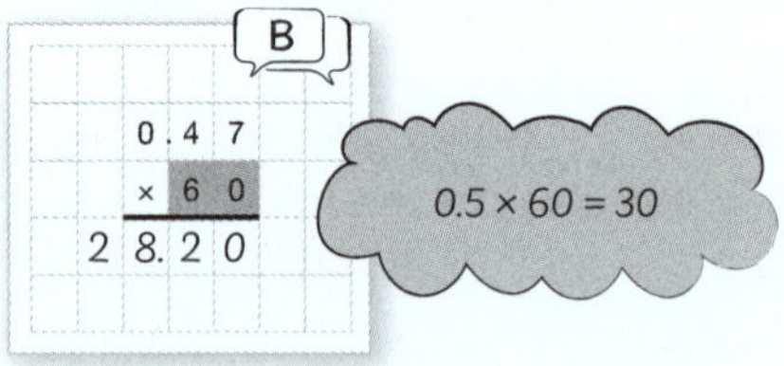

Have your child complete the other practice problems in the same way. Have her work down each column, and have her estimate each product (by rounding the decimal to the greatest non-zero place) before she finds the exact product.

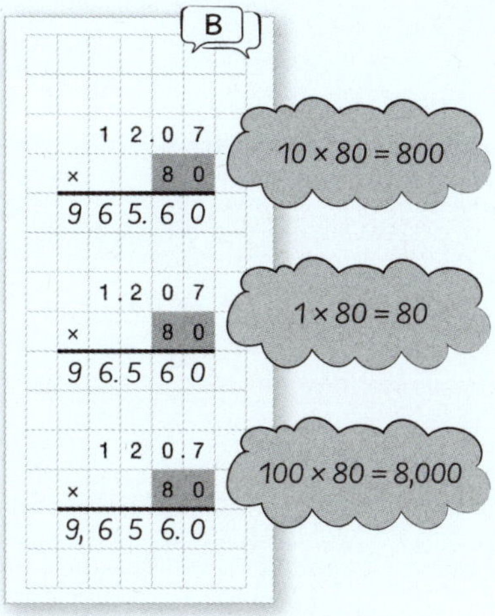

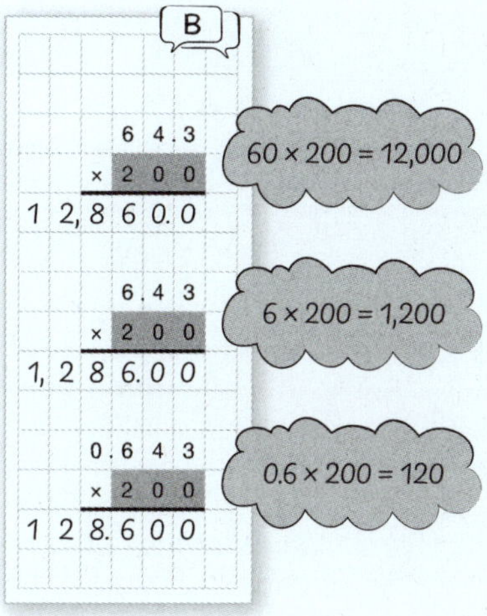

Independent Practice and Review

Have your child complete the Lesson 14.7 Practice and Review workbook pages.

Lesson 14.8
Multiply Decimals by Two-Digit Whole Numbers

Purpose	Materials
• Practice using the multiplication algorithm to multiply multi-digit numbers • Use the multiplication algorithm to multiply decimals by whole numbers	• None

Memory Work	
	• **What do we call the digits to the right of the decimal point?** *Decimal digits.* • **What do we call zeros that come before the first non-zero digit in a number?** *Leading zeros.* • **What do we call zeros that come after the final non-zero digit in a number?** *Trailing zeros.*

Warm-up (A): Review How to Multiply Multi-Digit Numbers with the Multiplication Algorithm

In Unit 3, we reviewed how to use the multiplication algorithm to multiply numbers with 2 or more digits. Have your child multiply to solve the problems in part A.

A

2 4 1	1 4
482	3,208
× 35	× 16
2410	19248
+ 14460	+ 32080
16,870	51,328

Remind your child as needed of the steps in the whole-number multiplication algorithm.

- Multiply the top number by the ones-place of the bottom number. Ignore the digit in the bottom number's tens-place for now.
- Write a zero in the ones-place of the second partial product.
- Multiply the top number by the tens-place of the bottom number. Ignore the digit in the bottom number's ones-place.
- Add the two partial products.

Activity (B): Multiply Decimals by Whole Numbers with the Multiplication Algorithm

Today, you'll learn how to use the written multiplication algorithm to multiply decimals by whole numbers. Just like in the last lesson, you multiply like usual and then decide where to put the decimal point.

Read aloud the first example problem. **We multiply $5.42 times 12 to find the cost of 12 baseballs.**

- **First, we multiply the digits like usual with the multiplication algorithm.**
- **Then, we count the decimal digits in the decimal factor. How many decimal digits does 5.42 have?** *2.*

- **5.42 has 2 decimal digits, so the product must have 2 decimal digits, too. We place the decimal point so that the product has 2 decimal digits. $5.42 times 12 equals $65.04. 12 baseballs cost $65.04.**

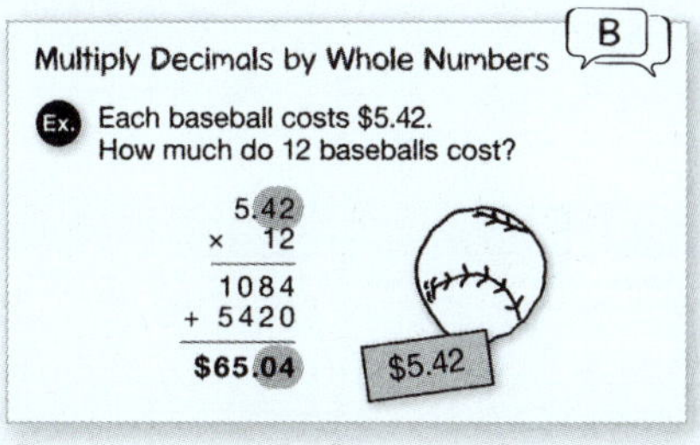

Does that seem like a reasonable answer? Why or why not? *Sample answer: Yes, because 5 times 12 is 60.* **$5.42 rounded to the nearest dollar is $5. $5 times 12 is $60, so that seems like a reasonable answer.**

> If your child needs a more concrete way to understand why this process works, encourage him to think about the equivalent problem with cents instead of dollars. **$5.42 equals 542 cents. 542 cents times 12 equals 6,504 cents, or $65.04.**

Read aloud the second example problem. **Each baseball only weighs 0.079 kilograms! That's only 79 thousandths of a kilogram. In the U.S. customary system, that's a little less than 3 ounces.** Discuss the example problem in the same way as you discussed the first example.

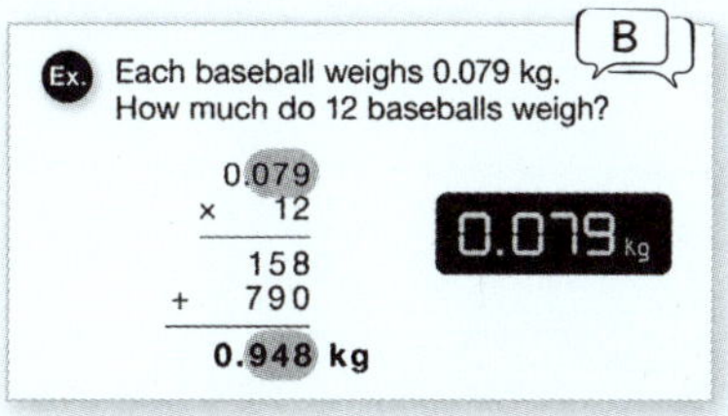

> These printed examples do not show the traded digits so that your child can focus on counting the decimal digits.

Activity (C): Play Pop the Product (1-Player Game)

Explain to your child how to play Pop the Product. Then, have him complete this one-player game. Encourage him to use estimation as he places the factors in the problems.

Pop the Product

Materials: None

Object of the Game: Write factors in the multiplication problems so that each problem yields the target product in the balloon above it.

For each problem, choose a number from the boxes on the left. Write the number in a multiplication problem so that the problem's product matches the description in the balloon above it. Then, solve the problem to check whether you are correct. If you are correct, draw an X on the balloon to "pop" it. Repeat until you've popped all the balloons.

Directions continued on next page.

Answer Key:

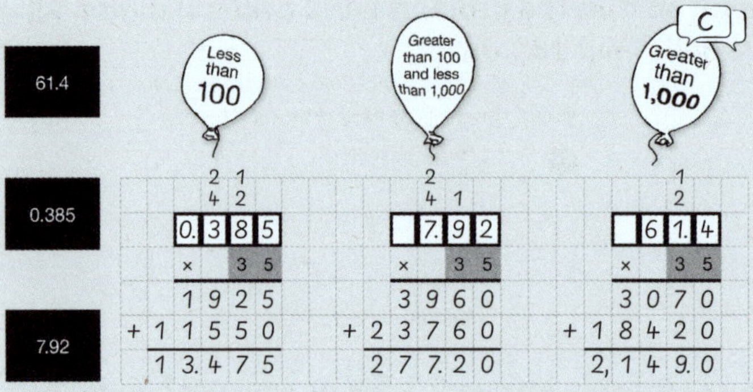

Independent Practice and Review

Have your child complete the Lesson 14.8 Practice and Review workbook pages.

Your child already solved many multi-digit multiplication problems on the Lesson Activities page, so the Practice page mostly focuses on placing the decimal point in the correct position and estimating products.

Lesson 14.9
Enrichment (Optional)

Purpose

- Practice memory work
- Learn mental math tricks
- Multiply decimals to find the cost of making a large batch of food
- Summarize what your child has learned and assess your child's progress

Materials

- *How Many Guinea Pigs Can Fit on a Plane?: Answers to Your Most Clever Math Questions*, by Laura Overdeck
- Grocery store flyer or website
- Family recipe that makes a large batch

Warm-up: Review Memory Work

Quiz your child on any of the memory work items that she struggled with during this unit.

Math Picture Book: *How Many Guinea Pigs Can Fit on a Plane?*

Read pages 124-125 in *How Many Guinea Pigs Can Fit on a Plane?*

Enrichment Activity: Find the Total Cost of a Large-Batch Recipe

In everyday life, we often multiply decimals to figure out how much things cost. If we buy more than one of an item, we multiply the number of items by the price of each item to find the total cost.

Show your child a family recipe that makes a large batch. (Or, use the recipe below.) **Let's find out how much it costs to make this recipe.** Find the price of each item in a grocery store flyer or on a grocery store website.

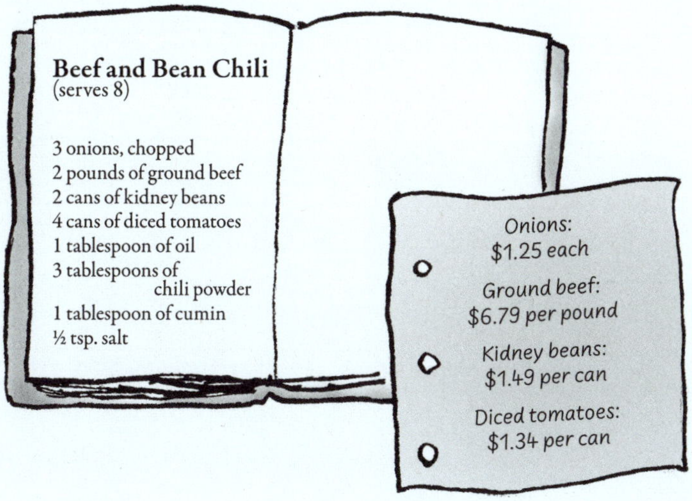

Then, have your child find the total cost of making the recipe. (Ignore small quantities of pantry staples like oil or spices.) Encourage her to use multiplication to find the cost of multiples of the same item. Then, have her add to find the total cost.

<u>*Onions*</u>

```
   1
  1.25
×    3
------
 $3.75
```

<u>*Ground beef*</u>

```
   1 1
   6.79
×     2
-------
 $13.58
```

<u>*Kidney beans*</u>

```
   1
  1.49
×    2
------
 $2.98
```

<u>*Diced tomatoes*</u>

```
   1 1
   1.34
×     4
-------
  $5.36
```

```
   3.75
  13.58
   2.98
×  5.36
-------
 $25.67
```

Unit Wrap-Up

Have your child complete the Unit 14 Wrap-Up.

Unit 14 Answer Key

14.1 Practice

Practice Complete the chart.

Standard Form	Number of Decimal Digits	Number of Leading Zeros	Number of Trailing Zeros
0.850	3	1	1
8.050	3	0	1
0.008	3	3	0
80.50	2	0	1
0.8	1	1	0
0.085	3	2	0
0.85	2	1	0
0.800	3	1	2

Complete the circles with <, >, or =.

0.8 (<) 0.85	0.85 (=) 0.850	0.8 (>) 0.085
8.050 (<) 80.50	0.085 (<) 0.850	0.800 (=) 0.8

Write a decimal point in each number to match the description.

Has 1 decimal digit	4 1 8.3	Has 1 decimal digit	7 0 9.0
Has 2 decimal digits	4 1.8 3	Has 2 decimal digits	7 0.9 0
Has 3 decimal digits	4.1 8 3	Has 3 decimal digits	7.0 9 0
Equals 3	3.0 0 0	Is less than 7 and greater than 6	6.1 3 5
Equals 30	3 0.0 0	Is less than 70 and greater than 60	6 1.3 5
Equals 300	3 0 0.0	Is less than 700 and greater than 600	6 1 3.5

14.1 Review

Review Find the products.

$42 \times 3 = 126$ $\quad$ $215 \times 7 = 1{,}505$ $\quad$ $1{,}407 \times 90 = 126{,}630$ $\quad$ $864 \times 200 = 172{,}800$

Rewrite each problem as a multiplication problem and solve. Simplify your answer if needed.

$\frac{5}{8} \div 2$	$\frac{4}{5} \div 3$	$\frac{9}{10} \div 3$
$\frac{5}{8} \times \frac{1}{2} = \frac{5}{16}$	$\frac{4}{5} \times \frac{1}{3} = \frac{4}{15}$	$\frac{9}{10} \times \frac{1}{3} = \frac{9}{30} = \frac{3}{10}$
$3 \div \frac{1}{8}$	$4 \div \frac{1}{3}$	$6 \div \frac{1}{4}$
$3 \times 8 = 24$	$4 \times 3 = 12$	$6 \times 4 = 24$

Write each number in the place-value chart.

tens	ones	tenths	hundredths	thousandths	
	0	8			8 tenths
	0	0	5		5 hundredths
	0	0	0	9	9 thousandths
	0	4	5		45 hundredths
	0	0	3	8	38 thousandths
	0	9	9	9	999 thousandths
	7				7 ones
7	0				7 tens

Find the missing angles in each triangle.

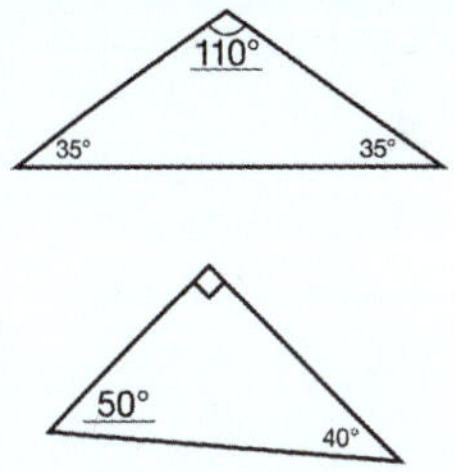

14.2 Practice

Practice Complete the chart. Color the decimal squares to match the rest of the row.

Decimal Squares	Words	Fraction	Mixed Number (if applicable)	Decimal
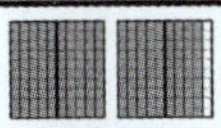	19 tenths	$\frac{19}{10}$	$1\frac{9}{10}$	1.9
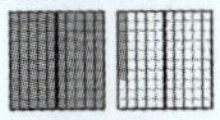	107 hundredths	$\frac{107}{100}$	$1\frac{7}{100}$	1.07
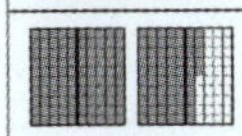	165 hundredths	$\frac{165}{100}$	$1\frac{65}{100}$	1.65
	500 thousandths	$\frac{500}{1,000}$	×	0.500
	70 thousandths	$\frac{70}{1,000}$	×	0.070

Write each number in the place-value chart.

tens	ones	tenths	hundredths	thousandths	
	0	0	0	8	8 thousandths
	0	0	8		8 hundredths
	0	8			8 tenths
	0	7			7 tenths
	7				70 tenths
7	0				700 tenths

tens	ones	tenths	hundredths	thousandths	
	0	0	4	5	45 thousandths
	0	4	5		45 hundredths
	4	5			45 tenths
	0	9	5		95 hundredths
	9	5			95 tenths
9	5				95 ones

14.2 Review

Review Find the products.

$$\begin{array}{r} 72 \\ \times\ 31 \\ \hline 72 \\ +\ 2{,}160 \\ \hline 2{,}232 \end{array} \qquad \begin{array}{r} 485 \\ \times\ 63 \\ \hline 1{,}455 \\ +\ 29{,}100 \\ \hline 30{,}555 \end{array}$$

Match equal numbers.

$\frac{1}{4}$ — 0.25
$\frac{1}{2}$ — 0.5
$\frac{3}{4}$ — 0.75

Draw a line to connect the numbers in order from Start to End. Follow the rule.

Rule: Add 0.3 (Start → 0.3 → 0.6 → 0.9 → 1.2 → 1.5 → 1.8 → 2.1 → 2.4 → 2.7 → 3.0 END)

0.3	0.4	0.5	2.9	3.1
0.6	0.7	1.3	2.7	3.0
0.9	1.1	2.1	2.4	2.8
1.2	1.5	1.8	2.0	2.6
1.4	1.7	1.9	2.2	2.5

Rule: Add 0.05 (Start → 0.05 → 0.10 → 0.15 → 0.20 → 0.25 → 0.30 → 0.35 → 0.40 → 0.45 → 0.50 END)

0.05	0.01	0.25	0.30	3.5
0.10	0.15	0.20	0.35	3.0
1.5	0.02	2.5	0.40	4.5
0.70	0.75	3.0	0.45	0.50
0.08	0.09	0.80	0.05	0.65

Find the products. Write your answers in simplest form. If the answer is an improper fraction, convert it to a mixed number or whole number.

$3 \times \frac{1}{10}$	$3 \times \frac{3}{10}$	$3 \times \frac{7}{10}$
$\frac{3}{1} \times \frac{1}{10} = \frac{3}{10}$	$\frac{3}{1} \times \frac{3}{10} = \frac{9}{10}$	$\frac{3}{1} \times \frac{7}{10} = \frac{21}{10} = 2\frac{1}{10}$
$3 \times \frac{1}{100}$	$3 \times \frac{3}{100}$	$3 \times \frac{7}{100}$
$\frac{3}{1} \times \frac{1}{100} = \frac{3}{100}$	$\frac{3}{1} \times \frac{3}{100} = \frac{9}{100}$	$\frac{3}{1} \times \frac{7}{100} = \frac{21}{100}$

Unit 14 Answer Key

14.3 Practice

Roll and Flip (2-Player Game)

Player 1	Player 2
___ × ___ = ___	___ × ___ = ___
___ × ___ = ___	___ × ___ = ___
___ × ___ = ___	___ × ___ = ___
___ × ___ = ___	___ × ___ = ___
Sum: ___	Sum: ___

Practice Find the product.

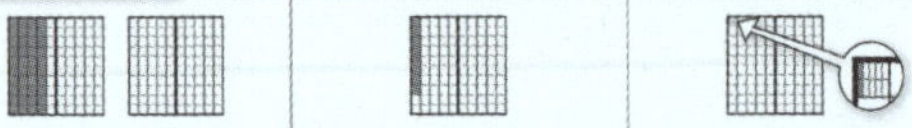

3 × 0.4 = 1.2 | 4 × 0.08 = 0.32 | 4 × 0.002 = 0.008

Circle the problems that equal the number in the star.

1.5	0.24	2	0.030
(5 × 0.3)	8 × 0.3	(4 × 0.5)	(6 × 0.005)
5 × 0.03	(8 × 0.03)	4 × 5	3 × 0.1
3 × 5	(4 × 0.06)	5 × 0.04	(3 × 0.01)
(3 × 0.5)	4 × 0.6	(5 × 0.4)	(5 × 0.006)

Solve. Write the equations you use.

Each bag of pretzels weighs 0.9 lb. How much do 5 bags of pretzels weigh?

5 × 0.9 = 4.5 lb.

The red wire is 0.07 m long. The blue wire is 4 times as long as the red wire. How long is the blue wire?

4 × 0.07 = 0.28 m

14.3 Review

Review Circle the best estimate for each sum or difference. You do not need to find the exact sum or difference.

3.07 + 6.894	0.07 + 0.935	0.007 + 0.001
8 (10) 12	0 (1) 2	(0) 1 2

6.1 − 1.87	5.394 − 0.43	3.13 − 2.977
3 (4) 5	3 4 (5)	(0) 1 2

Choose the more sensible measurement for each item.

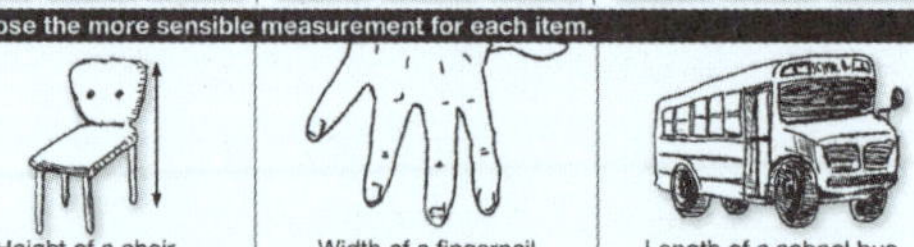

Height of a chair	Width of a fingernail	Length of a school bus
0.97 cm (0.97 m)	0.7 mm (0.7 cm)	(12.1 m) 12.1 km

Capacity of a water bottle	Weight of a kangaroo	Weight of a banana
1.1 mL (1.1 L)	88.4 g (88.4 kg)	0.115 g (0.115 kg)

Solve. Write the equations you use. Simplify your answer if needed.

Sonia has $\frac{1}{2}$ L of paint. She divides the paint equally into 5 smaller containers. How much paint is in each container?

$\frac{1}{2} \div 5$

$\frac{1}{2} \times \frac{1}{5} = \frac{1}{10}$ L

Ben has a board 5 m long. He saws the board into pieces that are each $\frac{1}{2}$ m long. How many pieces does he make?

$5 \div \frac{1}{2}$

5 × 2 = 10 pieces

14.4 Practice

Practice Find the product.

3.2 × 8 = 25.6	7.32 × 5 = 36.60	0.68 × 7 = 4.76	71.28 × 4 = 285.12
9.1 × 6 = 54.6	0.16 × 8 = 1.28	54.9 × 9 = 494.1	2.195 × 3 = 6.585

Round the decimal to the nearest whole number and estimate the product. Then, circle the better estimate for each problem. You do not need to find the exact product.

5 × 3.27	4 × 6.9	8 × 1.704
(15) 20	24 (28)	8 (16)

2 × 9.101	6 × 5.1	5 × 4.632
(18) 20	(30) 36	20 (25)

Solve. Write the equations you use.

The Gateway bike trail is 4.7 km long. The Torpedo trail is 5 times as long as the Gateway trail. How long is the Torpedo trail?

4.7 × 5 = 23.5 km

Each t-shirt costs $14.79. How much do 8 t-shirts cost?

14.79 × 8 = $118.32

14.4 Review

Review Find the product. Write your answers in simplest form. If the answer is an improper fraction, convert it to a mixed number or whole number.

$10 \times \frac{1}{10}$	$10 \times \frac{1}{100}$	$10 \times \frac{1}{1{,}000}$
$\frac{10}{1} \times \frac{1}{10} = \frac{10}{10} = 1$	$\frac{10}{1} \times \frac{1}{100} = \frac{10}{100} = \frac{1}{10}$	$\frac{10}{1} \times \frac{1}{1{,}000} = \frac{10}{1{,}000} = \frac{1}{100}$
$100 \times \frac{1}{10}$	$100 \times \frac{1}{100}$	$100 \times \frac{1}{1{,}000}$
$\frac{100}{1} \times \frac{1}{10} = \frac{100}{10} = 10$	$\frac{100}{1} \times \frac{1}{100} = 1$	$\frac{100}{1} \times \frac{1}{1{,}000} = \frac{100}{1{,}000} = \frac{1}{10}$

Label the numbers on the number line.

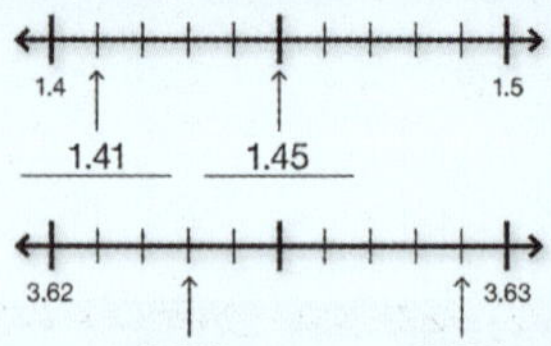

1.4 — 1.41, 1.45 — 1.5

3.62 — 3.623, 3.629 — 3.63

Write 10, 100, or 1,000 in the blank to make the equations true.

47 × 10 = 470
47 × 1,000 = 47,000
47 × 100 = 4,700
206 × 100 = 20,600
206 × 1,000 = 206,000
206 × 10 = 2,060

Write whether each triangle is equilateral, isosceles, or scalene. Then, write whether each triangle is acute, right, or obtuse.

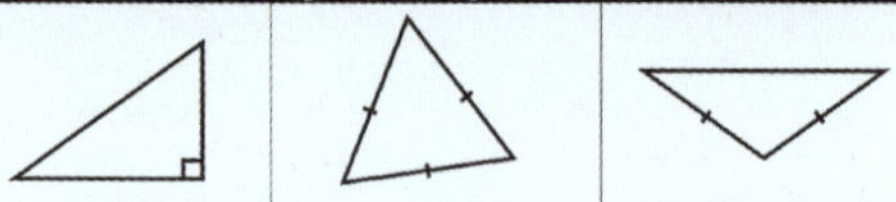

scalene	equilateral	isosceles
right	acute	obtuse

Unit 14 Answer Key

14.5 Practice

Practice Write the products on the place-value chart.

thousands	hundreds	tens	ones	tenths	hundredths	
			2.	0	7	2.07 × 1
		2	0.	7		2.07 × 10
	2	0	7			2.07 × 100
2,	0	7	0			2.07 × 1,000

hundreds	tens	ones	tenths	hundredths	thousandths	
		0.	6	0	1	0.601 × 1
		6.	0	1		0.601 × 10
	6	0.	1			0.601 × 100
6	0	1				0.601 × 1,000

Move the decimal point to find the product.

4.325 × 10 = 43.25
4.325 × 100 = 432.5
4.325 × 1,000 = 4,325

0.75 × 10 = 7.5
0.75 × 100 = 75
0.75 × 1,000 = 750

3.5 × 10 = 35
3.5 × 100 = 350
3.5 × 1,000 = 3,500

Write 10, 100, or 1,000 to complete the equations.

4.1 × 10 = 41
0.97 × 1,000 = 970
6.132 × 10 = 61.32

★ 0.004 × 1,000 = 4
★ 0.004 × 10 = 0.04
★ 0.004 × 100 = 0.4

Solve. Write the equations you use.

Carpenter ants are about 0.9 cm long. If 100 carpenter ants lined up (without any gaps between them), how many centimeters long would the line be?

0.9 × 100 = 90 cm

A paper clip is 2.8 cm long. If you lined up 1,000 paper clips (without any overlaps or gaps between them), how many centimeters long would the line be?

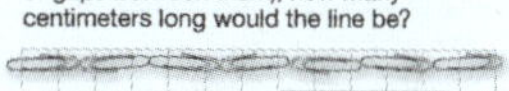

2.8 × 1,000 = 2,800 cm

14.5 Review

Review Complete the charts.

cm	mm
1	10
7	70
25	250
80	800
104	1,040
290	2,900

m	cm
1	100
4	400
8	800
11	1,100
250	25,000
450	45,000

kg	g
1	1,000
3	3,000
15	15,000
36	36,000
90	90,000
155	155,000

Write a fraction to complete each division problem. If needed, simplify the fraction, or convert to a whole number or mixed number.

$3 \div 4 = \frac{3}{4}$

$1 \div 6 = \frac{1}{6}$

$5 \div 5 = \frac{5}{5} = 1$

$4 \div 3 = \frac{4}{3} = 1\frac{1}{3}$

$6 \div 1 = \frac{6}{1} = 6$

$0 \div 5 = \frac{0}{5} = 0$

Use bar models to solve. Write the equations you use.

Cameron bought a bike lock and bike helmet. The lock cost \$18. It cost $\frac{3}{5}$ as much as the helmet. How much did the helmet cost?

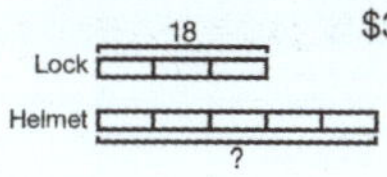

\$30

18 ÷ 3 = 6

6 × 5 = 30

Helmet: \$30

How much did Cameron spend in all?

\$48

30 + 18 = 48

14.6 Practice

Practice Complete the charts. Move the decimal point to multiply each number by the conversion factor.

cm (× 10)	mm
30	300
6	60
2.5	25
0.7	7
0.34	3.4
0.08	0.8

m (× 100)	cm
25	2,500
9	900
1.89	189
0.4	40
0.07	7
0.078	7.8

km (× 1,000)	m
5	5,000
3.186	3,186
3.15	3,150
3.1	3,100
0.652	652
0.004	4

kg (× 1,000)	g
38	38,000
16.357	16,357
1.5	1,500
0.892	892
0.49	490
0.4	400

L (× 1,000)	mL
2	2,000
3.7	3,700
0.65	650
0.081	81
0.07	70
0.001	1

Solve. Write the equations you use.

The rhino's horn is 0.87 m. How many centimeters equal 0.87 m?

0.87 × 100 = 87 cm

The giraffe is 5.08 m tall. How many centimeters equal 5.08 m?

5.08 × 100 = 508 cm

The poison dart frog weighs 0.003 kg. How many grams equal 0.003 kg?

0.003 × 1,000 = 3 g

The meerkat weighs 0.86 kg. How many grams equal 0.86 kg?

0.86 × 1,000 = 860 g

14.6 Review

Review Rewrite as a multiplication problem and solve.

$\frac{1}{5} \div 4$

$\frac{1}{5} \times \frac{1}{4} = \frac{1}{20}$

$4 \div \frac{1}{5}$

$4 \times 5 = 20$

$\frac{1}{6} \div 2$

$\frac{1}{6} \times \frac{1}{2} = \frac{1}{12}$

$2 \div \frac{1}{6}$

$2 \times 6 = 12$

$\frac{1}{4} \div 3$

$\frac{1}{4} \times \frac{1}{3} = \frac{1}{12}$

$3 \div \frac{1}{4}$

$3 \times 4 = 12$

Complete.

317 × 10 = 3,170
317 × 100 = 31,700
317 × 1,000 = 317,000

3.17 × 10 = 31.7
3.17 × 100 = 317
3.17 × 1,000 = 3,170

0.317 × 10 = 3.17
0.317 × 100 = 31.7
0.317 × 1,000 = 317

Find the missing angles.

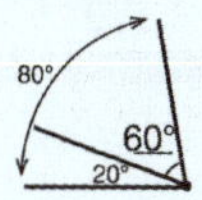

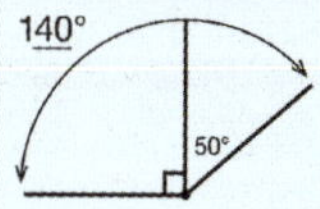

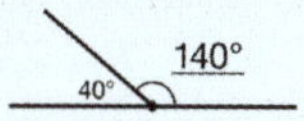

Find the perimeter and area.

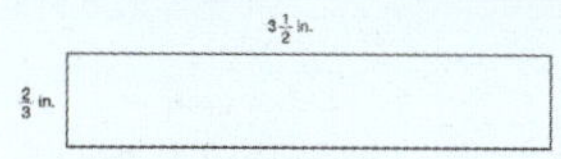

Perimeter: $8\frac{1}{3}$ in.

Area: $2\frac{1}{3}$ sq. in.

$3\frac{1}{2} + 3\frac{1}{2} + \frac{2}{3} + \frac{2}{3} = 8\frac{1}{3}$

$\frac{2}{3} \times 3\frac{1}{2}$

$\frac{2}{3} \times \frac{7}{2} = \frac{14}{6} = 2\frac{2}{6} = 2\frac{1}{3}$

Unit 14 Answer Key

14.7 Practice

Practice Find the product.

- 0.91 × 70 = 63.70
- 31.04 × 60 = 1,862.40
- 27.1 × 800 = 21,680.0
- 3.8 × 90 = 342.0
- 7.016 × 40 = 280.640
- 0.084 × 500 = 42.000

Write the decimal point in the correct position in these products.

- 0.29 × 70 = 20.30
- 4.518 × 90 = 406.620
- 0.738 × 200 = 147.600
- 8.6 × 40 = 344.0
- 0.047 × 50 = 2.350
- 21.55 × 300 = 6465.00

Solve. Write the equations you use.

Each rubber duck weighs 1.9 oz. How many ounces do 30 rubber ducks weigh?

1.9 × 30 = **57.0 oz.**

Each rubber duck is 7.94 cm long. If you lined up 30 rubber ducks in a line (with no gaps or overlaps), how long would the line be?

7.94 × 30 = **238.20 cm**

14.7 Review

Review Complete. Write the equations you use.

- 0.35 m = 35 cm — $0.35 \times 100 = 35$
- 2.1 L = 2,100 mL — $2.1 \times 1{,}000 = 2{,}100$
- 0.018 kg = 18 g — $0.018 \times 1{,}000 = 18$
- 1.05 km = 1,050 m — $1.05 \times 1{,}000 = 1{,}050$

Complete.

- $\frac{1}{10}$ of 30 = 3
- $\frac{3}{10}$ of 30 = 9
- $\frac{5}{10}$ of 30 = 15
- $\frac{7}{10}$ of 30 = 21
- $\frac{10}{10}$ of 30 = 30

Use long division to solve. Write the remainder as a fraction. Use the example to help.

Example: $73 \div 6 = 12\frac{1}{6}$ (1 ← remainder, 6 ← divisor)

- $142 \div 5 = 28\frac{2}{5}$ (− 10, 42, − 40, 2)
- $137 \div 2 = 68\frac{1}{2}$ (− 12, 17, − 16, 1)
- $104 \div 3 = 34\frac{2}{3}$ (− 9, 14, − 12, 2)

Solve. Write the equations you use. Write any fractions in simplest form.

Keegan makes 13 cups of soup. He divides the soup equally into 6 bowls. How many cups of soup are in each bowl?

$13 \div 6 = \frac{13}{6} = 2\frac{1}{6}$ **cups**

Zoe uses 20 feet of string to make 3 woven bracelets. How many feet of string does she use for each bracelet?

$20 \div 3 = \frac{20}{3} = 6\frac{2}{3}$ **ft.**

14.8 Practice

Practice Write the decimal point in the correct position in these products.

- 3.9 × 75: 195 + 2730 = 292.5
- 46.17 × 39: 41553 + 138510 = 1800.63
- 0.873 × 54: 3492 + 43650 = 47.142

Circle the most reasonable estimate for each product.

Problem	Choices	Answer
9.76 × 57	57, 570, 5,700	570
97.6 × 57	57, 570, 5,700	5,700
0.976 × 57	57, 570, 5,700	57
41.2 × 19	8, 80, 800	800
0.412 × 19	8, 80, 800	8
4.12 × 19	8, 80, 800	80

Solve. Write the equations you use.

Rosa has a hamster and a cat. Her hamster weighs 0.29 lb. Her cat weighs 32 times as much as her hamster weighs. How many pounds does her cat weigh?

0.29 × 32 = **9.28 lb.**

Each can holds 0.085 kg of cat food. How many kilograms of cat food do 24 cans hold?

0.085 × 24 = **2.040 kg**

14.8 Review

Review Cross out the shape that does not fit the category.

Trapezoids · Parallelograms · Rhombuses · Squares · Rectangles · Quadrilaterals

Julia wants to make $2\frac{1}{2}$ times this slime recipe. Multiply the amount for each ingredient by $2\frac{1}{2}$ to find how much of each ingredient she needs. Write your equations in the work space.

STRETCHY SLIME

- $\frac{3}{4}$ cup white glue
- $\frac{1}{2}$ teaspoon baking soda
- $\frac{3}{4}$ cup water
- $1\frac{1}{2}$ Tablespoons contact lens solution

STRETCHY SLIME ($2\frac{1}{2}$ times the original recipe)

- $1\frac{7}{8}$ cup white glue
- $1\frac{1}{4}$ teaspoon baking soda
- $1\frac{7}{8}$ cup water
- $3\frac{3}{4}$ Tablespoons contact lens solution

WORK SPACE

$2\frac{1}{2} = \frac{5}{2}$

$\frac{5}{2} \times \frac{1}{2} = \frac{5}{4} = 1\frac{1}{4}$

$\frac{5}{2} \times \frac{3}{4} = \frac{15}{8} = 1\frac{7}{8}$

$\frac{5}{2} \times \frac{3}{2} = \frac{15}{4} = 3\frac{3}{4}$

$\frac{5}{2} \times \frac{3}{4} = \frac{15}{8} = 1\frac{7}{8}$

Unit 14 Answer Key

14.9 Unit Wrap-Up A

Unit Wrap-Up Circle the words or problems that equal the number in the star.

0.6	1.8	3	0.040
(6 tenths)	(18 tenths)	6 × 0.05	(8 × 0.005)
6 hundredths	18 hundredths	(6 × 0.5)	4 × 0.1
(60 hundredths)	(180 hundredths)	5 × 0.006	(4 × 0.01)
60 thousandths	180 thousandths	(5 × 0.6)	5 × 0.08

Move the decimal point to find the product.

2.769 × 10 = 27.69
2.769 × 100 = 276.9
2.769 × 1,000 = 2,769

0.29 × 10 = 2.9
0.29 × 100 = 29
0.29 × 1,000 = 290

4.8 × 10 = 48
4.8 × 100 = 480
4.8 × 1,000 = 4,800

Use the conversion factors to convert the measurements. Write the equations you use.

kilometers → × 1,000 → meters → × 100 → centimeters → × 10 → millimeters

kilograms → × 1,000 → grams

liters → × 1,000 → milliliters

3.105 kg = 3,105 g
3.105 × 1,000 = 3,105

2.1 kg = 2,100 g
2.1 × 1,000 = 2,100

0.64 L = 640 mL
0.64 × 1,000 = 640

0.83 m = 83 cm
0.83 × 100 = 83

9.8 cm = 98 mm
9.8 × 10 = 98

4.55 km = 4,550 m
4.55 × 1,000 = 4,550

14.9 Unit Wrap-Up B

Unit Wrap-Up Write the decimal point in the correct position in these products.

17.4 × 8 = 139.2

0.387 × 6 = 2.322

0.64 × 83: 192 + 5120 = 53.12

2.506 × 31: 2506 + 75180 = 77.686

0.96 × 70 = 67.20

24.52 × 40 = 980.80

Peter is helping his dad buy snacks for the soccer team. Solve. Write the equations you use.

Each pouch of fruit snacks weighs 0.8 oz. There are 90 pouches in the box. What is the total weight of the fruit snacks in the box (in ounces)?

0.8 × 90 = 72.0 oz.

Each granola bar is 9.5 cm long. There are 60 granola bars in the box. If you lined up the granola bars end to end, what would be the total length of the granola bars (in centimeters)?

9.5 × 60 = 570.0 cm

Each bottle of sports drink holds 0.354 L. There are 18 bottles in each case. How many liters of sports drink are in one case?

0.354 × 18: 2832 + 3540 = 6.372 L

Each banana weighs about 0.115 kg. Peter and his dad buy 25 bananas. How many kilograms do the bananas weigh?

0.115 × 25: 575 + 2300 = 2.875 kg

Unit 14 Checkpoint

What to Expect at the End of Unit 14

By the end of Unit 14, most children will be able to do the following:

- Use place-value thinking to write decimals as groups of tenths, hundredths, and thousandths or multiply simple decimals by whole numbers.
- Move the decimal point to multiply decimals by 10, 100, or 1,000. Many children will still need help solving problems that involve tacking on trailing zeros.
- Convert metric measures by moving the decimal point. Some children will solve these problems mentally, while others will need to write out the multiplication problems.
- Multiply decimals by whole numbers with the written multiplication algorithm. Most children will be able to confidently place the decimal point in their answers. Many children will still make an occasional mistake with the steps in the multiplication algorithm or multiplication facts.
- Estimate answers to decimal multiplication problems and tell whether answers are reasonable
- Solve decimal multiplication word problems, including problems with money.

Is Your Child Ready to Move on?

In Unit 15, your child will learn how to divide decimals by whole numbers.

Your child does not need to have fully mastered multiplying decimals by whole numbers before moving on to Unit 15.

Unit 15
Divide Decimals by Whole Numbers

Overview

Your child will learn how to divide decimals by whole numbers, both with mental math and with long division. She will also learn to move the decimal point to divide numbers by 10, 100, or 1,000 and convert measurements within the metric system.

In *Sixth Grade Math with Confidence,* your child will learn how to divide decimals by decimals.

What Your Child Will Learn

In this unit, your child will learn to:

- Divide decimals by 10, 100, or 1,000
- Divide to convert metric measures
- Divide decimals by whole numbers with mental math or long division (and round the answer to a given place, if needed)
- Estimate answers to decimal division problems
- Solve decimal division word problems, including problems with money

Lesson List

Lesson 15.1	Use Place-Value Thinking to Divide Decimals by Whole Numbers
Lesson 15.2	Divide Decimals by 10, 100, or 1,000
Lesson 15.3	Move the Decimal Point to Convert Metric Measures
Lesson 15.4	Divide Decimals by Whole Numbers with Long Division
Lesson 15.5	Tack on Trailing Zeros Before Dividing
Lesson 15.6	Enrichment (Optional)

Extra Materials Needed for Unit 15

- For optional Enrichment Lesson:
    - *How Many Guinea Pigs Can Fit on a Plane?: Answers to Your Most Clever Math Questions,* by Laura Overdeck. Feiwel & Friends, 2017.
    - Grocery store flyer or website

Teaching Math with Confidence: Expressing Decimal Quotients with a Given Number of Digits

In this unit, your child will learn how to divide decimals by whole numbers. The unit follows the same general sequence as Unit 14. First, your child will use place-value thinking to divide simple decimals by whole numbers and divide decimals by 10, 100, and 1,000. Then, she will learn how to use written long division to divide decimals by whole numbers.

Most children find it very straightforward to divide decimals by whole numbers, since the process is nearly identical to the process for whole numbers. You divide the digits like usual, and then place the decimal point in the quotient directly above its location in the dividend. This ensures that each digit is in the correct place. (Note that when you divide decimals by decimals, placing the decimal point in the quotient is more complex. Your child will learn this skill in sixth grade.)

Ex. 3 bags of pretzels cost $8.25. How much does each bag cost?

```
   2.75
3|8.25
 -6
  22
 -21
   15
  -15
    0
```

Each bag costs $2.75.

Placing the decimal point in the quotient directly above its place in the dividend ensures that each digit is in the correct place.

At the end of your unit, your child will learn how to use long division to divide a whole number by a whole number to yield a decimal quotient. These problems are similar to the problems your child solved in Unit 13 when she divided a whole number by a whole number to yield a fractional quotient.

$3 \div 4 = \frac{3}{4}$

```
  0. 7 5
4|3. 0 0
 - 2 8
     2 0
   - 2 0
       0
```

Two ways to divide 3 by 4.

Your child needs to pay attention to two extra details in these problems. First, when she sets up each division problem, she needs to tack on trailing zeros after the decimal point to match the number of decimal digits she wants in the quotient.

At the farmers market, 8 zucchinis cost $3. What is the unit price for each zucchini? Write your answer with 2 decimal digits.

8|3.00

This problem asks for 2 decimal digits in the answer, so you tack on 2 trailing zeros after the decimal point when you set up the problem.

Then, after she completes the long division steps for all the digits (including the tacked-on zeros), she needs to check whether there is a remainder. If there is a remainder, she needs to tack on one more zero and divide one more time. Even though she doesn't need to include this digit in the quotient, it tells her whether to round the previous digit up or down.

```
   0.37
 8|3.00
 - 2 4↓
    60
  - 56
     4  ← Remainder
```

There is a remainder of 4 after you divide to the hundredths-place. So, you need to tack on another trailing zero and divide one more time.

```
   0.375
 8|3.000
 - 2 4↓|
    60 |
  - 56↓
     40
```

$0.3\underline{7}5 \approx \mathbf{0.38}$

Dividing one more time tells you the next digit in the quotient so that you know whether to round up or down. You do not have to complete the remaining long division steps after you find this digit.

Lesson 15.1

Use Place-Value Thinking to Divide Decimals by Whole Numbers

Purpose	Materials
• Color pictures to introduce decimal multiplication • Use mental math to divide decimals by whole numbers	• Base-ten blocks

Memory Work	
	• **What do we call the number to be divided?** *The dividend.* • **What do we call the number we divide by?** *The divisor.* • **What do we call the result when we divide two numbers?** *The quotient.*

In this lesson, your child will use mental math to divide simple decimals by whole numbers. In Lesson 15.4, your child will learn how to use long division to divide more-complex decimals by whole numbers.

Warm-up (A): Introduce Decimal Division

In Unit 14, you learned how to multiply decimals by whole numbers. In this unit, you'll learn how to divide decimals by whole numbers.

In the first picture, the large ball of clay weighs 0.9 kilograms. We want to split the large ball of clay into 3 smaller balls. We divide 0.9 by 3 to find the weight of each smaller ball.

Let's use base-ten blocks to model the problem. Place 9 rods on the table. **Each rod represents 0.1, or one-tenth of a flat.** Split the rods into 3 groups of 3. **9 divided by 3 equals 3, so what does 0.9 divided by 3 equal?** *0.3.* Write 0.3 in the blank and have your child draw a hand on the right-hand scale to show 0.3 kg.

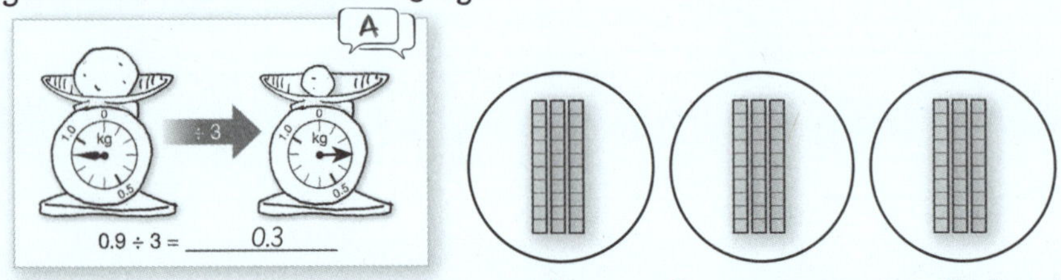

The water bottle in the second picture has 0.8 liters of water in it. We'll divide the water equally between the 2 empty bottles. Place 8 rods on the table. Split the rods into 2 groups of 4. **8 divided by 2 equals 4, so what does 0.8 divided by 2 equal?** *0.4.*

Write 0.4 in the blank. Have your child color both bottles up to the 0.4 line.

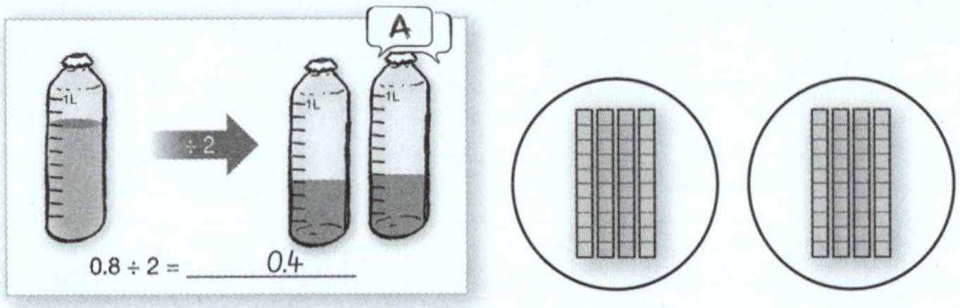

Point to both completed equations. **The divisors in these equations are 3 and 2. In both equations, the divisor tells the number of equal groups. All of the division problems in this unit will use this interpretation of division.**

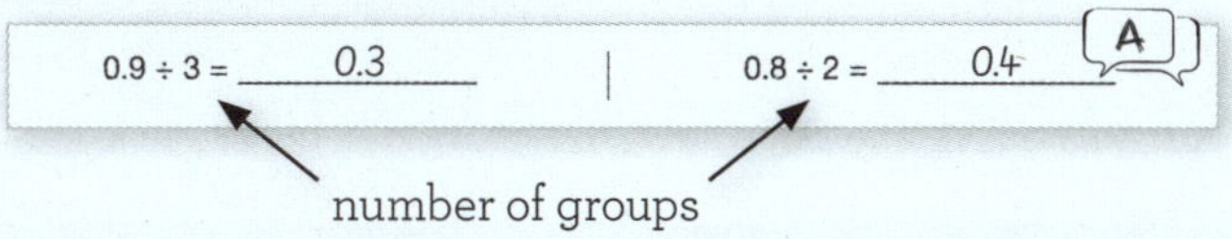

Activity (B): Use Place-Value Thinking to Divide Whole Numbers by Decimals

Today, you'll learn how to use place-value thinking to divide decimals by whole numbers. It's a lot like how we use place-value thinking to divide whole numbers.

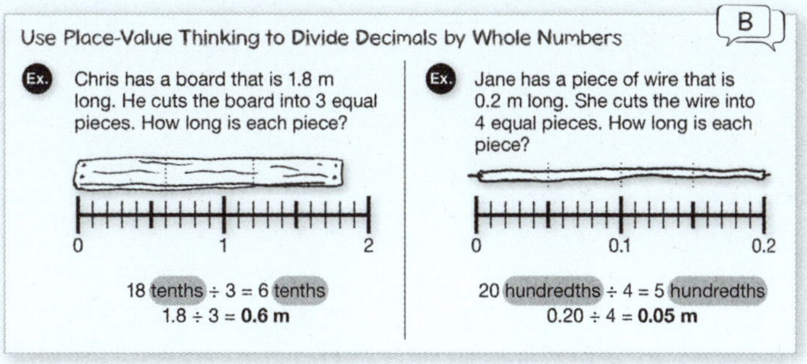

Read aloud the first example word problem.

- **The first example shows how to divide 1.8 by 3.** Place 1 flat and 8 rods on the table.
- **1.8 equals how many tenths?** *18.* Trade the flat for 10 rods (so you have a total of 18 rods).
- **18 tenths divided by 3 equals 6 tenths, or 0.6.** Split the rods into 3 groups of 6. **Each piece is 0.6 meters long.**

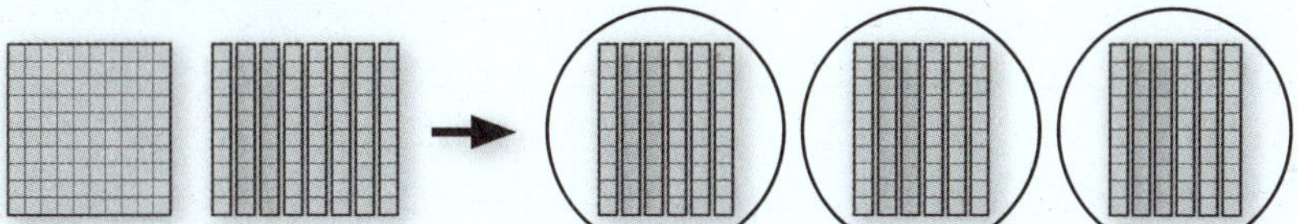

Read aloud the second example word problem.

- **The second example shows how to divide 0.2 by 4.** Place 2 rods on the table.
- **2 isn't divisible by 4. So, we think of 2 tenths as 20 hundredths instead.** Trade the 2 rods for 20 unit cubes.
- **20 hundredths divided by 4 equals 5 hundredths, or 0.05.** Split the unit cubes into 4 groups of 5. **Each piece is 0.05 meters long.**

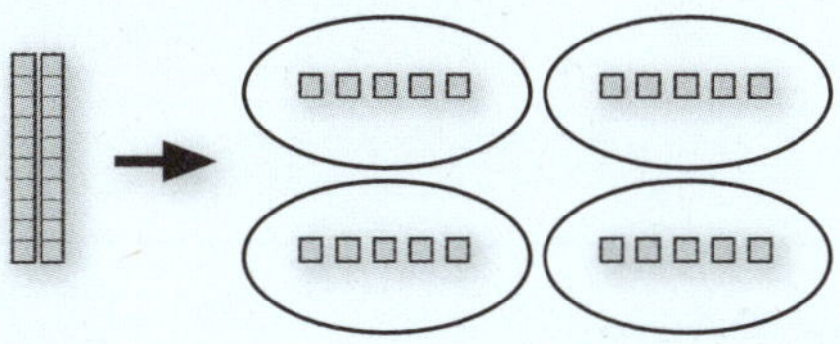

Have your child use place-value thinking to solve the practice problems. Use base-ten blocks to model the problems as needed.

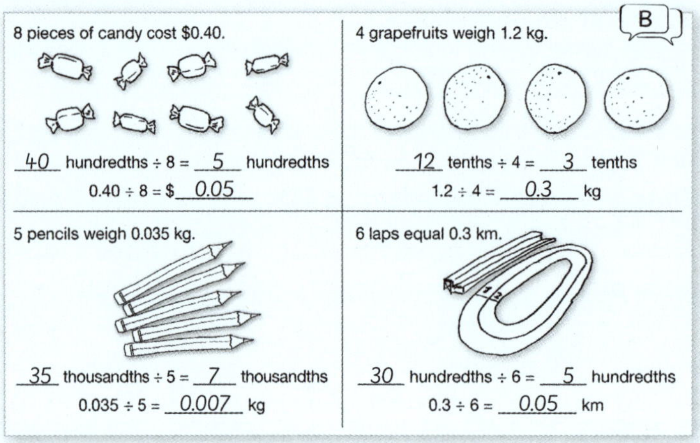
B

8 pieces of candy cost \$0.40.

40 hundredths ÷ 8 = 5 hundredths

0.40 ÷ 8 = \$ 0.05

4 grapefruits weigh 1.2 kg.

12 tenths ÷ 4 = 3 tenths

1.2 ÷ 4 = 0.3 kg

5 pencils weigh 0.035 kg.

35 thousandths ÷ 5 = 7 thousandths

0.035 ÷ 5 = 0.007 kg

6 laps equal 0.3 km.

30 hundredths ÷ 6 = 5 hundredths

0.3 ÷ 6 = 0.05 km

Activity (C): Play Four in a Row

Play Four in a Row.

Four in a Row

Materials: 12 counters per player, with a different color for each player

Object of the Game: Be the first player to place counters in 4 boxes in a row, either horizontally, vertically, or diagonally.

On your turn, choose one of division problems in a light-colored box on the game board. Find the matching quotient in a dark-colored box. Use 2 counters to cover both boxes. For example, if you choose 1.6 ÷ 4, cover that box and the box with 0.4. Play then passes to the other player.

Continue until one player covers 4 boxes in a row, either horizontally, vertically, or diagonally.

Answer Key:

- 1.6 ÷ 4 = 0.4
- 0.2 ÷ 5 = 0.04
- 0.21 ÷ 7 = 0.03
- 2.5 ÷ 5 = 0.5
- 0.042 ÷ 6 = 0.007
- 8.1 ÷ 9 = 0.9
- 0.36 ÷ 4 = 0.09
- 0.54 ÷ 9 = 0.06
- 4.9 ÷ 7 = 0.7
- 0.045 ÷ 9 = 0.005
- 0.64 ÷ 8 = 0.08
- 5.6 ÷ 8 = 0.7
- 0.4 ÷ 8 = 0.05

Independent Practice and Review

Have your child complete the Lesson 15.1 Practice and Review workbook pages.

Lesson 15.2
Divide Decimals by 10, 100, or 1,000

Purpose	Materials
• Practice dividing whole numbers by 10, 100, or 1,000 • Divide decimals by 10, 100, or 1,000 by moving the decimal point • Use division to find a unit price	• Base-ten blocks • Decimal Place-Value Chart (Blackline Master 6)

Memory Work	
	• **What is an acute triangle?** *A triangle with 3 acute angles.* • **What is a right triangle?** *A triangle with a right angle.* • **What is an obtuse triangle?** *A triangle with an obtuse angle.*

Warm-up (A): Divide Decimals by 10, 100, and 1,000 on the Place-Value Chart

In Unit 1, you learned how to divide numbers by 10, 100, and 1,000.

- **3,000 divided by 1 equals 3,000. What is 3,000 divided by 10?** *300.* Write 300 in the place-value chart. **Dividing by 10 is the same as shifting the 3 one place to the right on the place-value chart.**
- **What is 3,000 divided by 100?** *30.* Write 30 in the place-value chart. **Dividing by 100 is the same as shifting the 3 two places to the right on the place-value chart.**
- **What is 3,000 divided by 1,000?** *3.* Write 3 in the chart. **Dividing by 1,000 is the same as shifting the 3 three places to the right on the place-value chart.**

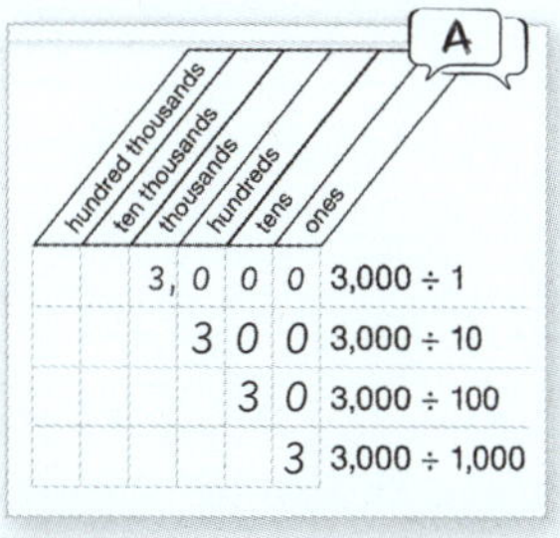

If your child has trouble with these questions, write the problems out horizontally as in Lesson 6.8. Remind him that we can cancel common zeros when dividing numbers with trailing zeros.

$3{,}00\cancel{0} \div 1\cancel{0} = 300$ $3{,}0\cancel{0}\cancel{0} \div 1\cancel{0}\cancel{0} = 30$ $3{,}\cancel{0}\cancel{0}\cancel{0} \div 1{,}\cancel{0}\cancel{0}\cancel{0} = 3$

We can use the same approach to divide a decimal number by 10, 100, or 1,000. We'll use base-ten blocks to see how.

Place 2 flats in the ones-column on the Decimal Place-Value Chart. **We have 2 wholes. 2 divided by 1 equals 2. When we divide 2 wholes by 10, each whole is divided by 10. Each flat becomes a rod.** Shift the 2 flats to the tenths-column and replace them with 2 rods. **We shift the 2 one place to the right. 2 divided by 10 equals 0.2.** Write 0.2 in the place-value chart. **We fill in a leading zero in the ones-place.**

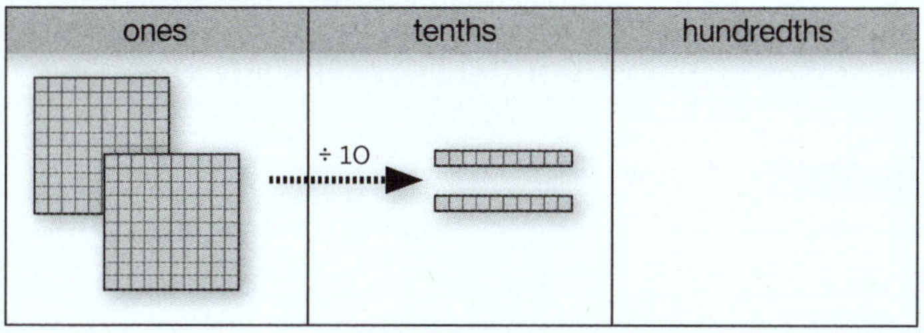

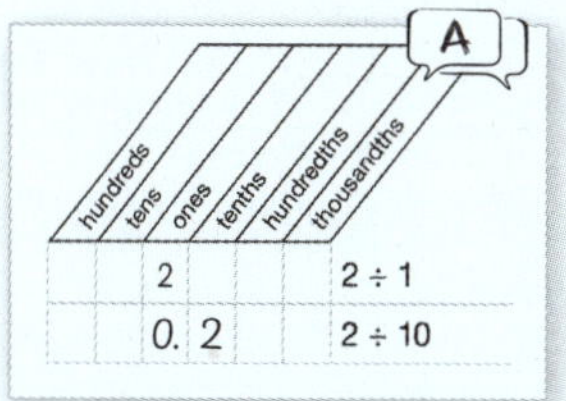

Clear the Decimal Place-Value Chart. Then, place 2 flats in the ones-place again. **When we divide 2 by 100, each whole is divided by 100. Each flat becomes a unit block.** Shift the 2 flats to the hundredths-column and replace them with 2 unit blocks. **We shift the 2 two places to the right. 2 divided by 100 equals 0.02.** Write 0.02 in the place-value chart. **We fill in two leading zeros.**

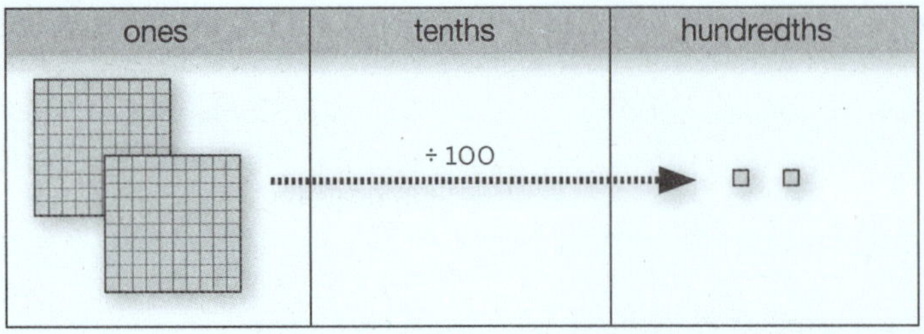

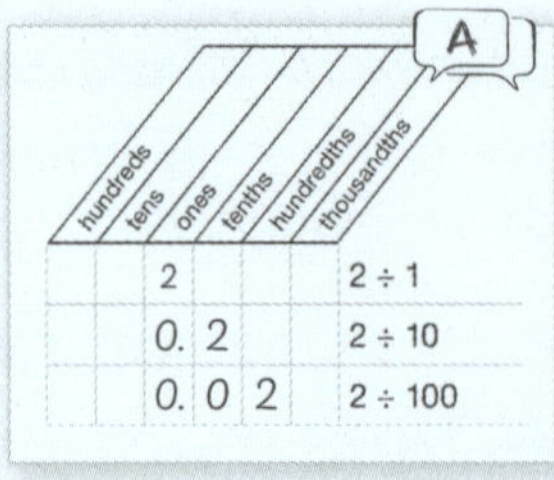

Clear the Decimal Place-Value Chart. Then, place 2 flats in the ones-place again. **When we divide 2 by 1,000, each whole is divided by 1,000. We shift the 2 three places to the right. 2 divided by 1,000 equals 0.002.** Write 0.002 in the place-value chart. **We fill in three leading zeros.**

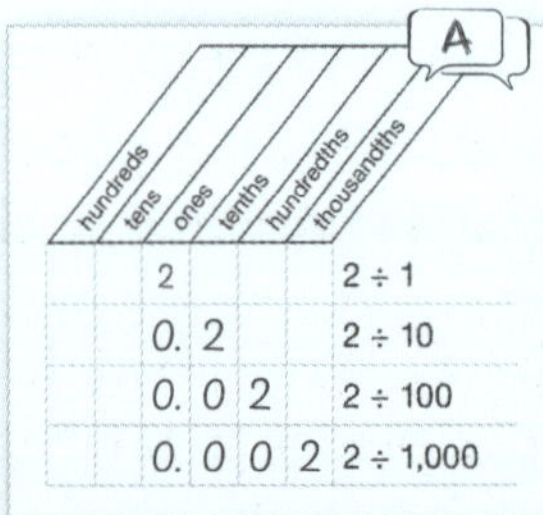

Your child may also find it helpful to see that fraction division yields the same answer as place-value thinking. For example, for 2 ÷ 100: **2 divided by 100 equals 2 hundredths, or 0.02.**

$2 \div 10 = \frac{2}{10} = 0.2$ $\quad 2 \div 100 = \frac{2}{100} = 0.02$ $\quad 2 \div 1{,}000 = \frac{2}{1{,}000} = 0.002$

Activity (B): Move the Decimal Point to Divide Decimals by 10, 100, or 1,000

In Lesson 14.5, you learned how to move the decimal point to multiply decimals by 10, 100, or 1,000. Today, you'll learn how to move the decimal point to divide numbers by 10, 100, or 1,000. Instead of moving the decimal point to the right, we move it to the left. Have your child read the text box aloud.

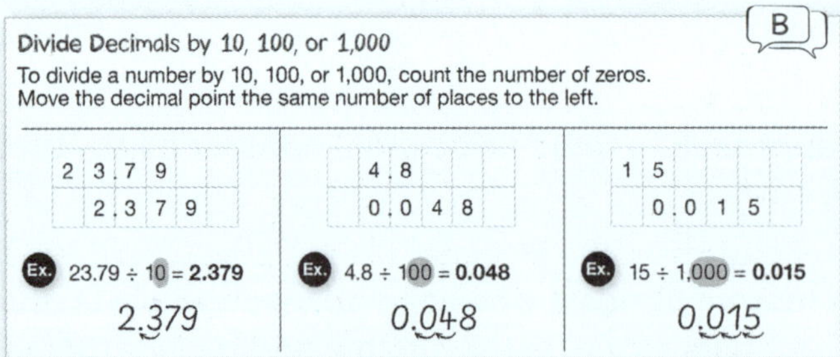

The first example shows how to divide 23.79 by 10.

- **First, we copy the number without the decimal point.**
- **10 has 1 zero. We put the pencil at the decimal point's original position, between the 3 and 7. 10 has 1 zero, so we move the pencil 1 place to the left and write the decimal point there.**
- **23.79 divided by 10 equals 2.379.**

We could also use estimation to check that this answer makes sense. What's 23.79 rounded to the tens-place? *20.* **What's 20 divided by 10?** *2.* **2.379 is a little more than 2, so that's a reasonable answer.**

If we put the decimal point in the wrong place, we might get an answer of 0.2379 or 237.9. Those answers don't make sense.

Discuss the other examples in the same way.

- For 4.8 ÷ 100, point out that you need to fill in leading zeros so that the digits are in the correct place: **We fill in a leading zero in the tenths-place. Otherwise, it would look like the 4 is in the tenths-place. We also fill in a leading zero in the ones-place to make the number easier to read.**
- For 15 ÷ 1,000, point out that the decimal point's original position is after the ones-place, even though there's no printed decimal point: **The decimal point always goes to the right of the ones-place. So, we put our pencil to the right of the 5 and then move 3 places to the left.**

Have your child follow the steps to solve the practice problems.

B

248 ÷ 10 = 24.8	485.6 ÷ 10 = 48.56	3.1 ÷ 10 = 0.31
248 ÷ 100 = 2.48	485.6 ÷ 100 = 4.856	3.1 ÷ 100 = 0.031
248 ÷ 1,000 = 0.248		

Activity (C): Divide and Round to Find Unit Prices

When carnivals and arcades buy prizes, the prizes often come in large boxes of 100 or 1,000 prizes. We can use division to find how much each prize costs. The cost of each item is called the unit price.

Read aloud the first word problem. Have your child write and solve a division problem to find the cost of each bouncy ball. **You found that each bouncy ball costs 0.3486 dollars. We don't usually use any decimal places beyond the hundredths-place for money amounts. Instead, we round the answer to the nearest hundredth. What's 0.3486 rounded to the hundredths-place?** *0.35.* **So, each bouncy ball costs about 35 hundredths of a dollar, or 35 cents.**

Repeat with the final word problem.

C

Each case of 100 bouncy balls costs $34.86. What is the unit price for 1 bouncy ball? Round your answer to the hundredths-place.

34.86 ÷ 100 = 0.3486

0.3486 ≈ 0.35

$0.35

Each case of 1,000 plastic frogs costs $51. What is the unit price for 1 plastic frog? Round your answer to the hundredths-place.

51 ÷ 1,000 = 0.051

0.051 ≈ 0.05

$0.05

Independent Practice and Review

Have your child complete the Lesson 15.2 Practice and Review workbook pages.

Lesson 15.3
Move the Decimal Point to Convert Metric Measures

Purpose	Materials
• Practice converting whole-number measurements in the metric system • Move the decimal point to convert measurements within the metric system	• None
Memory Work	• **What is the sum of the angles in a triangle?** *180°.*

Warm-up (A): Practice Dividing to Convert Metric Measures

In Lesson 14.6, you learned how to multiply by 10, 100, or 1,000 to convert metric measures. Today, you'll learn how to divide by 10, 100, or 1,000 to convert metric measures.

This chart is the same chart we used in Lesson 14.6. It shows the conversion factors for metric measurement units. Conversion factors are the numbers we multiply or divide by to convert measurements. We'll divide to convert measurements today, so the arrows point from the smaller units to the larger units.

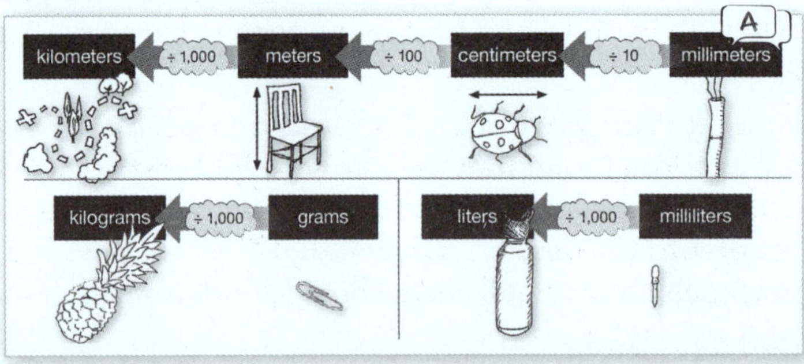

Use the following questions to review metric prefixes and practice converting whole-number metric measures.

- **What does the prefix kilo- mean?** *Thousand.* **There are 1,000 meters in a kilometer. So, if we want to convert meters to kilometers, we divide the number of meters by 1,000. 8,000 meters equal how many kilometers?** *8.*
- **What does the prefix centi- mean?** *Hundredth.* **Each centimeter is one-hundredth of a meter, and there are 100 centimeters in a meter. To convert centimeters to meters, we divide the number of centimeters by 100. 500 centimeters equal how many meters?** *5.*
- **What does the prefix milli- mean?** *Thousandth.* **Each millimeter is one-thousandth of a meter. There are 10 millimeters in each centimeter. To convert millimeters to centimeters, we divide the number of millimeters by 10. 120 millimeters equal how many centimeters?** *12.*
- **There are 1,000 grams in a kilogram. So, if we want to convert grams to kilograms, we divide the number of grams by 1,000. 15,000 grams equal how many kilograms?** *15.*
- **Each milliliter is one-thousandth of a liter. There are 1,000 milliliters in each liter. To convert milliliters to liters, we divide the number of milliliters by 1,000. 2,000 milliliters equal how many liters?** *2.*

Activity (B): Move the Decimal Point to Convert Metric Measures

In the last lesson, you learned how to move the decimal point to divide by 10, 100, or 1,000. When we convert from a smaller unit to a larger unit in the metric system, we divide by 10, 100, or 1,000. So, we can move the decimal point to perform the division. Have your child read the text box aloud.

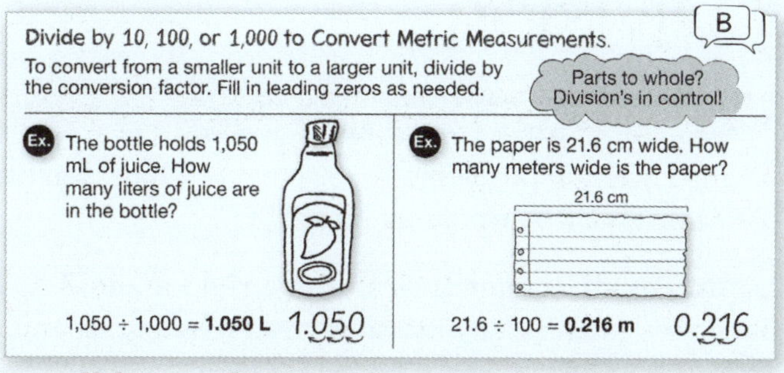

- **There are 1,050 milliliters of juice. How many milliliters equal 1 liter?** *1,000.* **So, we divide by 1,000 to convert milliliters to liters.**
- **What's 1,050 divided by 1,000?** *1.050.* **We divide by 1,000, so we move the decimal point 3 places to the left. The bottle holds 1.050 liters of juice.**
- **The paper is 21.6 cm wide. How many centimeters are in 1 meter?** *100.* **So, we divide by 100 to convert centimeters to meters.**
- **What's 21.6 divided by 100?** *0.216.* **We divide by 100, so we move the decimal point 2 places to the left. The paper is 0.216 meters wide.**

Have your child complete the practice problems. Have her write out a division problem for each conversion and then move the decimal point to find the answer. If she has trouble remembering the conversion factors, encourage her to use the chart in part A.

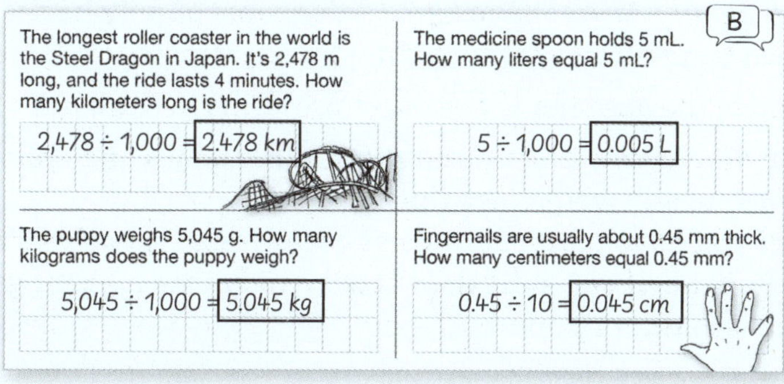

Independent Practice and Review

Have your child complete the Lesson 15.3 Practice and Review workbook pages.

Lesson 15.4
Divide Decimals by Whole Numbers with Long Division

Purpose	Materials
• Estimate answers to decimal division problems • Use long division to divide decimals by whole numbers	• Base-ten blocks (optional)

Memory Work	
	• **What do we call a quadrilateral with 4 right angles?** *A rectangle.* • **What do we call a quadrilateral with 4 right angles and 4 equal sides?** *A square.* • **What do we call a quadrilateral with 4 equal sides?** *A rhombus.* • **What do we call a quadrilateral with 2 pairs of parallel sides?** *A parallelogram.* • **What do we call a quadrilateral with exactly 1 pair of parallel sides?** *A trapezoid.*

Warm-up (A): Estimate Answers to Decimal Division Problems

We'll warm up today by estimating answers to decimal division problems. We'll find the exact answers later in the lesson.

What's 13.44 rounded to the nearest whole number? *13.* **If we divide 13 by 6, will the answer be less than 1 or greater than 1?** *Greater.* **How do you know?** *Sample answer: 13 divided by 6 is 2, with a remainder of 1.* **If you have 13.44 kilograms of jelly beans and divide them into 6 equal bags, each bag will weigh more than 1 kilogram.** Circle "Greater than 1."

Have your child estimate the answers to the other problems in the same way.

- For 4.285 ÷ 5: **If you have 4.285 pounds of gummy bears and split them into 5 equal groups, each group will weigh less than 1 pound.**
- For 0.078 ÷ 2: **If you have 0.078 pounds of cotton candy, you're starting with much less than 1 pound. So, if you split the cotton candy into 2 equal groups, each group will still weigh less than 1 pound.**

A

13.44 ÷ 6		4.285 ÷ 5		0.078 ÷ 2	
Less than 1	(Greater than 1)	(Less than 1)	Greater than 1	(Less than 1)	Greater than 1

Activity (B): Use Long Division to Divide Decimals by Whole Numbers

Today, you'll learn how to use long division to divide decimals by whole numbers. You divide like usual. Then, you write the decimal point directly above its original location so that each digit in the quotient is in the correct place. Have your child read the text box aloud.

B

Divide Decimals by Whole Numbers with Long Division

1. Divide like usual. Ignore any leading zeros.
2. Place the decimal point in the quotient directly above its place in the dividend. Fill in leading zeros as needed.

Ex. 3 bags of pretzels cost \$8.25. How much does each bag cost?

```
  2.75
3)8.25
 -6
  22
 -21
   15
  -15
    0
```

Each bag costs \$2.75.

Read aloud the example problem. **We need to divide $8.25 by 3 to find the cost of each bag of pretzels.**

- **First, we divide the digits with long division. The first step is to divide 8 dollars by 3. 8 dollars divided by 3 equals 2 dollars, with a remainder of 2, so we write a 2 directly above the 8. Then, we continue with the usual long division steps until we've divided all the digits.**
- **Then, we write the decimal place in the quotient directly above the decimal point's position in the dividend. This makes sure that each digit is in the correct place.**
- **8.25 divided by 3 equals 2.75, so each bag of pretzels costs $2.75.**

If your child has trouble understanding why you place the decimal point in this way, use base-ten blocks to model the problem. Place 8 flats, 2 rods, and 5 unit blocks on the Decimal Place-Value Chart. Then, use the base-ten blocks to model each step in the long division algorithm (as in the warm-up in Lesson 1.4.) Or, use play money.

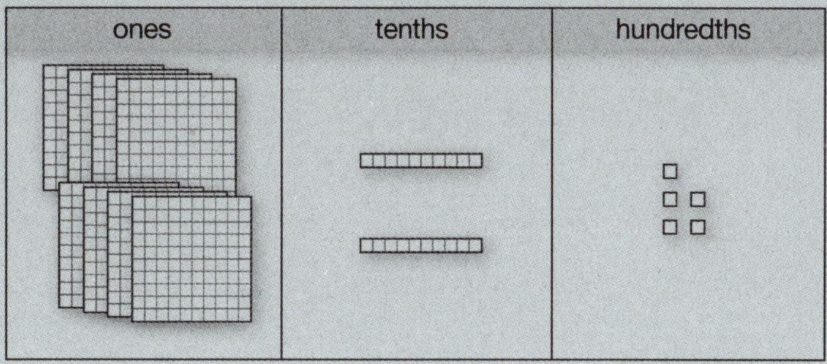

Have your child solve the practice problems in the same way. For 0.078 ÷ 2, point out that he should ignore the leading place-holder zeros in 0.078: **Seven-hundredths divided by 2 equals 3 hundredths with a remainder of 1. We write the 3 in the hundredths-place, directly above the 7.**

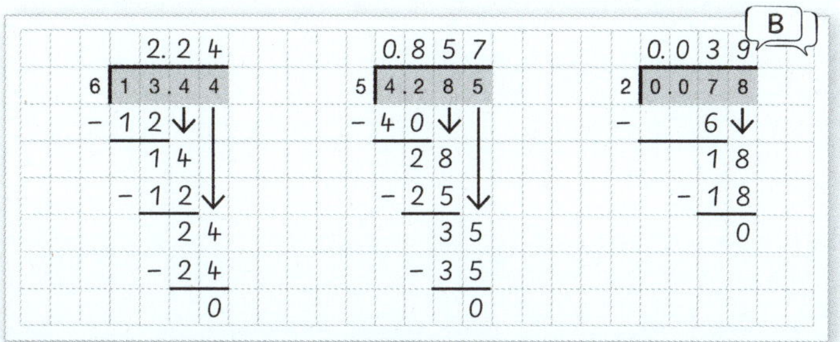

After your child completes the division problems, compare the answers to the estimates in part A. For example: **You found that 13.44 divided by 6 equals 2.24. You predicted the quotient would be greater than 1, so you were right.**

Activity (C): Play Decimal Division Least to Greatest (One-Player Game)

Explain the rules of Decimal Division Least to Greatest to your child and have him play. Encourage him to use estimation as he decides where to place the division problems.

Decimal Division Least to Greatest

Materials: None

Object of the Game: Write the division problems on the board so that the quotients are in order from least to greatest.

Choose where to write the 3 division problems on the game board. Try to place them so that their quotients will be in order from least to greatest.

Then, divide to find the quotients. You win the game if the quotients are in order from least to greatest.

Answer Key:

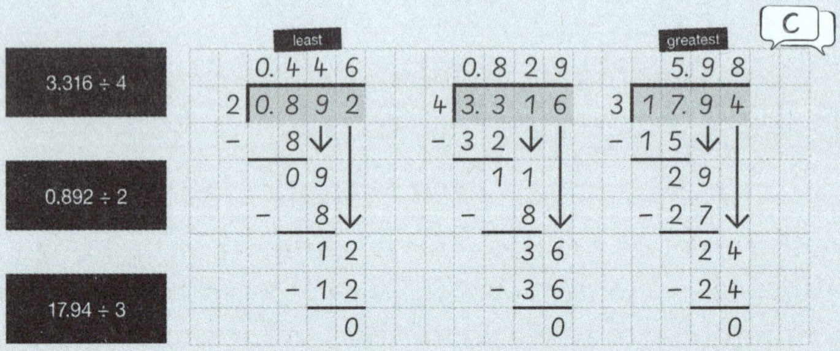

Independent Practice and Review

Have your child complete the Lesson 15.4 Practice and Review workbook pages.

Lesson 15.5
Tack on Trailing Zeros Before Dividing

Purpose	Materials
• Practice using long division to divide decimals by whole numbers • Tack on zeros to the dividend to solve decimal long division problems • Express decimal quotients with a given number of decimal digits (and round if needed)	• None

Memory Work	
	• **What do we call the horizontal axis?** *The x-axis.* • **What do we call the vertical axis?** *The y-axis.* • **What do we call the (0,0) point?** *The origin.* • **What is an ordered pair?** *A pair of numbers that identify the location of a point.* • **In an ordered pair, what do we call the first number?** *The x-coordinate.* **What does it tell?** *The point's horizontal distance.* • **In an ordered pair, what do we call the second number?** *The y-coordinate.* **What does it tell?** *The point's vertical distance.*

Your child will learn how to express quotients with a given number of decimal digits in this lesson. See the Unit 15 **Teaching Math with Confidence** for the two key details your child needs to attend to as she solves these problems.

Warm-up (A): Practice Using Long Division to Find Unit Prices

In the last lesson, you learned how to use long division to divide decimals by whole numbers. You divide like usual, and then decide where to put the decimal point.

One way we use decimal division in everyday life is to find unit prices. Point to the signs in part A.

- **The sign says that peaches are "3 for $2.49." This means that 3 peaches cost $2.49. Does 1 peach cost more or less than $1?** *Less.* **How do you know?** *Sample answer: If each peach cost $1, 3 peaches would cost $3. 3 peaches cost less than $3, so the unit price must be less than $1.*
- **Pears are 4 for $5.32. Does 1 pear cost more or less than $1?** *More.* **How do you know? Sample answer:** *If each pear cost $1, 4 pears would cost $4. 4 pears cost more than $4, so the unit price must be more than $1.*

Have your child write and solve long division problems to find the exact unit price for each type of fruit. Help as needed with setting up the long division problems. For example: **We know the total cost for 3 peaches. So, we divide the total cost by 3 to find the cost of 1 peach.**

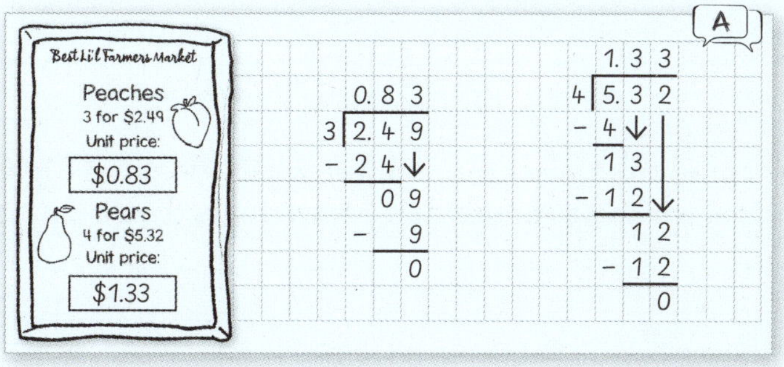

Activity (B): Tack on Trailing Zeros to Express Quotients with a Given Number of Decimal Places

At farmers markets, total prices are often given in numbers of whole dollars. To find an exact unit price with long division, we need to tack on trailing zeros in the price's tenths-place and hundredths-place.

Let's study the steps and the example to learn how to do this. Read aloud the example problem. **The problem says to express the answer with 2 decimal digits. This means that the answer should have digits in the first 2 decimal places, which are the tenths-place and hundredths-place. That makes sense, since we usually express prices with 2 decimal digits.**

Have your child read aloud step 1. **We want to find the unit price of each zucchini, so we divide $3 by 8. We want 2 decimal places in our answer, so we write a decimal point after the 3 and tack on 2 trailing zeros.** Point to the highlighted zeros in 3.00.

Tack on Zeros to Divide Whole Numbers by Whole Numbers

1. Set up the long division problem. Tack on trailing zeros in the dividend to match the number of decimal digits you want in your answer.

Ex. At the farmers market, 8 zucchinis cost $3. What is the unit price for each zucchini? Write your answer with 2 decimal digits.

8⟌3.00

Have your child read aloud step 2. **Next, we follow the long division steps and place the decimal point in the quotient directly above its place in the dividend. This is just like what we did in the last lesson.**

2. Follow the long division steps. Place the decimal point in the quotient directly above its place in the dividend.

```
   0.37
8⟌3.00
 − 2 4↓
     60
   − 56
      4
```

Have your child read aloud step 3. **After we divide to the hundredths-place, we still have a remainder of 4. We don't know if we should round our answer up or down.**

So, we tack on one more trailing zero and divide one more time to find the next digit in the quotient. We only need to find the next decimal digit in the quotient, so we don't have to complete the multiply, subtract, or bring down steps for the final digit. Point to the highlighted zero in 3.000.

```
   0.37            0.375
8⟌3.00          8⟌3.000
 − 2 4↓    →     − 2 4↓
     60              60
   − 56            − 56↓
      4              40
```

If your child finds it unsatisfying to leave the long division steps unfinished, it's fine for her to complete them when she solves practice problems.

We want to have 2 decimal digits in our answer, so we round the quotient to the hundredths-place. 0.375 rounded to the hundredths-place is 0.38. Each zucchini costs 38 cents.

0.375 ≈ **0.38**
Each zucchini costs $0.38.

In this problem, we wanted to express our answer with 2 decimal digits. When we divided to the hundredths-place, we had a remainder. So, we tacked on a zero and divided to the thousandths-place.

If you wanted to express this answer with just 1 decimal digit, you would divide to the hundredths-place, and then round the answer to the tenths-place.

Help your child follow the steps to find the unit prices for the peppers, cucumbers, and eggplants. Remind her as needed to divide the total price by the number of items to find each unit price.

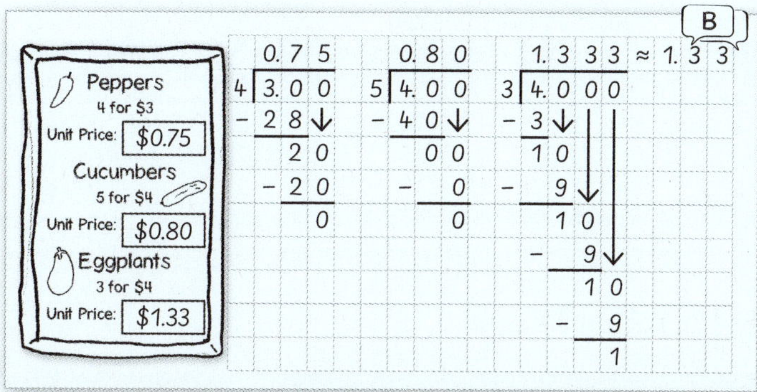

For the cucumbers and peppers, there is no remainder after you divide to the hundredths-place. So, your child doesn't need to tack on a zero in the thousandths-place for these problems.

Independent Practice and Review

Have your child complete the Lesson 15.5 Practice and Review workbook pages.

In the bottom part of the practice page, your child will extend her decimal division skills to measurements. Explain as needed that she can use the same approach to these problems as she used for finding unit prices. For example, for the first problem: **Zion has 2 liters of soda, and he splits it into 5 glasses. So, divide the total amount by the number of glasses to find how much soda is in each glass.**

Lesson 15.6
Enrichment (Optional)

Purpose	Materials
• Practice memory work • Learn mental math tricks • Find unit prices at the grocery store or farmers market • Summarize what your child has learned and assess your child's progress	• *How Many Guinea Pigs Can Fit on a Plane?: Answers to Your Most Clever Math Questions*, by Laura Overdeck • Grocery store flyer or website

Warm-up: Review Memory Work

Quiz your child on any of the memory work items that he struggled with during this unit.

Math Picture Book: *How Many Guinea Pigs Can Fit on a Plane?*

Read pages 126-127 in *How Many Guinea Pigs Can Fit on a Plane?*

Enrichment Activity: Compare Unit Prices for Grocery Store Items

In this unit, you've learned how to divide to find unit prices. In everyday life, we often use unit prices to compare prices and decide what to buy.

Packaged foods like crackers, cookies, and cereal often come in different sizes. We use the unit price for each ounce to figure out which size is the best value. The unit price is usually less expensive if you buy a larger size.

With your child, choose a packaged food that your family often buys and that comes in multiple sizes. Use your grocery store's flyer or website to find the weight (in ounces) and cost of each size. For example: **The regular-size box of cereal weighs 12 ounces and costs $5.19. The family-size box of cereal weighs 18 ounces and costs $5.59.** If needed, round each weight to the nearest whole ounce.

Then, have your child use long division to find the unit price for each ounce of the food. Have him round each unit price to the nearest hundredth of a dollar. For example: **The regular-size box of cereal costs $0.43 per ounce. The family-size box of cereal costs $0.31 per ounce.**

$$\begin{array}{r} 0.432 \\ 12\overline{)5.190} \\ -4\,8 \\ \hline 39 \\ -36 \\ \hline 30 \end{array}$$

$0.4\underline{32} \approx \$0.43$

	× 12
1	12
2	24
3	36
4	48
5	60
6	72
7	84
8	96
9	108

$$\begin{array}{r} 0.310 \\ 18\overline{)5.590} \\ -5\,4 \\ \hline 19 \\ -18 \\ \hline 10 \end{array}$$

$0.3\underline{10} \approx \$0.31$

	× 18
1	18
2	36
3	54
4	72
5	90
6	108
7	126
8	144
9	162

If the numbers of ounces have more than one digit, have your child make a quick multiplication table (as shown) to help with the long division problems.

If you live in a country that uses the metric system, find the unit cost per serving rather than the unit cost per ounce.

Many grocery stores list unit prices along with the total price on the shelf. Point them out the next time you go to the grocery store with your child.

Unit Wrap-Up

Have your child complete the Unit 15 Wrap-Up.

Unit 15 Answer Key

15.1 Practice

Four in a Row (2-Player Game)

1.6 ÷ 4	0.09	0.2 ÷ 5	0.5	0.21 ÷ 7
0.03	2.5 ÷ 5	0.06	0.042 ÷ 6	0.05
8.1 ÷ 9	0.08	0.36 ÷ 4	0.04	0.54 ÷ 9
0.005	4.9 ÷ 7	0.007	0.045 ÷ 9	0.7
0.64 ÷ 8	0.4	5.6 ÷ 8	0.9	0.4 ÷ 8

Practice Find the quotient.

1.4 ÷ 2 = 0.7

0.006 ÷ 3 = 0.002

0.1 ÷ 5 = 0.02

1.5 ÷ 3 = 0.5

0.72 ÷ 9 = 0.08

0.2 ÷ 5 = 0.04

0.64 ÷ 8 = 0.08

0.018 ÷ 3 = 0.006

0.01 ÷ 5 = 0.002

Solve. Write the equations you use.

Maria makes 2.4 lb. of pizza dough. She divides the dough into 4 equal balls. How much does each ball of dough weigh?

2.4 ÷ 4 = 0.6 lb.

6 pieces of paper weigh 0.03 kg. How much does 1 piece of paper weigh?

0.03 ÷ 6 = 0.005 kg

15.1 Review

Review Round to the underlined digit.

3.908 ≈ 4

3.908 ≈ 3.9

3.908 ≈ 3.91

Write 10, 100, or 1,000 in the blank to make the equations true.

390 ÷ 10 = 39

39,000 ÷ 1,000 = 39

3,900 ÷ 100 = 39

Plot the points on the coordinate grid. Then, connect the points to form a quadrilateral.

(1,0) (3,0) (4,5) (2,5)

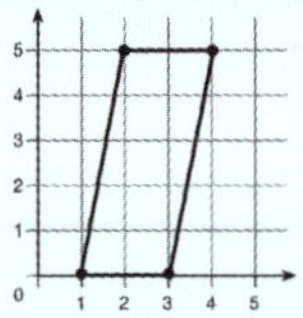

(1,5) (2,1) (4,1) (5,5)

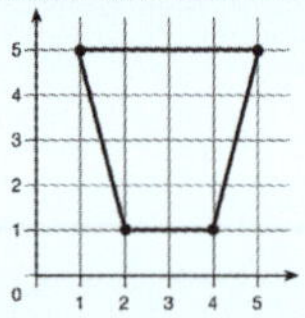

Solve. Write the equations you use. Write your answers as fractions or mixed numbers in simplest form.

3 friends share 4 candy bars. If they split the candy bars equally, how many candy bars will each person get?

$4 \div 3 = \frac{4}{1} \times \frac{1}{3} = \frac{4}{3} = 1\frac{1}{3}$ candy bars

Will has $\frac{1}{4}$ L of glue. He divides the glue equally into 5 smaller containers. How much glue is in each container?

$\frac{1}{4} \div 5 = \frac{1}{4} \times \frac{1}{5} = \frac{1}{20}$ L

Each pack of ramen noodles weighs $2\frac{1}{2}$ oz. There are 8 packs in a case. What is the total weight of all 8 packs?

$2\frac{1}{2} \times 8$

$\frac{5}{2} \times \frac{8}{1} = \frac{40}{2} = 20$ oz.

Elise has 4 cups of powdered lemonade mix. It takes $\frac{1}{8}$ c. of lemonade mix to make one serving. How many servings can she make?

$4 \div \frac{1}{8}$

$\frac{4}{1} \times \frac{8}{1} = \frac{32}{1} = 32$ servings

15.2 Practice

Practice Write the quotients on the place-value charts.

hundreds	tens	ones	tenths	hundredths	thousandths	
		9				9 ÷ 1
		0	9			9 ÷ 10
		0	0	9		9 ÷ 100
		0	0	0	9	9 ÷ 1,000

hundreds	tens	ones	tenths	hundredths	thousandths	
2	0	9				209 ÷ 1
	2	0	9			209 ÷ 10
		2	0	9		209 ÷ 100
		0	2	0	9	209 ÷ 1,000

Move the decimal point to find the quotient.

106 ÷ 10 = 10.6
106 ÷ 100 = 1.06
106 ÷ 1,000 = 0.106

999 ÷ 10 = 99.9
999 ÷ 100 = 9.99
999 ÷ 1,000 = 0.999

527 ÷ 10 = 52.7
527 ÷ 100 = 5.27
527 ÷ 1,000 = 0.527

8.7 ÷ 10 = 0.87
0.7 ÷ 10 = 0.07
0.39 ÷ 10 = 0.039

20.7 ÷ 100 = 0.207
8.9 ÷ 100 = 0.089
0.4 ÷ 100 = 0.004

333 ÷ 1,000 = 0.333
33 ÷ 1,000 = 0.033
3 ÷ 1,000 = 0.003

Solve. Write the equations you use.

100 stickers cost $12.56. What is the unit price of 1 sticker? Round your answer to the hundredths-place.

12.56 ÷ 100 = 0.1256
$0.13

100 yo-yos cost $347. What is the unit price of 1 yo-yo?

347 ÷ 100 = $3.47

Eli buys 3.65 m of wire. He cuts the wire into 10 equal pieces. How long is each piece?

3.65 ÷ 10 = 0.365 m

The elephant weighs 6,200 kg. It weighs 1,000 times more than the sloth. How much does the sloth weigh?

6,200 ÷ 1,000 = 6.2 kg

15.2 Review

Review Complete the charts.

mm	cm
10	1
40	4
80	8
100	10
120	12
450	45

cm	m
100	1
400	4
800	8
1,000	10
1,200	12
1,500	15

g	kg
1,000	1
3,000	3
4,000	4
6,000	6
10,000	10
23,000	23

Write the decimal point in the correct place in the products.

4.7 × 8 = 37.6

1.65 × 70 = 115.50

9.5 × 56: 570 + 4750 = 532.0

0.194 × 63: 582 + 11640 = 12.222

Find the area. Write your answer as a mixed number in simplest form.

4 in. by $\frac{3}{5}$ in.

$\frac{4}{1} \times \frac{3}{5} = \frac{12}{5} = 2\frac{2}{5}$ sq. in.

2 m by $\frac{9}{10}$ m

$\frac{2}{1} \times \frac{9}{10} = \frac{18}{10} = 1\frac{8}{10} = 1\frac{4}{5}$ sq. m

Rewrite as a multiplication problem and solve. Simplify your answer if needed.

$\frac{3}{10} \div 10$

$\frac{3}{10} \times \frac{1}{10} = \frac{3}{100}$

$5 \div \frac{1}{10}$

$5 \times 10 = 50$

$6 \div \frac{1}{2}$

$6 \times 2 = 12$

$\frac{8}{10} \div 2$

$\frac{8}{10} \times \frac{1}{2} = \frac{8}{20} = \frac{2}{5}$

$1 \div \frac{1}{5}$

$1 \times 5 = 5$

$\frac{9}{10} \div 3$

$\frac{9}{10} \times \frac{1}{3} = \frac{9}{30} = \frac{3}{10}$

Unit 15 Answer Key

15.3 Practice

Practice: Complete the charts. Move the decimal point to divide each number by the conversion factor.

mm (÷ 10)	cm
24	2.4
17	1.7
2.6	0.26
0.8	0.08
0.45	0.045
0.03	0.003

cm (÷ 100)	m
224	2.24
130	1.30
97	0.97
5	0.05
0.7	0.007
0.1	0.001

m (÷ 1,000)	km
5,001	5.001
2,250	2.250
945	0.945
64	0.064
8	0.008
1	0.001

g (÷ 1,000)	kg
2,700	2.700
1,111	1.111
642	0.642
101	0.101
75	0.075
4	0.004

mL (÷ 1,000)	L
4,075	4.075
1,375	1.375
250	0.250
80	0.080
42	0.042
6	0.006

Solve. Write the equations you use.

The bald eagle's wingspan is 170 cm. How many meters equal 170 cm?

170 ÷ 100 = **1.70 m**

The hummingbird weighs 15 g. How many kilograms equal 15 g?

15 ÷ 1,000 = **0.015 kg**

The chipmunk weighs 90 g. How many kilograms equal 90 g?

90 ÷ 1,000 = **0.090 kg**

The ant is 0.6 cm long. How many meters equal 0.6 cm?

0.6 ÷ 100 = **0.006 m**

15.3 Review

Review: Use long division to solve. Use the multiplication table to help with the last problem.

```
   7.8
9)70.7
 -63
   77
  -72
    5

    8.16
8)65.32
 -64
    13
   - 8
     52
    -48
      4

      1.41
28)39.70
  -28
   117
  -112
     50
    -28
     22
```

× 28	
1	28
2	56
3	84
4	112
5	140
6	168
7	196
8	224
9	252

Complete.

0.4 × 6 = 2.4
0.03 × 9 = 0.27
0.7 × 10 = 7
0.8 × 5 = 4.0
0.007 × 9 = 0.063
0.08 × 6 = 0.48

0.049 ÷ 7 = 0.007
1.4 ÷ 2 = 0.7
0.45 ÷ 9 = 0.05
0.03 ÷ 6 = 0.005
0.72 ÷ 8 = 0.09
6.4 ÷ 8 = 0.8

Use the clues to complete the chart. Write the equations you use in the work space.

- Pam's paper airplane flew 1.5 m farther than Kevin's.
- Angela's paper airplane flew 2 times as far as Kevin's.
- Angela's paper airplane flew 2.8 m farther than Dwight's.

WORK SPACE

8.7 + 1.5 = 10.2
8.7 × 2 = 17.4
17.4 − 2.8 = 14.6

Paper Airplane Distance

Name	Distance (m)
Kevin	8.7 m
Pam	10.2 m
Angela	17.4 m
Dwight	14.6 m

15.4 Practice

Practice: Circle the words that best describe the answer to each division problem.

6.80 ÷ 4: Less than 1 / **Greater than 1** (circled)

0.351 ÷ 3: **Less than 1** (circled) / Greater than 1

25.35 ÷ 15: Less than 1 / **Greater than 1** (circled)

Use long division to solve. Use the multiplication table to help with the last problem.

```
   1.70
4)6.80
 -4
  28
 -28
   00
  - 0
    0

   0.117
3)0.351
  - 3
    05
   - 3
     21
    -21
      0

     1.69
15)25.35
  -15
   103
  - 90
    135
   -135
      0
```

× 15	
1	15
2	30
3	45
4	60
5	75
6	90
7	105
8	120
9	135

Solve. Use the completed problems above to find your answers.

Jake has 6.80 kg of clay. He divides the clay into 4 equal balls. How much does each ball weigh?

1.70 kg

4 apples cost $6.80. What is the unit price for 1 apple?

$1.70

15 packs of candy weigh 25.35 oz. How much does each pack of candy weigh?

1.69 oz.

The scientist makes 0.351 L of a chemical solution. She divides it equally into 3 test tubes. How many liters are in each test tube?

0.117 L

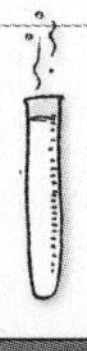

15.4 Review

Review: Complete.

12.5 → ×10 → 125 → ×10 → 1,250 → ×10 → 12,500

0.634 → ×10 → 6.34 → ×10 → 63.4 → ×10 → 634

15.6 → ×10 → 156 → ×10 → 1,560 → ×10 → 15,600

397 → ×10 → 3,970 → ×10 → 39,700 → ×10 → 397,000

Find the missing angles in the parallelogram.

Given: 110°. Answers: 70°, 110°, 110°, 70°

Complete the circles with <, >, or =.

4.6 (=) 4.60
1.03 (=) 1.030
2.1 (>) 2.010
0.050 (=) 0.05
0.07 (=) 0.070

Complete.

$\frac{1}{2}$ of 100 = 50
$\frac{1}{4}$ of 100 = 25
$\frac{1}{10}$ of 100 = 10
$\frac{2}{2}$ of 100 = 100
$\frac{3}{4}$ of 100 = 75
$\frac{3}{10}$ of 100 = 30

$\frac{1}{2}$ of 200 = 100
$\frac{1}{4}$ of 200 = 50
$\frac{1}{10}$ of 200 = 20
$\frac{2}{2}$ of 200 = 200
$\frac{3}{4}$ of 200 = 150
$\frac{3}{10}$ of 200 = 60

Unit 15 Answer Key

15.5 Practice

Practice Find the unit price for each item. Express your answers with 2 decimal digits.

Farmers Market Specials

STRAWBERRIES
4 baskets for $5
Unit price: $1.25

ASPARAGUS
3 bundles for $8
Unit price: $2.67

AVOCADOS
7 avocados for $5
Unit price: $0.71

WORK SPACE

```
   1.25          2.666          0.714
4|5.00        3|8.000        7|5.000
 -4            -6             -49
  10            20              10
 - 8           -18             - 7
   20            20              30
 - 20          -18             -28
    0            20               2
               -18
                 2
```

Solve. Write the equations you use in the work space.

Zion has 2 liters of soda. He divides it equally into 5 glasses. How many liters of soda are in each glass? Write your answer with 1 decimal digit.

0.4 L

Ava has 1 pound of walnuts. She divides the walnuts equally into 6 bags. What is the weight of each bag? Write your answer with 2 decimal digits.

0.17 lb.

The engineer has 7 cm of wire. He divides the wire into 8 equal pieces. How many centimeters long is each piece? Write your answer with 3 decimal digits.

0.875 cm

WORK SPACE

```
   0.4           0.875          0.166
5|2.0         8|7.000        6|1.000
 -20           -64            - 6
   0             60             40
               -56            -36
                 40             40
               -40            -36
                  0              4
```

15.5 Review

Review Complete.

47 mm = 4.7 cm	3,200 mL = 3.2 L	207 cm = 2.07 m
47 ÷ 10 = 4.7	3,200 ÷ 1,000 = 3.2	207 ÷ 100 = 2.07

Find all factor pairs for each number. Then, use the lists to find the greatest common factors.

Factor Pairs of 12	Factor Pairs of 15	Factor Pairs of 16
1 × 12	1 × 15	1 × 16
2 × 6	3 × 5	2 × 8
3 × 4		4 × 4

GCF of 12 and 15: 3 GCF of 12 and 16: 4 GCF of 15 and 16: 1

Find the volume of each pan. Write your equations in the work space.

8 in. × 8 in. × 2 in.	9 in. × 5 in. × 3 in.	13 in. × 9 in. × 2 in.
Volume: 128 cu. in.	Volume: 135 cu. in.	Volume: 234 cu. in.

WORK SPACE

8 × 8 × 2	9 × 5 × 3	13 × 9 × 2
64 × 2	45 × 3	117 × 2
128	135	234

15.6 Unit Wrap-Up A

Unit Wrap-Up Solve. Then, find the blank that matches the answer. Write the matching letter in the blank to solve the riddle.

! 0.35 ÷ 7 = 0.05	Y 0.064 ÷ 8 = 0.008	A 3.6 ÷ 9 = 0.4
E 8.1 ÷ 9 = 0.9	H 0.81 ÷ 9 = 0.09	T 0.081 ÷ 9 = 0.009
H 2.0 ÷ 4 = 0.5	A 0.30 ÷ 5 = 0.06	I 4.0 ÷ 5 = 0.8
Y 0.44 ÷ 10 = 0.044	L 3.6 ÷ 100 = 0.036	V 23 ÷ 1,000 = 0.023
E 6 ÷ 10 = 0.6	A 7 ÷ 1,000 = 0.007	N 8 ÷ 100 = 0.08
S 325 g = 0.325 kg	A 450 g = 0.450 kg	O 850 mL = 0.850 L
W 567 mm = 56.7 cm	T 567 cm = 5.67 m	P 567 m = 0.567 km

Why should you never argue with decimals?

T	H	E	Y
0.009	0.5	0.9	0.008

A	L	W	A	Y	S
0.450	0.036	56.7	0.06	0.044	0.325

H	A	V	E	A
0.09	0.007	0.023	0.6	0.4

P	O	I	N	T	!
0.567	0.850	0.8	0.08	5.67	0.05

15.6 Unit Wrap-Up B

Unit Wrap-Up Solve.

```
   0.19          8.95          4.9           0.064
5|0.95        3|26.85       7|34.3        6|0.384
 - 5           -24           -28            -36
   45            28            63             24
 - 45          -27           -63            -24
    0            15             0              0
               -15
                 0
```

Solve. Write the equations you use in the work space.

Anna's family buys 0.984 pounds of fudge. They split the fudge into 6 equal pieces. How much does each piece weigh? Write your answer with 2 decimal digits.

0.16 lb.

3 funnel cakes cost $10. What is the unit price for 1 funnel cake? Write your answer with 2 decimal digits.

$3.33

Sven's family buys a bag of taffy that weighs 0.8 lb. They divide the taffy into 6 smaller bags. What is the weight of each bag? Write your answer with 2 decimal digits.

0.13 lb.

WORK SPACE

```
   0.164          3.333          0.133
6|0.984        3|10.000       6|0.800
 - 6            - 9            - 6
   38             10             20
 - 36           -  9           -18
    24            10             20
  - 24          -  9           -18
     0            10              2
                -  9
                   1
```

Unit 15 Checkpoint

What to Expect at the End of Unit 15

By the end of Unit 15, most children will be able to do the following:

- Use place-value thinking to divide simple decimals by whole numbers.
- Move the decimal point to divide decimals by 10, 100, or 1,000. Many children will still need help solving problems that involve filling in leading zeros.
- Convert metric measures by moving the decimal point. Some children will solve these problems mentally, while others will need to write out the division problems.
- Divide decimals by whole numbers with long division. Most children will be able to confidently place the decimal point in their answers. Many children will still make an occasional mistake with the long division steps.
- Tack on zeros to the dividend to find quotients to a given place. Many children will still need help deciding how many digits to tack on and when to stop dividing.
- Estimate answers to decimal division problems and tell whether answers are reasonable.
- Solve decimal division word problems, including problems with money. Some children will still need help deciding which number is the divisor and which is the dividend in unit price problems.

Is Your Child Ready to Move on?

In Unit 16, your child will learn how to find the mean and median for a small data set. You will also review what your child has learned and celebrate completing the book!

Your child does not need to have fully mastered dividing decimals by whole numbers before moving on to Unit 16.

Unit 16
Data

Overview

Your child will learn how to find the mean and median for a data set. He'll also use these statistics to compare and contrast two sets of data and draw conclusions about them. In the final lessons, you and your child will review the major concepts and skills he has learned this year and celebrate completing the book.

What Your Child Will Learn

In this unit, your child will learn to:

- Find the mean and median for a data set
- Use the mean to find a missing value in a data set
- Use the mean and median to draw conclusions and compare two data sets

Lesson List

Lesson 16.1	Find the Mean	Lesson 16.5	Enrichment (Optional)
Lesson 16.2	Use the Mean to Find a Missing Value	Lesson 16.6	Review Whole Numbers and Decimals
Lesson 16.3	Find the Median	Lesson 16.7	Review Fractions
Lesson 16.4	Use the Mean and Median to Draw Conclusions	Lesson 16.8	Review Geometry, the Coordinate Plane, and Data

The optional enrichment lesson for this unit is in the middle of the unit so you can wrap up your study of data before beginning the end-of-year review lessons. This enrichment lesson involves conducting a survey and finding the mean and median of the results. If you'd like to complete Lesson 16.5 in one day, have your child conduct the survey before you teach Lesson 16.5. See Lesson 16.5 (page 527) for directions on how to help your child choose a survey question and conduct the survey.

Extra Materials Needed for Unit 16

- Stopwatch or stopwatch app
- For optional Enrichment Lesson:
  - *How Many Guinea Pigs Can Fit on a Plane?: Answers to Your Most Clever Math Questions*, by Laura Overdeck. Feiwel & Friends, 2017.

Teaching Math with Confidence: Understanding Mean and Median

In this unit, you'll teach your child how to find the mean and median for a data set. Both the mean and median are ways to describe the center of a data set. They are sometimes called "summary statistics," because they provide a single number that gives an overall understanding of the data.

The mean of a data set is simply the average. You and your child reviewed how to find averages in Unit 1: add up all the values in the data set and then divide by the number of values. Your child will also learn how to use the mean to do more sophisticated problem-solving in this unit.

7 values

Mean:

$7 + 8 + 7 + 6 + 10 + 6 + 5 = 49$

$49 \div 7 = 7$

Mean is another word for average. The mean number of eggs is 7.

Mathematicians use the word mean rather than average because it is more precise. For example, if someone says, "I spend an average of 30 minutes reading each day," they probably mean that 30 minutes is a typical amount, not that they recorded the number of minutes and calculated the exact average.

The median of a data set is the "middle" value. If you list all the values in order from least to greatest, the median is the value that is in the middle of the list. (If there are an even number of values in the list, you find the mean of the two values in the middle.)

Median:

5, 6, 6, (7), 7, 8, 10

The median is the value in the middle of the data set when the values are listed in order. The median number of eggs is 7.

In the sample egg data above, the mean and median are equal to each other. However, that's not always the case. Sometimes the mean and median are quite different from each other, especially if the data set contains outliers, values that are far away from the rest of the values. In general, the mean is affected more by outliers than the median is.

For example, in Lesson 16.4, your child will investigate data sets about children balancing on one foot with their eyes closed. Each value represents one attempt and tells the length of the attempt in seconds. The data set below shows that Calvin tried balancing 6 times. He was able to balance for 35 seconds one time, but the other 5 of his 6 attempts lasted less than 20 seconds. The 35-second attempt is an outlier, because it is far away from the other values.

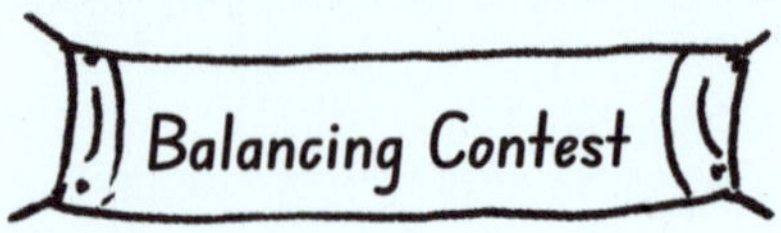

Calvin: 6, 9, 35, 4, 8, 16

↑ outlier (35)

When you calculate the mean, the outlier value of 35 seconds increases the sum significantly, which then increases the mean. But when you calculate the median, the outlier value doesn't have as much impact.

Mean:	**Median:**
$6 + 9 + 35 + 4 + 8 + 16 = 78$	4, 6, (8, 9), 16, 35
$78 \div 6 = 13$	$8 + 9 = 17$
	$17 \div 2 = 8.5$

This unit provides a brief introduction to the relationship between the mean and median for a data set. Your child will study these concepts in greater depth in *Sixth Grade Math with Confidence.*

Lesson 16.1
Find the Mean

Purpose	Materials
• Practice finding the average • Understand that "mean" is another word for average • Use a given total to find the mean	• None

Memory Work	• **What is a prime number?** *A number with exactly 2 factors.* • **What is a composite number?** *A number with more than 2 factors.*

Warm-up (A): Find the Average

Earlier this year, we reviewed how to find an average. How do we find an average? *Add up all the values and divide by the number of values.*

Read aloud the word problem. Have your child add to find the total number of books in the bookcase. Then, have her divide the sum by 6 to find the average number of books on each shelf.

What's the average number of books on each shelf? *12.* **Do any of the shelves actually have 12 books on them?** *No.*

The average is one way to describe the "center" of the data set. None of the shelves have 12 books. But, if you took all the books off the bookshelf and then divided them evenly on the shelves, you'd put 12 books on each shelf.

Activity (B): Find the Mean

On average, how much time do you spend on your math lesson each day? *Sample answer: 40 minutes.* **You spend more time on math some days and less time on other days, but that's the usual amount of time you spend on math. Did you add up a bunch of numbers and divide by the number of numbers to tell me your answer?** *No.* **Instead of doing calculations, you just told me your usual lesson length. And that's fine! In everyday conversation, we sometimes use the word "average" to mean something that's usual or typical.**

Mathematicians usually use the word "mean" instead of average, because it has a more precise meaning. The mean is the exact number you get when you add up all the numbers and then divide by the number of numbers. Have your child read the text box and example aloud.

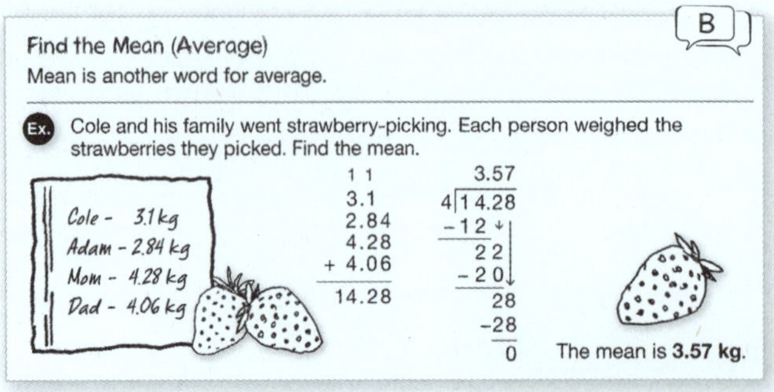

Use these questions to discuss the example.

- **How many kilograms of strawberries did Cole's family pick in all?** *14.28 kilograms.*
- **How many people helped pick strawberries?** *4.*
- **What is the mean?** *3.57 kilograms.*
- **If Cole's family combined all the strawberries and then split them evenly into 4 baskets, how many kilograms of strawberries would be in each basket?** *3.57 kilograms.*

Read aloud the first word problem. Have your child find the mean. If she's not sure, remind her to add the dollar amounts and then divide by the number of dollar amounts (4).

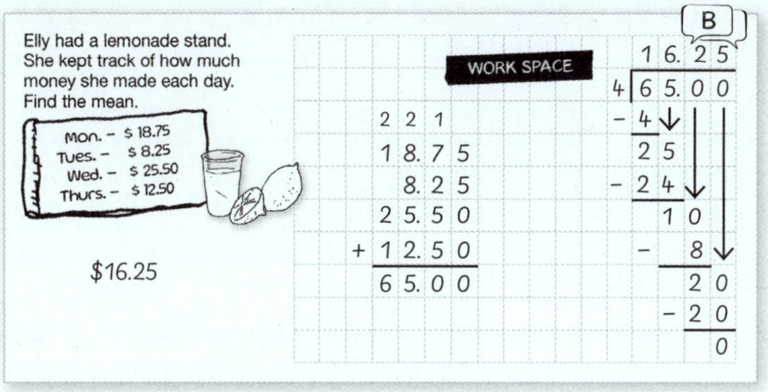
Elly had a lemonade stand. She kept track of how much money she made each day. Find the mean.

Mon. - $18.75
Tues. - $8.25
Wed. - $25.50
Thurs. - $12.50

$16.25

Use these questions to discuss her answer.

- **What's the mean?** *$16.25.* **If she had made the same amount each day, she would have earned $16.25 per day.**
- **Which days did she earn more than the mean?** *Monday and Wednesday.*
- **Which days did she earn less than the mean?** *Tuesday and Thursday.*

Read aloud the second word problem. **This problem is a little different than the first one. The problem tells you the total number of pages Gideon read. So, you don't need to find the sum first. Instead, you just divide 200 by 7 to find the average number of pages he read each day.**

Have your child divide 200 by 7 to find the average number of pages. Remind her as needed to tack on a zero in the tenths-place, divide to the tenths-place, and then round to the nearest number of whole pages.

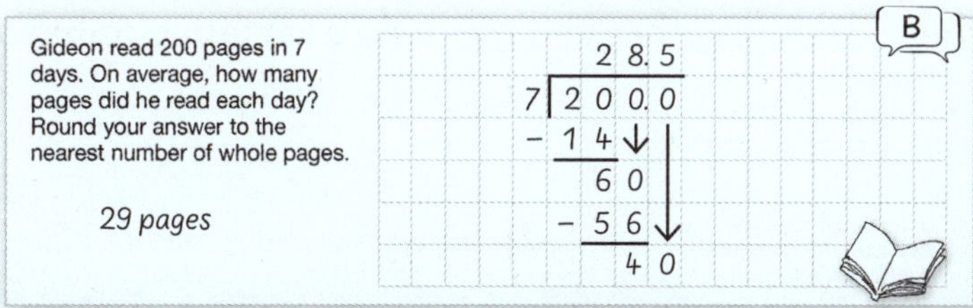
Gideon read 200 pages in 7 days. On average, how many pages did he read each day? Round your answer to the nearest number of whole pages.

29 pages

Some of the problems in this unit require a lot of space, especially the long division problems. If your child runs out of room in the work space, have her write her equations on scrap paper.

Independent Practice and Review

Have your child complete the Lesson 16.1 Practice and Review workbook pages.

Lesson 16.2
Use the Mean to Find a Missing Value

Purpose	Materials
• Practice finding the mean • Use the mean to find a missing value in a data set	• None

Memory Work

- **What is the mean of a data set?** *The sum of the values divided by the number of values.*

In the last lesson, your child found the mean by dividing the sum of the values in a data set by the number of values. In this lesson, he'll apply this concept in reverse as he uses the mean to find a missing value in a data set.

Warm-up (A): Practice Finding the Mean

In the last lesson, you learned how to find the mean for a data set. Read aloud the word problem and have your child find the mean. Have your child write out the equations on a separate piece of paper if he needs more space.

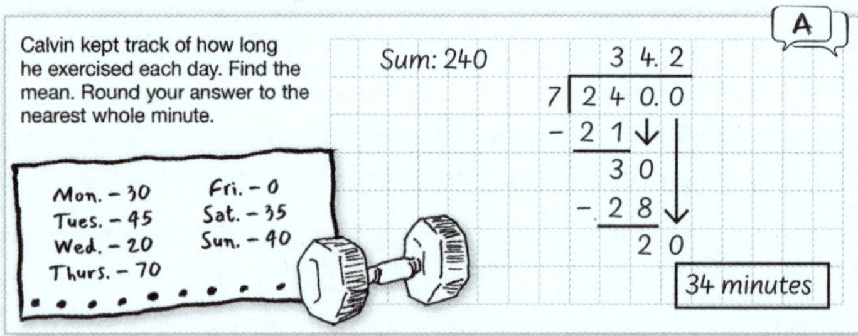

Activity (B): Use the Mean to Find a Missing Value in a Data Set

Today, you'll learn how to use the mean to find a missing value in a data set.

Sometimes, people try to do an activity for a certain number of minutes per day. For example, they might try to exercise for 30 minutes per day or practice the piano for 20 minutes per day. Is there anything that you try to do a certain number of minutes per day? *Answers will vary.*

Have your child read aloud the text box.

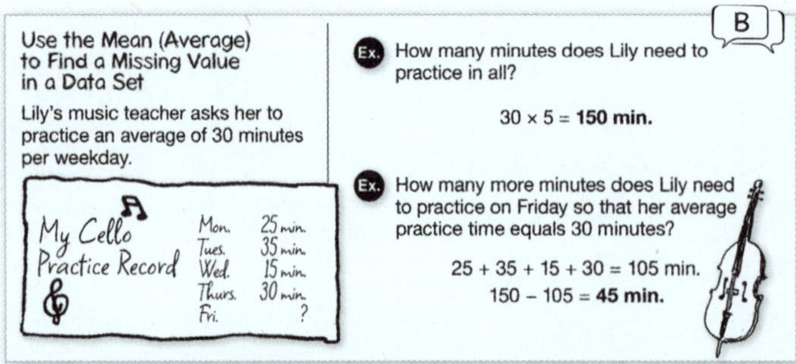

Use the following questions to discuss the example.

- **Lily is supposed to practice an average of 30 minutes per weekday. Which days did she practice fewer than 30 minutes?** *Monday and Wednesday.*
- **Which days did she practice exactly 30 minutes?** *Thursday.*
- **Which days did she practice more than 30 minutes?** *Tuesday.*

- **How many weekdays are there in one week?** *5.*
- **We multiply 30 times 5 to find the total number of minutes she is supposed to practice each week. What's 30 times 5?** *150.*
- **How do we find how many minutes she has already practiced this week?** *Add up her practice minutes so far.* **25 plus 35 plus 15 plus 30 is 105, so she's already practiced 105 minutes.**
- **How do we find how many more minutes she needs to practice?** *Subtract 105 from 150.* **How many minutes does she need to practice on Friday?** *45 minutes.*

Have your child use the same process to answer the word problem. If he runs out of space, have him write his equations on scrap paper.

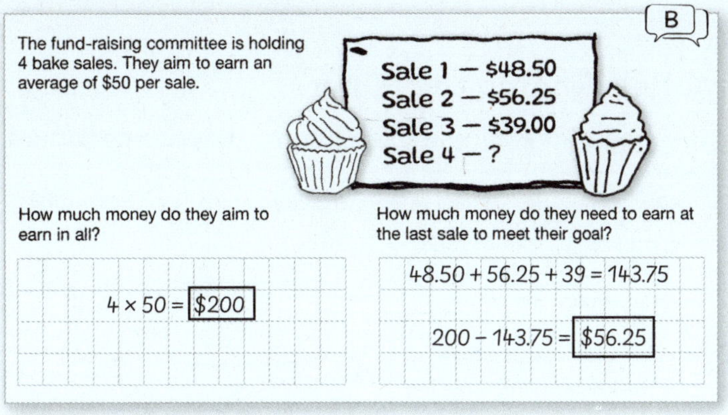

Independent Practice and Review

Have your child complete the Lesson 16.2 Practice and Review workbook pages.

Lesson 16.3
Find the Median

Purpose	Materials
• Practice finding the mean • Find the median for a data set	• Playing cards

Memory Work • **What is the mean of a data set?** *The sum of the values divided by the number of values.*

Warm-up (A): Practice Finding the Mean

Have your child find the mean for each data set. Have her write her equations on scrap paper.

A

Jo lives in Minnesota. She kept track of the temperature at noon for 5 days. Find the mean. Round to the nearest whole degree.

44° 49° 52°
56° 66°

Sum: 267 267 ÷ 5 = 53.4
53.4 ≈ 53°

Luke lives in Florida. He kept track of the temperature at noon for 6 days. Find the mean. Round to the nearest whole degree.

77° 80° 81°
77° 81° 78°

Sum: 474
474 ÷ 6 = 79°

Activity (B): Find the Median for a Data Set

In the last two lessons, you found the mean for different data sets. To find the mean, you added up the values and then divided the sum by the number of values. Today, you'll learn how to find the median for a data set. The median is another way to describe the center of a data set. Have your child read the top of the text box aloud.

B

Find the Median

The median is another way to describe the "center" of a data set.

1. Write the values in order from least to greatest.
2. Choose the value in the middle.

Ex. Find the median for Jo's temperatures.

44°, 49°, 52°, 56°, 66°

The median temperature is **52°**.

Jo recorded 5 temperatures. When you write the temperatures in order, 52 degrees is in the middle of the list. So, the median is 52 degrees.

In part A, you found that the mean of Jo's temperatures is 53 degrees. Are the mean and median equal? *No.* **They're close, but they're not exactly the same.**

Have your child read the bottom of the text box aloud.

B

If there are an even number of values, find the mean of the two values in the middle.

Ex. Find the median for Luke's temperatures.

77°, 77°, 78°, 80°, 81°, 81°

78 + 80 = 158
158 ÷ 2 = 79
The median temperature is **79°**.

Luke recorded 6 temperatures. When you write the temperatures in order, both 78 and 80 are in the middle, so you find the mean of these two values. The mean of 78 and 80 is 79, so the median temperature is 79 degrees.

In part A, you found that the mean of Luke's temperatures is 79 degrees. In this case, the mean and median are exactly equal.

Activity (C): Play Median War

Play Median War.

In some rounds, you and your child will need to find the mean of the two numbers in the middle. Find the mean mentally or write out the equations on scrap paper.

If your child has trouble finding the middle number in each round, have her cross out the number furthest to the left and furthest to the right. Repeat until only one or two numbers are left.

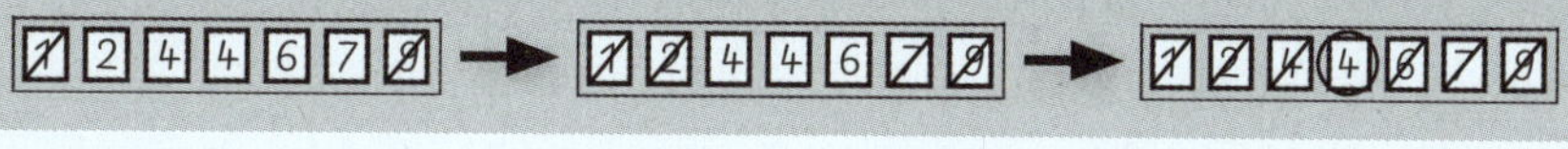

Median War

Materials: Deck of playing cards with jacks, queens, and kings removed (40 cards total)

Object of the Game: Win more points by having the greater median.

Shuffle the cards and place them in a face-down pile.

Median War has 5 rounds. In each round, both players take as many cards from the top of the deck as are needed to complete the blanks on their score card. Then, they arrange the cards in order from least to greatest. They write the numbers on the cards on their score card and find the median. Whoever has the greater median wins a point. (Aces count as 1s.)

For example, for the first round, each player flips over 3 cards. If you turn over a 2, 4, and 7, your median is 4.

Player 1		Player 2	
Numbers	Median	Numbers	Median
2 4 7	4	1 5 8	5

Sample first round. Player 2 wins the point, since 5 is greater than 4.

If you run out of cards, shuffle the cards in the discard pile and add them to the face-down pile.

Play until you have completed all 5 rounds. Whoever wins more points wins the game.

Advanced Version: Take one more card than there are blanks in each round. (For example, for the first round, take 4 cards.) Discard one card before you write your numbers on your score card and find the median.

Independent Practice and Review

Have your child complete the Lesson 16.3 Practice and Review workbook pages.

Lesson 16.4

Use the Mean and Median to Draw Conclusions

Purpose	Materials
• Measure how long you can balance on one foot and find the mean and median for the data • Practicing finding the mean and median • Explore how the range of values in a data set affect the mean and median • Use the mean and median to compare data sets and draw conclusions	• Stopwatch or stopwatch app

Memory Work

- **What is the mean of a data set?** *The sum of the values divided by the number of values.*
- **What is the median of a data set?** *The middle value when the values are in order from least to greatest.*

In this lesson, your child will explore the relationships between the values in a data set and their mean and median. This lesson is meant as a gentle introduction to these relationships, and it's fine if your child doesn't fully understand them. See the Unit 16 **Teaching Math with Confidence** for more on the relationship between the mean and median.

Warm-up (A): How Long Can You Balance on One Foot?

In the last few lessons, you've learned how to find the mean and median. Today, we're going to do an experiment. We'll see how long you can balance on one foot with your eyes closed. You'll balance 5 times, and then we'll find the mean and median for your times.

Have your child balance on one foot 5 times with his eyes closed. Use a stopwatch or stopwatch app to record how long he balances. Round each time to the nearest second and record it in the chart.

Attempt	1	2	3	4	5
Seconds	7	9	12	5	15

Sample times.

For this activity, your child may balance on either foot. He should keep the other foot in the air, and it may not touch the standing leg. Start the timer once he closes his eyes. Stop the timer once the foot in the air touches the ground. If your child balances for longer than 30 seconds, end the attempt and record 30 seconds in the chart.

If your child is not able to balance on one foot, modify this activity by having him sit in a chair and use one hand to keep a balloon afloat in the air for as long as possible.

What's the longest length of time you balanced? *Sample answer: 15 seconds.* **What's the shortest length of time you balanced?** *Sample answer: 5 seconds.*

Have your child find the mean and median for his data. (Have him round his answers to the nearest tenth of a second, if needed.)

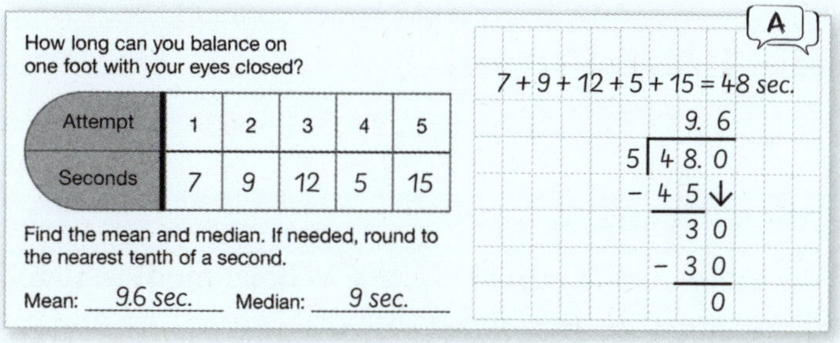

Sample mean and median.

Activity (B): Find the Mean and Median for Balancing Data

These data sets show how long four children balanced on one foot with their eyes closed. Each child recorded how many seconds he or she balanced during each attempt.

Take a look at the children's times. Who do you think is the best balancer? Why? *Sample answers: Calvin, because he balanced for the longest time. Latte, because she had a few long times.* Accept any reasonable answer.

Calculating the mean and median help us compare different data sets, especially when the data sets have different number of values. The children made different numbers of attempts. How many attempts did Gavin make? *5.* If your child's not sure, have him count the number of values. Repeat for the other data sets.

Let's calculate the mean and median for each data set to see who the best balancer is. Point to Gavin's data set. **What is the greatest value in Gavin's data set?** *19 seconds.* **What is the least value in Gavin's data set?** *4 seconds.* Have your child find the mean and median for Gavin's times. Have your child write his equations in the work space.

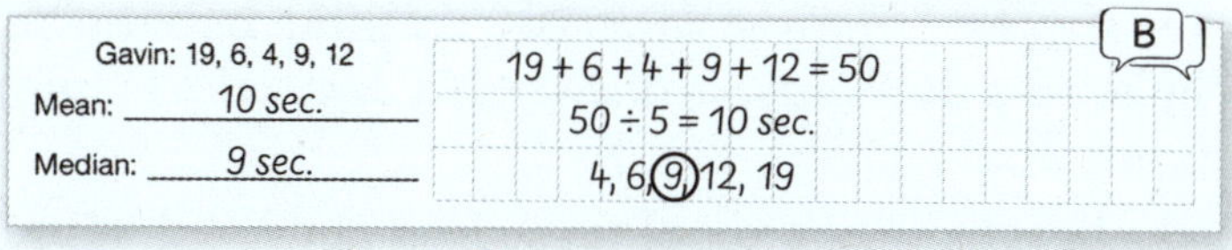

Point to Lily's data set. **Do you predict Lily's mean and median will be greater or less than Gavin's mean and median?** *Sample answer: Greater.* **Why?** *Her numbers are mostly higher than Gavin's numbers.* Have your child find the mean and median for Lily's times.

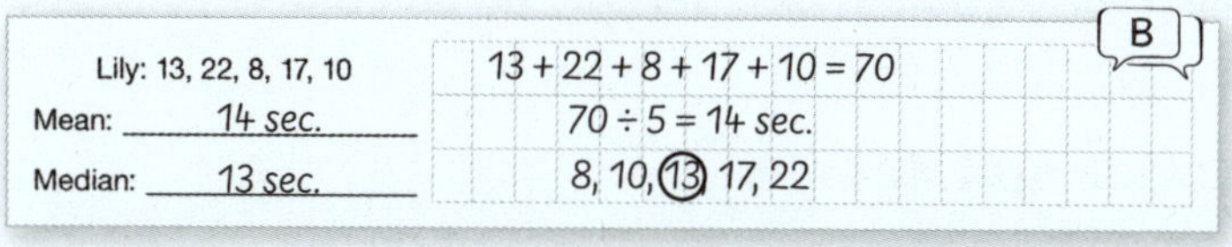

Whose mean is higher, Lily's or Gavin's? *Lily's.* **Whose median is higher?** *Lily's.* **Lily's times are mostly higher than Gavin's, so her mean and median are higher as well.**

Point to Latte's data set. **Do you predict Latte's mean and median will be greater or less than Lily's mean and median?** *Sample answer: Greater.* **Why?** *Her values are pretty high, even though one value is lower than any of Lily's values.* Have your child find the mean and median for Latte's times.

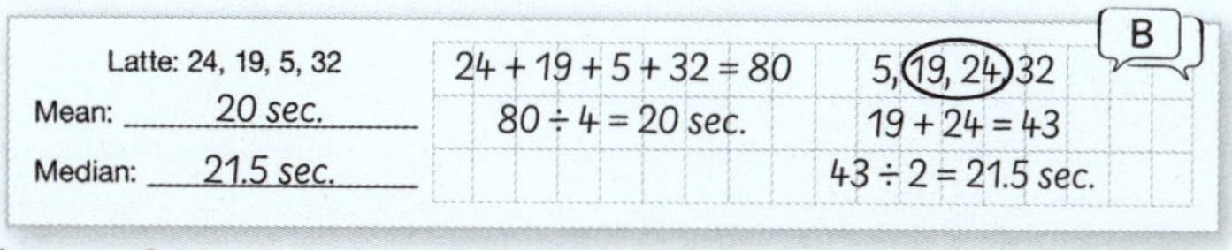

Whose mean is higher, Lily's or Latte's? *Latte's.* **Whose median is higher?** *Latte's.* **Latte's values are mostly higher than Lily's. Even though she had one low value, her other values are mostly higher than Lily's.**

Point to Calvin's data set. **Do you predict Calvin's mean and median will be greater or less than Latte's mean and median?** *Sample answer: Less.* **Why?** *His values are mostly lower than Latte's, even though he has one value that's higher than any of Latte's times.* Have your child find the mean and median for Calvin's times.

B

Calvin: 6, 9, 35, 4, 8, 16	6 + 9 + 35 + 4 + 8 + 16 = 78	
Mean: *13 sec.*	78 ÷ 6 = 13 *sec.*	4, 6, (8, 9), 16, 35
Median: *8.5 sec.*		8 + 9 = 17 17 ÷ 2 = 8.5 *sec.*

Whose mean is higher, Latte's or Calvin's? *Latte's.* **Whose median is higher?** *Latte's.* **Latte's values are mostly higher than Calvin's. Even though Calvin had one high value, his other values are mostly lower than Latte's.**

Calvin's mean is 4.5 seconds higher than his median. Why do you think his mean is so much higher than his median? *Sample answer: The 35-second time makes the mean higher.* **Calvin's 35-second value is a lot higher than his other values. When you calculate the mean and find the sum of the values, the 35-second value adds a lot to the sum. As a result, it raises the mean.**

> Values that are far away from the rest of the values in the data set are called *outliers.* Outliers generally have more of an effect on the mean than on the median. See the Unit 16 **Teaching Math with Confidence** for more on outliers.

Activity (C): Use the Mean and Median to Draw Conclusions

Have your child read aloud the questions and answer them.

C

Who balanced for the longest length of time?	Who had the highest mean?	Who had the highest median?
Calvin	*Latte*	*Latte*

Calvin balanced for the longest length of time. Do you think he's the best balancer out of these 4 children? Why or why not? *Sample answer: No, because he only had one long time. His other times were pretty low.*

Who do you think is the best balancer out of these four children? Why? *Sample answer: Latte, because she has the highest mean and median.* Accept any reasonable answer.

Calvin had the best time out of the four children, but his times weren't very consistent. Latte was more consistently good at balancing. She had one time that was low, but the rest were high.

Independent Practice and Review

Have your child complete the Lesson 16.4 Practice and Review workbook pages.

> Lesson 16.5 (an optional enrichment lesson) involves conducting a survey and finding the mean and median of the results. If you'd like to complete this lesson in one day, have your child conduct the survey before you teach it. See Lesson 16.5 (page 527) for directions on how to help your child choose a survey question and conduct the survey.

Lesson 16.5
Enrichment (Optional)

Purpose	Materials
• Practice memory work • Learn a mental math trick • Perform a survey and find the mean and median • Summarize what your child has learned and assess your child's progress	• *How Many Guinea Pigs Can Fit on a Plane?: Answers to Your Most Clever Math Questions*, by Laura Overdeck

Warm-up: Review Memory Work

Quiz your child on any of the memory work items that she struggled with during this unit.

Math Picture Book: *How Many Guinea Pigs Can Fit on a Plane?*

Read pages 128-129 in *How Many Guinea Pigs Can Fit on a Plane?*

Enrichment Activity: Find the Mean and Median for Survey Results

In this activity, you get to conduct a survey. Then, you'll find the mean and median of your results. What would you like to survey people about? *Answers will vary.* Discuss possibilities with your child and help her choose a question with a well-defined, numerical answer. For example:

- How many pets do you have?
- How many pockets are in the outfit you're wearing right now?
- How many seconds can you balance on one foot with your eyes closed?

Help your child create a list of 8-10 people to survey, and plan how she will conduct her survey. Choose people who are easy to reach, such as family members or neighbors, and help your child contact them and record their answers.

After your child completes the survey, have her find the mean and median of the responses.

> If you don't have time to conduct a survey, write down the number of children in 8-10 families you know. Then, have your child find the mean and median number of children.

Unit Wrap-Up

Have your child complete the Unit 16 Wrap-Up.

Lesson 16.6
Review Whole Numbers and Decimals

Purpose	Materials
• Celebrate what your child has learned about whole number and decimal arithmetic this year • Practice mental multiplication and division with whole numbers and decimals	• Counters • Die

Memory Work	
	• **What is the mean of a data set?** *The sum of the values divided by the number of values.* • **What is the median of a data set?** *The middle value when the values are in order from least to greatest.*

In the daily routine of lessons, it can be easy to forget how much progress your child has made since the start of the year. The final three lessons give both you and your child a chance to look back and celebrate how much he has learned.

Warm-up: Celebrate What Your Child Has Learned About Whole Number and Decimal Arithmetic

Today, we'll celebrate how much you've learned about whole number and decimal arithmetic this year. In Unit 2, you reviewed place-value in whole numbers and decimals, and you learned how to add and subtract decimals. With your child, flip through the Unit 2 workbook pages.

If you no longer have the workbook pages, flip through the matching lessons in the Instructor Guide and have your child look at the workbook answer keys instead.

You extended what you knew about multiplication and long division to multiply and divide whole numbers with more digits. You also learned more strategies for mental multiplication and division. Page through the Unit 3, Unit 6, and Unit 7 workbook pages.

Then, in Units 14 and 15, you learned how to multiply decimals by whole numbers and divide decimals by whole numbers. Page through the Unit 14 and Unit 15 workbook pages. **Next year, you'll learn how to multiply and divide decimals by decimals. You'll also learn how to use decimals to solve problems that involve percentages.**

Briefly discuss any concepts that were especially difficult for your child, and remind him how far he has come in his math learning. For example: **You worked really hard to practice mental division in Unit 6!**

Activity (A): Make Your Own Mental Math Board Game

We've played a lot of math games this year. Today, you get to make your own math game! Show your child the blank game board in part A. Have him choose numbers for the multiplication and division problems on the board. Encourage your child to choose a variety of whole numbers and decimals. He should choose numbers that are slightly challenging to solve mentally, but not frustrating.

For the blank squares, have your child choose and write an action. For example, he might choose actions such as the following:

- Go forward 3 spaces.
- Go backward 1 space.

- Lose a turn.
- Take an extra turn.
- Do 3 jumping jacks.
- Spin in a circle while you solve the next problem.

Make Your Own Math Game

START	40 × 300	1.2 ÷ 4	3,000 × 50
			0.6 ÷ 2
7 × 0.003	2,000 ÷ 40	0.6 × 4	Do 3 jumping jacks

Sample start of the game board.

If you have time, your child may choose a theme and decorate the game board as well. For example, he might draw tennis rackets and balls for a tennis theme, or he might draw planets and stars for an outer space theme.

Once he finishes the game board, use the following rules to play the game.

Make Your Own Math Game

Materials: 2 different-colored counters to use as game tokens; die

Object of the Game: Be the first player to reach the End square.

Each player chooses a counter to use as a game token and places it on the Start square.

On your turn, roll the die and advance your token the corresponding number of squares. If there is a math problem on the square, say the answer to the problem. If there is an action on the square, complete the action.

The first player to reach End wins the game.

Independent Practice and Review

Have your child complete the Lesson 16.6 Practice and Review workbook pages.

Lesson 16.7
Review Fractions

Purpose	Materials
• Celebrate what your child has learned about fractions • Practice adding, subtracting, multiplying, and dividing fractions	• 2 dice

Memory Work	
	• **What is the mean of a data set?** *The sum of the values divided by the number of values.* • **What is the median of a data set?** *The middle value when the values are in order from least to greatest.*

Warm-up: Celebrate What Your Child Has Learned About Fractions

We spent *a lot* of time on fractions this year! Today, we'll celebrate how much you've learned about fractions.

In Unit 5, you studied fractions and mixed numbers. You learned how to add and subtract fractions and mixed numbers with different denominators. With your child, flip through the Unit 5 workbook pages.

In Unit 8, you learned how to simplify fractions and find fractions of sets. You solved lots of word problems about fractions of sets. Page through the Unit 8 workbook pages.

Then, in Units 10 and 11, you learned how to multiply fractions and mixed numbers. You also used fraction multiplication to find area and to scale recipes up or down. Page through the Unit 10 and Unit 11 workbook pages.

Finally, in Unit 13, you learned how to divide fractions by whole numbers and how to divide whole numbers by unit fractions. You'll learn more about fraction division next year. Page through the Unit 13 workbook pages.

Briefly discuss any concepts that were especially difficult for your child, and remind her how far she has come in her math learning. For example: **Remember how hard it was to understand fraction multiplication at first! You kept at it, and now you understand what it means to find a fraction of a fraction.**

Activity (A): Play Fraction Roll

Play Fraction Roll.

Fraction Roll

Materials: 2 dice

Object of the Game: Win the most points.

Fraction Roll has 3 rounds. On your turn, roll 2 dice and use the table to look up the fraction or mixed number that matches the sum of the dice. Roll both dice again and look up the matching fraction or mixed number.

Directions continued on next page.

- In round 1, find the sum of the fractions or mixed numbers.
- In round 2, find the difference between the fractions or mixed numbers.
- In round 3, find the product of the fractions or mixed numbers.

Write the matching equation in the scorecard. Use the work space as needed to find the answer. For example, if you roll a 6 and 9 in the first round, the matching mixed numbers are 1 1/6 and 2 1/4. Their sum is 3 5/12.

The other player then takes a turn in the same way. Whoever has the greater result wins a point for that round.

	Round 1 Find the sum.
Player 1	$1\frac{1}{6}+2\frac{1}{4}=3\frac{5}{12}$
Player 2	$2\frac{2}{3}+1\frac{2}{5}=4\frac{1}{15}$

Sample round 1. Player 1 rolled a 6 and 9. Player 2 rolled an 8 and 5. Player 2 wins a point, since 4 1/15 is greater than 3 5/12.

Continue until you have completed all 3 rounds. Whoever has won more points wins the game.

Independent Practice and Review

Have your child complete the Lesson 16.7 Practice and Review workbook pages.

Lesson 16.8
Review Geometry, the Coordinate Plane, and Data

Purpose	Materials
• Celebrate what your child has learned about geometry, the coordinate plane, and data • Practice identifying points on the coordinate plane	• 2 dice • Counters

Memory Work	
	• **What is the mean of a data set?** *The sum of the values divided by the number of values.* • **What is the median of a data set?** *The middle value when the values are in order from least to greatest.*

Warm-up: Celebrate What Your Child Has Learned About Geometry, the Coordinate Plane, and Data

Today, we'll celebrate how much you've learned about geometry, the coordinate plane, and data.

In Unit 4, you studied volume. You learned how to find the volume of rectangular prisms. With your child, flip through the Unit 4 workbook pages.

In Unit 9, you learned how to plot points and graph number patterns on the coordinate plane. Page through the Unit 9 workbook pages.

In Unit 12, you studied triangles and quadrilaterals, and you learned how to find missing angles. Page through the Unit 12 workbook pages.

Last, in this unit, you learned how to find the mean and median for a data set. Page through the workbook pages for Lessons 16.1 – 16.5.

Activity (A): Play Coordinate Plane Tic-Tac-Toe

Play Coordinate Plane Tic-Tac-Toe.

Coordinate Plane Tic-Tac-Toe

Materials: 2 dice, counters

Object of the Game: Place counters on 3 points in a row, either horizontally, vertically, or diagonally.

On your turn, roll 2 dice. Use the numbers to create an ordered pair and place a counter on that point. For example, if you roll 4 and 3, you may place a counter on (3,4) or (4,3). If your opponent already has a counter on a point that matches your roll, you may replace their counter with one of your counters. If you already have a counter on both matching points, play passes to the other player.

Take turns rolling the dice and placing counters. The first player to place 3 counters in a row (either horizontally, vertically, or diagonally) wins the game.

Activity (B): Reflect on the Year

Read aloud the reflection questions in part B. Discuss each question and have your child answer each question.

B

What was your favorite math activity this year?	What math topic was most interesting to you this year?
building triangles	*coordinate plane*
What math skill did you work hardest to learn this year?	What do you hope to learn in math next year?
multiplying fractions	*negative numbers*

Sample responses.

Independent Practice and Review

Have your child complete the Lesson 16.8 Practice and Review workbook pages.

Unit 16 Answer Key

16.1 Practice

Practice: Find the mean for each data set. Write the equations you use in the work space.

Ben counted how many eggs his chickens laid each day.

Number of Eggs: 7 8 7 6 10 6 5

WORK SPACE

```
  7
  8
  7
  6
 10
  6
+ 5
 49
```

49 ÷ 7 = 7

Mean: 7 eggs

Lena went fishing and weighed each of the fish she caught.

Weights (kg): 0.96 1.23 1.04 0.85

```
  0.96
  1.23
  1.04
+ 0.85
  4.08
```

4.08 ÷ 4 = 1.02

Mean: 1.02 kg

Solve. Write the equations you use.

There are 5 people in Kalee's family. They work together to plant 80 flowers in the garden. On average, how many flowers does each family member plant?

80 ÷ 5 = 16 flowers

★ The bag of potatoes weighs 3 lb. There are 8 potatoes in the bag. What is the average weight of each potato? Round your answer to the nearest tenth of a pound.

```
   0.37
8 )3.00
 - 24
    60
  - 56
     4
```

0.4 lb.

16.1 Review

Review: Complete.

100 ÷ 50 = 2	100 ÷ 25 = 4	100 ÷ 20 = 5
200 ÷ 50 = 4	200 ÷ 25 = 8	200 ÷ 20 = 10
400 ÷ 50 = 8	400 ÷ 25 = 16	400 ÷ 20 = 20
700 ÷ 50 = 14	700 ÷ 25 = 28	700 ÷ 20 = 35
1,000 ÷ 50 = 20	1,000 ÷ 25 = 40	1,000 ÷ 20 = 50

Write each fraction or mixed number in simplest form. If the fraction or mixed number is already in simplest form, circle it.

$\frac{20}{40} = \frac{1}{2}$	$\frac{15}{20} = \frac{3}{4}$	($\frac{5}{12}$) circled
($1\frac{1}{3}$) circled	$3\frac{12}{18} = 3\frac{2}{3}$	$2\frac{48}{56} = 2\frac{6}{7}$

Complete the chart.

Meters	2.743	3.25	0.05	1.40	0.07	3.07
Centimeters	274.3	325	5	140	7	307

Solve. Write the equations you use.

Max orders a pizza and covers $\frac{3}{4}$ of it with pepperoni. Then, he cuts the part with pepperoni into 5 equal pieces. What fraction of the whole pizza is each slice?

$\frac{3}{4} \div 5$

$\frac{3}{4} \times \frac{1}{5} = \frac{3}{20}$ of a pizza

At a pizza party, 8 people eat 3 whole pizzas. On average, what fraction of a pizza does each person eat?

$3 \div 8 = \frac{3}{8}$ of a pizza

16.2 Practice

Practice: Use the goals and data sets to answer the questions. Write the equations you use.

Laura's goal: Save an average of $5 per week for 6 weeks.

Week 1 - $4, Week 2 - $3, Week 3 - $6, Week 4 - $5, Week 5 - $7, Week 6 - ?

How much money does Laura need to save in all to achieve her goal?

6 × 5 = $30

How much money does Laura need to save during Week 6 to achieve her goal?

```
  4
  3
  6
  5
+ 7
 25
```

30 − 25 = $5

Gavin's goal: Earn an average score of 220 at the archery tournament.

Round 1 - 208 points, Round 2 - 214 points, Round 3 - ?

How many points does Gavin need to earn in all to achieve his goal?

220 × 3 = 660 points

How many points does he need to earn in the third round to achieve his goal?

```
  208
+ 214
  422

  660
- 422
  238
```

238 points

Solve. Write the equations you use.

The soccer team scored a total of 36 goals this season. On average, each player scored 3 goals. How many players are on the team?

36 ÷ 3 = 12 players

Freya played the piano for an average of 45 minutes each day this week. How many minutes did she practice the piano in all?

```
  45
×  7
 315
```

315 min.

16.2 Review

Review: Match.

0.56 × 100	56	56 ÷ 10 …
0.56 × 10	5.6	560 ÷ 10
0.056 × 10	0.56	5.6 ÷ 10
0.56 × 1,000	560	5.6 × 100
	0.056	5.6 ÷ 10

Matches: 0.56 × 100 → 56 ← 560 ÷ 10; 0.56 × 10 → 5.6 ← 56 ÷ 10; 0.056 × 10 → 0.56 ← 5.6 ÷ 10; 0.56 × 1,000 → 560 ← 5.6 × 100.

Find all factors of each number. Then, answer the questions.

Factors of 100: 1, 2, 4, 5, 10, 20, 25, 50, 100

1 × 100, 2 × 50, 4 × 25, 5 × 20, 10 × 10

Factors of 90: 1, 2, 3, 5, 6, 9, 10, 15, 18, 30, 45, 90

1 × 90, 2 × 45, 3 × 30, 5 × 18, 6 × 15, 9 × 10

What factors do 100 and 90 have in common?

1, 2, 5, and 10

What is the greatest common factor of 100 and 90?

10

Solve. Write the equations you use. Write your answers as fractions or mixed numbers in simplest form.

There are 100 students in the drama school. 30 of the students are performing in the musical. What fraction of the students are performing in the musical?

$\frac{30}{100} = \frac{3}{10}$ of the students

Mark buys a bag of potting soil that weighs 11 pounds. He divides the potting soil equally into 3 pots. What is the weight of the soil in each pot?

$11 \div 3 = \frac{11}{3} = 3\frac{2}{3}$ lb.

Unit 16 Answer Key

16.3 Practice

Practice Find the median for each data set.

5 3 4 4 2
2, 3, (4), 4, 5
Median: 4

6 5 3 3 2 5 5 3
2, 3, 3, (3, 5), 5, 5, 6
3 + 5 = 8   8 ÷ 2 = 4
Median: 4

6 7 10 7 8 4 9
4, 6, 7, (7), 8, 9, 10
Median: 7

30 40 25 20 45 60
20, 25, (30, 40), 45, 60
30 + 40 = 70   70 ÷ 2 = 35
Median: 35

450 425 425 425 500 475 450
425, 425, 425, (450), 450, 475, 500
Median: 450

500 700 800 800 900 900 800 700
500, 700, 700, (800, 800), 800, 900, 900
800 + 800 = 1,600   1,600 ÷ 2 = 800
Median: 800

5 6 6 5 6.5 7.5 9 5.5
5, 5, 5.5, (6, 6), 6.5, 7.5, 9
6 + 6 = 12   12 ÷ 2 = 6
Median: 6

3.6 3.07 4.1 3.82 3.9
3.07, 3.6, (3.82), 3.9, 4.1
Median: 3.82

Cross out one number in each data set so that the remaining numbers have the given median. (The numbers are in order from least to greatest.)

Median: 4
2 3 3 4 5 6 7 ~~X~~

Median: 41
~~38~~ 39 40 41 46 48

Median: 0.6
~~0.4~~ 0.48 0.56 0.6 0.63 0.82

★ Median: 4.5
2 3 4 4 5 5 5 6 ~~X~~

Sample answers.

16.3 Review

Review Circle the problems that equal the number in the star.

0.18	3.0	0.027	0.4
6 × 0.3	6 × 0.05	0.3 × 9	8 × 0.005
(6 × 0.03)	(6 × 0.5)	0.03 × 9	(8 × 0.05)
3 × 6	(0.6 × 5)	(3 × 0.009)	8 × 0.5
(3 × 0.06)	0.06 × 5	(0.003 × 9)	8 × 5

Find the products. Write your answers in simplest form. If the answer is an improper fraction, convert it to a mixed number or whole number.

$4 \times 1\frac{2}{5}$: $\frac{4}{1} \times \frac{7}{5} = \frac{28}{5} = 5\frac{3}{5}$

$1\frac{2}{3} \times 1\frac{2}{5}$: $\frac{5}{3} \times \frac{7}{5} = \frac{35}{15} = 2\frac{5}{15} = 2\frac{1}{3}$

$\frac{7}{10} \times \frac{5}{6}$: $\frac{7}{10} \times \frac{5}{6} = \frac{35}{60} = \frac{7}{12}$

Solve. Write the equations you use.

A 5-pound bag of flour costs $4.79. What is the unit price for 1 pound of flour? Write your answer with 2 decimal places. Round if needed.

$4.790 ÷ 5 = 0.958 (5 into 4.790: − 45, 29, − 25, 40, − 40, 0)

$0.96

Paul earns $30 for baby-sitting for 4 hours. How much does he earn per hour? Write your answer with 2 decimal places. Round if needed.

30.0 ÷ 4 = 7.5 (− 28, 20, − 20, 0)

$7.50

16.4 Practice

Practice Paisley, Ezra, and Colton went bowling and kept track of their scores for four games. Find the mean and median for each person's scores. If needed, round your answers to the nearest tenth of a point. Then, answer the questions.

Paisley: 90, 86, 95, 65
Mean: 84
Median: 88

Ezra: 73, 107, 80, 64
Mean: 81
Median: 76.5

Colton: 87, 85, 94, 82
Mean: 87
Median: 86

WORK SPACE

90 + 86 + 95 + 65 = 336   336 ÷ 4 = 84
86 + 90 = 176   176 ÷ 2 = 88
73 + 107 + 80 + 64 = 324   324 ÷ 4 = 81
73 + 80 = 153   153 ÷ 2 = 76.5
87 + 85 + 94 + 82 = 348   348 ÷ 4 = 87
85 + 87 = 172   172 ÷ 2 = 86

Who had the highest mean?
Colton

Who had the highest median?
Paisley

Who had the highest score for one game?
Ezra

Which bowler would you most want to have on your bowling team? Why?
Colton. His average is highest.

Sample answer. Answer may vary.

16.4 Review

Review Complete the chart.

Liters	2.6	0.74	0.125	0.398	1.075	2.400
Milliliters	2,600	740	125	398	1,075	2,400

Write whether each triangle is equilateral, isosceles, or scalene. Then, write whether each triangle is acute, right, or obtuse.

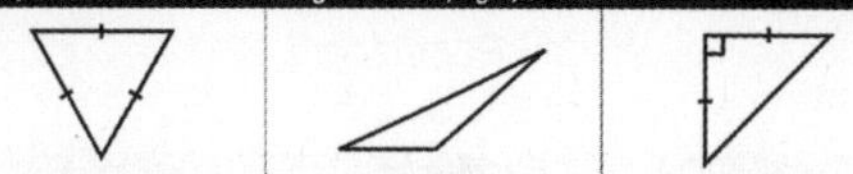

equilateral, acute | scalene, obtuse | isosceles, right

Rewrite each problem as a multiplication problem and solve. Simplify your answer if needed.

$\frac{1}{3} \div 4$: $\frac{1}{3} \times \frac{1}{4} = \frac{1}{12}$

$\frac{3}{5} \div 2$: $\frac{3}{5} \times \frac{1}{2} = \frac{3}{10}$

$2 \div \frac{1}{10}$: $2 \times 10 = 20$

Solve. Write the equations you use.

Ivan has $10. Then, he buys 3 pounds of grapes. Each pound of grapes costs $2.39. How much money does Ivan have left?

2.39 × 3 = 7.17
10.00 − 7.17 = **$2.83**

Valentina buys 3 pizzas and 4 bottles of juice. Each pizza costs $12.89. Each bottle of juice costs $3.17. How much money does she spend in all?

12.89 × 3 = 38.67
3.17 × 4 = 12.68
38.67 + 12.68 = **$51.35**

Unit 16 Answer Key

16.5 Unit Wrap-Up A

Unit Wrap-Up Find the mean and median for each data set. If needed, round your answers to the nearest tenth.

18 15 10 23 16

Mean: 16.4

Median: 16

$18 + 15 + 10 + 23 + 16 = 82$; $82 \div 5 = 16.4$

9 6 7 6 8 6

Mean: 7

Median: 6.5

$9 + 6 + 7 + 6 + 8 + 6 = 42$; $42 \div 6 = 7$; $6 + 7 = 13$; $13 \div 2 = 6.5$

Solve. Write the equations you use.

Oliver's goal is to run an average of 5 km per day.

Monday: 4.2 km
Tuesday: 5.2 km
Wednesday: 6 km
Thursday: 3.5 km
Friday: 4.5 km
Saturday: 8 km
Sunday: ?

How many kilometers does Oliver need to run each week to meet his goal?

$5 \times 7 = $ **35 km**

How many kilometers does Oliver need to run on Sunday to meet his goal for this week?

$4.2 + 5.2 + 6 + 3.5 + 4.5 + 8 = 31.4$

$35.0 - 31.4 = $ **3.6 km**

8 people work together to pack 320 boxes of food for the food pantry. On average, how many boxes does each person pack?

$320 \div 8 = $ **40 boxes**

The baseball team scored a total of 90 runs this season. On average, each player scored 6 runs. How many players are on the team?

$90 \div 6 = $ **15 players**

16.5 Unit Wrap-Up B

Unit Wrap-Up Claire asked some adults and children to try balancing on one foot with their eyes closed. She recorded how long each person balanced. Use her results to answer the questions.

Child Data (seconds)	Adult Data (seconds)
Santiago – 8	Mom – 12
Violet – 9	Dad – 17
Gael – 10	Aunt Ellen – 23
Alice – 15	Uncle Brian – 26
Ayla – 6	Aunt Sally – 19
Jaxon – 13	Grandma – 8
Kamila – 9	Grandpa – 7
Ian – 10	

Which child balanced the longest? How long did they balance?

Alice
15 seconds

Which adult balanced the longest? How long did they balance?

Uncle Brian
26 seconds

What is the median for the children's data?

6, 8, 9, (9, 10), 10, 13, 15

$9 + 10 = 19$ $19 \div 2 = 9.5$ sec.

What is the median for the adults' data?

7, 8, 12, (17), 19, 23, 26

17 sec.

What is the mean for the children's data?

$8 + 9 + 10 + 15 + 6 + 13 + 9 + 10 = 80$

$80 \div 8 = 10$ sec.

What is the mean for the adults' data?

$12 + 17 + 23 + 26 + 19 + 8 + 7 = 112$

$112 \div 7 = 16$ sec.

Do you think adults or children are better at balancing on one foot with their eyes closed? Why?

Adults, because their mean and median were higher.

Sample answer.

16.6 Practice

Practice Write one number that fits each description. (Many answers are possible for some of the descriptions.)

Sample answers.

Multiple of 7: 14

Factor of 36: 6

Divisible by 4: 16

LCM of 7 and 2: 14

7: 7, (14)

GCF of 36 and 12: 12

$1 \times (12)$, 2×6, 3×4

Divisible by 4 and 3: 12

Use long division to solve. Use the multiplication table to help.

$2{,}348 \div 35 = 67$ R 3

$2348 - 2100 = 248$; $248 - 245 = 3$

	× 35
1	35
2	70
3	105
4	140
5	175
6	210
7	245
8	280
9	315

Evaluate.

$4 \times 6 \times 25$

100×6

600

$7 + 8 \times (5 - 2)$

$7 + 8 \times 3$

$7 + 24$

31

Solve.

$1.48 + 2.392 = 3.872$

$3.5 - 0.742 = 2.758$

4.68×39: $4212 + 14040 = 182.52$

$2.892 \div 6 = 0.482$ ($28 - 24 = 4$; $49 - 48 = 1$; $12 - 12 = 0$)

16.6 Review

Review Find the mean and median for each data set.

10 5 10 8 7 7 7 10

Mean: 8

Median: 7.5

$10 + 5 + 10 + 8 + 7 + 7 + 7 + 10 = 64$

WORK SPACE

$64 \div 8 = 8$

$8 + 7 = 15$

$15 \div 2 = 7.5$

6 6 6 6 6 6

Mean: 6

Median: 6

$6 \times 6 = 36$

$36 \div 6 = 6$

4.2 9.1 8 12.4 11.3

Mean: 9

Median: 9.1

$4.2 + 9.1 + 8.0 + 12.4 + 11.3 = 45.0$

$45 \div 5 = 9$

Use mental math to complete.

$800 \div 4 = 200$

$800 \div 80 = 10$

$800 \div 2 = 400$

$800 \div 40 = 20$

$800 \div 8 = 100$

$800 \div 200 = 4$

Complete.

$1\frac{2}{3} = 1\frac{8}{12}$

$+\ 2\frac{3}{4} = 2\frac{9}{12}$

$3\frac{17}{12} = 4\frac{5}{12}$

$5\frac{1}{2} = 5\frac{4}{8}$ (rewritten as $4\frac{12}{8}$)

$-\ 3\frac{7}{8} = 3\frac{7}{8}$

$1\frac{5}{8}$

Use bar models to solve. Write the equations you use.

Mariella read 50 pages on Saturday. She read $\frac{2}{3}$ as many pages on Saturday as on Sunday. How many pages did she read on Sunday?

Saturday (50)
Sunday (?)

$50 \div 2 = 25$

$25 \times 3 = $ **75 pages**

Unit 16 Answer Key

16.7 Practice

Practice Find the sum, difference, product, or quotient. Write your answers as fractions or mixed numbers in simplest form. Then, find the blank that matches the product. Write the matching letter in the blank to solve the riddle.

N: $\frac{1}{5}+\frac{3}{5}$ → $\frac{4}{5}$

H: $\frac{3}{4}+\frac{5}{8}$ → $\frac{6}{8}+\frac{5}{8}=\frac{11}{8}=1\frac{3}{8}$

H: $\frac{2}{3}+\frac{3}{5}$ → $\frac{10}{15}+\frac{9}{15}=\frac{19}{15}=1\frac{4}{15}$

T: $\frac{5}{6}-\frac{1}{6}$ → $\frac{4}{6}=\frac{2}{3}$

I: $\frac{2}{3}-\frac{1}{12}$ → $\frac{8}{12}-\frac{1}{12}=\frac{7}{12}$

Y: $\frac{4}{5}-\frac{1}{2}$ → $\frac{8}{10}-\frac{5}{10}=\frac{3}{10}$

T: $\frac{3}{4}\times\frac{1}{4}$ → $\frac{3}{4}\times\frac{1}{4}=\frac{3}{16}$

G: $\frac{2}{3}\times 4$ → $\frac{2}{3}\times\frac{4}{1}=\frac{8}{3}=2\frac{2}{3}$

E: $5\times\frac{7}{8}$ → $\frac{5}{1}\times\frac{7}{8}=\frac{35}{8}=4\frac{3}{8}$

H: $\frac{1}{3}\div 4$ → $\frac{1}{3}\times\frac{1}{4}=\frac{1}{12}$

R: $\frac{7}{8}\div 2$ → $\frac{7}{8}\times\frac{1}{2}=\frac{7}{16}$

E: $4\div\frac{1}{5}$ → $4\times 5=20$

Which king loved fractions?

H ($\frac{1}{12}$) E ($4\frac{3}{8}$) N ($\frac{4}{5}$) R ($\frac{7}{16}$) Y ($\frac{3}{10}$) T ($\frac{2}{3}$) H E

E (20) I ($\frac{7}{12}$) G ($2\frac{2}{3}$) H ($1\frac{4}{15}$) T ($\frac{3}{16}$) H ($1\frac{3}{8}$)

16.7 Review

Review Circle the better estimate for each product or quotient.

Problem	Choices	Circled
6 × 1.29	0.6, 6	6
20 × 0.998	2, 20	20
8 × 0.432	3.2, 32	3.2
10.3 ÷ 5	0.2, 2	2
5.921 ÷ 2	0.3, 3	3
1.9 ÷ 3	0.6, 6	0.6

Use mental math to solve.

0.49 × 10 = 4.9
0.49 × 100 = 49
0.49 × 1,000 = 490

3 × 0.04 = 0.12
3 × 0.004 = 0.012
3 × 0.4 = 1.2

4 × 0.005 = 0.020
4 × 0.5 = 2.0
4 × 0.05 = 0.20

327 ÷ 10 = 32.7
327 ÷ 100 = 3.27
327 ÷ 1,000 = 0.327

0.36 ÷ 9 = 0.04
3.6 ÷ 9 = 0.4
0.036 ÷ 9 = 0.004

0.2 ÷ 4 = 0.05
0.02 ÷ 4 = 0.005
2.0 ÷ 4 = 0.5

Solve. Write the equations you use.

The flower festival is 4 days long. The organizers' goal is that an average of 200 people will attend the festival each day.

Flower Festival Attendance
Thursday — 157 people
Friday — 189 people
Saturday — 234 people
Sunday — ?

How many people need to attend the flower festival in all for the organizers to meet their goal?

200 × 4 = **800 people**

How many people need to attend the flower festival on Sunday for the organizers to meet their goal?

157 + 189 + 234 = 580

800 − 580 = **220 people**

16.8 Practice

Practice Complete the missing information for each rectangular prism. All measurements are in inches.

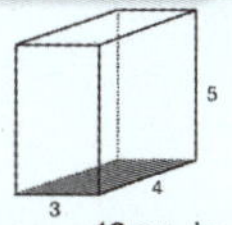
5
4
3

Base Area: 12 sq. in.
Height: 5 in.
Volume: 60 cu. in.

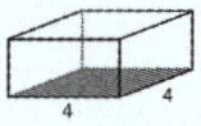
4
4

Base Area: 16 sq. in.
Height: 2 in.
Volume: 32 cu. in.

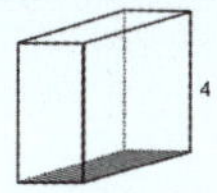
4

Base Area: 12 sq. in.
Height: 4 in.
Volume: 48 cu. in.

Use the information to complete the chart. Then, use the chart to make a line graph.

Taylor starts with $30. Then, she spends $3 per day on a snack.

Day	Money ($)
0	30
1	27
2	24
3	21
4	18
5	15
6	12

Taylor's Money

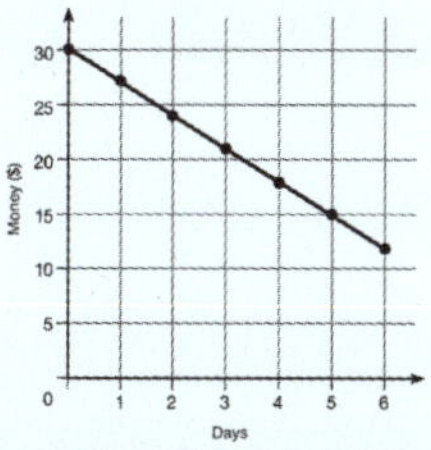
30
25
20
15
10
5
0
1
2
3
4
5
6
Money ($)
Days

Find the missing angles.

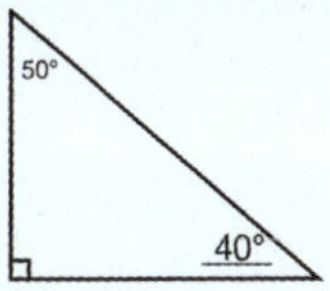
50°
40°

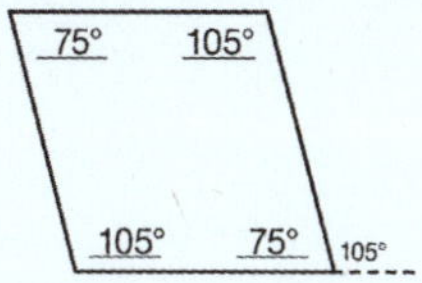
75°
105°
105°
75°
105°

16.8 Review

CONGRATULATIONS!

Presented to

____

for successfully completing

Fifth Grade Math with Confidence

__________ Date

__________ Signature

Unit 16 Checkpoint

What to Expect at the End of Unit 16

By the end of Unit 16, most children will be able to do the following:

- Find the mean for a data set by adding the values and dividing by the number of values. Some children will still need help rounding to the correct place if the mean is a decimal.
- Use the mean to find a missing value in a data set.
- Find the median for a data set. Some children will need to be reminded to find the mean of the middle two values if the data set has an even number of values.
- Use the mean and median to draw conclusions and compare two data sets.

Congratulations!

Congratulations on finishing *Fifth Grade Math with Confidence*! Give yourself a pat on the back for all that you've taught your child this year.

Memory Work

Review Memory Work

Throughout the year, your child will review the memory work she learned in *Fourth Grade Math with Confidence*. If your child did not use *Fourth Grade Math with Confidence*, she will gradually memorize these items over the course of the year. She does not need to fully master every item the first time it appears.

Topic	Memory Work
Numbers and Operations	• **What do we call the result when we add numbers together?** *The sum.* • **What do we call the result when we subtract a number from another number?** *The difference.* • **What do we call the result when we multiply two numbers?** *The product.* • **What do we call the numbers in a multiplication equation that we multiply together?** *Factors.* • **What do we call the number to be divided?** *The dividend.* • **What do we call the number we divide by?** *The divisor.* • **What do we call the result when we divide two numbers?** *The quotient.* • **What do we call an amount that is left over after division?** *The remainder.* • **Name 4 factors of X.** (Replace X with any number from 1 to 50.) *Answers will vary. Some numbers do not have 4 factors.* • **Name 4 multiples of X.** (Replace X with any number from 1 to 10.) *Answers will vary.* • **How do you know if a number is divisible by 2?** *It is even. It has 0, 2, 4, 6, or 8 in the ones-place.* • **How do you know if a number is divisible by 5?** *It has a 0 or 5 in the ones-place.* • **How do you know if a number is divisible by 10?** *It has a 0 in the ones-place.* • **What is a prime number?** *A number with exactly 2 factors.* • **What is a composite number?** *A number with more than 2 factors.* • **What's zero times any number?** *Zero.* • **What's zero divided by any other number?** *Zero.* • **What's any number divided by zero?** *Undefined.*
Measurement	• **How many inches equal 1 foot?** *12.* • **How many feet equal 1 yard?** *3.* • **How many inches equal 1 yard?** *36.* • **How many feet equal 1 mile?** *5,280.* • **How many ounces equal 1 pound?** *16.* • **How many fluid ounces equal 1 cup?** *8.* • **How many millimeters equal 1 centimeter?** *10.* • **How many centimeters equal 1 meter?** *100.* • **How many meters equal 1 kilometer?** *1,000.* • **How many grams equal 1 kilogram?** *1,000.* • **How many milliliters equal 1 liter?** *1,000.*

Topic	Memory Work
Fractions	• **What do we call the top number in a fraction?** *The numerator.* • **What does the numerator tell?** *The number of parts.* • **What do we call the bottom number in a fraction?** *The denominator.* • **What does the denominator tell?** *How many equal parts the whole was split into.* • **What do we call fractions that look different but have the same value?** *Equivalent fractions.* • **What do we call numbers that have a whole number and a fraction?** *Mixed numbers.*
Area and Perimeter	• **What does perimeter measure?** *The distance around the outside edge of a shape.* • **What does area measure?** *The amount of space that a shape covers.*
Geometry	• **What do we call an angle with a measure less than 90 degrees?** *Acute.* • **What do we call an angle with a measure equal to 90 degrees?** *Right.* • **What do we call an angle with a measure greater than 90 degrees and less than 180 degrees?** *Obtuse.* • **What do we call an angle with a measure equal to 180 degrees?** *Straight.* • **What do we call a quadrilateral with 4 right angles?** *A rectangle.* • **What do we call a quadrilateral with 4 right angles and 4 equal sides?** *A square.* • **What do we call a quadrilateral with 4 equal sides?** *A rhombus.* • **What do we call a quadrilateral with 2 pairs of parallel sides?** *A parallelogram.* • **What do we call a quadrilateral with exactly 1 pair of parallel sides?** *A trapezoid.* • **What is an acute triangle?** *A triangle with 3 acute angles.* • **What is a right triangle?** *A triangle with a right angle.* • **What is an obtuse triangle?** *A triangle with an obtuse angle.*

New Memory Work

Your child will gradually learn these memory work items over the course of the year. Not all units have new memory work.

Unit	Memory Work
1	• **What are the four basic operations?** *Addition, subtraction, multiplication, and division.* • **What is an equation?** *A number sentence with an equals sign.* • **What is an expression?** *Part of a number sentence without an equals sign.* • **What is the order of operations?** *Parentheses, multiply or divide from left to right, add or subtract from left to right.*
3	• **What does LCM stand for?** *Least common multiple.*
4	• **What does volume measure?** *The amount of space a solid occupies.* • **What is the formula for the volume of a rectangular prism?** *Multiply length times width times height.*

Unit	Memory Work
5	• **What do we call a fraction whose numerator is greater than or equal to its denominator?** *An improper fraction.*
6	• **How do you know if a number is divisible by 3?** *The sum of its digits is divisible by 3.* • **How do you know if a number is divisible by 4?** *When you divide it by 2, the quotient is even.* • **How do you know if a number is divisible by 6?** *It is even and divisible by 3.* • **What does GCF stand for?** *Greatest common factor.*
9	• **What do we call the horizontal axis?** *The x-axis.* • **What do we call the vertical axis?** *The y-axis.* • **What do we call the (0,0) point?** *The origin.* • **What is an ordered pair?** *A pair of numbers that identify the location of a point.* • **In an ordered pair, what do we call the first number?** *The x-coordinate.* **What does it tell?** *The point's horizontal distance.* • **In an ordered pair, what do we call the second number?** *The y-coordinate.* **What does it tell?** *The point's vertical distance.*
12	• **What is an equilateral triangle?** *A triangle with 3 equal sides.* • **What is an isosceles triangle?** *A triangle with 2 equal sides.* • **What is a scalene triangle?** *A triangle with no equal sides.* • **What is the sum of the angles in a triangle?** *180°.* • **What are opposite angles in a parallelogram?** *Angles that are across from each other.* • **What are adjacent angles in a parallelogram?** *Angles that are next to each other.*
14	• **What do we call the digits to the right of the decimal point?** *Decimal digits.* • **What do we call zeros that come before the first non-zero digit in a number?** *Leading zeros.* • **What do we call zeros that come after the final non-zero digit in a number?** *Trailing zeros.*
16	• **What is the mean of a data set?** *The sum of the values divided by the number of values.* • **What is the median of a data set?** *The middle value when the values are in order from least to greatest.*

Scope and Sequence

Unit	Objectives
Unit 1 Review and Order of Operations	• Review mental multiplication and division strategies • Review the written process for multiplying a multi-digit number by a one-digit number • Review how to use long division to divide a multi-digit number by a one-digit number • Review how to interpret line plots and find an average • Review how to multiply or divide to convert measurements • Find missing numbers in simple addition, subtraction, multiplication, and division equations • Use the order of operations to evaluate expressions with parentheses
Unit 2 Place Value and Decimals	• Understand whole-number place value to the billions-place • Round large numbers to any place • Add and subtract numbers to the billions-place • Understand decimal place value to the thousandths-place • Compare decimals to the thousandths-place • Write decimals in expanded form • Write decimals as mixed numbers or fractions with base-ten denominators (i.e., understand that 4.372 equals 4 372/1,000) • Round decimals to any place • Add and subtract decimals to the thousandths-place
Unit 3 Whole Number Multiplication	• Find the least common multiple (LCM) for a pair of numbers • Use the "multiply and adjust" strategy to mentally multiply • Use doubling to mentally multiply by 2 or 4 • Use the associative property to multiply three or more factors • Multiply numbers with trailing zeros, either mentally or with the multiplication algorithm • Use the box method to multiply two- or three-digit numbers • Extend the multiplication algorithm to larger numbers (up to four-digit times two-digit or three-digit times three-digit)
Unit 4 Volume	• Understand that volume is the amount of space a solid takes up • Use volume formulas (length × width × height or base area × height) to find volume • Divide to find a missing dimension of a rectangular prism • Divide to find the base area or height of a rectangular prism • Split solids into rectangular prisms and add to find the total volume • Solve volume word problems
Unit 5 Add and Subtract Fractions and Mixed Numbers with Different Denominators	• Review how to convert mixed numbers to fractions and fractions to mixed numbers • Review how to multiply to create equivalent fractions and find missing numbers in pairs of equivalent fractions • Use common denominators to compare fractions with different denominators • Add and subtract fractions or mixed numbers with different denominators • Solve fraction and mixed number word problems • Estimate the answers to mixed number addition and subtraction problems

Unit	Objectives
Unit 6 Mental Division	• Mentally divide by 15, 25, and 35 • Use divisibility rules to tell whether numbers are divisible by 2, 3, 4, 5, or 6 • Mentally divide by 2 by splitting numbers in half • Mentally divide by 4 by dividing by 2 twice • Use the "multiply and adjust" strategy to mentally divide two-digit numbers by one-digit numbers • Use mental division and divisibility rules to find all factors of numbers to 100 • Find the greatest common factor (GCF) of two numbers • Mentally divide by multiples of 10 or 100 (for example, 600 ÷ 30 or 3,000 ÷ 500)
Unit 7 Long Division	• Review how to use long division to divide by one-digit numbers • Use long division to divide by multiples of 10 and two-digit numbers • Use long division to solve word problems
Unit 8 Fractions of Sets and Simplest Form	• Describe part of a set with a fraction • Write fractions in simplest form • Describe part of a set or measurement unit with a fraction and find fractional parts of measurement units • Find the number of objects in a fractional part of a set • Use bar models to solve find-the-part, comparison, and find-the-whole fraction word problems
Unit 9 The Coordinate Plane and Line Graphs	• Identify and plot points on the coordinate plane (positive coordinates only) • Identify the slope of lines on the coordinate plane as upward, downward, horizontal, or vertical • Create and interpret line graphs based on real-world data • Make a table of values based on a real-life number pattern, plot the resulting ordered pairs, and use the graph to draw conclusions about the number pattern
Unit 10 Multiply Fractions	• Multiply to find a fraction of a fraction • Reason about fraction multiplication and compare products of fraction multiplication • Solve fraction multiplication word problems • Multiply to find the area of rectangles with fractional lengths
Unit 11 Multiply Mixed Numbers	• Multiply whole numbers by fractions or mixed numbers to find the total of equal groups • Multiply to find fractions of whole numbers or mixed numbers • Estimate products of mixed numbers and products of whole numbers and mixed numbers • Reason about fraction multiplication and predict whether a product will be greater than, less than, or equal to one the factors • Solve multiplication word problems that involve multiplying fractions, whole numbers, or mixed numbers • Multiply fractions, whole numbers, or mixed numbers to find the area of rectangles

Unit	Objectives
Unit 12 Geometry	• Review how to measure and draw angles with a protractor • Identify acute, right, and obtuse triangles • Identify equilateral, isosceles, and scalene triangles • Categorize triangles based on both their angles and sides • Find the measure of a missing angle in a triangle • Identify quadrilaterals • Build and draw triangles and quadrilaterals • Find the measure of missing angles in parallelograms and rhombuses
Unit 13 Divide Fractions	• Understand that the fraction bar is another way to represent division • Divide small whole numbers by small whole numbers and write the result as a fraction or mixed number (for example, 6 ÷ 5 = 1 1/5 or 3 ÷ 4 = 3/4) • Write remainders as fractions • Divide fractions by whole numbers (for example, 2/3 ÷ 4) • Divide whole numbers by unit fractions (for example, 3 ÷ ½) • Solve word problems that involve dividing fractions and whole numbers
Unit 14 Multiply Whole Numbers by Decimals	• Write decimals as groups of tenths, hundredths, or thousandths • Use place-value thinking to mentally multiply whole numbers by simple decimals • Move the decimal point to multiply decimals by 10, 100, or 1,000 • Multiply to convert metric measures • Multiply whole numbers by decimals with written multiplication • Estimate answers to decimal multiplication problems • Solve decimal multiplication word problems, including problems with money
Unit 15 Divide Decimals by Whole Numbers	• Divide decimals by 10, 100, or 1,000 • Divide to convert metric measures • Divide decimals by whole numbers with mental math or long division (and round the answer to a given place, if needed) • Estimate answers to decimal division problems • Solve decimal division word problems, including problems with money
Unit 16 Data	• Find the mean and median for a data set • Use the mean to find a missing value in a data set • Use the mean and median to draw conclusions and compare two data sets

Materials List

What You'll Need in Your Math Kit

You'll use the following materials regularly in *Fifth Grade Math with Confidence*. Stash them in a box or basket and always keep them ready for your next lesson. (See page 9 in the Introduction for more detailed descriptions of each item.)

- 30 small counters (15 each of 2 different colors)
- Fraction bars
- Fraction circles
- Base-ten blocks (30 unit blocks, 20 rods, 12 flats)
- 30 centimeter cubes (if you don't own base-ten blocks)
- Play money (20 one-dollar bills, 20 ten-dollar bills, 10 hundred-dollar bills)
- 1-foot (or 30-centimeter) ruler
- Protractor
- 2 packs of playing cards
- 2 dice
- Blank paper
- Pencils
- Highlighter
- 1 plastic page protector
- Dry-erase marker

Other Supplies

Besides your Math Kit, you'll also need the following household items. You'll only need most of them once or twice, so you don't need to gather them ahead of time or store them separately. Check the unit overviews for the specific household items you'll need for each unit.

Items marked with an asterisk are needed for the optional enrichment lessons at the end of each unit.

- *Travel brochures or internet access, optional
- World map, optional
- *8-10 jars of spices, labeled in ounces
- *Calculator or calculator app
- 1 extra die (to play a game that calls for 3 dice)
- 3 small boxes of different sizes (like boxes of pasta or rice)
- Measuring tape
- *Pillows, blankets, and furniture for building a fort
- Paper clip
- *Ingredients and supplies to make vegetable soup, optional
- 4 small slips of paper
- *Map app
- 5 craft sticks or writing utensils
- *Collection of 20-30 objects

- Colored pencils or markers
- *World map or globe with latitude and longitude lines, optional
- 3 paper half-circles
- Scissors
- Paper square foot
- 10 in. by 8 in. paper rectangle
- Rectangular object whose length and width are less than 1 foot (such as a book or picture)
- *Rectangular chocolate bar with lines that split it into fractional parts (such as a Hershey bar or Cadbury Dairy Milk bar)
- Measuring cups and spoons, optional
- 4 one-inch paper squares
- *Recipe with fractions and mixed numbers
- *Small piece of cardstock or cardboard (about 3 inches square)
- *Black marker
- *Colored pencils, markers, or watercolor paints
- *Grocery store flyer or website
- *Family recipe that makes a large batch, optional
- Stopwatch or stopwatch app

Guide to the Blackline Masters

Digital Copies of Blackline Masters

Prefer to print the Blackline Masters rather than copy them from the book? **Download digital copies of all Math with Confidence Blackline Masters at welltrainedmind.com/mwc.**

Reference Blackline Masters

Families often find it helpful to have the Memory Work pages (Blackline Master 1) available for easy reference. If possible, post these pages near your lesson area to help your child gradually memorize the items over the course of the year.

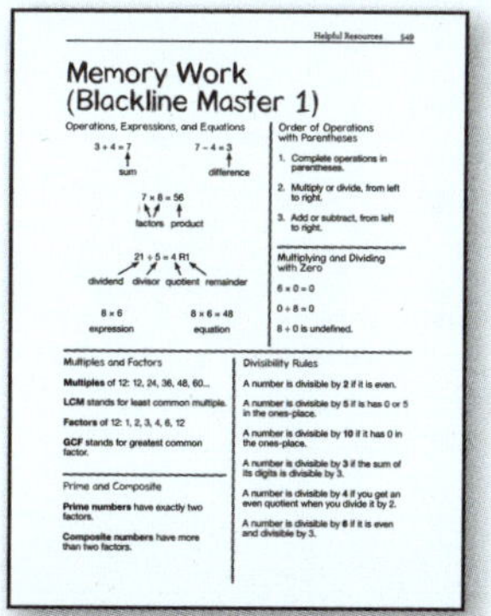

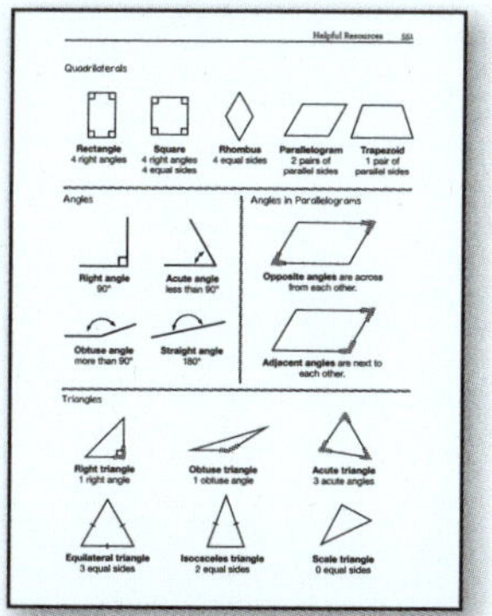

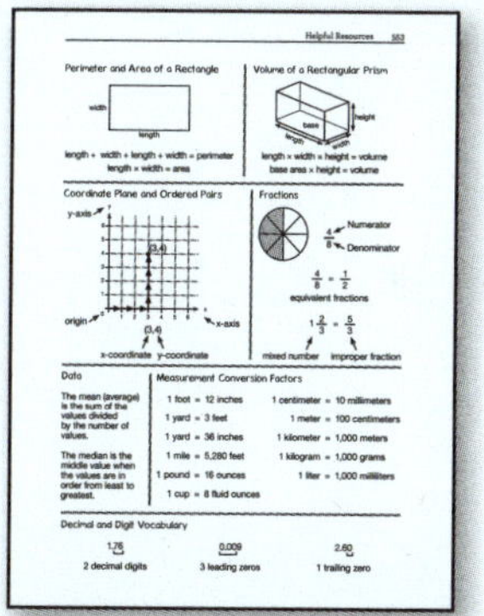

If slow multiplication fact recall is causing frustration or making the lessons long and tedious, keep the Multiplication Chart (Blackline Master 4) nearby and allow your child to use it as needed. For some children, using the chart for a few months makes a big difference in helping them solidify their multiplication fact fluency. See the Unit 1 Checkpoint (page 51) for more on multiplication fact fluency.

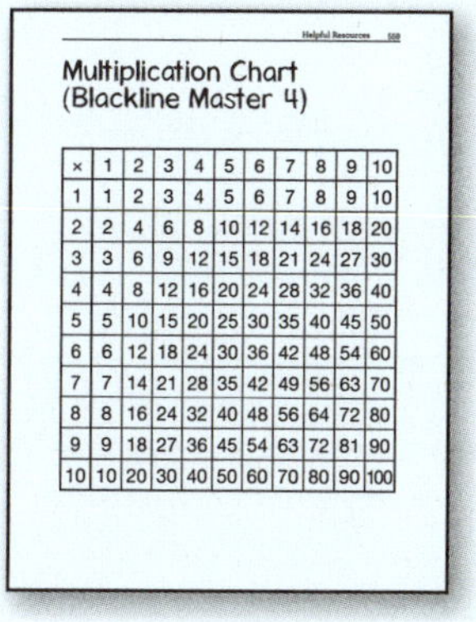

Multiplication Chart
(Blackline Master 4)

×	1	2	3	4	5	6	7	8	9	10
1	1	2	3	4	5	6	7	8	9	10
2	2	4	6	8	10	12	14	16	18	20
3	3	6	9	12	15	18	21	24	27	30
4	4	8	12	16	20	24	28	32	36	40
5	5	10	15	20	25	30	35	40	45	50
6	6	12	18	24	30	36	42	48	54	60
7	7	14	21	28	35	42	49	56	63	70
8	8	16	24	32	40	48	56	64	72	80
9	9	18	27	36	45	54	63	72	81	90
10	10	20	30	40	50	60	70	80	90	100

Short-Term-Use Blackline Masters

You will use these Blackline Masters for only a few lessons. You do not need to save them after you finish the corresponding unit.

- Decimal Cards (Blackline Master 5), used in Units 2 and 14 only
- Decimal Place-Value Chart (Blackline Master 6), used in Units 2 and 14 only
- Decimal Squares (Blackline Master 7), used in Unit 2 only
- Fraction Cards (Blackline Master 9), used in Units 5 and 10 only
- Paper Strips (Blackline Master 10), used in Unit 12 only
- Triangles for Folding (Blackline Master 11), used in Unit 12 only
- Paper Parallelogram (Blackline Master 12), used in Unit 12 only
- Paper Chocolate Bars (Blackline Master 13), used in Unit 13 only

Optional Blackline Masters

The Multiplication Assessment (Blackline Master 2) and Multiplication Review Games (Blackline Master 3) are optional for assessing and improving your child's multiplication fact recall. See the Unit 1 Checkpoint (page 51) for details on whether or not you need them.

The following Blackline Masters are provided in case you do not own real fraction bars, fraction circles, base-ten blocks, or play money.

- Fraction Bars (Blackline Master 8)
- Fraction Circles (Blackline Master 14)
- Base-Ten Blocks (Blackline Master 15)
- Play Money (Blackline Master 16)

Memory Work (Blackline Master 1)

Operations, Expressions, and Equations

3 + 4 = 7 (7: sum)

7 − 4 = 3 (3: difference)

7 × 8 = 56 (7, 8: factors; 56: product)

21 ÷ 5 = 4 R1 (21: dividend; 5: divisor; 4: quotient; 1: remainder)

8 × 6 — expression

8 × 6 = 48 — equation

Order of Operations with Parentheses

1. Complete operations in parentheses.
2. Multiply or divide, from left to right.
3. Add or subtract, from left to right.

Multiplying and Dividing with Zero

6 × 0 = 0

0 ÷ 8 = 0

8 ÷ 0 is undefined.

Multiples and Factors

Multiples of 12: 12, 24, 36, 48, 60...

LCM stands for least common multiple.

Factors of 12: 1, 2, 3, 4, 6, 12

GCF stands for greatest common factor.

Prime and Composite

Prime numbers have exactly two factors.

Composite numbers have more than two factors.

Divisibility Rules

A number is divisible by **2** if it is even.

A number is divisible by **5** if it has 0 or 5 in the ones-place.

A number is divisible by **10** if it has 0 in the ones-place.

A number is divisible by **3** if the sum of its digits is divisible by 3.

A number is divisible by **4** if you get an even quotient when you divide it by 2.

A number is divisible by **6** if it is even and divisible by 3.

Quadrilaterals

Rectangle
4 right angles

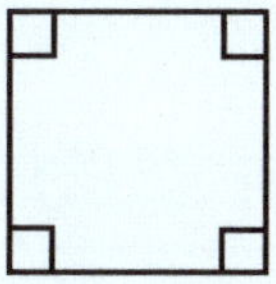

Square
4 right angles
4 equal sides

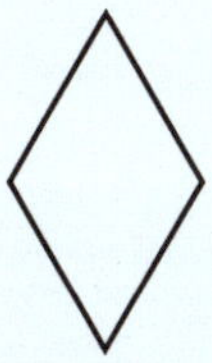

Rhombus
4 equal sides

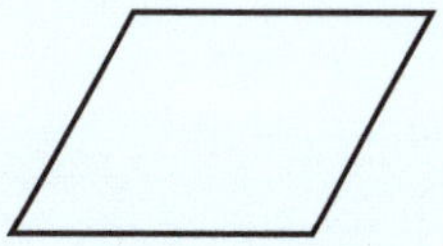

Parallelogram
2 pairs of parallel sides

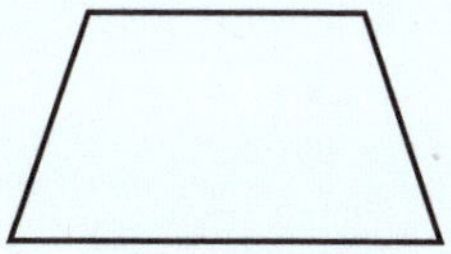

Trapezoid
1 pair of parallel sides

Angles

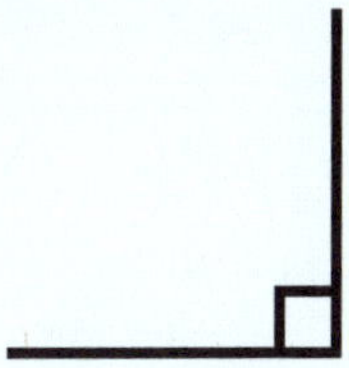

Right angle
90°

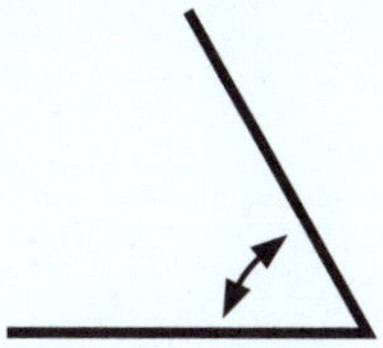

Acute angle
less than 90°

Obtuse angle
more than 90°

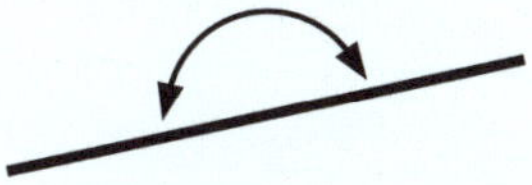

Straight angle
180°

Angles in Parallelograms

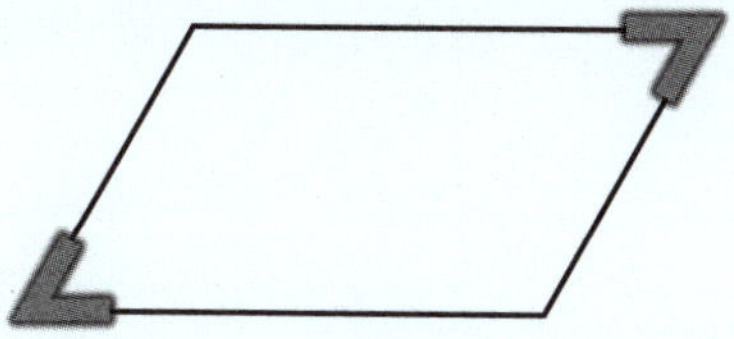

Opposite angles are across from each other.

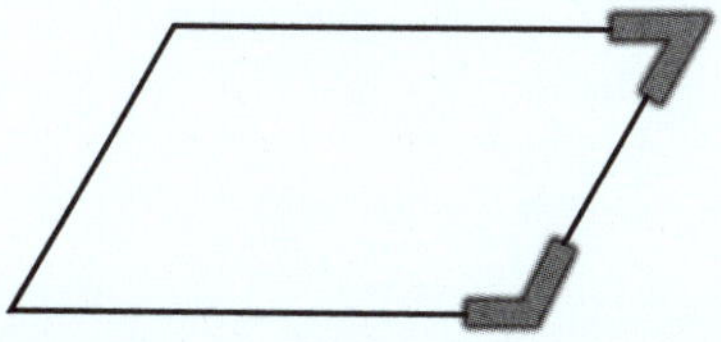

Adjacent angles are next to each other.

Triangles

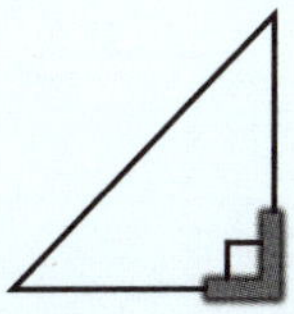

Right triangle
1 right angle

Obtuse triangle
1 obtuse angle

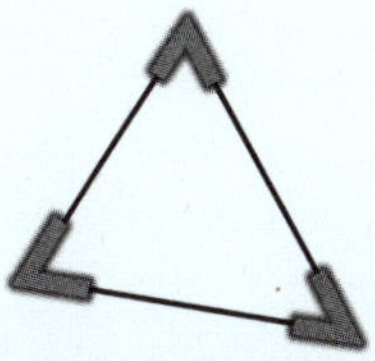

Acute triangle
3 acute angles

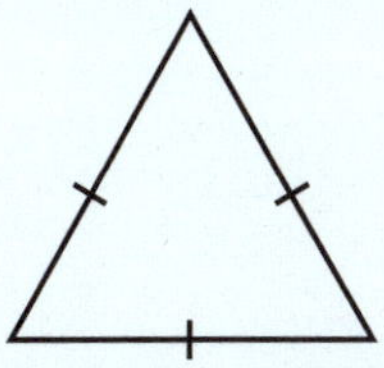

Equilateral triangle
3 equal sides

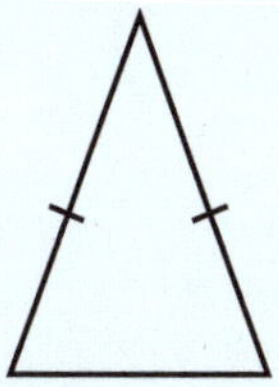

Isosceles triangle
2 equal sides

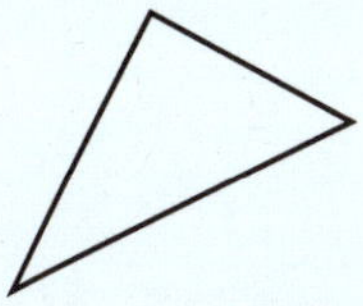

Scalene triangle
0 equal sides

Perimeter and Area of a Rectangle

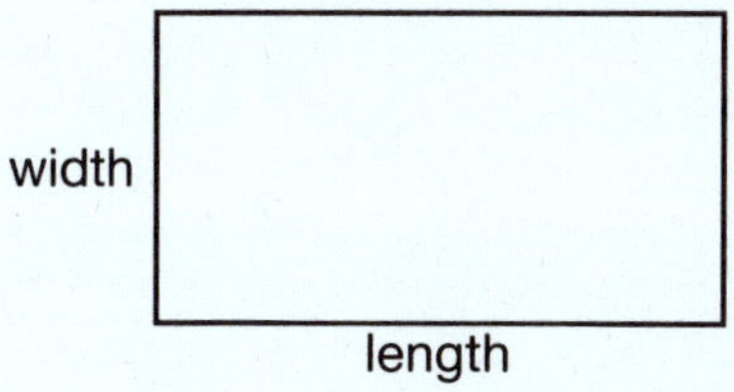

length + width + length + width = perimeter

length × width = area

Volume of a Rectangular Prism

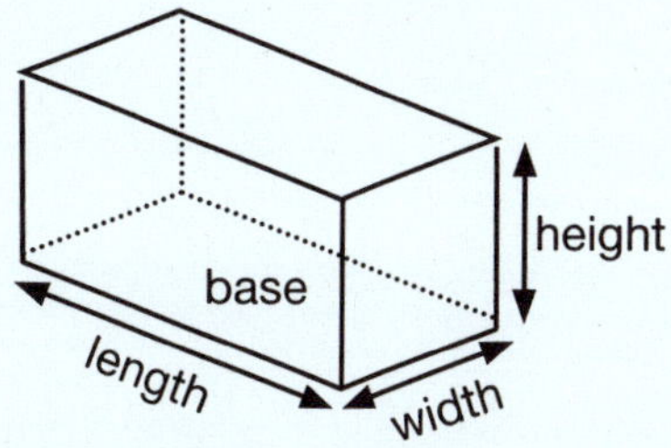

length × width × height = volume

base area × height = volume

Coordinate Plane and Ordered Pairs

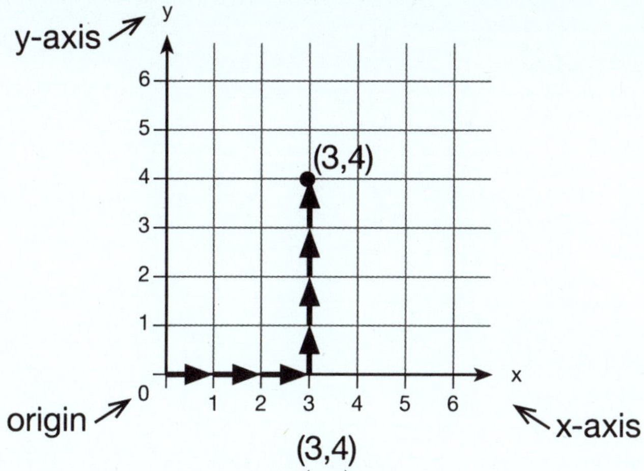

Fractions

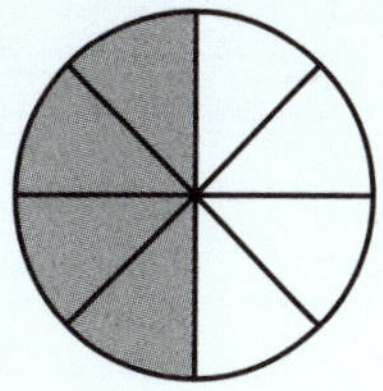

$\frac{4}{8}$ ← Numerator (4), Denominator (8)

$\frac{4}{8} = \frac{1}{2}$

equivalent fractions

$1\frac{2}{3} = \frac{5}{3}$

mixed number ↗ improper fraction ↖

Data

The mean (average) is the sum of the values divided by the number of values.

The median is the middle value when the values are in order from least to greatest.

Measurement Conversion Factors

1 foot = 12 inches	1 centimeter = 10 millimeters
1 yard = 3 feet	1 meter = 100 centimeters
1 yard = 36 inches	1 kilometer = 1,000 meters
1 mile = 5,280 feet	1 kilogram = 1,000 grams
1 pound = 16 ounces	1 liter = 1,000 milliliters
1 cup = 8 fluid ounces	

Decimal and Digit Vocabulary

1.76	0.009	2.60
2 decimal digits	3 leading zeros	1 trailing zero

Multiplication Assessment (Blackline Master 2)

How to Give the Assessment

Use this multiplication assessment to assess how well your child knows the multiplication facts. Make sure to give the assessment at a time when your child is fresh and focused so that the results are as accurate as possible.

- Ask your child each math fact **orally**. Encourage her to respond with the answer as quickly as possible, without repeating the question. For example: **6 times 1?** *6.*
- Ask questions across the page *horizontally*, not vertically. Start by moving from left to right across the first row, then the second row, and so on.
- Mark the problem as correct (✓) if your child says the correct answer within 3 seconds. Mark the problem as incorrect (×) if your child doesn't know the answer, takes longer than 3 seconds, or counts to find the answer.

Children who process information very quickly may be able to name the answers in less than 1 second, but children who are slower processors may always need a few seconds. As a general rule, aim for no more than **3 seconds** per fact, but adjust this guideline based on your individual child.

9 × 1 = **9** ☐	3 × 2 = **6** ☐	8 × 3 = **24** ☐	5 × 4 = **20** ☐	1 × 10 = **10** ☐
4 × 1 = **4** ☐	5 × 2 = **10** ☐	6 × 3 = **18** ☐	7 × 4 = **28** ☐	8 × 10 = **80** ☐
1 × 6 = **6** ☐	2 × 9 = **18** ☐	3 × 5 = **15** ☐	4 × 4 = **16** ☐	10 × 6 = **60** ☐
1 × 1 = **1** ☐	4 × 2 = **8** ☐	3 × 3 = **9** ☐	6 × 4 = **24** ☐	9 × 10 = **90** ☐
3 × 1 = **3** ☐	2 × 2 = **4** ☐	9 × 3 = **27** ☐	3 × 4 = **12** ☐	7 × 10 = **70** ☐
5 × 5 = **25** ☐	6 × 9 = **54** ☐	7 × 3 = **21** ☐	8 × 8 = **64** ☐	4 × 10 = **40** ☐
9 × 5 = **45** ☐	10 × 2 = **20** ☐	6 × 8 = **48** ☐	7 × 1 = **7** ☐	10 × 10 = **100** ☐
5 × 7 = **35** ☐	8 × 9 = **72** ☐	2 × 7 = **14** ☐	8 × 4 = **32** ☐	5 × 10 = **50** ☐
8 × 1 = **8** ☐	6 × 2 = **12** ☐	7 × 6 = **42** ☐	9 × 7 = **63** ☐	3 × 10 = **30** ☐
5 × 1 = **5** ☐	7 × 7 = **49** ☐	2 × 8 = **16** ☐	8 × 5 = **40** ☐	6 × 5 = **30** ☐
1 × 2 = **2** ☐	6 × 6 = **36** ☐	9 × 9 = **81** ☐	9 × 4 = **36** ☐	8 × 7 = **56** ☐

How to Interpret the Results

- If your child can find answers to most of the facts but takes longer than 3 seconds, he needs more practice to build his speed. Play one of the multiplication review games from Blackline Master 3 a few times per week (either at the beginning of a lesson or at a separate time of day) as you move forward in the program. Encourage your child to respond as quickly as possible as he names the products in the games.
- If your child has just a few facts that stump him, choose 3 of the tricky facts. Write them on a piece of paper and post them in your math lesson area. Have him practice these 3 facts at the beginning of each lesson until he has memorized them. Then, choose 3 new facts to focus on.
- If your child has trouble finding answers to many of the multiplication facts, he likely needs more practice with them to be successful with *Fifth Grade Math with Confidence. Multiplication Facts That Stick* (also available from Well-Trained Mind Press) provides a systematic approach to mastering the facts. Use the activities from *Multiplication Facts That Stick* for 5-10 minutes per day outside of your regular math time.

If you find that your child's lack of fluency with the multiplication facts makes lessons long and frustrating, **allow him to use the multiplication chart** (Blackline Master 4) as he completes lessons in *Fifth Grade Math with Confidence*. This will allow him to continue to make progress with new concepts while he works to solidify the multiplication facts.

Multiplication Review Games (Blackline Master 3)

Multiplication War

Materials: Deck of playing cards with jacks, queens, and kings removed (40 cards total)

Object of the Game: Win the most cards.

Shuffle together the cards. Deal them face down into two piles.

On your turn, flip over the top two cards in your pile. Find the product of the numbers. For example, if you flip over a 6 and a 7, the product is 42. Then, the other player flips over their top two cards and finds the product of the cards. Whoever has the greater product wins all 4 cards.

If the products are equal, leave the cards face-up on the table and have both players flip over another two cards from their piles. Whoever has the greater product wins all the face-up cards.

Play until the piles run out. Whoever has won more cards wins the game.

Challenge Version: Use only the 5s, 6s, 7s, 8s, and 9s from 2 decks of cards to give your child lots of practice with challenging multiplication facts like 7 × 8 or 9 × 6.

Multiplication Greatest to Least

Materials: 2 decks of cards, with jacks, queens, and kings removed (80 cards total)

Object of the Game: Win the most cards.

Shuffle the cards and deal 5 cards to both players. Place the rest of the deck in a face-down pile.

Choose who will go first. Player 1 chooses two cards from his hand, places them face-up on the table, and names the product. For example, if you play a 4 and a 9, the product is 36. Then, Player 1 picks up two new cards to replenish his hand.

Player 2 chooses any two cards from her hand whose product is less than Player 1's product. (The products may not be equal.) She places her cards on top of Player 1's cards, names their product, and takes 2 new cards to replenish her hand. For example, if Player 1 played a 4 and a 9, Player 2 can play any two cards with a product less than 36.

Continue alternating turns until one player can no longer play a lower product. The player who last played takes all of the face-up cards. The player who was unable to play new cards starts a new round.

Play until you have used all the cards. Whoever has won more cards wins the game.

Cooperative Version: Take turns playing pairs of cards. Try to play as many cards as possible before one player can no longer play a lower product. Count how many cards both players played, and see if you can play more cards in the next round.

Multiplication Chart (Blackline Master 4)

×	1	2	3	4	5	6	7	8	9	10
1	1	2	3	4	5	6	7	8	9	10
2	2	4	6	8	10	12	14	16	18	20
3	3	6	9	12	15	18	21	24	27	30
4	4	8	12	16	20	24	28	32	36	40
5	5	10	15	20	25	30	35	40	45	50
6	6	12	18	24	30	36	42	48	54	60
7	7	14	21	28	35	42	49	56	63	70
8	8	16	24	32	40	48	56	64	72	80
9	9	18	27	36	45	54	63	72	81	90
10	10	20	30	40	50	60	70	80	90	100

Decimal Cards (Blackline Master 5)

Directions: Cut out along the lines.

0.1	0.2	0.3
0.4	0.5	0.6
0.7	0.8	0.9
0.01	0.02	0.03
0.04	0.05	0.06

0.07	0.08	0.09
0.001	0.002	0.003
0.004	0.005	0.006
0.007	0.008	0.009

Decimal Place-Value Chart (Blackline Master 6)

ones	tenths

hundredths	thousandths

Decimal Squares (Blackline Master 7)

Directions: Put this page in a plastic page protector so you can write on it with a dry -erase marker.

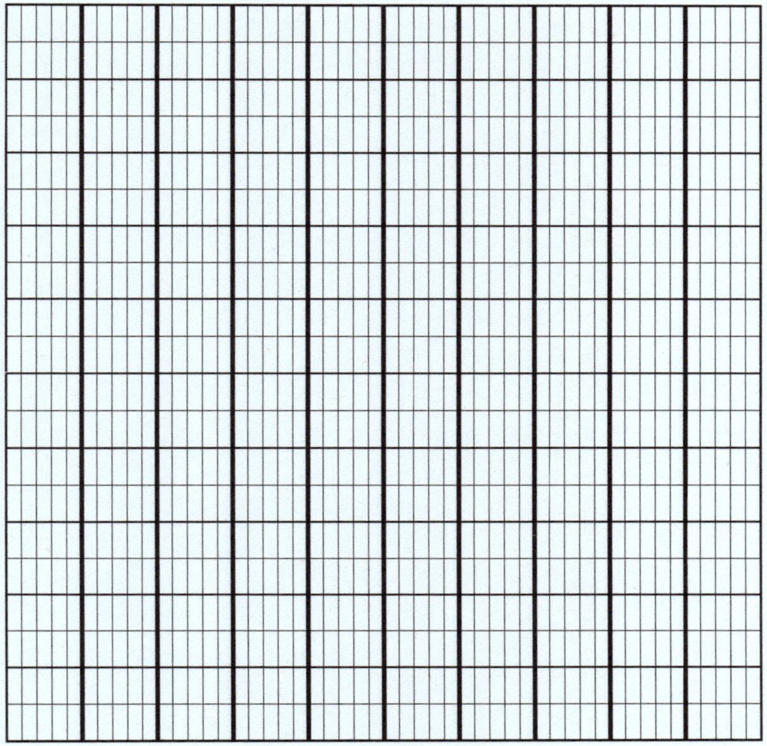

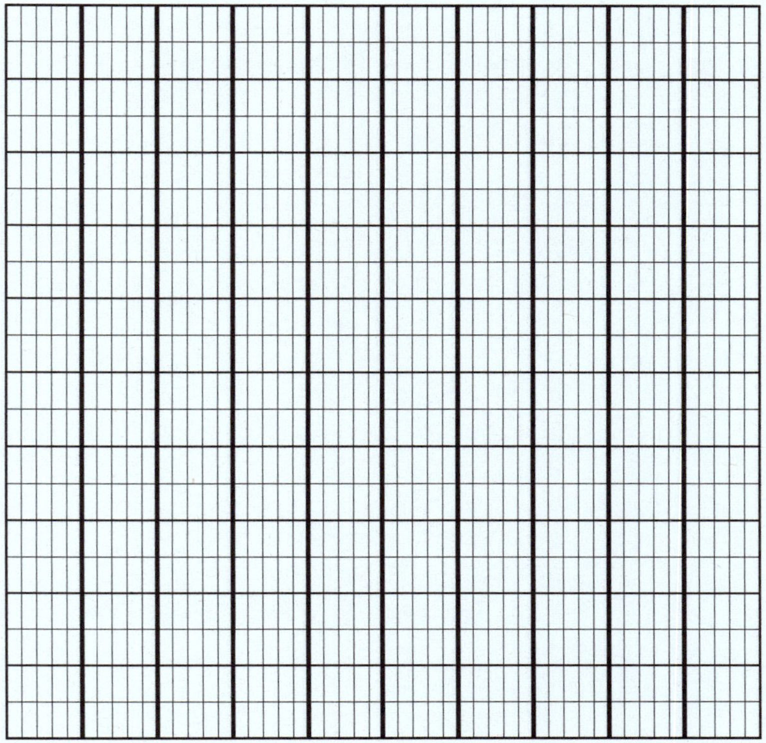

Fraction Bars (Blackline Master 8)

You do not need these if you have real fraction bars.

Directions: Use the following key to color the fraction bars. Then, cut out the fraction bars along the lines.

- 1 whole: red
- 1/2: orange-red
- 1/3: orange
- 1/4: yellow
- 1/5: light green
- 1/6: green
- 1/8: light blue
- 1/10: blue
- 1/12: purple

1

$\frac{1}{2}$ | $\frac{1}{2}$

$\frac{1}{3}$ | $\frac{1}{3}$ | $\frac{1}{3}$

$\frac{1}{4}$ | $\frac{1}{4}$ | $\frac{1}{4}$ | $\frac{1}{4}$

$\frac{1}{5}$ | $\frac{1}{5}$ | $\frac{1}{5}$ | $\frac{1}{5}$ | $\frac{1}{5}$

$\frac{1}{6}$ | $\frac{1}{6}$ | $\frac{1}{6}$ | $\frac{1}{6}$ | $\frac{1}{6}$ | $\frac{1}{6}$

$\frac{1}{8}$ | $\frac{1}{8}$ | $\frac{1}{8}$ | $\frac{1}{8}$ | $\frac{1}{8}$ | $\frac{1}{8}$ | $\frac{1}{8}$ | $\frac{1}{8}$

$\frac{1}{10}$ | $\frac{1}{10}$ | $\frac{1}{10}$ | $\frac{1}{10}$ | $\frac{1}{10}$ | $\frac{1}{10}$ | $\frac{1}{10}$ | $\frac{1}{10}$ | $\frac{1}{10}$ | $\frac{1}{10}$

$\frac{1}{12}$ | $\frac{1}{12}$ | $\frac{1}{12}$ | $\frac{1}{12}$ | $\frac{1}{12}$ | $\frac{1}{12}$ | $\frac{1}{12}$ | $\frac{1}{12}$ | $\frac{1}{12}$ | $\frac{1}{12}$ | $\frac{1}{12}$ | $\frac{1}{12}$

Fraction Cards (Blackline Master 9)

Directions: Copy on sturdy paper. Cut out along the lines.

$\frac{1}{2}$	$\frac{1}{3}$	$\frac{2}{3}$
$\frac{1}{4}$	$\frac{2}{4}$	$\frac{3}{4}$
$\frac{1}{5}$	$\frac{2}{5}$	$\frac{3}{5}$
$\frac{4}{5}$	$\frac{1}{6}$	$\frac{2}{6}$
$\frac{3}{6}$	$\frac{4}{6}$	$\frac{5}{6}$

$\frac{1}{8}$	$\frac{2}{8}$	$\frac{3}{8}$
$\frac{4}{8}$	$\frac{5}{8}$	$\frac{6}{8}$
$\frac{7}{8}$	$\frac{1}{10}$	$\frac{2}{10}$
$\frac{3}{10}$	$\frac{4}{10}$	$\frac{5}{10}$
$\frac{6}{10}$	$\frac{7}{10}$	$\frac{8}{10}$

$\frac{9}{10}$	$\frac{1}{12}$	$\frac{2}{12}$
$\frac{3}{12}$	$\frac{4}{12}$	$\frac{5}{12}$
$\frac{6}{12}$	$\frac{7}{12}$	$\frac{8}{12}$
$\frac{9}{12}$	$\frac{10}{12}$	$\frac{11}{12}$

Paper Strips (Blackline Master 10)

Directions: Cut out along the dark lines.

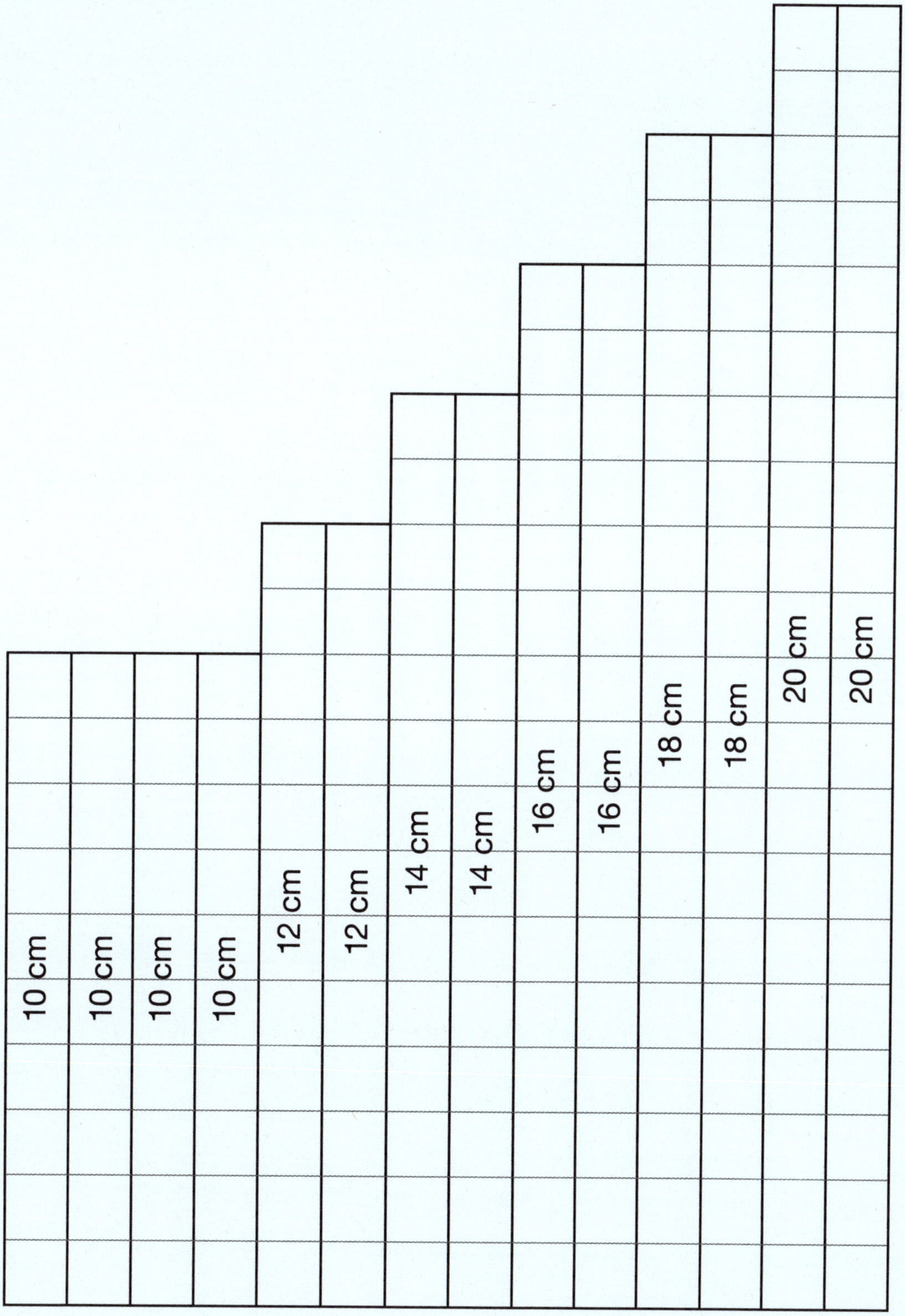

Triangles for Folding (Blackline Master 11)

Directions: Cut out the triangles.

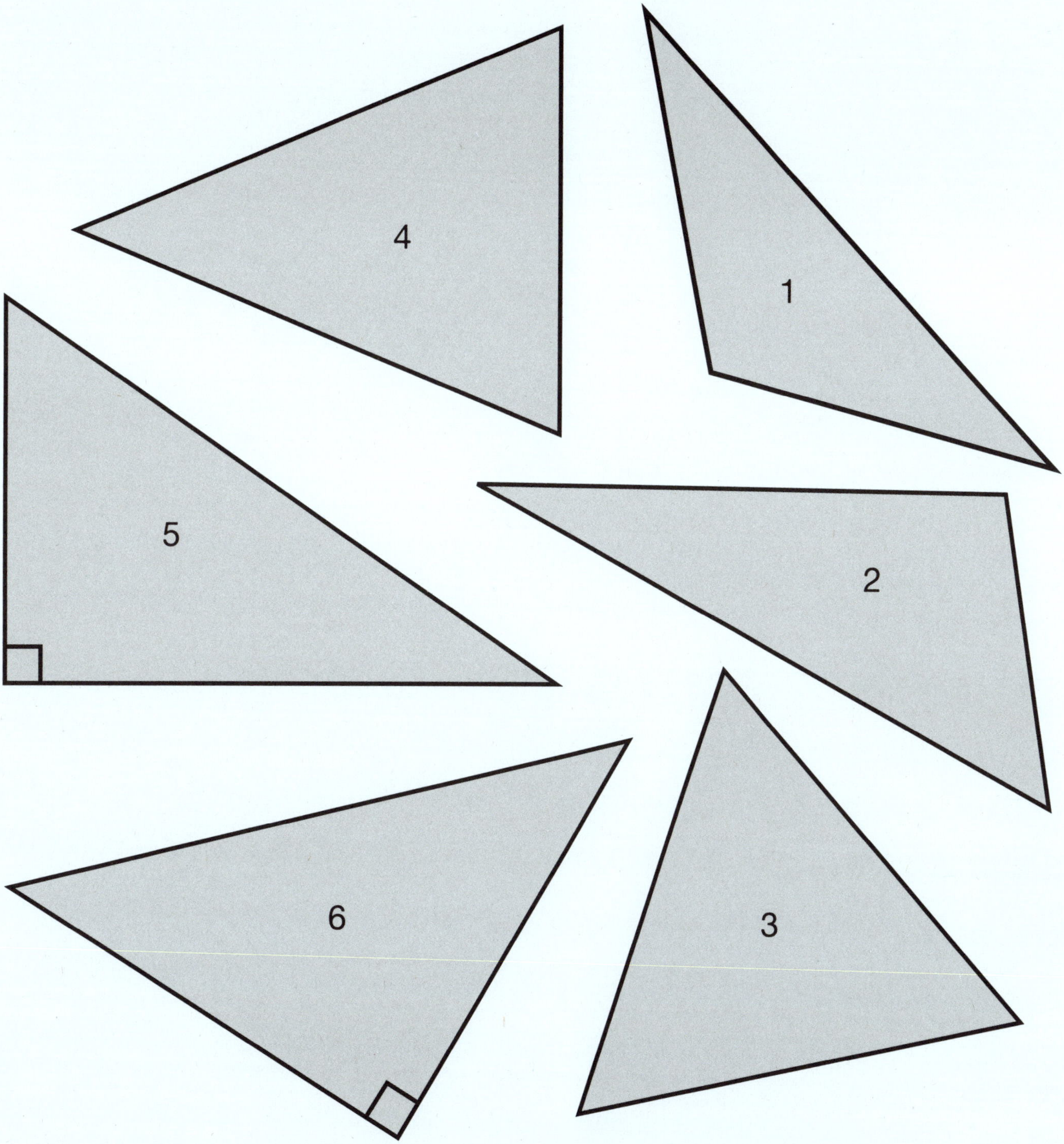

Paper Parallelogram (Blackline Master 12)

Directions: Cut out along the dark lines.

Paper Chocolate Bars (Blackline Master 13)

Directions: Cut out the chocolate bars along the dark lines.

Fraction Circles (Blackline Master 14)

You do not need these if you have real fraction circles.

Directions: Use the following key to color the fraction circles. Then, cut out the fraction circles along the lines.

- 1 whole: red
- 1/2: orange-red
- 1/3: orange
- 1/4: yellow
- 1/5: light green
- 1/6: green
- 1/8: blue
- 1/10: purple
- 1/12: brown

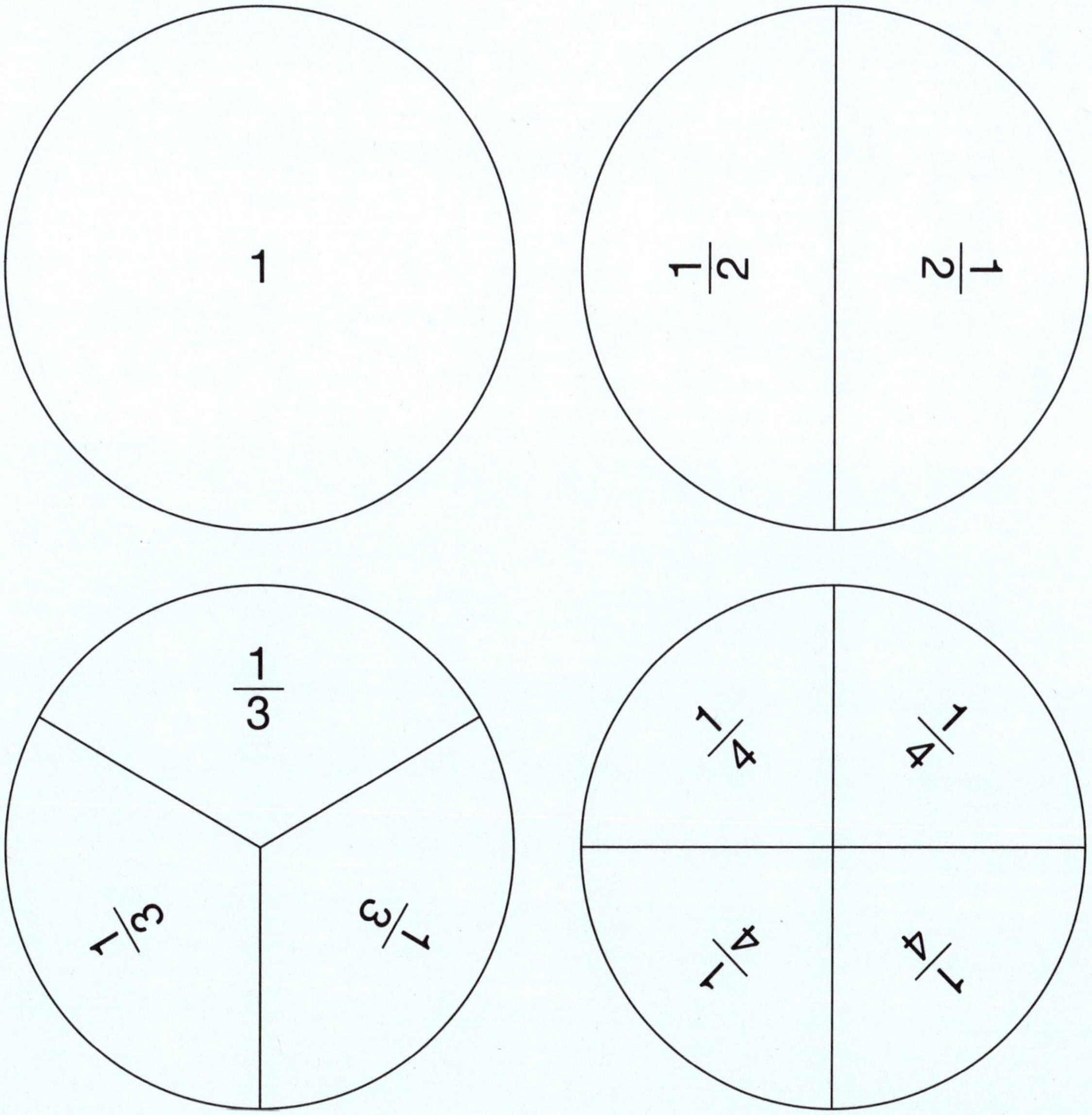

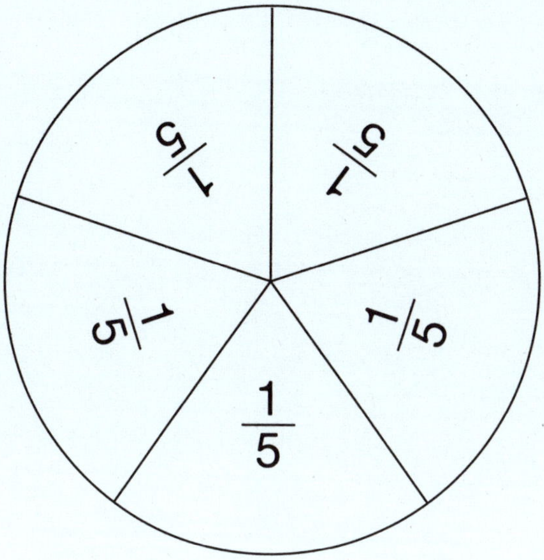
1/5
1/5
1/5
1/5
1/5

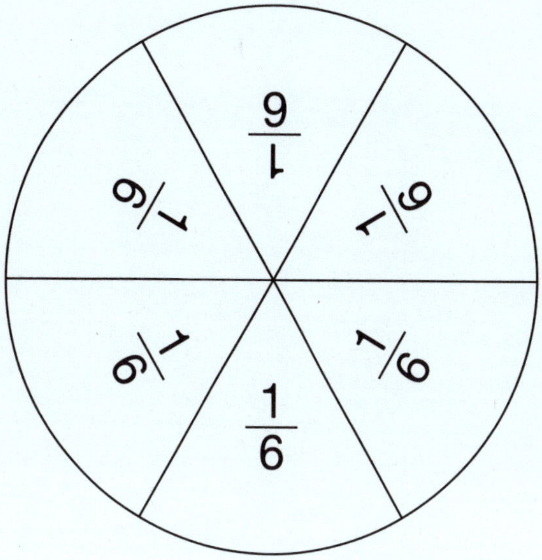
1/6
1/6
1/6
1/6
1/6
1/6

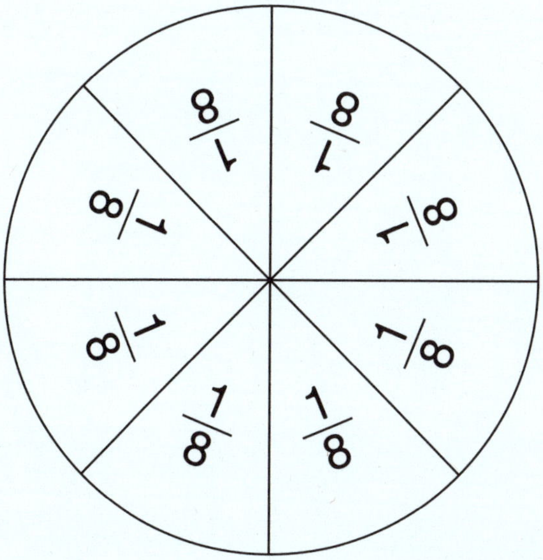
1/8
1/8
1/8
1/8
1/8
1/8
1/8
1/8

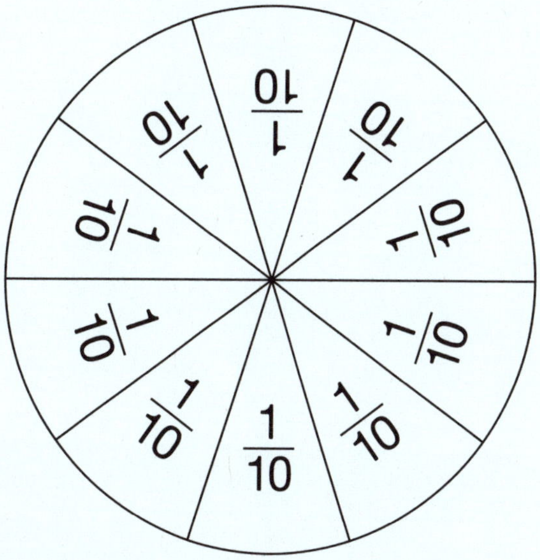
1/10
1/10
1/10
1/10
1/10
1/10
1/10
1/10
1/10
1/10

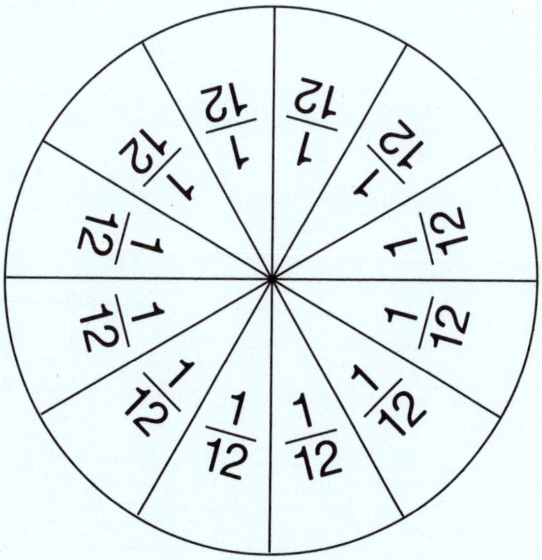
1/12
1/12
1/12
1/12
1/12
1/12
1/12
1/12
1/12
1/12
1/12
1/12

Base-Ten Blocks (Blackline Master 15)

You do not need these if you have real base-ten blocks.

Directions: Make 6 copies of this page on sturdy paper. Cut out the blocks on the dark lines.

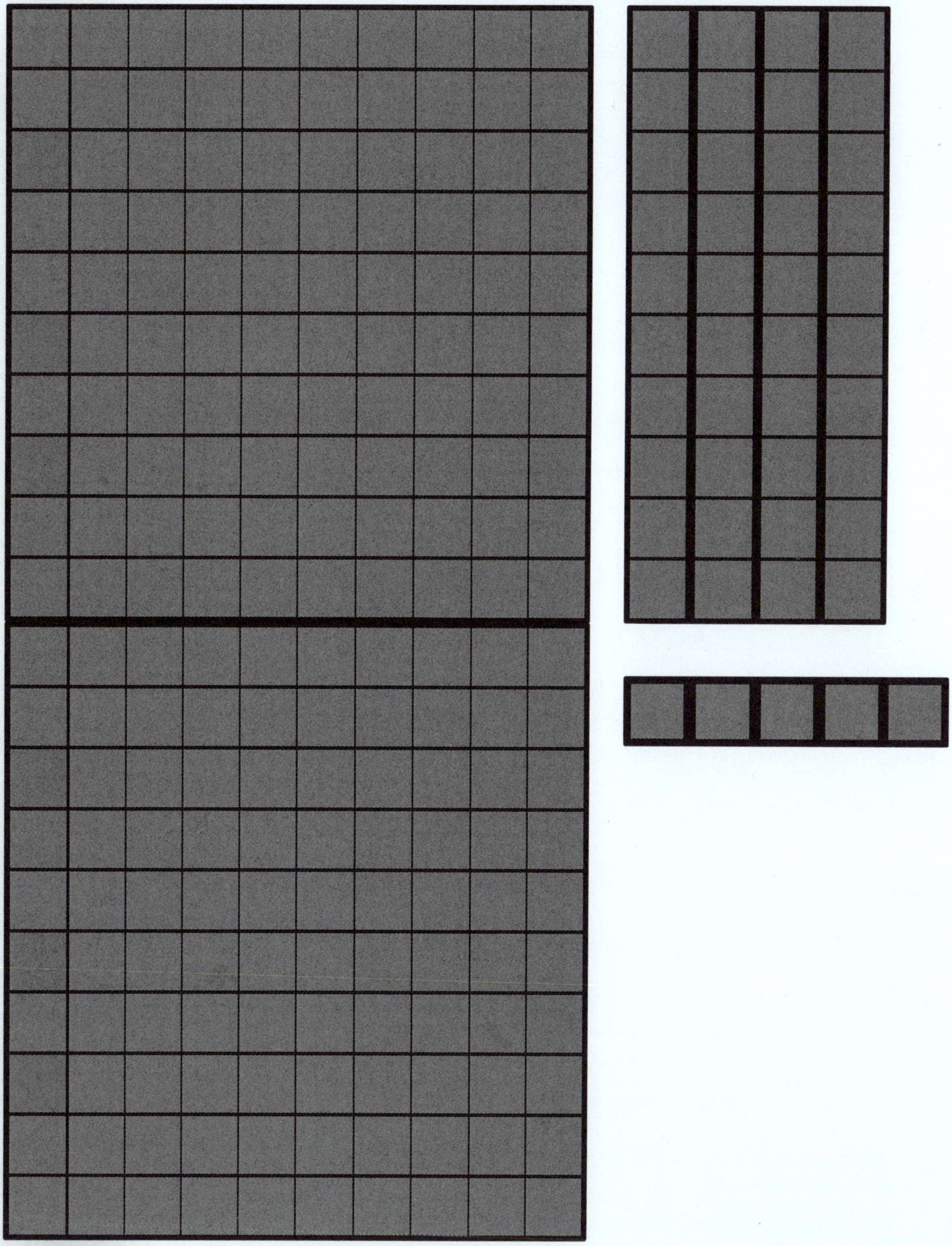

Play Money (Blackline Master 16)

You do not need these if you have other play money, either from a toy cash register or board game.

Directions: Make 2 copies of this page on sturdy paper and cut out the paper bills.

Acknowledgements

Thanks to Itamar Katz, whose design and illustration skills transform my Word document and messy sketches into this easy-to-use Instructor Guide and colorful, engaging Student Workbooks. These books wouldn't be the same without your insightful design suggestions and wonderful drawings, Itamar!

To my assistant Donna Hunter, for her diligent and skillful help throughout the year, especially with the answer keys. To Melissa Moore, both for her expert project management and for her steadfast support and encouragement. To Justin Moore, for his thoughtful clarifying questions and indefatigable copy-editing. And to Susan Wise Bauer, for her guidance and advice as I honed the vision for the *Math with Confidence* series.

To Shane Klink, who designed the beautiful covers for the series. To Rachael Churchill, whose thorough editing improved the clarity of the Instructor Guide and cleaned up my typos and mistakes.

Finally, many thanks to the members of the *Fifth Grade Math with Confidence* pilot-test group. Thank you for finding the activities that didn't work, the workbook pages that were too long, and the lessons that needed a little more fun! This program is better because of you, and I appreciate all the time you spent giving me feedback, answering my questions, and helping me understand how your kids responded to the lessons. Beyond these practical matters, thank you for your generous encouragement and support. Your commitment to giving your kids an excellent math education motivates and inspires me, and it is an honor to be part of that journey with you.

Aleicia Maness
Alicia McCain
Allicia Muxlow
Amanda Moffitt
Amanda Troxell
Amy Lerner
Angela Reams
Apollos
Ashley Scofield
Bethany Haugen
Bridget Camp
Carrie Hickman and Family
Chialin K.
Crystal and Noah Rivera-Silva
Diana Jensen
Domanique Glazier
Dorene Powell
Duski Van Fleet
Elizabeth Wenzel
Emily Kuhl
Evelyn Hakimian
Harper and Stephanie Edwards
Heather R.
Holly Merryman
Jade and Juniper Buchanan
Jami McCreary
Janelle Jones
Jenna and Lila Rice
Jennifer and Lillian Tierney
Jess Karimeddini
Jessica Grime
Jill Gray
Johanna Tomlinson
Julie Barnett
Julie Gatewood
Kara Walker
Karen and Peter Shiffler
Kathleen and Niall Santos
Kathryn Bitner
Katie Peterson
Katie Schulteis
Kelly and Madeline Russell
Kim O'Connor
Kristi Mikkelsen
Kristy Griggs
Kylee Feagan
Laura Peterson
Laura Sandiford
Lauren Funnell
Lindsay Partridge
Lisa Ertmer
Lisa Healy
Liz Jones
Mageda Merbouh-Bangert
Mandi Davidson
Mary Ann Glenn
Megan Preedin
Meghan Shaffer
Melissa Cragg
Melissa Jones
Melissa Mackey
Nancy Bradford
Rachel King
Rachel Sohn
Rebecca Matheson
Sabrina Koogler
Sally Metcalfe
Sandy Lorraine Tad-y
Sarah Aiken
Sarah Montgomery
Shannon Smith
Shelley Scoll
Stacy Whitaker
Susan Harmon
Tawheeda and Khadija
The Hansen Family
The Herman Family
The Klackle Family
The Mackie Family
The Martoncik Family
Tosin Olaiya